Tenth Edition

CRIMINAL BEHAVIOR

A PSYCHOLOGICAL APPROACH

Tenth Edition

CRIMINAL BEHAVIOR
A PSYCHOLOGICAL APPROACH

Curt R. Bartol

Anne M. Bartol

Boston Columbus Indianapolis New York San Francisco Upper Saddle River
Amsterdam Cape Town Dubai London Madrid Milan Munich Paris Montréal Toronto
Delhi Mexico City São Paulo Sydney Hong Kong Seoul Singapore Taipei Tokyo

Vice President and Executive Publisher: Vernon Anthony
Senior Acquisitions Editor: Gary Bauer
Assistant Editor: Tiffany Bitzel
Editorial Assistant: Tanika Henderson
Media Project Manager: Karen Bretz
Director of Marketing: David Gesell
Marketing Manager: Mary Salzman
Senior Marketing Coordinator: Alicia Wozniak
Production Manager: Pat Brown
Creative Director: Jayne Conte
Cover Design: Suzanne Duda
Cover Illustration/Photo: Fotolia
Full-Service Project Management/Composition: Abinaya Rajendran,
    Integra Software Services Pvt. Ltd.
Printer/Binder: Courier/Westford

Library of Congress Cataloging-in-Publication Data
Bartol, Curt R.
    Criminal behavior: a psychological approach/Curt R. Bartol, Anne M. Bartol.—10th ed.
       p. cm.
    ISBN-13: 978-0-13-297319-9 (alk. paper)
    ISBN-10: 0-13-297319-7 (alk. paper)
    1. Criminal psychology.   2. Criminal behavior—United States.   I. Bartol, Anne M.   II. Title.
    HV6080.B37 2014
    364.3—dc23

                                                                    2012033342

10 9 8 7 6 5 4 3 2 1

ISBN-13: 978-0-13-297319-9
ISBN-10:   0-13-297319-7

To Kai, who never ceases to wonder, to create, and to care.

CONTENTS

Chapter 3   ORIGINS OF CRIMINAL BEHAVIOR: BIOLOGICAL FACTORS   57

xvi   Contents

PREFACE

Criminal Behavior: A Psychosocial Approach is a textbook about crime from a psychological perspective. More specifically, this text portrays the criminal offender as embedded in and continually influenced by multiple systems within the psychosocial environment. We believe that meaningful theory, well-executed research, and skillful application of knowledge to the "crime problem" require an understanding of the many levels of events that influence a person's life course—from the individual to the individual's family, peers, schools, neighborhoods, community, culture, and society as a whole.

We do not consider all offenders psychologically flawed, and only some are mentally disordered. Many offenders do have substance abuse problems, and these may co-occur with mental disorders. However, offenders as a group are not mentally disordered, although some become so as a result of their incarceration. In addition, emotionally healthy people break the law, and sometimes emotionally healthy people end up on probation or in jails and prisons. Like earlier editions of this text, this edition too views the offender as existing on a continuum, ranging from the occasional offender who offends at some point during the life course, usually during adolescence, to the serious, repetitive offender who usually begins his or her criminal career at a very early age, or the one-time, serious offender.

In recent years, the psychological study of crime has taken a decidedly developmental approach, while retaining its interest in cognitive-based explanations for antisocial behavior. Scholars from various academic disciplines have engaged in pathways-to-crime research, for example. A very common conclusion is that there are multiple pathways to criminal offending; some begin to offend very early while others begin offending in adulthood. In addition, a variety of risk factors enable antisocial behavior, and protective factors insulate the individual from such behavior. The pathways approach does not always focus on psychological factors, but it coexists very well with psychological theories of child and adolescent development. In addition to developmental and cognitive research, much contemporary work is focusing on biopsychology and crime, or the way in which a range of genetic and biological factors may affect one's behavior.

Thus, the book reviews the contemporary research, theory, and practice concerning the psychology of crime as comprehensively and accurately as possible. The basic organization of the text continues to run from the broad, theoretical aspects of crime in the first half of the book to specific offense categories in the second. The early chapters discuss individual and social risk factors, developmental principles, and the psychology of aggression, including its biological basis. We include a complete chapter on psychopathy, because it is arguably one of the most heavily researched topics in the psychology of crime.

NEW TO THIS EDITION

The tenth edition was completed with the help of extensive reviews of the previous edition. The most significant changes reflect recent theoretical developments in criminology as well as the ongoing research on the psychology of crime. Every chapter includes updated citations. We have retained the 16-chapter structure used in the ninth edition. However, some topics have been deleted and others added, as we explain below.

- We have provided more coverage of contemporary antisocial behavior, including bullying, cyberbullying, and cyberstalking. Proposed legislation relating to these social problems is covered, as well as research on the effects of bullying and stalking.

- New sections have been added to almost every chapter. For example, we have expanded on such topics as home invasion, identity theft, synthetic marijuana, callous-unemotional traits, general theory of aggression, the I-cubed theory of aggression, behavior genetics, three-path model of sexual offenders, stereotypical child abductions, cybercrime, and the dynamic cascade model.
- We have added a significant amount of material about Laurence Steinberg's theory of adolescent development, one of the most provocative and heuristic theories in delinquency today.
- We have greatly expanded and reorganized the sections on the five types of profiling, and added sections on sexual assault victimization factors and Internet-facilitated sexual offending.
- The book includes updated examples and illustrations of the crimes and concepts being discussed, but retains illustrations of past events that reflect many of the psychological concepts discussed (e.g., hostage taking, school shootings, sniper events). Over half of the illustrations used refer to recent events, such as the fatal and nonfatal shootings in Tucson, mass killings in Norway, and child abductions.
- Nine boxes have been added to the book. They highlight contemporary concerns such as bias crimes, identity theft, bullying, and child pornography on the Internet.
- Reference to the revised *DSM* (*DSM-5*) is made at various points in the book, particularly in Chapter 8. Because *DSM-5* changes are only proposed at this point, we have retained the *DSM-IV* categories and definitions when relevant. However, readers are reminded to be aware that changes are proposed, including changes to the diagnoses relevant to the material presented.

In addition to the above-mentioned changes in this edition, readers familiar with previous recent editions of the text may want to take note of the following:

- As in the ninth edition, there is less information on the juvenile justice process and the history of juvenile justice, and there is little delinquency material in Chapter 1.
- Also as in the ninth edition, we do not discuss psychologically relevant issues relating to prisons and jails, such as overcrowding, violence, and conditions of confinement. Nevertheless, in light of their importance, we hope professors will find a way to incorporate these topics in their course content.
- Reviewers often ask for fewer statistics. We recognize the limits of statistical data but believe they cannot be ignored. We reduced statistics significantly in the ninth edition; in this edition, we have updated them and shifted some to tables. Students wanting more data should know where to obtain them from the sources provided.
- We removed the section on public order offenses, including prostitution, exhibitionism, voyeurism, and gambling, among others. We have included expanded material on human trafficking and integrated it into the chapter on sexual offending.
- Material on sexual predators now focuses on legislation aimed at preventing sex crimes; it is included in a box in Chapter 12. It is important to emphasize though that sexual predators are often not clinically mentally disordered.

The above represent only a few of the many changes made in this edition.

INSTRUCTOR RESOURCES

- Instructor's Manual
- MyTest
- PowerPoint Lecture Presentation

To access supplementary materials online, instructors need to request an instructor access code. Go to www.pearsonhighered.com/irc, where you can register for an instructor access code. Within forty-eight hours of registering you will receive a confirming e-mail including an instructor access code. Once you have received your code, locate your text in the online catalog and click on the Instructor Resources button on the left side of the catalog product page. Select a supplement and a log in page will appear. Once you have logged in, you can access instructor material for all Prentice Hall textbooks.

Criminal Behavior is designed to be a core text in undergraduate and graduate courses in criminal behavior, criminology, the psychology of crime, crime and delinquency, and forensic psychology. The material contained in this book was classroom-tested for over thirty years. Its emphasis on psychological theory and concepts makes it distinctive from other fine textbooks on crime, which are more sociologically based. The book's major goal is to encourage an appreciation of the many complex issues surrounding criminal behavior by citing relevant, contemporary research. Reviewers sometimes maintain that the text is too complex and should be stripped to its essentials; although we understand their concerns, we have resisted a more simplistic treatment. As one reviewer commented, "There is a lot of material in here, but my students and I adapt." Another wrote, "Better more than too little." Crime is complex, and simple explanations should be avoided. If, after studying the text with an open mind, the reader puts it down seeking additional information, and if the reader has developed an avid interest in discovering better answers, then this text will have served its purpose well.

Once again, we have benefited from the encouragement and help of many individuals. We cherish our main sources of emotional support—Gina and Jim; Ian and Soraya; and Kai, Madeleine, Darya, and Shannon. We are awed by their goodness, their sense of humor, the love they display, and their many accomplishments. On the professional side, we are most grateful to the production staff at Pearson Education/Prentice Hall, particularly Project Manager Jessica Sykes, and Assistant Editor of Criminal Justice Tiffany Bitzel. We appreciate as well the good work of Project Manager Abinaya Rajendran, from Integra-PDY. Finally, we wish to thank the following professors and scholars who reviewed the ninth edition and provided many helpful suggestions for improvement: Mike Butera, Bellevue University; Herb Stock, Naugatuck Valley Community College; Corajean A. Gregory, Mott Community College; Edward C. Keane, Ph.D., Housatonic Community College; Jane Younglove, California State University, Stanislaus; Tomasina L. Cook, Erie Community College; Jennifer Younkin, Old Dominion University; J. Michael Dwyer, Gulf Coast Community College; and Deborah Jean Harding, Ph. D., Amarillo College.

Curt R. Bartol
Anne M. Bartol

Introduction to Criminal Behavior

CHAPTER OBJECTIVES

- Define criminal behavior and juvenile delinquency.
- Stress that such behavior has multiple causes, manifestations, and developmental pathways.
- Introduce various theories that may help explain crime.
- Identify the different perspectives of human nature that underlie the theoretical development and research of criminal behavior.
- Emphasize that the study of criminal behavior and delinquency, from a psychological perspective, has shifted from a personality focus toward a more cognitive and developmental focus.
- Introduce the reader to the various measurements of criminal and delinquent behavior.

Crime intrigues people. Sometimes it attracts us, sometimes it repels us, and occasionally, it does both at once. It can amuse, as when we hear about capers that *presumably* do not harm anyone. However, even those who are cheered on in their attempts to evade the law leave victims in their wake. Colton Harris-Moore, called "the barefoot bandit" because he occasionally left prints of his bare feet at the scenes of his crimes, was arrested in 2010 after a two-year crime spree that included burglaries and vehicle thefts, even crossing international borders. Harris-Moore, who began his illegal activities as a juvenile, was sentenced to six and a half years in federal prison in January 2012. While his crimes were being investigated, "fan clubs" emerged on the Internet, and well-wishers expressed hopes that he would never be caught. His victims lost property, suffered emotional distress, and faced numerous inconveniences that accompany being victims of a crime. Crime harms.

Crime can frighten, particularly if we believe that what happened to one victim might happen to us or those we love. Crime can also anger, as when a beloved community member is brutally killed, a child is subjected to heinous abuse, or individuals have been deprived of their life savings by fraudulent schemes.

What is crime? Legally, it is defined as conduct or failure to act in violation of the law forbidding or commanding it, and for which a range of possible penalties exist upon conviction. Criminal behavior, then, is behavior in violation of the criminal code. To be convicted of crime, a person must have acted intentionally and without justification or excuse. For example, even an intentional killing may be justified under certain circumstances, as in defense of one's life. Although there is a very narrow range of offenses that do not require criminal intent (called strict liability offenses), the vast majority of crime requires it. Obviously, this legal definition encompasses a great variety of acts, ranging from murder to petty offenses.

While interest in crime has always been high, understanding why it occurs and what to do about it has always been a problem. Public officials, politicians, "experts," and many people in the general public continue to offer simple and incomplete solutions for obliterating crime: more police officers on the streets, video cameras and state-of-the-art surveillance equipment, street lights, sturdy locks, self-defense classes, stiff penalties, speedy imprisonment, or capital punishment. Some of these approaches may be effective in the short term, but the overall problem of crime persists. As in most areas of human behavior, there is no shortage of experts and opinions, but there are few all-encompassing and effective solutions.

Our inability to prevent crime is partly because we have trouble understanding criminal behavior and identifying its many causes. Because crime is complex, explanations of crime require complicated, involved answers. Psychological research indicates that most people have limited tolerance for complexity and ambiguity. People apparently want simple, straightforward answers, no matter how complex the issue. Parents become impatient when psychologists answer questions about child rearing by saying, "It depends"—on the situation, on the parents' reactions to it, on any number of possible influences. This preference for simplicity helps to explain the popularity of do-it-yourself, 100-easy-ways-to-a-better-life books. Today, the preference for simplicity is aided by the vast array of information available on the Internet. Search engines provide instant access to a multitude of both reputable and questionable sources. The discerning student is well served by this information explosion; he or she can find up-to-date research on virtually all topics covered in this book, for example. However, many people acquire information—but not necessarily knowledge—by clicking links, entering chat rooms, reading blogs, and following friends and "friends" who may or may not be providing legitimate data. Thus, the selective and careful use of information technology is a critical skill for all students to acquire.

This text presents criminal behavior as a vastly complex, sometimes difficult-to-understand phenomenon. Readers looking for simple solutions will have to reorient their thinking, set the text aside, or read it in dismay. There is no all-encompassing psychological explanation for crime, any more than there is a sociological, anthropological, psychiatric, economic, or historic one. In fact, it is unlikely that sociology, psychology, or any other discipline can formulate basic "truths" about crime without help from other disciplines and well-designed research. Criminology needs all the interdisciplinary help it can get to explain and control criminal behavior. An integration of the data, theories, and general viewpoints of each discipline is crucial. To review accurately and adequately the plethora of studies and theories from each relevant discipline is far beyond the scope of this text, however. Our focus is the *psychological perspective,* although other viewpoints are also described.

Our primary goal is to review and integrate recent scholarship and research in the psychology of crime, compare it with traditional approaches, and discuss strategies that have been offered to prevent and modify criminal behavior. We cannot begin to accomplish this task without first calling attention to philosophical questions that underlie any study of human behavior, including criminal behavior.

THEORIES OF CRIME

In everyday conversation, the term *theory* is used loosely. It may refer to personal experiences, observations, traditional beliefs, a set of opinions, or a collection of abstract thoughts. Almost everyone has personal theories about human behavior, and these extend to criminal behavior. To illustrate, some people have a personal theory that the world is a just place, where one gets what one deserves. "Just-worlders" believe that things just do not happen to people without a reason that is closely related to their own actions; for example, individuals who experience financial difficulties probably brought these on themselves. In 2008–2009, when many homeowners in the United States were facing foreclosure because they could not afford high mortgage payments, a just-worlder would be likely to say this was more their own fault than the fault of bank officers who enticed them into paying high interest rates. Just-worlders also believe good people are ultimately rewarded and bad people are ultimately punished. If you work hard and honestly, good things will happen to you. Laziness and dishonesty, on the other hand, will lead to limited success and potential poverty. In reference to crime, just-worlders may believe that burglary victims did not protect their property sufficiently or that battered spouses must have provoked their beatings, especially if there is no other available reason for explaining such behaviors.

The above beliefs represent individual theories or assumptions about how the world works. However, psychologists have also developed a somewhat more elaborate scientific theory based on just-world ideas and developed a scale to measure one's just-world orientation (Lerner, 1980; Lerner & Miller, 1978). A variety of hypotheses—sometimes discussed under the umbrella term **just-world hypothesis**—have been proposed and tested. For example, just-worlders have been hypothesized and shown to favor capital punishment and to hold politically conservative views. Interestingly, the most recent research on just-world theory has also identified two tracks: belief in a general just-world—described above—and belief in a personal just-world (Dalbert, 1999; Sutton & Douglas, 2005). Belief in a personal just-world ("I usually get what I deserve") is considered adaptive and helpful in coping with dire circumstances in one's life. For example, Dalbert and Filke (2007) found that prisoners with a high personal just-world orientation evaluated their prison experiences more positively and reported better overall well-being than those without such an orientation.

Scientific theories like the above are based on logic and research, but they vary widely in complexity. A scientific theory is "a set of interrelated constructs (concepts), definitions, and propositions that present a systematic view of phenomena by specifying relations among variables, with the purpose of explaining and predicting the phenomena" (Kerlinger, 1973, p. 9). A scientific theory of crime, therefore, should provide a general explanation that encompasses and *systematically* connects many different social, economic, and psychological variables to criminal behavior, and it should be supported by well-executed research. Moreover, the terms in any scientific theory must be as precise as possible, their meaning and usage clear and unambiguous, so that it can be meaningfully tested by observation and analysis. The process of theory testing is called **theory verification**. If the theory is not verified—indeed, if any of its propositions is not verified—the end result is falsification (Popper, 1968). For example, a theory that includes the proposition that all sex offenders were sexually abused as children would be falsified as soon as one nonabused sex offender was encountered.

The primary purpose of theories of crime is to identify the causes or precursors of criminal behavior. Some theories are broad and encompassing, whereas others are narrow and specific. Basically, theories of criminal behavior are summary statements of a collection of research findings. Perhaps more importantly, they provide direction for further research. If one component of a theory is falsified or not supported, the theory is not necessarily rejected outright, however. It can be modified and retested. In addition, each theory of crime has implications for policy or decisions made by society to prevent crime.

Theories of crime have been around for centuries. During the eighteenth century, the Italian philosopher Cesare Beccaria (1738–1794) developed a theory that human behavior is fundamentally driven by a choice made by weighing the amount of pleasure gained against the amount of pain or punishment expected. Beccaria argued that in order to reduce or stop criminal offending in any given society, the punishment should be swift, certain, and severe enough to deter people from the criminal (pleasure-seeking) act. If people realized in advance that severe punishment would be forthcoming, and coming soon, regardless of their social status or privileges, they would choose not to engage in illegal behavior. This theoretical thinking, which emphasizes free will as the hallmark of human behavior, has become known as **classical theory**. Both criminal and civil law are rooted in the theory that individuals are masters of their fate, the possessors of free will and freedom of choice. As one federal appellate court put it, "our jurisprudence...while not oblivious to deterministic components, ultimately rests on a premise of freedom of will" (*U.S. v. Brawner*, 1972, p. 995). It should be noted that many crime-prevention approaches are consistent with classical theory, or in its modern form, **deterrence theory** (Nagin, 2007). For example, surveillance cameras on the streets and harsh sentences assume that individuals choose to commit crime but may be persuaded not to under the threat of being discovered or being punished with long prison time.

Another thread of theoretical thought is called **positivist theory**, which is closely aligned with the idea of determinism. It is the theory that antecedents—prior experiences or influences—determine present behavior. According to this line of theoretical thinking, human behavior is governed by causal laws, and free will is undermined. In its extreme form, determinism asserts that all behavior is determined by antecedent events and that all human behavior, therefore, is fundamentally lawful. "Lawful" in this context refers to predictability and not the laws established by society. Many contemporary theories of criminology are positivist because they search for causes beyond free will.

In summary, the classical view of crime and delinquency holds that the decision to violate the law is largely a result of free will. The positivist or deterministic perspective argues that most criminal behavior is a result of social, psychological, and even biological influences. It does not deny the importance of free will, and it does not maintain that individuals should not be held responsible for their actions. However, it maintains that these actions can be explained by more than "free will." This latter perspective, then, seeks to identify causes, predict and prevent criminal behavior, and rehabilitate (or habilitate) offenders.

Theoretical Perspectives on Human Nature

All theories of crime have underlying assumptions about or perspectives on human nature. Three major ones can be identified. The **conformity perspective** views humans as creatures of conformity who want to do the "right" thing. To a large extent, this assumption represents the foundation of the humanistic perspectives in psychology. Human beings are basically "good" people trying to live to their fullest potential.

An excellent example of the conformity perspective in criminology is **strain theory**, which originated in the work of Robert K. Merton (1957) and continues today in the theory of Robert Agnew (1992, 2006) and his followers. Merton's original strain theory argued that humans are fundamentally conforming beings who are strongly influenced by the values and attitudes of the society in which they live. In short, most members of a given society desire what the other members of the society desire. In many societies and cultures, the accumulation of wealth or status is all important, representing symbols that all members should strive for. Unfortunately, access to these goals is not equally available. While some have the education, social network, personal contacts, and family influence to attain them, others are deprived of the opportunity. Thus, Merton's strain theory predicted that crime and delinquency would occur when there is a perceived discrepancy between the materialistic values and goals cherished and held in high esteem by a society and the availability of the legitimate means for reaching these goals. Under these conditions, a strain between the goals of wealth and power and the means for reaching them develops. Groups and individuals experiencing a high level of this strain are forced to decide whether to violate norms and laws to attain some of this sought-after wealth or power, or give up on their dream and go through the motions, withdraw, or rebel. Note that, although the original strain theory was formulated on American society, it can be applied on a global basis.

In more recent years, strain theorists have emphasized that crimes of the rich and powerful also can be explained by strain theory. Even though these individuals have greater access to the legitimate means of reaching goals, they have a continuing need to accumulate even greater wealth and power and maintain their privileged status in society (Messner & Rosenfeld, 1994).

In developing his General Strain Theory (1992), Agnew used the word *strain* in a slightly different way, seeing strains as events and conditions that are disliked by individuals. The inability to achieve one's goals was only one such condition; others were losing something of value, or being treated negatively by others (2006). General Strain Theory, which has attracted much research and commentary, is continually being tested and evaluated; the point we make here is that it remains under the umbrella of a strain theory, representative of the conformity perspective on human nature.

A second perspective—the **nonconformist perspective**—assumes that human beings are basically undisciplined creatures who, without the constraints of the rules and regulations of a given society, would flout society's conventions and commit crime indiscriminately. This perspective sees humans as fundamentally "unruly" and deviant, needing to be held in check. For example, the biological and neurobiological theories discussed in Chapter 3 identify genetic or other biological features or deficiencies in some individuals that predispose them to antisocial behavior like aggressive actions. Another good illustration of the nonconformist perspective is Travis Hirschi's (1969) social control theory, which is discussed in several chapters. **Social control theory** contends that crime and delinquency occur when an individual's ties to the conventional order or normative standards are weak or largely nonexistent. In other words, the socialization that usually holds one's basic human nature in check is incomplete or faulty. This position perceives human nature as fundamentally "bad," "antisocial," or at least "imperfect." These innate tendencies must be *controlled* by society. Years after developing social control theory, Hirschi teamed with Michael Gottfredson to develop a **General Theory of Crime** (GTC; Gottfredson & Hirschi, 1990). This theory, one of the most prominent in criminology today, suggests that a deficit of self-control or self-regulation is the key factor in explaining crime and delinquency.

The third perspective—the **learning perspective**—sees human beings as born neutral (neither inherently conforming nor unruly). This perspective argues that humans learn virtually all their behavior, beliefs, and tendencies from the social environment. The learning perspective is exemplified most comprehensively by **social learning theory**, to be a main topic in Chapter 4, and Edwin H. Sutherland's (1947) **differential association theory**. Social learning theory emphasizes such concepts as imitation of models and reinforcements one gains from one's behavior. According to differential association theory, criminal behavior is learned, as is all social behavior, through social interactions with other people. It is not the result of emotional disturbance, mental illness, or innate qualities of "goodness" or "badness." Rather, people learn to be criminal as a result of messages they get from others who were also taught to be criminal. Consequently, an excess of "messages" favorable to law violation over unfavorable messages promotes criminal activity. The conventional wisdom that bad company promotes bad behavior, therefore, finds validity in differential association theory. **Table 1-1** summarizes these three perspectives and provides examples of each.

From the mid-twentieth century to the present, many criminologists have embraced a developmental approach, viewing crime and other antisocial activity as behavior that begins in early childhood and proceeds to and sometimes through one's adult years. Developmental criminology cannot be placed firmly in any of the above three categories, although it would seem to be most at home in the learning perspective. Nevertheless, aspects of each perspective can be detected in the research and writing of developmental criminologists (e.g., Le Blanc & Loeber, 1998; Moffitt, 1993a, b; Patterson, 1982). We discuss these theories in some detail in Chapter 6.

Another way of looking at human nature is the **difference-in-degree** and the **difference-in-kind** perspective. The difference-in-degree perspective holds that human beings may be placed along a continuum consisting of all the animals in the known universe. According to this perspective, humans are intimately tied to their animal ancestry in important and significant ways. For example, this perspective might argue that human aggression and violence is a result of innate, biological needs to obtain sufficient food supplies, territory, status, or mates. In many ways, this approach is similar to the nonconformist point of view. In recent years, some criminologists have emphasized the importance of biological influences on behavior, not as exclusive determinants of behavior but rather as factors that should be taken into consideration (DeLisi, 2009).

TABLE 1-1 Perspectives of Human Nature		
Perspectives of Behavior	**Theory Example**	**Humans Are...**
Conformity perspective	Strain Theory (Merton) General Strain Theory (Agnew)	Basically good; strongly influenced by the values and attitudes of society
Nonconformist perspective	Social Control Theory (Hirschi) Biological Theories of Crime General Theory of Crime	Basically undisciplined; individual's ties to social order are weak; innate tendencies must be controlled by society; individual lack of self-control
Learning perspective	Differential Association Theory (Sutherland) Social Learning Theory (Rotter, Bandura) Developmental Criminology	Born neutral; behavior is learned through social inter actions with other people; changes over the life span affect behavior

The rapidly developing field of evolutionary psychology generally subscribes to this approach as well. Evolutionary psychology claims that human cognitive and emotional processes have been selected in our evolutionary environment as devices for solving particular adaptive problems faced by the Pleistocene hunter-gatherers (Bereczkei, 2000; Buss & Shackelford, 1997). Evolutionary psychologists stress that Darwinian theory provides ultimate explanations of many types of antisocial behavior (Quinsey, Skilling, Lalumière, & Craig, 2004).

The difference-in-kind perspective, on the other hand, argues that humans are distinctly different from other animals—spiritually, psychologically, and mentally. Noteworthy neurobiologists and pioneer brain researchers, such as Sir John Eccles (Eccles & Robinson, 1984), Roger Sperry (1983), and Wilder Penfield (1975), have concluded that humans differ radically in kind from all other animals. According to the difference-in-kind viewpoint, we will understand crime better if we study and build theories based on those human qualities that differ significantly from subhuman features. Consequently, this perspective sees antisocial or criminal behavior as a unique human attribute generated primarily by human cognitive processes. A resurgence of interest in such concepts as religiosity, compassion, and empathy as they relate to criminality illustrates this perspective.

DISCIPLINARY PERSPECTIVES IN CRIMINOLOGY

Criminology is the multidisciplinary study of crime. Many disciplines are involved in the collection of knowledge about criminal action, including psychology, sociology, psychiatry, anthropology, biology, neurology, political science, and economics. Over the years, the study of crime has been dominated by three disciplines—sociology, psychology, and psychiatry—but other disciplines or subdisciplines, such as economics and the biological sciences, are becoming more actively involved.

Although our main concern in this text is with *psychological principles,* concepts, theory, and research relevant to criminal behavior, considerable attention is placed on the research knowledge of the other disciplines, particularly sociology, psychiatry, and biology. Again, criminology needs all the help it can get in its struggle to understand, explain, prevent, and change criminal behavior.

It is not easy to make sharp demarcations between disciplines, because they often overlap in focus and practice. For example, what distinguishes a given theory as sociological, psychological, or psychiatric is sometimes simply the stated professional affiliation of its proponent. The reader should also realize that condensing any major discipline into a few pages hardly does it justice. To obtain a more adequate overview, the interested reader should consult texts and articles within those disciplines. **Table 1-2** summarizes these disciplinary perspectives.

Sociological Criminology

Sociological criminology has a rich tradition in examining the relationships of demographic and group variables to crime. Variables such as age, race, gender, socioeconomic status, and ethnic-cultural affiliation have been shown to have significant relationships with certain categories and patterns of crimes. Sociological criminology, for example, has allowed us to conclude that young African American males from disadvantaged backgrounds are disproportionately overrepresented as both perpetrators and victims of homicide. Juveniles as a group are overrepresented in nonviolent property offenses. White males are overrepresented in political and corporate crimes. The many reasons for this are reflected in the various perspectives and research findings that are

TABLE 1-2 Major Perspectives in Criminology

Perspective	Influence	Focus
Sociological criminology	Sociology	Examines relationships of demographic and group variables to crime; focuses on groups and society as a whole and how they influence criminal activity
Psychological criminology	Psychology	Focuses on individual criminal behavior; the science of the behavior and mental processes of the criminal
Psychiatric criminology	Psychiatry	The contemporary perspective examines the interplay between psychobiological determinants of behavior and the social environment; traditional perspective looks for the unconscious and biological determinants of criminal behavior

covered in the book. Sociological criminology also probes the situational or environmental factors that are most conducive to criminal action, such as the time, place, kind of weapons used, and the circumstances surrounding the crime.

A major contribution of sociological criminology, however, is the attention it directs to topics that reflect unequal distribution of power in society. This often takes the form of examining how crime is defined and how laws are enforced. It also addresses the underlying social conditions that may encourage criminal behavior, such as inequities in educational and employment opportunities. Conflict theories in sociology are particularly influential in questioning how crime is defined, who is subject to punishment, and in attempting to draw attention to the crimes of the rich and powerful.

Psychological Criminology

Psychology is the science of behavior and mental processes. **Psychological criminology**, then, is the science of the behavior and mental processes of the person who commits crime. While sociological criminology focuses primarily on groups and society as a whole, and how they influence criminal activity, psychological criminology focuses on individual criminal behavior—how it is acquired, evoked, maintained, and modified.

In the psychology of crime, both social and personality influences on criminal behavior are considered, along with the mental processes that mediate that behavior. Personality refers to all the biological influences, psychological traits, and cognitive features of the human being that psychologists have identified as important in the mediation and control of behavior. Recently, psychological criminology has shifted its focus to a more *cognitive, neuropsychological,* and *developmental* approach to the study of criminal behavior, although interest in personality differences among offenders continues. **Cognitions** refer to the attitudes, beliefs, values, and thoughts that a person holds about the social environment, interrelations, human nature, and himself or herself. In serious criminal offenders, these cognitions are often distorted. Beliefs that children must be severely physically disciplined or that victims are not really hurt by burglary are good examples of cognitions that may lead to criminal activity. Prejudice is also a cognition that involves distortions of social reality. They include erroneous generalizations and oversimplification about others. Hate or bias crimes—highlighted in **Box 1-1**—are generally rooted in prejudice and cognitive distortions held by perpetrators. Serial rapists also distort social reality to the point where they may assault

BOX 1-1
Hate or Bias Crimes

Crimes committed against individuals out of bias, hatred, or racial and ethnic prejudice are nothing new; they are well documented in the history of virtually every nation. What is relatively new in the United States is the effort to keep track of such crimes and impose harsh penalties on those who commit them.

Toward the end of the twentieth century, the U.S. Congress and many states began to address the crucial problem of crimes—especially violent crimes—committed out of hatred, prejudice, or bias against someone because of their race, religion, sexual orientation, or ethnicity. Eventually, characteristics such as gender, physical or mental disability, advanced age, or military status were added to the list of protected categories. Laws were passed requiring the gathering of statistics on these offenses and/or allowing enhanced sentences for someone convicted of a hate or bias crime. The first such federal law, the **Hate Crime Statistics Act** of 1990, required the collection of data on violent attacks, intimidation, arson, or property damage that are directed at people because of their race, religion, sexual orientation, or ethnicity. The law was amended in 1994 to include crimes motivated by bias against persons with disabilities, and in late 2009 to include crimes of prejudice based on gender or gender identity (Langton & Planty, 2011). The National Crime Victimization Survey (NCVS) also asks respondents whether they have been victims of hate crimes.

A victim of a hate crime may be a person, a business, or an institution, but hate crimes against individuals receive the most attention. These crimes often have long-term psychological and social repercussions that are extremely destructive to victims and their families. During the 1990s, race-related and sexual identity–related crimes were the most likely to be publicized.

Two horrendous instances were the Texas killings of James Byrd Jr. and Matthew Shepard. Byrd, a 49-year-old African American man, was walking home from a family party when he was offered a ride by three white men, all of them known white supremacists. The men—Lawrence Russell Brewer, John William King, and Shawn Berry—drove Byrd to a remote dirt road where they severely beat him. Then Byrd was chained to their pickup truck by the ankles and dragged along the road, which tore his body to pieces. Brewer and King have since been executed; Berry was spared the death penalty but given a life sentence. Shepard, a young gay university student in Wyoming, was kidnapped, beaten, tied to a fencepost, and left to die. He was found, hospitalized in a comatose state, and died shortly thereafter. The two men responsible for his death, Aaron McKinney and Russell Henderson, are serving terms of life imprisonment without parole.

Since the attacks of September 11, 2001, people of Arab or Muslim descent, or anyone with a "Middle Eastern look" (Rabrenovic, 2007), have increasingly been victims of hate crimes (Hendricks, Ortiz, Sugie, & Miller, 2007). In the most recent UCR statistics, 47.3 percent of bias-motivated crimes had a racial bias, 19.3 percent were motivated by sexual orientation bias, and 12.8 percent by bias against ethnicity or national origin. The remainder was motivated by religious bias (20%) or disability (0.6%) (see **Figure 1-2** at page 21.).

Relatedly, the Southern Poverty Law Center (SPLC) recently reported significant increases in hate groups in the United States. Hate groups are those whose beliefs or practices attack or malign an entire class of people, such as immigrants or members of a given race, ethnicity, or sexual orientation. The activities of hate groups are not necessarily criminal; in fact, they are more likely to involve rallies, marches, meetings, and distributing leaflets rather than perpetrating violence. Nevertheless, their message is disturbing, and individual members of those groups have engaged in serious crimes. The gunman who opened fire in a Sikh Temple in Wisconsin in August 2012, killing six people and wounding others, was associated with a neo-Nazi skinhead group. The SPLC identified 602 hate groups in the year 2000; by 2011, the number had increased to 1,018 (www.splcenter.org).

In a recent publication on hate crime victimizations from 2003 to 2009, derived from both NCVS and UCR data, Langton and Planty (2011) report the following:

- More than 4 in 5 hate crime victimizations involved violence; about 23 percent were serious violent crimes.
- In about 37 percent of violent hate crimes the offender knew the victim; in violent nonhate crimes, half of all victims knew the offender.

(continued)

- Eight hate crime homicides occurred in 2009.
- In nearly 90 percent of hate crime victimizations occurring between 2003 and 2009, the victim suspected the offender was motivated by racial or ethnic prejudice or both.
- Fewer than 1 in 10 hate crime victims stated that the offender left hate symbols at the crime scene; however, nearly all hate crime victims said that the offender used hate language.
- Police were notified of fewer than half (45%) of all hate crime victimizations.

- Generally, victims targeted because of a disability were least likely to report the hate crime to people.
- In 2009, according to UCR data, 85.9 percent of the law enforcement agencies participating in the Hate Crime Statistics Program reported that no hate crimes occurred in their jurisdiction.

The last bullet point should lead readers to be very cautious in accepting uncritically official reports of crime. Psychological concepts that might help us to understand why individuals would perpetrate these offenses are discussed in Chapter 4.

only victims who they perceive "deserve it." Some sex offenders even persuade themselves that they are not harming their victims, and white-collar offenders sometimes justify their crimes as what they have to do in order to stay in business. The importance of offender cognitions in understanding criminal behavior will be stressed throughout the book.

The neuropsychology of criminal behavior is a specialty that combines the scientific study of the nervous system with psychology and crime. This perspective studies to what extent damage, deficits, or abnormality of the brain may be related to antisocial behavior, particularly violent behavior. We will find in various sections of the book that compromised neuropsychological functioning may be associated with aggression and violent behavior. For example, a traumatic brain injury (TBI), such as one that might occur in a traffic accident, may produce personality changes, including increased aggressive behavior (Gurley & Marcus, 2008). In addition, we will learn that practices designed to improve neuropsychological functioning and prevent neuropsychological impairment early in life are likely to be major steps in understanding and reducing antisocial behavior.

Another area that is extremely important in understanding criminal behavior is learning how it develops. A **developmental approach** examines the changes and influences across a person's lifetime that may contribute to the formation of antisocial and criminal behavior. These are usually called "risk factors." Examples are poor nutrition, the loss of a parent, early school failure, or substandard housing. However, the developmental approach also searches for "protective factors," or influences that provide individuals with a buffer against the risk factors. A caring adult mentor and good social skills are examples of protective factors. If we are able to identify those changes and influences that occur across the developmental pathways of life that divert a person from becoming caring, sensitive, and prosocial, as well as those that steer a person away from a life of persistent and serious antisocial behavior, we gain invaluable information about how to prevent and change delinquent and criminal behavior. Consequently, psychological criminology develops, examines, and evaluates strategies and interventions that have the potential to prevent or reduce criminal behavior.

In the past, psychologists assumed that they could best understand human behavior by searching for stable, consistent personality **dispositions or traits** that exerted widely generalized effects on behavior. A trait or disposition is a relatively stable and enduring tendency to behave in a particular way, and it distinguishes one person from another. For example, one person may be extroverted and have a consistent tendency to socialize and meet others, while another may be shy and introverted and demonstrate a tendency to socialize with only very close friends. In recent years, researchers (e.g., Frick & White, 2008) have given considerable attention to some traits—collectively termed callous-unemotional traits—that are often associated with psychopathy. Callous-unemotional traits are characterized by a lack of empathy and concern for the welfare of others, and they often lead to a persistent and aggressive pattern of antisocial behavior. These traits will be discussed in more detail in later chapters. Trait theories hold that people show consistent behavior across time and place, and that these behaviors characterize personality. Many psychologists studying crime, therefore, assumed they should search for the personality traits or variables underlying criminal behavior. They paid less attention to the person's environment or situation. Presumably, once personality variables were identified, it would be possible to determine and predict which individual was most likely to engage in criminal behavior.

As you will learn, however, the search for any *single* personality type of the murderer, rapist, abuser, or burglar has not been fruitful. Contemporary perspectives in the psychology of crime still include personality or behavior traits in their explanations of crime, as we will see in our discussion of callous-unemotional traits, but they also include cognitions, neuropsychology, and developmental factors in these explanations. Thus, while trait psychology standing alone has lost favor, some aspects of this approach have survived, often in **criminal or offender profiling**, an enterprise that attracts much attention today in the entertainment media as well as coverage of sensational crimes. It is the process of identifying personality traits, behavioral tendencies, geographic location, and demographic variables of an offender based on characteristics of the crime (Bartol & Bartol, 2008, 2013). The "profiler" offers *statistical probability* about some *demographic and behavioral patterns* of certain offenders, and predictions concerning the possibility of the individual offending again. For example, the profiler may suggest that a rapist is *probably* young, white, unemployed, from the area, and so forth. He or she may also offer possible motives for the attack, based on research findings and accompanied by the necessary warnings that this particular offender may not fit those criteria.

To a very large extent, the profiling process is dictated by a database collected on previous offenders who have committed similar offenses. Basically, profiling is a form of behavioral assessment and prediction. It is important to emphasize that criminal profiling is not restricted to serial murder or serial sexual assaults, but has considerable value when applied successfully to other crimes, including arson, burglary, shoplifting, and robbery. Various forms of profiling are covered in more detail in Chapter 10.

Psychiatric Criminology

The terms *psychology* and *psychiatry* are often confused by the layperson and even by professionals and scholars in other disciplines. Many psychiatrists, like psychologists, work in a variety of settings that bring them into contact with persons accused of or convicted of crime. They assess defendants, provide expert testimony in court, and offer treatment in the community or in correctional facilities. Psychiatrists and psychologists who are closely associated with the courts and other legal arenas are often referred to as forensic psychiatrists or forensic psychologists.

Psychiatric concepts and theories are often believed to be accepted tenets in the field of psychology. However, the two professions often see things quite differently and approach explanations of criminal behavior along a different course. Part of this difference is due to the dissimilarity in the educational requirements for the two professions. Unlike psychologists, who have earned a PhD (doctor of philosophy), PsyD (doctorate in psychology), or, in some cases, an EdD (doctorate in education), and who often complete specialized training in research and some area of psychology, psychiatrists first earn a medical degree (MD or a DO [doctor of osteopathy]) and complete a medical internship, as other physicians do. Then, during an average four-year residency program in psychiatry, they receive specific training in psychiatry, often focusing on the diagnosis and treatment of individuals in forensic settings, such as court clinics or mental hospitals with special units for mentally disordered individuals accused of crime. Understandably, this medical training encourages a biochemical and neurological approach to explanations of human behavior, and this is often reflected in the psychiatric theories of criminal behavior.

By contrast, many psychologists receive a one-year internship focusing on clinical training, which is often followed by a one- to three-year postdoctoral program focusing on both research and practice. In a majority of cases, the psychologist completes these training steps before practicing professionally. The emphasis of this training is usually far more on the cognitive (thought processes), developmental, and learned behavior of human action and less on the biochemical or neurological influences. Nevertheless, some psychologists do pursue training that is more biologically focused.

Traditionally, psychologists have not been permitted by law to prescribe medication to patients. However, this distinction between the two professions is beginning to disappear. In 2002, New Mexico became the first state in the United States to allow psychologists with specified training to prescribe psychoactive drugs (drugs designed to treat psychological problems). Louisiana became the second state, in 2004; those qualified to prescribe are called "medical psychologists." Psychologists in the military also have prescription privileges. Twelve states have rejected such privileges, however, and at this point there appears to be a lull in additional efforts to gain the privileges. The powerful medical establishment has often fought these prescription privileges, saying they would lead to abuse and would decrease the quality of patient care. Even psychologists themselves disagree on this issue. Surveys suggest that most psychologists are in favor of extending privileges to those who want them and are suitably trained (Baird, 2007). Nevertheless, some worry that this could lead to a heavier reliance on medication for the treatment of mental disorder than is warranted.

Psychoanalytic Tradition

American psychiatric criminology has *traditionally* followed the Freudian, psychoanalytic, or psychodynamic tradition. The father of the psychoanalytical theory of human behavior was the physician-neurologist Sigmund Freud (1856–1939), whose followers are called Freudians. Many contemporary psychoanalysts subscribe to a modified version of the orthodox Freudian position and are therefore called neo-Freudians. Still other psychoanalysts follow the tenets of Alfred Adler and Carl Jung, who broke away from Freud and developed different theories about the human condition. A very influential psychoanalyst in recent times is Erik Erikson, who developed a theory of development that included eight stages. According to Erikson, ego identity is gradually achieved by facing positive goals and negative risks during eight stages across the life span. The degree of achievement in ego identity—or the progress one has made in reaching the various stages—may influence the tendency to commit crime, a topic we will return to later in the book.

Collectively, all psychoanalytic positions form the psychodynamic approach, which explains behavior in terms of motives and drives. This perspective views human nature as innately antisocial, similar to the nonconformist perspective and the difference-in-degree orientation discussed earlier. That is, humans are biologically driven to get what they want when they want it unless they are held in check by internal (conscience) and external (society) forces. Without an organized society with rules and laws, humans (especially men because of their biology) would aggress, plunder, steal, and even kill at will.

The psychoanalytic position assumes that we must delve into the abysses of human personality to find unconscious determinants of human behavior, including criminal behavior. Consider the following comments by two psychiatrists influenced by the psychoanalytic tradition: "The criminal rarely knows completely the reasons for his conduct" (Abrahamsen, 1952, p. 21). "Every criminal is such by reason of unconscious forces within him" (Roche, 1958, p. 25). Psychoanalytic and psychodynamic theories acknowledge that behavior varies across situations. However, they conclude that there are enduring and generalized underlying dynamic or motivational dispositions that account for this diversity. "Surface" behaviors indirectly signal or symbolize dynamic, underlying attributes. Psychological defenses distort and disguise the "true" meaning of external or observed behaviors. The trained clinician, therefore, must interpret the significance of these external behaviors, since the actor is not aware of their purpose.

The Freudian, psychoanalytic, and psychodynamic positions strongly endorse the view that the prime determinant of human behavior lies within the person, and that after the first few years of life, the environment plays a very minor role. Consequently, criminal behavior is believed to spring from within, primarily dictated by the biological urges of the unconscious. The environment, culture, or society cannot be held responsible for crime rates; biopsychological needs and urges within the individual are the culprits.

It would be unfair, however, to simply classify *contemporary* psychiatric criminology as heavily Freudian, psychoanalytical, or psychodynamic in perspective. Contemporary **psychiatric criminology** is far more diverse, increasingly research based, and is considerably less steeped in a belief that criminals are acting out their uncontrolled animalistic, unconscious, or biological urges. Therefore, *traditional* psychiatric criminology is distinguished from *contemporary* psychiatric criminology throughout the text. The traditional psychiatric view represents the biologically unconscious urges that drive humans, whereas the contemporary psychiatric view of crime represents the diverse and rich knowledge gained through research and clinical experience. Whenever possible, we rely on the more contemporary view when discussing psychiatric criminology in this text.

DEFINING AND MEASURING CRIME

As defined at the beginning of the chapter, *crime is intentional behavior that violates a criminal code, intentional in that it did not occur accidentally or without justification or excuse.* Since crime encompasses so many types of behavior, should we restrict ourselves to a legal definition and study only those individuals who have been convicted of behaviors legally defined as crime? Or should we include individuals who indulge in antisocial behaviors but have not been detected by the criminal justice system? Perhaps our study should include persons predisposed to be criminal, if such persons can be identified. As a review of criminology textbooks and literature attests, there is no universal agreement as to what group or groups should be targeted for study.

If we abide strictly by the legal definition of crime and base research and discussion only on those people who have committed crimes, do we consider only those who have been convicted and incarcerated or serving a sentence in the community, or do we include those who have "probably" broken the criminal law but have not been convicted? Even by conservative estimates, 16 percent to 18 percent of the total U.S. population has arrest records for nontraffic offenses (U.S. Department of Justice, 1988). While some of these individuals are "truly criminal," an undetermined number of others were arrested but were not truly guilty. And, as is becoming more apparent in recent years, the innocent are sometimes convicted and sent to prison. A national database of wrongful convictions assembled by law school faculty and students at the University of Michigan and Northwestern University indicates that 873 individuals were wrongfully convicted of serious crimes since 1989. Researchers are aware of almost 1,200 other cases of exonerations for which less data are available. Thus, over 2,000 offenders have been exonerated, often on the basis of DNA evidence (Associated Press, 2012). Finally, how can we include individuals who violate the law but escape detection or those who come to the attention of law enforcement officials but are never arrested?

In sum, trying to study crime and criminal behavior presents many problems for social scientists. The subjects of study are most typically captive, such as prisoners or delinquents in institutions. They are not necessarily representative of the true criminal population. With respect to obtaining data on the incidence, prevalence, and characteristics of crime, there are many pitfalls. Crime is usually measured in one of three ways, and none is perfect:

1. Official police reports of reported crime and arrests, such as those tabulated and forwarded to the Federal Bureau of Investigation for publication in its annual national statistical report on crime, the **Uniform Crime Reports (UCR)** and its accompanying **National Incidence Based Reporting System (NIBRS)**.
2. Self-report studies, whereby members of a sample population are asked what offenses they have committed and how often.
3. National or regional victimization studies, which sample a population of households or businesses asking respondents how often they have been victims of specified crimes.

Uniform Crime Reporting System

The Federal Bureau of Investigation's (FBI) **Uniform Crime Reports (UCR)** compiled since 1930, is the most-cited source of U.S. crime statistics. The UCR Program publishes an annual document containing accounts of crimes known to police and information on arrests received on a voluntary basis from local and state law enforcement agencies throughout the United States. The UCR data are available on the FBI website (www.fbi.gov), from which one should search for "Crime in the United States" followed by the relevant year. Interestingly, federal law enforcement agencies do not report through the traditional UCR Program, but they do through the NIBRS, to be described below.

The first UCR data were published with fewer than a thousand agencies reporting. More recent data include statistics from over 17,000 agencies, representing about 95 percent of the U.S. population (Federal Bureau of Investigation, 2011a (preliminary report)). The UCR Program is the only major data source permitting a comparison of national data broken down by age, sex, race, and offense. A *Supplementary Homicide Report* contains data on victim and offender demographics, the offender–victim relationship, the weapon used, and the circumstances surrounding the homicide. Additionally, the FBI provides special reports, such as those on hate crimes, campus crimes, and law enforcement officers killed in the line of duty. A special report was also prepared to cover the events of September 11, 2001.

The UCR provides a variety of information relating to crimes that come to the attention of police, and the city and region where the crime was committed. Arrest data include the age, gender, and race of persons arrested. Prior to 2004, the UCR labeled serious crimes as index crimes, or **Part I crimes**, and nonserious crimes as nonindex crimes, or **Part II crimes**. Index crimes were considered to be "indicators" of the crime problem in the United States. However, this distinction was found to be misleading. For instance, larceny-theft, which includes shoplifting, was categorized as an index crime, whereas fraud and drug offenses were classified as nonindex crimes. Moreover, larceny-theft makes up 60 percent of the total reported crime, and the enormous volume of these offenses overshadows more serious but less frequently committed offenses (Federal Bureau of Investigation, 2008). Consequently, since 2004, the term *index crime* has disappeared, but the Part I and Part II designations have remained (see **Table 1-3** for definitions of these crimes). Part I crimes are subdivided into violent and property offenses.

TABLE 1-3 Definitions of Part I and Part II Crimes in Uniform Crime Reports	
Part I Crime	
Murder and nonnegligent manslaughter	The willful (nonnegligent) killing of one human by another
Rape	The carnal knowledge of a female against her will. Attempts or assaults with intent to rape are included, but statutory rape is not included. (These are included in *arrest* statistics under sexual offenses, however.) Beginning in 2012, the definition will change, and the UCR will collect data on rape involving male victims.
Robbery	The taking or attempting to take anything of value from the care, custody, or control of a person or persons by force or threat of force or violence and/or by putting the victim in fear
Aggravated assault	An unlawful attack by one person on another for the purpose of inflicting severe or aggravated bodily injury; attempts to inflict injury are also included
Burglary	The unlawful entry of a structure to commit a felony or theft
Larceny-theft	The unlawful taking, carrying, leading, or riding away with of property from the possession or constructive possession of another; includes crimes such as shoplifting, pocket picking, purse snatching, thefts from motor vehicles, and bicycle thefts
Arson	Any willful or malicious burning or attempt to burn, with or without intent to defraud, a dwelling house, public building, motor vehicle or aircraft, or personal property of another
Common Part II Crimes	
Simple assaults	Assaults and attempted assaults in which no weapon is used and which do not result in serious or aggravated injury to victim
Forgery and counterfeiting	Making, altering, uttering, or possessing, with intent to defraud, anything false in the semblance of that which is true
Fraud	Fraudulent conversion and obtaining money or property by false pretenses
Embezzlement	Misappropriation or misapplication of money entrusted to one's care, custody, or control

(continued)

TABLE 1-3 continued

Common Part II Crimes

Stolen property	Buying, receiving, and possessing stolen property, including attempts to do so
Offenses against the family and children	Unlawful nonviolent acts by a family member that threaten the physical, mental, or economic well-being or morals of another family member; does not include assault or sex offenses
Sex offenses	Statutory rape, offenses against chastity, common decency, and morals
Drug abuse violations	State and/or local offenses relating to the unlawful possession, sale, use, growing, and manufacture of drugs
Gambling	Promoting, permitting, or engaging in illegal gambling
Vandalism	Willful or malicious destruction, injury, disfigurement, or defacement of any public or private property, real or personal, without the consent of the owner or persons having custody or control

Source: Federal Bureau of Investigation (2008).

Violent crime comprises four offenses: murder and nonnegligent manslaughter, forcible rape, robbery, and aggravated assault. The term *forcible rape* is redundant, because by definition all rape is forcible. However, the FBI uses the term to distinguish it from consensual sexual activity when one individual is an under-age female—the latter is called statutory rape. Interestingly, rape of male victims has not been included in forcible rape statistics until very recently; sexual assaults of males have been counted either as aggravated assaults or as other sexual offenses, depending on the circumstances and the extent of the injury. In 2012, it was announced that henceforth the rape of male victims will be included in the Part I rape data. Because this change is still being implemented, it is unclear when statistics on male victims will be available. Each of the four Part 1 violent offenses involves force or the threat of force. The Part 1 property crimes are burglary, larceny-theft, motor vehicle theft, and arson. The primary objective of the offender in property crime is the taking or destruction of money or property. Arson is included in property crime because it involves the destruction of property, but it may result in the loss of life or serious injury.

For all Part I crimes, the UCR provides information on the crime known to police (reported crime or crimes they have observed in progress), as well as arrests. Only arrest data are provided for Part II crimes. Thus, in order to appear in the UCR as a Part I crime, a crime must, at a minimum, meet the following requirements:

- Be experienced by the victim or observed by someone else
- Be defined as a crime by the victim or the observer
- In some way become known to a law enforcement agency as a crime
- Be defined by that law enforcement agency as a crime
- Be accurately recorded by the law enforcement agency
- Be reported to the FBI compilation center

It should be emphasized that the UCR provides *crime rate* data on only the eight Part I crimes listed above. The crime rate is the percentage of crime known to police per 100,000 population. For example, in 2010, the murder rate was 4.8, meaning there were 4.8 murders known to police for every 100,000 population. Because the UCR keeps track of trends in offending, the FBI was able to report that the 2010 murder figure represented a 15 percent decrease in the murder rate since 2001 (Federal Bureau of Investigation, 2011a). Part II offenses, for which only arrest data are provided, encompass all crimes, except traffic violations, which are not classified as Part I offenses. If a victim reports a simple assault (a Part II crime), that assault would not be included in the *crime rate*. However, the *arrest* of one or more individuals for that simple assault would appear in the UCR. Arrest data are also included for all Part I crimes.

On a regular yearly basis, if we look at crimes known to police, the property crime of larceny-theft, which usually comprises approximately 60 percent of the Part I crimes, is the most frequently occurring of all Part I crimes (see **Figure 1-1**). The violent crime of murder occurs the least frequently of all Part I crimes, accounting for only 0.1 percent of the total Part I crimes. In addition, again looking at crimes known to police, recent data indicate that in 2010 violent crimes were down approximately 13 percent from a decade ago, and the property crime rate was 19.6 percent below the 2001 rate (Federal Bureau of Investigation, 2011a). These are of course national figures. If we examine UCR breakdowns for different regions or metropolitan areas, we see variations in crime rates and trends.

The UCR also reports the **clearance rate** of all Part I crimes. An offense is cleared when at least one person is arrested, charged with the commission of the offense, and remanded to the court for prosecution (Federal Bureau of Investigation, 2005b). An offense may also be cleared by exceptional means when something happens to an offender outside the control of the reporting law enforcement agency. For example, if a person about to be arrested for rape commits suicide, the crime will likely be cleared. As another example, when a youth is required to appear in juvenile court or before other juvenile authorities, the incident is considered cleared by arrest, even though a physical arrest may not have occurred. In 2010, 47.2 percent of violent crimes in the United States and 18.3 percent of property offenses were cleared by arrest or exceptional means. Usually, murder has the highest clearance rate. In 2010, law enforcement agencies cleared 64.8 percent of murders; by contrast, burglary and motor vehicle theft have low clearance rates (12.4% and 11.8%, respectively). (See **Table 1-4** for illustrations of other clearance rates.)

TABLE 1-4 2010 Clearance Rates for Part I Crimes	
Violent Crime	**47.2%**
Murder	64.8%
Rape	40.3%
Robbery	28.2%
Aggravated assault	56.4%
Property Crime	**18.3%**
Burglary	12.4%
Larceny-theft	21.1%
Motor vehicle theft	11.8%
Arson	19.0%

Source: Federal Bureau of Investigation (2011a).

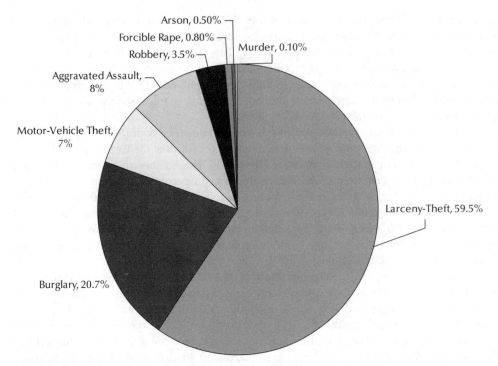

FIGURE 1-1   Percent Distribution of Part I Crimes, 2010   *Source*: Federal Bureau of Investigation (2011a).

Finally, arrest data should be distinguished from reported crime and clearance data. The UCR includes arrest data for 28 offenses, counting one arrest for each separate instance in which a person is arrested, cited, or summoned for an offense. Therefore, the number of arrests as reported in the UCR does not reflect the number of persons arrested, because one individual may be arrested multiple times. In 2010, the highest number of arrests were for drug abuse violations and larceny-theft. Recent arrest trends show decreases in violent crime, property crime, and arrests of both juveniles and adults. Males accounted for 80.5 percent of persons arrested for violent crime and 62.4 percent of those arrested for property crime. In 2010, 69.4 percent of all persons arrested were white, 28 percent were black, and 2.6 percent were listed as of other races (Federal Bureau of Investigation, 2011a.). It should be noted that although juveniles (under 18) are included in UCR statistics when they are arrested for criminal offenses, as of 2010 the program no longer collected data on runaways.

UCR Problems

UCR data are not without problems. One of the most frequently mentioned shortcomings is the **hierarchy rule**, which stipulates that when a number of offenses have been committed during a series, only the most serious offense is included in the UCR data. For example, if a person breaks into your apartment, steals money, kicks your cat, kills your roommate, and runs off in your car, only the murder will appear in the UCR. The exception to the hierarchy rule is arson, which is always reported even if accompanied by a violent offense (e.g., murder).

The compilation center also relies on the accuracy and compliance of local and state agencies to report crime statistics. The data also do not consider early discretionary decision making by law enforcement officers, such as a decision not to "found" a crime when it is reported by a member of the public or a decision not to arrest an individual. In addition, the Part I category emphasizes street crime to the neglect of the equally serious "white-collar" crime, which includes a wide variety of offenses such as corporate, political, and professional crimes. Very often these crimes are federal offenses and thus would not appear in the UCR.

Official crime statistics, like those of the UCR Program, are generally believed to underestimate most criminal offenses and are routinely criticized for errors and omissions. The overall number of criminal offenses that go undetected or are unknown by law enforcement agencies, known as the **dark figure**, is difficult to estimate, but data from an early victimization survey conducted by the U.S. Census Bureau suggest that out of every 100 offenses committed, 72 are never recorded in the official statistics (Skogan, 1977). However, Skogan also notes that most unreported violations appear to be minor property offenses rather than more serious crimes. As we see shortly, though, more recent victimization studies indicate that many serious crimes are not reported to police.

The National Incident-Based Reporting System

During the late 1970s, the law enforcement community called for the expanded use of the UCR and more detailed information on crime than the statistics offered in the UCR. In response, the NIBRS was initiated as a supplement to the UCR. Although the NIBRS was initially intended to replace the UCR, this has not yet happened and is unlikely to in the near future. It is also important to note that while federal law enforcement agencies are required to report through this system, states do so only on a voluntary basis.

Through NIBRS, the FBI collects data on two categories of offenses: Group A, which includes 46 serious offense categories such as arson, assault, homicide, fraud, embezzlement, larceny-theft, and sex offenses; and Group B, which includes 11 less serious offenses, such as passing bad checks, driving under the influence of alcohol, engaging in disorderly conduct, drunkenness, nonviolent family offenses, and liquor law violations (see **Table 1-5** for a list of Group A offenses).

In the *Group A Incident Report* information, a crime is viewed along with all its aspects. For example, the report of a crime includes information about the victim, weapon, location of the crime, alcohol/drug influence, type of criminal activity, relationship of victim to alleged offender, residence of victims and arrestees (if someone was arrested), and a description of property and its value. Presumably, this added information is an indispensable tool for law enforcement agencies and researchers because it provides them with detailed data about when and where specific types of crime take place, what forms they take, and the characteristics of their victims and perpetrators. Like the Part II crimes in the UCR, the crimes in Group B include only information about the arrestee and the circumstances of the arrest.

The benefits of the NIBRS are primarily through the more precise information it provides to researchers and investigators about when and where crime takes place, its form, and the characteristics of its victims and offenders. Another primary objective of NIBRS is to get a better handle on the nature and extent of crimes involving illicit drugs.

TABLE 1-5 National Incident-Based Reporting System (NIBRS) Group A Offenses	
Arson	*Homicide offenses*
Assault offenses	Murder/nonnegligent manslaughter
Aggravated assault	Negligent manslaughter
Simple assault	Justifiable homicide
Intimidation	*Kidnapping/abduction*
Bribery	*Larceny-theft offenses*
Burglary/breaking and entering	Pocket picking
Counterfeiting/forgery	Purse snatching
Destruction/damage/vandalism of property	Shoplifting
Drug/narcotic offenses	Theft from building
Drug/narcotic violations	Theft from coin-operated machines
Drug/equipment violations	Theft from motor vehicle
Embezzlement	Theft of motor vehicle parts/accessories
Extortion/blackmail	Motor vehicle theft
Fraud offenses	Pornography/obscene materials
False pretenses/swindle/confidence game	*Prostitution offenses*
Credit card/ATM fraud	Prostitution
Impersonation	Assisting or promoting prostitution
Welfare fraud	*Robbery*
Wire fraud	*Sex offenses, forcible*
Gambling offenses	Forcible rape
Betting/wagering	Forcible sodomy
Operating/promoting/assisting gambling	Sexual assault with an object
Gambling equipment violations	Forcible fondling
Sports tampering	*Sex offenses, nonforcible*
	Stolen property offenses
	Weapon law violations

Source: Based on information from *The National Center for the Analysis of Violent Crime, Annual Report, 1992* (Quantico, VA: FBI Academy, 1992), p. 22.

Among the additional crime categories now followed by the FBI but not *traditionally* included in the Uniform Crime Reporting System or the NIBRS reports are hate or bias crimes and terrorist activities. (See **Box 1-1** for information about hate crimes; terrorism and terrorist activities are covered in Chapter 11.)

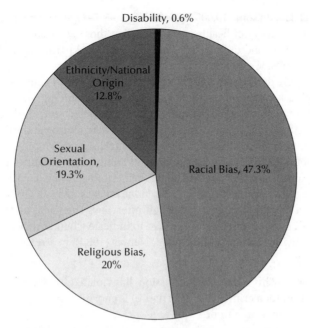

FIGURE 1-2   Bias-Motivated Offenses Percent Distribution,
2010   *Source*: Federal Bureau of Investigation (2011a).

Self-Report Studies

Many researchers believe that self-report (SR) studies provide a more accurate estimate of actual offenses than do UCR statistics, which are based on data provided by law enforcement. In self-report research, people report their own criminal or otherwise antisocial activity to researchers. Although respondents may inflate or deflate reports of their own criminal activity, proponents of this research strategy maintain that self-report offers a better approximation of criminal activity. In a dated but revealing SR survey (Wallerstein & Wyle, 1947), 1,698 persons were asked to indicate on a list of 49 criminal offenses which, if any, they had committed. The list included felonies and misdemeanors but excluded traffic violations. Of the nearly 1,700 respondents, 91 percent admitted they had committed one or more offenses for which they might have received jail or prison sentences. The average number of offenses for each person was 18. None of the sample had served an actual prison sentence. This study suggests that most people have broken the criminal law at some point in their lives.

In another classic study by Short and Nye (1957), three thousand high school students, with a guarantee of anonymity, were administered questionnaires about their unlawful actions. Results confirmed the high incidence of unlawful behavior such as was reported by the Wallerstein and Wyle study. Additionally, the study demonstrated that the unlawful conduct was evenly distributed across all socioeconomic classes. Even if the offenses were not serious ones, if these SR studies are representative, violations of the law are common across all levels of society, at least among young people. The Wallerstein and Wyle study did not address the issue of social class.

Most SR investigations focus on delinquency rather than adult offending. One study that is receiving extensive research attention is the National Longitudinal Study of Adolescent Health, which collected initial data on some 19,000 students in grades 7–12 at 132 schools. The self-reported information related to a variety of health issues, including those associated with criminal activity (e.g., illegal drug possession and use). A subgroup of the original participants, about 15,000, were recontacted as young adults. We discuss this research in Chapter 16.

When SR studies are done with adults, however, they are primarily adults who are incarcerated. Researchers frequently ask inmates about the extent of their past offending, and some of these studies will be cited throughout the book. Not all respondents are convicted individuals, however. In a classic study of employee theft, for example, researchers found that about one-third of employees who returned surveys admitted to stealing from their employers (Hollinger, 1986). A self-report survey of income tax evasion found 10 percent of the respondents admitting to cheating on their taxes (Tittle, 1980). College students also are often queried about their criminal behavior, including drug use and sexual assaults. These studies will be discussed later in the book as well.

Self-report data are gathered either through interviews (personal or telephone) or questionnaires. In most SR measures, subjects are asked to indicate whether they have engaged in any of the listed illegal activities and, if so, how often. Nettler (1984), in a review of the SR research, concluded the following:

- Almost everyone, by his or her own admission, has violated some criminal law.
- The amount of "hidden crime" (the dark figure) is enormous.
- Most of the infractions are minor.

The last point is an important one because it is the basis for much of the criticism directed at SR studies. Most of the offenses included in a majority of SR questionnaires are relatively minor ones—so minor that they are likely to distort one's impressions of criminal offending unless the content of the questions is known. For example, the questionnaire used by Short and Nye was a 23-item delinquency scale that included such questions as whether one has ever defied his or her parents' authority (to their face). Other items included whether one had ever skipped school without a legitimate excuse; taken little things (worth less than $2); bought or drank beer, wine, or liquor; had sexual relations with persons of the opposite sex or the same sex; run away from home; or gone hunting or fishing without a license. Note that some of the above items (e.g., skipping school and running away) relate to offenses that are against the law only for juveniles, called "status offenses." More "serious" violations listed were engaging in fist fights, gang fights, taking a car for a drive without the owner's (including parents') knowledge, use of narcotic drugs, theft (over $50), and vandalism.

Recent SR studies, responding to the criticisms of earlier investigations, have directed their questions at more serious criminal activities. Still, we must be careful about drawing far-reaching conclusions based on the information from SR research unless the nature of the questions is known, as well as who was asked, why, and how. Most importantly, because some people are likely not to be honest in reporting their own antisocial activities, we must be guarded in reviewing the data obtained from SR studies. The best studies recognize this problem themselves and include reliability checks in their methodology—such as by cross-checking the information against other sources. At this point, SR studies do suggest that minor criminal activity is extensive and widespread, at least among youth. Furthermore, SR studies continually show that the number of individuals involved in serious crimes is relatively small, but those few who do engage in serious criminal activity commit many crimes. Moreover, persistent, repetitive offenders do not specialize in any one crime (such as larceny) but show considerable versatility in criminal involvement, committing a wide variety of offenses, violent as well as nonviolent. We discuss this behavioral pattern in more detail in the next chapter.

Drug Abuse Self-Report Surveys

Several nationwide self-report surveys collect data on drug abuse in the United States. The major surveys are the *National Household Survey on Drug Abuse (NHSDA)*, the **Monitoring the Future Study (MFS)**, and the *Arrestees Drug Abuse Monitoring Program (ADAM and ADAM II)*.

NHSDA is an ongoing survey of the noninstitutionalized population of the United States, 12 years old or older. The survey has been conducted by the federal government since 1971 and is the primary source of statistical information on the use of illegal drugs in the United States. It is designed to estimate the rates of drug use, the number of users, and other aspects related to illicit drugs, alcohol, and tobacco products. The survey collects data by administering questionnaires to a representative sample of the population at their places of residence across all 50 states and the District of Columbia. The sample includes residents of households, noninstitutional group quarters (e.g., shelters, rooming houses, dormitories), and civilians living on military bases. Beginning in 1999, the NHSDA interview has been carried out using a computer-assisted interviewing methodology. Computers are used both for personal interviewing conducted by the interviewer and audio computer-assisted self-interviewing. Nationally, nearly 69,000 persons were interviewed in 2001.

The MFS is a nationwide survey of high schoolers in the United States conducted at the Institute for Social Research at the University of Michigan and sponsored by research grants from the National Institute of Drug Abuse. Each year, since 1991, a total of fifty thousand 8th, 10th, and 12th grade students are surveyed. The MFS also conducts a follow-up survey of each graduating class for a number of years after their initial participation. The mission of the MFS is to predict future trends of drug abuse based on current youth drug use. We describe these surveys and their informative results in more detail in Chapter 16 along with the ADD Health Survey referred to above.

The ADAM II is a continuation of a National Institute of Justice program—ADAM—that collected data from adult males and females who were arrested in 35 sites in the United States between 2000 and 2003, when it was terminated for lack of funding. In 2007, ADAM II, sponsored by the federal Office of National Drug Control Policy (ONDCP), took up the data collection, focusing on 10 sites. The ADAM II utilizes both urinalysis and self-report data to identify the level of recent drug use by the arrestees. The individuals arrested provide information about the types of drugs they use as well as how they obtained them. The urinalysis provides a validity check on the openness of the arrestees in providing information about their drug abuse. Urine specimens are analyzed for the presence of 10 substances (ONDCP, 2011). The urine tests are provided for 11 drugs and self-report information is collected for 15 drugs. The ADAM projects, both ADAM and ADAM II, offer invaluable insight into drug use of persons arrested in representative areas of the country. Again, latest findings are discussed in Chapter 16.

Victimization Surveys

Additional sources of data on criminal offending are victimization surveys. The main source of victimization data on crime is the **National Crime Victimization Survey (NCVS)**, originally called the National Crime Survey (NCS). Workers for the Bureau of the Census interview—in person or by phone—a large national sample of households (approximately 42,000) representing over 76,000 persons over the age of 12. The same households are interviewed every six months for a period of three years, and during each session, they are asked about crime they had experienced over the past six months. Persons living in group quarters such as dormitories, rooming houses, and religious group dwellings are included, but persons in institutions or in military barracks are not. Crimes committed against children below age 12 are not counted for privacy reasons and because the designers of the survey believe that younger respondents, compared with adults, are not as likely to provide accurate information. Additionally, because young children may be victims of crime within their own households, the topic would be too sensitive to broach. The NCVS provides the largest national forum for victims to describe the impact of crime and characteristics of violent offenders. Its reports, including detailed information about the methodology used to conduct the interviews and analyze the data, are available on the Bureau of Justice Statistics (BJS) website, http://www.bjs.gov.

The survey is currently designed to measure the extent to which households and individuals are victims of rape and other sexual assault, robbery, aggravated assault, simple assault, household burglary, motor vehicle theft, and theft. It also provides many details about the victims (such as age, race, sex, marital status, education, income, and whether the victim and the offender were related to each other) and about the crimes themselves. Recent versions of the NCVS also ask respondents whether they perceived they were victims of a hate crime. Among other things, the NCVS interviewer wants to know the following about all victimization:

- Exactly what happened
- When and where the offense occurred
- Whether any injury or loss was suffered
- Whether the crime was reported to the police and if not, why
- The victim's perception of the offender's gender, race, and age

According to the NCVS, victimization incidents have decreased in recent years (see, generally, BJS 2012). In 2009, about five and one half million total violent victimizations were experienced, while just under 5 million were experienced in 2010. By far the greatest number was for simple assault, with about three and a half million experienced in 2009 and 3,241,148 in 2010.

There are several possible explanations for these downward trends. The most optimistic is that victimizations are indeed decreasing, which in itself could be attributed to numerous factors. However, many crime victims are reluctant to report victimizations to police, to workers from the Census Bureau (which conducts the NCVS), or to private researchers. Again, there are numerous reasons for this: they may know who victimized them and not wish to implicate the individual; they may not want the attention; they may be embarrassed; they may not trust the agents of government; they may believe nothing can be done. In recent years, many undocumented workers are reluctant to come forward and report victimization out of fear of being deported.

The NCVS data consistently show demographic differences in victimization rates. Males and American Indian or Alaskan Native are victims of violent crime at rates greater than those of whites and persons of other races (Rennison & Rand, 2003; Truman, 2011) (See **Table 1-6**). For the first time since the NCVS began reporting victimizations by sex, males and females had similar rates of victimization. Persons age 12–24 sustain violent victimization at rates higher than individuals of all other ages, with the 18–20 age group being especially vulnerable. Persons age 18–20 experienced overall violence, rape/sexual assault, and assault overall at rates higher than rates for persons in other age categories. However, we also know that much abuse suffered by younger children—as well as by the elderly—is hidden. These patterns have continued in recent years, as we will see later in the book when specific crimes are covered.

Relationship patterns are also important in understanding victimization, particularly violent victimization. Females are most often victimized by someone they know, while males are more likely to be victimized by strangers (Rennison & Rand, 2003; Truman, 2011). Female victims

TABLE 1-6 Violent Victimizations per 1,000 Persons Age 12 or Older

Demographic Characteristics of Victim	Total	Rape/Sexual Assault	Robbery	Aggravated Assault	Simple Assault
Total	14.9	0.7	1.9	2.8	9.5
Sex					
Males	15.7	0.11	2.4	3.4	9.7
Female	14.2	1.3	1.4	2.3	9.2
Race/Hispanic Origin					
White	13.6	0.7	1.4	2.6	9.0
Black	20.8	1.11	3.6	4.7	11.4
Hispanic	15.6	0.81	2.7	2.3	9.8
American Indian or Alaskan Native	42.2	0.0	4.3	19.5	18.3
Asian or Pacific Islander	6.3	0.6	1.1	0.5	4.0
Two or more races	52.6	1.2	8.0	8.5	34.9
Age (years)					
12–14	27.5	2.7	0.7	5.8	18.3
15–17	23.0	1.7	2.7	5.8	18.3
18–20	33.9	1.1	5.9	6.9	20.0
21–24	26.9	1.5	3.7	8.0	13.7
25–34	18.8	1.3	2.5	3.3	11.7
35–49	12.6	0.6	1.5	1.9	8.6
50–64	10.9	0.0	1.3	2.1	7.6
65 or older	2.4	0.1	0.6	0.2	1.5

Source: data derived from Truman (2011).

report that most offenders are friends and acquaintances, followed by intimate partners or former intimates. By contrast, male victims report that strangers are the most likely perpetrators, followed by friends or acquaintances. Very few males report being victimized by intimate partners. These patterns have been consistent, varying slightly from survey to survey. Specific statistics will be provided in later chapters.

As suggested above, a good amount of victimization occurs at the hands of intimate partners. In 2000, Rennison & Welchans noted that every year, about 1 million violent crimes are committed against persons by their current or former spouses, boyfriends, or girlfriends. This **intimate partner violence (IPV)** is committed primarily against women. Black women are subject to intimate partner violence at a rate 35 percent higher than white women and approximately

2.5 times higher than the rate for women of other races. However, women in many ethnic groups are reluctant to report such violence, as we will learn in Chapter 9.

The NCVS, similar to all national surveys, has its problems in accurately portraying victimization data. As described earlier in this section, the NCVS samples households or group living facilities, but does not usually include the experiences of homeless individuals or those living in institutional settings such as battered persons' shelters (Rennison & Welchans, 2000). Consequently, the extent of intimate partner violence experienced by the homeless or those persons residing in shelters remains largely unknown. For example, a survey conducted by the U.S. Conference of Mayors indicated that intimate partner violence was the primary cause of homelessness for women (U.S. Conference of Mayors, 1998). Another study suggested that as many as 50 percent of homeless women and children became homeless after fleeing abuse (Zorza, 1991). If these individuals are not represented in the NCVS, the prevalence of intimate partner violence is underestimated.

Despite their shortcomings, victimization surveys are considered a good source of information about crime incidents, independent of data collected by law enforcement agencies throughout the country. Often the offending trends reported through NCVS data procedures differ substantially from those found in police data (Ohlin & Tonry, 1989). Although we have focused on the government-conducted NCVS to illustrate victimization data, be aware that independent researchers also survey victims of crime, often with grants from government agencies or private foundations. One noteworthy example is the National Violence Against Women Survey, conducted by the Center for Policy Research (Tjaden, 1997), which included an examination of the extent and nature of violence and stalking in American society. That survey and others like it will be covered later in the text.

Juvenile Delinquency

The definitions of crime and the methods of gathering crime data discussed above relate to both adults and juveniles. As we will learn in Chapter 6, which is devoted exclusively to juvenile delinquency, juveniles commit a disproportionate amount of crime, but it is not necessarily the most serious offenses. Furthermore, crimes committed by juveniles may be treated very differently from those committed by adults. In addition to the focus on delinquency in Chapter 6, we include special sections devoted to juvenile offenders and victims in other chapters. At this point, however, it is important to mention a few other preliminary distinctions.

First, not all offenses committed by juveniles are technically crimes. Some behaviors—referred to as **status offenses**—are forbidden only to juveniles because of their age. The prime examples are running away from home, curfew violations, underage drinking, skipping school on a regular basis (truancy), and—in some states—"incorrigibility." Many criminologists argue that status offenses should not be criminalized in the same way that true crimes are for various reasons. For example, status offenses label children delinquents for behavior that is not harmful to others, and they are often indicative of problems in the child's environment (e.g., the runaway child may be running away from victimization). Other criminologists argue that it is important to keep track of status offenders in order to provide them with help that they may need; additionally, some, though not all, status offenders commit "real crimes" like burglary and theft. What to do with status offenders is a controversial area, as we will see in Chapter 6. As noted earlier, the UCR is no longer collecting data on juvenile runaways.

Another distinction between adult and juvenile criminal behavior is that data gathering on juvenile offending is even more imperfect than data gathering on adult crime. The nature and extent of delinquent behavior—both what is reported and what is unreported to law enforcement agencies—is essentially an unknown area (Krisberg, 1995). Nonetheless, information from a variety of sources, including the UCR, self-report, court records, and data from juvenile corrections, provides us some insight into the nature and extent of juvenile offending.

Third, much of the crime (and status offenses) committed by juveniles may be regarded as a "rite of passage" to adulthood. Self-report data indicate that offending among juveniles is more widespread than among adults but—as with adult offending—most people eventually stop. In the case of juveniles, most stop committing crime once they reach adulthood and have a stake in prosocial behavior. Juveniles may act out in high school or slightly beyond, but then they get full-time jobs, go to college, get married, join the military. From a psychological perspective, however, we need to be particularly concerned with two groups of juveniles: those who continue offending, particularly serious offending, well into their adult years; and those who commit a very serious crime during their juvenile years. The former group typically demonstrated problem behavior very early in their lives. The latter group—those who commit a one-time, very serious offense—receives extensive media attention (e.g., juvenile school shooters or juvenile murderers), but this type of one-time offending is rare. Continued serious offending, though, is more problematic. Many theories of crime describe antisocial behavior as having its origins in childhood. Over the past few decades, developmental psychologists in particular have conducted extensive research on children and adolescents who begin offending early and continue into adulthood. This is the main topic of Chapter 2.

RECAP: DEFINING CRIME AND DELINQUENCY

A major challenge faced by the authors in preparing this book has been striking the balance between antisocial behavior and criminal behavior, or between antisocial individuals and legally defined criminals. Some scholars have argued (e.g., Sellin, 1970; Tappan, 1947)—and the law agrees—that one who engages in undetected criminal activity is not a criminal in the strictest or operational sense, because a criminal is by definition one who has been detected, arrested, and convicted. However, from a psychological point of view, we encounter problems when we limit ourselves to studying persons legally defined as criminals or behavior legally defined as crime. Legal classifications are determined by that which society, at some point in time, considers socially harmful. It may or may not also be considered morally wrong. Therefore, because each society has a different and changing set of values, what may be judged a criminal act in one may not meet the criteria in another, or even in the same society at a later time. Many states in the United States differ significantly in their criminal codes and are continually revising them. Chemical (drug) possession, prostitution, and dissemination of obscene material are examples of activities that generate ever-changing statutes, and if not changing statutes, selective enforcement. In recent years, use of cell phones or text messaging while driving has been banned in some jurisdictions, with criminal penalties sometimes prescribed. Although we do not condone text messaging while driving, we are not interested in focusing on the psychology of the text messager. The more serious crimes, those we are most concerned with in this text, are more likely to be universally recognized as unacceptable. Nevertheless, we also pay attention to offenses that may not be seen as serious or even wrong, but that can have psychological implications for offenders and victims. Shoplifting, minor fraud, and juvenile prostitution are examples.

Furthermore, members of every society (and consequently every society's legal system) perceive and process violators of the criminal code with some disparity, so that the offender's background, social status, personality, motivation, sex, age, race, and legal counsel, as well as the circumstances surrounding the offense, may all affect the criminal justice process. It is highly likely that individuals who have been arrested, convicted, and punished represent a distinctly different sample from those who participate in illegal activity but avoid detection, conviction, or punishment.

Approximately one-fifth of those arrested go to trial, according to Sarbin (1979), who describes the legal process of becoming a criminal. First, the agents of social control (usually the police) label the individual as a suspect. Next, the agents may decide that the suspect should be arrested. Third, the arrested party may be charged with a crime, at which point he or she becomes a defendant. Fourth, the defendant may plead guilty or be tried and convicted, at which point he or she becomes an offender (a felon or a misdemeanant, depending on the seriousness of the crime). Finally, the offender may be incarcerated in a correctional facility and be labeled a convict, inmate, prisoner, or criminal. Alternately, the offender may be placed on probation, effectively serving a sentence in the community. At each step in the process, there is a funneling effect that shows that fewer and fewer individuals reach each subsequent step in the criminal justice process. This funneling process is prominently displayed in numerous criminal justice texts to illustrate how the system operates.

One reason is the error and subjectivity that cannot realistically be removed from determinations of whether or not someone is guilty of a crime. Both judges and juries can be influenced by factors other than the strength of the evidence. For example, it has been demonstrated that the characteristics of the victim may influence how much punishment is assigned to the offender. In classic research, Landy and Aronson (1969) reported evidence that if the victim was a respectable citizen (i.e., successful and altruistic), the offender would receive a stiffer sentence than if the case involved an "unrespectable" victim (i.e., despicable and dishonest). In another classic study, Jones and Aronson (1973) found that defendants who raped a married woman or virgin were more likely to receive longer sentences than defendants who raped a divorced woman. Although these were early experiments in social psychology, later studies also confirmed that subjective factors have considerable influence on judge and jury decision making (Maeder, Dempsey, & Pozzulo, 2012; Rogers & Davies, 2007).

It is generally acknowledged, therefore, that those individuals sentenced to jail or prison are not representative of the "true" criminal population, because many true criminals go undetected and/or unpunished. Furthermore, as we have long suspected but only recently documented with the increasing availability of DNA evidence or reinvestigation of cases, convicted persons are not even necessarily true criminals (Associated Press, 2012). Yet, researchers studying the "criminal mind" often use as participants those individuals who have reached the final stage of the legal process—inmates in correctional institutions or convicted offenders serving their sentences in the community. Consequently, if we discuss only legally determined criminals, we will be neglecting a considerable segment of the population that actually breaks the law. To some extent, we have little choice but to do just that. Because this book is based on research, the kinds and amounts of available empirical data dictate to a great extent what will be covered.

Additionally, if we discuss only behavior that is legally defined as crime, we omit a sizable segment of behavior that is clearly relevant to our concerns. For example, a vast body of psychological research deals with topics like aggression and antisocial behavior. Because of their implications for the eventual development of behavior that is legally defined as crime, we will be covering these areas in the text.

The great majority of crime in the United States and other countries is not violent. In 2010, the highest numbers of arrests were for drug abuse violations, driving under the influence, and larceny-theft. The great majority of offenders are not serious offenders (Federal Bureau of

Investigation, 2011a). Psychological criminology, however, is most concerned about the minority. Therefore, the main focus of the book is the persistent, repetitive *offender*—or the persistent, repetitive antisocial *behavior*—whether detected or undetected by the criminal justice system. In other words, in this text, we concentrate on the individual who has frequently committed serious crimes or antisocial acts over an extended period of time (at least several years). Nevertheless, we also spend time on the one-time serious offender—the mass murderer, for example, or the juvenile offender who commits a heinous crime.

For all of the above reasons, many psychologists and other mental health professionals prefer the term *antisocial behavior* to *crime* or *criminal behavior* to refer to the more serious habitual actions that violate personal rights, laws, and/or widely held social norms. **Antisocial behavior** includes both the legal designation delinquency and criminal behavior, and the actions that violate standards of society but are undetected by law enforcement. Although arrest *may be* a valid indicator of antisocial behavior, it isn't enough. Many antisocial behaviors—probably most—go undetected or escape the attention of law enforcement. Consequently, we use antisocial behavior frequently throughout the text, especially when discussing the development of behavior that has not yet been legally designated delinquent or criminal behavior but is likely to lead to such designation.

Key Concepts

Antisocial behavior
Classical theory
Clearance rate
Cognitions
Conformity perspective
Criminal or offender profiling
Criminology
Dark figure
Deterrence theory
Developmental approach
Difference-in-degree
Difference-in-kind
Differential association
    theory

Dispositions or traits
General Theory of Crime
Hate Crime Statistics Act
Hierarchy rule
Intimate partner violence (IPV)
Just-world hypothesis
Learning perspective
Monitoring the Future
    Study (MFS)
National Crime Victimization
    Survey (NCVS)
National Incidence Based
    Reporting System (NIBRS)
Nonconformist perspective

Part I crimes
Part II crimes
Positivist theory
Psychiatric criminology
Psychological
    criminology
Social control theory
Social learning theory
Sociological criminology
Status offenses
Strain theory
Theory verification
Uniform Crime Reports
    (UCR)

Review Questions

1. Briefly explain the difference between psychological criminology and sociological criminology.
2. Define and provide examples of the conformity, nonconformist, and learning perspectives of human nature.
3. Identify and provide one example of each of the three predominant methods of measuring crime.
4. How does the NIBRS differ from the UCR?

5. List the strengths and weaknesses of self-report surveys.
6. What are status offenses and how do they differ from other juvenile offenses?
7. Compare and contrast the FBI's Uniform Crime Reports and the National Crime Victimization Survey, focusing on (a) how the data are obtained and (b) what type of information is available from each.

2

Origins of Criminal Behavior: Developmental Risk Factors

CHAPTER OBJECTIVES

■ Identify social, family, and psychological developmental risk factors that lead to delinquency and crime.

■ Demonstrate how early preschool experiences can lead to a life of antisocial behavior.

■ Emphasize the influence of peer rejection on child and youth behavior.

■ Stress the connection between cognitive abilities and delinquency and crime.

■ Introduce attention deficit hyperactivity disorder (ADHD), conduct disorder (CD), and oppositional defiant disorder (ODD) as possible contributors to delinquent behavior.

As a preschooler, Josh was the child most known for shoving other children, stepping on their toes, and refusing to comply with the instructions of his teachers. In grade school, he became the classroom bully; at age eight, he began to steal—from other children, from storekeepers, from teachers, and from his parents. By middle school, he was experimenting with drugs. He was suspended from high school on four separate occasions, all relating to violent behavior. Josh was convicted of robbery at age 19.

Antisocial behavior, including criminal behavior, in adults can often be traced to their childhoods. If we look back at the childhoods of offenders, for example, we typically see signs portending problems in adulthood, although this is not invariably so. As noted in Chapter 1, many theories of criminology propose that the roots of serious criminal behavior appear in childhood or early adolescence. This highlights the importance of identifying both factors that put children at risk of becoming antisocial and those that might protect vulnerable children from this fate.

Each person follows a different **developmental pathway**, the characteristics of which often can be identified at a very early age. The developmental perspective views the life course of all humans as following a pathway (or trajectory) that may be littered with risk factors. Some risk factors can be described as experiences that are common factors in the background of offenders, such as school failure, abuse of alcohol, or childhood victimization. In studies of both adult and juvenile offenders, researchers are beginning to identify a number of different pathways, which we will cover in later chapters. For example, some children follow a pathway leading to serious delinquency and crime, while others follow a pathway that may lead to minor juvenile offending. For some children, there is no offending at all. Along each developmental path, a child may be exposed to a variety of risk factors, and some children are exposed to many more than others. Some experts believe that the more risks a person is exposed to, the greater the probability that he or she will participate in antisocial behavior throughout his or her lifetime (Wasserman & Seracini, 2001). Contemporary researchers also stress the value of a nurturing environment to protect children against the onslaught of potential risk factors in their lives (Biglan, Flay, Embry, & Sandler, 2012).

Protective factors, characteristics, or experiences found in a nurturing environment can shield children from serious antisocial behavior. Warm and caring parents and a high-quality educational experience are examples. In general, a nurturing environment minimizes biologically and socially toxic conditions that influence healthy development (Biglan *et al.*, 2012). Though we recognize the importance of protective factors, the goal in this chapter is to pinpoint the origins and causes of delinquency and criminal behavior; thus, the focus is on factors that place individuals at risk for offending. Nevertheless, when we discuss intervention approaches later in the book, protective factors will be carefully considered.

The risk factors we are most concerned with in this chapter are individual attributes and developmental social, family, and psychological experiences that are believed to increase the probability that an individual will engage in persistent criminal behavior. In Chapter 3 we will focus again on individual attributes, but they will be biologically based. Examples of *social risk factors* are poverty and limited resources, antisocial peers, peer rejection, and preschool or school experiences. *Parental and family risk factors* include faulty or inadequate parenting, sibling influences, and child maltreatment or abuse. Examples of *psychological risk factors* are inadequate cognitive and language ability, inadequate self-regulation skills, and poor interpersonal and social skills. Psychological risk factors that are more biologically based, such as a troublesome temperament, will be discussed in Chapter 3.

It is important that we learn about these risk factors and how they influence the developmental pathway, especially during the early stages of development. Early identification will help improve the effectiveness of prevention and intervention programs designed to eliminate or, at least, reduce delinquent and criminal behavior. As noted by Terrie Moffitt (2005a, 2005b), we know that certain risk factors are closely linked to delinquency and criminal behavior, but how or why they are linked is largely unknown.

We must be careful not to imply that all criminal behavior has its origins in childhood, however. Pathways researchers emphasize that some individuals begin their criminal offending in adulthood (Farrington, Ttofi, & Coid, 2009) and that this may or may not be precipitated by childhood experiences. For example, some researchers have documented a pathway consisting of adult-onset female offenders whose criminal careers began when they engaged in dysfunctional relationships with male offenders (Salisbury & Van Voorhis, 2009). Nonetheless, risk factors are so often present in the childhoods of both juvenile and adult offenders that we must give them careful attention.

SOCIAL RISK FACTORS

Poverty

Poverty refers to a situation in which the basic resources to maintain an average standard of living within a specific geographic region are lacking. This typically includes the absence of sufficient income to meet basic necessities of life. In the United States, one out of five children lives in official poverty (households with incomes below the federal poverty line), and the numbers are growing (Yoshikawa, Aber, & Beardslee, 2012). In some cities, 50% of the children live in homes below the poverty line. The research literature is substantial in underscoring the adverse effects of poverty on child development. As Blair and Raver (2012) note, "It is well established that the material and psychosocial contexts of poverty adversely affect multiple aspects of development in children" (p. 310). The effects on human development are often severe. Moreover, the effects of poverty are cumulative in that the effects at one stage can hinder development at later stages (Yoshikawa *et al.*, 2012). There is also little doubt that poverty has a strong connection to persistent, violent offending, as measured by official, victimization, and self-report data on both adult and juvenile offenders. The connection between poverty and nonviolent offending is not quite as strong, but still existent. Accumulating research evidence indicates that poverty is one of the most robust predictors of adolescent violence for both males and females (Beyers, Bates, Pettit, & Dodge, 2003; Stouthamer-Loeber, Loeber, Wei, Farrington, & Wilkström, 2002), and the indigence of defendants processed in criminal courts is well documented. However, we must be careful both in interpreting these data and in making decisions about how to prevent future offending. Furthermore, it should be emphasized that this strong connection holds whether we are referring to victims or offenders. Children and youth living under dire economic conditions are more likely to be victims as well as offenders. Preschool children living in a low-income family characterized by poor housing and unemployment are especially at high risk to become delinquent and/or to become victimized (Dodge, 1993; Farrington, 1991). Adults living in substandard housing are more likely to be victims of crime than those living in more advantageous conditions.

The exact nature of the relationship between poverty and violence is not well understood. This is because poverty is intertwined with a large number of influences that are called poverty co-factors (Yoshikawa, *et al.*, 2012). For example, poverty is often accompanied not only by inequities in resources, but also by discrimination, racism, family disruption, unsafe living conditions, joblessness, social isolation, and limited social support systems (Evans, 2004; Hill, Soriano, Chen, & LaFromboise, 1994; Sampson & Lauritsen, 1994). Youth living under poverty conditions are more likely to attend inadequate schools, drop out of school, be unemployed, carry a firearm, be victimized, and be a witness to a variety of violent events. Therefore, many factors other than one's economic situation come into play.

Poverty influences the family in many ways, not the least of which is the impact on parents' behavior toward children. For instance, the stress caused by poverty in urban settings is believed to diminish parents' capacity for supportive and consistent parenting (Blair & Raver, 2012; Dodge, Greenberg, Malone, and Conduct Problems Prevention Research Group, 2008; Hammond & Yung, 1994). This situation may lead to coercive and highly aggressive methods of child rearing. Living in conditions where lack of social support, lack of resources, and lack of opportunity are prevalent make it difficult for some parents to avoid harsh and inconsistent discipline with their young children. Coercive methods are direct, immediate, and easy to administer. They require less time and energy to administer, compared with parenting that emphasizes sensitivity, interpersonal skills, and patient understanding. It is much "easier" to slap a child than it is to utilize more thoughtful parenting strategies, but the consequences of slapping can be severe. A pattern of slapping or hitting a child to punish or to maintain control promotes a negative self-concept in the child. Furthermore, parenting that utilizes aggressive and violent tactics often provides models and a violent context that can carry the cycle of violence into the next generation. Living in a disadvantaged environment accompanied by physical punishment may also lead to the belief that economic survival and social status depend greatly on being aggressive and violent to others.

Important caveats must be offered in any discussion of serious delinquency and economic status, however. First, the connection between low socioeconomic class and delinquency does not mean that poverty causes or inevitably leads to serious, chronic offending. *The great majority of poor children and adults are law-abiding citizens, and children and adults from families of high economic status do engage in serious delinquency and crime.* Both self-report and victimization data indicate that sexual assault, serious drug use, theft, and fraud are perpetrated by juveniles and adults across all social classes. Second, in many communities, children from the lower socio-economic class are targeted by law enforcement practices more than are children of the middle and upper classes. They are more likely to be taken into custody by police, referred to juvenile courts, and adjudicated delinquent. Thus, they appear in the government statistics that serve as the official measures of crime. Additionally, children of the poor are taken into a system that may itself promote delinquent behavior or adult crime, particularly when they are institutionalized with other offenders. Children of the middle and upper classes, by contrast, are more likely to be handled informally, provided with legal assistance, or placed by their parents in private facili-ties for the treatment of their problem behavior (Chesney-Lind, 2002; Chesney-Lind & Shelden, 1998; Schwartz, 1989).

Peer Rejection and Association with Antisocial Peers

Developmental researchers have continually found that children's peer relations make unique and essential contributions to each child's social and emotional development (Bagwell, 2004; Newcomb, Bukowksi, & Pattee, 1993). During adolescence, there is an increase in susceptibility to peer influence and a decline in susceptibility to parental influence (Mounts, 2002). In addition, numerous investigators have found that peer influence is a strong predictor of adolescent substance use and delinquent behavior (Coie & Miller-Johnson, 2001; Mounts, 2002). Not surprisingly, many members of most societies believe that this connection is obvious. The folk wisdom to "avoid bad companions" has long been the traditional admonishment from parents and other concerned adults. The link between childhood peer *rejection* and antisocial behavior and delinquency is not so obvious, however, and requires a closer examination.

One of the strongest predictors of later involvement in antisocial behavior is early rejection by peers (Dodge, 2003; Parker & Asher, 1987; Trentacosta & Shaw, 2009). In elementary school, being liked and accepted by the peer group is a crucial developmental task, generally leading to healthy psychological and social development (Rubin, Bukowski, & Parker, 1998). Social rejec-tion by peers in the elementary school grades, on the other hand, presents a very powerful risk factor for delinquency in adolescence and antisocial behavior throughout the life course (Laird, Jordan, Dodge, Pettit, & Bates, 2001). Research has consistently demonstrated that peer rejec-tion by first-grade peers is significantly linked to the development of antisocial behavior by the fourth grade (Cowan & Cowan, 2004; Miller-Johnson *et al.*, 2002). Furthermore, those children who were rejected for at least two or three years by second grade had a 50 percent chance of displaying clinically significant antisocial behavior later in adolescence, in contrast with just a 9 percent chance for those children who managed to avoid early peer rejection (Dodge & Pettit, 2003). Some researchers also find evidence of a "cascade effect," whereby conduct disorders lead to peer rejection and then to depressive symptoms in elementary school children (Gooren, van Lier, Stegge, Terwogt, & Koot, 2011).

Interestingly, the quality of parent–child and marital relationships seems to play a significant role in whether a child is rejected or not by peers early in his or her life. Research by Cowan and Cowan (2004) demonstrates that "negative qualities in marital- and parent-child relationships in both prekindergarten and kindergarten are risk factors for low social skills, aggressive behavior, and rejection in the early years of elementary school" (p. 173).

Peer-rejected children frequently interact with one another or gravitate to antisocial peers (Laird, Pettit, Dodge, & Bates, 2005). During the adolescent years, involvement with antisocial peers shows a robust and consistent relationship to delinquency, drug use, and a range of other problematic behaviors (Laird *et al.*, 2005). Consequently, we would expect that both peer rejection *and* involvement with antisocial peers would be characteristic of those youngsters exhibiting antisocial or delinquent behavior early in their social development.

WHY ARE SOME CHILDREN REJECTED BY THEIR PEERS?   Children are often rejected by their peers for a variety of reasons, but their own aggressive behavior appears to be a prominent reason. Children tend to reject those peers who frequently use forms of physical and verbal aggression as their preferred way of dealing with others. These findings prompted many social scientists to conclude that aggressive children are more likely than nonaggressive children to be rejected by peers. Ongoing research indicates, however, that the relationship may not be that straightforward. First, peers also may reject peers whom they perceive as shy and socially withdrawn. Second, not all aggressive children are rejected by peers; some are liked, accepted, and sought as friends. In fact, research finds that many popular youngsters are often dominant, arrogant, and physically and relationally aggressive (Cillessen & Mayeux, 2004; Rose, Swenson, & Waller, 2004). Thus, if the children are rejected, it is not *always* because they are aggressive.

On the other hand, aggression *combined with* peer rejection does appear to lead to serious antisocial or delinquent behavior. Children who are *both* physically aggressive and socially rejected by their peers have a high probability of becoming serious delinquents during adolescence and violent offenders during early adulthood. Researchers Coie and Miller-Johnson (2001), for example, conclude from their extensive review of the research literature that "those aggressive children who are rejected by peers are at a significantly greater risk for chronic antisocial behavior than those who are not rejected" (p. 201).

WHICH CHILDREN ARE PRONE TO PEER REJECTION?   An important question still remains: Why are certain aggressive children rejected in the first place? Coie (2004) points out that there are three important differences between peer-rejected boys and nonrejected boys. First, peer-rejected, aggressive boys are more impulsive and have problems sustaining attention and staying on task. Consequently, they are more likely to be disruptive of ongoing activities in the classroom or during group play. Second, peer-rejected, aggressive boys are aroused to anger more readily and probably have more difficulty calming down. This emotional rage is more likely to result in physical and verbal attacks on peers, which in turn encourages peers to avoid them altogether. Third, rejected, aggressive youngsters have fewer social and interpersonal skills for making friends and maintaining positive relationships with peers. In addition, they probably have acquired fewer social and interpersonal skills because they have had limited opportunities to practice these skills on nonrejected peers.

In summary, peer-rejected children often, though not invariably, are aggressive, but they also tend to be more argumentative, inattentive, and disruptive than others, and generally have poorer social skills. These behaviors are characteristic of attention deficit/hyperactivity disorder (ADHD), which will be discussed in more detail later in the section "Psychological Risk Factors." The observation that peer-rejected boys demonstrate inattentive, impulsive, disruptive behavior suggests that ADHD may contribute to some of the peer rejection. A study by Erhardt and Hinshaw (1994) underscores this possibility.

The study involved 25 boys with ADHD and 24 other boys who participated in a summer school program, all of whom did not know one another at the beginning of the program. The boys ranged in ages from 6 to 12 years old. As early as the first day of social interactions between the two groups, the ADHD and comparison boys showed clear differences in social behaviors, with the ADHD youngsters displaying socially noxious and noncompliance-disruptive behaviors. More important, within the first day, the ADHD youngsters were overwhelmingly rejected by their peers. Other studies have found similar results, with ADHD symptoms and aggression showing a close link to eventual antisocial behavioral patterns (Coie, 2004; Miller-Johnson *et al.*, 2002). Again, this topic is discussed in more detail later in the chapter.

GENDER DIFFERENCES IN PEER REJECTION   It should be noted that, to date, most of the research and theoretical work examining the effects of peer rejection, aggression, and delinquent behavior has focused on boys. Among girls, little is known about the combined effects of aggression and peer rejection. In one of the few studies focusing on girls, Prinstein and La Greca (2004) found that the development of antisocial and delinquent behavior in girls, as in boys, can be predicted by early involvement in aggressive behavior with peers. However, in a national sample of 413 children and adolescents, Higgins, Piquero, and Piquero (2011) found high peer rejection was related to high delinquency and crime in males but not in females.

There is also some evidence to suggest that relationally aggressive girls are more likely than nonaggressive girls to be peer rejected (Crick, 1995). Relational aggression is the tendency to hurt others and diminish their social status by words, shunning, or other nonphysical methods. Prinstein and La Greca discovered—as did Crick—that peer rejection among girls in elementary school not only increased aggression but also was associated with increased substance abuse and other delinquent behaviors during adolescence. On the other hand, peer acceptance reduced and even eliminated the risk of aggression and other delinquent behaviors later on. More specifically, the effects of childhood aggression and antisocial behavior were mollified under conditions of high acceptance by peers.

GANG OR DEVIANT GROUP INFLUENCES ON REJECTED YOUTH   There are three major perspectives on the influence of peer groups on antisocial and delinquent behavior. One perspective argues that youngsters become delinquent as a direct result of association with deviant peer groups. According to this view, almost any child is susceptible to the negative influences of participating in a deviant peer group. A second perspective contends that antisocial, peer-rejected youths seek out greater contact with similar peer-rejected and socially unskillful peers. A third perspective is somewhat between these two positions. Peer-rejected, antisocial children are drawn to deviant groups with members similar to themselves, and this encourages and amplifies *already existing* antisocial tendencies. Current research evidence is in favor of the third perspective. It appears that childhood peer rejection encourages children to participate in deviant peer groups that then *amplify* tendencies to become more deviant and antisocial. Put another way, deviant group membership or gangs encourage and increase the already existing antisocial patterns in children and adolescents. As noted by Coie (2004), "The impact of deviant peer group influences on the *crystallization of an antisocial developmental trajectory* [emphasis added] has been solidly documented" (p. 257).

Although the bulk of the evidence supports the third perspective of amplification of already existing deviant tendencies, there is some evidence that deviant group membership appears to encourage some nondelinquent children to participate in *minor* delinquent actions. For example, while following the social development of youngsters, ages 11–17, Elliott and Menard (1996) discovered that nondelinquent youths were more inclined to engage in minor delinquent activity after joining a deviant peer group than before. And Thornberry, Krohn, Lizotte, and Chard-Wierschem (1993) report that nondelinquent youths who joined gangs were more likely to engage in minor delinquent behavior while gang members but decreased or terminated their delinquent behavior when they left the group. These findings suggest that many children and adolescents join deviant groups for protection or because this is expected in their social environment; the desire to participate in antisocial acts is not a priority. Given the opportunity to join a prosocial group and to develop in a socially healthy environment, they would probably choose the prosocial group.

Preschool Experiences

Over the past 30 years, children as a group have been shifted gradually from home to center-based day care or nursery school. The proportion of mothers participating in the workforce has increased substantially in recent years; because mothers have traditionally been the primary care-takers, this is a significant change. The percentage of mothers with children under age six work-ing outside the home increased from 12 percent in 1947, to 31 percent in 1975, to 64 percent in 1997 (Tran & Weinraub, 2006). In 2003, more than half the mothers with infants less than one year old were in the labor force (Tran & Weinraub, 2006). The most recent data indicate that over 60 percent of children under the age of five are in some form of day-care or nonparental care on a regular basis (Morrissey, 2009; U.S. Bureau of the Census, 2002). About 15 percent of young children are in two or more child-care arrangements during a typical week (Morrissey, 2009).

While there are obviously numerous exceptions, out-of-home child care in the United States is, on average, mediocre. The quality of child care provided by day-care centers is highly variable, in large part due to low wages and high staff turnover in many facilities. Nonetheless, licensed day-care centers, which are expected to meet minimal standards for nutrition, program-ming, and staffing, are often more adequate than individual care providers whom some parents must rely upon. However it occurs, poor-quality child care has been reported to put children's development at risk for poorer language, poor cognitive development, and lower ratings of social and emotional adjustment (Tran & Weinraub, 2006). Unfortunately, children from families with single employed mothers and low incomes are more likely to be found in lower-quality care.

The reality of multiple child-care arrangements has only recently come to attention. The nation's economic crisis of 2009 resulted in many parents assuming second jobs—such as low-paying part-time work on weekends—to keep the family financially afloat. This may necessitate "juggling" child care duties among day-care centers, relatives, babysitters, and neighbors. Unfortunately, recent research suggests that these multiple arrangements have negative impacts on children's social adjustment (Morrissey, 2009). Being placed in different homes, day-care centers, classrooms, or peer groups on a weekly basis increases problem behavior and decreases prosocial behavior. This is especially the case for young children with difficult temperaments (to be discussed in Chapter 3) and young girls.

More encouragingly, there is evidence that improving out-of-home care for children can have long-term beneficial effects. Low-income children who experience high-quality infant and preschool care show better school achievement and socialized behavior in later years than similar children without preschool child-care experience or with experience in lower-quality care. For low-income children, quality child care offers learning opportunities and social and emotional supports that many would not experience at home. Again, this is not to say that low-income parents do not or cannot offer these opportunities to their children; however, the stress associated with maintaining the household under stringent economic conditions may make it difficult to do so. Income is not the determining factor in providing enrichment experiences, however. Parents in upper income brackets may also be overwhelmed by personal problems, long hours, and stressful work situations that affect their relationships with their children and the opportunities they provide them. In this sense, out of home, high-quality, preschool experiences benefit all children, regardless of the family's economic circumstances.

Behavioral problems in preschool children can be problematic, both for the children displaying them and for the children witnessing them, however. According to Goldstein, Arnold, Rosenberg, Stowe, and Ortiz (2001), day-care teachers worry about aggression in toddlers more than any other behavioral problem, and they report disruptive behavior as their greatest classroom challenge. These concerns may be important, as aggressive tendencies at three years of age predict aggressive behavior later in life (Goldstein *et al.*, 2001). Moreover, accumulating evidence indicates that the amount of exposure that a child has to aggressive peers in day care or preschool is predictive of later child aggressive behavior, perhaps because of modeling effects (Dodge & Pettit, 2003).

After-School Care

The quality of after-school care has been closely associated with the development of antisocial behavior (Flannery, Williams, & Vazsonyi, 1999; Posner & Vandell, 1999; Vandell & Posner, 1999). In the 1990s, the term *latch-key children* was applied to children who returned from school to an empty house and remained on their own until their parents or guardians finished their own workday. Children who spend fairly large amounts of time in unsupervised after-school self-care in the early elementary grades are at elevated risk for behavior problems in early adolescence (Pettit, Laird, Bates, & Dodge, 1997). Moreover, such children are more likely to spend time in unsupervised activity with peers in early adolescence (Colwell, Pettit, Meece, Bates, & Dodge, 2001). Antisocial children seek out niches that involve association with antisocial peers and environments with minimal adult supervision (Snyder, Reid, & Patterson, 2003). Day-care centers that open their doors to children after school hours or community groups that offer after-school programs in troubled neighborhoods can make a positive difference.

School Failure

Early school failure is also linked to antisocial development and delinquency (Dodge & Pettit, 2003). Interestingly, research indicates that retention in kindergarten and in the early school grades has long-term detrimental effects on development, in spite of its immediate academic benefits (Dodge & Pettit, 2003; Holmes, 1989; Sameroff, Peck, & Eccles, 2004). On the other hand, delaying entry into kindergarten does not appear to have the same effects. It is the "staying back" label that prompts retained children to be seen negatively and socially rejected and ridiculed by their peers (Plummer & Graziano, 1987).

In fact, early school failure seems to be more strongly associated with delinquency than low intelligence (Hinshaw, 1992). Some researchers discovered that the odds of severe delinquent behavior in eight-year-old male children who were failing in school were nearly double those of other male children (Loeber, Farrington, Stouthamer-Loeber, & Van Kammen, 1998).

Regardless of race or ethnic background, reading achievement appears to play a prominent role in school failure. In fact, not only is poor reading achievement closely associated with school failure, but it also predicts later arrest and criminal activity in boys (Petras *et al.*, 2004). On the other hand, a high level of reading achievement seems to prevent at-risk youth from engaging in later antisocial behavior. More specifically, a high level of reading achievement brings more acceptance from mainstream peers, greater attachment to school, enhanced job prospects in young adulthood, and better cognitive resources for anticipating the negative consequences of engaging in criminal activity (Petras *et al.*, 2004).

In summary, the most prominent social risk factors that have been identified in the development of criminal behavior include the many disadvantages of living in poverty, peer rejection combined with association with antisocial peers, poor-quality child care during the preschool years, and school failure. The more social risk factors a child experiences during his or her early life, the higher the probability a child will follow a developmental pathway toward delinquent and criminal behavior. Parental and family risk factors may play an even more prominent role in the development of antisocial behavior.

PARENTAL AND FAMILY RISK FACTORS

In the past decade, social science researchers have given extensive attention to the role of the family in providing a healthy environment for children and adolescents (see, generally, Biglan *et al.*, 2012 for an excellent review of this literature). Much of this attention is directed at identifying aversive events, such as abuse, criticism, insults, and coercive interactions among parents and children and among family members as a group. Once the events have been identified, treatment programs or interventions are attempted, with the goal of establishing a nurturing family environment. As Biglan *et al.* note, "Reducing aversive conditions such as harsh and inconsistent discipline and parental rejection is a core component of virtually every experimentally evaluated parenting intervention" (p. 259).

Single-Parent Households

According to the last completed official census (2001) figures, over 12 million American families with children are maintained by only one parent (U.S. Bureau of the Census, 2001). In 2004, 26 percent of all children in the United States lived with one parent; 88 percent of these children were with their mothers (Kreider, 2008). In 2010, 23 percent of children lived with only their mothers, 3 percent lived with only their fathers, and 4 percent lived with neither of their parents (ChildStats.gov, 2012). Early studies based on official data found that delinquents were more likely than nondelinquents to come from homes where parents were divorced or separated (Eaton & Polk, 1961; Glueck & Glueck, 1950; Monahan, 1957; Rodman & Grams, 1967). This led to conclusions that the single-parent home—or the "broken home" as it was called—could be blamed for much delinquency and thus could be considered a risk factor. Beginning in the 1970s, when self-report data indicated that delinquent behavior was widespread, criminologists began to question these conclusions. Today, researchers are more likely to examine accompanying factors such as the quality of the parent–child relationship, the family's economic status, and the degree of emotional support provided to the family by other adults, such as extended family members or community agents.

A wide variety of circumstances can lead to a single-parent home. The home may have started that way, as when an unmarried woman gives birth to or adopts a child. Additionally, two-parent homes may be "broken" by a wide variety of circumstances—death, desertion, divorce, or separation. Such separations do not affect all families the same way. Furthermore, there is evidence that children from single-parent homes that are relatively conflict-free are less likely to be delinquent than children from conflict-ridden "intact" homes (Gove & Crutchfield, 1982). The composition of the home (e.g., grandparents, stepparent, relatives, significant others, or friends) also must be considered. The "nontraditional" family has become a fixture in today's society. Many researchers define family as individuals related by blood or by legal arrangements (i.e., marriages, adoptions, legal guardianships, civil unions). Others point out that individuals who live together in long-term committed relationships—either as friends or as sexual partners—and who may be caring for their own or other people's children, are also family.

While the relationship between single-parent homes and delinquency continues to be commonly reported, we are far from explaining it—and it may be pointless to try. If the single-parent home is a risk factor, it is probably influenced by other interacting variables. Rather than concentrating on the *structure* of the family, a focus on the *process* is far more desirable. As Flynn (1983, p. 13) asserts, "One point is indisputably clear in the literature: A stable, secure, and mutually supportive family is exceedingly important in delinquency prevention." However family is defined, it should include at least one competent, caring adult with responsibility for the well-being of the child.

Parental Practices and Styles

Parental practices and styles pertain to the ways in which parents or caregivers interact with their children. Some parental (or caregiver) practices and styles appear to be more likely than others to lead to delinquency, and thus can be called risk factors. **Parental practices** are strategies employed by parents to achieve specific academic, social, or athletic goals across different contexts and situations (Hart, Nelson, Robinson, Olsen, & McNeilly-Choque, 1998). That is, the practices used by parents are intended to influence some particular aspect of the child's behavior (Mounts, 2002). Giving a child a weekly allowance with the hope of teaching her to manage money is an example of a practice. Reading with children, attending their sports events, or serving as room parents in school are other examples. Parenting practices have a direct effect on the development of specific child behaviors (from table manners to academic performance) and characteristics (such as acquisition of particular values or high self-esteem). Unfortunately, some parental practices are misguided at best, and at worst may constitute child neglect or abuse.

While parental practices refer to parental behavioral patterns, **parental styles** refer to parent–child interactions characterized by parental *attitudes* toward the child and the emotional climate of the parent–child relationship (Baumrind, 1991a; Mounts, 2002). Behaviors such as gestures, tone of voice, or the spontaneous expression of emotion are examples of parental style. For example, responsive parent–child interactions are described as warm, playful, accepting, and engaging. Studies reveal that a responsive parenting style often leads to social competence, peer acceptance, and less antisocial behavior (Hart *et al.*, 1998).

FOUR TYPES OF PARENTAL STYLES   Diana Baumrind (1991a) identified four parental styles: (1) authoritarian; (2) permissive; (3) authoritative; and (4) neglecting (see **Table 2-1**). Those parents who use an **authoritarian style** try to shape, control, and evaluate the behavior of their children in accordance with some preestablished, absolute standard. The authoritarian household has numerous rules and regulations which must be rigidly observed, often without question or explanation. Authoritarian parents discourage any verbal exchanges that imply equality between parent and child; the parent is the authority in all important matters, as well as many unimportant ones. Authoritarian parents expect their children to be obedient and unquestioningly respectful of authority. These parents are often referred to as "running a tight ship." Deviations and transgressions are met with punitive, forceful measures, which may or may not include physical punishment.

TABLE 2-1 Summary of Baumrind's Parental Styles	
Style	**Intent**
Authoritarian	To shape and control child's life
Permissive	No control and extremely few restrictions
Authoritative	To be rational and apply reasonable restrictions
Neglecting	Detached and unengaged in child's life

Years ago, a student who was the youngest in a family of five children, revealed to the class one of the most memorable experiences of his childhood. An older brother—then a high school junior—had arrived home shortly after midnight, heavily under the influence of alcohol. The father of the family woke each of the younger children and had them watch as he placed the oldest son face down across a chair and whipped his backside. He then told the other children, "This is what will happen to you if I ever see you come home like this." Asked about the outcome of this incident, the student said, "We all turned out fine; we knew our father loved us and we still know it now." Obviously, many of us would not agree with this approach, but despite this, the authoritarian parent is not the one most closely associated with criminal behavior in his or her offspring.

Parents who adopt a **permissive style** display tolerant, nonpunitive, accepting attitudes toward their children's behavior, including expressions of aggressive and sexual impulses. Permissive parents generally avoid asserting authority or imposing social controls or restrictions on the child's behavior. In this type of family, parents see themselves as "resource persons" to be consulted if needed. Permissive parents allow children to set their own time schedule for eating, sleeping, watching television, playing video games, leaving the home, and meeting with friends, and they employ little parental monitoring. They are, in essence, ineffectual in their socializing roles. While this may seem a harsh appraisal, and while these parents may suggest that children learn from their own mistakes, research indicates that permissiveness is not the recommended approach (Jackson & Foshee, 1998).

In the **authoritative style**, parents try to direct their children's activities in a rational, issue-oriented manner. There are frequent decision-making exchanges and a general spirit of open communication between parents and children. The hallmark of the family led by authoritative parents is reasoned discussion punctuated with social controls. Authoritative parents expect age-related "mature" behavior from the child, and they apply firm, consistent enforcement of family rules and standards. At the same time, they encourage independence and individuality. In the illustration given above, an authoritative parent might have allowed the high school junior to go to bed—perhaps even tucked him in—but would likely have reasoned with the son the next day and applied some penalty to the unacceptable behavior.

Finally, in the **neglecting style**, parents demonstrate detachment and very little involvement in their children's life or activities. They are neither demanding nor responsive. "They do not structure or monitor, and are not supportive, but may be actively rejecting or else neglect their childrearing responsibilities altogether" (Baumrind, 1991b, p. 62). Basically, the parent or parents respond minimally to either the child's needs or the child's behavior (Brenner & Fox, 1999). They are far more than permissive; they simply have no interest in controlling the child's behavior or monitoring the child's activities. In its extreme form, this style of parenting qualifies as child neglect. It should come as no surprise that Hoeve *et al.* (2007) found neglecting parenting was one of the strongest risk factors identified with delinquency and a life of crime. Baumrind (1991b) found that adolescents from unengaged families were far more likely than their adolescent peers to be antisocial, lacking self-regulation, social responsibility, and cognitive competence.

Baumrind's parenting types are not without their problems. Many parents, for example, vacillate between permissiveness and authoritativeness, and some vary their styles according to the age of the child. Authoritative parents may allow their children to set their own eating and sleeping schedules and choose their modes of dress, but may demand extensive input into decisions related to school, careers, or work. Likewise, some parents may be generally permissive in style, but suddenly erupt into anger and demand that their children abide by a newly announced rule. Despite its shortcomings, "Baumrind's conceptualization of parenting style has produced a remarkably consistent picture of the type of parenting conducive to the successful socialization of children into the dominant culture of the United States" (Darling & Steinberg, 1993, p. 487).

ENMESHED AND LAX PARENTAL STYLES   James Snyder and Gerald Patterson (1987) conclude that two parental styles contribute directly or indirectly to delinquency. They label the two styles "enmeshed" and "lax," and these are very similar to Baumrind's authoritarian and permissive styles. In the **enmeshed style**, parents see an unusually large number of minor behaviors as problematic, and they use ineffective, authoritarian strategies to deal with them. "These parents don't ignore even very trivial excessive behaviors. They issue more and poorer commands, use verbal threats, disapproval, and cajoling more frequently, but fail to consistently and effectively back up these verbal reprimands with nonviolent, nonphysical punishment" (Snyder & Patterson, 1987, p. 221). The ineffective use of coercive punishment sets up a reverberating pattern of family interactions "which elicits, maintains, and exacerbates the aggressive behavior of all family members" (p. 221). When one family member in this coercive interaction acts aversively, other family members react the same way, escalating the exchange. Cathy reacts strongly to her brother's loud music by suddenly yelling at him to turn it off. He yells back at her to "stick it." Cathy bangs violently on his door. He screams louder. The father screams at both, telling them to "shut up" or else. Cathy yells louder and proceeds to kick in her brother's door. She throws a vase at him, just missing. He runs after her, throwing a book. Eventually, the child sometimes "wins" this escalating confrontation when parents "give in" to demands, reinforcing this highly aversive interpersonal strategy. For example, father kicks a chair and "orders" the brother to turn the loud music off. Thus, parents and children "teach" each other that this harsh tactic works in social interactions, a pattern that soon extends to members outside the family.

Enmeshed parents also sometimes dispense authoritarian, harsh punishment, although it is inconsistent and ineffective. However, they probably do not have the energy to apply punishments to each and every behavior they perceive as problematic. Consequently, there are many instances where aversive behavior goes unpunished, such as in the preceding example. This pattern results in an intermittent, inconsistent punishment schedule that, in the long run, does little to discourage antisocial behavior.

The **lax style** employs strategies that are the opposite of the above. According to Snyder and Patterson (1987), lax parents are not sufficiently attuned to what constitutes problematic or antisocial behavior in children. Consequently, they allow much of it to slip by, without disciplinary actions. For a variety of reasons, they fail to recognize or accept the fact that their children are involved in deviant, antisocial, or even violent actions. They simply do not believe it is happening, or they convince themselves that there is very little they can do about it. Lax parents may pretend they are unaware that their son is hosting a drug fest in the back field or fail to see the danger in the weaponry he is collecting.

It appears that overcontrolling parental behaviors—those associated with enmeshed and authoritarian styles—are closely connected to the development of aggression and antisocial behavior in children and adolescents (Blitstein, Murray, Lytle, Birnbaum, & Perry, 2005; Ruchkin, 2002). By contrast, an authoritative style has the opposite effect. Blitstein *et al.* (2005) report evidence that violent behavior and antisocial behavior among girls may be buffered by the presence of a warm, responsive (i.e., authoritative) mother, although the same result was not found for boys. In short, authoritative mothers seem to play a more significant role for the prevention of antisocial behavior in girls than in boys (Hollister-Wagner, Foshee, & Jackson, 2001).

Of all the parenting styles discussed in this section, neglecting style is most closely associated with antisocial behavior and delinquency. Although this is not surprising, having a neglecting parent does not automatically lead to serious antisocial behavior. Alternative adult role models, such as relatives, teachers, coaches, or mentors, may be available. Other parental styles, though, are also tied to delinquency. These include Baumrind's permissive and Snyder and Patterson's lax style. The children brought up with these styles often have very low levels of self-reliance and great difficulty controlling their impulses. Permissive parents have long been faulted both for lack of discipline and lack of supervision. They may treat their children as adults, pushing them into adult behaviors or responsibilities far before they are ready and without needed direction from adult authority figures.

Parental Monitoring

Closely related to parental styles and antisocial behavior is the issue of parental supervision or monitoring. **Parental monitoring** "refers to parents' awareness of their child's peer associates, free-time activities, and physical whereabouts when outside the home" (Snyder & Patterson, 1987, pp. 225–226). The amount and quality of parental monitoring is influenced by a number of things. For example, divorce, serious financial distress, loss of job, parental psychological disorders, substance abuse, or death may significantly affect family dynamics and parental or caregiver monitoring. Monitoring appears to be especially important from about age nine to mid-adolescence, an observation that has received substantial support from several studies (Laird, Pettit, Bates, & Dodge, 2003). Parental anecdotes often support this as well. As one mother expressed, "I couldn't afford to be a stay-at-home Mom throughout my kids' childhoods, so I chose to do it when my oldest got to middle school. That's when they needed me home the most." However, monitoring does not necessarily require the physical presence of the parent. Other adult caretakers or after-school programs also could provide suitable monitoring. The working mother in the above example could still be an effective monitor by being aware of her children's activities and alert to their needs. In addition, we cannot underestimate the importance of *neighborhood* monitoring. For example, some researchers have found lower rates of delinquency and crime in communities where adults monitor the actions of young people and speak up when they see misbehavior (Sampson, Morenoff, & Gannon-Rowley, 2002). As has been frequently asserted, "It takes a village to raise a child."

The bulk of the available research also has concluded that the amount and quality of parental monitoring is a strong predictor of antisocial behavior during later childhood and adolescence (Kilgore, Snyder, & Lentz, 2000). Other studies have found significant evidence that poor parental monitoring and supervision are related to higher levels of violent behavior (Singer *et al.*, 1999) and drug abuse (Webb, Bray, Getz, & Adams, 2002). Some studies have indicated that poor parental monitoring and supervision increase the risk of delinquency two and a half times over those youth who experienced better supervision (Browning & Loeber, 1999).

Interestingly, still more research reports that some children and adolescents are easier to monitor and supervise than others, largely because of their willingness to cooperate in the monitoring process (Kerns, Aspelmeier, Gentzler, & Grabill, 2001). Although this in itself is not surprising, the researchers did document that youths who have a secure and responsive relationship with parents are more willing to be monitored, highlighting once again the importance of a positive parent–child relationship.

Influence of Siblings

Siblings imitate each other, and most often younger children imitate their older siblings rather than the reverse (Garcia, Shaw, Winslow, & Yaggi, 2000). Since siblings generally spend so much time together, it is reasonable to assume that they play a role in shaping the development of aggression and antisocial behavior. This area has not been researched as heavily as other peer influences, but the few studies available indicate that adolescents with high rates of delinquency are also more likely to have siblings with high rates of delinquency (Coie & Miller-Johnson, 2001). Rowe and Gulley (1992) suggest that older siblings who engage in delinquent behavior reinforce antisocial behavior in younger siblings when there is a close and warm relationship between the youths. If the siblings are not close, the opposite effect may occur. That is, the nonaggressive younger sibling may make it a point not to be like his or her older aggressive or antisocial sibling. In addition, the risk of delinquency is higher when the delinquent sibling is closer in age than those siblings spaced further apart (Rowe, Rodgers, & Meseck-Bushey, 1992).

Parental Psychopathology

Children of parents who are clinically depressed—especially mothers—are at increased risk for a range of socioemotional and behavioral problems, including antisocial behavior, emotion dysregulation, and poor cognitive development (Bennett, Bendersky, & Lewis, 2002; Mazulis, Hyde, & Clark, 2004; Nelson, Hammen, Brennan, & Ullman, 2003). As they grow older, children whose mothers were depressed during their infancy continue to display behavioral problems and often engage in various kinds of criminal behavior. Mothers are singled out because they tend to be the dominant caretakers. However, the risk for developing problem behaviors appears to be magnified if both parents are depressed during early childhood.

Parental alcoholism elevates risk for a variety of negative child outcomes, including behavioral difficulties, antisocial behavior, and subsequent alcoholism (Loukas, Zucker, Fitzgerald, & Krull, 2003; Zucker *et al.*, 2000). Interestingly, Loukas and her colleagues (2003) found that the presence of paternal alcoholism in the family may be more important than maternal alcoholism in contributing to a son's antisocial behavior and maladjustment.

The aggressive behavior that is demonstrated in domestic violence is clearly a form of parental psychopathology. However, this topic is discussed more fully in Chapter 9 under multiassaultive families and family violence.

Lack of Attachment

According to John Bowlby (1969), the early relationship between an infant and a caregiver largely determines the quality of social relationships later in life. Bowlby's **attachment theory** has been discussed extensively in the psychological literature and may be extended to the study of criminal behavior. It fits in well with the family and parental issues discussed above.

Some infants, when placed in a strange and unfamiliar environment, show *secure attachment*. They play comfortably in their mother's presence and demonstrate curiosity about their new and challenging environment. When the mother leaves, the child becomes distressed, but when she returns, the child beams with sheer delight. These infants use their mother or caregiver as a secure base from which to explore. Other infants may show an *insecure attachment*, which is often divided into two attachment styles: *anxious/ambivalent* and *avoidant*. The anxious/ambivalent-attached child becomes intensely distressed and anxious by separation, and in new environments, they often cling anxiously to their mother without much exploration (Ainsworth, 1979). When the mother returns after separation, they may become indifferent and even hostile toward the mother. These infants may push the returning mother away, stiffen up, or cry when picked up. The *avoidant attachment* style is characterized by little distress on the part of the infant, whether the mother is present or not. They rarely cry during separation or reunion. Avoidant attachment in infancy and childhood is associated with dismissing attachment in adulthood (Adshead, 2002).

Mary Ainsworth (1979) observed that caregivers who are sensitive, affectionate, and responsive, and who create in their babies a basic trust of the world, typically have securely attached infants. Children with a secure attachment base usually develop into psychologically healthy children. As adults, they form good relationships, empathize with others, and generally show good self-regulation (Ansbro, 2008). "Later on, they emerge as more competent and more sympathetic in interaction with peers" (Ainsworth, 1979, p. 936). Most infants in the United States are regarded as having a secure attachment to their mothers or caregivers (Thompson, 1998). It is also commonly believed that our attachments in infancy play a powerful role in romantic relationships as adults.

According to Ainsworth and her colleagues (1979), infants with avoidant attachment style often have parents who are aloof, distant, and prefer to avoid intimacy with their children. Consequently, these children as adults have difficulty forming intimate relationships. Infants with anxious/ambivalent attachment usually have parents who are overbearing and inconsistent in their affection and intimacy. These infants never know when and how their parents will respond to their needs. As adults, they want to have close relationships but continually worry about their partners and friends returning the affection. They tend to become obsessive and preoccupied with their relationships, especially with spouses and romantic partners.

Ward and his associates (Ward, Hudson, Marshall, & Siegert, 1995) hypothesize that many sex offenders probably had parents who were inconsistently affectionate and poor at identifying their child's needs. In essence, the sex offenders demonstrate the dismissing (avoidant) attachment style in their adult relationships. Adshead (2002) reports evidence for insecure attachment in her study of violent offenders. She notes that many victims of interpersonal violence are part of the violent offender's attachment network: a child, a parent, a partner, or expartner. Fear of loss or separation can generate strong feelings of anxiety and rage in the offender, often resulting in violent actions. Adshead found that a majority of offenders showed a dismissing attachment style, suggesting a diminished capacity for empathy toward their victims or relationships.

Discussion of the attachment process serves as a good link between the social risk factors reviewed in this section and the psychological factors about to be covered. (For a summary of all of the developmental risk factors, see **Table 2-2**.) While it has a connection with parenting styles,

TABLE 2-2 Developmental Risk Factors for Delinquency

Social Risk Factors
Poverty*
Early peer rejection
Association with antisocial peers
Inadequate preschool child care
Inadequate after-school care
School failure

Parental and Family Risk Factors
Single-parent household*
Permissive or lax parental style
Minimal parental monitoring
Parental psychopathology
Physical and emotional abuse/neglect
Domestic violence and/or substance abuse
Antisocial siblings

Psychological Risk Factors
Cognitive and language deficiencies
Low IQ scores or psychometric intelligence
Attention deficit hyperactivity disorder* (ADHD)
Conduct disorder (CD)
Oppositional Defiant Disorder (ODD)

*Must be accompanied by other factors in order to be considered strong risk.

the attachment process also reflects a characteristic of the individual offender. Although attachment may be an important component, it is only one of many and is unlikely to be a major factor. Furthermore, the factors covered below have received more research attention with respect to the development of antisocial behavior.

PSYCHOLOGICAL RISK FACTORS

Lack of Empathy

Anyone observing a group of children playing together can notice differences among them if one child gets hurt and begins to cry. Some children will ignore the crying child and continue with their play; others will become solicitous and want to be sure the child is alright. Although this is a simplistic example, we could say that the children in the second group are more empathetic than those in the first.

In practice and research, empathy is perceived as existing along two dimensions: affective and cognitive. Affective empathy is "an emotional response characterized by feelings of concern for another and a desire to alleviate that person's distress" (Young, Fox, & Zahn-Waxler, 1999, p. 1189). Cognitive empathy refers to the ability to understand a person from his or her frame of reference or point of view rather than simply from one's own point of view. Jolliffe and Farrington (2007) note that affective empathy is the ability to *experience* another person's emotions, whereas cognitive empathy is the ability to *understand* another's emotions. These terms are not mutually exclusive, however. In other words, one can possess both affective and cognitive empathy.

Deficiencies in empathy have long been considered characteristic of persistently aggressive and antisocial individuals (Cohen & Strayer, 1996; Hastings, Zahn-Waxler, Usher, Robinson, & Bridges, 2000). For example, low affective empathy is hypothesized to be a central ingredient of psychopathy, which is a combination of psychological and behavioral factors related to an increased tendency to engage in antisocial and violent behavior. Interestingly, psychopaths are believed to be able to understand the emotions of others (cognitive empathy), but show a remarkable inability to experience them. We return to the topic of psychopathy in greater detail in Chapter 7.

Girls generally show both dimensions of empathy earlier than boys, beginning in the second year of life and continuing at least through adolescence (Eisenberg & Fabes, 1998; Hastings *et al.*, 2000). The relationship between a lack of empathy and antisocial or excessively aggressive behavior is discernible in children during the early to middle elementary school years (Hastings *et al.*, 2000; Tremblay, Vitaro, Gagnon, Piche, & Royer, 1992), and seems to become stronger with age (Miller & Eisenberg, 1988). Children who demonstrate little empathy in the third grade exhibit even less in the eighth grade.

Researchers who have distinguished between the two dimensions of empathy have generally found that a deficiency in affective (or emotional) empathy appears to be most strongly related to violence and persistent criminal behavior (Jolliffe & Farrington, 2007; de Kemp, Overbeek, de Wied, Engels, & Scholte, 2007; Schaffer, Clark, & Jeglic, 2009). "It…appears that it is the inability to experience the emotions of others which is related to violence for both males and females rather than the inability to understand other people's emotions" (Jolliffe & Farrington, 2007, p. 281). In addition, "Both high-frequency male and female offenders showed lower affective empathy (but not cognitive empathy) than low-rate offenders" (Jolliffe & Farrington, 2007, p. 281). Essentially, people who engage in violence and/or a large variety of serious offenses appear to have a significant inability to feel the pain of their victims.

Some research has shown an interesting association between lack of empathy and animal cruelty. A bumper sticker proclaims, "People who abuse animals rarely stop there." Research supports this aphorism with respect to both children and adults. Cruelty to animals, defined as "socially unacceptable behavior that intentionally causes unnecessary pain, suffering, or distress to and/or death of an animal" (Guymer, Mellor, Luk, & Pearse, 2001, p. 1057), is a behavior that demonstrates a lack of empathy; if it occurs in childhood, it can signify serious problem behavior. The swatting of flies or the destruction of insects does not qualify as cruelty (although torture of insects does qualify), but cruelty to dogs, cats, and other household pets is considered significant. Cruelty as defined here does not refer to chasing the family cat and playfully pulling its tail, but swinging the cat by the tail or setting its ears on fire is another matter.

Several studies have found a strong association between animal cruelty and violent behavior toward humans. For example, Stouthamer-Loeber and her associates (2004) followed young males from the ages of 13–25 and discovered that cruelty to animals was one of the strongest predictors of serious, violent criminal behavior. Lucia and Killias (2011) discovered, in their sample of 3,600 Swiss students (grades 7–9), that 12 percent admitted animal cruelty (17% of boys and 8% of girls). More importantly, the researchers found that youths who have been cruel to animals were three times more likely to have committed serious interpersonal violence, compared to youths with no reported history of animal cruelty. Wright and Hensley (2003) found a possible link between childhood cruelty to animals and later serial murders. In fact, the five serial murderers studied by Wright and Hensley, which included the infamous Jeffrey Dahmer, used the same method of torture and killing on their human victims as they had used on their animal victims. Merz-Perez, Heide, and Silverman (2001) reported a similar finding.

Cognitive and Language Deficiencies

Cognitive and language impairments increase the risk of antisocial behavior, at least in boys (Brownlie *et al.*, 2004). For example, a high percentage of children and adolescents diagnosed and treated for antisocial behavior and conduct disorders demonstrate language impairments (Cohen *et al.*, 1998; Giddan, Milling, & Campbell, 1996). **Language impairment** usually refers to problems expressing or understanding language, and some research has even traced these problems as far back as very early childhood. In an important study of Swedish children, Stattin and Klackenberg-Larsson (1993) discovered that poor language development during the second year of life was a significant predictor of adult criminal behavior. Brownlie *et al.* (2004) also found that boys diagnosed with a language impairment at age five were far more likely to exhibit delinquent behavior at age 19 than a group of boys without early indications of a language impairment. This relationship held even when controlling for verbal IQ, demographics, and family variables. Brownlie *et al.* speculated, though, that the association may be largely due to the negative impact that language impairments have on the child's schooling and academic performance in general. In addition, language-impaired children are often rejected by peers and are frequently viewed negatively by their teachers. In essence, language deficiency often makes school a painful and unappealing enterprise, leading to poor or disinterested performance on academic tasks.

Language problems also increase frustration levels in children who have difficulty expressing their points of view, which is so necessary for reasonable resolutions of conflict. This frustration, if not self-regulated, is likely to lead to aggressive and disruptive behavior at home and at school.

Intelligence and Delinquency

For some time, criminologists (and many psychologists) have been eager to label the relationship between intelligence and delinquency and crime as misguided and unsubstantiated. Even to mention the connection may prompt a derisive reaction. As Hirschi and Hindelang (1977, p. 572) wrote some years ago, "Textbooks in crime and delinquency ignore IQ or impatiently explain to the reader that IQ is no longer taken seriously by knowledgeable students simply because no differences worth considering have been revealed by research." Hirschi and Hindelang maintained that these textbooks were misleading, because the delinquency literature consistently reported that delinquents do, as a group, score lower on standard intelligence tests than nondelinquents.

In their 1977 paper, Hirschi and Hindelang hypothesized that an *indirect* causal relationship exists between IQ and delinquency. That is, a low IQ leads to poor performance and negative attitudes toward school, which in turn leads to school failure and ultimately to delinquency. Low IQ does not directly lead to delinquency. A high IQ, on the other hand, leads to good performance and positive attitudes toward school, which in turn leads to the internal acceptance of conventional values and conformity (nondelinquency). The essential point, according to Hirschi and Hindelang, is that the inverse relationship between IQ scores and delinquency continues to be documented by research.

Why does this relationship exist? To address this question, it is necessary to consider the meaning of IQ and to stress that it is not identical to "intelligence." The term *IQ* is an abbreviation of *intelligence quotient*, derived from a numerical score on a so-called *intelligence* test. The term *IQ* originated out of what is now called the **psychometric approach**. The word *psychometric* means "psychological measurement." Traditionally, the psychometric approach has searched for unique differences in persons through the use of psychological tests, including intelligence tests, scholastic aptitude tests (e.g., SAT), school achievement tests, personality inventories, and other specific abilities tests. The various tests are used for many purposes, such as selection, diagnosis, and evaluation. The psychometric approach continues to be widely used by practicing psychologists and mental health professionals. However, the term *psychometric intelligence* **(PI)**—which was preferred by some psychologists (Neisser *et al.*, 1996) in the 1990s—has not caught on. Consequently, the traditional term *IQ* continues to be used with great frequency today.

Satisfactory performance on a vast majority of intelligence tests depends greatly on language acquisition and verbal development. Usually, a person must have considerable experience using and defining words—particularly English words—to do well on most IQ tests. The examinee must be able to make conventional connections and see distinctions between verbal concepts. The examinee must also know the facts that the test designer deems important to know within mainstream culture. At the very least, almost all intelligence tests measure some aspect of academic skills that are taught in school or that predict success in school. A vast majority of psychologists today would agree that IQ scores are strongly influenced by social, educational, and cultural experiences. In short, all intelligence tests are culturally biased.

More importantly, IQ scores and the concept of intelligence should not be confused. The term *IQ* merely refers to a standardized score from a test. *Intelligence, on the other hand, is a broad, all-encompassing ability that defies any straightforward or simple definition.* It means many things to different people. *Intelligence* includes ability ranging from musical talent to logical mathematical skills. The term may also include wisdom, intuition, judgment, and even humor. While delinquents, as a group, do score lower on intelligence *tests,* this observation should not be construed as documenting that delinquents are less intelligent than nondelinquents. For example, Brazilian street children are masters at doing the math required for survival in their street business even though they have failed mathematics in school (Carraher, Carraher, & Schliemann, 1985; Neisser *et al.*, 1996). Likewise, institutionalized delinquents often display artistic and verbal skills and a wry sense of humor that are not tapped by traditional IQ scores.

Nevertheless, the relationship between IQ test scores and school performance is strong and consistent. "Wherever it has been studied, children with high scores on tests of intelligence tend to learn more of what is taught in school than their lower-scoring peers" (Neisser *et al.*, 1996, p. 82). Schools help develop certain intellectual skills and attitudes. Quality schools generally have positive effects on IQ. Preschool programs (e.g., Headstart) show significant positive effects on children during their early school years, and recent research shows that these gains do not fade when the program is over, provided there is periodic intervention during the child's middle school years.

IQ AND ETHNICITY   Average IQ scores do vary among racial and ethnic groups. For example, many studies using different tests and samples typically show African Americans scoring significantly lower than whites (Neisser *et al.*, 1996). Studies show, however, that this IQ gap has been consistently decreasing since 1980 (Nisbett, 2005; Vincent, 1991). Asian Americans and whites, on average, score about the same on IQ tests; Native Americans score slightly lower than other groups on verbal skills, but this slight difference may be the result of chronic middle-ear infections common among Native American children (McShane & Plas, 1984a, 1984b). Latinos, who make up the second largest and fastest-growing minority group in the United States, typically score somewhere between African Americans and whites. It is unclear what these reported differences mean, and we emphasize that this research was conducted some years ago. However, there is no evidence to support the view that racial or ethnic differences in psychometric intelligence are due to genetics or biological factors. Although genetics may play a role in *individual* differences in psychometric intelligence, there is little evidence for ethnic *group* differences.

In the decade since these studies were published, considerable change has occurred, though the quality of many inner-city schools is still deplorable. Furthermore, the election of an African American U.S. president and the accompanying conversations on race and ethnicity should have positive effects on the cultural mainstream. Blacks as well as individuals of other races and ethnicities are involved prominently in leadership positions in politics, education, business, and the arts. For this reason, children from various racial and ethnic groups should be increasingly less likely to feel alienated from what may have been perceived as the dominant culture.

Other factors—such as poor nutrition, inadequate prenatal care, lack of adequate childcare facilities, and inaccessibility to occupational and training opportunities—also play critical but largely unknown roles on intelligence. IQ scores are crude indices of mainstream language skills that are heavily influenced by experience. In general, rich and varied experiences increase IQ scores, and limited experience decreases them (Garbarino & Asp, 1981; Neisser *et al.*, 1996). School experiences, if positive, may increase language skills; if negative, they may stagnate, or even decrease, language skills. IQ scores are also strongly influenced by the type of test used, its content, the many characteristics of testing situations, and the training and skill of the examiner.

Still, even with these many variations, the inverse relationship between IQ scores and the tendency toward delinquency is consistently reported (e.g., Binder, 1988; Quay, 1987; White, Moffitt, & Silva, 1989). As IQ scores go down, the probability of misconduct increases, and vice versa. Children with low IQ scores are at a higher risk for delinquent behavior, and as Anne Crocker and Sheilagh Hodgins (1997, p. 434) write, "To our knowledge, no study has failed to confirm this relation." The relationship is particularly strong for verbal IQ scores (Culberton, Feral, & Gabby, 1989; Kandel *et al.*, 1988). Furthermore, as noted by Crocker and Hodgins (1997), the relationship between low IQ scores and delinquency appears to be independent of socioeconomic status, race, and detection by the police (Lynam, Moffitt, & Stouthamer-Loeber, 1993; Moffitt, 1990b). Moreover, it should be emphasized that this relationship is not specific to delinquency; it is equally robust for adult offenders. Interestingly, it has been suggested that many adult onset offenders had low intelligence but did not offend as juveniles because they were protected by supportive families or schools. As these cognitively limited individuals reached adulthood, they were unable to transition successfully to adult roles (Thornberry & Krohn, 2005).

IQ AND ADULT OFFENDERS   Very low IQ scores, those that indicate mental disability, are of particular concern. Recent estimates indicate that at least 4 percent of the U.S. prison population qualify as being intellectually or cognitively disabled (Ashford, Sales, & Reid, 2001). Jails are believed to hold an even higher percentage. It should be noted that this disability (also referred to as mental deficiency, developmental disability, or retardation) is distinct from mental disorder or mental illness. Intellectual disability is a cognitive impairment that cannot be reversed, although persons with this disability can be educated, trained, and supported to lead productive lives. Mental disorder or illness is emotional, and it may or may not have a biological basis. It can be addressed with therapy or medication, but psychologists as a group far prefer the former. These conditions as they relate to criminal behavior will be discussed in more detail in Chapter 8.

SUMMARY   What does the relationship between IQ scores and delinquency and crime mean exactly? It probably means that delinquents *as a group,* particularly serious delinquents, have had limited experiences in mainstream society, ineffective parenting, restricted cognitive and language development, and poor school experiences, but it does not necessarily mean that they are not intelligent. An undetermined proportion of delinquents are cognitively impaired to the extent that they could be called "mentally deficient" or "intellectually challenged," but so many factors are involved in an ultimate IQ score that a simple causal connection between low IQ and delinquency is unwarranted.

Related to the IQ question is the issue of *learning disabilities*, a term that is also not synonymous with intelligence. Educational psychologists have identified a variety of learning disabilities, including some that may be associated with brain injuries and perceptual difficulties. Many, if not most, children with learning disabilities are not cognitively impaired. However, there is considerable empirical evidence that juvenile delinquents have a far greater incidence of learning disabilities than nondelinquents (Brier, 1989; Lombardo & Lombardo, 1991; Scaret & Wilgosh, 1989). While learning disabilities clearly exist, it is believed that they are overdiagnosed or misdiagnosed in many children who then acquire a label that may follow them through the educational system. Like the IQ question, it is very unclear what the relationship between delinquency and learning disability truly means.

Attention Deficit Hyperactivity Disorder

Children are born with a wide range of genetic influences, neurological predispositions, and different temperaments, although the social and physical environments may alter them. These are all biological factors, and some appear to play a major role in the development of crime and delinquency.

The term *hyperactive syndrome* (also called minimal brain dysfunction, hyperkinesis, attention deficit disorder, or currently **Attention Deficit Hyperactivity Disorder [ADHD]**) includes a variety of behaviors. The central three are (1) inattention (does not seem to listen, or is easily distracted); (2) impulsivity (acts before thinking, shifts quickly from one activity to another); and (3) excessive motor activity (cannot sit still, fidgets, runs about, is talkative and noisy).

ADHD is the leading psychological diagnosis for American children (Beike & Zentall, 2012; Molina *et al.*, 2012; Staller, 2006). Educators note that ADHD children have difficulty staying on task, remaining cognitively organized, sustaining academic achievement in the school setting, and maintaining control over their behavior. Although the common belief is that one eventually outgrows hyperactivity, the evidence is that the key symptomatic features of hyperactivity persist into adulthood (Klinteberg, Magnusson, & Schalling, 1989; Thorley, 1984). It should be emphasized, however, that many children diagnosed with ADHD grow up to lead highly successful lives, and most do not follow a life course of serious delinquency and crime. There is a long list of scientists, entertainers, politicians, artists, musicians, athletes, and other public figures that were once diagnosed with or are now suspected of having had ADHD, including Albert Einstein, Dwight D. Eisenhower, Whoopi Goldberg, Bill Gates, Bill Cosby, Michael

Phelps, Steven Spielberg, Walt Disney, John Lennon, Ann Bancroft, Terry Bradshaw, Richard Byrd, Andrew Carnegie, Robin Williams, Agatha Christie, and Ludwig Beethoven.

ADHD affects an estimated 7.8 percent of school-age children in the United States (Centers for Disease Control, 2005). It occurs more often in boys than in girls, usually in a ratio of 5 to 1. In the general adult population, the incidence is also about 5 percent (Kessler *et al.*, 2006). Furthermore, ADHD is diagnosed more frequently in children who have a close biological relative with ADHD than in the general population, suggesting there may be a significant biological component involved. ADHD appears to be largely a disorder of self-control and emotional regulation related to problems in brain functioning (Connor, Ford, Chapman, & Banga, 2012). Antisocial and aggressive behavior stemming from ADHD is most often impulsive and a reaction to frustration or perceived threat (Connor *et al.*, 2012). Boys with ADHD are at increased risk for engaging in delinquent and antisocial behavior. "As they grow older, children with untreated ADHD...may abuse drugs or alcohol, engage in antisocial behavior, and suffer physical injury at higher rates that the general population" (Stern, 2001, p. 1).

ADHD is a puzzling problem, the cause of which is largely unknown. Some scientists contend that ADHD children are born with a biological predisposition toward hyperactivity; others maintain that some children are exposed to environmental factors that damage the nervous system. Rolf Loeber (1990) demonstrates how exposure to toxic substances during the preschool years often retards children's neurological development or otherwise influences it in a negative way, often resulting in symptoms of ADHD. For example, children exposed to low levels of lead toxicity (e.g., from paint or contaminated soil) are more hyperactive and impulsive, and are easily distracted and frustrated. They also show discernible problems in following simple instructions. The causal factors of ADHD are probably multiple and extremely difficult to identify.

Some researchers observe that ADHD children do not possess effective strategies and cognitive organization with which to deal with the daily demands of school. ADHD children also seem to lack cognitively organized ways for dealing with new knowledge. The core problem appears to center around executive functions, or what can be termed *self-regulation skills* (Douglas, 2004). **Self-regulation** refers to the ability to control behavior. According to Virginia Douglas (2004), it is not so much "not knowing" as "not doing." Attention, inhibition, and organizing are ways of "doing" or working on cognitive processes. Stimulant drugs, Douglas argues, enable ADHD children to improve on self-regulation processes. These drugs themselves, though, are extremely controversial and are themselves widely believed to be overprescribed.

Although many behaviors have been identified as accompanying ADHD, another overriding theme is that ADHD children are perceived as annoying and aversive to those around them. Although ADHD children are continually seeking and prolonging interpersonal contacts, they eventually manage to irritate and frustrate those people with whom they interact (Henker & Whalen, 1989). They are often rejected by peers, especially if they are perceived as aggressive (Henker & Whalen, 1989). This pattern of peer rejection appears to continue throughout the developmental years (Reid, 1993). As noted earlier in the chapter, peer rejection is a strong predictor of delinquent behavior.

ADHD and Criminal Behavior

Some researchers (e.g., Pfiffner, McBurnett, Rathouz, & Judice, 2005) estimate about one-fourth of all children with ADHD engage in serious antisocial behavior during childhood and adolescence and criminal behavior as adults. Terrie Moffitt (Moffitt, 1993b; Moffitt & Silva, 1988) observes that a very large number of ADHD children self-report delinquent behaviors by early adolescence. She also found that children between the ages of five and seven who demonstrate the characteristics of both ADHD and delinquent behavior not only have special difficulty with social relationships but also have a high probability of consistent serious antisocial behavior into adolescence and beyond (Moffitt, 1990b). Experts generally agree that the most common problem associated with ADHD is delinquency and substance abuse. The data strongly suggest that youth with symptoms of both ADHD and antisocial behavior are at very high risk for developing lengthy and serious criminal careers (Moffitt, 1990b; Satterfield, Swanson, Schell, & Lee, 1994). David Farrington (1991), in his well-cited research, also found that violent offenders often have a history of hyperactivity, impulsivity, and attention-deficit problems.

It should be noted that "the prevalence rates for ADHD are 3–10 times higher in secure correctional facilities than are found in the general population" (Connor *et al.*, 2012, p.727). More specifically, ADHD rates are between 11.7 percent and 45 percent for incarcerated males, and 10 percent and 18.5 percent for incarcerated females, compared to around 5 percent in the general population (Connor *et al.*, 2012). In addition, incarcerated individuals with ADHD are more likely to engage in disruptive, rule-violating, and impulsive aggressive behaviors than others in secure correctional facilities. "ADHD youth in juvenile justice and secure treatment settings are at risk for rehabilitative failure, academic failure, occupational failure, continued antisocial behavior, substance abuse, comorbid psychiatric and learning disorders, and impulsive aggression" (Connor *et al.*, 2012, p. 743).

Conduct Disorder

ADHD frequently co-occurs with a diagnostic category called "conduct disorders" (Connor *et al.*, 2012; Offord, Boyle, & Racine, 1991; Reid, 1993), but the two should be considered separate entities. However, it should also be mentioned that the often observed progression from childhood ADHD to early-onset conduct disorder is accounted for, in part, by ineffective and coercive parenting (Beauchaine, Hinshaw, & Pang, 2010; Meier, Slutske, Heath, & Martin, 2009). Research demonstrates that certain disorders occur together often as a result of psychological and biological vulnerabilities interacting with environmental conditions, such as the quality of parenting.

The term *conduct disorder* (CD) represents a cluster of behaviors characterized by persistent misbehavior. Youth conduct problems frequently result in significant disruptions at home and school, and can lead to violence and other serious crimes (McMahon, Witkiewitz, Kotler, & The Conduct Problems Prevention Research Group, 2010). Examples of this misbehavior include stealing, fire setting, running away from home, skipping school, destroying property, fighting, frequently telling lies, and cruelty to animals and people. According to the *Diagnostic and Statistical Manual-IV-Revised* (DSM-IV-R), published by the American Psychiatric Association (2000), the central feature of conduct disorder is the *repetitive* and *persistent* pattern of behavior that violates the basic rights of others. CD can range from mild forms of expression (such as minimal harm to persons or property) to severe forms of behavior, such as substantial harm to persons, and significant damage to property.

It should be noted that the DSM is undergoing a fifth revision, with the DSM-5 expected in May 2013. Since the publication of the 4th edition in 1994, a plethora of studies have been conducted, leading to suggested changes in diagnoses and classifications of disorders, including those related to children. Among the most controversial are proposed changes involving conduct disorder, ODD, and autism. Researchers have expressed concern that changes are premature and that more evidence-based findings are warranted before drastic modifications in classification occur (Moffitt, Arsenault, *et al.*, 2008). In our discussion here, we employ characteristics mentioned in the 4th edition (American Psychiatric Association, 1994, 2000) as well as research conducted by academics and clinicians. Although it is possible that changes will occur relative to criteria for assigning these conditions, the condition itself, and its association with antisocial behavior, remains the focus of our concern. Proposed changes in the DSM will be covered again in Chapters 6 and 8.

Behavioral indicators of a conduct disorder can be observed in the context of interactions with parents well before school entry (Reid, 1993). For instance, children who are aggressive, difficult to manage, and noncompliant in the home at age three often continue to have similar problems when entering school. Furthermore, these behaviors show remarkable consistency through adolescence and into adulthood. CD children frequently have significant problems with school assignments, a behavioral pattern that often results in their being mislabeled with a "learning disability." It is important to note that genuinely learning-disabled students are not necessarily conduct disordered, however. In other words, the two designations may overlap, but each is also a distinct categorization. Aggressive CDs are at high risk for strong rejection by their peers (Reid, 1993). This rejection generally lasts throughout the school years and is very difficult to change (Reid, 1993). Children who are consistently socially rejected by peers miss critical opportunities to develop effective interpersonal and social skills. Lacking effective interpersonal skills, these youths are forced to get their needs met through more aggressive means, including threats and intimidation.

The *DSM-IV-R* (American Psychiatric Association, 2000) identifies two subtypes of conduct disorders based on the onset of the repetition and persistence of the misbehavior: the *childhood-onset type* and *adolescent-onset type*. According to the *DSM-IV-R*, childhood-onset type occurs when the pattern begins prior to age 10. The adolescent-onset type, on the other hand, is characterized by the absence of any pattern before age 10. The *DSM-IV-R* also notes that if the CD pattern begins before age 10, the prognosis is not good, compared with a more favorable prognosis for a later onset. In fact, Hodgins, Cree, and Mak (2008) found that if a CD pattern is present prior to age 15, it is strongly associated with an increased risk of violent behavior into middle age. This finding holds for both males and females.

There is some recent research suggesting that individual maladjustment and family influences are more highly associated with childhood-onset conduct disorders, whereas ethnic minority status and exposure to deviant peers is more highly associated with adolescent-onset conduct disorders (McCabe, Hough, Wood, & Yeh, 2001). The researchers also found that those children who exhibit childhood-onset conduct disorders are more likely to commit more serious or aggressive offenses than adolescent-onset conduct disorders, although the results were not as strong as the first finding.

Overall, between 2 percent and 8 percent of children and adolescents in the United States show behavioral patterns that may be diagnosed as a conduct disorder (Eddy, 2003; Frick, 2006). Boys outnumber girls by about four-to-one before adolescence, and by about two-to-one during adolescence (Frick, 2006). In addition, CD is the diagnostic label most often placed on youths who appear before the juvenile courts (Lahey *et al.*, 1995). A study by Anna Bardone and her colleagues (Bardone, Moffitt, & Caspi, 1996) found that CD patterns in girls are a strong predictor of a lifetime of problems, including poor interpersonal relations with partners/spouses and peers, criminal activity, early pregnancy without supportive partners, and frequent job loss and firings. Similar to CD boys, CD girls appear destined for a life of interpersonal conflict with the social environment.

OPPOSITIONAL DEFIANT DISORDER

Conduct disorder, along with **oppositional defiant disorder (ODD)**, are often classified as a **disruptive behavior disorders (DBD)**. Sometimes ADHD is also included as a disruptive behavior disorder. The DSM-IV-R describes the child with ODD as negative, hostile, and defiant, more than is expected for his or her age, and lasting for at least six months. According to the DSM, children and adolescents with ODD display a persistent pattern of angry outbursts, arguments, vindictiveness, resentment, and disobedience. These behavioral patterns may be directed at parents, teachers, siblings, classmates, friends, and other authority figures. The DSM-IV assumes that ODD is always present in youth who are diagnosed with conduct disorder (Burke, Waldman, & Lahey, 2010). However, many clinicians disagree. In clinical practice, CD sometimes occurs without the accompanying characteristics of ODD. Furthermore, although ODD is a challenging condition during childhood, it is a diagnosis that is not highly associated with *lasting* conduct or behavioral problems. To some, ODD is just "normal teenage behavior." In general, the symptoms of ODD appear to decline as the child gets older (Maughan, Rowe, Messer, Goodman, & Meltzer, 2004). Although there is some research that suggests that early signs of ODD predict early onset of CD, it is largely unknown if ODD predicts criminal behavior over the long run (Burke *et al.*, 2010). The complex relationship between ADHD, CD, ODD, and criminal behavior is perhaps best summarized by the following quote:

> ... delinquent adult boys usually traverse a developmental pathway that begins with severe hyperactive/impulsive behaviors as early as toddlerhood, followed by ODD in preschool, early-onset CD in elementary school, substance abuse disorders (SUDs) in adolescence, and antisocial personality in adulthood. (Beauchaine *et al.*, 2010, p. 328)

Finally, as noted earlier in the chapter, a cascade effect that includes peer rejection may be at work as well (Gooren *et al.*, 2011). That is, conduct disorder may precipitate peer rejection, which may then result in depression and antisocial behavior.

Summary and Conclusions

In recent years, developmental psychologists have been extremely active in studying the life course of individuals who participate in persistent juvenile and adult offending. They have examined developmental pathways or trajectories that lead to little or no offending, minor juvenile offending that ends around mid- to late adolescence, or serious offending into adulthood, among other things. In addition, psychologists have searched for effective intervention strategies for children and families, with a goal to promoting a healthy, nurturing environment.

Researchers can now point with confidence to a large list of risk factors associated with juvenile delinquency and criminal behavior. Unfortunately, effective treatment strategies are more elusive, although approaches such as reducing coercive family interactions have had promising results (Biglan *et al.*, 2012). With respect to risk factors, no single variable is particularly at fault. In this chapter, we began to examine some of the social and psychological risk factors associated with crime and delinquency, including peer and family influences, preschool and school influences, cognitive ability, ADHD, and conduct disorders.

Many theories of criminology trace the roots of offending to childhood and early adolescence. An adverse economic environment must be considered within the context of the many influences that impinge on young lives. Features often associated with poverty—discrimination, inadequate schools, unsafe living conditions, joblessness, social isolation, and opportunities to learn law-violating behaviors from peers—all play roles in the formation of crime and delinquency.

One risk factor that appears increasingly in the literature on delinquency is early peer rejection, even during the elementary school years. This can occur regardless of a child's socioeconomic status. Children who are rejected by peers are often aggressive, but aggression alone is not the major explanation. Rather, they also tend to be disruptive, impulsive, and/or have few interpersonal skills. Research has demonstrated consistently that antisocial adolescents, particularly those who displayed highly aggressive behavior, experienced significant peer rejection during their childhoods. In girls, substance abuse and other delinquent behaviors in adolescence have been associated with peer rejection in elementary school.

Preschool experiences are also increasingly being recognized as possible risk factors. Poor-quality child care places children at risk for poorer language and cognitive development, as well as deficiencies in social skills. Unfortunately, inadequate child care is often associated with low socioeconomic class, but it can be a problem for upper-income families as well. Thus, high-quality day care improves the chances that all children will do well both behaviorally and in school settings.

It is important to stress that delinquency is clearly not limited to youths from the lower class. Self-report data suggest that social class differences become smaller when youths are asked to report their own offending. If poverty and the conditions it generates are not an issue for these youth, we must look to other risk factors, such as parenting styles and practices, the influence of antisocial peers, and the more individual factors such as conduct disorders, ADHD, intelligence, and gender.

Among the parental and family risk factors discussed in the chapter are single-parent households, which have too often been blamed for antisocial behavior of children. We stressed that process variables rather than structure variables were more likely risk factors. For example, researchers have found associations between certain parental styles and antisocial behavior in children. Styles are typically identified as authoritarian, permissive, authoritative, or neglecting (Baumrind, 1991a) or as enmeshed or lax (Snyder & Patterson, 1987). Although many parents may well vary their styles across situations and as children get older, in general, one style dominates. The permissive and lax styles—characterized by little or no control over the children and extremely few restrictions—are highly correlated with delinquent behavior. In similar fashion, parental monitoring or supervision of the child's activities, particularly from the ages of nine to mid-adolescence, is crucial to the development of prosocial behavior. In addition, community or neighborhood monitoring should be promoted.

We covered psychological risk factors—those that are unique to the child—as factors on the road to delinquency. Low IQ scores have consistently been associated with delinquency, not necessarily directly but more likely because children with low scores do not do well in school, and school failure is also commonly associated with antisocial behavior. We stressed, though, that a low score on an "intelligence" test does not mean that a child is not intelligent. In addition, we know not only that many delinquents are intelligent despite scoring below normal on IQ tests, but also that other delinquents score high on IQ tests. Therefore, the IQ–delinquency connection must be expressed cautiously.

Children with ADHD are at some risk of antisocial behavior both as juveniles and adults. This disorder apparently affects 3 percent to 5 percent of school-age children, though in some communities the percentages are even higher, leading to questions about misdiagnoses. ADHD appears to be a disorder affecting social relationships—the children have difficulty staying on task, they get easily distracted, are impulsive, display excessive motor activity, and are annoying to others. These features often lead to peer rejection. Although ADHD is routinely treated with medication, this in itself is a controversial issue, and critics recommend the use of other approaches, including physical exercise and outdoor activities. Untreated, ADHD children are at risk for delinquency and substance abuse.

Conduct disorder is somewhat of a catch-all category that is characterized by persistent misbehavior, including stealing, running away, fighting, telling lies, and cruelty. Different sub-classifications and criteria for CD are proposed for the new edition of the DSM, a fact that has prompted controversy among many researchers and treatment providers. Signs of conduct disorder may occur as early as age three; when children reach school age, they are often mislabeled with a "learning disability" or with ADHD, but the three are distinct categories. Not surprisingly, conduct disorder is also associated with peer rejection. Finally, ODD is often associated with antisocial behavior, but not everyone agrees that it merits the attention it has received. The association between ODD and ongoing criminal activity has not been established.

Key Concepts

Attachment theory
Attention Deficit
   Hyperactivity
   Disorder (ADHD)
Authoritarian style
Authoritative style
Conduct disorder (CD)
Developmental pathways

Disruptive behavior
   disorders (DBD)
Enmeshed style
Language impairment
Lax style
Neglecting style
Oppositional defiant
   disorder (ODD)

Parental monitoring
Parental practices
Parental styles
Permissive style
Psychometric approach
Psychometric
   intelligence (PI)
Self-regulation

Review Questions

1. What three categories of risk factors are covered in this chapter? Name and explain briefly any two factors falling into each category.
2. Discuss the relevance of peer rejection to ongoing antisocial behavior.
3. Explain the difference between ADHD and conduct disorder.
4. Describe the features of ADHD that create problems for the child who has this disorder.
5. In what ways may preschool experiences influence a life of delinquency and crime?
6. Describe each of Baumrind's four parental styles.
7. What is attachment theory, and how may it relate to juvenile delinquency and adult criminal behavior?

3

■ ■ ■ ■ ■

Origins of Criminal Behavior: Biological Factors

CHAPTER OBJECTIVES

■ Explore the genetic and biological aspects of criminal behavior.

■ Provide an overview of behavior genetics and molecular genetics as they pertain to antisocial behavior.

■ Provide an overview of twin and adoption studies and their relation to theories of crime.

■ Identify environmental risk factors that play a role in the psychobiological aspects of criminal behavior.

■ Discuss temperament and its effects on the behavior of children and their caretakers.

■ Summarize recent research on adolescent brain development, especially executive functions and risk-taking behavior, and their relationship to antisocial and criminal behavior.

Cross the threshold of any preschool or kindergarten classroom, and you are likely to encounter a flurry of activity—little people scurrying or trying to scurry around the room, or restless and energetic tykes eager to move to a different location or position. You are also likely to observe a fair amount of pushing and shoving, despite a teacher's efforts to keep these behaviors under control. "Josh," described at the beginning of Chapter 2, was probably not that atypical as a preschooler or even as an early grade school student.

A common research finding is that many, if not most, children (and especially boys) exhibit high levels of physical aggression in preschool or kindergarten, but in most cases, they typically show significant reductions of these behaviors during the early school years due to the effects of socialization and parenting (Bongers, Koot, van der Ende, & Verhulst, 2003; Séguin, Nagin, Asaad, & Tremblay, 2004). The pushing and shoving observed in kindergarten should dissipate within the next few years. Another common finding, however, is that certain brain and biochemical abnormalities appear to *predispose* some children to exhibit higher levels of aggression than that exhibited by their peers, and if these abnormalities are not neutralized by socialization and competent parenting, many of these children grow up to follow a life path characterized by high levels of aggression and violence. Youngsters who follow an early onset of persistent antisocial behavior often exhibit biological/neurological abnormalities or deficits, while late-onset offending appears to be more influenced by social factors (Moffitt, Lynam, & Silva, 1994; Rutter, 1997; Rutter, Giller, & Hagell, 1998).

Thus, many—perhaps most—contemporary criminologists would agree that genetics may play some role in criminality, but the social environment is the most important determinant of criminal behavior. Greed, desire for power, the glorification of violence, poverty, high unemployment, poor education, faulty parenting, and group values that deviate from society's norms are often considered the major culprits in producing crime. Heredity-based or physiologically based components have been traditionally scoffed at, and their possible role as causal agents in criminality is often dismissed. In recent years, however, as more research on biological factors is conducted, the interaction between genes and the environment is receiving more positive attention (Wright & Boisvert, 2009). To adopt a phrase heard frequently in the political arena, views on this issue are evolving.

Adrian Raine (2008), a prominent biopsychologist, has remarked: "Despite strong resistance in many quarters, there is now little scientific doubt that genes play a significant role in antisocial behavior" (p. 323). According to Raine, the more challenging questions today are twofold: (1) determining how much of antisocial behavior is influenced by genes and (2) deciding which specific genes predispose a person to which kinds of antisocial behavior. The first question is probably best answered by twin and adoption studies, using methods developed by behavior genetics. Twin studies generally provide more support for the heritability of antisocial behavior than adoption studies. When one identical twin demonstrates antisocial behavior, there is a significant probability that the other twin will demonstrate similar behavior, even when they are reared apart. Nevertheless, both twin and adoption studies have the potential of providing a more convincing case for the relative influence of genetic and environmental factors. To answer Raine's second question—which specific genes predispose a person to which kinds of antisocial behavior—researchers are beginning to investigate the association between certain polymorphisms (e.g., DAT1 and 5HTT) and chronic criminal behavior or low self-control. We focus on each of these questions below.

Biopsychologists (psychologists who study the biological aspects of behavior) try to determine which genetic and neurophysiological variables play a part in criminal behavior, how important they are, and what can be done to modify them. Biopsychologists do not believe that genetic or neurophysiological components are the sole or even primary causal agents of human behavior. Most would say that understanding the social environment is as important as understanding the biological one. In the words of one group of biopsychologists, "The social world, as well as the organization and operation of the brain, shapes and modulates genetic and biological processes, and accordingly, knowledge of biological and social domains is necessary to develop comprehensive theories in either domain" (Cacioppo, Berntson, Sheridan, & McClintock, 2000, p. 833). In this chapter, we concentrate on the biological relationships to criminal behavior, while, at the same time, continually appreciating the enormous influence of the social environment on the neurological and biological processes.

The chapter first explores the genetic aspects of crime, including findings from twin and adoption studies and from molecular biology. We then move on to discuss physiological and environmental health factors that can lead to antisocial behavior.

GENETICS AND ANTISOCIAL BEHAVIOR

Over the past three decades, two methods and analytical procedures have had enormous influence on genetic research: **behavior genetics** and **molecular genetics**. Behavior genetics focuses on examining the role genes play in the formation and development of human and other animal behavior. It is the branch of biology that investigates the relationship between genes and the environment in determining individual differences in behavior. It has the advantage of "clearly distinguishing genetic from environmental influences and estimating their relative magnitudes" (Rhee & Waldman, 2011, p. 143). The method used in behavior genetics is especially powerful for disentangling genetic from environmental influences in twin and adoptive studies.

Molecular genetics is the field of biology that studies the structure and function of genes at the molecular level. Contemporary molecular biology has focused on specific genes as foundations for certain patterns of behavior. Further, "a central precept of molecular biology is that all the information needed to construct a mammalian body, whether human or mouse, is contained in the approximately 100,000 genes of mammalian DNA and that a set of master genes activates the DNA necessary to produce the appropriate proteins for development and behavior" (Cacioppo *et al.*, 2000, p. 833). Molecular genetics studies how the genes are transferred from generation to generation. Research in this area generally concentrates on the long polymers of deoxyribonucleic acid or DNA.

Behavior Genetics

Traditional behavior genetics views behavioral differences as springing from three genetic or environmental sources: (1) influences attributable to genetic effects; (2) environmental influences shared by siblings (e.g., family environments); and (3) influences that arise from unshared environmental experiences that makes siblings differ from one another (Dick & Rose, 2002). The magnitude of these genetic and environmental influences is usually obtained from statistical analyses that compare identical twins with fraternal twins, who like ordinary siblings share one-half their genes. Therefore, one way to determine the role of genetics in criminality is to compare the incidence and type of delinquency or criminal convictions among identical (monozygotic) and fraternal (dizygotic) twins. **Dizygotic (DZ) twins** (also called **fraternal twins**) develop from two different fertilized eggs and are no more genetically alike than nontwin siblings. **Monozygotic (MZ) twins** (or **identical twins**) develop from a single egg; they are always of the same sex and share the same genes. Presumably, then, if genes are determinative, identical twins should display highly similar behavior. If they do not, then we may infer that the behavioral differences are due to environmental factors. Because MZ twins share 100 percent of their genes, it can be inferred that a child's genetic risk for antisocial behavior is high if his or her co-twin shows antisocial behavior and low if the MZ co-twin does not.

However, to complicate matters a bit, approximately two-thirds of monozygotic twins are monochorionic (share the same chorion), and one-third of the monozygotic pair is dichorionic (two different chorions) (Rhee & Waldman, 2002). The chorion is the outer membrane enclosing the embryo. Therefore, some identical twins develop in slightly different prenatal environments, which may contribute to some individual differences that may emerge as the twins develop into maturity. In fact, several studies have found that monochorionic, monozygotic twins are more similar in personality and cognitive ability than dichorionic, monozygotic twins (Rhee & Waldman, 2002). Theoretically, however, by comparing fraternal twins and identical twins, researchers should be able to identify the relative contributions of genes compared with environmental factors in the development of personality, cognitive ability, and behavior in general.

Twin Studies

Over 100 twin (and adoption) studies involving a total of more than 77,000 families have examined the relationship between genes and antisocial behavior (Moffitt, 2005a, 2005b; Raine, 2008). The research has included as many as 800,000 pairs of twins (Johnson, Turkheimer, Gottesman, & Bouchard, 2009). The data from these studies have allowed researchers to conclude that genes influence approximately 50 percent of the population variation in antisocial behavior, indicating that genetics plays a very significant role in its development. Similar results have been reported for specifically aggressive and violent behavior (Rhee & Waldman, 2011) and for serious, chronic juvenile offenders (Barnes, Beaver, & Boutwell, 2011). The presence of genetic influences does not mean, however, that genes directly *cause* the behavior to the exclusion of other influences (Johnson *et al.*, 2009). Genes are not fixed, static, and immutable. Environmental influences early in human development can directly change gene expression, in turn altering brain functioning and resulting in antisocial and other forms of deviant behavior; or environmental influences can have the opposite effect, producing a positive change on genes that might otherwise be problematic. Psychosocial influences can result in structural modifications to DNA that have profound influences on neuronal functioning and behavior.

Moreover, if genes influence half of the total variation in antisocial behavior, this still leaves considerable room for environmental influences on the formation of behavior. Peer and sibling interactions, child neglect and abuse, social modeling, and brain injuries or disease can also have negative influences. On the positive side, warm, supportive parenting can effectively neutralize or shift a child's behavior toward more prosocial and non-antisocial behavior, even in those children who are most genetically vulnerable toward criminal behavior (Kim-Cohen & Gold, 2009).

Several concepts should be recognized before a good understanding of twin and adoption studies can be achieved. They are shared environments, nonshared environments, and concordance.

SHARED AND NONSHARED ENVIRONMENTS   **Shared environments**, sometimes referred to as common environments, include prenatal and life experiences affecting both twins in the same way. For example, twins raised by the same biological parents share a common hereditary and home environment. Shared environments in this sense are apt to promote high trait or behavioral similarity between twin pairs, especially for identical twins. This is especially the case for antisocial behavioral patterns, even in siblings who are not twins (Kendler, Prescott, Myers, & Neale, 2003; Moffitt, 2005a). Antisocial-prone parents tend to produce antisocial-prone offspring. Compared to genes that account for about 50 percent of the variation in antisocial behavior, shared environments contribute about 15 percent to 20 percent of the variation (Moffitt, 2005a; Rhee & Waldman, 2002).

Nonshared environments, on the other hand, include living experiences that are different for each twin, such as being raised in a different home environment, participating in different activities, or even attending different schools. Parents sometimes want to preserve the uniqueness of each twin by encouraging them to join separate groups or pursue separate hobbies. Therefore, in order to determine the relative influence of genes on behavior, compared with the environment, shared and nonshared aspects must be considered. The available research suggests that nonshared environments account for approximately 30 percent of the variation in antisocial behavior (Moffitt, 2005a). However, research suggests that developmental factors also play a critical role. For example, twin research indicates that, for a variety of traits, the magnitude of genetic and nonshared environmental influences increases as a person gets older, whereas the magnitude of shared environmental influences decreases (Loehlin, 1992; Plomin, 1986; Rhee & Waldman,

2002). That is, as the child begins to spend more time outside the family circle, especially when he or she becomes a young adult, the influence of the shared environment (family) tends to wane, whereas the influence of genetics and nonshared environments (e.g., peers) becomes more discernible. Rhee and Waldman (2002) describe a longitudinal study by Matheny (1989) that revealed that the temperaments (e.g., emotional tone, fearfulness, approach or avoidance toward others) became more similar for identical pairs than for fraternal pairs as they grew older. Thus, we might expect that developmental age of the participants in any twin study may play an important role in determining the influences of genetics compared with the environment. We return to this point shortly.

Some investigators suggest that identical twins are so physically alike that they probably elicit similar social responses from their environment (shared environment), more so than fraternal twins. In this sense, they are more likely to develop similar personalities. There may be merit to this viewpoint, but research does not yet support it. When reared together, identical twins or their parents may make a conscious effort to accentuate their individual identities, whereas when reared apart, they may have less need to be different.

CONCORDANCE   A key concept in twin study research, **concordance** is the genetics term for the degree to which related pairs of subjects both show a particular behavior or condition. It is usually expressed in percentages. Assume that we want to determine the concordance of intelligence among 20 pairs of identical twins and 20 pairs of fraternals. If we find that 10 pairs of the identical twins have approximately the same IQ score, but only five pairs of the fraternals obtain the same score, our concordance is 50 percent for identicals and 25 percent for fraternals. The concordance for identicals would be twice that of fraternals, suggesting that hereditary factors play an important role in intelligence. If, however, the two concordances were about the same, we would conclude that genetics is irrelevant, at least as represented in our sample and measured by our methods.

Numerous early twin studies using this concordance method have indicated that heredity may be a powerful determinant of intelligence, schizophrenia, depressions, neurotic disorders, alcoholism, and criminal behavior (Claridge, 1973; Hetherington & Parke, 1975; McClearn & DeFries, 1973; Rosenthal, 1970, 1971). The first such study relative to criminality was reported by the Munich physician Johannes Lange (1929) in his book *Crime as Destiny* (Christiansen, 1977; Rosenthal, 1971). The title reflects Lange's conviction that criminal conduct is a predetermined fate dictated by heredity. He found a criminality concordance of 77 percent for 13 pairs of adult identical twins and only 12 percent for 17 pairs of adult fraternal twins. Auguste Marcel Legras (1932) then found a 100 percent criminal concordance for five pairs of identicals. Note that both of these studies used small samples. Subsequent studies, using more sophisticated designs and methods of twin identification and sampling, continued to find a substantially higher criminal concordance for identical twins when compared with fraternals. The levels were not as high as those reported by either Lange or Legras, however. Although these tabulated investigations differed in method and definitions of criminality, the combined concordance levels demonstrate that, where criminal behavior is concerned, identical twins seem better matched than fraternal twins.

The Twins' Early Development Study

One of the most closely watched series of twin studies is the longitudinal research now being conducted in the United Kingdom with a large sample of twins born in 1994, 1995, and 1996 in England and Wales. Called the **Twins' Early Development Study (TEDS)**, it explores behavior problems as well as problematic development in language, cognition, and academic abilities from early childhood through adolescence (Oliver & Plomin, 2007; Trouton, Spinath, & Plomin, 2002). Although there has been some attrition since data were first collected, over 13,000 pairs of twins have remained involved in the research. The ongoing project is based at King's College London and is under the leadership of Professor Robert Plomin.

As we have indicated throughout this chapter, both nature and nurture contribute to human behavior, and—not surprisingly—this is supported in TEDS research studies. However, TEDS research indicates that nature has considerable influence over some behavior problems (e.g., those associated with ADHD). With respect to antisocial behavior, which is our main concern, the TEDS data suggest heritability plays a modest role. Nevertheless, at least one personality feature that has been associated with antisocial behavior—the callous-unemotional trait—shows very high heritability and little shared environmental influence (Oliver & Plomin, 2007; Viding, Blair, James, Moffitt, & Plomin, 2005).

In a study facilitated by the TEDS database, Jaffee and her colleagues (2005) used monozygotic (MZ) and dizygotic (DZ) twin pairs to study the interplay between genetic and environmental risks on the development of antisocial behavior in a cohort of 1,116 five-year-old twin pairs and their families. These participants are members of the Environmental Risk (E-Risk) Longitudinal Twin Study. The Jaffee researchers ascertained the children's antisocial behavior through interviews with parents, assessments of the children, and questionnaires administered to teachers. The environmental risk factor in the study was the amount of maltreatment the child reportedly received from parents, because research shows that early maltreatment often leads to antisocial behavior (Lansford *et al.*, 2002). Not surprisingly, Jaffee *et al.* (2005) discovered that the effect of maltreatment on the risk to develop antisocial behavior was strongest among those at higher genetic risk. In other words, those children with a genetic predisposition to become troublesome and antisocial were especially likely to be that way if they were mistreated. These findings, and the findings of many other studies, continue to support the general consensus that environmental changes turn genetic influences on and off during the developmental years, and that biological factors and environmental influences do interact (Raine, 2002). As mentioned in this chapter, there is emerging evidence that suggests the social environment (e.g., parenting) can affect people who are at genetic risk more strongly than previously appreciated (Moffitt, 2005b).

These environmental influences seem to wane somewhat as a person moves into adulthood, however. For example, there is emerging evidence that the magnitude of familial or parental influences on aggressive behavior decreases with increasing age, and genetic factors increasingly play a prominent role in the stability of aggression and antisocial behavior across the life span (Rhee & Waldman, 2002; van Beijsterveldt, Bartels, Hudziak, & Boomsma, 2003). This effect seems to be particularly strong in males. Female aggressive behavior, on the other hand, seems to be more strongly affected by the family environment (van Beijsterveldt *et al.*, 2003). In other words, family influences appear to be more powerful in the inhibition of antisocial behavior in girls than in boys, particularly as the girls approach adolescence and early adulthood.

Twin Study of Child and Adolescent Development (TCHAD)

Another longitudinal research project is the Twin Study of Child and Adolescent Development (TCHAD), using data from the Swedish Twin Registry. Tuvblad, Eley, and Lichtenstein (2005), studying 1,226 twin pairs, employed a well-researched behavioral scale to measure parental-reported aggression in children ages eight and nine. They then asked the same group of children to report their own delinquent behavior eight years later. The researchers used both monozygotic and dizygotic twins in their effort to disentangle genetic factors from environmental factors. They found that genetic factors played an important role in the early onset of aggressive behavior in children, but appeared to play a less important role in the development of delinquent behavior as reported by male adolescents. A similar finding was reported by Taylor, Iacono, and McGue (2000), who found that genetics played a more prominent role in early-onset delinquency (life-course-persistent offenders), whereas the social environment (e.g., delinquent peers) was more influential in late-onset delinquency (adolescent-limited offenders). The participants in the study were all boys. Surprisingly, genetics appeared to play a much more prominent role in development of *both* aggressive behavior and delinquency in girls in the Tuvblad *et al.* (2005) study. These results appear to be in contrast to the study of Rhee and Waldman (2002), who concluded that the magnitude of genetic and environmental influences on antisocial behavior is equal for both genders. It is clear from these two contrasting studies that further research on the relative influence of genes on gender differences in antisocial behavior is warranted.

Adoption Studies

Another method used to identify crucial variables in the interaction between heredity and environment is the adoption study, which helps identify environments most conducive to criminality. The adoption study capitalizes on the assumption that adoptive parents and their adopted children are not genetically related (Jaffe, Strait, & Odgers, 2012). There have been exceedingly few such investigations, however, and those few have been fraught with methodological problems.

One of the first adoption studies was carried out in Denmark by Schulsinger (1972), who explored the incidence of psychopathy in the biological relatives of adopted adults. Schulsinger compared 57 adopted adults whom he diagnosed psychopathic to a control group of 57 nonpsychopathic adopted adults. The two groups were matched for sex, age, social class, and age of transfer to the adopting family. The study's direct implications for criminal behavior are questionable, because Schulsinger defined psychopathy by his own loose criteria. Individuals who were impulse ridden and who exhibited acting-out behavior qualified. As we will see in Chapter 7, these descriptions do not necessarily connote either psychopathy or criminality. Nevertheless, impulsivity is associated with some forms of criminal behavior, so the study has some relevance.

Schulsinger found that 3.9 percent of the biological relatives of psychopathic adoptees could also be classified as psychopathic, whereas only 1.4 percent of the control group's biological relatives could. The results just failed to reach statistical significance, indicating that we should be very cautious about accepting their implications. It is interesting, though, that psychopathy—even given its loose definition—was about two and a half times greater in the family backgrounds of acting-out adoptees.

Crowe (1974) conducted a better-designed study, a follow-up of 52 persons relinquished for early adoption by female offenders. Ninety percent of the biological mothers were felons at the time of the adoptive placement, the most common offenses being forgery and passing bad checks. Twenty-five of the adoptees were female, and all were white. Another 52 adoptees with no evidence of criminal family background were selected as a control group and matched for sex, race, and age at the time of adoption.

For the follow-up phase of the study, Crowe selected 37 index and 37 control subjects who had by then reached age 18. (Index subjects in research are those subjects who are of major concern.) Seven of the index adoptees had arrest records: As adults, all seven had at least one conviction, four had multiple arrests, two had multiple convictions, and three were felons. Of the 37 matching controls, two had adult arrest records and only one of these had been convicted. Each subject's personality was diagnosed by three clinicians based on test results and data gathered in an interview; no family background was included. The clinicians made their diagnoses independently of one another and without knowing the subject's group. Six of the adoptees born of female offenders were labeled "antisocial personality"; one control group subject was labeled "probable antisocial personality."

Crowe found a positive correlation between the tendency of the index group to be antisocial and two other variables: the child's age at the time of adoptive placement and the length of time the child had spent in temporary care (orphanages and foster homes) prior to that placement. The older the child of an offender upon adoptive placement and the longer the temporary placement, the more likely the child would grow up antisocial. The control group members were not affected by these conditions. This suggests either that the two adoptee groups responded differently to similar environmental conditions or that the adoption agency placed the offspring of female offenders in less desirable homes—and there was no indication that this selective placement had occurred.

Hutchings and Mednick (1975) also conducted a study examining the effects of genetics and environment. They reasoned that if there is a genetic basis for criminality, then there should be a significant relationship between the criminal tendencies of biological parents and those of their children who were adopted by someone else. In 1971, using Copenhagen adoption files, Hutchings and Mednick identified 1,145 male adoptees, who were by then 30–44 years old. They were matched with an equal number of nonadoptee controls on sex, age, occupational status of fathers, and residence. The researchers learned that 185 adoptees (16.2%) had criminal records, compared with 105 nonadoptees (8.9%). A check on the biological fathers of the adoptees revealed that they were nearly three times more likely to be involved in criminal activity than were either the adoptees' adoptive fathers or the fathers of the nonadopted controls. Furthermore, there was a significant relationship between the criminality of the sons and that of the fathers. Where the biological father had a criminal record and the adoptive father had none, a significant number of adoptees still became criminal (22%), but where the biological father had no record and the adoptive father had a criminal record, the number of adoptees who pursued criminal activities was lower (11.5%). If both the biological and adoptive fathers were criminal, the chances were much greater that the adoptee would also be criminal than if only one man was criminal. Hutchings and Mednick concluded that genetic factors continue to exert strong influences in the tendency toward criminality, even though environmental factors also play important roles.

One serious limitation to the Hutchings-Mednick data, as well as to any adoption study, is that agencies often try to match the adopted child with the adoptive family on the basis of the child's biological and sometimes socioeconomic background as well. The Crowe study involving the children of offenders found no evidence of this, but the Danish agency used in the Hutchings-Mednick investigation confirmed that this was done. To their credit, the researchers not only recognized this problem, but also admonished that extrapolations to American society should be made cautiously, since Danish society at the time was more homogeneous in cultural values and race.

The most comprehensive adoption study to date was conducted by Mednick, Gabrielli, and Hutchings (1984, 1987). These researchers compared the court convictions of 14,427 adoptees (adopted between the years 1927 and 1947) in a small European country with conviction records of their biological and adoptive parents. The study showed a significant relationship between the conviction history of the adoptees (for both males and females) and their biological parents. Specifically, if either biological parent had been convicted of a crime, the risk of criminality in the adoptee (the biological child) increased significantly. This relationship was especially strong for male adoptees who were chronic or persistent offenders. As we might expect, chronic offenders accounted for a disproportionate share of the total offending for the entire cohort. Interestingly, there was no evidence that the type of crime committed by the biological parent had any relation to the type of crime committed by the biological child. Both the biological parent and biological child tended to engage in crime but selected different kinds of crime. There was also no indication that the adopted children knew about the criminality of their biological parents. The researchers concluded that some factor transmitted by criminal parents increased the probability that their children would engage in criminal behavior. Elsewhere, Gabrielli and Mednick (1983, p. 63) commented, "It is reasonable... to conclude that some people inherit biological characteristics which permit them to be antisocial more readily than others."

In summary, both twin and adoption studies suggest that genetic components may contribute moderately to a tendency to become criminal, but they have also found that environment is highly important (Raine, 2002). According to biopsychologists, the available data so far indicate that some people may be born with a biological predisposition to behavior that runs counter to social values and norms, but environmental factors may either inhibit or facilitate it. For example, adoptees at genetic risk for antisocial behavior because their biological parents were antisocial are more likely to become antisocial themselves if their adoptive parents provided stressful home environments, such as by abusing them (Johnson, 2007; Raine, 2002). Genes may not influence criminal behavior directly, but genes may act to influence people's susceptibility or resistance to environmental risk factors.

Molecular Genetics

As pointed out by Adrian Raine (2008), molecular genetics attempts to answer such question as, "Which genes predispose to which kinds of antisocial behavior?" (p. 323). Some answers are beginning to emerge. For example,

> If the monoamine oxidase A (MAOA) gene is knocked out (neutralized) in mice, they become highly aggressive, becoming 'knock-out' fighters themselves. Knock the gene back in, and they return to their normal behavior patterns. (Raine, 2008, p. 323)

The **MAOA** gene appears to play an instrumental role in preventing antisocial behavior in humans (Kim-Cohen *et al.*, 2006). Interestingly, the low activity form of the MAOA gene (abbreviated MAOA-L) which has been commonly linked to aggression and violence, has been nicknamed "the warrior gene" by some researchers in the field (McDermott, Tingley, Cowden, Frazzetto, & Johnson, 2009). It is estimated that **MAOA-L** is carried by roughly one-third of the population in Western societies and usually comes into play after some form of provocation (McDermott *et al.*, 2009). In a recent study, those persons with the MAOA-L gene who were exposed to adversity in their childhoods were significantly more likely to report offending in late adolescence and early adulthood (Fergusson, Boden, Horwood, Miller, & Kennedy, 2012). Again, this study highlights the importance of considering the effects of the environment on genes rather than simply assuming that genes directly cause behavior.

Raine further notes that at least seven genes have been identified by molecular genetic research to be associated with antisocial behavior in humans. In most cases, these genes appear to contribute to impairments in brain structure and function which, in turn, result in antisocial or abnormal aggressive behavior. Structural or functional problems in the prefrontal cortex are associated with impulsively violent offenders. For example, some research has discovered reduced glucose metabolism in the prefrontal cortex of convicted murders (Raine, Buschsbaum,

& LaCasse, 1997) and a reduction of gray matter in the prefrontal cortex of criminal psycho-paths (Yang *et al.*, 2005). Both studies found no obvious evidence that these brain abnormalities were due to trauma or disease, but seemed to reflect the influence of genes.

PSYCHOPHYSIOLOGICAL FACTORS

Psychophysiology is the study of the dynamic interactions between behavior and the autonomic nervous system. The autonomic nervous system is the subdivision of the peripheral nervous system that regulates involuntary functions, such as heartbeat, blood pressure, breathing, and digestion, and is closely connected to the genetic makeup of the individual. Heart rates (cardio-vascular activity) and electrical conductance in the skin (electrodermal activity) are the usual measures of psychophysiological investigations examining the relationship between antisocial behavior and autonomic activity. Autonomic arousal theory of crime hypothesizes that persis-tent, chronic offenders compared with those with no or little offending history, will exhibit low levels of autonomic arousal across a wide variety of situations and conditions. Presumably, low levels of arousal predispose a person to crime because this produces some degree of fearlessness, and also because it encourages antisocial stimulation (excitement) seeking (Raine, 2002). That is, persistent offenders experience little anxiety and fear and are not troubled about getting caught and punished. Furthermore, they find certain aspects of crime exciting and challenging. On the other hand, high levels of autonomic arousal, in light of the amount of fear and anxiety involved, encourage childhood socialization because of fear of disapproval and punishment. According to DeLisi, Umphress, and Vaughn (2009), the **amygdala** is a brain structure that is particularly important to consider in light of its role in regulating fear and other emotional responses. (See **Figure 3-1** for a view of the structure of the brain.) The amygdala, they contend,

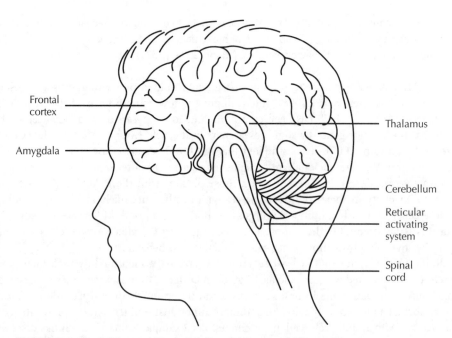

FIGURE 3-1 Brain Diagram Displaying Frontal Cortex and Amygdala

is crucially related to psychopathy and to the callous-unemotional traits that are often associated with persons who engage in chronic antisocial activity.

Some studies reveal that antisocial boys and criminal psychopaths do appear to have lower levels of physiological arousal (as measured by electrodermal and cardiovascular activity) than their non-antisocial counterparts (Raine, 2002; Raine, Venables, & Williams, 1995, 1996). We cover this in more detail when we discuss the psychopath in Chapter 7.

TEMPERAMENT

A child's **temperament**—defined as a "natural" mood disposition determined largely by genetics and biological influences—may offer important clues about criminal behavior. How we approach and interact with our social environment influences how that environment will interact with us. This is true even of infants and very young children. Parents, teachers, physicians, and caretakers know very well that infants and young children differ in activity, emotionality, and general sensitivity to stimuli. A smiling, relaxed, socially interactive child is apt to initiate and maintain a different social response than a fussy, tense, and withdrawn one. A consistently ill-tempered child—assuming the ill temper cannot be attributed to physical discomfort such as hunger or pain—may become so frustrating to his parents that they feel overwhelmed and helpless in dealing with him. The parents' resulting irritability may feed into the behavior of the child in a reciprocal fashion, producing a serious disruption in the parent–child relationship. Frustration may progress into physical or emotional abuse or neglect by the parent(s). In essence, parents (or caregivers) and the child are active agents, who, by continuous transactions, co-create their emerging relationship (Kochanska, Friesenborg, Lange, & Martel, 2004). The overwhelming consensus among experts is that parental responsiveness, nurturance, and warmth have emerged as critical core determinants of the early parent–child relationship (Kochanska *et al.*, 2004).

One of the most influential perspectives on temperament was developed by Thomas and Chess (1977). They contend that temperament is an innate readiness to respond to events and objects across a variety of situations. In addition, it is continually evolving and is strongly influenced by family, parental styles, and the social environment in general. Thomas and Chess systematically studied temperament by asking parents to report on nine characteristics of their infants: (1) rhythmicity of biological functions, such as regularity of bowel movements, sleep cycles, and feeding times, (2) activity level, (3) approach toward or withdrawal from new stimuli, (4) adaptability, (5) sensory thresholds, (6) predominant quality of mood, (7) intensity of mood expression, (8) distractibility, and (9) attention span or persistence. Based on these data, the researchers were able to classify child temperament into three styles: (1) the easy child, (2) the difficult child, and (3) the slow-to-warm-up child.

Table 3-1 summarizes the characteristics of each style. The easy child is characterized by high rhythmicity, positive moods, high approachability, high adaptability, and low intensity of mood expression. The difficult child shows the opposite patterns: irregular biological functioning, initial aversion, and slow adaptability to environmental changes, high intensity of emotional expression, and generally a negative mood. The slow-to-warm-up child displays high activity, withdrawal from new stimuli and people, low adaptability, negative mood, and low intensity. Difficult children, according to Thomas and Chess, represent a specific cluster of inborn temperamental attributes that make child rearing more challenging for many parents or caregivers.

It is suggested here that temperament increases or decreases the *probability* of antisocial behavior, not that it determines directly whether an individual will or will not engage in antisocial

TABLE 3-1 Thomas-Chess Categories of Child Temperaments			
Behavioral Characteristics	**Easy Child**	**Difficult Child**	**Slow-to-Warm-up Child**
Rhythmicity	Regular	Irregular	Regular
Moods	Positive	Negative	Negative
Approach to others	High	Low	Low
Adaptability	Rapid	Slow	Slow
Intensity	Low	High	Low

Source: Based on information from Thomas and Chess (1977).

behavior. That is, the concurrence of these temperaments and certain kinds of family environments and parenting style may lead to delinquent or criminal outcomes. Studies have continually discovered significant *links* between children's "difficult" temperament and the occurrence of persistent antisocial behavior (e.g., Bates, Pettit, Dodge, & Ridge, 1998; Rubin, Burgess, Dwyer, & Hastings, 2003; Shaw, Owens, Giovannelli, & Winslow, 2001).

Features of Temperament

As it is currently used in the research and scholarly literature, "temperament" is assumed to (1) have a constitutional or biological basis, (2) appear in infancy and continue throughout life, and (3) be influenced by the environment (Bates & McFadyen-Ketchum, 2000). Most developmental experts today believe that temperament has biological underpinnings that are best identified at birth (Bates *et al.*, 1998; Dodge & Pettit, 2003; Lahey & Waldman, 2003). Else-Quest, Hyde, Goldsmith, and Van Hulle (2006) write, "Temperament reflects biologically based emotional and behavioral consistencies that appear early in life and predict—often in conjunction with other factors—patterns and outcomes in numerous other domains such as psychopathology and personality" (p. 33). Most of the contemporary research on temperament, therefore, focuses on the infant, because the connection between temperament and behavior seems uncomplicated at this stage and becomes more complex as the child matures and interacts with the psychosocial environment.

Currently, most developmental experts agree that activity and emotionality are two of the behaviors that are strong indicators of temperament. Activity, the most widely studied, refers to gross motor movement across a variety of settings and times, such as the movement of arms and legs, squirming, crawling, or walking. Emotionality refers to such features as irritability, sensitivity, soothability, and general intensity of emotional reactions. Self-regulation (a technical term for controlling impulsivity) is another behavior that is often included in descriptions of temperament. Self-regulation refers to the extent that a child controls his or her own behavior, independent of the control of others and the social environment. Highly impulsive and unmanageable children (poor self-regulators) move into (and often against) their environments at a higher pace and more aggressively than less impulsive children. Research has shown a strong connection between poor self-regulation and antisocial behavior across different social situations (Olson, Sameroff, Kerr, Lopez, & Wellman, 2005).

Failure to acknowledge these dispositional or temperamental variables may leave researchers and practitioners with an incomplete picture of the development of antisocial behavior, especially in cases of individuals who demonstrate a persistent pattern of violent or serious offending. Else-Quest *et al.* (2006) report that girls temperamentally seem better able than boys to manage and regulate their attention and inhibit their impulses (self-regulation). Henry, Caspi, Moffitt, and Silva (1996) found that children considered temperamentally explosive and lacking in self-control were more likely to become violent adolescents compared with their more temperamentally stable peers. In a recent study, Honomichl and Donnellan (2012) found that preschoolers with difficult temperaments (characterized by negative moodiness and low soothability) demonstrated a significantly higher incidence of antisocial problems and reckless risk taking at age 15 compared to their peers. However, although temperament is present at birth, it must be emphasized that its manifestations can be modified by the social environment, especially by parents and significant caregivers. As noted in this section, difficult temperaments can be challenging, but a nurturing and warm parenting style, in which rules are firmly laid out and appropriate self-regulation is encouraged, can prevent, change, or eliminate antisocial behavior in children (Moffitt, 2005b; Veenstra, Lindenberg, Oldehinkel, De Winter, & Ormel, 2006). On the other hand, a difficult temperament combined with parental rejection or parental coercion offers a high risk for antisocial behavior (Dekovic, Janssens, & Van As, 2003; Veenstra *et al.*, 2006).

Likewise, the temperament of parents must also be considered as a possible component in the development of the criminal behavior. Moffitt (1993b) suggests that parents and their offspring often resemble each other in temperament and personality. An irritable, temperamental child may have a high probability of being born to highly irritable, temperamental parents. Thus, parents of difficult children often lack the necessary psychological and emotional resources to cope effectively with a difficult child. Cultural differences may also play a role in the interaction between parenting and temperament, but the research on the parent–child temperament interaction is relatively too recent to make advanced, even tentative, conclusions (Porter *et al.*, 2005; Russell, Hart, Robinson, & Olsen, 2003).

In the next section, we will take a closer look at additional environmental factors that may facilitate or inhibit antisocial tendencies. These factors include prenatal influences, postnatal diseases and experiences, and inadequate nutrition and medical care.

ENVIRONMENTAL RISK FACTORS

In addition to genetic and temperamental factors, in utero experiences may also play a role in the predisposition toward criminal behavior. During pregnancy, the fetus is exposed to various influences that may adversely affect development, leading to potential risks for serious antisocial behaviors later in life. Exposure to a toxic or diseased prenatal environment is one example. "Fetuses exposed to opiates or methadone are at heightened risk for conduct problems 10 to 13 years later, as are fetuses exposed to alcohol, marijuana, and cigarette by-products during pregnancy" (Dodge & Pettit, 2003, p. 351). Fetal alcohol spectrum disorder (FASD) is another example. FASD is a broad term for serious medical conditions that result from prenatal exposure to alcohol (Brown, Connor, & Adler, 2012). Youth with FASD are linked to a high rate of self-regulation problems, antisocial behavior, and conduct disorders (Brown *et al.*, 2012).

Substance use is not the only provider of a toxic environment, however. Much research in recent years has focused on exposure to lead, both before and after birth. Research is very clear that abnormal levels of lead predict a variety of academic and cognitive problems in children (Biglan, Flay, Embry, & Sandler, 2012). Citing a number of studies, Biglan *et al.* (p. 260) conclude that "lead exposure is associated with an increased lifetime burden of special education, attention deficit disorder, crime, and even homicide." Before and after birth, lead poisoning found in old paint cans lead to long-term conduct problems in adolescence and young adulthood (Dodge & Pettit, 2003).

Lead has been found in a variety of other products, including toys, fuel, writing instruments, and products that come into contact with food. During the years 1999–2002, approximately 2 percent of children aged 1–5 had blood lead levels above 10 µg/dl (micrograms per deciliter) (Federal Interagency Forum on Child and Family Statistics, 2005). Children aged 1–5 are particularly affected because of frequent hand-to-mouth behavior. Although 10 micrograms per deciliter is considered elevated according to federal safety standards, significant and troubling behavioral and health effects have been shown to occur at lower levels (Biglan *et al.*, 2012; Federal Interagency Forum on Child and Family Statistics, 2005). Childhood exposure to chips or dust from lead-based paint has been shown to contribute to learning and cognitive development problems (e.g., Braun *et al.*, 2006; Canfield *et al.*, 2003), which increases the risk for antisocial and delinquent behavior. Fortunately, since the 1970s, lead exposure has declined primarily because of the removal of lead from gasoline and the drastic reduction in the use of lead-based paint. Nevertheless, lead can also be present in soil, air, and water (Narag, Pizarro, & Gibbs, 2009). It is estimated that 1.7 million youth in their teenage years have blood lead levels greater than the level of safety established by the Centers for Disease Control (CDC) (Narag *et al.*, 2009).

Many children have blood lead levels at or above 5 µg/dl, and these children are predominantly in homes with incomes below poverty level (Dietrich, Ris, Succop, Berger, & Bornschein, 2001; Needleman, McFarland, Ness, Fienberg, & Tobin, 2002). Some racial and ethnic groups may be particularly susceptible (e.g., African American children, 19%; Mexican American children, 7%). Bone lead levels have been shown to be related to antisocial behavior in adolescents (Dietrich *et al.*, 2001; Needleman *et al.*, 2002; Stretesky & Lynch, 2001, 2004). To what extent lead exposure leads *directly* to antisocial behavior is unknown, and the data so far are only suggestive. Still, parents and caregivers are urged to avoid exposing young children to paint chips, dust, and other substances containing lead if at all possible. Airborne lead or lead in water systems or soil is an environmental hazard that needs broader public attention.

Birth Complications

Birth complications are also associated with violent and persistent offending, but usually the relationship is most significant when *combined* with other psychosocial risks. The most common psychosocial risks are maternal separation, maternal rejection, marital discord, parental mental health problems, and paternal absence. For example, Raine, Brennan, and Mednick (1997) followed the criminal offending history of over four thousand Danish babies to age 34. Birth complications, when combined with early maternal rejection, predicted careers of violent crime. Interestingly, the relationship did not hold for *nonviolent* criminal careers, such as burglary, theft, shoplifting, and drug distribution. Another study (Neugebauer, Hoek, & Susser, 1999) found that maternal malnutrition during pregnancy in combination with adverse caregiving conditions may also be closely linked to violent behavior in the offspring.

The relationship between birth or pregnancy complications and a disadvantaged familial environment found in the Denmark study has also been replicated in four other countries (Sweden, Finland, Canada, and the United States) (Raine, 2002). It should be emphasized that birth or pregnancy complications by themselves are not enough to trigger violent crime and serious antisocial behavior. The relationship seems to require the presence of negative environmental circumstances and heightened psychosocial risks in general. For example, one study

(Arseneault, Tremblay, Boulerice, & Saucier, 2002) discovered that obstetrical complications (preeclampsia, chronic fetal hypoxia, placenta problems, umbilical cord prolapse, and induced labor) increased the risk of being violent at both 6 and 17 years of age among boys who grew up in highly adverse familial environments (early maternal rejection or a disadvantaged familial environment).

Birth and pregnancy complications, in combination with a faulty psychosocial environment, are most likely to have a negative impact on children's abilities to learn to self-regulate their behavior. Neurological deficits (such as brain damage) due to birth and pregnancy problems—if not modified and buffered by a stable home environment—are apt to lead to antisocial behaviors characterized by poor impulse or self-control and limited verbal ability because the child lacks the patience to develop socially appropriate verbal skills.

Nicotine, Alcohol, and Drug Exposure

There is substantial literature on the effects of prenatal exposure to drugs on child development. However, the prenatal effects of substance and alcohol abuse on antisocial behavioral development have received relatively little attention and firm conclusions are difficult to make. A few studies have examined these effects, however. According to Raine (2002, p. 317), "The effects of fetal exposure to alcohol in increasing risk for conduct disorders is well known, but recently a spate of studies has established beyond reasonable doubt a significant link between smoking during pregnancy and later conduct disorder and violent offending." As mentioned earlier in the chapter, youth with FASD (fetal alcohol spectrum disorder) are far more likely to exhibit aggressive behavior, violence, and other conduct problems than the general youth population (Brown *et al.*, 2012). In fact, some studies suggest that "a large percentage of youth in confinement suffer from undiagnosed FASD" (Brown *et al.*, 2012, p. 773).

The evidence for the relationship between maternal smoking during pregnancy and antisocial behavior in her children is quite strong for boys, but weak for girls (Wakschlag & Hans, 2002). In addition, women who quit smoking during their pregnancy give birth to children who demonstrated lower levels of antisocial behavior in life than women who do not quit smoking (Jaffee, Strait, & Odgers, 2012; Robinson *et al.*, 2010). One study (Brennan, Grekin, & Mednick, 1999), using a birth cohort of 4,169 males, found a strong connection between adult violent offending and smoking by their mothers during their pregnancy. On average, the mothers smoked 20 cigarettes a day. This relationship was especially strong (increasing by fivefold) when the offspring were both exposed to nicotine and had birth complications. In another study that used a large sample from the general population of Finland, Räsänen *et al.* (1998) found that, compared with the sons of mothers who did not smoke, the sons of mothers who smoked during pregnancy had more than a twofold risk of having committed a violent crime or having repeatedly committed crimes. This finding held even when other biopsychological risk factors were controlled. The available evidence suggests that smoking during pregnancy may contribute to brain deficits that have been frequently found in adult offenders (Raine, 2002). However, Jaffee *et al.* (2012) caution that, despite the consistency across studies, it remains difficult to firmly conclude that maternal smoking causes antisocial behavior in children. They point out that mothers who smoke during pregnancy are different in many aspects from those who do not. Mothers who smoke tend to have less income and less education, are of lower socioeconomic status, and experience more stress in pregnancy than nonsmoking mothers. In addition, smokers are more likely to have a history of antisocial behavior compared to nonsmokers (Jaffee *et al.*, 2012). It is possible, therefore, that there may be other factors besides smoking that contribute to the eventual antisocial behavior of these children. It is clear, though, that the infants of smoking mothers have significant health problems, including slower brain development (Roza *et al.*, 2007; Shah & Bracken, 2000).

Maternal substance abuse during pregnancy does show a link to substance abuse by their offspring during adolescence, but it is difficult to determine whether this link is due to a shared genetic predisposition between parent and child, the child modeling the parents' behavior, or the in utero effects of the substances themselves (Allen, Lewinsohn, & Seeley, 1998). Identifying the differential effects of maternal substance abuse of specific drugs is also daunting because the drug-abusing mother rarely uses a drug in isolation. That is, abusers usually use multiple substances. Nonetheless, there is some strong evidence to suggest that prenatal cocaine use by mothers adversely affects emotional and attention regulation in infants and preschool-aged children (Mayes, 1999). This finding is significant because cocaine or crack continued to be used by some pregnant women at least into the 1990s. For example, in some inner-city populations, nearly 50 percent of women giving birth reported or tested positive for cocaine use at the time of delivery (Mayes, 1999).

Brain Development

Neurological and brain dysfunction due to faulty brain development is clearly linked to serious and violent antisocial behavior (Ishikawa & Raine, 2004). It appears this connection is particularly relevant in the case of pathological violence (such as impulsive violence occurring in the context of emotional arousal and provocation) (Siever, 2008). The link is especially strong if the brain dysfunction is located in the frontal lobe, which comprises about one-third of the front part of the human brain (see **Figure 3-1**). Organized thought, planning, and self-regulation are located in this area.

The importance of the frontal portion of the brain was revealed in the classic case of Phineas Gage. In September 1848, Gage worked as a construction foreman for the Rutland & Burlington Railroad in Vermont. The work crew was blasting rock while clearing the roadbed for a new rail line outside the town of Cavendish. But during the preparation for the next blast, something suddenly went wrong. A premature explosion sent an iron rod, used for tampering the gunpowder into the blasting hole, into Gage's head. The 3-foot iron, which Gage was using, entered the side of his face, shattering the upper jaw, passing through the frontal lobe, out the top of his head, and flew another 50 feet in the air. The frontal lobe area of his brain was badly damaged. Surprisingly, Gage spoke within a few minutes after the blast, walked with little or no assistance, and sat in a cart that took him to the town doctors. Although Gage lived for another 12 years, the accident dramatically changed his personality. Prior to the accident, Gage was controlled, playful, friendly, and competent. He was a responsible and dependable employee for the railroad. After the accident, he became hostile, ill-tempered, profane, highly unreasonable, and showed poor social judgment. He demonstrated uncontrolled anger, a pattern that led to his inability to hold down a job. Although one could argue that anyone having experienced this trauma might display some personality changes, the extent of the changes and their radical nature were attributed to the physical damage to his brain.

We do not have to go back more than a century to find other examples of individuals with frontal lobe damage and subsequent personality change, however. Traumatic brain injury (TBI) is widely believed to affect one's personality, not infrequently leading to increased aggression (Barash, Tranel, & Anderson, 2000). Researchers studying Vietnam war veterans found that those with head injuries scored higher than those without such injuries on tests of violence (Grafman *et al.*, 1996). Numerous studies indicate that veterans of later conflicts, such as Operation Enduring Freedom (OEF) and

Operation Iraqi Freedom (OIF), were even more likely to experience and survive traumatic brain injuries (see, e.g., Christy, Clark, Frei, & Rynearson-Moody, 2012, and references therein). Based on available research, it has been clearly established that individuals with frontal lobe damage are far more likely to use physical intimidation and violence in conflict situations (Grafman *et al.*, 1996; Siever, 2008). This is especially the case in impulsive violence, where self-regulation and self-control appear to be lacking.

While brain damage due to accidents and physical trauma can result in a propensity toward impulsive violence, the quality of the prenatal environment is also clearly important in brain development. The brain is highly vulnerable to intrinsic hazards (cell development gone wrong) and to external insults resulting from viral infection, drug or alcohol exposure, malnutrition, or other teratogens. Nutritional adequacy is crucial for both prenatal and postnatal brain development because of the growing brain's reliance on folic acid, iron, vitamins, and other nutrients. Malnutrition is a biological hazard to which the developing infant brain is especially vulnerable. Other hazards include fetal exposure to maternal viruses like HIV and rubella, illicit drugs such as cocaine and heroin, maternal alcohol ingestion, exposure to environmental toxins (e.g., DDI, lead, mercury, and PCB) and other teratogens. The developing brain's vulnerability to many of these hazards continues throughout the early years after birth. As we learned in the beginning of this section, unsafe lead levels found in the paint of older homes or in the environment may be a contributing factor in the development of serious antisocial behavior.

Another area of the brain, the *limbic system*, which consists of a diverse group of loosely connected brain structures and circuitry, has also emerged as an important component associated with impulsive violence. The most important brain structure in the limbic system involved in aggressive behavior is the **amygdala** (see **Figure 3-1**). The amygdala is a small, almond-shaped group of nerve cells that appears to play a major role in learning, memory, and the experience of emotions. Impulsive aggression and violence appear to be related to activity in the amygdala (DeLisi, Umphress, & Vaughn, 2009; Jones, Laurens, Herba, Barker, & Viding, 2009; Siever, 2008). Developmental influences that adversely affect the amygdala (and the limbic system generally) are very likely to affect various emotional responses, especially anger.

BRAIN PLASTICITY   After birth, early experiences are crucial in shaping the cultivation and pruning of neural synapses that underlie the functional capabilities of the developing brain (Thompson & Nelson, 2001). Recent studies of humans and other species have made it clear that the developing brain is profoundly responsive to experience (Nelson & Bloom, 1997). Both structure and function are affected by experience, a phenomenon known as **plasticity**. In fact, the plasticity and compensational capacities of the developing brain is perhaps the most remarkable discovery found in the developmental sciences to date (Lidzba & Staudt, 2008).

Among the most important of early experiences in the developing infant is nurturant, sensitive care. Although there are few relevant human neuroscience data, parents and caregivers are encouraged to talk and sing to, play with, read to, and sensitively nurture young children because of how these contingent sensory experiences provide stimulation for the brain (Thompson & Nelson, 2001). On the other hand, when caregivers are unable to provide these multisensory stimulations, brain development is likely to be delayed, either temporarily or permanently depending on the timing and quality of the intervention.

The first three to four years of life are significant in the prevention of antisocial behavior and persistent, serious criminal behavior throughout life, but other developmental periods are also important. There is some evidence, for example, that by the fourth year of life, the plasticity of the brain for language development begins to decrease (Chilosi *et al.*, 2008), suggesting that language stimulation of the developing brain is most important during the first four or five years of life. But this does not mean that brain stimulation after age five is not necessary for brain growth and development. Research demonstrates that the brain retains its capacity to grow throughout life (Thompson & Nelson, 2001). Brain development can be facilitated not only during the first four years but also at other developmental stages. This point suggests that early deprivation and harm can be treated and modified during later years, even in adults.

Hormones and Neurotransmitters

Neurotransmitters are chemicals, manufactured in the brain, that are intimately involved in biochemical activity and transmission of messages in the nervous system. Research has consistently suggested that the neurotransmitter **serotonin** may play the most significant role in aggression and violence (Coscina, 1997; Lesch & Merschdorf, 2000; Loeber & Stouthamer-Loeber, 1998; Moffitt *et al.*, 1997; Vaughn, DeLisi, Beaver, & Wright, 2009). Serotonin exists in large amounts in the frontal lobe, which we have learned is involved in planning and self-regulation. The evidence to date suggests that deficiencies of serotonin in the frontal regions of the brain result in disinhibition of aggression upon provocation (Siever, 2008). There is also some evidence that levels of serotonin may explain to some extent the general differences in physical aggression between men and women (Verona, Joiner, Johnson, & Bender, 2006).

Some additional preliminary but inconclusive findings suggest that humans who become violent after drinking alcohol (Virkkunen & Linnoila, 1993), and children who torture animals (Kruesi, 1979; Kruesi *et al.*, 1990), appear to be abnormally low in concentrations of serotonin. Other research suggests that low levels of brain serotonin encourage impulsive forms of aggressive or violent behavior (Kruesi & Jacobsen, 1997).

If certain neurotransmitters are implicated in aggressive behavior, it is not too far-fetched to consider drug regimens for control. Neurotransmitters are strongly affected by drugs. However, since neurotransmitters are the basic chemicals for all behavior, any modification of their levels in the nervous system is likely to affect a large range of behavior and emotions, not only the behavior that researchers are seeking to control. Therefore, although the considerable potential of drugs in controlling and reducing aggression cannot be overlooked, their peripheral effects must be considered.

Some researchers believe that the differential hormonal effects may partly explain why males overwhelmingly display higher levels of aggression and commit more violent crimes than do females. Some studies report that high testosterone levels in males may be associated with violent crimes, such as murder (Dabbs, Carr, Frady, & Riad, 1995; Dabbs, Riad, & Chance, 2001). Despite the progress in the last few years, the link between hormones and violence remains largely speculative and inconclusive (Ramirez, 2003). We underscore, however, that learning and social expectations and cognitions play an extremely powerful role in any statistics that indicate gender or age differences in criminal behavior.

NEUROPSYCHOLOGICAL FACTORS

As described in the previous sections, neuropsychological deficits, especially those associated with executive function problems in the frontal lobe, are reasonably well-established risk factors for antisocial behavior in children, adolescents, and adults (Raine, 2002). **Executive function** refers to the higher levels of cognitive processes that organize and plan behavior, including reasoning, logic, and abstract reasoning. Executive function also prioritizes the steps necessary for solving problems and is also closely involved in self-control. Several studies of school-age children and adolescents have found a significant relationship between deficits in executive functions and antisocial behavior (Morgan & Lilienfeld, 2000; Syngelaki, Moore, Savage, Fairchild, & Van Goozen, 2009; Tremblay, 2003). Acting without thinking is also believed to be closely associated with deficits in executive function (Romer, 2010; Romer *et al.*, 2011). Acting without thinking is "characterized by hyperactivity without evidence of deliberation or attention to the environment" (Romer, 2010, p. 265). Acting without thinking is a form of impulsiveness that is the focus of neurobehavioral theories of early risk for substance abuse problems and other types of risk-taking behavior in adolescents.

Terrie Moffitt (1993a) has argued that neuropsychological deficits in combination with certain family risk factors are often found in persistent, serious, violent offenders. Liu, Raine, Venables, and Mednick (2004) report from their investigations that malnutrition at age three predisposes a child to neurocognitive deficits, which in turn predispose a child to persistent antisocial behaviors throughout childhood and adolescence. The authors believe that early malnutrition negatively affects brain growth and development and that the brain impairments may promote antisocial and violent behavior by affecting cognitive executive functions. Morgan and Lilienfeld (2000) concluded after an extensive review of the research literature that there is a robust and statistically significant relationship between antisocial behavior and executive function deficits.

Risk Taking

Adolescence is a time of heightened risk taking and unchecked recklessness. Parents often wonder why teenagers take unnecessary risks and make imprudent decisions even though they appear to know better. Adolescent risk taking involves substance abuse, binge drinking, cigarette smoking, reckless driving (often while intoxicated), attempted suicide, and risky sexual behavior. We discuss risk taking in more detail in this section because it is a major factor leading to delinquent, antisocial, and violent behavior, and it involves cognitions, executive functions, arousal, impulse control, and many other concepts discussed thus far. As noted by Sunstein (2008), "adolescent risk-taking leads to seriously impaired lives and even premature deaths" (p. 145). Adolescents are especially vulnerable to considerable risk when they are in a group of their friends or peers, and this vulnerability appears to be the case for both males and females. In fact, crimes committed by adolescents in groups are seldom premeditated (Steinberg, Cauffman, Woolard, Graham, & Banich, 2009).

The high level of vulnerability to risk taking is believed to be the result of high levels of sensation or reward seeking and low impulse control, a condition most prevalent during mid-adolescence (Steinberg, 2010a). As teenagers get older, risk-taking behavior slowly decreases, but continues to some extent until around age 25. For some, risk-taking behavior continues throughout their lives. Laurence Steinberg (2008, 2010a) maintains that high risk taking during adolescence has a lot to do with brain development. "Indeed, it appears that the brain changes characteristic of adolescence are among the most dramatic and important to occur during the human lifespan" (Steinberg, 2010b, p. 160). In fact, many of these changes occur in the prefrontal area (Gogtay & Thompson, 2010; Paus, 2010).

Based on considerable developmental and neurological research, Steinberg (2010a, 2010b) has developed a theory that states that impulsive risk taking and self-control develop along different timetables and have different neurological influences during adolescence and into young adulthood. The theory is called the **dual systems model of adolescent risk taking**. According to Steinberg's perspective, risky behavior in adolescence is the product of an interaction between developmental changes within two brain systems: a socioemotional system located in the limbic system, including the amygdala and prefrontal areas; and a cognitive control system, which is found mainly in the prefrontal and parietal regions (Steinberg, 2010a). In essence, the socioemotional system is a processing center for reward seeking, social information, and emotional reactions that is more sensitive and easily aroused during puberty (Steinberg, 2007). The cognitive control system is highly similar to executive function. According to this dual system, the socioemotional system, which is largely responsible for increases in reward, emotional arousal, and stimulation seeking, matures around age 14 for most adolescents; whereas the cognitive control system, which is responsible for self-regulation and impulse control, gradually matures into young adulthood. This means that young adolescents not only possess a heightened sensitivity to emotions and stimulation seeking but also can cognitively process and retain considerable amounts of information: "By age 16, adolescents' general cognitive abilities are essentially indistinguishable from those of adults, but adolescents' psychosocial functioning, even at the age of 18, is significantly less mature than that of individuals in their mid-20s" (Steinberg et al., 2009, p. 592). According to Steinberg (2010a), the temporal gap between the development of the socioemotional systems and the maturation of the cognitive control "creates a period of heightened vulnerability to risk-taking during middle adolescence" (p. 216). In other words, the two systems do not become balanced and coordinated until the mid-20s for most individuals. In this sense, adolescents may exhibit adultlike levels of maturity in some areas by the time they are about 15, but show continual immaturity well beyond this point in other areas, especially self-control (Steinberg et al., 2009). "From this perspective, middle adolescence (roughly 14-17) should be a period of especially heightened vulnerability to risky behavior, because sensation seeking is high and self-regulation is still immature" (Steinberg, 2010b, p. 162). In other words, neuroscience research (as have many parents) strongly supports the view that adolescence is characterized by dramatic increases in various appetites that remain largely unchecked until self-regulatory systems mature.

Self-report studies find that about 90 percent of teenage boys surveyed admit to committing criminal offenses for which they could be incarcerated (Scott & Steinberg, 2008). Unfortunately, and as many experts know, educational programs designed to reduce adolescent risk taking and criminal activity are largely ineffective. "The problem is not what they know, but what they do" (Sunstein, 2008, p. 147). That is, teenagers know a lot but have difficulty controlling their behavior at times. Most systematic research on educational programs designed to reduce risky behavior in adolescents and young adults show that the programs are far more successful in changing their *knowledge* about risks than in alternating their *behavior* (Steinberg, 2008, 2004). "Although adolescents conceptually understand the risk associated with their behaviors by about the age of 14, the inhibitory mechanisms required to assist those risky behaviors are not equivalent to adults until approximately 20 years of age" (Pharo, Sim, Graham, Gross, & Hayne, 2011, p. 971). Steinberg (2010b) brings up an interesting question: How much is self-regulation influenced by the social environment? If the development of self-regulation is also dependent on experience, it is important to find out which experiences matter most. Systematic research has yet to answer that question.

Summary and Conclusions

Realizing that crime, like all human behavior, may result from an interaction among heredity, neurophysiology, and the environment, we have in this chapter looked at the research on the genetic and biological makeup of persons who engage in persistent antisocial behavior, particularly that which is defined as criminal. The biopsychological approaches of today are far more sophisticated compared with very early efforts to link biology with criminal behavior. These early efforts associated criminal activity with (for example) the size of one's skull or one's physique. Contemporary biopsychologists assert that, while some people may be predisposed toward aggressive behavior or behavior that indicates a need for stimulation, socialization or medication can keep inappropriate expressions of those behaviors in check. However, although the past decade has seen a resurgence of interest in this biosocial perspective, many criminologists resist any notion of biological or genetic predispositions. Some, while veering away from predispositions, do agree that factors like toxins, hormones, or brain injuries can influence one's behavior, however.

The genetic factor has been explored in twin and adoption studies and in the work of molecular biologists. Despite the continuing research, such as the TEDS and TCHAD twin studies discussed in the chapter, it is difficult to draw firm conclusions about the magnitude of genetic and environmental influences on antisocial behavior. Some empirical studies, however, have found a high concordance rate between identical twins engaged in crime, lending some credence to genetic predisposition. These studies have shown that even when separated at birth, identical twins tend to be similar in their pursuit of criminal careers. However, researchers continually have difficulty separating the social environment (shared or nonshared) from the nature–nurture equation, and it is becoming increasingly clear that the social and biological approaches to understanding human behavior are complementary rather than antagonistic (Cacioppo *et al.*, 2000). There have been relatively few adoption studies conducted, primarily because of the inaccessibility of records. Researchers in this area, who say their research supports the genetic viewpoint, admonish that the social environment can either stimulate or inhibit any inborn tendency toward criminality.

In the field of molecular genetics, researchers have isolated genes that they believe are particularly significant in predisposing individuals to violent or other antisocial behavior. The prominent biopsychologist Adian Raine has stated that at least seven genes are associated with antisocial behavior. For example, a low form of the MAOA gene (known as MAOL-L) is associated with aggression, and some polymorphisms are associated with low self-control.

Considerable research also has explored temperament, a mood disposition determined largely by genetics and biological influences, and its relationship with antisocial or criminal behavior. Temperament appears in infancy and continues throughout one's life. An irritable baby, according to these researchers, is a challenge to parents or caretakers who may become highly frustrated dealing with him. Likewise, a child who is impulsive is a poor self-regulator who often comes into conflict with the environment. On the other hand, nurturing and warm caretakers can override the effects of such difficult temperaments.

The structure of the brain, and specifically the amygdala, also has been scrutinized. The frontal lobe of the human brain, which includes the amygdala, is the location for organized thought, planning, and self-regulation. Faulty brain development in utero or trauma to the brain in childhood may predispose someone to behaviors linked with criminality, including low impulse control, callous-unemotional traits, or poor self-regulation. Some environmental hazards that have been studied include exposure to lead and other toxic substances, maternal smoking and alcohol use, and malnutrition. Brain injuries in later life, which have received increasing attention in recent years because of survival rates of veterans who have experienced such trauma, can also contribute to aggressive behavior.

Nevertheless, even "normal" brain development has been associated with antisocial behavior, particularly in adolescents. The research of Lawrence Steinberg, for example, demonstrates persuasively that much of the "acting out" behavior characteristic of adolescence is related to the risk taking that occurs because of lack of maturation in certain developmental milestones. For example, Steinberg's research demonstrates that many adolescents are cognitively capable at age 16, but have not reached socioemotional maturity until their mid-20s.

We emphasize that most studies in this area, with respect to adult criminality, focus on violent crime or aggressive antisocial behavior and, with just a few exceptions, have not focused on nonviolent crimes.

The interest is mainly on exploring the relationship between "violence and the brain." However, assigning a *major* role in the causation of such behavior to diverse neurological deficits and nervous system functioning is unwarranted. While biopsychology and neurophysiological factors may play some role in the formation of criminal behavior—specifically by affecting brain development—it is far more likely that violent and nonviolent antisocial behavior develops as a result of a series of complicated interactions with significant others in the social environment.

Key Concepts

Amygdala
Behavior genetics
Biopsychologists
Concordance
Dual systems model of
    adolescent risk taking
Executive function
Fraternal twins (dizygotic twins)

Identical twins
    (monozygotic twins)
MAOA
MAOA-L
Molecular genetics
Neurotransmitters
Nonshared environments

Plasticity
Psychophysiology
Serotonin
Shared environments
Temperament
Twins' Early Development
    Study (TEDS)

Review Questions

1. Briefly describe behavior genetics and how it differs from molecular genetics.
2. In what ways has behavior genetics contributed to our knowledge about the role genetics play in criminal behavior?
3. Summarize the findings of adoption studies on the interaction between heredity and environment.
4. Define and explain the significance of the following: concordance, plasticity, serotonin, and executive function.

5. What is meant by the term *shared environment* and why is it important in genetic research on crime?
6. Explain how temperament plays a role in the development of antisocial behavior.
7. Provide examples of any three environmental hazards that have been linked with aggressive behavior.
8. Describe Steinberg's dual systems model of adolescent risk taking.

4

■ ■ ■ ■ ■ ■ ▬▬▬▬▬▬▬▬▬▬▬▬▬▬▬▬▬▬▬▬▬▬▬▬▬▬▬▬▬▬▬▬▬▬▬▬▬▬

Origins of Criminal Behavior: Learning and Situational Factors

CHAPTER OBJECTIVES

■ Present learning and cognitive factors as key elements in the development of delinquent and criminal behavior.

■ Review the historical background of behaviorism and its contributions to understanding how delinquent and criminal behavior is learned.

■ Define and describe classical conditioning, operant conditioning, and social learning.

■ Review the fundamental principles of social learning and its contributions to understanding antisocial behavior.

■ Introduce frustration-induced crime.

■ Describe the power of the social situation, authority, and deindividuation in instigating criminal actions.

When people experience brain injuries or suffer seizures or strokes, it is not unusual for them to have short-term memory loss. They may, for example, continue to ask the same question repeatedly, both not realizing that they just asked it and not knowing the answer. Individuals with dementia, of course, also experience memory loss. As a general principle, though, people do not come into situations empty-headed. They remember what just happened and what has happened in the past. They also have an infinite store of living experiences and an extensive repertoire of strategies for reacting to events. Up to this point, we have not highlighted these cognitive strategies, concentrating instead on various individual, family, and social risk factors that can contribute to the development of criminal behavior.

A basic premise of this text is that criminal behavior is learned. Traditionally, psychologists have delineated three major types of learning: **classical** or **Pavlovian conditioning**, **instrumental learning** or **operant conditioning**, and **social learning**. The reader with a background in introductory psychology will recall Ivan Pavlov's famous experiments with dogs that learned to salivate at the sound of a bell, because the bell had been associated with the arrival of food. Even when the food was not presented, the dogs salivated when the bell was rung. When classical conditioning is applied to people, it suggests that they, too, can "learn" if they have been rewarded or punished for behavior. Biological factors, such as those discussed in Chapter 3, appear to account in part for individual differences in susceptibility to classical conditioning (Eysenck, 1967). The classical conditioning perspective presumes, however, that the human being is an automaton and acts in a monotonous routine manner without active intelligence. Pair a neutral stimulus with a closely following rewarding or painful event and the alert, intact robot will eventually, and automatically, connect the stimulus with the reward or the pain. This sequence may be a powerful factor in some behaviors, but certainly not in all or even most. Conditioning is only one of several factors involved in the acquisition (or avoidance) of criminal behavior. We will discuss classical conditioning again later in the chapter.

In instrumental learning, the process is quite different. Here, the learner must do something to the environment in order to obtain a reward or, in some cases, to avoid punishment. Instrumental learning is based on learning the consequences of behavior: if you do something, there is some probability that a certain rewarding event (or perhaps an avoidance of punishment) will occur. A child may learn, for example, that one parent will give her a piece of candy to quell a temper tantrum; the other parent will not yield. The child will eventually learn to use temper tantrums when the first parent is around but not the other.

Social learning is more complex than either classical conditioning or instrumental learning, because it involves learning from watching others and organizing social experiences in the brain. Of the three types of learning, social learning is the most representative of contemporary psychology. It enables us to integrate knowledge from varied aspects of a person's environment and to consider—not only the biological and social environment that was discussed in the previous chapters—but also the cognitive environment. In this chapter, we will revisit classical and instrumental learning, but we focus primarily on social learning.

In order to understand criminal behavior in some depth, it is crucial that we regard all individuals—whether or not they violate the rules of society—as *active* problem solvers who perceive, process, interpret, and respond uniquely to their environments. For the moment, think of unlawful behavior as subjectively adaptable rather than deviant. In this sense, unlawful conduct or antisocial behavior is a response pattern that a person has found to be effective, or thinks will be effective, in certain circumstances.

Violent crimes like aggravated assault and homicide are sometimes called "irrational," "uncontrollable," "explosive," or "motiveless," and therefore are believed to resist or defy analysis (e.g., President's Commission on Law Enforcement and Administration of Justice, 1967). On the other hand, we know that some violent crimes (e.g., a carefully planned murder) do not meet any of those characteristics. Violent crimes, including terrorist acts, are often carefully controlled. Later in this text, we will find that different types of violence can be placed into different theoretical frameworks. The decision to act violently may be a quick one, but the violent behavior—including but not limited to terrorist acts—is usually not irrational or uncontrollable. If we consider individual violence, such as a domestic assault, we can say that some people have poor self-regulation skills, but most individuals can control their behavior, regardless of their excuses. Furthermore, it is almost impossible to determine what is rational or irrational unless we examine the psychological processes of the offender.

Engaging in criminal behavior might be one person's way of adapting or surviving under physically, socially, financially, or psychologically dire conditions. Even behavior that can be attributed to a severe mental disorder may be adaptive, though it may not be legally culpable. Another person might decide that violence is necessary to defend honor, protect self, or reach a personal goal. In either case, the person is choosing what he or she believes is the best alternative for that particular situation (although real choice may be illusory in the case of the person who is severely mentally disordered). It is not, of course, the alternative that others would choose, nor what society condones. The mass murderer Anders Breivik, convicted of killing 77 individuals in Norway in 2011, did not want the judicial system to find him legally insane. He insisted he committed his actions to protect his country from European liberalism. Breivik was found guilty and sentenced to the maximum term, but he expressed satisfaction with the verdict and said he did not regret his actions.

As noted above, violent acts can be placed in a variety of theoretical frameworks, and they will be discussed again in later chapters. In a very general sense, learning—both operant (or instrumental) and social learning—is an extremely important component to understanding violent behavior. Because these concepts spring from the school of psychological thought called behaviorism, we will begin our discussion there.

BEHAVIORISM

Behaviorism officially began in 1913 with the publication of a landmark paper by John B. Watson (1878–1958), "Psychology as the Behaviorist Views It." The paper, which appeared in the journal *Psychological Review*, is considered the first definitive statement on behaviorism, and Watson is acknowledged as the school's founder. However, Watson was by no means the first to discuss the basic elements of behaviorism. Its roots can be traced back at least to Aristotle (Diserens, 1925). Watson's behaviorism represents a recurring phase in the cyclical history of psychology. A psychology of consciousness or mind is followed by a psychology of action and behavior (behaviorism), from which a psychology of mind and consciousness reemerges. Today psychology is immersed once again in a psychology of mind, especially cognitive processes and the neuropsychological aspects of the brain. **Cognitive processes** are those internal mental processes that enable humans to imagine, to gain knowledge, to reason, and to evaluate information. Although some theorists have suggested that cognitive psychology does not sufficiently recognize the importance of self-reflectiveness or self-agency (Bandura, 2001), to others cognitive psychology does encompass these aspects. Interestingly, contemporary psychology also is embracing biological and developmental influences on human behavior, as we learned in Chapter 3. For the moment, however, let's return to Watsonian behaviorism, which has heavily influenced psychological interpretations of criminal behavior.

Watson frequently declared that psychology was the science of behavior. He believed that psychologists should eliminate the "mind" and all of its related vague concepts from scientific consideration because they could not be observed or measured. He was convinced that the fundamental goal of psychology was to understand, predict, and control human behavior, and that only a rigidly scientific approach could accomplish this.

Watson was greatly influenced by Pavlov's famous research on classical conditioning, alluded to briefly above. Pavlov (1849–1936) was a Russian physiologist interested in studying the digestive system. His subjects were dogs, which he strapped in a harness, placed different types of food in their mouths, and then measured the flow of saliva through a tube he surgically placed in their cheek. During these experiments, he began to notice a curious fact. The dogs began to salivate *before* they received the food. He observed that some began to salivate at the mere sight of the container where their food was kept, and some salivated at the sight of the caretaker who normally fed the dogs. Dog owners will easily recognize this pairing. A dog will become excited, and the less dignified will start slobbering as you begin opening a bag of dog chow or shaking a box of dog biscuits. Pavlov quickly recognized the importance of this connection and spent the rest of his life studying it. (We should note that other household pets display similar characteristics, but because Pavlov studied dogs we must resist the temptation to add illustrations in praise of the family cat or guinea pig.)

Pavlov expanded his laboratory conditions by controlling the dog's associations between events or things and the delivery of food. He began to present a neutral event (an event not previously associated with food) just before food delivery. In his well-known laboratory conditions, he presented a bell just before meat powder. The meat powder was termed the *unconditioned stimulus* because its ability to produce salivation was innate and did not depend on the dog's having to learn the response. Likewise, the salivation was an unconditioned response because it too does not depend on learning. The bell became the *conditioned stimulus*, because the dog quickly learned that the sound of the bell (or even the presence of the bell) preceded the treat. Similarly, salivation to the bell became the *conditioned response* because the association was learned. As we will learn in later chapters, classical conditioning is relevant to the understanding of some crimes, particularly some sexual offenses.

Watson thought that psychology should focus exclusively on the interplay between stimulus and response. A **stimulus** is a person, object, or event that elicits behavior. A **response** is the elicited behavior. Watson was convinced that all behavior—both animal and human—was controlled by the external environment in a way similar to that described by Pavlov in his initial study—stimulus produces response (sometimes called S-R psychology). Therefore, for Watson, classical (or Pavlovian) conditioning was the key to understanding, predicting, and controlling behavior, and its practical applicability was unlimited.

The chief spokesperson for behaviorism for several decades was B. F. Skinner (1904–1990), who was the most influential psychologist in the United States in the twentieth century. The Skinnerian perspective especially dominated the application of behavior modification or behavior therapy in the correctional system and in many institutions for the developmentally disabled or mentally disordered. Patients or offenders earned rewards for good behavior or lost items or points when good behavior was not forthcoming. As the history of institutionalization demonstrates, there were many abuses associated with these practices; for example, some rewards were basic necessities, such as adequate food or clothing, which should have been provided regardless of one's behavior (Rothman, 1971). In addition, "good behavior" within an institutional setting did not necessarily carry over to the outside world.

Some contemporary theories on criminal behavior (e.g., Akers, 1985) try to integrate Skinnerian behaviorism with sociological perspectives. Concepts associated with behaviorism are entrenched in many other theories as well. It is worthwhile, therefore, to spend some time sketching the Skinnerian approach to human behavior in general before assessing its impact on the study of criminal behavior.

Skinner's Theory of Behavior

Like Watson, Skinner believed that the primary goal of psychology is the prediction and control of behavior. And like Watson, he believed that environmental or external stimuli are the primary— if not the sole—determinants of all behavior, both human and animal. The environmental stimuli become **independent variables**, and the behaviors they elicit the **dependent variables**. In the behavioral sciences, a **variable** is any entity (or behavior) that can be measured. A behavior (or response) is called "dependent" because it is under the control of (or dependent on) one or more independent variables. The consistent relationships between independent and dependent variables (stimulus and response) are scientific laws. Thus, according to Skinner, the goal of behavioristic psychology is to uncover these laws, making possible the prediction and control of human behavior, including antisocial behavior.

Unlike Watson, Skinner did not deny the existence and sometimes usefulness of private mental events or cognitive processes. He emphasized, however, that these stimuli are not needed by a *science* of behavior, since the products of mental activity can be explained in ways that do not require allusion to unobserved mental states. Specifically, mental activity can be explained by observing what a person does, and it is what a person does that matters. Watson, remember, insisted that consciousness and mind simply do not exist. Thought, to Watson, was little more than tiny movements of the speech apparatus. To Skinner, thought and cognitive processes existed, but studying them is unlikely to lead to the "hard" science of behavior. Consequently, in order to understand and modify antisocial or criminal behavior, the thoughts, values, decisions, and intentions of a criminal mind are irrelevant. According to Skinner, to understand the development of delinquency and criminal behavior, we must focus on environmental stimuli, observable behavior, and rewards.

BEHAVIORISM AS A METHOD OF SCIENCE   At this point, we must emphasize the need to distinguish between behaviorism as a *method of science* and as a *perspective on human nature*. As a method of science, behaviorism posits that knowledge about human behavior can be best advanced if scientists use referents that have a physical basis and can be *publicly observed* by others. Since private events that happen inside our heads cannot be seen by others, they cannot be subjected to the rules of science. According to Skinner, behavioral science data must be comparable to be verified or disconfirmed. Otherwise, psychology would remain a philosophical exercise steeped in armchair speculation and untestable opinions. Self-proclaimed experts could continue to assert that shoplifting is an addiction, just like alcoholism, without being taken to task about the validity of their statements. Only a well-executed, systematic study in which the terms *shoplifting* and *addiction* are clearly spelled out and rigorously tested will advance our knowledge about the accuracy of the shoplifting-addiction connection. Therefore, every psychological experiment, every sentence written into a psychological report, should be anchored to something that we can all observe, or that is testable by another professional. Rather than merely saying that someone is anxious or angry, we must identify the precise behaviors that prompt us to make these interpretations. This offers a basis for others, including the person being observed, to agree or disagree with us.

BEHAVIORISM AS A PERSPECTIVE OF HUMAN NATURE   Concerning behaviorism as a perspective of human nature, Skinner—and a majority of psychologists with a strong behavioristic leaning—embraced the view that humans differ only in degree from their animal ancestry. The behavior of humans follows the same basic natural laws as that of all animals. Like Darwin, Skinner saw no radical differences between humans and animals. Even human language and conceptual thinking are nondistinctive. Verbal behavior "is a very special kind of behavior, but there is nothing by way of processes involved that would distinguish it from nonverbal behavior and hence [verbal behavior] would not distinguish man from the [other] animals" (Skinner, 1964, p. 156). To Skinner, therefore, research on subhumans such as monkeys, rats, and pigeons had great value; if carefully done, it would reveal lawful relationships between all organisms and their environments.

Clearly, Skinner was also a strong situationist. **Situationism** refers to the belief that all behavior is at the mercy of stimuli in the environment, and individuals have virtually no control or self-determination. Independent thinking and free will are myths. Animals, including humans, react, like complicated robots, to their environments. The environmental stimuli and the range of reactions are complex and infinite, but with careful research, this complexity is not unmanageable. Complex human behavior can be broken down into more simple behavior, a procedure sometimes referred to as **reductionism**. In other words, complicated behavior can be best understood by examining the simplest stimulus-response chains of behavior. This point brings us to the issue of operant conditioning.

OPERANT LEARNING   Skinner accepted the basic tenets of classical conditioning, but asserted that we need an additional type of conditioning to account more fully for all forms of behavior. In Pavlov's experiments on classical conditioning, the dogs did not operate on their environments to receive rewards; the event (food) occurred regardless of what they did. Skinner called this "responding conditioning" and contrasted it with a situation in which a subject does something that affects the situation. In other words, subjects behave in such a way that reinforcement is forthcoming. To uncover this operant conditioning principle, Skinner established an association between *behavior* and its *consequences*. He trained pigeons (apparently less troublesome and less expensive than dogs) to peck at keys or push levers for food. The pecking or pushing are operations on the environment. Operant conditioning, then, is learning to either make or withhold a particular response because of its consequences. Operant conditioning (or operant learning) is a fundamental learning process that is acquired (or eliminated) by the consequences that follow the behavior. Recall the child who learned the effectiveness of the temper tantrum in the company of one parent but not the other. Children often operate on their environments in this way, "learning" the effectiveness of certain behaviors as they go along—but so do adults. You may have learned that complimenting a co-worker improves the quality of your day, while being the office grump drives people away. If you prefer to be a loner, however, the office grump strategy could be effective.

The learning that comes about through operant conditioning was described before Skinner's time, but he is credited with drawing contemporary attention to it. In the late eighteenth and early nineteenth centuries, for example, philosophers like Cesare Beccaria and Jeremy Bentham observed that human conduct was controlled by the seeking of pleasure and the avoidance of pain. In essence, this is what is meant by operant learning. It assumes that people do things solely to receive rewards and avoid punishment. The rewards may be physical (e.g., material goods, money), psychological (e.g., feelings of importance or control over one's fate), or social (e.g., improved status, acceptance).

REINFORCEMENT   Skinner called rewards **reinforcement**, defining that term as anything that increases the probability of future responding. Furthermore, reinforcement may be either positive or negative. In **positive reinforcement**, we *gain* something we desire as a consequence of certain behavior. We spend hours practicing a difficult piece on the keyboard or perfecting a ski jump and are rewarded by our own feeling of accomplishment, praise from listeners, or a gold medal in the Olympics. In **negative reinforcement**, we *avoid* an unpleasant event or stimulus as a consequence of certain behavior. For example, if as a child you were able to avoid the unpleasantness of certain school days by feigning illness, your malingering was negatively reinforced. Therefore, you were more likely to engage in it again at a future date, under similar circumstances—high school dress-up day, class discussion day in a difficult college course, or the day the district supervisor was scheduled to visit the office. Thus, both positive and negative reinforcement can increase the likelihood of future behavior.

PUNISHMENT AND EXTINCTION   Negative reinforcement is to be distinguished from punishment and extinction. In **punishment**, an organism receives noxious or painful stimuli as consequences of behavior, such as being slapped or hit for "being bad." In **extinction**, a person or

TABLE 4-1	Skinner's Basic Principles of Operant Learning	
	Goal	**Action**
Positive reinforcement	Increases a desired behavior	Introduction of a pleasant stimulus following a desired behavior
Negative reinforcement	Increases a desired behavior	Removal of aversive stimulus following a desired behavior
Punishment	Decreases undesired behavior	Introduction of aversive stimulus following undesired behavior
Extinction	Eliminates undesired behavior	No reinforcement or punishment for undesired behavior

animal receives neither reinforcement nor punishment (see **Table 4-1**). Skinner argued that punishment is a less effective way to eliminate behavior, because it merely suppresses it temporarily. At a later time, under the right conditions, the response is very likely to reoccur. Extinction is far more effective, because once the organism learns that a behavior brings no reinforcement, the behavior will be dropped from the repertoire of possible responses for that set of circumstances.

According to Nietzel (1979), C. R. Jeffrey (1965) was one of the first criminologists to suggest that criminal behavior was learned according to principles of Skinnerian operant conditioning. Shortly afterward, Burgess and Akers (1966) agreed with this, and further hypothesized that criminal behavior was both acquired and maintained through operant conditioning. But, as Nietzel points out, most of the direct evidence for this claim comes from experiments with nonhuman animals. Evidence that the same occurs in humans is scarce and replete with possible alternative interpretations.

Nevertheless, neither Jeffrey nor Burgess and Akers relied exclusively on Skinnerian theory. Rather, they combined sociologist Edwin Sutherland's principles of social learning with operant conditioning, particularly the reinforcement aspect, to suggest explanations for criminal behavior (Williams & McShane, 2004). We will return to Sutherland's theory shortly.

OPERANT LEARNING AND CRIME   The premise that operant conditioning is the basis for the origin of criminal behavior is deceptively simple: Criminal behavior is learned and strengthened because of the reinforcements it brings. According to Skinner, human beings are born neutral—neither good nor bad. Culture, society, and the environment shape behavior. Therefore, behavior will be labeled "good," "bad," or "indifferent," as society chooses. What is judged "good" behavior in one society or culture may be labeled "bad" in another. Members of one group in a society may believe that it is "bad" for a child to masturbate or to pretend that a block of wood is a toy truck and "good" to hit the child to stop these behaviors. To others, the behavior of the adults who hit the child is "bad." Depending on the severity of the punishment, it may also be aggravated assault.

Skinner was convinced that searches for individual dispositions or personalities that lead to criminal conduct are fruitless, because people are ultimately determined by the environment in which they live. He did not completely discount the role of genetics in the formation of behavior, but he saw it as a very minor one; the dominant player is operant conditioning. According to Skinner and his followers, if we wish to eliminate crime, we must change society through behavioral engineering based on a *scientific* conception of humans. Having agreed on rules and regulations (having defined what behaviors constitute antisocial or criminal offenses), we must design a society in which members learn very early that positive reinforcement will not occur if they transgress against these rules and regulations, but will occur if they abide by them.

This is a tall order, since the reinforcements for antisocial behavior are already occurring, are not always obvious, and may actually be highly complex. Property crimes such as shoplifting and burglary, or violent crimes such as robbery, appear to be motivated in many cases by a desire for physical rewards. However, they may also be prompted by a desire for social and psychological reinforcements, such as increased status among peers, self-esteem, feelings of competence, or simply for the thrill of it. It is a safe bet that much criminal behavior is undertaken for reinforcement purposes, positive or negative. The problem then becomes, how do we identify those reinforcements and how do we prevent them from happening, or at least minimize their value?

Contemporary psychology still embraces a behavioristic orientation toward the *scientific* study of behavior, but has grown very cool toward the Skinnerian perspective of human nature. All behaviorists are not Skinnerians. Many (if not most) find Skinner's brand of behaviorism too limiting and find the many facets of social learning—discussed below—far more appealing. While they agree that a stimulus can elicit a reflexive response (classical conditioning) and that a behavior produces consequences that influence subsequent responding (operant conditioning), they are also convinced that additional factors must be introduced to explain human behavior.

This brings us to the topic of mental states and cognitive processes, which Skinner urged all behavioral scientists to shun. In recent years, many psychologists have been examining the roles played by self-reinforcement, anticipatory reinforcement, vicarious reinforcement, and all the symbolic processes that occur within the human brain. To avoid confusion, we must now begin to distinguish Skinnerian behaviorism from other forms, including social behaviorism (social learning) and differential association-reinforcement.

SOCIAL LEARNING

Early learning theorists worked in the laboratory, using nonhumans as their primary subjects. Pavlov's, Watson's, and Skinner's theories, for example, were based on careful, painstaking observations and experiments with animals. The learning principles gleaned from their work were generalized to a wide variety of human behaviors. In many cases, this was a valid process. Few psychologists would dispute the contention that the concept of reinforcement is one of the most soundly established principles in psychology today.

However, behaviorists also suggested that since all human behavior is learned, it can also be changed, using the same principles by which it was acquired. This generated a plethora of behavior therapies or behavior modification techniques. Use learning principles to establish conditions that change or maintain targeted behaviors and therapeutic success would follow. The apparent simplicity of the procedures and methods was especially appealing to many clinicians and other professionals working in the criminal justice system, and behavior modification packages sometimes guaranteed to modify criminal behavior were rushed to various institutions, including facilities for juveniles. As noted above, patients as well as prisoners (and juveniles) would be rewarded for good behavior with such incentives as cigarettes, canteen privileges, or an extra shower.

But oversimplification is dangerous when we deal with human complexity. Human beings do respond to reinforcement and punishment, and behavior therapy based on learning principles can change certain elements of behavior. Moreover, humans can be classically conditioned, although there are individual differences in their susceptibility. When we lose sight of the person and overemphasize the environmental or external determinants of behavior, however, we may be overlooking a critical level of explanation. Remember that human beings are, in large part, active problem solvers who perceive, encode, interpret, and make decisions on the basis of what the environment has to offer. Thus, internal factors, as well as external ones, may play significant roles in behavior. This is the essence of **social learning theory**, which suggests that to understand criminal behavior we must examine perceptions, thoughts, expectancies, competencies, and values. Each person has his or her own version of the world and lives by that version.

To explain human behavior, social learning theorists place great emphasis on cognitive processes, which are the internal processes we commonly call thinking and remembering. Classical and operant conditioning ignore what transpires between the time the organism perceives a stimulus and the time it responds or reacts. Skinnerian behaviorists claim, "If we can account for the facts by using observable behavior, why worry about the labyrinths of internal processes?" Social behaviorists, however, counter that this perspective offers an incomplete picture of human behavior.

The term *social learning* reflects the theory's strong assumption that we learn primarily by observing and listening to people around us—the social environment. In fact, social learning theorists believe that the social environment is the most important factor in the *acquisition* of most human behavior. Humans are basically social creatures. These theorists do accept the necessity of reinforcement for the *maintenance* of behavior, however. Criminal behavior, for example, may initially be acquired through association and through observation, but whether or not it is maintained will depend primarily upon reinforcement (operant conditioning). For example, if a boy sees someone he admires (i.e., a role model) successfully pilfering from the local sporting goods store, the boy may try some pilfering of his own. Whether he continues that behavior, however, will depend on the personal reinforcement or value it assumes. If no reinforcement is forthcoming (he fails to pocket a baseball because someone else walked into the store, or he finds that the gym shorts he stole do not fit), then the behavior will probably drop out of his response repertoire (extinction). If the behavior brings aversive results (punishment), this might inhibit or suppress future similar behavior, but the suppression or inhibition is unlikely to be long lasting.

Several clusters of psychologists are enrolled in the social learning school of thought. Additionally, the discipline of sociology has its own social learning school. We will focus first on the work of two prominent representatives, psychologists Julian Rotter and Albert Bandura, since they seem to have the most to offer to the study of criminal behavior from the social learning perspective.

Expectancy Theory

Julian Rotter is best known for drawing attention to the importance of expectations (cognitions) about the consequences (outcomes) of behavior, including the reinforcement that will be gained from it. In other words, before doing anything, we ask, "What has happened to me before in this situation, and what will I gain this time?" According to Rotter, whether a specific pattern of behavior occurs will depend on our expectancies and how much we value the outcomes. To predict whether someone will behave a certain way, we must estimate that person's expectancies and the importance he or she places on the rewards gained by the behavior. Often, the person will develop "generalized expectancies" that are stable and consistent across relatively similar situations (Mischel, 1976). **Expectancy theory**, therefore, argues that a person's performance level is based on that person's *expectation* that behaving in a particular way will lead to a given outcome.

The hypothesis that people enter situations with generalized expectancies about the outcomes of their behavior is an important one for students of crime. Applying Rotter's theory to criminal behavior, we would say that when people engage in unlawful conduct, they *expect* to gain something in the form of status, power, security, affection, material goods, or living conditions. The violent person, for example, may elect to behave that way in the belief that something will be gained; the serial murderer might believe that God has sent him on a mission to eliminate all "loose" women, and thus by doing so he pleases God; the father who physically abuses his children thinks they will comply with his wishes or learn to respect adults; the woman who poisons an abusive husband looks for an improvement in her life situation. Simply to label a violent person "impulsive," "crazy," or "lacking in ego control" fails to include other essential ingredients in the act. Although self-regulation and moral development are involved, people who act unlawfully perceive and interpret the situation and select what they consider to be the most effective behavior under the circumstances. Usually, when people act violently, they do so because that approach has been used successfully in the past (at least they believe it has been successful). Less frequently, they have simply observed someone else gain by employing a violent approach, and they try it for themselves. This brings us to Bandura's imitational model of social learning.

Imitational Aspects of Social Learning

An individual may acquire ways of doing something simply by watching others do it; direct reinforcement is not necessary. Bandura (1973b) introduced this idea, which he called **observational learning** or **modeling**, to the social learning process. Bandura contends that much of our behavior is initially acquired by watching others, who are called models. **Models** are those significant persons in the social environment that provide cues for how to do something. For example, a child may learn how to shoot a gun by imitating television or video characters. He or she then rehearses and fine-tunes this behavioral pattern by practicing with toy guns. The behavior is likely to be maintained if peers also play with guns and reinforce one another for doing so. Even if the children have not pulled the triggers on real guns, they have acquired a close approximation of shooting someone by observing others do it. It is likely that just about every adult and older child in the United States knows how to shoot a gun, even if they have never actually done so: "You aim and pull the trigger." Of course, shooting safely and accurately is much more complicated, but the rudimentary know-how has been acquired through **imitational learning** (also called modeling or observational learning). The behavioral pattern exists in our repertoires, even if we have never received direct reinforcement for acquiring it.

According to Bandura, the more significant and respected the models, the greater their impact on our behavior. Relevant models include parents, teachers, siblings, friends, and peers, as well as symbolic models like literary characters or television, video, or movie personages. Rock stars and athletes are modeled by many young people, which is one reason we are exposed to so many public figures touting smart phones, weight-loss programs, reverse mortgages, and brands of underwear. Well-known individuals also appear in public service announcements, such as those promoting a drug-free life. Interestingly, these public service advertisements often miss the point. In observational learning, it is not so much what the model says as what the model does that is effective. If sports stars actually avoided the use of drugs in their daily lives, their messages to youth might be more effective. The observed behavior of the model is more likely to be imitated if the observer sees the model receive a reward, such as fame plus millions of dollars per year. It is less likely to be imitated if the model is punished. Thus, according to social learning principles, convictions of sports and entertainment figures charged with crimes like domestic violence, substance abuse, rape, assault, tax evasion, and animal abuse would suggest that the behaviors will not be imitated. On the other hand, if they serve little or no time and write a widely purchased book about their experiences, an observer might not perceive this as a punishment. Bandura believes—much like Rotter—that once a person decides to use a newly acquired behavior, whether he or she performs or maintains it will depend on the situation and the expectancies for potential gain. This potential gain may come from outside (the praise of others, financial gain) or it may come from within (self-reinforcement for a job the individual perceives as well done).

Much of Bandura's original research was directed at the learning of aggressive and violent behavior through modeling. We will be returning to his theory, therefore, in Chapter 5 on aggression and violence. At this point, however, be aware that a substantial body of experimental findings gives impressive support to his theory. In a classic study, preschool children who watched a film of an adult assaulting an inflated plastic rubber doll were significantly more likely to imitate that behavior than were a comparable group who viewed more passive behavior (Bandura & Huston, 1961; Bandura, Ross, & Ross, 1963). Many studies employing variations of this basic procedure report similar results, strengthening the hypothesis that observing aggression leads to hostility in both children and adults (Walters & Grusec, 1977). In more recent years, this research has been extended to viewing media violence and playing violent video games (Dodge & Pettit, 2003). While the research in these areas is not totally conclusive (Azar, 2010), the growing evidence is that people who observe aggressive acts not only imitate the observed behavior but also become generally more hostile and aggressive themselves (Anderson & Prot, 2011; Bryant & Zillman, 2002; Bushman & Gibson, 2011; Huesmann, Moise-Titus, Podolski, & Eron, 2003). This is most likely to be the case for individuals who are already prone to violence or have excessive exposure to the most violent images.

To some extent, social learning, as it is discussed by Rotter and Bandura, humanizes the Skinnerian viewpoint, because it provides clues about what transpires inside the human brain, especially the cognitive processes involved. It draws our attention to the cognitive aspects of behavior, while classical and operant conditioning focus exclusively on the environment. Social learning theorists use environment in the social sense, which includes the internal as well as the external environment. Skinnerians prefer to limit relevant stimuli to external surroundings.

Differential Association-Reinforcement Theory

Ronald Akers (1977, 1985; Burgess & Akers, 1966) proposed a social learning theory of deviance that tries to integrate the core ingredients of Skinnerian behaviorism, the social learning theory as outlined by Bandura, and the differential association theory of criminologist Edwin H. Sutherland (1947). Akers called his theory **differential association-reinforcement (DAR)**. Briefly, the theory states that people learn to commit deviant acts through interpersonal interactions with their social environment.

To understand DAR theory, we must grasp Sutherland's differential association theory, which dominated the field of sociological criminology for over four decades. It was first set forth in the third edition (1939) of Sutherland's *Principles of Criminology* and restated in 1947. Although Sutherland died in 1950, the theory was left intact in Donald R. Cressey's subsequent revisions of the original text (Sutherland & Cressey, 1978; Sutherland, Cressey, & Luckenbill, 1992).

Sutherland, a sociologist, believed that criminal or deviant behavior is learned the same way that all behavior is learned. The crucial factors are with whom a person associates, for how long, how frequently, how personally meaningful the associations, and how early they occur in the person's development. According to Sutherland, in our intimate personal groups, we all learn definitions, or normative meanings (messages or values), favorable or unfavorable to law violation. A person becomes delinquent or criminal "because of an excess of definitions favorable to violation of law over definitions unfavorable to violation of law. This is the principle of differential association" (Sutherland & Cressey, 1974, pp. 80–81).

Note that criminal behavior does not invariably develop out of association or contacts with "bad companions" or a criminal element. The messages, not the contacts themselves, are crucial. Furthermore, in order for the person to be influenced toward delinquent behavior, the deviant messages or values from the "bad companions" must outweigh conventional ones. Therefore, Sutherland also believed that criminal behavior may develop even if association with criminal groups is minimal. For example, law-abiding groups—such as parents—may communicate subtly or bluntly that it is all right to cheat, or that everyone is basically dishonest. This is an extremely important point that will be reiterated when we discuss moral disengagement later in the chapter. Nevertheless, contemporary reviews of differential association theory emphasize that the associations with deviant peer groups have a major effect on illegal behavior (Williams & McShane, 2004). What is not known is which comes first: the behavior or the associations (Williams & McShane, 2004).

Sutherland's theory is probably popular among social scientists because, as one writer put it some time ago, "it attempts a logical, systematic formulation of the chain of interrelations that makes crime reasonable and understandable as normal, learned behavior without having to resort to assumptions of biological or psychological deviance" (Vold, 1958, p. 192). However, the theory is also ambiguous; because of this feature, it did not at first draw much empirical research (see Gibbons, 1977, pp. 221–228). How are a person's contacts to be measured and weighed? Also, as Cressey (Sutherland & Cressey, 1974) admits, the theory does not specify what kinds of learning are important (e.g., operant, classical, modeling). Neither does it adequately consider individual differences in the learning process. Among some sociologists, however, differential association theory remains popular and continues to attract research interest (Williams & McShane, 2004).

Akers (1985) tries to correct some of the problems with differential association theory by reformulating it to dovetail with Skinnerian and social learning principles. He proposes that most deviant behavior is learned according to principles outlined in Skinner's operant conditioning, with classical conditioning playing a secondary role. Furthermore, the strength of deviant behavior is a direct function of the amount, frequency, and probability of reinforcement the individual has experienced by performing that behavior in the past. The reinforcement may be positive or negative in the Skinnerian meanings of the terms.

Crucial to the Akers position is the role played by *social* and *nonsocial reinforcement*, the former being the more important. "Most of the learning relevant to deviant behavior is the result of social interactions or exchanges in which the words, responses, presence, and behavior of other persons make reinforcers available, and provide the setting for reinforcement" (Akers, 1985, p. 45). It is also important to note that most of these social reinforcements are symbolic and verbal rewards for participating or for agreeing with group norms and expectations. For example, doing something in accordance with group or subcultural norms is rewarded with "Way to go," "Great job," a pat on the back, a high five, or a friendly grin. Nonsocial reinforcement refers primarily to physiological factors or material acquisition that may be relevant for some crimes, such as drug-related offenses or burglary.

Deviant or antisocial behavior, then, is most likely to develop as a result of social reinforcements given by significant others, usually within one's peer group. The group first adopts its own *normative definitions* about what conduct is good or bad, right or wrong, justified or unjustified. These normative definitions become internal, cognitive guides to what is appropriate and will most likely be reinforced by the group. In this sense, normative definitions operate as **discriminative stimuli**—social signals transmitted by subcultural or peer groups to indicate whether certain kinds of behavior will be rewarded or punished within a particular social context.

According to Akers, two classes of discriminative stimuli operate in promoting deviant behavior. First, positive discriminative stimuli are the signals (verbal or nonverbal) that communicate that certain behaviors are encouraged by the subgroup. Not surprisingly, they follow the principle of positive reinforcement: The individual engaging in them gains social rewards from the group. The second type of social cue, *neutralizing* or *justifying discriminative stimuli*, neutralizes the warnings communicated by society at large that certain behaviors are inappropriate or unlawful. According to Akers, they "make the behavior, which others condemn and which the person himself may initially define as bad, seem all right, justified, excusable, necessary, the lesser of two evils, or not 'really' deviant after all" (Akers, 1977, p. 521). Statements like "Everyone has a price," "I can't help myself," "Everyone else does it," or "She deserved it" reflect the influence of neutralizing stimuli.

The more people define their behavior as positive or at least justified, the more likely they are to engage in it. If deviant activity (as defined by society at large) has been reinforced more than conforming behavior (also defined by society), and if it has been justified, it is likely that deviant behavior will be maintained. In essence, our behavior is guided by the norms we have internalized and for which we expect to be continually socially reinforced by significant others.

Akers accepts the validity of Bandura's modeling as a necessary factor in the initial acquisition of deviant behavior. But its continuation will depend greatly on the frequency and personal significance of *social reinforcement*, which comes from association with others.

Akers's social learning theory has received its share of criticism. Some scholars consider it circular and difficult to follow: Behavior occurs because it is reinforced, but it is reinforced because it occurs. Kornhauser (1978) asserted that there was no empirical support for the theory. During the 1980s and 1990s, though, Akers himself—along with research colleagues—published a number of studies supportive of his theory, particularly as it related to drug use (e.g., Akers & Cochran, 1985; Akers & Lee, 1996; Krohn, Akers, Radosevich, & Lanza-Kaduce, 1982). Like Sutherland's differential association theory, Akers's approach retains respectability within sociological criminology.

FRUSTRATION-INDUCED CRIMINALITY

Several learning investigators (e.g., Amsel, 1958; Brown & Farber, 1951) have noted that when organisms—including humans—are prevented from responding in a way that had previously produced rewards, their behavior often becomes more energetic and vigorous. Animals bite, scratch, snarl, and become irritable; humans may snarl and become irritable and rambunctious (and may also bite and scratch). Researchers assume that these aroused responses result from an aversive internal state of arousal that they call **frustration**.

Thus, when behavior directed at a specific goal is blocked, arousal increases, and the individual experiences a drive to reduce it. Behavior is energized, but more significantly the responses that lead to a reduction in the arousal may be strengthened or reinforced. This suggests that people who employ violence to reduce frustration will, under extreme frustration, become more vigorous than usual, possibly even resorting to murder and other violent actions. It also suggests that violent behavior directed at reducing frustration will be reinforced, since it reduces unpleasant arousal by altering the precipitating event or stimuli.

The Socialized and Individual Offender

Leonard Berkowitz (1962) conducted numerous studies relating frustration to criminality. He divided criminal personalities into two main classifications: the **socialized** and the **individual**

offender. You have already met socialized offenders. We have discussed them throughout this chapter as products of learning, conditioning, and modeling. They offend because they have learned to, or expect rewards, as a result of their interactions with the social environment. The individual offender, by contrast, is the product of a long, possibly intense series of frustrations resulting from unmet needs. According to Berkowitz, both modeling and frustration are involved in the development of criminal behavior, but one set of life experiences favors a particular criminal style. "Most lawbreakers may have been exposed to some combination of frustrations and aggressively antisocial models, with the thwartings being particularly important in the development of 'individual' offenders and the antisocial models being more influential in the formulation of the 'socialized' criminals" (Berkowitz, 1962, p. 303).

Berkowitz adds an important dimension to frustration, suggesting that it is particularly intense if an individual has high expectancy of reaching a goal (Berkowitz, 1969). People who anticipate reaching a goal, and who feel they have some personal control over their lives, are more likely to react strongly to interference than those who feel hopeless. In the first case, delay or blockage may generate intense anger and even a violent response, if the frustrated individual believes that type of response will eliminate the interference. The power of frustration may well have been what Maslow (1954) was referring to when he stated that crime and delinquency represent a legitimate revolt against exploitation, injustice, and unfairness. The frustration hypothesis also fits neatly into theories offered by radical or conflict criminologists. Individuals who feel suppressed by the power elite and feel they have a right to reap society's benefits may well experience intense frustration at continuing domination. These criminologists would prefer, though, that the focus be on those who commit crime while holding the power rather than on those who commit crime out of possible frustration.

Frustration-Induced Riots

The frustration-induced theory helps to explain the behavior of looters during unexpected events like floods, fires, urban riots, or electrical blackouts, but such illegal activity does not invariably occur, and it often does not occur when it is expected.

An often cited instance of frustration-induced criminality is the period between April 30 and May 3, 1993, when businesses in Los Angeles were burned and looted by individuals who were angry at a jury's acquittal of four white LA police officers in the March 1991 beating of African American motorist Rodney G. King. (Later, a federal jury convicted two of the four officers on federal charges.) Fifty-eight people were killed in the four days of rioting, and damage was estimated to be at least $1 billion. Although many of the looters were African Americans, not all were. People of all ages and racial or ethnic backgrounds were stealing everything from food and alcohol to firearms and stereos. The rioting triggered smaller uprisings in several other cities, including San Francisco, Atlanta, Seattle, Las Vegas, and Miami. Authorities concluded that the riots were brought on by frustrations with economic, social, and political inequalities found in many sectors of American society, including the court system. The Los Angeles riot was similar to the August 1965 uprising of the Watts section of LA, when 34 were killed and one thousand were injured. The riot was prompted by deeply felt frustrations with the same perceived inequalities in American society. Since, there have been at least five major city riots in the United States, mostly started in the wake of reports of police violence and perceived inequities.

Following Hurricanes Katrina and Rita in 2005, there were reports of property crime and some violence. Many commentators noted that this was a reflection of the frustration residents of New Orleans and other communities felt at the failure on the part of federal and state agencies to provide a quick, humane, and efficient response to this natural disaster. Nevertheless, despite the frustration, the vast majority of residents did not engage in criminal activity. In fact, they were more likely to be resilient and to help one another in their time of need.

The frustration-induced theory also would suggest that individuals who commit larceny under these situations have materialistic goals (e.g., their fair share of middle-class goods) that they have not yet attained. Society blocked the goals, and the individuals became impatient and frustrated. When the opportunity to loot arises, they are there to take it. Demographic profiles of the 2,706 adults arrested and charged with looting during the New York City blackout of 1977 support this theory. The defendants had stronger community ties and higher incomes than the average defendant in the criminal justice system (*New York Times*, August 14, 1977). Only about 10 percent were on some form of public assistance; approximately half were gainfully employed. Sixty-five percent of those arrested were African American and 30 percent were Hispanic. These data indicate that these defendants were, in general, eager to eliminate further delays in meeting their expectancy for a better life.

On the other hand, there have been numerous accounts of peaceful demonstrations and protests after a perceived injustice, even when major disruptions or even riots had been feared. In the fall of 2011 the Occupy Wall Street movement that began in New York City spread rapidly across the United States as well as in other countries. It was fueled by intense disenchantment with financial markets and corporate greed. Despite the large numbers of individuals who turned out for these protests, there was no widespread looting or violence, although there were reports of minor vandalism, disruption of traffic, and property damage. There is no question that frustration played a large role in prompting the protests. Nevertheless, the frustration aggression hypothesis would not be supported.

Frustration and Crime

In summary, the role of frustration in criminal behavior can be complex, and it may be a matter of degree. Berkowitz hypothesizes that the more intense and frequent the thwartings or frustrations in a person's life, the more susceptible and sensitive the person is to subsequent frustration. Thus, the individual who frequently strikes out at society in unlawful or deviant ways may have encountered numerous severe frustrations, especially during early development, but has not given up hope. In support of this argument, Berkowitz cites the research findings on delinquency (e.g., Bandura & Walters, 1959; Glueck & Glueck, 1950; McCord, McCord, & Zola, 1959), revealing that delinquent children, compared with nondelinquents, have been considerably more deprived and frustrated during their lifetime.

Berkowitz also suggests that parental neglect or failure to meet the child's needs for dependency and affection are internal, frustrating circumstances that germinate distrust of all others within the social environment. This generalized distrust is carried into the streets and school, and the youngster may exhibit a "chip on the shoulder." The frustration of not having dependency needs met prevents the child from establishing emotional attachments to other people. The individual may thus become resentful, angry, and hostile toward other people in general.

Current psychological approaches to delinquency would not disagree, but would place far less blame on the parent. They are more likely to recognize the restrictions that parents face as a result of social problems like racism and economic inequality. It has been observed, for example, that over 20 percent of children under the age of 18 in the United States live in households below the official poverty line, and another 20 percent are near poor (Yoshikawa et al., 2012). The negative effects of poverty on the mental, emotional, and behavioral health of children are well recognized, as we noted in Chapters 2 and 3. In addition, contemporary psychologists recognize the influences of other social systems in the juvenile's life, including peers and the educational system.

SITUATIONAL INSTIGATORS AND REGULATORS OF CRIMINAL BEHAVIOR

Most contemporary theories and research support the view that human behavior results from a mutual interaction between personality and situational variables. However, several behavioral and social scientists (e.g., Alison, Bennell, Ormerod, & Mokros, 2002; Gibbons, 1977; Mischel, 1976) complain that much crime research and theory neglects situational variables in favor of dispositional factors. They contend that criminality in many cases may simply reflect being in the wrong place at the wrong time with the wrong people. For example, Gibbons comments, "In many cases, criminality may be a response to nothing more temporal than the provocations and attractions bound up in the immediate circumstances out of which deviant acts arise" (Gibbons, 1977, p. 229). Skinner, of course, exemplifies the position that behavior is controlled by environmental contingencies and events.

Haney (1983) discusses **fundamental attribution error**, which refers to a common human tendency to discount the influence of the situation and explain behavior by referring to the personality of the actor instead. Fundamental attribution error is a concept that applies to making attributions about others, not ourselves. For example, when correctional counselors were asked why inmates had committed the crimes that put them in prison, the counselors attributed the causes almost exclusively to dispositional or personality factors (such as laziness, or meanness) rather than to environmental factors (such as upbringing, poverty, or social factors) (Saulnier & Perlman, 1981). The inmates, on the other hand, said that factors they believed landed them in prison were largely external in nature, such as poverty, poor employment opportunities, and physical and sexual abuse. When it comes to ourselves, we engage in **self-serving biases**, in which we tend to attribute good things about ourselves to dispositional factors, and bad things to events and forces outside ourselves. For example, when we do well on an exam, we tend to attribute the cause to our intelligence and study habits. On the other hand, when we do poorly, we tend to attribute the cause to a poorly designed or unfair exam. The professor asked "trick questions" or did not post suitable notes on the student study site.

Haney believes that personality or internal states account very little for how we act. He contends that the important determining influence is the situation in which we find ourselves. In essence, Haney is arguing that, given the appropriate circumstances, anyone might engage in culpable criminal behavior—that we all have our price.

Situations are rarely static. Our behavior influences them to some extent, and they in turn influence our behavior. This reciprocal interaction between person and environment is one reason students of crime are beginning to pay more attention to victimology—victims often influence the course of criminal actions, particularly violent ones. **Victimology** is the scientific study of the causes, circumstances, individual characteristics, and social context of becoming a victim of a crime. Although victimologists are very careful not to blame victims for the crimes perpetrated against them, they do note that certain actions can facilitate, precipitate, and sometimes even provoke others to commit crime (Karmen, 2009). Examples are leaving one's car door unlocked, thus facilitating theft, and throwing the first punch in a brawl, thus provoking a stabbing incident.

At this point we will turn our attention to two situational factors that are often overlooked but seem to play a particularly important role in antisocial behavior: obedience to authority, and deindividuation.

Authority as an Instigator of Criminal Behavior

Sometimes, people behave illegally because someone with power told them they must, even though the actions do not "set right" with their own principles. Kelman and Hamilton (1989) refer to this phenomenon as **crimes of obedience**. "A crime of obedience is an act performed in response to orders from authority that is considered illegal or immoral by the larger community" (Kelman & Hamilton, 1989, p. 46). The classic example of the influence of authority is the military order to kill indiscriminately or to commit some other atrocity, such as Lieutenant William Calley's carrying out the massacre of villagers at My Lai in the Vietnam War. An example of crimes of obedience in a political/bureaucratic context is the Watergate scandal, when, on June 17, 1972, a group of men under the auspices of the Nixon administration burglarized the Democratic National Headquarters in the Watergate apartment complex. The concept also came to mind in the midst of scrutinizing the interrogation tactics and the treatment of detainees in the wake of September 11. Crimes of obedience also appear to be widespread in the corporate world, an issue we deal with in more detail in Chapter 11.

In an attempt to delineate some of the variables involved in obedience to authority, Stanley Milgram (1977) designed a series of experiments, using as subjects persons who volunteered (for money) in response to a newspaper ad. The experiments, which eventually received intensive public scrutiny and are now cited in nearly every introductory psychology textbook, studied the amount of electrical shock people were willing to administer to others when ordered to do so by an apparent authority figure.

The subjects were adult males, ages 20–50, who represented a cross section of the socio-economic classes. They were told that the researchers were studying the effects of punishment on memory. The experiment required a "teacher" and a "victim." Unknown to the volunteers, the victim was part of the experiment, a confederate who had been trained to act in a certain manner as part of the experimental design. In a rigged coin toss, the naive subject (the volunteer) always became the teacher and the confederate the victim. The victim-learner was taken to an adjacent room and strapped into a wired in the presence of the "naive" teacher.

Next, the teacher was led back to a room where he saw a simulated shock generator—a frightening apparatus with 30 toggle switches presumably capable of delivering 30 levels of electric shock to the learner in the adjacent room. Each level was marked in volts ranging from 15 to 450 and accompanied by a switch. In addition, labels indicated "slight shock," "danger: severe shock," and beyond, to an "XXX" level. Each time the learner gave an incorrect answer to a learning task, the teacher was instructed to administer a stronger level of shock. The victim, who did not of course receive any shock at all, purposefully gave incorrect answers; he had also been trained to scream in agony, plead with the subject to stop, and pound on the wall when the higher levels of shock were administered.

Milgram wanted to discover how far people would go under the orders of an apparent authority figure (the experimenter). He may have found more than he bargained for. Almost two-thirds of the subjects obeyed the experimenter and administered the maximum shock levels. Interestingly, when Milgram originally asked mental health experts to predict the outcome of this experiment, the majority of them thought that only a pathological few would obey the experimenter's commands to incrementally increase the shock to dangerous levels (Tsang, 2002). The experts apparently discounted the enormous pressures that the experiment placed on subjects and committed the fundamental attribution error, assuming that "the obedient person who obeys evil commands is sadistic and ill" (Tsang, 2002, p. 27).

Many of Milgram's subjects, while obeying the experimenter's instructions, demonstrated considerable tension and discomfort. Some stuttered, bit their lips, twisted their hands, laughed nervously, sweated profusely, or dug their fingernails into their flesh, especially after the victim began pounding the wall in protest (Milgram, 1963). After the experiment, some reported that they wanted to stop punishing the victim but continued to do so because the experimenter would not let them stop. Milgram (1977, p. 118) concluded, "The individual, upon entering the laboratory, becomes integrated into a situation that carries its own momentum."

In subsequent studies, Milgram modified the procedure to include women and to determine more precisely what conditions inhibited or promoted this extreme obedience. For example, he varied the psychological and physical distance between the subject and the victim. To increase the psychological distance between the two, Milgram eliminated the cries of the victim that had been programmed into the original experiment. In another experiment, to minimize the physical and psychological distance between them, the subject sat next to the victim.

In general, Milgram found that the subjects obeyed the experimenter less as physical, visual, and auditory contact with the victim increased. However, the nearer the *experimenter* got to the "teacher," the more likely the teacher was to obey. Milgram found no evidence of significant personality or gender differences in the studies as far as shocking behavior was concerned, but he did find that female teachers were more distressed about their task than their male counterparts.

The psychological and physical distance variable suggests some interesting implications. If we were to analogize between Milgram's studies and violent actions, we would expect that the more impersonal the weapon or situation (psychological and physical distance), the greater the likelihood for destruction and serious violence. Certainly, killing someone with a firearm at a distance versus killing someone point-blank are two different tasks. And both methods differ from choking someone to death with one's bare hands. It would appear that the firearm offers a more impersonal and possibly easier way to eliminate someone, and thus is more likely to lead to violent behavior actually being carried out. Admittedly, this suggestion makes some quantum jumps from a psychological experiment in an artificial setting, but it is a point worth considering when we discuss the relationship between weapons and violence in Chapter 9.

In assessing the profound influence of commands from an authority figure, we should also pay close attention to the reactions of the subjects in Milgram's study. As noted above, individual differences were detected in the way the subjects reacted to the situation, but not in their actual willingness to shock. Although some subjects refused to continue with the experiment when they believed that they were hurting the victim, most (about 65%) administered the full range of shock levels. Most also displayed anxiety and conflict.

Milgram noted a curious dissociation between word and action. Many subjects said they could not go on, but nevertheless they did. Some justified their action by concluding that the experimenter would not permit any harm to come to the victim. "He must know what he is doing." Other subjects expressed different interpretations and expectancies, such as the belief that the scientific knowledge gained in the experiment justified the method. It is interesting to note that people who have not undergone the ordeal are quite convinced that they would be members of the defiant group who refused to deliver the extreme levels of shock. Later studies conducted both in the United States and abroad confirmed Milgram's findings, however (Burger, 2009; Penrod, 1983).

Milgram hypothesized that the subject's obedient behavior could be explained by a shift in the perceived role played by the subject. He referred to this shift in role as an "agentic state," where "a person sees himself as an agent for carrying out another's wishes" (Milgram, 1974, p. 133). In other words, the subject believes he is no longer acting on his own accord but for another authorized agent. Tsang (2002, p. 28) notes that Bandura (1999) also theorizes "that many individuals in an obedient situation have a shift in attention from their responsibility as moral agents to their duty as obedient subordinates." Similar points of view have been expressed by Kelman and Hamilton (1989) and Blumenthal (1999).

Milgram suggested that our culture may not provide adequate models for disobedience to authority. Likewise, Kelman and Hamilton (1989) argued that it was important for schools to provide *all* children with opportunities to develop leadership skills and encourage them to be critical thinkers and to question authority in an effective manner. Milgram admonished (1977, p. 120) that his studies raise the possibility that human nature or, more specifically, the kind of character produced in American democratic society, cannot be counted on to insulate its citizens from brutality and inhumane treatment at the direction of malevolent authority. A substantial proportion of people do what they are told to do, irrespective of the context of the act and without limitations of conscience, so long as they perceive that the command comes from a legitimate authority.

Recently, Jerry Burger (2009) replicated Milgram's study in an effort to discover if people today would still obey commands from authority figures if they were uncomfortable about doing what was asked. He discovered that obedience rates were only slightly lower than those Milgram had found 45 years earlier. In addition, contrary to expectations, participants who witnessed another person refusing to obey the experimenter's instructions obeyed just as often as those who did not witness another person refusing to obey. Moreover, men and women did not differ in their rates of obedience. The findings suggest that the same situational factors appear to be operating today. Burger also found that individuals who were high in empathy expressed a reluctance to continue to obey earlier than those who were low in empathy. However, even though they expressed reluctance, these participants continued to follow procedure nonetheless.

Milgram's original experiment was controversial for a number of reasons, but most particularly for deceiving its participants and not adequately deprogramming them after the experiment had ended. Over the years, some participants have stated that they suffered emotionally as a result of their willingness to harm others, even though they were told the shocking had been a ruse. In his replication, Burger (2009) took a few additional precautions. He excluded people with a history of psychological or emotional problems from the study. He also stopped the experiment at 150 volts for all participants. In addition, participants who had at least three college-level psychology classes were excluded because there was high probability they would know the results of the original experiment.

Milgram's theory—supported by Burger's research—may account to some extent for immoral or despicable acts committed under the influence of authority. At the beginning of his presidency, President Barack Obama announced the closing of the military detention center at Guantanamo Bay in Cuba, although this has yet to occur. The executive order was issued after extensive publicity about interrogation tactics and humiliating treatment used at Guantanamo and other locations, and it accompanied the president's condemnation of torture. Some of the soldiers who were guards came forward to reveal actions they took under orders from supervisors. Many military psychologists work in these settings, although they are typically not directly involved in interrogation. Nevertheless, with the realization that some psychologists were complicit with or did not disapprove of these approaches, the Board of Directors of the American Psychological Association issued a policy statement condemning the participation of psychologists in questionable interrogation tactics (APA, 2009). The policy "prohibits psychologists from working in national security detention settings that operate in violation of international law or the U.S. Constitution, with a few noted exceptions" (p. 10). The policy also prohibits psychologists from participating in torture or any cruel or inhuman interrogation procedures. Most recently, on its website, the APA reiterated its position, adding that there are no exceptions. Although generalizations from the psychological laboratory to the real-world scenarios of destructive or violent obedience must remain tentative for the time being, the relevance of the Milgram-type studies to actual situations cannot be overlooked.

Milgram appeared convinced that situational factors normally override individual factors, and he would probably find personality or the morality of the individual fundamentally irrelevant in the explanation of the behavior. Other theorists, however, argue that it is precisely personality or moral development that account for resistance to authority. Kelman and Hamilton (1989) suggested that one's behavior in high authority situations most likely is a result of an interaction between one's personality characteristics and the roles played. Philip Zimbardo (1970, 1973; Haney & Zimbardo, 1998), on the other hand, is more closely aligned with Milgram, believing that the situation—including the overwhelming power of roles—is the most likely determinant of the behavior. Zimbardo demonstrated this in the famous Stanford Prison Experiment, and more broadly in his concept of deindividuation, which we discuss below. In addition, in recent years, Zimbardo, along with other researchers, has focused on moral disengagement, which we also discuss in this chapter.

Deindividuation

Deindividuation theory is based on the classic crowd theory of Gustave Le Bon. The theory, formulated in Le Bon's book *The Crowd: A Study of the Popular Mind* (1885/1995) was introduced into mainstream social psychology by Festinger, Pepitone, and Newcomb in 1952 (Postmes & Spears, 1998). Deindividuation, according to Festinger *et al.* (1952), refers to the observation that in crowds or groups, many people lose their sense of individuality, remove self-imposed controls, and neutralize their internalized moral restraints. Thus, "deindividuation was closely associated with the feeling of not being scrutinized or accountable when submerged in the group" (Postmes & Spears, 1998, p. 240). Philip Zimbardo (1970) extended and further developed deindividuation theory in a number of well-known research projects. For Zimbardo, deindividuation involved feelings of reduced self-observation, and he sought to identify the things that could induce that state (Postmes & Spears, 1998).

Deindividuation, Zimbardo hypothesized, usually follows a complex chain of events. First, the presence of many other persons encourages feelings of anonymity. Then the individual feels he or she loses identity and becomes part of the group. Under these conditions, he or she can no longer be singled out and held responsible for his or her behavior. Apparently, this feeling then generates a "loss of self-awareness, reduced concern over evaluations from others, and a narrowed focus of attention" (Baron & Byrne, 1977, pp. 581–582). When combined, these processes lower restraints against antisocial criminal behavior and appear to be basic ingredients in mass violence. However, they also may be at work in nonviolent offenses, such as looting.

In one early experiment, Zimbardo (1970) purchased two used cars, left one abandoned on a street in Manhattan, New York, and the other on a street in Palo Alto, California (about 55,000 population in the late 1960s). Zimbardo's deindividuation hypothesis predicted that, due to the large population of New York, people would more likely lose their identity and feel less responsible for their actions. Consequently, New Yorkers would be more likely to loot the abandoned vehicle. This is exactly what happened. Within 26 hours, the New York car was stripped of battery, radiator, air cleaner, radio antenna, windshield wipers, side chrome, all four hubcaps, a set of jumper cables, a can of car wax, a gas can, and the only tire worth taking. Interestingly, the looting was not done by delinquents or members of a criminal subculture; all the looters were well-dressed, middle-class individuals. On several occasions, the looting was done by entire families: children and parents together in a family enterprise.

On the other hand, the car in Palo Alto was untouched during the seven days it was left abandoned. At one point during a rainstorm, a passerby actually lowered the hood to prevent the motor from getting wet. Why such a dramatic difference?

Zimbardo suggests that the anonymity of the New York residents worked in combination with situational cues, implying that they could get by without repercussions. Zimbardo's hypothesis contends that in high population areas, who cares what you are doing as long as you are not bothering others or damaging a concerned party's property? Passersby in New York even stopped and chatted with the looters. In Palo Alto, people could be more easily identified. Moreover, a person engaging in this kind of behavior would expect to be the target of social disapproval or gossip.

Deindividuation is a commonly used concept to explain various expressions of collective behavior such as violent crowds, mindless hooligans, and the lynch mob, as well as social atrocities such as genocide (Postmes & Spears, 1998). As we saw from the car experiment, deindividuation is not necessarily associated with crowds. Nor is a massive population required. The effect may be achieved by a disguise, a mask, or a uniform also worn by others, or it may be achieved by darkness (Zimbardo, 1970). Research data suggest that people may be more abusive, aggressive, and violent when their identity is hidden. This phenomenon *might* explain why, throughout history, war paints, masks, and costumes have been donned by warriors preparing for battle (Watson, 1973). Even contemporary soldiers, guerrillas, and military advisors are deindividuated by their uniforms. Deindividuation also helps explain the apparent ease with which members of groups such as the Ku Klux Klan regressed from being apparently respectable citizens by day to violent, hooded terrorizers by night. Again, however, it is too simplistic to assume that no dispositional or other factors are at work.

In one widely cited experiment, Zimbardo manipulated two variables: feelings of anonymity and features about the victim. He randomly assigned female college students to deindividuation and "identifiable" groups. Subjects in the deindividuation group wore shapeless white lab coats and hoods over their heads and worked in dimly lit conditions. The experimenters avoided using their names. By contrast, participants in the identifiable groups felt anything but anonymous. They wore large name tags, were greeted by name, worked under fully illuminated conditions, and wore their own clothes with no added lab coats or hoods.

Subjects were told the project was set up to study empathy. The real purpose, of course, was to study the relationship between deindividuation and aggression. Each subject listened to a five-minute recorded interview between her future "victim" and the experimenter. Some victims were portrayed as warm, sincere, honest persons, while others were obnoxious, self-centered, conceited, and critical. After each interview, the subjects were allowed to administer shock to the interviewees they had heard on tape. They were allowed to observe the reactions of their victims by way of a one-way mirror. Aggressive behavior of the subjects was measured by the length of time a painful electrical shock was administered. "Victims"—who actually received no shock—were trained to writhe, twist, and grimace.

Recall now that Zimbardo was manipulating two variables: anonymity (loss of personal identity) and features of the victim (environmental stimuli). Thus, some subjects were hooded, others were well identified. Some victims were pleasant and likable, others were obnoxious. Zimbardo reasoned that members of the deindividuation group would administer shocks of longer duration because of the diffusion of responsibility and loss of personal identity. He also hypothesized that victim features would be irrelevant, because the heightened arousal experienced under deindividuation would interfere with the ability to discriminate between the victims. Put another way, the excitement and resulting arousal engendered by shocking someone without the threat of any repercussions would prevent discernment of the target (the person receiving the shock).

One additional hypothesis was tested. Zimbardo predicted that subjects in the deindividuation group would administer longer shocks as the experiment progressed. He believed the act of administering shock without responsibility would be exciting and reinforcing for its own sake (what he called "affective proprioceptive feedback"). Zimbardo predicted that members of the deindividuation group would increase the duration of shock administered to the victim as the experiment progressed. In brief, the person finds that doing the antisocial behavior feels "so good" each time she does it that the behavior builds on itself in intensity (vigor) and frequency.

Results of the experiment supported all three hypotheses. The deindividuation group shocked victims twice as long as the identifiable group. The deindividuation group also administered the same levels of shock, regardless of the victim's personality features. And, finally, this group shocked for longer periods as the experiment progressed. Zimbardo argued that deindividuated aggression is not controlled by the social environment; it is unresponsive to both the situation and the state or characteristics of the victim.

Zimbardo's research design, like that of Milgram, has been criticized extensively for its questionable use of subject deception and shock (albeit simulated) and its focus on the negative aspects of human behavior. In a sense, these types of experiments constitute a form of psychological entrapment. Would people really act this way if not prompted by an experimenter? In the wake of such experiments, the National Institute of Mental Health, the American Psychological Association, and other organizations have adopted ethical guidelines that are applied to the funding and approval of research. Experiments like Zimbardo's, therefore, are unlikely to be replicated, although we learned above that Milgram's experiment was replicated with modifications that rendered it more ethically acceptable. Moreover, the possible implications of the results of these research studies cannot be ignored.

The Stanford Prison Experiment

The disguise aspect of deindividuation was vividly illustrated in still another sobering Zimbardo experiment (1973) known as the Stanford Prison Experiment. Zimbardo and his colleagues simulated a prison environment in the basement of the psychology building at Stanford University, with physical and psychological trappings supposedly representative of an actual prison: bars, prison uniforms, identification numbers, uniformed guards, and other features that encouraged identity slippage. (The facility actually represented a jail more than a prison. Furthermore, as critics of the experiment have noted, the simulation lacked authenticity in a number of ways, including the sack-like uniforms and stocking caps worn by the "prisoners" and the mirrored sunglasses worn by "guards" [Johnson, 1996]. Corrections officers in real prisons and jails also undergo training and, though they hold power over inmates, they are not given the unlimited power that Zimbardo placed in the hands of his experimental subjects.)

Student volunteers were screened through clinical interviews and psychological tests to ensure that they were emotionally stable and mature. According to Zimbardo, the subjects finally selected were "normal," intelligent college students from middle-class homes throughout the United States and Canada. They were paid $15 a day for participating.

The experiment required two roles, guard and prisoner, which were assigned by random coin toss. The randomization assured that there were no significant differences between the two groups. The "prisoners" were unexpectedly "arrested" and brought to the simulated prison in a police car. There they were handcuffed, searched, fingerprinted, booked, stripped, "deloused," given a number, and issued a prison uniform. Each prisoner was then placed in a six-by-nine-foot cell with two other inmates.

The guards wore standard uniforms and mirrored sunglasses to encourage deindividuation, but as noted, they were not representative of the attire worn by real correctional officers. In addition, they carried symbols of power: a night stick (which many real officers do not carry), keys to the cells, whistles, and handcuffs. Before the prisoners could do even routine things (e.g., write a letter, smoke a cigarette), they had to obtain permission. Guards drew up their own formal rules for maintaining law and order in the prison (16 rules in all) and were free to improvise new ones.

Within six days, both guards and prisoners had completely absorbed their roles:

Three prisoners had to be released during the first four days because of hysterical crying, confusion in thinking, and severe depression. Many others begged to be paroled, willing to forfeit the money they had earned for participating in the experiment.

About a third of the guards abused their power and were brutal and demeaning. Other subjects did their jobs as tough but fair correctional guards, but none of these supported the prisoners by urging the brutal guards to ease off. The realism of the prison was apparently striking. "The consultant for our prison...an ex-convict with sixteen years of imprisonment in California's jails, would get so depressed and furious each time he visited our prison, because of its psychological similarity to his experiences, that he would have to leave". (Zimbardo, 1973, p. 164)

The situation became such that Zimbardo decided to terminate the experiment during the sixth day, instead of proceeding through the planned two weeks.

The experiment prompted him to conclude, "Many people, perhaps the majority, can be made to do almost anything when put into psychologically compelling situations—regardless of their morals, ethics, values, attitudes, beliefs, or personal convictions" (1973, p. 164). Much the same conclusion had been reached by Milgram with respect to the influence of authority figures. Although the Stanford Prison Experiment underscores the crucial importance of situational variables in determining behavior, there were still significant individual differences in the way the subjects responded to the conditions. Recall that only one-third of the guards became brutally enthralled with their power. Rather than making far-reaching conclusions on the basis of how a total of 21 subjects (both guards and prisoners) responded, it would be much more fruitful to give some attention to individual variables. For example, it would have been helpful to examine the values, expectancies, competencies, and moral development of the participants, in combination with the situational factors. What developmental factors most likely predisposed individuals to act the way they did, and exactly how did they perceive the situation? What did they expect to gain by their behavior?

Moral Disengagement

Bandura (1990, 1991) has proposed the concept of **moral disengagement** to explain why people do immoral or heinous acts that are against their own moral judgment when ordered to do so by some higher authority or under high social pressure. At times the acts are not universally recognized as immoral, but are more in keeping with their occupational roles, such as part of the military or law enforcement communities. According to Bandura, individuals, through social learning, internalize moral principles that bring self-worth when they are maintained and self-condemnation when they are violated, and they act accordingly, exercising what he refers to as "moral agency." Consequently, it is not simply the power of the situation that determines a person's actions. Additionally, people's moral principles and the ease with which they can become detached from them strongly influence the extent to which they will follow immoral or illegal orders. Bandura further supposes that before one can engage in behaviors that violate one's moral principles, he or she has to *disengage* his or her own moral sanctions to avoid self-condemnation. Specifically, "effective moral disengagement...frees one from the restraints of self-censure experience as anticipative guilt from detrimental conduct" (Bandura, Caprara, Barbaranelli, Pastorelli, & Regalia, 2001, p. 125). For example, Bandura, Barbaranelli, Caprara, and Pastorelli (1996) found that delinquents used various methods of moral disengagement, relying most heavily on moral justification and dehumanization of victims. The delinquents could justify certain antisocial behavior by relying on habitual and various forms of moral disengagement from the social standards of conduct. Dehumanization refers to the process of maintaining beliefs that strip people of human qualities or invests them with demonic or bestial qualities (Bandura *et al.*, 2001). "The victims are then seen as subhuman, without the same feelings or hopes as the perpetrators, and thus one can rationalize that normal moral principles do not apply" (Tsang, 2002, p. 41). Dehumanization is covered in more detail in Chapter 11.

Bandura and associates (Bandura *et al.*, 2001) discovered that male adolescents, compared with female adolescents, were "more prone to disengage moral self-sanctions from detrimental conduct, were quicker to rouse themselves to anger through hostile rumination, and were less prosocially oriented" (p. 131). These results, the researchers conclude, lend support to the influence of social learning as a major determinant of the frequently reported gender differences in detrimental or immoral conduct. "Girls are substantially more consoling, sharing, helpful, and affectionately demonstrative" (Bandura *et al.*, 2001, p. 131). Boys, on the other hand, tend to be far less likely to engage peers in discussions of their negative feelings and hostility toward others. Bandura's studies underscore the importance of considering the situation *and* the personal attributes of the person in understanding why people do what they do.

Moral disengagement has remained a provocative topic for contemporary researchers, many of whom focus, like Bandura, on adolescents (e.g., Gini, 2006; Paciello, Fida, Tramontano, Lupinetti, & Caprara, 2008; Shulman, Cauffman, Piquero, & Fagan, 2011). There are interesting exceptions. For example, Osofsky, Bandura, and Zimbardo (2005) studied moral disengagement among prison personnel in facilities where the death penalty was carried out. They included executioners, support teams for the condemned inmates and their families, and corrections officers who were not directly involved in the execution process. They found that the executioners displayed the highest levels of disengagement, as well as dehumanization of the condemned prisoners and justification for their work. Members of the support teams were the least likely to display moral disengagement.

Studies of disengagement among adolescents indicate that it often declines with age, and this finding is associated with an accompanying decline in antisocial behavior (Paciello *et al.*, 2008). Thus, in their longitudinal study of 1,169 adolescent felony offenders, Shulman *et al.* found that as the youths grew older, their attitudes toward wrongdoing also changed in a positive direction—that is they were less likely to condone it—and their offending behavior desisted. The reasons for this, the authors note, remain to be explored, although some preliminary research is available. "Understanding what contributes to this change in delinquent youths' attitudes toward wrongdoing is a worthwhile aim for future studies" (Shulman *et al.*, 2011, p. 1630).

Deindividuation and Crowd Violence

The powerful effects of crowds on individual behavior has interested social scientists since the early 1900s. Crowd influence is usually studied under the rubric *collective behavior*, which includes riots, gang rapes, panics, lynchings, demonstrations, and revolutions. For our purposes, we are concerned with collective behavior only as it affects the instigation and maintenance of violence. Recall that earlier in the chapter we discussed the role of frustration as a possible instigator of riots or other antisocial behavior displayed in group situations. Here, we focus on a different component, the likelihood that in a crowd individuals may lose their individual identity and adopt the behavior of those around them.

One of the first theorists of collective behavior was Gustave Le Bon. As noted earlier, his 1896 book *The Crowd* is regarded as the classic study of groups. Because his views were colored by the French Revolution, Le Bon did not take kindly to individual behavior swayed by the crowd. Humans in a crowd are like a herd of animals, he said, easily swayed or frightened. Le Bon believed that those who normally are nonviolent and law abiding are still capable of excessive violence, intolerance, and general cruelty. The person enmeshed in the mob loses sensibility and the ability to reason, and forfeits his or her own mind to the crowd. The collective mind is dangerously brutal and destructive to people and property. According to Le Bon, even educated people become simpleminded and irrational under its influence. Essentially, Le Bon claimed, each person comes under the control of the reflexive "spinal cord" rather than the cerebral cortex.

Most of us have seen dramatizations of a "berserk" mob clamoring for the destruction of some political, social, or physical institution or for swift "justice" for an individual or group. Descriptions of mob actions often liken them to brush fires that grow in intensity and are quickly out of control. There are numerous anecdotal accounts of vandalism and assaults that occur in some communities, often alcohol related and associated with festivals or celebrations. In some cases, fans have displayed antisocial behavior after sports events (both when their teams won and when their teams lost). However, since true mob actions are naturally occurring and spontaneous events, it is difficult to place them under the scrutiny of scientific, systematic investigation. The processes involved in mob action are still not well understood. Some social psychologists (e.g., Diener, 1980; Zimbardo, 1970) have attempted laboratory studies of mob or group violence, generally by approximating conditions that might bring out aggression and positing that, if allowed to continue, the aggression would likely result in violence. Obviously, they must stop far short of actual violence, so whether it would have occurred remains speculative. Zimbardo (1970) believed that deindividuation accounts for much of the tendency of otherwise "tame" individuals to engage in antisocial, violent behavior. Recall that deindividuation includes a reduction in feelings of personal distinctiveness, identifiability, and personal responsibility. Furthermore, in a crowd, the threshold of normally restrained behavior is lowered. In other words, people feel anonymous, less responsible for their behavior, and less inhibited. According to Zimbardo, these conditions encourage the antisocial behavior associated with selfishness, greed, hostility, lust, cruelty, and destruction.

Diener's (1980) perspective is a bit different. According to Diener, because deindividuated individuals do not pay attention to their internal processes, including their self-regulatory capabilities, they depend more on environmental cues for behavioral direction. Thus, when aggressive and violent cues are present, they are far more likely than usual to engage in violence. It is Diener's contention that if the victim of a mob action could, in some way, be "humanized," the crowd might stop its brutality. In other words, the perpetrators' attention should be directed toward the suffering or fear expressed by the victim rather than the violence being displayed by other actors. Diener also believes that participants in a mob action can be made to pay closer attention to their own internal regulation norms. His hypothesis deserves to be tested by further research. Of course, whether the cries and pleas of the victim during an attack actually could alter the crowd behavior is a question unlikely to be answered by laboratory research. Furthermore, because the theories of Zimbardo and Diener are based on laboratory studies, we cannot conclude that they generalize to actual situations. They do, however, suggest possible explanations for violent mob behavior.

Summary and Conclusions

This chapter has led us away from the biologically oriented approaches of Chapter 3 to the perspective that all behavior, including antisocial behavior, is learned as a result of interactions with the environment—after, not before birth. According to the theories discussed in this chapter, people are not born with a predisposition to violence, rather they become that way as a result of social experiences. Furthermore, criminal behavior, again like all behavior, is an individual's way of adapting to his or her environment.

We have reviewed Skinnerian behaviorism, a theory based on the psychology of J. B. Watson and Ivan Pavlov. Together, Skinnerian, Watsonian, and Pavlovian psychology provided the field with some of its most fundamental concepts, such as classical conditioning, operant conditioning, reinforcement, punishment, and extinction. Today, most behaviorists may applaud the basic premise that stimuli elicit responses (classical conditioning), and behavior produces consequences that influence subsequent responses (operant conditioning). However, they also believe other factors must be introduced to explain human behavior. Thus, social learning theorists have focused on cognitions, attitudes, beliefs, and other mental processes that must be taken into consideration.

We covered the expectancy theory of Rotter, the observational learning theory of Bandura, and the social learning theories of Sutherland and Akers to illustrate these mental processes. Sutherland, a sociologist with antipathy toward psychology, probably would not want to be included in this group, but his is still a learning theory. Berkowitz's frustration theory, and Zimbardo's concept of deindividuation and accompanying research were also discussed. Each

of these emphasizes to varying degrees the importance of learning in the development *and maintenance* of criminal behavior. Most of them also outline the external reinforcements involved in this maintenance, or alternately, its cessation. People who engage in persistent antisocial behavior get tangible rewards, as well as social and psychological ones. Collectively, external reinforcements that bring us material, social, or psychological gain are called positive reinforcements. Behaviors that enable us to avoid unpleasant circumstances are negatively reinforced.

Also included in the regulation of behavior is vicarious reinforcement, which consists of both observed reward and observed punishment. When we observe others (models) receiving rewards or punishments for certain behavior, we tend to alter our behavior correspondingly. Models are extremely important in the acquisition and regulation of criminal behavior. They are reference points for what we should and can do in a particular set of circumstances. Therefore, models may act as inhibitors or facilitators of behavior. People internalize the actions and philosophies of significant models, thereby making them part of their own behavioral repertoire and cognitive structure. Research in recent years has focused extensively on the models available in the media, violent video games, and Internet sites. There is growing evidence that some individuals who observe aggressive acts to a great degree themselves become more violent and aggressive.

In addition to models, situational factors can be important contributors to criminal behavior. To some theorists, frustration plays a significant role in violent criminality. When children are frustrated at not having their needs met by parents or caretakers, for example, this promotes distrust of other adults and prevents the forming of emotional attachments. Individuals who strike out at society have encountered severe frustration, according to this approach.

We also discussed the influence of authority figures and the environmental factors involved in the process of deindividuation. People sometimes engage in illegal or violent conduct because they are told or ordered to do so, as Milgram's classic shocking experiment demonstrated. It is interesting that Burger (2009) found results very similar to Milgram's. There are many anecdotal illustrations as well in the military, in law enforcement, and in places of business. Some psychologists have searched for individual differences that might predict the extent to which a person will or will not obey an order perceived to be immoral or illegal, such as differences in personality or moral development, a topic that will be covered in Chapter 11. In recent years, researchers have focused on moral disengagement, a process by which people are able to separate themselves from their normal codes of conduct in order to engage in illegal or morally ambivalent behavior. On the other hand, other researchers point to the powerful influence of roles, which is illustrated by Zimbardo's Stanford experiment. In still other instances, one's personal sense of identity appears to be lost in the excitement of the crowd. Under these deindividualized conditions, people—again, not all—may do things they normally would not do.

Key Concepts

Behaviorism	Frustration	Positive reinforcement
Classical conditioning (Pavlovian conditioning)	Fundamental attribution error	Punishment
	Imitational learning	Reductionism
Cognitive processes	Independent variable	Reinforcement
Crimes of obedience	Individual offender	Response
Deindividuation	Models	Self-serving biases
Dependent variable	Moral disengagement	Situationism
Differential association-reinforcement (DAR)	Negative reinforcement	Social learning theory
	Observational learning (modeling)	Socialized offender
Discriminative stimuli		Stimulus
Expectancy theory	Operant conditioning (instrumental learning)	Variable
Extinction		Victimology

Review Questions

1. Describe the process of operant conditioning and give an example of how criminal behavior is acquired.
2. Explain the difference between differential association theory and differential association-reinforcement theory.
3. Explain the concept of deindividuation and illustrate by describing any one experiment in social psychology.
4. What is "frustration-induced criminality"? Provide an illustration.
5. Briefly explain Bandura's theory of moral disengagement.
6. Compare and contrast the behaviorism promoted by B. F. Skinner with the modern behaviorism promoted by Bandura.
7. Describe and discuss the situational factors that can influence criminal behavior. In addition to those mentioned in this chapter, what others might be identified?
8. What is meant by crimes of obedience? Give examples.
9. Explain the concept of moral disengagement and discuss its relevance to antisocial or morally ambivalent behavior.

5

Human Aggression
and Violence

CHAPTER OBJECTIVES

- Explore the vast array of problems in defining and identifying aggressive behavior.
- Review the major theories on the development of aggression and violence.
- Emphasize the importance of cognitive processes in aggressive behavior.
- Explore the interactions of biology and cognitive processes in aggressive behavior and violence.
- Outline the important key concepts in understanding aggression and violence, such as hostile attribution bias, weapons effect, contagion effect.
- Introduce the General Aggression Model and I^3 Theory.
- Illustrate common occurrence of aggression with a discussion of road rage and aggressive driving.
- Review the effects of electronic and other media on aggression and violence.

There is ample evidence of the long history of human involvement in aggression and violence. The 5,600 years of recorded human history, for example, include 14,600 wars, a rate of more than 2.6 per year (Baron, 1983; Montagu, 1976). Today, many people fear a terrorist attack such as that which occurred in 2001 or on public transportation systems in Spain and England in 2005 and India in 2006. Acts of terrorism on a smaller scale continue today. Nevertheless, violence is more likely to occur in people's homes or in high-crime areas on the streets.

Violence and aggression go hand in hand, but—as will be demonstrated in this chapter—not all aggression is violent in the physical sense of that word. Some writers argue that aggression has been instrumental in helping people survive. Through centuries of experience, humans learned that aggressive behavior enabled them to obtain material goods, land, and treasures; to protect property and family; and to gain prestige, status, and power. Although some might wonder whether the human species could have survived had it not used aggression, others are quick to point out that both historically and in the present, aggressive behavior is at the root of numerous social and individual problems.

Aggression—a psychological concept that we will define shortly—warrants an entire chapter because it is the basic ingredient in violent crime. By studying aggression, psychologists have made substantial contributions to society's efforts to understand both violent and nonviolent crime, as well as violent behavior that may not necessarily be defined as crime (e.g., legitimate uses of force). Is human aggression instinctive, biological, learned, or some combination of these characteristics? If it results from an innate, biological mechanism, the methods designed to control, reduce, or eliminate aggressive behavior will differ significantly from methods used if aggression is learned.

Perspectives of human nature emerge very clearly from the scholarly and research literature on aggression. Some writers and researchers believe that aggressive behavior is basically biological and genetic in origin, a strong residue of our evolutionary past. This physiological, genetic contention is accompanied by compelling evidence that explanations of human aggressive behavior may be found in the animal kingdom from which it originated. On the other hand, researchers who subscribe to the learning viewpoint believe that, while some species of animals may be genetically programmed to behave aggressively, human beings learn to be aggressive from the social environment. The learning position also offers cogent evidence to support its theory. Other researchers remain on a theoretical fence, accepting and rejecting some aspects of each argument. Research does indicate, however, that the level of aggressive behavior demonstrated by an eight-year-old appears to remain largely unchanged well into adulthood for many children, regardless of gender (Kokko & Pulkkinen, 2005).

If aggression and violence represent a built-in, genetically programmed aspect of human nature, we may be forced, as Baron (1983) suggests, toward a pessimistic conclusion. At best, we can only hope to hold our natural, aggressive urges and drives temporarily in check. Furthermore, we should design the environment and society in such a way as to discourage violence, including administering immediate and aversive consequences (punishment) when it is displayed. Even better—and setting aside ethical or legal considerations for the moment—we might consider psychosurgery, electrode implants, and drug control—all effective methods for the reduction, if not the elimination, of violence.

If, on the other hand, we believe that aggression is learned and is influenced by a wide range of situational, social, and environmental variables, we can be more optimistic. Aggression is not an inevitable aspect of human life. Once we understand what factors play major roles in its acquisition and maintenance, we will be able to change human behavior by manipulating these factors. There are, of course, both positive and negative aspects of human aggression. Many individuals who play in competitive sports, hunt for sport, serve in the military, and work for law enforcement engage in socially permissible forms of aggression that may be necessary or that enhance their quality of life as well as that of others. To some extent, aggression is also valued in politics and in the corporate world. What we are concerned with in this chapter is the inappropriate expression of aggression, particularly as displayed in violent behavior. In other words, the focus in this chapter is on the negative aspects, or the forms of aggression that are not socially permissible.

By most accounts, animal aggression reflects the biological programming carried in the genes to ensure the survival of the species. Humans, with their enormously complex and sophisticated brain (cerebral cortex), rely heavily on thought, associations, beliefs, and learning; these become primary determinants of behavior. Theorists differ over the degree to which genetic programming contributes to human behavior. Thus, are people aggressive and violent because their animal instincts continue to promote this particular behavior? And, if the evolutionary aggressive drives still reside within the subcortical structures of the brain (below the cortex in the "old" brain), as some writers tell us they do, are they modifiable? If not, how can we best prevent people from attacking and killing one another? On the other hand, a difference-in-kind perspective suggests that genetic predispositions, or biological precursors of aggression, have a minimal influence on human behavior, if they have any influence at all. After defining aggression, we will return to these different points of view.

DEFINING AGGRESSION

The task of defining human aggression is surprisingly difficult, as many social psychologists have discovered. Forcibly jabbing someone in the midsection is certainly defining it by example—or is it? Now what about jabbing someone more softly, in jest? Would everyone consider football and boxing aggressive behaviors? If someone pointedly ignores a question, is that an example of aggression? What if someone spreads malicious gossip? If a burglar breaks into your home and you reach for your trusty but rusty rifle, aim it at the intruder, and pull the trigger, is yours an act of aggression? Is it any less so if the rifle does not fire? If someone sits passively on a doorstep and blocks your entry, is this aggression?

Some social psychologists define aggression as the intent and attempt to harm another individual, physically or socially, or, in some cases, to destroy an object. This definition seems adequate for many situations, but it has several limitations. Refusing to speak does not fit well, since it is not an active attempt to harm someone, nor is blocking someone's entry. Most psychologists place these two behaviors in a special category of aggressive responses and call them **passive-aggressive behaviors**, since they are generally interpreted as aggressive in intent, although the behavior is passive and indirect.

As fascinating as passive-aggressive behavior may be, it is generally irrelevant when we discuss crime, since the aggression we are concerned about is the type that manifests itself directly in violent or antisocial behavior. We might stretch the point by suggesting that the doorstep sitter is trespassing, in which case he or she might be charged with a criminal offense. Likewise, there are other situations in which passive-aggressive behavior could lead to various types of crime. Refusing to file income tax because one is intensely dissatisfied with the policies of the government is one example. In general, however, the aggressive behavior we wish to focus on in this chapter is not of the passive-aggressive kind.

In an effort to conceptualize the many varieties of human aggression, Buss (1971) tried to classify them based on the apparent motivation of the aggressor, although his classification does not refer specifically to motivations (see **Table 5-1**). You may easily find exceptions and overlapping categories in the Buss scheme, but that emphasizes how difficult it is to

TABLE 5-1	Varieties of Human Aggression			
	Active		**Passive**	
	Direct	**Indirect**	**Direct**	**Indirect**
Physical	Punching Hitting	Practical joke Booby trap	Obstructing passage	Refusing to perform a necessary task
Verbal	Insulting the victim	Malicious gossip	Refusing to speak	Refusing consent

Source: Based on information from Buss (1971).

compartmentalize human aggressive behavior. It also epitomizes the many definitional dilemmas that hamper social psychologists studying aggression.

Hostile and Instrumental Aggression

Before finally settling on a satisfactory definition of aggression (and we will get there), it may be useful to recognize two types of aggression, **hostile or expressive aggression** and **instrumental aggression**, a distinction first made by Feshbach (1964). They are distinguished by their goals, or the rewards they offer the perpetrator. Hostile aggression, which we are most concerned with in this chapter, occurs in response to anger-inducing conditions, such as real or perceived insults, physical attacks, or one's own failures. The aggressor's goal is to make a victim suffer. Most criminal homicides, rapes, and other violent crimes directed at harming the victim are precipitated by hostile aggression. The behavior is characterized by the intense and disorganizing emotion of anger, with anger defined as an arousal state elicited by certain stimuli, particularly those evoking attack or frustration. (See **Box 5-1** for discussion of a contemporary case relevant to this issue.)

BOX 5-1

Aggression in the Trayvon Martin Case

In February 2012, 17-year-old Trayvon Martin, a black youth, was walking in a gated community in Sanford, Florida, unarmed and carrying a box of Skittles and a bottled iced tea he had just purchased from a convenience store. What happened next is still being debated. What we know is that 28-year-old George Zimmerman, a white (Hispanic) Neighborhood Watch volunteer, pursued Martin after calling 911 to report what he believed to be a suspicious individual. Despite being advised by the 911 dispatcher not to follow Martin, Zimmerman did so. Martin also made a phone call to his girlfriend, indicating that someone was after him. At some point a scuffle ensued and Trayvon Martin was fatally shot in the chest at close distance.

Following extensive media publicity about the case, Zimmerman was arrested six weeks after the shooting and charged with second-degree murder. Second-degree murder indicates an intention to kill but no premeditation, whereas first-degree murder involves both premeditation and intention.

Although it is not known at this point how this case will proceed, Zimmerman first claimed that he feared for his safety and shot Martin in self-defense. Under the laws of most states, we have the right to defend ourselves if a reasonable person, in a similar situation, would perceive him or herself to be in immediate danger of grave bodily harm and unable to flee. (The obligation to flee does not apply if one is in one's own home.) In addition, the force used in self-defense should not be disproportionate to the force with which one is faced. As an example, a gun should not be used to defend oneself against a fist. This in itself is controversial, however, because fists can be lethal. Although the specific wording of self-defense rules may vary slightly from state to state, these are common elements.

In Florida, however, as in several other states, there is a "Stand-Your-Ground" Law, over and above the usual rules of self-defense. Stand your ground laws essentially broaden the concept of self-defense; they do not involve the obligation to flee. Although they vary in terminology from state to state, they do not always refer to grave danger of serious bodily harm or to the use of disproportionate force. Critics argue that these laws encourage confrontation and promote violence. Supporters say they deter violent crime. The relative merits of these arguments are not ours to address here, but readers should recognize that concepts discussed in this chapter are relevant to these laws.

We use the Trayvon Martin case, not to attribute blame, but to illustrate many of the concepts discussed in the chapter. Regardless of how this case turns

(continued)

out—Zimmerman's trial date is set for Spring 2013—but the matter could be resolved before then—the following statements can be made with confidence:

- The two young men were involved in a physical fight. Bruises were found on both of them and one, of course, died. Therefore, the case illustrates *violence*.
- In accordance with Buss's typology, *direct, active aggression* of a *physical* sort occurred. It is likely that there was *direct, active, verbal aggression*, as well, but we do not know this without more information.
- *Hostile aggression* occurred—and each individual was both a victim and a perpetrator. Recall that hostile aggression does not equate to crime.
- It is likely that Bushman and Anderson's (2001) continuum of aggression is involved; that is, some of the aggression used may have been more *automatic* than controlled.

In addition, the following concepts from the chapter might be relevant to this case. You may agree or disagree.

- Territoriality: According to classic ethological theory, Zimmerman's pursuit of Martin could illustrate his belief that Martin did not belong in this gated community. It should be noted, though, that the ethological perspective, including the concept of territoriality, has not been sufficiently generalized to humans.
- Weapons effect: The sight of a gun in Zimmerman's hands could have prompted Martin to act aggressively, either in anger or in self-defense.
- Cognitive scripts: Both young men had ample cognitive scripts that might be associated with violence. As a Neighborhood Watch volunteer (and criminal justice major) Zimmerman was familiar with scenarios that might predispose him to play out a scene whereby he would capture someone he perceived to be "up to no good." Martin, as a young black male, knew that young black males are often wrongfully profiled and sometimes harmed physically. He could easily envision a scenario whereby his life was in danger.
- Hostile attribution bias: It is possible that each individual attributed hostile intentions to the other. Hostile attribution bias is an individual personality characteristic, however, and we have no knowledge that it could be a factor for either of them.

In addition to the above, you may well find other connections. Consider, for example, the possible relevance of covert aggression, reactive aggression, excitation–transfer theory, and displaced aggression theory, all discussed in this chapter.

Instrumental aggression begins with competition or the desire for some object or status possessed by another person—jewelry, money, territory. The perpetrator tries to obtain the desired object regardless of the cost. Instrumental aggression is usually a factor in robbery, burglary, larceny, and various white-collar crimes. The perpetrator's obvious goal in a robbery is to obtain items of value. Usually, there is no intent to harm anyone. However, if someone or something interferes with the perpetrator's objective, he or she may feel forced to harm the victim or risk losing the desired goal. In that sense, a robbery may lead to murder, but the aggression represented is still instrumental. Instrumental aggression is also usually a feature of calculated murder committed by a hired, impersonal killer. Although psychologists make the distinction between hostile and instrumental aggression, the law does not, insofar as responsibility for the crime is concerned. However, certain factors associated with hostile aggression (e.g., if the crime is committed in a particularly heinous fashion) can affect the criminal sentence. On the other hand, a contract killer's instrumental aggression may also bring a longer sentence if information about prior offenses comes to light at sentencing.

It should be mentioned, however, that some scholars (e.g., Bushman & Anderson, 2001) find fault with a strict hostile-instrumental dichotomy. Bushman and Anderson point out that this two-category division fails to take into account that many aggressive acts have multiple motives. Furthermore, they say, aggressive acts can be better understood if they are placed somewhere along a continuum that runs from controlled aggression at one pole to automatic (impulsive or thoughtless) aggression at the other pole. Bushman and Anderson believe that, although the dichotomy was useful during the early stages of theory development, it is time to move to a more cognitive approach to understanding the various types of aggressive behavior. This is discussed more fully in the section on the cognitive models of aggression later in the chapter.

Interpretation by Victim

As Bandura (1973a) noted, most definitions of aggression imply that aggression revolves around the behaviors and intentions residing within the perpetrator (or performer). Going a step further, he suggests that an adequate definition of aggression must consider both the "injurious behavior" of the perpetrator and the "social judgment" of the victim. Thus, a soft poke in the belly may qualify as aggression if it is both done derisively and the recipient interprets it that way. A textbook on criminal behavior, however, must focus on aggression as manifested in conduct, not as it is perceived by a victim; it is the actions of the perpetrator that are critical. For our purposes, therefore, we define aggression as *behavior perpetrated or attempted with the intention of harming another individual physically or psychologically (as opposed to socially) or to destroy an object*. The psychological harm would cover aggressive actions that do not involve physical force but are still criminally accountable, such as intimidation, threats, or stalking. This definition encompasses all the behaviors described in Buss's typology. Note, however, that aggressive behavior will not *always* qualify as criminal. A law enforcement officer using *reasonable* force against a criminal suspect is displaying aggressive behavior, but it is not criminal. A hunter shooting a deer (in season) falls into the same category. A person who reasonably perceives him or herself in grave danger of serious bodily harm and defends him or herself against an aggressor, *without using disproportionate force*, is not a criminal.

Furthermore, we define violence as *destructive physical aggression intentionally directed at harming other persons or things*. Violence may be methodical or random, sustained or fleeting, intensive or uncontrolled. It always harms or destroys the recipient or is intended to do so (Daniels & Gilula, 1970). Therefore, all violent behavior is aggressive behavior, but not all aggressive behavior is violent. Spreading malicious, false information about someone or stalking are cases in point. Both are aggressive, one is also criminal in most jurisdictions, but neither is violent per se, although both may lead to violence.

THEORETICAL PERSPECTIVES ON AGGRESSION

Behavioral and social scientists have debated for over a half century whether humans are born aggressive and naturally violent, or born relatively free of aggressive tendencies. Several theories have been developed that try to provide some answers to the debate. A theory is an integrated set of principles that describes, predicts, and explains some phenomena. It also guides research. The aggression debate, part of a wider controversy about the respective merits of nature and nurture, touches every school of thought in human behavior. According to the first perspective, humans are programmed aggressive to defend themselves, family, and territory from intruders. According to the second, humans become violent by acquiring aggressive models and actions from society. In this section, the topics will move from the instinctive and biological perspectives to the more learning-based perspectives.

Psychoanalytical/Psychodynamic Viewpoint

Psychodynamic theorists assume that humans, by their very nature, will always be prone to aggressive impulses and hence are likely to commit violent acts if these impulses are not appropriately managed or held in check. Sigmund Freud, the father of psychoanalysis and a physician by training, was convinced that human beings are susceptible from birth to a buildup of aggressive energy, which must be dissipated or drained off before it reaches dangerous levels. This is known as the **psychodynamic or hydraulic model** since it bears a close resemblance to pressure build-up in a container. If excessive pressure accumulates in the container—the human psyche—an explosion is likely to occur, as demonstrated by tirades that may involve violence. According to the traditional Freudian perspective, people who have tirades are blowing off the excess steam of aggressive energy.

Freud suggested that violence in all of its forms is a manifestation of this aggressive energy discharge. Internal energy accumulates to dangerous levels when people have not discharged it appropriately through a process called catharsis, one of the most important concepts in psychoanalytic psychotherapy. Catharsis may be accomplished by actual behavior (e.g., playing football) or may occur vicariously (watching football). The Freudian-psychodynamic position predicts that children who participate in or avidly watch school sports will ultimately be less aggressive than children who do not. Freudian psychodynamic followers also maintain that people who engage in violent crime (particularly hostile aggression) have not had sufficient opportunity to "blow off steam" and keep their aggressive energies at manageable levels.

According to the psychoanalytical viewpoint, if violent crime is to be controlled, the human animal must be provided with multiple but appropriate channels for catharsis (e.g., adequate recreational facilities). In this way, children and adults presumably learn to dissipate aggression in socially approved, appropriate ways. Psychotherapy is one such channel, encouraging catharsis under the guidance of a therapist.

Ethological Viewpoints

Ethology is the study of animal behavior in relation to the animal's natural habitat, and it compares that behavior to human behavior. In the mid-1960s, a number of ethologists published books and articles about aggression that interested and appealed to the general public. Three especially popular books were Konrad Lorenz's *On Aggression* (1966), Robert Ardrey's *The Territorial Imperative* (1966), and Desmond Morris's *The Naked Ape* (1967). Before his death, Lorenz was the chief spokesperson for a theoretical formulation of ethology as it relates to aggression.

A Nobel laureate in biology, Lorenz believed that aggression is an inherited instinct of both humans and animals. One of its main purposes is to enable the animal—and the human being—to defend "staked out" territory, a territory that ensures sufficient food, water, and space to roam and reproduce. If this space is violated, Lorenz argued, the instinctive or genetically programmed response is to attack, or at least to increase aggressive behavior toward the intruder, thus preventing further territory violation. The tendency to attack space violators is referred to as **territoriality**. Lorenz believed it is an innate propensity developed through the lengthy, complex process of evolution. This innate aggressive behavior among members of the same animal species (intraspecific aggression) prevents overcrowding and ensures the best and most powerful mates for the young.

The more deadly the animals' evolutionarily developed weaponry (e.g., fangs, claws, size, and strength), the more intense the innate inhibitions against engaging in physical combat with members of its own species. This innately programmed inhibition is a form of insurance for species survival, Lorenz believed, since constant intraspecific physical combat would eventually extinguish the species. Intraspecies aggression is accomplished, therefore, not by actual combat but by complicated displays of force and superiority, such as a show of teeth, size, or color array. These displays are referred to as **ritualized aggression** and they are seen throughout the animal kingdom. Through an intricate communication system, the animals transmit signals, after which the more powerful, dominant animal generally wins out. The losing animal demonstrates defeat by various appeasement behaviors, such as rolling over on its back (characteristic of puppies), lowering its tail or head, and emitting cries of defeat. The weaker animal then leaves the territory of the dominant one.

What does all of this have to do with human aggression? Lorenz and other ethologists believe that it is important to understand animal aggression before we try to understand human aggression, since humans are part of the animal world and probably follow many of its basic principles. In other words, ethologists subscribe to the **difference-in-degree** Darwinian perspective, discussed briefly in Chapter 1. Efran and Cheyne (1974), for example, observed after studying invasion of personal space among humans that "human society may operate through mechanisms which are less uniquely human than is currently fashionable to suggest" (p. 225).

Lorenz raises another issue that, if valid, is more significant to criminal behavior, however. He maintained that human beings have outdistanced the evolutionary process of inhibiting aggression. Instead of developing natural weapons and the species-preserving function of ritualized aggression, humans have developed technological weaponry. Thus, he and many other ethologists believe they can provide at least a partial answer to why human beings wantonly maim and kill members of their own species: They have not developed the ability to engage in the species-preserving behavior of ritualized aggression. Instead, through superior learning ability, they have developed the capacity to annihilate.

The ethological position is intriguing, but it has not been supported by human aggression research (Bandura, 1983; Montagu, 1973; Zillmann, 1983). Zoologists, biologists, and psychologists have tried with little success to apply the Lorenzian tenets to humans. One problem is that the ethological position relies on a strong analogy between animals and humans. Lorenz argued, for example, that the Greylag goose is remarkably similar to the human species (Berkowitz, 1973). However, the human brain makes us remarkably unlike the Greylag goose and considerably less likely to rely on instinct for determining behavior. Research has yet to delineate any instinctive or invariant genetically programmed behavior determinant in humans. Furthermore, "the capacity to exercise control over one's own thought processes, motivation, and action is a distinctively human characteristic" (Bandura, 1989, p. 1175).

Ethologists also fail to acknowledge and interpret the vast body of existing scientific research that has tested their position and found it wanting. This curious response—or nonresponse—undermines the validity of their whole presentation. Some critics have referred to ethological theorizing as "scientific-sounding misinformation" (Leach, 1973). To date, therefore, there is little evidence to justify portraying humans as *innately* dangerous and brutal or as controlled by instinct. Some contemporary theories do adopt a biological perspective on violence, however, as we discuss later in the chapter.

The ethological perspective has evolved into what is referred to today as **evolutionary psychology**. Evolutionary psychology is the study of the evolution of behavior using the principles of natural selection. It argues that human evolutionary history provides the fundamental framework for understanding human cognition and behavior. An important point to remember here is that evolutionary psychology does not see aggression as pathology, but something that is normal, especially for men (Spallone, 1998).

Frustration–Aggression Hypothesis

Around the time of Freud's death in 1939, a group of psychologists at Yale University proposed that aggression is a direct result of frustration (Dollard, Doob, Miller, Mowrer, & Sears, 1939). According to John Dollard and his colleagues, people who are frustrated, thwarted, annoyed, or threatened will behave aggressively, since aggression is a natural, almost automatic response to frustrating circumstances. Moreover, people who exhibit aggressive behavior are frustrated, thwarted, annoyed, or threatened. "Aggression is always a consequence of frustration" (Dollard *et al.*, 1939, p. 1).

Because of its simplicity and important implications, the **frustration–aggression hypothesis** drew much research, along with much criticism. Psychologists found it difficult not only to decide what frustration was but also to determine how it could be measured accurately. Researchers also learned that aggression was a much more complex phenomenon than Dollard and his associates had postulated. Frustration does not always lead to aggression, and aggressive behavior does not always signify "frustration." Experiments indicated that people respond to frustration and anger differently. Some do indeed respond with aggression, but others display a wide variety of responses.

Led by Leonard Berkowitz (1962, 1969, 1973), whose general views on some of the causes of criminality were presented in Chapter 4, researchers began to propose a revised, contemporary version of the frustration–aggression hypothesis. According to Berkowitz, frustration increases the probability that an individual will become angry and soon act aggressively. In short, frustration facilitates the performance of aggressive behavior. The behavior may be overt (physical or verbal) or implicit (wishing someone dead). Anger, however, is not the only emotion that potentially leads to aggression. Aversive conditions, such as pain, or pleasant states, such as sexual arousal, may also lead to aggressive behavior (Berkowitz, 1973). We will return to this subject shortly.

As we learned in Chapter 4, an important component of the revised frustration–aggression hypothesis is the concept of anticipated goals or expectations. When a behavior directed at a specific goal is thwarted, frustration is more likely to result. Thus, the person must have been expecting or anticipating the attainment of a goal or achievement. Mere deprivation of goods will not necessarily lead to frustration. People who are living under deprived conditions may not be frustrated unless they actually expect something better. Moreover, aggression Berkowitz says, is only one possible response to frustration. The individual may learn others, like withdrawal, doing nothing, or trying to alter the situation by getting out of the situation completely or by compromising. With this approach, Berkowitz not only emphasizes the importance of learning but also stresses the role of individual differences in response to frustrating circumstances.

The revised frustration–aggression hypothesis, therefore, suggests the following steps: (1) the person is blocked from obtaining an expected goal, (2) frustration results, generating anger, and (3) anger *predisposes* or readies the person to behave aggressively. Whether the person actually engages in aggressive actions will depend in part on his or her learning history, interpretation of the event, and individual way of responding to frustration. It will also depend, however, on the presence of aggression-eliciting stimuli in the environment.

WEAPONS EFFECT   Berkowitz notes that the presence of aggressive stimuli in the external environment (or internal environment represented by thoughts) increases the probability of aggressive responses. A weapon is a good example of such a stimulus. Most people in our society associate firearms with aggression, even if violence does not occur. Consider the public outrage that erupted in the summer of 2009 when a man carried a handgun to a speech by President

Obama. The individual did not threaten the president, but the fact that he had a gun on his person was disconcerting. Berkowitz (1983) likens the firearm to a conditioned stimulus in that the weapon conjures aggressive associations, facilitating overt aggression. A gun, even when not used, is more likely to generate aggressive action than is a neutral object. "The mere sight of the weapon might elicit ideas, images, and expressive reactions that had been linked with aggression in the past" (Berkowitz, 1983, p. 124).

In one experiment designed to test this hypothesis (Berkowitz & LePage, 1967), angry male subjects were more likely to engage in aggressive action in the presence of a gun than a comparable group of angry subjects in the presence of a badminton racket. This suggests that a visible weapon (such as a law enforcement officer might carry) may actually facilitate, rather than inhibit, a violent response in some people. This is not to say that sworn law enforcement officers should not carry weapons. However, the carrying of weapons by others—such as private citizens, neighborhood watch volunteers, campus police in some colleges and universities, and private security officers—is often a controversial issue. Although the U.S. Supreme Court has ruled that the Second Amendment right to bear arms is a private right (District of Columbia v. Heller, 2008), restrictions on that right are possible.

The Berkowitz-LePage finding generated much controversy as to whether weapons actually do provoke aggressive behavior. A number of studies tried to replicate the finding, but failed to find evidence of a **weapons effect** (Penrod, 1983). Some researchers believed that many of the participants used in some of the studies "saw through" the purpose of the study and performed the way they thought the experimenter wanted them to, a research flaw called demand characteristics. However, a comprehensive review of the research literature found strong evidence that the weapons effect does exist (Carlson, Marcus-Newhall, & Miller, 1990). Carlson *et al.* concluded, "Aggression-related cues present in experimental settings act to increase aggressive responding. This cue effect occurs more strongly when subjects have been negatively aroused before their exposure to aggression-facilitating cues" (p. 632). The weapons effect has also been found in other countries, including Belgium, Croatia, Italy, and Sweden (Berkowitz, 1994).

Berkowitz (1989) emphasized two important components to the frustration-aggression equation. Aggressive behavior will be generated (1) to the extent that a person perceives the mistreatment as intentional and (2) to the degree that the frustration experienced is aversive. According to Berkowitz, people "... are much more likely to become openly aggressive at someone's blocking their goal attainment if they believe their frustrater had deliberately and unjustifiably attempted to keep them from reaching their goal than if they think the thwarting had not been intentional or had not been directed at them personally" (Berkowitz, 1989, p. 68). Thus, self-restraint comes into play when people think they have not been deliberately mistreated or that the blocking of the goal was legitimate. On the other hand, people become angry and aggressive when they perceive that they have been treated unfairly or were personally attacked.

Berkowitz also postulates that thwartings or frustrations generate a negative affect, which refers to an emotional state people typically seek to lessen or eliminate. Furthermore, an unexpected interference is more apt to provoke an aggressive reaction than is an anticipated barrier to goal attainment, because the former is usually much more unpleasant. That is, an unexpected interference has a more negative effect.

Cognitive-Neoassociation Model

In his reformulation of the frustration–aggression hypothesis, Berkowitz has emphasized the importance of cognitive factors. Currently, it is called the **cognitive-neoassociation model**. It operates in the following manner: During the earlier stages, an aversive event produces a negative affect (discomfort). This negative affect may be due to physical pain or psychological discomfort. Physical pain as an aversive circumstance is clear, but psychological discomfort needs further elaboration. Being verbally insulted is a good example. While there is no physical pain, personal insults or demeaning comments engender anger, depression, or sadness—all negative affects—in just about everyone. Unpleasant feelings or negative affects presumably then give rise, almost automatically, to a variety of feelings, thoughts, and memories that are associated with flight (fear) and fight (anger) tendencies. During this early stage, mediating cognitive processes have little influence beyond the immediate appraisal that the situation is aversive. Some people may act quickly on the basis of these initial emotions without further deliberation or forethought, sometimes engaging in violence. Berkowitz emphasizes that any unpleasant feeling or arousal can evoke aggressive, even violent responses. A teenager frustrated with school may be prone to vandalize a school bus, or a worker who receives a negative evaluation from his supervisor may be inclined to rip a sink off the wall in the men's room.

Most of us get past the initial stages, however. During the later stages, cognitive appraisal may go into operation and substantially influence the subsequent emotional reactions and experiences after the initial, automatic responses. These cognitions mediate and evaluate a proper course of action. During the later stages, aroused people make causal attributions about the unpleasant experience, think about the nature of their feelings, and perhaps try to control their feelings and actions. Thus, what began as an angry reaction to someone's critical comments develops into a careful consideration of their merits or a conclusion that they are not worth being concerned about.

Excitation Transfer Theory

Zillmann (1988) has proposed a theory to explain how physiological arousal can generalize from one situation to another. Called **excitation transfer theory**, it is based on the assumption that physiological arousal, however produced, dissipates slowly over time. For example, a person who receives some anger-producing criticism at work is likely to have some residual arousal from that criticism when he or she arrives home later that evening. Encountering some annoying event at home, the person is apt to "fly off the handle" and overreact to the minor home incident. "You're taking it out on me," or "You're taking it out on the kids" are familiar statements in some homes. Consequently, the combination of preexisting arousal, plus anger generated by the irritation at home, may increase the likelihood of aggression. The transfer of arousal from one situation to another is most likely to occur if the person is unaware that he or she is still carrying some arousal from a previous situation to a new, unrelated one.

Displaced Aggression Theory

Closely related to the excitation transfer theory is **displaced aggression theory**, especially the recent model proposed by Bushman, Anderson, Miller, and their colleagues (Anderson & Bushman, 2002; Bushman, Bonacci, Pederson, Vasquez, & Miller, 2005; Miller, Pedersen, Earleywine, & Pollack, 2003). According to Bushman *et al.* (2005), "Aggression is *displaced* when the target is innocent of any wrongdoing but is simply in the wrong place at the wrong time" (p. 969). Displaced aggression can occur when an individual cannot aggress against a source of provocation, such as a boss at work, but feels less constrained about being aggressive toward an innocent, nonprovoking, or mildly provoking individual (or pet). However, the displaced aggression is probably more likely to be directed at a person (or pet) who emits a mildly annoying act—the cat that tips over the water dish, for example. Bushman *et al.* refer to this phenomenon as *triggered displaced* *aggression*: "Following an initial provocation, the target commits a minor provocation, the triggering event, which in turn prompts an aggressive response" (p. 970). The "displaced" aggressive response is usually far in excess of what might be expected to be directed at the minor provocation but probably is in proportion to the perceived severity of the initial provocation. One may believe the boss deserves a good kick for not appreciating one's hard work on a project; since one can't kick the boss, the cat bears the brunt of the anger.

Bushman *et al.* (2005) take the model one step further by working into the equation the concept of rumination. **Rumination** refers to self-focused attention toward one's thoughts and feelings. In other words, the person keeps thinking about the incident long after it is over. More importantly, ruminative thought can harbor and maintain angry feelings over a period of time, far removed from the initial provocation. It is, according to Bushman *et al.*, the ruminative thoughts that can promote subsequent aggression against someone who is mildly annoying but not highly deserving of an aggressive attack.

Aggressive Driving and Road Rage

Aggressive driving and road rage illustrate the previous displaced aggression-arousal theory very well. Before we proceed, however, it is important to note that although aggressive driving and road rage are sometimes used interchangeably, many experts consider them distinct phenomena (Asbridge, Smart, & Mann, 2006). **Road rage**, a term coined by the media in the late 1980s (Roberts & Indermaur, 2005), is defined as an incident in which an angry, impatient, or aroused motorist *intentionally* injures or kills, or tries to injure or kill, another motorist, passenger, or pedestrian, in response to a traffic dispute, altercation, or grievance (Joint, 1995; Mizell, 1995). The provocation may be real or imagined. It is also considered road rage when an aroused, upset motorist drives his or her vehicle into a building or other structure or property (Mizell, 1995). Examples of road rage include chasing another vehicle, driving straight at another vehicle when angered, extreme tailgating, and trying to edge another car off the road (Galovski & Blanchard, 2004).

Aggressive driving, on the other hand, is usually considered less serious. Generally, aggressive driving is the result of a motorist becoming impatient or frustrated, and it is often not the direct result of the behavior of another motorist. In other words, aggressive driving is often the result of the triggered displaced aggression discussed in the previous section. The aggressive driver was already angry at someone or something and "takes out" this anger on the road. Common examples of aggressive driving include tailgating, cutting in and out of lanes, excessive speed, illegal passing, horn blowing, flashing headlights, refusing to yield right of way, slow driving with intent of blocking other vehicles, and running red lights. In contrast, road rage is most often the result of interpreting the actions of other motorists as personal affronts which require retaliating to vindicate one's self-esteem (Neighbors, Vietor, & Knee, 2002). Aggressive driving, on the other hand, is most often caused by traffic congestion, travel impedance, and time urgency (Neighbors *et al.*, 2002). Both aggressive driving and road rage are particularly problematic in the United States, but they appear to be growing worldwide problems (Asbridge *et al.*, 2006; Fierro, Morales, & Álvarez, 2011; Junger, West, & Timman, 2001; Krahé, 2005). It is estimated that an average of over 1,500 men, women, and children are injured or killed each year in the United States as a direct result of aggressive driving or road rage, and this is increasing at a rate of about 7 percent per year (Yu, Evans, & Perfetti, 2004).

An interesting survey of drivers in 20 major U.S. cities was conducted by Prince Market Research for Auto Vantage, an automobile membership club offering travel services (Associated Press, 2006). Two thousand adult drivers who regularly commuted within each city were asked to rate the amount of road rage and "rude" driving in their metropolitan area. The survey found that

Miami drivers reported the most incidents of road rage and rude driving during 2006. Phoenix was second in the road rage and rude driving, followed by New York City, Los Angeles, and Boston. Nashville and Minneapolis reported the fewest incidents. The drivers were also asked what driving behavior most incites road rage in themselves. Thirty-nine percent said being "cut off," 30 percent said tailgating, and 23 percent reported slow driving. There were no significant gender differences in the survey.

WHO ARE THE ROAD RAGERS?   A growing number of studies reveal that the majority of road ragers are young males (ages 18–35) who have criminal and violent histories, psychiatric problems, and drug or alcohol problems (Asbridge *et al.*, 2006; Mizell, 1995; Smart, Asbridge, Mann, & Adlaf, 2003). For example, Galovski and Blanchard (2002) report that nearly half of the motorists referred by a traffic court to a program specifically designed for highly aggressive drivers (mostly road ragers) had one of more convictions for driving under the influence of alcohol. In reference to the relationship between criminal history and aggressive driving, Junger *et al.* (2001) examined the criminal histories of a random sample of 1,531 persons involved in traffic accidents in the Netherlands. The researchers discovered that those motorists involved in traffic accidents due to risky or highly aggressive driving (according to the police) were far more likely to have a police record for violent crime, vandalism, property crime, and similar traffic accidents in the past. However, aggressive drivers and road ragers come from all walks of life, across a variety of socioeconomic levels and occupations. Celebrities are not immune. "In California, Oscar winner Jack Nicholson believed that a driver of a Mercedes-Benz cut him off in traffic. The [then] 57-year-old actor grabbed a golf club, stepped out of his car at a red light, and repeatedly struck the windshield and roof of the Mercedes" (Mizell, 1995, p. 5).

In another study by Fierro, Morales, and Álvarez (2011), not only were individuals who were under the influence of alcohol more likely to be engaged in road rage incidents but so were those individuals under the influence of marijuana. This was a surprise. The researchers write: "Although it is known that alcohol has disinhibitory effects, thus contributing to aggressive behavior, cannabis is rarely associated with aggression; on the contrary, it tends to produce calm and passivity" (p. 191). However, no explanation for this finding was offered. The study is an interesting one but needs replication.

WHO ARE THE VICTIMS?   Research suggests that some drivers are repeatedly victims of road rage (Mann *et al.*, 2007). This observation suggests that road rage incidents may result from an interactive process of escalating aggression in which the victim and perpetrator both contribute to the incident. Victims, for example, may have irritating driver habits that provoke anger in other drivers, such as driving too slowly in fast lane traffic or carelessly driving in dangerous situations by cutting another driver off. In some cases, the victim was the perpetrator of angry driving in the beginning of an incident, but provoked another driver to the point where the roles became reversed. The perpetrator–victim interactions in road rage incidents underscore the dynamic, changing characteristics of aggression in general.

WEAPONS USED   The weapons most commonly used by road ragers are firearms (37%) and the vehicle itself (35%). In fact, some research suggests that having a gun in the car is linked to high levels of aggressive behavior behind the wheel (Miller, Hennenway, & Solop, 2002). Other weapons used are tire irons, jack handles, baseball bats, hurled projectiles, defensive sprays, fists, and feet. Mizell (1995, p. 8) writes, "While the event that sparks the incident may be trivial, in every case there exists some reservoir of anger, hostility, or frustration that is released by the triggering incident." In one case, a man was attacked by fellow motorists because he could not turn off the antitheft alarm on his rented jeep. Surprisingly, it is not unusual for angry drivers to use their motor vehicles to attack law enforcement personnel and vehicles.

PRECIPITATING FACTORS IN ROAD RAGE   Domestic violence or domestic disputes are very common factors in both aggressive driving and road rage, when upset spouses and intimate partners vent their anger on the highway. Under these conditions, the gender differences in aggressive driving are not as great as might be expected. In one survey, 54 percent of the women admitted to aggressive driving behavior compared with 64 percent of men (Joint, 1995). In that survey, respondents reported that aggressive tailgating (62%) was the most common form of aggressive driving, followed by headlight flashing (59%), obscene gestures (48%), deliberately obstructing other vehicles (21%), and verbal abuse (16%).

However, the immediate, precipitating causes of road rage are largely minor misunderstandings that are perceived and interpreted by the other drivers as aggressive, aversive, or directed personally at them. It also appears that a major factor in the road rage reaction is frustration, followed by emotional arousal that detaches the angry driver from his or her usual cognitive control of appropriate behavior. In many instances, the road rager is already primed for aggressive or violent action due to an incident that happened before reaching the highway (Connell, 1996). A quarrel with a loved one, some difficulty on the job, problems making financial ends meet, or any number of previous events can contribute to the arousal factor. The stimulus that sets off the aggression, as Berkowitz might argue in his cognitive-neoassociation model, is the annoying behavior of another driver. The available weapon is the motor vehicle. Thus, the necessary components of a negative affect and the appropriate stimuli are in place for aggression to occur. Obviously, not all drivers in these circumstances react with rage. In the following section, we focus more on the factors that might distinguish one person's reactions from that of another.

SOCIAL LEARNING FACTORS IN AGGRESSION AND VIOLENCE

Why do some people behave aggressively when intensely frustrated, while others change their tactics, withdraw, or seem not to be affected? One major factor may be past learning experiences. The human being, as we noted in Chapter 4, is very adept at learning and maintaining behavior patterns that have worked in the past, even if they only worked occasionally. This learning process begins in early childhood. Children develop many behaviors merely by watching their parents and significant others in their environment, a process we have called modeling or observational learning. A child's behavior pattern, therefore, is often acquired through the modeling or imitation of other people, real and imagined, in the child's environment (Bandura, 1973a). In fact, available research reveals that the conditions most conducive to the learning of aggression are those in which the child (1) has many opportunities to observe aggression, (2) is reinforced for his or her own aggression, or (3) is often the object of aggression (Huesmann, 1988).

Suppose Harris's father returns home feeling harried after a hot and humid day during which he accomplished nothing (frustration). He finds an official-looking letter from the IRS in the mailbox. He opens it, perhaps muttering mild obscenities under his breath, and finds that the IRS apparently suspects he has shortchanged the U.S. government by several hundred dollars, although he knows he has not (more frustration). He is invited for an audit (even more frustration). In response, he slams his fist on the table, exclaims "Damn it!" or some colorful variation, and kicks the nearest chair (just enough not to damage his toe, since he has learned the painful consequences from past similar episodes). Unknown to father, Harris has observed this whole scenario. An hour later, when his block tower crumbles, little Harris pounds his fist, kicks the living room chair, and curses, "Damn it!"

Modeling

Many years ago, Albert Bandura (1965) conducted what is now considered a classic study in psychology. Sixty-six nursery school children (33 girls and 33 boys) were divided into three groups and shown one of three five-minute films. All three films depicted an adult verbally and physically assaulting a Bobo doll, a large plastic, inflatable clown with a sand base that bounces back after being pushed down. (A common toy in the 1950s and 1960s, the Bobo doll has now morphed into inflatable Spiderman or X-MEN characters that are available on the toy market of today.) In the film, the adult punched, kicked, and hit the clown with a mallet. One group saw the adult model being rewarded with candy and a soft drink after displaying aggressive behavior. A second group observed the model being spanked (with a rolled-up magazine) and reprimanded verbally. A third group witnessed a situation in which the model received neither punishment nor reward.

After the children saw the film, they were permitted to free play for 10 minutes in a playroom of toys, including a Bobo doll. The group that had witnessed the adult model being rewarded for aggressive behavior exhibited more aggression than the other two groups. In addition, boys were more aggressive than girls. The group that saw the adult model being punished exhibited the lowest amount of aggression in the playroom.

Bandura's subsequent research, which included variations on this basic study design, consistently demonstrated this modeling effect. Furthermore, numerous follow-up studies not only replicated his findings but also suggested that media violence (TV, movies, video games) may have a strong influence on real life in many situations (Baron, 1977).

When a child's imitative behavior is reinforced or rewarded by praise and encouragement from significant models, the probability that the behavior will occur in the future is increased. There is evidence that American parents (consciously or inadvertently) encourage or reinforce aggressive behavior in their children, particularly in their sons. For example, the behavior of Harris described above might have been reinforced if Dad or Mom drew attention to it—"Isn't that cute?"—or if they laughed. In a future episode, the kicking behavior might be directed at the family cat. Furthermore, while kicking chairs and towers may seem relatively mild, the same behavior becomes very sobering if the parent's anger is taken out on a family member, as too many Harrises in our society have observed and experienced. Other children are "merely" expected or encouraged to be hard-hitting linebackers and to hold their own against neighborhood bullies, providing they are approximately the same size. They learn that the child who aggresses successfully against others is often rewarded by status, prestige, and the most attractive toys or material goods.

Types of Models

Bandura (1983) identifies three major types of models: family members, members of one's subculture, and symbolic models provided by the mass media. As we noted in Chapter 2, family members, particularly parents, can be very powerful models up until early adolescence. Beginning in early adolescence, peer models are likely to dominate. Not surprisingly, the highest incidence of aggression is found in communities and groups in which aggressive models abound and fighting prowess is regarded as a valued attribute (Bandura, 1983; Lacourse, Nagin, Tremblay, Vitaro, & Claes, 2003; Thornberry & Burch, 1997).

The mass media, including television, movies, magazines, newspapers, and books, provide abundant symbolic models. Video games and the Internet have vastly expanded this collection. Television pervades the life of the growing child, even the very young one, and offers hundreds of potentially powerful aggressive and violent models in a variety of formats, ranging from Saturday morning cartoon film festivals to triple-X-rated cable movies. The effects these models have on children are a highly debated issue, and one we cover later in this chapter.

Since parents are powerful models, we would expect aggressive or antisocial parents to have aggressive or antisocial children. In an old but classic study, Sears, Maccoby, and Levin (1957) interviewed four hundred mothers of kindergarten children about their disciplinary techniques, their attitudes about children's aggressiveness, and the children's expressions of aggression toward peers, siblings, and parents. One of the major findings was that physical punishment by parents was related to aggressiveness in the children. This was especially true when physical discipline was supplemented by high permissiveness toward aggression. In support of this finding, some researchers found that preschoolers played more aggressively when they were watched by a permissive adult than when no adult was visible (Siegel & Kohn, 1959).

Bandura (1973a) argues persuasively that aggressive behavior can be most productively understood and modified if we give attention to the learning principles like those alluded to earlier. As psychologists learn more about human behavior, many are beginning to agree with him.

Social learning theory hypothesizes that the rudiments of aggressive behavior are initially acquired through observing aggressive models or on the basis of direct experience; aggression is then gradually refined and maintained by reinforcement. Therefore, people may have an aggressive behavioral pattern, but may rarely express it if it has no functional value or is not condoned by significant others in their social environment. The social learning system acknowledges that biological structures can set limits on the types of aggressive responses that can be learned, and that genetic endowment influences the rate at which learning progresses (Bandura, 1973a). Biology does not program the individual to specific aggressive behavior, however. These behaviors are learned by observation, either deliberately or inadvertently; they become refined through reinforced practice.

Observation Modeling

In addition, mere exposure to aggressive models does not guarantee that the observer will try to engage in similar aggressive action at a later date. First, a variety of conditions may prevent observational learning from even taking place. Individuals differ widely in their ability to learn from observation. Some people may fail to notice the essential features of the model's behavior or may have a poor symbolic or visual memory. Alternately, they may not wish to imitate the model. Bandura suggests also that one important component of observational learning may be the motivation to rehearse what has been observed. He notes that a mass murderer, for example, may get an idea from descriptive accounts of another mass killing. The incident remains prominent in his mind long after it has been forgotten by others. He continues to think about the crime and to rehearse the brutal scenario mentally until, under appropriate conditions, it serves as a script for his own murderous actions.

Another restriction on observational learning is what happens to the observed model. If the model is reprimanded or punished either during or immediately after an aggressive episode, this will probably inhibit the observer's behavior. The "bad guy" should not get away with violence, if we are to discourage antisocial behavior via the entertainment media.

If aggressive behavior is to be maintained, it needs periodic reinforcement. According to social learning theory, aggression is maintained by instrumental learning. In the initial stage of learning, observation is important, but in the later stages, reinforcement is essential. The reinforcement may be positive, as when the individual gains material or social rewards, or it may be negative, if it allows the individual to alter or avoid aversive conditions. If aggressive behavior brings rewards in either of these ways, the person is likely to continue it. Research has consistently discovered that aggressive children anticipate more positive outcomes and fewer negative outcomes following their aggressive acts (Hubbard, Dodge, Cillessen, Coie, & Schwartz, 2001). "When compared with average peers, aggressive children are more likely to believe that aggression will produce tangible rewards, reduce aversive treatment by others, make themselves and peers feel good, increase self-esteem, and help to avoid a negative image" (Hubbard *et al.*, 2001, p. 268).

A youngster subjected to unmerciful harassment or bullying because of his unusual name or where he lives may be able to stop the teasing with his fists. The reinforcement he gets from his newly found aggressive behavior is negative, but it is still rewarding. Aggression can also allow the individual to feel in control of a situation if things have not been going his or her way. A more extreme example is when a student who is constantly bullied by peers decides to put a stop to the aversive circumstances by using a firearm on all those who are perceived as participants. The psychological reinforcement offered by feeling in control is an extremely powerful component in any human behavior, especially aggressive or violent behavior.

COGNITIVE MODELS OF AGGRESSION

Recent cognitive models for learning aggression have hypothesized that, while observational learning is important in the process, the individual's cognitive capacities and information processing strategies are equally important. Two major cognitive models have emerged in recent years. One that has been proposed by Rowell Huesmann (1997) is a hypothesis called the **cognitive scripts model**. The other model has been developed by Kenneth Dodge and his colleagues (Dodge, 1986; Dodge & Coie, 1987) and is called the **hostile attribution model**.

Cognitive Scripts Model

According to Rowell Huesmann (1988), social behavior in general, and aggressive behavior in particular, is controlled largely by cognitive scripts learned and memorized through daily experiences. "A script suggests what events are to happen in the environment, how the person should behave in response to these events, and what the likely outcome of those behaviors would be" (Huesmann, 1988, p. 15). Scripts may be learned by direct experience or by observing significant others (Bushman & Anderson, 2001). Once learned, the script is usually followed. Each script is different and unique to each person, but once established it becomes resistant to change and may persist into adulthood. For a script to become established, it must be rehearsed from time to time. With practice the script will not only become encoded and maintained in memory but also be more easily retrieved and utilized when the individual faces a problem. "Scripts can be viewed as cognitive programs that have been acquired over time and are stored in a person's memory and are used as guides for behavior and social problem solving" (Huesmann, Dubow, & Boxer, 2011, p. 128). Furthermore, the individual's "evaluation of the 'appropriateness' of a script plays an important role in determining which scripts are stored in memory, in determining which scripts are retrieved and utilized, and which scripts continue to be utilized"

(Huesmann, 1988, p. 19). Emotions play a role too, as they influence script selection and the evaluation of scripts. For example, script selection is likely to be different when the person is angry compared to when that same person is happy. Parents also play an important role. "In the short run, when children see their parents behave aggressively, schemas, scripts, and normative beliefs associated with aggression are primed in the children's minds" (Huesmann *et al.*, 2011, p. 131). Since parents provide suitable models, children are likely to mimic their parents' aggressive behaviors almost immediately, as we saw in the example with Harris and his block tower. However, children do not simply mimic the immediate behavior; they tend to encode into their own repertoire of scripts their parents' scripts, as well as their parents' views and beliefs about the world. As the child grows older, the evaluation process includes the confidence that he or she has in predicting outcomes of the script, the extent to which an individual judges himself or herself capable of executing the script, and the extent to which the script is seen as congruent with the person's self-regulating internal standards. Scripts that are inconsistent or violate one's internalized standards are unlikely to be stored or utilized. An individual with poorly integrated internal standards against aggression, or who is convinced that aggressive behavior is a way of life, is more likely to incorporate aggressive scripts for behavior. Importantly, the aggressive child is apt to instigate aggressive reactions from others, confirming his or her beliefs about the aggressiveness of human nature in a circular, perpetuating fashion.

Hostile Attribution Model

Kenneth Dodge and his colleagues discovered that highly aggressive and violent youth often have a **hostile attribution bias**. That is, youth (and adults) prone toward violence are more likely to interpret ambiguous actions as hostile and threatening than are their less aggressive counterparts (Dodge, 1993). For example, a foot casually and innocently positioned near a school desk may be interpreted as a deliberate attempt to trip. As Dill, Anderson, Anderson, and Deuser (1997, p. 275) put it, people described as having hostile attribution bias "tend to view the world through blood-red tinted glasses." Children with a hostile attribution bias are twice as likely as average children to see aggressive actions from others where there are none (Hubbard *et al.*, 2001). As noted by Dodge (2011), "when a respondent infers that the act was committed with hostile intent (*a hostile attribution*), the probability that the respondent will react aggressively is high (about .76), whereas when the same respondent infers that the act was committed benignly, the probability of an aggressive behavior is low (about .25)" (p. 165). In addition, the hostile attribution bias is present in both boys and girls (Vitale, Newman, Serin, & Bolt, 2005).

Research consistently indicates that violent youth "typically define social problems in hostile ways, adopt hostile goals, and seek few additional facts, generate few alternative solutions, anticipate few consequences for aggression, and give higher priority to their aggressive solutions" (Eron & Slaby, 1994, p. 10). Similarly, Serin and Preston (2001, p. 259) conclude, "Aggressive juvenile offenders have been found to be deficient in social problem-solving skills and to espouse many beliefs supporting aggression. Specifically, they tend to define problems in hostile ways, adopt hostile goals, seek less confirmatory information, generate fewer alternative solutions, anticipate fewer consequences for aggressive solutions, and choose less effective solutions."

Research indicates that this hostile attribution bias begins to develop during the preschool years and seems to be a stable attribute that is still present into adulthood (Dodge, 2011; Dodge *et al.*, 2002; Nigg & Huang-Pollock, 2003). Dodge (1993) reports that when children were followed from elementary school to middle school, a child's tendency to attribute hostile intentions to others showed a significant relationship between peer rejection during elementary school and increased aggression during middle school. Coie (2004) asserts, "The fact that rejected, aggressive males show persistently higher tendencies toward hostile attribution biases, as well as other social cognitive deficits related to aggression, fits with their pattern of higher involvement in violent delinquent acts in adolescence and their tendency to persist in violent behavior into the early adult years" (p. 255).

There is further research to suggest that some children are especially primed to develop hostile expectations of peers because of earlier exposure to family abuse and maltreatment (DeWall, Twenge, Gitter, & Baumeister, 2009; Dodge, Bates, & Pettit, 1990; Hubbard *et al.*, 2001). "Children develop basic trust through interaction with caring adults, and violation of that trust through extreme or ongoing maltreatment is hypothesized to lead to schemas, scripts, knowledge structures, and working models that others will act maliciously" (Dodge, 2011, p. 173). Studies have revealed that children exposed to maltreatment early in their lives become "hypervigilant toward hostile social cues, perceptually ready to perceive hostility in others' intentions, and quick to generate aggressive retaliatory responses to even mild provocations" (Dodge, 2001, p. 65). In addition, peer-rejected children with hostile attribution bias are frequently targets of physical assault by others, prompting them to be more suspicious of the motives of others (Coie & Miller-Johnson, 2001). These children appear to be especially quick at developing hostile attribution biases against a wide range of peers, including new acquaintances. "These children come to have a generalized set of social cognitions that dispose them to draw hostile inferences from the behavior of new peer acquaintances more quickly than their peers do" (Hubbard *et al.*, 2001, p. 277). Some other children, although prone to hostile attribution bias, tend to be specific in who they identify as hostile, probably due to certain behavioral patterns or interests they find threatening.

Ronald Blackburn (1998) also reports research evidence that suggests that persistent lawbreaking by adults represents attempts to master a social environment perceived as hostile and threatening. Blackburn hypothesizes that serious, repeat offenders approach the world with a well-developed hostile-dominance interpersonal style. That is, rather than be simply a reflection of deficits in conscience or self-control, frequent criminal behavior may represent an ongoing attempt to control and dominate others in the social environment. According to Blackburn, chronic criminality can be understood as "an attempt to maintain status or mastery of a social environment from which they feel alienated" (1998, p. 174). The well-rehearsed cognitive script of persistent, lifelong offenders, therefore, is to dominate—often in a hostile manner—social environments they perceive as hostile.

Blackburn's observations have been recently supported by research by Vitale *et al.* (2005) who investigated the amount of hostile attribution in 150 incarcerated males. The researchers discovered that psychopaths were significantly more likely to exhibit hostile attribute bias than nonpsychopaths in a variety of situations. The study also supported the hypothesis that there may be different antisocial pathways associated with hostile attributions. That is, hostile attribution bias was also prevalent in those prisoners who held negative thoughts about themselves, other people, and the world in general.

In summary, hostile attribution bias involves the tendency to view the behavior of others as provocative, harmful, hostile, or wrongful. Some individuals demonstrate this tendency more strongly than others. Consequently, attribution bias or style should be viewed as existing along a continuum. At its extreme level, the bias represents a cognitive deficit in processing that distorts social information so dramatically that the individual is literally unable to process that information accurately (Fontaine, 2008). In some cases, some people may engage in extreme violence toward others they interpret as trying to do them harm. In the chapters on criminal homicide (Chapters 9 and 10), we will return to this topic as it applies to murder, including serial and mass murder.

Aggressive Behavior: Simple and Easy to Use

Aggression is a simple, direct way of solving immediate conflicts. If something is not going your way, approaching the social environment in a threatening, hostile manner is the most direct way (not necessarily the most effective in the long run) of confronting your tormentors. On the other hand, prosocial solutions and alternative nonaggressive scripts are less direct and more complex than aggressive solutions. In essence, they are more difficult to apply. Theoretically, the more cognitively "simple" individual would be more inclined to pursue simplistic and direct solutions to problems. In addition, because prosocial solutions are more complicated and more difficult to apply, they also require effective social skills. However, the development of effective social skills takes time, and those skills will have a spotty reinforcement history until perfected. Aggressive behavior, on the other hand, often receives immediate reinforcement for the aggressor, and therefore is more likely to be retained in one's arsenal of strategies for immediate solutions of conflictful situations.

After a 22-year longitudinal study, Eron and Huesmann (1984) concluded that diminished intellectual competence and poor social skills have an early effect in increasing the likelihood that a child will adopt characteristically more aggressive styles of behavior to conflict resolution. For example, research has repeatedly documented the fact that juveniles who are serious sexual offenders have significant deficits in social competence, such as inadequate social skills, poor peer relationships, and social isolation from peers (Righthand & Welch, 2001). Further, the evidence indicates that this aggressive style will persist across situations and time and become a preferred style throughout adulthood. But the relationship is not simply one way, with limited intellectual competence and inadequate skills promoting aggressive behavior. Rather it appears to be interactive. Aggressive behavior may interfere with positive social interactions with teachers and peers for intellectual and social advancement, perpetuating a chain of mutually influencing events: aggressive behavior influencing the social environment, and the social environment, in turn, influencing aggressive behavior.

Dolf Zillmann (1988) proposes a similar idea to the cognitive script theory, but, like Berkowitz, emphasizes the importance of physiological arousal and its interaction with cognitions. Zillmann agrees with Hebb (1955, p. 249) that arousal "is an energizer, but not a guide, an engine but not a steering gear." Cognition provides the steering and direction to the energizing effects of anger, fear, or frustration. A long-standing observation in the study of animal and human aggression is that when the organism recognizes or perceives a threat to its welfare and well-being, it can either fight or flee. Following this "recognition of endangerment," physiological arousal quickly sets in, preparing the organism for fight or flight. The "recognition of endangerment," Zillmann reminds us, can be immediate, and the response can be reflexlike. What happens then is also highly dependent on cognition, especially in humans. Very likely, this is when cognitive scripts come in.

If the arousal is moderate, the individual with skills and well-integrated standards of prosocial values will probably pursue nonaggressive scripts, even though the person may have been angry or threatened at first. However, very *high* levels of arousal interfere with the complex cognitive processes that mediate our consideration of our internal codes of conduct, as well as our ability to assess the intentions of others and the mitigating circumstances around the incident

(Zillmann, 1988). Think of a very stressful or frightening situation that has happened to you, and how difficult it was to think clearly. Or think of a time when you became extremely angry and said or did things you wish you hadn't. At high levels of arousal, our cognitions seem to become narrower and more restricted, almost incapacitated at times. Generally, under these high states of arousal, we resort to strongly established habits to guide and dominate our behavior. In essence, we become "impulsive" and largely unthinking, and cognitions that mediate the diminution of hostile or even violent actions are substantially reduced. However, if we have practiced or rehearsed nonviolent or nonaggressive behaviors as solutions, these cognitive scripts are likely to be the habits we resort to under high stress, fear, and high arousal.

THE GENERAL AGGRESSION MODEL

In an attempt to integrate the common features of previous theories of aggression, Nathan DeWall and Craig Anderson (DeWall & Anderson, 2011, DeWall, Anderson, & Bushman, 2011) propose the **general aggression model (GAM)**. According to DeWall and Anderson (2011), "GAM provides the only theoretical framework of aggression and violence that explicitly incorporates biological, personality development, social processes, basic cognitive processes, short-term and long-term processes, and decision processes" (p. 255). Although the model attempts to include most if not all the factors that can influence aggression and violence, it draws heavily on social-cognitive and social learning theories that have been developed over the past 40 years by social, personality, cognitive, and developmental psychologists. According to the model, aggression and violence depend on how an individual perceives and interprets the social environment, expectations about the likelihood of various outcomes, knowledge and beliefs about how people usually respond in certain situations, and the degree to which a person believes he or she has the ability to respond effectively. Although the cognitive process is initially complicated, judgments and choices in the process become automatized through cultural teachings and repeated experiences. Ultimately, they require little mental effort or conscious awareness. For instance, through repeated experiences and cultural teachings, some individuals quickly and thoughtlessly interpret that others—because of their appearance, religion, or national origin—are hostile and pose a physical threat.

GAM also posits that violence often occurs because of an escalation cycle, which begins with an initial triggering event that may be serious or relatively benign "The triggering event can influence any kind of dyad, including two people, two groups, two religions, or two nations" (DeWall & Anderson, 2011, p. 23). In these situations, one person or group considers retaliation to the incident to be justified or mild, whereas the other group believes the retaliation to be unjustified and severe. The person or group who believes the retaliation was unjustified often retaliates back. The cycle often persists through several iterations of violent actions. DeWall and Anderson hypothesize that one explanation for the persistence of the retaliation cycle is fundamental attribution error, discussed in Chapter 4. In fundamental attribution error—you will recall—people ascribe the negative behaviors of others to dispositional factors (he's mean), while their own negative behavior is due to situational factors (it was the right thing to do, considering the circumstances). DeWall and Anderson (2011) write: "people become caught in a web in which members perceive the other party as acting out of malice or evil and perceive their own behavior as appropriate responses to the situation at hand" (p. 24).

Beyond the escalation cycle, DeWall and Anderson contend that aggression and violence spring from a wide range of factors. "If you want to create people who are predisposed to aggression and violence, begin by depriving them of resources necessary to meet basic needs—physical, emotional, psychological, and social" (p. 26). Then, provide them with multiple examples and models of aggression and violence, especially examples that appear to work. And then, provide them with cognitive beliefs and values that dehumanize potential human targets, especially groups of people who are unlike the in-group. Then expose them to various forms of violence and destruction to the point where they become desensitized to it. Finally, provide the proper behavioral-cognitive scripts, and you should have the desired level of violence (DeWall & Anderson, 2011).

I³ THEORY

In an expansion of the GAM, **I³ theory** (pronounced "I-cubed theory") has been recently developed. Similar to GAM, I³ theory is designed to provide an organized structure for understanding: (a) the process by which a given factor promotes aggression, and (b) how multiple risk factors interrelate to create or reduce aggression (Slotter & Finkel, 2011). I³ theory organizes the many aggression risk factors into three categories: (1) *instigating* triggers, which are discrete incidents that arouse tendencies or predispositions that are conductive to aggression; (2) *impelling* forces, which are forces that increase the likelihood of an aggressive action following the instigating trigger; and (3) *inhibiting* forces, which are factors that increase the likelihood that aggression will be mitigated or contained (Shaver & Mikulincer, 2011). I³ theory differs from GAM in that it incorporates recent research on self-regulation as a core emphasis of the theory, and it specifies different, novel ways in which aggression risk factors produce aggression and violence (Slotter & Finkel, 2011).

GAM and I³ theory represent the new, emerging meta-theories on aggression that have been formulated to organize and integrate the many mini-theories that have been discussed in earlier sections of the chapter. Both provide an excellent frame of reference for future research on human aggression and violence.

OVERT AND COVERT ACTS OF AGGRESSION

Rolf Loeber and Magda Stouthamer-Loeber (1998) recommend that researchers on aggression and violence be mindful of two types of aggressive actions: overt and covert. According to Loeber and Stouthamer-Loeber, the two forms of aggression are different in (1) behavior patterns, (2) emotions, (3) cognitions, and (4) development. *Behaviorally*, overt aggression usually involves direct confrontation with victims and the administration of physical harm or threats of physical harm. Covert aggression, on the other hand, does not involve direct confrontation but relies on concealment, dishonesty, or sneaky behavior. It is similar to the passive-aggressive behavior discussed earlier in the chapter. In many instances, overt aggression decreases with age, while covert aggression increases with age (Loeber, Lahey, & Thomas, 1991; Stanger, Achenbach, & Verhulst, 1997). However, children who exhibit serious forms of overt aggression (violence) tend to increase their violence as they get older and often commit both violent and property crimes as adults (Loeber & Stouthamer-Loeber, 1998).

Emotionally, anger is usually an important ingredient in most overt acts of aggression, while more neutral emotions are characteristic of covert actions. Violent actions are usually accompanied by high levels of arousal brought on by anger. Covert actions, on the other hand, tend to be less emotional in nature, such as fraud, theft, embezzlement, burglary, and other white-collar or property offenses (see **Table 5-2**).

TABLE 5-2	Overt and Covert Aggressive Actions			
Aggression	Behavior Patterns	Emotions	Cognitions	Development
Overt	Direct confrontation with victims; generally decreases with age	Anger, high level of arousal and violence	Lacks social cognitions for coming up with nonaggressive solutions	Aggression begins early, especially in boys
Covert	Concealment, dishonesty, sneaky behavior; increases with age	Less emotion; crimes such as fraud, larceny, and theft	Relies on cognitive capabilities, such as planfulness, deceitfulness	Can evolve as well-learned strategy to escape punishment

Covert and overt aggression can also be distinguished on the basis of the *cognitions* that accompany them. As we explained in this chapter, violent persons (overt aggression) tend to have cognitive deficiencies that make it difficult for them to come up with nonaggressive solutions to interpersonal conflicts and disputes. Overt aggressors also have hostile attributional biases that contribute to violence-prone cognitive processing. On the other hand, people who use covert aggression as a preferred strategy do not demonstrate the degree of cognitive deficiencies in solving their interpersonal problems, nor do they manifest a hostile attributional bias. "Instead, it is postulated that most covert acts are facilitated by specific cognitive capabilities, such as planfulness (i.e., casing situations prior to theft), preoccupations with consumables and property, and lying to escape detection" (Loeber & Stouthamer-Loeber, 1998, p. 250). Occupationally related crimes, for instance, such as theft of company property, the misuse of information, or software piracy, are often committed with planning and forethought. Some crime committed through the use of computers, called **cybercrime**, is also a good example of covert actions of aggression. Examples are cyberstalking and cyberbullying, both discussed more fully in Chapter 15.

Developmentally, overt aggression generally begins early, especially in boys, as seen, for example, in the case of life-course-persistent offenders. However, Loeber and Stouthamer-Loeber suggest that development of overt aggressive behavior does not necessarily parallel the development of covert actions. Instead, "some children have never been socialized by their parents to be honest and to respect the property of others. This is common among neglectful parents or parents who hold an indistinct or a weak moral stance in these respects" (1998, p. 251). Honesty and respect for the property of others are instilled by the teaching provided by parents or primary caregivers and the prosocial models they offer their children. Some covert actions, especially lying, can also evolve as a well-learned strategy that serves to minimize the chances of detection and punishment by adults.

It should be emphasized that not all overt aggressors who engage in violence start early. As Loeber and Stouthamer-Loeber note, "It is necessary to account for the emergence of violence in individuals during adulthood who do not have a history of aggression earlier in their lives" (1998, p. 246). These *late-onset types* represent a minority of adult violent offenders, but the hypothesis does suggest that not all highly aggressive and violent individuals manifested aggression in childhood.

Reactive and Proactive Forms of Aggression

Kenneth Dodge and his colleagues (Dodge, Lochman, Harnish, Bates, & Pettit, 1997) have suggested that another way of classifying aggression in children (and adults) is to make a distinction between reactive aggression and proactive aggression. **Reactive aggression** includes anger expressions, temper tantrums, and vengeful hostility, and more generally "hot-blooded" aggressive acts. **Proactive aggression**, on the other hand, includes bullying, domination, teasing, name-calling, and coercive acts—in other words, more "cold-blooded" aggressive actions. Reactive aggression appears to be a reaction to frustration and is associated with a lack of control due to high states of arousal. In general, reactive aggression is a hostile act displayed in response to a perceived threat or provocation. Proactive aggression, by contrast, is less emotional, and more driven by expectations of rewards. "Proactive aggression is unprovoked, deliberate, goal-directed behavior used to influence or coerce a peer" (Hubbard *et al.*, 2001, p. 269). Reactive aggression has its theoretical roots in the frustration–aggression model proposed by Berkowitz (1989) discussed earlier. The theoretical roots of proactive aggression are found in social learning theory which, as we learned previously, states that aggression is acquired behavior that is controlled and maintained by reinforcement. It is highly similar to the concept of instrumental aggression. Reliable observations of these two forms of aggression have been found in children (as young as 3–6 years of age) through teacher ratings, peer ratings, clinical psychiatric records, and direct observations of peer interactions by researchers (Dodge & Coie, 1987; Dodge *et al.*, 1997; Poulin & Boivin, 2000).

Reactively aggressive children, compared with proactively aggressive children, display greater problems in social and psychological adjustment (Dodge *et al.*, 1997). Psychological adjustment problems include a lack of emotional control when angry, accompanied by sleep disorders, depressive symptoms, and personality disorders. On average, these problems emerged around age 4–5. In addition, reactive aggression is related to the tendency to overattribute hostile intent to peers in ambiguous provocation situations (hostile attribution bias) (Hubbard *et al.*, 2001). That is, when a reactive aggressive child interprets a peer's behavior as intentionally harmful or aggressive, he is far more likely to respond with angry retaliation or even violence.

Dodge (1991) proposed that reactive and proactive aggression originate from different social experiences and develop independently. According to Dodge, reactive aggression develops in reaction to a harsh, threatening, and unpredictable environment or abusive or cold parenting (Vitaro, Brendgen, & Barker, 2006). Proactive aggression, on the other hand, develops as a result of exposure to aggressive role models who value the use of aggression to resolve conflict or advance personal interests (Vitaro *et al.*, 2006). However, Vitaro *et al.* are quick to point out that proactive and reactive aggression may not only be fostered by different social environments but may also be influenced by differences in temperamental and genetic factors. That is, reactive aggression appears to be associated with a temperamental disposition toward anxiety, angry reactivity, emotional impulsiveness, and inattention. Proactive aggression appears to be less affected by temperament and is more based on beliefs that aggressive behavior will bring rewards and positive outcomes. Furthermore, preliminary research results suggest that reactive aggression develops earlier in the life span than proactive aggression, and the two types of aggression seem to follow different developmental trajectories (Vitaro & Brendgen, 2005).

Gender Differences in Aggression

While boys engage in more overt aggression and direct confrontation as they grow up, it is not clear if boys are generally more aggressive than girls. It is clear that *physical* aggression is more prevalent among males than females and that this consistent finding holds across hundreds of studies and across nations (Archer, 2004; Campbell, 2006), but what about other forms of aggression?

The current work of cognitive psychologists suggests that there may be socialized differences in the way girls and boys construct their worlds. Social learning theorists have long held that girls are "socialized" differently than boys, or taught not to be overtly aggressive. Anne Campbell (1993, p. 19) argues that "boys are not simply more aggressive than girls; they are aggressive in a different way." Other researchers concur with this observation (Hawkins, Pepler, & Craig, 2001; Lumley, McNeil, Herschell, & Bahl, 2002; Wood, Cowan, & Baker, 2002). According to Campbell, boys and girls are born with the potential to be equally aggressive, but girls are socialized not to be overtly aggressive, whereas boys are encouraged to be overtly aggressive to defend themselves.

Interestingly, research indicates that boys and girls are equally physically aggressive toward their peers when they are toddlers, but that this pattern soon changes as they get older and enter their elementary school years (Xie, Farmer, & Cairns, 2003). Loeber and Stouthamer-Loeber (1998, p. 253) conclude from their review of the research that "in general, gender differences in aggression, as expressed by frustration and rage, are not documented in infancy." They note that only in the preschool period (3–5 years of age) do observable gender differences begin to emerge, with boys displaying more overt aggression than girls. Overt aggression becomes especially prominent in boys from elementary school age onward. Boys are taught to be tough, not to cry, and to take on the bullies and physically defend themselves. However, many researchers report that girls are more likely to engage in relationship or interpersonal forms of aggression rather than the physical forms of pushing and hitting (Casey-Cannon, Hayward, & Gowen, 2001; Crick & Zahn-Waxler, 2003; Prinstein, Boergers, & Vernberg, 2001). For example, researchers (Björkqvist, Lagerspetz, & Kaukianinen, 1992; Cairns, Cairns, Neckerman, Ferguson, & Gariépy, 1989) find that girls and women tend to use more covert, indirect, and verbal forms of aggression, such as character defamation and ostracism. Other researchers report that girls are far more likely to employ *relational aggression*, such as abandoning one friend in favor of another, spreading malicious gossip, or ridiculing another's physical traits (e.g., their facial features, weight, or general demeanor) (Crick, 1995; Crick & Grotpeter, 1995; Crick & Zahn-Waxler, 2003; Garside & Klimes-Dougan, 2002; Loeber & Stouthamer-Loeber, 1998).

In conclusion, there is growing recognition that gender differences in aggression are not simply due to biology, but are primarily due to cultural and socialization processes that promote different kinds of aggression. Environmental cues are also important in cognitive scripts and in the aggressive strategies individuals employ for various situations. Which script or strategy an individual employs is dependent on which environmental cues are present.

EFFECTS OF MEDIA VIOLENCE

Youth today are growing up in a media-saturated environment (Gentile & Walsh, 2002), and much of this environment has a violence theme. In the first nationwide survey of video game play in the United States, researchers learned that 97 percent of adolescents (ages 12–17 years) play computer, Web, portable, or console video games (Lenhart et al., 2008; Willoughby, Adachi, & Good, 2011). Ninety-nine percent of boys and 94 percent of girls play the games (Lenhart et al., 2008). Nearly half of the teens play video games on a mobile device, such as a cell phone, tablet, or other handheld system. Nearly a third play on a daily basis, and another 21 percent play at least several times a week. An estimated 80 percent of teens play five or more different game genres, and 40 percent play eight or more types of games (Lenhart et al., 2008). Most significantly for this chapter, over half of the adolescents surveyed said they play violent video games on a regular basis. With the variety of portable, wireless devices available today, youth and adults have access to games at all times, unless they are in a location where use is restricted.

Violence is a common theme in the movie, TV, and video game media. Even before the video game explosion, surveys estimated that the average American child sees more than 100,000 violent episodes and some 20,000 murders on television before reaching adolescence (Myers, 1996). Other studies estimated there were four scenes of violence portrayed on network television to every one scene expressing affection. Note that this does not include the huge range of "non-network" programming that offers an increasing number of options for viewers. A three-year study (1994–1997) by four universities on violence on American television revealed that 90 percent of movies shown on television include violence (National Cable Television Association, 1998). Violence was found most frequently on subscription television (85% on premium cable and 59% on basic cable), while the lowest incidence of violence (18%) was found on Public Broadcasting Service (PBS) stations. Across three years of the study, nearly 40 percent of the violent incidents on television were initiated by "good" characters, who are likely perceived as attractive role models. In 67 percent of the programs, violence was portrayed within a humorous context. In general, the study found that most media violence is glamorized and that the long-term negative consequences of violent behavior are rarely depicted. Nearly three-quarters of violent scenes contain no remorse, criticism, punishment, or emotional reactions from the perpetrators. Overall, the survey found that the percentage of programs on television that contain some violence remained unchanged over the three-year period of study. In a special report, the Parents Television Council (2007) concluded that television violence increased between the years 1998 and 2006 by 309 percent, and there is reason to believe the amount of violence has further increased in recent years.

The research community is sharply divided on the long-term effects of violent media on aggressive behavior. To date, however, the overwhelming bulk of the research suggests that portrayals of violence on television and movies may have a significant effect on the frequency and type of aggressive behavior expressed by America's youth. Over the past 45 years, research has periodically demonstrated that media violence viewing is a contributing factor on the development of aggression and violence in children, adolescents, and young adults (Huesmann, Moise-Titus, Podolski, & Eron, 2003). Moreover, media violence appears to influence children more strongly than adults, as they seem to be more susceptible to its long-term effects. Interestingly, the Huesmann *et al.* (2003) study discovered that violent films and TV programs that have the most deleterious effects on children are not always the ones that adults perceive as the most violent. Research suggests that violent scenes in which children can identify with the perpetrator of the violence, and those in which the perpetrator gets rewarded for the violence, have the greatest negative impact on children. It is not necessarily the level of violence per se.

Although the largest body of research on media violence has concentrated on televised violence, the research community in recent years has shifted its attention to violent video games (Murray, 2008). Similar to studies on violent film and TV programs, recent research consistently suggests that heavy exposure to violent video games may be significantly linked to increases in aggressive behavior, aggressive thoughts, aggressive feelings, and decreases in helping behavior (Anderson 2004; Anderson & Bushman, 2001; Anderson *et al.*, 2008; Dill & Dill, 1998). As we see shortly, not all researchers agree with these conclusions.

Before proceeding with this discussion, it is important to distinguish between short-term and long-term effects of violent media on aggressive behavior. Research indicates that different cognitive processes are involved (Huesmann, 2007). Although there is compelling evidence that exposure to violent electronic media has both short-term and long-term effects, we are particularly concerned here about long-term effects. They occur as a result of observational learning, desensitization, and storing violent and aggressive material into the thought process. Young children are especially open to new learning, and these early experiences often have a greater impact during the early development years than learning events that occur during adulthood. Thus, if young children learn that violence or aggressive behavior is acceptable, this information is likely to follow them to and through adulthood. To this effect, Huesmann *et al.* (2003) write, "In recent theorizing, long-term relations have been ascribed mainly to acquisition through observation learning of three social-cognitive structures: schemas about a hostile world, scripts for social problem solving that focus on aggression, and normative beliefs that aggression is acceptable" (p. 201). Over time, and with frequent exposure to aggressive behavior, children develop beliefs (schemas) that the world is basically a hostile place, that aggression is an acceptable social behavior, and that the best way to solve conflicts and to get things is to be aggressive. These aspects may actually become part of the personality over the long run.

Research by Krahé and Möller (2004) supports these hypotheses. They found that adolescents were more likely to condone aggression and to display hostile attribution bias toward ambiguous cues if they were frequently exposed to violent electronic games. Another study (i.e., Funk, Baldacci, Pasold, & Baumgardner, 2004) demonstrated that high exposure to violent electronic games is associated with lower levels of empathy and more positive attitudes toward violent behavior in general. This study also indicated that violent video games may have greater impact than other forms of violent entertainment media, such as films or television programs. This is likely due to the interactive component of video games, whereby the individual is a virtual participant rather than a passive observer of the violence.

Huesmann and his colleagues (2003) report strong long-term effects of media violence observed in early childhood appears to carry over into adulthood. They conclude the following:

> Overall, these results suggest that both males and females from all social strata and all levels of initial aggressiveness are placed at increased risk for the development of adult aggressive and violent behavior when they view a high and steady diet of violent TV shows in early childhood. (p. 128)

The effects of violent video or electronic games on the development of aggressive behavior received considerable scrutiny after a series of school shootings by avid players of such games occurred during the late 1990s and early 2000s. In April 1999, public concern was especially strong after 13 persons were murdered and 23 wounded during a shooting spree by two students at Columbine High School in Colorado. The two assailants were considered social outcasts and seemed preoccupied with the violence presented in the media, music, and video games. Reports indicated that the two were especially fascinated by the bloody video game *Doom*, one of the earliest and most successful of all electronic games. It is interesting to note that the Marine Corps in 1998 adapted *Doom II* to train soldiers for combat, and called it *Marine Doom*. The video game, consisting of a team leader, two riflemen, and a machine gunner, was designed to teach teamwork, coordination, and effective decision making. Although the game is no longer used by the military, it has been released for public use.

Lt. Col. (Ret.) David Grossman, a former Airborne Ranger, West Point psychology professor, and a leading expert on the psychology of killing, has written several books that pertain to the subject of violence in the media. The school shootings prompted the books *On Killing* and *Stop Teaching Our Kids to Kill*. In the latter, Grossman and DeGaetano (1999) point out that the training methods used by the military, which includes brutalization, classical conditioning, operant conditioning, and role modeling, can be found in many of the violent video games found on the market today. They argue that video game publishers unethically train children in the use of weapons and, more importantly, harden them emotionally to the act of murder by simulating the killing of hundreds or thousands of opponents.

The impact of violent electronic games is not restricted to the United States. It occurs in other countries also, such as Japan (Anderson, 2004; Anderson *et al.*, 2008). In another example, Krahé and Möller (2004) describe an incident that occurred in Germany in April 2002, in which 17 people were killed in a shooting spree by an expelled student who had spent much of his time playing violent electronic games.

However, similar to the effects of TV and movies, the research community is divided about the long-term effects of violent video games, and the empirical evidence has been challenged at many levels. Some scholars argue that many of the studies on video games are inconclusive and can be criticized on methodological grounds (Ferguson *et al.*, 2008; Grimes & Bergen, 2008; Gunter, 2008; Savage, 2008; Savage & Yancey, 2008). Certainly, the overwhelming majority of individuals who play violent video games do not commit violent acts. Therefore, the oversimplified position that violent video media or games cause or even promote violence must be tempered. It may well be that exposure to media violence does increase violence and aggressive behavior for individuals who are already aggressive and prone toward violence. Media violence may not do the same for those individuals less prone toward physical aggression and violence.

In October 2002, 10 people in Washington, D.C., were killed at random over a 23-day period. One of the shooters was 17-year-old Lee Malvo. Malvo's defense team argued that the youth had been brainwashed and trained to kill while playing violent video games depicting sniper attacks, such as *Halo*, *Tom Clancy's Ghost Recon*, and *Tom Clancy's Rainbow Six: Covert Ops* (Olson, 2004). While this may appear to be anecdotal evidence that extensive exposure to violent video games is harmful, it should also be noted that Malvo had been exposed to a wide variety of risk factors throughout his early life, including apparent rejection by his biological father and instability in his home life. He had also demonstrated a variety of antisocial actions, such as cruelty to animals, including apparently killing at least 20 cats (Olson, 2004).

Thus, if there is a research consensus emerging, it is that violent video games may be one risk factor, and when coupled with other risk factors, it may contribute to antisocial or even violent behavior. It is unlikely that video games contribute directly to make a child grow up to be a killer or even become excessively aggressive. "A review of both aggregate studies and experimental evidence does not provide support for the supposition that exposure to media violence causes criminally violent behavior" (Savage & Yancey, 2008, p. 786). However, a recent review of the research literature concluded: "The evidence strongly suggests that exposure to violent video games is a causal risk factor for increased aggressive behavior, aggressive cognition, and aggressive affect and for decreased empathy and prosocial behavior" (Anderson *et al.*, 2010, p. 151). Willoughby *et al.* (2011) found that adolescents who play violent video games across their high school years demonstrated steeper increases in aggression over time compared to those who reported less violent video game playing, The authors concluded that "violent video game play may influence an individual's level of direct aggression by promoting aggressive beliefs and attitudes and creating aggressive schema, aggressive behavioral scripts, and aggressive expectations" (p. 11). Adding to the controversy, one study (Willoughby, Adachi, & Good, 2011) found that it was the video game competitiveness—not the violent content—that may be responsible for encouraging aggressive behavior, at least in the short term.

Whether the exposure directly leads to increased *violence* remains an unanswered question. Willoughby *et al.* speculate that the long-term relationship between violent video play and aggression may be different for adolescents and adults (25 year or older) because of changes in brain development during adolescence and into young adulthood. As we learned in Chapter 3, brain development and self-regulation maturation are not complete until sometime after age 25 and beyond. These brain changes are likely to reduce violent behavior patterns as one gets older, for most but not all. One aspect that demands further investigation, however, is the possibility that certain personalities may be significantly more susceptible to the effects of violent media than others, regardless of age (Bettencourt, Talley, Benjamin, & Valentine, 2006).

Contagion Effect

To this point we have focused upon the effects of violence in the entertainment media. However, even news reports of violence may be problematic. Like entertainment media, the news media may provide aggressive models or may produce a **contagion effect or copycat effect**. This is a tendency in some people to model or copy an activity portrayed in the entertainment or news media. Contagion effect is said to occur when action depicted in the media is assessed by certain individuals as a good idea and then mimicked. An ingenious bank robbery, dramatized on television, might be imitated. The contagion effect is not simply restricted to media portrayals of violence, however. For example, a study by Joiner (1994) illustrates how depression in a college classmate may be contagious. A classmate who is depressed can lower the mood of friends, family, and others who associate with the depressed person and try to help. The contagion effect also has been cited in reports of teen suicide, as in a recent case in which four girls from one high school committed suicide over the course of an academic year.

Another tragic illustration of the copycat effect can be found in a series of school shootings, discussed briefly above, that began in 1997. In October of that year, a 16-year-old, having just stabbed his mother to death, arrived at the high school in Pearl, Mississippi, and began randomly shooting his classmates, killing two and wounding seven. Less than two months later, a 14-year-old boy opened fire on a group of fellow high school students participating in a prayer circle in West Paducah, Kentucky. He killed two schoolmates and wounded five others. The West Paducah incident received worldwide media coverage for several weeks, accompanied by extensive stories about the shooter. A few months later, on March 24, 1998, two boys, ages 13 and 11, armed with seven handguns and three rifles, opened fire on their classmates as they gathered on the school playground in Jonesboro, Arkansas, killing four very young girls and their teacher and wounding 10 others. Of the 15 killed or wounded, only one was male, suggesting that the young shooters were aiming specifically at girls.

After Jonesboro and exactly one month later, a 14-year-old male student in Edinboro, Pennsylvania, began shooting during a school dance, killing a teacher. This incident was followed by another shooting less than a month later in Fayetteville, Tennessee, resulting in the death of a student. A week later, a 15-year-old male in Springfield, Oregon, walked into the high school cafeteria and began randomly shooting at fellow students, firing 50 rounds from a .22-caliber semiautomatic rifle in less than a minute. As he stopped to reload, the young shooter was tackled and disarmed by a varsity wrestler. During that one minute, however, he managed to kill two classmates and wounded 22 others. He had also shot both his parents prior to leaving for school. Less than two weeks later, on June 15, 1998, a 14-year-old student, armed with a .32-caliber semiautomatic handgun, opened fire in the hallway of a high school as students took final exams, wounding a basketball coach and a volunteer aide. All of these young shooters had an inordinate interest in guns, had troubled backgrounds, knew the details of the previous school shootings, and had a strong fascination with violence presented through the media. Thus, both media violence and the contagion effect seem to be implicated, but these were not the only commonalities.

The contagion effect seems to be very strong with reference to Columbine; in some sense the horrific incident set up a cultural script for others to imitate (Larkin, 2009). As mentioned earlier, on April 20, 1999, two teenagers, Eric Harris and Dylan Klebold, in Littleton, Colorado, entered Columbine High School and killed 13 people and injured dozens of others before taking their own lives. Since the Columbine shooting, researchers studying school shootings have found that a significant number of them have been modeled after the Columbine incident (Larkin, 2009). In a recent incident in Salt Lake City in January, 2012, police arrested two youths who had allegedly planned to plant bombs in their school; they learned that one of the youths had actually traveled to Littleton to interview the principal of Columbine to learn more about the attack.

In summary, exposure to media-portrayed violence does not automatically promote aggression. Some individuals are affected more than others. It is clear that no one causal factor alone accounts for more than a small proportion of variance of individual differences in aggressive behavior (Bartholow, Sestir, & Davis, 2005; Huesmann, 1998). Researchers have found evidence that positive parental models are likely to override violent models on television (Goldstein, 1975; Huesmann *et al.*, 2003). Moreover, television violence seems to have substantially less effect on families in which the parents do not rely on aggressive behavior for solving problems (Wright *et al.*, 2001).

Summary and Conclusions

In this chapter, we reviewed the major psychological perspectives on aggression and violence. Answers to what can be done about aggression and violent crime rest ultimately on one's perspective of human nature. If one believes that aggression is innate and part of our evolutionary heritage, a position held by mainstream psychoanalytic and ethological thought, then the conclusion must be that aggression is part of life, and that little can be done to alter this basic ingredient of human nature. Clues for reducing aggression are found in the behavior demonstrated throughout the animal kingdom. If, on the other hand, one believes that human aggression is acquired, then the key becomes principles of human learning and thought, and hope that one can change this acquired behavior for the betterment of humankind. The distinction between the innate and learning viewpoints has been somewhat oversimplified, but most contemporary theories on aggression fall within one or the other

camp. At this point, the learning perspective has garnered considerably more empirical support than the innate perspective. Cognitive factors are especially important in explanations of human aggression.

Complicating the above, though, is the increasing amount of research being done in the biological sciences, most particularly relating to the brain and to human genetics. Ninety-five percent of everything we know about the human brain has been learned within the last 15 years. Researchers are acquiring extensive information about the contribution of genes to physical characteristics and susceptibility to medical problems. Many believe that they will eventually link genes to a variety of behavioral problems and mental disorders as well. It is crucial to keep in mind, though, that although some genes may *predispose* individuals to certain disorders that may lead to violence or other antisocial behavior, genes do not *determine* behavior.

Furthermore, as more research data are published, even the *learning* perspective becomes increasingly complex, and additional factors must be considered. For one thing, physiological arousal certainly plays a major role in aggressive and violent behavior, as suggested by Berkowitz (1989). High levels of arousal seem to *facilitate* (again, not cause) aggressive behavior in certain situations. Extremely high arousal seems to interfere with our sense of self-awareness and internal control, rendering us more susceptible to environmental cues and to mindless or habitual behaviors. In this sense, under very high arousal, we may not stop to consider the consequences of our violent behavior. The discussion of road rage and aggressive driving in the chapter illustrates this very well.

The different classifications of aggressive behavior were also emphasized in this chapter. Overt and covert forms of aggression must be considered in any discussion of crime. Overt aggressors are more likely to be involved in violent crimes, whereas covert aggressors are more prone to be involved in property offenses. And although the conventional wisdom has been that boys are more likely to commit highly aggressive crimes, the evidence suggests that girls may be equally involved in aggressive behavior of a different kind. Gender differences in aggressive behavior are believed to be mainly due to socialization factors.

Situational and neurophysiological factors also contribute significantly to aggressive behavior. Aggressive stimuli, including weapons, crowds, pollution, temperature, smells, and central nervous system pathology all must be entertained as possible contributors. Social learning theorists also note that the media and the models they provide substantially affect our attitudes, values, and overall impressions about violence as well as our behavior. Attitudes, beliefs, and thoughts refer to the cognitive processes that are beginning to emerge as contenders for a leading role in the psychological explanation of criminal behavior. Operant and classical conditioning remain important, but they do not adequately address the many intricacies of criminal behavior.

The controversial topic of violence in the entertainment and news media was addressed. In light of rapid developments in technology, it is impossible to shelter children and adolescents from violent images in a realistic manner, though it is possible to place limits on that exposure. Media violence, though, is only one of many risk factors in the development of violent behavior. Nevertheless, for some children, excessive exposure to such images can have significant negative effects on their development. With children and adolescents increasingly exposed to video games, including violent games, researchers are avidly exploring the effects of this exposure. The overwhelming evidence points to negative effects for some children and adolescents. These effects include both aggressive behavior and an insensitivity or indifference to violence. Although there are individual differences in reactions to violent images and games, research results thus far suggest there is cause for concern that excessive exposure to violence of this sort cannot be good for the emotional health of children and adolescents.

We end the chapter with a concise summary statement by Rowell Huesmann who, after reviewing the research literature, concludes, "No one causal factor by itself explains more than a small portion of individual differences in aggressiveness" (1997, p. 70). He hastens to add, however, that "early learning and socialization play a key role in the development of habitual aggression" (1997, p. 70).

Key Concepts

Aggressive driving	Cybercrime	Excitation transfer theory
Cognitive-neoassociation model	Difference-in-degree	Frustration–aggression hypothesis
Cognitive scripts model	Displaced aggression theory	General aggression model
Contagion effect (copycat effect)	Evolutionary psychology	(GAM)

Hostile attribution bias
Hostile (expressive) aggression
Hostile attribution model
I^3 theory (I-cubed theory)
Instrumental aggression

Passive-aggressive behaviors
Proactive aggression
Psychodynamic model (hydraulic
   model)
Reactive aggression

Ritualized aggression
Road rage
Rumination
Territoriality
Weapons effect

Review Questions

1. What physiological factors have been associated with aggression?
2. What accounts for gender differences in aggression? Cite relevant research findings.
3. Define cognitive scripts and how they may be applied in situations where spontaneous violence could occur.
4. Define weapons effect and discuss how it may account for some of the violence in today's society.
5. Define hostile attribution bias and discuss how it might explain chronic aggression in young children.
6. Explain the difference between each of the following: overt and covert acts of aggression, cognitive scripts model and hostile attribution model, and reactive and proactive aggression.
7. Review the research presented in this chapter on the effects of the mass media on violence.

6

Juvenile Delinquency

CHAPTER OBJECTIVES

▪ Contrast legal, social, and psychological definitions of delinquency.

▪ Identify five major categories of juvenile offending.

▪ Describe Moffitt's developmental theory of delinquency.

▪ Describe Patterson's coercion developmental theory.

▪ Introduce callous-unemotional traits as features of serious delinquency.

▪ Review treatment strategies for juveniles as a group.

▪ Summarize features of effective treatment programs.

▪ Highlight Multisystemic Therapy (MST) as an effective community-based approach.

Juveniles may well be the most maligned age group in our society. Myths abound about their contribution to crime and the extent of damage for which they are responsible. During the last quarter of the twentieth century, it was common to read accounts of skyrocketing juvenile crime, young superpredators in our midst, declining morality in youth, and the woeful state of family life that was seen as a major contributor to juvenile vandalism, drug use, thievery, and violence. To some extent, these accounts were supported by statistics, particularly during the 1980s and early 1990s. However, fears were also fueled by atypical illustrations of juvenile crime, such as a particularly heinous account of a murder committed by a juvenile or those associated with a number of school shootings.

The first decade of the new century continued to see such atypical accounts, including school shootings, the case of the 11-year-old who shot his father's pregnant girlfriend (with a rifle he was given as a Christmas present), or the 16-year-old who stabbed his father during a dispute over a case of beer. Most recently, bullying and cyberbullying have attracted media scrutiny. There is reason to be concerned about these activities and juvenile crime in general, although the behaviors may be less widespread than they appear to be based on media accounts. We will discuss cyberbullying in more detail in Chapter 15.

Juvenile crime is troubling, but it is not intractable. Since the mid-1990s, we have seen a decrease in crime committed by youths across most crime categories, including both property and violent crime,

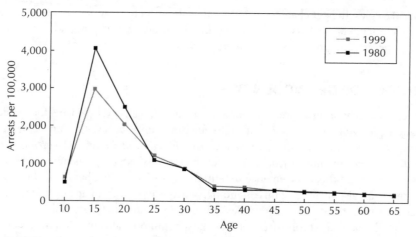

FIGURE 6-1 Property Crime Arrests per 100,000 *Source:* data from Snyder (2000), p. 7.

but there are periodic upward spikes. For example, from 1985 through 1997, the number of delinquency cases handled by juvenile courts climbed steadily by 61 percent (Sickmund, 2009). However, from 1997 through 2005, the number of cases handled dropped 9 percent (Sickmund, 2009). In addition, drug use has seen significant increases. Juveniles as a group are responsible for a small percentage of arrests compared with adults, although they are arrested disproportionately compared with other age groups. (See **Figures 6-1** and **6-2**.) Moreover, the typical juvenile is far more likely to be the victim than the perpetrator of a violent crime. Nevertheless, a significant number of juveniles do victimize one another, drug use persists, and the problem of youth violence has not disappeared. Thus, though we have made strides in understanding the factors leading to these behaviors and developing strategies for prevention and treatment, much work remains to be done.

In this chapter, we review the incidence, prevalence, and nature of delinquency and the developmental theories that have been proposed to explain it. We also discuss prevention and

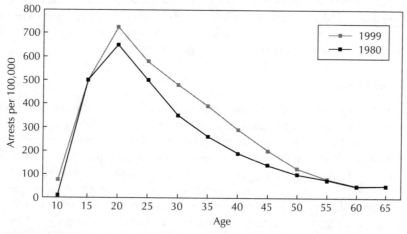

FIGURE 6-2 Violent Crime Arrests per 100,000 *Source:* data from Snyder (2000), p. 6.

treatment strategies. In later chapters, we give some attention to treatment issues relating to specific juvenile offenders, such as juveniles who kill, juveniles with psychopathic characteristics, juvenile fire setters, and juvenile sex offenders.

DEFINITIONS OF DELINQUENCY

"Juvenile delinquency" is an imprecise, nebulous, social, clinical, and legal label for a wide variety of law- and norm-violating behavior. At first glance, a simple legal definition seems to suffice: *Delinquency is behavior against the criminal code committed by an individual who has not reached adulthood, as defined by state or federal law.* But the term *delinquency* has numerous definitions and meanings beyond this one-sentence definition. As we noted in Chapter 1, the legal definition in some states also includes status offending, which is not behavior against the criminal code but is behavior prohibited only for juveniles. For example, running away, violating curfew laws, and truancy, all qualify as **status offenses**. The most common status offenses in recent years are incorrigibility, followed by running away (Sickmund, 2004). The status offense that has increased substantially in frequency in recent years is underage drinking.

Even age is not a simple issue in the definition of delinquency. Although no state considers anyone above 18 a delinquent, some have provisions for "youthful offenders," who are older, and some use 16 as the cutoff age. A minority of states give criminal courts, rather than juvenile courts, automatic jurisdiction over juveniles at age 16 or 17. Furthermore, all states allow juveniles—some as young as age seven—to be tried as adults in criminal courts under certain conditions and for certain offenses. Under federal law, juveniles may be prosecuted under the criminal law at age 15. Increasingly, however, more and more young offenders are moved to adult court in this manner. Under the legal definition of delinquency, the youths transferred to criminal courts are not delinquents.

Many states do not have a legally defined age of criminal responsibility, that is, minimum age of arrest for children (Snyder, Espiritu, Huizinga, Loeber, & Petechuk, 2003). The minimum age will also indicate at which point the child may be brought before a juvenile court for delinquency proceedings. When the minimum *is* specified, it varies from age six to age ten, depending on the state. Another interesting and rarely mentioned issue is that of the developmentally disabled individual. The shoplifter or exhibitionist with a mental age of 10 and a chronological age of 33 is not eligible for delinquency status, yet his mental abilities resemble those of children far more than those of adults. On the other hand, an eight-year-old "genius" with a mental age of 25 could presumably not be tried in criminal court simply because of his mental age, though he could be tried on the basis of the crime he was alleged to have committed.

Child Delinquents

At the turn of the twenty-first century, the term *child delinquent* came into vogue. **Child delinquents** are juveniles between ages 7 and 12, who have committed a delinquent act according to criminal law (Loeber, Farrington, & Petechuk, 2003). Child delinquents often attract the attention of the mass media and public officials, especially after some especially violent incident that involves a very young offender. During the past decade, the number of child delinquents handled by juvenile courts has increased 33 percent, generating some concern in criminal justice circles and society in general. Overall, children younger than age 13 make up about 9 percent of all juvenile arrests (Snyder, Espiritu, *et al.*, 2003). According to Loeber *et al.* (2003), child delinquents are two or three times more likely to become serious, violent, and chronic offenders than adolescents who begin offending in their teens.

Social Definitions of Delinquency

Social and psychological definitions of delinquency may overlap considerably, just as each overlaps with legal definitions. Social delinquency consists of a wide variety of youthful behaviors considered inappropriate, such as aggressive behavior, truancy, petty theft, vandalism, or drug abuse. The behavior may or may not have come to the attention of the police. It is not unusual for "social delinquents" to be referred to community social service agencies or to juvenile courts, but they never legally become delinquents until and unless they are found in a hearing to have committed the crime for which they are charged. For example, a juvenile court intake officer may place a juvenile on "informal probation," giving him a second chance to be supervised in the community rather than formally referred to juvenile court where he faces the possibility of being adjudicated delinquent. Other options for dealing with social delinquents are diversion programs, whereby juveniles are steered away from formal court proceedings if they admit their offenses and participate in various programs, such as substance abuse treatment, restitution, or community service.

Psychological Definitions

Psychological definitions of delinquency usually include conduct disorder and antisocial behavior. In other words, from a psychological perspective, a "delinquent" would have a conduct disorder or would display some form of serious antisocial behavior. **Conduct disorder**—as we discussed in Chapter 2—is a diagnostic term used to represent a group of behaviors characterized by *habitual* misbehavior, such as stealing, setting fires, running away from home, skipping school, destroying property, fighting, being cruel to animals and people, and frequently telling lies. Like the social delinquent, the psychological delinquent may or may not have been arrested for these behaviors. Some of the behaviors, in fact, are not even against the criminal law. The term *conduct disorder* is more fully described in the *American Psychiatric Association's Diagnostic and Statistical Manual* (1994, 4th ed.), and its slightly revised edition, the *DSM-IV-R* (2000).

As mentioned in Chapter 2, the *DSM* is undergoing still another revision, with the 5th edition due in May 2013. It is expected that classifications of conduct disorder will change significantly, along with criteria for assigning that diagnosis. The 4th edition separates conduct disorders into two categories, depending on the onset of the misbehaviors. If the misconduct began in childhood (before age 10), it is called *conduct disorder: childhood-onset type*. If the misconduct began in adolescence, it is called *conduct disorder: adolescent-onset type*. It is unclear whether these two divisions will remain in the new edition. By the time you read this textbook, you may be able to answer this question.

The clinical term **antisocial behavior** is usually reserved for more serious *habitual* misbehavior, especially a behavioral pattern that involves direct and harmful actions against others. It is to be distinguished, however, from the term *antisocial personality disorder,* a diagnostic label reserved primarily for *adults* who displayed conduct disorders as children or adolescents, and continue serious offending well into adulthood. We discuss antisocial personality disorders in more detail in Chapter 7.

THE NATURE AND EXTENT OF JUVENILE OFFENDING

Approximately 1.2–2.0 million juveniles under age 18 are arrested yearly by law enforcement officers in the United States. **Table 6-1** gives an overview of the Part I crimes for which they were taken into custody in 2010, the most recent data available. **Figure 6-3** provides an overview of percentage distribution of all crimes committed by juveniles.

TABLE 6-1	Estimated Juvenile Arrests for Part I Crimes, 2010		
Offense	Under Age 18	Under Age 15	Under Age 10
Total All Crimes	1,288,815	349,695	8,205
Murder	784	135	0
Forcible Rape	2,196	717	7
Robbery	21,110	3,936	36
Aggravated Assault	35,001	10,917	302
Burglary	51,298	14,019	498
Larceny-Theft	223,207	63,254	1,097
Motor Vehicle Theft	12,268	2,465	20
Arson	3,576	2,105	204

Source: Federal Bureau of Investigation (2011a).

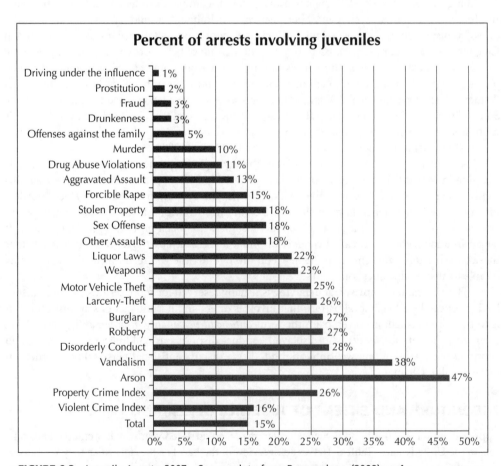

FIGURE 6-3   Juvenile Arrests, 2007   *Source:* data from Puzzanchera (2009), p. 4.

Other revealing figures are those related to delinquency cases in juvenile courts. Between 1960 and 2008, delinquency caseloads in these courts increased more than 300 percent, from 400,000 to over 1,600,000 (Puzzanchera, Adams, & Sickmund, 2011). Nonetheless, juvenile crimes declined over the past decade, and court caseloads decreased 12 percent from their peak in 1997 to 2008 (Puzzanchera *et al.*, 2011). On average, nearly two-thirds of the cases involve youths age 15 or younger at the time of referral. Trends (between 1985 and 2008) also indicate a decrease in property offending cases but an increase in offenses against person, drug offenses, and public order offenses. Juvenile courts also have seen an increase in female delinquency cases, up from 19 percent in 1985 to 27 percent in 2008. We will discuss gender issues in delinquency below.

The nature and extent of delinquent behavior—both what is reported and what is *unreported* to law enforcement agencies—are essentially an unknown area (Krisberg & Schwartz, 1983; Krisberg, 1995), even more so than adult crime. We simply do not have complete data on the national incidence of juvenile delinquency, broadly defined. We do have some statistics collected by law enforcement agencies (e.g., through the UCR system), the courts, and facilities for delinquents. The government regularly publishes reports on juvenile court statistics and on children in custody in both detention and treatment facilities. Nevertheless, as for adult crime, there is a huge dark figure. As Barry Krisberg (1992, p. 2) notes, "Put simply, the amount of crime committed by juveniles is unknown and perhaps unknowable."

Usually, unlawful acts committed by delinquents are placed into the following five major categories, which are defined in **Table 6-2**:

1. Unlawful acts against persons
2. Unlawful acts against property
3. Drug offenses
4. Offenses against the public order
5. Status offenses

The first four categories in the list are comparable in definition with crimes committed by adults and are discussed shortly. Before we turn to these criminal acts, it is important to focus briefly on the fifth category, the troubling issue of status offending.

TABLE 6-2   Categories of Juvenile Offending

Unlawful Acts	Definition
Unlawful acts against persons	Violent crimes, similar to those crimes committed by adults, such as aggravated assault, robbery, sexual assault
Unlawful acts against property	Property crimes, similar to those crimes committed by adults, such as burglary, larceny-theft, vandalism
Drug offenses	Possession, distribution, and/or manufacture of drugs
Public order offenses	Nuisance crimes against society, such as noise violations
Status offenses	Acts only juveniles can commit, such as violation of curfew, running away, school truancy

Status Offenses

Status offenses are acts that only juveniles can commit and that can be adjudicated only by a juvenile court. As mentioned earlier, typical status offenses range from misbehavior, such as violations of curfew, running away from home, and truancy, to offenses that are interpreted subjectively, such as unruliness, unmanageability, or incorrigibility. However, only four status offenses are tabulated by the National Center for Juvenile Justice (2003): running away, truancy, ungovernability (also known as incorrigibility or being beyond the control of one's parents or guardians), and underage liquor law violations (e.g., a minor in possession of alcohol, underage drinking). Although a number of other behaviors are often considered status offenses (e.g., curfew violations, tobacco offenses), they are usually not discussed in governmental reports.

The juvenile system has historically supported differential treatment of male and female status offenders. Adolescent girls, for example, have often been detained for incorrigibility or running away from home, when the same behavior in adolescent boys was ignored or tolerated. Until recently, about three times as many girls were detained for status offenses as boys (U.S. Department of Justice, 1988). In recent years, as a result of suits brought on behalf of juveniles, many courts have put authorities on notice that this discriminatory approach is unwarranted. Even so, relatively recent figures indicate that girls are still more likely than boys to be arrested as runaways (National Center for Juvenile Justice, 2003; Snyder, Sickmund, & Poe-Yamagata, 2000). Beginning in January 2011, the UCR program discontinued the collection of arrest data for the category of runaways, and the category will be excluded from all tables in the annual publication *Crime in the United States*. The National Incident Based Reporting System (NIBRS) will continue to report runaway data using the Group B Arrest Report (Code 90I).

It has been argued that, because status offenses lend themselves to so much subjectivity, they should be removed from the purview of all state juvenile courts (American Bar Association, 1979). Some states have clearly moved in this direction. On the other hand, while many states do not label status offenders "delinquents," they do allow their detention and/or supervision because they are presumed to be in need of protection either from their own rash behavior or the behavior of others. The statutes allowing this are usually referred to as PINS or CHINS laws (person or child in need of supervision). Under these laws, runaways or incorrigible youngsters are subject to juvenile or family court jurisdiction, sometimes at the instigation of their parents, even though they may not have committed an act comparable with a crime. These statutes also allow these specialized courts to address the needs of neglected and dependent children, so a child who has been labeled a "CHINS" has not necessarily displayed problem behaviors.

In this text, although status offending and minor delinquent crime are considered, our focus is on violent offending and more serious property offending. We are particularly interested in the developmental trajectories that lead to serious delinquency. In recent years, developmental psychologists have conducted extensive research on this topic, as we note shortly.

The Serious Delinquent

Both self-report studies and official data indicate that only a small percentage of the juvenile population engages in serious delinquent behavior, whether it is defined legally, socially, or psychologically. Nevertheless, those who do commit a variety of antisocial behaviors often escape detection. An early self-report study (Weis & Sederstrom, 1981) indicated that only about 3–15 percent of serious offenses ever result in "police contact." Likewise, Elliott, Dunford, and Huizinga (1987) suggest that serious, repetitive juvenile offenders escaped detection 86 percent of the time over a five-year period. These figures further suggest that the incidence of offending may be substantially underestimated by official arrest data. In other words, a small percentage of youth are committing a substantial amount of offenses that do not come to the attention of police. Research also suggests that this group of youths—when they do enter the justice system—tend to be high in recidivism, or repeat offending (Bartol & Bartol, 1998). In addition, frequent offenders do not specialize in any one particular kind of offending, such as theft or larceny. Instead, they tend to be involved in a wide variety of offenses, ranging from minor property crimes to highly violent ones. Longitudinal research also indicates that repetitive offenders as a group were unusually troublesome in school, earned poor grades, and had inadequate or poor social skills. Furthermore, these troublesome behaviors often began at an early age, and the more serious the offender, the earlier these childhood patterns appeared. Serious or habitual juvenile offenders rarely restrict their behaviors to one type of offense category.

A number of pessimistic conclusions about serious delinquents have been challenged as a result of an ongoing, longitudinal study of 1,354 predominately male, serious juvenile offenders for seven years after their conviction (Mulvey, 2011). The highly cited and continuing "Pathways to Delinquency" research sponsored by the Office of Juvenile Justice and Delinquency Prevention (OJJDP) indicates that most serious offenders reduce their offending over time, particularly when monitored in the community after short-term incarceration. As a general principle, long incarceration is ineffective at reducing recidivism among young offenders. The research, which followed youth in two metropolitan areas in Phoenix, Arizona, and Philadelphia County, Pennsylvania, also indicated that substance abuse treatment was effective in reducing both substance use and criminal offending. In the words of chief investigator Edward P. Mulvey, "The most important conclusion of the study is that even adolescents who have committed serious offenses are not necessarily on track for adult criminal careers" (2011, p. 3).

GENDER DIFFERENCES IN JUVENILE OFFENDING

As a general rule, boys far outnumber girls in most types of offending, but most particularly in violent offending. Victimization data, self-report data, and official data (both police records and court statistics) all support this gender gap. In addition, the reported ratios of males to females for most crimes remained basically the same for decades, apparently regardless of cultural or societal changes. In fact, males were so overrepresented in violent crimes (approximately a 9–1 ratio) that some theorists suggested that hormonal and biological factors, including the presence of testosterone in males, were the most logical explanation for these gender differences (Wilson & Herrnstein, 1985).

The most recent data on juvenile arrests suggest, however, that the gender gap may be closing for some offenses. Between 1996 and 2009, arrests of juvenile females generally increased more (or decreased less) than male arrests in most categories (Puzzanchera & Adams, 2011; Snyder, 2008; Zahn, Hawkins, Chiancone, & Whitworth, 2008). In 2009, girls accounted for 30 percent of the juvenile arrests (Puzzanchera & Adams, 2011). They accounted for 18 percent of arrests for juvenile violent crime, 38 percent of arrests for juvenile property crime, and 45 percent of juvenile larceny-theft arrests. Furthermore, as noted above, the proportion of female delinquency case heard in juvenile courts rose from 19 percent in 1985 to 27 percent in 2008 (Puzzanchera et al., 2011).

It is important to realize that we know far too little about girls' crime, the reasons it is committed, and the social and developmental factors that precipitate it (Broidy et al., 2003; Chesney-Lind & Shelden, 1998). Even contemporary studies based on large samples, such as the Pathways study referred to above, either do not include girls or study them in much smaller numbers. (The

Pathways study followed 1,170 males and 184 females.) Partly to rectify this imbalance, and partly in response to rising arrest rates of female juveniles in the 1990s, the Office of Juvenile Justice and Delinquency Prevention convened the *Girls Study Group* (GSG) in 2004. This is a comprehensive research project designed to gain a better understanding of girls' delinquency and recommend effective prevention programs directed specifically at girls, a population whose needs are too often overlooked. The GSG consists of an interdisciplinary group of scholars and practitioners from the fields of sociology, psychology, criminology, and gender studies as well as legal practitioners and girls' program development coordinators.

In addition to investigating the extent of delinquency, the GSG seeks to answer the following questions: Which girls become delinquent? What factors protect girls from delinquency? What factors put girls at risk of delinquency? What developmental pathways lead to girls' delinquency? What factors are most effective in preventing girls' delinquency?

One of the earliest studies from the group focused on whether violence is increasing among girls. The GSG (Zahn, Brumbaugh, *et al.*, 2008) found, based on arrest victimization and self-report data, that "although girls are arrested more for simple assault than previously, the actual incidence of being seriously violent has not changed much over the past two decades" (p. 15). The Group concluded that "there is no burgeoning national crisis of increasing serious violence among adolescent girls" (p. 15).

The Group surmised that the increases in arrests for girls *may* be attributed more to changes in enforcement policies than to changes in girls' behavior. For example, as a result of mandatory arrest policies in domestic violence, girls involved in family altercations may be more likely to be arrested than to be provided with mediation services (Zahn, Hawkins, *et al.*, 2008). Based on existing research literature, the GSG (Zahn, Brumbaugh, *et al.*, 2008, p. 15) further concluded that when girls' violence did occur, it was usually for the following reasons:

- **Peer violence**. Girls come to blows with peers to gain status, for self-defense against sexual harassment, to defend themselves against bullying, or to defend their sexual reputation.
- **Violence within schools**. Fighting by girls in school may represent anger against teachers or school administrators, or may reflect a general feeling of hopelessness. Furthermore, schools' zero-tolerance policies probably increases the number of arrests and referrals for fights involving girls (Zahn, Hawkins, *et al.*, 2008). Although these policies may increase the likelihood of arrests for both boys and girls, the effects seem to be stronger for girls.
- **Violence within disadvantaged neighborhoods**. Under these conditions, girls may become violent to protect themselves from being victimized.
- **Girls in gangs**. Girls join gangs for a variety of reasons. Violent behavior may be an expectation, or girls in gangs may fight for any of the reasons listed under peer violence.
- **Family violence**. It appears that girls fight more frequently at home with parents than do boys. Girls fight with parents for a variety of reasons. For some, it represents striking back against what they perceive as an overly controlling parental style; for others, it is defense or anger reaction to some form of abuse (emotional, physical, and/or sexual) by members in the household. It is important to note that some status offenses involving a domestic dispute between a girl and her parent or sibling—and which formerly might have been labeled "incorrigibility"—could now be classified as a simple assault and could result in an arrest (Zahn, Hawkins, *et al.*, 2008).

The Group also has studied the many intervention programs offered for girls by the juvenile justice system. Although there were positive findings, for the great majority of programs there was insufficient evidence to conclude that they were effective or ineffective. In addition, there were not enough resources available for conducting rigorous evaluations of these programs (Zahn, Hawkins, *et al.*, 2008). Additional material on the work of the GSG is available at http://girlsstudygroup.rti.org.

A Further Word on Status Offenses

As noted earlier in the chapter, girls traditionally have been taken into custody by police for status offending (particularly running away and curfew violations) more often than boys. It appears, also that when theft is involved, the value of the items stolen by girls is less than the value of those stolen by boys (Chesney-Lind & Shelden, 1998). The connection between juvenile running away and prostitution is a sobering one. Recent arrest figures indicate that the runaway figures are about equal for girls and boys (Puzzanchera, 2009; Snyder, 2008). Nevertheless, girls are believed to be far more likely than boys to run away because of victimization in the home and ultimately to take up prostitution to survive. In fact, a history of violent victimization, in or outside the home, seems to haunt both juvenile and adult female offenders (Acoca & Austin, 1996) and is apparent in much of the current literature on women's pathways to offending (Salisbury & Van Voorhis, 2009). According to one study (Acoca & Dedel, 1998), 92 percent of juvenile female offenders reported that they had been subjected to some form of emotional, physical, and/or sexual abuse. Twenty-five percent reported they had been shot or stabbed one or more times.

Research by developmental psychologists has shed considerable light on the gender difference in juvenile offending. There is growing recognition that biology is *not* a significant factor in explaining the gender differences in offending, including violent offending (Adams, 1992; Pepler & Slaby, 1994). Research by Eleanor Maccoby (1986), for example, indicates that girls and boys learn different types of prosocial behavior, with girls being more accommodating than boys. The current work of cognitive psychologists suggests that there may be socialized and cultural differences in the way boys and girls perceive their worlds. Social learning theorists have long held that girls are "socialized" differently from boys, or taught not to be aggressive. Anne Campbell (1993, p. 19) is representative of much of the current thinking when she notes that boys and girls are born with the potential to be equally aggressive, but girls are socialized not to be overtly aggressive, whereas boys are encouraged to be aggressive. The slight change in the ratio of violent offending, coupled with the overall decrease in juvenile violent crime discussed earlier in the chapter, suggests that the socialization of girls and boys is becoming more comparable. On the one hand, girls today are likely receiving the same aggression-supporting messages as boys (e.g., from media), and also have fewer restrictions on their behavior than they have had in the past. On the other hand, both genders are being encouraged to make good decisions and look for socially acceptable ways of channeling aggressive tendencies.

It remains to be seen whether the gender gap in offending will close even more, increase, or remain stable in the years ahead. In addition to psychosocial development, numerous societal factors affect the patterns of offending for both juveniles and adults. The GSG, discussed above, concluded that risk factors for delinquency are the same for boys and girls (Zahn, Hawkins, *et al.*, 2008). These include the economy, community disorganization, the actions of police, the quality of schools, the resources available to courts and to correctional agencies, and the adequacy of health and social services, to name but a few. In addition, however, girls may experience risk factors over and above those experienced by boys, such as a greater likelihood of sexual victimization and issues of self-esteem.

DEVELOPMENTAL THEORIES OF DELINQUENCY

It should be clear by now that a considerable amount of contemporary research has focused on understanding the *developmental processes* leading to aggression, antisocial behavior, and delinquency during the elementary school years and into adolescence. Contemporary research has consistently demonstrated that the offender population consists of various distinct subgroups, each following an identifiable developmental pathway that is associated with different risks and outcomes (Wiesner & Windle, 2004).

As we learned in Chapter 2, studying the developmental process of individuals requires an examination of the trajectory of that development. A trajectory in this sense refers to the developmental changes a person shows over his or her lifetime. Examining differences in developmental trajectories or pathways of individuals over time adds a deeper understanding of delinquency than focusing on differences among individuals at any one point in time. A developmental trajectory or pathway reflects the changes in an individual's cognitive, emotional, and social growth as he or she grows into adulthood. Included in the pathways are numerous experiences that may be encountered, such as early childhood victimization or the loss of a parent during preadolescence. However, protective factors—those that cushion the path—are also crucial to consider. In a recent study published by the GSG discussed above, researchers found that girls who reported having caring adults in their lives were less likely to report committing crimes, status offenses, and membership in gangs during adolescence (Hawkins, Graham, Williams, & Zahn, 2009). Theories that use developmental trajectories as models can identify a sequential chain of events that suggest how antisocial behavior is shaped and sustained (Kazdin, 1989).

Research has led to the striking consensus that children and adolescents follow different developmental pathways in their offending or nonoffending careers. Some children engage in stubborn, defiant, and disobedient behavior at very young ages, progressing to mild and then more severe forms of violence and criminal behavior during adolescence and young adulthood (Dahlberg & Potter, 2001). Some children exhibit cruelty to animals, aggressive behavior toward peers, bullying, and substance abuse at a very early age and continue this antisocial pathway far into adulthood. Other children show very few signs of antisocial behavior at very young ages, but during adolescence, they engage in various forms of delinquent behavior. Still others avoid engaging in any significant antisocial behavior over their lifetimes.

Despite these different developmental pathways, there is good evidence that most serious, persistent delinquency and crime patterns usually begin early and worsen with age, although as the Pathways study (Mulvey, 2011) indicates, we cannot assume that serious juvenile offenders will continue their criminal activity into adulthood. *Some* serious juvenile offenders will not continue into adulthood, but many will do so. Researchers have noted early childhood differences in impulsiveness, social skills, and feelings for others among those children who become seriously antisocial and those children who stay on a prosocial life course. Contemporary developmental psychologists have begun targeting the development of antisocial behavior even during the preschool years.

Moffitt's Developmental Theory

The major impetus for the developmental perspective as an explanation for delinquency has been the theory and ongoing research of psychologist Terrie Moffitt (1993a, 1993b, 2003, 2006) and her colleagues. Originally, Moffitt's developmental theory identified two developmental paths. On one path, the Moffitt group placed a small group of children who begin a lifelong pattern of delinquency and adult crime at a very early age, probably around age three or even younger.

Moffitt (1993a, p. 679) writes, "Across the life course, these individuals exhibit changing manifestations of antisocial behavior: biting and hitting at age four, shoplifting and truancy at age ten, selling drugs and stealing cars at age sixteen, robbery and rape at age twenty-two, and fraud and child abuse at age thirty." These individuals, whom Moffitt calls **life-course-persistent (LCP) offenders**, continue their antisocial ways across all kinds of conditions and situations. Moffitt reports that many of these LCP offenders exhibit neurological problems during their childhoods, such as difficult temperaments as infants, attention deficit/hyperactive disorder (ADHD) as children, and learning problems during their later school years. These early indicators of LCP offenders will be covered in the next chapter. Judgment and problem-solving deficiencies are often apparent when LCP children reach adulthood. LCP offenders generally commit a wide assortment of aggressive and violent crimes over their lifetimes.

LCPs as children miss opportunities to acquire and practice prosocial and interpersonal skills at each stage of development. This is partly because they are rejected and avoided by their childhood peers, and partly because their parents, teachers, and caretakers become frustrated and give up on them (Coie, Belding, & Underwood, 1988; Coie, Dodge, & Kupersmith, 1990; Moffitt, 1993a). According to Moffitt (1993a, p. 684), "If social and academic skills are not mastered in childhood, it is very difficult to later recover from lost opportunities." Furthermore, as noted previously, disadvantaged homes, inadequate schools, and violent neighborhoods are factors that are very likely to exacerbate the ongoing and developing antisocial behavioral pattern of LCPs.

LCPs are plagued by various psychological and antisocial problems throughout their lifetimes. To paraphrase Jaffee *et al.* (2005), early-onset antisocial behavior appears to be associated with pervasive mental (Moffitt, Caspi, Harrington, & Milne, 2002), physical (Farrington, 1995), economic (Caspi, Wright, Moffitt, & Silva, 1998), and interpersonal (Moffitt *et al.*, 2002) problems across the life span. Wiesner, Kim, and Capaldi (2005) write, "Developmental theories posit that antisocial behavior that onsets early in childhood is likely to lead to a cascade of secondary problems, including academic failure, involvement with deviant peers, substance abuse, depressive symptoms, health risk sexual behavior, and work failure" (p. 252). It appears as though LCPs become entrapped in a deviant lifestyle right out of the developmental gate. They are embedded in a social context that further increases their risk status (van Lier, Vuijk, & Crijen, 2005). Other researchers have consistently reported that a small minority of children (about 5–10%) follow a high antisocial developmental trajectory (Fontaine, Carbonneau, Vitaro, Barker, & Tremblay, 2009; van Lier *et al.*, 2005; van Lier, Wanner, & Vitaro, 2007). They are almost exclusively males. Recent research suggests that only about 1–2 percent of girls show this persistent, early-onset pattern (Fontaine *et al.*, 2009). In addition, the level of antisocial behavior of LCPs seems to diverge from their less antisocial counterparts across time (van Lier *et al.*, 2005). In other words, LCPs actually increase their offending as they grow older. The reasons for this may be due, at least in part, to their exposure to the learning, practicing, and reinforcement of antisocial behavior through the affiliation with similarly diverging antisocial peers. Basically, antisocial youth progressively affiliate with similarly antisocial peers (van Lier *et al.*, 2005).

The great majority of juvenile offenders are those individuals who follow a second developmental path: They begin offending during their adolescent years and generally stop offending somewhere around their eighteenth birthday. Moffitt labels these youths **adolescent-limited (AL) offenders**. Their developmental histories do not demonstrate the early and persistent antisocial problems that members of the LCP group manifest. However—and this point is important—the frequency, and in some cases, the violence level of offending during the teen years, may be as high as that of the LCP youth. In effect, the teenage offending patterns of the AL and that of the LCP may be highly similar during the adolescent years (Moffitt, Caspi, Dickson,

Silva, & Stanton, 1996). "The two types cannot be discriminated on most indicators of antisocial and problem behavior in adolescence; boys on the LCP and AL paths are similar on parent-, self-, and official records of offending, peer delinquency, substance abuse, unsafe sex, and dangerous driving" (Moffitt *et al.*, 1996, p. 400). Accordingly, mental health workers and criminal justice experts could not easily identify the group classification (AL or LCP) simply by examining juvenile arrest records, self-reports, or the information provided by parents during the teen years.

Nevertheless, the AL delinquent is most likely, during the teen years, to be involved in offenses that symbolize adult privilege and demonstrate autonomy from parental control. Examples include vandalism, drug and alcohol offenses, theft, and "status" offenses such as running away or truancy. In addition, AL delinquents are likely to engage in crimes that are profitable or rewarding, but they also have the ability to abandon these actions when prosocial styles become more rewarding. For example, the onset of young adulthood brings on opportunities not attainable during the teen years, such as leaving high school for college, obtaining a full-time job, and entering a relationship with a prosocial person. AL delinquents are quick to learn that they have something to lose if they continue offending into adulthood. During childhood, in contrast to the LCP child, the AL youngster has learned to get along with others. It should also be emphasized that "the theory of AL antisocial behavior regards it as an adaptation response to modern teens' social context, not the product of a cumulative history of pathological maldevelopment" (Moffitt & Caspi, 2001, p. 370). They normally have a satisfactory repertoire of academic, social, and interpersonal skills that enable them to "get ahead." Therefore, the developmental histories and personal dispositions of the AL youth allow him or her the option of exploring new life pathways, an opportunity not usually afforded the LCP youth. In short, Moffitt's theory hypothesizes that most young persons who become adolescence-limited delinquents are able to desist from crime when they age into maturity, turning gradually to a more conventional lifestyle (Moffitt & Caspi, 2001).

Interestingly, in a follow-up study, Moffitt *et al.* (2002) discovered that many ALs, at age 26, were still in trouble. "Although AL men fared better overall than LCP men, they fared poorly relative to the 'unclassified' men, who represented males with no remarkable delinquency history" (Moffitt *et al.*, 2002, p. 199). The researchers found that AL men accounted for twice their share of the property and drug convictions during adulthood, compared with men without a delinquency history. It seemed as though some AL men relied on crime to supplement their incomes. The researchers further state that "the very name 'adolescence-limited' reveals that this much offending by AL men at age 26 was not anticipated by our theory" (p. 200). The researchers, in an effort to explain the discrepancy, speculated that perhaps adulthood in contemporary society may begin after 25 years of age. Therefore, this new developmental stage, called "emerging adulthood," prolongs the crime-promoting conditions of adolescence. "This stage is characterized by roleless floundering, in which young people neither perceive themselves to be adults, nor choose to occupy any adult roles historically favored by people in their twenties (e.g., parenthood, marriage)" (Moffitt *et al.*, 2002, p. 200). This would suggest that they too will cease offending just as did their AL counterparts who did not continue. On the other hand, Moffit *et al.'s* (2002) finding has prompted some researchers to hypothesize that there may be still another classification needed to account for the persistent offending found in adults. That is, some persistent offenders begin their antisocial ways during their adolescent years rather than their childhood years. This pattern appears to be especially the case for female offenders (Fontaine *et al.*, 2009). Emerging research now refers to early-onset and adolescent-onset persistent offending. However, it is also important to consider AL offenders who offend into adulthood but stop earlier than the LCP. Thus, we would have four categories of frequent offending: (a) the AL offender, (b) the AL who continues into early adulthood but then stops, (c) the early-onset LCP, and (d) the late-onset LCP. **Table 6-3** summarizes the major differences between LCP and AL offenders.

TABLE 6-3	Comparisons between LCPs and ALs	
	Life-Course-Persistent (LCP)	**Adolescent Limited (AL)**
Crime or antisocial behavior begins...	early (perhaps as early as age three)	later (usually during the early adolescent years)
Criminal behavior...	continues throughout the offender's life	usually stops after reaching early adulthood
Types of criminal behaviors...	assortment	assortment
Developmental backgrounds...	often show neurological problems, ADHD, conduct problems	usually normal and without neurological problems
Academic skills...	usually below average	usually average to above average
Interpersonal and social skills...	usually below average	usually average to above average

GENDER DIFFERENCES As mentioned earlier in this section, Moffitt's theory has been developed primarily on the developmental trajectories of males. It was also mentioned that females demonstrate similar patterns. Moffitt and Caspi (2001) report evidence that the developmental typology fits both genders. However, the LCP pattern of behavior is far more likely to be followed by males than females (approximately 10 males to 1 female), whereas the gender difference is negligible for the AL pattern (approximately 1.5 males to 1 female). These findings are consistent with other studies (Kratzer & Hodgins, 1999; Mazerolle, Brame, Paternoster, Piquero, & Dean, 2000). In other words, the vast majority of female delinquents *appear* to fit the AL pattern. On the other hand, in a study of 820 girls, Côté, Zoccolillo, Tremblay, Nagin, and Vitaro (2001) found that only 1.4 percent of the girls followed the LCP profile. Other researchers have found approximately the same percentage of early-onset, persistent offenders among females (Fontaine *et al.*, 2009).

According to Moffitt (2003), an ongoing association with delinquent peers appears to be an important factor in the onset of delinquency among adolescent girls. An intimate relationship with a male delinquent is also closely connected to delinquency in adolescent girls (Moffitt, Caspi, Rutter, & Silva, 2001).

Although many studies have indicated that only a small percentage of girls become early-onset persistent offenders, a few studies suggest that girls may be more vulnerable to early onset of serious antisocial behavior than previously thought. Brennan, Hall, Bor, Najman, and Williams (2003) found that girls in their sample displayed the same pattern as boys. In the Brennan *et al.* study, 9 percent of the boys and 7.4 percent of the girls in the high-risk sample were classified as displaying *early-onset* persistent aggressive behavior. However, Silverthorn and Frick (1999) maintain that girls tend to engage in serious antisocial behavior for the first time at later ages—and generally in adolescence—than boys. According to Silverthorn and Frick, antisocial behavior in girls is delayed because of such factors as parental and school-based socialization practices that encourage them to restrict their outward aggressive tendencies during middle childhood. Nevertheless, McCabe, Rodgers, Yeh, and Hough (2004) offer some evidence that a high percentage of antisocial girls began their antisocial behavior before the age of 10. Similar results were reported by Leve and Chamberlain (2004), who found that 23 percent of serious antisocial girls were arrested before age 11, and 71 percent before age 14. These results suggest that per-haps a larger portion of girls can be considered early-onset delinquents than previously believed, and that they may well follow the same developmental trajectory as early-onset boys. These researchers identified parental transitions (separation, divorce, death, incarceration) and biologi-cal parental criminality as the strongest predictors of early-onset offending in girls.

Studies further suggest that girls and women who follow an early and persistent trajectory of antisocial behavior exhibit these behaviors throughout the life span and tend to manifest a variety of maladjustment problems in adulthood (Fontaine, 2008; Fontaine *et al.*, 2009; Odgers *et al.*, 2008). Interestingly, there is some evidence to indicate that even girls who begin offending during adolescence may have a life of difficulty. Odgers and her colleagues (2008) report that—although adolescent-onset female offenders do not experience the same degree of problems as the LCP female offenders—they still were at risk of poor outcomes, especially financial, physical health, and mental health difficulties. In sum, persistent antisocial behavior, whether it begins in childhood or adolescence, is often a precursor of other problems well into adulthood.

Gorman-Smith and Loeber (2005) report, based on extensive data from the National Youth Survey, that girls tend to follow the same developmental pathways toward antisocial behavior and delinquency as boys. Although fewer girls engage in antisocial or delinquent behavior compared with boys, those that do show similar pathways. In other words, serious antisocial and delinquent involvement in girls showed early-onset antisocial patterns similar to boys. However, Gorman-Smith and Loeber did learn that the risk factors for girls may be somewhat different from those for boys. For example, because girls are more invested in interpersonal relationships than boys, they are more likely to get involved in or be affected by parental conflict and transitions, a find-ing similar to that reported in the Leve and Chamberlain (2004) study. Peer influences may also be different for boys and girls. Girls may be more likely to be pulled into delinquency through involvement in intimate relationships with delinquent men rather than through involvement with delinquent gangs. Therefore, while the developmental pathways may be similar, the fam-ily and peer risk factors may be different for boys and girls. Because research so often identifies unique risk factors, it has been argued that the pathways themselves are unique and that girls' and women's pathways to crime should be studied and considered separately from those of boys and men (Salisbury & Van Voorhis, 2009). In fact, Fontaine and colleagues (2009) write, "…the review of the literature suggests that the development of antisocial behavior in females may be more heterogeneous and complex than some theoretical models have suggested" (p. 376).

Coercion Developmental Theory

Similar to Moffitt's theory, Gerald Patterson (1982, 1986; Patterson, Forgatch, & DeGarmo, 2010) also believes that early starters are at greater risk of more serious criminal offending. However, the major difference is that Patterson places a greater emphasis on the role of parenting rather than focusing on the specific characteristics of the child. The coercion developmental theory contends that poor parental monitoring of child activities, disruptive family transitions (e.g., divorce), and inconsistent parental discipline are major psychosocial contributors to early-onset delinquency (Brennan *et al.*, 2003; Patterson, 1982). The theory argues that the key predictor of early-onset offending is the family environment in which the child learns to use coercive behaviors, such as temper tantrums and whining, to escape parental discipline and authority. In line with his theory, Patterson and his colleagues conduct ongoing research and family treatment programs to reduce the amount of coercion exercised by parents (Patterson *et al.*, 2010).

Coercion theory acknowledges that some children are more likely than other children to elicit inept parenting strategies. For example, a child with an irritable temperament who is constantly whining is more likely to provoke coercive parenting than a pleasant, constantly smiling child. In the coercive cycle, the parent and child each behave in a way that is annoying to the other in an attempt to control the other's behavior. As the child's behaviors increase in intensity and frequency, the parent eventually acquiesces, unwittingly reinforcing the behavior. As the child becomes increasingly irritating, the parent further escalates power-assertion techniques and, presumably, the level of hostility displayed toward the child.

Coercion becomes the child's primary interpersonal strategy, and this generalizes to environments outside the home. According to coercion theory, antisocial behavior is seen as progressing from faulty parent–toddler interactions to similar interactions with teachers, peers, and others in the child's environment. The coercion developmental model is largely based on social learning theory. According to the theory, "Developmental trajectories for antisocial behavior are initiated, maintained, and diversified as a result of cumulative daily social experiences with parents, siblings, and peers that are highly aversive, inconsistent, and unsupportive" (Snyder, Reid, *et al.*, 2003, p. 31).

DEVELOPMENTAL TRAJECTORIES The theory identifies two developmental trajectories or pathways toward antisocial behavior, each characterized by an orderly sequence of stages (Patterson & Yoerger, 2002). "One trajectory leads to early arrest (prior to age 14) and adult crime and the other to late-onset arrests and desistance from adult crime" (Patterson & Yoerger, 2002, p. 147). However, the theory takes the position that both the early- and late-start trajectories represent variations of the same basic processes. That is, social-environmental influences, such as divorce, poverty, and parental depression, work in combination with inept parenting and deviant peer socialization to produce two different levels of delinquent and antisocial behavior. There are three variables that separate early- from late-onset trajectories: (1) the early-onset process begins during the preschool years, whereas the late onset begins in midadolescence, (2) the inept parenting is more severe for the early onset compared with the late onset, and (3) the levels of social incompetence are more pronounced for the early as compared with the late-onset delinquency. The inept parenting is often characterized by parents who use ineffective discipline practices, such as physical punishment, and who themselves tend to display antisocial behavior and be plagued by frequent marital transitions and discord.

Because of these differences, early-onset delinquents tend to demonstrate limited levels of social skills, more disruptive peer relations, and lower self-esteem. The late-onset delinquents exhibit similar deficiencies, but not to the degree of early onsets. Basically, late-onset delinquents are less antisocial than the early-onset delinquents but more antisocial than nondelinquents. Research finds that the likelihood of arrest as a young adult for early onsets is high, whereas that for late onsets is relatively low (Patterson & Yoerger, 2002). For example, the majority (71%) of late-onset boys desisted before becoming involved in adult crime (Patterson & Yoerger, 2002), while 74 percent of early-onset offenders are arrested by the time they become young adults (age 21–29) (Stattin & Magnusson, 1991).

GENDER DIFFERENCES According to the coercive development perspective, gender differences in aggression are well in place by age five and persist throughout childhood and adolescence (Snyder, Reid, *et al.*, 2003). These early differences are largely in favor of aggressiveness in boys. The coercive perspective further posits that gender differences in antisocial behavior are the result of the different environmental experiences and reinforcements encountered by boys and girls. Boys and girls evoke different responses from parents, and each gender responds differently to the same parenting conditions. Parents tend to be more coercive toward boys compared with girls, and this difference appears to be more pronounced for highly aggressive boys and girls (Snyder, Reid, *et al.*, 2003). The coercive development model hypothesizes, therefore, that girls display less antisocial behavior because they are less frequently involved in coercive parent–child interactions.

Peer socialization factors begin to play a significant role as the child moves into preschool and kindergarten. Boys and girls demonstrate a strong preference for interaction with same-gender children beginning at age three. Boys tend to ignore girls who try to enter their play groups, even though an individual boy will play with one or two girls. There are more challenges, noncompliance, and rough-and-tumble play among boys, whereas there tends to be more cooperation, verbal exchange, compliance, and mutual accommodation among girls. Unlike for boys, for girls there are fewer highly antisocial, same-gender peers to model or with whom they can associate and exchange deviant talk. Consequently, when girls do begin to show antisocial behavior, it most often occurs during the adolescent years, and appears to be somewhat tied to pubescence. During adolescence, the preference for same-gender peers diminishes and a broad array of peer affiliates becomes available, including antisocial ones.

Callous-Unemotional Trait Theory

Do some people, including children, possess personality traits that render them particularly susceptible to antisocial behavior? Some researchers seem to think so. Among the most carefully studied is a group of traits collectively referred to as **callous-unemotional (CU)**, identified by Paul Frick and his colleagues (Barry *et al.*, 2000; Frick, Barry, & Bodin, 2000). These researchers conducted a series of research projects to determine if they could detect childhood precursors to adult psychopathy (discussed in more detail in Chapter 7). They were able to identify a group of children who were diagnosed with conduct disorders but who demonstrated particularly severe and chronic patterns of antisocial behavior beyond what is normally seen in other children with conduct disorders. After a series of studies, they found that a subgroup of children and adolescents showed a lack of empathetic concern for others, limited capacity for guilt, and a poverty of emotional expression (Frick, Bodin, & Barry, 2000; Frick, O'Brien, Wootton, & McBurnett, 1994). These traits are highly characteristic of behavioral patterns typically found in adult psychopaths.

A considerable body of contemporary research continues to support the validity and reliability of the CU trait cluster. Contemporary research has found, for example, that children with CU traits are not afraid of being punished for their aggressive actions and view aggression as an effective means for dominating others (Pardini & Byrd, 2012). The CU children in the study tended to minimize the extent to which aggression caused victim suffering, and they openly acknowledged caring little about distress and suffering in others. The title of their research publication captures Pardini and Byrd's findings well: "I'll show you who's boss, even if you suffer and I get into trouble." Additional recent research has found that CU traits in childhood and adolescence are strongly predictive of psychopathy in adulthood (Kahn, Frick, Youngstrom, Findling, & Youngstrom, 2012). Furthermore, CU traits are predictive of severe aggressive patterns of behavior for both boys and girls, and for children as young as ages 3 and 4 (Kahn *et al.*, 2012). Perhaps more disturbing, the level of severity of the aggressive behavior found in CU children and adolescents is considerably beyond that typically found for most juvenile offenders. Essentially, CU traits in childhood are predictive of lifelong serious, violent offending.

As noted above, one of the proposed revisions of the *DSM* involves re-classifications and criteria for a diagnosis of conduct disorders. Among the proposals is that the classification "with significant callous unemotional traits" be added (Kahn *et al.*, 2012) as one subtype of CD. To meet this criterion, a child or adolescent would have to exhibit two of the following traits over at least a 12-month period: "lack of remorse or guilt, callous-lack of empathy, unconcerned about performance at school or work, and shallow or deficient affect" (Kahn *et al.*, 2012, p. 272). Critics of this change have argued that, although the research on CU traits is fascinating, it has not developed sufficiently to warrant such a major change in CD criteria (Moffitt *et al.*, 2008).

The number of children and adolescents with high CU traits has been estimated to be between 13 percent and 36 percent in incarcerated antisocial juveniles, to a range of 10 percent and 32 percent in a community sample of children diagnosed with conduct disorder (Kahn *et al.*, 2012). In a mental health clinic sample, who were referred because of troubling problems, between 21 percent and 50 percent of children and adolescents with conduct disorder exhibited CU traits (Kahn *et al.*, 2012). It should be emphasized that a diagnosis of conduct disorder is not a necessary condition for possessing CU traits. More specifically, some children and adolescents referred to the mental health clinic in the Kahn *et al.* study exhibited a high level of CU traits, but did not have the diagnosis of conduct disorder. Interestingly, cruelty to animals was one of the indicators designating CU traits in the Kahn *et al.* investigation.

A growing body of research *suggests* that significant and sustained reductions in CU traits in children and adolescents can be accomplished through sophisticated, multimodal cognitive-behavioral treatment approaches (Kolko & Pardini, 2010; Salekin, 2010). This approach, combined with parental factors such as increased warmth and low levels of harsh discipline, appears to date to offer the most promising results over time (Pardini, Lochman, & Powell, 2007; Kolko & Pardini, 2010).

We will return to the discussion of CU traits in Chapter 7, because they are highly similar to the core behavioral patterns of psychopathy. They will be particularly pertinent to material on juvenile psychopathy.

Other Developmental Theories

Other researchers using a developmental perspective have identified more than the early- and late-onset trajectories discussed above. For example, Loeber and Stouthamer-Loeber (1998) and Chung, Hill, Hawkins, Gilchrist, and Nagin (2002) were able to identify five developmental pathways. Nagin and Land (1993), Côté *et al.* (2001), and Shaw, Gilliom, Ingoldsby, and Nagin (2003) have all found four trajectories that lead to antisocial, delinquent, or criminal behavior. Wiesner and Windle (2004) suggest there may be as many as six different developmental pathways to delinquency and crime. Regardless of the number of paths, a distinguishing feature of all developmental models is that the age of onset of the serious antisocial behavior is crucial, as is the severity and persistence of the offending as the child grows into adolescence or young adulthood. Still to be established are the risk and protective factors that may distinguish the pathways and whether these differ according to gender.

PREVENTION, INTERVENTION, AND TREATMENT OF JUVENILE OFFENDING

Treatment and Rehabilitation Strategies

Each year, more than 2 million youth come into contact with the juvenile justice system (Kinscherff, 2012). By some accounts, a substantial number of these youths (65% to 70%) have at least one diagnosable mental health need, and 20–25 percent have serious emotional problems (Kinscherff, 2012; Langton, 2012). One well-cited study (Shufelt & Cocozza, 2006) estimates that 55 percent of males and females involved in the juvenile justice system probably could receive at least two co-occurring mental health diagnoses. In addition, disruptive behavior disorders are diagnosed in approximately 45 percent of the males and just over half (51%) of the females who are involved in the juvenile justice system (Kinscherff, 2012). Substance abuse disorders are also common, occurring in at least half of the youth involved in the system. Research in general has consistently linked substance abuse with serious juvenile offending (Mulvey, Schubert, & Chassin, 2010).

Substance abuse may or may not co-occur with mental health needs, however. Furthermore, it is important to stress that many youth who come into contact with the juvenile justice system do not merit a mental health diagnosis; our main concern in this text is those who do. In addition, we cannot ignore youths who are *at risk* of mental health needs, based on the many risk factors discussed in previous chapters. For example, peer rejection, inadequate parenting, physical abuse, toxic environments, and school failure can lead to serious depression along with antisocial behavior.

The number of prevention, intervention, and treatment programs that have been tried with juvenile offenders and children at risk or already involved in the juvenile justice system is overwhelming. Unfortunately, few programs designed to reduce delinquent or predelinquent behavior have been effective or shown lasting effects (Tarolla, Wagner, Rabinowitz, & Tubman, 2002; Zigler, Taussig, & Black, 1992). Many have never been evaluated scientifically, based on sound research principles. As the Girls Study Group remarked, there are simply not enough resources available to conduct rigorous program evaluations (Zahn, Hawkins, *et al.*, 2008).

Serious forms of antisocial behavior in school-age children and adolescents have been particularly resistant to change (Borduin *et al.*, 1995; Shaw *et al.*, 2003). Serious juvenile offenders are especially prone to have low motivation for altering their antisocial behaviors and to display a lack of trust, noncompliance, and high levels of anger and impulsiveness (Tarolla *et al.*, 2002). Although programs aimed at their conduct are many, most do not have significant positive effects because they begin too late in the developmental sequence. "By the time children reach these programs, often after referral by court personnel, they are already entrenched in a long history of antisocial interaction with parents, schools, and community that is not easily reversed" (Zigler *et al.*, 1992, p. 997). It is no wonder, then, that the most highly touted programs are those that focus on early intervention, particularly within the context of the family environment (Biglan *et al.*, 2012).

Although the above conclusions are discouraging, it is noteworthy that positive changes have been occurring. Some programs are emerging as highly successful in eliminating antisocial behavior and reducing delinquent behavior, even in children with serious behavior problems and even in institutionalized delinquents. Others show considerable promise. Before discussing those programs, though, we identify what exactly is meant by a successful program.

CHARACTERISTICS OF SUCCESSFUL PROGRAMS

Effective prevention and treatment programs for serious juvenile offenders share common features. In some cases, programs do not necessarily have to target serious offenders; they may be of benefit to all children. For example, Zigler *et al.* (1992) concluded in their review that delinquency can be prevented by *early* childhood intervention programs that promote competence (social, interpersonal, and academic) in children across multiple systems in which they are embedded (family, school, peers, and community). These programs can be made available to children in various community settings, such as schools or child-care facilities. By contrast, crisis-oriented programs emphasizing counseling or social casework chiefly to deal with a presenting problem have been ineffective, largely because they focus on a single setting or competency and often are applied too late. Successful and promising prevention and treatment programs have the following characteristics.

They Begin Early

Seriously antisocial children often can be identified when they are as young as four or five years old on the basis of their aggressive, disruptive, and noncompliant behaviors across home and preschool or school settings. As we learned earlier in the chapter, Terrie Moffitt (1993a; Moffitt *et al.*, 1996) provides convincing evidence that the life-course-persistent delinquent manifests discernible indicators of antisocial behavior as early as age three. Consequently, some researchers (e.g., Guerra, Huesmann, Tolan, Van Acker, & Eron, 1995) recommend that prevention preferably begin no later in life than the first grade and definitely before age eight. Because seriously antisocial children are likely to progress in a spiral of escalating and more severe antisocial and violent behaviors over time, early intervention is critical if it is to be effec-tive (Conduct Problems Prevention Research Group, 2004). In addition, there appears to be a mysterious jump in antisocial behavior between the first and second grade for many children, and, therefore, prevention programs enacted later than the first grade will probably need to be more intensive. Guerra *et al.* (1995) have observed that aggressive and antisocial behav-ior begin to develop even earlier in children living in the most economically deprived urban neighborhoods, an observation that appears to hold for both boys and girls (Tolan & Thomas, 1995). In addition, as we learned earlier in the book, there is considerable evidence to suggest that the earlier the signs of antisocial behavior, the more serious or violent the antisocial or criminal behavior will be in later life (Tolan & Thomas, 1995).

Early antisocial indicators often forecast a life of crime. As noted by Rolf Loeber (1990, p. 6), "there is considerable continuity among disruptive and antisocial behavior over time, even though they may manifest themselves differently at different ages." Loeber further finds that as children and adolescents progress toward more serious delinquent behavior, they tend to move toward diversification, rather than moving from one specific deviant behavior to another. Thus, it is clear that without early intervention, many children who are at risk of delinquency are more likely to engage in increasing levels of serious, chronic offending as they grow older, while still exhibiting less serious problems. That is, the adolescent who participates in a gang beating or a drive-by shooting will still use drugs and steal electronic equipment.

They Follow Developmental Principles

Prevention programs that are effective are soundly based on child developmental principles obtained from well-designed research (Dodge, 2001). As we noted earlier in the chapter, differ-ent developmental pathways can lead to serious violence and delinquency, and the age of onset of these behaviors can vary considerably. In designing programs to prevent violence and chronic antisocial behavior, it is critical to understand the factors that place youths on a developmental trajectory of serious delinquency. Further, it is equally important to understand how these fac-tors interact with the social environment. As persons move through life, they enter and exit a series of developmental stages (Dahlberg & Potter, 2001). Interestingly, data from the Rochester Youth Study (Thornberry, Huizinga, & Loeber, 1995) indicate that protective factors must be con-stantly present at transition from early to late adolescence and not simply in place at a single point in childhood or adolescence (Conduct Problems Prevention Research Group, 2004). "Although the negative impact of early risk factors may be buffered by the provision of protective support services during the grade school years, the risk factors themselves may continue to influence developmental trajectories during adolescence" (Conduct Problems Prevention Research Group, 2004, p. 193). This point is especially relevant when the child or adolescent continues to live in a dangerous social, physical, and emotional environment.

In an extensive review, Tremblay, LeMarquand, and Vitaro (1999) examined 50 prevention programs and discovered that 20 of them had been evaluated under carefully designed test conditions. Those programs that were most effective were based on sound child developmental research (Dodge, 2001). Linking the appropriate prevention program with the developmental stage of the youth is paramount for significant, long-term success in delinquency prevention.

They Focus on Multiple Settings and Systems

Successful intervention programs must not only begin as early as possible, but also must be skillfully directed at as many causes and negative influences as possible. Targeting multiple potential risk or protective factors rather than one or two in isolation greatly increases the likelihood of positive adjustment and the significant reduction of antisocial and violent behavior (Tedeschi & Kilmer, 2005). Programs that have shown long-term success have utilized multipronged approaches concentrating on treating children through their broad social environment, including improving relationships with family and peers and helping them to develop better academic skills for school success (Biglan *et al.*, 2012). In addition, effective intervention programs include prenatal and perinatal medical care and intensive health education for pregnant women and mothers with young children (Coordinating Council on Juvenile Justice and Delinquency Prevention, 1996). These services reduce the delinquency risk factors of head and neurological injuries, exposure to toxins, maternal substance abuse, nutritional deficiencies, and perinatal difficulties. For example, research (Dietrich, Ris, Succop, Berger, & Bornschein, 2001; Needleman, McFarland, Ness, Fienberg, & Tobin, 2002) has discovered a strong relationship between high levels of lead in the bones of children and violence and delinquency in adolescence. Recall that in Chapter 2, we emphasized the significance of environmental contamination for healthy brain development.

There is little doubt that living conditions in poorest inner-city neighborhoods are extremely harsh and that—for many children—the daily onslaught of violence, substance abuse, child abuse, and hopelessness is highly disruptive to normal development, even if they experience these conditions only indirectly. For the child who is directly exposed to an adverse family life and inadequate living arrangements with little opportunity to develop even the rudiments of social, interpersonal, and academic skills for dealing effectively with his or her environment, the damage may be almost irreparable. Clearly, the longer a child is exposed to an adverse environment, the more difficult it will be to modify his or her life course away from crime and delinquency.

They Acknowledge and Respect Cultural Backgrounds

Although some urban neighborhoods contain numerous risk factors, these same neighborhoods also may be rich in values and traditions that, if acknowledged, would qualify as crucial protective factors. For example, various ethnic and racial groups place great value on the extended family, a particular style of music, or certain holiday traditions and celebrations. Even ways of communicating often vary among groups; some stress the importance of eye contact, for example, while others consider it disrespectful. These cultural markers can affect the development of antisocial behavior, sometimes promoting it but often suppressing it. Effective programs, then, are sensitive to a family's cultural background and heritage and they promote its positive aspects.

Even poverty may affect individuals differently on the basis of their ethnicity and the *meaning* of poverty within a given cultural context (Guerra *et al.*, 1995). For example, whereas one group may regard being poor as matter of fact and to be expected—albeit something to be overcome—another group may view it as a sign of oppression by another dominant group in a society. In some cultural groups, stealing brings shame upon one's family; in others, stealing may be the norm, as long as the target of the theft is limited to those outside the group. This is not to suggest that individual members of these groups will necessarily act in accordance with the group's values and expectations, however. Effective treatment providers are constantly aware of the cultural background of the juveniles they deal with, as well as the caveat that they cannot assume that the culture will inevitably determine or regulate the juveniles' behavior.

They Focus on the Family First

Research has continually shown that the most successful interventions concentrate first on improving parenting and the family system in general, followed by improving peer relations and academic skills. It is clear that certain family relationships and parenting practices strongly promote serious and violent delinquency, while other practices and relationship discourage it (Patterson, Forgatch, & DeGarmo, 2010). Some family characteristics seem to be linked to delinquency regardless of ethnic or socioeconomic status (Gorman-Smith, Tolan, Huesmann, & Zelli, 1996). The family characteristics most closely connected to serious delinquency are poor parental monitoring and supervision of the child's activities, poor and inconsistent discipline, and a lack of family closeness or cohesion.

Recall that in Chapter 2 we discussed risk factors for antisocial behavior, including many associated with the family. In that chapter we emphasized, as well, that contemporary researchers are focusing on the treatment approaches that will foster nurturing, healthy family environments (Biglan *et al.*, 2012). (See **Box 6-1**, describing a promising approach to address family risk factors.) According to Dishion and Andrews (1995), studies have consistently revealed that negative, coercive exchanges between parents and children are predictive of child antisocial behavior (e.g., Patterson, 1986), delinquent behavior (e.g., Bank & Patterson, 1992), and adolescent substance abuse (e.g., Dishion & Loeber, 1985). Research also indicates that emotional closeness and family cohesion, where the child receives emotional support, adequate communication, and love, are essential in the prevention of antisocial behavior and delinquency (Gorman-Smith *et al.*, 1996).

Peer systems are critically important, and research has shown that negative peer associations are significant predictors of both substance abuse and delinquency (O'Donnell, Hawkins, & Abbott, 1995). Thus far, though, intervention programs have been *unsuccessful* in utilizing peer

---

BOX 6-1
Working with Families and Schools: The LIFT Project

Throughout the chapter we have cited the research of Gerald Patterson and his colleagues at the Oregon Social Learning Center (OSLC). The Patterson group has not only conducted a series of longitudinal studies, but also offer direct services, including therapy, to children and families who may be at risk of future offending.

An interesting project undertaken by the group focuses on prevention efforts during the elementary school years (Reid & Eddy, 2002). Called Linking the Interests of Families and Children (LIFT), the project is an example of primary or universal prevention, discussed in this chapter. LIFT operates under the assumption that *all* children can benefit from intervention early in their school years. Developing positive interactions among children and their social environments—peers, teachers, caregivers—is crucial. As Reid and Eddy comment, "The most convenient way to access a child's universe of teacher and peer relationships is to work directly in the school and home settings with all children" (p. 223).

(continued)

LIFT is an extension of the Oregon Youth Study (OYS), pioneered by the Patterson group. The study was conducted in public schools in neighborhoods with higher than average delinquency rates. The LIFT project targeted all children in first and fifth grades. Both home intervention and school intervention were used, and collaboration between these settings was emphasized.

In the home intervention component, groups of parents met weekly for six weeks in the school setting. Times were varied, and free child care was offered to encourage maximum participation. Parents and caregivers participated in role play activities, heard brief lectures, and saw videos on effective parenting practices. "Parents of first graders were taught coaching skills to assist children in the development of positive peer relationships, and parents of fifth graders were taught problem-solving skills helpful in dealing with the problems of adolescence" (p. 225). Group leaders sometimes visited homes to deliver the curriculum if parents were unable to attend, and were available to answer questions between meetings. Teachers were involved by sending home a weekly newsletter and suggesting activities that complemented what had been learned in the weekly sessions.

The classroom intervention component was delivered in 30-minute sessions twice a week for 10 weeks. Children were taught listening skills, emotion management, and prosocial behaviors, and the fifth graders were taught study skills. The school component also included playground intervention, where positive and aversive behaviors during recess were addressed, again for all first and fifth graders.

Reid and Eddy (2002) provide an excellent overview of the LIFT project as well as a review of the research evaluating it. They note that preliminary results are encouraging. Physical aggression on the playground diminished, with aggressive children showing marked decreases in antisocial behavior. Maternal discipline style improved, with those mothers who had displayed aversive behaviors showing the largest immediate reductions in those behaviors. Teaching rating data also indicated a positive impact on children's behavior in the classroom. These improvements were seen for both first and fifth graders, suggesting to the researchers that the LIFT curriculum was appropriate as a universal prevention strategy across the elementary school years.

groups as effective change agents in modifying these antisocial behaviors. Interventions that are peer focused can actually have unintended negative effects if they require increased contact with antisocial peers (Vitaro & Tremblay, 1994). Similarly, Dishion and Andrews (1995) found that placing high-risk teens into groups together encouraged escalations in tobacco use and problem behaviors in school. Dishion and Andrews further discovered that bringing high-risk peers together may have actually served to increase contact with deviant peers and, in the long run, exacerbated their antisocial involvement. They recommended that intervention programs that use antisocial peers as change agents be discouraged unless very carefully designed. Likewise, research indicates that group homes for delinquents may increase delinquent behavior (Chamberlain, 1996). The assumption is that antisocial peers tend to model and encourage other antisocial peers.

In summary, effective prevention and treatment programs begin early, are based on child development principles, deal with multiple systems, recognize the cultural influences interacting on the child, and focus on the family and parental skills. When working directly with the developing antisocial child, the effective program focuses on improving positive social and prosocial skills, enhancing academic and learning skills, and promoting self-esteem and confidence.

CLASSIFICATION OF PREVENTION AND INTERVENTION PROGRAMS

As mentioned earlier, many prevention, intervention, and treatment programs have been tried with children and adolescents over the past 30 years, but few have been submitted to rigorous evaluation. For those that have been evaluated, most have failed if we use future offending or long-term, lasting positive outcomes as criteria. That is to say, the programs were not demonstrated to be effective at reducing antisocial behavior significantly. In some cases, though, other improvements (e.g., in behavior, self-esteem, or interpersonal relationships) were found. It is also clear that—for those juveniles with substance abuse problems—addressing and treating these problems significantly reduces the likelihood of continued offending (Mulvey, 2011).

Because of the large number of programs available for juveniles, we will only cover those that are well known or that have been notably successful or promising. Some treatment programs targeting specific juvenile offenders (e.g., juvenile sex offenders or juvenile murderers) will be covered in later chapters.

In order to provide some structure to this array of programs, we will organize the remainder of the chapter into three main sections: (1) primary prevention (also called universal prevention in the literature), (2) selective prevention (also called secondary prevention), and (3) treatment or intervention (also called tertiary prevention). These three categories are similar to the public health model of prevention originally proposed by Gordon (1983), and elaborated upon further by Guerra, Tolan, and Hammond (1994) and Mulvey, Arthur, and Reppucci (1993) among others. Although this classification provides structure for the purpose of discussing programs, there is often overlap between these convenient divisions because many programs target a mixture of populations. For example, Project Headstart—which was originally designed to provide a "catch-up" educational program for economically disadvantaged families and was considered a primary prevention program—has evolved into a broader program that helps a wider socioeconomic spectrum. Furthermore, because some of the children in Headstart may qualify as seriously "at-risk" children, for them, the program could be considered a selective program. Likewise, Multi-Systemic Therapy (MST), because it focuses on the family unit, may include both serious delinquents and their siblings who could be considered at risk of future offending.

Primary (or universal) prevention is designed to prevent delinquent behavior before any signs of the behavioral pattern emerge. Primary prevention programs are most often implemented early in the developmental sequence of children, preferably before the ages of seven or eight. Typically, they are conducted in the school or preschool setting, and focus on large groups of children, *regardless of possible differences in risk of delinquency.* In most instances, primary prevention programs target all children within a particular geographic area or setting (e.g., a school or school grade) without any further selection criteria (Offord, Chmura Kraemeer, Kazdin, Jensen, & Harrington, 1998). Many of these programs require the promulgation of far-reaching policies and procedures, which often involve legislative authorization and funding. Examples include widespread programs to enhance prenatal care, maternal and infant care and nutrition, and family management programs for preschool children (Committee on Preventive Psychiatry, 1999). Another excellent example of this approach is the development of resilience or protective factors in young children before school entry or soon after entry. We discuss this far-reaching but powerful approach in more detail shortly.

Selective or secondary prevention consists of working with *specific* children and adolescents who are at *high risk* and who display some *early signs of antisocial behavior* but have not yet been classified or adjudicated delinquent by the court. The basic assumption in selective prevention is that early detection and early intervention will prevent the youngster from graduating into more serious, habitual offending. A good example of this type of prevention is the Perry Preschool Project started in 1962. The project was an organized educational program directed at the cognitive and social development of young children considered at *high risk* of delinquency and school failure (Berrueta-Clement, Schweinhart, Barnett, & Weikart, 1987). Another well-known example of this prevention strategy is juvenile diversion, which diverts first-time offenders from formal court processing but places them in short-term programs that presumably will discourage them from reoffending. An advantage of selective prevention programs is that they focus on those youth who should benefit most from the services. That is, the effort is more concentrated on those at risk rather than on an entire group of children, many of whom may show no risk factors at all. A disadvantage is that secondary prevention programs isolate and label children as potential problems, possibly creating a self-fulfilling prophecy: "I'm in this special program, therefore I'm different (and bad). So I might as well *be* bad."

The third approach (**tertiary prevention**) is generally referred to as **treatment** (or intervention) in the delinquency literature. We prefer to use the term *treatment*, because it can be argued that primary and selective prevention are also forms of intervention. Furthermore, although there is some overlap between selective prevention and treatment—in the sense that juveniles in selective prevention programs also often receive treatment—we reserve "treatment" to apply to those programs designed to reduce serious, habitual delinquent or antisocial behavior by adjudicated delinquents. Usually, those fully involved delinquents or highly antisocial children have been referred for psychological care in the community or have been placed in residential correctional facilities, training schools, or rehabilitation centers.

PRIMARY PREVENTION

In the past, prevention and treatment programs tried to focus on reducing or eliminating *risk* factors that children and adolescents face during their formative years. In recent years, however, a discernible shift has taken place that emphasizes the development and enhancement of *protective* factors. While both approaches are important, in this chapter, we focus on protective factors through the development of resilience. We contend that the development of resilience is an extremely effective method for primary and selective prevention of delinquency in children and adolescents and also has enormous potential as an effective treatment strategy. Consequently, we begin the primary prevention section by describing how resilience can come into play across all three classifications of prevention and treatment.

The Enhancement and Development of Resilience

With increasing awareness of the protective factors that promote resilience in children and adolescents, theorists, researchers, and policy makers are now attempting to apply this knowledge toward the prevention of antisocial behavior, particularly in children considered at moderate to high risk. Prevention and treatment programs that are designed to foster and maintain resilience in youth are also known as strength-based programs. It should be emphasized that resilience is made up of ordinary rather than extraordinary processes, and that the average child can be taught to become resilient (Smith, 2006). Prevention programs that promote cognitive and social competencies in the child or adolescent, improve childrearing practices in the family, and foster the development and maintenance of effective social support systems are most likely to be effective in the long run.

Strategies for developing resilience include the enhancement of a child's strengths and interests, as well as the reduction of risk or stressors, and the facilitation of protective processes. Overall, the rallying cry for many programs focusing on enhancing resilience has become, "Every child has talents, strengths, and interests that offer the child potential for a bright future" (Damon, 2004, p. 13). These attitudes reflect a major transformation in conceptualizing the prevention of antisocial behavior and other childhood problems over the past few decades. This is partly because the many risk factors that were described in Chapters 2 and 3 are often very difficult to change, particularly in juvenile treatment programs (Hawkins *et al.*, 2009).

Children who are at risk of engaging in serious antisocial behavior have been exposed to aversive events, which often cannot be reversed. These can include dire economic situations, abuse (physical or emotional), rejection by peers, or trauma such as the sudden loss of a parent or sibling, alone or in combination. This is why some researchers advocate that we must help youth learn how to manage their risk, such as by effectively dealing with the trauma of childhood physical and sexual abuse (Ruffolo, Sarri, & Goodkind, 2004). There is no single means of maintaining equilibrium following highly aversive events, but rather there are multiple pathways to resilience (Bonanno, 2004), as there are multiple pathways on the road to delinquency. For example, McKnight and Loper (2002) found that the most prominent resilience factors in adolescent girls at risk of delinquency were an academic motivation and a desire to go to college, absence of substance abuse, feeling loved and wanted, belief that teachers treat students fairly, parents trusting adolescent children, and religiosity. In a study using ADD Health data, however, Hawkins *et al.* (2009) found that religiosity was *not* a protective factor with one exception: girls reporting high levels of religiosity reported lower incidents of selling drugs. Connectedness to school also did not serve as a protective factor, although success in school was protective for some forms of delinquency, such as assault and status offenses. Interestingly, "girls who were successful in school were more likely to commit a property offense during late adolescence and young adulthood" (Hawkins *et al.*, 2009, p. 5). Hawkins *et al.* also found that the strongest protective factor was the extent to which a girl felt she had caring adults in her life. The presence of caring adults reduced the likelihood that girls would engage in several forms of antisocial behavior.

Waaktaar, Christie, Borge, and Torgerson (2004) conducted a study to explore how resilience or protective factors could be used to help at-risk youths. The youth averaged 12.3 years of age, and slightly over one-third were girls. They represented a medley of cultural and ethnic backgrounds, including the West Indies, Far East, Central Asia, the Arab world, and northeast Africa. All the participants had experienced serious and/or multiple life stresses, and—at the time of the study—they were not receiving "satisfactory help" through "psychiatric" intervention.

The researchers targeted four resilience factors for therapeutic intervention: positive peer relations, self-efficacy, creativity, and coherence. Positive peer relations were defined as prosocial interactions, peer acceptance, and support. Self-efficacy is the belief that one can achieve desired goals through one's own actions (Bandura, 1989, 1997). Hundreds of studies have supported the observation that self-efficacy leads to a range of positive outcomes, and it is regarded as central to resilience (Lightsey, 2006). Creativity in this context refers to individual talent to create an artistic or other communicative product, such as a song, dance, film, play, poem, or short story. This approach requires that children be encouraged to express themselves and their experiences symbolically. Coherence refers to the ways in which people evaluate themselves and their circumstances both cognitively and emotionally. It involves "helping young people to find a coherent meaning to their past, present, and future life through positive thinking, accepting the reality of their bad experiences, avoiding self-blame for uncontrollable circumstances and finding adaptive paths forward" (Waaktaar *et al.*, 2004, p. 173). The researchers discovered that child therapy that focuses on these four concepts has the potential to enhance resilience significantly.

An excellent illustration of a culturally sensitive program developed for resilience development is Project SELF, a school curriculum designed to promote self-esteem, self-efficacy, and improved problem-solving skills in inner-city fourth-grade children through a culturally based curriculum (Hampson, Rahman, Brown, Taylor, & Donaldson, 1998). The researchers write, "Using a pre/post evaluation design with a control group, we demonstrated that students who received the program exhibited greater improved knowledge of the curriculum, elevated self-esteem, a greater sense of self-efficacy, and improved long-term consequential thinking skills as compared to controls" (Hampson *et al.*, 1998, p. 24). What really made the difference, the researchers concluded, was the program's focus on "the students' own ancestral history, biology, beliefs and values, choices and potential" throughout the curriculum (Hampson *et al.*, 1998, p. 27). In order to improve resilience, the researchers reasoned, children must touch base with their cultural or ethnic identity.

SELECTIVE PREVENTION

Selective (or secondary) prevention is directed at children and adolescents who are believed to be "at risk" of engaging in delinquency on the basis of any number of risk factors (e.g., low self-concept, highly dysfunctional family situation, conduct disorder). In a comprehensive review of the research literature, Tremblay and Craig (1995) concluded that selective prevention programs with at-risk youths tend to be successful mainly when the intervention aims at more than one risk factor (e.g., children's disruptive behavior, aggressive behavior, and parenting), lasts for relatively long periods of time (at least one year), and is implemented before adolescence. The time must be quality time, and the more intensive the intervention, the better. Like much of the research alluded to thus far, the programs identified by Tremblay and Craig were especially effective when implemented during the preschool or the early elementary school years. In the case of some selective prevention programs, such as juvenile diversion, such early intervention is not possible.

Nevertheless, diversion programs can be effective, depending on what approach is being taken. Diversion from standard prosecution for both adults and juveniles is now a standard part of the criminal justice process; with respect to juveniles, diversion is often accompanied by substance abuse treatment or mental health treatment. Recall the statistics cited earlier in the chapter regarding juveniles with mental health needs in the juvenile justice system. Concerns about these increasing numbers of juveniles prompted the National Center for Mental Health and Juvenile Justice (NCMHJJ) to fund initiatives to divert these juveniles from prosecution (Colwell, Villarreal, & Espinosa, 2012). Colwell *et al.* studied juveniles with mental health needs who were assigned to specialized supervision as a diversionary approach and a comparison group of juveniles without the specialized supervision. The youth with mental health needs were significantly less likely to be adjudicated delinquent and were also more likely to improve in problem-solving skills and interpersonal relationships. Although the study was a preliminary one, it suggests an efficient use of this particular diversionary program for juveniles with mental health needs.

Selective prevention programs increasingly are provided primarily to those children identified as showing *early* signs of developing serious and persistent antisocial behavior. It is clear that high-risk children can be identified with reasonable accuracy in early life, at least by the beginning of elementary school (Dodge & Pettit, 2003; Hill, Lochman, Coie, & Greenberg, 2004; Lochman & Conduct Problems Prevention Research Group, 1995). As noted by Dodge and Pettit (2003), the effectiveness of early screening has major consequences for public policy. Schools can play a more active role than they have in the past in identifying young children who could benefit from a prevention program. In addition, selective prevention programs can be more focused, more efficient, and more intensive than universal prevention programs (Hill *et al.*, 2004). It should also be mentioned that prevention with young children offers far more hope than prevention with adolescents who may be already down the path of persistent antisocial behavior. However, prevention methods must span from childhood to adolescence because new risk factors emerge at each new developmental stage (Dodge & Pettit, 2003). That is to say that the child must be followed through his or her developmental years. According to the Carnegie Council on Adolescent Development (1995), approximately 25 percent of American youth ages 10–17 are *highly* vulnerable to the negative consequences of multiple high-risk behaviors, such as substance abuse, school failure, and delinquency. About 7 million youth are particularly vulnerable to delinquency, gang activity, criminal activities, and violence (see Smith, 2006). An additional 7 million adolescents are at moderate risk of dropping out of school, for either bullying or being bullied in school, and/or committing suicide (Carnegie Council of Adolescent Development, 1995). We do not know, of course, how many of these children would have been identified as high risk in their preschool years.

The Fast Track Experiment

The Fast Track Project is a multisite, multicomponent prevention program for young children at high risk of long-term antisocial behavior (Conduct Problems Prevention Research Group, 1999). It is based on developmental pathway theory (e.g., Moffitt, 1993a) and is longitudinal in design. Fast Track is a two-pronged project. Participants in the program include both high-risk children (selective or secondary prevention) and all the children in school grades one to five (primary or universal prevention) within a particular school. The children in the high-risk group began to show persistent and serious antisocial behavior in early childhood (before first grade), as reported by parents and teachers. The Fast Track Project is guided by developmental theory that posits that multiple influences interact in the development of antisocial behavior (Conduct Problems Prevention Research Group, 2004).

The program is divided into two major phases: the elementary school (grades 1–5) and adolescent periods (grades 6–10). The elementary school phase addresses six areas of risk and protective factors: parenting, child social problem-solving and emotional coping skills, peer relations, classroom atmosphere and curriculum, academic achievement with a focus on reading, and home–school relations (Conduct Problems Prevention Research Group, 2004). The families of the children were invited to participate in weekly parent/child groups, plus home visits, tutoring, and school follow-up. The adolescent phase focuses on four areas associated with successful adolescent adjustment: peer affiliation and peer influence, academic orientation and achievement, social cognition and identity development, and parent and family relationships (Conduct Problems Prevention Research Group, 2004). The protective role of parental supervision and monitoring was also emphasized.

Children in the program were compared with a group of high-risk children (the control group) who did not participate in the program. Early results indicated that the participating children, relative to the children in the control condition, progressed significantly in their acquisition of most of the skills deemed to be critical protective factors (Conduct Problems Prevention Research Group, 1999). The high-risk experimental group children, compared with the control high-risk children, exhibited improvements in their social, emotional, and academic skills, especially their reading skills. Their peer relationships also improved significantly. The results were equally effective for both boys and girls. Parents who participated in the program displayed more warmth, appropriate and consistent discipline, self-efficacy, and positive school involvement. Evaluations of the program's effectiveness were taken at the end of first and third grades.

The primary prevention effects of Fast Track were equally impressive. Classrooms that participated in the program were found to have lower peer-rated aggression and lower peer-related hyperactive-disruptive behaviors than were those classrooms that did not participate in the program (the control groups). Ratings by research observers in the classrooms indicated that prevention classrooms had better classroom atmosphere, students were better able to express their feelings appropriately (self-regulation), and the classroom as a whole was better able to stay focused and on task.

Fast Track provides an example of how a carefully articulated developmental model that accounts for the change and accumulation of risk factors and protective factors throughout the development period starting with children at school entry and continuing through adolescence in high school can be effective (Conduct Problems Prevention Research Group, 2004). However, designers of Fast Track faced many challenges and discovered how difficult it is to overcome the effects of dangerous, crime-ridden neighborhoods and the influences of impoverished families in which parental psychopathology and substance abuse are too common.

TREATMENT APPROACHES

The effectiveness of most treatment approaches has not been established. In many cases, the treatments have not been empirically investigated or evaluated (Zahn, Day, Mihalic, & Tichavsky, 2009). Nevertheless, some meta-analyses are available, and these have added considerably to this body of information (Hanson, Bourgon, Helmus, & Hodgson, 2009). For example, treatment programs that concentrate on self-regulation skills and changing thought processes hold considerable promise if the treatment programs also include the family, school, peers, and community. It has also become apparent—from a psychological perspective—that the most effective treatment strategies for both juveniles and adults are based on the RNR (risks, needs, responsivity) approach (Andrews, Bonta, & Hoge, 1990; Bonta & Andrews, 2007). Cognitive-behavioral programs fit nicely into RNR principles. We discuss RNR in more detail in Chapter 13.

A wide range of treatment methods have been tried specifically with juvenile delinquents. In a common scenario, the juvenile court refers a persistent delinquent youth to an outpatient mental health clinic for counseling and psychotherapy. The traditional approach relies on a one-on-one strategy of providing psychotherapy to an individual, though group treatment also may occur. Most commonly, the relationship with the therapist is the primary medium through which change is achieved (Kazdin, 1987). Presumably, the treatment provides a corrective experience by providing insight and exploring new ways of behaving (Kazdin, 1987). In some instances, the delinquent youth may receive individual counseling from a member of the juvenile court staff (Borduin, 1994). Delinquent youth who require a more restrictive setting are usually placed in a residential facility where group therapy is more common than individual counseling.

It is important to realize, though, that research has continually demonstrated that individual-based psychotherapy has not been shown to be effective when used in isolation (Committee on Preventive Psychiatry, 1999; Tarolla *et al.*, 2002). In other words, simply applying any form of psychotherapy to a child or adolescent already on a developmental path leading to serious delinquency without involving the social environment is, in most cases, a waste of time, money, and energy. Letourneau and Miner (2005) make the observation that "the developmental literature suggests that treatments that focus primarily on changing the individual characteristics (e.g., cognitions and behaviors) of youthful offenders, without also targeting relevant factors with caregivers (e.g., monitoring), peers (e.g., improving ties with prosocial peers), and school (e.g., increasing and improving caregiver-teacher communications) might be of limited usefulness" (p. 306).

Restrictive interventions for serious juvenile offenders, such as residential treatment and incarceration, have also not been effective and are extremely expensive (Henggeler, 1996; Mulvey, 2011). Moreover, any prevention or treatment program that focuses on only one risk factor is unlikely to lead to long-lasting change in delinquency because multiple other forces act to support antisocial development (Dodge & Pettit, 2003). According to Henggeler (1996, p. 139), "Restrictive out-of-home placements neither address the known determinants of serious antisocial behavior nor alter the natural ecology to which the youth will eventually return. Indeed, data show that incarceration may not even serve a community protection function."

There are some additional points to note before proceeding. The characteristics of treatment programs may be different for those juveniles who receive treatment while confined in an institution compared with those who receive treatment in a noninstitutional setting. Not only is the setting different, but the participants may also differ in terms of offending history and the seriousness of the offending. For example, those offenders who are in an institution are likely to be considered dangerous or a high risk to reoffend. There are likely to be gender and age differences also.

Furthermore, it is difficult to make conclusions about wide-range effectiveness of intervention programs under the auspices of juvenile corrections because there are so many different treatment programs with different policies, procedures, staff training, and outcome measures. For example, Krisberg and Howell (1998) remarked that in juvenile corrections, "there are training schools, detention centers, camps, ranches, wagon trains, environmental institutes, group homes, boot camps, residential programs for emotionally disturbed youths, chemical dependency programs, correctional sailing shills, and independent living arrangements" (p. 347). Juvenile corrections also involve a wide range with respect to size, locations, and security levels.

Traditional treatment programs for the life-course-persistent offenders (LCPs) or serious delinquent offenders have had little success historically, whether provided in community or residential settings (Borduin, 1994). Treatment programs that have worked on mild or adolescent-limited offenders have been unsuccessful when applied to LCPs or serious delinquency. In most instances, as soon as youths leave the therapeutic milieu and return to their natural social environment, the chronic antisocial behavior reemerges. In fact, the poor track record with LCPs has prompted some professionals and policy makers to resist providing rehabilitative or treatment services to the serious offender (Borduin, 1994).

However, an examination of these failures reveals that rehabilitation and treatment services have often been too simplistic or narrowly focused, such as by focusing only on the individual. As noted, many programs have failed to include or even recognize the many influences (family, peers, school, community) that unwittingly promote and contribute to antisocial behavior. Not only must effective treatment approaches be multisystemic and address the multidimensional causes of juvenile offending, they must also be intensive and long lasting if they are going to have an impact on juvenile offenders who have already become deeply entrenched into their antisocial behavioral patterns. The behaviors of hard-core juvenile offenders are often severe, pervasive, and well learned. While treatment for them is by no means hopeless, LCP delinquents require innovation and extreme patience for the many frustrating setbacks that will certainly occur over the long haul. With the above cautions in mind, we discuss below some of the treatment approaches that have been used with delinquents. We begin with treatments tried in residential settings, then proceed to those based in the community.

Traditional Residential Treatment

The traditional form of **residential treatment** is the juvenile "training school" or "rehabilitation center," where youths are incarcerated for extended periods of time, sometimes even until they reach adulthood. These institutional settings are typically physically secure and may represent the "last stop" for youths with whom less restrictive community settings have been tried. On the other hand, a juvenile found to have committed a one-time serious crime—such as a murder or a rape—may also be placed in such a setting. As a group, youths in residential treatment have high rates of substance abuse, emotional disturbance, and low academic achievement.

The evaluation research on institutional treatment is not encouraging. Studies have even demonstrated that incarcerated juvenile offenders who receive residential treatment have higher rates of criminal involvement after release than their counterparts who received intensive family and community-based treatment (Tarolla et al., 2002).

Lipsey and Wilson (1998) examined the effectiveness of two hundred treatment programs for serious juvenile offenders. The analysis included 83 studies of the effects of treatment with *institutionalized* offenders, 74 of which involved juveniles in the custody of juvenile justice institutions, and 9 that involved residential institutions administered by mental health or private agencies. The analysis also included 117 treatment programs for *noninstitutionalized* juveniles, most of whom were on probation or parole. Although the results were mixed and confusing, with no one particular treatment program showing superiority, the average program for both institutionalized and noninstitutionalized offenders produced a 12 percent reduction in subsequent reoffense rates. The most effective programs (e.g., teaching family home, interpersonal skills development, and other broad-based interventions) were able to produce a 40 percent reduction rate, a promising result, while some other programs (e.g., Wilderness/Challenge, vocational programs, milieu therapy) were largely ineffective by most measures. The most effective programs included key components, such as focusing on social skills training, parent management, and family support.

Nontraditional and Community Treatment

BOOT CAMPS   Boot camps for juveniles were modeled after the adult correctional model that emerged in the 1980s (MacKenzie & Hebert, 1995). Also called "shock incarceration," the boot camp was a short-term, intensive, military-style program intended for generally nonviolent offenders. Juvenile boot camps were intended to be more rehabilitative in nature, offering, for example, substance abuse treatment, along with community follow-up, sometimes glibly referred to as "after-shock." Critics expressed grave doubts that the boot camp model would be effective, particularly for girls (Chesney-Lind & Shelden, 1988).

By the early 1990s, about 10 states had opened boot camps for young offenders. In light of the public interest in these approaches, the Office of Juvenile Justice and Delinquency Prevention (OJJDP) funded demonstration projects at three sites to develop and evaluate a model boot-camp program for male juveniles, ages 13–18.

The ambitious goals of these boot-camp programs, as reported by Bourque *et al.* (1996), were as follows:

- Serve as a cost-effective alternative to institutionalization
- Promote discipline through physical conditioning and teamwork
- Instill moral values and a work ethic
- Promote literacy and increase academic achievement
- Reduce drug and alcohol abuse
- Encourage participants to become productive, law-abiding citizens
- Ensure that offenders are held accountable for their actions

In the three OJJDP-funded demonstration sites, the boot-camp experience included a 90-day residential program that was heavily focused on military drills, discipline, and physical conditioning. The regime included uniforms, military jargon, and an exhausting daily routine from 5:30 or 6:00 a.m. until 9:00 or 10:00 p.m. To a lesser extent, rehabilitation activities such as remedial education, life-skills education and counseling, and substance abuse education were included.

Youth in the programs had committed a wide range of offenses, including property, drug, and other felonies, but excluding violent offenses. In all three sites, the programs demonstrated short-term success during the residential phase; at least 80 percent of the boys "graduated" from boot camp. The boys improved in educational performance, physical fitness, and behavior, and the staff noted their improvements in respect for authority, self-discipline, teamwork, and physical appearance. The youths themselves rated their experience positively, noting that they believed they had significantly changed the direction of their lives. The positive results were short lived, however.

The aftercare components of the program were discouraging, and they began to raise important questions about the effectiveness of boot camps for juvenile offenders. A variety of aftercare services were made available, depending on the site. These included specially created aftercare centers, mainstreaming into local boys clubs, academic instruction, drug counseling, and support services. In a one-year follow-up, all three sites reported high rates of noncompliance, absenteeism, and new arrests. "No site graduated more than 50 percent of its aftercare participants, and terminations were most commonly caused by new arrests in two sites" (Bourque *et al.*, 1996).

Despite these shortcomings and the research evidence against them, the growth of juvenile boot camps in many states continued unabated (Tyler, Darville, & Stalnaker, 2001). In Texas alone, the Board of Texas Juvenile Probation, in 1998, approved 18 proposals to construct juvenile boot-camp facilities across the state. By 2008, there were approximately 50 public and privately administered juvenile boot camps in the United States (Weis & Toolis, 2008), with the great majority privately operated. Although there are three identifiable styles of boot camps that have evolved over the years (the military drilling style, the rehabilitative approach, and the educational/vocational model), a majority of the current juvenile boot camps still concentrate on the military drill which focuses on strict discipline as their central theme (Benda, 2005; Tyler *et al.*, 2001).

Interestingly and relevantly, documented instances of extreme abuse led to the closure of juvenile boot camps in Arizona, Georgia, and Maryland (Bottcher & Ezell, 2005). In 2000, Maryland disbanded its juvenile boot camps and fired top juvenile justice officials after publicity surrounding allegations of physical and emotional abuse of juveniles. Florida disbanded its camps after a boy died from staff beatings.

In addition to these concerns about how juveniles are treated in boot camp settings, critics note that their effectiveness has not been demonstrated. The research literature has continually reported that juvenile boot camps are ineffective in reducing recidivism (Benda, 2005; MacKenzie, Layton, Soural, Sealock, & Bin Kashen, 2001), even when intensive aftercare is provided (Bottcher & Ezell, 2005). Today, juvenile boot camps still exist, but they seem to have gone under the research radar. The OJJDP website lists no publications under that topic, and it is likely that many, if not most, juvenile justice scholars and policy makers consider them an idea whose time should never have come. It should not be surprising to anyone that a short-term residential program for juvenile offenders that is so discipline oriented is unlikely to produce positive long-term results.

Community Treatment: MST with Serious Offenders

Scott Henggeler and his colleagues have designed a treatment approach—**multisystemic therapy (MST)**—for serious juvenile offenders, which is responsive to many of the social systems influencing the child's delinquent behavior (Henggeler & Borduin, 1990; Henggeler, Melton, & Smith, 1992; Scherer, Brondino, Henggeler, Melton, & Hanley, 1994). "Consistent with the known causes of adolescent criminal behavior and substance abuse, MST addresses the multidetermined nature of antisocial behavior in adolescents at individual, family, peer, school, and community levels" (Henggeler, 2011, p. 376). The major focus of MST, however, is the family, and a major ingredient of the treatment is that the family must be actively involved in the program. The program addresses the cognitive and systemic (i.e., family, peer, and school) factors that are associated as risk factors for antisocial behavior (Schaeffer & Borduin, 2005). Together, counselors and family collaborate to develop pertinent treatment goals, as well as appropriate plans to meet these goals (Henggeler, 1996). Barriers and impediments to the plan, such as uncooperative family members, teachers, and school administrators, are worked with directly and actively. MST is an action-based treatment program in that it tries to get the involved family members to take "action" (behaviorally do something) rather than just talking. Since its modest beginnings in the late 1970s, there are more than 450 MST programs operating in over 30 states and 11 nations, serving more than 15,000 adolescents with serious antisocial behavioral problems (Henggeler, 2011).

MST is an intensive time-limited form of intervention where trained therapists have daily contact with the adolescent and his or her family for approximately 60 hours over four months. The caseload of the therapist is small, averaging four to six families per counselor. MST therapists identify both strengths and problem areas within the individual, the family, and the other social systems, such as peers, school, social service agencies, and parents' workplace. To a large extent, MST is based on the systems model developed by Bronfenbrenner (1979).

Basically, MST focuses on the strengths of the family. The program tries to identify family strengths and provide the parent(s) with the resources needed for effective parenting and for developing a better functioning and cohesive family unit. For example, the therapists might work with the parents on improving communication and problem-solving skills, being less susceptible to manipulation by the child, enhancing their consistency in administering discipline and rewards, helping them find ways to reduce stress, and reducing parental drug and alcohol abuse.

MST therapists also work with the targeted youth to remediate deficits in interpersonal skills that hinder acceptance by prosocial peers. Youth and therapist may work on modifying thought processes and coping mechanisms that may interfere with the family, peer, school, and neighborhood microsystems. Other MST strategies include decreasing the teenager's antisocial peer contacts and increasing affiliation with prosocial peers and activities. Another approach is to develop tactics to monitor and promote the youth's school performance. For example, the therapist would work toward opening and maintaining effective communication lines between parents, teachers, and administrators.

One of the first studies concerning the effectiveness of MST was conducted with a population of youths from Simpsonville, South Carolina, who had at least three nonviolent arrests or one violent arrest and who were living with at least one parent. The participants in the study averaged 3.5 arrests and had spent an average of 9.5 weeks in lockup in a correctional facility. Their average age was 15.2 years. The results showed that those youths receiving MST were less likely to be arrested and reduced incarceration by 64 percent during a 59-week follow-up, compared with a control group of youths who received usual services (court-ordered curfew and/or referral to a community agency). They were also reportedly less aggressive with peers compared with the control group. The lower rearrest rates held for at least 2.5 years after treatment (Henggeler *et al.*, 1993).This is a relatively long follow-up compared with most intervention studies and demonstrates that the program has considerable promise.

In another study, Borduin *et al.* (1995) examined the long-term effects of MST compared with individual therapy on the prevention of criminal behavior and violent offending among 176 juvenile offenders at high risk of committing more serious crimes. A four-year follow-up of rearrest data revealed that MST was more effective than individual therapy in preventing future criminal behavior, including violent behavior. The MST program reduced rearrests for violent and other serious crime by 63 percent over the four-year follow-up.

In a follow-up of the Borduin *et al.* (1995) study, Schaeffer and Borduin (2005) followed the original 176 participants for nearly 14 years. The data showed that MST participants had significantly lower recidivism rates at follow-up than did those participants who received individual therapy (50% vs. 81%, respectively). Recidivism, depending on the study, refers to rearrest, reconviction, or incarceration after an initial juvenile arrest, conviction, or incarceration. Furthermore, MST offenders, compared with individually treated offenders, had 54 percent fewer arrests and 57 percent fewer days of confinement in adult correctional facilities. Some recent research on MST continues to support its effectiveness, in this case specifically with adolescent sex offenders (Borduin, Schaeffer, & Heiblum, 2009).

To date, approximately 21 studies have been published; most of them have focused on serious juvenile offenders, such as violent offenders, sex offenders, and drug-abusing offenders (Henggeler, 2011). A vast majority has shown MST to be effective. "Numerous clinical trials have established the capacity of MST to reduce youth criminal behavior, substance abuse, psychiatric symptoms, and out-of-home placements while improving family relations and school performance" (Henggeler, 2011, p. 376).

Current research has identified two key factors as critical to the program's success for dealing with antisocial behavior: changes in caregiver discipline practices and a reduction in youth associations with deviant peers (Henggeler *et al.*, 2009; Tighe, Pistrang, Casdagli, Baruch, & Butler, 2012). Deković and associates (Deković, Asscher, Manders, Prins, & van der Laan 2012) found that one of the important aspects targeted by MST for improvement in parental discipline practices is parental sense of competence. The researchers were able to show that increases in parental competence enhance parents' faith in their own ability to parent adequately, especially in terms of warmth, affection, parental supervision, and appropriate discipline. "The increases in sense of competence may motivate parents to be more persistent in attaining their goals, following through their discipline efforts, and thus becoming more consistent in their behavior toward the adolescent" (Deković *et al.*, 2012, p. 10). This chain of events reduced the adolescent's negative and antisocial behavior. Interestingly, the MST program has also been extended to treat youth with serious and chronic health conditions, such as poorly controlled diabetes and obesity.

In the longest follow-up and most comprehensive study to date on the effects of MST (Sawyer & Borduin, 2011), it was found that, after 22 years, the positive impact of the therapy was still significant. More specifically, MST participants were significantly less likely to be arrested for felony crimes than participants of other therapies (34.8% vs. 54.8%, respectively) over the span of 22 years. It should be emphasized that the original participants in this study were 176 violent juvenile offenders who averaged 3.9 arrests for serious crimes. At the beginning of the project all participants were originally randomized either to MST or other types of therapy (i.e., individual therapy). In conclusion, Sawyer and Borduin (2011) write, "the present findings provide additional support for the efficacy and applicability of MST with serious and violent juvenile offenders, whose high recidivism rates are of great concern to policymakers" (p. 650).

Summary and Conclusions

The crimes committed by juveniles get considerable media attention, particularly if they are unusual or when they are committed by groups. Gang activity in particular raises public concern, but many gang members have reached the age of adulthood and therefore do not qualify for delinquent status. The unlawful acts committed by youth are usually placed in five categories: unlawful acts against person, unlawful acts against property, drug offenses, offenses against the public order, and status offenses. Of the five, crimes against persons are the least predominant in arrest statistics. Juvenile courts, however, are least likely to handle drug cases, compared with property, public order, and crimes against persons, respectively.

We began the chapter with a brief discussion of status offenses, those behaviors that would not be considered crimes if committed by adults. Researchers have long focused on studying these behaviors; there are gender differences in enforcing them, status offenses often signify deeper problems in a youth's life, and some but not all status offenders move on to commit more serious crimes. Of all the status offenses, running away is probably the most troubling. Both boys and girls run away, but girls are more likely to have run away because of victimization in the home and are also more likely to become involved in prostitution to survive. Research on adult female offenders finds these patterns in many of their backgrounds.

We discussed other gender differences in juvenile offending, noting that girls traditionally have been far less present than boys in juvenile offending statistics. In the 1990s, we began to see a closing of this gender gap, though girls still represent a lower proportion of the delinquency statistics for most offenses, with the exception of runaway. The gender gap for drug offending—and to a lesser extent for violence—is also getting smaller. We reviewed some of the findings of the Girls Study Group (GSG), comprised of scholars and practitioners from different fields, which is conducting ongoing research to identify which girls become delinquent, how they got that way, and what factors are effective in preventing girls' delinquency.

The chapter is most concerned with serious delinquency and the developmental pathway that leads to that point. Serious delinquents typically begin their antisocial behavior patterns at an early age, and as they grow older, they rarely restrict their behavior to any one offense. As the Pathways study (Mulvey, 2011) demonstrates, however, we cannot assume that even serious offenders do not desist from criminal offending. The developmental theory of Terrie Moffitt is particularly instructive in understanding serious offending. Moffitt's conceptualization of the life-course-persistent (LCP) offender and the adolescent limited (AL) offender has spurred extensive research interest in these two developmental tracks. Later researchers, including Moffitt herself, have recognized that additional tracks are needed to account for offending behavior. Nevertheless, the LCP juvenile is of keen interest from a psychological

perspective. LCP offenders have not acquired prosocial and interpersonal skills and are often plagued by psychological problems well into adulthood. Most juveniles, however, confine their offending to their early years and move on to prosocial lives.

We also discussed Patterson's coercion developmental theory, which attributes much serious delinquency to parenting practices, particularly poor monitoring. Although Patterson does not reject the notion that individual differences in the child affect his or her behavior, he sees the family environment as setting the stage for later antisocial behavior, which is facilitated by the coercive style learned from parents. Patterson and his colleagues continue to offer and evaluate treatment programs for families whose children are at risk of delinquency.

At a time when much of the public fears crime and is skeptical about the prospect of reforming offenders, research results on some approaches to treating even serious juvenile offenders are promising. We highlighted characteristics that programs with good results have in common. Not surprisingly, effective programs begin early in a child's life, they are conscious of key principles of child and adolescent development, they focus on multiple settings in a child's life (e.g., the child, family, school), they acknowledge and respect cultural backgrounds, and they focus on the family first, with a goal of improving parental skills. With regard to the last characteristic, it is easy to give up on some families that seem highly dysfunctional. However, in many situations, the family is what is familiar to the child. If not sensitive to this, some therapists may overlook or underestimate the love and sense of belonging that exists.

Prevention and intervention programs in juvenile justice were classified according to a tripartite model: primary or universal prevention, secondary or selective prevention, and treatment or intervention (also called tertiary prevention). We provided illustrations of each category, focusing most on treatment programs. Primary prevention programs are intended for all children in a given group, whether or not they are "at risk" of engaging in delinquency. Prenatal services, tactics to encourage resilience, and school nutrition programs are examples of such programs. Although research on such programs is positive, because of their universal nature it is difficult to conduct adequate follow-up studies to determine whether children do engage in delinquent behavior. Secondary programs are aimed at "at-risk" children: those with demographic or individual features suggesting that they are likely to engage in delinquency. We discussed the Fast Track Project as a prime illustration of this secondary approach.

The focus on treatment, or tertiary prevention, highlighted a variety of programs that have yielded favorable research results, both in institutional settings and in the community. Research on institutional treatment is discouraging at best. The rehabilitation approaches tried have often been simplistic and narrowly focused; alternatively, they have not been submitted to empirical research, so we cannot know whether they were effective. Adolescents who have received either traditional or nontraditional (e.g., boot camps) institutional treatment fare less well than those receiving intensive community treatment. Within the institutions, however, some programs may be more promising than others. Juvenile sex offender treatment is a case in point.

One promising approach is multisystemic therapy, the community-based, intensive therapy approach for serious offenders outlined by Henggeler and his associates (1992; Schaeffer & Borduin, 2005). A fundamental premise of MST is that youths—even those who committed violent crimes—are better served in their own homes, away from the influences of institutional life. MST offers intensive treatment that focuses on all of the juvenile's social systems: the family, the school, the neighborhood, and the peer group, to the extent that these are relevant. MST therapists—psychologists, social workers, and counselors—have very small caseloads and are able to focus extensively on developing resources to support the existing family unit.

Although community-based programs like MST are promising, even for some violent juveniles, it would be naïve to believe that all serious juvenile offenders can be treated in the community. Unless we do away with the juvenile justice system and place all juveniles in the custody of "adult" corrections, there will always be a need to hold some in secure residential settings. The challenge, therefore, is to develop effective treatment programs for the small group of adolescents who cannot benefit from less restrictive community alternatives.

Key Concepts

Adolescent-limited (AL)
   offenders
Antisocial behavior
Boot camps
Callous-unemotional
   (CU) traits
Child delinquents

Conduct disorder
Life-course-persistent
   (LCP) offenders
Multisystemic therapy (MST)
Primary prevention
   (universal prevention)

Residential treatment
Selective prevention (secondary
   prevention)
Status offenses
Tertiary prevention
   (treatment)

Review Questions

1. Summarize the differences between LCP and AL offenders; discuss why more than two tracks or pathways to offending might be needed.
2. Discuss significant findings from the Girls Study Group and from the Pathways to Desistance studies.
3. Describe Gerald Patterson's coercion developmental model.

4. What are status offenses? What has research found relating to gender differences in these offenses?
5. Identify the three categories of delinquency prevention programs and give an illustration of each.
6. What are the strengths of MST as an approach to serious delinquents?

7

Criminal Psychopathy

CHAPTER OBJECTIVES

- Present a special type of offender (the criminal psychopath) who is different emotionally, cognitively, and behaviorally from other offenders.
- Review the various measures of psychopathy.
- Examine the neurobiological aspects of psychopathy.
- Review the evidence for juvenile psychopathy.
- Identify the ethical dilemmas that juvenile psychopathy presents.
- Discuss representative research on treatment strategies used with adult psychopaths and juveniles with psychopathic features.

"Given its relation to crime and violence, psychopathy is arguably one of the most important psychological constructs in the criminal justice system." (Porter *et al.*, 2000, p. 227). It is relevant to most topics discussed in this text. Psychologist Paul Frick (2009), a prominent researcher in psychopathy, writes, "the construct of psychopathy is important to the legal system (for example, defining offenders who are a high risk for recidivism), to the mental health system (for example, defining a group of antisocial people who have unique treatment requirements), and for research attempting to explain the cause of antisocial and aggressive behaviour (for example, defining a group of antisocial people with unique causal processes)" (p. 803). It is no surprise, then, that psychopathy has become a central focus of research in psychology, particularly as it relates to criminal behavior.

Most recently, *juvenile* psychopathy has become the subject of considerable interest and debate. Some researchers question its validity and implications, while others believe it is crucial that we identify psychopathic characteristics in juveniles in order to intervene at an early age. Juveniles who possess psychopathy-like characteristics, such as callous-unemotional (CU) traits, are believed to be particularly susceptible to antisocial behavior throughout their lives.

As we will see in the chapter, the psychopath is not identical to the person with an antisocial personality disorder, but some researchers and clinicians continue to confuse the two terms (Gacono,

Nieberding, Owen, Rubel, & Bodholdt, 2001). Because psychopathy is such an important topic in criminal psychology, we devote an entire chapter to describing the research and clinical characteristics of this interesting behavior.

WHAT IS A PSYCHOPATH?

The term *psychopath* is currently used to describe a person who demonstrates a discernible cluster of psychological, interpersonal, and neurophysiological features that distinguish him or her from the general population. Psychologist Robert Hare (1993), one of the world's leading experts on psychopathy, describes psychopaths as "social predators who charm, manipulate, and ruthlessly plow their way through life, leaving a broad trail of broken hearts, shattered expectations, and empty wallets. Completely lacking in conscience and empathy, they selfishly take what they want and do as they please, violating social norms and expectations without the slightest sense of guilt or regret" (p. xi).

Hare (1970) proposed a useful scheme to outline three categories of psychopaths: the primary, the secondary or neurotic, and the dyssocial. Only the **primary psychopath** is a "true" psychopath. The primary or "true" psychopath has certain identifiable psychological, emotional, cognitive, and biological differences that distinguish him or her from the general or criminal population. We discuss these differences in some detail throughout the chapter. The other two categories meld a heterogeneous group of antisocial individuals who comprise a large segment of the criminal population. **Secondary psychopaths** commit antisocial or violent acts because of severe emotional problems or inner conflicts. They are sometimes called acting-out neurotics, neurotic delinquents, symptomatic psychopaths, or simply emotionally disturbed offenders. Recent research indicates that the secondary psychopath demonstrates more emotional instability and impulsivity than the primary psychopath, and secondary psychopaths also appear to be more aggressive and violent (Kimonis, Skeem, Cauffman, & Dimitrieva, 2011). The researchers also discovered that secondary psychopathy, compared to primary psychopathy, is more rooted in parental abuse and rejection. The third group, **dyssocial psychopaths**, display aggressive, antisocial behavior they have *learned* from their subculture, like their gangs or families. In both cases, the label "psychopath" is misleading, because the behaviors and backgrounds have little, if any, similarity to those of primary psychopaths. Yet, both secondary and dyssocial psychopaths are often incorrectly called psychopaths because of their high recidivism rates.

Another term that should be distinguished from primary psychopathy is **antisocial personality disorder (APD)**. This term is used by psychiatrists and many clinical psychologists to describe "a pervasive pattern of disregard for, and violation of, the rights of others that begins in childhood or early adolescence and continues into adulthood" (American Psychiatric Association, 1994, p. 645). Antisocial personalities (ASPs) are further described as those persons who "fail to conform to social norms with respect to lawful behaviors. They may repeatedly perform acts that are grounds for arrest, such as destroying property, harassing others, stealing or pursuing illegal occupations" (American Psychiatric Association, 1994, p. 646). As we noted, the descriptions of the psychiatric term *antisocial personality disorder* follow very closely the descriptions of the psychological term *psychopathy*. However, the definition of APD is more narrow than primary psychopathy because it restricts its definition to behavioral indicators. Hare's definition of primary psychopathy also includes emotional, neurological, and cognitive aspects. Nevertheless, with each new publication of the American Psychiatric Association's *Diagnostic and Statistical Manual of Mental Disorders*—and the upcoming revision will likely be no exception (Gurley, 2009)—the characteristics used to describe the antisocial personality

(ASP) are increasingly similar to Hare's primary psychopathy in behavioral terms. It is easy to understand why clinicians and students often confuse the terms.

This text adopts Hare's scheme, considering "primary psychopath" an empirically and clinically useful designation. It is distinguished from secondary or neurotic psychopaths in its behavioral, cognitive, and neurophysiological features. From this point on, when we refer to the psychopath, we mean the primary psychopath. He or she is unique: not neurotic, psychotic, or emotionally disturbed, as commonly believed and portrayed by the entertainment media. Primary psychopaths are usually not volcanically explosive, violent, or extremely destructive. They are more apt to be outgoing, charming, and verbally proficient. They may be criminals—in fact, in general, they run in perpetual opposition to the law—but many are not. When they do engage in violent crimes like rapes and murders, however, their methods of assaulting and killing can be particularly brutal. The term **criminal psychopath** will be used to identify those primary psychopaths who do engage in repetitive antisocial or criminal behavior, though it is not necessarily violent.

An Example of a Psychopath

A good example of a nonviolent primary psychopath is Ferdinand Waldo Demara Jr.(1921–1982) the "Great Impostor," who forged documents and tried dozens of occupations without stopping to obtain a high school education. A brief description of some of his exploits may help put the psychopath in perspective (see Critchton, 1959, for a more complete version).

Demara frequently came into contact with the law during the 1940s and 1950s, primarily because he persisted in adopting fake identities. He once obtained the credentials of a Dr. French, who held a Harvard PhD in psychology. Demara was in the U.S. Navy at the time, awaiting a commission on the basis of other forged documents, but when he realized he was in danger of exposure via a routine security check, he decided he would prefer the Dr. French identity. He dramatized a successful suicide by leaving his clothing on the end of a pier with a note stating that "this is the only way out." Navy officials accepted his "death," and Demara became Dr. French. With his impressive credentials in hand, he obtained a dean of philosophy position in a Canadian college, successfully taught a variety of psychology courses, and assumed administrative responsibilities.

He developed a friendship with a physician, Joseph Cyr, and learned the basics of medicine from their long conversations. He eventually borrowed and duplicated Cyr's vital documents—birth, baptism, and confirmation certificates, school records, medical license—and obtained a commission in the Royal Canadian Navy as Dr. Cyr. He read extensively to nurture his growing knowledge of medicine.

During the Korean War, Demara/Cyr was assigned to a destroyer headed for the combat zone. The ship met a small Korean junk carrying many seriously wounded men, who were brought on board for emergency medical care. Three men were in such critical condition that only emergency surgery could save their lives. Although Demara had never seen an operation performed, he hurriedly reviewed his textbooks. With unskilled hands, he operated through the night. By dawn, he had not only saved the lives of the three men but had also successfully treated 16 others.

Demara/Cyr's deeds were broadcast over the ship's radio and disseminated, along with his photo, by the press. The real Dr. Cyr, shocked to see Demara's visage over his own respected name, immediately exposed him. Demara was discharged from the Canadian Navy, which, to save itself from additional embarrassment, allowed him to leave without prosecution. Demara's biography represents an example of a psychopath who did not engage in serious or lifelong violent crime.

Many psychopaths do commit violent crimes, though, some of them heinous and brutal. Neville Heath—charming, handsome, and intelligent—brutally and sadistically murdered two young English women (Critchley, 1951; Hill, 1960). Like Demara, Heath had an extraordinary career, much of it in the armed forces. Unlike Demara, his brushes with the law were serious and occasionally ended in imprisonment. He was commissioned and dishonorably discharged on three separate occasions, once each in the British Royal Air Force, the Royal Armed Service Corps, and the South African Air Force. He flew in a fighter squadron in the RAF until he was court-martialed for car theft at age 19. He then committed a series of thefts and burglaries and was sentenced to Borstal Prison. Pardoned in 1939, he joined the Royal Armed Service Corps but was dismissed for forgery. On his way home to England, he jumped ship and eventually managed to obtain a commission in the South African Air Force until his past caught up with him. When not in trouble, Heath was regarded as a daring, confident, and highly charming officer—and a rake. After the third court-martial, he developed a taste for sadistic murder.

You may be able to identify other examples of psychopaths at their worst. The notorious Charles Manson, who in the 1960s exhibited an uncanny ability to attract a devout cluster of unresisting followers, is one probable example. The fictional Hannibal Lechter, whose sadistic offenses and deadly charm have captivated readers and screen audiences, is another. It is not advisable, though, to see psychopaths around every corner, despite the frequent usage of this designation in popular media. When Joran Van der Sloot, the "Dutch playboy" was charged with one killing and suspected in the disappearance of a college student in 2010, headlines asked whether he was a psychopath. Every alleged violent criminal is not a psychopath. Moreover, as we note below, it is more likely that psychopathy exists on a continuum and that "full blown psychopaths" are rare. Throughout the remainder of this chapter, we examine in more detail their behavioral patterns, cognitive processes, interpersonal features, neuropsychological characteristics, and general backgrounds.

BEHAVIORAL DESCRIPTIONS

One pioneering authority on the behavioral characteristics of the psychopath was Hervey Cleckley, a well-known psychiatrist who died in 1984 at the age of 81. A large part of Cleckley's professional recognition came as a result of the nonfiction book *The Three Faces of Eve*, which he coauthored with Corbett Thigpen. The book, which is about the phenomenon of "multiple personality," was made into a very popular 1957 movie with the same title. However, his major professional contribution to the field of psychiatry can be found in his often-quoted text, *The Mask of Sanity* (first published in 1941). The book describes in clear and empirically useful terms the major behaviors demonstrated by the full-fledged or primary psychopath, as distinct from the other psychopathic types referred to previously. Cleckley was able to identify 16 characteristics he felt described the typical psychopath (see **Table 7-1**). We discuss some of these psychological characteristics identified by both Cleckley and Hare in more detail below.

Charming and Verbally Fluent

Superficial charm and average to above-average intelligence are two of the psychopath's main features, according to Cleckley, and they are both especially apparent during initial contacts. It should be emphasized, however, that a large portion of the psychopaths Cleckley worked with

TABLE 7-1   Psychopathic Behaviors Identified by Hare and Cleckley

Hare PCL Checklist	Cleckley's Primary Psychopath Description
Glibness/superficial charm	Superficial charm and good intelligence
Grandiose sense of self-worth	Pathological egocentricity
Pathological lying	Untruthfulness and insincerity
Cunning/manipulative	Manipulative
Lack of remorse or guilt	Lack of remorse or guilt
Shallow affect	General poverty of affective reactions
Callous, lack of empathy	Unresponsiveness in interpersonal relationships
Failure to accept responsibility for actions	Unreliability
Promiscuous sexual behavior	Impersonal sex life
Lack of realistic, long-term goals	Failure to follow any life plan
Poor behavioral controls	Impulsive
High need for stimulation/prone to boredom	Inadequately motivated antisocial behavior
Irresponsibility	Poor judgment Absence of delusions Absence of anxiety Bizarre behavior after drinking alcohol

were well educated and from middle- or upper-class backgrounds (Hare & Neumann, 2008), so they may not have been representative of psychopaths as a group. Nevertheless, many psychopaths impress others as friendly, outgoing, likable, and alert. They often appear well educated and knowledgeable, and they display many interests. They are verbally skillful and can talk themselves out of trouble. In fact, their vocabulary is often so extensive that they can talk at length about anything (Hare, 1991). However, systematic study of their conversation reveals that they often jump "from one topic to another and that much of their speech is empty of real substance, tending to be filled with stock phrases, repetitions of the same ideas, word approximations, abstract terms and jargon used in a superficial or inappropriate fashion, logically inconsistent statements and phrases, and half-formed sentences" (Hare, 1991, p. 57). As Hare (1996, p. 46) notes, "In some respects, it is as if psychopaths lack a central organizer to plan and keep track of what they think and say." However, since psychopaths are so charming and manipulative, these language short-comings are not readily apparent.

Readers should not conclude that psychopaths as a group are usually verbally and socially skillful at *successfully* manipulating others and the system. In a revealing study that followed a large number of psychopaths from age 8 to 48 (Ullrich, Farrington, & Coid, 2008), it was found that psychopathic traits did not lead to status or wealth, or successful intimate relationships. Apparently, the charm, deception, and impression management used by psychopaths does not lead to success in life.

Psychological Testing Differences

Psychometric studies (studies that use standard psychological tests as measures) indicate that psychopaths usually score higher on intelligence tests than the general population (Hare, 1970, 1996), particularly on individually administered tests. In fact, Hare wryly comments, the psychopaths who were the sample for his studies were probably the least intelligent of their ilk, since they were not quite bright enough to avoid being arrested and convicted for their offenses. (Hare at the time had conducted much of his research on imprisoned psychopaths.) Recent research (e.g., Ishikawa, Raine, Lencz, Bihrle, & Lacasse, 2001) has found that a useful dichotomy of psychopathy may be to divide psychopaths into "successful" psychopaths (those who have committed crimes but avoided arrest and conviction for offenses) and "unsuccessful" psychopaths (those who have been convicted and imprisoned). Overall, available research indicates that many psychopaths are bright, but some are not (Hare & Neumann, 2008).

Psychopaths and Mental Disorders

Psychopaths usually do *not* exhibit mental disorders, either mild or severe. Most lack any symptoms of excessive worry and anxiety, psychotic thinking, delusions, severe depressions, or hallucinations. Even under high-pressure conditions, they remain cool and calm, as did Ian Fleming's fictitious James Bond, probably a prime example. Feasibly, the doomed psychopath might enjoy a steak dinner (*au poivre*) with gusto just before being executed. The infamous multiple murderer Herman W. Mudget, alias H. H. Holmes, retired at his normal hour the evening before his execution, fell asleep easily, slept soundly, and woke up completely refreshed. "I never slept better in my life," he told his cell guard. He ordered and ate a substantial breakfast an hour before he was scheduled to be hanged. Until the moment of death, he remained remarkably calm and amiable, displaying no signs of depression or fear (Franke, 1975).

Psychologists usually do not consider psychopathy a mental disorder, but they do recognize that it has a biological basis, as we will discuss later in the chapter. Interestingly, representatives of the legal system may have some sympathy for the psychopath because of this biological aspect. In a recent study (Aspinwall, Brown, & Tabery, 2012), the researchers asked 181 criminal court judges to "sentence" someone convicted of a crime. All judges were told that a psychiatrist had diagnosed the defendant with psychopathy, but some were also told that psychopathy had a biological basis. Those judges given the biological information were significantly more likely to sentence the offender to a shorter term. In other words, they believed that this biological explanation for the behavior was a mitigating factor in sentencing.

Moreover, not everyone agrees with the view that psychopaths do *not* suffer from some mental disorder. Some clinicians argue that psychopathy and schizophrenia are part of the same spectrum of disorders (Hare, 1996), and Cleckley briefly considered psychopathy as a form of masked psychosis. Some forensic clinicians maintain that they occasionally see a mentally disordered offender who qualifies as both a psychopath and a schizophrenic (Hare, 1996). There is some evidence to suggest that it is not uncommon to find psychopaths who seem mentally disordered in maximum security psychiatric units for highly violent or dangerous patients. Other researchers have reported similar findings (Quinsey, Harris, Rice, & Cormier, 2006; Tengström, Hodgins, Grann, Långström, & Kullgren, 2004; Vitacco, Neumann, & Jackson, 2005). Tengström *et al.* found that individuals diagnosed with schizophrenia and who demonstrated many of the features of psychopathy had more severe histories of offending and violence than those persons diagnosed with schizophrenia alone.

Do Psychopaths Ever Commit Suicide?

Cleckley was under the impression that psychopaths rarely—if ever—committed suicide. Recent research and clinical experiences, however, have put Cleckley's observation in doubt. Hare, for instance, knows of several psychopaths who took their own lives when it became clear to them there was no other way out of what they perceived as an intolerable situation (Hare & Neumann, 2008). Intolerable situations include a very long prison term, incurable illness, or being surrounded by the police. "We suspect that at least some cases of 'suicide by cop' involved psychopaths who were trapped and wished to go out in a 'blaze of glory'" (Hare & Neumann, 2008, p. 228).

Verona, Patrick, and Joiner (2001) found that, among male inmates, psychopaths who were especially aggressive and impulsive did show some indicators of suicidality. *Suicidality* is a term used by clinicians to indicate there is a risk of suicide, usually inferred from suicidal thoughts or intent. In another study that examined psychopathy and suicidality in psychiatric patients, youthful offenders, jail detainees, and prison inmates, the researchers also found a significant relationship between psychopathy and suicidality (Douglas, Herbozo, Poythress, Belfrage, & Edens, 2006). However, the researchers also warned that the suicide–psychopathy relationship was highly complex and multifaceted, and required much more research to confidently establish it. In sum, research and clinical experience are beginning to find that some psychopaths who find themselves in desperate situations do commit suicide, especially if they are highly impulsive and violent.

Other Principal Traits

Other principal traits of the psychopath are selfishness and an inability to love or give affection to others. According to Cleckley, egocentricity is *always* present in the psychopath and is essentially unmodifiable. The psychopath is unable to feel genuine, meaningful affection for others. Psychopaths may be likable, but they are seldom able to keep close friends, and they have great difficulty understanding love in others. They may be highly skillful at pretending deep affection, and they may effectively mimic appropriate emotions, but true loyalty, warmth, and compassion are foreign to them. Psychopaths are distinguished by flat emotional reaction and affect. And since psychopaths have so little need to receive or give love, psychopaths, as a group, have relatively little contact with their families, and many change their residences frequently (Hare, 1991). In addition they do not usually respond to acts of kindness. They show capacity only for superficial appreciation. Paradoxically, they may do small favors and appear considerate toward others.

Psychopaths have a remarkable disregard for truth and are often called "pathological liars." They seem to have no internalized moral or ethical sense and cannot understand the purpose of being honest, especially if dishonesty will bring some personal gain. They have a cunning ability to appear straightforward, honest, and sincere, but their claims to sincerity are without substance.

Psychopaths are unreliable, irresponsible, and unpredictable, regardless of the importance of the occasion or the consequences of their impulsive actions. Impulsivity appears to be a central or cardinal feature of psychopathy (Hart & Dempster, 1997). This pattern of impulsive actions is cyclical, however. Psychopaths may, for months on end, be responsible citizens, faithful spouses, and reliable employees. They may experience great successes, be promoted, and gain honors, as did Demara and Heath. Skillfully as they have attained these socially desirable goals, they have an uncanny knack of suddenly unraveling their lives. They become irresponsible, and may pass bad checks, sabotage the company computers, or go on a drunken spree. They also tend to have a "bad temper" that flares quickly into an argument and attack. Psychopaths may later say they are sorry and plead for another chance—and most will probably get it. Invariably, if the psychopath is a young adult, the irresponsible behavior will return.

Even small amounts of alcohol prompt most psychopaths to become vulgar, domineering, loud, and boisterous and to engage in practical jokes and pranks. Cleckley noted that they choose pranks that have no appeal for most individuals, and that seem bizarre, inappropriate, and cruel. They lack genuine humor and, not surprisingly, the ability to laugh at themselves.

Although often above average in intelligence, psychopaths appear incapable of learning to avoid failure and situations that are potentially damaging to themselves. Some theorists suggest that the self-destructive, self-defeating deeds and attitudes reflect a need to be punished to mitigate the guilt they subconsciously experience, or more simply, that they are driven by a masochistic purpose. Evidence refuting these explanations is offered later in this chapter.

A cardinal fault of psychopaths is their absolute lack of remorse or guilt for anything they do, regardless of the severity or immorality of their actions and irrespective of their traumatic effects on others. Since they do not anticipate personal consequences, psychopaths may engage in destructive or antisocial behavior—such as forgery, theft, rape, brawls, and fraud—by taking absurd risks and for insignificant personal gain. When caught, they express no genuine remorse. They may readily admit culpability and take considerable pleasure in the shock these admissions produce in others. Whether they have bashed in someone's head, ruined a car, or tortured a child, psychopaths may well remark they did it "for the hell of it."

Psychopaths have little capacity to see themselves as others perceive them. Instead of accepting the facts that would normally lead to insight, they project and externalize blame onto the community and family for their misfortunes. Interestingly, educated psychopaths have been known to speak fluently about the psychopathic personality, quoting the literature extensively and discussing research findings, but they cannot look into their own troublesome antics or mount a reasonable attack on their actions. They articulate their regrets for having done something, but the words are devoid of emotional meaning, a characteristic Cleckley calls **semantic aphasia**. Johns and Quay (1962) remarked that psychopaths "know the words but not the music." Similarly, Grant (1977) notes that the psychopath knows only the book meaning of words, not the living meaning. Hare (1996, p. 45) concludes, "In short, psychopaths appear to be semantically and affectively shallow individuals."

Another important behavioral characteristic of psychopaths noted by Blair, Peschardt, Budhani, Mitchell, and Pine (2006) is their *excessive* use of instrumental aggression. Instrumental aggression, as discussed in Chapter 5, is purposeful and goal-directed aggression used to achieve a specific goal, such as the possessions of another person. It is distinguished from reactive aggression, which is considered spontaneous, unplanned, and done in response to an event or an action by another individual. However, the psychopath is inclined to achieve his or her goal regardless of who is hurt, damaged, or destroyed. Therefore, insensitive to others in achieving this goal, the psychopath may use reactive aggression if someone insults or attempts to block this goal achievement. Cornell and his colleagues (1996, p. 788) comment, "Consider an extreme example of an instrumental offender who unexpectedly encountered a man with a large sum of money, confronted the man to demand his money, became angry at the man's sarcastic response, and then beat him to death." Cornell *et al.* (1996) conclude that the distinction between instrumental and reactive violence is not clear-cut. Finally, an important behavioral distinction underlying much of Cleckley's description is what Quay (1965) refers to as the psychopath's profound and pathological stimulation seeking. According to Quay, the actions of the psychopath are motivated by an excessive *neuropsychological* need for thrills and excitement. It is not unusual to see psychopaths drawn to such interests as race car driving, skydiving, and motorcycle stunts. We will examine this alleged need for stimulation in the pages to follow.

In recent years, it has become useful for research purposes to focus on psychopaths who repeatedly commit crimes, collectively called criminal psychopaths. Concentrating on psychopaths who are violent or chronic offenders provides invaluable information about their backgrounds, learning history, and behavioral patterns. Such research also might offer key strategies for how to deal and potentially treat this challenging group of individuals.

THE CRIMINAL PSYCHOPATH

As stated repeatedly above, many psychopaths have no history of serious antisocial behavior, and persistent, serious offenders are not necessarily psychopaths. For our purposes here, the term *criminal psychopath* will be reserved for those psychopaths who demonstrate a wide range of *persistent* and *serious* antisocial behavior. As a group, they tend to be "dominant, manipulative individuals characterized by an impulsive, risk-taking and antisocial lifestyle, which obtain their greatest thrill from diverse sexual gratification and target diverse victims over time" (Porter *et al.*, 2000, p. 220). As noted at the beginning of this chapter, Porter and his colleagues consider psychopathy "one of the most important psychological constructs in the criminal justice system" (p. 227).

Contemporary theory and research consider psychopathic traits and predispositions as existing on a continuum. The entertainment media often portray the psychopath as an inhumane, vile, despicable person who enjoys violence. One is left with the impression that an individual is either a psychopath or a nonpsychopath. However, psychopathic traits and characteristics in adults and adolescents are best viewed today as occurring along a dimension or continuum, with some people demonstrating more psychopathic tendencies than others. As we will see shortly, someone is labeled as a psychopath after attaining a given cutoff score on tests to measure the construct. The accumulation of psychopathic characteristics is what determines the final diagnosis, and not everyone agrees on the required cutoff point. Therefore, the best perspective to take when studying the following material is that psychopathy exists on different levels rather than viewing people as either psychopaths or nonpsychopaths. Nevertheless, when we refer to percentages of psychopaths in a population, we are referring to the percentages that have met the cutoff criteria as defined by a particular research study.

Prevalence of Criminal Psychopathy

Overall, Robert Hare (1998) estimates that the prevalence of psychopaths in the general population is about 1 percent, whereas in the adult prison population, estimates range from 15 percent to 25 percent. Some researchers (e.g., Simourd & Hoge, 2000) wonder, however, whether these estimates are not somewhat inflated. Simourd and Hoge report only 11 percent of their inmate population could be identified as criminal psychopaths. The inmates used in the Simourd–Hoge study were not simply inmates in a medium security correctional facility. All 321 were serving a current sentence for violent offending, more than half of them had been convicted of a previous violent offense, and almost all of them had extensive criminal careers. Even so, few qualified as criminal psychopaths. Therefore, percentage estimates of criminal psychopathy within any given prison population should be tempered by the type of facility, as well as the cultural, ethnic, gender, and age mix of the targeted population. Interestingly, the American Psychiatric Association (1994) estimates that the overall prevalence of *antisocial personality disorder* (APD) in the community at large is about 3 percent in males and about 1 percent in females. In clinical samples (those receiving therapy for various disorders), the prevalence estimates vary between 3 percent and 30 percent, depending on the characteristics of the sample surveyed. Keep in mind, though, that APD is *not* identical to psychopathy, even though the *Diagnostic and Statistical Manual* confuses APD with psychopathy. As noted above, it appears that the next edition of the *DSM* (*DSM-5*) may continue to confuse the two diagnostic labels (Gurley, 2009).

Offending Patterns of Criminal Psychopaths

Criminal psychopaths are believed responsible for a disproportionate amount of crime in society, and they are considered to be the most violent and persistent offenders (Declercq, Willemsen, Audenaert, & Verhaeghe, 2012; Forth & Burke, 1998; Hart & Hare, 1997; Newman, Schmitt, & Voss, 1997; Saltaris, 2002). Gretton, McBride, Hare, O'Shaughnessy, and Kumka (2001, p. 428) point out that criminal psychopaths generally "lack a normal sense of ethics and morality, live by their own rules, are prone to use cold-blooded, instrumental intimidation and violence to satisfy their wants and needs, and generally are contemptuous of social norms and the rights of others." Hare (1996, p. 38) posits, "The ease with which psychopaths engage in…dispassionate violence has very real significance for society in general and for law enforcement personnel in particular." Hare refers to a report by the Federal Bureau of Investigation (1992) that found that nearly half of the law enforcement officers who died in the line of duty were killed by individuals who closely matched the personality profile of the psychopath. Moreover, the unlawful acts of psychopathic sex offenders are likely to be more violent, brutal, unconventional, and sadistic than those of other sex offenders (Hare, Clark, Grann, & Thornton, 2000; Porter, Birt, & Boer, 2001; Woodworth & Porter, 2002). Psychopathic sex offenders appear to be more motivated by thrill seeking and excitement rather than simply sexual arousal (Porter, Woodworth, Earle, Drugge, & Boer, 2003). Psychopaths as a group also appear to be significantly more sadistic than violent nonpsychopaths (Holt, Meloy, & Stack, 1999) and commit more diverse and severe forms of sexual homicides (Firestone, Bradford, Greenberg, & Larose, 1998; Porter, Woodworth, M., Earle, J., Drugge, J., & Boer, 2003). Porter and his colleagues (2003) found that in a sample of the male offenders incarcerated in two Canadian federal prisons for homicide, nearly half could be classified as sexual homicide offenders. (In order to be classified as a sexual homicide, there had to be physical evidence of sexual activity with the victim before, during, or after the homicide.)

Murderers described as excessively sadistic and brutal tend to have many psychopathic features (Hare *et al.*, 2000; Stone, 1998). Serial murderers who exhibit psychopathic features are especially sadistic and brutal in their murders. Collectively, the research suggests that psychopaths may be more likely than other offenders to derive pleasure from both the nonsexual and sexual suffering of others (Porter *et al.*, 2003).

Many of the murders and serious assaults committed by nonpsychopaths occurred during domestic disputes or extreme emotional arousal, thereby qualifying as reactive aggression. This pattern of violence is rarely observed for criminal psychopaths (Declercq *et al.*, 2012; Hare, Hart, & Harpur, 1991; Williamson, Hare, & Wong, 1987). Criminal psychopaths frequently engage in violence as a form of revenge or retribution, or during a bout of drinking. Many of the attacks of nonpsychopaths are toward women they know well, whereas many of the attacks of criminal psychopaths are directed toward men who are strangers. Hare *et al.* (1991, p. 395) observe that the violence committed by criminal psychopaths was callous and cold-blooded, "without the affective coloring that accompanied the violence of nonpsychopaths." Research also indicates that rapists who have psychopathic characteristics are more likely to have "nonsexual" motivations for their crimes, such as anger, vindictiveness, sadism, and opportunism (Hart & Dempster, 1997).

PSYCHOLOGICAL MEASURES OF PSYCHOPATHY

Currently, the most popular instrument for measuring criminal psychopathy is the 22-item **Psychopathy Checklist (PCL)** (Hare, 1980) and its 20-item revision (**PCL-R**) (Hare, 1991, 2003). The PCL-R has been published in a second edition, which includes new information on its applicability in forensic and research settings. In some circles, the PCL-R is regarded as the "gold standard" for the measurement of psychopathy (Vitacco *et al.*, 2005). The second edition also has been expanded for use with offenders in other countries and includes updated normative and validation data on male and female offenders. A 12-item short-form version has also been developed, called the **Psychopathy Checklist: Screening Version (PCL:SV)** (Hart, Cox, & Hare, 1995; Hart, Hare, & Forth, 1993). Other additions are the **Psychopathy Checklist: Youth Version (PCL:YV)** (Forth, Kosson, & Hare, 2003) and the *P-Scan: Research Version.* The PCL:YV is beginning to be researched more extensively and is covered in more detail in the section "Juvenile Psychopathy." The P-Scan is a screening instrument that serves as *rough* screen for psychopathic features and as a source of working hypotheses to deal with managing suspects, offenders, or clients. It is designed for use in law enforcement, probation, corrections, civil and forensic facilities, and other areas in which it would be useful to have some information about the possible presence of psychopathic features in a particular person. Of course, the P-Scan needs much more research before its results can be considered definitive. All five checklists are conceptually and—with the exception of the P-Scan—psychometrically similar.

The PCL scales are largely based on Cleckley's (1976) conception of psychopathy, but are specifically designed to identify psychopaths in male prison, forensic, or psychiatric populations. Cleckley's work was based primarily on psychiatric patients. Although several other personality scales for measuring psychopathy have been developed in recent years, the PCL-R is currently the most frequently used instrument for both research and clinical application; it will be the center of attention for the remainder of this section.

Some scholars (e.g., Skeem & Cooke, 2010a, 2010b) believe that the PCL-R has become so popular that it obscures the distinction between a measure and a theory. That is, the PCL-R is merely a limited measure of psychopathy, not a theory of psychopathy. More specifically, the PCL-R is heavily based on those psychopaths who are convicted criminals, not on psychopaths who are not criminal offenders. Consequently, the PCL-R may not be an adequate measure of psychopathy, and it certainly (according to Skeem and Cooke) does not qualify as a comprehensive theory of psychopathy that generates empirical study. Skeem and Cooke believe that some antisocial behavior seems essential to the interpersonal and emotional core of psychopathy, such as noncriminal manipulation of others for personal gain. Criminal behavior, on the other hand, refers to behavior that is officially sanctioned by the legal system. Criminal behavior represents illegal behavior, punishable by criminal sanctions. "Given individual differences in talents and opportunities, psychopathic tendencies may be manifested in one individual's criminality, in another individual's heroism, and in still another's worldly success" (Skeem & Cooke, 2010a, p. 435).

Hare and Neumann (2010) disagree with Skeem and Cooke's claim that criminality is an essential component of the PCL-R. They argue that antisocial behavior, not criminal behavior, is central to the concept and measurement of psychopathy. Hare and Neuman assert that "Although the PCL-R is not perfect, it works well enough to have generated many hundreds of empirical studies on psychopathy...and to have withstood unusually intense conceptual and statistical scrutiny" (p. 450).

The PCL-R

The PCL-R assesses the affective (emotional), interpersonal, behavioral, and social deviance facets of criminal psychopathy from various sources, including self-reports, behavioral observations, and collateral sources, such as parents, family members, friends, and arrest and court records which can help to establish the credibility of self-reports (Hare, 1996; Hare *et al.*, 1991). In addition, item ratings from the PCL-R, for instance, require some integration of information across multiple domains, including behavior at work or school; behavior toward family, friends, and sexual partners; and criminal or antisocial behavior (Kosson, Suchy, Mayer, & Libby, 2002). Typically, highly trained examiners use all this information to score each item on a 0–2 scale, depending on the extent to which an individual has the disposition described by each item on the checklist (0 = consistently absent; 1 = inconsistent; 2 = consistently present). Scoring is, however, quite complex and requires substantial time, extensive training, and access to a considerable amount of background information on the individual. In recent years, some researchers have been obtaining PCL-R scores from detailed records, without the interview component. Although there is some support for conducting such reviews (Gretton *et al.*, 2001), it appears that lower scores may result from using this approach (Hare, 2003).

A score of 30 or above usually qualifies a person as a primary psychopath (Hare, 1996). In some research and clinical settings, cutoff scores ranging from 25 to 33 are often used (Simourd & Hoge, 2000). Hare (1991) recommends that persons with scores between 21 and 29 be classified as "middle" subjects who show many of the features of psychopathy but do not fit all the criteria. As mentioned above, psychopathy is best conceptualized as occurring on a continuum; person with scores below 21 are considered "nonpsychopaths."

So far, the research has strongly supported the reliability and validity of the PCL-R for distinguishing criminal psychopaths from criminal nonpsychopaths, and for helping correctional and forensic psychologists involved in risk assessments of offenders (Hare, 1996; Hare & Neumann, 2008; Hare, Forth, & Stachan, 1992). In addition, the instrument provides researchers and mental health professionals with a universal measurement for the assessment of psychopathy that facilitates international and cross-cultural communication concerning theory, research, and eventual clinical practice (Hare *et al.*, 2000). Currently, the PCL-R is increasingly being used as a clinical instrument for the diagnosis of psychopathy across the globe, although it appears to be most powerful in identifying psychopathy among North American white males (Hare *et al.*, 2000).

Interestingly, Scott Lilienfeld and his colleagues (Lilienfeld, Gershon, Duke, Marion, & de Waal, 1999) have developed a psychopathy scale for chimpanzees, called the Chimpanzee Psychopathy Measure (CPM). Preliminary data indicate that the scale appears to be a reliable measure of psychopathic-like behavior in chimpanzees. According to the researchers, the psychopathic behavior of chimps include excessive displays of sexual activity, daring behaviors, teasing, silent bluff displays, and temper tantrums. While we do not suggest that chimp research is akin to research with humans, these data underscore the potential neuropsychological basis for psychopathy in humans.

Core Factors of Psychopathy

From the research on the PCL-R, it has become clear that psychopathy is multidimensional in nature. One statistical procedure designed to find different dimensions or factors in test data is **factor analysis**. When expert ratings of psychopathy on the PCL-R were submitted to a factor analysis, at least two behavioral dimensions or factors emerged (Hare, 1991; Harpur, Hakstian, & Hare, 1988;

Hart, Hare, & Forth, 1993). Many researchers note that more have been identified, and the two-factor position is becoming less accepted as a complete portrayal of psychopathy.

THE TWO-FACTOR POSITION   In the two-factor scheme, **Factor 1** reflects the interpersonal and emotional components of the disorder and consists of items measuring remorselessness, callousness, and selfish use and manipulation of others. The typical psychopath feels no compunctions about using others strictly to meet his or her own needs. **Factor 2** is most closely associated with a socially deviant or antisocial lifestyle, as characterized by poor planning, impulsiveness, an excessive need for stimulation, proneness to boredom, and a lack of realistic goals. Some researchers have found that Factor 1 appears to be associated with planned predatory violence, while Factor 2 appears to be related to spontaneous and impulsive violence (Hart & Dempster, 1997). Factor 1 is also linked to resistance and inability to profit from psychotherapy and treatment programs (Seto & Barbaree, 1999). Factor 2 appears related to socioeconomic status, educational attainment, and cultural/ethnic background, whereas Factor 1 may be more connected to biopsychological influences (Cooke & Michie, 1997). Research also suggests that Factor 1 *may* be a more powerful indicator of psychopathy than Factor 2 (Cooke, Michie, Hart, & Hare, 1999). In addition, while it is quite clear that Factor 1 does a better job of identifying psychopathy in general, there is some evidence that Factor 2 does a better job of predicting general recidivism and violent recidivism (Walters, 2003).

THE THREE-FACTOR POSITION   Psychopathic behavior may be too diverse to be captured in only two dimensions. With increasing sophistication of statistical methods (e.g., confirmatory factor analysis and model-based cluster analysis), contemporary research indicates that there may be at least three core behavioral or personality dimensions that best describe psychopathy (Cooke & Michie, 2001; Cooke, Michie, Hart, & Clark, 2004; Vitacco *et al.*, 2005). In an influential paper, Cooke and Michie (2001) challenged the traditional two-factor explanation of psychopathy and recommended that psychopathy be divided into the following core dimensions:

1. An arrogant and deceptive interpersonal style, which includes a grandiose sense of self-worth, glibness, superficial charm, lying, conning, manipulation, and deceitfulness. (This dimension is also referred to as impression management.)
2. Deficient affective or emotional experience characterized by low remorse, low guilt, a weak conscience, the absence of anxiety, fearlessness, callousness, little empathy, and a failure to accept responsibility for one's actions.
3. An impulsive and irresponsible behavioral style, including failure to think before acting, a lack of long-term goals, stimulation seeking, unsatisfactory work habits, and a parasitic lifestyle (living off others, including spouses, intimate partners, friends, and parents).

THE FOUR DIMENSIONS POSITION   Some researchers (e.g., Hare, 2003; Hare & Neumann, 2008; Salekin, Brannen, Zalot, Leistico, & Neumann, 2006; Vitacco *et al.*, 2005) have asserted that, in addition to disturbances in interpersonal, affective, and behavioral functioning, the definition of psychopathy should also include a fourth factor or dimension: antisocial behavior. Hare and Neumann (2008) write, "A number of recent studies…provide considerable support for a four-factor model of psychopathy across diverse and primarily very large samples of male and female offenders" (p. 232). The four-factor model has also been supported across various cultures, ethnic groups, young and adult offenders, and forensic patients (Jackson, Neumann, & Vitacco, 2007; Jones, Cauffman, Miller, & Mulvey, 2006; Neumann, Hare, & Newman, 2007; Neumann, Kosson, Forth, & Hare, 2006).

| TABLE 7-2 | Summary of the Four Hypothesized Core Factors of Psychopathy |

Factor	Core Features
Interpersonal (F1)	Lying, conning, manipulating others; superficial charm; promiscuous sexual behavior
Impulsive lifestyle (F2)	Irresponsibility; sensation seeking; lack of realistic goals, poor planning
Affective (F3)	Shallow emotions, callousness, little empathy; grandiose self-worth
Antisocial tendencies (F4)	Poor self-regulation; persistent criminal activity; antisocial behavior

The argument for a four-factor model is based on the finding that individuals manifesting psychopathic traits often exhibit violence and a large collection of other antisocial behavioral patterns that are more than the poor planning and impulsivity associated with Factor 2. Consequently, the argument contends that researchers and clinicians are missing a critical ingredient in the understanding and definition of the psychopath if measures of antisocial behavior are left out of the equation. It is also argued that much of the predictive power of psychopathy is enhanced if we take into consideration past criminal behavior (Salekin *et al.*, 2006). According to the four-factor perspective, the factors are as follows: (1) interpersonal, such as pathological lying and conning, (2) impulsive lifestyle, such as irresponsible behavior, sensation seeking, and impulsiveness, (3) affective (shallow affect or emotional reactions, lack of remorsefulness for their actions), and (4) antisocial tendencies, such as poor self-regulation and a wide array of antisocial behavior. **Table 7-2** summarizes these four factors.

Recidivism

Research studies report that the recidivism rate of psychopaths is very high. **Recidivism** refers to the tendency to return to criminal offending, although studies differ in how it is measured (e.g., arrests, convictions, self-reported crime). In other words, psychopaths commit crimes again and again, regardless of the methods used to stop or rehabilitate them. According to Porter *et al.* (2000), research suggests psychopaths reoffend faster, violate parole sooner, and perhaps commit more institutional violence than nonpsychopaths. In one study (Serin, Peters, & Barbaree, 1990), the number of failures of male offenders released on unescorted temporary absence programs (furloughs) was examined. The failure rate for psychopaths was 37.5 percent, while none of the nonpsychopaths failed. The failure rate during parole was also examined. While 7 percent of nonpsychopaths violated parole conditions, 33 percent of the psychopaths violated their conditions. In another study (Serin & Amos, 1995), 299 male offenders were followed for up to eight years after their release from a federal prison. Sixty-five percent of the psychopaths were convicted of another crime within three years, compared with a reconviction rate of 25 percent for nonpsychopaths. Quinsey, Rice, and Harris (1995) found that within six years of release from prison, more than 80 percent of the psychopaths convicted as sex offenders had violently recidivated, compared with a 20 percent recidivism rate for nonpsychopathic sex offenders. Recidivism was measured by either arrests or convictions for a violent offense. Richards, Casey, and Lucente (2003) found the PCL-R and the PCL:SV measures of persistent offending history, in conjunction with high scores on the PCL-R, are probably two of the most powerful predictors of violent recidivism available anywhere. In fact, the PCL-R is a strong predictor of recidivism even when the offender's criminal history is not known to the examiner (Hemphill & Hare, 2004; Hemphill, Hare, & Wong, 1998).

High recidivism rates are also characteristic of psychopathic adolescent male offenders. Shortly, though, we will discuss the controversy over whether juvenile psychopathy even exists. According to Gretton *et al.* (2001), these offenders are more likely than other adolescent offenders to escape from custody, violate the conditions of probation, and commit nonviolent and violent offenses over a five-year follow-up period. The high recidivism rates among adult and juvenile offenders have prompted some researchers to conclude that there is "nothing the behavioral sciences can offer for treating those with psychopathy" (Gacono, Nieberding, Owen, Rubel, & Bodholdt, 1997, p. 119). This is partly because psychopaths tend to "be unmotivated to alter their problematic behavior and often lack insight into the nature and extent of their psychopathology" (Skeem, Edens, & Colwell, 2003, p. 26). As we note below, other researchers are more optimistic.

THE FEMALE PSYCHOPATH

Overall, research suggests that there are significantly fewer female than male psychopaths, both in the general population and among persons convicted of crime (Bolt, Hare, Vitale, & Newman, 2004; Rogstad & Rogers, 2008). In the general population, the estimated prevalence of psychopathy among males is 1 percent (Hare, 2003), but the prevalence is significantly less among females (Nicholls, Ogloff, Brink, & Spidel, 2005). Salekin, Rogers, and Sewell (1997) reported that the prevalence rate of psychopathy for female offenders in a jail setting was 15.5 percent, compared with the 25 percent to 30 percent prevalence rate estimated for male offenders. In another study, Salekin, Rogers, Ustad, and Sewell (1998) found, using a PCL-R cutoff score of 29, that 12.9 percent of their sample of 78 female inmates qualified as psychopaths. In a more recent investigation involving 528 adult women incarcerated in the state of Wisconsin, Vitale, Smith, Brinkley, and Newman (2002) report that only 9 percent of their participants could be classified as psychopaths, using the recommended cutoff score of 30 on the PCL-R. Finally, Hare (2003) found that about 7.5 percent of female offenders and 15 percent of male offenders meet the recommended cutoff score of 30 on the PCL-R. All these studies consistently indicate that females generally score lower on the PCL-R than males.

Hare's PCL and PCL-R have been developed almost exclusively on male criminal psychopaths. Some studies using the PCL-R suggest that female criminal psychopaths may demonstrate different behavioral patterns than male criminal psychopaths (Nicholls & Petrila, 2005; Vitale, Smith, Brinkley, & Newman, 2002). Although the data are far from conclusive, female psychopaths, compared with male psychopaths, appear to demonstrate a lack of realistic long-term goals, have numerous marital relationships, engage in a wide range of crime, and show a greater tendency to be sexually promiscuous (Grann, 2000; Salekin *et al.*, 1997; Warren *et al.*, 2003). We urge caution in interpreting this last characteristic, because men and women are often judged differently on this criterion. Female psychopaths also may not express the same emotional processing abnormalities as male psychopaths (Sutton, Vitale, & Newman, 2002). It appears that the affective features of psychopathy are especially important in identifying female psychopaths, with high levels of callousness and low levels of empathy clearly distinguishing them from nonpsychopathic women (Jackson, Rogers, Neumann, & Lambert, 2002; Rogstad & Rogers, 2008).

There is also some evidence that female psychopaths are less aggressive and violent than male psychopaths (Mulder, Wells, Joyce, & Bushnell, 1994) and may begin their offending careers later than male psychopaths (Hart & Hare, 1997). Female psychopaths may also recidivate less often than male psychopaths (Salekin *et al.*, 1998). In fact, the evidence suggests that psychopathic female inmates may have recidivism rates that are no different than the recidivism rates reported for nonpsychopathic female inmates (Salekin *et al.*, 1998).

Similar to gender differences in criminality on the whole, the reported gender distinctions in psychopathy are probably due to a number of social influences and neuropsychological differences that occur across the developmental trajectory of males and females. Women and men arrive at crime via different pathways, and we must often look for different explanations for their crimes (Salisbury & Van Voorhis, 2009). As a result of these differences, females with psychopathic characteristics might rely on different tactics than males to reach the same goals (Nicholls & Petrila, 2005).

The more recent research utilizing the PCL-R shows considerable promise in identifying gender differences in psychopathy, but many researchers and experts urge caution before the instrument is adopted for clinical or diagnostic use with women (Nicholls *et al.*, 2005). Rogers (2000) admonishes that "psychologists are on safest ground if they limit their risk predictions on the PCL-R to White males with criminal histories" (p. 600). For the most part, however, there is emerging evidence that psychopathy as measured by the PCL-R has a significant relationship with antisocial behavior in adult females. To date, though, the research on female juvenile psychopaths is less convincing, as we will see shortly.

RACIAL/ETHNIC DIFFERENCES

Kosson, Smith, and Newman (1990) noticed that most measures of psychopathy have been developed using white inmates as subjects. In their research, they found that psychopathy, as measured by Hare's PCL, does exist in African American male inmates in a pattern that resembles white male inmates. However, Kosson *et al.* found one important difference. The African American criminal psychopaths tended to be less impulsive than white criminal psychopaths. This finding raises some questions as to whether the PCL is entirely appropriate to use with African American inmates. On the other hand, Jennifer Vitale *et al.* (2002) found no significant racial differences in the scores and distributions of female psychopaths. More specifically, Vitale *et al.* report that 10 percent of the 248 incarcerated Caucasian women who participated in their study reached the cutoff scores of 30 or higher on the PCL-R compared with 9 percent of the 280 incarcerated African American women who had similar scores.

A meta-analysis by Jennifer Skeem, John Edens, Jacqueline Camp, and Lori Colwell (2004) supports the conclusion that the differences between blacks and whites are minimal. They concluded that "Our finding that Blacks and Whites do not meaningfully differ in their levels of core psychopathic traits is consistent with community-based findings for self-report measures of psychopathy and clinical diagnoses of antisocial personality disorder" (p. 505). Recent research suggests that there are no significant differences between black and Hispanic inmates compared to white inmates (Neumann & Hare, 2008; Vachon, Lynam, Loeber, & Stouthamer-Loeber, 2012). Research has also found that there are no apparent differences between blacks and whites, convicted or nonconvicted, on PCL-SV scores, indicating that, in general, racial/ethnic difference in psychopathy scores are minimal (Vachon *et al.*, 2012).

Some researchers have raised the intriguing and serious issue of whether the stigmatizing diagnosis of psychopathy is likely to be used in a biased manner among minority or disadvantaged groups (Edens, Petrila, & Buffington-Vollum, 2001; Skeem, Edens, & Colwell, 2003; Skeem, Edens, Sanford, & Colwell, 2003). In essence, the consequence of being diagnosed with psychopathy is becoming more serious (Skeem, Edens, and Colwell, 2003). As pointed out by

Skeem, Edens, Sanford, & Colwell (2003), Canada and the United Kingdom use the diagnosis of psychopathy to support indeterminate detention for certain classes of offenders. Furthermore, "there is evidence that psychopathy increasingly is being used as an aggravating factor in the sentencing phase of U.S. death penalty cases, where it has been argued that the presence of these personality traits renders a defendant a 'continuing threat to society'" (Skeem, Edens, and Colwell, 2003, p. 17). Edens, Petrila, and Buffington -Vollum (2001) suggest that perhaps the PCL-R should be excluded from capital sentencing until more solid research on its ability to predict future dangerousness in minority and disadvantaged individuals is established.

JUVENILE PSYCHOPATHY

As we have seen, one of the serious shortcomings of the extensive research conducted on psychopathy is that it has focused almost exclusively on white, adult males (Frick, Bodin, & Barry, 2000). Consequently, research on juvenile (adolescent and child) psychopathy is limited, but it is rapidly growing. There is substantial evidence that male criminal psychopaths begin their offending patterns at a very early age (Frick, 2009; Rutter, 2005). However, attempts to apply the label "psychopathy" to juvenile populations "raise several conceptual, methodological, and practical concerns related to clinical/forensic practice and juvenile/criminal justice policy" (Edens, Skeem, Cruise, & Cauffman, 2001, p. 54). Some debate has focused on whether psychopathy can or should be applied to juveniles at all. Can features of adult psychopathy be found in children and adolescents in the first place? Others are concerned that—even if psychopathy can be identified in adolescents—the label may have too many negative connotations. More specifically, the label implies that the prognosis for treatment is poor, a high rate of offending and recidivism can be expected, and the intrinsic and biological basis of the disorder means little can be done outside of biological interventions. This may lead those working in the juvenile justice system to give up on the juveniles so labeled. A third debate contends that psychopathy assessments of youths must achieve a high level of confidence before they can be employed in the criminal justice system (Edens, Campbell, & Weir, 2007; Seagrave & Grisso, 2002). We will discuss these assessments shortly.

Can Juvenile Psychopathy be Identified?

Another major problem of identifying juvenile psychopaths is that psychopathy—if it exists in this age group—may be very difficult to measure reliably because of the transient and constantly changing developmental patterns across the life span. Many clinicians and researchers have resisted any trend to search for psychopathy in juveniles, noting that features of the adult psychopath simply represent normal adolescent development. In other words, adolescents often appear callous and narcissistic, sometimes to hide their own fear and anxiety. They are often impulsive and engage in sensation-seeking behaviors, and many are not particularly good at long-range planning. In reality, these and other psychopathic-like characteristics represent either a passing phase in the difficult transition to adulthood or the adolescent's "cover" to make himself or herself appear noncaring. For other children, psychopathic-like characteristics might be indicative of physical or sexual abuse. Children in abusive homes often demonstrate an abnormally restricted range of emotions that are similar to the emotional characteristics of psychopathy. Actually, these symptoms are the child's way of coping with a very stressful home environment (Seagrave & Grisso, 2002). Furthermore, "Some adolescent behavior may…appear psychopathic by way of poor anger control, lack of goals, and poor judgment, but is actually influenced by parallel developmental tasks encountered by most adolescents" (Seagrave & Grisso, 2002, p. 229). Going against the rules is part of many adolescents' attempts to gain autonomy from adult dominance, such as found in adolescent-limited offending.

Nevertheless, certain problem characteristics in children and adolescents—for example, conduct problems, hyperactivity, impulsivity, and attention difficulties—resemble features of the adult psychopath and suggest that the term *juvenile psychopath* may have some validity. On the other hand, these characteristics may simply represent disorders such as conduct disorder (CD) or oppositional defiant disorder (ODD) that are distinct from psychopathy. As Cruise, Colwell, Lyons, and Baker (2003) have emphasized, to be useful, the construct of juvenile psychopathy must be distinguished from other diagnoses. It appears, though, that current research is rapidly approaching a distinct construct. For example, a multidimensional model that identifies callous and unemotional traits (C/U), narcissism, and impulsivity has been proposed and tested as indicative of childhood psychopathy (Barry, Barry, Deming, & Lochman, 2008; Fite, Stoppelbein, & Greening, 2009; Frick, 2009; Pardini & Loeber, 2008).

A large amount of empirical research solidly supports the juvenile psychopathy construct (Asscher, *et al.*, 2011). Studies continually find support for its existence and validity, and it seems to remain stable from age 7 to at least age 24 (Lynam *et al.*, 2009; Lynam, Caspi, Moffitt, Loeber, & Stouthamer-Loeber, 2007).

Ethical Considerations

On the whole, though, there is considerable concern about misuse of labels suggesting psychopathy by juvenile justice professionals, including judges, youth detention workers, and treatment providers. Because of the widespread assertion that psychopaths are highly resistant to treatment, an adolescent "psychopath" accused of a crime—or even a youth demonstrating psychopathic characteristics—is more likely to be transferred to the adult court system rather than kept in the juvenile system. In the latter, treatment is more likely to be available once the youth has been adjudicated delinquent. Until very recently, a 16- or 17-year-old juvenile labeled a psychopath also was more likely to be sentenced to death in some states (Edens, Guy, & Fernandez, 2003). However, in 2005, the U.S. Supreme Court ruled that juveniles who committed their crimes at these ages could not be sentenced to death (*Roper v. Simmons*). The court had previously set 16 as the minimum age at which juveniles were eligible for the death penalty (*Thompson v. Oklahoma*, 1989). Nevertheless, juveniles who are tried in criminal courts continue to be subjected to lengthy punitive criminal sanctions.

Surprisingly, one study found no negative effects associated with the label in a juvenile court (Murrie, Boccaccini, McCoy, & Cornell, 2007). By contrast, Viljoen, MacDougall, Gagnon, and Douglas (2010) found that that juveniles whose cases indicated psychopathy received harsher treatment by juvenile courts, including being transferred to adult courts. Viljoen *et al.* remarked, "psychopathy evidence was commonly used to infer that a youth would be very difficult or impossible to treat" (p. 271). Recall, though, the study referred to earlier in the chapter (Aspinwall *et al.*, 2012), wherein judges gave shorter sentences to an adult identified as a psychopath when evidence of a biological basis to the condition was presented. One would think that a youth would receive a sentence that would be at least as favorable. Future researchers will likely continue to explore the impact of biological information on the actual sentences imposed by judges.

Even·when juveniles are kept in the juvenile system and placed in treatment centers the label "psychopath" may become a self-fulfilling prophecy with treatment providers who may be unlikely to expend considerable effort on a seemingly hopeless case. Supporters of the construct of juvenile psychopathy argue that treatment providers should have that information at their disposal, both to make management decisions regarding custody and programming and to fashion the type of treatment that could be effective. Others contend that it is important to identify psychopathy as early as possible to avoid the negative consequences to society and to help juveniles with psychopathic characteristics. Fortunately, researchers are beginning to identify promising treatment (Salekin & Lynam, 2010; Spain, Douglas, Poythress, & Epstein, 2004), as we discuss later in the chapter. In essence, if there is a distinct difference between psychopathic youth and nonpsychopathic youth, supporters claim it is critical that knowledge of this difference be communicated to those who work most closely with them. Additionally, it is helpful to identify and promote "protective factors" in a child's developmental sequence that might help insulate him or her from psychopathy (Salekin & Lochman, 2008). Supporters also believe there is wisdom in targeting for early intervention a subgroup of adolescents who otherwise might become career criminals (Skeem & Cauffman, 2003). This presumes, of course, that youth are correctly identified, which leads to the issue of reliability and validity.

Psychopathic assessments of youths must achieve a high level of confidence before they can be used in the criminal justice system, where individuals face dire consequences (Seagrave & Grisso, 2002). For example, if an assessment instrument is designed to measure juvenile psychopathy, then there must be considerable research to demonstrate that it, in fact, does measure what it says it measures. Many experts maintain that, with reference to "juvenile psychopathy," we are not near that point yet.

Even so, over the past 15 years, knowledge regarding the theoretical and empirical applicability of juvenile "psychopathy" has expanded at a fast pace (Salekin, Leistico, Trobst, Schrum, & Lochman, 2005). The research has demonstrated that the diagnostic label is linked to conduct disorder (Forth & Burke, 1998; Frick, 1998; Lynam, 1998) and higher levels of delinquency and police contacts (Corrado, Vincent, Hart, & Cohen, 2004; Falkenbach, Poythress, & Heide, 2003; Murrie, Cornell, Kaplan, McConville, & Levy-Elkon, 2004; Salekin, Ziegler, Larrea, Anthony, & Bennett, 2003). Only about 25 percent of juveniles with conduct disorders show psychopathic tendencies (Blair, Peschardt, Budhani, Mitchell, & Pine, 2006). Forth and Burke (1998) report that children and adolescents with psychopathic traits differ from other antisocial youngsters in terms of the age of onset of their behavior problems, the number of violent acts committed, the seriousness of their offenses, and their recidivism rates. Consequently, it appears that those youth who demonstrate psychopathic characteristics also seem to be heavily involved in antisocial behavior, at least hinting that the psychopathic label may have some validity.

Prevalence of Psychopathic Traits in Juvenile Delinquents

In a study examining the prevalence rate of psychopathic tendencies in children, Skilling, Quinsey, and Craig (2001) found that 4.3 percent of a sample of over 1,000 boys in grades 4–8 could be classified as psychopathic on every measure employed in the study. Dåderman and Kristiansson (2003) found that 59 percent of their sample of violent juvenile offenders qualified as psychopaths. Similarly, Brandt, Kennedy, Patrick, and Curtain (1997), using a sample of incarcerated adolescents with persistent violent offending histories, reported that they could identify 37 percent of the sample as psychopathic. By contrast, Campbell, Porter, and Santor (2004) discovered that only 9 percent of their sample of incarcerated adolescent offenders could be classified as psychopaths. These authors note, though, that the juveniles they studied were primarily nonviolent in nature, with only 15 percent having a history of violent offending. It is clear, therefore, that the sample used in a study, as well as the measuring instrument itself, will strongly influence the number of identifiable psychopathic traits within a given group of adolescents.

Measures of Juvenile Psychopathy

It is not surprising that the avid interest in psychopathy, including juvenile psychopathy, would lead to the development of a variety of instruments designed to measure it, or at least psychopathic characteristics. Several instruments for measuring juvenile psychopathy have been developed in recent years, including the *Psychopathy Screening Device*, or the PSD (Frick & Hare, 2001; Frick, O'Brien, Wootton, & McBurnett, 1994); the *Childhood Psychopathy Scale*, or the CPS (Lynam, 1997); the *Youth Psychopathic Traits Inventory*, or YPI (Andershed, Kerr, Stattin, & Levander, 2002); and the *Psychopathy Checklist: Youth Version*, or the PCL:YV (Forth, Kosson, & Hare, 2003). Although originally developed as research instruments rather than for diagnostic purposes in clinics or for the courts, they are now widely available to forensic clinical examiners for use in their private practice and their consulting work with the courts and the juvenile justice system.

All the measures have some difficulty because juvenile psychopaths—if they exist—are unlikely to give accurate or honest self-reports about their emotions, thoughts, or behavior. The PCL:YV relies on an interview that has some specific questions to ask, plus collateral and other written data. Because of the interview and collateral data requirement, the PCL:YV requires extensive training to administer and is time consuming. In addition, the PCL:YV is more research based and measures four dimensions of psychopathy. In contrast, the PCS and the YPI rely heavily on self-reports, while the APSD and CPS are designed to obtain information from teachers, parents, and the child or adolescent himself or herself.

The PCL:YV (youth version) is a 20-item rating scale adapted from the adult PCL-R (Hare, 1991, 2003) for use with juveniles. It adopts the four-factor model approach, scoring individuals on interpersonal, affective, behavioral, and antisocial factors. The PCL-YV has been subjected to extensive research, which suggests that it has adequate reliability and validity (for a review, see Vincent, 2006). However, caution is urged in its use. In particular, it appears to have limited ability to identify a meaningful relationship to psychopathy and antisocial behavior in adolescent girls (Odgers, Reppucci, & Moretti, 2005; Sevecke, Pukrop, Kosson, & Krischer, 2009; Vincent, Odgers, McCormick, & Corrado, 2008). It appears, therefore, that further investigations into the capacity of the PCL:YV to distinguish psychopathy in girls are critical before it can become a useful forensic tool.

There have been several attempts to compare various measures of juvenile psychopathy in terms of their validity and reliability (Farrington, 2005a). Preliminary research so far indicates that the measures do not have much in common, but more research needs to be done before conclusions can be drawn. One recent study shows considerable promise. Lynam and his colleagues (2007) were interested in discovering whether psychopathy scores on the CPS at age 13 predicted psychopathy scores on PCL:SV (short or screening version) at age 24. Surprisingly, the researchers determined that the CPS did a decent job of predicting PCL:SV scores. These results suggest that psychopathy not only appears stable across stages of development but also implies that juvenile psychopathy appears similar to adult psychopathy in many ways.

BIOLOGICAL FACTORS AND PSYCHOPATHY

There is belief among the general public that psychopathic tendencies are caused exclusively by social factors, such as abuse and poor upbringing. However, researchers have implicated a variety of biological factors as well. Contemporary research favors the view that psychopathic behavior results from a complex interaction between neuropsychological and learning or socialization factors.

Genetic Factors

There is emerging evidence that genetics may play a role in the development of psychopathy (Blonigen, Carlson, Krueger, & Patrick, 2003; Blonigen, Hicks, B. M., Krueger, R. F., Iacono, W. G., & Patrick, 2005; Viding, Blair, James, Moffitt, & Plomin, 2005). For example, some evidence suggests that temperament linked to low arousal and fear responses is associated with psychopathy (Frick & Morris, 2004). A temperament of this nature may disrupt the formation of guilt, conscience, or concern about punishment. It is also suggested that youth with psychopathic features may have brain abnormalities (Newman, Curtin, Bertsch, Baskin-Sommers, 2010) and that psychopathy may run in families (Viding & Larsson, 2010).

The overall influence of genetics on psychopathy is not large, but it seems large enough to draw the increasing attention of developmental and genetic researchers, especially those investigators interested in twin studies. Blair *et al.* (2006) believe that genetic contributions may play a significant role in the emotional dysfunction frequently found in psychopaths. That is, heredity may contribute significantly to the underarousal and low emotional responsiveness of psychopaths. However, at this point in our knowledge, we appear to be a long way off from a genetic account of psychopathy.

Neurophysiology and Psychopathy

Although the research on psychopaths in recent years has focused on the psychometric characteristics of psychopaths, the current trend in psychopathy research is the investigation of neuropsychological factors involved in determining their behavior (Gao, Glenn, Schug, Yang, & Raine, 2009; Vien & Beech, 2006). Neuropsychological indicators (called **markers**) have been repeatedly found in psychopaths, as reflected in electrodermal (skin conductance) measures and cardiovascular and other nervous system indices (Fishbein, 2001; Morgan & Lilienfeld, 2000). It is important, therefore, to become familiar with additional neuropsychological vocabulary and basic structures of the nervous system, some of which appeared in Chapter 3. The concepts presented here will also lay the foundation for topics in later chapters (e.g., Chapters 12 and 13 on sexual offenses and Chapter 16 on drugs) as well.

BASIC NEUROPHYSIOLOGICAL CONCEPTS AND TERMINOLOGY   The human nervous system can be divided into two major parts, on the basis of either structure or function. The structural division—the way it is arranged physically—is perhaps the clearest distinction. The central nervous system (CNS) and the peripheral nervous system (PNS) are the two principal parts. The CNS comprises the brain and spinal cord, and the PNS comprises all nerve cells (called neurons) and nerve pathways located outside the CNS (see **Table 7-3**). In other words, those nerves that leave the spinal cord and brain stem and travel to specific sites in the body belong to the peripheral (outside) nervous system. This includes all the nerves connecting the muscles, skin, heart, glands, and senses to the CNS.

The basic function of the PNS is to bring all the outside information to the CNS, where it is processed. Once the CNS has processed information, it relays the interpretation back to the PNS if action is necessary. When you place your finger on a hot object, the PNS relays these raw data (it is not yet pain) to the CNS, which interprets the datum as the sensation of pain, and in return, relays a command to the PNS to withdraw the finger. The PNS cannot interpret; it only transmits information to the CNS and carries communications back. In the following pages, we will consider the significance of each of these systems to the diagnosis of psychopathy.

TABLE 7-3	Divisions of the Human Nervous System

I. Central nervous system (CNS)
   A. Brain
   B. Spinal cord

II. Peripheral nervous system (PNS)
   A. Somatic nervous system (communicates with voluntary muscles)
   B. Autonomic nervous system
      1. Parasympathetic nervous system (relaxes and deactivates after emergencies)
      2. Sympathetic nervous system (activates for emergencies)

Central Nervous System Differences

Structurally, the CNS consists of the brain and spinal cord. Interpretation, thoughts, memories, and images all occur in the cerebral cortex (the highest center of the brain). It is the processing center for stimulation and sensations received from the outside world and the body via the PNS. The cerebral cortex, which is the outer surface of the human brain, contains more than 100 billion nerve cells (called neurons) (Hockenbury & Hockenbury, 2004; *Scientific American*, 1999). Each neuron has a complicated communication link to numerous other neurons, creating an extremely complex and poorly understood communications network. Although the physical structure of the brain does not directly concern us, the electrical circuitry and arousal properties of the cortex are relevant in understanding the neuropsychological characteristics of the psychopath.

Hemisphere Asymmetry and Deficiency

The human brain can be divided anatomically into two cerebral hemispheres—a right and a left. These two cerebral hemispheres seem to coexist in some sort of reciprocally balancing relationship in cortical functioning and information processing. For most individuals, the right hemisphere specializes in nonverbal functions, whereas the left specializes in verbal or language functions. Furthermore, the left hemisphere processes information in an analytical, sequential fashion. Language, for example, requires sequential cognition, and the left seems to be the best equipped for this operation. The right hemisphere, on the other hand, seems to process information holistically and more globally. For example, the right is involved in the recognition of faces, a complicated process requiring the processing of information all at once or simultaneously. Thus, the right and left hemispheres are two functionally differentiated information processing systems.

In addition to information processing, research is now finding that these two cerebral hemispheres also make different contributions to human emotions (Jacobs & Snyder, 1996; Tomarken, Davidson, Wheeler, & Doss, 1992). The right hemisphere appears to be particularly important in the understanding and communication of emotion (Kosson, *et al.*, 2002; Wheeler, Davidson, & Tomarken, 1993). The left seems to be closely tied to self-inhibiting processes, in contrast with the right, which appears to be more spontaneous and impulsive (Tucker, 1981). Furthermore, the two hemispheres must have a balance of contribution from each for normal judgment and appropriate self-control (Tucker, 1981), and self-regulation of emotion (Tomarken *et al.*, 1992). These control and judgment processes are especially prevalent in the frontal lobes (front sections of the brain).

Hare (Hare, 1998; Hare & Connolly, 1987; Hare & McPherson, 1984) hypothesizes that criminal psychopaths manifest an abnormal or unusual balance between the two hemispheres, both in language processing and in emotional or arousal states, which he calls **hemisphere asymmetry**. Hare notes that criminal psychopaths are often strikingly inconsistent with their verbalized thoughts, feelings, and intentions. Criminal psychopaths seem to be highly peculiar in the organization of certain perceptual and cognitive processes. Their left hemisphere seems, in some ways, deficient in linguistic processing because they do not rely on the verbal sequential operations to the extent that a majority of individuals do. Hare (1998) also hypothesizes that as the language task increased in complexity, nonpsychopathic persons rely more and more on the left hemisphere to process the information, while psychopaths rely more on the right hemisphere. Subsequent research supported this hypothesis (Lorenz & Newman, 2002).

There is also some research indicating that psychopaths are less accurate than nonpsychopaths at reading emotional expressions portrayed by faces. More specifically, psychopaths appear to be less accurate than nonpsychopaths in facial emotional recognition under conditions designed to promote reliance on left-hemisphere processing (Kosson *et al.*, 2002). These data are in support of the *left-hemisphere activation hypothesis* (Kosson, 1998), which states that psychopaths exhibit deficits on a variety of tasks that require activation of the left hemisphere.

Since language plays a very important role in the self-regulation of behavior, one of the contributing factors in the extremely impulsive, episodic behavior of psychopaths may reside in some deficiency in their use of internal language. This characteristic was pointed out some time ago by Flor-Henry (Flor-Henry, 1973; Flor-Henry & Yeudall, 1973), who was convinced that psychopathy is closely linked to left-hemispheric language dysfunction. There has been some research to suggest that the right hemisphere of psychopaths may be deficient as well (Herpertz & Sass, 2000). Research by Day and Wong (1996) and Silberman and Weingartner (1996), for example, suggests that many psychopaths have impairments in the right hemisphere that prevents them from experiencing emotions as strongly as the nonpsychopath population. Other researchers have found evidence that psychopaths exhibit an **emotional paradox**. "That is, psychopaths demonstrate normal appraisal of emotional cues and situations in the abstract (i.e., verbal discussion), but they are deficient in using emotional cues to guide their judgments and behavior in the process of living" (Lorenz & Newman, 2002, p. 91). In other words, psychopaths seem to be able to talk about emotional cues but lack the ability to use them effectively in the real world. This deficiency seems to be due to processing problems located in the left hemisphere (Bernstein, Newman, Wallace, & Luh, 2000; Lorenz & Newman, 2002). Nachshon (Nachshon, 1983; Nachshon & Denno, 1987) points out that many studies have found that a disproportionate percentage of violent, repetitive offenders have left-hemispheric dysfunction. Researchers in Germany had found similar results (Pillmann *et al.*, 1999).

Frontal Neuropsychological Studies

Some studies suggest that psychopaths may also suffer from frontal lobe problems or dysfunctions (Kiehl, 2006; Morgan & Lilienfeld, 2000; Sellbom & Verona, 2007). This observation is especially the case in many structural brain imaging studies that suggest psychopaths exhibit impairments in this region (Gao *et al.*, 2009). The frontal lobe refers to that section of the cerebral cortex we commonly call the forehead (**see Figure 3-1**, page 66). The frontal lobes (there are two) are believed to be responsible for the "higher level" cognitive functions of abstraction, decision making, cognitive flexibility, foresight, the regulation of impulses, and the control of appropriate behavior (Ishikawa *et al.*, 2001). In other words, the frontal lobes perform the "executive functions" of the human brain. Researchers tend to be more specific in their terminology and focus on the prefrontal cortex, the "front" area of the frontal lobe or cortex. **Executive functions** refer to higher-order mental abilities involved in goal-directed behavior. Executive functions include organizing behavior, memory, inhibition processes, and planning strategies. Research has been consistent in demonstrating that prefrontal damage results in poor decision making, reduced autonomic functioning, and a psychopathic-like personality (Yang *et al.*, 2005).

A growing amount of research indicates that psychopaths do appear to have defects in frontal lobe processing (Blair, 2007; Harenski, Kiehl, & Shane, 2010). A comprehensive review by Morgan and Lilienfeld (2000) concluded that psychopaths, as a group, do show executive function deficits, which may result in faulty impulse control, judgment, and planning under certain conditions.

In an interesting study, Cathy Widom (1978) found that psychopaths recruited from newspaper advertisements did not demonstrate the same level of frontal lobe deficits as incarcerated psychopaths. Widom speculated that "successful psychopaths" (community-based psychopaths who escaped conviction of their offenses and who answered the ad) probably had better functioning frontal lobes for controlling their behavior than the "unsuccessful" institutionalized psychopaths. Consistent with Widom's results, Ishikawa *et al.* (2001) discovered that successful psychopaths do not show the same psychophysiological or neuropsychological deficits as unsuccessful psychopaths. Overall, the researchers found that successful psychopaths exhibited stronger and better-organized executive functions than either the unsuccessful psychopaths or the controls used in the study.

Despite the increasing number of empirical studies on adult psychopaths, brain imaging studies on children and adolescents who show some psychopathic traits are rare (Gao *et al.*, 2009), but there are exceptions (e.g., Viding & Larsson, 2010, mentioned above). And, the few studies that have been conducted provide "some evidence supporting the speculation that the condition of psychopathy may, in part, be a result of neurodevelopmental abnormalities" (Gao *et al.*, 2009, p. 815). Furthermore, these neurodevelopmental abnormalities appear to occur very early in life. One study, for instance, found that individuals who incurred damage to the prefrontal cortex before the age of 16 months showed considerable similarity to psychopaths (Anderson, Bechara, Damasio, Tranel, & Damasio, 1999). The researchers noted that these patients were "characterized by a pervasive disregard for social and moral standards, consistent irresponsibility and a lack of remorse" (Anderson *et al.*, 1999, p. 1035).

At this point, the evidence suggests that the frontal lobes or prefrontal cortex may play an important role in explaining some of the observed behavioral differences between psychopaths and nonpsychopaths. Furthermore, frontal lobe dysfunction may not be simply limited to psychopaths but may be a feature that is characteristic of many other types of offenders (Raine, 1993).

Amygdala Dysfunction

Psychopaths clearly demonstrate some problems in emotional processing. The frontal lobe is most often associated with this observation, as we have seen. Some researchers are beginning to believe that another neurological structure responsible for this dysfunction may be the amygdala (Crowe & Blair, 2008; Kiehl, 2006). The amygdala is an almond-shaped cluster of neurons in the brain responsible for emotions such as fear, anger, and disgust) (see **Figure 3-1**, page 66). The amygdala is also involved in learning and short-term memory, especially in those learning situations involving high emotions. Some researchers have specifically tied the amygdala to psychopathy and the possession of callous-unemotional traits (DeLisi, Umphress, & Vaughn, 2009).

Kiehl *et al.* (2001) found that psychopaths exhibited lower amygdala activity during an emotional processing task when compared with criminal nonpsychopaths and noncriminal controls.

Similar findings were reported by others (Gao *et al.* 2009; Harenski *et al.*, 2010; Müller *et al.*, 2003). With further research, the relationship between amygdala and learning might emerge as a highly significant factor in understanding the emotional behavior of the psychopath.

Peripheral Nervous System (PNS) Research

The PNS is subdivided into a *somatic division*, comprising the motor nerves that innervate the muscles involved in body movement, and an *autonomic division*, which controls heart rate, gland secretion, and smooth muscle activity. Smooth muscles are those muscles found in the blood vessels and gastrointestinal system; they look smooth under a microscope in comparison with the muscles, which look striped or textured.

The autonomic segment of the PNS is extremely relevant to our discussion of the psychopath, because here, too, research has consistently uncovered a significant difference between the psychopath's and the general population's reactivity or responsiveness to stimuli. The autonomic division is especially important, because it activates emotional behavior and responsivity to stress and tension. It can be subdivided into the *sympathetic* and *parasympathetic systems* (see **Figure 7-1**).

The sympathetic system is responsible for activating or arousing the individual for fight or flight before (or during) fearful or emergency situations. As you will recall, the psychopath displays a James Bond–like coolness, even in stressful situations. We might explain this in one of two ways. Either the sympathetic nervous system does not react sufficiently to stressful stimuli or the parasympathetic system springs into action in the psychopath more rapidly than in nonpsychopaths. There is research support for both of these positions.

Before discussing in more detail the psychopath's autonomic nervous system, we should note the principles and techniques of measuring autonomic activity. Emotional arousal, which is largely under the control of the autonomic nervous system, can be measured by monitoring the system's activity, such as heart rate, blood pressure or volume, and respiration rate. The most commonly used physiological indicator of emotional arousal, however, is *skin conductance response* (SCR), also known as the *galvanic skin response* (GSR). Since *SCR* is the label most advocated by researchers (Lykken & Venables, 1971), it will be used throughout this chapter.

SCR is simply a measure of the resistance of the skin to conducting electrical current. Although a number of factors in the skin influence its resistance, perspiration seems to play a major role. Perspiration corresponds very closely to changes in emotional states and has, therefore, been found to be a highly sensitive indicator of even slight changes in the autonomic nervous system. Other things being equal, as emotional arousal increases, perspiration rate increases proportionately. Small changes in perspiration can be picked up and amplified by recording devices, known as polygraphs or physiographs. An increase in perspiration lowers skin resistance to electrical conductance. In other words, skin conductance (SC) increases as emotional arousal (anxiety, fear, etc.) increases.

We noted earlier that psychopaths lack the capacity to respond emotionally to stressful or fearful situations. Essentially, they give the impression of being anxiety free, carefree, and cool, and they display a devil-may-care attitude. We would expect, therefore, that compared with the normal population, the psychopath has a comparatively underactive, underaroused autonomic nervous system. What has the research literature revealed? Consistently, investigators have reported low SC arousal in psychopaths (Fishbein, 2001). "Deficits in measures of SC arousal are believed to be associated with low autonomic arousal levels which are, in turn, related to low emotionality, poor conditionability, lack of empathy and remorse, and ability to lie easily" (Fishbein, 2001, p. 51). We now turn our attention to the division of the nervous system most responsible for SC arousal.

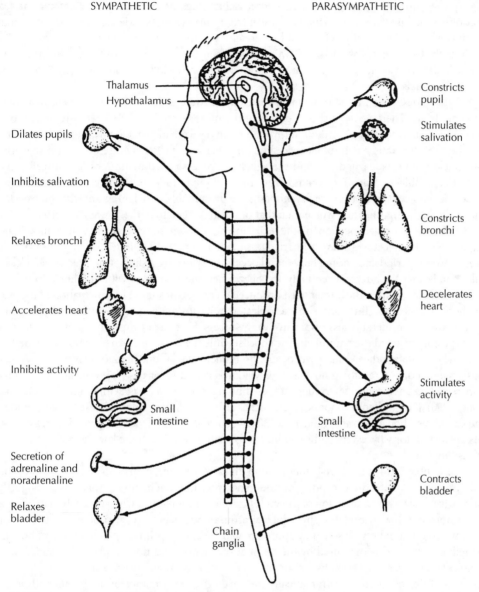

SYMPATHETIC

PARASYMPATHETIC

Thalamus
Hypothalamus

Constricts
pupil

Stimulates
salivation

Dilates pupils

Inhibits salivation

Constricts
bronchi

Relaxes bronchi

Decelerates
heart

Accelerates heart

Inhibits activity

Stimulates
activity

Small
intestine

Small
intestine

Secretion of
adrenaline and
noradrenaline

Contracts
bladder

Relaxes
bladder

Chain
ganglia

FIGURE 7-1 Illustration of the Sympathetic and Parasympathetic Subdivision of the Autonomic Nervous System

Autonomic Nervous System Research

A relatively large number of studies focusing on the autonomic nervous system of the psychopath have been conducted (Gao *et al.*, 2009). In a pioneering study, Lykken (1957) hypothesized that since anxiety reduction is an essential ingredient in learning to avoid painful or stressful situations, and since the psychopath is presumed to be anxiety free, then the psychopath should have special difficulty learning to avoid unpleasant things. Recall that two characteristic features of psychopaths are their inability to learn from unpleasant experiences and their very high recidivism. Lykken carefully delineated his research groups according to Cleckley's criteria. His psychopaths (both males and females) were drawn from several penal institutions in Minnesota and were classified as either primary or neurotic psychopaths. College students comprised a third group of normals.

Lykken designed an electronic maze that subjects were expected to learn as well as possible in twenty trials. There were 20 choice points in the maze, each with four alternatives, with only one being the correct choice. Although three alternatives were incorrect, only one of these would give the subject a rather painful electric shock. Lykken was primarily interested in discovering how quickly subjects learned to avoid the shock, a process called **avoidance learning**. He reasoned that avoidance learning would be rewarded by the reduction of anxiety on encountering the correct choice point, but since psychopaths are presumably deficient in anxiety, their performance should be significantly worse than that of normals. The hypothesis was supported.

Prior to the maze portion of the experiment, Lykken measured the skin conductance changes of each subject while he or she tried to sit quietly for 30–40 minutes. During this time, the subjects would periodically hear a buzzer and occasionally receive a slight, brief electric shock several seconds after the buzzer. Eventually, the buzzer became associated with the shock. In normal individuals, the sound of the buzzer itself produced an anxiety response in anticipation of the electric shock (classical conditioning) and was reflected by a substantial increase in SCR. Psychopaths, however, were considerably less responsive to this stress. Furthermore, psychopaths were incapable of learning to avoid the painful electric shocks, while the normals learned significantly better.

Lykken's data indicate that psychopaths do in fact have an underresponsive autonomic nervous system and, as a result, do not learn to avoid aversive situations as well as most other people. More recent research continues to support these findings (Gao et al., 2009; Gottman, 2001; Ogloff & Wong, 1990). Diminished autonomic reactivity has also been discovered in adolescents and children who exhibit psychopathic traits (Fung et al., 2005; Gao et al., 2009). Does this provide at least a partial explanation for why psychopaths continue to get into trouble with the law, despite the threat of imprisonment?

Schachter and Latané (1964) followed up on Lykken's work by using similar apparatus and basic procedures, with the exception of one major revision. Each subject was run through the maze twice, once with an injection of a harmless saline solution, once with an injection of adrenaline, a hormone that stimulates physiological arousal. Subjects were prisoners selected on the basis of two criteria: how closely they approximated Cleckley's primary psychopath and how incorrigible they were, as measured by the number of offenses and time in prison. Prisoners high on both criteria were psychopaths; prisoners relatively low were nonpsychopaths.

Injections of adrenaline dramatically improved the performance of the psychopath in the avoidance learning task. In fact, with adrenaline injections, the psychopaths learned to avoid shocks more quickly than did normal prisoners with similar injections. On the other hand, when psychopaths had saline injections, they were as deficient in avoidance learning as Lykken's psychopaths.

Since anxiety is presumed to be a major deterrent to antisocial impulses, the manipulation of arousal or anxiety states by drugs may suggest policy implications for the effective treatment of convicted psychopaths. Specific drugs apparently have the potential to increase the emotional level of psychopaths to a point equivalent to the level of the general population.

Subsequent research by Hare (1965a, 1965b) found that primary psychopaths have significantly lower skin conductance while resting than do nonpsychopaths. Other researchers have reported similar results (Herpertz & Sass, 2000; Lorber, 2004). In a major study, Hare (1968) divided 51 inmates at the British Columbia Penitentiary into three groups—primary psychopaths, secondary psychopaths, and nonpsychopaths—and studied them under various conditions, while constantly monitoring their autonomic functioning. The experimental conditions also permitted the observation of a complex physiological response known as the *orienting response* (OR).

The OR is a nonspecific, highly complicated cortical and sensory response to strange, unexpected changes in the environment. The response may take the form of a turning of the head, a dilation of the eye, or a decrease in heart rate. It is made in an effort to determine what the change is. Pavlov referred to the OR as the "what-is-it" reflex. It is an automatic, reflexive accompaniment to any perceptible change, and it can be measured by various physiological indices. The OR produces, among other things, an increase in the analytical powers of the senses and the cortex.

Hare found that not only did psychopaths exhibit very little autonomic activity (skin conductance and heart rate) but they also gave smaller ORs than did nonpsychopaths. His data suggest that psychopaths are less sensitive and alert to their environment, particularly to new and unusual events.

Hare later reported intriguing data relating to the heart or cardiac activity of the psychopath. The aforementioned conclusions were based on skin conductance data. When cardiovascular variables are considered, however, some apparent anomalies appear. While skin conductance is consistently low, cardiac activity (heart rate) in the psychopath is often as high as that found in the nonpsychopathic population (Hare & Quinn, 1971). Hare comments, "The psychopaths appeared to be poor electrodermal [skin conductance] conditioners but good cardiovascular ones" (Hare, 1976, p. 135). That is, although psychopaths do not learn to react to stimuli as measured by skin variables, it appears that they learn to react autonomically as well as nonpsychopaths when the heart rate is measured. Hare suggests that the psychopath might be more adaptive to stress when "psychophysiological defense mechanisms" are brought into play, thereby reducing the impact of stressful stimuli.

Hare and his colleagues designed experiments in which the heart rate could be monitored throughout the experimental session. In one experiment, a tone preceded an electric shock by about 10 seconds (Hare & Craigen, 1974). In anticipation of the shock, psychopaths exhibited a rapid acceleration of heartbeat, followed by a rapid deceleration of heart rate immediately before the onset of the noxious stimulus (a "normal" reaction is a gradual but steady increase in heart rate until the shock). However, their skin conductance remained significantly lower than that of nonpsychopaths. Therefore, psychopaths appear to be superior conditioners when cardiac activity is measured, indicating that they do indeed either learn or inherit autonomic adaptability to noxious stimuli. Hare suggests that this accelerative heart response is adaptive and helps the psychopath tune out or modulate the emotional impact of noxious stimuli. This, he speculates, may be the reason that skin conductance responses are relatively low in the psychopath.

Lykken (1955) also conducted experiments testing the performance of psychopaths on polygraph equipment. If psychopaths are generally underaroused, we would expect that lie detectors would be unable to differentiate their deceptive from their truthful responses, since polygraphs rely on physiological reactivity to questions. Also, psychopaths should have no trouble being deceptive, since they are typically adept at manipulating and deceiving others. Lykken's research confirmed these expectancies. Psychopaths emitted similar skin conductance responses, regardless of whether they were lying or telling the truth. Nonpsychopaths displayed significant differences in reactivity; their lie ratios, reflected by skin conductance, were larger than those of psychopaths. Because of the artificial atmosphere of the laboratory compared with real-life situations, particularly stressful ones, Lykken admonished against uncritical acceptance of his findings until further testing.

Few studies have since directly examined the relationship between psychopathy and lie detection. However, Raskin and Hare (1978) did reexamine the Lykken study, using more sophisticated equipment and better standardization for lie detection. Using 24 psychopathic prisoners and 24 nonpsychopathic prisoners, they found that both groups were equally easily detected at lying about a situation involving a $20 mock theft. This contradictory finding underscores the fact that fine-tuning is still needed if we are to understand the neurophysiological characteristics of the psychopath.

There is evidence, for example, that sufficiently aroused or motivated psychopaths will give physiological responses to interesting events that equal the responses of nonpsychopaths (Hare, 1968). On the other hand, when it comes to highly stressful, serious occasions, psychopaths appear to have incomparable skill at attenuating guilt or aversive reactions (Lykken, 1978). The simulated crime scene in the Raskin–Hare experiment was not only relatively unstressful but may also have been regarded by the psychopath as an interesting "game." The acid test for the lie detection hypothesis will rest with carefully designed experiments under real-life, highly stressful situations. The present data do not justify firm conclusions. Christopher Patrick and his colleagues (Patrick, Bradley, & Lang, 1993) conducted a study designed to test in what ways the startle reflex action in psychopaths differs from that of the normal population. An example of a startle response is the eye-blink reflex in response to a puff of air. These researchers note that psychophysiological research on the psychopath has relied almost exclusively on skin conductance and cardiovascular measures. The researchers found that criminal psychopaths (measured by Hare's PCL-R) exhibited much lower startle responses under aversive conditions than nonpsychopaths. Their findings confirm previous research showing that criminal psychopaths give smaller autonomic responses under aversive conditions than do other nonpsychopathic offenders. Hare (1993, 1996) postulates that psychopaths suffer from a general "hypoemotionality." That is, it appears that psychopaths fail to experience the full impact of any kind of emotion—positive or negative. Psychopaths may be born with this hypoemotionality and that may account for their lack of remorse throughout their lifetimes.

In summary, the research reviewed thus far allows us to make four tentative conclusions about the autonomic functioning of the psychopath. First, psychopaths appear to be both autonomically and cortically underaroused, both under rest conditions and under some specific stress conditions. They are much more physiologically "drowsy" than nonpsychopaths. Second, because they lack the necessary emotional equipment, psychopaths appear to be deficient in avoidance learning, which might account partially for their very high recidivism rates. Third, some data suggest that if emotional arousal can be induced, such as by adrenaline, psychopaths can learn from past experiences and avoid normally painful or aversive situations, such as prison, embarrassment, or social censure. And fourth, with adequate incentives, such as monetary rewards, psychopaths can learn from past experiences and avoid aversive consequences as well as anyone.

Adrian Raine, in his excellent review of the relevant research, finds that many of these psychophysiological indicators discussed for psychopaths may be characteristic of repetitive, violent offenders in general. In fact, in reference to resting heart rate levels in *noninstitutionalized offenders*, he concludes, "This is probably the best replicated and most robust biological finding on antisocial behavior reported to date" (1993, p. 190).

We noted earlier that psychopaths are often profoundly affected by alcohol, even in small amounts. Alcohol is a general CNS depressant, decreasing arousal levels in the nervous system. Research indicates that underaroused psychopaths are already half asleep and "half in the bag"; alcohol has the general effect of "bagging" them completely. Therefore, we would expect not only that the psychopath would get intoxicated more rapidly than the nonpsychopath of comparable weight but also would probably pass out sooner. We would also expect the psychopath to have few sleep difficulties. Steven Smith and Joseph Newman (1990) found that a higher percentage of criminal psychopaths have been polydrug users when compared with criminal nonpsychopaths. In addition, criminal psychopaths were particularly heavy alcohol abusers, and alcohol may have played a very significant role in prompting their extensive antisocial behavior.

Recent research has shown that adult psychopaths usually exhibit significant antisocial behavior in their childhoods (Seagrave & Grisso, 2002). It is reasonable, therefore, to expect researchers to begin searching the developmental trajectory of psychopathy in order to identify tomorrow's psychopaths. The next section examines what we currently know about the childhood of the psychopath. In light of our earlier discussion of juvenile psychopathy, though, we must be careful not to assume that adult psychopaths were necessarily psychopathic as juveniles.

CHILDHOOD OF THE PSYCHOPATH

We have discussed the behavioral descriptions and biopsychological components of psychopaths. Now, how did they get that way? Criminal behavior and other behavior problems are often assumed to be rooted in the home, usually in homes with conflict, inadequate discipline, or poor models. From our discussion of the biopsychological components of psychopaths, however, it is obvious that the answer is not that simple. Psychopathy seems to be a result of a highly complex interaction of biopsychological, social, and learning factors.

Cleckley (1976) was not convinced that any common precursors exist in the family backgrounds of psychopaths, even though relatively homogeneous classifications of psychopathy do exist. However, even if we accept that neurophysiological factors may be causal factors in the development of psychopathy, this does not mean they are hereditary. In fact, there is little evidence to support a *strong* genetic influence on psychopathy so far. It is possible, though, that psychopaths are born with a biological predisposition to develop the disorder and that this predisposition requires certain psychosocial factors before emerging, such as neglectful or abusive parenting. It could be that psychopaths have a nervous system that interferes with rapid conditioning and association between transgression and punishment. Because of this defect, the psychopath fails to anticipate punishment and, hence, feels no guilt (no conscience). As an alternative to the defect argument, it is possible that certain aspects of the psychopath's nervous system simply have not matured. Another possibility is that genetics, toxicity (e.g., lead paint or other sources of lead or other toxic substances) in utero or early childhood, birth difficulties, temperament, and other early developmental factors may affect certain processes in the nervous system, rendering some children vulnerable to develop conduct problems and psychopathic characteristics. We have learned in the chapter, for example, that early damage to the prefrontal cortex may contribute significantly to psychopathic trait development. These early contexts are especially prevalent for disadvantaged children. In addition, it should be emphasized that social factors play a major role in affecting these predispositions. "For example, a problematic temperamental predisposition at 6 months of age *and* low socioeconomic status at birth *and* early life experiences of physical abuse *and* peer rejection in early elementary school combine to predict clinically significant conduct-problem outcomes...in adolescence" (Dodge & Pettit, 2003, p. 354). Basically, persistent and serious offending that emerges early in life is driven partially by heritable influences that are strengthened or weakened during childhood and adolescence by parenting and other environmental factors (Tengström *et al.*, 2004).

Many researchers believe that psychopathy begins in childhood and continues throughout adulthood (Farrington, 2005b; Forth & Burke, 1998; Lynam, 1998), which has led to the intense interest in juvenile psychopathy (see Salekin & Lochman, 2008). According to the research, the childhood of the psychopath is littered with signals that something is amiss. Marshall and Cooke (1999) found that, compared with nonpsychopaths, psychopaths were more likely to have experienced family difficulties such as parental neglect, abuse, or even antipathy and indifference. They were also more likely to have experienced negative school experiences. Poor parental monitoring and discipline have also been identified in the backgrounds of psychopaths (Tolan, Gorman-Smith, & Henry, 2003). Lynam (1998) reports that children with symptoms of hyperactivity, impulsivity, and attention problems *and* conduct problems closely resemble psychopathic adults. The extensive research of Paul Frick (2009) supports these observations. We hasten to add, however, that while it may appear that all psychopaths have experienced all or some of these problems as children, this is not to say that children with similar problems are necessarily fledgling psychopaths.

"Few researchers have tried to investigate early childhood risk factors that might predict, influence, or cause psychopathy" (Farrington, 2005a, p. 493). Additionally, few researchers have conducted prospective longitudinal investigations of those risk factors (Farrington, 2005a). Some retrospective studies (Koivisto & Haapasalo, 1996; Patrick, Zempolich, & Levenston, 1997) and some longitudinal studies (Lang, af Klinteberg, & Alm, 2002; Weiler & Widom, 1996) have found that PCL-R scores appear to be related to early childhood abuse. In one prospective longitudinal study of 400 London boys, ages 8–10 years, it was found that physical neglect, poor parental supervision, a disrupted family, large family size, a convicted parent, a depressed mother, and poverty predicted psychopathy scores at age 48 (Farrington, 2005b).

A fruitful avenue for exploring the childhood of the psychopath would be close examination of the life-course-persistent (LCP) offender described by developmental theorists. Developmental theory postulates that LCP offenders manifest antisocial behaviors across all kinds of conditions and situations in their childhoods. Neurologically, LCPs demonstrate a variety of minor neuropsychological disorders, such as difficult temperaments as infants, attention-deficit disorders or hyperactivity as children, and learning problems as adolescents. Socially, LCPs are rejected by peers during their preteen years and are annoying to adults. Emotionally, these children display virtually no empathy or concern for others, show very little bonding to family, and often are sadistic and manipulative. They are highly impulsive and lack insight. A careful reading of LCPs' developmental histories often shows a striking resemblance to the symptomology of criminal psychopaths. It should be emphasized, however, that only a modest number of LCPs probably qualify as full-blown psychopaths.

TREATMENT OF PSYCHOPATHS

The treatment and rehabilitation of criminal psychopaths has been shrouded with pessimism and discouragement. Hare (1996, p. 41) asserts, "There is no known treatment for psychopathy." A long line of research documents that *adult* psychopaths are not responsive to treatment, whether in prisons, in psychiatric treatment centers, or in the community (e.g., Hare *et al.*, 2000). Some commentary has indicated that psychotherapy or intervention with psychopaths is basically a waste of time. Gacono *et al.* (2001) concluded from their review that "simply stated, at this time there is no empirical evidence to suggest that psychopathy is treatable" (p. 111). O'Neill, Lidz, and Heilbrun (2003) remarked that "to date, there is no treatment for psychopathy that has been established as effective" (p. 300). In fact, some forms of treatment (e.g., milieu therapy) have been linked to higher rates of violent recidivism in psychopaths (Rice, Harris, & Cormier, 1992). Several studies indicate that psychopaths are either completely nonresponsive to treatment or play the treatment game well, pretending to cooperate but in actuality "conning" the treatment provider (Hare, 1996; Porter *et al.*, 2000; Rice *et al.*, 1992). Farrington (2005a) states that "it seems to be generally believed that psychopaths are difficult to treat because (a) they are an extreme, qualitatively distinct category; (b) psychopathy is extremely persistent throughout life; (c) psychopathy has biological causes which cannot be changed by psychosocial interventions; and (d) the lying, conning, and manipulativeness of psychopaths make them treatment resistant" (pp. 494–495).

Indeed, based on the research examining the effectiveness of various treatment programs, there does not appear to be any effective treatment program for adult psychopaths in the criminal justice system today. Hare (1996, p. 41) admonishes, though, "This does not necessarily mean that the egocentric and callous attitudes and behaviors of psychopaths are immutable, only that there are no methodologically sound treatments or 'resocialization' programs that have been shown to work with psychopaths." Other researchers take a decidedly different perspective and believe that untreatability statements concerning the psychopath are unwarranted (Salekin, 2002; Skeem, Monahan, & Mulvey, 2002; Skeem, Poythress, Edens, Lilienfeld, & Cale, 2003; Wong, 2000). There is some evidence that psychopaths who receive larger "doses" of treatment are less likely to demonstrate subsequent violent behavior than those who receive less treatment (Skeem, Poythress *et al.*, 2003). It should be mentioned that a vast majority of the research has focused on recidivism rates of male psychopathic offenders, and very little is known about the recidivism rates of female psychopathic offenders.

It is usually difficult to evaluate properly the effectiveness of programs designed to treat psychopaths because of their ability to manipulate the system. For example, many psychopaths volunteer for various prison treatment programs, show "remarkable improvement," and present themselves as model prisoners. They are skillful at convincing therapists, counselors, and parole boards that they have changed for the better. Upon release, however, there is a high probability that they will reoffend. In fact, there is some evidence to suggest that psychopaths who participate in therapy are more likely to engage in violent crime following the treatment than those psychopaths who did not receive treatment. Rice *et al.* (1992) investigated the effectiveness of an intensive therapeutic community program offered in a maximum security facility. The study was retrospective in that the researchers examined records and files 10 years after the program was completed. The results showed that psychopaths who participated in the therapeutic community exhibited higher rates of violent recidivism than did the psychopaths who did not. The results were the reverse for nonpsychopaths. Nonpsychopaths who received treatment were less likely to reoffend than nonpsychopaths who did not receive treatment.

Some critics of this study have remarked that the therapeutic community referred to was highly atypical of treatment programs in correctional facilities and has limited generalizability. Furthermore, the researchers themselves cautioned that the psychopaths used in the study were an especially serious group of offenders. Eighty-five percent had a history of violent crimes. Whether less serious psychopathic offenders will show similar results is unknown. The researchers conclude, "The combined results suggest that a therapeutic community is not the treatment of choice for psychopaths, particularly those with extensive criminal histories" (Rice *et al.*, 1992, p. 408). Hare (1996) suggests that group therapy and insight-oriented treatment programs—both of which were features of the program reviewed above—may help the psychopath develop better ways of manipulating and deceiving others.

Treatment of Children and Adolescents with Psychopathic Features

As we noted in the previous section, the treatment and rehabilitation of adult criminal psychopaths has been cloaked with pessimism and discouragement. While there are exceptions, very few treatment approaches have been successful. Unfortunately, little is known about the effectiveness of prevention and treatment methods for child and adolescent psychopathy (Farrington, 2005a, p. 494) or, as many researchers and clinicians prefer to say, children and adolescents with psychopathic tendencies or characteristics. Recall from our discussion of juvenile psychopathy that this is an extremely controversial area, with many preferring not to place such a negative label on juveniles.

Logically, it makes sense to hypothesize that children and adolescents with psychopathic features would respond more positively than psychopathic adults to prevention and treatment strategies because of their malleability. Consequently, researchers have begun to evaluate the effectiveness of (a) treatment programs designed specifically for juveniles with psychopathic characteristics and (b) programs for youthful offenders that include those with psychopathic characteristics.

Studies have underscored the observations that children and adolescents with psychopathic features show distinct sets of emotional and cognitive deficits that lead to their violent and antisocial behavior. According to Salekin and Frick (2005), knowledge about these areas may be important for designing more individualized interventions for youths with psychopathic traits. For example, laboratory studies have revealed that children with conduct problems and high levels of callous-unemotional traits exhibit tendencies to respond better to reward-driven interventions and respond poorly to punishment-driven or fear-induced forms of intervention (Hawes & Dadds, 2005). These findings imply that children displaying high-reward drive and low fearful inhibitions should, compared with conduct-problem children *without* CU traits, respond well to parents who use reward-based strategies for changing behavior (e.g., praise, rewards, reinforcement tokens), but remain insensitive to other parental disciplinary practices (e.g., time-outs, forms of verbal or behavioral punishments, such as scolding or confiscating a favorite game). "The assessment of CU traits in addition to other established risk factors," Hawes and Dadds (2005) conclude, "may allow such children to be targeted with more individualized intervention" (p. 740).

Juveniles with psychopathic characteristics did not fare well in an outpatient *substance abuse* treatment program, however (O'Neill *et al.*, 2003). In this study, youths with higher scores on the PCL:YV were more likely to be rearrested and demonstrated higher attrition from the program, lower quality of participation, and more frequent use of alcohol and drugs while in the treatment program. The treatment program was based on a cognitive-behavioral model, whereby the adolescents would set goals and learn coping skills. They had daily group therapy sessions and twice-weekly one-hour sessions of individual therapy. While youths who scored low on the PCL:YV did benefit from the program, those with high scores did not. The reasons for the failure in this program are unknown.

On a more promising note, Salekin, Rogers, and Machin (2001) in their survey of over five hundred child clinical psychologists discovered that many of these clinicians reported that they were moderately to significantly successful in treating children and adolescents with psychopathic features. The treatment duration for these psychopathic youth averaged about 12 months. "After nearly 1 year of treatment these youths reportedly made marked improvement on such criteria as violence and recidivism" (Salekin *et al.*, 2001, p. 192). The clinicians estimated that approximately 42 percent of the boys and 45 percent of the girls made moderate-to-marked improvement in reducing their psychopathic symptomatology overall. "These findings are important," Salekin *et al.* conclude, "and indicate that psychopathy, at least in youth, may be less recalcitrant to treatment than previously thought" (p. 192).

Salekin (2002) also published a comprehensive review of 42 studies specifically directed at treating psychopathy. Despite some methodological shortcomings with many of the studies (e.g., small sample size, diverse definitions of psychopathy), cognitive-behavioral, psychodynamic, and eclectic interventions were shown to be effective. The most notable benefits included a reduction in psychopathic characteristics, such as a decrease in lying, an increase in remorse or empathy, and improved relations with others. Salekin specifically noted that one intensive action-oriented program was highly successful (88%) with youngsters showing psychopathic tendencies. Ingram, Gerard, Quay, and Levison (1970) devised a program specifically designed to address psychopathic behaviors in youth. The program was based on the sensation-seeking model that kept the 20 young participants interested in treatment throughout the sessions. The program was able to decrease institutional aggressive behavior and improved overall adjustment in the community. Those psychotherapies that proved most effective tended to be more intensive and often combined with other programs, such as group psychotherapy, pharmacotherapy, or the involvement of family members. "These results indicate, at least preliminarily," Salekin writes, "that for complex problems such as psychopathy, more elaborate and intensive intervention programs involving individual psychotherapy, treatment of family members, and input from groups (other patients/inmates) are beneficial and may enhance their overall effectiveness" (p. 105). The key for success with psychopaths may be the scope, type, intensity, and duration of the treatment, as well as the training of the staff applying the intervention. Salekin points out that those intervention programs that were less successful were characterized by little input by trained mental health professionals and extremely little one-to-one patient–psychologist contact. He further stated that early intervention is particularly important in working with children exhibiting psychopathic traits. Salekin concludes then, as he has more recently (Salekin & Lynam, 2010), that the therapeutic pessimism that surrounds the treatment of psychopathy and undermines motivation to search for effective modes of intervention for the disorder is unwarranted.

Summary and Conclusions

The primary psychopath should be distinguished from people who may be classified as psychotic, neurotic, or emotionally disturbed. The primary psychopath should also be distinguished from the sociopath, who is similar in many ways. However, the term *sociopath* usually refers to a person who *habitually* violates the law and who does not seem to learn from past experience. Another common term—*antisocial personality disorder* (APD)—also is distinct from *psychopathy*, even though these two terms are often confused by clinicians and researchers. This is understandable, because the diagnostic category "antisocial

personality disorder," as defined in the latest editions of the *DSM*, has many parallels to Robert Hare's concept of criminal psychopathy.

The psychopath as discussed here may or may not run afoul of the law. In addition, psychopaths demonstrate a variety of behavioral and neurophysiological characteristics that differentiate them from other groups of individuals. In this text, we are of course most interested in the psychopath who does run afoul of the law, particularly by way of persistent and/or violent offending. Hare has proposed the term *criminal psychopath* to describe this individual. In this sense, the criminal psychopath, the sociopath, and the person with antisocial personality disorder are very similar in their offending patterns.

Psychopaths most often function in society as charming, daring, witty, intelligent individuals, high on charisma but low on emotional reaction and affect. They appear to lack moral standards or the ability to manifest genuine sensitivity toward others. If criminals, they become the despair of law enforcement officials because their crimes appear to be without discernible or rational motives. Even worse, they show no remorse or ability to be rehabilitated.

We reviewed much of the neurophysiological research suggesting that the psychopath is different from the rest of the population on a number of physiological measures. The psychopath seems to be underaroused, both autonomically and cortically, a finding that may account for his or her difficulty in learning the rules of society. However, there is some evidence to suggest that with adequate incentives, psychopaths may learn societal expectations very well.

Studies on the childhood of psychopaths strongly suggest that they may have been ADHD as children, causing chaos for parents and teachers. It would be a folly to maintain, though, that the ADHD child of today is the psychopath of tomorrow. Perhaps because they are physiologically underaroused, psychopaths do not respond as well to admonishments, threats, or actual punishment as do their nonpsychopathic peers. They do not learn society's expectations and the rules of right and wrong, possibly because anxiety-inducing disciplinary procedures are not that anxiety-producing for them. In many respects, the criminal psychopath follows a developmental path highly similar to the life-course-persistent offender described by developmental theory, outlined in Chapter 2.

There are still numerous gaps in our knowledge of the psychopath, one being in the area of gender differences. Research on female psychopaths is scant. Some research suggests that behavioral characteristics for females are generally similar to those of male psychopaths, with slightly more emphasis among females on sexual acting-out behavior. This probably reflects a cultural bias, however, since women have been traditionally chastised more than men for behavior

deemed inappropriate according to sexual mores. However, research on female criminal psychopaths using Hare's PCL-R implies that their behavioral patterns may be somewhat different than those of male criminal psychopaths.

A highly controversial area relating to psychopathy is the measurement and existence of juvenile psychopathy. Researchers are very actively involved in developing scales to assess this construct and in comparing features of juvenile and adult psychopaths. Psychopathic characteristics in juveniles may be deceiving, however. Many youth, for example, are impulsive, seek stimulation, and appear to be noncaring; these features are often part of the normal turmoil of adolescent development. While it is worthwhile to study these characteristics, we must not rush to judgment and assume they are indicative of psychopathy.

The bulk of contemporary research acknowledges that some juveniles at least possess psychopathic characteristics, but concerns about the implications of labeling juveniles this way in the juvenile justice system remain. We do not want to condemn juveniles to a label that is frequently associated with defeat: Psychopaths do not feel remorse, therefore cannot be helped. Nonetheless, recent positive treatment approaches have been identified, so there is less pessimism in this regard than in the past.

Contemporary research on psychopathy is robust and shows few signs of abating. By now, it is quite clear that Hare's primary psychopath—as measured by the PCL—has many unique features and that it may involve more than the two factors originally identified. The four-factor model is rapidly gaining adherents. At the least, we can say that psychopathy includes distinctive cognitive and emotional styles and physiological indicators. Many psychopaths also had childhoods marked by parental deficiency and conduct problems. These features combine to render the psychopath highly resistant to treatment. This is particularly frustrating to clinicians working with criminal psychopaths, many of whom know how to play the clinical games that will make it appear that they have changed their behavior. It is not surprising, then, that researchers and clinicians place more hope in early intervention strategies.

Key Concepts

Antisocial personality disorder
(APD)
Avoidance learning
Criminal psychopath
Dyssocial psychopath
Emotional paradox
Executive functions
Factor analysis

Factor 1
Factor 2
Hemisphere asymmetry
Markers
Primary psychopath
Psychopathy Checklist (PCL
and PCL-R)

Psychopathy Checklist: Screening
Version (PCL:SV)
Psychopathy Checklist: Youth
Version (PCL-YV)
Recidivism
Secondary psychopath
Semantic aphasia

Review Questions

1. Briefly describe the core behavioral characteristics of the criminal psychopath.
2. What differences have been found between male and female psychopaths?
3. Name and describe briefly any five instruments used to measure psychopathy.
4. Define each of the following as proposed by Hare: primary psychopath, secondary psychopath, dyssocial psychopath, and criminal psychopath.

5. What has been learned about (a) recidivism and (b) treatment of the criminal psychopath?
6. Identify some of the ethical problems created as a result of labeling a child a "psychopath."
7. Describe the three- and four-factor models of psychopathy.
8. How is the psychopath different from the nonpsychopath on psychophysiology? Thoroughly discuss all relevant features.

8

Crime and Mental Disorders

CHAPTER OBJECTIVES

- Define mental disorders.
- Provide an overview of the *DSM* and the diagnoses that are most relevant to criminal behavior.
- Define and review issues relating to competency to stand trial.
- Review the insanity defense rules and standards.
- Discuss special defenses sometimes raised to absolve defendants of criminal responsibility.
- Discuss the prevalence of mental illness in incarcerated populations.
- Define risk assessment and identify various tests used for this purpose.

In January 2011 Congresswoman Gabrielle Giffords of Arizona was shot in the head by 23-year-old Jared Loughner, who also killed six other people, including a nine-year-old girl and a federal judge, and wounded 12 other people along with Congresswoman Giffords. The shootings occurred while Congresswoman Giffords was meeting with her constituents outside a supermarket in Tucson. Loughner was initially ruled **incompetent to stand trial (IST)** and was treated for severe mental disorders at a hospital in Missouri. Part of the treatment involved the administration of psychoactive medication, which were given against his will but with court approval. In August 2012, after being found competent to plead guilty, Loughner pled guilty to his crimes, apparently to avoid the death penalty.

In March 2012, Army Staff Sergeant Robert Bales allegedly left his barracks at nighttime, walked through two villages in southern Afghanistan, went into several homes, and shot to death many Afghans, including nine children. He was charged with 16 counts of murder, six counts of aggravated assault, and multiple violations of military law, including use of anabolic steroids. At the time of the shootings, Bales was in his fourth deployment, having served three tours in Iraq prior to his assignment in Afghanistan. At the time this book went to press he was scheduled to be tried in military court early November 2012. Although the defense strategy is not known at this time, commentators have suggested that traumatic brain injury or PTSD may be relevant to this case.

In the summer of 2011, eight-year-old Leiby Kletzky was abducted while walking home from a day camp in his Brooklyn neighborhood. His dismembered body was found less than three days later and a neighbor, Levy Aron, was arrested and charged. Aron's lawyers at one point announced that they would use the insanity defense, but Aron pled guilty, apparently to spare him a trial and a possible sentence of life without parole. (New York is not a death penalty state.) In late summer 2012, a year after the crime, Aron was sentenced to 40 years to life in prison. His attorneys have emphasized that he suffered from severe mental illness as a child and young adult.

Finally, in another shocking case that cannot be forgotten, 31-year-old Andrea Yates drowned her five children, ages six months to seven years, in a bathtub in 2001. Yates had a history of mental disorder; she had attempted suicide twice and had been hospitalized at least four times, apparently for depression. At her trial, Yates raised the insanity defense, citing in particular a severe case of postpartum psychosis. Her lawyers said she believed she was possessed by Satan and that her children would suffer in hell because she represented evil. To save them from that fate, she thought it was critical that they die now so that they could go to heaven; she herself would be executed for their deaths, as Satan demanded.

Yates was found guilty of the deaths of three of her children, but she was re-tried when an appeals court found significant errors in the prosecution of her case. In her second trial she was found **not guilty by reason of insanity (NGRI)**. She remains institutionalized today, receiving treatment in a secure hospital setting.

The Yates case created a national debate over the legal standards for mental disorders, and the Aron case, before it was resolved, raised similar questions, although it did not receive the same degree of national attention. The case involving Jared Loughner raised questions about the treatment of defendants found incompetent to stand trial, and the case in Afghanistan involving Robert Bales has already brought attention to PTSD and brain injury. In this chapter, we discuss many of the points and issues brought up by these and other cases.

Despite the tragedy of the above cases, brutal, violent, and apparently senseless crimes are not usually committed by people who are mentally ill or "sick." It is a common perception that someone who walks into a business establishment and randomly shoots its customers and employees must be mentally ill. Likewise, someone who sexually assaults, tortures, and kills a four-year-old child has to be sick. How else could these people do this? An alternate explanation focuses on the subhuman perspective: If not sick, they are less than human. Closely related is the view that these individuals are basically evil. Although these latter approaches are gaining ground, perhaps reflecting public impatience with perceived insanity loopholes in the law, there is still wide public subscription to a presumption of mental illness, particularly in the case of outrageous, inexplicable crimes. Nevertheless, brutal and violent crimes are not usually committed by people who are mentally ill, and the mentally ill do not usually commit such crimes.

The media have been instrumental in developing the connection between mental disorder and crime, particularly serious violent crime. Along with greed and revenge, mental illness is a basic motivation for criminality in the vast majority of crimes on television and other entertainment media (Surette, 1999). John Monahan (1992) cites an early survey (Gerbner, Gross, Morgan, & Signorielli, 1981) showing that on prime-time American television, 73 percent of all individuals characterized as mentally disordered also displayed some violent behavior. In a later analysis (Shain & Phillips, 1991), 86 percent of all print stories dealing with former mental patients focused on the violence of the patients, especially if the topics dealt with serial or mass murder. The plethora of profiling shows on cable television and the networks today tend to portray violent criminals, particularly murderers, as bizarre, often psychotic, and resistant to the efforts of the profilers to "get into their minds."

Many researchers today distinguish between mental illness in general and *serious mental illness* (SMI) in particular, and they focus their attention on the latter. SMI is not always defined the same way, but a common definition is "the class of disorders with psychotic features (e.g., Schizophrenia,...Major Depressive Disorder...) or other symptoms that have the potential to very substantially affect an individual's interpersonal and vocational functioning" (Heilbrun *et al.*, 2012, note 1). It is important to emphasize, as well, that people with SMI—when they do commit crimes—typically commit minor offenses rather than those highlighted at the beginning of the chapter. They are more likely to trespass, shoplift, or commit simple assault than to murder someone.

The challenge for the criminal justice system is how to "process" persons with SMI. Munetz and Griffin (2006) proposed a conceptual model—the Sequential Intercept Model (SIM)—to detail the points at which mental health and social interventions could be used to supplant or supplement the usual criminal justice process. For example, pretrial diversion programs, mental health courts, and postrelease programs for convicted offenders all have a place in the SIM (see, generally, Heilbrun *et al.*, 2012 for applications of the SIM). The challenge for researchers and clinicians is how to assess and treat such individuals.

DEFINING MENTAL ILLNESS

Mental illness is a disorder (some say a disease) of the mind that is judged by experts to interfere substantially with a person's ability to cope with life on a daily basis. It presumably deprives the person of freedom of choice, but it is important to note that there are degrees to this deprivation. In other words, even a seriously disordered individual has some decision-making ability. Mental illness is manifested in behavior that deviates notably from normal conduct. Serious mental illness, as we noted above, not only deviates from normal conduct, it also severely impedes, or has potential to impede, a person's functioning. However, the word *illness* encourages us to look for etiology, symptoms, and cures, and to rely heavily on the medical profession both to diagnose and to treat. It also encourages us to excuse the behavior of persons plagued with the "sickness." The term **mental disorder**, however, need not imply that a person is sick, to be pitied, or even necessarily less responsible for his or her actions. Therefore, although *mental illness* is still used in the psychological, psychiatric, and legal literature, as well as in both civil and criminal law, we prefer the less restrictive *mental disorder*. This is not to say that medication is not needed, and it is not to say that persons with mental disorder are always responsible for their behavior. It is also not to say that society should not be compassionate.

Another term that must be distinguished is **mental retardation**, professionally known as **developmental or intellectual disability**. This is a cognitive deficiency—measured by "IQ tests"— that cannot be cured. However, many developmentally disabled individuals can be provided training and support services to lead productive and independent lives. Even so, they are sometimes charged with primarily minor offenses that result in arrests, being detained in jail, and serving time. Dual diagnoses of mental retardation and substance abuse have been observed in a significant number of these individuals (Day & Berney, 2001). Misperceptions about the intellectually or developmentally disabled are perhaps not as strong as misperceptions about the mentally disordered, but they represent a population whose needs may go unrecognized by the criminal justice system. Thus, while the chapter focuses primarily on issues related to the mentally disordered, we will also give attention to unique problems faced by the intellectually disabled.

Mental disorders are manifested in a variety of behaviors, ranging in severity from dangerous, harmful acts to conduct that is essentially innocuous. In a classic work, Morse (1978) preferred the term *crazy behavior*, which he characterized as behavior that is obviously strange and unusual *and cannot be logically explained*. The person who walks onto the hotel elevator at the lobby level and faces the rear, staring blankly at the elevator's rear wall, while others are facing the front, is exhibiting strange behavior. However, if the elevator subsequently opens at the "back" door, there is a logical explanation: the person is a hotel guest or employee who is familiar with the elevator's setup. In the absence of such an explanation, the behavior becomes disconcerting to the other passengers and, if only mildly, "crazy." In this instance, some clinicians—again in the absence of a logical explanation—may see the behavior as symptomatic of an anxiety disorder or a dissociative disorder, depending on other aspects of the individual's behavior. However, the behavior, as described above, is not dangerous. On the other hand, a person who walks into a hotel lobby in a highly agitated state, brandishing a knife, and stating that hotel employees were all trained by Satan and must die for their sins is exhibiting both "crazy" and dangerous behavior. There is obviously a crucial distinction between the above scenarios.

The *DSM*

The concept of mental disorder, therefore, connotes a wide range of bizarre, dramatic, harmful, or mildly unusual behaviors whose classifications are published in the ***Diagnostic and Statistical Manual of Mental Disorders (DSM).*** Compiled by committees appointed by the American Psychiatric Association, the *DSM*—now in its fourth edition (*DSM-IV*) but in the process of revision—is the guidebook for clinicians seeking to define and diagnose specific mental disorders. It is used by virtually every mental health professional in the United States to guide diagnosis and to justify third-party reimbursement for treatment, although many do not agree with its classifications, and some use an alternate classification system. Regardless of the system used, diagnoses appear in official records, such as court documents and prison files.

The *DSM* is reviewed and revised periodically to conform to the contemporary, mainstream thinking of psychiatrists and other mental health professionals. The upcoming version, the long-awaited *DSM-5*, is expected to be based more on scientific advancements as well as clinical expertise and is now due out in 2013.

Some of the changes proposed for the fifth revision are controversial, however, and it remains to be seen how the controversies will be resolved. We mentioned some concerns about proposed changes in Conduct Disorder classifications in Chapter 2. Critics are also worried about the *DSM*'s increasing "medicalization" of behaviors—that is, the suggestion that they be treated with various drugs. In addition, the revision committee has proposed a "prepsychotic risk syndrome" applicable to young people. Changes related to PTSD are also expected. Several new behavioral addictions have been proposed, including sexual addiction, but thus far only one related to gambling has survived scrutiny. Also controversial is the proposed redefinition of the autism spectrum and the elimination of Asperger's syndrome. Because the *DSM-5* is not finalized at the time this book is going to press, readers should be careful about drawing any conclusions about any of these proposed changes.

We now turn to the specific disorders identified in the *DSM* that are most likely to be associated with criminal conduct, though not necessarily serious criminal conduct. It must be stressed, however, that (1) persons with these disorders are not "crime prone," and (2) even if an individual is diagnosed with these disorders, he or she still can be held responsible for criminal conduct.

For the present, the four categories of mental disorders most relevant are (1) schizophrenic disorders, (2) paranoid or delusional disorders, (3) mood disorders (serious depression), and (4) the personality disorder called "antisocial personality disorder." The first two fall into what was previously called the "psychotic" category. The third is considered in that psychotic category only if serious enough, such as bipolar depression. The fourth is a separate category under the general label "personality disorders." These four categories of disorders are relevant because they are most likely to be the diagnoses received by individuals charged with serious criminal, or antisocial behavior, assuming that a mental disorder is at issue. They are also the disorders most often cited to support an insanity defense to criminal charges. We review each of these disorders and then assess their relevance to criminal behavior. However, toward the end of the chapter, we discuss less common disorders that, when cited in courts, attract considerable media attention.

Schizophrenic Disorders

Schizophrenia is the mental disorder that people most often associate with "crazy behavior," since it frequently manifests itself in highly bizarre actions. It is a mental disorder that continues to be extremely complex and poorly understood (Andreasen & Carpenter, 1993; Sitnikova, Goff, & Kuperberg, 2009). The disorder generally begins early in life, often leads to social and economic impairment, and leaves traces on its victims for the rest of their lives (Andreasen & Carpenter, 1993). Behavioral manifestations of schizophrenia are varied, but there are some common characteristics.

Severe breakdowns in thought patterns, emotions, and perceptions are common. Spells of extreme social withdrawal from others are also typical. The thoughts and cognitive functioning of the person with schizophrenia become disorganized and fail to correspond to reality, and his or her speech will reflect this. The most common example is a loosening of associations, in which ideas shift between totally unrelated and only obliquely related subjects. Thought becomes fragmented and bizarre, and **delusions**—false beliefs about the world—are common. An example of a delusion is *believing* some alien from another universe is listening in on your cell phone conversations or sending you text messages and ultimately plotting against you.

The person with schizophrenia is typically inappropriate in emotion or affect (e.g., indiscriminate giggling or crying), or reflects emotional flatness, where very little—if any—emotional reaction is exhibited. The voice is monotonous, the face immobile and expressionless. The major disturbances in perception are various forms of **hallucinations**, which involve sensing or perceiving things or events that others do not sense or perceive. The most common hallucinations are auditory, with the individual hearing voices or sounds that no one else in the vicinity hears.

The proportion of violent crimes committed by people with schizophrenia is small; however, when they do commit violent crimes, the level of violence may be higher than that of the "typical" violent offender, particularly with respect to homicide or aggravated assault. At least one of the clinicians who evaluated Jared Loughner diagnosed him schizophrenic, a fact that was revealed at a hearing relative to his competency to stand trial. In a study of 125 homicide offenders diagnosed with schizophrenia (Laajasalo & Häkkänen, 2006), one-third were considered excessively violent. Excessive violence was most common among offenders with hallucination and delusions, rather than one or the other. Delusions, particularly persecutory ones, are particularly common in those schizophrenics who commit violent offenses. Other researchers (Marleau, Millaud, & Auclair, 2003; Taylor *et al.*, 1998) also have found that hallucinations alone (without delusions) are rare at the time of crime among homicide offenders. Interestingly, though, the strongest predictors of excessive violence in Laajasalo and Häkkänen's study were the offender's own history of violence and the presence of a cooffender at the scene.

The *DSM-IV* outlines five characteristic symptoms of schizophrenia, at least two of which must be manifested before a diagnosis can be entertained: (1) delusions, (2) hallucinations, (3) disorganized speech, (4) grossly disorganized behavior, and (5) inappropriate affect. Furthermore, the social interactions, self-care, and/or occupational life of the individual must show signs of being markedly below the level achieved prior to the onset. In addition, there must be continuous signs of the disturbance for at least six months.

The *DSM-IV* also recognizes five subtypes of schizophrenia: (1) disorganized, (2) catatonic, (3) paranoid, (4) undifferentiated, and (5) residual. Following is a brief summary of the essential features of each subtype:

1. *Disorganized type:* These individuals show inappropriate affect (flat, incongruous, or silly emotional responses) and marked incoherence and disorganization in thought patterns. Associated features include grimaces, strange mannerisms, complaints of nonexistent physical ailments, extreme social withdrawal, and other oddities of behavior.
2. *Catatonic type:* This type shows severe disturbances in muscular and voluntary movement. Extended periods of mutism are common. Parrotlike and senseless repetition of a word or phrase just spoken by another person is also common. Prominent grimacing is another frequent characteristic. The catatonic may assume a bizarre posture for long periods of time (usually several hours) and then fly into an overactive, agitated state of screaming and throwing things.
3. *Paranoid type:* These individuals are characterized by delusions and hallucinations (usually auditory hallucinations). A person with paranoid schizophrenia may be convinced that the world is inhabited by extraterrestrials who are plotting to take over the world. Another may hear voices commanding him to rid the world of red-haired individuals. Of all the schizophrenic types, the paranoid is the most frequently represented in criminal behavior.
4. *Undifferentiated type:* This type shows psychotic symptoms that cannot be classified into any of the foregoing categories. People with this type display active psychotic features, such as hallucinations, delusions, incoherent speech, or confused and disorganized behavior, but do not meet the specifications of the other types.
5. *Residual type:* These individuals have had at least one episode of schizophrenia, and there is evidence that some of the symptoms are continuing. For example, the person may still display blunted emotions or illogical thinking, but no other symptoms.

The *DSM-IV* identifies a sixth category, *schizophreniform disorder,* a behavioral pattern that shows at least two indicators of delusions, hallucinations, disorganized speech, grossly disorganized behavior, and emotional inappropriateness. It is a temporary disorder and underscores the difficulty in classifying schizophrenic disorders in general. In order to qualify for schizophreniform disorder, the symptoms must persist for at least one month but less than six months. If the symptoms continue more than six months, the clinician is encouraged to classify the disorder into one of the five longer-lasting types.

Delusional Disorders

The **delusional disorders** (also called **paranoid disorders**) are characterized by the presence of one or more *nonbizarre* delusions that persist for at least one month. The judgment of whether the delusion's systems are bizarre or nonbizarre is especially important in deciding between a delusional disorder and schizophrenia. In delusional disorder, the delusions are reasonably believable and not completely far-fetched. An example of a nonbizarre delusion is the belief that a neighbor is spying and attempting to poison one's dog, when there is no evidence to that effect. Even so, neighbors sometimes spy and sometimes do try to poison dogs. A bizarre delusion—more characteristic of schizophrenia—is the belief that the neighbor has disguised herself as a mosquito and is hovering outside one's window.

Delusional disorders often accompany other disorders like schizophrenia, organic mental disorder, paranoid personality disorder, and depressions. However, the essential feature of all delusional disorders is the delusional system, which most often includes persecutory beliefs about being spied on, cheated, conspired against, followed, drugged, maliciously maligned, harassed, or obstructed. Generally, anger, resentment, and sometimes violence accompany these false persecutory beliefs. Suspiciousness, either generalized or directed at one or more persons, is also common. The *DSM-IV* recognizes seven different types of delusional disorders, but the persecutory type is the one most closely associated with criminal conduct, especially violent criminal conduct. Thus, the individual who believes he is being followed by someone intending to do him harm may try to kill or otherwise harm his "persecutor."

Depressive Disorders

The disorders described in this section have a variety of names and diagnostic labels, such as affective disorders, mood disorders, and bipolar depressive disorders. The most common label is **major depressive disorder**. The symptoms include an *extremely* depressed state that lasts for at least two weeks and is accompanied by a generalized slowing down of mental and physical activity, gloom, despair, feelings of worthlessness, and perhaps frequent thoughts of suicide. Everyone has up and down periods, but these mood changes are extreme and the depression is deep and usually long-lasting. Persons with major depression describe themselves as down, discouraged, and hopeless. A less common form of depression is bipolar depression in which there are both periods of depression and periods of excessive euphoria called *mania*.

The role of depression in the development of criminal behavior has been studied now for many years. Preliminary data indicate that depression may be strongly associated with delinquency, especially in teenage girls (Kovacs, 1996; Obeidallah & Earls, 1999; Teplin, 2000). However, both boys and girls display depressive symptoms (Diamantopoulou, Verhulst, & van der Ende, 2011; Wareham & Dembo, 2007). Depression seems to render teenagers—both boys and girls—indifferent to their own personal safety and the consequences of their actions. They just don't care what happens to them, which may increase the likelihood of gravitating toward delinquency. On the other hand, delinquent behavior may lead to depression. In a longitudinal study of 3,604 adolescents (Kofler *et al.*, 2011), the researchers found more support for the former theory—that is, that early depressive symptoms predicted later delinquent behavior. This appeared to be the case especially for girls.

Depression also likely plays a significant role in mass murders, school shootings, workplace violence, and "suicide-by-cop" incidents in which a person sets up a situation wherein police are essentially forced to shoot. These incidents are discussed in greater detail in Chapters 9 and 10.

Antisocial Personality Disorder

The essential feature of a person with **antisocial personality disorder (APD)** is a history of continuous behavior in which the rights of others are violated. As mentioned in Chapter 7, the criteria closely follow Robert Hare's definition of the criminal psychopath. The individual must be at least 18 years of age and must have a history of some symptoms of conduct disorder before age 15. Recall that a diagnosis of **conduct disorder** is reserved for children and adolescents. Before a person can be diagnosed with APD, a pervasive pattern of disregard for and the violation of the rights of others must be indicated by at least three of the following behavioral patterns:

1. Failure to conform to social norms or the criminal law, as reflected by frequent performance of acts that are grounds for arrests
2. Irritability and unusual aggressiveness, as indicated by repeated physical fights or assaults

3. Consistent irresponsibility, as reflected in a poor work history or failure to honor financial obligations
4. Impulsivity or a failure to plan ahead (characteristic at all ages)
5. Deceitfulness, as reflected in frequent lying, use of aliases, or conning others for personal profit or pleasure
6. Reckless disregard for the safety of others or self
7. Lack of remorse or guilt for wrongdoings, as indicated by indifference to or rationalization of having hurt, mistreated, or stolen from another

Additional symptoms, as outlined in the *DSM-IV*, include stealing, fighting, truancy, and resisting authority—typical childhood symptoms. Antisocial personalities—often referred to as ASPs in the literature—lack empathy and tend to be callous, cynical, and contemptuous of the feelings, rights, and sufferings of others. Furthermore, they frequently exhibit precocious and aggressive sexual behavior, excessive drinking, and the use of illicit drugs. There is a markedly impaired capacity to maintain lasting, close, warm, and responsible relationships with family, friends, or sexual partners.

On average, ASPs fail to become independent, self-supporting adults. They spend most of their lives in institutions (usually correctional facilities) or remain highly dependent on their families. Other accompanying features include restlessness, an inability to tolerate boredom, and a belief that the world is hostile. ASPs often complain of tension and depression, but they do not usually meet the criteria for a diagnosis of depression. They are often impulsive and unable to plan ahead, and show deficits in executive functioning.

Antisocial personality disorder occurs more frequently in males than in females. It is estimated that about 3 percent of the American male population and about 1 percent of the American female population fall into this category (*DSM-IV*). Furthermore, the disorder is more common in lower-socioeconomic populations, partly because it is connected with impaired earning capacity and partly because of the greater likelihood of being raised in an economically disadvantaged, dysfunctional household with limited adequate role models and resources. Lastly, the *DSM* concludes that the disorder runs in families, possibly due to a genetic link that predisposes the child to antisocial behavioral patterns. Other perspectives would emphasize that family members share the disorder—not because of a genetic link—but because they also share the economic and social background that facilitates it. Nevertheless, in recent years many researchers are adopting a biopsychological perspective and finding an interaction between genes and the environment in many behaviors related to offending, including APD (see, e.g., Delisi, Beaver, Vaughn, & Wright, 2009).

Research dating from the 1970s has indicated that APD is a common diagnosis of criminal defendants and offenders. In an early study, Henn and his colleagues conducted an extensive series of investigations on all defendants referred by a St. Louis, Missouri, court for psychiatric assessment over a 10-year period (Henn, Herjanic, & Vanderpearl, 1976a). Focusing on a sample of 1,195 defendants accused of a variety of crimes and referred for psychiatric assessment, Henn and colleagues learned that the most frequent diagnosis was personality disorder, accounting for nearly 40 percent of all the diagnoses.

The pervasiveness of this diagnosis continues today. APD is frequently offered as a diagnosis in criminal courts and in corrections, sometimes serving as a catch-all category. Researchers have noted that when courts press for a diagnosis, many clinicians will oblige by concluding that an individual qualifies for APD (Melton, Petrila, Poythress, & Slobogin, 2007). In correctional facilities, rates of inmates considered APD range from 30 percent to 50 percent, and it is not unusual to find the diagnosis in over 50 percent of the correctional population (Gacono,

Nieberding, Owen, Rubel, & Bodholdt, 2001). APD is such a common diagnosis applied to persons both accused of and convicted of criminal offenses that some jurisdictions specifically exclude it from the list of mental disorders that can support an insanity defense.

COMPETENCY AND CRIMINAL RESPONSIBILITY

The above psychiatric diagnoses are often those that come into play when decisions must be made as to whether defendants who are mentally disordered are competent to stand trial or, if competent, are culpable enough to be held responsible for the crimes that occurred. In this section, we review these two very important legal constructs.

Incompetency to Stand Trial

Some persons charged with a crime are considered so intellectually and/or psychologically impaired that—were they to be tried—they would be present in body but not in mind. The U.S. Supreme Court has determined that the trial of such an individual violates the Constitution. Specifically, defendants are competent to stand trial if they have "sufficient present ability to consult with their lawyer with a reasonable degree of rational understanding...and a rational as well as factual understanding of the proceedings" (*Dusky v. United States*, 1960, p. 402). To protect the rights of the individual and to preserve the dignity of the court process, the law states that a person who is incompetent must not be tried.

Incompetence does not refer only to one's mental or emotional state, however. It may also refer to a lack of understanding of court proceedings, one's rights, or the functions performed by one's lawyer. Some criminal defendants, for example, may not understand the judge's role and may not know that they do not have to take the witness stand. Words and terms like "self-incrimination," "burden of proof," "stipulate," or even "plead" may be perplexing. This is especially, though not exclusively, a problem with relation to juveniles (Rogers *et al.*, 2012). Therefore, some efforts to restore individuals to competency involve educational strategies.

Competency is also an important issue in regard to defendants who are developmentally disabled. As Mumley, Tillbrook, and Grisso (2003, p. 343) noted, "Unlike psychotic defendants, persons with mental retardation often do not show obvious signs of poor understanding or reasoning, so that attorneys may be less capable of identifying those who are in need of AC (adjudicative competence) evaluation." Consequently, we have little information on the extent to which these defendants are referred for competency evaluation, and virtually no information on the proportion of IST defendants who are developmentally disabled.

In addition, the competency issue does not relate only to the actual trial. In fact, some scholars now prefer to use the term **adjudicative competence** rather than competence to stand trial (e.g., Bonnie & Grisso, 2000; Mumley *et al.*, 2003; Viljoen & Wingrove, 2007). The former term relates to the ability to participate in a wide variety of court proceedings and court-related activities, including plea bargaining, preliminary hearings, and other pretrial hearings related to one's case. It also encompasses two distinct concepts: (1) the competence to proceed (which implies understanding the purpose of the proceedings and being able to help one's attorney), and (2) decisional competence (which implies the ability to comprehend the significance of various decisions to be made) (Mumley *et al.*, 2003). If a criminal defendant is found incompetent to stand trial, the court has essentially determined that he or she cannot understand the process that is occurring or effectively participate in it. Interestingly, the issue of competence also extends to whether a mentally disordered defendant who is competent to stand trial is also competent to represent himself. In a 2008 case (*Indiana v. Edwards*), the U.S. Supreme Court ruled that a unitary standard for deciding these two issues was inappropriate. Although many questions were left unanswered in that case, for our purposes, it must be emphasized that just because defendants are competent to stand trial, this does not mean that they are competent to serve as their own attorney or to plead guilty.

The competency issue can be raised at any time during the actual proceedings. For example, a defendant may be competent up to and into the beginning phases of his trial; during a long and protracted trial, he may become incompetent. A defendant also may be competent before and during trial, but incompetent at the time of sentencing or during post-conviction proceedings, such as appeals.

Evaluations for **competency to stand trial** represent the most common referral for criminally related forensic assessments (Cruise & Rogers, 1998). Most typically, defendants referred for competency evaluation have a history of psychiatric care or institutionalization or exhibited signs of mental disorder at arrest or while detained in jail. Data indicate that approximately 25,000 criminal defendants nationwide, or about one in 15, are evaluated each year by state and federal courts for their competency to stand trial (Cruise & Rogers, 1998; Nicholson & Kugler, 1991). About four out of every five of these evaluated defendants—or roughly 20–30 percent depending upon the study—are found competent (Grisso, 1986; Nicholson & Kugler, 1991; Pirelli, Gottdiener, & Zapf, 2011; Roesch, Zapf, Golding, & Skeem, 1999).

It is important to emphasize the distinction between incompetence to stand trial (IST) and insanity, the legal concept to be discussed below. Although they may be related, the two concepts are distinct and should be assessed by clinicians separately—although this is not always done. In high-profile cases, competency and sanity are more likely to be kept distinct; for example, in ordering the competency evaluation of Jared Loughner, the judge in the case made it clear that the evaluation was to be limited to the issue of competency, not sanity. Criminal responsibility, which is at the core of the insanity defense, and competency to stand trial refer to a defendant's mental state/capacity at *two different points in time*. If a defendant pleads not guilty by reason of insanity, the law asks, "What was the defendant's state of mind at the time the offense was committed?" In competency considerations, the question becomes, "What is the defendant's state of mind at the present time, or at the time of the pretrial proceedings or trial?" An individual who was seriously mentally disordered at the time of an offense and whose criminal responsibility is questionable may have enough mental stability by the time of the trial to be competent to stand trial. On the other hand, a person may be of sound mind during the unlawful act, but may later become disordered or disoriented and be determined incompetent to stand trial.

If found incompetent to stand trial—a decision that must be made by the presiding judge—the defendant is typically sent to a mental institution until rendered competent, as was Jared Loughner mentioned at the beginning of this chapter. For those defendants who are restored to competency, some research suggests that the average time needed for restoration is about three months (Hoge *et al.*, 1996). In a survey of mental health program directors across the United States, Miller (2003) found that outpatient treatment to restore competency was rare. Outpatient *evaluations* of competency were on the increase, however. Most recently, though, some states are providing for more competency *restoration* in the community, particularly for juveniles who have been found incompetent to participate in court proceedings. In such states, inpatient treatment is considered only as a last resort.

Until the 1970s, the typical procedure for *evaluating* competency required that defendants be confined within a maximum security institution for a lengthy psychiatric-psychological evaluation (usually 60–90 days). Following evaluation, the defendant was granted a hearing on the matter of competency. If the court found the defendant unable to understand the charges or the judicial proceedings, or to help counsel in his or her defense, then the defendant would automatically be committed to a secure hospital for an indefinite period of time—until competent. Theoretically, this indefinite time period could extend—and sometimes did—into a lifetime of involuntary commitment.

In 1972, in *Jackson v. Indiana*, the Supreme Court declared that such an indefinite confinement violated the Constitution. While the court allowed the confinement, it specified that if no progress was made toward competence, the individual must be released or must be recommitted under civil, not criminal statutes. Today, individuals found IST with little likelihood of being restored to competency often have their cases dismissed if the charges were not very serious. However, in many jurisdictions, the prosecutor still retains the option of reinstituting charges if the person regains competency at some later time.

In recent years, ISTs have asserted additional constitutional rights in connection with their status, including the right to the "least restrictive or drastic alternative," specifically the right to be treated in a community setting rather than in an institution. As noted earlier, though, recent research suggests that community treatment is not the typical approach (Miller, 2003). In addition, because treatment is often offered in the form of psychoactive drugs, some defendants ruled IST—like Jared Loughner—have argued that they should not be forced to take these drugs. Psychoactive drugs are "those drugs that exert their primary effect on the brain, thus altering mood or behavior, or that are used in the treatment of mental disorders" (Julien, 1992, p. xii). Although these drugs have been improved considerably over the past few decades, many have side effects—including in some cases debilitating side effects—and are resisted by many patients.

In a Supreme Court ruling on this matter (*Sell v. United States*, 2003), the court ruled that, in a case that did not involve violence, courts must be wary of ordering such medication against a defendant's will. Sell, a former dentist charged with insurance fraud, had been found incompetent and was hospitalized for treatment. He had a history of mental disorder and had prior hospitalizations, during which he had received psychoactive drugs. Psychiatrists again prescribed psychoactive drugs in an effort to render him competent to stand trial, but Sell refused to take them. Both a trial judge and a federal court of appeals ruled against him, but the U.S. Supreme Court did not agree. The court noted that the trial court had not adequately weighed the advantages and disadvantages of the drugs, and it sent the case back to the court to do just that. However, for serious, violent crimes, where the government has a strong interest in bringing a defendant to trial, the court has been less sympathetic to the defendant, refusing to hear an appeal of an order for involuntary medication (*United States v. Weston*, cert. denied). Russell Eugene Weston, Jr. is the individual charged with the lethal shooting of two Capitol police officers in 1998 and the nonlethal shooting of two other individuals. In light of the nature of the crimes, Weston's long history of serious mental illness (he was a diagnosed paranoid schizophrenic with previous hospitalizations), and the government's strong interest in bringing him to trial, courts ruled in favor of the involuntary medication, saying he could be forced to take the medication. It should be noted, though, that the lower court in Weston's case had given careful consideration to the advantages and disadvantages of ordering the medication. Interestingly, over 10 years after the incident, Weston apparently remains in a federal psychiatric facility and has yet to be tried.

Several studies, including a recent meta-analysis covering 68 studies conducted between 1967 and 2008 (Pirelli *et al.*, 2011), have compared defendants found competent to stand trial to those found incompetent. Competent and incompetent defendants do not differ significantly on demographic variables such as race, gender, or marital status (Nicholson & Kugler 1991; Riley, 1998; Rosenfeld & Ritchie, 1998). They do differ, not surprisingly, on clinical variables. Thus, persons found incompetent are more likely to be diagnosed with a psychotic disorder or organic mental disorder (Warren, Rosenfeld, Fitch, & Hawk, 1997) or schizophrenia and affective disorders (Hoge *et al.*, 1997). Pirelli *et al.* found that those defendants with psychotic disorders were about eight times more likely to be found incompetent than those without such disorders. Pirellie *et al.* also found that defendants who were unemployed or had previous psychiatric hospitalizations were about twice as likely to be found incompetent as those who were employed or without previous psychiatric histories.

Criminal Responsibility

Given the widespread publicity associated with the insanity defense, most people are probably far more aware of defendants found not guilty by reason of insanity (NGRI) than those found incompetent to stand trial. Insanity is a legal term, not a psychiatric or psychological one; for our purposes, it should be used only in the context of a criminal offense. Insanity refers to a person's *state of mind at the time an offense was committed.* When an individual is found not guilty by reason of insanity, a judge or jury have determined that he or she was so mentally disordered at the time of the crime that the person should not be held responsible. This was the case for John Hinckley, the man who in 1981 shot President Ronald Reagan, wounding him along with three others, including press secretary James Brady, and for Andrea Yates, in her second trial. The law assumes that mental disorder *can* rob an individual of free will or the ability to make appropriate choices. Note that insanity should not be *equated* with mental disorder, even serious mental disorder. That is, a mentally disordered person can still be found responsible for committing a criminal offense. Likewise, an individual who is intellectually disabled can still be held criminally responsible.

Insanity defenses, especially if they are successful, receive extensive media coverage and commentary. When Hinckley was found NGRI by a federal jury, there was widespread public indignation accompanied by numerous demands for repeal of the insanity defense in both federal and state laws. Since the Hinckley acquittal by reason of insanity in June 1982, at least 34 states have made some kind of alteration to their insanity statutes (Steadman *et al.*, 1993). Moreover, in response to the public outcry against the Hinckley acquittal, the U.S. Congress passed the *Insanity Defense Act of 1984,* which is discussed below. Virtually, all these legal changes made it more difficult for defendants who wished to plead not guilty by reason of insanity. Incidentally, to this day, Hinckley remains hospitalized, although he has been allowed to leave the facility for overnight visits to his home for incrementally longer periods.

In the case of Andrea Yates, public outcry was much less vociferous. Recall that she was convicted in her first trial, but that conviction was overturned. She was then found not guilty by reason of insanity, in a bench trial. Between the two trials, there was extensive publicity about her background, her past institutionalizations, and the many warning signs about her serious disorder. Although there is no documented evidence to this effect, it is likely that the public had a better appreciation of the dire emotional state that led to the tragic circumstances of her children's deaths.

It is important to note that the number of insanity defenses raised in the United States is believed very small compared with the total number of criminal cases. Furthermore, despite the outcry after the Hinckley verdict, insanity defenses are rarely successful. In addition, we often hear that someone is planning to use the insanity defense but this does not necessarily come to pass. Amy Bishop, a biology professor at the University of Alabama, Huntsville, opened fire on colleagues in a department meeting in 2010, killing some and wounding others. Although her lawyers had indicated that she would use an insanity defense, she pled guilty on September 11, 2012. Levy Aron made the same decision. Unfortunately, there are no *systematic, nationwide* data on how often the insanity defense is actually used (McGinley & Paswark, 1989). County, state, and federal levels of government rarely share information about these issues (Steadman *et al.*, 1993). Steadman and his colleagues write, "County level information on insanity pleas, for example, is rarely, if ever, aggregated to the state level, meaning almost nothing is known about the earliest stages of the insanity defense process" (1993, p. 3). However, there are some good estimates based on studies conducted by independent and governmental researchers. These researchers estimate that insanity defenses are used in only 1 percent of all U.S. felony criminal cases (Callahan, Steadman, McGreevy, & Robbins, 1991; Golding, Skeem, Roesch, & Zapf, 1999).

HOW SUCCESSFUL IS THE INSANITY DEFENSE?   Data on acquittals suggest that the defense is typically not successful. In an eight-state study of 9,000 defendants who pleaded not guilty by reason of insanity, Callahan *et al.* (1991) found a 22–25 percent success rate. Other studies have reported wide statewide differences, with a high of 44 percent in Colorado and a low of 2 percent in Wyoming (McGinley & Paswark, 1989). Cirincione and Jacobs (1999) found a mean of only 33.4 insanity acquittals per year across 35 states over the period 1974–1995. More important, acquittals seem to be closely tied to the diagnosis placed on the defendant and, to some extent, on the crime charged (Cochrane, Grisso, & Frederick, 2001; Warren *et al.*, 1997). Cochrane *et al.* found that federal defendants with diagnoses of psychotic disorders, affective disorders, and mental retardation had higher rates of acquittal than those diagnosed with other disorders. Personality disorders were negatively correlated with a finding of insanity. More recently, researchers have found that jurors are favorably disposed toward defendants who provide neurological evidence, particularly evidence of traumatic brain injury (Gurley & Marcus, 2008). Such injury to the brain may be accompanied by increases in aggression, personality changes, and impaired ability to control one's emotions, among other consequences (Gurley & Marcus, 2008).

By contrast, some elements work against a defendant pleading not guilty by reason of insanity. For example, recall that many states specifically exclude antisocial personality disorder as a mental disorder to support an insanity defense. As we learned in Chapter 7, this is often the diagnosis placed on individuals who are believed to be psychopaths. Warren *et al.* (1997) found that defendants charged with violent crimes against others had the highest acquittal rates, while sex offenders significantly are more likely to be *convicted*. Nevertheless, the research literature strongly indicates that the clinical diagnosis, more than the offense, seems to be the critical factor. This also may explain the low acquittal of sex offenders, because these offenders are often not considered by clinicians to be mentally disordered.

In the United States, acquittals are far more difficult to obtain from juries (jury trials) than from judges (bench trials), a pattern that underscores the pervasive negative attitude the American public has toward the insanity defense. For example, in their eight-state study, Callahan *et al.* (1991) found that only 7 percent of the acquittals were handed down by juries. In another study, Boehnert (1989) found that 96 percent of defendants found not guilty by reason of insanity had gone before a judge. Thus, it seems wise for defendants who plan to use the insanity defense to have a bench trial (where the judge decides) rather than a jury trial. On the other hand, research suggests that, if jurors are informed of the consequences of an NGRI verdict—specifically that the defendant will likely be hospitalized for treatment—they may be more likely to acquit the defendant (Wheatman & Shaffer, 2001).

Callahan *et al.* (1991) found that successful NGRI defendants, compared with unsuccessful defendants, tended to be older, female, better educated, and single. They also had a history of prior hospitalization and were considered extremely disturbed. Furthermore, 15 percent of the acquitted defendants had not themselves raised the insanity defense, indicating that they were so disordered that an insanity verdict was essentially imposed on them.

WHEN IS THE INSANITY DEFENSE MOST OFTEN USED?   Defense attorneys generally do not recommend that their clients plead not guilty by reason of insanity unless they are charged with a serious offense and the evidence against them is overwhelming. Nevertheless, it is a mistake to think that defendants charged with misdemeanor offenses do not raise this defense; it is sometimes used to obtain treatment for mentally disordered individuals who might not otherwise be eligible for institutionalization. However, when the possible penalty is capital punishment or life imprisonment without parole, an insanity defense becomes more palatable to the defense. In many jurisdictions, however, insanity acquittees are immediately confined to a mental institution, where they are kept for as long as needed to produce substantial improvement in their condition and assure that they are not a danger to themselves or others. In fact, until recently, research indicated that persons found NGRI on average spent at least as much time in mental institutions or treatment facilities as they would have spent in prison if convicted (Golding et al., 1999). More and more, though, persons found NGRI are being institutionalized for shorter periods of time and then released, typically on a conditional basis, into the community where they can receive specialized treatment services (Vitacco et al., 2008). This also allows mental health authorities to monitor their progress and assure that they are taking the medication that presumably keeps them stabilized and their mental disorder in remission. Vitacco et al. (2008) found considerable success offering quality services to insanity acquittees in the community. Quality services often included alcohol and drug abuse treatment as well as close monitoring of both mental health symptoms and compliance with medication orders. In other words, someone should assure that the acquittees are "taking their meds" if these have been prescribed. Vitacco et al. found that most individuals who were returned to the institution were more likely to be sent back for rules violations than for criminal charges.

Community treatment orders are partially in response to a 1992 U.S. Supreme Court decision, *Foucha v. Louisiana*, which placed some limits on the hospital confinement of persons found not guilty by reason of insanity. In the *Foucha* case, the Court ruled that insanity acquittees may not be held in psychiatric facilities once they are no longer mentally disordered, even if it could be argued that they are dangerous. Foucha had been hospitalized for four years. While a committee of mental health practitioners found his mental illness to be in remission, they could not certify that he was no longer dangerous. Nevertheless, a divided Supreme Court (5–4) ruled that, if no longer mentally ill, he should be discharged. Critics of the *Foucha* decision maintain that the Court did not sufficiently recognize the recurring quality of serious mental disorders. They note that, while mental disorders may go into remission, persons suffering from them are not necessarily cured (Golding et al., 1999). On the other hand, it is difficult to justify holding an individual who is not disordered on the premise that at some point in the future, his or her disorder is likely to reappear and the person will commit a violent crime.

Thus far, we have discussed the consequences of a finding of not guilty by reason of insanity. In the following section, we cover a variety of standards that courts use to decide whether a person was insane.

INSANITY STANDARDS

The insanity defense has been recognized in English courts for over 700 years (Simon, 1983). Since the American legal system is derived from British law, American courts have generally recognized it as well. Standards or tests to determine insanity vary widely among the states, but they usually center around one of three broad models: the M'Naghten Rule, the Brawner Rule, or the Durham Rule. Moreover, all the insanity standards are fundamentally based on two criteria: irrationality and compulsion (Morse, 1986). If it can be established that a person was not in control of his or her mental processes (was thinking irrationally) and/or was not in control of his or her behavior (was driven by compulsion) at the time of the offense, then there are grounds for absolving that person of some or all responsibility for the offense. Jurisdictions, however, differ in the extent they accept both these criteria. That is, some jurisdictions accept both criteria, while others will accept only the irrationality component. It is important to note, as well, that in a recent insanity-related decision (*Clark v. Arizona*, 2006), the U.S. Supreme Court made it clear that states could determine their own insanity standards and that the Court would not establish a universal Constitutional standard that would apply to all (DeMatteo, 2007).

The M'Naghten Rule

The **M'Naghten Rule** has been around in some form since at least the nineteenth century. The current rule was formulated in 1843, after Daniel M'Naghten, a Scottish woodcutter, was acquitted of killing a man he believed to be the prime minister. M'Naghten thought he was being persecuted by the Tories and their leader, Prime Minister Sir Robert Peel. He fired a shot into a carriage transporting Peel's secretary, Edward Drumond, thinking Peel himself was in the carriage. There was no question that M'Naghten had committed the act, but the court believed he was so mentally deranged that it would be inhumane to convict him. Applying a "wild beast" test in use at the time, the court concluded it was clear he was not in control of his faculties. He was committed to the Broadmoor Mental Institution, where he remained until his death 22 years later. It was widely believed that M'Naghten "knew" his actions were wrong and that he should have been convicted. Therefore, the law was changed to prevent a similar "miscarriage of justice" in the future. Thus, the rule that bears M'Naghten's name is not the rule under which he was tried.

In 1851, the M'Naghten Rule was adopted in the federal and most state courts in the United States. It is deceptively simple, and therein lies its popularity. It states that a person is not responsible for a criminal act if, "at the time of committing the act, the party accused was labouring under such a defect of reason, from disease of the mind, as not to know the nature and quality of the act he was doing; or if he did know it...he did not know he was doing what was wrong" (*M'Naghten*, 1843, p. 718). Essentially, the rule states that if a person, because of some mental disease, did not know right from wrong at the time of an unlawful act, or did not know that what he or she was doing was wrong, that person cannot be held responsible for his or her actions.

Thus, the M'Naghten Rule, sometimes referred to as the **right and wrong test**, emphasizes the *cognitive elements* of (1) being aware and knowing what one was doing at the time of the illegal act, or (2) knowing or realizing right from wrong in the moral sense. The rule recognizes no degree of incapacity. You are either responsible for the action or you are not. There are no in-betweens.

Some states supplement M'Naghten with an irresistible impulse test, which has similarities to the "wild beast" test applied in the original M'Naghten case. The irresistible impulse test recognizes or assumes that people may realize the wrongfulness of their conduct, be aware of what is right or wrong in a particular set of circumstances, but still be powerless to do right in the face of overwhelming pressures from uncontrollable impulses. In other words, there are conditions under which people presumably cannot help themselves. The M'Naghten Rule alone would not cover those circumstances, since it requires that the person did not know right from wrong.

The Brawner Rule and the American Law Institute Rule

The **Brawner Rule**, which is largely based on an insanity rule suggested by the Model Penal Code (MPC), is another rule for determining insanity. The MPC was proposed in 1962 by a group of legal scholars associated with the American Law Institute (ALI). The Code was drafted to serve as a model for legislatures seeking to modernize and rationalize their criminal statutes. According to the Brawner Rule, "A person is not responsible for criminal conduct if at the time of such conduct as a result of mental disease or *defect* [italics added], he lacks substantial capacity either to appreciate the criminality [wrongfulness] of his conduct or to conform his conduct to the requirements of the law" (*United States v. Brawner*, 1972, p. 973). It must be demonstrated that the disease or mental defect *substantially* and directly (1) influenced the defendant's mental or emotional processes, or (2) impaired his or her ability to control behavior. The Brawner Rule, unlike M'Naghten, recognizes *partial* responsibility for criminal conduct, as well as the possibility of an irresistible impulse beyond one's control. It also excludes from the definition of mental disease or defect any repeated criminal or otherwise antisocial conduct, an exclusion we referred to earlier in the chapter. This provision (called the **caveat paragraph**) was intended to disallow the insanity defense for criminal psychopaths who persistently violate social mores and the law. Thus, psychopaths and persons with APDs cannot claim that their abnormal condition is a mental disorder, disease, or defect, even if they have been diagnosed with APD.

The Durham Rule: The Product Test

The **Durham Rule** was created in 1954 in *Durham v. United States* by the same court that later rejected it in favor of the Brawner Rule. Monte Durham, a 26-year-old resident of the District of Columbia, had a long history of mental disorder and petty theft. His crime of the moment was burglary, but he was acquitted because his unlawful act was considered to be "the product of a mental disease or mental defect" (*Durham v. United States*, 1954, p. 874). While the M'Naghten Rule focuses on knowing right from wrong (the mental element in a crime), Durham assumes that one cannot be held responsible if an unlawful action is the product of mental disease or defect.

There is nothing in the Durham Rule that relates directly to the person's mental judgment. If the person has a disease or defect, lack of culpability is easily assumed. The rule was later clarified in *Carter v. United States* (1957), which held that mental illness must not merely have entered into the production of the act, it must have played a necessary role.

Many states were attracted to the apparent simplicity of the Durham Rule, since it seemed more straightforward and comprehensible to juries. However, it soon became apparent that definitions of "mental illness" are vague and subjective, a situation that fostered the widespread discretionary power of psychiatry and considerable misuse of mental health experts during trial. Moreover, virtually any defendant could be excused once mental disease or defect had been established, and the Durham Rule quickly lost its popularity.

Until the 1980s, most jurisdictions adopted one of the above rules, with varying degrees of satisfaction. However, the well-publicized Hinckley acquittal sparked a public outcry for the elimination of the insanity defense and prompted legislative bodies and many professional organizations to reexamine it. The American Bar Association and the American Psychiatric Association, for example, proposed new, more restrictive standards (Steadman *et al.*, 1993). Nearly 100 different reforms in 34 jurisdictions occurred soon after Hinckley's acquittal, the most active insanity reform period in American history. In most instances, these reforms reflected a return to the M'Naghten Rule in a modified, more restrictive form (Steadman *et al.*, 1993). A small minority of states have abolished the insanity defense altogether. Other changes include (1) placing on defendants the burden of proving they were insane (where in the past prosecutors had been required to prove they were not insane), (2) restricting the role of clinical testimony, and (3) requiring persons found NGRI to prove they were no longer mentally ill before being released from a mental institution. Many of these changes were modeled after the federal law discussed below. Recall, though, as mentioned above, the U.S. Supreme Court has given wide latitude to the states in defining insanity and crafting their laws relating to it (DeMatteo, 2007).

The Insanity Defense Reform Act

Amid public clamors to abolish the insanity defense completely after the Hinckley acquittal, Congress passed the **Insanity Defense Reform Act of 1984**, which kept the defense in the federal law but modified it in important ways. Rita Simon and David Aaronson (1988, p. 47) assert, "The Hinckley verdict was unquestionably the decisive influence on congressional modifications to the insanity defense." Essentially, Congress made it more difficult for persons using the insanity defense in federal courts to be acquitted. The Insanity Reform Act changed the Brawner/ALI Rule—the rule that has been most consistently adhered to in all federal circuits (except the Fifth Circuit) since its adoption during the early 1970s—to one patterned more along the lines of the M'Naghten Rule. Specifically, a defendant cannot be held responsible if "at the time of the commission of the acts constituting the offense, the defendant, as a result of a severe mental disease or defect, was unable to appreciate the nature and quality or the wrongfulness of his acts. Mental disease or defect does not otherwise constitute a defense" (18 U.S.C., sec 20[a] [1984]).

In addition, the new federal standard changed the Brawner/ALI Rule in three principal ways (Simon & Aaronson, 1988). First, the act abolished the irresistible impulse test (commonly called the **volitional prong**) of the Brawner/ALI Rule. The inability to control one's actions because of mental defect was no longer acceptable as an excusing condition. Second, the act modified the "cognitive" requirement by replacing the phrase "lacks substantial capacity...to appreciate" with "unable to appreciate." The intention was to tighten the requirement to a total lack of ability to appreciate that what they did was wrong (Simon & Aaronson, 1988). Third, under the new law, the mental disease or defect must be severe, to emphasize that certain behavioral disorders (especially personality disorders) do not qualify as a defense. It should be noted that the federal law also bars mental health clinicians from expressing an opinion as to whether the defendant was insane. Clinicians may testify, report on the findings of their evaluations, and provide a diagnosis, but they may not express an ultimate opinion. This is to emphasize that insanity is a legal determination that must be made by the court. **Table 8-1** summarizes common standards for determining criminal responsibility in mentally disordered defendants.

Guilty but Mentally Ill

Also in response to disenchantment with the insanity defense, some states have introduced a new verdict alternative, **Guilty but Mentally Ill (GBMI)**. Michigan was the first to adopt this alternative in 1975, and by 1992, 11 other states had followed Michigan's lead. The GBMI option is intended as an alternative to, not a substitute for, the NGRI verdict. States differ in the standards and procedures associated with the GBMI verdict, and some use slightly different terminology, such as guilty except insane. In all, though, the major intention of the option is to reduce the number of insanity acquittals, hold the defendant blameworthy, but still recognize the presence of a mental disorder. Thus, GBMI allows the court to render a "middle-ground" verdict in the case of allegedly mentally disordered defendants. The verdict allows juries, for example, to reconcile their belief that a defendant who commits a crime should be held responsible with the belief that he or she also needs help.

TABLE 8-1 Standards for Criminal Responsibility

Standard	Year First Used	Description
M'Naghten Rule	1843	It must be clearly proved that at the time of committing the act, the party accused was laboring under such a defect of reason, from disease of the mind, as not to know the nature and quality of the act he was doing, or if he did know it, that he did not know he was doing what was wrong.
Durham Rule	1954	An accused is not criminally responsible if the unlawful act was the product of mental disease or mental defect.
Brawner/ALI Rule	1972	A person is not responsible for criminal conduct if at the time of such conduct, as a result of mental disease or defect, he lacks substantial capacity to either appreciate the criminality [wrongfulness] of his conduct or to conform his conduct to the requirements of the law.
Insanity Defense Reform Act	1984	A person charged with a criminal offense should be found not guilty by reason of insanity if it is shown that, as a result of mental disease or mental retardation, he was unable to appreciate the wrongfulness of his conduct at the time of his offense.
Guilty but mentally ill	1975	This holds the defendant blameworthy for the offense, but recognizes the presence of a mental disorder.

Research on the GBMI laws indicates that the intended purposes may not have been accomplished. An early study in Michigan found that insanity acquittals remained stable while guilty verdicts generally declined (Smith & Hall, 1982). The same finding was reported in other states that adopted the GBMI option (McGinley & Paswark, 1989). Furthermore, defendants found GBMI have received longer sentences and had longer confinements than "sane" defendants found guilty of similar charges (Callahan, McGreevy, Cirincione, & Steadman, 1992; Steadman *et al.*, 1993). In addition, research indicates that those individuals found GBMI are no more likely to receive psychotherapy or rehabilitative services than other mentally disordered defendants in the prison system (Borum & Fulero, 1999; Morse, 1985; Slobogin, 1985; Zapf, Golding, & Roesch, 2006). Thus, the promise of treatment that is implicit in the statutes remains unfulfilled. However, depending upon the wording of the statute, it may be read as creating a *right* to treatment for those defendants found GBMI (Cohen, 2008), although this is not the common approach. Interestingly, there is also evidence that defendants charged with a serious violent crime often elect the GBMI alternative as part of the plea-bargaining process. Defense attorneys may be more willing to accept this option than go to trial and risk their client's life (Steadman *et al.*, 1993). Considering the research strongly suggesting that GBMI statutes do not accomplish what was intended, virtually all of the scholarly writing on this issue has questioned the wisdom and efficacy of these laws (Cohen, 2008).

UNIQUE DEFENSES

Earlier in the chapter, we discussed some of the psychiatric diagnoses that are most likely to accompany a decision that a defendant is incompetent to stand trial or used to bolster an insanity defense. In this section, we discuss additional disorders or diagnoses that are less common but still cited by defense lawyers, either to absolve defendants completely or to support a claim of diminished capacity or responsibility. Most typically, these are not complete defenses but rather absolve individuals of some degree of responsibility, if they are successful. In addition, these unique conditions may help defendants obtain a more favorable plea bargain or more lenient sentencing.

Posttraumatic Stress Disorder

According to the *DSM-IV*, **posttraumatic stress disorder (PTSD)** is "the development of characteristic symptoms following exposure to extreme traumatic stress or involving direct personal experience of an event that involves actual or threatened death or serious injury, or other threat to one's physical integrity; or witnessing an event that involves death, injury, or threat to the physical integrity of another person; or learning about unexpected or violent death, serious harm, or threat of death or injury experienced by a family member or other close associate" (p. 424). The precipitating event would be substantially distressing to almost anyone, and it is "usually experienced with intense fear, terror, and helplessness" (p. 424).

PTSD was formally recognized as a distinct disorder in the 1980 edition of the *DSM-III* following efforts by veterans' groups to have mental health professionals recognize a "post-Vietnam syndrome" that led to a variety of disabling symptoms (Appelbaum *et al.*, 1993). Since being formally recognized, PTSD has been broadly applied to war veterans, survivors of the Holocaust, survivors of major disasters—such as the events of September 11, 2001—and victims and survivors of rape, child abuse, spousal abuse, and sexual harassment. Victims of human rights abuses around the globe are also susceptible to the symptoms associated with PTSD.

PTSD falls under the broader category of "anxiety disorders," which are characterized by persistent anxiety and worry. Other examples of anxiety disorders are panic attacks, agoraphobia, social phobia, obsessive compulsive disorder, and acute stress disorder. PTSD is one of the diagnostic categories slated for change in the revised *DSM*, and the proposed changes were controversial. For example, the *DSM-5* may include the subtypes of PTSD in preschool children and PTSD with prominent dissociative symptoms, with these subtypes not mutually exclusive. As we have cautioned throughout this chapter, readers are encouraged to consult the new edition of this diagnostic manual once it is released.

Studies have estimated that between 1 percent and 7 percent all Americans suffer from PTSD (Elhai, Grubaugh, Kashdan, & Frueh, 2008, 6.8%; Sutker, Uddo-Crane, & Allain, 1991, 1–2%). The prevalence of PTSD among military veterans is believed to be considerably higher than the prevalence in the general population, however. Kulka *et al.* 1991, estimated that PTSD affected 31 percent of all male and 27 percent of all female Vietnam veterans. More recently, it has been estimated that 16.6 percent of soldiers returning from Iraq and Afghanistan met criteria for PTSD within a year of their return (Hoge, Terhakopian, Castro, Messer, & Engel, 2007).

The symptoms of PTSD include "flashbacks," recurrent dreams or nightmares, or painful, intrusive memories of the traumatic event. A diminished responsiveness, a don't-care attitude, or psychological "numbing" to the external world are common, particularly during the weeks following the event. However, as suggested by the Hoge *et al.* research, the symptoms of PTSD may not emerge until considerable time has elapsed, six months to a year or more. In fact, the *DSM-IV* distinguishes among acute (symptoms last less than three months), chronic (symptoms last longer than three months), and delayed onset PTSD (when at least six months have passed since the traumatic event). Feelings of alienation or detachment from the social environment are also characteristic, a pattern that leads to difficulty in developing close, meaningful relationships with others. Other symptoms include sleep problems, being easily startled, considerable difficulty concentrating or remembering, and extreme avoidance of anything that reminds them of the event. Even anniversaries of the trauma are often enough to precipitate symptoms. Individuals with a diagnosis of PTSD tend to be moody, depressed, and difficult to be around or work with. They often move from job to job, relationship to relationship. In the case of veterans, those with PTSD diagnoses are significantly more likely than those without such diagnoses to be perpetrators of domestic violence and to be arrested for criminal activity (Friel, White, & Hull, 2008).

PTSD has been used to support a defense of NGRI, in both violent and nonviolent cases (Monahan & Walker, 1990, 1994). For example, PTSD has been used as an excusing condition for drug trafficking (e.g., *United States v. Krutschewski*, 1981). Evidence to date, however, shows that—while courts are willing to admit evidence of PTSD—using it to support an insanity defense is not likely to be successful (Appelbaum *et al.*, 1993; Friel *et al.*, 2008; Sparr, 1996). When the PTSD defense has been successful, it usually results in a finding of *diminished responsibility,* rather than the complete absolution of responsibility (NGRI) for the defendant. PTSD has also been cited in plea bargaining and in presentence reports (Monahan & Walker, 1990). That is, prosecutors may be more willing to accept a guilty plea to a reduced charge, and judges more willing to impose a lighter sentence, if evidence of PTSD exists. In a recent U.S. Supreme Court case (*Cone v. Bell,* 2009), the Court vacated the death sentence of a Vietnam veteran because the sentencing jury had not considered the fact that he suffered from PTSD as a mitigating factor in his crime. In cases involving veterans, PTSD may also be used as evidence for diminished responsibility in assigning cases to pretrial diversion, in plea bargaining, and in sentencing (Appelbaum *et al.*, 1993; Christy, Clark, Frei, & Rynearson-Moody, 2012). Indeed, in a study of the attitudes of prosecutors toward veterans with PTSD, Wilson, Brodsky, Neal, and Cramer (2011) found that the prosecutors perceived them as less criminally culpable and were more willing to be lenient, such as by referring these defendants to diversion programs, compared with defendants without PTSD.

The primary legal argument used by the defense is that the defendant was in a PTSD dissociated state when he committed the act. Although PTSD is not regarded as a dissociative disorder in the *DSM* (it is an anxiety disorder), it does have dissociative symptoms and therefore, those who suffer from it, could be considered to be at times in a **dissociated state**. This refers to symptoms in which the individual feels detached from him- or herself and his or her surroundings and basically loses some contact with reality. While in that state, a person typically does not remember what he or she has experienced or even his or her own identity. In *State v. Felde* (1982), the defendant—a Vietnam veteran who shot a police officer—"claimed that he was in a dissociative state and that he believed that he had been captured by the North Vietnamese at the time he shot the officer" (McCord, 1987, p. 65). In *Miller v. State* (1983), the defendant, charged with a prison escape, argued that he thought he was still in Vietnam and his only intention was to get back to the United States. When Robert Bales was charged with murders of Afghan civilians, there was suspicion that he would raise a PTSD defense; as noted earlier in the chapter, his military trial is imminent but the strategy to be used by the defense is not known.

PTSD has been used to excuse or mitigate criminal responsibility in cases involving battered women who maintain that they have **battered woman syndrome**, sometimes considered a variant of PTSD (Appelbaum *et al.*, 1993). This is a controversial area for at least two major reasons. First, there is not universal agreement in the psychological literature that there exists a battered woman syndrome. Second, advocates for battered women resist the implication that they have a mental disorder or that they are "insane." When PTSD is used, a battered woman may claim that the abuse was so extensive and brutal that, in a dissociative state brought about by the disorder, she killed the abuser. In this case, she is more likely to claim "temporary insanity" than "insanity," in the hope that acquittal will not be followed by commitment to a mental institution. However, PTSD in a battered woman also may be used to support a claim of self-defense rather than insanity, though courts have not been sympathetic to this approach (Slobogin, 1999). When used in this way, the defendant focuses on other symptoms of PTSD—for example, heightened fear, anxiety, depression—rather than on the dissociative state. In a different context, evidence that a rape victim shows the symptoms of PTSD has been accepted in some courts as proof that the victim has indeed been raped (Appelbaum *et al.*, 1993). Likewise, PTSD has been used in civil suits involving emotional or physical personal injury, such as sexual harassment suits or civil suits against former abusers.

In summary, evidence that an individual is suffering from PTSD is accepted in many courts, but it rarely absolves criminal defendants of total responsibility. Rather, it may support a diversion from prosecution—if the crime is not a serious one—and it may be helpful at the plea bargaining stage or in supporting a claim of diminished capacity. Evidence of PTSD has also contributed to lenience in sentencing; and, of course, in the hands of a sympathetic jury, it could lead to an acquittal.

Until recently, some legal scholars and researchers believed that there was no objective way to assess PTSD—its diagnosis depended almost exclusively on the self-report of the individual or the observations of those close to him or her. Consequently, there was considerable opportunity for malingering or faking the disorder. While malingering remains a concern, clinicians believe they have found better methods of discovering it (Resnick, 1995). In addition, several clinical methods of assessing PTSD itself have been developed and evaluated, including the Clinician-Administered PTSD Scale (CAPS; Blake, Weathers, & Nagy, 1995), which has been referred to as the "gold standard" for assessing the disorder (Friel *et al.*, 2008).

Dissociation

One of the most fascinating concepts in contemporary psychology is that of dissociation, which is believed to exist on a continuum from the normal to the pathological (Moskowitz, 2004). Most of us probably daydream, which is a "normal" form; in its most severe or pathological form, dissociation can refer to extreme amnesia for past events or even dissociative identity disorder (DID), which was formerly called multiple personality disorder (MPD). Each of these will be discussed in more detail below. The *DSM-IV* identifies five different dissociative disorders, including amnesia and DID, and defines dissociation as "a disruption in the usually integrated functions of consciousness, memory, identity, or perceptions of the environment" (APA, DSM-IV, 2000, p. 456). The more extreme or pathological forms of dissociation may be claimed when defendants are charged with violent offenses. As we saw in the section above, persons with PTSD charged with violent crimes may argue that they committed their criminal acts while in a dissociative state.

Dissociative Identity Disorder

The essential feature of **dissociative identity disorder (DID)** (formerly called **multiple personality disorder [MPD]**) is "the existence within the person of two or more distinct personalities or personality states that recurrently take control of behavior" (*DSM-IV*, p. 484). Furthermore, "each personality state may be experienced as if it has a distinct personal history, self-image, and identity, including a separate name" (*DSM-IV*, p. 484). Periodically, at least two personalities take full control of the individual's behavior. The change or transition from one personality to another is often very sudden (seconds to minutes), and is generally triggered by stress or some relevant environmental stimuli. Often, hypnosis can also bring about this shift into another personality.

According to the *DSM-IV*, each of the personalities may be aware of some or all the other personalities in varying degrees. There may be as many as a hundred different identities. The disorder occurs about three to nine times more frequently in females than in males. Persons who experience DID are highly suggestible and impressionable, and can be readily hypnotized either by themselves or others. Reported cases of what was then called MPD have historically been extremely rare. However, between 1980 and 1989, the number of cases diagnosed in the United States rose dramatically, from 200 to 6,000 (Slovenko, 1989). Part of this increase is due to the American Psychiatric Association officially recognizing the disorder in the *DSM-III*. In a review of the literature on dissociation and violence, Moskowitz (2004) reported that several prominent studies during that time period found violent "alters" in a significant number of persons who had been diagnosed with DID. Interestingly, however, Moskowitz maintains that varieties of dissociative disorders, not just DID, are often overlooked in criminal justice populations, particularly males.

On occasion, what was then called MPD was used successfully as an excusing condition for criminal responsibility (e.g., *State v. Rodrigues*, 1984; *State v. Milligan*, 1978). In general, however, MPD was not a successful defense (Slovenko, 1989). One of the more well-known cases in which the MPD defense was tried and failed involved serial killer Kenneth Bianchi, known as the Hillside Strangler (*State v. Bianchi*, 1979). The Hillside Strangler was given wide publicity because of the brutality and sadistic quality of his murders. The victims were young women who were raped and strangled, and whose nude bodies were conspicuously displayed on the hillsides in the Los Angeles area. The Hillside Strangler was responsible for at least a dozen murders during a one-year period (1977–1978).

Despite considerable evidence against him, Bianchi insisted that he was innocent, arguing that an alter personality, "Steve," had done the killings. He pleaded not guilty by reason of insanity. A team of experts appointed by the court found no basis for Bianchi's claim of MPD. Although Bianchi knew the "textbook version" of MPD (probably knowledge gained during a period of his life in which he had impersonated a psychologist), he was less than convincing on the more subtle aspects of the disorder recognized by the experts. The team concluded that Bianchi was a psychopath. Bianchi then quickly changed his plea to guilty in order to avoid the death penalty.

To this day, there is debate among practitioners and scholars as to whether MPD/DID actually exists. It has been referred to as the "UFO of psychiatry" (Ondrovik & Hamilton, 1991). In some instances, it may be **iatrogenic**—that is, unintentionally caused by clinicians or practitioners themselves. This means that practitioners who firmly believe in and are perceptually sensitive to DID look for and interpret a variety of behaviors as symptoms of the disorder. In effect, the practitioner may develop the syndrome in the patient, and the patient, in turn, learns to believe that he or she is afflicted with it. It has also been argued that implicit and explicit suggestions during hypnosis can shape segments of self into the appearance of MPD (Orne, Dinges, & Orne, 1984). Regardless of whether the syndrome is iatrogenic or whether it is possible for several personalities to "possess" a physical body, an important point must be made. The syndrome is *often subjectively real* to the patient, and the person who allegedly experiences it often plays each of the roles well and convincingly. Martin Orne and his colleagues (Orne *et al.*, 1984, p. 120) observe, "So striking are the behavioral differences between personalities that the assertion is often made that one would need to have the dramatic skills of Sarah Bernhardt or Sir Laurence Olivier, along with a detailed knowledge of psychiatry, to effectively simulate such radically different persons."

In summary, the validity of DID as a viable entity is very much open to debate by both the mental health and legal professions. Supporters of the concept maintain that diagnostic procedures among clinicians are more accurate today than in the past, and clinicians have at their disposal specific diagnostic tests to detect the disorder (Comer, 2004). At present, though, there is very little solid evidence that the syndrome, as a bona fide mental disorder in which one personality completely controls the other(s), actually exists, except possibly in rare situations. Nevertheless, it is not unusual to be in a roomful of clinicians who seem firmly convinced that DID is a significant problem encountered in their practices and one that mental health practitioners still fail to diagnose. According to this perspective, treatment is a highly complex and multistage process. It involves allowing the alter egos to emerge and enabling the client to confront them. Eventually, the "alters" are left behind, a process that can be frightening to the client. As one therapist commented, after a long period of treatment, the client had successfully confronted her problems and was ready to move on to a normal life. However, she was concerned about how she would handle financial matters, because "Ruth"—one of her alters—was the one who had always balanced the checkbook.

Amnesia

Amnesia refers to complete or partial memory loss of an event, series of events, or some segment of life's experiences, either due to physical trauma, neurophysiological disturbance, or psychological factors. According to the *DSM-IV*, "Individuals with an amnestic disorder are impaired in their ability to learn new information or are unable to recall previously-learned information or past events" (p. 156). Amnesia is not simply forgetting a name, a date, or an incident, but is reserved for severely impaired ability to remember past material (retrograde amnesia) or to acquire and retain new material (anterograde amnesia).

Some researchers have identified a classification of amnesia called **limited amnesia**, which is "a pathological inability to remember a specific episode, or small number of episodes, from the recent past" (Schacter, 1986, p. 48). Limited amnesia may be caused by emotional shock, alcohol or drug intoxication, or a blow to the head. Therefore, limited amnesia is not ongoing, nor does it involve extensive memory loss. Rather, the loss is temporary and restricted to a specific event or incident.

In general, the courts have not been receptive to amnesia as a valid condition in either the insanity defense, or as a condition that promotes incompetence to stand trial (Rubinsky & Brandt, 1986). The exception is in cases of brain injury, when a connection can be established between the injury and the memory loss. Paull (1993) notes that there have been cases in at least 20 states and five federal circuit courts where the court has held that amnesia per se does not render a defendant incompetent. One reason for this judicial "hard line" approach to amnesia is the suspicion that the defendant may be faking the memory loss. It is easy for people to simply say they cannot remember committing the crime, and it is difficult for psychologists to determine whether a person can or cannot remember. In recent years, though, psychologists have been able to fine-tune a number of instruments designed to measure malingering—or faking—of various symptoms, including symptoms of amnesia (Rogers, 1997). Additionally, some psychologists believe that amnesia can be evaluated with recognition tests that are tailored to the information that the client claims not to know (Frederick, 2000).

Amnesia associated with alcoholic intoxication presents a favorite excuse for reprehensible behavior, and is the most commonly invoked excusing condition in criminal cases. "When I drink

I go blank about some things" is the usual line. It is intriguing to note that 30–65 percent of persons convicted of criminal homicide claim they cannot remember the crime, usually because of alcoholic intoxication at the time of the offense (Schacter, 1986). A similar pattern exists for other violent crimes (e.g., rape) as well.

However, the courts have not been sympathetic to defendants who rely on excuses based on alcohol or other drug intoxication. This is because the courts hold the person blameworthy since he or she should have known, at the outset, the risks involved in drinking alcohol or taking drugs. Thus, attempts to use amnesia in this way have met with strong judicial resistance. For example, one court held that "insanity is the incapacity to discriminate between right and wrong while amnesia is simply the inability to remember" (Rubinsky & Brandt, 1986, p. 30). Therefore, amnesia per se fails to qualify as a mental disorder that robs a person of the ability to distinguish between right and wrong.

MENTAL DISORDER AND VIOLENCE

While the mental disorders described in this chapter may be associated with a variety of criminal offenses, it is the crimes of violence that are most disturbing. The depressed individual may embezzle funds in an effort to obtain a way out of his dire economic situation. The individual with a delusional disorder may break into a building to seek shelter from those who persecute him. The person with an antisocial personality disorder may perpetrate a series of economic scams on unsuspecting victims. Publicity is most likely to accompany criminal behavior when it is violent, however, and the public is most fearful of these offenses, despite the fact that we are far more likely to be victims of economic crimes than violent crimes. And as we learned above, the mere presence of a mental illness does not guarantee that a defendant will be found incompetent to stand trial or absolved of criminal responsibility. In some jurisdictions, this is even more true when defendants are accused of violent crimes than when they are accused of property offenses.

As a group, individuals who are mentally ill are no more likely to commit crimes than those who are not. Nevertheless, they do appear with some regularity in arrest records, in jails, in prisons, and on probation and parole caseloads, and they present special challenges to those who supervise them. Recent research indicates that community alternatives, including pretrial diversion into a specialized treatment program, may be a good approach for persons with severe mental illness who have been charged with crimes (Colwell, Villarreal, & Espinosa, 2012; Heilbrun et al., 2012). Colwell et al. found that assignment to such a program significantly reduced the likelihood of future adjudication.

The prevalence of mental disorders is more than three times higher in the criminal justice population than in the general population (Skeem, Emke-Francis, & Louden, 2006). Part of this is due to a decrease in the availability of inpatient care for mental health problems, as well as problems with homelessness and substance abuse. In recent years, researchers have searched for groups or classifications of seriously mentally ill offenders who may be particularly prone to involvement in the criminal justice system. Constantine et al. (2010), for example, found three arrest trajectories patterns for the seriously mentally ill: low chronic, high chronic, and sporadic. Their study of close to 4,000 participants with diagnoses of serious mental disorders did not separate violent from nonviolent offenses, although it did separate felonies from misdemeanors.

Long-term inpatient care or hospitalization of the mentally disordered has largely disappeared, particularly in public institutions. While these institutions still exist, they are generally intended for short-term crisis care and treat patients with drugs rather than psychotherapy. They typically do not hold most patients for more than three to six months, although there are exceptions. (One is the sexually violent predator, who is discussed in Chapter 12. Persons found not guilty by reason of insanity (John Hinckley, Andrea Yates) or incompetent to stand trial (Russell Weston)—if their crimes or alleged crimes were particularly serious—are other examples.) Although the mentally disordered may be discharged from these institutions with orders to continue taking medication, they may not be well supervised and may not participate in outpatient treatment services. The seriously mentally ill who do so are less likely to appear in official arrest records (Constantine *et al.*, 2010.)

Research on the Violence of the Mentally Disordered

Early research literature consistently supported the position that mentally disordered individuals—even the severely mentally disordered—are no more likely to commit serious crimes against others than the general population (Brodsky, 1973, 1977; Henn, Herjanic, & Vanderpearl, 1976a; Monahan, 1981; Rabkin, 1979). In other words, more recently, Heilbrun, Douglas, and Yasuhara (2009, p. 348) commented, "Despite the presence of literally hundreds of studies that address this question, it remains unclear whether mental illness is related to violence." Indeed, some recent research (Brennan, Mednick, & Hodgins, 2000; Klassen & O'Connor, 1988, 1990; Monahan, 1992; Silver, 2006) finds that a certain subset of the mentally disordered population may be at risk of committing violence. Specifically, male mentally disordered patients, *who have a history of at least one violent incident,* have a high probability of being violent within a year after release from the hospital. In fact, evidence is beginning to accumulate that individuals with schizophrenia are at increased risk of violent offending and even at higher risk to commit murder (Naudts & Hodgins, 2005). In addition, when offenders with schizophrenia do commit murder, they most often kill relatives, and many are exhibiting hallucinations and delusions at the time of the offense (Häkkänen & Laajasalo, 2006). As we noted earlier, however, delusions that are of a persecutory nature are particularly problematic. In a meta-analysis of 204 studies, psychosis also was found to increase the odds of violence by as much as 50–70 percent (Douglas, Guy, & Hart, 2009).

We cannot emphasize enough that a majority of people with mental disorders do *not* commit serious or violent offenses. For example, only 11.3 percent of the men and 2.3 percent of the women who developed schizophrenia committed violent offenses (Tengström, Hodgins, Grann, Långström, & Kullgren, 2004). In addition, those individuals with schizophrenia who commit violent crime constitute a very heterogeneous group. "Some display a history of antisocial behavior from a very early age; others begin engaging in antisocial behavior around the time of schizophrenia onsets; others commit only 1 violent attack in their lives, while others behave aggressively only when acutely psychotic" (Naudts & Hodgins, 2005, p. 1).

Research also finds that offenders with schizophrenia who have high scores on the Psychopathy Checklist-Revised (PCL-R) are usually convicted for more violent offenses than those with low scores on the PCL-R (Tengström *et al.*, 2004). The results suggest that PCL-R scores offer the strongest predictor of violent and chronic offending histories. Tengström *et al.* (2004) write, "These results indicated that among offenders with schizophrenia, as among non-mentally ill offenders, high PCL-R ratings are associated with more severe histories of offending and violence" (p. 385).

The Tengström *et al.* (2004) study underscores the fact that males who develop schizophrenia *and* exhibit antisocial behavior at an *early* age often demonstrate persistent and versatile patterns of criminal offending. Essentially, early-onset offenders with schizophrenia show a pattern very similar to life-course-persistent offenders (LCP), discussed earlier in the text.

In addition, there is further evidence that men who have both schizophrenia and a substance abuse problem are at an increased risk of violent offending. For instance, Räsänen *et al.*

(1998) report evidence that male schizophrenics with alcohol abuse problems are 25 times more likely to commit violent crimes than males with no mental disorders and no alcohol problems. Follow-up studies of patients with schizophrenia and substance abuse problems have frequently found them to be at risk of committing violent offenses (Appelbaum, Robbins, & Monahan, 2000; Tengström *et al.*, 2004).

John Monahan (1992) stresses two things about the research showing a connection between mental disorders and violence. First, the relationship refers only to people *currently* experiencing a *serious* mental disorder. People who have experienced a serious mental disorder in the past and are not showing symptoms currently are unlikely to engage in violent behavior. Second, it is still a fact that a great majority (over 90%) of the currently mentally disordered are not violent. Media portrayals of common psychotic killers driven berserk by bloodthirsty delusions are sensational, frightening, and perhaps entertaining, but in reality the phenomenon is rare. Finally, it must be emphasized not only that the mental disorder–violence link relates to the seriously mentally disordered (e.g., schizophrenics), but also that the relationship is also stronger for individuals who have a history of violent behavior. Recall that Laajasalo and Häkkänen (2006) found that the strongest predictors of excessive violence among their sample of schizophrenics convicted of homicide were a past history of violent behavior and the presence of a cooffender.

Furthermore, it is possible, as some clinicians believe, that the more bizarre violent offenses are committed by the mentally disordered, particularly those categorized as schizophrenic or paranoid. Moreover, the more extreme violence of schizophrenics is typically directed toward family members or acquaintances, and bizarre self-mutilation is more likely than mutilatory murders (Blackburn, 1993). However, Ronald Blackburn (1993, p. 274) admonishes, "Although there appears to be an increased risk in schizophrenia, particularly in paranoid schizophrenia, it must be reiterated that only a small minority of patients in this category are violent, and that the disorder itself is rarely sufficient to account for violent acts in instances where they occur."

Individuals experiencing affective (mood) psychoses are less likely to be violent. When affective psychoses are associated with violence, they are usually manifested in women within the context of extended suicide, in which the offender kills herself as well as others in the environment, including her immediate family (Blackburn, 1993). However, as is noted in Chapter 10, mass murders in public settings are often committed by men who feel hopeless and also have the signs of affective psychoses. In most cases, mass murderers plan to die or commit suicide at the site of their crime.

The MacArthur Research Network

Some of the best-known research on the potential violence of the mentally disordered has been conducted by the MacArthur Research Network (Monahan *et al.*, 2001; Steadman *et al.*, 1998). Researchers followed over 1,000 patients discharged from civil psychiatric hospitals in an effort to determine the extent to which they demonstrated aggressive behavior over a one-year period. The patients also had been measured on a wide range of "risk factors"—134 in all—while they were hospitalized. These included such factors as violent fantasies, history of abuse as a child, frequency of parents fighting with each other, and number of negative and positive persons in the social network, to name but a few. The data allowed the MacArthur researchers to develop a risk-assessment instrument, The Multiple Iterative Classification Tree (ICT), which they believe can help clinicians identify low, average, and high-risk individuals. They emphasize, however, that the instrument was developed on psychiatric inpatients in acute facilities who would soon be discharged, and should not be generalized to other contexts until validated on additional populations. It is worth noting that about half of the discharged patients in this study were in the low-risk group, while the remaining patients were about evenly divided between average and high-risk groups. However, no single risk factor was a significant predictor of violence. As Monahan *et al.* (2001, p. 142) stated, "The propensity for violence is the result of the accumulation of risk factors, no one of which is either necessary or sufficient for a person to behave aggressively toward others."

In later research, Monahan and his colleagues (Monahan *et al.*, 2005) used a new sample of patients discharged from psychiatric hospitals who had been classified as being at low risk (less than 9% likelihood of violence) or high risk (greater than 37 percent likelihood of violence). The patients were first assessed and interviewed during their hospitalization for follow-up; all high-risk patients and a random sample of low-risk patients and those who knew them were interviewed in the community at 10 and 20 weeks after the date of discharge. Arrest and rehospitalization records were also reviewed. The expected rates of violence were 1 percent for the low-risk group and 64 percent for the much smaller high-risk group; the observed rates of violence were 9 percent for the low-risk group and 49 percent for the high-risk group.

A SUMMARY STATEMENT

In sum, then, the research on the mentally disordered and violence allows us to conclude the following:

- Past mental disorder alone, even serious mental disorder, is not necessarily a good predictor of violence.
- The mental disorder most closely associated with violent and serious offenses is schizophrenia.
- Persons with schizophrenia who commit violent crimes—and most do not—consist of a very heterogeneous group.
- Males who have developed schizophrenia and who score high on the PCL-R have an increased risk of being violent.
- Males who develop schizophrenia *and* exhibit antisocial behavior at an *early* age often demonstrate persistent and versatile patterns of criminal offending.
- Violence is associated with *current* serious mental disorder, particularly when a history of violent behavior is also present.
- At least in civilly committed institutionalized patients, the classification system devised by the MacArthur Research Network is an efficient predictor of future violence in the community.
- While researchers have developed some instruments to assess the likelihood that a person will engage in violence, no one factor serves as strong predictor; violent behavior seems to be a result of an accumulation of risk factors, unique to each individual.

Police and the Mentally Disordered

As indicated in the previous section, some research documents that persons who are seriously mentally ill often appear in arrest records, charged with both felony and misdemeanor crimes (Constantine *et al.*, 2010). Early research documented that police may be more apt to arrest the mentally disordered (Teplin, 1984). In her classic study in which trained graduate students in psychology observed 1,382 police–citizen encounters, Teplin found police arrested 20 percent more individuals with symptoms of mental disorders than without such symptoms. Considering that many disordered individuals tend to have annoying symptoms, such as verbal abuse, belligerence, and disrespect, the slightly higher probability of arrest is hardly surprising. To some extent, police also may have taken some of these individuals into custody in order to provide them with shelter. However, police officers failed to recognize the behavior as representing a mental disorder in a large number of cases, believing the individuals were simply being disrespectful and asking for trouble.

In the nearly 30 years since Teplin's study, significant changes have occurred nationwide relative to law enforcement's handling of mentally disordered individuals. First, police academies are more likely to offer some training in both recognizing and dealing with mental disorders (Fields, 2006). In some communities, police have taken the initiative to appoint specially trained liaison officers to work with the disordered (Smith, 2002). Nonetheless, researchers continue to identify problems related to police and the mentally disordered. Redlich, Summers, and Hoover (2010), for example, found that persons who are mentally disordered are more likely than those who are not to give "false confessions" to police. In a later study on false confessions (Redlich, Kulich, & Steadman, 2011), it was found that the mentally disordered were asked more questions and were not surprisingly more confused by the interrogation experience. Second, communities across the nation are establishing specialized courts—mental health courts—that provide diversionary options to jailing and prosecuting the mentally disordered—and the developmentally disabled—who are charged with nonviolent offenses, or even minor violent crimes, such as simple assault. Rather than being held in jail, they are offered shelter and treatment or training services. Mental health courts are increasing across the nation and continue to be evaluated for their efficiency, cost-effectiveness, and quality of treatment (see, e.g., Redlich, Liu, Steadman, Callahan, & Robbins, 2012, and references therein).

MENTALLY DISORDERED INMATES

Mental disorders in those incarcerated in prison and jail are sometimes cited as evidence of a link between crime and abnormal behavior. Both the prevalence and the nature of disorder among these populations are difficult to determine, however, because statistics and descriptions vary widely. Furthermore, some data are based on the inmates' own self-report, while other data are based on clinical findings. Nonetheless, most contemporary research indicates that the percentage of mentally disordered inmates in the nation's jails and prisons is increasing (Althouse, 2010). In a study by James and Glaze (2006), it was estimated that half of all prison and jail inmates have a mental health problem (James & Glaze, 2006). This does not mean that they are seriously mentally disordered—rather, it suggests that they might benefit from mental health treatment. Female inmates have higher rates of mental health problems than male inmates (see **Table 8-2**). The most common problem reported is major depression, followed by psychotic disorders.

Other researchers have reported that 10–15 percent of persons in jails and federal and state prisons have *severe* mental disorders (Lamb, Weinberger, & Gross, 2004). It is difficult to determine to what extent these data include APDs; it is estimated that 40–80 percent of inmates carry that diagnosis (Steffan & Morgan, 2005). Nevertheless, both researchers and mental health professionals working with jail and prison inmates report significant increases in *serious* mental health problems (Ashford, Sales, & Reid, 2001).

It is obvious that jail and prison conditions, as well as conditions in juvenile facilities, can have deleterious effects on mental states. Therefore, an individual may become mentally disordered after being institutionalized, which may be reflected in these statistics. However, considerable evidence indicates that many inmates or prisoners were showing signs of mental disorders prior to incarceration (Bureau of Justice Assistance, 2000).

TABLE 8-2	Inmates Identified as Mentally Disordered, by Gender, Race/Hispanic Origin, and Age		
	Percent Identified as Mentally Disordered		
Offender Characteristics	**State Inmates**	**Federal Inmates**	**Jail Inmates**
All inmates	56.2	44.8	64.2
Gender			
Male	55.0	43.60	62.8
Female	73.1	61.2	75.4
Race/Hispanic Origin			
White	62.2	49.6	71.2
Black	54.7	45.9	63.4
Hispanic	46.3	36.8	50.7
Other	61.9	50.3	69.5

Source: Data from James & Glaze (2006).

Diagnoses of Mentally Disordered Inmates

It remains difficult to determine, however, the precise clinical diagnoses associated with these mental disorders. Many could have been diagnosed with antisocial personality disorder. Second, some data were collected by asking the inmates themselves about their mental conditions. Third, the reliability of psychiatric diagnoses, even in the general population, is often in doubt. Finally, we do not know whether the mental disorders reported are the result of being in prison or jail, or whether the individual entered the system with the existing disorder. Regardless, however, if the disorder exists, it is a problem.

In summary, it is very clear that prisons and jails today are facing increasing numbers of mentally disordered inmates whose problems will likely escalate if not sufficiently treated. This may be especially problematic in high-security, supermax facilities where inmates are kept in solitary confinement, sometimes for many years (see, generally, Toch, 2008). Even in the general population of prisons and jails, however, the prevalence of individuals in need of mental health services is sobering.

DANGEROUSNESS AND THE ASSESSMENT OF RISK

Up to this point in the chapter, we have covered a range of situations involving mentally disordered individuals, criminal courts, police, and prisons and jails. In many—but not all—of those situations, the courts and other agents of the criminal justice system were concerned about whether the disordered individual was also a danger to society.

The concept of dangerousness pervades much of the criminal law and appears in civil law as well. Defining dangerous behavior is a challenge faced by legislatures, courts, and clinicians. All states and all courts recognize that behavior that is likely to result in *physical harm* is dangerous. They begin to differ when behaviors that lead to property damage or psychological injury are involved. One example of psychological injury is the effect on victims of stalking, who may be continually shadowed, photographed, contacted online, sent text messages, and otherwise harassed. Some courts have ruled that this type of behavior can cause irreparable emotional damage. They conclude that a threat of "psychological trauma is...as much a menace to the health or safety of others as is possible physical injury" (Developments in the Law, 1974, p. 1237). This form of psychological damage has prompted many state legislatures to pass "stalking laws" that state that persons who continually follow and otherwise harass other individuals are dangerous and can be charged with a criminal offense.

It is fair to say, though, that dangerousness is used primarily in conjunction with violent behavior. Defendants charged with violent crimes are sometimes denied bail because they are judged dangerous, violent offenders are sentenced to long prison terms to prevent them from committing more crime, and some are sentenced to death because it is feared they will commit more violence. Decisions on whether to parole prisoners convicted of violent crimes are largely based on whether they are dangerous.

Risk Assessment

Implicit in the above decisions is the belief that it is possible to predict an individual's violent behavior. Although some clinicians believe they can do so with a high degree of confidence, most are far more modest about this ability. Since the 1990s, the research and professional literature have increasingly preferred the term *risk assessment* rather than prediction of dangerousness. Risk assessment suggests that clinicians and researchers are more proficient at *assessing the probability* that a given individual—or group of individuals—will engage in harmful behavior than they are at outrightly predicting that someone is dangerous or will be violent. We will return to this change in terminology shortly.

Controversy over the ability to predict, particularly predict violence, has been longstanding. Not surprisingly, it has often been fueled by highly publicized incidents. The April 2008 shootings at Virginia Tech were perpetrated by Seung-Hui Cho, who had a history of psychiatric treatment and periodic episodes of violence. A year later, 12 people were killed by Jiverly Voong, who entered an immigration center in Binghamton, New York, dedicated to helping immigrants adjust to life in the United States. Individuals who knew him said they were "not surprised," because he was isolated, had continuously voiced his disenchantment with his station in life, and complained that people ridiculed his lack of facility with the English language. Nevertheless, the above could characterize numerous individuals who do not go out and kill others.

We do not know whether either Cho or Voong had actually made threats against others. One who apparently did was Charles Whitman, a University of Texas student majoring in architectural engineering, who murdered his wife and his mother in 1966. Shortly thereafter, he carried his personal arsenal in a footlocker to the observation deck of the 307-foot-tall University Tower, where he loaded a number of high-powered, scope-equipped rifles and began randomly shooting at people near the observation deck and on the ground far below. Whitman managed to shoot 44 victims, killing 14, before a police officer and a citizen climbed to the tower and ended the tragedy by shooting Whitman himself.

An investigation revealed that the 25-year-old Whitman had consulted a psychiatrist five months before the incident, and, during a two-hour interview, had described "overwhelming violent impulses" and great fear of his inability to control them. He had also revealed a compelling need to "go up on the tower with a deer rifle and start shooting people." Whitman did not return for further consultation after the initial two-hour session. Nevertheless, when the news of his contact with a psychiatrist was disseminated, there was public outcry and many questions about why he was not treated, confined, or referred to the proper authorities. Similar questions were raised when the public learned that James Huberty, who killed 22 fast-food restaurant patrons in the summer of 1984, had also had contact with a mental health clinic. In Huberty's case, social workers had apparently tried without success to return his telephone calls.

The *Tarasoff* Case

A crime that occurred over 30 years ago in California continues to have reverberations among clinicians today. A young woman, Tatiana Tarasoff, was stabbed and killed by Prosenjit Poddar. An outpatient at a University of California, Berkeley, clinic, Poddar had revealed to his psychiatrist his fantasies about harming, or perhaps even killing, a woman whom he had met at a dance. The psychologist, who learned from one of his patient's friends that he planned to purchase a gun, became increasingly concerned. When the patient discontinued therapy, clinic officials wrote to the police requesting their help in getting the individual committed to a mental institution. Police investigated the case, interviewed Poddar, warned him to stay away from the woman, but did not pursue the commitment, apparently because California's new civil commitment law was difficult to interpret. After the murder, the victim's family sued the university clinic, claiming the psychologist had been negligent in not warning the young woman or the family of the danger.

The *Tarasoff* case, undoubtedly familiar to all clinicians, addressed directly the question of what duty therapists owe to third parties in warning them of possible harmful behavior from their clients. The California Supreme Court first ruled that when a therapist determines that a patient is a serious danger to another person, the therapist has a **duty to warn** that individual (*Tarasoff v. Regents*, 1974). Two years later (*Tarasoff v. Regents*, 1976), the Court redefined the role as a **duty to protect**. That is, the therapist need not directly warn the individual, but he or she should take some steps to protect the individual from harm. Following the California court's decisions, many other states—either through court decisions or by statute—adopted rules similar to those announced in the *Tarasoff* case. By the early twenty-first century, half the states had done so (Quattrocchi & Schopp, 2005), and two states had explicitly rejected the doctrine (DeMatteo, 2005). Whether or not there exists a statutory duty to warn/protect, many practitioners have interpreted the "spirit" of *Tarasoff* as a standard of practice, believing that the clinician has a professional obligation to take some steps to protect an identifiable potential victim (e.g., Litwack & Schlesinger, 1999). In some states the laws are broad, such as by requiring clinicians to protect even if information is derived from someone who is a relative of the patient, while in other states the clinician's obligations are no greater than meeting a standard of ordinary care and competence and/or are limited to cases where there is a clearly identifiable potential victim (Quattrocchi & Schopp, 2005).

In July 2012, 24-year-old James Holmes entered a theater in Aurora, Colorado, during a midnight premier of the Batman film *The Dark Knight Rises*. Holmes allegedly threw smoke bombs then began to fire weapons, killing 12 theater-goers. Approximately 70 other individuals were wounded or were hurt as they tried to escape. Police soon after learned that Holmes' apartment was wired with explosive devices that, if not detonated, would likely have killed someone going through his door. Holmes, a graduate student at the University of Colorado-Denver, had seen a mental health professional on campus prior to the incident, and the professional had apparently been concerned enough about his behavior that she called in a threat assessment team to consider how to handle the situation. However, Holmes withdrew from the university before the team took any action. We emphasize that there remain many unanswered questions about this incident, and no conclusions should be made or blame attributed. However, the case is relevant because it raises the question, can mental health professionals predict dangerous behavior?

Courts and legislatures that have adopted duty to warn/protect rules apparently believe that mental health professionals can predict with considerable accuracy who is or will be dangerous and who will not. The law has been relying on predictions of dangerousness for a long time, dating at least as far back as the sixteenth century (Morris & Miller, 1985). Yet, researchers and clinicians have long struggled both to define dangerousness and to predict its occurrence. After the *Tarasoff* case, dangerousness generated more controversy than even the insanity defense (Simon & Cockerham, 1977), and the standard that emerged from that case continues to be criticized in the legal and psychological literature (e.g., Quattrocchi & Schopp, 2005).

Today, as noted above, the psychological literature avoids the term *prediction of dangerousness* and has replaced it with *risk assessment*. Clinicians maintain that, at best, they can offer probabilities based on known factors relating to the individual, often based on data obtained from large groups. (Recall our earlier discussion of the MacArthur Risk Assessment Study with civilly committed psychiatric patients.) Regardless of the terminology, it is clear that some attempt at assessing/predicting the likelihood that an individual will commit violence is warranted; what is not clear as a result of *Tarasoff* is the steps that should be taken by the clinician, who is also bound by confidentiality in treating his or her patient.

There is little doubt that a person who has been violent in the past and indicates by word or deed that he or she plans to do serious harm to others is—in common terms—dangerous. Someone who has committed a series of murders, mutilations, or rapes, and who attests to planning to do more of the same, is a dangerous individual. Even so, clinicians prefer to stay within the realm of probabilities, such as by calling the person a "high risk." If a person has no history of violence and threatens harm, however, the situation becomes more problematic. Likewise, if a person has been violent in the distant past but has shown no recent signs of violent behavior, the situation is again problematic. In these contexts, clinicians would have difficulty reaching a consensus on who is "dangerous" and who is not. This is why current thinking favors using a list of "risk factors" to determine the likelihood that aggressive behavior will occur. Risk assessment—particularly the assessment of violence risk—is perhaps the most complicated and controversial issue in the entire field of forensic psychology (Borum, 1996). Many researchers and scholars (e.g., Heilbrun *et al.*, 2009; Steadman *et al.*, 1993) consider it one of the most important issues in both criminal and civil matters worldwide. A variety of instruments are available for clinicians engaging in the risk-assessment enterprise. As we will see, some of these instruments are chiefly actuarial in nature and may even be filled out just from case files, without an interview, although this is not generally recommended. Other instruments focus more on the interview process, but suggest questions to help the clinician to exercise structured clinical judgment.

The early research on prediction of dangerousness—before researchers shifted to risk assessment terminology—demonstrated that clinicians had a strong tendency to overpredict dangerousness, a pattern that held for criminal offenders as well as mentally disordered patients (Monahan, 1981, 1984). At a minimum, the most sophisticated predictive methods yield 60–70 percent false positives (people who were predicted to be dangerous but did not engage in harmful behavior) (Kozol, Boucher, & Garofalo, 1972; Rubin, 1972; Wenk, Robison, & Smith, 1972). In a 10-year follow-up investigation of 592 convicted male offenders, mostly sex offenders (Kozol, Boucher, & Garofalo, 1972), two of every three persons predicted dangerous were false positives, even after extensive background data and results of independent clinical exams by psychiatrists had been made available to those doing the predicting. Moreover, because of some flaws in the design of the study, the odds for accurate prediction were very much in the researchers' favor (Dix, 1980; Monahan, 1976; Steadman, 1976).

In the 1970s, classic studies that followed individuals after their release from mental institutions also documented the limitations of prediction. Steadman (1976) followed patients who were released from New York hospitals after a landmark U.S. Supreme Court case, *Baxstrom v. Herold* (1966). These "Baxstrom patients" had first been convicted of crimes and had then been transferred to civil mental institutions without hearings shortly before their prison sentences expired. On average, they had spent eight years in confinement beyond their prison sentence. The Baxstrom patients were predominantly nonwhite, lower socioeconomic class, middle-aged males. Although a vast majority had arrest records and many had previous convictions, only 58 percent had been convicted of violent crimes (Steadman, 1976). On the average, the patients had been institutionalized continuously for 14 years. In its *Baxstrom* decision, the Supreme Court noted that—like other individuals committed to civil mental institutions—the prisoners had a right to a hearing to determine whether they were mentally disordered and dangerous. As a result, many were released, often against the advice of clinicians who predicted that they were dangerous.

The Baxstrom patients were considered some of New York's most dangerous mental patients, but follow-up reports found that predicted dangerousness had been grossly overstated (false positives) (Monahan, 1976). Steadman and Cocozza (1974) followed up 85 Baxstrom patients and discovered that 20 percent were rearrested, but only 7 percent were convicted, usually for minor violations such as vagrancy and public intoxication. An examination of both in-hospital and community behaviors revealed that only 20 percent of the "extremely dangerous" patients were assaultive toward others during the four-year follow-up period (Steadman, 1976).

Risk Factors for Violence

For close to 50 years, scholars have debated the respective merits of statistically based assessment of risk versus the more subjective, clinically based methods, sometimes referred to as unstructured clinical judgment. The debate is also referred to as the actuarial versus clinical debate. Actuarial measures offer a compilation of risk or needs factors on which the individual is evaluated (e.g., past violence, age, criminal record, early onset of antisocial behavior). Risk measures have gone through four generations of development (Campbell, French, & Gendreau, 2009). *First generation measures* were based on unstructured clinical judgment, with little or no statistical basis. *Second generation measures* offered a more standardized method of assessing risk, using primarily static (nonchanging) variables, such as age, gender, and criminal history. In the *third generation*, developers of risk assessment instruments introduced criminogenic needs into the equation; that is, a way of identifying factors that could respond to treatment, and thus change. Put another way, they identified needs that could be targeted in order to reduce risk of offending. Examples of criminogenic needs are antisocial attitudes or substance use. *Fourth generation instruments* are more attuned to the treatment or rehabilitation process; like third generation tools, they identify both static and dynamic risks and needs, but they also are integrated into the whole process of managing risk and choosing treatment interventions (see Campbell *et al.*, 2009).

Research on the reliability and validity of these various instruments, particularly those of the latest generations, is ongoing. Whether they are equally effective with men and women is a question often posed in the literature. In general, however, actuarial instruments have consistently outperformed clinical judgments. In a recent meta-analysis (Ægisdóttir *et al.*, 2006), the researchers found that actuarial risk prediction was 17 percent better than its clinical counterpart. Nevertheless, for many reasons, many mental health practitioners have been and are reluctant to yield their professional judgments to actuarial models. Therefore, a separate category of measures, based on Structured Professional Judgment (SPJ), was developed "as a potentially reasonable, empirically defensible approach to risk assessment that did not have some of the perceived weaknesses of extant actuarial instruments or of unstructured clinical prediction" (Heilbrun *et al.*, 2009, p. 336). SPJ instruments involve some consideration of actuarial-based factors, but still allow clinicians to supplement these with their impressions or observations based on clinical experience.

It must be stressed that—although we discuss risk assessment in the chapter on crime and mental disorder—risk assessment is not limited to the mentally disordered. And it must be stressed, again, that the mentally disordered, as a group, are not dangerous. Overall, the best predictor of future behavior is *past behavior,* but even past behavior will not necessarily be repeated. The best predictor of criminal behavior is a history of criminal behavior, and past violence will suggest a probability of future violence. A history of criminal behavior is the best predictor of criminal recidivism regardless of whether the offender is mentally disordered or normal (Bonta, Law, & Hanson, 1998). But again, people change. Furthermore, the more frequently the behavior has occurred in a variety of situations, the more accurate will be the predictions. Someone who frequently manifests violence across many different situations will be far easier to predict than a person who is only occasionally violent in some situations.

Since the 1990s, researchers have made considerable strides in the ability to identify more factors that are associated with violence. In addition to criminal history, recent research strongly indicates that other predictors of criminal recidivism (not limited to violence) include some combination of age, juvenile delinquency, and substance abuse (Andrews & Bonta, 1994; Bonta *et al.*, 1998; Gendreau, Little, & Goggin, 1996). However, researchers have also warned that risk factors are unique for each individual, and that no one factor will necessarily predict violence or serious antisocial behavior in any one individual.

Summary and Conclusions

In this chapter, we focused on the relationship between mentally disordered individuals and crime. In order to understand this relationship, we must go beyond labels, which do not explain why someone behaves in a certain way.

Mental illness (or mental disorder) is a disorder or disease of the mind that interferes substantially with a person's ability to cope with life on a daily basis. Although it deprives someone of freedom of choice, this deprivation is rarely total. As noted in the chapter, even severely disordered individuals can have some decision-making ability. Mental illness should be distinguished from retardation or developmental disability. The former can be treated, cured, or held in remission; the latter cannot, although developmentally disabled individuals can be taught

to perform many tasks and supported in their desires to be self-sufficient.

We reviewed diagnostic categories that are most often associated with criminal behavior. For example, persons accused of crime may introduce these diagnoses to support an insanity defense. The main categories discussed were schizophrenic disorders, with particular emphasis on the paranoid type that is most frequently represented in criminal behavior; delusional disorders, with emphasis on the persecutory type; depressive disorders, which may play a major role in delinquency, mass murders, and workplace violence, among others; postpartum depression, with emphasis on the rare postpartum psychosis that can result in serious crime; and antisocial personality disorder, which most courts today do not accept in support of an insanity defense. The juvenile equivalent of APD is conduct disorder, and it is a frequent diagnosis of adolescents held in detention and treatment facilities.

The chapter also reviewed the legal constructs of competency and insanity. Criminal defendants are found incompetent if they are so disordered that they cannot understand the proceedings or help their attorneys in their own defense. Adjudicative competence is relevant to a wide range of proceedings, including a variety of pretrial hearings and the trial itself as well as the sentencing stage and beyond. The law says that an incompetent defendant is not present; therefore, before proceeding with prosecution, he or she must be rendered competent. As we noted, the common approach with incompetent defendants is to hospitalize them for treatment until they attain competency; alternately, the case against them is dismissed, particularly if the crime is not serious. A major issue today relating to incompetent defendants is the extent to which they can be medicated against their will. Courts have generally ruled that when the government has a strong interest in bringing the defendant to trial—such as in a serious crime—medication will be allowed.

Although it is the competency issue that affects the greatest number of defendants, it is the insanity issue that most intrigues the public. The truly insane individual is not responsible for his or her crime. Successful insanity defenses are rare, but even when they occur, they are no bargain. Persons found not guilty by reason of insanity are typically institutionalized, often for longer periods of time than they would have served in prison. We reviewed the various standards for establishing insanity, including the M'Naghten (right/wrong) Rule, the ALI/Brawner Rule, and the Durham Rule (product test). Since the 1980s, largely as a result of the acquittal of John Hinckley, many states and the federal government have passed more restrictive insanity statutes, making it even more difficult for defendants to be absolved of criminal responsibility. Some states also have adopted a "guilty but mentally ill" verdict form, which allows a judge or jury to find a defendant guilty, but also acknowledges that he or she needs treatment. Research indicates, though, that the treatment implied is rarely provided in correctional facilities.

We also discussed "special defenses" that are sometimes raised in criminal cases, either to absolve a defendant completely or to support a defense of diminished capacity: PTSD, dissociative identity disorder (DID; formerly called multiple personality disorder), and amnesia.

Individuals with mental disorders as a group are no more likely than the general population to commit crimes, including violent crimes. If we include the category antisocial personality disorder, the catch-all diagnostic category discussed in Chapter 7, the likelihood of committing crime increases somewhat. In addition, recent research documents that the subgroup of *currently* mentally disordered male patients, particularly with schizophrenic diagnoses, and who have a *history of violence*, does demonstrate far more violence than nondisordered members in the general population. According to Monahan (1996), this relationship is especially significant if a current mental disorder is accompanied by three symptoms: (1) feeling that others wish to do one harm, (2) feeling that one's mind is dominated by forces beyond one's control, and (3) feeling that others' thoughts are being put into one's head.

The visibility of the mentally disordered, as well as publicity given to the occasional sensational case in which a severely disordered individual kills a stranger, has led to questions about dangerousness and our ability to predict it. When the criminal justice system deals with a defendant charged with a violent crime or an offender convicted of one, whether or not the individual is disordered, the system wants to know if he or she is dangerous. For many years, mental health practitioners tried to answer this question with little success. Traditionally, clinicians overestimated the potential violence of this population, engendering debate about the proper criteria for assessing dangerousness. How many persons were forcefully confined, on the basis of dangerousness, without justification?

Recently, this enterprise has shifted to "risk assessment." Rather than trying to predict whether someone is dangerous and will commit a violent act, the clinician is now more likely to identify risk factors that may make it *more likely* that he or she will do so. In other words, the prediction of dangerousness has been transformed to an *assessment of the probability* that violence or other serious offending will occur in the future.

Key Concepts

Adjudicative competence

Amnesia

Antisocial personality disorder (APD)

Battered woman syndrome

Brawner Rule

Caveat paragraph

Competency to stand trial

Conduct disorder

Delusional disorders or paranoid disorders

Delusions

Diagnostic and Statistical Manual of Mental Disorders (DSM)

Dissociated state disorder

Dissociative identity disorder (DID)

Durham Rule

Duty to protect

Duty to warn

Guilty but mentally ill (GBMI)

Hallucinations

Iatrogenic

Incompetent to stand trial (IST)

Insanity Defense Reform Act of 1984

Limited amnesia

Major depressive disorder

Mental illness or mental disorder

Mental retardation or intellectual or developmental disability

M'Naghten Rule

Multiple personality disorder (MPD)

Not guilty by reason of insanity (NGRI)

Posttraumatic stress disorder (PTSD)

Right and wrong test

Schizophrenia

Volitional prong

Review Questions

1. What is meant by a "duty to warn" and a "duty to protect"? And to whom does it pertain?
2. What are the conditions under which mentally disordered people may become violent or seriously criminal?
3. Briefly describe four legal standards for insanity and their requirements.
4. Identify and include symptoms of the four diagnostic categories most relevant to criminal behavior.
5. What are guilty but mentally ill statutes? Why do many legal scholars oppose them?
6. Give an example of iatrogenic effects in counseling or psychotherapy.
7. Describe fully and evaluate any three of the unique defenses discussed in the chapter.
8. Thoroughly explain the difference between incompetence to stand trial (or adjudicative incompetence) and insanity. Include in your answer what researchers have learned about the individuals who receive those legal designations.

9

Homicide, Assault, and Family Violence

CHAPTER OBJECTIVES

- Define criminal homicide, negligent manslaughter, and aggravated assault.
- Review the demographics of homicide victims and offenders.
- Emphasize that criminal homicide is rare compared with other violent offenses.
- Review what we know about juvenile murderers and their victims.
- Present the research on family violence, its dynamics, and its causes.
- Summarize stereotypical child abduction data.

If the news and entertainment media are reasonably decent barometers of human interest, homicidal violence must be one of our most fascinating subjects and, along with sex, the most marketable. Usually, the more bizarre, senseless, or heinous the murder, the more extensive press coverage it receives, followed shortly thereafter by books, television specials, and movies. Unusual mass murders, serial murders, and so-called motiveless killings are especially popular. Yet on a national level, criminal homicide consistently accounts for only about 1 percent or 2 percent of all violent crimes reported in the FBI's Uniform Crime Reports (UCR).

The number of homicides reached an all-time high of 24,503 in 1991 and then fell quickly to 15,522 in 1999 (Cooper & Smith, 2011). Since that time, the number of homicides has remained relatively constant. A total of 14,748 such homicides were reported in 2010 (Federal Bureau of Investigation, 2011a). In the same year, an estimated 1.246 million violent offenses were reported to law enforcement agencies. If we consider its percentage distribution among all violent crimes, then, murder represents only 1.2 percent of the total (see **Figure 9-1**). Furthermore, a vast majority of these criminal homicides offer very little mystery or intrigue. In many cases, they involve angry friends, spouses, or acquaintances killing friends, spouses, or acquaintances. Gang and drug-related violence, where members of rival groups are killed or where other victims are caught in crossfire, account for other examples. During 2007, the relationship between the victims and the perpetrators was known in 54 percent of all of the homicides. Within those known relationships, 25 percent of the victims were

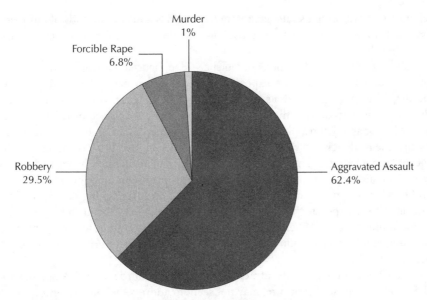

FIGURE 9-1 Violent Crime Distribution in the United States, 2010
Source: Federal Bureau of Investigation (2011a).

related to their killer, and 53 percent were acquainted with them. This does not make them less serious. It is simply a reminder that homicidal attacks of strangers are not the norm.

The disproportionate amount of attention paid to criminal homicides may be explained in a variety of ways. Obviously, this is a highly serious crime, with death being the ultimate victimization. However, another reason for the attention may be related to our fascination with the mysterious and the macabre. We crave science fiction, tales of terror, even haunted houses. Perhaps we need a certain amount of excitement and arousal to prevent our lives from becoming too mundane and boring. Psychologists have long known that novelty produces arousal and excitement and breaks monotony (Berlyne, 1960). This human need for stimulation and excitement is greater in some people (extraverts) than others (introverts) (Eysenck, 1967), and this may partly explain the appeal of roller coasters, skydiving, race car driving, bungee jumping, use of some drugs, and gambling. Stimulation seekers also may enjoy films featuring vampires, werewolves, and heavy violence—or these vicarious pleasures might be enjoyed by those not wishing to seek out this type of excitement directly. In any case, tales of murder, fictional or not, add zest to life. For the family that has been touched by murder, however, this vicarious response on the part of others must be difficult to understand and to accept.

The marketability of murder may also be explained by curiosity or exploratory behavior, which is very closely related to excitement and arousal. One purpose of curiosity is to allow organisms to adjust to their environments (Butler, 1954). An individual or an organism explores a new situation to satisfy this curiosity—which is theorized to be a physiological drive state—and in the process of discovering information, adapts to the new situation. Curiosity about murder might help us prepare for the possibility that a similar event could happen to us. Reading about bizarre, seemingly irrational homicides may help us to identify danger signals. Information about the incident gives clues about who murders, who gets murdered, and under what circumstances. To some extent, we can take preventive measures, even though there is no guarantee that such measures will keep us safe. Furthermore, families and close friends of murder victims would say that nothing can prepare someone for the devastation that is experienced when a loved one is murdered.

The above reactions to depictions of violence—experienced vicariously—may be regarded as adaptive or functional. Extensive exposure to violence also has a dysfunctional side, however. Specifically, it may immunize us from the horror of violence. Many social commentators have advanced cogent arguments that humans have become conditioned or jaded to cruelty and inhumane behavior and that people are desensitized to human suffering. In addition, the constant attention that the media give to violence, especially murder, also makes it seem more widespread and frequent than it really is. This phenomenon is called the **availability heuristic** by social psychologists. Heuristics refer to cognitive shortcuts that people use to make quick inferences about their world. When the media continually show graphic and frightening accounts of violence, people are likely to incorporate these vivid details into cognitive shorthand and have them readily *available* for future reference. When they think of violence at a later time, they remember the most frequently seen and horrific accounts, increasing their fear of violent crime and exaggerating its incidence in their minds.

To speculate about why we are attracted to accounts of murder and violence, or to wonder about the effects of repeated exposure, may not seem to address the main focus of this chapter, which is the violent offender. Speculation becomes relevant, however, when we shift the focus to the individual who is part of a society that seems to have an inordinate need to seek out stimulation or to know details of crimes. When that individual is insensitive to suffering and begins to create his or her own excitement by torturing and murdering, we have a social problem. Psychology, as we will see in this chapter, can offer some suggestions for understanding and solving this problem.

After defining our terms, we examine situational and dispositional factors that occur consistently in homicide and aggravated assault, beginning with statistical data on their incidence and prevalence and their demographic correlates. Thus far in the text, theoretical issues and potential causes of crime have been introduced with minimum application to specific offenses. Beginning here and throughout the remainder of the book, we interweave the research and concepts previously outlined with specific categories of criminal behavior. Thus, in this chapter, we focus on family violence.

DEFINITIONS

Criminologists generally study aggravated assault and homicide together, primarily because they view many aggravated assaults as failed homicide attempts (Doerner, 1988; Doerner & Speir, 1986). Dunn (1976) challenges this practice. He notes that the aggravated assault rate is at least 20 times that of homicide. "Given this disparity in rates, it is difficult to imagine that even one-quarter of all aggravated assaults were attempted homicides or would have been homicides except for the intervention of medical care" (Dunn, 1976, p. 10). Therefore, it may be unwarranted to consider aggravated assault as being in the same league as homicide; the two may differ in important variables, including the motives of the perpetrator. A purist, therefore, would try to maintain an aggravated assault–homicide distinction. And, of course, the distinctions are maintained in crime statistics, as well as in criminal law.

For our purposes, it is neither realistic nor desirable to maintain a definitive assault–homicide distinction. Not realistic, since much of the relevant research on offender *characteristics* collapses the categories into one, under the rationale that people who kill usually (but not invariably) have a history of assaultive behavior. It is not desirable, since, from a psychological point of view, the two types of behavior are comparable in many ways. On the other hand, certain kinds of homicide offenders—such as serial and mass murderers—have distinctive characteristics. These crimes will be covered in the next chapter. Often, though, the type of weapon used or the quality of medical care available determines the final outcome. The high-powered bullet, as an obvious example, is in most cases far more lethal than the knife, and rapid response to an assault can save a life. A stabbing or even a beating may represent behavior similar to that displayed in homicide with a small firearm. In law, the distinctions between murder and aggravated assault are crucial; in psychology, they are less so. The individual is displaying highly aggressive behavior in either situation. For this chapter, combining the discussion of homicide and aggravated assault as one form of violent behavior makes sense, although the statistics section will separate them briefly. In later chapters, we discuss other forms of violent behavior, including rape, armed robbery, and arson.

Criminal Homicide

Criminal homicide is causing the death of another person without legal justification or excuse. Legally, it is usually divided into two categories: **murder** and **nonnegligent manslaughter**. The term *murder* is reserved for the "unlawful killing of one human being by another with malice aforethought, either expressed or implied" (Black, 1990, p. 1019). "Malice aforethought" refers to premeditation, or the mental state of a person who thinks ahead, plans, and voluntarily causes the death of another, without legal excuse or justification. However, "premeditation" can occur in a very short period of time (even a minute); it does not require weeks of planning.

Homicide laws in most states have additional gradations or degrees. In many jurisdictions, murder is divided into two degrees, a statutory provision that allows courts to impose a more severe penalty for some murders than others. The degree system was once a useful and meaning-ful method of distinguishing between murder that was punishable by death and that which was not (Gardner, 1985). In more recent times, the distinctions between the degrees have been more blurred. Broadly, state statutes generally posit that murder of the first degree is a homicide that was committed with particularly vicious, willful, deliberate, and premeditated intent. Murder of the second degree is characterized by the intentional and unlawful killing of another but with-out the type of malice and premeditation required for first-degree murder. Examples of second-degree murder include "crimes of passion," such as an enraged father who strangles the drunken driver who just killed his son. Although there was no premeditation, the angry father still wanted to kill him. The Uniform Crime Reports include both murder and nonnegligent manslaughter under the rubric criminal homicide for reporting purposes. Deaths of others that occur as a result of negligence (negligent manslaughter) are not included. The essential difference between murder and nonnegligent manslaughter is that malice aforethought must be present for murder, whereas it must be absent for nonnegligent manslaughter.

Negligent manslaughter is killing another as a result of recklessness or culpable negli-gence. Some jurisdictions use the term *involuntary manslaughter*. Although there is no intent to kill, the law says you should have known that your actions could result in the death of another person. For example, a man who recklessly waves a gun around in jest, and the gun discharges and kills someone, is still responsible for that person's death even though he did not intend to take someone's life. A driver who turns to look at her passenger, crosses the center lane, and hits an oncoming car, killing its occupant, displayed negligent (not reckless) behavior, but would still be responsible for the death. What the above two individuals have in common is that they did not intend to kill anyone. As a recent example, Dr. Conrad Murray was convicted of involuntary manslaughter in the 2009 death of singer Michael Jackson. Murray had prescribed overdoses of the anesthetic propofol, supposedly to help Jackson sleep, but which was attributed as the cause of his death. The above situations are all different from nonnegligent manslaughter, which is covered along with murder in the UCR statistics. Nonnegligent manslaughter refers to an action that is more than negligent or reckless, but less than premeditated. It typically occurs in a highly aroused emotional state.

The person charged with murder (first or second degree) or with nonnegligent manslaughter intended that his victim die. In the case of nonnegligent manslaughter, the original intent may not have been to kill the victim. However, the person became so agitated and emotionally upset in a particular situation that he or she lost partial control of his or her self-regulatory system. A man who chokes a woman to death during rough sex would be an example. In some states, nonnegligent manslaughter would be similar to second-degree murder. The broad parameters of homicide law in the United States are highly similar to the laws of homicide found in other countries and cultures (Morawetz, 2002). This similarity is largely because maintaining some semblance of social order in any given society depends greatly on controlling reckless and widespread homicide. As pointed out by Morawetz (2002), "Homicide law…responds to a universal need to identify, deter, and punish intentional and reckless killings, a need that crosses borders. We all fear annihilation" (p. 400).

In line with UCR classifications, we combine both murder and nonnegligent manslaughter under the general term *homicide* in this chapter. We are not concerned with suicides, accidental deaths, negligent or involuntary manslaughter, or justifiable homicide (e.g., the justifiable killing of a person by a law enforcement officer in the line of duty). In other words, from a psychological point of view, these are not illustrative of the aggressive behavior we are concerned about in a book about criminal behavior. It should be emphasized, however, that the definitions of criminal homicide used in this chapter, and by governmental agencies and researchers in general, do not encompass the many legal definitions found in various jurisdictions.

Aggravated Assault

In most jurisdictions, **assault** is the intentional inflicting of bodily injury on another person, or the attempt to inflict such injury. It is important to qualify this definition, because in past years, assault and battery were considered two discrete crimes: State laws treated the *threat* of physical injury as an assault, and the completed act of physical contact or unlawful touching as battery. Although many states have gotten away from distinguishing the two, in some jurisdictions (e.g., Florida), assault is still the threat of injury, while the actual contact is battery. Furthermore, all jurisdictions continue to recognize some distinction of assault and battery, such as in their definitions of mayhem, malicious wounding, or felonious assault (Bacigal, 2002). For our purposes, we adopt the definitions used in the UCR.

An assault or attack becomes **aggravated assault** when the intention is to inflict serious bodily injury. Aggravated assault is often accompanied by the use of a deadly or dangerous weapon, such as a gun, knife, ax, or other sharp or blunt instrument. Simple assault is the unlawful, intentional inflicting of less than serious bodily injury without a deadly or dangerous weapon, or the attempt to inflict such bodily injury, again without a deadly or dangerous weapon. However, even one's fists can become a deadly weapon; thus, if a victim is seriously assaulted in a fistfight, the perpetrator will likely be charged with aggravated assault.

Aggravated assault will be covered in the domestic violence section of the chapter. The beginning sections of this chapter will focus on homicide, particularly homicide dealing with a single offender killing one person. Multiple murders will be covered in Chapter 10. We begin with briefly covering the demographics of homicide offenders and then proceed to the psychological characteristics of people who kill. The demographic characteristics most commonly studied in homicide research are race or ethnic origin, gender, social class, and the victim–offender relationship.

DEMOGRAPHIC FACTORS OF HOMICIDE

Researchers have found that a variety of demographic factors are strongly associated, or correlated, with criminal homicide. These factors may be characteristics of the offenders or the victims. We must emphasize, though, that the factors reported in the literature often refer to *arrests* for murder or nonnegligent manslaughter. Although the minimum standard for an arrest is probable cause that the individual committed a crime or is about to commit a crime, arrests do not necessarily result in conviction, or a finding of guilt. This is an important caveat whenever we consider the official police data which are cited in many research studies, though other studies focus on convictions. As we discuss the demographics of homicide, readers should keep in mind the distinctions between arrests, convictions, and victimizations.

Race/Ethnicity

One of the most consistent findings reported in the criminology literature is that African Americans in the United States are involved in criminal homicide—both as offenders and victims—at a rate that significantly exceeds their numbers in the general population. Although African Americans make up about 13 percent of the U.S. population, they accounted for approximately 53 percent of all arrests for homicide in 2007 (Federal Bureau of Investigation, 2008). The reported homicide offending rate for blacks is nearly eight times higher than the rate for whites (Cooper & Smith, 2011). The victimization rate for blacks is six times higher than the rate for whites (Cooper & Smith, 2011). Most murders are intraracial (whites kill whites; blacks kill blacks), although stranger homicides are more likely to cross racial lines (about 27%).

The disproportionate representation of African Americans in the arrest and conviction data for homicide probably reflect social inequities, such as lack of employment or educational opportunities, racial oppression in its many forms, discriminatory treatment at the hands of the criminal justice system, and law enforcement practices in inner-city areas where many African Americans reside. There is no evidence to suggest that a racial biological or neuropsychological predisposition plays a role in the consistently reported differences in violence rates over the years.

Furthermore, much more research needs to be done on the relationship between racial/ethnic minorities and crime. Using rigid categories such as black, Latino/Hispanic, Asian, Native Americans, and white represents an oversimplification of the multiethnic and multicultural mixtures across the nation. Cultures and subcultures are highly complex and multidimensional, and meaningful research on the ethnic/minority differences in violence—if it is to be conducted—requires a knowledgeable awareness of and sensitivity to this complexity.

Gender

The relationship between homicide and gender is also robust. UCR data consistently reveal that the annual arrest rates for murder run about 90 percent male, 10 percent female (Federal Bureau of Investigation, 2011a). Males represent 77 percent of homicide victims and 90 percent of offenders (Cooper & Smith, 2011).

Age

With monotonous regularity, national statistics from all sources continue to underscore the fact that about half of all those arrested for violent crime are between the ages of 20 and 29. Although this statistic refers to all violent crimes, it applies specifically to criminal homicide as well. Approximately one third of murder victims and almost half of the offenders are under age 25 (Cooper & Smith, 2011).

Socioeconomic Class

Research has consistently shown that children born into an adverse neighborhood and disadvantaged family context are at higher risk for violence, as either offenders or victims, than are children raised in a more propitious environment. As discussed in Chapter 3, poverty places children at risk for violence because of lack of resources, social support, and opportunity, a reality that highlights the crucial importance of social programs. Some researchers have observed that conditions of poverty make it difficult for parents or caregivers to avoid harsh and inconsistent discipline for their young children (Dodge, Greenberg, Malone, & Conduct Problems Prevention Research Group, 2008). Nonetheless, as a general principle, it is important to remember that warm, supportive parenting exists across all social classes. In addition, as we learned in earlier chapters, parenting or caretaking itself is not the only factor to take into account in trying to explain violence.

Circumstances

Recent data indicate that interpersonal arguments (including those preceding family violence) are the most frequently cited circumstances for murder (Cooper & Smith, 2011). Second are murders that occur in the process of committing felonies such as rape, robbery, burglary, arson, or drug trafficking (Federal Bureau of Investigation, 2008). Thirty-three percent involved other types of circumstances—some also involving felonies—such as brawls, sniper attacks, or juvenile and gang killers (see **Table 9-1** for recent statistics on circumstances accompanying murder).

TABLE 9-1   Murder Circumstances by Victim's Gender, 2010

Circumstances	Total Murder Victims	Male	Female	Unknown
Total	**12,996**	**10,058**	**2,918**	**20**
Felony type total	1,923	1,601	319	3
Rape	41	0	41	0
Robbery	780	696	83	1
Burglary	80	60	20	0
Larceny-theft	20	16	4	0
Motor vehicle theft	37	27	10	0
Arson	35	24	11	0
Prostitution	5	0	5	0

TABLE 9-1 (continued)

Circumstances	Total Murder Victims	Male	Female	Unknown
Other sex offenses	14	10	4	0
Narcotic drug laws	463	431	32	0
Gambling	7	7	0	0
Other—not specified	441	330	109	2
Suspected felony type	66	40	25	1
Other than felony-type total	6,351	4,648	1,697	6
Romantic triangle	90	72	18	0
Child killed by babysitter	36	21	15	0
Brawl due to influence of alcohol	121	103	18	0
Brawl due to influence of narcotics	58	44	14	0
Argument over money or property	181	153	28	0
Other arguments	3,215	2,316	897	2
Gangland killings	176	164	12	0
Juvenile gang killings	673	639	33	0
Institutional killings	17	15	2	0
Sniper attack	3	3	0	0
Other—not specified	1,781	1,118	660	3
Unknown	4,656	3,769	877	10

Source: Federal Bureau of Investigation (2011a).

WEAPONS USED IN VIOLENCE

Nationwide data indicate that firearms are used in approximately 67 percent of all homicides, while knives or cutting instruments were used in less than 13 percent of the homicides (Federal Bureau of Investigation, 2011a; Zawitz & Strom, 2000). Approximately 68 percent of firearm homicides are committed with handguns, 4 percent with shotguns, 4 percent with rifles, and 23 percent with unspecified firearms.

About every 14 minutes, someone in America dies from a gunshot wound. About half of those deaths are suicides, about 44 percent are homicides, and 4 percent are unintentional shootings (*Washington Post,* October 12, 1993; Zawitz & Strom, 2000). It is likely that most readers of this book are familiar with at least one incident in which a member of the community has been killed in such a tragic manner. A girl playing on her doorstep in daylight was killed when she was hit by a stray bullet fired from a gun in the possession of a young adult in the neighborhood; a boy was killed at a friend's home when the friend accidentally discharged a loaded rifle. These are anecdotes, but they are repeated in many communities across the nation.

After many years of public debate on the interpretation of the Second Amendment to the Constitution, the U.S. Supreme Court ruled in two separate cases that the right to bear arms is an individual right that neither the federal government nor state and local governments can abridge (*District of Columbia v. Heller*, 2008; *McDonald v. Chicago*, 2010). Both cases were close (5-4) decisions. Together, the cases indicate that citizens have a constitutional right to firearms but governments can place restrictions on ownership or regulate sales and purchases. Although the Supreme Court has thus far refused to hear cases seeking to answer questions left unanswered by the *Heller* and *McDonald* decisions, lower courts have allowed states to have waiting periods, require criminal and mental health background checks, and forbid ownership by felons or possession by juveniles, for example.

Guns do not *cause* violent crime, but accessibility of guns facilitates it. Hepburn and Hemenway (2004) found that where there are higher levels of gun ownership, homicides are substantially higher. Of course, where homicides are higher, individuals may be more likely to own guns for protection, and it is understandable that some wish to do this. Furthermore, many people—particularly in more rural areas—own guns for sport, and they clearly have a right to these weapons. It cannot be denied, however, that the availability of firearms is a major reason that homicides occur.

In Chapter 5, we discussed the **weapons effect**, where the mere sight of an aggressive stimulus can influence behavior. Because weapons are associated with violence, the visible presence of a handgun, a club, or a knife automatically brings violence-related thoughts (cognitions) to mind. The classic study of Berkowitz and LePage (1967) was among the first experiments to provide evidence of a strong link between aggressive thoughts engendered by the presence of a weapon and subsequent aggressive behavior. Hepburn and Hemenway's (2004) discovery that a high number of available weapons within a neighborhood promote more aggression in a vicious circle of violence may be partially due to the widespread presence of aggressive stimuli.

Juvenile Weapon Possession

The Violent Crime Control and Law Enforcement Act of 1974 made it a federal offense for any person to sell or transfer a handgun to a person under age 18; it is also a federal crime for a juvenile to possess ammunition of a handgun. Many states have similar laws. These are the types of restrictions that seem acceptable, even after the *Heller* and *McDonald* decisions, in which even Justices in the majority indicated that governments were entitled to regulate firearms in some respects. Yet, even with restrictions, there are multiple ways for juveniles to obtain firearms, and they report being able to do so with ease. For example, gangs often have a "community gun" well hidden on the street but easily accessible to gang members if needed. Some juveniles (about 28%) ask others, such as older siblings or friends, to buy guns for them (Braga & Kennedy, 2001). About 11 percent of juveniles buy them from a gun shop or pawnshop. Theft is also an important source of firearms for juveniles. It is estimated that about 500,000 guns are stolen each year, mostly from residences (Braga & Kennedy, 2001). It is further estimated that about 70 percent of the firearms used by offenders are obtained through theft (Wright & Rossi, 1994). As pointed out by Braga and Kennedy (2001), juveniles obtain guns through corrupt licensed dealers, unregulated dealers, gun shows, organized gun rings and fences, and criminal firearms trafficking. The above studies were conducted over a decade ago, but—though the statistics may change—their basic findings have not been disputed.

According to the 2010 UCR data, 29 percent of the total arrests for the illegal carrying or possession of a firearm were juveniles, and 11 percent of the total arrestees were under age 15. In self-report studies, males are four times more likely than females to report carrying a weapon. The weapons most often carried were knives or razors (55%), followed by clubs (24%), and firearms (21%). In a national survey of more than 16,000 students in grades 9–12, 18 percent said they had carried a weapon outside the home in the previous 30-day period (Lizotte & Sheppard, 2001). The percentages were higher (22%) for youths living in inner-city high schools. A more recent survey (PRIDE, 2003) reported that approximately 2 percent of middle school youths (grades 6–8) carried a gun to school on a regular basis during 2002–2003. Available data (e.g., Decker, Pennel, & Caldwell, 1997) suggest that more than two-thirds of juveniles who carry weapons say they do so primarily for self-protection.

PSYCHOLOGICAL ASPECTS OF HOMICIDE

The psychology of murder is a very complex subject. There is no universal set of homicide offenders who present developmental risk factors or personality characteristics which predict they are particularly prone to commit murder. Homicide is multidetermined and is associated with many risk factors, as are other crimes. As we learned in earlier chapters, the risk factors may be social, psychosocial, or even biological in nature. They include early onset of antisocial behavior, peer delinquency, peer rejection or victimization, early indications of conduct disorder, living in poverty, growing up in violent families and neighborhoods, and even birth complications, to name but a few. To a large extent, homicide is also situation specific. That is, it depends on a number of things, including the availability of a weapon, the amount of alcohol consumption, the nature of the provocation (if provocation is involved), the circumstances, the motivation, and the emotional and mental state of the offender at the time.

Because of the complexity and diversity of homicide offending, a typology of the various types of homicide will aid greatly in presentation of the psychological aspects of homicide. In contemporary psychology, the term **typology** refers to a particular system for classifying personality, motivations, or other behavioral patterns. Usually, the typology is used to organize a wide assortment of behaviors into a more manageable set of brief descriptions. A typology is not perfect and does not always reflect reality, but it does help in understanding an enormously complex phenomenon such as homicide. It should be mentioned that we will also utilize various typologies to explain other crimes throughout the remainder of the book.

The FBI *Crime Classification Manual* (Douglas, Burgess, Burgess, & Ressler, 1992, 2006) is the most widely known and used typology system used by law enforcement officials and some researchers. It is not without controversy: Critics maintain that its classifications have not been empirically derived (e.g., Canter, Alison, & Wentink, 2004). The manual describes four major categories of homicide based on the underlying motives of the offender. The manual also lists several subcategories of homicide motives under each category. The manual is the result of a 10-year study conducted by the Federal Bureau of Investigation's National Center for the Analysis of Crime. The four major homicide categories are as follows: (1) criminal enterprise murder, (2) personal cause murder, (3) sexual homicide, and (4) group cause homicide. *Criminal enterprise* murder refers to killings done for material gain, such as money, goods, territory, or favors. The category includes eight subcategories, such as contract killing, gang-motivated murder, kidnap murder, product tampering, insurance-motivated murder, and felony murder. Felony murder refers to a homicide committed during the commission of another serious crime, such as a robbery, burglary, or kidnapping. *Personal cause murder*, usually committed under emotional upheaval, conflict, or passion, is a homicide precipitated by a general altercation or argument. Personal cause homicide subsumes 11 subcategories, including domestic violence, argument murder, revenge killing, and hostage murder. *Sexual homicide* category is defined as a murder that has a sexual component in the situation or dynamic that leads to the murder. This category includes four subtypes: organized crime scene murder, disorganized crime scene murder, mixed crime scene murder, and sadistic murder. In most instances, serial killers represent this category. *Group cause homicide* is committed by two or more individuals who share common ideologies or belief systems. This category includes three subtypes: cult murder, extremists (political, religious, or socioeconomic murder), and group excitement. Terrorist activity most often represents this classification.

Although the *FBI Crime Classification Manual* presents an interesting breakdown of homicide categories and subcategories, it is too overwhelming and complicated to use as a framework for presenting homicide in this chapter. However, we will present many of the unusual types of homicide listed in the manual in the next chapter, particularly homicide involving multiple victims. Although there have been a number of other homicide typologies developed, most have focused on the more sensational murderers known as serial or mass killers. Very few typologies or classification systems have been developed on the "underclass" of homicide offenders—the more mundane, single homicide offender, which is the focus of this chapter. One meaningful exception has been the four distinct categories generated by Roberts, Zgoba, and Shahidullah (2007), who analyzed the patterns and motivations of 336 homicide offenders known to the New Jersey Department of Corrections. The four classifications are as follows:

1. Offenders who committed a homicide that was precipitated by a general altercation or argument, such as an argument over money or property, or verbal disputes that escalate into fight. Escalation of aggression refers to progressive increases of hostile or destructive behavior, often to the point of violence. It often stems from the need to reciprocate after being provoked by aggressive behavior from another person. Roberts *et al.* (2007) discovered that the altercation or argument was often over an exceedingly small amount of money (such as $4) or insignificant value of property (such as a bike). This category represented the largest group, accounting for 45 percent of the total homicide offenders. It is likely that this is the largest group that would be found in other jurisdictions as well.

2. Offenders who committed a homicide during the commission of a felony. In this situation, homicides are committed as a means to commit other crimes, such as robbery, burglary, grand theft, or kidnapping. Roberts *et al.* (2007) noted that a majority of these offenders had records of past criminal histories.

3. Offenders who committed a domestic violence–related homicide. The perpetrators in these instances were current or ex-spouses, cohabitating intimate partners, or girlfriends or boyfriends. The researchers found that these homicides were precipitated by "the complexities and fragilities in relations involving sex, love, and emotion" (Roberts *et al.*, 2007, p. 499). This group represented the second-largest group, accounting for 25 percent of the homicide offenders.

4. Offenders who were charged with a degree of homicide after an accident, usually involving automobiles. In most cases, the fatality was a result of driving under the influence of alcohol or drugs.

We begin with the first two classifications: (1) offenders who committed a homicide precipitated by a general altercation or argument, and (2) offenders who committed a homicide during the commission of a felony. The third classification, offenders who committed a domestic violence-related homicide, will be covered later in the chapter under family violence. The fourth category, offenders who were charged with a degree of homicide after an accident, will not be considered in this chapter. They are distinct from the other groups in that they did not intend to perpetrate harm against their ultimate victims.

General Altercation Homicide

General altercation homicide is a result of hostile aggression. As we learned in Chapter 5, hostile aggression is a form of reactive aggression, and it occurs in response to anger-inducing conditions, such as real or perceived insults, threats, physical attacks, or one's own failures. The ultimate goal is to make a victim or victims suffer. This reactive violence, as it is sometimes called, "...is hot blooded, emotionally charged, and enacted quickly for the purpose of harming a perceived provocateur or defending oneself" (Fontaine, 2008, p. 243). It usually involves little instrumental motivation (Fontaine & Dodge, 2006) and consequently is distinct from instrumental aggression or violence. Reactive violence is essentially identical to the Roberts *et al.* first category, which delineates the offender who impulsively and fatally retaliates to a perceived egregious provocation or threat.

Many general altercation offenders probably possess a strong **hostile attribution bias**, which promotes violence whenever they perceive provocations and threats, no matter how benign or minor. In other words, they see a threat even when a threat is not intended; they do not walk away. Fontaine (2008) describes these individuals as possessing dysfunctional thinking processes in the interpretation of ambiguous social stimuli. They seem to have a "hair trigger" toward others where the slightest and most benign provocation sets them off. Common descriptions of this behavior include impulsiveness and out-of-control behavior. A not atypical illustration is the office worker who lashes out in anger at a fellow employee for making an off-handed, harmless remark.

Impulsivity is a key concept in understanding violence. In most cases, impulsive violence is a result of faulty or inadequate self-regulation (also known as self-control) compounded by a hostile attribution bias and a simplistic belief of how to deal with perceived hostility or threats. **Self-regulation** is defined as the capacity to control and alter one's behavior and emotions. Note that the definition includes *both* behavioral and emotional control. One of the most important protective factors against developing violent behavior is success in developing self-regulation of emotions, impulses, and behavioral reactions at an early age (Alvord & Grados, 2005).

Recall the discussion of attachment theory in Chapter 2. Fontaine and Dodge (2006) point out that attachment theory is based on the observation that early life events have enduring and considerable influence on beliefs and biases, even more so than do later events. In fact, early events shape the manner in which later events are cognitively represented. It is highly likely that many general altercation offenders demonstrated inadequate self-regulation skills early in their developmental years (Krueger, Caspi, Moffitt, White, & Stouthamer-Loeber, 1996). Clear signs of self-regulation and self-control begin to emerge during the second year of life, as does the concern for others. During the third year, children are expected to become reasonably compliant with parental requests and to internalize the family standards and values for behavior. Girls, on average, tend to show earlier self-regulated compliance during childhood than boys (Feldman & Klein, 2003). Fortunately, most people are able to restrain their aggressive impulses so as to stop violence or severe aggressive behavior. However, alcohol has the property of impairing self-regulation and self-control, even in persons who have a reasonably developed self-regulatory system. Consequently, considerable violence is especially prevalent among those persons who are intoxicated (with alcohol or other substances) and have marginally developed self-regulation skills.

Another key concept in explaining reactive violence is emotional arousal. Cognitive or thinking processes are greatly impaired at extreme levels of emotional arousal (Zillmann, 1979, 1983). Under high excitement, such as anger, behavior normally controlled by reasonable thought becomes controlled by biases and habitual responses. If the individual has the well-learned habit of exploding, lashing out, or otherwise acting in a violent manner, he is especially likely to do this under highly emotional circumstances. High arousal inhibits cognitive processing to the point where one may not think before acting. Therefore, at very high levels of emotional upset, violence is apt to become impulsive, a term Zillmann associated with habit strength. The violent behaviors have been so well learned that they appear quickly and without thought on the part of the individual. They seem to be "mindless" actions.

Felony Commission Homicides

Felony commission homicides are motivated by instrumental aggression. Instrumental aggression—as we learned in Chapter 6—is aggression for the sake of obtaining some object, rewards, or status possessed by another person—jewelry, money, territory, or influence. It is compared with reactive aggression, which occurs in response to provocation or perceived provocation. When it comes to severe or violent aggression, we will call the term in this section proactive violence. Proactive violence is characterized by cold-blooded, nonemotional, and premeditated aggression for the purpose of personal gain, such as is characteristic of some robberies. This description falls within the category of some offenders who kill during the commission of a felony. However, the term fits only those who anticipated and were accepting of the death of a victim. It does not fit the individual who holds up a liquor store with no intention of killing, but the robbery goes horribly wrong and the robber kills in a state of panic. In that case, the violence is better classified as reactive.

Proactive violence is typified by insensitive, calculated acts of severe violence enacted in the course of a crime, such as robbery, burglary, and drug acquisition. This form of violence is less emotional compared with reactive violence and more likely driven by the expectation of reward (Dodge, Lochman, Harnish, Bates, & Pettit, 1997). Similar to reactive aggressive patterns, proactive forms of violence appear to start early. Dodge *et al.* (1997) discovered in their research that children who frequently demonstrated reactive aggression seemed not only to have self-regulation problems, but did not expect positive consequences for their behavior. Their reward was in hurting the victim. Proactively aggressive children, on the other hand, anticipated more positive consequences for aggressive actions based on previous social learning. The researchers concluded that "…the proactively violent group might be displaying its violence because of an acquired belief that such violence will lead to positive social consequences for them" (Dodge *et al.*, 1997, p. 49). These findings suggest that reactive violence is thoughtless and emotionally driven, whereas proactive violence is self-regulated and stems from a rewarding learning history. The self-regulation process requires the development and refinement of cognitions and concepts which stem from social learning at an early stage of development, but these children also learn that strongly aggressive actions and bullying lead to the acquisition of goods and status from others.

In conclusion, it should be emphasized that the division separating general altercation homicide offenders from felony commission homicide offenders is used here primarily to present some types of homicide into a manageable set of explanations. There is certainly overlap between the two classifications, as some felony commission offenders during a mugging or armed robbery, for example, lose self-control quickly if the victims do not cooperate fully. In addition, we all tend to lose self-regulatory function under certain conditions when we become angry. High levels of emotional arousal take our attention away from our usual internal mechanisms of control.

When we become extremely angry, for instance, we often say and do things we later regret. We feel upset, remorseful, and guilty, and we wish we could take back our words or actions. If we had carefully considered and evaluated the consequences of our behavior, we would probably have acted differently. But under the heat of emotion, our self-regulatory system, with all its standards, morality, and values, was held in abeyance. As we get older, however, we generally learn from experience to pay closer attention to our internal control mechanisms, and we engage in fewer impulsive outbursts. This "mellowing" feature may partly account for the lower rates of impulsive violence as age increases.

We should also mention that the Roberts *et al.* classification scheme does not entirely account for those offenders who have mental or behavioral disorders, such as severe depression and psychosis. In Western countries, it is estimated that 10 percent to 15 percent of those persons convicted of homicide have some form of psychotic disorders (Hodgins, 2001; Nordström, Dahlgren, & Kullgren, 2006), a topic that was covered in Chapter 8. It is highly likely, therefore, that a significant proportion of the 336 homicide offenders in the Roberts study had one or more psychological disorders. After all, hostile attribution biases are not far from well-developed delusional thinking, and poor self-control or impulse-control deficits are not far from an assortment of disorders characterized by emotional and mental dysfunction.

Juvenile Homicide Offenders

In January 2001, Robert Tulloch, age 17, and Jimmy Parker, age 16, arrived at the home of two Dartmouth College professors, Half and Susanne Zanter, under the guise of conducting an environmental survey. Half Zanter invited them in, led them to his study, and proceeded to answer some of their questions, even offering them help in wording them. At some point, the "survey" stopped and the professor was stabbed repeatedly. When his wife came running to his aid, she too was stabbed to death. With the rural New Hampshire community in shock, police began to search for a random killer or possibly even a disgruntled student. Clues at the scene eventually led them to suspect the two juveniles, and a warrant was issued for their arrest. They were located in Michigan after police were notified by a truck driver who had offered them a ride.

The Dartmouth murders—as they have come to be known—were atypical with respect to juvenile murders, most of which are believed to be the result of drive-by shootings or gang-related turf wars. Other juvenile murders are accompanied by severe family dysfunction, such as physical or sexual abuse. In this case, the two boys came from "average" families in their small New Hampshire community, were involved in school activities, and were not economically disadvantaged, although one family was better off financially than the other. The murders were planned—but it is not clear that the professors were the first targets. Neither did robbery appear to be a motive; the boys left the house without taking cash, jewelry, or valuable objects (Powers, 2002). The boys apparently wanted to see if they could successfully carry out a murder; one writer commented that they were going through the "apocalypse of adolescence" (Powers, 2002).

Both Tulloch's and Parker's cases were heard in criminal court, both pled guilty, and both are now serving sentences in the New Hampshire prison system. Tulloch is serving life without parole and Parker is serving 25 to life.

The above incident is atypical, just as are many other cases that receive extensive media attention. The Dartmouth murders do not correspond well with what is known about juvenile homicide offenders (commonly abbreviated JHOs). For example, studies (Cornell, 1989; Myers, Scott, Burgess, & Burgess, 1995; Shumaker & Prinz, 2000) reveal that a majority of homicide acts by juveniles took place during either general altercation episodes—including gang warfare—or the commission of a felony. These categories, of course, are basically the same as the first two categories outlined by Roberts and his associates.

The 2010 UCR data reveal that only 9 percent of offenders arrested for homicide were juveniles. A breakdown of the overall data by gender showed that 94 percent of the juvenile offenders who were arrested for murder were male and 6 percent were female. There appears to be significant gender differences when it comes to juvenile murder. Studies reveal that girls, compared to boys, are significantly more likely to kill family members, younger victims, female victims, intimate partners, and their offspring (Heide, Roe-Sepowitz, Solomon, & Chan, 2012). More specifically, "Female JHOs were 9 times more likely than male JHOs to kill intimate partners, 4 times more likely to kill children under age 5, and twice as likely to kill family members and female victims" (Heide *et al.*, 2012, p. 373). Boys are more likely to kill strangers, and to be involved in gang-related killings. Female JHOs are more likely to use knives or other weapons, whereas male JHOs prefer guns (Heide *et al.*, 2012; Heide, Solomon, Sellers, & Chan, 2011). When girls kill, they often do so to resolve a conflict; boys are more likely to be involved in crime-related homicides (Heide *et al.*, 2011).

From 1985 through 2000, the juvenile courts handled 1,700 juvenile murders, but the number of cases has steadily decreased since 1996 (Puzzanchera, Stahl, Finnegan, Tierney, & Snyder, 2004; Sickmund, 2009). To some extent, this reflects nationwide trends to transfer juveniles charged with serious crimes to criminal courts rather than process them in the juvenile system, discussed in Chapter 6.

Nonetheless, regardless of the courts in which they are processed, the number of juveniles age 15 or younger who murder is relatively small (Snyder, 2001). Between 1980 and 1997, about 2 percent (or 600 cases) of murders involved *child* delinquents (ages 7–12), and the annual rate of these homicides is relatively stable, averaging about 30 homicides per year (Loeber, Farrington, & Petechuk, 2003). Nearly all of the homicides committed by children (94%) involved a single victim, mostly male (70%). More than half (58%) of the murder victims of child delinquents were juveniles under age 18 and more than a third (38%) of the victims were under age 13 (Snyder, 2001). Rarely was the victim a parent. The killing of a parent by a juvenile is often precipitated by child maltreatment, especially psychological abuse and neglect (Heide, 1993). More than half (54%) of the victims of child delinquents were killed with firearms. Gun play is often a contributing factor when children kill other children (Goetting, 1993).

Demographics and Psychological Characteristics of Juvenile Murderers

To obtain more detailed information both about the crimes and about the backgrounds of the offenders, some researchers have conducted studies with small samples of juvenile offenders. In general, these offenders have committed the "typical" homicides, not those of the apparent callousness exhibited in the Dartmouth case. For example, Myers and Scott (1998) examined 18 male juvenile murderers between the ages of 14 and 17 who met the criteria for conduct disorder at the time of their crimes. Their homicides were committed either in relation to criminal activities (72%) or during interpersonal conflict (28%). Half of the victims were strangers, whereas the other half were acquaintances (39%) or family members (11%). The results revealed that 16 of the 18 (89%) juvenile murderers had histories of one or more psychotic episodes (especially paranoid ideation), and other forms of mental disorders. These results were remarkably similar to the prevalence rate in earlier studies examining the psychological characteristics of juvenile murderers (e.g., Lewis *et al.*, 1985, 1988).

Research has also revealed that juvenile murderers—and those juveniles who commit violent crimes in general—tend to have a history of severe educational difficulties compared with nonviolent juveniles (Heckel & Shumaker, 2001). Children who begin school with deficits in social and cognitive skills are at high risk to engage in antisocial and violent behavior (Dodge *et al.*, 2008). Myers, Scott, Burgess, and Burgess (1995) report that within their sample of 25 juvenile murderers, 76 percent demonstrated a learning disability and 86 percent had failed at least one grade. Verbal abilities evaluated by intelligence tests have also been found to be associated with antisocial behavior (Moffitt & Caspi, 2001). Significant language handicaps appear to be the most prominent learning problems among juvenile murderers (Heckel & Shumaker, 2001; Myers & Mutch, 1992). Again, none of the above was noteworthy in the backgrounds of Tulloch and Parker.

Another prominent factor in the backgrounds of juvenile homicide offenders is lack of parental monitoring. As shown in Chapter 2, parental monitoring refers to such things as knowing the child's whereabouts, being involved in the child's school activities and homework, and supervising time allocations for outside activities. Knowing the whereabouts and setting time limits for activities outside the home are especially important during the preteen and teenage years. Roe-Sepowitz (2007) reports that limited parental involvement and lack of supervision were present in many of the adolescent female murderers she followed. Hill, Castellino, *et al.* (2004) report that lack of parental involvement in school during the middle school years also appears to be critical. In Tulloch's and Parker's case, however, lack of parental involvement would be a difficult argument to make. They seemed to be no less supervised than other adolescents inching their way to independence, and the parents were apparently interested in and caring about their activities.

Other studies have reported that juvenile homicide offenders often have high rates of family abuse (Darby, Allan, Kashani, Hartke, & Reid, 1998; Lansford, Deater-Deckard, Dodge, Bates, & Pettit, 2004), substance use and alcohol abuse (DiCataldo & Everett, 2008; Roe-Sepowitz, 2007), and prior delinquency (Loeber *et al.*, 2005; Roe-Sepowitz, 2007) and peer delinquency (Loeber *et al.*, 2005). Many juvenile murderers also appear to have a variety of neurological abnormalities (Heckel & Shumaker, 2001), similar to what has been reported in the medical histories of life-course-persistent offenders. Myers and his colleagues (e.g., Myers, 1994; Myers & Mutch, 1992; Myers, Scott, Burgess, & Burgess, 1995) have continually noted the high incidence of conduct disorders in his samples of juvenile murderers, ranging from 84 percent to 88 percent. ADHD has also been identified with juvenile murderers with some regularity (Heckel & Shumaker, 2001).

In summary, although researchers have made headway in identifying factors that might explain murder committed by juveniles, some cases defy neat explanations. The complexity of crime is illustrated in the bizarre case introduced at the beginning of this section.

The Dynamic Cascade Model

The list of risk factors influencing antisocial behavior, as we have discovered throughout the book, is extensive and even overwhelming. Loeber and his colleagues suggest that the probability of individuals committing homicide is enhanced by their exposure to an *accumulation* of different risk factors during early development (Loeber *et al.*, 2005). They contend that violence-producing processes do not suddenly emerge; they accumulate over many years. The implications of the Loeber *et al.* position are that the higher the number of risk factors a child experiences, the greater the tendency to engage in violent acts during the life course.

Kenneth Dodge and his colleagues (2008) have advanced a theory that goes beyond the risks accumulation perspective, and helps us explain, organize, and understand how youth and adults get to the point of committing a homicide. It is called the **dynamic cascade model**. The model provides a coherent developmental story of how violent behavior grows across childhood and adolescence in a dynamic cascade. The model hypothesizes that each risk-factor group operates on antisocial and violent outcomes by directly influencing the next factor group in a developmental sequence. Dynamic cascade in this context refers to a succession of developmental skills or deficits, each of which enhances, affects, or determines the next skill or deficit along a life-course trajectory. The term *snowballing* effect could also be used to describing the cascading effect.

To illustrate, the model starts with children who are born into an adverse neighborhood or disadvantaged family context (not necessarily economically disadvantaged), where parents may feel they need to resort to harsh or inconsistent discipline in a desperate attempt to control their young children. Although a more comprehensive model would also include prenatal experience and temperament, Dodge and his colleagues stated that their research began when the children were age five; they did not examine their lives retrospectively before that time. Harsh and inconsistent parental disciplinary strategies for controlling their children have a high risk of preventing the child from acquiring social and cognitive skills that are necessary for school social and academic success. "These skill deficits include vocabulary deficits, poor social problem solving, hostile attributional biases, and emotion recognition deficits" (Dodge *et al.*, 2008, p. 1921). Lacking the necessary social and academic skills to achieve during the early school years, the child begins to show conduct problems soon after entry into school, signaling the early start of the life-course-persistent offender. Next in the cascade is school social and academic failure as a result of disinterest in school and conduct disorder. Peer rejection sets in during this time. As the youth approaches early adolescence, parental monitoring of his or her activities and whereabouts is virtually nonexistent, accelerating academic failure and poor relationships with nondelinquent peers. Consequently, deviant peer associates become important and highly influential, and this often leads to persistent antisocial and violent behavior. The Dodge *et al.* research team was also able to determine that girls follow largely similar developmental pathways toward violence as boys. The researchers recognized that males are more likely than females to become seriously violent due to biological and socialization differences. However, they found little evidence to support the view that females, as a group, take a different developmental path to violence from males. In other words, they did not find a gender-specific developmental pathway.

After describing the dynamic cascade model, Dodge and his associates conclude with this crucial statement:

> An important implication of the current findings is that it is premature to conclude that an early-starting antisocial 5-year-old is unequivocally destined for a life-persistent path toward violent outcomes. Although the risk is substantial, it is by no means certain. The findings reported here indicate that trajectories can be deflected at each subsequent era in development, through interactions with peers, school, and parents along the way. (Dodge *et al.*, 2008, p. 1922)

This emphasizes that there are many preventive and therapeutic ways to steer a child away from a developmental trajectory of violence and serious delinquency and crime. Thus, psychological treatment of juveniles who kill may be more realistic than treatment of adults who commit these crimes. The dynamic cascade model provides specific targets for prevention at specific periods in development. In addition, because new risks arise with each developmental period, prevention and intervention cannot be deemed completed until the child passes through adolescence.

Treatment of Juveniles Who Kill

Juvenile homicide is a complex, if rare, phenomenon, and it often defies categorization. Contrast, for example, school shooting cases, the Dartmouth murders, the case of a boy who kills his abusive father, the 13-year-old girl who kills her newborn infant, the gang member in a drive-by shooting, and the 14-year-old who smothers his younger cousin to death in the process of trying to rape her. Some juveniles who kill are mentally disordered or developmentally disabled, and some may have psychopathic traits, but clearly not all do. Very little research is available by which to document the percentages, however. Most of the treatment information of juvenile murderers is from clinical case reports of a few cases referred for treatment (Heide, 2003; Heide *et al.*, 2012). Juveniles who commit homicide—if not transferred to criminal courts—generally are placed in a juvenile facility where they do not always receive treatment tailored to the needs of the offender. In addition, the likelihood of juvenile murderers receiving intensive psychological treatment and intervention decreases as they enter adolescence (Heide, 2003; Myers, 1992). Older adolescent murderers are often placed in adult prisons, where they may be held in protective custody until old enough to be transferred to the general population. Mental health care in juvenile facilities is typically minimal because of financial constraints and limited awareness of the psychological needs of this population (Heide, 2003). Psychiatric hospitalization, although commonly used for young children who kill, is rarely done for adolescent murderers (Heide, 2003). There are, of course, exceptions.

Overall, young killers appear to make a satisfactory adjustment in a correctional facility and in the community after release from custody (Heide, 2003). This is especially true for those youths who have killed family members as an isolated act of violence (Hillbrand, Alexandre, Young, & Spitz, 1999). On the other hand, hard-core, persistent, violent delinquents who killed in the course of committing other crimes do not make a good adjustment and often continue offending on release. The evidence for successful treatment of those juveniles who committed homicide during an altercation is mixed.

FAMILY VIOLENCE

We will begin this section with the good news. As with most other crimes, both crime reports (e.g., UCR records) and victimization reports (e.g., NCVS) indicate that family violence has gone down since the early 1990s. This can be attributed to numerous factors, and each policy maker likely has his or her preferred explanation. A decline in crime rates is always welcome, but it does not obscure the fact that a significant portion of the population is still subject to victimization. Moreover, very recent victimization data show some increases (BJS, 2012).

As will be made clear throughout this section, research on this topic is extremely fragmented, due in large part to differences in terminology. For example, family violence is also called domestic violence, intimate partner violence, or spousal abuse, and within the category of domestic violence researchers refer to *child abuse, maltreatment, neglect, sibling violence*, and *elderly abuse*, to name but a few terms. The term *intimate partner violence* (IPV) is of relatively recent origin, but is increasingly being used to refer to physical, sexual, or psychological harm by a current or former partner or spouse, heterosexual or of the same sex. It is the definition used by the Centers for Disease Control and Prevention (CDC). Family violence refers to any assault, intimidation, battery, sexual assault, sexual battery, or any criminal offense resulting in personal injury or death of one family or household member by another who is or was residing in the same single-dwelling unit (Wallace & Seymour, 2001). The term *battering* is often used in a slightly more specific fashion to describe *physical violence* in intimate relationships, during a dating relationship, marriage or partnership, or separation and divorce.

Criminologists and treatment providers are not concerned only with the "violence" aspect, however. Many victims experience psychological harm, and in some cases, what occurs in this area is not necessarily physical harm—it may be only psychological. Stalking is a good illustration; it may involve no physical harm, yet some researchers include it under the term *domestic violence* (e.g., Perilla, Lippy, Rosales, & Serrata, 2011). Another example is ongoing verbal abuse, which is rarely studied (Perilla *et al.,* 2011). Thus, some researchers define family violence as "an ongoing, debilitating experience of physical, *psychological,* and/or sexual abuse in the home, associated with increased isolation from the outside world and limited personal freedom and accessibility to resources" [italics added] (Wallace & Seymour, 2001, p. 4). Nonetheless, however it is defined or whatever terminology is used, at the heart of family violence is usually the perpetrator's misuse of power, control, and authority (American Psychological Association, 2003). (See **Box 9-1** for related material on family violence.)

The conundrum created by using different terms continues to be alluded to in virtually all research on family violence or violence against women and children (see, generally, White, Koss, & Kazdin, 2011). Researchers today try to define their terms very specifically, and they sometimes mint new terms that will better capture what they intend to study. With respect to child abuse, for example, the prominent researcher David Finkelhor (2011, p. 10), notes, "My preferred solution is to call this field *childhood victimization* or *developmental victimology,* using the broader victimization concept instead of the terms *violence* or *abuse.*" As Finkelhor observes, the broader term allows us to focus on the areas that professionals are concerned about: conventional crimes against children; acts that violate child welfare statutes—such as neglect or abuse; victimizations of children by nonadults, such as bullying and peer and sibling violence. We will return to Finkelhor's approach below.

For our purposes, we use the term *family violence* because it has traditionally been most often used in the research literature. Nevertheless, virtually all professionals recognize that its

---

BOX 9-1
The Violence Against Women Act (VAWA)—Politics in 2012

The Violence against Women Act (VAWA), first passed by Congress in 1994 by a large margin, takes a comprehensive approach to domestic violence and sexual assault through a broad array of legal reforms. "The Act explicitly recognizes that domestic violence is a serious crime that harms not only its immediate victims, but also their families, children, and the larger community" (Campbell, 1996, p. 2). Among many provisions, the law extended rape shield laws to protect victims from abusive inquires about their private sexual conduct and provided funds for community services for victims of domestic violence. Over the years since its passage, the VAWA has been applauded for making a positive contribution to decreases in domestic violence across the nation.

The *Violence against Women Act of 2000* (often referred to as VAWA-2) expanded research and services to victims nationwide and focused on the role of courts in combating violence against women through training, education, and technical assistance for judges and other court personnel (Roberts, 2002). Like its predecessor, the VAWA-2 received widespread support across the political spectrum.

In 2012, the VAWA was again scheduled for reauthorization, but the political climate had changed. The U.S. Senate voted to reauthorize funds for the VAWA in April, adding protections for LGBT women. The bill also would facilitate the prosecution of those who perpetrate violence against Native American women living on reservations and make it easier for undocumented immigrants to report abuse without fear of retribution. The House of Representatives, however, passed its own version that did not include these changes. As of late 2012, the VAWA had yet to be re-authorized.

victims are not only *physically* harmed, they are harmed psychologically as well. Moreover, sometimes physical harm does not even occur. For example, some victims—both children and adults—are exposed to continual berating and to cruel but nonphysical punishments, such as being forced to witness the killing or maiming of a pet. Even child molestation is not always classified as *violent*, although legally the inappropriate touching of a child qualifies as sexual assault in most jurisdictions. And, in the case of corporal punishment—which is clearly violent—it is not the type of violence that raises widespread concern. In other words, despite disavowal of spanking by most professionals, the criminal justice system does not intercede unless it is carried to extremes. As Finkelhor (2011) succinctly states, "it is a crime for a man to hit his wife but not his child" (p. 19). Likewise, in any discussion of family violence, it is important to keep in mind that one form of violence or dysfunction is often accompanied by other forms. For example, child maltreatment and intimate partner violence commonly co-occur, with some estimates indicating that half of the families with maltreatment of children also involve IPV (Briggs, Thompson, Ostrowski, & Lekwauwa, 2011).

Prevalence

The ultimate family violence includes the death of one or more individuals. About one of every five murders and nonnegligent manslaughters in the United States—in which the victim–offender relationship is known—involves a family member killing another family member, with a majority (about 50%) involving spouse killing spouse (Durose *et al.*, 2005; Federal Bureau of Investigation, 2011a). Similar statistics have also been reported in Canada, although the spousal homicides rate is the lowest reported in three decades (Statistics Canada, 2011). Homicide within the family accounts for 45 percent of all murders in England and Wales (d'Orban & O'Connor, 1989; Home Office, 1986; Mirrless-Black, 1999). A neglected area of research in family violence is homicide followed by suicide, in which a family member kills other family members and then kills himself or herself. One reason for the neglect is that homicide-suicides are relatively rare, accounting for less than 2 percent of all homicides. Yet they are so sobering that they are almost invariably covered by national media. Research has consistently shown that a high proportion of homicide-suicides (usually well over 50%) involve spouses, especially ex-spouses.

Victims

In 1995, approximately 19 percent of all arrests made for aggravated assaults and 68 percent for simple assault involved family members (U.S. Department of Justice, 2000b). Children under 12 comprised 5 percent of victims of family aggravated assault and 4 percent of the victims of family simple assault. Infants (under one year old) are the most vulnerable victims of family violence. **Figure 9-2** shows the nature of offenses that occurred against infants during the years 2001–2003. Most often, the offense committed against infant victims is simple assault, and the second most common is aggravated assault (Federal Bureau of Investigation, 2005b). **Figure 9-3** shows the age of victims who were also present at the time of infant victimizations. Although infants make up the majority of victims, sometimes additional victims of other ages are present at the infant's victimization, demonstrating the multiple aspects of family violence. Infants are rarely the solitary victim in family violence.

Self-report victimization studies also suggest that at least 20 percent of simple or aggravated assaults involve family members (U.S. Department of Justice, 1989). Although these official statistics are woefully incomplete, they still underscore the considerable magnitude of family violence.

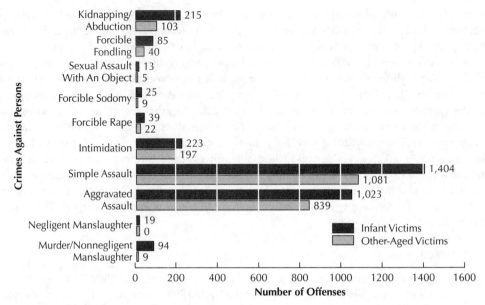

FIGURE 9-2 Offenses Related to Infant Victims   *Source*: Federal Bureau of Investigation (2005b), p. 359.

Some variant of family violence has probably existed for as long as individuals grouped together as families, both nuclear and extended. However, with the notable exception of intra-familial homicide, domestic or family violence has not traditionally been regarded as serious crime or worthy of criminal prosecution in this country. State governments and the courts have long claimed that family relationships require or deserve special immunity, including the views that parents have a right to discipline children physically, that a husband possesses the right to

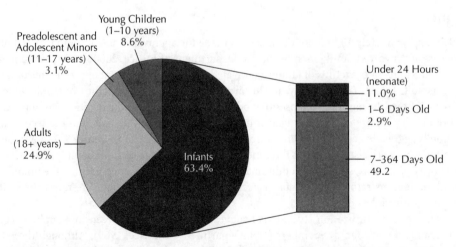

FIGURE 9-3 Age of Victims Present at Infant Victimization   *Source*: Federal Bureau of Investigation (2005b), p. 360.

have sexual access to his wife, or that nagging women or disobedient children often provoke and deserve the beatings they receive (Pleck, 1989). This view has been energetically challenged in recent years by various interest groups attempting not only to acquaint the public with the problem but also to activate lawmakers and the criminal justice system toward more stringent legal and social sanctions.

Research on family violence will be divided into four major questions: (1) how much family violence is there? (2) What are the common characteristics (or correlates) of the offenders and victims? (3) Is family violence fundamentally different from other kinds of violence (such as street violence)? (4) What are the causes of family violence? We will explore the research in these four areas, keeping in mind the critical problems in definition, sampling, and methodology just described. It should be pointed out that intrafamilial sexual abuse, although mentioned in the following sections, is discussed in greater detail in Chapter 13.

Incidence, Prevalence, and Demographics of Child Abuse and Neglect

In the United States, about 1 in 7 children (138 per 1,000) are maltreated at some time during their childhood (Finkelhor, Ormrod, Turner, & Hamby, 2005). Maltreatment refers to all forms of abuse and/or neglect and can be divided into five types: physical abuse, sexual abuse, emotional abuse, neglect, and family abduction (see **Table 9-2**). Finkelhor *et al.* (2005) discovered that emotional abuse (name calling or denigration by an adult) was the most frequent of the five types. Boys and girls experienced similar rates for maltreatment with the exception of sexual abuse. Girls are four times more likely to be sexually abused. Finkelhor and his associates also conducted a national survey of youths and caretakers regarding the experiences of over 4,500 children from 0 to 17 years. Called the National Survey of Children Exposed to Violence (NatSCEV) (Finkelhor, Turner, Ormrod, & Hamby, 2009), it revealed that almost half of these children had experienced a physical assault in the course of the previous year, often at the hands of their siblings and peers.

TABLE 9-2	Definitions of Child Abuse and Neglect
Type of Abuse	**Definition**
Physical abuse	Occurs when a parent willfully injures, causes injury, or allows a child to be injured, tortured, or maimed out of cruelty or excessive punishment.
Emotional abuse	Chronic pattern of behavior in which the child is belittled, denied love to promote specific behavior, or subjected to extreme and inappropriate punishment.
Emotional neglect	Failure to provide a child with appropriate support, attention, and affection.
Sexual abuse	Exploitation of a child or adolescent for another person's sexual and control gratification.
Child neglect	Chronic failure of a parent or caretaker to provide a child with basic needs such as food, clothing, shelter, medical care, educational opportunity, protection, and supervision.
Missing and exploited	Kidnapping a child from a custodial parent, child abduction by strangers, or child sexual exploitation for child pornography, child prostitution.

Source: Based on information from Whitcomb (2001).

Finkelhor and his colleagues also brought attention to the plight of poly-victims, those children who experience multiple victimizations over the course of their development (Finkelhor, Ormrod, & Turner, 2007)—such as parental abuse, bullying, physical victimization by caretaker, and sexual victimizations. In their national surveys, poly-victims were defined as youths who had experienced four or more victimizations over the course of a single year. "Analyses have suggested that poly-victimization is the pattern most associated with mental health problems and bad outcomes, and that poly-victims are the kids harboring the greatest amount of distress" (Finkelhor, 2011, p. 21). They note that children who experience a single kind of victimization are more able to recover than those who experience multiple kinds from multiple sources. For these latter children, victimization is more a condition than an event (Finkelhor, 2011, p. 22).

The prevalence of this victimization is approximately 12 per 1,000 children, a rate that has been relatively consistent over the past decade. The data also indicate that child protective services received approximately 2,672,000 reports of *possible* maltreatment in 2001 (U.S. Department of Health and Human Services, 2003). According to the U.S. Department of Health and Human Services (2003), approximately two-thirds (63%) of all victims were neglected, and about one out of five children (19%) experienced physical abuse. Approximately 10 percent were sexually abused, and another 8 percent were emotionally abused. There is a high probability that emotional abuse is substantially underreported. Over one-quarter of the victims were victims of more than one type of maltreatment. Definitions for each of these terms are found in **Table 9-2**.

The highest victimization rates were for the 0–3 age group, and rates declined as age increased. Child abuse/neglect perpetrators, defined as persons who have maltreated a child while in a caretaking relationship to the child, were mostly female (three-fifths). More than four-fifths (87.1%) of the victims were maltreated by one or both parents. The most common pattern of maltreatment was a child neglected by a female parent with no other perpetrators identified (44.7%). In cases involving sexual abuse, more than half (55.5%) of the victims were abused by known male adults.

Boys and girls are about equally neglected, physically, or emotionally abused, but, as mentioned earlier, girls are four times more likely to be sexually abused. In 2001, an estimated 1,300 children died of abuse and neglect, a rate of approximately 1.81 deaths per 100,000 children in the general population (U.S. Department of Health and Human Services, 2003). This child fatality figure due to maltreatment is very probably an underestimation, however. The figure is probably closer to 2,000 or more. Determining the actual number of children who die each year from maltreatment is exceedingly difficult. Child fatalities due to maltreatment are probably underreported because *some* deaths labeled as accidents, or sudden infant death syndrome (SIDS), might be attributed to child maltreatment if more comprehensive investigations were conducted.

Interestingly, research has found that pet abuse and child abuse commonly occur together in dysfunctional families (Arkow, 1998). Adults who are cruel and inhumane to children (and their spouses) are often cruel and inhumane to the family pet(s) as well. Abusers often threaten to harm or actually kill a pet to frighten a child into secrecy or to punish the child or to keep the spouse from reporting the abuse to authorities. In one study, more than half of the women at a shelter reported that their pets had been harmed or killed by their partner, and they delayed coming to the shelter for fear of harm to their pets (Ascione, 1997).

Missing, Abducted, Runaway, and Thrownaway Children

Each year, thousands of children run away, are abducted, or are thrown away. A thrownaway youth refers to one whom a parent or caretaker "throws" out of the home. Numerous children—some say a majority—who run away do so to escape neglect or abuse from their current home or living arrangement. Most of the nationwide data on these children are reported in the NISMART Bulletins. NISMART is an acronym for the National Incidence Studies of Missing, Abducted, Runaway, and Thownaway Children, a large nationwide survey of households, juvenile residential facilities, and law enforcement agencies conducted by the Office of Juvenile Justice and Delinquency Prevention. NISMART consists of several studies designed to estimate the size and nature of the missing children problem in the United States. A more recent study, the NISMART-2, covers the period 1997–1999. Much of the information in this section comes from the NISMART-2 report (U.S. Department of Justice, 2002a).

In 1999, an estimated 1,682,900 youth had a runaway or thrownaway episode (U.S. Department of Justice, 2002a). In most instances (71%), the runaway/thrownaway youth could have been endangered during the episode by virtue of such "street" factors as substance dependency, use of hard drugs, sexual or physical abuse, and their presence in places where criminal activity is prevalent. Recall that the UCR is no longer collecting data on runaways as of January 2012, although many states continue to do so. In addition, runaways are often taken into custody for curfew violations, so those statistics reflect the runaway problem to some extent.

Nonstranger child abduction can be another form of child abuse. In many instances, child abduction by a noncustodial parent or other family member from the custodial parent takes place. However, an undetermined number of child abductions are done by a parent who wants to protect the child or children from abuse by the other parent. Even a custodial parent may, in these circumstances, "abduct" the child, if the two parents share joint custody. According to the National Center for Missing and Exploited Children (NCMEC) an estimated 205,000 children were victims of family abduction in 2010 (Douglas, 2011), and nearly half are usually younger than six years of age (U.S. Department of Justice, 2002a).

Abduction of children by nonfamily members is less frequent. In this type of abduction, a nonfamily perpetrator takes a child by use of physical force or threat of bodily harm or detains the child for a substantial period of time (at least one hour) in an isolated place without lawful authority or parental permission. Nonfamily abductions are not typically the "stereotypical" stranger abductions highlighted in the media, where the primary motivation is depicted as sexual, however. They also may occur when a child younger than 15 is taken or detained or voluntarily accompanies a nonfamily person who conceals the child's whereabouts, demands a ransom, or expresses the intention to keep the child permanently. This last would include situations where a 20-year-old persuades his 14-year-old girlfriend to leave the state, or where a family acquaintance takes a child to protect the child from abuse. In 2010, approximately 58,200 children were abducted by nonfamily perpetrators, but this covered a very wide range of circumstances (Douglas, 2011).

Stereotypical Child Abductions

Stranger or slight-acquaintance abductions—every parent's nightmare—are relatively rare, although any number is too great. These cases are called **stereotypical abductions** because they often end in tragedy, have traumatizing effects on communities, and receive considerable attention from the national media. Overall, they are highly influential in forming public opinion about the risks and frequency of stranger abduction homicides. In every year since 2000, the number of high-profile stereotypical abductions is consistently estimated to be about 115 (Finkelhor, Hammer, & Sedlak, 2002), a number that is consistent with FBI estimates. Sixteen percent of these children are taken from the home, usually out of their bedroom. The abducted child is frequently sexually assaulted and then killed. An estimated 40 percent of all stereotypical abductions result in the death of the child, usually within the first 24 hours (Finkelhor *et al.*, 2002; Hanfland, Keppel, & Weis, 1997; Lord, Boudreaux, & Lanning, 2001). In another 4 percent of the cases, the child remains missing (U.S. Department of Justice, 2002a).

Investigators generally agree that the first three hours after abduction is the most critical (Hanfland *et al.*, 1997). It is estimated that about two-thirds of the abducted children are killed during that time frame, and nearly half of them are killed within the first hour. Another 32 percent of the surviving victims of stereotypical abduction receive injuries that require medical attention.

Sexual motivations appear to be a major factor in stereotypical abductions. Nearly half of all child victims of these stereotypical kidnappings were sexually assaulted by the perpetrator, and about one-third required medical attention for injuries (U.S. Department of Justice, 2002a). Over two-thirds of the victims of stereotypical kidnapping are female. The ages of the victims usually range between 6 and 14 years, and preschoolers are rarely targeted. Apparently, the age preference for those abductors who target females is around 11, largely because the abductors find them physically mature to be sexually desirable and vulnerable enough to be easily controlled and exploited (Hanfland *et al.*, 1997). In the summer of 2009 the nation was riveted to news that an 11-year-old girl abducted 17 years before was alive and living with her alleged abductor and his wife in a bizarre living arrangement that included a sheltered backyard structure. Now 28, the victim had apparently given birth to children fathered by this individual. In another high-profile similar case in the early 2000s, a teenage boy was found and returned to his family after having lived under an assumed name with his abductor for a number of years. Such returns are unfortunately very rare, however.

Most of the abductions of elementary school children occur in or around the victim's home, with the majority being abducted within one-quarter mile of their residence. The stereotypical abduction of middle school children took place in playgrounds, parks, wooded areas, shopping malls, and other areas of recreation. Rarely are children abducted from school grounds. Most children were taken into vehicles (45%) or to the offender's home (28%). Ransom is rarely demanded by the perpetrator(s) (less than 5% of all nonfamily or stereotypical abductions). The vast majority of abductors who are caught are under the age of 30, with an average age of 27 (Hanfland *et al.*,́ 1997). Only 10 percent are over 40. They are predominately unmarried men with poor social skills, marginal work habits, and have very few friends (Lord *et al.*, 2001).

Munchausen Syndrome by Proxy

An unusual but serious type of child abuse is called **Munchausen syndrome by proxy (MSBP)**. This is a form of child abuse in which the parent (usually the mother), or parents, *consistently* and *chronically* bring a child in for medical attention with symptoms falsified or directly induced by the parent or parents (Murray, 1997). Munchausen syndrome by itself is the chronic and relentless pursuit of medical treatment for combinations of symptoms that are either falsely reported or the results of consciously self-inflicted injury. In its proxy form, MSBP, another person, usually a child, is the victim. MSBP cases are found in homes of all socioeconomic levels (Pearl, 1995), and the victims are most often children between infancy and eight years of age (Jones *et al.*, 1986). Both male and female children may be victims. In most cases (about 98% of the time), the mothers are the offending parent, while the father is often unaware of what is happening. There does not seem to be a gender preference for the victim, as both male and female children are represented in equal numbers.

Very often, the offending mother is very knowledgeable about medical issues, has a fascination with medical details, has her own medical history of fabricated illnesses, and may be a health professional herself. In addition, the mother will be unusually attentive to the child and will be reluctant to leave the child's side during medical examination or treatment (although this could be said of most parents). A clearer symptom of MSBP is the child's series of reoccurring medical conditions that either do not respond to treatment or follow an unusual course that is persistent, puzzling, and unexplained. Another MSBP symptom is a series of physical or laboratory findings that are highly unusual, discrepant with medical history, or physically or clinically impossible. In extreme cases, the parent may initiate starvation in the child, nearly suffocate the child, inflict vaginal/rectal injuries in order to produce bleeding, add fat to stool collection to produce a lab abnormality, put her blood into child's urine sample before lab testing, or even inject contaminated material intravenously into the child's bloodstream (Murray, 1997; Pearl, 1995). The extreme forms of abuse certainly can lead to serious injury or even death. Unfortunately, the prevalence or incidence of MSBP is unknown at this time, probably partly due to the difficulty of identifying actual illnesses as opposed to the fabricated ones.

In some instances, the family pet may be the victim of MSBP, with the pet owner consistently taking the pet to the veterinarian for a variety of vague or fake symptoms. The pet owner often is trying to get sympathy and attention through the pet's misfortune.

Shaken Baby Syndrome

Another form of child abuse is **shaken baby syndrome (SBS)**, in which a parent or caretaker, usually in anger, shakes a baby so hard that serious head injury results. Although there are no accurate statistics regarding the frequency of this form of abuse, there is consensus that head trauma is the leading killer of abused children (over 50%) and that shaking is involved in many of these cases (Duhaime, Christian, Rorke, & Zimmerman, 1998; Showers, 1999; Smithey, 1998). Ellis and Lord (2001) estimate that 10 percent to 12 percent of all deaths due to abuse and neglect are attributable to SBS (see also National Information Support and Referral Service, 1998). In addition, available research suggests that 70 percent to 80 percent of the perpetrators of SBS are male, and most of the time they are the parent of the child (Child Abuse Prevention Center, 1998; Ellis & Lord, 2001). Both male and female babies appear to be equally victimized. And, of course, not all baby victims of SBS die, but many suffer significant brain damage, resulting in conditions such as cerebral palsy, blindness, deafness, seizures, learning disabilities, and coma.

Available research indicates that childhood abuse and neglect in general increase the odds of future delinquency and adult criminality by 40 percent. More specifically, being abused or neglected as a child increases the likelihood of arrest as a juvenile by over 50 percent, as an adult by 38 percent, and for a violent crime by 38 percent (Widom, 1992). More recent research by Widom (2000) confirms these data further. She states (2000, p. 5), "The odds of arrest for a juvenile offense were 1.9 times higher among abused and neglected individuals than among controls; for crime committed as adult, the odds were 1.6 times higher." In addition, psychological and emotional problems were prevalent among the abused and neglected sample. Specifically, the abused and neglected individuals were significantly more likely than the controls (a comparison group who had not experienced abuse or neglect) to have attempted suicide and to have met the criteria for antisocial personality disorder.

INFANTICIDE

In this section, the focus is on that form of child homicide that occurs when a person intentionally kills a child or infant, and *intends that the death occur*. That is, the homicide is not accidental or the incidental result of abuse or neglect. Although the term **infanticide** literally means the killing of an *infant,* it has become synonymous with the killing of a child by a parent. Some forms of infanticide can be traced back to ancient societies, including ancient Greece, Rome, China, India, and Europe. "In some instances, it took place as part of socially sanctioned religious sacrifice, was meant to dispose of physically defective infants, was a way to dispose of female infants when males were preferred, or was a form of population control (Smithey, 2002, p. 888).

An estimated 1,200–1,500 children are intentionally killed each year by a parent or other person, representing about 12 percent to 15 percent of the total homicides in the United States (Child Welfare Information Gateway, 2012; Emery & Laumann-Billings, 1998) (see **Figures 9-2** and **9-3**). There were 69 children under the age of 18 murdered in Canada, comprising 12 percent of the total homicides in that country in 2001 (Au Coin, 2003b). In the United States and Canada, about two-thirds of murdered children are killed by family members, mostly parents. Child homicide is not randomly distributed, but occurs with greater frequency across the globe in areas characterized by poverty, limited opportunity, and urbanization. A majority of child homicides across the globe are the result of parents killing their own child. Interestingly, the United States ranks fifth in homicides of infants under one year of age (with a rate of 5.4 per 100,000 live births) among 18 developed countries (Smithey, 2002). The majority of homicides of newborns and young children in the United States are committed by the biological mother (Porter & Gavin, 2010). This statistic should be approached with caution, because mothers are more likely than fathers to be responsible for care of the child on a day-to-day basis. Infants aged 12 months or younger have the highest homicide victimization rate of any single group in Australia, England and Wales, Canada, and the United States (Brookman & Nolan 2006). In England and Wales, for instance, children younger than one year are at least twice as likely to be a victim of homicide as any other age group (Brookman & Nolan, 2006). They are, in most cases, killed by a biological parent.

In Canada, between 1974 and 2001, children under age six were more likely to have been killed as a result of strangulation or a beating than by other methods (Au Coin, 2003b). In England and Wales, two-thirds of the infants are killed as a result of suffocation or nonspecific methods such as shaking (shaken baby syndrome) and physical abuse (Brookman & Nolan, 2006). Older Canadian children, on the other hand, were more likely to be killed by a firearm, with 32 percent of victims age 6–8 years and over 50 percent of victims 15–17 years of age dying of gunshot wounds (Au Coin, 2003b).

Several decades ago, Resnick (1970) recommended that the killing of one's children be divided into two separate categories, **neonaticide,** which refers to the killing of the newborn within the first 24 hours after birth, and **filicide,** which refers to the killing of a child older than 24 hours. Resnick's research indicated that neonaticide was more likely to represent an attempt to dispose of a problem, while filicide was more likely a reflection of parental depression or feelings of being overwhelmed. This distinction has now largely disappeared from the literature, but social concerns about neonaticide continue. An increasing number of jurisdictions, for example, now have laws that bar the prosecution of parents who leave newborns or infants in "safe harbors" such as hospitals, churches, or synagogues. The assumption is that if the parents have no such safe harbor, they might not sufficiently care for the infants or, worse, take the drastic step of ending their lives.

Neonaticide

The extent of neonaticide is difficult to determine because many go undetected and there is no national data depository for these cases (Beyer, Mack, & Shelton, 2008). The same situation holds for filicide (Koenen & Thompson, 2008). It is roughly estimated that approximately 150–300 incidents of neonaticide occur each year in the United States (Meyer & Oberman, 2001). A similar estimate has been advanced by researchers on filicide (Koenen & Thompson, 2008). In their investigation of existing neonaticide data at the FBI National Center for the Analysis of Violent Crime, Beyer and her colleagues (2008) discovered that many of the 40 women in their study gave birth unassisted to infants of normal birth weight. The women then killed the neonate, disposed of the body, cleaned up the crime scene, and remained undetected. "Many of the offenders are then able to engage in routine activities, immediately following the birth of the child, including attending classes, shopping, eating out, dancing, or returning to work" (Beyer *et al.*, 2008, p. 531).

Beyer *et al.* found very little evidence that the women who engaged in neonaticide had serious mental or psychological disorders, a finding consistent with previous studies (Dobson & Sales, 2000; Spinelli, 2001). However, several women did show some bizarre behaviors following the neonaticide, such as placing the infant's body in containers, driving around with the infant's body in the trunk of their car, or breastfeeding the dead infant. Similarly, Spinelli (2001) identified bizarre incidents following the neonaticide, such as returning to bed with the infant's corpse or keeping it under their clothes. In one case, "The putrefied corpse of one infant was found two weeks after delivery in a file cabinet in the office the subject shared with others" (Spinelli, 2001, p. 812). Such extreme measures likely were indicative of some mental disorder or postpartum psychosis precipitated by hormonal changes associated with the pregnancy and birth.

Beyer *et al.* report that virtually none of the women in the study had a criminal history, nor were arrested for crime against a child prior to the homicide. It is also interesting to note that several of the offenders had living biological children (ranging in number from one to four additional children) at the time of the homicide. Killing the newborn appears to reflect a desire to rid oneself of a problem. Most of the women who commit neonaticide are described as being sexually submissive, immature, childlike, and passive (Koenen & Thompson, 2008). However, there is so little research specifically on this topic that firm conclusions are unwarranted.

Filicide

Although severe mental disorders and suicide are rare in neonaticide, this is not the case in filicide. Some researchers contend that a majority of the women who commit filicide are demonstrating symptoms of affective disorders, a psychotic disorder, or a combination of the two (Lewis & Bunce, 2003). Traditionally, women who kill their children have been viewed by the legal system and the mental health profession as suffering from severe emotional problems, rendering them either insane (the legal system) or psychotic (the mental health profession). Men who kill their children are more likely to be viewed as evil and cruel (Wilczynski, 1997).

Resnick (1969, 1970) concluded that two-thirds of the mothers who committed filicide were psychotic, compared with only 17 percent of the women in the neonaticide group. As noted, Resnick found that a vast majority of the filicide group suffered from serious depression, while very few women in the neonaticide group exhibited this feature. Furthermore, suicide attempts accompany one-third of the filicides, but rarely accompany neonaticide.

More recent research sheds additional light on maternal murder of their young. In a cross-national comparison of British and Canadian filicidal women by McKee and Shea (1998), the data suggested that women who were charged with murdering their children usually suffered from a diagnosable mental disorder and were contending with many stressful events in their lives at the time of the murder. In another study, results showed that women suffering from a diagnosed mental disorder were more likely to use a weapon to murder their children than filicidal women not suffering from an apparent mental disorder (Lewis, Baranoski, Buchanan, & Benedek, 1998). The Lewis *et al.* study found that guns were used 13 percent of the time and knives 12 percent of the time.

Some studies have indicated that the prevalence of major depression among women who commit filicide is as high as 82 percent (Haapasalo & Petäjä, 1999). Most often, the clinical diagnosis is "postpartum depression," a depressive episode thought to be brought on by childbirth. However, it is important to realize that three categories of mental or emotional reactions may be apparent after childbirth: (1) postpartum blues, (2) postpartum depression, and (3) postpartum psychosis (Dobson & Sales, 2000). The most frequent is *postpartum blues*, characterized by crying, irritability, anxiety, confusion, and rapid mood changes. It is estimated that anywhere from 50 percent to 80 percent of women exhibit some minor features of postpartum blues about one to five days after delivery (Durand & Barlow, 2000). The symptoms may last for a few hours to a few days and are clearly associated with childbirth and the hormonal changes that accompany pregnancy and delivery. The connection between postpartum blues and neonaticide or filicide has not been supported by the research literature (Dobson & Sales, 2000).

The second category, *postpartum depression*, occurs during the weeks or months after childbirth. The symptoms include depression, loss of appetite, sleep disturbances, fatigue, suicidal thoughts, apathy about the newborn, and a general loss of interest in daily living. However, in contrast to postpartum blues, postpartum depression does not appear totally related to childbirth. Rather, it is more a clinical form of depression that is present before childbirth and probably is more a recurring depressive disorder—perhaps also partly brought on by hormonal changes—that has existed before the delivery; however, it is accelerated by late pregnancy, birth, and the subsequent physical exhaustion and overwhelming responsibility of caring for an infant. This form of mood disorder is usually not linked to filicide. The third category, *postpartum psychosis*, is a severe mental disorder that is rare, occurring in one out of every 1,000 women following delivery. Usually, the psychotic features are strikingly similar to symptoms of serious bipolar depression and appear directly associated with childbirth. Nevertheless, it is not unusual to find mental disorder in the woman's history, even before the pregnancy. Sometimes, this mental disorder is severe enough to lead to the mother's attempted suicide, together with an attempt to kill the infant (Kendall & Hammen, 1995). Dobson and Sales (2000) report that research indicates that many women (estimates range from 20% to 40%) who commit filicide are suffering from postpartum psychosis. In one noteworthy incident that occurred in the 1980s, the new mother had lowered the window shades of her home for several weeks after her baby's birth, sitting in darkened rooms, and resisting entreaties of her husband and other family members to get psychological help. On the day of the killing, she shot her infant to death in his crib. The prosecutor dismissed the case, supposedly because he could not find one clinician who would say she was *not* suffering from a severe form of postpartum psychosis.

Overall, though, few filicides are committed by mothers suffering from depression or psychosis, or some other serious mental disorder. Filicides can result from acts of omission, such as neglecting to supervise or monitor the child in a hazardous environment or dangerous situation, or acts of commission, such as shaking an infant or delivering a swift blow to silence persistent crying. The father or another male figure may also be the responsible party, but research on filicides tends to focus on the mother, who is usually the primary caretaker. In many cases, it is difficult to determine whether the child's death is due to an accident, carelessness, or an intentional act to murder.

Coramae Richey Mann (1993) investigated the patterns and characteristics of maternal filicide in six major U.S. cities (Chicago, Houston, Atlanta, Los Angeles, New York, and Baltimore) between 1979 and 1983. Although the data set for the study consisted of 296 cleared (or solved) homicide cases in which the offender was female, Mann restricted her research sample to 25 maternal filicides of preschool children (ages birth to five years). Because of the small sample size, any far-reaching conclusions must be drawn very cautiously.

Mann found that 40 percent of the women who killed their preschool children had arrest records. One offender had 15 misdemeanor arrests, while another had six felony arrests. Twenty-five percent had arrest records for violent crime. Moreover, 12 of the 25 filicide offenders had recorded child abuse histories where court or social service intervention had taken place. Most of the victims were killed in the bathroom (30%), or the bedroom (26%), usually on Sunday morning. Manual methods were used in 80 percent of the cases—hands or feet (52%), suffocation or strangulation (16%), or drowning (12%). The killing of older children (ages 4 or 5) tended to be more brutal.

While a majority of the offenders in the Mann study were initially charged with murder, only 19 percent were convicted of that charge. Forty percent of the women who killed their preschool children were sent to prison, most often on a conviction of manslaughter, and another 36 percent received a probation sentence. The remaining six cases were either not processed, dismissed, or received special treatment from the court, and their dispositions were sealed. A determination of a mental disorder of the offenders was apparently rare.

Dobson and Sales (2000) conclude, "There is certainly little evidence that women who kill their infant within the first 24 hours of birth are seriously mentally ill, and furthermore, many women who kill their infant after the first 24 hours do not exhibit symptomatology that meets the requirements for diminished capacity or insanity" (p. 1109). However, they also concluded that the potential role of psychosis in *some* women should not be underestimated in filicide. In some instances of filicide, such as observed by Resnick, some mothers are psychotic or otherwise seriously mentally disordered. This is one reason that the Andrea Yates case, discussed at the beginning of Chapter 8, was so intriguing to observers. Advocates for Yates insisted that there was a very clear pattern of severe mental illness that offered an explanation for the tragic circumstances surrounding the death of her children.

PARTNER AND OTHER FAMILY ABUSE

Intimate Partner Abuse: Prevalence, Incidence, and Nature

Intimate partner violence is the contemporary term used by researchers to characterize the physical, psychological, and sexual violence perpetrated by individuals in a present or past intimate relationship. While this form of abuse has usually been included in studies of family violence or domestic violence, focusing specifically on the intimate partnership has allowed the research microscope to examine same-sex relationships, dating relationships, and past relationships that may not have been considered in other studies. Since the turn of the twenty-first century, research on IPV has expanded dramatically, perhaps even more than research in other areas of family or domestic violence. Nevertheless, many criminologists and researchers continue to include IPV as a form of domestic violence, or even more broadly, of family violence. In a recent review, Perilla *et al.* (2011) use the term *domestic violence* to summarize what is known about IPV worldwide and in the United States in particular. Furthermore, most studies focus on women as victims and men as perpetrators, although female-against-male violence and same-sex violence are receiving more attention.

The National Family Violence Survey of 1995–1996 estimated that the prevalence of women battering in the United States ranged from 6 to 8.7 million annually (Roberts, 2002). This violence was presumably at the hand of intimate partners. It is further estimated that one in three murders every year are intimate partner homicides (Roberts, 2002). According to estimates from the National Crime Victimization Survey (NCVS), there were 691,710 nonfatal violent victimizations committed by current or former spouses, boyfriends, or girlfriends of the victims during 2001 (Rennison, 2003). Eighty-five percent of victimizations by intimate partners were against women. Overall, **intimate partner violence** comprised 20 percent of violent crime against women in 2001. In 2002, 32.1 percent of female murder victims were slain by their husbands, ex-husbands, or boyfriends, compared with 2.7 percent of the male murder victims who were killed by their wives, ex-wives, or girlfriends (Federal Bureau of Investigation, 2003).

Many years ago, psychologist Lenore Walker (1979) minted and developed the term **battered woman syndrome (BWS)** to characterize a cluster of behavioral and emotional features that were often shared by women who have been physically and psychologically abused over a period of time by the dominant male figure in their lives. Feelings of low self-esteem, depression, and learned helplessness are among the important components that frequently accompany the syndrome. During the 1980s, many researchers were able to document the syndrome, but others were not. Walker herself (1984) subsequently agreed that women who had been abused did not necessarily display the symptoms she had originally outlined, particularly helplessness. Nonetheless, it is clear that psychological damage is no stranger to individuals who have been abused.

Research on domestic violence finds that a great majority of battered women either remain in lifelong abusive relationships, leave the relationship, or are killed by their abusers. Very rarely do battering relationships get better. A small minority of abused women kill their abusers. Although evidence for the battered woman syndrome is being admitted into the trials of women who do kill their abusers (Schuller & Vidmar, 1992), it is rarely successful in bringing about an acquittal (Browne, 1987; Ewing, 1990).

Currently, there is considerable debate concerning the reliability, validity, and usefulness of the diagnosis "battered woman syndrome" (Bartol & Bartol, 2004). One of the major problems with the concept is the tendency for mental health and law professionals to regard it as a *single* entity representing some kind of mental or behavioral disorder displayed by all women who experience a severe abusive relationship. In addition, some theorists prefer to view the psychological effects of battering as a form of the posttraumatic stress disorder (PTSD) discussed in Chapter 8, rather than as a separate syndrome.

However, battered women demonstrate a wide range of behavioral patterns that often reflect survival skills and adaptation to serious, life-threatening situations rather than a psychological disorder. Many women simply do not exhibit discernible clusters of psychological maladjustment, depression, and helplessness as portrayed by the battered women syndrome or by PTSD, even though they may have experienced high degrees of coercion, domination, and abuse during a lengthy relationship (Stark, 2002). Some victims, regardless of the abuse, may not demonstrate any signs of a syndrome or mental health problems at all.

Same-Sex Domestic Violence

In recent years, the nature and extent of same-sex partnerships has received increased attention. With the increasing likelihood that more and more states will recognize the right of same-sex couples to marry, these partnerships will come under the same research microscope as heterosexual marriages, including scrutinizing their divorce rates, styles of parenting, and any presence of violence in their relationships. Some researchers (Potoczniak, Mourot, Crosbie-Burnett, & Potoczniak, 2003) already have discovered some strong similarities in the research literature comparing the violence cycles and stages of abuse between same-sex domestic violence (SSDV) and opposite-sex domestic violence (OSDV). For example, similar to OSDV perpetrators, SSDV perpetrators are extremely controlling, threatened by outside influences, are highly selfish, and blame their partners for the abuse. In addition, the SSDV victims show many of the same behavioral and thought characteristics of OSDV victims.

Turrell (2000) examined SSDV among lesbians, gay women, and gay men. In the survey, female participants were able to choose between the designations "lesbian" and "gay women." Turrell found a physical abuse prevalence rate of 44 percent for gay men, 58 percent for gay women, and 55 percent for lesbians in a past or present relationship. With increased attention relating to issues involving civil unions and same-sex marriages across the nation in recent years, it is obvious that a better understanding and skillful research attention to SSDV are important, especially pertaining to providing adequate domestic violence and psychological services to the victims and training criminal justice personnel to handle the incidents in a competent fashion.

Psychological and Demographic Characteristics of Abusers

As the section on battered woman syndrome indicates, most of the research on psychological characteristics in domestic violence has focused on the characteristics of the person being abused, particularly the woman in heterosexual relationships. It has been a traditional belief in some quarters that these battered women allow themselves to be battered (Frieze & Browne, 1989). Others have argued that victims of spouse abuse are masochistic, consciously and unconsciously precipitating the violence to which they are subjected (Megargee, 1982). Still others have depicted battered wives as lacking self-esteem, being highly passive and dependent on their husbands, and willing to place greater value on maintaining the marriage above their safety (Megargee, 1982).

Some researchers, though, have preferred to focus on the characteristics of the abusers. Abusive husbands, for example, have been depicted as extremely possessive and unreasonably jealous men who treat their wives like property coveted by other men. This depiction led to other assumptions about the inadequacy, incompetence, and low self-esteem of these abusive husbands who saw threats to their masculinity everywhere. Christine Rasche (1993) examined 155 "mate" homicides in Florida that occurred between 1980 and 1986. She was able to identify several motives for these intimate homicides, with possessiveness the most prominent. The list of motives and related percentages was as follows:

- Possessiveness (48.9%)
- Self-defense (15.5%)
- Abuse by victim (2.6%)
- Feelings arising out of arguments (20.7%)
- Other motives (9.7%)
- Unknown (7.7%)

Alcohol abuse is also often seen as part of the clinical picture. Similarly, men who abuse their children were seen as incompetent, immature individuals, overwhelmed and frustrated by the responsibilities of parenting. The violence of both the abusive husband and the abusive father was seen as irrational and expressive, precipitated by frustration and extreme anger. Some professionals have suggested that street violence is generally rational and instrumental, whereas family violence is predominately irrational and expressive (see Hotaling & Straus, 1989; Megargee, 1982).

The empirical evidence for these depictions is meager, equivocal, and confusing and no more persuasive than the depictions of battered women as passive and lacking in self-confidence. Some studies find some support for these correlates; others provide no support. Despite several attempts at psychological typologies for wife and child abusers (Megargee, 1982), there does not seem to be any evidence for typical psychological profiles for either the abusers or the abused. However, recent research results look promising for a typology that might help in the prevention, intervention, and treatment of abusers. In an extensive review of the research literature, Holtzworth-Munroe and Stuart (1994) identified three primary types of male spouse batterers: Type 1 batterers, who abuse family members only; Type 2 batterers, who abuse family members because of emotional problems; and Type 3 batterers, who are generally violent toward both family members and persons outside the family. Type 1 abusers are the most common, tend to be less aggressive than the other two, and also tend to be more remorseful for their actions. They are generally inadequate, passive men who are dependent on others. Type 2 batterers tend to be depressed, inadequate individuals who are emotionally volatile and who display indicators of personality disorders and psychopathology. Type 3 batterers are individuals who are antisocial, criminally prone, and violent across situations. They are more likely to abuse alcohol and are generally more belligerent toward almost everyone. They are also most likely to be involved in serious violence toward a spouse.

The search for demographic variables has been equally mixed and inconclusive (Hotaling & Straus, 1989; Weis, 1989). Wife and child abuse appears to cut across socioeconomic, religious, and ethnic lines. Even current research on gender does not reveal clear trends for women or men as assaulters of spouse, child, or parent.

The abuse of alcohol and drugs seems to play a role as an exacerbator, *but not as a cause*, of the family violence. Abusive men with severe alcohol or drug problems are apt to abuse their partners both when drunk and when sober. However, abusive husbands who drink heavily are violent more frequently, and inflict more serious injuries on their partners than do abusive men who do not have a history of alcohol or drug problems (Frieze & Browne, 1989). A similar pattern also holds for men who abuse their children. Many use alcohol as an excusing agent that allows them to escape some culpability for their antisocial or violent actions, as well as to avoid the full impact of legal sanctions. Babcock, Waltz, Jacobson, and Gottman (1993), in some very promising research, examined the interactions of marital power, interpersonal strategies, and communication skills as predictors of marital violence. They reasoned that husbands who are unable to affect their intentions through negotiation or general communication skills are more likely to resort to physical aggression—pushing, slapping, and beating—to achieve their intentions. This is especially the case if the wives are more verbally competent, more educated, or have better jobs than their husbands. For example, previous research suggests that women with jobs that are higher in status than their husband's jobs experience more life-threatening violence than wives who were occupationally similar to their husbands (Hornung, McCullough, & Sugimoto, 1981). Frustrated with some combination of power discrepancy between him and his wife, the husband's only effective expressive retort may be physical aggression. Moreover, husbands who battered their wives were more likely to be in relationships where their demands were met with their wives' withdrawal (e.g., defensiveness, passive inaction, "stonewalling," and the "silent treatment"). The researchers interpreted the withdrawal pattern as one of power (the individual has resources the other partner wants), whereas the demanding role represented a weak position (the individual wants something the other partner has). This research emphasizes the importance of studying the reciprocal interaction of a relationship if we are to understand family violence more fully.

Elderly Abuse: Prevalence, Incidence, and Nature

It is estimated that approximately 2.1 million older Americans are victims of abuse each year (American Psychological Association, 2012). Although these data are not of recent origin, representing information from 1996, updated official statistics are challenging to uncover. Elder abuse is characterized by the infliction of physical, emotional, or psychological harm on the older adult, usually defined as age 65 or older (Marshall, Benton, & Brazier, 2000). "The general concept involved in the numerous definitions of 'elder abuse' is that the victim is injured, neglected, or exploited because of vulnerabilities associated with age, such as impaired physical or mental capacities" (Klaus, 2000, p. 13).

Neglect in this instance is "the refusal or failure to fulfill any part of a person's obligation or duties to an elder" (Seymour, 2001, p. 4). More specific elder abuse definitions include "the refusal or failure to provide an elderly person with such life necessities as food, water, clothing, shelter, personal hygiene, medicine, comfort, personal safety, and other essentials included in the responsibility or agreement with an elder" (Seymour, 2001, p. 4). Although less acknowledged, the overmedication of adults, particularly in nursing home settings, can be regarded as a form of neglect as well. Abandonment may also be included in the definition of neglect, and is characterized by such things as the desertion of an elder at a hospital, a nursing facility, or other similar institution, or desertion of an elder at a public location (see **Table 9-3**).

The elderly appear to be maltreated in much the same way that children are maltreated—with one notable exception: financial exploitation (Pagelow, 1989). The likeliest candidates for elder abuse appear to be white women between the ages of 75 and 85, middle to lower class, Protestant, and suffering from some form of physical or mental impairment (Pagelow, 1989). Only 5 percent of the elderly are placed in institutions or rest homes, although 85 percent of them have at least one chronic illness (Hudson, 1986). Most elderly are living at home or in the homes of relatives. Abusive caretakers tend to lack resources, feel trapped, and may be abusing drugs or alcohol.

Spouses constitute the second-largest abuser category. Male caretakers are more likely to abuse the elderly physically, while female caretakers are prone to abuse them psychologically or neglect them. However, both men and women are equally likely to exploit them financially. The most common abuse is a combination of psychological abuse and neglect (Pagelow, 1989). About 20 percent of elder abuse cases are physical, and 45 percent involve neglect (Marshall, Benton, & Brazier, 2000).

Although there are similarities between the various types of family abuse, elder mistreatment is a more complex phenomenon that encompasses both aspects of interpersonal violence and the aging process (Wolf, 1992). That is, elder abuse and neglect are often a result of long-standing

TABLE 9-3 Estimated Incidence of Specific Types of Elder Abuse, 1996

Type of Abuse	Estimated Percentage
Neglect	58.50
Physical abuse	15.70
Financial exploitation	12.30
Emotional abuse	7.30
Sexual abuse	0.04
Other types	5.10
Unknown	0.06

Source: Data from National Center on Elder Abuse (1999).

troubled family dynamics and interpersonal processes that have been highly charged when the dependency relationship is altered, because of either illness or financial needs.

Estimates of the proportion of elderly persons (persons 65 or older) who are abused range from 4 percent to 10 percent, but it is difficult to make confident estimates because of a lack of reliable statistics (Klaus, 2000; Pagelow, 1989; Pillemer & Suitor, 1988). The first-ever National Elder Abuse Incidence Study, conducted by the National Center on Elder Abuse (1999), estimated that during 1996, at least one-half million older persons in domestic settings were abused and/ or neglected, or experienced self-neglect, and that for every reported incidence of elder abuse, neglect, or self-neglect, approximately five go unreported (Seymour, 2001). The same report found that female elders are abused at a higher rate than males, even after accounting for their larger numbers in the aging population. And two-thirds of the perpetrators of elder abuse are adult children or spouses. While there is no one single causal factor to fully explain why family members abuse their seniors, some explanations have focused on caregiver stress and dependency issues (either the caregiver's or the senior's) (Au Coin, 2003a).

Pillemer and Finkelhor (1988) focused on the Boston metropolitan area and found that 3 percent of the elderly suffered from one of three kinds of abuse: physical abuse, chronic verbal abuse, or neglect. Based on their findings, the researchers extrapolated that about 1 million elderly persons are similarly abused throughout the United States. A Canadian survey (Podnieks, Pillemer, & Nicolson, 1990) reported that about 4 percent of the elderly population living in private homes in Canada was subjected to abuse and neglect.

The violent crime committed against persons age 65 or older is most likely to be simple assault (Klaus, 2000). Nevertheless, there is ample evidence that they are also victims of more serious violent crimes. Recent statistics from two countries are illustrative. In Canada, 6 percent of the total homicide victims were older Canadians (65 or older), with a family member being responsible for over half of the cases (Au Coin, 2003a). The same statistic (6.4%) was reported in the United States for older Americans (Federal Bureau of Investigation, 2003). The term **eldercide** is usually reserved for the murder of a person age 65 or older. In Canada, when the incident involved a family member, a majority of older women were killed by a spouse or ex-spouse (53%), whereas older men were most often killed by an adult son (43%) (Au Coin, 2003a). The data are similar for American senior citizens (Klaus, 2000). In Canada, the most common cause of death for older victims of family-related homicides was beating (29%) and shooting (28%), followed by stabbing (23%) (Au Coin, 2003a). Although a similar family breakdown is not currently available in the U.S. data, the most common causes of death for all older victims were firearms (45%), followed by stabbing (20%), blunt objects (14%), and beatings with fists or feet (13%) (Federal Bureau of Investigation, 2003).

Sibling-to-Sibling Violence

Violence between siblings is believed to be the most common form of violence within families, but surprisingly little is known about it (Finkelhor, 2011; Gelles, 1997; Wallace, 1996). The violence and abuse a child or adolescent receives from a sibling is often overlooked and trivialized (Simonelli, Mullis, & Rohde, 2005). Sibling conflicts are generally seen as a normal part of growing up (Underwood & Patch, 1999). Mothers and fathers display a great tendency to deny the seriousness of the aggressive outburst of siblings or their children—including violence toward themselves—in order to perpetuate a "myth of family harmony" (Harbin & Madden, 1979). Yet in many cases, sibling conflict and violence involves punching, choking, beating up, threatening to use a weapon, and actually using a weapon. In addition, sibling violence appears to be linked to violence in dating relationships, family violence in adulthood, and nonfamily adult violence in general (Hoffman, Kiecolt, & Edwards, 2005). More severe forms of child-to-family violence involve murder, and have specific terms, such as **siblicide** (sibling killing sibling), **patricide** (killing one's father), **matricide** (killing one's mother), **sororicide** (killing one's sister), **fratricide** (killing one's brother), and **parricide** (killing one or more of one's parents).

Nearly 30 years ago, Steinmetz (1981) reported that two-thirds of the adolescent siblings in the family sample she studied—a sample characterized by family violence—used physical violence to resolve conflict. These findings have been recently supported by Hoffman *et al.* (2005) who found 70 percent of the adolescents in their sample (students) had committed at least one violent act against their closest-age sibling during their senior year of high school. Families having only sons consistently experience more sibling violence than do families with only daughters (Hoffman *et al.*, 2005). Hoffman *et al.* (2005) found that males perpetrated more violent acts against their brothers than against sisters or sisters against their siblings. In 2002, 72 percent of murders by siblings involved a brother killing a brother, and 14 percent involved a brother killing a sister (Durose *et al.*, 2005). An additional 14 percent of siblicides involved a sister killing a brother or sister. Among the 671 intrafamilial murders reported in 2002, 18 percent (or 119 murders) involved a sibling victim (Durose *et al.*, 2005).

Victims of the more extreme forms of sibling violence tend to be younger siblings. For example, Fehrenbach, Smith, Monastersky, and Deisher (1986) reported that over 40 percent of victims of adolescent sexual assault were younger siblings. Available data also suggest that 85 percent of siblicide offenders and 73 percent of siblicide victims are male (Dawson & Langan, 1994). Approximately 1 out of every 100 homicides in the United States is a siblicide (Federal Bureau of Investigation, 2005b; Underwood & Patch, 1999). In their analysis, Underwood and Patch (1999) reported that the most common circumstance of sibling homicide was some type of argument between the perpetrator and the victim. Interestingly, the same study uncovered very few incidents involving Asian Americans or Pacific Islanders in their data set. African Americans, on the other hand, were overrepresented in the data. In addition, firearms predominated as the weapon of choice in siblicides.

Child-to-Parent Violence

Child-to-parent violence and abuse has also become an important topic. In one early study (Gelles, 1982), approximately 4 adolescents (ages 15–17) in 100 were reported to kick, bite, punch, hit with an object, beat up, threaten, or use a gun or knife against a parent. Almost one-third of restraining orders issued in Massachusetts were requested by parents against their adolescent children (Pagani *et al.*, 2004). In a study using a nationally representative sample of American children, Ullman and Straus (2003) concluded that 10% of the adolescents (ages 10–17) participated in child-to-parent violence during the previous 12 months. Sixty percent of these youths had witnessed violence between their parents. In one longitudinal study involving 2,524 Canadian adolescents, Pagani *et al.* (2004) affirmed that 13 percent of the teenagers engaged in physical aggression toward their mothers, ranging from pushing and shoving, punching or kicking, throwing objects, to using a weapon.

In 2010, 25 percent of the family murder victims were killed by their children (Federal Bureau of Investigation, 2011a) (see **Figure 9-4**). The killing of parents, termed parricide, is most often committed by sons by a ratio of about 3 to 1 over daughters (Federal Bureau of Investigation, 2005b; Lubenow, 1983; Pagelow, 1989). Mothers are killed (matricide) far more often than fathers (patricide) by both adolescents and adult sons and daughters. Female parricide is exceptionally rare in all countries of the world (d'Orban & O'Connor, 1989). When daughters kill a parent or parents, they often secure the help of a male friend or sibling. In Britain, boys most often kill a parent (or

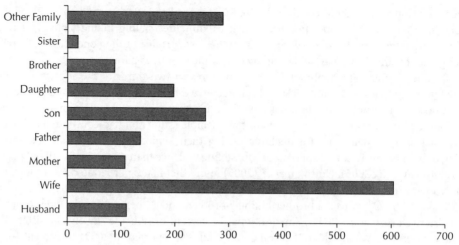

FIGURE 9-4 Number of Murders by Family Relationship *Source*: Federal Bureau of Investigation (2011a).

parents) with explosive violence in response to prolonged provocation and parental brutality and abuse (d'Orban & O'Connor, 1989). Heide (1993) identifies three types of youth parricide: (1) the severely abused child, (2) the severely mentally ill child, and (3) the dangerously antisocial child. The complex dynamics of families in which parricides occur often include multiassaultive family patterns, easy access to firearms, alcohol and drug abuse, and the youthful offender's strong feelings of helplessness in coping with the stresses at home. Sometimes the adolescent murderer, as well as other family members, feels a sense of relief that the parent(s) is (are) dead.

Figure 9-5 shows the overall percent distribution of murder by relationship to the victim. **Figure 9-6** displays the distribution of "other known" relationships found in the pie chart illustrated in **Figure 9-5**.

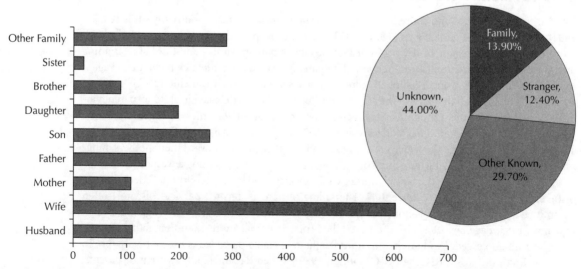

FIGURE 9-5 Murder Distribution by Relationship, 2010 *Source*: Federal Bureau of Investigation (2011a).

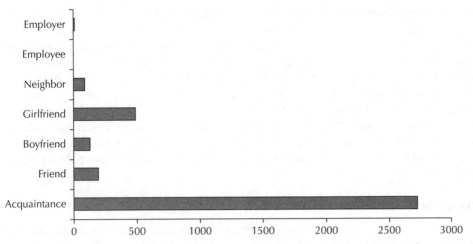

FIGURE 9-6 Murder by Other-Known Relationship, 2010   *Source*: Federal Bureau of Investigation (2011a).

Although males predominate in the more extreme forms of juvenile violence toward parents, the gender differences disappear at more moderate levels of violence (Pagani *et al.*, 2004). In addition, the risk of violence toward parents gradually increases during adolescence, peaking at age 15 and diminishing thereafter (Pagani *et al.*, 2004). This pattern corresponds to the peak age of adolescent violence toward nonrelated individuals noted by Loeber and Stouthamer-Loeber (1998). Most violent incidents between child and parents are associated with conflicts about home responsibilities, money, and privilege (Pagani *et al.*, 2004). Children and adolescents who displayed early and chronic forms of aggression and antisocial behavior are most likely to be aggressive toward parents (Pagani *et al.*, 2004). "As adolescents, those described as chronically aggressive by their (annually) different primary school teachers were (9 and 4) times at greater risk of engaging in verbal and physical aggression (respectively) toward their mothers in comparison to their persistently nonaggressive peers" (Pagani *et al.*, 2004, p. 534). In fact, violent predispositions during childhood, measured by teachers, are among the best predictors of later violence toward mothers. "Indeed," Pagani *et al.* (2004) concluded in their study, "teacher-rated disruptiveness during early childhood predicted the risk of engaging in physical aggression toward mothers during adolescence" (p. 220).

Multiassaultive Families

Some families, referred to as **multiassaultive families**, are characterized by continual cycles of intrafamilial physical aggression and violence. Siblings hit each other, spouses hit each other, parents hit the children, and the older children hit the parents. According to the available data, at least 7 percent of all intact families may be considered multiassaultive (Hotaling & Straus, 1989). As noted previously, child maltreatment often accompanies intimate partner violence (Briggs, Thompson, *et al.*, 2011).

Research supports the notion that assault is a generalized pattern in interpersonal relations that crosses settings and is used across targets beyond the immediate family (Hotaling & Straus, 1989). Men in families in which children and wives are assaulted are five times more likely to have also assaulted a nonfamily person than are men in nonassaultive families. A similar pattern holds for women from multiassaultive families, although the relationship is not as strong. Sibling violence is particularly high in families in which child assault and spouse assault are present, with boys displaying significantly more assaultive behavior (Hotaling & Straus, 1989). Moreover, children from multiassaultive families have an inordinately high rate of assault against nonfamily members (Hotaling & Straus, 1989). These children are also more likely to be involved in property crime, to have adjustment difficulties in school, and to be involved with police (Hotaling & Straus, 1989). It should be carefully noted that it is extremely difficult to tell what is causing what in this complicated web of interrelated variables. Nevertheless, it is quite clear that multiassaultive family members are violent and antisocial across a variety of settings, toward both family members and society in general, and may demonstrate this behavioral pattern throughout most of their lifetimes.

The Cycle of Violence

For some time, the scholarly and popular literature has concluded that both abusive parents and abusive spouses have themselves been the victims of family violence during their childhoods (Megargee, 1982). Some research suggests that highly violent offenders may have been subjected to more severe and frequent physical and psychological abuse and punitive parenting during their childhoods than other offenders (Hämäläinen & Haapasalo, 1996). Individuals grow up to be abusive because they were abused themselves, a belief referred to as the **cycle-of-violence hypothesis**.

According to social learning theory, those who receive harsh discipline learn that physical violence can be used to change the behaviors of others (Schwartz, Hage, Bush, & Burns, 2006). **Coercion development theory**, proposed by Patterson (1982) and discussed in Chapter 6, also posits that coercive and punitive tactics in parenting increase the likelihood of later aggressive behavior and potential domestic violence. Theories that view domestic violence as a tactic for gaining power and control in relationships are highly consistent with coercion theory. As noted by Schwartz *et al.* (2006), "Men involved in intimate violence have been found to have demand and/or withdraw patterns of communication with their partners and perceive themselves as lacking power in their relationships" (p. 212). Consequently, abusing spouses and other family members is one way, in the abuser's eyes, of gaining and maintaining control over those in their immediate social environment. There is also accumulating evidence that males who experience parental neglect during their childhoods are more likely to engage in dating violence, a behavior that is a precursor to spousal abuse (Chapple, 2003; Simons, Lin, & Gordon, 1998).

Nevertheless, violence does not necessarily beget violence. The cycle of violence and the presumed overall consequences of abuse and neglect do not take into account the resilience of human beings, which rules out any simple cause-and-effect relationship between maltreatment and future violent behavior (Garbarino, 1989). In many cases, rather than finding that abusive parenting is the logical consequence of being victimized as children, the opposite sequence is likely to take place. Realizing and sensitive to the enormous psychological and social costs of family violence, many victims of child abuse may be even less likely than their nonabused peers to commit aggressive acts as adults within their families. Garbarino (1989, p. 222), for example, writes, "Many victims of child abuse, probably most, survive it and avoid repeating the pattern in their own child rearing."

On the other hand, children who are maltreated are at risk of further *victimization* as adults; this is particularly true, but not exclusively, of children who were sexually abused. The revictimization is usually through intimate partner violence (Briggs, Thompson, *et al.*, 2011). Thus, while the cycle of violence may be broken in the sense that the child victim does not, as adult, victimize others, the thread of violence continues because the child is revictimized as an adult.

The Effects of Family Violence on Children

Domestic violence is recognized as a serious problem in our society today, but how such violence affects the children who are exposed to it did not appear in the research literature until the 1980s. Children who are exposed to violence between adults in their homes have often been referred to as the "silent," "forgotten," and "unintended" victims of domestic violence. These children were initially referred to as simply "witnesses" or "observers," but recent research literature has discovered that some not only are directly involved victims themselves but also suffer some troubling consequences.

Children experience domestic violence through a bewildering array of events. Most often, children see or hear the violence, and they are often directly targeted, sometimes fatally. In a recent incident, a 13-year-old boy was the only survivor in a family mass shooting during which the father shot his mother and two younger siblings before turning the gun on himself. The father had shot at the 13-year-old, but missed. According to news reports, the boy ran around the garage with his hands lifted in the air in a surrender gesture before fleeing to the home of a neighbor. Other children experience family violence by trying to intervene or calling 911 (Edleson, 1999). Additional examples include the assaulter taking the child hostage to force the mother's return, using a child as a physical weapon against the victim, forcing the child to watch the violence, forcing the child to participate in the abuse, and using the child as a spy or questioning the child about the mother's activities (Ganley & Schechter, 1996). In another recent incident, a man tied up and brutally sexually assaulted his wife in front of their three children. Any of these experiences can leave lasting imprints on a child or adolescent.

Experiencing the aftermath of the violence may be equally traumatic for children (Edleson, 1999). Examples include the child seeing the mother with physical injuries and possibly in need of medical help, observing maternal emotions (such as anxiety, depression, stress), and having the family move to a shelter for battered women to escape further abuse. If the family has pets, leaving the pet behind can be intensely traumatizing for the child—and often the pet is abused as well. The aftermath of violence can also include a father alternating between physical violence and loving care, as well as police intervention that could result in the removal of the father from the home. In some instances, removal of the children from the home by child welfare agencies is also a terrifying possibility.

The number of children exposed to domestic violence in the United States each year is largely unknown, despite the fact that domestic violence appears to be on the decrease (Finkelhor, 2011). Straus (1991, p. 136) estimates that "at least a third of Americans have witnessed violence between their parents, and most have endured repeated instances." This estimation is based on Straus and Gelles's (1990) national survey that discovered that the 30 percent of parents who admitted domestic violence existed in their home also reported that their children had witnessed at least one violent incident during the length of the marriage.

Early research found that 13 percent to 27 percent of adults recall witnessing physical violence during their childhood years between their parents (Forrstrom-Cohen & Rosenbaum, 1985). Recent research indicates that nearly one-third of children living with two parents have witnessed domestic violence between their parents (Margolin & Vickerman, 2011). Police arrest data from five U.S. cities revealed that children were directly involved in adult domestic violence incidents about 27 percent of the time (Fantuzzo, Boruch, Abdullahi, Atkins, & Marcus, 1997). Fantuzzo *et al.* also found that younger children were disproportionately represented in households where domestic violence occurred. Another study (Silvern *et al.*, 1995) found that exposure to domestic violence may be even higher in some populations. Silvern and colleagues found that 118 (41.1%) of the 287 college women and 85 (32.2%) of the 263 college men surveyed had witnessed abuse by one parent against the other.

Explanations about how domestic violence affects a child must include an assortment of already existing risk factors. The child's age, the nature and severity of the violence, socioeconomic status, and parental substance abuse all must be entered into the equation.

The child's behavioral and emotional functioning is the area that has received the most attention from researchers. According to Margolin and Vickerman (2011, p. 63), frequent exposure to domestic violence between their parents represents "one of the most common and severe adverse events during childhood." Overall, studies report the consistent finding that children exposed to domestic violence exhibit many behavioral and emotional problems when compared with other children. For instance, studies using the Child Behavior Checklist (Achenbach & Edelbrock, 1983) and similar measures have found that children who are exposed to domestic violence display more aggressive and antisocial behaviors as well as fearful and inhibited behaviors (Fantuzzo et al., 1991; Hughes, 1988; Hughes, Parkinson, & Vargo, 1989), and show lower social competence and interpersonal skills than other children (Adamson & Thompson, 1998; Fantuzzo et al., 1991; Hughes, 1988). More aggressive and antisocial behaviors are often referred to as "externalized" behaviors, while fearful and inhibited behaviors are referred to as "internalized" behaviors (Carlson, 1991; Edleson, 1999; Stagg, Wills, & Howell, 1989).

Domestic violence has also been shown to have dramatic negative effects on children's emotional health and overall adjustment. Both boys and girls in families with spousal violence demonstrate far more depression and aggression (McClosky, Figueredo, & Koss, 1995; Wolfe, Jaffe, Wilson, & Zak, 1985) and lower self-esteem (Hughes & Barad, 1983) compared with other children. In addition, children who are exposed to violence between parents are more likely to show anxiety, depression, trauma symptoms, and temperamental problems (Hughes, 1988; Maker, Kemmelmeier, & Peterson, 1998).

Another consequence of experiencing violence within the home is the overall effects it has on the child's immediate and long-term cognitive functioning and attitudes about how to deal with violence and conflict resolution in their own lives. Many researchers conclude that children's exposure to adult domestic violence may generate attitudes justifying their own use of violence to solve problems and deal with frustrations. For example, Spaccarelli, Coatsworth, and Bowden's (1995) study found support for such an association by showing that, among a sample of 213 adolescent boys incarcerated for violent crimes, those boys who had experienced family violence were more likely to subscribe to the viewpoint that "acting aggressively enhances one's reputation or self-image" (p. 173). And Carlson (1991) reports that in a sample of 101 adolescents, boys who witnessed domestic violence were significantly more likely to approve of violence than were girls who had witnessed domestic violence.

In conclusion, the empirical evidence reveals that children's exposure to domestic violence is a serious and widespread problem. Such violence affects children indirectly through its effect on the parenting relationship, as well as directly affecting children's behavioral, emotional, cognitive, psychological, and social adjustment.

Cessation of Family Violence

Although theories of family violence are underdeveloped, the effectiveness of various procedures or strategies to reduce family violence can still be tested. Unfortunately, up to the last years of the twentieth century there were few systematic evaluations of the effectiveness of particular strategies in combating family violence (Elliott, 1989). Furthermore, coordinated efforts at gathering data and assessing methods of preventing and treating family violence in general and child victimization in particular were lacking.

In the late twentieth century, the National Center on Child Abuse and Neglect (NCCAN) funded the collaborative effort, LONGSCAN, which is intended to follow and track over 1,000 children and their families from early childhood years through adolescence. Preventive and support services are offered through social service agencies, and data are collected that should aid in both identifying the causes of family violence and the provision of effective services.

Much of the contemporary work and commentary has been directed at reducing wife abuse or male abuse of female intimate partners. Fagan (1989) hypothesizes that a large segment of the rewards and support men receive for abusing women derives from a long-standing cultural stereotype that men must be dominant and show women who is boss. One very "masculine" way of achieving and maintaining this expected dominance is through physical aggression and, if necessary, some violence. Some of the reinforcement comes from the satisfaction of maintaining this physical dominance and the positive social status that accompanies domination over women, particularly wives, advocated by one's peer group and subculture. Accordingly, men subscribing to this subculture socialize together, drink together, and participate in male-oriented recreation activities, generally excluding their wives from these activities. This male subculture provides a social milieu that supports and encourages traditional male dominance in male–female relationships, even if it requires violence now and then. Frequent contacts with this exclusive male subculture by the husband, combined with increasing social isolation of the wife, are particularly associated with the more severe forms of wife abuse (Bowker, 1983; Fagan, 1989). Presumably, the more deeply immersed into this subculture a man is, the more likely he is to batter his wife.

To what extent some women also support this male-dominating tradition is largely unknown, but knowledge about the degree to which women explicitly or implicitly favor this belief system may be extremely important in a deeper understanding of the dynamics of the relationship. This is not to imply that a subculture that supports male domination in a marriage necessarily advocates violence in carrying out this dominance, but research does suggest that many wife batterers manage to isolate their families socially while receiving considerable encouragement and support for physical aggression from their social network of friends.

An effective way of breaking the wife- or female partner–abuse cycle, therefore, is to change the abuser's attitudinal system and social network of friends who support or at least condone physical male domination of family relationships. Obviously, this strategy will not be easy to apply in many abusive behavioral patterns. Abusers have had a lifelong learning experience in developing belief systems, and probably have had considerable reinforcement history for their aggressive actions toward women from their subculture. "Leaving the subculture is not unlike leaving the world of the addict or the alcoholic" (Fagan, 1989, p. 408).

Initiating motivation to change a behavioral pattern of abuse often requires establishing a series of situations where the psychological costs for the abuse outweigh its psychological benefits. Legal sanctions may be one way, but many batterers realize that these sanctions are normally weak and without teeth. However, serious attempts by the criminal justice system to put some bite into these legal sanctions (such as arrests, criminal charges, and conviction) may begin to prove effective over the long haul, provided that they are accompanied by community support systems for the woman. It is important to note that it is unlikely that any one arrest or single event will promote a wish to change. It is more likely that a series of aversive and costly events, such as strong legal sanctions, combined with social sanctions from the community (public disclosure, visits by social agencies) and emotional sanctions from the victim (reporting the abuse to authorities, leaving the home, separating, threatening divorce) will wear the abuser down to a point at which he makes a decision to change his behavioral patterns.

However, the more severe and protracted the violence is, the more difficult it may be to stop, despite formal external interventions—legal or otherwise (Fagan, 1989). Legal and social sanctions for spouse abuse may work for less chronic and severe situations. However, legal sanctions, regardless of the nature and strength of the sanction, may not only be ineffective for the more serious cases, but could possibly lead to escalation in violence. Therefore, social, legal, and emotional sanctions may be more effective with individuals who do not have an extensive history of repetitive and serious violence.

Summary and Conclusions

In this chapter, we began to narrow our focus to consider specific offenses. Previous chapters were broader, in that they dealt with general theoretical orientations to crime. Here, we reviewed the major sociological data on violence and summarized empirical and clinical research on family violence.

Sociological and official data indicate that homicides are rare compared with the total incidence of violent crime. In the United States, violent crime is often committed by young males living in environments that implicitly or explicitly advocate violence for the resolution of conflict. Guns (especially handguns) are commonly used in the crime. Certain minority groups are overrepresented in violent crime statistics, but there are a number of explanations for this that have nothing to do with racial or ethnically based individual factors. Statistics indicate also that, when the relationship of victim and offender is known, the homicide victim and the offender are usually family members, friends, or acquaintances. The relationship is known in between half to two-thirds of the offenses. While assaults are far more common than homicide, the same sociological features appear, particularly for aggravated assault.

While many of the psychological characteristics of offenders are similar in crimes of assault and homicide, some homicides deserve separate attention. These include the homicides that will be covered in the next chapter, and juvenile murders, which were covered here. Juvenile murders are rare, but when they occur they attract both media and research attention. Researchers have learned that juvenile murderers who act on their own or in a dyad (as opposed to killing as gang activity) often have no significant history of violence, but often come from dysfunctional families, have poor peer relationships, and have emotional and sometimes biological deficiencies—such as brain damage. The Dartmouth murder illustration used in this chapter seems atypical; the psychopathic features discussed in Chapter 7 might be relevant in that case, but we stress that not enough information is available to draw firm conclusions.

Family violence is a very broad subject that encompasses child abuse, spouse or partner abuse, elder abuse, sibling abuse, and child-to-parent abuse. Researchers increasingly use the term *intimate partner abuse* to convey that victims and perpetrators can occupy separate households or be former intimate acquaintances. Abuse comes in many forms, including physical, psychological, or sexual abuse. Family violence is found across ethnic, racial, and socioeconomic classes. Women are disproportionately subject to spousal violence and the dire economic situations that may lead to both victimization and victimizing. Children are particularly vulnerable targets for family violence and maltreatment, enduring physical maltreatment, sexual exploitation, medical and emotional neglect, and psychological trauma—all of which are usually lifelong in their consequences. In this chapter, we focused not only on "typical" forms of child abuse, but also on statistics and research relating to child abductions, shaken baby syndrome, Munchausen syndrome by proxy, and infanticide. For the child who survives abuse, the psychological consequences can nevertheless be devastating. Though he or she does not necessarily become an abuser, perpetuating the cycle of abuse, emotional scars relating to one's self-concept and the ability to trust others are often very deep and longlasting.

In addition to the obvious physical injuries and deaths that result, family violence is often cited in research and clinical studies as contributing to other individual, family, and societal problems. Most of all, family violence and maltreatment highlight the importance of considering a victimological approach for the complete understanding of violent crime and underscore the fact that the family is far

from being a safe haven for many. Factors such as family instability and violence have been consistently found to be prevalent among juveniles who engage in sexually abusive and violent behavior (Righthand & Welch, 2001). Many studies conclude that abused children have trouble recognizing appropriate emotions in others, have less empathy for others, and have difficulty taking another person's perspective (Knight & Prentky, 1993). It is very likely that many of the life-course-persistent (LCP) offenders discussed elsewhere in the text spring from families characterized by abuse, violence, and neglect.

Key Concepts

Aggravated assault
Assault
Availability heuristic
Battered woman syndrome
    (BWS)
Coercion development theory
Criminal homicide
Cycle-of-violence hypothesis
Dynamic cascade model
Eldercide
Filicide

Fratricide
General altercation homicide
Hostile attribution bias
Infanticide
Intimate partner violence (IPV)
Matricide
Multiassaultive families
Munchausen syndrome
    by proxy (MSBP)
Murder
Negligent manslaughter

Nonnegligent manslaughter
Neonaticide
Parricide
Patricide
Shaken baby syndrome
Self-regulation
Siblicide
Sororicide
Stereotypical abductions
Typology
Weapons effect

Review Questions

1. What is the availability heuristic? How might it account for our perception of violence?
2. What are the psychological effects of (a) child abuse and (b) other domestic violence on children?
3. Define "battered woman syndrome" and briefly state the controversy associated with it.
4. Define each of the following: neonaticide, parricide, infanticide, filicide, eldercide, homicide.
5. Define "weapons effect" and how it might contribute to violence in our society.

6. What is the cycle-of-violence hypothesis?
7. Explain how juvenile homicide is different from adult homicide.
8. Compare and contrast shaken baby syndrome and Munchausen syndrome by proxy as specific forms of child abuse.
9. Discuss eldercide as a form of family violence, including its prevalence, perpetrators, and etiology.

10

Multiple Murder, School Violence, and Workplace Violence

CHAPTER OBJECTIVES

▪ Define and review research on investigative psychology and profiling.

▪ Describe the five types of profiling and their relevance to investigating serious crime.

▪ Summarize what is known about serial killers and their victims.

▪ Summarize what is known about mass murderers and their victims.

▪ Discuss crime that can lead to multiple murder, such as school and workplace violence.

This chapter takes a more detailed look at criminal homicide, including several psychology-related investigative methods commonly used to identify offenders. We will revisit criminal homicide, but focus more on serial murder, mass murder, and the violence at schools and the workplace that ends in death. Terrorism, which often involves multiple killings, will be covered in some detail in the next chapter. Although the homicides covered in this chapter are relatively rare, the social and emotional impact they have on a community—and on a society as a whole—is considerable. The fear and terror they engender can alter the lifestyles of thousands. Moreover, they draw extensive media coverage; some of it is accurate, but much of it lacks a solid understanding of the psychosocial aspects involved in the crime. Therefore, it is important that we give some attention to what we know—and do not know—about these well-publicized offenses. Finally, we end the chapter by discussing some of the current psychological theories and research that try to explain contemporary violence.

INVESTIGATIVE PSYCHOLOGY

Before discussing the various categories of multiple murder, it is important that we consider contemporary research on psychology's efforts to shed some light on this phenomenon. In recent years, considerable public attention has been given to topics like profiling and investigative psychology. Readers are undoubtedly familiar with popular movies and television shows (e.g., *Silence of the Lambs, Criminal Minds*) that feature these activities. In one season of *CSI*, we learned that the team leader—played then by actor Laurence Fishburne—formerly taught courses on the psychology of homicide. In an early episode, he was seen introducing his class—via webcam—to an imprisoned serial killer, allowing them to pose questions in order to help them understand the mind of a killer. The popular series *Criminal Minds* includes actors portraying behavioral scientists who work within the FBI's Behavioral Science Unit (BSU). Although the various types of profiling are not restricted to the serious crimes that are the subject of this chapter, profilers often focus on those serious, and sometimes sensational, crimes.

In the professional and academic world, the word *profiling* is often avoided. There are many reasons for this. First, because the activity is unregulated in the United States, persons with minimum degrees or experience can call themselves profilers; some have attained celebrity status, appearing for media interviews and writing in ongoing blogs. At times their "predictions" have been extremely inaccurate. Second, these profilers tend to rely on "hunches" rather than on scientific data. While hunches based on clinical experience are understandable, those without data to back them up are problematic. We discuss this in more detail below. Third, some profilers in the past have written self-serving personal accounts of their experiences that minimize the imperfect nature of their art. And finally, depictions of profilers in novels or entertainment media too often suggest they are infallible and can solve most crimes. For these reasons, to bring more respectability to the profiling enterprise, some professionals prefer to call themselves "behavioral analysts" or "investigative psychologists" rather than profilers.

Investigative psychology, a term coined by David Canter, the director of the Centre for Investigative Psychology at the University of Liverpool in England, refers to the application of psychological research and principles to the investigation of criminal behavior. Investigative psychology tries to answer three fundamental questions that are crucial in criminal investigations (Canter & Alison, 2000, p. 3):

1. What are the important behavioral features of the crime that may help identify and successfully prosecute the perpetrator?
2. What inferences can be made about the characteristics of the offender that may help identify him or her?
3. Are there any other crimes that are likely to have been committed by the same person?

These questions are central to investigative psychology, and they are rapidly being addressed in the United States as well as the United Kingdom, where it is fair to say that this *scientific* approach to criminal investigation—from a psychological perspective—originated. In recent years psychologists worldwide have embraced the need to accumulate data based on empirical research in order to consult with investigators looking to solve crimes. In the United States, for example, members of the Society for Police and Criminal Psychology as well as members of the Police and Public Safety Section of Division 18 of the American Psychological Association conduct research relevant to investigative psychology and consult with the law enforcement community.

In this chapter, because the term *profiling* remains in widespread use, we will retain it in our discussion of the various forms of profiling as well as the research on its effectiveness. However, as in other published work (Bartol & Bartol, 2013), we subdivide profiling into five distinct types. It should be emphasized, though, that the investigation of crime may involve more than one of these forms.

PROFILING

The term *profiling* is used to describe the gathering of various kinds of information about a person or persons. It can be divided into five somewhat overlapping categories, not all of which are equally relevant to the topic of this chapter: (1) psychological profiling; (2) suspect-based profiling;

TABLE 10-1	Summary of Primary Investigative Methods Used by Five Types of Profiling
Type of Profiling	**Primary Investigative Method**
Crime scene	Information from the scene of the crime
Psychological	Risk assessment methods and procedures
Geographic	Computer models of typical spatial behavioral patterns of offenders
Suspect-based	Base-rate information of previous offenders
Equivocal death analysis	Interview and background information

(3) geographic profiling; (4) crime scene profiling; and (5) equivocal death analysis. Although we give attention to each type, the last one is the least likely to be relevant to multiple murders.

Each of these profiling methods—and the investigators who employ these methods—relies on different ways to analyze the person, the crime scene, or the incident. **Table 10-1** summarizes the primary investigative methods used in the different forms of profiling.

Some of the profiling categories rely on either the **clinical** or **actuarial** approach. The clinical approach is *case focused* and tries to infer characteristics of an offender from the analysis of evidence gathered from a specific crime or series of crimes (Alison, West, & Goodwill, 2004). The method concentrates on the description, understanding, and prediction of a *single* offender based on the material gathered on an *individual* case. It is based on the premise that every case is unique, and often emphasizes discovering the motivation for the crime as a basic understanding of the offender. The clinical approach relies heavily on experience and training, and is often supplemented by intuition, subjectivity, and sometimes "gut feelings."

On the other hand, the actuarial approach concentrates on a database gathered from groups of offenders who have committed similar crimes or engaged in similar incidents. This profiling tactic is based on how groups of offenders who have committed similar crimes have acted in the past. The accumulated data from these groups of behavioral patterns are called the **base rates**. Base rate is defined as "the unconditional, naturally occurring rate of a phenomenon in a population" (VandenBos, 2007, p. 103). If, for example, 65 out of 100 killers move the body from the crime scene, the profiler can conclude that it is more likely than not that the body was moved. If 90 out of 100 moved the body, there is a high probability that the body was moved.

Psychological Profiling

Psychological profiling is an assessment practice designed to help in the identification and prediction of behavior in individuals. As a general concept, it is not limited to negative characteristics. For example, psychological profiling may be used to predict positive characteristics in candidates for law enforcement or even for public office (Bartol & Bartol, 2013). For our purposes, however, we focus on profiling of negative characteristics, such as those that may be associated with criminal behavior. In that sense, psychological profiling consists of two basic approaches: threat assessment and risk assessment. Threat assessment is the process of determining the validity and seriousness of threat being carried out by a person or group of persons. In most cases, the threat has already been made and is generally directed at a person, facility, institution, organization, or group of persons. Therefore, threat assessment might be employed in the case of a high school student who has indicated online that he plans to "take out" the school, or an employee who displays uncharacteristic, bizarre behavior. Each of these situations will be discussed later in the chapter.

Risk assessment—which was covered in Chapter 8—comes into play even if no direct threat has been made. Risk assessment is a process to evaluate "individuals who have violated social norms or displayed bizarre behavior, particularly when they appear menacing or unpredictable" (Hanson, 2009, p. 172). The primary goal of risk assessment is to estimate the probability that a particular person will harm self or others, and more importantly, to suggest what can be done to prevent the harm.

Suspect-Based Profiling

Suspect-based profiling, also known as prospective profiling, refers to identifying the psychological and behavioral features of persons who may commit a particular crime, such as school violence, terrorist activities, stalking, drug trafficking, shoplifting, or skyjacking. For example, is there a "profile" of a school shooter? We address this question later in the chapter. Suspect-based profiling is built on the systematic collection of behavioral, personality, cognitive, and demographic data on previous offenders who committed similar crimes. Therefore, suspect-based profiling is largely actuarial because it uses statistical methods rather than clinical skills to arrive at conclusions about who is likely to commit the crime.

Suspect-based profiling is often used at airports and border crossings to interdict drugs and out of concern for terrorist activities. Recently, the U.S. Transportation Safety Administration (TSA) has trained behavioral detection officers (BDOs) to observe air passengers for behavior clues—presumably identified by systematic research—that may indicate intentions to harm. Unfortunately, this type of profiling is susceptible to racial or ethnic profiling, though the TSA stresses the focus is on behavior, not race or ethnicity. Racial profiling is defined as "police-initiated action that relies on the race, ethnicity, or national origin rather than the behavior of an individual or information that leads the police to a particular individual who has been identified as being, or having been, engaged in criminal activity" (Ramirez, McDevitt, & Farrell, 2000, p. 3).

Racial profiling is an illegal practice, though it is difficult to prove that it occurred. However, it is a practice that accounts in part for the fact that racial and ethnic minorities are disproportionately represented in arrest statistics. Furthermore, racial profiling illustrates the dangers and inaccuracies of the profiling enterprise that could affect many in the population.

Racial profiling is not new, but it was not until the 1990s that it began to be seen as a nationwide problem. Apparent incidents of racial profiling were experienced so commonly by people of color that they began to label the phenomenon "driving while black" or "driving while brown" (commonly abbreviated DWB), as a play on the legally accepted term *DWI* (driving while intoxicated or impaired). Since the terrorist attacks of September 11, 2001, increased scrutiny of persons of Muslim backgrounds has been reported. As we noted earlier in the book, bias crimes against these individuals have increased as well.

Geographic Profiling

Geographic profiling is a technique that can help locate where a serial offender resides, or other locations that serve as a base of operations of an offender , such as a bar, place of work, or significant other's home. Geographic profiling depends, in most cases, on computer software programs to complete the analysis. Currently, there are three popular ones: Rigel, Crimestat, and Dragnet. Rigel was developed out of the work of D. Kim Rossmo, who was the first police officer in Canada to obtain a PhD in criminology.

In 1995, Rossmo completed a doctoral dissertation on the method of geographic profiling that has emerged as a promising tool for serial offender identification. He also developed a computer program called "Criminal Geographic Targeting," or CGT, which was designed to analyze the geographic or spatial characteristics of an offender's crimes. The CGT generates a three-dimensional map that assigns statistical probabilities to various areas that seem to fall into the offender's territory. The three-dimensional map is then placed over a street or topographical map where the crimes have occurred. The program considers known movement patterns, possible comfort zones, and victim-searching patterns of the offender. Ultimately, the objective of the program is to pinpoint the location of the offender's residence and/or base of operations. The CGT program has been incorporated into the Rigel and Rigel Analyst software applications (Rich & Shively, 2004). Crimestat was developed by Ned Levine and Associates (2000, 2002) and was funded by the National Institute of Justice. Dragnet was developed by David Canter (2008).

Rossmo's research has focused heavily on serial offenders, particularly those who offend against persons. He identified four "hunting patterns" violent serial offenders use in their search for victims: (1) hunter, (2) poacher, (3) troller, and (4) trapper. Rossmo (1997) wrote, "Hunters are those criminals who specifically set out from their residence to look for victims, searching through the areas in their awareness space that they believe contain suitable targets" (p. 167). The hunters are geographically stable in that their crimes usually occur near the offender's residence or neighborhood. Poachers are more transient, traveling some distance from their neighborhood in their search for suitable victims. The troller, on the other hand, does not specifically search for victims but depends on random encounters during the course of other activities. The trapper creates situations (traps) to entice victims to come to him.

Geographic profiling, therefore, can help in any criminal investigation of an unknown offender by locating the approximate area in which he or she lives, or by narrowing the surveillance and stakeouts to places where the next crime by the offender is most likely to occur. The process can be highly complex and technical, involving far more than placing push-pins on a map. This type of profiling basically tries to identify the geographic territory the offender knows well, feels most comfortable in, and prefers to find or take victims in (Rossmo, 1997). Although a *criminal* profile hypothesizes about the demographic, motivational, and psychological features of the crime and offender, a geographic profile focuses on the location of the crime and how it relates to the residence and/or base of operations of the offender. Nevertheless, motivational and psychological features may be taken into account. Geographic profiling is useful not only in the search for serial violent offenders but also in the search for property offenders, such as serial burglars and serial arsonists. It is important to realize, however, that geographic profiling is essentially an investigative tool that does not necessarily solve crimes, but should help in identifying appropriate areas for surveillance, patrol saturation, stakeouts, and monitoring.

Crime Scene Profiling

Crime scene profiling, also called criminal profiling, offender profiling, crime scene analysis, or criminal investigative analysis, is the process of identifying personality traits, behavioral patterns, geographic habits, cognitive tendencies, and demographic features of an *unknown* offender based on *characteristics of the crime*. It can be considered a skill or an activity that is a part of the investigative psychology described earlier. Therefore, while investigative psychology is the broad application of psychological research and principles to solving crimes, crime scene profiling is the narrower activity that focuses on the traits, features, and habits of an unknown offender. Because it is highly relevant to many of the topics in the book, as well as to the material in the present chapter, crime scene profiling will be discussed in some detail here.

Descriptions or profiles of the general characteristics of a person on the basis of a limited amount of information were used long before the FBI employed such methods (Canter & Alison, 2000). In fact, the history of crime scene profiling can be traced at least as far back as Jack the Ripper, the serial killer who brutally murdered five prostitutes in separate incidents in London's East End in 1888. Although the case was never solved, the chief forensic pathologist, Dr. George Baxter Phillips, attempted to help police investigators by inferring personality characteristics based on the nature of the wounds inflicted on the victims (Turvey, 2012). That is, he noticed that the wounds were inflicted with considerable skill and knowledge, suggesting that the killer had a sophisticated knowledge of human anatomy. Interestingly, the fictional detective Sherlock Holmes, first created by Sir Arthur Conan Doyle in 1887, consistently employed a form of criminal profiling in his intriguing search for the offender. Since then, virtually every detective or mystery novel has the main characters engaging in some variant of criminal profiling.

Crime scene profiling was developed in the United States by the Behavioral Science Unit of the FBI during the 1970s. During its early development, it was used primarily to provide investigative assistance to law enforcement in cases of serial homicide and serial rape (Homant & Kennedy, 1998). In 1984, the National Center for the Analysis of Violent Crime (NCAVC)—located in the FBI Academy in Quantico, Virginia—was created and within it the Behavioral Analysis Unit (BAU) and the Violent Criminal Apprehension Program (ViCAP). Today, most of the crime scene profiling is conducted under the auspices of the BAU, although the BSU remains a separate unit that sponsors research and training, and works closely with the NCAVC. The approach of crime scene profiling during its early development was clinical.

John Douglas is a former FBI agent and former head of the Behavioral Science Unit of the FBI. He has published extensively on investigative methods and profiling. According to Douglas and Corinne Munn (1992a), three important features of offender behavior may be evident at the scene of a crime: (1) the *modus operandi*, (2) the personation or signature, and (3) staging. *Modus operandi* (the MO) refers to the actions and procedures an offender engages in to commit a crime successfully. It is a behavioral pattern that the offender learns as he or she gains experience in committing the offense. Since the offender generally changes the MO until he or she learns which method is most effective, or changes the MO to mislead investigators, some professional profilers believe that investigators may make a serious error if they place too much significance on the MO when linking crimes, however (Douglas & Munn, 1992c).

Anything that goes beyond what is necessary to commit the crime is called the **personation** or the **signature**. For example, a serial offender may demonstrate a repetitive, almost ritualistic behavior from crime to crime, an unusual pattern that is not necessary to commit the offense. The signature may involve certain items that are left or removed from the scene, or other symbolic patterns, such as writings on the wall. If the victim is murdered, the signature may include unusual body positions or mutilations. In very rare instances, the signature may involve a "DNA torch," where the offender pours gasoline over the genital areas of the victim and sets the victim and the structure or motor vehicle on fire in an effort to destroy any evidence of sexual assault. A signature may also involve the repetitive acts of domination, manipulation, and control used by a serial rapist (Douglas & Munn, 1992b). Or it may be revealed by physical evidence found at the crime scene, such as the type of ligature used or the personal items taken from the victim by a serial rapist. The signature is often thought to be related to the unique cognitive processes of the offender and, in this sense, may be more important to an investigator than the MO. In most cases, signature behaviors often establish the theme of the crime for investigators, as they often reveal the psychological and emotional needs of the offender (Turvey, 2008).

Staging refers to the intentional alteration of a crime scene prior to the arrival of the police, and it is sometimes done by someone other than the perpetrator. As Douglas and Munn (1992a) note, staging is usually done for one of two reasons: either to redirect the investigation away from the most logical suspect, or to protect the victim or the victim's family. Staging is frequently done by someone who has an association or relationship with the victim. For example, staging done by the family with the intent to protect the victim may be seen in autoerotic fatalities. **Autoeroticism**, a term coined by Havelock Ellis, refers to self-arousal and self-gratification of sexual desire without a partner.

In some instances, the method of autoeroticism may result in the death of the individual, such as by self-strangulation or hanging. Douglas and Munn (1992a) assert that in about one-third of autoerotic fatalities, the victim is nude, and in about another one-third, the victim is clothed in a costume, such as a male in female clothing. Under these conditions, friends or family members may alter the scene to make the victim more "presentable" to the authorities. In some instances, they may even stage a criminal homicide, including ransacking the house or specific rooms to give the impression of a burglary gone wrong.

In some instances, an offender may engage in **undoing**, a behavioral pattern found at the scene in which the offender tries to psychologically "undo" the murder. For example, the offender may wash and dress the victim, or place the body on a bed, gently placing the head on a pillow and covering the body with blankets. This pattern typically occurs in offenders who become especially distraught about the death of the victim. Very often, the offender has a close association with the victim. In other cases, an offender may try to dehumanize the victim by engaging in actions that obscure the identity of the victim, such as excessive facial battery. Other offenders may employ more subtle acts of dehumanization, such as covering the victim's face with some material or object, or placing the victim facedown. Note that the difference between undoing and staging is the reason behind the action; in staging, the offender or someone else is trying to alter the crime scene in order to divert suspicion. In the classic case, the offender wipes fingerprints from a weapon and positions it close to the body in such a way that a death looks like a suicide.

Crime scenes and offenders are also sometimes classified as organized, disorganized, or mixed (see **Tables 10-2** and **10-3**). As we note shortly, however, this is not necessarily a valid classification as it pertains to offenders, although it is still used in profiling circles. An **organized crime scene** indicates planning and premeditation on the part of the offender. The crime scene shows signs that the offender maintained control of himself and the victim. Often, the victim is moved from the abduction area to another secluded area, and perhaps the body is moved to still another area. Furthermore, the offender in an organized crime usually selects victims according to some personal criteria. The infamous serial killer Ted Bundy, for example, selected young, attractive women who were similar in appearance. He was also successful in the abduction of these young women from highly visible areas, such as beaches, campuses, and ski lodges, indicating considerable planning and premeditation (Douglas, Ressler, Burgess, & Hartman, 1986).

A **disorganized crime scene** demonstrates that the offender very probably committed the crime without premeditation or planning. The crime scene indicators suggest the individual acted on impulse or in rage, or under extreme excitement. The disorganized offender obtains his victim by chance, often without specific criteria in mind. Generally, the victim's body is found at the scene of the crime. The **mixed crime scene** has ingredients of both organized and disorganized crime aspects. For example, a crime may have begun as carefully planned, but deteriorated into a disorganized crime when things did not go as planned. In fact, the mixed crime scene is likely the most common type.

TABLE 10-2	Profile Characteristics of Organized and Disorganized Murderers as Classified by the FBI
Organized	**Disorganized**
Average to above-average intelligence	Below average intelligence
Socially competent	Socially inadequate
Skilled work preferred	Unskilled work
High birth order status	Low birth order status
Father's work stable	Father's work unstable
Sexually competent	Sexually incompetent
Inconsistent childhood discipline	Harsh discipline as a child
Controlled mood during crime	Anxious mood during crime
Use of alcohol with crime	Minimal use of alcohol
Precipitating situational stress	Minimal situational stress
Living with partner	Living alone
Mobility (car in good condition)	Lives/works near crime scene
Follows crime in news media	Minimal interest in news media
May change job or leave town	Significant behavior change

Source: Federal Bureau of Investigation (1985), p. 19.

TABLE 10-3	Crime Scene Differences Between Organized and Disorganized Murderers as Classified by the FBI
Organized	**Disorganized**
Planned offense	Spontaneous offense
Victim a targeted stranger	Victim/location known
Personalizes victim	Depersonalizes victim
Controlled conversation	Minimal conversation
Crime scene reflects control	Crime scene random and sloppy
Demands submissive victim	Sudden violence to victim
Restraints used	Minimal use of restraints
Aggressive acts prior to death	Sexual acts after death
Body hidden	Body left in view
Weapon/evidence absent	Weapon/evidence often present
Transports victim or body	Body left at death scene

Source: Federal Bureau of Investigation (1985), p. 19.

Although the organized–disorganized classification system seems intuitively logical, it appears to have very limited usefulness as an investigative tool (Canter, Alison, Alison, & Wentink, 2004; Kocsis, Cooksey, & Irwin, 2002). In fact, Snook, Cullen, Bennell, Taylor, and Gendreau (2008) report that, at this point, there is no convincing evidence to support the dichotomy. It may be more realistic to assume that crime scenes fall along a continuum, with the organized description at one pole and the disorganized description at the other pole, but with few crimes being at either pole.

The practice of crime scene profiling is utilized by police agencies across the world (Snook et al., 2008). Many police investigators and detectives indicate they find it useful in their investigations of certain crime. In one survey reported by Snook et al. (2008), 8 out of 10 police officers in the United Kingdom found criminal profiling helpful in their investigations and said they would seek profiling help again. In an exploratory Internet survey of forensic psychologists and psychiatrists, Torres, Boccaccini, and Miller (2006) found that 40 percent of these professionals thought that criminal profiling was scientifically reliable and valid. Unfortunately these perceptions are not supported by the research, as we will see shortly.

Profiling appears to be particularly useful in serial sexual offenses, such as serial rape and serial sexual homicides (Pinizzotto & Finkel, 1990). This is because we have a more extensive research base on sexual offending than we do on homicide. In addition, profiling of serial offenders is most successful when the offender demonstrates some form of psychopathology at the crime scene, such as torture, evisceration, postmortem slashing and cutting, and other mutilation (Pinizzotto, 1984). However, profiling is largely ineffective at this time in the identification of offenders involved in fraud, burglary, robbery, political crimes, theft, and drug-induced crime because of the limited research base, although significant gains in some of these areas have been made in recent years.

Research on Crime Scene Profiling

There has been very little published research on the utility, reliability, and validity of crime scene profiling in general (Alison, Smith, & Morgan, 2003; Woodworth & Porter, 2001), although some studies have attempted to assess its accuracy. One pioneering study was conducted by Pinizzotto and Finkel (1990). The study involved four trained FBI experts, six trained police detectives, six experienced detectives without training, six clinical psychologists naive about crime scene profiling, and six untrained undergraduate students. The results, in general, were not strongly supportive of profile accuracy. Trained experts were somewhat more accurate in profiling the sexual offender, but were not much better than the untrained groups in profiling the homicide offender. The researchers also tried to identify any qualitative differences in the way experts and nonexperts processed the information provided. Overall, the results showed that experts did not process the material any differently than the nonexperts. This finding suggests that the cognitive methods and strategies used by expert profilers are not discernibly different from the way nonexperts process the available information about the crime. The artificiality of the experiment and the quality of information given by the groups may have been influential factors in this observation, however. What the researchers did find is that some trained profilers were more interested and skillful in certain areas than other profilers. Some profilers, for example, were good at gaining information from the medical reports, whereas others were better at gaining clues from the crime scene photos. This finding indicates that group profiling by a team of trained experts may be more effective than utilizing one single profiler.

Despite media portrayals of highly successful and probing profilers employing sophisticated techniques and thoughtful strategies for identifying the offender, reality is far more sobering. Contemporary researchers on profiling (Alison, Bennell, Omerod, & Mokros, 2002; Alison & Canter, 1999) point out that there are two basic flaws in modern-day profiling. One flaw is the assumption that human behavior is *consistent* across a variety of *different* situations. The other flaw is the assumption that offense style or evidence gathered at the crime scene is directly related to specific personality characteristics. Psychology has consistently found that behavior varies according to situations or the social context, especially if the social contexts are significantly different. Moreover, there is little empirical data that link crime scene characteristics to personality or other psychological features of the offender. Snook *et al.* (2008) write,

> Criminal profilers do not seem to recognize that a consensus began to emerge in the psychological literature some 40 years ago that to rely on traits or personality dispositions as the primary explanation for behavior was a serious mistake. Situational factors contribute as much as personality dispositions to the prediction of behavior. (p. 1261)

There are other problems with profiling as well. Some studies point out that a large proportion of the conclusions and predictions contained within profile reports are both ambiguous and unverifiable (Alison, Smith, Eastman, & Rainbow, 2003; Alison, Smith, & Morgan, 2003; Snook, Eastwood, Gendreau, Goggin, & Cullen, 2007). Many of the statements are so vague that they are open to a wide range of interpretations. Compounding the problem is the tendency for police investigators to interpret the ambiguous information contained within the profile report to fit their own biases and hunches about the case or the suspect. They select those aspects of the report that they see as fitting their own cognitive sketch of the suspect while ignoring the conclusions and predictions in the report that do not fit. This powerful tendency is known in psychology as **confirmation bias**. We are all subject to confirmation bias to some extent, but being aware of it may lessen its impact.

The above points underscore the fact that many individuals who call themselves profilers are prone to rely on outdated personality theory and psychological principles, and are basically unfamiliar with the current research literature on profiling and human behavior in general. Some believe that profiling is best done on "gut feelings" and "instinct" based on many years of experience of crime scene investigations. On the other hand, some professional profilers indicate that their profiling strategies are effective and are founded on extensive databases and clinical expertise (Dern, Dern, Horn, & Horn, 2009). The potential usefulness of crime scene profiling is too critical to be relegated to the entertainment media and questionable applications by law enforcement. It is important, therefore, that we learn how reliable and valid the various profiling methods currently utilized are, and how they can be improved to allow meaningful application in forensic settings.

Contemporary Perspectives on Crime Scene or Offender Profiling

To summarize, crime scene profiling is not about entering "the evil mind of the serial offender." The primary goal of a professional profiler is to provide information to investigators and law enforcement that is based on solid behavioral science (Rainbow & Gregory, 2011). Profilers are expected to offer advice and information that is based on empirical research on criminal behavior and up-to-date psychological principles. Recent research on profiling finds that it is more helpful to investigators if the profiler focuses on discovering how victims are chosen, how they are treated, the distance and routes traveled by the offender, and the nature of the forensic evidence left at the crime scene, especially if the evidence is unknowingly left by the offender. For example, there is a difference between a crime-scene signature and a psychological signature (Bartol & Bartol, 2013). As described earlier, a serial offender may demonstrate a repetitive, distinguishing behavior from crime to crime, an unusual pattern that is not necessary to commit the offense. The offender *intentionally* engages in this behavioral pattern to leave behind his or her trademark, the crime-scene signature. However, there is also a psychological signature left at the scene, which represents a habitual or repetitive behavioral pattern that an offender unknowingly leaves behind. A **psychological signature** is subtle but distinctive ways of speaking, thinking, behaving, and even problem solving *beyond the person's awareness*. It is the psychological signature that potentially provides keys to linking crimes and identifying aspects about the offending that ultimately may be helpful to investigators.

David Canter and his associates (Canter, 2000a, b) believe that an offender's style of committing a crime is a reflection of the offender's general lifestyle, not some special, unusual aspect of it. For example, how the offender treats the victim provides critical clues for the profiling process. That is, the manner in which the victim is treated and the role the offender assigns to the victim provide a distinctive pattern of how he treats others in his daily life. Offender actions that exhibit a distinctive theme and that are relatively unusual will provide the best clues for differentiating this crime from those committed by other offenders. More specifically, it is far more helpful to investigators if the offender's behavioral patterns differ from the broad database committed by other offenders who have committed similar crimes. Before this is possible, however, there must be a significant and systematic database of similar offender behavioral patterns. Some of the distinguishing clues are so subtle, however, that their identification takes a skillful and knowledgeable profiler to discover them. Furthermore, there should be some consistencies in the manner in which the offender carries out the crime from one incident to another, regardless of how indistinguishable it seems at first glance. And the consistencies may or may not be found in the modus operandi.

In summary, much more research needs to be done on profiling accuracy, usefulness, and processing before any tentative conclusions can be advanced in the area. Some positive steps have being made in that direction in recent years. Contrary to popular perceptions, crime scene profiling is not and should not be restricted to serial murder and serial sexual assaults. It has considerable potential value when applied competently to crimes such as arson, burglary, shoplifting, and robbery. Contemporary research has found situational factors to be critically important in profiling and predicting criminal behavior. Bennell and Canter (2002) and Bennell and Jones (2005) report in their studies of commercial and residential burglary that a high level of consistency exists when burglars choose the sites for their crimes. They found, for instance, that the distance between two crime locations was a very effective linking feature in that shorter distances between burglaries reliably signaled an increased likelihood that the same person committed the burglaries. Method of entry and items stolen, on the other hand, were not useful as profile indicators. The Bennell research demonstrates that some subsets of behavior do reveal consistent criminal patterns and may be very useful in the development of empirically based profiling methods and typologies.

Equivocal Death Analysis

Equivocal death analysis, also called **reconstructive psychological evaluation**, is the reconstruction of the emotional life, behavioral patterns, and cognitive features of a deceased person. In this sense, it is a postmortem psychological analysis and therefore is frequently referred to simply as a **psychological autopsy** (Brent, 1989; Ebert, 1987; Selkin, 1987). The psychological autopsy was first used to help medical officials determine the cause of deaths that were classified as ambiguous, uncertain, or equivocal (Shneidman, 1994). Today, equivocal death analysis or the psychological autopsy is most often done to determine whether the death was a suicide, and if it was a suicide, the reasons why the person did it. In other words, the individual conducting the autopsy tries to "reconstruct" what was in the mind of the decedent. In practice, equivocal death analysis usually relies on both clinical and actuarial approaches, depending on the investigator.

Equivocal death analysis (EDA) is only peripherally relevant to the subject of this chapter. It is usually relevant in the case of *single* murders, if there is question whether an individual committed suicide or was murdered. However, in some mass death situations, psychological autopsies have been conducted on individuals who also died in the incident in an effort to attribute blame. Perhaps the most noteworthy illustration of this is the explosion aboard the USS *Iowa* in 1989, which caused the death of 47 naval personnel. There was question whether the explosion was accidental or had been deliberately caused by a midshipman who was said to have been despondent and purposefully set off a detonation device. A psychological autopsy of the midshipman was conducted, and initially concluded that he had committed suicide, taking 46 others with him. Congressional committees, however, heard testimony from other psychologists who expressed concerns about the validity of the psychological autopsy and suggested the explosion was accidental.

In sum, the psychological autopsy involves the discovery and reconstruction of a deceased person's life based on the evidence left behind by that person. It is an investigation that entails revisiting the person's lifestyle, thought processes, and recent emotional and behavioral patterns prior to his or her death. It can be valuable in various forensic situations and circumstances, including insurance benefit determinations, worker's compensation cases, testamentary capacity cases, product liability determinations, malpractice cases, and criminal investigations. Its importance in criminal investigations refers to determinations of whether a person's death was due to a homicide, an accident, or suicide.

The reliability and validity of the psychological autopsy, however, has yet to be demonstrated and remains open to debate, although process is being made, especially pertaining to attempts to standardize how autopsies are conducted (Knoll, 2008, 2009; Portzky, Audenaert, & van Heeringen, 2009; Snider, Hane, & Berman, 2006). At this point in our knowledge, the quality of the psychological autopsy depends largely on the training, knowledge, experience, and clinical orientation of the investigator (Knoll, 2008).

MULTIPLE MURDERERS

One of the most frightening and perhaps incomprehensible types of homicide is the random killing of groups of people, either in one episode (mass murders) or individually (serial murders) over a period of time. Although multiple murders are still rare occurrences, when discovered they remain etched in the public consciousness. Some are decades old.

The slaughter of 21 patrons at a McDonald's restaurant in San Ysidro, California, in July 1984, by James Oliver Huberty is a case in point. Another is the mass murder of 22 patrons at Luby's Cafeteria in Killeen, Texas, on October 16, 1991. Many people still recall the planned, separate murders of 33 young men and boys whose bodies were found in the cellar of the suburban Chicago home of John Wayne Gacy during the late 1970s. Between 1978 and 1991, Jeffrey Dahmer lured at least 17 boys and young men into his apartment in Milwaukee, where he drugged, killed, and dismembered them. The public was shocked to learn the details of how Dahmer ate the victims' flesh and had sex with the corpses. Other notorious multiple murderers include David Berkowitz, known as the infamous Son of Sam; Kenneth Bianci, the Hillside Strangler; Albert DeSalvo, believed to be the Boston Strangler (although this has never been confirmed); Gary Ridgeway, the Green River Killer; Elaine Wuornos, one of the few female serial killers to have been identified and put to death; Donald Harvey, the nursing-care killer; Dennis Rader, the BTK killer; and Theodore Bundy.

England was the setting for the notorious Jack the Ripper and, more recently, Peter Sutcliffe, the Yorkshire Ripper who killed 13 women in the red-light districts of Northern England. Dennis Nilsen became England's first serial killer to prey on homosexuals, committing at least 15 known murders (Jenkins, 1988).

The list of older mass murders can be augmented by more recent incidents. In 2009, a 19-year-old entered the grounds of a school and killed 16 people, including 13 teachers, in the suburbs of Stuttgart, Germany. In the same week, in the United States, a 28-year-old allegedly killed ten people, including his mother, relatives, and neighbors before killing himself. Two weeks later, a gunman opened fire in a North Carolina nursing home, killing eight and wounding several others. And in Binghamton, New York, a heavily-armed man who had recently lost his job, had relationship difficulties, and claimed to be ridiculed because of his difficulty with the English language, entered a building that served as a community service center for immigrants. He killed 14 people before killing himself. Other individuals barricaded themselves in the basement for several hours before police were able to enter and secure the building and assure that the shooter was no longer at large.

Recently, in Norway in 2011, Anders Breivik killed 77 people in a bombing and gun rampage. Eight of these victims were killed by a bomb Breivik planted in Oslo, while 69 were teens and young adults at a Youth Labor Camp. The camp was situated on an island, and some of the victims were shot in the water while attempting to escape the gunfire. Breivik acknowledged his actions but refused to plead guilty or not guilty by reason of insanity, claiming that he was defending his country against Muslim immigration and European liberalism. And, in another recent incident in March 2012, staff sergeant Robert Bales left his barracks on two separate occasions, walked through villages in Afghanistan, and allegedly killed 17 Afghan civilians in their homes. Also in 2012, James Holmes allegedly killed twelve people and wounded many others in a mass shooting in a movie theater in Aurora, Colorado, and a gunman shot six people in a Sikh temple in Wisconsin, before himself being shot to death.

These are but illustrations of tragic incidences that occurred—sometimes over a short period of time—both in the United States and in other nations. However, as can be seen from the above examples, some of which will be discussed in more detail below, not all multiple murders can be categorized in the same way.

Definitions

Serial murder is usually reserved for incidents in which an individual (or individuals) kills two or more victims in separate events (Federal Bureau of Investigation, 2005a). Some experts and legislation (Protection of Children from Sexual Predators Act, 1998) have defined serial murder as three or more victims in separate incidents, but more recently the FBI has defined it as two or more. The FBI argues that the lower number of victims allows law enforcement more flexibility in committing resources to a potential serial murder investigation (Federal Bureau of Investigation, 2005a). The time interval between serial murders—sometimes referred to as the cooling-off period—may be days or weeks, but it is more likely months or years. The cooling-off period is the main difference between serial murders and other multiple murders. The murders are premeditated and planned, and the offender usually selects victims with specific characteristics, such as young age, certain hair color, or occupation. **Spree murder** normally refers to the killing of three or more individuals without any cooling-off period, usually at two or more locations. A bank robber who kills some individuals within the bank, flees with hostages, and kills a number of people while in flight during a statewide chase would be an example of a spree murderer. However, some experts are not convinced that spree murder represents a meaningful separate category of multiple murder (Federal Bureau of Investigation, 2005a). This is understandable; some murders that would be characterized as spree share characteristics of serial murders; others seem to be more like multiple murders, without the single location. Essentially, the spree-murder designation does not provide any real benefit to law enforcement. **Mass murder** involves killing four or more persons at a single location with no cooling-off period between murders. There are various kinds of mass murder, including those sponsored by some governmental authority, such as genocide designed to exterminate large groups of people, often on the basis of religion or ethnicity. Another type is mass murder by terrorists, such as occurred in New York City on September 11, 2001, when nearly 3,000 persons were killed. Mass murder committed by terrorists will be discussed in more detail in the next chapter. In this section, we focus on mass murder by individuals acting on their own initiative.

Investigators have traditionally identified two types of mass murder by individuals: classic and family (Douglas *et al.*, 1986). An example of a **classic mass murder** is when an individual barricades himself or herself inside—or walks into—a public building, such as a fast-food restaurant, randomly killing the patrons and any other individual he or she has contact with. The 1984 shootings of patrons at the San Ysidro's McDonald's restaurant in San Diego and 1991 shootings at Luby's cafeteria in Killeen, Texas, mentioned earlier, are examples. In May 2012 a man walked into a Seattle café, shot to death four people and seriously wounded a fifth, killed a woman and hijacked her car, then shot himself in the head when police were closing in. The 2007 Virginia Tech murders in Blacksburg, Virginia, the 2008 Northern Illinois University killings in Dekalb, the 2009 killings in Binghamton, New York, and the 2012 rampage in the Aurora theater are other recent examples of classic mass murder. In these instances, the shooters entered buildings or classrooms claiming most victims at random and sometimes killing themselves. To return to the point made above about classification difficulty, however, the Virginia Tech killings could also be classified as spree murders, because they were spread throughout the day, with no "cooling off" period and did not occur in one location.

Some mass murders that have features of classic mass murders seem to require a separate classification, however. Although the victims may seem to be chosen at random, they are often perceived by the perpetrator to belong to a particular group or to be representative of a threatening group, despite the unreasonableness of the threat. For example, in the Norway killings, Breivik railed against "multicultural forces" and most of his victims were young people at a camp for members of the Youth Labor Party; Marc Lepine, the Montreal shooter, expressed intense hatred for "feminists." He walked into a classroom at the University of Montreal, ordered male students to leave, and shot female students. Jared Loughner opened fire on a politician and the constituents who came out to greet her.

A **family mass murder** is when at least three family members are killed (usually by another family member). Very often, the perpetrator kills himself or herself, an incident that is classified as a mass murder/suicide.

SERIAL MURDERERS

The U.S. Department of Justice estimated that there were about 35–40 serial murderers active at any given point in the United States during the 1970s and 1980s (Jenkins, 1988). Hickey (2006) makes similar estimates on the more recent number of active and unapprehended serial killers. Realistically, though, there are no accurate data on the prevalence and number of serial murderers active at any one time in the United States or internationally (Brantley & Kosky, 2005). There are some recent estimates that suggest the number of serial murders has decreased in the United States during the years 1970 to 2009 (Quinet, 2011).

It is equally difficult to estimate the annual number of serial murder victims. Many serial offenders are adept at hiding their victims, and some inflate the number of their victims. Gary Ridgway, the Green River Killer, confessed to killing 48 women, and he skillfully hid their bodies. The long-haul truck driver Keith Hunter Jesperson, known as the Happy Face Killer because of the smiley face he drew on his many letters to the media, claimed to have killed 160 persons in multiple states, although he later recanted these assertions. He took great pride in the fact that he had been killing for over a year before any of the bodies were discovered (Quinet, 2007). In one case of a serial murder described by Wolf and Lavezzi (2007), the offender hid the bodies of eight women in the house inhabited by his parents and sister. Some of the bodies were found in the crawl space of the basement, and others were found comingled in the attic.

Many serial killers select victims that apparently are not missed or, if missed, they are given up as runaways or adults who have left of their own volition. An examination of the victim selection of known serial murderers will reveal that killers prefer the group of people offering easy access, transience, and a tendency to disappear without seeming to cause much alarm or concern. Victims are often prostitutes, runaways, young male drifters, and itinerant farm workers. Young women in or near a university or college campus or the elderly and solitary poor appear to be the groups next preferred. The strongest determining factor in victim selection for both groups—the factor that victims seem to have in common—is their vulnerability or easy availability. Serial murderers rarely break in and kill middle-class strangers in their homes, for example, despite media portrayals. It should be pointed out, however, that although serial killers begin their murderous careers by selecting highly vulnerable victims, they may, as their killings continue, gain substantially more confidence in their ability to abduct more "challenging" victims. Fortunately, very few serial killers become this successful before they are arrested.

Although serial killers are similar in some background characteristics to the single-victim killers discussed in the previous chapter, there are notable differences in the victims they choose and their method of committing the crimes. For example, the victims of single-victim murderers are most often family, friends, and acquaintances. Serial murderers most often kill strangers with no apparent consensual relationship between the offender and the victim. The lack of a relationship in serial murders makes identifying suspects especially difficult.

The preferred method of killing also is often different for the two groups. Serial offenders tend to prefer more hands on killing through strangulation or beating with hands or feet, while single-victim offenders prefer guns (Kraemer, Lord, & Heilbrun, 2004). As we learned in the previous chapter, single offenders kill most often out of anger and lack of control stemming from interpersonal conflict and provocation. Some, of course, kill in accordance with a carefully thought-out plan, but this is believed to be the exceptional case. Serial homicides, on the other hand, are often deliberate, premeditated, sexually predatory in nature, and are not usually precipitated by interpersonal disagreements or provocation. Serial homicide offenders also exhibit more planning by moving the victim or body from one location to another, by using restraints, and by disposing of the body in a remote location (Kraemer *et al.*, 2004). Single-victim offenders tend to be much less skillful in disposing of the body.

Psychological Motives and Causes of Serial Killings

A frequent question asked is, what risk factors predispose a person to become a serial murderer? Serial murderers like all human beings are products of their genetic makeup, their upbringing, their social environment, and ultimately the developmental path that circumstances lead them to take. There is no single identifiable causal factor in the development of a serial killer. As we have discussed throughout the book, criminal behavior develops from a complicated mixture of various factors and influences. The same factors and influences that lead to violence very likely play a significant role in serial homicide, although others are certainly added. For example, and as noted above, the motives of many serial killers appear to be based on some combination of psychological rewards, such as control, domination, media attention, and personal or sexual excitement rather than identifiable material gain. Their actions are predictably planned, organized, and purposeful, and they seem to take delight in playing games with the law enforcement community and the public at large.

Many serial homicide offenders are especially drawn to committing murders that attract media interest, send spine-chilling fear into the community, and are incomprehensible to the public. Keith Hunter Jesperson apparently became so irritated that his killings were not highly publicized that he began writing letters to the media in 1994, signing his letters with a smiling happy face, and thus earning the nickname the Happy Face Killer. Dennis Rader, who could be classified as both a serial and mass murderer, also sent letters to police and newspapers. In his communications, he suggested a number of names for himself; one that eventually stuck was BTK, an acronym for "bind, torture, and kill."

The evidence does not support any notion that serial killers kill on the basis of some compulsion or irresistible urge. Rather, the murder appears to be more a result of opportunity and the random availability of a suitable victim. It is a mistake, therefore, to assume that serial murderers are seriously mentally disordered or emotionally disturbed according to traditional clinical or psychiatric standards. Some are, but most are not.

Nor should it be assumed that serial killers are social misfits who have trouble fitting into the local community. The BTK killer, Dennis Rader, killed ten victims in and around Wichita, Kansas. He was married for 33 years, had two children, and was a Boy Scout leader. He was a long-time and dedicated church member who had held elected office in his church council. He was employed as a local government official and served on several community boards. The Green River Killer, Gary Ridgway, who confessed to killing 48 women over a 16-year period in the Seattle Washington area, read the Bible at work and tried to save others by talking about religion with coworkers. At one time, he went door to door for a Pentecostal church trying to save souls. He liked to hunt, fish, work around the yard, and take trips with his wife in their RV. He had been married three times, had a son, and was married at the time of his arrest. He worked as a truck painter for a company for 32 years. Robert Lee Yates, Jr., who murdered 13 women, worked as a corrections officer in the state Penitentiary in Walla Walla, Washington, and was a well-decorated helicopter pilot during his 19 years of military service.

Although the cognitive processing and values of serial murderers may be considered extremely aberrant when it comes to sensitivity and concern for their victims, a vast majority of serial killers fail to qualify as seriously mentally disordered in the traditional diagnostic categories of mental disorders discussed in Chapter 8. As a group—and there are always exceptions—they would not be diagnosed paranoid schizophrenic, delusional, or psychotic, for example. However, some would likely qualify as having "antisocial personality disorder," a category that is virtually indistinguishable from psychopathy, which was discussed in Chapter 7. Serial killers have developed versions of the world that facilitate repetitive murder, often in a brutal, demeaning, and cold-blooded manner, but they are not necessarily *seriously mentally disordered* in the clinical use of this term. This is a difficult concept to comprehend, because most of us are probably attuned to believe that anyone who kills in this manner "must be crazy."

Research on Backgrounds

The backgrounds of serial killers are varied and underscore the importance of the many risk factors discussed earlier in the book. Similar to violent offenders in general, serial killers have frequently experienced considerable abuses and deprivations within their families growing up (Delisi & Scherer, 2006). McKenzie (1995) discovered in her examination of 20 serial killers that 80 percent were reared in homes characterized by family violence and severe abuse, and parental alcoholism; 93 percent had been exposed to inconsistent and chaotic parenting. For example, Henry Lee Lucas, who claimed to be responsible for an unlikely 600 murders, was severely abused as a child. He was regularly beaten by his mother who at one point struck him so hard with a piece of wood that he was in a coma for three days. He eventually killed her. Coral Eugene Watts, who is suspected of killing 100 women, was continually abused and berated by his stepfather, and was persistently bullied and socially rejected in school.

In his study of serial killers in England, Jenkins (1988) found that—unlike the typical violent individual who demonstrates a propensity for violence at an early age—serial murderers generally begin their careers of repetitive homicide at a relatively late age. He concluded that most started their careers between the ages of 24 and 40. Interestingly, the median age of arrested serial murderers in Jenkins's sample was 36. Arrests typically occurred about four years after they began killing. The serial murderers did have extensive police records, though, but the records reflected a series of petty theft, embezzlement, and forgery, rather than a history of violence (Jenkins, 1988). Surprisingly, they did not have extensive juvenile records. Jenkins concluded that the English cases did not provide any early indicators or predictors of eventual murderous behavior. When British serial murderers committed their first murder, about half were married, had a seemingly stable family life, and had usually lived in the same house for many years. A majority had stable jobs, and, disconcertingly, a good number had been former police officers or security guards.

Female Serial Killers

Although relatively rare, there have been at least three dozen female serial murderers in U.S. history. Hickey (1991) identified 34 documented female serial murderers, with 82 percent of them acting after 1900. Moreover, there are some discernible differences between female and male serial murderers. For example, only about one-third of the female offenders killed strangers, in contrast to males who almost exclusively killed strangers (Holmes, Hickey, & Holmes, 1991).

Interestingly, the available research indicates that female serial murderers are active longer than their typical male counterparts, averaging around 8 to 11 years (Farrell, Keppel, & Titterington, 2011; Kelleher & Kelleher, 1998). According to Farrell *et al.* "On average, they operate within a different victim pool, enjoy longer active periods, and amass more victims than their male counterparts" (p. 229). Farrell *et al.* report that the average number of victims murdered by female offenders is nine, a figure supported by research by Eric Hickey (2010). The average number of victims of male serial killers is unknown. However, Hickey (2010) estimates that although a few have high body counts, the majority have fewer victims than do female serial killers. Most victims of female serial killers are husbands, former husbands, or suitors. For example, Belle Gunness murdered an estimated 14–49 husbands or suitors in La Porte, Indiana (Holmes *et al.*, 1991). Nannie Doss killed a combination of 11 husbands and family members in Tulsa, Oklahoma. The second largest group of victims murdered by female serial killers are those who are weak and dependent on them, such as children and the elderly (Farrell *et al.*, 2011; Kelleher & Kelleher, 1998).

The first known female serial killer was Lucretia Patrica Cannon, who was active in Delaware between 1802 and 1829 (Farrell *et al.*, 2011). Perhaps the most notorious female serial killer in our time was Aileen Wuornos, who killed seven men in Florida in 1989 and 1990, when she was in her thirties. Wuornos had a pathetic, devastating childhood and adolescence, littered with the risk factors we discussed in early chapters. She was pregnant at 13 and became a prostitute at 15. She had a lengthy criminal record, mostly for nonviolent offenses, but she was also frequently victimized. She was generally well known to the criminal justice system even before her first murder. Wuornos is unusual insofar as female serial killers go, because her victims were strangers or brief acquaintances rather than husbands or persons of whom she was in charge. She argued that the men she killed had raped her or attempted to rape her, or that her crimes were in self-defense. Psychiatrists diagnosed her with borderline personality disorder, but it was almost universally believed that she would be convicted, and she was. Wuornos was executed by lethal injection in October 2002. She was the subject of several documentaries and the movie *Monster*, in which—despite the film's title—she was portrayed somewhat sympathetically by Charlize Theron.

Traditionally, female serial killers murder primarily for material or monetary gain, such as insurance benefits, will allocations, trusts, and estates. Furthermore, the method of killing is through poisons (usually cyanide) or overdoses of pills. Approximately half of the female serial killers had a male accomplice. Some women murdered because of involvements in cults or with a male serial murderer. For example, Charlene Gallego, the common-law wife of serial killer Gerald Gallego helped him select, abduct, and murder at least 10 individuals (Holmes *et al.*, 1991).

Over the past two decades, several female health care workers who have killed patients have been identified, although males—including a physician—have also been identified. Some research suggests that as many as 17 percent of female serial killers are nurses (Stark, Paterson, Henderson, Kidd, & Godwin, 1997). A female health worker may have been responsible for the deaths of 28 patients at two hospitals in The Hague, Netherlands. Her victims were either children or elderly patients, and her method of killing involved injections of various substances. She was arrested in December 2001 and was later convicted of four counts of first-degree murder and three counts of attempted murder.

The motivations of health care workers' serial killings are variable: recognition, attention, revenge, power, and control (Brantley & Kosky, 2005). Some of these health care workers admitted that the killings relieved tension, stress, and frustration (Linedecker & Burt, 1990). Some also maintained that they killed to put the patients out of their misery and that these were essentially mercy killings.

The Victimological Perspective in Understanding Serial Killers

Jenkins (1993) contends that the current popular image of the serial murderer—a white male who kills for sexual motives—may be an inaccurate one. He argues that lack of a **victimological perspective** encourages confusion and distorted information. He suggests that our current knowledge about serial murderers is strongly influenced by two factors: availability of the victims and the attitudes of law enforcement agencies toward those victims. Rather than strictly focusing on individual and personality attributes of the offender, he believes we should also examine the *social opportunity* to kill. In other words, what we know about serial murder may be strongly influenced by the nature and type of the potential victims.

To illustrate, Jenkins (1993) provides the case of Calvin Jackson, who was arrested in 1974 for murder committed in a New York apartment building. Actually, Jackson was a serial murderer, but none of his victims led the police to suspect a serial killer. Jackson's killings took place in a single-occupancy hotel where the guests were poor, socially isolated, largely forgotten, and mostly elderly. Time after time, the police were called to the hotel to deal with cases of death or injury due to alcohol, drugs, or old age. When foul play was suspected, the police never considered it the work of a serial murderer, because the victims did not fit the stereotypic profile. Since there was no evidence of grotesque sexual abuse of the victim (the victim stereotype), there was little reason for the police to entertain the possibility of a serial murderer. Other serial murderers may set up situations where murders resemble drug-related homicides. Therefore, our current knowledge of serial murderers may be restricted to a certain category of offender.

Geographical Location of Serial Killing

Most serial killers have specific preferences for the location of their killings. They frequently commit their killings within comfort zones that are often defined by an anchor point, such as their residence, employment, or the residence of a relative. Geographic profiling data continue to support this observation. Very few serial murderers travel interstate to kill (Federal Bureau of Investigation, 2005a). Those that do travel interstate for their murders are often truck drivers, those in military service, transients, or itinerant individuals who move from place to place. Hickey (1997) estimates that 14 percent of serial killers use their homes or workplaces as the preferred location, whereas another 52 percent commit their murders in the same general location or region, such as the same neighborhood or city. This tendency suggests that geographic profiling may be an invaluable aid in the identification of serial killers.

Perhaps an effective method for reducing serial murder is to identify and protect specific high-risk groups and regions and to take whatever social measures are needed to reduce their vulnerability. Focusing on the offender through crime scene profiling and other investigative measures is usually of limited usefulness because most serial killers are apprehended by a mixture of fortuitous events and carelessness by the offender.

Ethnic and Racial Characteristics

The widespread belief that only whites are serial killers and blacks and other minorities never commit this type of crime is basically a myth (Walsh, 2005). Walsh found that approximately 21.8 percent of the serial killers in the United States have been black, and was able to document 90 black serial killers during the post–World War II era. Research on Latino and other minority serial killers is virtually nonexistent.

The number of victims black killers admitted killing does not differ significantly from white serial killers either. Jake Bird, for instance, was verified to have killed 44 victims, just 4 victims short of the white killer Gary Ridgeway's (the Green River Killer) record-setting 48. And some are equally chilling. Walsh (2005) describes the methods of black serial killer Maury Travis when he writes, "Travis had a secret torture chamber in his basement, where police found bondage equipment, videotapes of his rape and torture sessions, and clippings relating to police investigations of his murder victims (mostly prostitutes and crack addicts). Travis hanged himself in jail after confessing to 17 murders" (p. 274).

We may have assumed that serial killings are perpetrated almost exclusively by whites because of how serial murder is identified and investigated. For example, law enforcement agencies may be less prone to investigate some crimes as serial murders if victims are found in a rundown apartment complex located in a poverty-stricken, crime-infested neighborhood. Under these circumstances, law enforcement officials are more likely to conclude that the victim is simply another fatality in the long stream of never-ending violence found in parts of inner cities. This point was made by Jenkins (1993) in the previous section.

Also, as Walsh (2005) has observed, the media tend to cover the sensational serial killings by whites but fail to cover in any detail those offenses committed by blacks and other minorities. "The extensive media coverage of Bundy, Gacy, and Berkowitz cases have made these killers almost household names, but African Americans such as Watts, Johnson, Francois, and Wallace are practically unknown, despite having operated within the same general time framework (1980s and 1990s)" (Walsh, 2005, p. 274). Similar disparity in media coverage of other crimes has occurred. In many communities, it is not unusual to see extensive coverage of the disappearance or murder of a white child and very little attention given to a similar tragedy involving a black victim. Because violent crime, on the whole, is interracial rather than intraracial (Federal Bureau of Investigation, 2005a), it follows that lack of attention might favor the nonwhite perpetrators of these offenses.

Juvenile Serial Murderers

Serial murder by children and adolescents is an exceedingly rare event, and scientific information is extremely sparse. Myers (2004) could only identify six serial cases involving juveniles over the past 150 years, after an exhaustive search of periodicals, newspapers, books, legal references, and Internet sources on crime. According to Myers (2004), serial murders by juveniles are a complex phenomenon, with psychological, family, social, cultural, and biological factors playing a role. Myers believes that many of the same motives manifested by adult serial killers hold for child and adolescent serial killers.

MASS MURDERERS

Surprisingly, little research has been directed at mass murderers, especially in comparison with the attention directed at serial murderers. Perhaps this is because mass murder, while frightening, is not as intriguing or mysterious as serial murder. Furthermore, mass murder happens quickly and unpredictably without warning—then the killing is usually over. It is often clear who the offender is, and his or her life is usually ended on the spot, either when they kill themselves or when they are shot by the police. If arrested, they are almost invariably convicted. Serial murders, on the other hand, occur over a period of weeks, months, or years, and the identity of the offender is unknown.

In this section, we will focus on mass murder by the individual. As we referred to earlier in the chapter, there are two types of mass murder by the individual: classic mass murder and family mass murder. This section will concentrate on the classic type.

Classic Mass Murder

Mass murderers tend to be frustrated, angry people who feel helpless about their lives. They are usually between the ages of 35–45, and they are convinced there is little chance that things will get better for them. Their personal lives have been a failure by their standards, and they have often suffered some tragic or serious loss, such as a loss of meaningful employment. George Hennard, for example, the 35-year-old who shot to death 22 patrons in a cafeteria in Texas, had lost his cherished job as a merchant marine. Anders Breivik, the Norway mass killer, claimed to have attempted and failed at six business enterprises. Breivik, disgruntled with society and government, bombed the government buildings in Olso in July 2011, killing eight. He then proceeded to go on mass shooting at a camp of the Workers Youth League, killing 69, mostly teenagers.

Mass murders are usually carefully planned, sometimes over very long periods of time. For example, on November 2, 1991, Gang Lu, a former graduate student at the University of Iowa, sought six specific professors he felt kept him from getting a $1,000 award for his doctoral dissertation. He managed to kill five of the six within 10 minutes before taking his own life. Lu had written five separate letters to people detailing his plans prior to the murder. Likewise, Hennard had apparently planned his onslaught for many months, even studying video documentaries of previous mass murders.

As mentioned above, the targets selected by mass murderers are often—perhaps even most often—deliberate. They are either symbolic of their discontent (such as their workplace) or are hated or blamed for the perpetrator's misfortunes. George Hennard had a lifelong hatred of women; 14 of his 22 victims were women. At Luby's Cafeteria, he moved from victim to victim, frequently selecting women, and methodically shot each victim in the head at close range as he shouted "bitch." Marc Lepine, who killed primarily female students, had a three-page suicide note in his pocket in which he complained that feminists had always ruined his life. James Oliver Huberty, the McDonald's killer, selected a fast-food restaurant in a Hispanic community (San Ysidro) because he apparently disliked Hispanics and children.

There is little question that Anders Breivik targeted those he killed. Breivik spoke vociferously against European liberalism and Muslim immigration, and he clearly stated during his court appearances that he did not regret his actions. He would do them again, he said, to defend his country against multicultural forces.

Mass murderers often take a very active interest in guns, especially semiautomatics that maximize the number of deaths in a short period of time. In large measure, the availability of high-powered semiautomatic or automatic weaponry accounts for the increasingly large death toll in recent mass murders. Moreover, mass murderers usually plan to die at the scene, either by committing suicide or by being shot down by law enforcement. There are of course exceptions, as we see in the cases of Breivik and Holmes.

Also, mass murderers are often socially isolated and withdrawn people who are without a strong social network of friends or supports. Breivik lived with his mother, and he apparently spent many hours playing the online game "World of Warcraft." Their isolation is probably due to some combination of an active dislike of people and their inadequate interpersonal and social skills. The mass murder is their chance to get even, to dominate others, to take control, to call the shots, and to gain recognition. The 41-year-old individual who killed at the immigration center in New York had a history of interpersonal and work problems. He was apparently bitter and angry, and had stated that the United States was a terrible place. An immigrant himself, he had obtained his citizenship and had lived in the United States for most of his adult life; however, he had considerable trouble learning English and maintained that people ridiculed his speech. Many who knew him said they were not surprised at his actions.

A Mass Murder Typology

James Alan Fox and Jack Levin (2003) proposed a five-category typology based on the motivations for mass killings. The five categories are revenge, power, loyalty, profit, and terror. According to Fox and Levin, many—if not most—mass killings are motivated by *revenge*, either against specific individuals or specific groups. Usually, the killer seeks to get even with a group of people he dislikes. Fox and Levin bring up the concept of "murder by proxy" in which victims are chosen because they are associated, by the killer, with a primary target against whom revenge is sought. For example, 25-year-old Marc Lépine's long-term hatred against feminists ignited his murderous rampage at the Université de Montréal. Although some of his victims may have not considered themselves feminists, he considered all women, by proxy, feminists.

Another recent example of the revenge mass killer occurred on March 10, 2009, when Michael McLendon, age 28, went on a rampage in southern Alabama. The gunman, who killed 11 people including himself, had a list of people he had worked with who had allegedly done him wrong. He began the day of the shooting by burning down his mother's house (her body and four dead dogs were later found inside), and shot most of his victims at a sausage plant where he had stopped working just days before the rampage.

The second type identified by Fox and Levin (2003) is the killer who seeks *power* and domination over his victims. They enjoy and crave the fear in others they engender and the immense control they have over their victims. Usually, the need for revenge and power go together. The power killer is seeking both revenge and control over his tormentors. Fox and Levin observe that the thirst for power and control inspire this type of mass murderer to dress in military fatigues and combat gear, and carry assault weapons packed with considerable firepower. Some investigators refer to them as pseudocommando killers. Another example of this type of mass killer is James Huberty, who could also fit into the revenge category because of his dislike of Hispanics and children. The third type is inspired to kill by a warped sense of love and *loyalty*, usually based on a desire to save their loved ones from misery and hardship. Many family massacres stem from this motivation. "Typically, a husband/father is despondent over the fate of the family unit, and takes not only his own life, but also those of his children and sometimes his wife, in order to protect them from pain and suffering in their lives" (Fox & Levin, 2003, pp. 59–60).

The fourth motivation for mass murder is *profit*. The intention in this murder is to eliminate victims and witnesses to a crime, such as a robbery. Drug war between organized crime groups is also sometimes involved. This type of mass murder also sends the message to other potential witnesses that the same thing could happen to you if you try to testify to authorities.

The fifth and final motivation for mass murder is *terror*. In this situation, the perpetrator wants to send a message through a horrific murder. One of the more infamous examples of this type is represented by Charles Manson, who led a quasi-commune located in southern California in the 1960s. Manson, who likely would qualify as a charismatic psychopath, desired to send a message of terror to communities in southern California. He was a devout listener to Beatles music, and was especially influenced by the song "Helter Skelter," a composition found on the Beatles' *White Album*, which he interpreted as prophesying an apocalyptic war between blacks and whites. Manson apparently wanted to start a race war by having his followers commit horrific mass murders of wealthy whites and have them blamed on angry blacks. Manson had the grandiose delusion of world domination (Deal & Hickey, 2003). He believed that once Helter Skelter started, blacks would eventually kill all whites except for himself and his family because they would hide in the desert (Deal & Hickey, 2003). On August 9, 2009, Manson told four of his followers that it was time for Helter Skelter. He instructed them to commit brutal mass murder and to "leave a sign and do something witchy" to ignite fear and terror within the white community. The site they selected was the home of well-known actress Sharon Tate and film director Roman Polanski, located in a prominent Los Angeles neighborhood. The group brutally murdered five people at the house that night, including Tate, who was eight and one-half months pregnant. Polanski was out of the country at the time. After the killing, they wrote the message "pig" on the front door of the house in the blood of one of the victims.

The next night, six Manson followers set out—again per Manson's instructions—to murder Leno LaBianca, a wealthy supermarket executive, and his wife Rosemary, a successful dress shop co-owner. After Leno was killed, one of the followers carved "war" on the man's abdomen. The group also left frightening messages in three different places in the house, "death to the pigs," "rise," and "Healter (sic) Skelter," all in the victims' blood. Manson was eventually arrested, convicted of accessory to murder, and sentenced to death. However, his sentence was commuted to life in prison in 1976 after the Supreme Court of California temporarily eliminated that state's death penalty. One of Manson's followers, Tex Watson, allegedly found God in prison. Another member, Lynette "Squeaky" Fromme, was paroled and later reimprisoned after threatening the life of President Ronald Reagan. In 2009 she was again released from prison. Still another follower, Susan Atkins, died of cancer in prison in Fall 2009. Other members of the Manson family have been paroled or remain incarcerated.

The Manson slayings demonstrate the power that a charismatic figure—and in this case probably a psychopath—can have over vulnerable individuals. Manson himself was not directly involved in the killings; his followers did precisely what he wanted them to do, providing unquestioned obedience to his commands.

The remainder of the chapter addresses some specific offenses that have been, or possess the strong possibility of becoming, mass murder. School violence and workplace violence do not necessarily result in death, of course, but when they do, the deaths may be multiple. These crimes have drawn extensive media coverage, and some research interest, in recent years.

SCHOOL VIOLENCE

In the late 1990s a rash of school shootings made headlines. As discussed briefly in Chapter 5, the most infamous case was the mass murder of 12 students and one teacher at Columbine High School in Littleton, Colorado, in April 1999. The two teenage boys who did the shootings committed suicide during the incident. Twenty more students were injured. Although there had been a number of school shootings prior to Columbine (there were at least 10 school shootings between 1996 and 1999), the Columbine shooting prompted a great deal of alarm and concern nationwide. In addition, the media and some experts were quick to make gross generalizations about the school violence problem.

However, even prior to these violent incidents, anecdotal and media accounts of children being victimized at school by other children prompted researchers to study the issue to document the magnitude of the problem. Violence in schools is more than school shootings. Violence in schools includes aggravated and simple assaults, sexual assaults, and robbery. As long ago as 1974, the U.S. Congress funded a three-year study to evaluate the nature and extent of crime, violence, and disruption in the nation's schools. The studies have continued periodically over the years. Today, the National Center for Education Statistics (Robers, Zhang, Truman, & Snyder, 2012) has published the most comprehensive study available.

The report indicated the following:

- In 2010, the number of students (ages 12–18) who reported being victims of crime was 828,000. Keep in mind, however, that the total number of students enrolled in prekindergarten through 12th grade during the 2009–10 school year was approximately 49 million.
- During the same year, there were 359,000 reported violent victimizations, of which 91,400 were serious ones.

- Of the 33 student, staff, and nonstudent school-associated violent deaths occurring between July 2009 and June 2010, 25 were homicides, 5 were suicides, and 3 were legal interventions (involving a law enforcement officer). During that same time period, 17 of the homicides were school-age youth (ages 5–18) while at school.
- In 2009, 8 percent of the students in grades 9–12 reported being threatened or injured with a weapon, such as a gun, knife, or club, on school property.
- Eight percent of the secondary school teachers and 7 percent of the elementary school teachers reported being threatened with injury by a student. In addition, 6 percent of elementary school teachers and 2 percent of secondary school teachers reported being physically attacked by a student.
- Six percent of students (ages 12–18) reported being cyber-bullied in 2009.

Students were more likely to be victims of serious violence or homicide away from school, occurring at a rate of 12 crimes per 1,000 students away from school. Over the years, the percentage of youth homicides occurring at school remains at less than 2 percent of the total number of youth homicides, indicating youths are more likely to be murdered away from school (Robers *et al.*, 2012). Still, national statistics indicate that about one out of 10 students in secondary schools fear that they will be attacked or harmed while at school (Verlinden, Hersen, & Thomas, 2000).

School Shootings

Although school shootings are understandably frightening and are of deep concern, statistically they are rare. O'Toole (2000, p. 4) lists the usual wrong or unverified impressions of school shooters often promoted by the news media. Among these myths are the following:

- School violence is an epidemic.
- All school shooters are alike.
- The school shooter is always a loner.
- School shootings are exclusively motivated by revenge.
- Easy access to weapons is the most significant factor.
- Unusual or aberrant behaviors, interests, or hobbies are hallmarks of the student destined to become violent.

Investigations of school shooters have consistently found that the two characteristics that emerge are peer rejection and social rejection. The Columbine High School shooter, Dylan Klebold, wrote in his diary how lonely he was without friends and was especially tortured by his failures with girls (Meadows, 2006). The other shooter, Eric Harris, wrote in his diary how everyone continually made fun of him. A vast majority of shooters have poor social and coping skills and felt picked on or persecuted (Verlinden *et al.*, 2000). They expressed anger about being teased or ridiculed and vowed revenge against particular individuals or groups. Moreover, as a group, "they lacked social support and prosocial relationships that might have served as protective factors" (Verlinden *et al.*, 2000, p. 44). Cruelty to animals was prominent in the backgrounds of at least half of the shooters (Verlinden *et al.*, 2000). Their backgrounds also revealed a keen interest in guns and other weaponry, and they often had easy access to firearms (see **Table 10-4**). Most of these assailants expected to be killed or planned suicide during or immediately after the attacks. All the attacks seemed to be carefully planned and thought out beforehand.

TABLE 10-4	School Homicides, 1994–1999	
Type of weapon	**Number**	**Percent**
Total	172	100
Firearm	119	69
Handgun	89	52
Rifle	18	11
Unknown	12	7
Sharp object	31	18
Beating	12	7
Strangulation	5	3
Other	5	3

Source: Data from Perkins (2003), p. 11.

In virtually all school shootings, investigators discovered that the violent intentions of the assailants were repeatedly made clear to others, particularly peers, often including the time and place. It is estimated that at least 50 percent of school shooters let their intentions known to others, a phenomenon that become known by investigators as *leakage*. Documents show that the Columbine school shooters repeatedly dropped hints at school about their murderous intentions (Meadows, 2006). However, peers rarely reported these threats to the authorities. The reasons for this lack of reporting behavior are not well understood, but fear seems to play a major role. A survey by the Safe School Coalition of Washington State (1999) (cited in Verlinden *et al.*, 2000) revealed that fear of not being believed, fear of retribution, and fear for what might happen to the youth threatening the school violence were the most frequently reported concerns of peers. Verlinden *et al.* (2000) concluded that the risk for school violence is high when there are multiple warning signs and risk factors. "The more signs there are and the greater the opportunity, motivation, and access to weapons, the greater the possibility that the child may commit a violent act" (Verlinden *et al.*, 2000, p. 47).

So far, we have talked about school-age shooters killing classmates and teachers. Adults unaffiliated with the school are also involved in school shootings. In recent years, adult males have barged into school buildings, killing students. Perhaps one of the more horrific occurred in West Nickel, Pennsylvania, where, on October 2, 2006, 32-year-old Charles Carl Roberts carried three guns into Nickel Mines School, an Amish one-room schoolhouse. The gunman took hostages, all girls, and sent the boys and adults outside. He barricaded the doors and then opened fire on a dozen girls, killing five and seriously wounding five before committing suicide. His motivation was unclear, but he indicated that his actions were not directly related to school or the Amish community, but was driven by events in his childhood. More likely, "he may have viewed himself as powerless or his own life circumstances as hopeless and acted out in a school environment that was simple, peaceful—and completely at his mercy" (Gerler, 2007, p. 2).

A week earlier, 53-year-old Duane Roger Morrison, armed with an assault rifle and carrying a backpack full of explosives, walked into Platte Canyon High School located in Bailey, Colorado. He took six female students hostage and sexually assaulted five of them. He then released four of them. When a SWAT team broke into the classroom, Morrison shot and killed a 16-year-old girl before turning the gun on himself. The motive of this adult attacker remains unclear.

Psychological Characteristics of School Shooters

Leary, Kowalski, Smith, and Phillips (2003) examined the psychological characteristics of juvenile offenders involved in 15 school shootings between 1995 and 2001. They discovered that social rejection was involved in most cases of school shootings. Most of the rejected shooters experienced an ongoing pattern of teasing, bullying, or ostracism, and a few were subjected to a recent romantic rejection. In many cases, the victims of the violence were those who rejected or humiliated the shooter. But social rejection alone did not seem to be enough to prompt the killing of classmates. In addition to the social rejection, perpetrators showed at least one of the following three risk factors: psychological problems, an interest in guns or explosives, or a morbid fascination with death. The psychological problems centered around low impulse control, lack of empathy for other people, serious depression, aggressiveness, and antisocial behavior. Many of the shooters had been in trouble for aggressive behavior toward peers, and some had abused animals. Depression appears to be especially important in identifying potential school shooters. In one comprehensive study, three-fourths of school shooters had expressed thoughts of suicide or attempts at suicide before the attack (Vossekuil, Fein, Reddy, Borum, & Modzeleski, 2002).

Fascination with firearms, bombs, and explosives is also a common theme. They seem to be comfortable with instruments of destruction. Wike and Fraser (2009) note that police in Plymouth Meeting outside of Philadelphia arrested a 14-year-old school dropout who, with his parents' assistance, had collected swords, guns, grenades, bomb-instructional manuals, black powder used in bomb making, and videos of the Columbine massacre. According to police—who acted on a tip from students—this alienated student had plans to attack his former school.

The third observation is that shooters tend to be highly fascinated with death and dark lifestyles and themes. They are not as horrified by sadistic and brutal carnage as most of their peers. Jeffrey Wiese, a 16-year-old at Red Lake High School in Minnesota, killed his grandfather and his grandfather's girlfriend, and then drove to the high school and fatally shot a security guard, a teacher, and five students. He wounded six others before shooting himself. Weise, who had been hospitalized for suicidal behavior, left many dark themes on websites, dressed in black, and wrote stories about school shootings and zombies (Weisbrot, 2008). However, these dark themes may be more characteristic of depression, thoughts of suicide, and anger at society than a central lifestyle. Eric Harris and Dylan Klebold, the Columbine High School shooters, are often referred to as devout believers of the macabre, but the evidence does not hold up that this was clearly the case. Rather, it appears that they were both angry young men. In a vast majority of school shootings, the perpetrator apparently had very little attachment or bonding to their schools, teachers, or peers (Wike & Fraser, 2009). School attachment and bonding appear to be crucial in any strategy designed to reduce school violence. Some investigators have found that school attachment plays an important role in producing high levels of academic achievement and in reducing substance use, violence, and high risk sexual behavior (Catalano, Haggerty, Oesterle, Fleming, & Hawkins, 2004; Wike & Fraser, 2009).

In a national study of school violence, Gottfredson, Gottfredson, Payne, and Gottfredson (2005) report that schools in which students find the rules fair and in which discipline is managed consistently experience less violence and disorder. This is regardless of the type of school and community. They also found that schools characterized by high teacher morale, focus, strong leadership, and high teacher involvement are protected from school crime and violence. Their conclusions: The school climate makes a significant difference in reducing the overall crime, disorder, and violence that occur within the school building.

One key conclusion made by Leary *et al.* (2003) is, "The typical shooter is a male student who has been ostracized by the majority group at his school for some time, and has been chronically taunted, teased, harassed, and often publicly humiliated." Being the victim of vicious and public bullying by peers consistently emerges in the school experiences of shooters. We now turn our attention to the topic of bullying.

School Bullying

School bullying came under intense public and media scrutiny after the shootings at Columbine High School in 1999 and Santana High School in Santee, California, in early 2001 (Ericson, 2001). In both cases, there was evidence that the shooters had been bullied to various degrees. Considerable research-based literature on the topic has emerged over the past decade, much of it prompted by conclusion that school shooters were often socially rejected and bullied, and eventually took their revenge through violent actions on their schools and peers. Seung-Hui Cho, the shooter who killed 31 students and professors at Virginia Tech in 2007, was said to have been bullied in high school and ridiculed about his accent to the point that he resisted speaking to others.

Bullying is commonly defined as a form of peer aggression in which one or more individuals repeatedly physically, verbally, and/or psychologically harass a weaker victim (Olweus, 1997; Vijoen, O'Neill, & Sidhu, 2005). Examples of physical bullying include hitting, spitting, kicking, punching, pushing, and taking or destroying personal items. Verbal bullying includes name calling, taunting, malicious teasing, and verbal threats. Psychological bullying includes spreading rumors and engaging in social exclusion, extortion, or intimidation.

Bullying is a common and significant problem for a large number of children throughout the world. Over half of school children have reported being victimized and over half have taken part in bullying (Jolliffe & Farrington, 2006). It commonly occurs on playgrounds, on school buses, in school hallways, neighborhoods, and homes. According to some research, both the victims and the bullies themselves are highly disliked and socially rejected by peers (Eslea *et al.*, 2003; Veenstra, Lindenberg, Oldehinkel, De Winter, Verhulst, & Ormel, 2005). Other research suggests that this may not be the case; some bullies are admired, and children who are bullied are liked by others and find adult mentors and peer support (see **Box 10-1**). While the playground or school bus or school halls is where bullying traditionally has occurred, technology has expanded the problem to the borderless cyberworld (Diamanduros, Downs, & Jenkins, 2008). Cyberbullying is fast emerging as having the same devastating psychological effects on its victims as persistent traditional bullying. It is especially troubling for its intended victim because the perpetrator is often unknown. Cyberbullying will be covered in more detail in Chapter 15.

It is clear from research that bullying has negative effects on both the victim and the bully, though, as noted above and in **Box 10-1**, the research is not unequivocal. It is important to note that in a survey of middle and high school students in the United States, two-thirds of the bullying victims believed school professionals responded poorly to the bullying incidents (Office of Justice Programs, 2011).

Victims of persistent bullying are more likely to perform significantly more self-destructive actions and are more likely to bring weapons to school to protect themselves (Henry & Sanders, 2007). A deeply troubled youth, however, after many years of being victimized by bullying, may decide he has no alternative but suicide, or worse, a massive school shooting accompanied by suicide (Burgess, Garbarino, & Carlson, 2006). And the victims of the shooting may be the bullies themselves. At least two-thirds of school shooters were teased, taunted, or bullied by peers (Vossekuil *et al.*, 2002). Nevertheless, it is important to remember that many children who are bullied survive the experience, usually with help from adult mentors or peers.

In ending this section, it should be emphasized that chronic bullies themselves and those that have been both bullied and became bullies often demonstrate little empathy for others

BOX 10-1
Bullying—A Different Perspective

Helene, age 11, is half-way through her first year in middle school. Her close-knit family comprises a father, whose sales work takes him away from home for days at a time, a mother, who works part-time to supplement a meager family income, and three older brothers. They live in a rural area, and Helene's older brothers were her primary playmates in her early childhood. She is shy, she dresses like a boy, and she has no girlfriends. In elementary school, compared with middle school, she was sometimes the victim of crude remarks, particularly on the school bus. However, the school was a small one, she had a few girlfriends, and several adults took an active interest in her and engaged her in school activities. Middle school, by contrast, is a disaster for Helene; there are numerous unfamiliar students, and like her schoolmates, she moves from room to room. She is taunted, is the object of mean and obscene gestures, and is not part of any definable group.

Barry is nine. He is pudgy and pale, and he has no interest in the sports activities that seem to consume so many of his classmates. Like Helene, he comes from a close-knit family of modest economic means. His two siblings are both younger, and his best friend, a boy who lives across the street, is homeschooled. Barry reads voraciously and is sensitive about all living things. Coming upon a group of boys who were terrorizing a cat, Barry began to cry. Since then, these boys have pushed him against the school wall and called him derogatory names.

Bullying—also referred to as peer victimization—is typically defined as intentional harm-doing, carried out repeatedly over time. It occurs within an interpersonal relationship that is characterized by an imbalance of power, and it may take several forms, including physical or verbal victimization, rejection, and cyberbullying (Seeley, Tombari, Bennett, & Dunkle, 2011). Helene and Barry are both victims of bullying. Interestingly, many successful, well-educated adults also report being bullied as children.

In a recent report, Seeley *et al.* (2011) summarize results of three bullying-related studies funded by the Office of Juvenile Justice and Delinquency Prevention (OJJDP). One study was quantitative, asking 1,000 students in the sixth grade whether they were engaged in their school and whether they had experienced specific kinds of bullying. The other two studies

were qualitative. In one the researchers interviewed high-achieving high school students and incarcerated young inmates who had been bullied about their past experience. In the second, they asked teachers for their appraisals of bullying programs, as well as how schools should respond to bullying.

Among the key findings from the three reports are the following:

- Bullying does not have a direct effect on truancy; that is, students who are bullied will not necessarily stay away from school.
- Truancy will be likely to occur if bullied students are not engaged, so engaging bullied students in academics or extracurricular activities will help them overcome the negative effects of bullying.
- The change in school structure, from elementary to middle school, often makes bullied students feel more isolated.
- Responsible adults are crucial support for bullied students.
- Schools should teach students how to care for others, and they should provide opportunities for their students to participate in community service; bullies and their victims are on equal ground when they are participating in such activities. Said another way, bullies do not hold the upper hand when they are out of their environment.
- Prefabricated programs or curricula to prevent and address bullying are often not effective. Teachers do not like them, and the lessons they teach do not stay with the students.

The above summary, as well as the full report (available from the OJJDP website), gives reason to hope. Despite much of the research on the negative effects of bullying, many children who are bullied find caring adult mentors and engage in meaningful activities, even becoming high achievers in high school and beyond.

However, the OJJDP research also highlights the pitfalls that may be inherent in the very structure of the middle school system, whereby students must transition from a close-knit elementary school community to an impersonal, hectic environment with no consistent adult mentor available. This is something to think about for parents preparing to send their children to middle schools.

(Jolliffe & Farrington, 2006), cruelty to animals (Henry & Sanders, 2007), and many engage in a life of antisocial and violent behavior long after they leave school (Henry & Sanders, 2007). However, although bullying remains a problem for children and adolescents, the perpetrators are far more likely than the victims to engage in antisocial behavior in their adulthood.

WORKPLACE VIOLENCE

Defining Workplace Violence

Many terms and behaviors have been subsumed under the rubric of workplace violence. In the public mind, workplace violence usually means a worker killing his or her coworkers or supervisors. Commentators, researchers, and experts, on the other hand, have used workplace violence to refer to a wide range of aggressive actions, such as gossip, assaults, sexual assaults, robberies, and murders. For our purpose, it is worthwhile to distinguish between workplace aggression and workplace violence. **Workplace aggression** is "a general term encompassing all forms of behavior by which individuals attempt to harm others at work or their organizations" (Neuman & Baron, 1998, p. 393). Workplace aggression may range from subtle and hidden actions to active confrontations or direct destruction of property (Hepworth & Towler, 2004). **Workplace violence**, on the other hand, refers to incidents in which the offender intends to cause *serious* physical or bodily harm to an individual or individuals within an organization or to the organization itself.

In 2009, 521 persons, age 16 or older, were murdered at the workplace (Harrell, 2011). The highest workplace violence occurs for law enforcement officers, security guards, and bartenders (Harrell, 2011). Although the impression derived from media reports over the past two decades is that workplace violence is expanding, it must be emphasized that a large majority of workplace homicides do *not* involve murder between coworkers or supervisors *within* an organization but occur in robberies and related crimes by people *outside* the organization (Neuman & Baron, 1998) (See **Tables 10-5**

TABLE 10-5	Workplace Homicides of Victims, Age 16 or Older, by Known Offender Type, 2005–2009
Offender Type	**Percent of Workplace Homicide (%)**
Total	100.0
Robbers and other assailants	70.3
Robbers	38.3
Other assailants	32.0
Workplace associates	21.4
Coworker, former coworker	11.4
Customer, client	10.0
Relatives	4.0
Spouse	2.9
Other relatives	0.8
Other personal acquaintances	4.3
Current or former boyfriend or girlfriend	2.0
Other acquaintances	2.3

Source: Data from Harrell (2011).

TABLE 10-6	Victim–Offender Relationship for Victims of Workplace Violence, by Sex, 2005–2009

	Percent of Workplace Violence	
Victim–Offender Relationship	**Male (%)**	**Females (%)**
Total	100.0	100.0
Intimate partner	0.8	1.7
Other relatives	0.6	0.7
Well-know/casual acquaintances	11.7	18.9
Work relationships	25.5	31.7
Customer/client	3.9	6.5
Patient	1.5	6.0
Current or former	—	—
Supervisor	1.2	3.3
Employee	2.6	1.7
Coworker	16.3	14.3
Do-not-know relationship	8.5	6.1
Stranger	52.9	40.9

Source: Data from Harrell (2011).

and 10-6). That is, young convenience store clerks or fast-food restaurant workers are often the victims of robbery and other forms of violence while working. Between 2005 and 2009, approximately 28 percent of the workplace homicides involved victims in retail sales and related occupations, and about 17 percent victims were in protective service occupations (e.g., law enforcement officers, security officers) (Harrell, 2011). Shootings accounted for 80 percent of the workplace homicides.

Examples of Workplace Violence

Gregorie (2000, pp. 2–3) outlines four types of offenders who commit violence at the workplace, in an effort that is very useful for understanding this phenomenon. The classification system or typology was first identified by the California Division of Occupational Safety and Health in *Guidelines for Workplace Security* (1995). The four types of offenders are as follows:

- *Type I.* This offender has no legitimate relationship to the workplace or the victim and usually enters the workplace to commit a criminal action such as a robbery or theft. Common victims of Type I offenders are small, late-night retail establishments, including convenience stores and restaurants, and taxi drivers. This type of workplace violence also includes terrorist and hate crimes such as the World Trade Center and Alfred P. Murrah Federal Building bombings, as well as attacks on women's health centers or immigration centers.
- *Type II.* This offender is the recipient of some service provided by the victim or workplace and may be either a current or former client, patient, or customer.

- *Type III.* This offender has an employment-related involvement with the workplace. The act of violence is usually committed by a current or former employee, supervisor, or manager who has a dispute with another employee of the workplace. This type of workplace violence offender is usually referred to as the "disgruntled employee" and is often someone who has been fired, demoted, or lost benefits. When death results from the violence, if the victim or victims were of higher authority than the perpetrator, the crime may be called **authority homicide**.
- *Type IV.* This offender has an indirect involvement with the workplace because of a relationship with an employee. The offender may be a current or former spouse or partner, someone who was in a dating relationship with the employee, or a relative or friend. This type of violence follows the employee into the workplace from the outside.

The first of these categories, depicting violence by someone not connected to workplace, accounts for the vast majority of violence and homicides, perhaps as high as 80 percent of the total (Critical Incident Response Group, 2001). The motive is usually robbery, and in many cases, the offender or offenders are carrying a gun or other weapon, greatly increasing the likelihood that the victim (most often, the victims) will be killed or seriously wounded. However, the attacker may be striking out directly at the workplace itself and its inhabitants. Workers who exchange cash with customers as part of the job, work late-night hours, and work alone are at greatest risk for Type I workplace violence when robbery is the motive. In California, for example, the majority (60%) of workplace homicides involved a person entering a small, night-retail establishment, such as a liquor store, gas station, or convenience food store, to commit a robbery (Southerland, Collins, & Scarborough, 1997). Taxi drivers, security guards, and proprietors of "mom-and-pop" stores are also vulnerable to this type of workplace violence.

Type II workplace violence usually involves health care workers, police officers, counselors, schoolteachers, college professors, social workers, and mental health workers. An example of Type II workplace violence is provided by the University of Iowa Injury Prevention Research Center (2001, p. 7):

> Rhonda Bedow, a nurse who works in a state-operated psychiatric facility in Buffalo, NY, was attacked by an angry patient who had a history of threatening behavior, particularly against female staff. He slammed Bedow's head down onto a counter after learning that he had missed the chance to go outside with a group of other patients. Bedow suffered a concussion, a bilaterally dislocated jaw, an eye injury, and permanent scarring on her face from the assault.

In the 1970s and 1980s, a number of social workers were assaulted—and sometimes killed—by individuals who were furious because their children were removed from the family home or because they lost custody based on social worker recommendations. These tragedies prompted many state agencies to erect barricades between clients and the workers and, in many cases, to hire private security officers to screen those entering the offices. Likewise, after similar incidences in which family court judges and lawyers were threatened, shot at, or stabbed, family court proceedings—which had traditionally been held rather informally—were formalized and the courtrooms themselves subjected to heightened security.

The Type III workplace violence offender probably is regarded by the media as the most sensational and receives a bulk of its coverage. As noted by the Critical Incident Response Group (2001, p. 11), "mass murders in the workplace by unstable employees have become media-intensive events." An example of Type III violence occurred on August 20, 1986, when a part-time letter carrier, facing possible dismissal after a troubled work history, walked into the Edmond, Oklahoma, post office where he worked and shot 14 people to death before killing himself. In the previous three years, four postal employees were slain by present or former coworkers in separate shootings in South Carolina, Alabama, and Georgia (Critical Incident Response Group, 2001). Similar mass murders in the workplace by emotionally disturbed employees have drawn considerable media scrutiny and—because they initially came to attention with the post office crimes—the term *going postal* was introduced into the American lexicon. The Critical Incident Response Group (2001) has identified a number of additional examples, including four state lottery executives killed in Connecticut by a lottery accountant (1998), seven coworkers killed by a Xerox technician in Honolulu (1999), seven murdered by a software engineer at the Edgewater Technology Company in Massachusetts (2000), four killed by a 66-year-old former forklift driver in Chicago (2001), three killed by an insurance executive at Empire Blue Cross and Blue Shield in New York City (2002), three murdered by a plant worker at a manufacturing plant in Missouri (2003), and six killed by a plant worker at Lockheed–Martin aircraft plant in Mississippi (2003). The Chicago, New York, Mississippi, and Connecticut shooters killed themselves during the incident. The Honolulu and Massachusetts shooters went to trial, both raised the insanity defense, but both were convicted.

Type IV workplace violence represents a spillover of domestic violence or intimate partner violence into the workplace, and usually women are the victims. As noted earlier, homicide is the leading cause of workplace death for women, accounting for 41 percent of all female worker fatalities (Kelleher, 1997). A good example of Type IV workplace violence is provided by the University of Iowa Injury Prevention Research Center (2001, p. 11):

> Pamela Henry, an employee of Protocall, an answering service in San Antonio, had decided in the summer of 1997 to move out of the area. The abusive behavior of her ex-boyfriend, Charles Lee White, had spilled over from her home to her workplace, where he appeared one day in July and assaulted her. She obtained and then withdrew a protective order against White, citing her plans to leave the country. On October 17, 1997, White again appeared at Protocall. This time he opened fire with a rifle, killing Henry and another female employee before killing himself.

Perpetrators of Workplace Violence

According to the FBI (Southerland *et al.*, 1997), the workplace homicide offender whose motivation is not robbery is often a disgruntled employee (Type III) who believes the job is (or was) his life, is a loner, has few friends, and lacks a support system. The target of the attack may be a person or persons working within a building or structure or for an organization that symbolizes the authority (Douglas *et al.*, 1992). However, it should be emphasized that there is no precise "profile" or litmus test that will provide clear signs that an employee will become violent. Rather, it is important for employees and employers to remain alert to unstable or problematic behavior that, in combination with threatening behavior, could result in violence (see **Table 10-7**).

A vast majority of Type III victims are killed (often randomly) by disgruntled employees who were fired or felt mistreated by the company or agency. It seems that a particular autocratic work environment, such as found in large, impersonal bureaucratic organizations, can be a problem. However, as the examples provided by the Critical Incident Response Group (2001) indicate,

TABLE 10-7	Identifying Problematic Behaviors in Coworkers Which Might Lead to Violence

- Increasing belligerence
- Ominous specific threats
- Hypersensitivity to criticism
- Recent acquisition/fascination with weapons
- Apparent obsession with a supervisor or coworker or employee grievance
- Preoccupation with violent themes
- Interest in recently publicized violent events
- Outbursts of anger
- Extreme disorganization
- Noticeable changes in behavior
- Homicidal/suicidal comments or threats

Source: Based on information from Critical Incident Response Group (2001), pp. 21–22.

no workplace seems immune. As we discussed previously, when an employee feels frustrated and angry, he or she may be more likely to strike out, and this could occur even in a benevolent work environment.

Similar to mass murderers in general, offenders who commit authority homicide—in which a figure in authority, such as a supervisor, is killed—tend to be white males who have few social supports, are socially isolated, and blame others (externalize) for their problems and misfortune. They are often seriously depressed. Very often, the offender expects to die at the scene, either at his own hands or by the police. Authority offenders also tend to be preoccupied with weapons, accumulating a number of them over a period of time with eventual revenge or "occupational martyrdom" in mind. The weapons are often of maximum lethality, such as automatic assault weapons (e.g., AK-47) (Douglas *et al.*, 1992). In most instances, the offender is middle-aged (over 30 and under 60) (Kelleher, 1997). There is also evidence that workplace offenders tend to have a history of violent behavior, and alcohol or drug abuse, and will vocalize, or otherwise act out, their violent intentions prior to the authority homicide (Kelleher, 1997).

Summary and Conclusions

In this chapter, we have taken a closer look at types of homicides that are relatively rare but have significant impact on large numbers of victims, both directly and indirectly. Multiple murders can be divided into three main categories: serial, spree, and mass killings, but the spree murder category is losing favor with criminologists and investigators. Mass killings are often divided into classic and family mass murders. We focused on the classic form here, having discussed family violence in Chapter 9. In classic mass murders, the victims are most often strangers, though they may be acquaintances or persons with whom the murderer interacts on a frequent basis, such as in a workplace situation. The victims of classic mass murder also often represent a group toward which the perpetrator has hostility, such as women or members of a certain ethnic group. The deaths that occur as a result of terrorism, a distinct form of mass murder, are discussed in Chapter 11. In addition, the present chapter reviewed non-homicidal actions that have received attention in recent years, including school violence, bullying, and workplace violence.

Many of the crimes that are covered here are often investigated by police with the help of investigative psychology, loosely referred to as "profiling." Because *profiling* is the commonly used term, we employ it in the chapter, but have divided it into five areas: psychological profiling, suspect-based profiling, geographic profiling, crime-scene profiling, and equivalent death analysis. Investigative psychology, which refers to the application of psychological research and principles to the investigation of criminal behavior, is used particularly in crime-scene profiling, but it can occur in all forms. It typically includes crime scene investigative methods, such as reviewing features of the modus operandi, the personation or signature, and staging. Crime scene profiling focuses more on the offender, identifying personality traits, behavioral patterns, demographic features, and sometimes geographic habits, such as the distance offenders travel from their homes.

Crime scene profiling is a strategy widely used in law enforcement, particularly for multiple murders or sex crimes. In serial murders, for example, profiling is helpful particularly if the offender demonstrates some psychopathology, such as a specific method of torture. However, it may also be very useful for nonviolent crimes, such as burglaries or arsons. Profiling is a complex enterprise, though, and unfortunately it is often based on hunches or anecdotal information. However, with increasingly larger databases made available to professional profilers, along with scientifically rigorous methods applied to the techniques they use, there is hope that the enterprise will gain validity. Rarely does a profile provide the specific identity of an offender, but it is not intended to. As Douglas *et al.* (1986) noted, profiling tries to narrow the field to a manageable number of suspects.

The form of multiple murder that most terrorizes a community is the serial killing, particularly because it may appear that anyone can be a potential victim. Serial killers generally choose their victims for their specific characteristics, however. For example, victims may be women in their twenties, transients, preadolescent and adolescent boys, prostitutes, or, in the case of female serial killers, husbands, suitors, or individuals dependent on them for care. Research indicates that the great majority of serial killers are males; however, prior assumptions that they were invariably white males may be unwarranted. Serial killers are rarely juveniles.

There are many descriptions and illustrations of mass murder but few empirical studies. In the classic form of mass murder, an individual enters a scene and opens fire on a group of people, such as in a restaurant, a place of worship, or a place of work. This form of mass murder is usually carefully planned, and the victims are often symbols of the murderer's discontent (e.g., the workplace or a group of women). Alternately, the group of victims includes one or more individuals whom the killer hates or blames for his misfortunes. Mass murderers are typically socially isolated and withdrawn and have inadequate interpersonal and social skills.

We discussed unique crimes that have the potential of becoming mass murders, such as school and workplace violence. School violence is a widespread problem in the educational system, although it rarely ends in death. In the 1990s, however, an inordinate number of school shootings were reported, the most noteworthy being the Columbine incident in Littleton, Colorado, in 1999. Investigations of school shootings consistently find that peer rejection and social rejection in general were factors contributing to the eruption of violence. Bullying, discussed briefly in Chapter 6, was covered here as well because of sobering evidence that adolescent school shooters were often the targets of bullying. However, other factors, such as cruelty to animals and fascination with guns and other weaponry, often appeared in the background of school shooters. Virtually all had communicated their intentions to other students, sometimes in specific terms.

The chapter ends with coverage of workplace violence, another phenomenon that may or may not end in mass murder. Offenders are divided into four categories: those having no connection to the workplace, those who have received some service provided by the organization, those who currently or formerly worked there, and those who have some relationship with one or more employees. The vast majority of violence is perpetrated by the first category, those who come into the workplace from the outside, such as the convenience store robber who kills its employees. Most psychological research has focused on the third type, the disgruntled employee who kills supervisors and/or fellow workers. These individuals are not only angry but also usually socially isolated and seriously depressed. Typically, they expect or plan to die at the scene.

Key Concepts

Actuarial profiling
Authority homicide
Autoeroticism
Base rate
Classic mass murder
Clinical profiling
Confirmation bias
Crime scene profiling
Disorganized crime scene
Equivocal death analysis
Reconstructive psychological
    evaluation

Family mass murder
Geographic profiling
Investigative psychology
Mass murder
Mixed crime scene
Organized crime scene
Personation
Psychological autopsy
Psychological profiling
Psychological signature

Serial murder
Signature
Spree murder
Staging
Suspect-based profiling
Undoing
Victimological
    perspective
Workplace aggression
Workplace violence

Review Questions

1. Briefly describe the difference between an organized and disorganized crime scene. Discuss the profile characteristics of each.
2. Identify and discuss the five-category typology based on the motivations for mass killings provided by Fox and Levin.
3. Define geographic profiling, and identify in what ways it is useful to law enforcement.
4. Why is the victimology perspective important in understanding serial murder?
5. Define staging, and give examples of when it is most likely to occur.
6. Define investigative psychology.
7. List and define the types of multiple murder, and provide an illustration of each.
8. List and briefly define each of the four categories of workplace violence.
9. What are the psychological characteristics of mass murderers, according to the available research?
10. According to the available research, what characteristics are school shooters most likely to have in common?

11

Psychology of Terrorism

CHAPTER OBJECTIVES

- Examine the many definitions of terrorism.
- Evaluate the motives of terrorists and goals of terrorist groups.
- Describe the lone-wolf terrorist.
- Identify the social contexts that spawn and promote terrorism.
- Introduce a typology of terrorism in order to emphasize the multidimensional features of persons who engage in it.
- Identify psychological concepts that contribute to the understanding of terrorist activity.

> "Terrorist acts are defined to a large degree by their impact, and especially their psychological effects" (Ditzler, 2004, p. 189).
>
> Without a doubt, "the September 11 attack had achieved its purpose: to create a global psychological state of fear, uncertainty, and terror" (Marsella, 2004, p. 39).
>
> "Terrorism, like a shark attack, wields tremendous psychological impact" (Victoroff, 2005, p. 33).

As the above quotes indicate, the nature of terrorism is basically psychological; its aim is to create crippling fears and psychological debilitation in a civilian population (Levant, 2002). Given the nature of terrorism, it is clear that psychology has an important role to play in understanding it, counteracting it, and treating its traumatizing effects (Levant, Barbanel, & DeLeon, 2004). Not until September 11, 2001, however, did psychologists demonstrate more than a passing interest in investigating, studying, and writing about terrorism (Marsella, 2004).

On that day, an entire nation and much of the world were stunned by the destruction of life and property, when two planes struck the World Trade Center in New York City, a third airliner was flown into the Pentagon in the nation's capital, and a fourth crashed into a field in Somerset County, Pennsylvania. The plane that crashed in Pennsylvania was believed to be heading for the White House, but heroic passengers on board took over the plane, preventing it from remaining on its original course. At the World Trade Center, 2,823 were killed (including five children under the age of five); at the

Pentagon, 184 lives were lost; and all 40 passengers died in the Pennsylvania crash. Nineteen terrorists (all under the age of 35) were directly involved in the airline hijacking (10 at the World Trade Center, 5 at the Pentagon, and 4 in Pennsylvania) (Federal Bureau of Investigation, 2002). Since that day, there has been an enormous increase in books, articles, and commentary on the psychological foundations of modern-day terrorism by psychologists, psychiatrists, and other mental health professionals.

Terrorists are often described as abnormal individuals, sometimes by using terms like *evil, psychologically insane, immoral, seriously mentally disordered,* or *psychopathic killers.* Indeed, the outrageous, inhumane attacks on innocent civilians challenge the view that terrorists are rational, emotionally stable individuals. However, there is very little evidence that members of terrorist organizations are mentally unstable, irrational, or psychopathic (Maikovich, 2005; Monahan, 2011; Sarangi & Alison, 2005). In fact, many studies report that terrorists are psychologically much healthier and considerably more stable than other violent criminals (Silke, 2008). There are exceptions, as we will note later in the chapter. Essentially, though, people who demonstrate mental or emotional disorders do not make good terrorists. "They lack the discipline, rationality, self-control and mental stamina needed if terrorists are to survive for any length of time" (Silke, 2008, p. 104). In fact, well-organized terrorist groups are said to expel individuals from their ranks who are emotionally unstable, primarily because they represent a security threat (Post & Gold, 2002). As we learned in Chapter 5, much of the aggression displayed by violent criminals is spontaneous or reactive; terrorists go to great lengths preparing for their attacks, and any breach of their plans seriously compromises their goals. In summary, terrorism is most often a rational behavior based on the belief that violence is morally justified and necessary to further political goals (Ruby, 2002). In the present chapter, we explore these themes in greater detail.

DEFINITIONS AND EXAMPLES

Throughout this book, and most particularly in Chapters 9 and 10, we have encountered individuals who terrorized others through their criminal activity. Serial killers, for example, terrorize communities, and a home invader may terrorize a family. However, to terrorize is not to be a terrorist in the context of this chapter. Furthermore, holding a community ransom to fear that still another person will be killed is not to engage in terrorism in the context of this chapter. How then do we define *terrorism*? According to Sternberg (2003), terrorism is simply "the systematic use of terror, especially as a means of coercion" (p. 299). Hallett (2004) defines the term as a theatrical crime against person or property in which only symbolic or psychological satisfaction to the perpetrators is gained. Using these definitions, however, serial killers would qualify as terrorists.

In federal law, terrorism is defined as "the unlawful use of force or violence against persons or property to intimidate or coerce a government, the civilian population, or any segment thereof, in furtherance of political or social objectives" (Code of Federal Regulations, 18 U.S.C § 2331(1)). In accordance with this more elaborate conception, terrorism may be either domestic or international, depending on the origin, base, and objectives of the terrorist organization (U.S. Department of Justice, 2000a). In the United States, domestic terrorism refers to groups or an individual based and operating entirely within the United States or its territories without foreign direction. A well-known example occurred on April 17, 1995, when a truck bomb destroyed the Alfred P. Murrah Federal Building in Oklahoma City, killing 167 (19 were children) and injuring 684 persons. Timothy McVeigh, a U.S. citizen and former soldier, was convicted and eventually executed for this crime. His coconspirator, Terry Nichols, pled guilty in both federal and state courts to avoid the death penalty. The Oklahoma City attack remains the deadliest *domestic* terrorist incident ever committed on U.S. soil.

Most recently, on November 5, 2009, Army Major Nidal Hasan killed 13 people and wounded 32 others at Fort Hood, Texas. All but two were military personnel. Although we could consider this an illustration of mass murder of the workplace violence variety discussed in Chapter 10, the circumstances of the shooting—including words shouted by Hasan as he opened fire—led the Department of Defense (DoD) to consider this a form of domestic terrorism. An independent review was undertaken to address possible deficiencies in DoD's force protection and identify employees who could potentially pose credible threats to themselves or others (Monahan, 2011). However, Hasan could also be considered a "lone-wolf" terrorist, a topic to be discussed later in the chapter.

Other illustrations of domestic terrorism include actions by members of far-right extremist groups, including political and religious white supremacists, such as Aryan Nations and neo-Nazi organizations. For example, members of the so-called Army of God claimed responsibility for bombings of women's health centers where abortions were performed and an alternative lifestyle nightclub in Atlanta. This form of domestic terrorism is increasingly gaining attention in the scholarly literature (see, generally, Freilich, Chermak, & Caspi, 2009 and references cited therein), and some law enforcement authorities consider it a greater threat to national security than international terrorism (Chermak, Freilich, & Shemtob, 2009).

International terrorism refers to violent acts or acts dangerous to human life that are a violation of the criminal laws of the United States or any state and under the direction of a foreign government, group, organization, or person. Although terrorist activities are widespread and affect people throughout the world, the most vivid example of international terrorism and the one most covered by the media and the research literature is that represented by the events that occurred on September 11, 2001. With that exception, most international terrorism aimed at U.S. property or citizens occurs in other countries. For example, in the late twentieth century, groups in Columbia targeted American interests, kidnapped seven U.S. citizens, and carried out multiple bombings against oil pipelines used by American companies (U.S. Department of Justice, 2000a). Another example involves the American embassies in Nairobi, Kenya, and Dar es Salaam, Tanzania, where in August 1998, both embassies were bombed almost simultaneously. The truck bombings killed 224, including 12 American citizens, and injured over 4,500 located in or near the embassies. **Figures 11-1** and **11-2** illustrate data gathered by the National Counterterrorism Center (NCTC) on global attacks in 2008. And, just as this book is going to press, the nation is mourning the deaths of Christopher Stevens, the U.S. ambassador to Libya, and three other Americans who were staff and security personnel at the consulate in Benghazi. In what is now recognized as a terrorist attack, they were killed on September 11, 2012.

Despite these sobering incidents and numbers, Americans living, working, or visiting abroad are no more likely to be victimized by terrorist activities than are citizens of other nations. Terrorist activities were a fact of life in other parts of the world long before September 11, 2001, and they have continued since then. Japan, the United Kingdom, Spain, Indonesia, Israel, Palestine, Sri Lanka, and Saudi Arabia have all been targeted. On March 11, 2004, a series of coordinated bombings directed at the commuter train system of Madrid, Spain, was carried out by an al-Qaeda–inspired terrorist group. The attacks killed 191 people and injured 1,900. On July 7, 2005, the first Islamist suicide bombings in Europe occurred in London (Silke, 2008). Four suicide bombers detonated explosives during the morning rush hour, killing 52 persons and injuring 700 (Silke, 2008). And on October 1, 2005, terrorists believed to be associated with the terrorist network Jemaah Islamiah detonated bombs at two sites in Bali, Indonesia, killing 26 and injuring about 120 persons. Terrorism frightens and touches people worldwide.

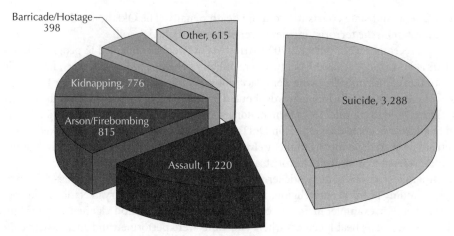

FIGURE 11-1   Deaths by Method in Global Attacks, 2008   *Source*: National Counterterrorism Center (April 2009).

A quick scan of the literature reveals there are multiple additional definitions, and many illustrations, of terrorism. Victoroff (2005) found at least 109 definitions within the academic literature alone. He asserts that the lack of consensus is probably inescapable, considering the heterogeneity of terrorist behaviors and the wide variety of declared or assumed motivations, justifications, and goals. As Monahan (2011, p. 15) asks succinctly, "(I)s it plausible to expect that the risk factors for joining the Irish Republican Army are the same as the risk factors for joining the Taliban?" Trying to reach a comprehensive definition is complicated by the maxim, "One person's terrorist is another person's freedom fighter" (Marsella, 2004, p. 15).

Despite the vast and sometime overwhelming array of definitions, Marsella (2004) finds some common ground in all of them, although—as in the definitions above—it may be implicit. "Terrorism is broadly viewed as (a) the use of force or violence (b) by individuals or groups (c) that is directed toward civilian populations (d) and intended to instill fear (e) as a means of coercing individuals or groups to change their political and social positions" (p. 16). These five elements are common to the illustrations used in this chapter. Note that the fifth element in particular discourages any temptation to call a serial killer a terrorist. Marsella further notes that any comprehensive definition of terrorism also requires thoughtful consideration of the psychosocial context, motives, and consequences of the act.

Although terrorism is not a new phenomenon, terrorism today offers a much greater threat of violence to the world than ever before. This is because of the globalization of commerce, travel, and the rapid flow of information, "...which puts economic disparities and ideological competition in sharp relief and facilitates cooperative aggression by far-flung but like-minded conspirators" (Victoroff, 2005, p. 3). Victoroff (2005) also notes that, because of this rise in globalization, religious fundamentalism has ascended as an aggrieved competitor with the market-economic, democratic, and secular trends of the rapidly changing modern world. Furthermore, this expanding globalization has been instrumental in the emergence of the first *multinational* terrorist group of the twenty-first century, called al-Qaeda (Hellmich, 2008), the group responsible for the attacks of September 11.

In response to these attacks, the United States launched strong military forces into Afghanistan in an effort to weed out al-Qaeda cells in that country. Soon thereafter, the United

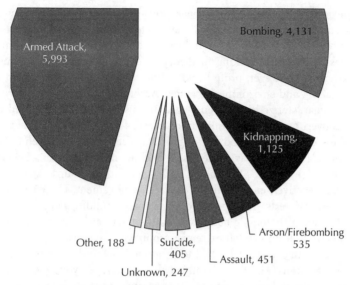

FIGURE 11-2   Primary Methods Used in Global Attacks, 2008
Source: National Counterterrorism Center (April 2009).

States invaded Iraq on the premise that it contained weapons of mass destruction (WMD) and in apparent pursuit of al-Qaeda–sponsored organizations. Critics argued forcefully—and events since then have documented—that the invasion of Iraq was unjustified. Furthermore, many people believe that such aggressive military responses are rarely successful in preventing future attacks because they do not address the root conditions that spawn terrorism (Marsella, 2004). Instead, "there must be a response to prevent its emergence and its growth and development as an appealing option" (Marsella, 2004, p. 34). "(T)errorism may be contained but never defeated as long as there are real or perceived threats or injustices that foster widespread hatred and revenge. There may be small and large military successes, but eventually there must be coming to grips with the strengths and weaknesses of the human psyche and the cultural milieu in which it is fostered" (Moghaddam & Marsella, 2004b, p. 4).

CLASSIFICATION OF TERRORIST GROUPS

In addition to the domestic and international classifications, there are several other ways to classify terrorism and those who engage in it. The FBI classifies terrorists according to political leanings. For example, *right-wing terrorists* are extremist groups or individuals that generally adhere to an antigovernment or racist ideology and often engage in a variety of hate crimes and violence. They may be prompted to become active by the passage of legislation or by government policy in opposition to their beliefs, such as laws placing restrictions on gun ownership or taxation or laws granting civil rights to minority groups. As noted above, far-right organizations are receiving considerable research scrutiny. Freilich *et al.* (2009) note that, though the domestic far right is not easily defined, it is composed of individuals or groups that are fiercely nationalistic, antiglobal, suspicious of centralized federal authority, and reverent of individual liberty, such as the right to own guns or be free from taxes. They also believe in conspiracy theories, believe attacks to national sovereignty and/or personal liberty are imminent, and consequently participate in paramilitary training in survival skills.

Left-wing extremist groups have also been prevalent in American history. Although less likely to be labeled "terrorists," their actions may qualify them for that designation when they move from political activism to violent activities. Historically, left-wing extremism developed from working-class movements seeking in theory to eliminate class distinctions. More modern left-wing extremists, however, protest and politically agitate against certain governmental policies, discrimination, and environmental issues. According to Smith and Morgan (1994), the extreme left "...is characterized by extreme egalitarianism, an extreme hatred of racism and capitalism, and an overt opposition to militarianism" (p. 44). Examples of American radical left groups include the Weather Underground—originally called the Weathermen (taken from a line in a Bob Dylan song). The group was created as an offshoot of Students for a Democratic Society (SDS) to promote social change. SDS—along with many other groups—strongly opposed the Vietnam War and later actively engaged in the civil rights movement. The Weathermen, however, went beyond peaceful protests. They bombed government buildings and some banks, though they always tried to warn the public before the bombings in an effort to preserve human life. Another powerful and well-known left extremist group was the Black Panther Party, an African American organization that was established to promote black influence through militant-type protests and demonstrations. The Black Panthers also encouraged young African Americans to be proud of their heritage and sponsored various programs to help the black community, including recreational and nutritional programs. The organization was most active in the United States from the mid-1960s to the mid-1970s. Law enforcement organizations were highly suspicious of the group's intentions and went to great lengths to discredit and destroy the organization. Among the most controversial law enforcement activities was the raid on Black Panther headquarters that included the fatal shooting of two Panthers, Fred Hampton and Mark Clark.

Another FBI classification is **special interest extremists**, whose activities revolve around one issue about which they are passionate. The predominant representatives of this group are violent antiabortion groups that firebombed women's health centers during the 1990s. This category also includes **radical environmental groups**, such as the Earth Liberation Front (ELF). The ELF organization received particular attention during the late 1990s by destroying homes, earth-moving equipment, power lines, computer systems, and buildings that they believed damaged the earth's ecology. In its own words, the organization's primary mission was to "speed up the collapse of industry, to scare the rich, and to undermine the foundations of the state."

During the past several decades, fear of **nuclear/biological/chemical (NBC) terrorism** has apparently accelerated. The thought of being exposed to an invisible or undetectable agent can be more frightening to the general public than the prospect of physical injury or death caused by conventional weapons. Furthermore, the threat of NBC terrorism is more realistic today because terrorists are able to take advantage of the greater availability of information and weapons technology.

Nuclear terrorism includes the use of nuclear bombs or dirty bombs that make use of radioactive material and thus far has not been known to occur. The public is periodically told, however, of thwarted attempts to plant dirty bombs in various global locations. Most recently, in the Spring of 2012, an al-Qaeda plot to place a bomb in an airline departing from Yemen and heading for the United States was stopped; the "terrorist"—instructed to place a bomb in his underwear—was a CIA undercover agent who had infiltrated a terrorist training ground and kept U.S. officials apprised of the plan. By design, he was "arrested" before the plot unfolded.

Unknown and unforeseen attacks with chemical agents or biological agents, on the other hand, have happened. The use of sarin, a deadly nerve agent, in the subway system of Tokyo, Japan, in 1995, provides a horrifying example. The attacks were carried out by the doomsday cult

Aum Shinrikyo (Supreme Truth Sect) and resulted in the deaths of 11 people and injuries to more than 5,000. It is estimated that about 375 pounds of sarin is enough to kill over 50,000 persons. The use of biological agents in this context is sometimes referred to as **bioterrorism**. It involves the use of bacteria, viruses, germs, and other agents such as anthrax, bubonic plague, and smallpox (Marsella, 2004). A recent example of domestic bioterrorism is represented by the anthrax attacks that occurred in the United States less than a month after 9/11/2001. The bioterrorist(s) sent the anthrax by letter to various persons in the eastern sections of the United States, including the Washington offices of Senators Patrick Leahy and Tom Daschle, and the New York office of former CBS anchor Dan Rather. Anthrax is an acute infectious disease caused by the spore-forming bacterium *Bacillus anthracis*. Although anthrax is most commonly found in hoofed mammals, it can also infect humans. Symptoms of the disease vary depending on how the disease was contracted, but they usually occur within seven days after exposure. The serious forms of human anthrax are inhalation anthrax, cutaneous (skin) anthrax, and intestinal (ingestion) anthrax. Inhalation (pulmonary) anthrax starts with inhalation of anthrax spores and has a mortality rate of around 95 percent, even with treatment. Cutaneous anthrax starts with the spore colonizing the skin through an abrasion, cut, or wound. The mortality rate of cutaneous anthrax ranges from 20 percent to 25 percent without treatment and is less than 1 percent with treatment. Intestinal anthrax, by far the worst, is usually transmitted through eating contaminated meat. It has a mortality rate of 95 percent, even when treated.

The bioterrorist(s) sent letters containing both inhalation and cutaneous anthrax to the victims. (The FBI believes the anthrax mailer was a microbiologist, Dr. Bruce Ivins, who committed suicide on August 1, 2008, before formal charges were filed.) The anthrax spores were mixed with a light powder in the folds of the letters. The first known case of the anthrax letter attack killed a photo editor of a newspaper in Boca Raton, Florida, in October 2001. In total, the bioterrorist letters resulted in at least five deaths due to inhalation anthrax infections; another eight cases of nonfatal cutaneous anthrax infections were reported during 2001. Bioterrorism, if delivered under the right conditions and by using a highly infectious biological agent, could be devastating.

A TERRORIST TYPOLOGY

In addition to categorizing terrorist groups on the basis of their interest, researchers have also attempted to provide typologies of individuals within the groups based on their motives. In most cases, the motivation can be generalized to the group as a whole. Ditzler (2004) describes a terrorist typology promulgated by the U.S. Army Command and General Staff College (Terrorism Research Center, 1997). The typology also incorporates some of the research conducted at RAND (Hoffman, 1993). The typology identifies three motivational categories: (1) the rationally motivated terrorist, (2) the psychologically motivated terrorist, and (3) the culturally motivated terrorist.

The *rationally motivated terrorists* are those who consider the goals of the organization and the possible consequences of their actions. They develop well-defined and theoretically achievable goals that may involve political, social, economic, or other specific objectives. In many cases, rationally motivated terrorists try to avoid loss of life but focus instead on destroying infrastructures, buildings, and other symbolic structures to get their message across. Note that this classification does not suggest that the behavior of the group is rational or logical; rather, they believe it is, and they typically carry out carefully planned activities. An example of this motivation was the Weather Underground described earlier.

Psychologically motivated terrorists are driven by "a profound sense of failure or inadequacy for which the perpetrator may seek redress through revenge" (Ditzler, 2004, p. 202). The attraction to terrorism is usually based on the psychological benefits of group affiliation and collective identity. They are especially drawn to terrorist groups that have a charismatic leader. One variation of the psychologically motivated terrorist, though, is the lone-wolf operation, "for whom the validation of the self is not derived through group affiliation, but through the sense of power, mastery, and autonomy that attends to the ability to make unilateral decisions" (Ditzler, 2004, p. 203). An example of this type of terrorist may be Theodore Kaczynski, known as the Unabomber. Often, **lone-wolf terrorists** have strong feelings of social alienation, anger, and extreme antigovernment ideology. In most instances, they view themselves as victims of the "system." We will return to the lone-wolf terrorist, including Kaczynski, later in the chapter.

Culturally motivated terrorists are driven by fear of irreparable damage to their way of living, national heritage, or culture done by an organization, foreign country, or powerful factions. Most often, religion is the aspect that generates the fervor or passion in the group as well as the individual. National or cultural groups that are largely governed or socially defined by a particular system of faith are often constantly vigilant for forces that may eradicate their religious way of life or cultural identity. Ditzler gives the example of Afghanistan under the Taliban, where "Islam provided not only a system of religious faith as understood in the West, but the entire system of civil and criminal law, political organization, and social behavior" (2004, p. 203). Under such conditions, a perceived threat to the faith would be cause for alarm and a threat to the group's existence. However, as we know from the millions of law-abiding and peaceful Islamics, most members of the religious group do not respond to threats to their way of life with acts of terrorism. One of the most troubling outcomes of the events of September 11 was the widespread and unjustified distrust of those of Islamic faith.

FOLLOWERS AND LEADERS: WHO JOINS AND WHO LEADS

Overall, terrorists are a very heterogeneous group, and the range of people who become involved in terrorism may be placed on a wide spectrum (Silke, 2008). They may differ in educational levels, family background, intelligence, gender, socioeconomic class, and religious conviction. Although young men make up the majority of terrorists, some are women, and a few men are much older than the average group member. In his investigation of 242 jihadi terrorists in Europe, Bakker (2006) was able to identify five women recruits. Bakker (2006) also found that most of the terrorists were in their teens to mid-twenties, but some were also in their fifties.Over 70 percent of al-Qaeda members were married, including many who carried out suicide attacks (Sageman, 2004; Silke, 2008). Many married al-Qaeda members also had children.

Sageman (2004) found in a survey of extremist Islamist groups, over 60 percent had some higher levels of education, and three-quarters of them came from upper- or middle-class backgrounds. The 9/11 pilots included the middle-aged, middle-class urban planner Mohammad Atta and the wealthy and educated Ziad Jarrah, who enjoyed discos and beer (Victoroff, 2005). Although a significant number of terrorist members come from well-established or well-heeled family backgrounds, many come from the poorer and less-advantaged people of the world (Miller, 2006). Many terrorists come from backgrounds where, " . . . menial work gives little satisfaction, political freedom is sparse or nonexistent, avenues of recreational escapism are few, and social mobility and hope for a better life is little more than a fantasy" (Miller, 2006, p. 126). For instance, the typical Palestinian terrorist comes from a large family with an impoverished background and low educational achievement, although in recent years there is a trend for more professionals and middle-class individuals to be among the Palestinian terrorist groups (Victoroff, 2005).

In a summary of the literature on risk factors for terrorism, Monahan (2011) confirms the above. He notes that the mean age for terrorists is between 20 and 29, the preponderance are male, and the majority appear to be unmarried. Their backgrounds indicate no evidence of major mental illness. With respect to social class, "the evidence thoroughly contradicts the common belief that terrorists are disproportionately of lower social class.... In terms of occupation, income, and educational level, terrorists appear to be largely indistinguishable from the local population" (p. 10).

Why Do They Join?

When people lack the skills and strategies to modify at least some of their social situations, feelings of helplessness usually result. This may explain why some individuals engage in terrorist activities, but by no means all. These feelings are in turn likely to provoke one of two response patterns: approach (attack) or avoidance (withdrawal). The withdrawal response, as theorized by Martin Seligman (1975), is often called **reactive depression** or **learned helplessness**. The person feels there is nothing that can be done about his or her predicament, so why bother? This response pattern is vividly illustrated by powerless people living under dire poverty conditions, who perceive that they have little opportunity for change—a life without hope. On the other hand, an alternative response is to attack, to lash out in desperation, especially if a person believes this response pattern will be effective in improving his circumstances, or the circumstances of his family or community. If people have next to nothing or little hope for a better future, "the only thing you cannot take away from them is their religious or political or philosophical belief" (Miller, 2006, p. 126). This is especially so if that belief tells them that, despite their hardships, their God is ultimately just and things will work out for them either in this world or in the next.

It has also been hypothesized that young people lacking self-esteem and a sense of self may be primary candidates for joining terrorist groups. Many Irish and European terrorists, for instance, say they became politically violent primarily to seek a sense of purpose and self-worth (Victoroff, 2005). This perspective fits well with Erik Erikson's theory that adolescents reach a stage of identity formation during which ideologies are most likely to have a significant and potentially lasting impact. Erikson viewed identity and the sense of self as central themes in anyone's life course. Arena and Arrigo (2005) point out that some scholars have suggested that many terrorists have failed to effectively negotiate Erickson's eight stages and consequently have assumed a negative identity. The negative identity encourages these persons to turn to extremist organizations to finally experience purpose and meaning in their lives. To what extent terrorists have failed to successfully manage Erickson's stages has not been researched enough to make any conclusions, but it is an interesting hypothesis.

Social learning theory also provides some insight into the psychological processes that influence members to join a terrorist organization. Victoroff (2005) writes, "Teenagers living in hotbeds of political strife may directly witness terrorist behaviors and seek to imitate them or, even more commonly, learn from their culture's public glorification of terrorists—for example, the 'martyr posters' lining the streets of Shi'a regions of Lebanon and Palestinian refugee camps or the songs celebrating the exploits of the PIRA" (p. 18). However, although the theory has strong explanatory power for why they join, it does not completely explain why more young teenagers living within these social contexts do not become terrorists.

Although most do not, some international terrorists volunteer for suicide missions. For Western societies, suicide is often associated with despair, depression, or a disordered mind (Miller, 2006). However, members of terrorist groups are *not* necessarily depressed nor do they see things as hopeless. Rather, upon entering a terrorist organization, they see themselves doing something worthwhile with their lives; and if they participate in a suicide mission, they see themselves as martyrs, bringing honor to their families and communities (LoCicero & Sinclair, 2008). Terrorists on suicide missions firmly believe that their death is for a just cause and that the act provides a ticket to another form of eternal life. Al-Qaeda portrayed martyrdom as a highly desirable goal in the training camps of Afghanistan, and many recruits were willing to volunteer for suicide missions (Busch & Weissman, 2005). After reviewing several studies on the suicidality of terrorists involved in suicide bombings, Monahan (2011) noted that they are not otherwise suicidal—that is, were it not for their mission, they would not likely be candidates for suicide.

A majority of terrorists lack the early developmental antisocial patterns found in chronic *violent* criminal offenders. They are often young men in their teens or twenties who have been good students and model citizens and participants in their communities or families. In general, they come from stable, religious families who may even support their cause and their supreme sacrifice, although some are outcasts from their communities. Their willingness to sacrifice themselves comes from the rage and resentment they have for the unjust persecutions and humiliations they perceive as originating from outside groups, governments, or societies.

Finally, Monahan (2011) posits, there is no evidence that terrorists have personality disorders or problems with substance abuse. In addition, "The search for personality traits that distinguish terrorists from nonterrorists with any degree of reliability has a long and frustrating history" (p. 12). Citing several researchers, Monahan notes that that search has been more or less abandoned.

Becoming a Terrorist: The Process of Radicalization

In the context of terrorism, radicalization is defined as an individual's indoctrination to fully embrace a terrorist group's ideology and mission and to gradually embrace the level of violence necessary to reach the group's goals. Becoming a terrorist is for most people a gradual process (Horgan, 2005). It takes time to become a full-fledged member of a terrorist organization, and the process usually involves many steps, activities, and commitments. The change is frequently achieved by a gradual disengagement of self-censure. The process usually involves small groups engaging in long periods of intense social interactions (Silke, 2008). Within the group, individuals gradually adopt the beliefs of the extreme members in a psychological process called risky shift (Silke, 2008). **Risky shift** refers to the tendency of groups to develop beliefs and make decisions that are more extreme than the initial inclination of its members. It should be emphasized, however, that group discussions do not usually change the members' initial beliefs into the opposite direction, but serve to make more extreme their initial views. For example, the members may find their religious faith and commitment more important and more intense after group discussions.

Once they formally join the terrorist organization, the process is so gradual, the recruits may not even recognize the transformation they are undergoing (Bandura, 2004). The recruits become deeply immersed in the ideology of the organization and may even be expected to perform unpleasant acts to discover if they can tolerate hardships and cognitive dissonance without much self-censure. The social modeling of the more-experienced peers becomes an integral part of the indoctrination process. "The training not only instills the moral rightness and importance of the cause for militant action; it also creates a sense of eliteness and provides social rewards of solidarity and group esteem for excelling in terrorist exploits" (Bandura, 2004, p. 140).

Another common factor in the backgrounds of many jihadi recruits is social marginalization (Silke, 2008), but as noted above, this is not necessarily the case. A majority of the recruits who joined al-Qaeda groups were socially isolated from friends, family, and cultural origins at the time they volunteered. One of the major attractions of terrorist groups is the psychological benefits of group affiliation (Ditzler, 2004). In fact, the opportunity to become a member of a meaningful, close-knit organization often holds much stronger attraction than the stated political objectives of the organization.

From a developmental perspective, ease of recruitment may depend to some extent on the fact that the youth being recruited are developmentally less competent decision makers than adults due to both cognitive and psychosocial factors (LoCicero & Sinclair, 2008). Peer influence is often cited as the primary reason for joining a terrorist group (Victoroff, 2005). Increased social standing among family and friends is also listed as a principal reason. Once young recruits become members of the group, charismatic leaders have a very strong impact on their decision making as well as on the development of their value system.

One psychological element that may be helpful in understanding why someone would become a terrorist is the cognitive construct. Constructs are mental representations of the social environment; they are our mental summaries of what we know and understand about the world, especially the social world. They allow flexibility of thought and increase our ability to anticipate future events and to alter a course of action based on unanticipated events. Some people possess more cognitive constructs and knowledge about the world than others. That is, some people are more cognitively complex and their decision making considers all gray areas. People who possess many sophisticated constructs are able to evaluate behavior and world events in more complex ways than people with few, crude constructs. In essence, a construct is an element of knowledge, which varies with age. As experiences and learning with the environment accumulate, the number, quality, and organization of these constructs normally change. It is likely that those who engage in terrorism as followers have fewer sophisticated constructs, but this cannot necessarily be assumed of leaders.

As pointed out by Commons and Goodheart (2007), "Individuals who operate at a more complex stage are less likely to respond with violent, non-empathic behavior" (p. 96). Therefore, leaders of terrorist organizations try to recruit young men who are enthusiastic but who operate at a relatively low level of cognitive complexity. This does not mean they look for individuals with low intelligence, only that they are naïve and idealistic.

Fail-Safe Procedures

Laurence Miller (2006) notes that many terrorist organizations develop a fail-safe procedure to ensure that the suicide mission is completed. Terrorists eventually have the difficult task of coping with the realization that they must kill people, most often innocent people, including children. This realization can become psychologically stressful to maintain a terrorist lifestyle during the early stages of membership. Consequently, the organization must focus on intense indoctrination of the members who will carry out the mission, and restricts the tactical details of the mission to the leaders of the organization. As the suicide mission approaches, the organization will have those selected to complete the mission engage in a series of "point-of-no-return rituals" to ensure compliance. "These include having members write last letters to friends and relatives, videotaping a goodbye narrative, saying final prayers, and so on" (Miller, 2006, p. 131). These commitments make it increasingly difficult for the "living martyr" to back out. In those cases where the organization believes the martyr may back out, they arrange for a remote control detonation, just in case (Silke, 2003).

Terrorist Leaders

Leaders of terrorist organizations often have some level of charisma (Ditzler, 2004; Staub, 2004). Many are seen by their followers as profoundly significant and influential. Consequently, many recruits of terrorist organizations want to attain some degree of the leader's significance for themselves (Ditzler, 2004), or submit themselves to powerful leaders (Staub, 2004). In terrorist groups, there is often a strong hierarchy, chain of command, and strong expectation of obedience to authority (Staub, 2004). It is instructive for our purposes in this section, to examine in more detail al-Qaeda and its leader Osama bin Laden, who was captured and killed in 2011. Despite his death, al-Qaeda continues on, although in what is considered a weakened and modified form.

Al-Qaeda's decentralized, multifaceted organization with multiple, different activities reflected a high level of cognitive complexity in its leader in the domain of organizational competence (LoCicero & Sinclair, 2008). The complicated organizational structure of al-Qaeda—at least in the years immediately following the September 11 attacks—strongly suggests that bin Laden's organization skills were more advanced than most people realize. Bin Laden was able to organize al-Qaeda on the basis of semiautonomous groups who operated somewhat independently (Staub, 2004). For example, the 19 terrorist hijackers who carried out the attacks of 9/11 were in control of what they were doing and had the power over its execution (LoCicero & Sinclair, 2008). This indicates that the al-Qaeda followers were able to work together without an authoritarian leader and were functioning in a fairly advanced manner. Bin Laden began his quest as a young son of a wealthy Saudi magnate and at some point decided to commit himself to the Afghan resistance (Borum & Gelles, 2005). With his own wealth, bin Laden hired workers and bought equipment, and with his executive skills created and maintained a sophisticated system to reach and sustain Muslims across the globe to unite in a holy war against what they considered to be communist suppression (Borum & Gelles, 2005).

Together with his friend and confidant Ayman al-Zawahiri, bin Laden began to recognize that Islamic discontent, fueled by globalization, Soviet repression of Islam, and anti-Islamic governmental policies, was brewing in various parts of the world (Borum & Gelles, 2005). Perhaps more importantly, they realized that their greatest and most enduring weapon was its anti-American ideology. From this ideological platform, al-Qaeda eventually was able to progress into a web of affiliated networks that coordinated terrorist recruitment, training, and operations.

Prior to bin Laden's death, Borum and Gelles (2005) observed that "al-Qaeda has evolved from a group, to an organization, to a network, and ultimately—in its current form—to an international jihadist movement that embraces and promotes a virulent and militant anti-Western ideology" (p. 481). Although it is sometimes remarked that al-Qaeda has been decimated since bin Laden's death, it is more likely that it has been weakened but not decimated. However, bin Laden's demise may affect the inspirational level of al-Qaeda (DeAngelis, 2011).

Hellmich (2008) reports some experts believed bin Laden was a mentally disordered man without any systematic or logical ideology. However, mentally disordered people usually make poor leaders, incapable of complex technical operations, and are usually incompetent communicators (Hellmich, 2008). Perhaps a more realistic appraisal is that bin Laden operated more like a venture capitalist than a simple-minded, hate-filled fanatic (Hoffman, 2002; LoCicero & Sinclair, 2008). Bin Laden succeeded in creating a high degree of unity and cohesion with his network and was able to develop smaller, independent, but loyal cells over a number of continents (Busch & Weissman, 2005).

Until very recently, there have been strong indications that much of the world, particularly Western nations, did not truly understand the roots of international terrorism. One scholar noted, for example, "Thus far, Al Qaeda is winning the war of exploitation: they understand us and our weaknesses far better than we understand them" (Hellmich, 2008, pp. 120–121). Political leaders in the United States and other democratic countries frequently spoke of the war on terrorism and—in throwing suspicion on individuals of Arab or Muslim descent—alienated a very large part of the world. In the first year of his administration, President Barack Obama stated, "The Muslim world is not our enemy," and the phrase "war on terrorism" began to be downplayed. Nevertheless, the President gave the order to kill bin Laden, and has vowed to pursue terrorists who took lives in Benghazi. Terrorist threats are taken seriously, but the interests of national security are not at odds with diplomacy and a willingness to listen to the grievances of other nations.

Lone-Wolf Terrorists

Although we most often associate terrorism with 9/11, most of the terrorist attacks in the United States have actually been carried out not by international terrorist groups but by one, sometimes two or three, "lone wolves." Moreover, the United States appears to be especially vulnerable to this type of terrorism; available data suggest that, between the years 1968 and 2007, 42 percent of the identified lone-wolf attacks in the world occurred in the United States (COT, 2007).

The "lone-wolf" terrorists are generally psychologically different from conventional terrorists who belong to a more organized extremist group, network, or organization as discussed above. The lone-wolf operators do not rely on group or organization affiliations to validate their mission. They basically operate on their own; they design their own plans, select their own targets, choose their own *modus operandi*, and make their own decisions. Based on their unique interpretations of the world, they perceive injustices that they wish to bring to public attention. Alternately, they adopt the ideological or philosophical leanings of an extremist or outside group, even when the group itself does not engage in terrorist activities. Eric Rudolph, to be discussed below, is a good example of this. **Table 11-1** summarizes the key characteristics of lone-wolf terrorists.

Lone-wolf terrorists present a greater threat in some ways than conventional terrorist organizations. They are more difficult to track and predict, and gathering intelligence on them is a challenge. Explosives tend to be their main weapon of choice, followed by firearms (COT, 2007), and they principally target civilians. The attacks are premeditated, usually carefully planned, and self-financed. Unlike conventional terrorists who are affiliated with organized groups, they usually do not plan to die during their attacks, and they often escape arrest for long periods of time.

One primary example of a lone-wolf terrorist is Theodore Kaczynski, the Unabomber who carried out a campaign of 16 mail bombings over a 17-year period that resulted in 3 deaths and

---

TABLE 11-1 Main Characteristics of Lone-Wolf Terrorists

1) They operate individually.
2) They do not belong to an organized terrorist group, network, or organization.
3) They act without the direct influence of a leader or hierarchy.
4) They may *claim* to be acting on behalf of an interest group.
5) Their attacks are premeditated and carefully planned.
6) They are more likely than other terrorists to be emotionally disturbed.
7) They demonstrate poor interpersonal and social skills.

23 injuries. He apparently wanted to draw attention to a list of societal problems, including technology, the destruction of the environment, and the worldwide industrial system in general. The targets of his mail bombings, therefore, were usually individuals he identified as involved in some aspect of technology, such as in university research facilities. Kaczynski was a highly educated individual who was a loner during much of his life and eventually withdrew from society and lived simply in a wooded cabin. Though he is widely believed to have been seriously mentally disordered, he ferociously resisted an insanity defense. However, he was apparently persuaded to plead guilty to avoid a death sentence, and he entered into a plea agreement whereby he was sentenced to life in prison with no possibility of parole. In a radio interview in May 2009, Kaczynski's younger brother David stated that, although family members continue to write to him in prison, he has never responded. David Kaczynski said that his older sibling was in two prisons, one in the penal system and the other in his own mind.

Timothy McVeigh, the Oklahoma City bomber, is often used as another classical example of a lone-wolf terrorist. Although Terry Nichols provided some tactical support for the bombing and at least one other individual apparently knew of the plan, McVeigh did the planning, target selection, and decision making in the bombing of the Alfred P. Murrah Federal Building in Oklahoma City that resulted in the deaths of 168 people. As mentioned earlier in the chapter, the Oklahoma City bombing was the deadliest attack of terrorism in the United States prior to the September 11, 2001, attacks. McVeigh's motivation was revenge against what he perceived was a tyrannical U.S. government. Another often-cited example of a lone-wolf terrorist is Eric Rudolph—also known as the Olympic Park bomber—who committed a series of bombings in Georgia and Alabama in his campaign against health centers where abortions were performed and gay nightclubs. He had no known coconspirators, and apparently planned and carried out the bombings on his own. Rudolph likely identified with antiabortion activist groups and with groups opposed to equal rights regardless of sexual orientation, although the majority of these groups did not condone his actions. He maintained a socially isolated existence and was eventually captured in 2003 near a trash container as he was foraging for food.

The ideological motivation of most lone-wolf attackers in the United States centers around white supremacy, antiabortion, or antigovernmental issues (COT, 2007). They are often associated with "hate groups," which are increasing in number as we noted early in the book (see Box 1-1, p. 9), even though the groups may disassociate themselves from the actions of these members. In other countries, nationalism, cultural divisions, and religious conflicts are among the more prevalent motivations.

In sum, a majority of lone-wolf terrorists demonstrate poor interpersonal and social skills and adopt an isolationist attitude, staying away from much direct contact with society. Although conventional terrorists who are affiliated with a terrorist organization do not demonstrate behavioral patterns of emotional instability, the rate of psychological problems appears to be significantly higher among lone-wolf terrorists (COT, 2007; Hewitt, 2003).

THE PSYCHOSOCIAL CONTEXT OF TERRORISM

The psychosocial context refers to those social and psychological circumstances that encourage certain behaviors to develop and expand. The psychosocial context is a cognitively constructed world that is sustained through the socialization process associated with each culture. Culture in this sense may be as broad as an entire country or as narrow as a small group of individuals. Thus, there is psychosocial context relevant to both the entire society and the subcultural components of that society.

Ervin Staub (2004) postulates that certain cultural characteristics are conducive to the emergence of terrorist groups. One characteristic is what he calls **cultural devaluation**, a process that occurs when a group or culture is selected by another group or culture as a scapegoat or an ideological enemy. "It might consist of beliefs that the other is lazy, or of limited intelligence, or manipulative, or morally bad, or a dangerous enemy that intends to destroy society or one's own group" (Staub, 2004, p. 158). The United States itself is often seen this way. Many groups and individuals see the United States as being indifferent to the world's suffering and insensitive to global cultural diversity and local identity (Marsella, 2004). Many are convinced that this indifference contributes to the political suppression of the poor and the disadvantaged on a global basis (Marsella, 2004). In addition, some believe American culture is a real and tangible threat to cultural identities, religious affiliation, and ways of life (Marsella, 2004).

It is also worth noting that in the United States, persons associated with racial, ethnic, or religious groups often believe the "dominant" values of American society are inconsistent with the values of their own subgroups. The vast majority of these individuals either accepts this discrepancy or works within the system to change the dominant views. However, some individuals may take a terrorist approach. Thus, although Staub (2004) discusses what are well recognized as *terrorist groups*, the principle of cultural devaluation can also apply to individuals or groups who engage in terroristlike activities but who are not always considered terrorists. Persons who in the 1980s and 1990s firebombed women's health clinics where abortions were provided along with other health services are a case in point.

A second characteristic noted by Staub involves perceptions of *inequality, relative deprivation,* and *injustice.* Disadvantaged, powerless, and shunned people are sometimes more likely to join violent or terrorist groups, not only to get some of their basic needs met but also to gain a sense of identity and community that the terrorist group offers. Staub (2001) calls such situations *difficult life conditions* characterized by hunger, sickness, no sense of community, and lack of shelter for oneself and one's family. "People with few material resources, having little to lose, are prime candidates for joining extremist organizations that promise better living conditions as soon as the haves are removed from power" (Wagner & Long, 2004, p. 211). Not only is there promise of better physical living conditions but also promise of feeling a sense of belonging. Taylor and Louis (2004) make a similar point when they argue that, in addition to disadvantaged economic and political factors, the need for psychological identity draws some individuals into terrorist groups. They assert, "What makes terrorist groups particularly attractive is their simplistic worldview that offers recruits a clear collective identity" (p. 184). To this end, terrorist groups also fill a necessary psychological void. Some individuals, however, may also join because they "have moral principles that lead them to identify with those who are affected by difficult conditions or are unjustly treated" (Staub, 2004, p. 159).

A third characteristic is that many—perhaps most—terrorist groups have a strong hierarchy, sometimes with leaders who are described as all-powerful, convincing, and charismatic. Staub calls this psychosocial characteristic a *strong respect for authority*. Some persons who join simply wish to relinquish their unfulfilled selves and submit themselves to powerful leaders and chain-of-command organizations. They feel most comfortable in hierarchical social structures organized for a challenging or exciting mission. Overall, these real or perceived conditions are apt to be productive areas for terrorist recruitment when promises of a better life beckon.

In summary, terrorism is a learned form of political action that is facilitated by the social and cultural context and maintained by intrinsic rewards, group influences, and indoctrination processes (Ruby, 2002).

PSYCHOLOGY OF TERRORIST MOTIVES AND JUSTIFICATIONS

Despite the efforts discussed earlier in the chapter to neatly classify terrorists and terrorist groups according to motives, there is no single motive for engaging in terrorism. The motives are multiple and complex, ranging from revenge and anger, to attaining paradise, status, respect, and life everlasting (Marsella, 2004). "The roots of terrorism are complex and reside in historical, political, economic, social and psychological factors. Of all of these, psychosocial factors have been among the least studied and the least understood, but arguably the most important" (Moghaddam & Marsella, 2004a, p. xi).

Contemporary researchers are attempting to identify individual risk factors for engaging in terrorism, in an effort to alert investigators to possible activities of this nature. Risk assessment of terrorism is a relatively new enterprise for the psychological community, but several studies have been conducted with this goal in mind. Reviewing this research, Monahan (2011) notes that there is little evidence of risk factors at this point beyond the nontrivial factors (e.g., age, gender) mentioned above. Risk factors for what Monahan calls "common violence" (e.g., a history of violence) do not typically apply to terrorists. Nevertheless, "promising candidates include ideologies, affiliations, grievances, and moral emotions" (p. 29). That is, the extant research suggests that terrorist have strong beliefs in the rightness of their causes and are willing to act on those beliefs; they associate with other terrorists; they have some grievance against a group or a government; and they experience strong moral emotions, such as contempt or disgust. As Monahan emphasizes, it is premature to assume the validity of these risk factors without additional research.

Bandura (2004) skillfully takes the explanation for motives of terrorism into the cognitive realm. He posits that terrorists justify their horrific acts through **cognitive restructuring**, a psychological process that involves moral justifications, euphemistic language, and advantageous comparisons.

Moral justification enables people to engage in reprehensible conduct by telling themselves that their actions are socially worthy and have an ultimate moral and good purpose. Bandura writes,

> The conversion of socialized people into dedicated fighters is achieved not by altering their personality structures, aggressive drives, or moral standards. Rather, it is accomplished by cognitively redefining the morality of killing, so that it can be done free from self-censuring restraints. Through moral sanction of violent means, people see themselves as fighting ruthless oppressors who have an unquenchable appetite for conquest or as protecting their cherished values and way of life, preserving world peace, saving humanity from subjugation to an evil ideology, and honoring their country's international commitments. (2004, p. 124)

The second cognitive restructuring process of **euphemistic language** is based on the well-known research finding that language shapes thought patterns on which people base many of their actions. Importantly, people can display more cruelty or at least can feel better about what they are doing when their conduct is given a sanitized or neutral label. Consequently, they use terms such as *waste* people rather than kill them, or *collateral damage* to designate civilians who are killed in bombings. Among the colorful metaphors and euphemisms offered by Bandura to emphasize his point are bombing missions referred to as "serving the target," and bombs themselves called "vertically deployed anti-personal devices." The third cognitive restructuring process is **advantageous comparison**, where terrorists are convinced that their way of life and fundamental cultural values are superior to those they attack. Advantageous comparison is further advanced when the terrorists are told and come to believe that the enemy engages in widespread cruelties and inhumane treatment of the people the terrorists represent. The United States, for example, is seen by many people in Arab countries as blameworthy for their problems because of a variety of U.S. policies and practices (Staub, 2004), thus providing a fertile atmosphere for terrorist recruitment. Advantageous comparison methods draw heavily on history to justify violence. For example, terrorist leaders will indoctrinate their followers about the many oppressive policies and tyrannical tactics their targeted organization or country has employed on them in the past. Many people believe, for example, that the United States has historically and consistently supported repressive governments in the Arab world and elsewhere. Terrorist recruiters take these beliefs a step further and turn them into a hatred of the repressors.

ADDITIONAL DISENGAGEMENT PRACTICES

Bandura states that other disengagement practices are also at play in developing motivations, such as dehumanization, displacement of responsibility, and diffusion of responsibility. **Dehumanization** is based on the premise that mistreating or randomly killing *humanized* or known persons significantly increases the risks of self-condemnation. It is easier to mistreat (and kill) strangers who are divested of human qualities. "Once dehumanized, they are no longer viewed as persons with feelings, hopes, and concerns but as subhuman forms" (Bandura, 2004, p. 136). Now they can justifiably be called "savages," "gooks," "degenerates," "monsters," "the unwashed masses," "evil cowards," and so on.

In displacement of responsibility, terrorists may view their actions as stemming from the dictates of authorities and leaders rather than from their own personal responsibility. Consequently, they avoid self-condemning reactions because they are not personally responsible for their conduct; they are only following orders, perhaps even from their god. Some serial killers (e.g., "Son of Sam") have used similar justifications for their actions. Diffusion of responsibility is similar to the concept of **deindividuation**, discussed in Chapter 5. Terrorism often requires the services of many people in the organization, all pulling together to achieve some ultimate purpose. Bandura points out that each person in the organization often performs relatively small, fragmentary jobs that, taken individually, seem harmless, and out of the limelight. The collective sense of identity that results allows members of the group to participate in being part of horrific or heinous actions that individually they may resist doing themselves.

PSYCHOLOGICAL NATURE OF TERRORISM

After the attacks of September 11, 44 percent of the adults in a national survey said they experienced significant amount of stress, and 90 percent said they had some degree of stress following the attack (Schuster *et al.*, 2001). However, it has also been shown that ethnic background, gender, and age influence the psychological reactions to terrorism (Walker & Chestnut, 2003). Many participants in the Walker and Chestnut survey thought that the United States has been overly involved in the affairs of other countries and that those countries were now retaliating. In addition, participants felt that the United States had developed a false sense of security in believing terrorist groups would not retaliate for the policies the United States has used on other countries and cultural groups.

Although psychologists or other mental health professionals provide psychological services to those persons adversely affected by terrorism, it is equally important to try to prevent it. One important point that was made in the beginning of this chapter bears repeating: "The overwhelming majority of evidence indicates that responding to violence with violence only provokes further violence" (Wagner & Long, 2004, p. 215). Aggressive military action is rarely the solution, unless it is in response to an imminent, documented threat to a country and its inhabitants. International terrorism is unlikely to be reduced until the root causes of the violence are addressed and corrected: "These causes often include real or imagined injustice in meeting basic human needs for coping with difficult life conditions, insecurity, lack of self-determination, and disrespect for one's social identity" (Wagner & Long, 2004, p. 219).

Cognitive Restructuring

As mentioned in Chapter 1, social psychologists have observed that many people believe the world is a just place, where one gets what one deserves and deserves what one gets (Lerner, 1980). People who have a just-world bias perceive a connection between what people do, are, or believe in and what happens to them. According to the just-world bias, for the sake of cognitive consistency, many people cannot believe in a world governed by a schedule of random events. The suffering of innocent or respectable people—those who have done nothing to bring about their own grief—would be too unacceptable and unjust (Lerner & Simmons, 1966). Thus, when tragedy strikes, believers in a just world tend to blame the victims, concluding that these victims must have deserved their fate in some way. Maikovich (2005) links the same process to the thinking patterns of terrorists. She writes, "When terrorists view the current sociopolitical situation through the lens of a just world bias, their attack victims are not unjustly hurt or killed, but rather deserve these fates either because of what they did personally or, more commonly, because of what their government did" (Maikovich, 2005, p. 383). In this sense, killing the identified enemy is seen as right and moral (Staub, 2004). For example, after the September 11, 2001, terrorist attacks, al-Qaeda leader Osama bin Laden proclaimed that al-Qaeda's attacks were justified against the aggressive, intrusive, and unjust United States.

Terrorist organizations are typically extremely hierarchical, so that those who actually commit the violent acts can nearly always be said to be following orders of some higher authority (Maikovich, 2005). Psychologists have discovered that many people disengage their personal standards from their conduct when they are told to do something reprehensible by a legitimate authority. Terrorist organizations are designed so that their leaders are unquestionably legitimate, commanding of respect, and powerful (Maikovich, 2005). When someone who possesses legitimate power or perceived power commands someone to do something, the person who is commanded is, in a sense, relieved of personal responsibility for the conduct, even if the conduct is alien to his or her personal standards. This concept is called displacement of responsibility by Bandura (2004), strong respect for authority by Staub (2004), or obedience to authority by Milgram (1974).

Bandura (1983) lists six common disengagement practices we use for dealing with our own reprehensible, antisocial conduct. It is instructive to examine each of these strategies, because they help us understand the psychology of terrorism as applied to those who are carrying out these activities. Although somewhat repetitive, they serve as a good summary of much of what we have discussed in this chapter.

First, people do not ordinarily engage in antisocial conduct until they have justified to themselves the rightness or morality of their actions. Even reprehensible acts can be made honorable through cognitive restructuring. Thus, a distressed father, convinced that he must save his family from the evil of the world, kills his children, his wife, and then himself. In essence, he reconstructed his construct system to fit what he believed was the right thing to do under the circumstances. Another example—though certainly not reprehensible—is the moral young man who believes very strongly that killing is wrong but voluntarily goes to war to protect his country. At first, the actions of these two individuals may seem to have nothing in common; and we condemn the actions of the first and condone or praise the actions of the second. However, in both instances, cognitive restructuring has occurred.

A second disengagement practice—related to the first—is that of people convincing themselves that their violent acts are really trivial and not all that bad compared with what others have done. In war, we convince ourselves that the atrocities committed by the enemy are far worse than anything we do. The concept of advantageous comparison, discussed with reference to cognitive reconstructing by terrorists, is similar. A third strategy involves the power of language. One of the costs of human intellectual ability is the considerable power of words; they allow us to justify our actions with relative ease. We use euphemisms to neutralize reprehensible behavior. For example, intelligence manuals use words like *neutralize* and *terminate* instead of *assassinate* and *kill*. The euphemisms carry less onus and cause less disruption to moral beliefs.

A fourth strategy—one most commonly found in group violence—is the diffusion of responsibility. Statements that best typify this practice include "I was just following orders," "I was just following the crowd," and "The executive board decided that it was in the best interest of the economy (and the company) to continue production, despite some risk to the health of others." These assertions have the effect of displacing responsibility for one's actions to others, or to forces outside oneself.

A fifth strategy is to not even think about the consequences of one's actions. Here, people convince themselves that the consequences are not important. Alternately, they manage to detach themselves from the aftermath of violent actions. For example, the bombardier or the person who pushes the button that will release lethal chemicals onto a civilian population is not only following orders (diffusion of responsibility) but also probably not allowing himself to think about the tragedy that will result.

Finally, the sixth practice is to dehumanize the victim. "She was loose and got what she deserved." "He was scum." The enemies are labeled "gooks" or something akin to vicious animals. Dehumanization, as discussed earlier, removes all the human, dignifying qualities from the victim or intended victim. As Bandura (1983, p. 32) points out: "Many conditions of contemporary life are conducive to dehumanization. Bureaucratization, automation, urbanization, and high social mobility lead people to relate to each other in anonymous, impersonal ways." These impersonal, dehumanizing aspects of life facilitate violence and make living with it possible. Dehumanization of the enemy is frequently cited as a factor allowing killing (LoCicero & Sinclair, 2008).

Moral Development

One of the most difficult aspects to understand about terrorism is the willingness of supposedly capable leaders to sacrifice the lives, not only of their enemies but also of the individuals they recruit. Often, innocent lives of those close to the recruits are lost as well. For example, in a recent illustration of a suicide bombing, a woman walked into a marketplace with a bomb strapped to her person, holding the hand of her six-year-old daughter. Terrorist groups are known to arm children with explosives that are guaranteed to take the life of the child when detonated. How can a leader who is apparently so skillful at running a complex, multinational organization be able to brutally and, with little empathy, kill so many civilians, including children? How could Timothy McVeigh be willing to bomb a building with a child care center on its premises?

For answers to these questions, some psychologists look to the study of moral development, a construct closely related to cognitive complexity and a bit different from the cognitive restructuring discussed above. Moral development refers to the gradual development of a person's concepts of right and wrong, conscience, ethical and religious values, social attitudes, and behavior. A person who is highly cognitively complex is usually at a high level of moral development. However, we are beginning to learn that people who show cognitive complexity and skill in one domain—such as leadership—may not show cognitive complexity (or moral development) in another domain. Nevertheless, it is unlikely that cognitively complex individuals who engage in reprehensible violence against innocent victims can do so unless they are able to justify to themselves the morality of their actions—thus, one would argue that they have convinced themselves of the morality of their cause. In developmental psychology, investigations centering on moral development have been primarily focused on moral judgment and reasoning. The Swiss psychologist Jean Piaget (1948) was an early pioneer in studying how people mentally symbolize social rules and how they make judgments based on the social rules. He hypothesized that morality develops in a series of steps and stages. Each moral stage depends on previous stages, along with the intellectual and cognitive abilities and the social experiences of the individual. The developmental psychologist Lawrence Kohlberg (1976) revised the Piagetian formulation substantially and generated a considerable amount of research interest on the topic. Kohlberg believed that the morality process is fundamentally concerned with justice and fairness and is a process that continues throughout one's lifetime.

Similar to Piaget, Kohlberg postulated that moral development evolves in a sequence of stages (see **Table 11-2**). The sequence is invariant: Each individual must develop the features, skills, and judgments of a lower moral stage before attaining a higher one. Kohlberg identifies three primary stages: preconventional morality, conventional morality, and postconventional morality. Within each primary stage, there are two additional stages that we will refer to as early and late. During the early preconventional stage, one behaves solely on the basis of obtaining rewards and avoiding punishment. The individual has not yet developed any notion of right or wrong and, therefore, is not moral at all. This orientation toward reward and punishment and unquestioning deference to superior powerful others are principally characteristic of children under age seven, and unfortunately some adults.

During the late preconventional stage, the right action consists of that which satisfies one's own needs. This stage reflects a selfish orientation that considers the needs of others only to the extent that favors will be returned: "You scratch my back and I'll scratch yours." According to Kohlberg (1976), human relationships are viewed similarly to those in a marketplace, not of loyalty, gratitude, or justice, but of using others to gain something. The person develops some understanding that in order to obtain rewards, one has to work with others. Note that the emphasis is still on meeting one's own needs.

TABLE 11-2	Kohlberg's Stages and Motives for One's Behavior
Stage	**Focus**
Early preconventional	Avoid punishment
Late preconventional	Fair exchange; get something in return
Early conventional	Approval from others
Late conventional	Duty, obedience to rules
Early postconventional	Rules important, but can be broken if questionable
Late postconventional	Universal principles of justice and ethics apply

The early conventional morality stage is referred to as the "good boy" or "good girl" orientation. The individual's behavior is directed toward gaining social approval and acceptance, and there is much conformity to stereotyped images of what the majority regards as good behavior. During this stage, the conscience, or the ability to feel guilt, begins to emerge. At the late conventional stage, the orientation is to do things out of duty and to respect the authority of others. The person becomes especially aware that certain rules and regulations are necessary to ensure the smooth functioning of society or of terrorist organizations. Socially approved behavior is motivated by anticipation of dishonor and blame if one is derelict in performing one's duty. Guilt feelings arise principally out of doing concrete harm to others. It is at this stage—an average level of moral development—that many young recruits of al-Qaeda and other terrorist organizations probably begin their journey.

The final and highest stage of moral development—the postconventional—is probably reached by only a small sector of the world population. It requires the ability to be reasonably abstract and possess good cognitive ability. During the early postconventional stage, correct action is determined by an understanding of the general rights of the individual as compared with the standards that have been critically examined and agreed upon by the whole society. In this stage, one must also consider the rightness or wrongness of behavior on the basis of personal values. The early postconventional person sees flexibility in the laws of any given society.

The late postconventional person demonstrates an orientation "toward the decision of conscience and toward self-chosen ethical principles appealing to logical comprehensiveness, universality, and consistency" (Kohlberg, 1977, p. 63). The moral principles are abstract and ethical, and they reflect universal principles of justice and of the reciprocity and equality of human rights. These principles also require considerable cognitive complexity. The person relies on his or her own personally developed ethical principles and shows respect for the dignity of human beings as individual persons.

People progress through the stages at different rates and at different ages in their lives, and many never reach the postconventional stage. However, there have been a number of critiques of Kohlberg's theory. Many argue that it emphasizes a justice perspective to the exclusion of empathy or other moral values, such as caring and sensitivity to others. In addition, Kohlberg focused on males to the exclusion of females. It is now established that females outperform males on most measures of moral development, especially pertaining to empathy and prosocial behavior (Spinrad, Eisenberg, & Bernt, 2007). Still, Kohlberg's theory provides an interesting framework for understanding the morality of the leadership and followers of terrorist organizations.

Terrorists often experience considerable social and moral support for their actions among their community. They may be regarded by some as heroic freedom fighters and religious martyrs. Terrorist groups generally assert that their cause is righteous and moral and that their intentions are noble and just (Stevens, 2005). The morality of al-Qaeda, for instance, rests on lofty collection of ideologies that rely on justice to the people, freedom from oppression, duty to God, or retribution for crimes against "our" people (Kruglanski & Fishman, 2006). They rely on moral imperatives to justify their cause and overall mission. And they firmly believe in these values and their own morality. Consequently, they view the world through the lens of their religious beliefs—in their own eyes, and the eyes of their supporters, they are likely high in moral development.

Whether we can apply Kohlberg's stages to their morality is another question. Kohlberg developed his stages of moral development within the social context of Western civilization's concept of justice. To what extent this theory applies to Islamic fundamentalism is debatable and well beyond the scope of currently available empirical evidence. Nevertheless, fundamentalist groups exist in a number of contexts, and a small minority engages in terrorist activities. One of the major approaches of fundamentalism is the dogmatic ability to see the world in black-and-white terms. Al-Qaeda groups tend to have a very narrow definition of what constitutes a proper Muslim, and generally reject Shi'as, Sufi Muslims, and Sunnis (Piazza, 2009). Similar points can be made about other terrorist groups or individuals discussed in this chapter. The Armies of God believe they are right on social issues like abortion and gay marriage, and ecoterrorists believe they must protect the environment by violent means, if necessary.

As we have seen, terrorists justify their acts of violence under the premise that they are accomplishing a greater good, like freeing a society from tyrannical rule or Corruption. Even lone-wolf terrorists may adopt this perspective. Persons of high moral development have often broken laws on the basis of ethical principles; in its purest form, for example, civil disobedience involves the breaking of a law that one considers unjust. Henry David Thoreau refused to pay poll taxes, and Martin Luther King, Jr. and countless followers defied laws that prescribed separate water fountains and seats on public buses for racial minorities. In another form, civil disobedience involves breaking a law that is not in itself unjust, but the law is broken to bring attention to what the individual considers a greater evil. Thus, a person may trespass or burglarize in order to gain access to a research facility that injects toxins into monkeys. Although we may not agree with their tactics, we often do not question the moral development of many individuals who practice civil disobedience. However, we tend to draw the line at the use of violence or threats of violence to accomplish one's goals. It is extremely difficult, therefore, to conceptualize terrorists as individuals advanced in moral development, although they believe themselves to be.

Summary and Conclusions

In the latter part of the twentieth century, the typical textbook in criminology paid scant attention to the topic of terrorism. The events of September 11, 2001, drastically changed that. Although terrorist activities had been occurring, both in the United States and worldwide, long before the attacks on the World Trade Center and the Pentagon, that date marked a radical shift in public attention and fear, law enforcement activity, and psychological interest. By definition, terrorism involves the unlawful use of force or violence, so by definition, terrorist activities are criminal.

Scholarly literature, government documents, public policy writings, and the media have proposed numerous definitions and categories of terrorism. We adopted the definition used in federal documents, seeing terrorism as unlawful force or violence used to intimidate or coerce a government or population in furtherance of political or social objectives. Terrorism may be either domestic or international, depending on the origin, base, and objectives of the

terrorist organization. We covered the FBI's classifications of terrorist *groups*—according to their political leanings—and psychology's classifications of terrorist *motivations*. The groups include the right-wing terrorists, the radical environmental, the special interest extremists, and the nuclear/biological/chemical group. Note that these categories best characterize domestic terrorism; while the al-Qaeda terrorists would probably be classified in the right-wing group, they are far different in organization, skills, and motivations from Timothy McVeigh or Theodore Kaczynski. Classifications of psychological motives are better able to capture terrorism in all its facets, despite the fact that we discussed only three *categories*: rationally motivated, psychologically motivated, and culturally motivated terrorists.

The chapter also covered the psychosocial context of terrorism, specifically those social and psychological characteristics of a society or a group that are conducive to the emergence of terrorist groups. When a society or a group devalues another, the devalued other can be seen as a scapegoat or an ideological enemy and thus can become the target of terrorist attacks. Abortion providers became the targets of terrorist attacks because their activities were seen as morally bad. Symbols of power in the United States—the World Trade Center and the Pentagon—were attacked by al-Qaeda because the United States was seen as a dangerous enemy. Perceptions of inequity, relative deprivation, or injustice are also conducive to the emergence of terrorist groups. While most individuals and groups with these perceptions do not terrorize others, those who do terrorize often harbor those perceptions. Finally, the hierarchical command structure evident in many terrorist groups suggests that strong belief in authority and respect of a charismatic leader may facilitate terrorist activity, when the group is already predisposed to that type of action.

While there is no single motive for terrorism, most terrorist acts, because of their horrifying nature, involve some cognitive restructuring. As Bandura has observed, individuals who engage in terrorism justify their actions in a variety of ways. These include using techniques of moral justification, whereby they convince themselves that their actions are socially worthy and have an ultimate moral purpose—the ends justify the means. Terrorists also use euphemistic language and advantageous comparison to restructure their cognitions; thus, their own actions are seen as harmless compared with the actions of the targets of their activities. Finally, terrorists may dehumanize their targets and lose their own identities—and their individual responsibility—by deindividuating. That is to say, it is the collective not the individual identity that is responsible. The disengagement tactics outlined by Bandura can also apply to criminal behavior in a variety of contexts, not just the violence exhibited by terrorist groups.

Key Concepts

Advantageous comparison
Bioterrorism
Cognitive restructuring
Cultural devaluation
Dehumanization
Deindividuation

Euphemistic language
Learned helplessness
Lone-wolf terrorist
Moral justification
Nuclear/biological/chemical
    terrorism

Radical environmental
    groups
Reactive depression
Risky shift
Special interest extremist

Review Questions

1. How are terrorist groups classified?
2. Summarize the terrorist typology present in the chapter.
3. What are the main characteristics of the lone-wolf terrorist?
4. Define moral justification and how it may play a part in terrorist acts.
5. Define cognitive restructuring, with particular emphasis on how advantageous comparisons play an important role in the development of terrorism.

6. Define euphemistic language, and identify how it is linked to terrorism and other acts of violence.
7. Define dehumanization and describe its role in brutal, demeaning acts of violence.
8. Summarize Kohlberg's stages of moral development.

12

Sexual Assault

CHAPTER OBJECTIVES

- Define rape and sexual assault.
- Discuss the impact of sexual assault on victims.
- Examine risk factors for sexual assault.
- Describe risk factors that influence the development of sexually assaultive behavior in men.
- Introduce the Knight and Sims-Knight three-path model of sexual offending.
- Describe in detail the Massachusetts Treatment Center's classification system of rapists to highlight the heterogeneity of rape offenders.
- Describe the Groth typology of rape offenders.

Sexual behavior in many societies is a subject fraught with moral codes, taboos, norm expectations, religious injunctions, myths, and unscientific conclusions. In the mid-twentieth century, research published by Albert Kinsey and his colleagues helped dispel myths and correct fallacies about sexual behavior in both men and women (Kinsey, 1948, 1953). Many myths and misconceptions still linger, including those about sex offenders, who are frequently viewed as a homogenous class of individuals.

Research shows, however, that sex offenders differ in personal attributes such as age, background, personality, race, religion, beliefs, attitudes, and interpersonal skills (Knight, Rosenberg, & Schneider, 1985; Parent, Guay, & Knight, 2011). *There is no single profile that encompasses even a majority of sex offenders.* The features of the crimes also differ markedly among offenders, including time and place, the gender and age of the victim, the degree of planning the offense, and the amount of violence used or intended (Knight *et al.*, 1985). In addition, sex offenders often commit a variety of crime beyond sexual offenses, although this is more likely to be the case with rapists than with child molesters (Harris, Mazerolle, & Knight, 2009). Research also indicates that sexual reoffending by sex offenders is not as prevalent as previously assumed. In fact, there is considerable evidence to show that adult sexual offenders are more likely to be convicted for nonsexual offenses than they are for sexual offenses, both before and after a conviction for a sexual offense (Smallbone & Wortley, 2004).

DEFINITIONS AND STATISTICS

Although the words *rape* and *rapist* continue to be widely used, and will often be used in this chapter, many researchers and policy makers prefer to use the more inclusive term *sexual assault*. In addition, about half of the 50 states do not use the word *rape* in their penal code involving sexual assault or sex offenses (Langan, Schmitt, & Durose, 2003). As noted in Chapter 1, *forcible rape* is the term that has traditionally been used by the FBI in the gathering of crime reporting and arrest statistics for Part I crimes. The term is redundant, because by definition all rape is forcible. However, "consensual" sexual intercourse between an adult and an underage individual is a crime, so the FBI uses the term *statutory rape* for the latter offense, as we will note below. Accordingly, **forcible rape** has long been defined as "the carnal knowledge of a female forcibly and against her will" (Federal Bureau of Investigation, 2005b, p. 27). This includes attempts to commit rape by force or threat of force. Recall, however, that the definition has now been changed. The new definition of forcible rape is as follows: The penetration, no matter how slight, of the vagina or anus with any body part or object, or oral penetration by a sex organ of another person, without the consent of the victim (Holder, 2012). This new definition broadens the type of sexual assault to be included in the UCR rape statistics. The definition further includes *any gender* of the victim or perpetrator, and includes instances in which the victim is incapable of giving consent because of temporary or permanent mental or physical incapacitation, for example, due to the influence of drugs or alcohol. Thus, force is presumed, even if the individual does not resist. Prior to this change, the rape of males was a Part II offense. Because these changes will take several years to be fully implemented, readers should be aware that UCR statistics reported in this chapter still rely on the old definition.

Both the new and old definitions distinguish forcible rape from statutory rape or rape by fraud. These are included in the list of Part II crimes, for which arrest data are collected. **Statutory rape** has been defined as the carnal knowledge of a girl under the age of consent, the age at which individuals are considered competent to give consent to sexual behavior. It pertains exclusively to consensual intercourse, as opposed to other types of sexual contact (Langan *et al.*, 2003). With the UCR changes described above, the definition will be gender neutral in that both girls and boys will be included. The critical factor for statutory rape is the age of the victim, an arbitrary legal cutoff point below which a youth is believed not to have the maturity to consent to intercourse or understand the consequences. Age limits vary from state to state, but most set the limit at 16 or 18. Also, it is generally understood that an age span must exist between the two individuals, typically two years. Thus, if a 25-year-old male engages in sexual relations with a minor female, he may be convicted of statutory rape, even if he argues that she "consented." An 18-year-old male engaging in sexual relations with a 16-year-old female would not have the same problem. **Rape by fraud** is having sexual relations with a consenting adult female under fraudulent conditions. One of the most frequently cited examples is that of the psychotherapist who has sexual intercourse with a patient under the guise of offering treatment. Another rape category that is beginning to receive some attention is **marital rape**, although it is not treated separately in UCR statistics. During the past four decades, there have been dramatic changes in marital rape laws in the United States. In 1970, marital rape was not a crime in any state, but by 1993, all 50 states had passed laws criminalizing it (Martin, Taft, & Resick, 2007). It is estimated that about 10–14 percent of married women have experienced marital rape (Martin *et al.*, 2007), but like all rape statistics it is likely that much of it goes unreported.

Many in the general population (including at times the victims themselves) do not define sexual attacks as rape unless the assailant is a stranger. Thus, if the victim is sexually assaulted by a husband or a boyfriend, she may not report the incident. Criminal justice officials, as well as the general public, often feel that marital or date rapes are unimportant because they are believed to happen so rarely, compared with stranger rape, or to be less psychologically traumatic to the victim. Some criminal prosecutors, for example, admit they are reluctant to prosecute marital or date rape cases because of concerns that juries will not believe that a woman could be raped by a husband or male friend (Kilpatrick, Best, Saunders, & Veronen, 1988). However, in a survey of the general population conducted by Kilpatrick and colleagues (1988), subjects who had been raped identified their husbands as assailants in 24 percent of the cases and male friends in 17 percent of the cases. These data suggest that over 40 percent of the rapes were committed by husbands or dates, a significant and frequently overlooked statistic in the tabulation of rape. A growing recognition of sexual assault by spouses and acquaintances has led many scholars to prefer the term *intimate partner violence*, which includes sexual as well as physical assaults.

Date or Acquaintance Rape

Date rapes (sometimes called acquaintance rapes) may be far more common than generally realized, perhaps as high as 60 percent of all rapes. Some data suggest that up to one-third of young adults between the ages of 16 and 24 have reported being involved in at least one abusive dating incident (Lingren, 2001). **Date rape** refers specifically to a sexual assault that occurs within the context of a dating relationship. In a survey conducted by Frintner and Rubinson (1993) of 925 college women, over one-fourth of the respondents had experienced sexual assault or attempted sexual assault. Nearly 83 percent of the college women who had been sexually assaulted said the attacker had been someone they knew and that most of these incidents had happened during their freshman year.

Dating patterns have changed dramatically in the twenty-first century. Many couples meet on the Internet, and both women and men initiate a first "date." Whereas males might feel less entitled to "payback" than before—when they paid expenses and provided transportation—other factors (e.g., alcohol, other drugs, sexual mores) can facilitate a rape. Date rapes also occur in the context of a casual encounter at a party or a bar. Women who are raped by acquaintances still often blame themselves for the attack or are blamed by others for arousing the date or placing themselves in vulnerable situations. In addition, sexual assault by a date or acquaintance may be more traumatizing than assault by a stranger because of the implicit trust involved.

One traumatizing aspect of date rape relates to a phenomenon pointed out by Karmen (1996), who identifies a distinction made by some people between a "real rape" and a date rape. In a real rape—again, a redundant term—the presumption is that the woman is clearly assaulted if she is ambushed as an unsuspecting victim by a blitz attack by a complete stranger. It is even more convincing if the attacker is armed, leaps out of the darkness, enters her home uninvited, or imposes serious physical injury, such as knife wounds. A date rape, on the other hand, is often not considered a real rape since it occurred on an arranged date with someone she knew, agreed to go out with, or met in a social situation. Thus, the victim is less likely to be believed and more likely to be blamed (Ullman, 1999). As Ullman (2007, p. 412) observes, "These negative reactions are harmful to women's psychological functioning and may lead to or reinforce their own self-blame for being raped." We return to the topic of date rape in Chapter 16 where "date rape drugs" are discussed.

Incidence and Prevalence of Rape

In many parts of the globe, violence—including violence against women—is underplayed and underreported. Saudi Arabia, Afghanistan, Somalia, Chile, and India are only some countries where sexual abuse of women and girls may be rampant (UNFPA, 2009). In 2012, the world has been riveted to the civil war in Syria, where rapes and murders of women and children are regularly reported, but where other nations are reluctant to intervene.

In the United States, an estimated 84,767 rapes were reported to law enforcement agencies nationwide in 2010 (Federal Bureau of Investigation, 2011a). This figure represents a rate of approximately 54.2 per 100,000 female inhabitants. Rapes by force account for 93.0 percent of reported rape offenses, and attempts or assaults to commit rape comprised 7.0 percent. Keep in mind that these figures are based on the UCR's traditional definition, which recognizes only women and girls as victims of rape. Some research, based on self-report surveys or victimization data, suggests that about 10 percent of the rapes in this country do not conform to the traditional UCR definition (Chaiken, 1998a). For example, it is estimated that in about 9 percent of rapes, the victim was male (Sampson, 2011; Turchik & Edwards, 2011). These data probably underestimate the extent of this problem as men may be just as reluctant or even more reluctant than women to report sexual assault. The sexual abuse scandal that shook the Catholic Church in the 1990s and 2000s also illustrates the difficulty in obtaining valid statistics on this crime (Terry, 2008). Most recently, the Boy Scouts of America have come under fire for not investigating or reporting instances of sexual assault by some scout masters. Sexual abuse of children in institutional settings, such as juvenile detention and treatment centers, is often uncounted. Furthermore, the reality of prison rape is seldom considered in official statistics, including victimization data.

Research data that are available indicate that 18 percent of women in the United States have been raped at some point in their lifetimes (Kilpatrick, Resnick, Ruggiero, Conoscenti, & McCauley, 2007; Post, Biroscak, & Barboza, 2011). Kilpatrick *et al.* defined rape to include forcible rape, incapacitated rape, and drug-facilitated rape. In the United States, children and college students, persons with disabilities, and incarcerated individuals are the most vulnerable to be raped (Carbon, 2010).

Female college students are the most extensively studied populations pertaining to sexual violence (Post *et al.*, 2011), even though they may not be the most representative group of victims. The Campus Sexual Assault (CSA) study of 5,446 college women found that 28.5 percent reported having experienced an attempted or completed sexual assault before or since entering college (Krebs, Lindquist, Warner, Fisher, & Martin, 2007). Kilpatrick *et al.* (2007) found that 11.5 percent of undergraduate women selected from a representative national list of four-year colleges and universities said they had been raped during their lifetime, including forcible sexual penetration (8.7%) and incapacitated rape (6.4%).

Between the years 1992 and 2000, it is estimated that only 36 percent of rapes, 34 percent of attempted rapes, and 26 percent of other sexual assaults were reported to law enforcement or medical personnel (Rennison, 2002). These estimates are supported by other data as well (Lisak, Gardinier, Nicksa, & Cote, 2010; Lisak & Miller, 2002). The military is not immune to the problem of sexual assault, and these assaults, too, often go unreported. Only 20 percent of unwanted sexual contacts in the U.S. military are reported to military authorities (Carbon, 2010, U.S. Department of Defense, 2009).

In summary, the actual rape rate is greatly underestimated, partly because of some of the definitional problems listed in the previous sections, and partly because of the ordeal victims must go through just to report the incident. In addition, in some settings (e.g., the church and the Boy Scouts) decisions are made to handle these assaults internally to guard the reputation of the institution or the individual perpetrator, "This was a pillar of the community; we just allowed him to resign." Victimization studies offer a revealing contrast to the police data. A study based on data collected in the National Violence Against Women Survey (NVAWS) estimates that the number of attempted or completed rapes is four times greater than even the NCVS estimates (Tjaden & Thoennes, 2006). Recall that the NCVS is the government's official victimization survey.

For the greater part of this chapter we focus on the offenders: their characteristics, possible motivations, and risk factors associated with their behavior. Thus we will return to offenders shortly. Prior to this it is important to consider the victims of sexual assault, particularly the psychological effects they experience as a result.

IMPACT ON VICTIMS

Regardless of the sex offender's characteristics, motivations, and method of attack or coercion, the social and psychological costs to victims and their families are immeasurable and often devastating. An early but often-cited survey of 3,132 households in the Los Angeles Epidemiologic Catchment Area (ECA) illustrates this very well. Researchers found that over 13 percent of the individuals interviewed had been victims of sexual assault at least once in their lifetimes (Burnam *et al.*, 1988; Siegel, Sorenson, Golding, Burnam, & Stein, 1987; Sorenson, Stein, Siegel, Golding, & Burnam, 1987). Two-thirds of the sexually assaulted subjects reported two or more assaults. Moreover, lifetime sexual assault was more frequently reported by women (16.7%) than men (9.4%). In a sobering finding, 13 percent of the victims were first assaulted between the ages of 6 and 10, 19 percent between 11 and 15, 34 percent between 16 and 20, and 15 percent between 21 and 25. The experience of being sexually assaulted was associated with substantially higher risks for later onset of serious, self-destructive depression, substance abuse, numerous fears and inhibiting anxieties, and a variety of major interpersonal problems. Overall, the ECA project found that both male and female victims of sexual assault are two to four times more likely than nonvictims to develop serious psychological problems.

Psychological Effects on Victims

It is often said that rape victims are victimized twice, once by the perpetrator and again by the criminal justice system during the investigation of the crime and, if a suspect is arrested, during the prosecution phase. Victims also may be victimized by media scrutiny and by a public that may question whether the incident happened, or denigrate the victims and attribute some blame to them.

Upon reporting the assault, they are expected to recall and describe personally stressful and humiliating events in vivid detail for law enforcement personnel. Today, increasingly more police departments take steps to ease the victim's ordeal. These include having victim advocates present, having women officers available for female rape victims, and/or providing rape sensitivity training for both male and female officers. In addition to the interview with representatives of law enforcement, the victim is required to undergo a medical examination to establish physical evidence of penetration and use of physical force. It is no wonder that many people who have been raped prefer the term *survivor* to victim because of its more positive connotation. To be a rape survivor suggests that one is in control and that the rapist, the criminal justice system, and the public have not succeeded at totally demolishing one's self-concept.

If the victim is able to withstand these stressful conditions, which are sometimes exacerbated by negative reactions from parents, spouses, partners, family members, friends, and even by threats from the assailant, the victim must then prepare for the courtroom, where her or his privacy is invaded and credibility may be attacked. Rape trials are usually covered extensively by the press, although many news organizations do not reveal the victims' names. In recent years, particularly with revelations about clergy abuse, victims have spoken out by filing civil suits against their abusers or the churches or other institutions that often shielded them.

Traditionally, in criminal cases, victim credibility was so much at issue that defense lawyers concentrated on the prior sexual history of a victim. In one highly cited study, 92 percent of the prosecutors asserted that victim credibility was one of the most important elements in convincing juries to convict for rape (Chappell, 1977). The strategy of disparaging the victim came under attack in the 1970s and 1980s, and many states revised their evidentiary rules in an attempt to limit the use of a victim's sexual history. By the turn of the twenty-first century, virtually all states had enacted "rape shield" laws that restricted, to varying degrees, the admissibility of the victim's sexual history into the courtroom (Kilpatrick, Whalley, & Edmunds, 2000). In addition, victim assistants—whose function it is to offer support, give direct services, and advocate for victims—have been instrumental in easing the victim's burden. In tight economic times, however, these services are often severely limited. Furthermore, rape shield laws do not always provide the protection for which they were designed (Ross & Bachar, 2002); they vary from state to state (Kinports, 2002). Consequently, many victims are surprised and dismayed when they are asked questions about their social and sexual histories during adjudication, something they believed would not happen (Ross & Bachar, 2002). The Violence Against Women Act (VAWA) covered in Chapter 9 (see **Box 9-1**, page 264) addressed many of these problems by encouraging more uniformity in rape shield laws and protecting victims of violence nationwide.

In sum, those who survive sexual assaults are prone to suffer psychological consequences, most of which are probably never acknowledged. Research documents that the consequences are real. Raped women represent the largest proportion of PTSD sufferers in the United States (Leiner, Kearns, Jackson, Astin, & Rothbaum, 2012). In addition, rape victims are four times more likely than nonvictims to contemplate suicide, and 13 percent of them actually attempt suicide (Carbon, 2010).

Physical Injury of Victim

As noted above, rape and other sexual assaults are most likely to be perpetrated against women and girls; male victims are fewer in number, but the psychological and physical injury they experience cannot be overlooked. Most of the research thus far has focused on female victims, however.

Women's fears about being physically harmed in rape are not unfounded. While weapons, especially firearms and knives, are used in only about 25 percent of the reported assaults (U.S. Department of Justice, 1988), about one-fourth of all rape victims sustain injury serious enough to warrant medical attention or hospitalization. *Severe physical injury,* however, is relatively rare, with about 5 percent receiving serious, lasting injury (Williams & Holmes, 1981). Another 39 percent receive minor injuries, and 23 percent receive a variety of cuts and bruises (Williams & Holmes, 1981). Further study suggests that women receive more physical and psychological trauma from sexual assault by husbands than by strangers (Kilpatrick *et al.*, 1988). In addition, the psychological damage is apparently longer lasting and more damaging, resulting in serious depression, extensive fears, and problems of sexual adjustment. Later in the chapter we will discuss the topic of rape resistance, which is associated with characteristics of rape offenders. For the moment, it is important to note that in the past, women were advised not to resist a rape attempt in order to minimize the risk of other physical harm, possibly even death. With growing evidence that passive resistance was not necessarily related to the amount of harm experienced, advice has changed (Ullman, 2007; see also **Box 12-2** later in the chapter). However, it should be emphasized that physical resistance is not *required* to demonstrate lack of consent.

SEXUAL ASSAULT VULNERABILITY FACTORS

Investigations examining the causes of sexual assault and general violence against women have generally focused on one of two issues: the behavior, cognitions, and the tactics of offenders, and the risk factors faced by the victims (Siegel & Williams, 2001). It should be emphasized at the onset that the responsibility for the violence against women clearly rests with the offenders. But it is also important to examine the vulnerability factors that put victims at risk so that prevention and intervention strategies can be implemented. "Vulnerability factors are those that increase women's risk of experiencing sexual assault" (Ullman & Najdowski, 2011, p. 152). We first examine the victim vulnerability factors, and then we will turn our attention to the characteristics of the sexual offenders.

"Certain places and situations may put women at a greater risk of rape and affect their ability to effectively resist an attacker" (Ullman, 2007, p. 416), and these may differ according to whether the perpetrator is a stranger or an acquaintance. Sexual assaults by acquaintances most often occur indoors or in isolated locations. With respect to strangers, bars are especially risky settings for women if drinking alone. Fraternity parties also sometime put women at risk. In addition, use of alcohol or drugs by one or both parties, women initiating a date, or men paying for a date—though still a common practice—all are contributing factors in developing a risky situation. Nevertheless, while women should be cognizant of these risky settings, the crime is the fault of the perpetrator, not the one who is attacked.

Age

If one looks only at victimization data, rape appears to be a crime primarily committed against youth. The National Women's Study (Tjaden & Thoennes, 1998b) reported the following statistical data concerning the age of victims:

- 29 percent of all forcible rapes occurred when the victim was less than 11 years old.
- 32 percent occurred when the victim was between the ages of 11 and 17.
- 22 percent occurred between the ages of 18 and 24.
- 7 percent occurred between the ages of 25 and 29.
- 6 percent occurred when the victim was older than 29 years old.

According to these data, nearly two-thirds of the known victims of sexual assault are 17 or younger. Additional research has found similar results. Basile and Smith (2011) report that 71 percent of female victims were first raped before the age of 18 years. Tjaden and Thoennes (2000) discovered that, of the 17.6 percent of all women surveyed who indicated they had been the victim of a completed or attempted rape at some time in their life, 21.6 percent said they were younger than age 12 when they were first raped. Another 32 percent said they were between the ages of 12 and 17 when first raped.

Relationship Factors

Kilpatrick *et al.* (2000, p. 12) report cogent evidence that most of the rapists of adult victims are intimate partners and not strangers. They list the following victimization information on adult women gathered from the National Women's Survey:

- 24.4 percent of the rapists were strangers.
- 21.9 percent were husbands or ex-husbands.
- 19.5 percent were boyfriends or ex-boyfriends.
- 9.8 percent were relatives.
- 14.6 percent were other nonrelatives, such as friends or neighbors.

Victim surveys also indicate that the most commonly used methods of force during date rapes are verbal persuasion, alcohol, or drugs. While weapons are rarely used, physical overpowering is commonly reported (Kanin, 1984). Furthermore, data suggest that date rapes occur most frequently in the male's apartment or room, with the next likely location being the female's apartment or room. Very few occur in a car or outside. About 7 percent of rape/sexual assault involved multiple offenders who were strangers to the victim (Greenfeld, 1997).

Consumption of Alcohol

With reference to situational characteristics, alcohol plays a major role in both incapacitated and coerced sexual assaults. Incapacitated sexual assault is defined as "any unwanted sexual contact occurring when a victim is unable to provide consent or stop what is happening because she is passed out, drugged, drunk, incapacitated, or asleep, regardless of whether the perpetrator was responsible for the substance use or whether substances were administered without her knowledge" (Krebs *et al.*, 2007, p. ix). The Campus Sexual Assault Study (Krebs *et al.*, 2007) found that the vast majority of incapacitated sexual assault victims (82 percent) reported drinking alcohol and being drunk prior to being victimized compared to physically forced victims who reported being drunk (13 percent). Drug use was relatively rare for either incapacitated victims or physically forced victims, at least among college students. Not surprisingly, a large number of incapacitated sexual assault victims said they were at a party when the incident happened.

Alcohol use also plays a significant, multifaceted role in sexually coercive behavior (Knight & Sims-Knight, 2011). The victim is especially vulnerable if she has been drinking heavily (Ullman & Najdowski, 2011).

The effect of alcohol is seen on the offender as well. Alcohol impairs self-control, contributes to communication misinterpretations, and disrupts decision-making ability. About half of the sexual offenders and one-half the victims in adult rapes had been drinking alcohol prior to the assault (Abbey, Zawacki, Buck, Clinton, & McAuslan, 2004). Alcohol also appears to affect the severity of the assault. Offender alcohol abuse is believed to increase the level of violence for both rapists and child molesters (Abbey, Clinton-Sherrod, McAuslan, Zawacki, & Buck, 2003; Knight & Sims-Knight, 2011).

History of Victimization

For some unexplained reason, having a history of victimization is associated with individual women's vulnerability to sexual assault (Testa, Hoffman, & Livingston, 2010; Ullman & Najdowski, 2011). More specifically, "…research suggests that child sexual abuse victims who are revictimized as adolescents are more likely than others to experience addition revictimization as adults" (Ullman & Najdowski, 2011, p. 154). The reasons for this phenomenon appear to be highly complex and multifaceted, and despite the growing research literature on the topic we have yet to have answers about why it occurs.

Risk Taking Behaviors

The tendency to engage in risky or impulsive sexual behavior increases the chance of being sexually assaulted, such as accepting a ride with a stranger, heavy drinking at parties, or hitchhiking alone. Risky sexual behavior appears to be especially prevalent at the time of high school graduation and during the first semester of college (Testa *et al.*, 2010). As discussed in the delinquency chapter, adolescents (both males and females) are prone to take unnecessary risks in their daily lives, even though they cognitively know better. Having many prior sexual partners also seems to increase the risk of sexual assault (Testa, VanZile-Tamsen, & Livingston, 2007).

Closely related to risk taking behavior are failures to perceive risk in a situation or the ability to detect danger cues associated with increased vulnerability to sexual assault (Ullman & Najdowski, 2011). Researchers have identified two kinds of risk recognition failure in vulnerable women: global and specific (Gidycz, McNamara, & Edwards, 2006; Nurious, 2000). In **global risk recognition failure**, women are aware of the prevalence of sexual assault, but they believe they are at a significantly lower risk to be victimized than their peers (Norris, Nurious, & Graham, 1999).

In **specific risk failure** (sometimes referred to as situational), some women, for a variety of reasons, do not recognize that the situation they are in poses a threat. Alcohol usually plays a prominent role in this form of risk-recognition failure. In addition, risk recognition is more difficult when the potential offender is an acquaintance or a presumed friend because the threat often emerges incrementally. Also in these situations there is a high degree of ambiguity because the woman must decide between social, friendship concerns and safety (Nurious, Norris, Young, Graham, & Gaylord, 2000). Training programs designed to help women identify risk factors and to better defend themselves are increasingly being developed, researched, and implemented in recent years (Gidycz *et al.*, 2006).

RAPE OFFENDER CHARACTERISTICS: WHO OFFENDS?

The causes of sexual offending are neither simple nor straightforward. As the knowledge from systematic study accumulates, it is clear that this behavior is influenced by multiple, interactive factors. Past learning experiences, cognitive expectations and beliefs, conditioning, environmental stimuli, and reinforcement contingencies (both rewards and punishments) are all involved.

Some studies (e.g., Revitch & Schlesinger, 1988) reveal that many sex offenders are not prone to violence or physical cruelty, but rather are timid, shy, and socially inhibited. This is particularly correct for a large segment of pedophiles—those who offend against children—as will be discussed in the next chapter . It is far less likely to be correct with respect to rapists, whose attacks often have strong aggressive features in addition to the violence that defines the act itself. That is, by definition, rape is a violent, aggressive act. Other sex offenders are exhibitionists and never physically touch their victims. In reality, not all sex offenders are alike, which is a research finding that is often not recognized by the general public. Over the past 30 years, public approbation of sex crimes has produced many punitive laws aimed at deterring sexual offending (see **Box 12-1**.) Some of these laws apply to sex offenders as a group rather than to individual types.

BOX 12-1
Sex Offender Legislation

Over the past two decades, several federal laws and many state laws have been enacted that strongly influence how the federal and state governments view sex offenders. National data suggest that there are approximately 234,000 sex offenders under the care, custody, or control of correction agencies on any given day

(Chaiken, 1998b). We caution, though, that the term *sex offender* ranges from rapists to exhibitionists and it includes people who are in detention centers, jails, prisons, prison hospitals, and in the community on probation or parole. Not all of these individuals are violent. In fact, sex offender researchers often emphasize that the dangerousness associated with these offenders is overpredicted (Hanson & Morton-Bourgon, 2005; Harris & Lurigio, 2010). Yet a highly publicized, brutally violent attack perpetrated by a convicted-but-released sex offender will understandably provoke public outrage and will often result in the passage of legislation aimed at preventing further instances.

Among the most noteworthy are the laws that attempt to keep track of sex offenders by requiring them to register their whereabouts on a continuing basis when they are released from prison or as a condition of remaining in the community. Collectively, these are known as sex offender registration and notification (SORN) laws. Federal laws, often named after the victims of child abductions (e.g., Jacob Wetterling, Megan Kanka, Amber Hagerman, Adam Walsh), called for a variety of restrictions on offenders or, in the case of the Amber Alert, provided a means for quick circulation of information when a child disappeared. Many of the laws provide for notification to schools, daycare centers, social service agencies, and in some cases the general community, if a sex offender is living in the neighborhood. In some jurisdictions, convicted sex offenders are prohibited from residing in certain districts or obtaining employment in occupations where they would come into frequent contact with children. Most recently, sex offenders in some jurisdictions have been prohibited from participating on social media sites on the Internet, a prohibition that has been challenged on First Amendment grounds.

Some laws require yearly registration for 10 years, while others require registration throughout one's life. In the early part of the twenty-first century the federal government encouraged states to revise their systems pertaining to the classification of sex offenders to make registration and notification more consistent across the country (Harris, Lobanov-Rostovsky, & Levenson, 2010). This helped create a national database for use by law enforcement authorities. Furthermore, information about sex offenders has now become so widely available that it is commonly on the Internet. In some communities, cable stations carry pictures of offenders along with some details of their crimes, including the ages of their victims.

In 2006, in what is perhaps the most comprehensive piece of legislation related to sex offenders, the Adam Walsh Child Protection and Safety Act 9 (AWA) was signed into law. The Act is named after the eight-year-old boy who was abducted from a shopping mall in 1981 and was found murdered 16 days later. His father, John Walsh, later founded the National Center for Missing and Exploited Children and became host of the long-running Fox network show *America's Most Wanted*. The AWA preserves the three-tier offender categorization that was initiated in earlier federal laws, such as Megan's Law. AWA requires that Tier 3, the most serious offenders, update their whereabouts every three months for the rest of their lives. Tier 2 offenders must update every six months for 25 years, and Tier 1 every 12 months for 15 years. Failure to register and to update is a federal felony. Among other provisions, the AWA also sets up a national database and registry system for consistent reporting by states and increases the penalties for sex trafficking of children and engaging children in child prostitution. Since its passage, portions of the law—particularly the required provisions relating to lower tier offenders—have been challenged, and many critics believe it overbroad. At this point, however, at least one federal appeals court (the 11th circuit) has upheld its registration provisions.

Although laws aimed at the prevention of sex offending are meritorious on their face, many criminology researchers fear that they are unwise public policy, particularly as they relate to lower level sex offenders (Burchfield & Mingus, 2008; Tewksbury, 2005). Some argue that they may be counterproductive, even interfering with treatment goals, particularly for those sex offenders who are also mentally ill (Harris, Fisher, Veysey, Ragusa, & Lurigio, 2010). Others note that residency requirements provide false confidence, because sex offenders "travel" to obtain their victims (Duwe, Donnay, & Tewksbury, 2008).

Although sex offender registration and notification continues to be challenged in the courts, the courts—including the U.S. Supreme Court in 2002—have upheld various provisions of these laws. It is likely that SORN laws will remain on the books in some form well into the future.

In this chapter we are most concerned with the crimes of rapists. Their sexual aggression can be divided into at least two major categories: instrumental and expressive. **Instrumental sexual aggression** is when the sexual offender uses just enough coercion to gain compliance from his victim. In **expressive sexual aggression**, the offender's primary aim is to harm the victim physically as well as psychologically. In some cases, the expressive aggression is "eroticized" in that the offender becomes sexually aroused in the presence of physical or psychological brutality. As you will see later in the chapter, these two simple categorizations are not sufficient for understanding the rapist, however. Criminologists and researchers in psychology have proposed a number of more complex typologies.

What kind of a person rapes? How did he get that way? Why does he do it? Can the "rapist personality" be easily identified? Are rapists mentally disordered? Generally speaking, sexual socialization and social learning play a crucial role in the rapist's perceptions of what the rape accomplishes and what is "masculine." It is important to realize that sexual socialization (or sexual training) is rarely acquired entirely from home or school; much of it comes from peers, friends, the entertainment media, and experimentation. Some of it may be due to biological factors interacting with developmental influences and the social environment. Most of us, even as children, were fed misconceptions, taboos, and strategies for dealing with the opposite sex. Males often learn it is "manly" to take the sexual initiative and to persist, even against resistance.

In this section, we will cover what we know about rape-prone men, including risk factors. Risk factors pertain to environmental, biological, psychological, and other characteristics associated with an increased probability or likelihood that a person will become sexually aggressive and ultimately sexually assaultive.

Age

The most consistent demographic finding is that rapists tend to be young. According to UCR data for 2010, 43 percent of those *arrested* for forcible rape were under age 25, and 14 percent were actually under age 18 (Federal Bureau of Investigation, 2011a). Four percent of the total arrests for forcible rape and 11 percent of the total arrests for other sex offenses were under age 15. In Canada, rates of sexual offending were highest among juveniles ages 12 to 17 (Worling & Langton, 2012). The percentage of juvenile arrests for rape has largely been the same for years. The UCR data, however, represent an underestimation. As reported earlier, some studies indicate that at least 30 percent of the rapes in the United States are committed by juveniles (Cellini, 1995). In a survey of high school students, nearly half (48%) of the females reported experiencing sexual aggression, and one-third (34%) of the males admitted committing this type of offending (Maxwell, Robinson, & Post, 2003).

Other research has reported that adolescent males commit 20–30 percent of all rapes and 30–50 percent of all child molestations (Becker & Johnson, 2001). Surprisingly, 70 percent of these adolescent sex offenders come from two-parent homes, most attend school and achieve average grades, and very few suffer from major mental disorders (Becker & Johnson, 2001). Researchers also have begun to focus on sexual offending by girls, a subject that until recently was virtually ignored (Becker & Johnson, 2001). There is also considerable evidence that prepubescent children—both boys and girls—may commit sexual offenses at a rate much higher than commonly supposed. Several studies have reported sexual aggression in children as young as three or four years of age (Araji, 1997), although their aggressive actions do not qualify as crimes because children at these ages cannot form the necessary criminal intent. In addition, a surprisingly large number of preadolescent girls are reported to be sexually aggressive toward other children, and these girls often engage in behaviors that are just as aggressive as boys' behaviors (Araji, 1997). Victims of preadolescent offenders are generally very young (averaging between ages 4 and 7), most often are female (when the offender is a male), and typically are siblings, friends, or acquaintances (Righthand & Welch, 2001).

Offending History

Many men accused of and convicted of rape have been in perpetual conflict with society, long before the current rape offense. In a sample of 114 convicted rapists studied by Scully and Marolla (1984), 12 percent had a previous conviction for rape or attempted rape, 39 percent had previous convictions for burglary and robbery, 29 percent for kidnapping and abduction, 25 percent for sodomy, and 11 percent for first- or second-degree murder. Overall, 82 percent had a prior criminal record, but only 23 percent had been convicted of sexual offenses.

Juvenile sex offenders (JSO), who rape and sexually assault frequently, engage in a wide range of other criminal and antisocial but nonsexual behaviors (Caldwell, 2007, 2010; Carpentier & Proulx, 2011; Seto & Lalumière, 2010). They tend to shoplift, steal, engage in firesetting, bully and intimidate, display cruelty to animals, and physically assault others. This behavioral pattern also is typical of adult sex offenders (Hanson & Morton-Bourgon, 2005). In addition, JSOs who rape are more likely to commit the sexual offense along with a co-offender, commit a nonsexual offense in conjunction with the sexual assault, and have a previous arrest record (Hunter, Figueredo, Malamuth, & Becker, 2003). On the other hand, while many would fit the life-course-persistent (LCP) offender category discussed in previous chapters, others apparently do not offend sexually into adulthood. In one Canadian study involving 351 adolescents who had sexually offended, the researchers discovered that almost half of the sample had been charged with a new offense eight years later (Carpentier & Proulx, 2011). Perhaps more revealing was the finding that only 10 percent had been charged with a sexual offense during that follow-up period. As a result of this growing awareness, many researchers are seeking valid and reliable risk assessment measures for predicting which juveniles will and will not reoffend (Viljoen, Elkovitch, Scalora, & Ullman, 2009).

In a follow-up study of 3,115 rapists released from prison, 1.3 percent of the rapists were rearrested for a new sex crime within six months of release (Langan *et al.*, 2003). At the end of three years after release, 5 percent of the rapists were rearrested for another sex crime (rape or sexual assault). Forty-one percent were arrested for another, nonsexual crime within three years after release. Fifteen percent were rearrested for a violent crime (other than rape or sexual assault). Thus, rapists in this large sample had a low recidivism rate for *sexual* offenses but a very high rate for offenses *in general*.

Research on juvenile sex offenders suggests that one of the strongest risk factors that lead juveniles to recidivate is paternal (father) abandonment, especially if the abandonment occurs over a long period of time (Carpentier & Proulx, 2011). The investigators also reported that sexual victimization was significantly related to an increase in sexual, violent, and overall recidivism. "In all, half of the sexual recidivists in this study had been victims of hands-on sexual abuse, compared with slightly less than one-third of nonrecidivists" (Carpentier & Proulx, 2011, pp. 445–446). A comprehensive study by Seto and Lalumière (2010) also reported evidence that sexual abuse is associated with sexual offending, but it seems to be more related to the early onset of sexual offending rather than its frequency. One factor that did emerge from the Seto and Lalumière study that appeared to be significantly related to juvenile sex offending was atypical sexual interests. That is, research suggests that juvenile sex offenders show unusually high levels of sexual arousal toward children and depictions of coerced sexual assaults on peers and adults. They also appear to have an extensive fantasy life based on these depictions.

Attitudes That Support Rape

Undoubtedly, a major explanatory factor for many rapes is the attitudes about women and rape itself held by the perpetrators. Some researchers go so far as to say that these attitudes also are held by many individuals in the general population. Koss and Dinero (1988) conducted a well-designed survey of approximately 3,000 male students at 32 U.S. colleges and universities. Students were asked questions about the extent of verbal coercion and physical force they had used to become sexually intimate with women without their consent. They were also questioned about attitudes and habits. The results indicated that highly sexually aggressive men expressed greater hostility toward women, frequently used alcohol, frequently viewed violent and degrading pornography, and were closely involved with peer groups that reinforce highly sexualized and dominating views of women. In addition, the more sexually aggressive the student, the more likely he was to believe that force and coercion are legitimate ways to gain compliance in sexual relationships. The researchers concluded, "In short, the results provided support for a developmental sequence for sexual aggression in which early experiences and psychological characteristics establish conditions for sexual violence" (p. 144).

In summary, most rapists seem to subscribe to attitudes and ideology that encourage men to be dominant, controlling, and powerful, whereas women are expected to be submissive, permissive, and compliant. For example, one recent study found rape-prone men strongly endorse rape-supportive statements, such as that most women like to be dominated, a woman cannot be raped unless she wants to be, or women who say no are usually lying (Blake & Gannon, 2010).

Such an orientation seems to have a particularly strong disinhibitory effect on sexually aggressive men, encouraging them to interpret the ambiguous behavior of women as come-ons, to believe that women are not really offended by coercive sexual behaviors, and to perceive rape victims as desiring and deriving gratification from being sexually assaulted (Lipton, McDonel, & McFall, 1987).

The role played by fantasy and imagination in the development of sexually aggressive behavior is becoming an increasingly important topic (Knight & Sims-Knight, 2011). Self-reports by sexual offenders find that frequent imagery and fantasy of sexually aggressive scenes play a major role in motivating and guiding overt sexual aggression. Interestingly, in a self-report survey of 114 college men conducted by Greendlinger and Byrne (1987), over one-third indicated they fantasize about aggressively raping a woman and 54 percent fantasize about "forcing a woman to have sex."

As far back as the 1970s, research demonstrated that aggressive fantasies are particularly exciting to men convicted of rape. Abel and his associates (Abel, Barlow, Blanchard, & Guild, 1977; Abel, Becker, Blanchard, & Djenderedjian, 1978) found that rapists show high and nearly equal sexual arousal to audiotaped portrayals of both rape and consenting sexual acts. The degree of sexual arousal was indicated by the subject's penile tumescence, which is measured by a device called a plethysmograph. Male nonrapists, on the other hand, show significantly less penile tumescence to rape depictions. In fact, convicted rapists became highly aroused by rape depictions in which the victim experiences abhorrence and pain rather than sexual pleasure. Encouraged by these findings, Abel developed a physiological measure called the "rape index." The index is arrived at by dividing the average percentage of full penile erection to rape stimuli by the average percentage of full penile erection to consenting sexual stimuli. Avery-Clark and Laws (1984) have developed a similar indicator for pedophiles called the *Dangerous Child Abuser Index*. Today, many investigators use this measure in the diagnosis and treatment of rapists, as well as child molesters. Generally, research suggests that rapists tend to have a higher rape index than nonrapists. The overall accuracy of the penile plethysmograph and its sensitivity to extraneous factors and faking remain very much in question, however. Furthermore, some clinicians and researchers have moral objections to using this approach.

Abel and his group also discovered that some rapists became highly sexually aroused even to scenes of *nonsexual aggression,* such as a man beating a woman with his fists. Thus, it appears that some men strongly associate aggression and violence toward women with sexual arousal, a pattern very similar to that of the sexual aggressive rapist described later in the chapter. In fact, in rapists, the intensity of this deviant arousal has been found to be positively related to the number of rapes committed and the degree of injury inflicted on victims (Abel *et al.*, 1978). Some rapists apparently find scenes that show women being beaten exciting and pleasurable. In addition, male spouse abusers may, in part, be motivated by such arousal. On the other hand, a majority of men (70%) in the general population find the presence of aggression inhibiting to sexual arousal (Malamuth, Check, & Briere, 1986). Interestingly, men in the general population who are sexually aroused by force also are more accepting of an ideology that justifies male aggression against, and dominance over, women. These men also admit that they would probably rape if the opportunity were presented (Malamuth *et al.*, 1986). Related to the role played by fantasy in the development of sexual deviance is the role played by masturbation. The intrinsically physiological pleasure and arousal generated by masturbation can serve as a strong bonding agent, particularly if paired repeatedly with some fantasized object or person. Also, it is important to realize that there are two powerfully reinforcing processes in masturbatory activity: sexual arousal and the reduction of that arousal at orgasm. Fantasized or actual behaviors that are sexually arousing and that result in sexual satisfaction (i.e., orgasm) are likely to increase in strength and frequency. This process is known as "masturbatory conditioning" (Marshall & Barbaree, 1988). On the basis of clinical studies (e.g., George & Marlatt, 1989; Groth, 1979; Marshall, 1988), it appears that masturbatory conditioning may play an integral part in the development of both normal and deviant sexual behavior.

In sum, the evidence to date indicates overwhelmingly that rapists learn to be rapists and that much of the teaching is done by equally naive peers, parents, significant social models, and the entertainment media. Rape springs from a culture, characterized by violence that communicates a dominant ideology that degrades women and justifies coercive sexuality. Fortunately, most males eventually acquire a close approximation of sexual sophistication and some understanding of the needs of others. Many rapists, however, seem to remain sexually and, in some ways, socially immature.

Rape Myths

Rape myths have received considerable research attention during the past four decades. **Rape myths** are "attitudes and beliefs that are generally false but widely and persistently held, and that serve to deny and justify male sexual aggression against women" (Lonsway & Fitzgerald, 1994, p. 134). They stem from the traditional view of masculinity that men should be strong, assertive, sexually dominant, and heterosexual (Davies, 2002). Rape myths essentially are the false beliefs that women must be dominated and coerced into sexual activity.

Rape myths and misogynistic (hatred of women) attitudes appear to play a major role in sexual assault. Many—but not all—rapists and violently sexually aggressive men tend to hold them. Research indicates that men who subscribe to rape myths are hostile toward women in general (Forbes, Adams-Curtis, & White, 2004; Suarez & Gadalla, 2010). Furthermore, attitudes that promote the denigration of women may be widespread. There is distressing evidence that rapists may reflect the explicit and implicit beliefs held by many others. Recall that in one study, 35 percent of male college students on several different campuses felt there was some likelihood that they would rape if they could be sure of getting away with it (Malamuth, 1981). In another study, 60 percent of a group of 352 male undergraduates indicated there was some likelihood they would rape or force a female to perform a sexual act against her will if given the opportunity (Briere, Malamuth, & Ceniti, 1981).

Malamuth (1989) cautions, however, that one should not conclude that subjects who indicate they would sexually force a woman are necessarily "potential rapists." The scale used in his research, Attraction to Sexual Aggression (ASA), is designed to measure the belief that actually engaging in sexual aggression would be an arousing, attractive experience. Whether they would act on that belief is dictated by a myriad of factors across a wide spectrum of influences, including the degree of motivation to commit the act, the internal and external inhibitions present, and the opportunity to commit the act.

There is some recent evidence that some false beliefs and rape myths are beginning to change—at least among college students. Ferro, Cermele, and Saltzman (2008) report that today's college students are less likely to hold false beliefs about rape, and are generally sympathetic toward rape victims. However, the students still hold rape myths concerning marital rape. The participants found it difficult to believe that rape occurs in a married relationship since a higher level of intimacy is expected between married couples. They were also reluctant to believe that the act was a violation of the wife's rights or that she would be psychologically damaged from the experience.

Cognitive-Perceptual Distortions in Communication

Some men have strong cognitive-perceptual biases that lead to misconceptions of women's verbal and nonverbal communications (Knight & Sims-Knight, 2003, 2011). Overall, a subgroup of men, who are inclined to be sexually aggressive and coercive, perceive more sexual intent in women's behavior than women perceive in their own behavior or the behavior of other women (Farris, Treat, Viken, & McFall, 2008). For example, some men perceive friendly behavior (verbal and nonverbal) from a woman as seductive and assertive behavior as hostile and attacking. A simple touching of the arm may be interpreted as sexual interest. Furthermore, men who believe that rape is justifiable in certain situations and who blame women for victimization appear to have considerable difficulty distinguishing between when a woman is sexually interested and when she is not (Farris, Viken, Treat, & McFall, 2006). Alcohol certainly compounds the situation by influencing judgment and perceptual processing.

According to Farris et al., these men appear to have particular difficulty decoding sexual interest from disinterest based on clothing style. That is, some men believe that clothing choice is used by women specifically to signal their sexual interest. The researchers also discovered that sexually aggressive men tend to have particular difficulty making snap judgments. For example, "it appears that provocative clothing was particularly distracting to aggressive men when judgments had to be made quickly" (Farris et al., 2006, p. 874).

The Influence of Pornography

The relationship between rape and pornography is shrouded with confusion and surrounded by debate. Two presidential commissions established to study the effect of pornography on crime and human behavior reached opposite conclusions. The first and most comprehensive, established in 1967, was directed not to issue recommendations unless the effects were clear-cut. Because of the complexity it uncovered, the commission could not conclude whether explicit sexual material contributed significantly to sex crimes, prompting then-president Richard M. Nixon to remark that the commission was "morally bankrupt." Many have used this conclusion to support their contention that pornography is not harmful. The second National Commission on Obscenity and Pornography, which issued a report in 1984, recommended widespread restrictions of pornographic material. This commission has been extensively criticized for its lack of scientific objectivity.

Part of the problem is determining exactly what is meant by pornography. Seto, Maric, and Barbaree (2001) offer some help. First, there is the distinction between erotica and pornography. Erotica refers to "sexually explicit material that depicts adult men and women consensually involved in pleasurable, nonviolent, nondegrading, sexual interactions" (Seto *et al.*, 2001, p. 37). Pornography may be described as depictions of sexual contact where one of the participants is portrayed as powerless or nonconsenting, or is little more than an object for the pleasure of the other participant or participants. Pornography may be further described as either physically violent or degrading and humiliating to one of the participants, usually the woman if the parties are of different sexes. Both forms of the pornography portray sexual interactions as impersonal and without affection or consideration of the actors as individuals.

Overall, Seto *et al.* (2001) were able to conclude from their critical review of the research literature that there is little support for a direct causal link between pornography use and sexual aggression. However, some research evidence has suggested that under *certain* conditions, pornography facilitates aggressive, sexual behavior. Studies by Donnerstein (1983) and Malamuth (Malamuth & Check, 1981; Malamuth, Haber, & Feshbach, 1980; Malamuth, Heim, & Feshbach, 1980) indicate, for example, that a general statement that pornography does not negatively influence people needs several qualifiers. In a series of ongoing experiments, Donnerstein found evidence that three factors influence the relationship between pornography and human aggression: (1) the level of arousal elicited by pornographic films, (2) the level of aggressive content, and (3) the reactions of the victims portrayed in these films and photographs. Donnerstein and others (e.g., Meyer, 1972; Zillman, 1971) angered male subjects in a variety of ways, then found that pornography shown to these aroused subjects significantly increased their aggressive behavior toward others. Because of their arousing properties, the pornographic stimuli apparently may promote aggression under certain conditions. This finding accords with Berkowitz's theory (discussed in Chapter 5) on the relationship between arousal and aggression. Anything—sexual or not—that increases the arousal level of an already aroused subject will increase aggressive behavior in situations where aggression is the dominant behavior. The increased arousal may also draw the subject away from his own internal control or self-regulatory mechanisms, thereby allowing him to be less concerned about the consequences of his behavior. Furthermore, pornography investigations reveal that if the subject was angered by a woman, he would be even more aggressive toward other women after being exposed to a pornographic image or film. These findings corroborate the frequent clinical observation that prior to a rape, many rapists had been angered, upset, humiliated, or insulted, often by a woman (e.g., Groth, 1979).

Extremely violent stimuli, both pornographic and nonpornographic, can also facilitate aggression toward women, even in nonangered males, under certain conditions. The level of violence in the film appears significant. Portrayals of women being assaulted, even nonsexually, can increase subsequent aggressive behavior by men toward women, even when the males are not angry. Therefore, highly aggressive and violent acts depicted in the media may facilitate the rape act for some males. Since many rapists regard their act as a direct aggressive attack on women, seeing films where women are physically abused may encourage and support their own violent inclinations. Seto *et al.* (2001) make the point, though, that individuals who are already predisposed to sexually offend are the most likely to demonstrate the strongest effects of pornographic materials on their sexual and aggressive behavior. Men who are not predisposed toward aggressive sexual behavior are unlikely to be affected by pornographic materials.

The reactions of the victims portrayed in films also seem crucial. Films or photographs that depict the female victim enjoying rape (common in pornography) encourage acceptance of the rape myth and promote violence against women (Allen, Emmers, Gebhardt, & Giery, 2001; Malamuth & Check, 1981). In fact, Allen and his colleagues (2001) found that as the level of coercion depicted in the pornographic material goes up, so does the acceptance of the rape myth. If, on the other hand, the victim finds the rape both painful and abhorrent (negative aggressive pornography), male observers are disinclined to act aggressively. However, several qualifiers must be attached to this finding. If the male observer is already angered (aroused), seeing the victim suffer may make him more aggressive, since any arousal increase in an already aroused subject will increase subsequent aggressive behavior. The specific content of the film becomes irrelevant, as long as it meets the minimum criterion of being somehow arousing. On the other hand, males who are not upset or aroused before seeing a female victim suffer are less likely to aggress against women.

For some individuals, however, due to their conditioning history, pain cues are reinforcing if they are repeatedly associated with sexual gratification. Precisely how they react to various pornographic portrayals is unclear, but it seems reasonable to suggest that they would find depictions of pain both highly arousing and supportive of their belief that pain and sexual gratification go together. They might also conclude that the pain–pleasure relationship is inherently characteristic of everyone's sexual gratification and that women really enjoy being "roughed up."

The relationship between violent pornography and sexual aggression remains complex and troubling. Although sexually arousing nonviolent pornography should be available in a free society and arguably has social value, it can also be argued that *violent* pornography has no redeeming value. Its harmful effects, however, are difficult to document except as they relate to a subgroup of individuals. Some studies do indicate, however, that there is a significant relationship between violent pornographic consumption and attitudes supporting violence against women (Hald, Malamuth, & Yuen, 2010). This relationship appears to be especially strong for men who are considered at high risk for sexual aggression and rape (Malamuth Huppin, & Paul, 2005; Vega & Malamuth, 2007). Based on the majority of studies to date, it is reasonable to assume that if all violent pornography were eradicated today, sex crimes would likely decrease. Similar arguments could be made to support universal confiscation of handguns and rifles, or random, unannounced drug testing of the citizenry, both of which violate the U.S. Constitution. The extent to which a society should be asked to barter freedom in exchange for security remains a topic about which reasonable people consistently disagree. The commercial sexual exploitation of children by distributors via media and Internet pornographic materials is a very different story, and producing, possessing, and distributing depictions of children engaged in sexually explicit activity is a criminal offense. Nevertheless, prosecutors have been known to be overzealous in pursuing individuals who take pictures of their naked children or collect items depicting children in suggestive poses, when evidence of exploitation of actual children is meager. If it is clear that children are being used in these depictions it is another matter. The number of sexually exploited children through prostitution and sex trafficking in the United States and across the globe is astounding, and resources might better be spent fighting this serious problem. We will cover this topic in the next chapter on the sexual assault of children and youth. In that chapter, we will also cover the topic of psychological treatment of sex offenders in general. As you will learn, there is increasing evidence that the principles of psychological treatment that are effective with moderate and high-risk offenders in general (Andrews, Bonta, & Hoge, 1990) are also effective with sex offenders (Hanson, Bourgon, Helmus, & Hodgson, 2009).

THE KNIGHT AND SIMS-KNIGHT THREE-PATH MODEL

Raymond Knight and Judith Sims-Knight (2003) have proposed a **three-path model** that identifies major causal pathways in the development of sexual coercive behavior. The model helps explain the development of sexual coercive behavior in both adult and juvenile offenders (Knight & Sims-Knight, 2004). The model proposes that three personality traits define the three paths that lead to sexually violent behavior: (1) sexual drive/preoccupation; (2) antisocial behavior; and (3) callousness/unemotionality. The three traits are strengthened, in part, by two forms of early childhood abuse: physical/verbal and sexual abuse. According to Knight and Sims-Knight, early childhood physical/verbal abuse appears to strongly influence two paths toward sexual coercion. First, it enhances the development of arrogance, deceitfulness, and emotional detachment. Research has consistently shown that juvenile and adult sexual offenders are far more callous and unemotional than other offenders (Caputo, Frick, & Brodsky, 1999). This trait cluster is similar to some of the characteristics found in psychopaths.

Concerning the second path, physical/verbal abuse provides a model for some individuals to amplify aggressive behavior, a high-level of antisocial behavior, sensation seeking, alcohol and drug abuse, and impulsive acting out. These individuals tend to engage in a wide range of offending behaviors, with sexual violence being only one of them. This path strongly resembles the life-course-persistent offender described by Moffitt (1993a, 1993b), and discussed in the delinquency chapter.

Childhood sexual abuse influences a third path. Childhood sexual abuse appears to be especially prevalent in the backgrounds of juvenile sexual offenders (Zkireh, Ronis, & Knight, 2008). This form of abuse often leads to sexual preoccupation and compulsivity, which increases the risk of aggressive and coercive sexual fantasies and behavior (Knight & Sims-Knight, 2004) (See **Figure 12-1**). It should be emphasized that physical/verbal abuse and sexual abuse do not automatically lead to the traits and associated behaviors described above.

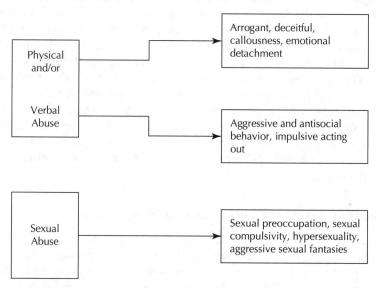

FIGURE 12-1 Knight and Sims-Knight Three-Path Model of Sexual Offending.

As pointed out throughout the book, it takes a combination of risk factors and biological predispositions to result in antisocial and criminal offending. Abuse is just one of those risk factors, but it does frequently show up in the backgrounds of sex offenders.

Research to date indicates that early traumatic physical and sexual abuse play an important role across the board in the development of the personality traits. According to Knight and Sims-Knight (2004), these traits "play a critical role across the life span for sexually coercive males, are critical in assessing risk of recidivism, and should be targets of therapeutic intervention" (p. 49). Moreover, "the consistent predictive potency of this model across criminal and community samples supports the hypothesis that a unified theory of sexual coercion can be generated" (Knight & Sims-Knight, 2011, p. 132). The model, as the authors admit, still needs refinement and perhaps modification. However, this empirically based model holds considerable promise in becoming a unified theory for understanding sexual assault and providing a framework for intervention and treatment.

CLASSIFICATION OF RAPE PATTERNS

Since such a wide variety of sexual offenders are involved in rape, some interesting attempts have been made to categorize rapists according to their behavioral patterns. Researchers at the Massachusetts (Bridgewater) Treatment Center (Cohen, Garafalo, Boucher, & Seghorn, 1971; Cohen, Seghorn, & Calmas, 1969; Knight & Prentky, 1987; Prentky & Knight, 1986) recognized that rape involves both sexual and aggressive features and tried to formulate a behavioral classification system that takes these elements into consideration.

Before we proceed, however, it is important to remind readers that classification systems are permeated with numerous problems and drawbacks. One obvious problem is that individuals do not fit neatly into a category. Furthermore, there may not be many who do. As astutely noted by Gibbons (1988), classification systems or typologies generally consist "of criminological foundations that assume that real life persons can be found in significant numbers who resemble the descriptions of offenders in the various typologies that have been put forth...researchers have often failed to uncover many point-for-point real-life cases of these hypothesized types of offenders" (p. 9). However, as we have noted earlier in the book, typologies or classification systems are valuable in organizing an otherwise confusing array of behaviors. They can also be useful in correctional facilities for risk management, such as deciding where to place an inmate, or in treatment programming, such as deciding what particular treatment modality might be most beneficial for an inmate. It should be stressed, however, that rape is not a unified behavior pattern but rather is a complicated, often poorly understood, individualized behavior that appears to be precipitated by a variety of internal and external stimuli. (See **Box 12-2** for a discussion of the relevance of offender typologies to victim resistance.)

Massachusetts Treatment Center Classification System

The Massachusetts Treatment Center (MTC) originally identified four major categories of rapists: (1) displaced aggression, (2) compensatory, (3) sexual aggressive, and (4) impulsive rapists. Although these major categories still exist—with slight changes in nomenclature—MTC researchers have refined the classification system to include various subcategories, as will be noted shortly. **Displaced aggression rapists** (also called in other classification systems

BOX 12-2
Victim Resistance

A frequently asked question about sexual assault of women is, to what extent should a woman fight back and try to resist the attack? In the past, women were often encouraged to take a passive role, under the assumption that resistance would infuriate the offender and increase the risk of further injury, even death. However, this created a double bind, because courts then required evidence that the victim had struggled. As noted in the chapter, contemporary legal thought does not equate failure to resist with consent. Thus, a victim should not be blamed because she did or did not resist.

However, with increasing awareness of the psychological trauma experienced by many women who have survived a completed rape (Ullman, 2007), researchers began to search instead for effective strategies that could be used against perpetrators. Recent research indicates that some rape resistance strategies can be effective.

In an interesting study, Sarah Ullman and Raymond Knight (1993) examined the police reports and court testimonies of 274 women who were either raped or who avoided rape by violent stranger rapists. They found that forceful resistance (fighting, screaming, fleeing, or pushing the offender) was more effective for avoiding rape than nonresistance. This strategy was especially effective in cases in which the offender had a weapon. However, although the victim avoided being raped or sexually assaulted, she often received more physical injury when the offender had a weapon, even if the weapon was not used. On the other hand, nonresistance strategies—pleading, crying, or trying to reason with the offender—were largely ineffective in avoiding rape or physical injury. In fact, victims who used these nonresistant strategies were more likely to be sexually and physically assaulted than women who strongly resisted.

More recent research continues to support the view that women who fight back forcefully are more likely to avoid completed rape (see Ullman, 1997, 2007). One thing to keep in mind is that the Ullman and Knight (1993) study focused on violent, stranger offenders who were committed to the Massachusetts Treatment Center (MTC) as sexually dangerous offenders. Whether the same results would occur when examining another type of offender is unclear. Moreover, the MTC rape categories make it fairly clear that compensatory rapists and impulsive rapists—and possibly many sexual aggressive

rapists—will be deterred by a victim who struggles. However, the displaced aggression rapists may respond with more violence if the victim resists. Nevertheless, it is unrealistic to think that a victim would be able to detect this one type of rapist and decide not to resist because of this. And, as Ullman (2007) writes, "More research is needed, but concerns that sadistic rapists or other specific rapist types (e.g., pervasively angry, opportunistic, nonsadistic sexual, vindictive) will inflict more injury on victims who forcefully resist remain unfounded to date" (p. 420).

In an earlier comprehensive review of the research, Rosenbaum, Lurigio, and Davis (1998) identified four basic strategies of resistance to rape: (1) forceful physical resistance, (2) forceful verbal resistance, (3) nonforceful physical resistance, and (4) nonforceful verbal resistance. Forceful physical resistance involves hitting, kicking, biting, using fingernails, or a weapon. Research suggests that using this method of resistance generally helps reduce the probability of severe sexual abuse or rape completion, but it also increases the risk that the victim will be attacked and physically injured. Forceful verbal resistance includes screaming, calling for help, or threatening the attacker. While this strategy reduces the probability of a rape completion, the degree of physical injury inflicted on the victim is unclear from the research evidence. The third strategy, nonforceful physical resistance, includes trying to flee the scene, pushing the attacker away, or shielding oneself. This type of resistance reduces the probability of rape completion but has little or no effect on the amount of injury received by the victim. Like the Ullman and Knight research that followed it, Lurigio et al. found that nonforceful verbal resistance, such as pleading, crying, or trying to reason with the attacker, generally leads to an increased probability of rape completion, and has no effect in reducing physical injury.

Overall, it appears that some type of forceful resistance is most effective in reducing a violent sexual attack and avoiding the completion of a rape. To the question, "Should the victim forcefully resist, scream, or try to run?" therefore, the answer is in the affirmative, though unfortunately these responses are not always possible. However, pleading for mercy or not forcefully resisting (verbally or physically) is more likely to result in a completed rape.

displaced anger or **anger-retaliation rapists**) are primarily violent and aggressive in their attack, displaying minimal or total absence of sexual feeling. These men use the act of rape to harm, humiliate, and degrade the woman. The victim is brutally assaulted and subjected to sadistic acts like biting, cutting, or tearing. In most instances, the victim is a complete stranger who happens to be the best available object or stimulus for the violence, although she may possess characteristics that attract the assailant's attention. The assault is not sexually arousing for the displaced aggression rapist, and he often demands oral manipulation or masturbation from the victim to become tumescent. Available evidence suggests that resisting this type of rapist only makes him more violent. However, this is not meant to suggest that someone *not* resist.

According to Knight and Prentky (1987), an offender must demonstrate the following characteristics during the attack in order to be assigned to the displaced aggression category:

1. The presence of a high degree of nonsexualized aggression or rage expressed either through verbal and/or physical assault that clearly exceed what is necessary to force compliance of the victim.
2. Clear evidence, in verbalization or behavior, of the intent to demean, degrade, or humiliate the victim.
3. No evidence that the aggressive behavior is eroticized or that sexual pleasure is derived from the injurious acts.
4. The injurious acts are not focused on parts of the body that have sexual significance.

Although many of these rapists are married, they are usually ambivalent toward the women in their lives (Cohen *et al.*, 1971), and their relationships with women are often characterized by frequent irritation and periodic violence. They perceive women as being hostile, demanding, and unfaithful. In addition, they often select as their targets for sexual assault women whom they consider active, assertive, and independent. The occupational history of these assailants is stable and often shows some level of success. Usually, the work is "masculine," such as truck driving, carpentry, construction, or mechanics. The attack typically follows an incident that has upset or angered the rapist, particularly about women and their behavior. The term *displaced aggression* is derived from the fact that the victim rarely has played any direct role in generating the aggression and arousal. This offender often attributes his offense to "uncontrollable impulses."

Compared with other rapists, the childhood of the displaced aggression offender is often chaotic and unstable. Many were physically and emotionally neglected. A large number were adopted or placed in foster homes. About 80 percent were brought up in single-parent homes.

Compensatory rapists rape in response to an intense sexual arousal initiated by stimuli in the environment, often quite specific stimuli. This type of rapist is sometimes referred to in the clinical and research literature as the "power-reassurance," "sexual aim," "ego dystonic," or "true" sex offender. Aggression is not a significant feature here; the basic motivation is a desire to prove sexual prowess and adequacy. In their day-to-day lives, compensatory rapists tend to be extremely passive, withdrawn, and socially inept. They live in a world of fantasy that centers on images of eagerly yielding victims who will submit to pleasurable intercourse and find the rapist's performance so outstanding that they will plead for a return engagement. The compensatory rapist's fantasies or personal versions of the world may so distort his view of the victim that he may seek further contact with her, even if she strongly resisted the sexual assault.

Although his victim is usually a stranger, the compensatory rapist has probably seen her frequently, watched her, or followed her. Specific stimuli associated with her probably excite him. For example, he may be drawn to college women but may feel the attraction would not be mutual if he approached them via a socially accepted route. He cannot face the prospect of rejection. However, if he can prove his sexual prowess, the victim will appreciate his value. If the victim vigorously resists the compensatory rapist, he is likely to flee; if she submits passively, he will rape without much force or violence. This sexually aroused passive assailant will often ejaculate spontaneously, even on mere physical contact with the victim. In general, he does not demonstrate other kinds of antisocial behavior.

The compensatory rapist is often described by others as a quiet, shy, submissive, lonely nice man. Although he is a reliable worker, his withdrawn, introverted behavior, lack of self-esteem, and low levels of need for achievement usually preclude academic, occupational, or social success. His rapes—or attempts at rape—are efforts to compensate for his sense of inadequacy, hence the category to which he is assigned. More recent research by Knight and Prentky (1987) questions the incompetence issue. They found that, compared with the other rapist types, the compensatory rapist evidenced the best heterosexual adaptation and achieved the highest employment skill level. Consequently, the term *compensatory rapist* has been replaced with the term *sexual gratification*, nonsadistic type.

The **sexual aggressive** or **sadistic rapist** is the one in whom sexual and aggressive features seem to coexist at equal or near equal levels. In order for him to experience sexual arousal, it must be associated with violence and pain, which excite him. He rapes, therefore, because of the combination of violence and sexual features in the act. He is convinced that women enjoy being forcefully raped and being dominated and controlled by men. This, he believes, is part of women's nature. Anger and aggression are not always present during the early stages of the assault, which may actually begin as a seduction. In this sense, the sexual aggressive rapist considers the victim's resistance and struggle a game, a form of protesting too much; what she really wants is to be sexually assaulted and raped. This belief appears deeply ingrained and widely accepted in many Western societies (Edwards, 1983). Consider the following remarks made by a Scottish attorney general: "M.P.s would do well to remember that rape involves an activity which was normal . . . it was part of the business of men and women that they hunted and were hunted and said 'yes' and 'no' and meant the opposite" (Edwards, 1983, p. 114).

Sexual aggressive offenders are often married, but because they display little commitment or loyalty, they also often have a history of multiple marriages, separations, and divorces. They also may be frequently involved in domestic violence. In fact, their backgrounds include antisocial behaviors beginning during adolescence or before and ranging from truancy to rape-murder. They have been severe management problems in school. Throughout their childhood, adolescence, and adulthood, they exhibit poor behavior controls and a low frustration tolerance. Their childhoods are characterized by physical abuse and neglect.

In the extreme, these rapists engage in sexual sadism much like the displaced aggression rapists: Their victims may be viciously violated, beaten, and even killed. The difference between the two types is that the sexual aggressive rapist derives intense sexual satisfaction from aggression, pain, and violence. In order to qualify for assignment to this category, the offender needs to demonstrate (1) a level of aggression or violence that clearly exceeds what is necessary to force compliance of the victim, and (2) the explicit, unambiguous evidence that aggression is sexually exciting to him.

A fourth type of rapist, the **impulsive** or **exploitative rapist**, demonstrates neither strong sexual nor aggressive features, but engages in spontaneous rape when the opportunity presents itself. The rape is usually carried out in the context of another crime, such as robbery or burglary. The victims simply happen to be available, and they are sexually assaulted with minimum extra-rape violence or sexual feeling. Generally, this offender has a long history of criminal offenses other than rape. In order to be assigned to this group, the offender must show (1) callous indifference to the welfare and comfort of victim, and (2) the presence of no more force than is necessary to gain the compliance of the victim.

The MTC:R3

The Massachusetts Treatment Classification scheme offers a rough framework for conceptualizing and simplifying the behaviors and motives involved in rape. However, it needs refinement and reconstruction, a process the group has been pursuing for a number of years (e.g., Knight, 1999; Knight & Prentky, 1990). After a series of analyses and further development, the new Massachusetts Treatment Classification scheme (called the MTC:R3) finds that rape offenders can now be classified into *four* major types and *nine* subtypes. Although the basic four offender types—displaced aggression, sexual gratification (formerly compensatory), sexual aggressive, and impulsive—are still in the equation, the researchers have also discovered there are subtle differences within the original four types. The researchers decided that four primary *motivations* for rape could improve the MTC significantly: *opportunity, pervasive anger, sexual gratification,* and *vindictiveness* (Knight, 1999; Knight, Warren, Reboussin, & Soley, 1998). Knight and his colleagues (Knight *et al.*, 1998) concluded that these four motivations appeared to describe enduring behavioral patterns that distinguished most rapists. The **opportunistic types** (Types 1 and 2) are similar to the impulsive rapist described earlier. Their sexual assaults appear to be impulsive, predatory acts as a result of being in a situation where the opportunity for the sexual attack arises, and they are not primarily driven by sexual fantasy or explicit anger at women. However, analysis of offender data showed that the opportunistic type can be subdivided on the basis of their social competence (see **Figure 12-2**). Type 1 offenders are higher in social competence and first exhibited their impulsive sexual tendencies in adulthood. Type 2 offenders, on the other hand, are lower in social competence and first demonstrated their impulsive sexual actions during adolescence.

The **pervasive anger type** (Type 3) is similar to displaced aggression rapists but with the difference that his generalized anger pervades all areas of his life. Their pervasive anger is not simply directed at women but at everyone. Consequently, they often have a long history of antisocial, violent behavior of all kinds, and they tend to inflict high levels of physical injury on their victims, especially their rape victims. In many ways, they manifest behaviors similar to the life-course-persistent offender. **Sexual gratification** motivations characterized four subtypes of rapists in the newly developed MTC classification scheme (Types 4, 5, 6, and 7; see **Figures 12-2**). The sadistic rapists (Types 4 and 5) are subdivided into overt and muted types "on the basis of whether their sexual-aggressive fantasies are directly expressed in violent attacks or are only fantasized" (Knight *et al.*, 1998, p. 58). The nonsadistic sexual rapists (Types 6 and 7) are subdivided on the basis of their social competence; they are similar to the compensatory rapist described earlier in the chapter.

The new MTC:R3 also includes **vindictive offender** types (Types 8 and 9), characterized by anger directed exclusively at women. These types are also highly similar to the displaced aggressive type described in the original MTC. "The sexual assaults of these men are

MTC:R3

PRIMARY MOTIVATION

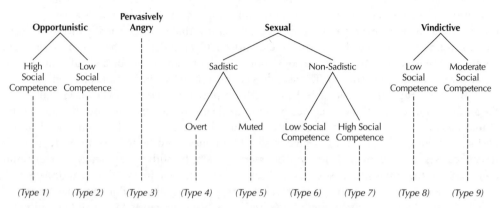

FIGURE 12-2   Breakdown of Four Categorizations of Rapist Type into Subtypes.
Source: R. A. Knight *et al.* Criminal Justice and Behavior, Vol. 25. p. 57, Fig. 2. Copyright © Sage 1998 by Publications, Inc. Reprinted by permission of Sage Publications, Inc.

distinguished by behaviors that are explicitly intended to harm the woman physically, as well as to degrade and humiliate her" (Knight *et al.*, 1998, p. 58). Like the opportunistic and nonsadistic rapists, the vindictive types can be subdivided into high social competence and low social competence people.

Knight *et al.* (1998) postulate that these nine rape-offender classifications can help substantially in providing additional clues in crime-scene investigations. With refinement and continuing research, the MTC:R3 should ultimately enable investigators to identify "type" based on parameters gathered at the crime scene. The MTC:R3 also underscores the multiple strategies and cognitive beliefs possessed by rapists and discourages dogmatic proclamations about why rape occurs. The MTC:R3 increases the understanding of the etiology of sexual offending and helps mental health professions predict recidivism. Knight (1999) cautions, though, that while the MTC:R3 provides a useful way of classifying the many motivations of rapists, it may need considerable refinement and research to establish its validity and ultimate utility. In a recent study, Goodwill, Alison, and Beech (2009) found that the MTC:R3 does appear to have predictive validity in criminal profiling.

The Groth Typology

Groth (1979) has developed a typology with many similarities to the MTC scheme. The Groth proposal is based on the presumed motivations and aims that underlie almost all rapes. Rape is seen as a "pseudo-sexual act" in which sex serves merely as a vehicle for the primary motivations of power and aggression. Groth asserts, "Rape is never the result simply of sexual arousal that has no other opportunity for gratification....Rape is always a symptom of some psychological dysfunction, either temporary and transient or chronic and repetitive" (p. 5). Later, he states, "Rape is always and foremost an aggressive act" (p. 12). Consequently, Groth divides rape behavior into three major categories: anger rape, power rape, and sadistic rape.

In **anger rape**, the offender uses more force than necessary for compliance and engages in a variety of sexual acts that are particularly degrading or humiliating to the woman (such as sodomy or urinating on her). He also expresses his contempt for the victim through abusive and obscenity-laced language. Thus, for the anger rapist, rape is an act of conscious anger and rage toward women, and he expresses his fury physically and verbally. Sex is actually dirty, offensive, and disgusting to him, and this is why he uses it to defile and degrade the victim. Very often, his attacks are prompted by some previous conflict with or humiliation by a significant woman (often a wife, a boss, or a mother). The assault is characterized by considerable physical brutality.

In **power rape**, the assailant seeks to establish power and control over his victim. Thus, the amount of force and threat used depends on the degree of submission shown by the victim. "I told her to undress and when she refused I struck her across the face to show her I meant business" (Groth, 1979, p. 26). His goal is sexual conquest, and he will try to overcome any resistance. Sexual intercourse is his way of asserting identity, authority, potency, mastery, and domination rather than strictly sexual gratification. Often the victim is kidnapped or held captive in some fashion, and she may be subjected to repeated assaults over an extended period of time. The sexual assault is sometimes disappointing to the power rapist because it fails to live up to his frequent fantasies of rape. "Everything was pleasurable in the fantasy, and there was acceptance, whereas in the reality of the situation, it wasn't pleasurable, and the girl [sic] was scared, not turned on to me" (Groth, 1979, p. 27).

The third pattern of rape, **sadistic rape**, includes both sexual and aggressive components. In other words, aggression is eroticized. The sadistic rapist experiences sexual arousal and excitement in the victim's maltreatment, torment, distress, helplessness, and suffering. The assault usually involves bondage and torture, and he directs considerable abuse and injury on various areas of the victim's body. Prostitutes, women he considers promiscuous, or women representing symbols of something he wants to punish or destroy often incur the wrath of the sadistic rapist. The victim may be stalked, abducted, abused, and sometimes murdered.

Groth (1979) reports that over half of the offenders evaluated or treated by his agency (Connecticut Sex Offender Program) were power rapists, 40 percent were anger rapists, and only 5 percent were sadistic rapists. There are many similarities between Groth's scheme and the MTC typology. The anger rapist is similar to the displaced aggression rapist, the sadistic rapist is similar to the sexual aggressive rapist, and the power rapist shows many commonalities with the compensatory rapist. However, the MTC typology is far more extensive and based on ongoing research.

Summary and Conclusions

The very serious crime of rape is widely believed to be the most underreported crime. When we consider the psychological toll it takes on its victims—or rape survivors—it is not surprising that the vast majority of rapes never come to the attention of police. We noted early in the chapter that many researchers, as well as statutes, now use the term *sexual assault,* which can encompass both penetration and a variety of behaviors that fall short of that ultimate violation.

Traditionally, both rape and other sexual assaults have been considered almost exclusively a male enterprise, both in their perpetration and victimization. In the 1990s, researchers began to question this assumption. Although it is still a fact that men and boys commit the great majority of sexual offenses, we can no longer ignore the reality that women and girls also commit them. Because most theory building and typologies have been developed on males, we have used the male pronoun to refer to offenders throughout the chapter. In similar fashion, victims of sexual assault in the literature are generally believed to be female, but this too is changing with increasing focus on victimization of boys and men, including those incarcerated, by both men and women. In addition, future UCR reports will tabulate rape in a different manner, including assaults of male as well as female victims.

We reviewed statistics on rape and sexual assault, as well as available demographic information about both offenders and victims. Research indicates that some individuals may be more vulnerable to being raped than others, either by nature of their demographic characteristics, such as age, or situational characteristics, such as use of alcohol or victimization history. Despite some interest in studying victimization in this manner, researchers are quick to point out that the blame for rape is on the perpetrator, not the victim.

With respect to offenders, they commit their crimes for a variety of reasons. A major motivation appears to be to harm, derogate, or embarrass the victim. In some situations, the rapist may interpret his behavior as harmless, believing that his victims enjoy being "roughed up." Nevertheless, the effect is invariably the opposite. The psychological and social damages to the victim are incalculable. Sexual assaults by husbands, dates, and intimate friends are more frequent than commonly supposed and there is indication that the psychological damage may be even greater than in stranger rape.

Most rapists are young and often show a history of rape and other violent actions. Several attempts at typologies or classification systems of sex offenders have been made, the most notable being those developed by the Massachusetts Treatment Center and Nicholas Groth. Of the two, the MTC classification system, which encompasses both types of rapists and their motivations, is the most widely used and has been the one most submitted to empirical research. MTC researchers also have developed a three-path model, which identifies personality traits that are associated with sex offenders: sexual preoccupation, antisocial, and callous-unemotional.

Rape and other sexual behavior appear to be due, in part, to the type of socialization experiences the offender has had. The offender has constructed, from information received from a variety of sources and models, a belief and value system that encourages and justifies the aggressive behavior. Furthermore, most rapists have attitudes and an ideology that encourage men to be dominant, controlling, and powerful, while expecting women to be submissive, permissive, and compliant. This attitudinal pattern may be much more prevalent in society in both men and women than commonly realized. It is also a global phenomenon.

We also learned that under high levels of arousal, any consideration of the rightness of a sexual assaulter's behavior or its consequences may be obliterated. As we saw with reference to homicide and assault, high levels of arousal reduce attention to private self-awareness and personal standards of appropriate conduct. Under high levels of excitement, along with the influence of alcohol or other drugs, some normally law-abiding persons may become rapists, or at least use the high excitement as a justification for their rape behavior. Of course, some people possess a value system that justifies rape or the resolution of interpersonal conflict through violence, regardless of their arousal level.

This chapter also includes a brief discussion of the role of pornography in facilitating aggressive sexual behavior. In a free society, pornographic material obviously cannot be banned (although restrictions can be and are placed on the pornography that exploits children). Considering the appeal of pornography, it is clear that there is no direct causal link to rape or other sexual assault. However, research does indicate that individuals who are predisposed to commit such assault often use pornography as a stimulus. Furthermore, *violent* pornography has been shown to increase violent tendencies even in some males who were not otherwise predisposed. Thus, the effect of violent pornography on aggressive behavior is troubling. We return to this topic in the next chapter.

Key Concepts

Anger rape

Compensatory rapist

Date or acquaintance rape

Displaced aggression rapists/
displaced anger/anger-
retaliation rapists

Expressive sexual aggression

Forcible rape

Global risk recognition failure

Impulsive rapist/exploitative
rapist

Instrumental sexual aggression

Marital rape

Opportunity rapist

Pervasive anger rapist

Power rape

Rape by fraud

Rape myths

Sadistic rape

Sexual aggressive rapist/sadistic
rapist

Sexual gratification rapist

Specific (or situations) risk
recognition failure

Statutory rape

Three-path model

Vindictive offender

Review Questions

1. Define date or acquaintance rape, and summarize the research on estimated incidence.

2. Define and provide examples of rape myths.

3. How did Groth classify rapists? Be sure to describe all of his classifications.

4. What are the known offender characteristics of rapists?

5. Describe the rape offender classification system developed at the Massachusetts Treatment Center.

6. Does pornography play a crucial role in sex crimes against women and children? Briefly support your answer with reference to research findings.

13

Sexual Assault of Children and Youth and Other Sexual Offenses

CHAPTER OBJECTIVES

- Define pedophilia and related concepts.
- Outline the demographic and other characteristics of child molesters.
- Review the research literature on classification systems of child molesters.
- Summarize what is known about the recidivism rates of adult and juvenile child molesters.
- Discuss contemporary research on Internet-facilitated child pornography.
- Identify treatment approaches to reducing sex offender recidivism.

In 2009, the world was shocked at the revelation that an Austrian citizen, Josef Fritzl, had held his own daughter as a sexual captive in the basement of the family home in St. Poelten, Austria, for 24 years. She had borne him seven children, who had apparently been raised as her younger brothers and sisters. Later that year, he confessed to a range of sexual crimes against his daughter and his other children. In 2012, reverberations from clergy-abuse scandals that were publicized in the 1990s continue, with victims coming forward and more claims made against adults who participated or covered up the crimes. Also in 2012, Penn State University was reeling from the case involving former football coach and defensive coordinator Jerry Sandusky of 45 counts of child molestation. Sandusky was convicted of abusing 10 boys over a 15-year-period. The University faces civil suits alleging that some officials failed to investigate Sandusky's behavior and engaged in complicity to cover it up.

Pedophilia (from the Greek word for child lover) is the clinical term for the more commonly used terms *child molestation* and *child sexual abuse*. We must emphasize at the outset, however, that the clinical condition is not necessarily accompanied by action. When criminal action *is* involved, even though we may refer to the offender as a **pedophile**, this is not the official term; that is, the person is prosecuted for child sexual assault, child molestation, child sexual exploitation, producing and distributing child pornography, or any one of a number of other sexual crimes against children.

Pedophilia is defined in a variety of ways. The *DSM-IV* (1994) defines it as a condition in which "over a period of at least six months, recurrent, intense sexually arousing fantasies, sexual urges, or behaviors involving sexual activity with a prepubescent child or children (generally age 13 years or younger) occur" (p. 528). The *DSM-IV* further specifies that some pedophiles are sexually attracted only to children (the exclusive type), whereas others are sexually attracted to both children and adults (nonexclusive type).

According to Finkelhor and Araji (1986), pedophilia is an adult's conscious sexual interest in prepubertal children. One of two behaviors signifies that interest. Either the adult has had some sexual contact with a child (touched the child or had the child touch him—pedophiles are usually males—with the purpose of arousing him sexually) or the adult has masturbated to sexual fantasies or images involving children. Although the second behavior is not a crime, criminal behavior may have been involved in the procuring of the images, a topic we will address later in the chapter. Occasionally, researchers extend the definition to include ages 13 through 15, but most literature uses the term **hebephilia** for sexual contact by adult males with young adolescents. However, the distinction between hebephilia and pedophilia does not appear to be clinically meaningful (Blanchard, Klassen, Dickey, Kuban, & Blak, 2001), so hebephilia is usually not considered a distinct, diagnostic category.

Traditionally, most definitions of pedophilia were restricted to sexual contact between an adult and child who are not closely related. Sexual acts between members of a family when at least one participant is a minor has traditionally been labeled incest or **intrafamilial child molestation** and is most commonly perpetrated by men who molest their sexually immature daughters or stepdaughters (Rice & Harris, 2002). Sexual contact with immature family members by individuals from outside the family is called **extrafamilial child molestation**. See **Table 13-1** for terms and definitions.

Some mental health professionals argue that pedophilia and child molestation should refer to two different things, with the former limited to fantasies or sexual attraction to children and

TABLE 13-1 Terms Used in Research on Child Molestation	
Term	**Definition**
Extrafamilial child molestation	Sexual contact with a minor child by someone *outside* the immediate family.
Intrafamilial child molestation	Sexual contact with a minor child by someone *within* the immediate family.
Pedophilia	For some researchers and clinicians, the term refers to strong sexual *attraction* toward children. Others use the term to refer to sexual *contact* with children. In this text, it will refer to the latter.
Pedophile	Someone with strong sexual attraction toward children, or someone who has frequent sexual contacts with children.
Child molester	Largely accepted term for someone who has sexual contact or sexually abuses a minor child. In this text, it will be used interchangeably with pedophile.
Hebephilia	Sexual contact by adult males with young adolescents.
Paraphilia	Sexual disorders in which sexual arousal occur almost exclusively in the presence of inappropriate objects or individuals.

the latter referring to the act itself (Bartol & Bartol, 2008). In other words, as noted above, pedophilia is the condition, not the behavior. Other professionals prefer the all-encompassing term **paraphilia**, which covers other cognitions and behaviors in addition to those relating to children. The essential features of paraphilia "are recurrent sexually arousing fantasies, sexual urges, or behaviors generally involving (1) nonhuman objects, (2) the suffering or humiliation of oneself or one's partner, or (3) children or other nonconsenting persons, that occur over a period of at least 6 months" (American Psychiatric Association, 1994, p. 522). In this chapter, however, we will continue to use the term pedophilia when referring to illegal sexual actions on children, ranging from sexual touching to penetration.

INCIDENCE AND PREVALENCE OF PEDOPHILIA

As with sexual offenses in general, a caveat pertaining to the statistics is necessary. Data on pedophilia are difficult to obtain, since there are no central or national objective recording systems for tabulating sexual offenses against children. Sex crimes as a group have the lowest rates of reporting of all crimes (Terry & Tallon, 2004). Most estimates of the distribution of pedophiles in the general population are derived from arrest or prison data. However, as noted at the beginning of the chapter, offenders may be arrested and prosecuted under a variety of statutes and for a variety of offenses, including child rape, aggravated assault, sodomy, incest, indecent exposure, or lewd and lascivious behavior. Furthermore, although the UCR lists sex offenses other than forcible rape and prostitution in its statistics on Part II crimes, it does not differentiate pedophilia from the mixture of these other possible sexual offenses. *Pedophilia* is a clinical term, not a legal one.

From a national survey of about 1,200 American males (Finkelhor & Lewis, 1988), it is estimated that between 5 percent and 10 percent of the male population has engaged or will engage in child sexual abuse at some time in their lives. In one anonymous survey, about 4 percent of college-aged men admitted having sexual contact with a prepubescent girl (Ahler, Schaefer, *et al.*, 2011). It is important to note, however, that these figures may include a one-time incident that—although still to be condemned—may not represent the offender's usual behavior and would not qualify him as a pedophile for purposes of this chapter. For example, a 14-year-old babysitter who sexually fondles a three-year-old might self-report that behavior to researchers out of guilt. Nevertheless, these and other data indicate that children are sexually victimized at levels that far exceed those reported for adults (see Finkelhor & Dziuba-Leatherman, 1994). In a more recent review, Michael Seto (2008a) estimates an upper-limit prevalence of pedophilia is about 5 percent in the general male population.

Prison data also give us an indication of the extent of the problem. Two-thirds of all prisoners in state prisons convicted of rape or sexual assault had committed their crime against a child, and in most cases the victim was female (Greenfeld, 1996). Approximately 60 percent of those convicted of child molestation had attacked victims aged less than 13 years.

Nationwide tabulations of the number of victims are equally difficult to obtain. For example, the National Crime Victimization Survey only collects data from victims older than age 12, thus neglecting the victimization of young children. However, a variety of retrospective surveys of the general population indicate that from a quarter to a third of all females and a tenth or more of all males have indicated that they were molested during childhood (Finkelhor & Lewis, 1988; Peters, Wyatt, & Finkelhor, 1986). Moreover, only 35 percent of the children who are sexually victimized report it to anyone (Finkelhor, 1979). Russell (1984) found that in her survey sample, only 2 percent of all incestuous abuse cases and 6 percent of all cases of extrafamilial abuse of girls under 18 had ever been reported to the police. In a nationally representative sample of 2,030 children ages 2–17

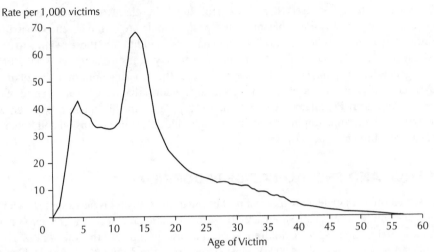

Rate per 1,000 victims

FIGURE 13-1 Age Distribution of Victims of Sexual Assault *Source*: Data from Snyder (2000).

years, Finkelhor, Ormrod, Turner, and Hamby (2005) discovered that 1 in 12 children or youth had experienced a sexual victimization during the year of the survey (see **Figure 13-1**). Sexual assaults were substantially more common against girls than boys. The survey also found that the great majority of sexual victimizations were perpetrated by acquaintances. And, in a recent survey of juveniles held in public facilities, about 14 percent who stayed from 7 to 12 months reported sexual victimization (Beck, Harrison, & Guerino, 2010).

The National Incident-Based Reporting System (NIBRS), as described in Chapter 1, has the potential to provide better information on the prevalence of sexual assaults on young children. Using NIBRS data between 1991 and 1996, Snyder (2006) found that 34 percent of the victims of sexual assault reported to law enforcement were under age 12. Most disturbing was the finding that one of every seven victims of sexual assault (14% of the victims) was under age six.

It is well recognized in the criminology literature that female adolescents and adults with persistent antisocial behavior have often experienced child sexual abuse (Ullman, 1999, 2007). Among nonoffenders, the figures are also sobering. Russell (1984) surveyed 930 randomly selected female residents of San Francisco during 1978. The purpose of the project was to obtain an estimate of the incidence and prevalence of rape and other forms of sexual assault, including the amount of sexual abuse respondents experienced as children. Twelve percent of the women said they had been sexually abused by a relative before the age of 14. Twenty-nine percent reported at least one experience of sexual abuse by a nonrelative before reaching the age of 14. Overall, 28 percent of the 930 women reported at least one incident of sexual abuse before reaching the age of 14 (see **Figure 13-1**).

The reports of perpetrators themselves indicate that numerous children are affected. Abel and his colleagues (Abel, Becker, Murphy, & Flanagan, 1981) reported that incarcerated homosexual pedophiles had, on the average, 31 victims, while heterosexual pedophiles had an average of 62 victims. A Dutch study (Bernard, 1975) reported that at least half of its respondents claimed sexual contacts with at least 10 or more children. Fourteen percent of the sample—which included both arrested and nonarrested pedophiles—admitted to sexual contacts with more than 50, and 6 percent to contacts with between 100 and 300 children. Fifty-six percent of this sample indicated they had one or more "regular" sexual contacts with children. Fully 90 percent asserted that they did not want to stop their pedophilial activities.

While some of the above studies may appear dated, nothing in the recent research literature suggests that this problem has been attenuated. A recent meta-analysis found that one in ten adults in the United States had experienced sexual abuse before age 18 (Pérez-Fuentes *et al.*, 2012). In a study of worldwide prevalence, child sexual abuse is estimated to be 11.8 percent or 118 per 1,000 children (Stoltenborgh, van Ijzendoorn, Euser, & Bakermans-Kranenburg, 2011). The global estimated prevalence for girls is 18 percent and about 8 percent for boys. Similar worldwide prevalence rates were reported by Pereda, Guilera, Forns, and Gómez-Benito (2009), who found a child sexual abuse prevalence of 19.2 percent for girls and 9.9 percent for boys. In summary, the amount of sexual abuse and violence against children is staggering.

Situational and Victimization Characteristics

The offender, or pedophile, is almost always male, but the victim may be of either gender. As noted earlier, however, research is beginning to focus more on the sexual offending of women (Becker & Johnson, 2001; Ellis, 1998; Sandler & Freeman, 2007). Although the predominant view remains that men far outnumber women as perpetrators, there is growing recognition that women are not immune to committing this type of crime. Research to date, however, suggests that pedophilia may manifest differently in women (Seto, 2008a, 2012a). We will discuss this topic again later in the chapter.

Heterosexual pedophilia—male adult with female child—appears to be the more common type, with available data indicating that three-quarters of pedophiles choose female victims exclusively (Langevin, 1983; Lanyon, 1986). Homosexual pedophilia—male adult preference for male child—appears to be substantially less frequent (about 20%–23% of the reported cases). A small minority of pedophiles choose their victims from both sexes, a phenomenon referred to as crossover. **Crossover**, in offender research, denotes the extent the offender is consistent selecting specific types of victims or targets. If the offender selects a wide range of victims or targets, he or she is demonstrating crossover. For example, in one study (Abel, Becker, Cunningham-Rathner, Mittelman, & Rouleau, 1988), 20 percent of the offenders reported offending against both male and female victims and 42 percent said they had victims from several age groups (less than 14 years old, 14–17, and some more than 17). They also selected victims from inside and outside the family. Sim and Proeve (2010) found a considerable amount of crossover in their study of 128 adult male child sexual offenders. More than half of the offenders exhibited crossover in at least one of three domains: victim age, gender, or relationship to the offender. Their data highlight the point that crossovers are not rare among adult offenders who sexually molest children. The researchers discovered the highest degree of crossover (48%) occurred in the victim age domain, similar to the Abel *et al.* (1988) research. They also found 20 percent crossover for gender type and a 30 percent crossover for relationship to victim domain. Sim and Proeve conclude the following: "It is unclear whether crossover in victim type is consistent with offenders' sexual preferences, or that they crossover victim type because their preferred victim type is not available and another type of victim is available" (p. 411). It is clear that crossover research is one area that needs further investigation, as it has implications for understanding pedophilic behavior.

Types of Sexual Contact

The behavior of the pedophile or child molester is usually limited to caressing the child's body, fondling the child's genitals, and/or inducing the child to manipulate the adult's genitals. Penetration is apparently involved in only a small proportion of the total number of offenses (Seto, 2008b).

The form of the sexual contact seems to depend on three factors: the degree to which the offender had previous nonsexual interactions with children, the nature of the relationship between the child and the offender, and the age of each. Offenders who have had limited interaction with children are more likely to perform or to expect genital–genital and oral–genital contact, rather than to indulge only in caressing or fondling. Furthermore, the more acquainted the offender and the victim are with one another, the greater the tendency for genital–genital or oral–genital contact.

There is some disagreement about the extent to which child molesters harm the child physically or use physical force. According to most research, pedophiles do not usually use overt physical coercion. McCaghy (1967) found no evidence of any kind of coercion, verbal or physical, in three-fourths of the child molestation cases he examined. Research by Groth and his colleagues (Groth, Hobson, & Gary, 1982) supports these findings. Lanyon (1986), summarizing the research, concluded that violence is involved in about 10 percent to 15 percent of child sexual abuse cases.

Some research documents more force and violence, however. Hall, Proctor, and Nelson (1988) report that 28 percent of a sample of convicted pedophiles (122 nonpsychotic patients of a state mental hospital) were officially identified as having used physical force or the threat of force beyond what was necessary to gain the victim's compliance. Marshall and Christie (1981) found that in a sample of 41 pedophiles incarcerated in Canadian federal penitentiaries, 29 had used physical force. In an earlier study of 150 pedophiles, Christie, Marshall, and Lanthier (1979) had reported that 58 percent used excessive force in their attack and 42 percent of the child victims had sustained notable injuries. The researchers suggested that the offenders in their sample were highly sexually aroused by physical violence, significantly more so than other nonaggressive sex offenders. The reported differences in the use of violence and force by pedophiles appear to be explained by the sample used. Studies reporting a high incidence of violence or aggression focus on incarcerated, relatively hard-core offenders, while those reporting little or no violence sampled less-criminal or nonincarcerated pedophiles, generally those on probation.

Groth *et al.* (1982) recommend that the few offenders using violence or force and causing physical harm to the child should be labeled "child rapists." On the other hand, those offenders only using psychological pressures should be considered child molesters or pedophiles. Although Groth's suggestion has merit, researchers in this area have used *pedophile* or *child molester* as umbrella terms to cover all child sexual abusers, including those who rape their victims.

Psychological Effects of Child Sexual Victimization

Research offers strong support for the assumption that any form of sexual abuse in childhood produces long-term psychological problems in many children (Briere, 1988). Reports of depression, guilt, feelings of inferiority, substance abuse, suicide ideation, anxiety, chronic tension, sleep problems, and fears and phobias are common. Depression is the symptom most commonly reported among adults who were molested as children.

The extent of psychological damage to the child produced by sexual abuse is dependent on several factors. Groth (1978) contends that the greatest trauma occurs in children who have been victims for long periods of time, are victimized by a closely related person (such as a father or stepfather), when the victimization involves penetration, and when it is accompanied by aggression. In their careful review of the research literature on pedophilia, Browne and Finkelhor (1986) concluded that (1) younger children appear to be somewhat more vulnerable to trauma than older children, (2) the closer the relationship between offender and victim, the greater the trauma, and (3) the greater the force used the greater the trauma. They also maintained, however, that there is no conclusive support for the contention that the longer and more frequent the abuse, the greater the trauma. Nor is there any clear evidence that traumas are related to the type of sexual abuse (e.g., penetration, fondling, fellatio, cunnilingus). This suggests that "mild" abuse may be as traumatizing as penetration, especially if the victim is young and closely related to the offender.

OFFENDER CHARACTERISTICS

Many aggressive pedophiles demonstrate a large number of similarities to rapists and the prison population in general (Knight, Rosenberg, & Schneider, 1985). The most notable commonalities are the following: (1) they have problems with alcohol, (2) they have a high rate of high school failure and dropout, (3) they *tend to* have unstable work histories in unskilled occupations, and (4) they *tend to* come from the low socioeconomic class. Alcohol abuse is frequently a problem in sex offenders. While about one-third to one-half of convicted rapists have serious problems with alcohol, about one-quarter to one-third of convicted pedophiles have such problems (Knight *et al.*, 1985).

Prentky, Knight, and Lee (1997) conclude from their extensive research on the subject that the classification and diagnosis of child molesters are complicated by a high degree of variability among individuals in reference to personal characteristics, life experiences, criminal histories, and reasons or motivations for offending. Essentially, there is no single "profile" that accurately describes all child molesters, or for that matter, all sex offenders. With this caveat in mind, we proceed with some commonly observed characteristics of those who offend against children in this way.

Gender of the Offender

Pedophilia is primarily committed by males, but it is not exclusively a male offense. The National Center on Child Abuse and Neglect (2000) reported that 46 percent of the abusive sexual experiences encountered by children included a female perpetrator. This figure is misleading, however, in that it includes any female caretaker who "permitted acts of sexual abuse to occur" (Russell & Finkelhor, 1984). In other words, leaving the child with a boyfriend as a babysitter who in turn molests the child would be considered sexual abuse by the mother. The mother who fails to report her suspicions that her husband is sexually abusing her daughter may also be included in the statistic. If only those women who *committed* child sexual abuse themselves are included, the percentage of female offenders drops to 13 percent (of all cases) when the victims are female and 24 percent when the victims are males (Russell & Finkelhor, 1984). More recent data suggest that 8 percent of all *arrests* for sexual assault were female (Freeman & Sandler, 2008). UCR 2010 data reveal that females account for 1 percent of those arrested for sexual assault (Federal Bureau of Investigation, 2011a). The number of arrests of females for sexual offenses in any given year probably represents a low figure. In cases that involved female sexual abuse, either the abuse is not reported for many years or, if reported, it is often dismissed or disbelieved (Strickland, 2008).

Utilizing a matched sample of 780 female and male sex offenders in New York state, Freeman and Sandler (2008) determined that female sex offenders were more likely to victimize males, whereas male sex offenders were more likely to victimize females. In addition, the researchers found that male sex offenders have a far more extensive criminal history than female sex offenders. This criminal history included both sexual and nonsexual offenses. Similarly, most of the female sex offenders investigated by Vandiver and Walker (2002) had a history of only one sex offense and no other criminal history.

Findings in others studies indicate that women who become sexual abusers have themselves experienced more physical, emotional, and sexual abuse than female nonsexual offenders (Mathews, Hunter, & Vuz, 1997; Strickland, 2008). In addition, they are more likely than nonsexual offenders to come from severe deprived backgrounds, such as poor living conditions, food deprivation, and lack of medical care. These conditions of extreme deprivation and abuse are likely to sharply affect appropriate coping and interpersonal skills, self-regulation skills, emotional maturity, and feelings of self-worth. As noted by Strickland (2008), females who suffered family violence, sexual abuse, and severe deprivation may have greater difficulty in developing and maintaining appropriate interpersonal relationships. Similar findings are found in the backgrounds of male child sex abusers, especially sexual abuse (Simons, Wurtele, & Durham, 2008). To a large extent, these forms of trauma may induce women who sexually abuse to find intimate relations with young children and adolescents.

Female sex offenders are beginning to receive considerable research and clinical attention (e.g., Freeman & Sandler, 2008; Gannon & Rose, 2008; Sandler & Freeman, 2007; Vandiver & Kercher, 2004). Since most of the documented sexual offenses committed by females involve infant, child, or adolescent victims (Strickland, 2008), female sex offenders are covered in this chapter rather than in the previous chapter on general sexual assault.

Age

Although there is considerable age variability, it is well documented that male pedophiles tend to be older, on average, than male rapists (Hanson, 2001). While about 75 percent of convicted male rapists are under 30, about 75 percent of convicted male child molesters are over that age (Henn, Herjanic, & Vanderpearl, 1976b). By contrast, Sandler and Freeman (2007) found that the average female sex offender was in her early thirties, and they most often target victims just under age 12 years. The age at which they commit their first sexual offense may also differ according to gender. Vandiver and Walker (2002) report the majority of female sex offenders committed their first sexual offense at around age 31. Groth (1978) notes that all the male child molesters he and colleagues have worked with had committed their first child molestation offense before age 40. Over 80 percent were first offenders by age 30, and about 5 percent had committed their first sexual assault before they reached adolescence. However, in addition to the statistical finding that child molesters tend to be older than most other sexual offenders, there seems to be a pattern of victim preference as a function of age. Older pedophiles (over 50) seek out immature children (age 10 or younger); younger pedophiles (under age 40) prefer girls between the ages of 12 and 15 (Revitch & Weiss, 1962). The latter offenders are technically classified as hebephiles.

The above data refer to adult sexual offenders. Contemporary research demonstrates very clearly that sexual offending by juveniles is not uncommon, however. We will return to juveniles in a separate section later in this chapter.

Attitudes Toward Victims

Perhaps because of the extremely negative attitude society displays toward child molesters, pedophiles almost always resist taking full responsibility for their offenses (McCaghy, 1967). They are motivated to disguise their thoughts and feelings about their sexual beliefs and attraction toward children. Many claim that they went blank, were too intoxicated to know what they were doing, could not help themselves, or did not know what came over them. They show a strong preference to attribute the cause of their behavior to external forces or motivating factors largely beyond their personal control.

Self-control emerges as a critical variable in cognitions of pedophiles. As outlined by Hanson (2001), low self-control refers to the tendency to respond impulsively to temptation, have little consideration of the consequences, and engage in high-risk behaviors. However, pedophiles appear to have significantly better self-control than rapists (Hanson, 2001), leading to the conclusion that pedophiles' claims that their behavior is outside of their control may have very little validity.

Cognitive Functions

In an important study, Cantor, Blanchard, Robichaud, and Christensen (2005) found that adult males who commit sexual offenses score significantly lower in IQ measures than adult males who commit nonsexual offenses. However, IQ differences between sexual and nonsexual offenders do not occur uniformly across sexual offender subtypes. That is, offenders who commit rape against *adults* did not differ in IQ from the nonsexual offenders. Overall, the results revealed that the younger the victim, the lower the intelligence of the offender. Furthermore, the observed difference in intelligence for sexual offenders and nonsexual offenders appears to be largely due to the scores of child molesters. In fact, the IQ scores of pedophiles were, on average, about 10 IQ points below the general population average. Cantor *et al.* (2005) admonish that the results do not indicate that low IQ scores *cause* pedophilia, only that something may have happened during early childhood to limit their cognitive functioning. Seto and Lalumière (2010) found in their review of the research literature that adolescent sex offenders had significantly more learning problems and disabilities than nonsex offenders. In addition, emerging research suggests that problems in executive, neurocognitive functioning and prefrontal processing may play a significant role in explaining the sexual-deviant behavior for some pedophiles (Eastvold, Suchy, & Strassberg, 2011; Kruger & Schiffer, 2011; Schiffer & Vonlaufen, 2011). The researchers speculated that neurodevelopmental damage may have occurred at some point early in their lives. These results suggest that some pedophiles commit their crimes against children partly because of poor judgment and impulse control due to problems in brain functioning. Alternatively, individuals with lower cognitive skills or brain deficits may be more likely to be rejected sexually by peers and consequently more likely to turn to children for sexual gratification (Seto & Lalumière, 2010).

Lower levels of intellectual and cognitive functioning in pedophiles are associated with a stronger sexual attraction for male children and a greater interest in younger children compared with pedophiles with higher levels of intelligence (Blanchard *et al.*, 1999). Lower intelligence may limit the individual from appreciating the nature of the sexual assault or its long-term consequences. Seto and Lalumière (2010) write: "Persons with lower cognitive abilities may have poorer judgment or impulse control and thus may be more likely to commit sexual offenses opportunisitically" (p. 531).

Interpersonal and Social Skills

Prentky *et al.* (1997) assert that the more an offender's sexual preference is limited to children, the less socially competent the offender tends to be. In this context, social competence refers to the offender's social and sexual relationships with adults. Several studies (e.g., Hunter, Figueredo, Malamuth, & Becker, 2003; Marshall, Barbaree, & Fernandez, 1995; Marshall & Mazzucco, 1995) have revealed that, on average, pedophiles are inadequate socially, lack interpersonal skills, are unassertive, and have poor self-esteem. Adolescent pedophiles are also found to be significantly below average in social skills, compared to other adolescent offenders (Seto & Lalumière, 2010). We have also seen the same social, interpersonal, self-worth, and confidence factors among female sex offenders (Strickland, 2008). (See **Table 13-2** for a comparison of pedophile and rapist characteristics.)

TABLE 13-2	General Comparisons Between Pedophiles and Rapists on Important Variables		
Common Characteristic*	**Pedophiles**	**Rapists**
Cognitive functioning	Below average	Average
Interpersonal skills	Below average	Average
Education level	Low	Average
Employment	Unstable	Stable
Age	Older	Younger
Self-control	Average	Low
Sexual recidivism	Unknown, but likely high for a small group	Lower
Offending history	Largely restricted to pedophilia	Variable and extensive
Alcohol use	Frequent problem	Less of a problem

*This table is intended to provide only the typical findings from the available research. It should be emphasized, however, that there are many individual exceptions to these comparisons.

Similar to other sexual offenders, the classification, diagnosis, and assessment of pedophiles are complicated by a high degree of variability among individuals in reference to personal characteristics, life experiences, criminal histories, and motives for offending (Prentky *et al.*, 1997). "There is no single 'profile' that accurately describes or accounts for all child molesters" (Prentky *et al.*, 1997, p. v). The best way to highlight the complex nature of pedophilia is through a discussion of two well-known classification systems or typologies. Like the rape typologies described in the previous chapter, they were developed by the Massachusetts Research Center and by Groth, with the former being more research based and the latter more clinically based. In addition, like the rapist typologies discussed in the previous chapter, they have been formulated primarily on information gathered on male offenders.

CLASSIFICATION OF CHILD OFFENDER PATTERNS

The Massachusetts Treatment Center (MTC) (Cohen, Seghorn, & Calmas, 1969; Knight, 1988; Knight *et al.*, 1985) has developed a widely cited typology of pedophile behavioral patterns. Four major pedophiliac patterns have been identified: (1) the fixated type, (2) the regressed type, (3) the exploitative type, and (4) the aggressive or sadistic type.

The **fixated (or immature) pedophile** demonstrates a long-standing, exclusive preference for children as both sexual and social companions. He has never been able to develop a mature relationship with his adult peers, male or female, and he is considered socially immature, passive, timid, and dependent by most people who know him. He feels most comfortable relating to children, whom he seeks out as companions. Sexual contact usually occurs only after the adult and child have become well acquainted. Fixated pedophiles rarely marry, and their social background lacks much evidence of dating peers or even any sustained, long-term friendship with an adult (outside of relatives). This pedophile wishes to touch, fondle, caress, and taste the child. He rarely expects genital intercourse, and very rarely does he use physical force or aggression.

The fixated pedophile generally has average intelligence. His work history is steady, although it is often work that is below his ability. His social skills are adequate for day-to-day functioning. Probably most troubling about the fixated or immature pedophile is that he is not concerned or disturbed about his exclusive preference for children as companions, nor can he see why others are concerned. Therefore, he is difficult to treat and is most likely to recidivate.

The **regressed pedophile** had a fairly normal adolescence and good peer relationships and sexual experiences, but later developed feelings of masculine inadequacy and self-doubt. Problems in the individual's occupational, social, and sexual lives followed. The regressed child offender's background commonly includes alcohol abuse, divorce, and a poor employment record. Each pedophilial act is usually precipitated by a significant jolt to the offender's sexual adequacy, by either female or male peers. For example, the pedophile may perceive other males as being more successful with women after a female acquaintance rejects him in favor of another man. Unlike the immature (or fixated) child offender, the regressed child offender usually prefers victims who are strangers and who live outside his neighborhood. The victims are nearly always female. Also unlike the fixated pedophile, he seeks genital sex with his victim. Because he feels remorseful and expresses disbelief after that act, clinicians usually find him a good prospect for rehabilitation. As long as stressful events are kept to a minimum and he learns to cope adequately with those he does have, he is unlikely to reoffend. We return to this later in the chapter when we discuss principles of effective treatment.

The **exploitative pedophile** seeks children primarily to satisfy his sexual needs. He exploits the child's weaknesses any way he can and tries various kinds of strategies and tricks to get him or her to comply. He is usually unknown to the child and commonly tries to get the child isolated from others and his or her familiar surroundings. If necessary, he will use aggression and physical force to get the child to comply with his wishes. The exploitative offender does not care about the emotional or physical well-being of the child, but only sees the victim as a sexual object.

The exploitative offender exhibits a long history of criminal or antisocial conduct. His relationships with peers are unpredictable and stormy. He is unpleasant to be around and is often avoided by others who know him. He tends to be highly impulsive, irritable, and moody. His markedly defective interpersonal skills may be the principal reason that he chooses children as victims (Knight *et al.*, 1985). Clinicians find him difficult to treat, as his deficiencies extend to all phases of his daily life. Nevertheless, and again as will be discussed later, treatment based on certain principles may be effective.

The **aggressive** (or **sadistic**) **pedophile** is drawn to children for both sexual and aggressive reasons. Pedophiles in this group are apt to have a long history of antisocial behavior and poor adaptation to their environments. Since the primary aim is to obtain stimulation without consideration for the victim, this group often assaults the child viciously and sadistically. The more harm and pain inflicted, the more this offender becomes sexually excited. Aggressive or sadistic pedophiles are most often responsible for child abductions and murders. Clinicians find this type not only dangerous to children but also among the most difficult to treat. Fortunately, this type is rare. Although rare, this is the type frequently portrayed in the media and is most associated—though wrongfully so—with the image of the child molester.

An example of an aggressive pedophile was Albert Fish (1870–1936), whose background is discussed by Nash (1975). Fish, called the "Moon Maniac," admitted sexually molesting more than 400 children over a span of 20 years. In addition, he confessed to six child murders and made vague reference to numerous others. He was eventually convicted of murdering a 12-year-old girl and was electrocuted in 1936. A more contemporary example might well be John Wayne Gacy Jr., who sadistically murdered 33 teenage boys and young men and buried their bodies in the cellar of his suburban Chicago home.

Fish thought the conditions of his childhood led to a "perverted" life of crime. He was abandoned at an early age and placed in an orphanage, where he first witnessed and experienced brutal acts of sadism. Fish was quoted as saying, "Misery leads to crime. I saw so many boys whipped it ruined my mind." He apparently began his career of child molesting in earnest when his wife deserted him for another man. This suggests that, like regressed offenders, aggressive offenders may begin their crimes in response to precipitating events involving rejection and feelings of sexual inadequacy.

The above are two quite distant examples of the individuals who committed a multitude of heinous acts over periods of time. Both were subjected to sensational media coverage, as were the child abduction cases referred to in previous chapters. Sensational media coverage also occurred in the Sandusky case in 2012, where both victims and other witnesses testified to crimes that occurred in the locker room shower and the basement of Sandusky's home. The more typical cases that receive less public attention, often because offenders plead guilty instead of going to trial, are no less troubling. Persons familiar with court and social service records (e.g., lawyers, social workers, treatment providers, juvenile justice professionals) offer chilling information about the behaviors engaged in by pedophiles and the effects on their victims. An eight-year-old girl told the court about the sexual game her stepfather played on the bed with her and her younger sister every Friday evening. In another incident, a teacher suspected a problem because a young child's leg jumped up and down with great anxiety as the end of the school day approached. It was learned that the child was being sexually abused by an after-school caretaker. Other children are forced to engage in sexual activities with their siblings or are threatened with death or grievous harm if they reveal what is occurring.

The MTC:CM3

Like the Massachusetts Treatment Center classification scheme for rapists, the MTC classification system of child molesters has also undergone some refinement in recent years. In an effort to depict more accurately the complexity involved in classifying pedophiles, the MTC:CM3 (referring to Massachusetts Treatment Center: Child Molester, Version 3) includes tentative changes to the original scheme described earlier. Specifically, three significant changes are recommended: (1) Divide the regressed and fixated types into three separate factors—degree of fixation on children, the level of social competence achieved, and the amount of contact an offender has with children, (2) incorporate into the scheme a new narcissistic offender type, and (3) partition the violence of the sexual assault into physical injury and sadistic components (Knight, 1989).

The researchers discovered that, although the regressed pedophile classification is a valid one, it was also more complicated than originally supposed. Researchers found that the regression classification could be further subdivided into the molester's style of offending, his interpersonal relationships with children, the intensity of the offender's interest, and the level of social competence achieved by the offender. For example, offenders could be classified according to their level of fixation and social competence. Level of fixation refers to the strength of an offender's sexual interest in children (Knight, Carter, & Prentky, 1989). In other words, to what extent are children the major focus of the offender's thought and attention? If children are the central focus of the offender's sexual and interpersonal fantasies and thoughts for more than six months, then the offender qualifies for high fixation. Social competence refers to the degree to which the offender can participate effectively in daily living. An offender would have high social competence if he has demonstrated at least two of the following behaviors: (1) has had a single job lasting three or more years, (2) has had a sexual relationship with an adult for at least one year, (3) has assumed responsibility in parenting a child for three or more years, (4) has been an active member in an adult-oriented organization (e.g., church group, business group) for one or more years, or (5) has had a social friendship with an adult for at least one year. The dimensions of fixation and social competence result in four types of child molesters: high fixation, low social competence (type 0); high fixation, high social competence (type 1); low fixation, low social competence (type 2); and low fixation, high social competence (type 3). The regressed type was dropped in MTC:CM3 in favor of the term *low fixation*.

Research further revealed that pedophiles can also be distinguished on the basis of how much daily contact with children they seek (see **Figure 13-2**). A high-contact offender demonstrates regular contact with children in both sexual and nonsexual contexts (Knight *et al.*, 1989). Offenders of high contact often become involved in an occupation or recreation that brings them in considerable contact with children, such as bus drivers, schoolteachers, Boy Scout leaders, and Little League coaches. Research data revealed there are two kinds of offenders who seek more extensive involvement with children beyond their sexual offenses. The first high-contact type, the *interpersonal offender* (type 1), seeks the extensive company of children for both social and sexual needs. He sees the child as an appropriate companion in a relationship and believes the friendship is mutually satisfying. The second type, the *narcissistic offender* (type 2), solicits the company of children only to increase his opportunities for sexual experiences. Like exploitative offenders, these offenders typically molest children they do not know, and their sexual acts with children are typically genitally oriented (Knight, 1989). Furthermore, there is little or no concern about the needs, comfort, or welfare of the child (Knight *et al.*, 1989).

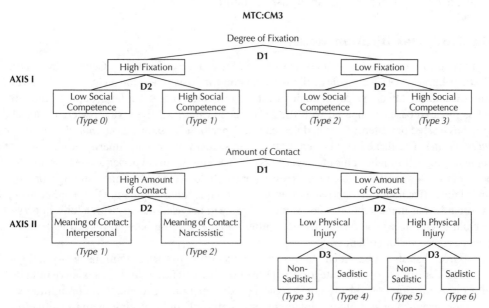

FIGURE 13-2 Flow Diagram of the Decision Process for Classifying Child Molesters on Axis I and Axis II on the MTC:CM3 *Source*: R. A. Knight *et al. Journal of Interpersonal Violence*, Vol. 4. p. 8, Fig. 1. Copyright © 1989 by Sage Publications, Inc. Reprinted by permission of Sage Publications, Inc.

Another group of pedophiles are low-contact seekers. Low-contact offenders' only contacts with children are in the context of sexual assault. Low-contact offenders are classified according to the amount of physical injury they administer to their victims. Two types of low-contact seekers tend to administer very little *physical* injury to their victims: the exploitative type and the muted sadistic type. Low injury refers to the absence of physical injury to victim and the presence of such acts as pushing, shoving, slapping, holding, and verbal threats. None of the acts of low injury results in a lasting injury. The *exploitative, nonsadistic offender* (type 3) uses no more aggression or violence than is necessary to secure victim compliance. Furthermore, the assault does not reveal evidence that sadistic actions engender sexual arousal in the offender. The *muted* or *symbolic sadistic offender* (type 4) engages in a variety of distressing, painful, and threatening acts, none of which causes significant physical injury to the child.

Finally, the MTC:CM3 classifies two offenders who have often administered a high amount of physical injury to their victims: the aggressive offender and the sadistic offender. High injury is characterized by hitting, punching, choking, sodomy, or forcing the child to ingest urine or feces (Knight *et al.*, 1989). The *aggressive, nonsadistic offender* (type 5) is similar to the aggressive pedophile described earlier except that sadism is not a primary aim of the assault. This offender is extremely angry about all things in his life and is generally violent toward people in his life, including children. The *sadistic offender* (type 6) obtains sexual pleasure from the pain, fear, and physical harm he inflicts on the child.

The newly developed MTC:CM3 helps identify offender type based on crime scene information and perhaps presents a more refined classification system of child molester or predator types. However, research beyond the MTC population is needed before investigators feel comfortable about adopting this promising scheme. Looman, Gauthier, and Boer (2001) were able to replicate the MTC:CM3 Classification System with a Canadian sample of child molesters, suggesting that the system has applicability across cultures.

The Groth Classification Model

In a classification system similar to that of the Massachusetts Treatment Center, Groth (1978; Groth & Burgess, 1977) classifies child offenders on the basis of the longevity of the behavioral patterns and the offender's psychological aims. Like Groth's rape offender groupings, though, it is less research based compared with the MTC classifications. If the sexual preference for children has existed persistently since adolescence, the person is classified as an *immature* or *fixated child offender*. The fixated child offender has been sexually attracted primarily or exclusively to younger people throughout his life, regardless of what other sexual experiences he has had. Groth believes that this fixation is due to an arresting of psychological maturation, resulting from unresolved formative issues that persist and underlie subsequent development. On the other hand, if the offender has managed to develop some normalcy in his relationships with adults, but resorts to child offending when stressed or after suffering a devastating blow to his self-esteem, he is called a *regressed* child offender.

Groth has also subdivided child offenders according to their intentions or psychological aims. He identifies two basic categories: (1) sex pressure offenders, and (2) sex force offenders. In sex pressure offenses, the offender's typical modus operandi is to entice children into sexual behavior through persuasion or cajolement, or to entrap them by placing them in a situation in which they feel indebted or obligated. A child may feel he owes something to the person who taught him to swim or bought him a bike. The sex force offense, on the other hand, is characterized by threat of harm and/or the use of physical force in the commission of the offense. The offender either intimidates the child—by exploiting the child's relative helplessness, naiveté, and awe of adults—or attacks and physically overpowers his victim.

Groth finds he can further subdivide the sex force group into the *exploitative type*, in which the threat of force is used to overcome victim resistance, or the *sadistic type*, who derives great pleasure in hurting the child. The exploitative type typically employs verbal threats, restraint, manipulation, intimidation, and physical strength to overcome any resistance on the part of the child. His intent is not necessarily to hurt the child but to obtain compliance. The sadistic type, which fortunately is rare, eroticizes physical aggression and pain. He uses more force than is necessary to overpower the victim and may commit a so-called lust murder. Therefore, the physical and psychological abuse and/or degradation of the child is necessary for him to experience sexual excitement and gratification. Often, the child is beaten, choked, tortured, and violently sexually abused.

Certainly the Groth typology has strong commonalities with the MTC typology. The immature and the regressed child offenders display features of the sex pressure offender, and the aggressive child offender shows strong similarities to the sex force offender. It may be more appropriate at the present time to classify the child offender according to the degree of coercion or force he uses rather than according to personality features. The first method focuses on offender behavior, a criterion that is more objective and clearcut. The second focuses on "understanding" the behavior by assuming a variety of personality constructs. We have too little information about child offenders at this point to do that with total confidence.

Female Sex Offender Typology

Donna Vandiver and Glen Kercher (2004) have proposed a clinically useful and research-meaningful typology of female sex offenders. Utilizing 471 registered adult female sexual offenders in Texas, the researchers identified six types:

1. Heterosexual nurturers
2. Noncriminal homosexual offenders
3. Female sexual predators
4. Young adult child exploiters
5. Homosexual criminals
6. Aggressive homosexual offenders

Heterosexual nurturers were the largest group. This group victimized only males with an average age of 12. The offenders are generally in mentorship, care-taking, or teacher roles, such as the teacher–lover category in which a teacher engages in a "romantic" relationship with one of her students or a counselor with one of her clients. Many of the offenders in this group do not perceive the relationship as abusive or psychologically damaging to the child. These females appear to be motivated by a desire for intimacy to compensate for unmet emotional and social needs, and may not recognize or want to recognize the inappropriateness of the relationship. This group had a low recidivism rate.

Noncriminal homosexual offenders represented the second largest group. This group primarily preferred early adolescent females as victims (average age of 13). This offender group appeared to have many of the same characteristics as heterosexual nurturers but their victim preferences were females. Similar to heterosexual nurturers, these offenders were unlikely to have a criminal record or to recidivate.

Female sexual predators victimized both male (60 percent) and female children (40 percent) who averaged 11 years of age. This group resembled other female criminals, and their sexual offending may be an offshoot of other criminal activity. In other words, they are repeat offenders committing a variety of crimes. They also had a high probability of committing another sexual offense.

Young adult child exploiters most often committed sexual assault. Their victims were frequently young with an average age of seven, and involved both genders. These offenders themselves were the youngest of the six offender groups, with an average age of 28. About half of the victims were related to the offender, sometimes the offender's own child.

The fifth group, homosexual criminals, had an extensive history of antisocial behavior. Their victims were usually female with an average age of 11. Their sexual crimes included committing acts of indecency with a child and compelling the child into prostitution or child pornography. Most of these offenders are motivated by profit rather than sexual ambitions.

Aggressive homosexual offenders represent the smallest group and were also the oldest. Their victims were generally adult females and therefore are not relevant to the topic of this chapter. They appeared to be representative of homosexual women involved in a domestically violent relationship.

In their sample of 390 female sex offenders in New York state, Sandler and Freeman (2007) also identified six categories. In addition, their sample was very similar to Vandiver and Kercher's on demographic variables, such as offender age and race. However, Sandler and Freeman did not entirely support some of the characteristics reported in the Vandiver and Kercher typology. This is to be expected, considering that typologies that attempt to classify female sex offenders are in early stages of development.

Sandler and Freeman did find support for the heterosexual nurturer and young adult child exploiter categories found by Vandiver and Kercher, but some characteristics of the four other categories were different. One of the major differences was the gender of the victims. Sandler and Freeman discovered that many of the female sex offenders did not *consistently* victimize one gender more than the other. Because the cluster analysis did not highlight a strong victim preference as found in the Vandiver-Kercher analysis, Sandler and Freeman felt it was appropriate to label only one group as homosexual, which they called the homosexual child molester. This group, which emerged as the smallest, almost exclusively targeted female victims (91%).

Some of the differences in results of the two studies may be due to the substantially different criminal codes or registry requirements for sex offenders between states. In addition, the Vandiver and Kercher sample included females who may or may not have served time in prison, and their offenses were considered serious enough to warrant arrest and prosecution (Gannon & Rose, 2008). Although their sample was a forensic population, it represented a very wide range of female sexual offenders.

Although the two studies significantly advance our knowledge pertaining to female sex offenders, neither study was able to obtain additional data relating to co-offenders (Gannon & Rose, 2008). In other words, did the females offend alone or with a co-offender, such as a male partner? Gannon and Rose (2008) emphasize that this shortcoming limits strategies and programs for treating female sex offenders. In addition, neither Sandler and Freeman's nor Vandiver and Kercher's typologies examine psychological variables, such as mental health status or the victimization histories of the offenders themselves. In general, the research on female sexual offenders has focused on the demographics and the very basic details of their offending characteristics, which is extremely helpful. However, as Gannon and Rose (2008) note, there is very little research on the sexual interests, empathy, intimacy deficits, and self-regulation of female sex offenders. This research needs to be done if we are to get a better understanding of the female sex offender.

JUVENILE SEX OFFENDERS

A significant number of sexual offenses in the United States are committed by juveniles. According to the latest UCR, 14 percent of arrests for forcible rape and 18 percent for arrests for other sex offenses (other than forcible rape or prostitution) were persons under the age of 18. The actual numbers are probably higher. As much as 30 percent to 50 percent of child molestation offenses (known and unknown) may be committed by adolescents (Cellini, 1995). Van Wijk, van Horn, Bullens, Bijleveld, and Doreleijers (2005) discovered that juvenile child molesters represent a very different group compared with juvenile rapists. These researchers found that juvenile child molesters demonstrate significantly more social isolation because of poorly developed social skills and very limited interactions with peers. This and other research indicates that those youngsters who molest children (individuals at least four or five years younger in age than the perpetrator) were introverted and rejected by peers from an early age. The majority of their victims (more than 60%) are younger than 12, and two-thirds of these young victims are younger than 6 (Veneziano & Veneziano, 2002). Ryan, Miyoshi, Metzner, Krugman, and Fryer (1996) found that 63 percent of the victims of juvenile molesters were younger than age nine. Adolescent rapists, on the other hand, are more likely to select victims their own age or older (Veneziano & Veneziano, 2002). A study investigating incest cases reported that sibling offenders are more likely to have molested younger children than are nonsibling offenders (Worling, 1995).

Juvenile molesters are far more likely than juvenile rapists to have been sexually abused themselves in early childhood (Prentky, Harris, Frizzell, & Righthand, 2000). Juveniles who sexually offend against children display lower self-efficacy and self-esteem, and higher levels of depression, anxiety, and pessimism than found for other juvenile sex offenders (Hunter & Figueredo, 1999; Hunter et al., 2003). They view themselves as socially inadequate and anticipate peer ridicule and rejection (Hunter et al., 2003). They also show greater deficits in psychosocial functioning than other juvenile sex offenders, are less aggressive, and are more likely to offend against victims to whom they are related (Hunter et al., 2003).

Female Juvenile Sex Offenders

According to the latest UCR statistics, juvenile females accounted for only 8 percent of all juveniles arrested for sex offenses (excluding rape, where their rates are lower, and prostitution, where their rates are higher) (Federal Bureau of Investigation, 2011a). However, the actual prevalence of juvenile female sexual offending is unknown.

First, most of the research on female sex offending has focused on adult female offenders (Bumby & Bumby, 1997). Second, as noted earlier, when female juveniles sexually offend, the victim is usually a child younger than themselves by five years or more, suggesting it is undiscovered or unlikely to be reported to protect the victim from additional trauma. Finally, research on girls who have committed sex offenses has been sparse, and existing investigations have been limited to small sample sizes and other methodological shortcomings (Becker, Hall, & Stinson, 2001; Righthand & Welch, 2001).

Fehrenbach and Monastersky (1988) found that most adolescent girls who sexually victimized young children did so while doing child care or babysitting. The victims of the 28 female sex offenders they studied were 12 years old or younger. They were mostly acquaintances (57%), followed by siblings (29%) and other relatives (14%). Mathews, Hunter, and Vuz (1997) provided data on 67 female adolescent sex offenders who ranged in age from 11 to 18. More than 90 percent of their victims were acquaintances or relatives. Each of the above two studies also found that a high percentage of the abusers (50% and 77.65%, respectively) themselves had a history of being sexually abused. These findings suggest that female juveniles who sexually offend are far more likely to have been sexually abused themselves than male juvenile sex offenders. Similarly, Bumby and Bumby (1997) found that adolescent female sex offenders tend to be depressed, have a poor self-concept, have a suicide ideation, and have most often been sexually abused during childhood.

RECIDIVISM OF PEDOPHILES

If pedophilia is learned, we would expect a fairly high incidence of recidivism. Like the national recidivism rates for most offenses, however, pedophile recidivism rates are difficult to obtain. Moreover, the second time around, the pedophile is undoubtedly more careful about detection. On the other hand, he is also more closely monitored by the criminal justice system or may be in treatment. Interestingly, therefore, some research suggests low repeat offending, particularly for nonviolent pedophiles. In general, though, research on recidivism must still be described as uncovering mixed results.

Hanson (2001) examined the recidivism rates of over 4,500 sexual offenders from diverse settings (Canada, the United States, and the United Kingdom). The data revealed a 19 percent sexual recidivism rate for extrafamilial pedophiles, compared with a sexual recidivism rate of 17 percent for rapists during an average follow-up time of five years. These figures seem low compared with the findings of other researchers. For example, in a follow-up investigation of 4,295 child molesters released from prison in 1994, Langan, Schmitt, and Durose (2003) found that 39 percent were rearrested within three years after release. However, this figure represents rearrest for any type of offense, not just sexual offenses. If we examine rearrest data for sex crime against a child, only 3.3 percent of the child molesters were rearrested within the three-year follow-up. Thus, Langan's rates are actually lower than those of Hanson. In another study conducted in the United Kingdom, it was found that 12 percent of 413 child molesters had recidivated within two to four years after treatment (Beech, Mandeville-Norden, & Goodwill, 2012). A majority (59%) of the repeat offenders committed sexual offenses, ranging from very serious offenses such as rape to less serious (noncontact) sexual offenses, such as indecent exposure. It is unclear, however, how many of the repeat offenders in the study actually had sexual contact with children.

Other types of data, including research on treatment dropout, suggest that recidivism is a significant problem. Repeat offending is especially troublesome when child molesters demonstrate not only deviant sexual interests involving children but also exhibit features of psychopathy (Seto, 2008b; Strassberg, Eastvold, Kenny, & Suchy, 2012). Strassberg *et al.* (2012) make the case that their findings suggest two types of child molesters. One is the typical pedophile whose main interest is sexual contacts with children; whereas the other is the psychopathic child molester whose main sexual interest is not children. "For those who are self-centered, impulsive, uncaring for others, manipulative, and free of conscience, all typical psychopathic qualities, many kinds of antisocial acts become more likely, including the sexual abuse of children" (Strassberg *et al.*, 2012, p. 381).

Abel and colleagues (Abel *et al.*, 1988) report that of the 192 nonincarcerated child offenders who voluntarily participated in a treatment program, the men most likely to drop out of treatment were those with a history of considerable and varied pedophilic behavior. That is, 70 percent of the frequent child offenders who demonstrated no gender or age preference (child or adolescent) dropped out of treatment, usually early in the process. The treatment program consisted of 30 group sessions of 90 minutes given weekly and directed at decreasing deviant arousal, developing cognitive restructuring of distorted sexual attitudes and beliefs, and increasing the offenders' social competence with adults. Interestingly, those who managed to complete the program, and who had varied child offending behaviors and multiple victims, were the ones who were most likely to recidivate within one year after treatment. This should not suggest that treatment is ineffective, however. Further indications of recidivism rates of child offenders can be garnered from the 13-year outpatient treatment program described by Marshall and Barbaree (1988). This Canadian project offered psychological treatment of deviant sexual behavior on a voluntary basis to a variety of sexual offenders. Forty percent of the child offenders refused treatment. The project had access to official records (charges and convictions) throughout North America, as well as to information from "unofficial" files of local police departments and Children's Aid Societies in the towns where the offenders lived. Thirty-two percent of the untreated child offenders reoffended, compared with 14 percent of the treated offenders (a somewhat more optimistic appraisal of the effectiveness of treatment). The average follow-up period for both groups was approximately 3.5 years. Of the 26 men who recidivated, only 11 were identified "officially" (charges and convictions), whereas the remainder were identified through the "unofficial" information. Even so, the unofficial measures of recidivism were still collected by public agencies, leaving us to wonder how high the "true" unofficial recidivism rates for child offenders really are.

Recidivism of Juvenile Sex Offenders

Some investigators (Alexander, 1999; Hunter & Becker, 1999) have reported that juvenile sex offenders are significantly less likely to reoffend than adult offenders. In general, studies have reported that the juvenile offender recidivism rate for sex offenses ranges between 2 percent and 14 percent (Reitzel, 2003; Rubinstein, Yeager, Goodstein, & Lewis, 1993; Sipe, Jensen, & Everett, 1998; Waite *et al.*, 2005). Alexander (1999) found an overall sexual recidivism rate (based on rearrest) of 7 percent, with juvenile rapists having the highest sexual reoffending rate of all juvenile sex offenders. There is also considerable evidence that juvenile sex offenders who are highly impulsive and demonstrate poor self-regulation are far more likely to reoffend than those juvenile sex offenders who are evaluated as less impulsive (Waite *et al.*, 2005).

If juveniles do indeed reoffend less than adult sex offenders, this may be due to a variety of factors, including the aging out process and the availability of effective treatment. As we will note later in the chapter, extensive attention has been given to sex offender treatment in juvenile facilities, as well as in community placements. It is possible—though still speculative—that this attention is bearing fruit. As juveniles get older and move out of their living situations, they also are more likely to develop consensual sexual relationships with persons within their own age group. Thus, they neither need nor have the same opportunity for contact with younger children.

THEORIES ON POTENTIAL CAUSES

Most explanations of pedophilia focus on a single factor as the principal cause of sexual and social preferences for children by adults. One clinical hypothesis, for example, suggests that pedophiles select children as sex objects because they are haunted by feelings of masculine and sexual inadequacy in adult relationships (e.g., Groth *et al.*, 1982). They are terrified of being ridiculed in their sexual and social behavior by the adult world. In the world of the child, they can be safely curious, awkward, and inexperienced. This observation might help explain why pedophiles rarely engage in intercourse with adults. Although this inadequacy hypothesis appears to have some validity, it fails to explain the full range and diversity of pedophilic behavior.

Finkelhor and Araji (1986) find four basic explanations for pedophilia in the research and clinical literature: emotional congruence, sexual arousal, blockage, and disinhibition theories

TABLE 13-3	Four Theoretical Explanations for Pedophilia
Theory	**Basic Premise**
Emotional congruence	Pedophiles see themselves as children with childish emotional needs and interests, and therefore feel most comfortable with children.
Sexual arousal	Pedophiles become unusually sexually aroused to stimuli not typical of the other adults.
Blockage	Pedophilia is the result of unattainable sexual and emotional gratification with adults, usually because of inadequate interpersonal and social skills. They feel more comfortable socially and sexually with children.
Disinhibition	Pedophilia is the result of poor self-regulation or self-control.

(see **Table 13-3**). The most common is the *emotional congruence theories.* These theories try to explain why a person would think that relating sexually to a child is emotionally gratifying and congruent with their needs. They convey the idea of a fit between the adult's emotional needs and the child's characteristics. Most congruence theories are psychoanalytic in origin and focus on "arrested psychological development." According to this perspective, pedophiles see themselves as children with childish emotional needs and dependency, and consequently they feel most comfortable with children. A similar version focuses on the low self-esteem and loss of efficacy pedophiles experience in their daily lives. Relating to a child is congruent, because the inadequate adult finally feels powerful, omnipotent, and in control of a relationship. In short, relating to a child provides a sense of mastery and control in their lives.

The second group of theories, the *sexual arousal theories*, try to explain why pedophiles become sexually aroused by certain characteristics of children. Sexual arousal is typically measured by penile tumescence to the presence of children or to sexual fantasies of children. This perspective contends that pedophiles become sexually aroused to stimuli (features of children) that, for a variety of reasons, do not generate sexual arousal in normal males. One set of theories within this group posits that it is a common childhood experience to engage in sexual play with playmates. For the pedophile, the childhood sexual play may have been particularly vivid, rewarding, stimulating, and even possibly the most sexually exciting experience he has ever had. Adult sexual play, by comparison, was less arousing, satisfying, or rewarding, perhaps even nonexistent. The pedophile's shyness, for example, may have precluded adult sexual contacts. Under these conditions, he probably took the most available sexual avenue, masturbation. The powerful reinforcing role of masturbatory behavior (masturbatory conditioning) has been demonstrated in clinical studies of most sexual offenses (Marshall, 1988). During masturbation, the pedophile's fantasies may focus on the satisfying sexual experiences he had during childhood. Repetitive masturbatory activity, therefore, reinforces the immature level of sexual behavior associated with childhood. Whereas masturbation of itself may be a normal outlet for sexual tension, for the pedophile it becomes an act that reinforces his attraction to children. Continual association between the pleasurable masturbatory activities and fantasies about childhood sexual experiences results in a strong bond between sexual arousal and children. Eventually, the children become sexual stimuli capable of arousing high levels of sexual excitation.

Another version of the sexual arousal perspective links traumatic sexual victimization to pedophilic behavior. Many researchers have found unusually high amounts of childhood sexual victimization in the background of pedophiles (Bard *et al.*, 1987). It is unclear, however, how sexual trauma, which is aversive, becomes conditioned or associated with the presumed sexual pleasures of pedophilia.

Blockage theories assume that pedophilia is the result of blockage of normal sexual and emotional gratification from adult relationships. Frustrated in his quest for normal channels of sexual gratification, the offender seeks the company of children. Blockage theories emphasize the unassertive, timid, inadequate, and awkward personalities of the pedophile, arguing that these social deficiencies make it nearly impossible for him to develop normal social and sexual relationships with adult women. When the marital relationship breaks down, for example, the pedophile may turn to his daughter as a substitute.

The fourth set of explanations focus on the loss of self-control and personal constraints on behavior. *Disinhibition theories* outline a variety of circumstances that presumably propel the offender to his deeds. Poor impulse control, excessive use of alcohol and drugs, and an assortment of stressors could all lead him over the brink to his favorite deviant sexual practices. As mentioned earlier, many pedophiles refuse to take blame, but attribute the cause of their pedophilic behavior to forces outside themselves. "I couldn't help myself" or "I don't know what came over me" are frequent pleas.

Which theoretical perspective has the inside track for the explanation of pedophilia? By itself, none can account for the multiple causes and the full range of learning experiences, beliefs, motivations, and attitudes of pedophiles. Theories that focus on cognitive aspects appear to be the most promising, just as treatment based on cognitive principles holds the most promise for preventing recidivism. Nonetheless, as Walters, Deming, and Elliott (2009, p. 1025) observe, "Cognitive factors have not received the attention they deserve from researchers in the field of sex offending."

In recent years, however, much research attention has been given to the cognitions and beliefs of child molesters, especially pertaining to their cognitive distortions. The cognitive distortion hypothesis states that child molesters hold "well-established and generalized offense-related beliefs that facilitate sexual offenses against children" (Gannon & Polaschek, 2006, p. 1001). An example would be the core belief that children are fundamentally sexual beings who enjoy and often seek out sex with adults (Ward, 2000). Another example would be the belief that children are relatively unaffected by sexual activities with adults (Gannon & Polaschek, 2006).

Gannon and her colleagues have critically examined the research and theory relating to cognitive distortions by child molesters (Gannon & Polaschek, 2006; Gannon, Ward, & Collie, 2007). Although clinical treatment of child molesters has run ahead of scientific knowledge, they conclude that there continues to be considerable confusion about the nature of these cognitive distortions. Consequently, researchers have yet to develop a comprehensive theory to explain child molesters and their motivations and beliefs.

INTERNET-FACILITATED SEXUAL OFFENDING

In recent years, there has been increasing attention directed at online sexual offending, particularly child pornography offending. Online sexual offending refers to "the use of Internet and related digital technologies to obtain, distribute, or produce child pornography, or to contact potential child victims to create opportunities for sexual offending" (Seto, Hanson, & Babchishin,

2011, p. 125). The possession, distribution, and production of child pornography is illegal under federal laws and laws in all 50 states (Wolak, Finkelhour, & Mitchell, 2005).

It should be noted that Congress initially passed a law, the Child Pornography Protection Act (CPPA) of 1996 that defined child pornography very broadly (18 U.S.C. §2256). Under that law child pornography was any visual depiction, including any photograph, film, video, or computer or computer-generated image or picture, whether made or produced by electronic, mechanical or other means, of sexually explicit conduct, *that may or may not involve actual children*. Whereas some aspects of this law were not controversial (e.g., using an actual minor engaging in sexually explicit conduct), others were (e.g., using an adult pretending to be a minor). Consequently, the U.S. Supreme Court struck down provisions of the law (*Ashcroft v. Free Speech Coalition*, 2002). Congress then passed the PROTECT Act (Prosecutorial Remedies and Other Tools to end the Exploitation of Children Today) in 2003. That law was most recently upheld by the U.S. Supreme Court in *U.S. v. Williams* (2008). (See **Box 13-1** for more discussion of these cases.)

BOX 13-1

Child Pornography, the Internet, and the Courts

Obscenity and pornography are two different things. Obscenity, though difficult to define ("I know it when I see it," one Supreme Court Justice famously wrote) is not protected by the First Amendment. People can be charged with producing it or distributing it. In reality, despite a careful attempt by the Court to define it, people are rarely prosecuted for violating obscenity statutes today.

By contrast, pornography, whether hard core or soft core, is protected, except in the case of children. Put another way, the law has carved out an exception to account for cases in which pornography involves the exploitation of children. Courts, including the U.S. Supreme Court, have ruled that states and the federal government can prosecute people for the possession, production, and distribution of child pornography, even if it does not meet the criteria for obscenity (*N.Y. v. Ferber*, 1982). Consequently, with increasing accessibility of child pornography on the Internet, Congress and the legislatures of many states have passed laws addressing this social problem. One such law was the Child Pornography Prevention Act (CPPA) of 1996.

Readers will appreciate that technology today can create images that are representations of people, not actual people. Thus, someone can make "virtual child pornography"—a computer image of what appears to be two children engaging in sexual activity, but no children are really involved in the creation of the image. Alternately, a producer of child pornography could use youthful-looking adults and present them as children.

The CPPA prohibited these enterprises. The Free Speech Coalition, a loose assortment of businesses involved in the adult-entertainment trade, challenged the CPPA and won both in lower courts and the U.S. Supreme Court. In 2002, the U.S. Supreme Court surprised and angered many observers when it invalidated key parts of this federal law, specifically because the law applied even when actual children were not involved (*Ashcroft v. Free Speech Coalition*). Those who applauded the Court's decision noted that the law was too broad, and that the Supreme Court had made the correct call in striking down its most troublesome provisions, which tread unacceptably on the freedoms guaranteed by the First Amendment.

Following the Free Speech Coalition decision, Congress immediately passed a modified law, which has come to be called the PROTECT Act. This law focuses on both the possession and the "pandering" of child pornography. The pandering aspect applies to any person "who knowingly advertises, promotes, presents, distributes, or solicits" child pornography.

Enter Michael Williams. Following the passage of the PROTECT law, Williams signed in to an Internet chat room with a suggestive screen name. He unknowingly began a conversation with a Secret Service agent who was posing as someone interested in child pornography. The agent focused on Williams because he had previously posted a message:

"Dad of toddler has 'good' pics of her an [sic] me for swap of your toddler pics, or live cam."

Williams later posted that he had photographs of men molesting his four-year-old daughter, and eventually also appended to his messages a hyperlink that led to seven pictures of actual children engaging in sexually explicit conduct, although none apparently of his daughter. The Secret Service, armed with a search warrant, seized two hard drives containing at least 22 images of real children engaged in sexually explicit conduct, some of it sadomasochistic (facts outlined in *U.S. v. Williams*, 2008).

Williams pleaded guilty both to pandering child pornography and to possessing it, but he reserved the right to challenge the pandering charges, and he did. His lawyers maintained that he never had provided the agent with the pictures—that, in fact, there were no such pictures of his daughter.

The U.S. Supreme Court, however, said a person could be prosecuted for knowingly offering child pornography—even if it didn't exist—as well as for being willing to purchase it, even if they do not actually receive it. Greenhouse (2008) notes that as a result of the Supreme Court's decision, people offering child pornography can be convicted under the federal law if they believe that what they are offering depicts real children or for trying to convince the would-be recipient that it does (Greenhouse, 2008). Williams fell into the latter category.

What do we learn from the Williams case? The legal lessons are multiple, and it is not our intention to focus on them here. With respect to the study of criminal behavior, we are given a real-world illustration, but no explanation, of one person's egregious behavior. Williams was given a five-year prison sentence for his crimes, but it is unknown whether the cognitions and other risk factors that contributed to his offense have ever been addressed.

Who Are the Offenders?

The producers of child pornography are often persons who have legitimate access to the child, such as parents/guardians (22%), relatives (10%), family friends (47%), babysitters, and coaches (U.S. Sentencing Commission, 2012). Our focus in this section, however, will be on those offenders who access or possess rather than produce child pornography.

One of the key goals of researchers in child pornography is to determine the risks that online offenders pose to actual sexual contact with children. In other words, do those persons interested in child pornography online also seek physical sexual contact with children? Many studies indicate that the majority of online offenders have no prior *official* contact sexual offense history (Seto *et al.*, 2011). Many do not even have any prior criminal history of any kind. However, one study discovered that a majority of online offenders (85%) admitted to contact crimes (unofficially) while undergoing treatment or during a polygraph examination (Bourke & Hernandez 2009). That study has been criticized for having several serious methodological shortcomings. In a more comprehensive study, conducted by Seto *et al.* (2011), the data revealed that approximately one in eight online offenders had a known contact sexual offense history, based on official records of arrests, charges, or convictions. The ratio was higher when self-report information (rather than official records) was used, revealing that about a half of the online offenders admitted to a contact sexual offense. Seto and his colleagues conclude the following: "Many of the online offenders in our study are likely to be sexually interested in children, but only half are known to have acted on these sexual interests" (p. 140). However, the Seto *et al.* study did find that the recidivism rate for contact sexual offense was quite low (5%) for the majority of online sex offenders.

Although there is no typical profile of the child pornography offender, online offenders are likely to be non-Hispanic white, single, and unemployed (Babchishin, Hanson, & Hermann, 2011). They tend to be slightly younger than contact sex offenders (Babchishin *et al.*, 2011). Moreover, online offenders, compared to contact sex offenders, appear to have greater empathy for their victims, have greater ability to control acting on their child-oriented sexual interests, and usually restrict their sexual interests to online activity (Seto & Hanson, 2011).

Who Are the Child Victims?

The emergence of Internet technology lowered the costs of producing commercially circulated pornographic material, substantially increased its availability, and reduced the risk of detection connected to production, distribution, and possession (Quayle & Jones, 2011). The Internet's rapid expansion also has meant more focus on the Internet sex offender (Quayle, 2009). The victims depicted in the commercial child pornographic media are typically white, prepubescent girls (ages 8–12 years) (Quayle & Jones, 2011). The second most often used child victim category was Asian prepubescent girls. Female children outnumber male children in the sexualized photographic media images by about four to one.

In an extensive study called the *National Juvenile Online Victimization Study*, Wolak *et al.* (2005) examined the information on Internet-related child pornography offenders who had been arrested over a 12-month period, beginning July 1, 2000. Wolak *et al.* described 40 percent of offenders as "dual offenders" because they not only had child pornography in their possession but also had a history of sexually abusing minors. Relatively few of the offenders had prior arrests for nonsexual offending (22%). Ninety-one percent of those arrested were non-Hispanic whites.

Eighty-three percent of those arrested had sexual images of children between the ages of 6 and 12, and 39 percent had images of three- to five-year-old children. Nineteen percent had images of toddlers or infants younger than three years of age. Sixty-two percent had pictures of mostly girls, and 14 percent possessed pictures of mostly boys. Perhaps more revealing was the finding that 21 percent had images of children in violent scenes, such as bondage, rape, and torture. Most of these graphic photos involved images of children who were gagged, bound, blindfolded, or otherwise enduring some form of sadistic sex. Thirty nine percent of the arrestees possessed moving images in digital or other videos formats. These images were discovered by investigators in 2000 and 2001; recent technological advances (e.g., smartphones, ipads, sophisticated encryption formats) now make it easier for offenders to collect and store child pornography. New technological tools also have enhanced offenders' ability to evade detection by law enforcement (Collins, 2012). In addition, advances in technological communication systems allow persons to find others who share their interests, which, in turn, encourage the development of peer, supportive communities.

Online Sex offenders Interested in Adolescents

Although this section was primarily concerned with online child pornography offenders drawn to prepubescent children, we should briefly describe online offenders who are interested in adolescent pornography or actual sexual encounters with teens. Briggs, Simon, and Simonsen (2011) conducted an exploratory study designed to examine offender differences between noncontact online sexual offenders and those online offenders who activity seek out opportunities to have sex with adolescents. Some online offenders engage in the process of exploitation, luring, and enticement of the teenager to meet with them. The offender may communicate with several adolescents at once via various chat rooms, thinking he is doing so anonymously. However, police officers have been active over the past two decades in their attempts to apprehend these offenders by posing as juveniles online (Mitchell, Wolak, & Finkehor, 2005).

Briggs and his colleagues identified two types of men who use the Internet to gain sexual gratification via adolescent victims. One type utilizes live online chat rooms to entice male or female teenagers into an offline sexual relationship. The other is the fantasy-driven offender who uses the Internet as "a sexual medium to connect with teens for the purpose of cybersex and masturbation" (Briggs *et al.*, 2011, p. 87). For these latter, socially isolated adults, the Internet provides an impersonal social and sexual outlet without the risk of face-to-face rejection. They usually have no interest in an actual physical contact with the teenager.

SEX TRAFFICKING

During the past two decades, much attention has focused away from prostitution—which was often referred to as a victimless crime—toward a related topic, human trafficking, an activity that typically involves forced prostitution. Human trafficking has become a highly lucrative criminal market in the United States (Finckenauer & Schrock, 2000) and includes children as well as adult victims. According to some experts (e.g., Schauer & Wheaton, 2006), the United States ranks as the world's second largest destination country (after Germany) for women and children trafficked for purposes of sexual exploitation in the sex industry. Examples include women who agree to come to this country as food service workers, hotel employees, or dancers, but then are forced into prostitution until they are able to pay off the debt incurred through a smuggling fee. In some countries, parents "sell" their children to traffickers who take them to other parts of the world, including the United States, and profit from their sexual exploitation. Violence, intimidation, and brutality are particularly common with trafficking victims brought in for the sex industry. Human trafficking often involves a variety of additional illicit activities, including fraud, extortion, racketeering, money laundering, bribery of public officials, drug use, document forgery, and gambling (Finckenauer & Schrock, 2000; Richard, 1999).

Arguments for the decriminalization or legalization of prostitution are often appealing, particularly if one believes that the present laws are selectively enforced against women, or that prostitution is essentially a victimless crime. However, such decriminalization or legalization approaches must find an alternative way to address the exploitation of juveniles and the many abuses that occur as a result of human trafficking.

Those who engage in sexual trafficking are rarely studied by researchers from a psychological perspective. They are more likely to be perceived as economic offenders than as sex offenders. In fact, in previous editions of this text, we placed human trafficking in the next chapter—Chapter 14—on economic crimes. Nevertheless, although the traffickers themselves may not be directly participating in sexual abuse, they are facilitating it and thus arguably could be referred to as sex offenders as well. It is even possible that future research could uncover a link between sexual exploitation of this nature and direct sexual abuse.

TREATMENT OF SEX OFFENDERS

While the research is mixed with respect to recidivism rates among sex offenders, as a general principle, they are often highly resistant to changing their deviant behavior patterns. As noted above, there are exceptions both across offender types and within an offender population.

A wide variety of treatment programs have been tried, but early reviews were not optimistic. A 1994 survey of therapeutic services for sex offenders revealed that there were 710 adult and 684 juvenile treatment programs (Longo, Bird, Stevenson, & Fiske, 1995), compared with 297 adult and 346 juvenile treatment programs in 1985 (Knopp, Rosenberg, & Stevenson, 1986). Despite the increase in treatment programs, the success ratio remains disappointingly low (Camilleri & Quinsey, 2008; Thakker, Collie, Gannon, & Ward, 2008). One of the most devastating early reviews was produced by Furby, Weinrott, and Blackshaw (1989, p. 27), who concluded after assessing research on a range of therapeutic approaches, "There is as yet no evidence that clinical treatment reduces rates of sex reoffenses in general and no appropriate data for assessing whether it may be differentially effective for different types of offenders." However, and more optimistically, meta-analyses have demonstrated that treatment programs based on cognitive-behavioral approaches have shown positive results, as we will note below.

Furthermore, many psychologists who work with sex offenders say the situation is far from hopeless. Most of the optimism comes from those working with child molesters (Thakker *et al.*, 2008). First, many clinicians believe that the most effective interventions, or treatment methods, are those that follow the **principles of risk, need, and responsivity** (**RNR**) identified by James Bonta, Robert Hoge, and Don Andrews (see, e.g., Andrews, Bonta, & Hoge, 1990; Bonta & Andrews, 2007). Second, they believe that these principles can be applied to sex offenders. Camilleri and Quinsey (2008), for example, conclude from their extensive review of treatment for child molesters that treatment so far has been ineffective because no one has developed "a method that can durably alter the central criminogenic need factor in pedophilia—sexual preference for children" (p. 203).

Before discussing how RNR principles relate to sexual offending, it is worthwhile to overview them briefly. According to Hanson *et al.* (2009, p. 867), "...treatments are most likely to be effective when they treat offenders who are likely to reoffend (moderate or higher risk), target characteristics that are related to reoffending (criminogenic needs), and match treatment to the offenders' learning styles and abilities (responsivity; cognitive-behavioral interventions work best)."

Interestingly, offenders who are considered low risks of reoffending are also not considered good targets for psychological treatment. This is both because they do not need the intensive attention and because scarce resources can best be applied to offenders who need them the most. Low-risk offenders can benefit from support services in the community (e.g., help with finding employment or improving social skills). Moderate and high-risk offenders, on the other hand, can benefit by psychological treatment that focuses on their criminogenic needs, defined as factors in their lives that make it more likely that they will engage in criminal activity. Examples of criminogenic needs are substance abuse problems or episodes of violent behavior. The responsivity principle is met if the treatment offered recognizes the individual strengths and abilities of the offender. Cognitive behavioral programs have fared very well when measured against this last criterion because they seek to engage the offender actively in his or her own treatment. In a meta-analysis involving 69 studies and covering close to 10,000 sexual offenders, Lösel and Schmucker (2005; Schmucker & Lösel, 2008) found that treatment programs based on cognitive behavioral principles had positive effects. Likewise, Hanson *et al.* (2009) found in another meta-analysis that a program's faithfulness to RNR principles was associated with lower recidivism in sex offenders.

Prentky *et al.* (1997) conclude that sex offender therapy can be categorized into four broad approaches. One approach is **evocative therapy**, a treatment that focuses on (1) helping offenders to understand the causes and motivations of their sexual behavior and (2) increasing their empathy for the victims of the sexual assault. Evocative therapy may include individual, group, couples/marital, and family counseling. A second approach is **psychoeducational counseling**, which utilizes a group or class setting to remedy deficits in social and interpersonal skills. Psychoeducational strategies include anger management, the principles of relapse prevention, and other topics such as human sexuality, dating, and myths about sexuality and relationships. A third approach is **drug treatment**. This approach concentrates on "reducing sexual arousability and the frequency of deviant sexual fantasies through the use of antiandrogen and antidepressant medication" (Prentky *et al.*, 1997, p. 13). The fourth approach is **cognitive behavior therapy**. The behavioral component focuses on sexual preference, while the cognitive component focuses on changing beliefs, fantasies, attitudes, and rationalizations that justify and perpetuate sexually violent behavior. Child molesters appear to have far more cognitive distortions than men who sexually assault adult women (Camilleri & Quinsey, 2008). Prentky *et al.* (1997) suggest that the most effective approach probably resides in using some combination of the four, although which specific combination remains unclear. They agree, however, that cognitive-behavioral approaches (complemented on occasion with some medication) continue to offer the most effective technique in the temporary cessation of deviant sexual behavior in motivated individuals. Cognitive-behavior therapy argues that maladaptive sexual behaviors are learned according to the same rules as normal sexual behavior, by means of classical and/or instrumental conditioning, modeling, reinforcement, generalization, and punishment. They are, therefore, modifiable. Cognitive-behavioral therapy, compared with traditional verbal, insight-oriented therapy, has demonstrated short-term effectiveness in eliminating exhibitionism and fetishism (Kilmann, Sabalis, Gearing, Bukstel, & Scovern, 1982), some forms of pedophilia (Hall, 1995; Marshall & Barbaree, 1988), and sexual aggression and arousal (Quinsey & Marshall, 1983).

A major problem, however, is not with getting the motivated offender to stop his deviant sexual pattern, but with preventing his relapse across time and situations. This is especially the case with pedophilia. It is analogous to dieting. Most diet regimens do work in getting the motivated individual to lose weight. However, they offer little help in preventing people from eventually relapsing into old eating habits. This is why ongoing therapeutic supervision of sex offenders is critical. Although some success with cognitive-behavioral therapy with sex offenders has been established, the effects of the treatment often do not last (Brecklin & Forde, 2001; Camilleri & Quinsey, 2008).

A treatment approach showing some promise in the treatment of sex offenders is called **relapse prevention (RP)**. "RP is a self-control program designed to teach individuals who are trying to change their behavior how to anticipate and cope with the problem of relapse" (George & Marlatt, 1989, p. 2). The program emphasizes self-management; clients are considered responsible not for the cause but for the solution of the problem. And as the name implies, the program concentrates on preventing a *relapse* of deviant sexual behavior. Therefore, RP distinguishes treatment from maintenance. As stated earlier, cognitive-behavior therapy is effective in the temporary cessation of the behavior, but additional steps must be taken to make the change permanent. Cognitive behavioral therapists are well aware of this, and some employ RP to achieve this goal.

RP is specifically designed to be effective in helping the individual *maintain* the "cure." Distinctions are made between the terms *relapse* and *lapse*. "Relapse is a violation of a self-imposed rule or set of rules governing the rate or pattern of a selected target behavior" (George & Marlatt, 1989, p. 6). A *lapse* on the other hand, refers to "a single instance of violating the rule" (p. 6). "With sex offenders, the term relapse will refer to any occurrence of a sexual offense, thus connoting full-scale reestablishment of the problematic behavior. The term lapse will refer to any occurrence of willful and elaborate fantasizing about sexual offending or any return to sources of stimulation associated with the sexual offense pattern, but short of performance of the offense behavior" (p. 6).

RP, as a system of maintenance-oriented principles and interventions, has two central objectives: It teaches individuals (1) to cope effectively with "high-risk situations" (HRSs) and (2) to identify and respond to early warning signals of urges and "apparently irrelevant decisions" (AIDs). An HRS is any situation that poses a threat to the individual's sense of control over his behavior and consequently increases the probability of lapse or relapse. Examples of

HRSs that may predispose an individual toward relapse include negative emotional states, such as anger and depression, interpersonal conflict, and various social pressures (George & Marlatt, 1989). Research by Pithers and associates (Pithers, Kashima, Cumming, Beal, & Buell, 1988; Pithers, Beal, Armstrong, & Petty, 1989) has found that rapists often experience anger and use alcohol or other drugs before engaging in sexual aggression. Pedophiles, on the other hand, often experience anxiety or depression before seeking a child. A feeling of low self-esteem is experienced by both groups. These precursors reflect the beginning stages of an HRS. In other words, they psychologically predispose the individual toward a relapse.

Relapse seems to follow a sequence of events, all representing HRSs (George & Marlatt, 1989; Pithers, Marques, Gibat, & Marlatt, 1983). First, an urge, fleeting thought, or dream about committing an offense occurs. This is followed by elaborations of fantasies about committing the offense. Then, the aroused individual engages in masturbation coupled with fantasies and/or pornography related to the imagined sexual activity. The individual then plans how he is going to commit the act. Finally, the individual engages in the act. RP provides a framework within which a variety of behavioral, cognitive, educational, and skill-training techniques are used to train sex offenders to recognize and interrupt these chains of events (Marshall & Barbaree, 1988).

Critical to RP treatment intervention is the motivation of the offender. Without motivation, the program will not work. Remember, RP is aimed primarily at *maintaining* a cessation of the deviant behavior, not cessation itself. Therefore, a behavior therapy program or other conventional treatment intervention that stops the behavior must precede RP. The treatment phase normally takes a relatively short period of time. Another important point outlined by George and Marlatt (1989) is that incarceration without treatment will not prevent reoffending. They offer three reasons for this. First, externally imposed, forced control does little to encourage an offender to seek help in changing his ways. Second, the offender can still maintain attachment to his offense pattern through fantasy. Third, it is conceivable that an offender could continue to actually engage in some semblance of his offense patterns even during confinement.

RP is a relatively recent development and its long-term success has yet to be established (Marques, Wiederanders, Day, Nelson, & Van Ommeren, 2005). Some have questioned its application to sexual offenders, since it was originally designed for treatment of sexual abusers without an adequate research basis (Laws, Hudson, & Ward, 2002). However, it does have substantial promise for the elimination of deviant behavior in offenders motivated to change. And as noted by Prentky *et al.* (1997, p. 14), "Continuity of treatment is considered a critical factor in managing sex offenders. Maintenance is forever, and Relapse Prevention never ends. Community-based clinical management must be supportive, vigilant, and informed by current wisdom about maximally effective maintenance."

Treatment of Juvenile Sex Offenders

While juvenile sexual offenders (JSOs) may also be treated in community settings—in fact, it is preferable that this be done—we focus here on the serious offenders who are most likely to be held in restrictive institutional settings. Nevertheless, it is important to keep in mind that juvenile sexual offenders—like adult sexual offenders—are often viewed as a homogeneous class of individuals. Research shows, however, that they vary widely in the frequency and type of sexual activity they engage in, and they differ in personal attributes, such as age, background, personality, race, religion, beliefs, attitudes, and social skills. There is no profile of the juvenile sex offender.

The foundation of treatment for JSOs is grounded on the premise that their deviant sexual behaviors are associated with distorted thought patterns that serve to deny, justify, minimize, and rationalize their actions (Eastman, 2004; Worling & Langton, 2012). Research reveals that sexually aggressive male juveniles subscribe to attitudes and ideology that encourage males to be dominant, controlling, and powerful, whereas females are expected to be submissive, permissive, and compliant. Such a cognitive orientation seems to have a particularly strong disinhibitory effect on sexually aggressive juveniles, prompting them to interpret ambiguous behaviors of girls or women as come-ons, to believe that they are not really offended by coercive sexual behavior, and to perceive victims as desiring and deriving gratification from being sexually assaulted (Lipton, McDonel & McFall, 1987). Thus, it would seem that cognitive behavioral programs, aimed at encouraging the offender to modify these misperceptions, would hold considerable promise.

Consequently, treatment approaches to JSOs have traditionally included treatment of denial, past victimization, attitudes and values, social skills, and arousal patterns (Kahn & LaFond, 1988; Sciarra, 1999). In addition, these treatment programs have been modeled after treatment programs designed for adult sex offenders. However, few studies have examined whether these same programs are effective in the treatment of JSOs until recently.

Currently, there is considerable ongoing research evaluating treatment programs for juveniles (Veneziano & Veneziano, 2002). These programs designed for JSOs are different from those that target adult sexual offenders. This is primarily because contemporary research suggests that juveniles are far more changeable than adults, are more influenced by the social environment, and appear to be at lower risk for sexual recidivism (Veneziano & Veneziano, 2002).

Worling and Langton (2012), in an article reviewing the assessment and treatment of juvenile sex offenders in residential settings, note that there have been few published studies in recent years in which researchers used a treatment and a comparison group. However, overall "there is a growing body of evidence that specialized treatment programs result in lower recidivism rates" (p. 827). "Unfortunately," they continue, "there is very little guidance from the published research at this time regarding which treatment components are effective for which youth" (p. 827). Worling and Langton summarize a number of treatment goals that are common to sex offender treatment programs in the United States and Canada. They include, among others, enhancing accountability for one's crimes; enhancing healthy sexual interests, prosocial sexual attitudes, and awareness of victim impact; establishing plans to prevent future offending; and involving parents and caregivers. Worling and Langton also observe that these confined settings very often produce sexual victimization of both sex offenders and nonsex offenders. They cite the sobering statistic reported by Beck, Harrison, and Guerino (2010) that 2 percent of youth in their survey reported victimization by youth and approximately 12 percent reported victimization by staff within the first year they were held in custody. An alarming 81 percent of the youth who were victimized reported being victimized more than once, and 43 percent had been victimized by more than one individual. The longer the youth was held in custody, the more likely was the sexual victimization.

Summary and Conclusions

Following upon the chapter on sexual assaults of adults, the present chapter has focused upon sexual offenses against children. We used the term *pedophilia* to characterize these offenses but noted that the legal terms include but are not limited to *child molestation, child sexual assault,* and *child rape.* Individuals are not arrested and charged with *pedophilia*; this is a clinical term that covers a range of sexually related offenses against children. However, the term *pedophile* is now commonly used by the public and in media accounts.

Sexual assaults against children—covering a range of offenses—are disturbingly too common, although accurate statistics are difficult to obtain. Much of our information is derived not only from arrest and conviction data but also from the reports of adults who say they were victimized as children and from the perpetrators themselves. Arrest data indicate that 34 percent of all victims of sexual assault reported to law enforcement in the early 1990s were under age 12. In a related finding, some research indicates that approximately two-thirds of convicted rapists in state prisons committed their crimes against children. By their own accounts, offenders admit to molesting not one but many children, sometimes over a period of years. Other research suggests that from a quarter to a third of all women and one-tenth of men say they were sexually abused during childhood. As we discussed in the chapter, the long-term psychological effects of this victimization are often, if not typically, devastating.

We reviewed a variety of offender characteristics, including both demographic and psychological features. Aggressive pedophiles—not all are—show similarities to men who rape adults, including problems with alcohol, high rates of school failure, unstable work history, and low socioeconomic status. Pedophiles as a group tend to be older than rapists, although the great majority apparently commits the first offense before age 30. Although increasingly more attention is being given to female pedophiles, pedophilia is still predominantly a male phenomenon.

The cognitive skills of pedophiles are typically lower than those of the general population. They often lack social skills and adequate self-control mechanisms. They rarely take responsibility for their offenses, preferring to attribute their behavior to external forces beyond their control. Although there have been successful treatment programs for pedophiles, program dropout rates are often high. However, many clinicians maintain that pedophiles are far easier to treat than rapists.

The Massachusetts Treatment Center has developed classification systems for the behavioral patterns of both rapists and child molesters, as we noted in this and the previous chapter. Both systems have undergone revision to further specify and refine some of their categories and to incorporate crime scene information. We reviewed the MTC systems in some detail, focusing on the MTC:CM3, the latest version. Similar but less elaborate classification systems proposed by Groth for both rapists and child molesters were covered as well. The MTC classification systems are the most widely used and have been the most submitted to empirical research.

We discussed some of the available research on juvenile sex offending, which is clearly a major challenge to the juvenile justice system. Distinctions are often made in the literature between juvenile molesters and juvenile rapists. For example, molesters almost invariably choose children younger than they are as victims, while rapists choose victims of about the same age or older. Molesters are also more likely than rapists to have been victims of child sexual abuse and to view themselves as socially inadequate. The topic of female juvenile sex offending is increasingly making an appearance in the literature. These offenders typically have been abused themselves and often commit their abuses while babysitting or otherwise caring for children.

A variety of explanatory theories were covered, but it is clear that no one theory or no one factor would account for the behavior of all offenders. We cannot say, for example, that all pedophiles engage in their actions because they are haunted by feelings of sexual inadequacy with adults. Theories have been placed in one of four major groups: the emotional congruence, the sexual arousal, the blockage, and the disinhibition theories. While pedophilia appears to be motivated by both sexual desire and an expectation of sexual adequacy that would not occur in sexual congress with another adult, it is engaged in for a variety of reasons by a variety of offenders.

Thus, we must guard against referring to a common "molester profile." Each has his own construct system and beliefs about his behavior and motivations. Some offenders, for whatever reason, are vicious and violent; others are passive, relatively meek people who enjoy the companionship of children. It appears from the research that many, if not most, pedophiles are the latter. They apparently see themselves as sexually and interpersonally inept adults who feel more comfortable interacting with children.

Perhaps the most unstudied sex offenders are those whose crimes are facilitated by the widespread availability of child pornography on the Internet and those who engage in human trafficking. Child pornography is not protected by the First Amendment; it is a crime to produce it, distribute it, and possess it. We discussed the U.S. Supreme's Court's latest ruling on federal laws designed to prevent the exploitation of children. Some who procure child pornography also directly victimize children and adolescents, but we cannot draw firm conclusions on the basis of the limited amount of research available. Children, adolescents, and adults also are victimized by human trafficking, an activity that almost invariably includes forced prostitution.

Although reviews of the treatment literature are not encouraging, particularly programs aimed at the most serious offenders, treatment of sexual offending can be successful if the offender's motivation to change is evident. Successful treatment strategies must focus not only on the cessation of the antisocial sexual conduct but on maintenance of prosocial behaviors as well. Thus, both relapse prevention and continual monitoring or supervision should be a part of the treatment regimen. Recent meta-analyses indicate that cognitive-behavioral treatment based on risk, needs, and responsivity (RNR) principles is most promising with respect to both sex offenders and offenders in general.

Key Concepts

Aggressive (sadistic) pedophile
Cognitive behavior therapy
Crossover
Drug treatment
Evocative therapy
Exploitative pedophile

Extrafamilial child molestation
Fixated (immature) pedophile
Hebephilia
Intrafamilial child molestation
Paraphilia
Pedophile

Pedophilia
Psychoeducational counseling
Regressed pedophile
Relapse prevention (RP)
Risk, needs, responsivity
    principles (RNR)

Review Questions

1. Discuss the difficulty in obtaining reliable data about sexual offending against children, particularly with respect to official measures of crime.
2. What are the major differences between extrafamilial pedophiles and intrafamilial pedophiles?
3. Although there is no common profile of a pedophile, some demographic and personality characteristics are often found. Provide examples of these characteristics.
4. Outline the pedophile typologies of the MTC and the Groth system. Which is better supported by the research literature?

5. List some of the justifications that pedophiles use for their sexual behavior.
6. Identify and describe the four theoretical explanations for pedophilia.
7. In what major way does a fixed pedophile differ from a regressed pedophile?
8. What three treatment principles are represented in the acronym RNR? Briefly define each.

14

Property Crime

CHAPTER OBJECTIVES

- Provide an overview of property crimes.
- Sketch burglary, including property cues, motives, demographics, and cognitive processes of burglars.
- Discuss the psychological effects of burglary on victims.
- Describe the nature of home invasions.
- Describe identity theft and its psychological consequences.
- Examine motor vehicle theft, including carjacking, and the motives and decision making of offenders.
- Discuss the prevalence of shoplifting along with motives and other psychological factors involved.
- Review the definitions and typologies of "white-collar crime."

This chapter deals with a wide variety of criminal activity that at first glance would appear to have little in common. However, for the most part, the offenses in this chapter are radically different from the criminal behavior we have discussed up to this point. What they all have in common is a lack of physical aggression—or violence—in the perpetration of the act itself, although in some cases—for example, carjacking and certain home invasion—violence may be a by-product. The crimes discussed here will implicate different psychological concepts from those thus far covered. Whereas we have spent considerable time on learning, classical conditioning, self-esteem, frustration, and of course aggression in the previous chapters, we will see a de-emphasis on these concepts in this chapter, despite the fact that they may still be relevant. On the other hand, we will place more emphasis on such concepts as self-reinforcement, expectations, justifications, and motivations than we did in previous chapters.

Property crimes generally involve the illegal acquisition of money and material goods, or the illegal destruction of property for financial gain. According to the UCR, the four major property crimes (all Part I) are larceny, burglary, arson, and motor vehicle theft. Of the four, arson is the most complex to categorize because it is not always committed for profit. For example, it may simply reflect the desire to destroy property, or it may be committed to cover up another crime, even murder. Although property crimes do not typically involve physical aggression, they are similar to the violent offenses discussed in earlier chapters in one important psychological aspect: Most of them involve a dehumanization of the victim, albeit in a different sense from the dehumanization that often occurs in violence.

As we learned in Chapter 11, **dehumanization** occurs when a person or group of persons sees and treats certain individuals as objects, rather than as human beings. When a person is not responding to the human qualities of other people, it becomes much more possible to act inhumanely toward them. Therefore, offenders find it easier to see their victims as objects rather than as people. In most economic or property crimes (such as larceny and burglary), the offenders avoid confronting their victims directly. Although there are exceptions, they usually do not directly observe or experience the economic, social, and psychological discomfort of their victims. The victim is absent or just observed fleetingly, as in a purse snatching. Therefore, internal values and social constraints are less effective, allowing the offender to repress, deny, or justify the crime more easily. As Gresham Sykes (1956) puts it, the individual's internal sentiments are more easily neutralized by the physical absence of the victim. The offender does not have to think of the effects his or her actions have on the victim, because the offender often does not know the victim as a human being, only as a target.

We might have included robbery in this chapter, not because it is strictly a property crime (it isn't), but because robbers have more in common with the crimes discussed in this and the next chapter than with those discussed up to this point. Robbery is classified as a violent crime against persons in the UCR because it involves the threat or the use of force. A robber points a gun at a store clerk and orders her to empty the cash drawer. Two young robbers accost a third youngster on the street and, at knifepoint, force him to remove his new boots and leather jacket, but do not harm him physically. Physical aggression is clearly implicated in these actions, but it is of a different nature from the aggression of the assaulter, the rapist, or the murderer. However, a substantial proportion of robberies do amount to physical harm to the victim, thus the topic will be covered in Chapter 15. Nevertheless, the psychological principles involved in robbery are close to those involved in burglary and other economic crimes.

Table 14-1 gives a percentage breakdown of the UCR Part I property crimes for 2010. As you can see, larceny-theft accounted for about two-thirds of the property crime, followed by burglary at almost one-quarter of the property offenses. For the violent offenses (not shown here), robbery accounted for 29.5 percent.

In addition to the crimes specified above, the chapter will also cover identity theft, a crime reaching near-epidemic proportions. We also cover "white-collar" offenses and discuss the difficulty defining that concept. Specific crimes like fraud and embezzlement will be presented.

TABLE 14-1 Part I Property Crimes, 2010

Offense	Number of Offenses	Percent of Part I Property Crime
Total property	9,139,712	100
Larceny-theft	6,185,867	67
Burglary	2,159,878	23
Motor vehicle theft	737,142	8
Arson	56,825	2

Source: Federal Bureau of Investigation (2011a).

Obviously, most people engage in economic and property crime for the money, or for other tangible rewards that meet biological, psychological, or social needs. Sykes (1956) notes, however, that this does not tell us why some people commit economic crime under certain social conditions, while others do not. Explanations based strictly on economic necessity and the satisfaction of basic human needs do not go far enough. Sykes proposes the concept of **relative deprivation** as one additional factor. To assess the economic want associated with economic crime, we should consider not what the person has or is making in personal income, but rather how great the discrepancy is between what he or she has and what he or she would like to have. Specifically, relative deprivation is the psychological distance between what people perceive they have now and what they feel they can realistically attain. In another sense, relative deprivation refers to a pervasive sense of injustice that develops between the "haves" and "have nots." Relative deprivation does not mean that one will necessarily commit economic crime, of course. The awareness of the economic gap between the wealthy and those less privileged can also lead to social action or demands for change. This was the major message given by the Occupy Wall Street movement and its spin-offs in 2011 and 2012. Thus, though relative deprivation is an interesting concept, it would require empirical documentation to make it a likely explanatory factor for criminal behavior.

From a psychological perspective, then, economic crimes cannot be simply explained by biological needs, material wants, or relative deprivation. Powerful cognitive motivators must also be considered. These cognitive factors are in the form of outcome expectations and the capacity to predict and appreciate future consequences of one's behavior. Furthermore, the cognitive forces may be relatively independent of external reinforcements like tangible rewards or even social and status rewards. Self-reinforcements, including self-rewards and self-punishments, may represent a major motivating factor in many property crimes. That is, the offender may receive pleasure and self-satisfaction in the completion of a crime and from doing it well.

Cognitive factors are also extremely important in another sense: They allow the offender to justify his or her behavior. A strong theme of this chapter is the tendency of economic offenders to minimize, distort, or deny misconduct or reprehensible behavior. As mentioned above, the fact that the victim is absent or observed only fleetingly helps them to do this. We expand on these psychological issues of motivation and justification throughout the following pages.

BURGLARY

Burglary is a crime that often affects large segments of the population and can cause extensive economic and emotional distress to victims. It is defined as the unlawful entry of a structure, with or without force, with intent to commit a felony or theft. The FBI classifies burglary into three categories: (1) forcible entry, (2) unlawful entry where no force is used, and (3) attempted forcible entry. Approximately 2.2 million burglaries occurred in the United States during 2010 (Federal Bureau of Investigation, 2011a). During 2010, 190,440 persons were arrested for burglary. Nationwide, the residential burglary rate is 29.6 per 1,000 inhabitants (Catalano, 2005).

Characteristics of Burglary

About one-third of burglaries do *not* involve forced entry. That is, the offenders entered through an unlatched window or unlocked door or used a key "hidden" in an obvious place, such as under a doormat. Another 6.3 percent of the 2010 burglaries were *attempts* at forcible entry.

Consistently, year after year, about two-thirds of all reported burglaries involve residential property, while the remaining one-third involves commercial establishments. To be considered residential burglary, the structure entered need not be the house itself. Illegal entry of a garage, shed, or other structure on the premises also constitutes a residential burglary. Burglaries of residences occur more frequently during the daytime, whereas burglaries of businesses and nonresidential property mostly occur at night.

Burglaries are more likely to occur during the warmer months, especially July and August, apparently because people are more likely to be outdoors or away on vacation and are more likely to leave doors and windows open, making their residences vulnerable. An early study by Langer and Miranksy (1983) reveals that a large segment of the population does not take responsibility for burglary prevention. Approximately half of the New York City residents questioned admitted they did not lock all their doors when away from home, even if they had been burglarized before. Interestingly, while 66 percent believed that burglary could be prevented, 61 percent of these subjects did not use all their locks. They believed that it was the responsibility of others (e.g., the police, the landlord, the building superintendent) to guard the premises, rather than their own personal responsibility. We must be very careful not to blame victims for *any* criminal offenses, however. It is one thing to alert people and make them aware of steps they can take to protect themselves from crime; it is quite another to fault them for not taking the steps. In the above study, those who thought their neighborhoods were unsafe and burglary-prone were less likely to use locks than those who considered their neighborhoods safe and less burglary-prone. Possibly, people in burglary-prone areas are convinced that if someone decides to burglarize their homes, there is not much they can do about it, locks or no locks. Another factor, though, is that good locks cost money. If one lives on a tight budget, buying a lock may be seen as a low priority.

Who Commits Burglary?

Like many other criminal offenses, burglary seems to be primarily a crime committed by the young. About 58 percent of those arrested in 2010 were under 25, with the average age being about 22 (Federal Bureau of Investigation, 2011a). Approximately 22 percent were under 18. To some extent, this arrest ratio may reflect the lack of sophistication of younger burglars who, because of their inexperience, are more likely to be detected. However, researchers have noted that, with increasing age, some burglars find they are not as nimble and athletic as they once were. Crawling through small open windows and climbing fences take their toll, and these strenuous activities become more burdensome with age. Thus, many older burglars turn to shoplifting (Cromwell, Olson, & Avary, 1991). Shoplifting—to be discussed again shortly—is considerably easier, less risky, and more cost efficient. Shoplifted items are more easily converted to cash and are more profitable than items gained through burglary, because they are new, untraceable, and have their price tags attached. Furthermore, the criminal penalties are significantly less for shoplifting than they are for burglary.

Burglary is largely a male enterprise, with only 16 percent of those arrested being women in 2010. Although 67.4 percent of those arrested in 2010 were white, nonwhites were overrepresented in proportion to their numbers in the general population (Federal Bureau of Investigation, 2011a).

As noted earlier, about two of every three burglaries are residential, and burglary of residences usually occurs during the daytime and on weekdays. Daytime burglary by juveniles is closely associated with truancy (Scott, 2004). Commercial establishments are usually burglarized late at night and on weekends (Cromwell *et al.*, 1991; Pope, 1977b). This is not surprising, since burglary is a passive crime; the offender selects times and places that will minimize the possibility of an encounter with victims. Almost all *experienced* burglars (well over 90%)

assert they will not even enter a residence when the occupants are believed to be at home (Cromwell *et al.*, 1991). Homes occupied during the day most commonly are occupied by a parent providing child care or by retired individuals. However, burglars know that occupants develop predictable patterns regarding the use of discretionary time for the purposes of shopping, errands, or visiting friends or relatives. Individuals who work outside the home during weekdays also show similar patterns on weekends. Parents also usually develop predictable patterns of taking children back and forth to school, nursery programs, and recreational activities.

Of all property crimes, burglary probably offers the greatest probability of success with the least amount of risk. Not only is it a crime without victim contact and probability of identification, but also it does not require weapons. Furthermore, the penalties usually are less severe than those for robbery.

Burglary Cues and Selected Targets

The identification of situational cues is especially important in successful burglary. Nee and Taylor (1988) found that there are at least four broad categories of relevant cues used by experienced residential burglars. They are as follows:

1. *Occupancy cues*, such as letters or newspapers visible in mailbox; motor vehicles present; windows, blinds, and curtains shut or open
2. *Wealth cues*, such as the appearance of the house, the neighborhood, the quality of the landscaping, the make(s) of car(s) driven, and visible furnishings
3. *Layout cues*, such as how easy it would be to gain access to the house or building, as well as escape
4. *Security cues*, such as alarm systems, window locks, and dead bolt locks

Taylor and Nee (1988) designed a study that tested the possible differences in identifying these cues between burglars and home owners. The burglars consisted of a group of 15 experienced burglars serving time in Cork Prison in Ireland, and the home owners consisted of 15 Irish home owners. Each subject was requested to explore a simulated environment made up of slides and maps of five different houses. The researchers found that burglars were better able to discern security provisions and were more concerned about escaping successfully from the scene than were home owners. Most surprising, however, was the high amount of agreement between burglars and home owners on which houses were most vulnerable to burglary.

Burglars tend to prefer single-family homes, primarily because they can be entered directly from the street, and because they often have multiple access and escape points (Bernasco, 2006). Neighborhood residents who are not affiliated with or are isolated from their neighbors (called anonymous environments) are also preferred because the neighbors will less likely be alarmed by unusual or suspicious events (Bernasco, 2006). Corner homes offer an attractive target, as they offer many escape routes, have fewer neighbors nearby, and are more difficult for neighbors to watch (Rengert & Groff, 2011).

Rengert and Groff (2011) note that antiques displayed in a window or somewhere outside are important cues for some burglars. Antiques indicate that the residents are probably collectors, and burglars often assume that they may find valuable coins, stamps, old guns, and other collectibles inside the house.

Burglars have a number of strategies for determining if a targeted house is unoccupied. One strategy, for example, is surveying funeral notices published in newspapers (Rengert & Groff, 2011). "Burglars realize that this is a time when family and friends of the deceased are likely to be at the funeral" (Rengert & Groff, 2011, p. 161). Another method is gathering information about the targeted house while performing a legitimate occupation, such as landscaping and lawn care, sales, or cable television installation. Still another method is for the burglar to check Facebook or other online networking portals. Many people post that they are on vacation or are planning to go on vacation, often listing the exact dates. (Interestingly, Facebook postings have worked in the other direction as well: a news story recently reported the antics of juveniles who bragged about their burglarizing exploits on Facebook, and even began posting where they would strike next. Police were waiting for them and caught them in the act.)

Some burglars simply knock on the door. If someone answers the door, they use the excuse that they were looking for directions, were out of gas, or are having car problems. They may also glance around the inside of the house, given the opportunity, to assess whether there is likely to be items worth taking in the future. Leaving the garage door open of an attached garage and no vehicle in sight is a clear invitation to a burglar, but we stress that the burglary, if it occurs, is not the fault of the victim.

Burglar Cognitive Processes

Bennett and Wright (1984) conducted an extensive three-year project involving convicted burglars confined in various prisons throughout southern England. The study is about 30 years old, but it is one of the few qualitative studies that focused on the cognitions of the burglars themselves, through semistructured interviews. The researchers' primary interest was to learn the decision-making processes and perceptions of the residential burglars at the time of the crime. Although a majority of the burglars had committed a variety of other economic crimes, almost all of them considered burglary their main criminal activity. Therefore, most of them probably qualify as professionals rather than amateurs.

Bennett and Wright discovered that almost all the burglaries were planned. Many other studies have arrived at the same conclusion (Vaughn, DeLisi, Beaver, & Howard, 2008). Very few were the result of spur-of-the-moment decisions, nor were there any constant or irrepressible urges to burglarize. More than likely, though, those burglaries that appeared to be impulsive or opportunity-driven are probably the result of well-learned cognitive scripts. **Cognitive scripts** are mental images and plans of how one will act and react in certain situations. The more one rehearses these scripts, behaviorally and mentally, the more habitual they become under similar conditions.

The two main aspects that went into the planning of burglars in the Bennett and Wright investigation were the situational cues of surveillability and occupancy. Surveillability cues were related to the amount of cover or openness around the house, whether it was overlooked by neighboring houses, the availability of access to the rear, and the presence or proximity of neighbors. Occupancy cues were similar to the ones reported by Nee and Taylor, such as a car in the driveway, lights on in the house, the presence of mail, whether the walks were shoveled or the lawn was cut, and so forth. Experienced burglars said that "occupancy proxies" were the major deterrents in attempts to burglarize. Specifically, burglar alarms and dogs were extremely important in the prevention of burglary. This was also a consistent finding of Cromwell and colleagues (1991). In fact, Cromwell and colleagues found that the dog does not have to be a large one, and it does not have to be the unfairly maligned pit bull. Any dog will do, since a large one poses a physical threat, and the small dog will be noisy. Cats do not seem to qualify.

Cromwell and his associates also found that dead bolts caused burglars considerable difficulty in entry, even though some of the experienced burglars claimed such locks would not be any problem. However, Cromwell and colleagues not only obtained self-report data from experienced burglars, but also had them demonstrate their claims. Security locks and dead bolts caused all kinds of trouble, even for highly experienced burglars—and even though they had maintained that the locks would not be a deterrent. Much of the research on burglary, on the other hand, finds that increased police patrols and other such strategies have very little influence on decisions to burglarize, or on its success rate. This is primarily because the patrols cannot last indefinitely, and police cannot be everywhere at once. However, curious neighbors—those always peeking out their windows or finding yard chores to do when there is different activity next door—do tend to be strong deterrents for burglars. This observation is supported by both experienced burglars and crime statistics.

Recent Research on Occupancy Cues

Research data suggest that, although burglary is a "planned" behavior, burglars identify a large number of potential targets, and then select the most vulnerable. Cromwell and his colleagues caution, however, that even though much of the research on burglary suggests that a high percentage of burglars make carefully planned, highly rational decisions based on a detailed evaluation of environmental cues, the critical factor seems to be finding the right opportunity from an array of potential targets. In other words, burglary is not generally an impulsive crime, but it isn't usually planned to precise detail either. For example, an offender may target a specific house at a particular time. On the day of the planned burglary, the homeowner is unexpectedly home; the burglar then selects a different target. There is considerable research showing that cues indicating occupancy of the home often act as a deterrent, thus reducing the risk of burglary victimization (Snook, Dhami, & Kavanagh, 2011). There is also contemporary research evidence indicating that professional burglars use less, but more relevant, information about their targets than amateur or novice burglars, who are influenced by irrelevant information (Garcia-Retamero & Dhami, 2009). That is, professional burglars make their decisions to burglarize a residence on only one or two cues of occupancy based on their previous experience. For example, if no car is parked outside and the curtains are closed at ground level, these two cues would indicate to the professional burglar that the residence is unoccupied. In fact, Snook *et al.* (2011) found that "vehicle cue" was the most important for burglars in deciding occupancy. Essentially, it seems that professionals do not clutter their minds with complicated strategies compared to novices who tend to rely on more cognitively complex strategies. As emphasized by Snook *et al.*, "this growing body of research on burglars' decision making appears to contradict criminological theories of rational choice that portray offenders as employing compensatory decision strategies that weigh and integrate information" (p. 323). Skillful burglars apparently use simple, fast, and frugal decisions based on previous experiences.

Entry Strategies

Cromwell and his colleagues (1991) found in their systematic study of experienced burglars that one of the most popular entry methods was through sliding glass patio doors. Burglars said that these doors are easily popped out of their sliding tracks by hand or with aid of a crowbar or screwdriver. Entry is therefore quick and noiseless. Another common method is to remove, cut, or gently break a windowpane and crawl through the open window. A skillful burglar will carefully remove the pane, crawl through, and then replace the pane in a professional manner. Other commonly preferred methods for residential burglary include forcing the rear door open with a pry tool or kicking it down, or opening the garage door and forcing open the door between the garage and the house.

A more modern entry method for professional burglars is to use a bump key. Most doors can be opened with a **bump key**—usually made of brass—which fits into the keyway of the lock. Bumping is a method of pin manipulation within the lock by using a key made specifically designed for most commonly used door locks. That is, one bump key is usually sufficient for unlocking a majority of the locks made by a certain manufacturer. Although bump keys are produced for certified locksmiths, a competent professional burglar can purchase online a set of 11 bump keys that fit most of all the commonly used locks. In some cases, a bump hammer must also be purchased. Bump keys allow burglars to enter a house without any signs of damage or signs of entry, and it may be days before anything is noticed missing. An electronic keypad would be one way to deter this method of illegal entry. Once in the house, burglars check easy escape routes in case someone arrives home. Then they usually go to the master bedroom where many valuables are located. As pointed out by Rengert and Groff (2011), the master bedroom also provides a good container for carrying valuables—the pillowcase. After the bedroom, the burglar often turns his or her attention to the dining area, looking for silverware, candlesticks, and silver service. Kitchens are usually avoided. If available, a study or home office is a good place to locate stamp and coin collections, and portable electronic items.

How Far Do Burglars Travel?

National research data on arrested burglars in the United States indicate that a large proportion commit the offense near their own residence. Both classic and more recent research supports this. The Santa Clara Criminal Justice Pilot Program (1972) found that over one-half of the apprehended offenders traveled no more than a mile from their own home to commit the offenses. More recently, in a study of serial burglars who operated in a small town in southern England, Barker (2000) found that these offenders tended to live surprisingly close to the areas they burglarized. She discovered, however, that the mean home-to-offense distance increased during the later stages of burglary. For example, the average home-to-first-offense distance was 2.16 kilometers, the average distance from home to the middle offense in the series was 3.57 kilometers, and the average distance from home to the last offense in the series was 5.52 kilometers. It is difficult to generalize from these data, however, because apprehended burglars are presumably less skillful and thus more detectable than burglars who succeed. It is possible that successful burglars operate farther away from home. However, in general, burglars are probably less likely to travel distances because they are less familiar with unknown and uncharted territory. Eskridge (1983) found that those who burglarized commercial establishments were more willing to travel much greater distances. Interestingly, Bennell and Jones (2005) found that both commercial and residential burglars select distinct geographical areas to commit their crimes, and they appear to return to those selected areas until they have exhausted the suitable targets.

Gender Differences in Methods and Patterns

In their study of male and female burglars, Decker, Wright, Redfern, and Smith (1993) found that the offending patterns of female burglars were very similar to those of males. One major exception was that male burglars often stole cars in addition to burglarizing residences or commercial establishments, whereas the female burglars did not. Decker and his colleagues found that they could divide the female burglars into two major groups: accomplices and partners. Accomplices committed the burglary because of their subservience to others—usually men—during their burglaries. Partners, on the other hand, participated as equals in the commission of burglary. Although some of these females co-offended with males, they did not take orders from them.

Use of Alcohol and Other Substances

Although the well-known Santa Clara 1972 project concluded that burglars are rarely under the influence of alcohol and other drugs at the time of their crime, the more recent data reported by the Cromwell and associates (1991) study indicates this is not so. Ninety-three percent of the professional burglars studied by the Cromwell group said they "fixed" or "got high" before entering a residence. These experienced, professional burglars admitted they needed to lower their anxiety levels and reduce their fear prior to the burglary. The vast majority of these burglars reported that moderate amounts of alcohol or drugs simply made them better burglars, because these substances increased their alertness, vigilance, and improved their nerve to stay in the residences long enough to search for and locate a variety of items to steal. Female burglars do the same thing (Decker *et al.*, 1993). Specifically, the calming effects of certain drugs and alcohol enabled them to focus more on environmental cues related to risk, as well as valuable items hidden in the house that they normally would not find. Psychologically, this observation makes sense because high levels of arousal do narrow one's attention span and reduce one's focus on environmental cues under certain pressure situations (Easterbrook, 1959). Also, the Cromwell study found that heroin-using burglars tend to be more rational, more professional, and less likely to be arrested than burglars using cocaine or speed (or more generally, stimulants). Moreover, the heroin user was able to exercise considerable control over the amount of the drug used for maximum proficiency in burglarizing. In addition, many offenders commit burglary to support their drug habit.

Property Taken and Disposed

The items that burglars usually take from homes are jewelry, gold, valuable household ornaments, stamp and coin collections, and computers—both desktops and laptops—followed by tools (Schneider, 2005). Non-garden-type power tools are especially popular, including cordless drills, saws, snap-on tools, and generators. High-quality televisions, video players, electronic equipment, and all types of alcohol are also desired items. Most recently, prescription medications and even diabetic test strips are in high demand. Burglars usually do not spend the time looking for cash, unless they suspect that there are substantial quantities hidden somewhere in the house. Garden tools that are in good shape, such as mowers, trimmers, and hedge cutters, may be taken if the burglar has readily available transportation. Credit cards and wallets are not sought by most burglars.

Being easy to sell is the most common reason provided for stealing certain items (Schneider, 2005). Some very expensive items, such as valuable paintings, may be avoided because they may be very difficult to sell. The ease in carrying or removing the item is the second reason for stealing it.

Amateur burglars usually take money or personal items that they need, whereas the professional takes items with excellent resale value, such as electronics, cameras, cash, guns, jewelry, and furs (Rengert & Groff, 2011; Vetter & Silverman, 1978). The professional usually has access to a **fence**, whereas the amateur rarely has that kind of contact. Amateurs usually sell their stolen items to pawn shops or friends. A fence, an integral component in the professional burglary cycle, is a person who knowingly buys stolen merchandise for the purpose of resale. Professional burglars also have individually distinctive methods and not infrequently leave their mark (their signature) to goad the investigators they have foiled. Many professional burglars prefer retail stores over residential homes.

The Cromwell and associates (1991) research raises serious questions about the extent to which professional fences are used today, however. In their investigation of experienced burglars operating in an urban Texas metropolitan area of 250,000, they found considerable diversity in the channels through which stolen property was distributed. Some burglars sold their stolen property to pawnshops, others to friends and acquaintances, and still others traded their property for drugs. Some resold the merchandise to legitimate businesses or strangers. The researchers, therefore, suggest that the "professional fence may have been displaced by a more diverse and readily accessed market for stolen property" (p. 73). Stolen property today, for example, is often disposed of via Internet sites.

However, Schneider (2005) found that selling stolen property to handlers or fences was the preferred method for disposing of merchandise acquired through burglary, especially by persistent or professional burglars. After fences, the second choice was to sell to friends or trade the stolen items for drugs. In some instances, the burglar keeps the stolen property for himself or herself, but this choice increases the chances of being detected.

Motives

As you might expect, the motives for burglary are varied, but the primary factor for professionals is undoubtedly monetary gain. When performed competently, burglary is a lucrative business with low risks and with monetary rewards far surpassing those the burglar might earn in the "straight" world. In addition, burglars make a rough estimation on whether the expected financial gain outweighs the effort and the risk of detection (Bernasco, 2006).

David (1974) learned that a husband and wife team he interviewed made, on the average, $400 to $500 a day; a solitary offender in his sample made about $500 per week. These figures will obviously be substantially higher in today's market. Many professionals also conceive of their behavior as a challenging skill to be continually developed and refined. Some even said they get a "rush" of excitement during the planning and commission of the crime, especially if they are good at it (Cromwell *et al.*, 1991). In this sense, burglary is highly adaptive and represents an instrumental behavior supported by strong reinforcement. For many burglars, however, a simple conclusion that they participate in their crimes as their sole profession or lucrative business may be unwarranted. A vast majority of burglary is committed to supplement the offender's incomes and to improve their quality of life (Rengert & Wasilchick, 1985). The income gained from burglary enables the offender to buy drugs, alcohol, expensive goods, and, more broadly, to be able "to party." Alternatively, it may be used, like the profits from other economic crimes, to finance a college education or a gambling habit or to pay a debt. Subsistence needs are often met through other sources of income, such as a regular job.

Some burglars may burglarize the same place again, or even repeatedly, in a pattern called **repeat burglary**. Burglars that participate in repeat burglary do it because of the efficiency in time, planning, and risk involved (Farrell, Phillips, & Pease, 1995). Residential locations are especially vulnerable because residents do not necessarily change the layout or make entry more difficult after a burglary. In other words, the burglar knows the layout of the target well, was successful the first time, and may even have seen valuables the first time around that prompted a return visit. In addition, researchers have identified a phenomenon called **near-repeat** offending (Bernasco, 2008; Sagovsky & Johnson, 2007), which refers to the likelihood of additional burglary in a neighborhood after one house has been successfully burglarized. Usually, these near-repeat crimes occur within the first few weeks of the original crime (Sagovsky & Johnson, 2007). The near-repeat phenomenon also has been found for other crimes, such as shootings, robbery, and car theft (Youstin, Nobels, Ward, & Cook, 2011).

Shover (1972) discusses some of the outstanding features of the competent professional burglar, whom he calls the **good burglar**. This burglar demonstrates technical skill, maintains a good reputation for personal integrity among colleagues in the criminal subculture, gets most of his income from burglary, and has been at least relatively successful at the crime. A good reputation means that the burglar is closemouthed, does not cooperate with police if questioned, and is sympathetic to the criminal way of life.

The professional burglar, then, is primarily motivated not only by money but also by self-satisfaction and accomplishment. When self-satisfaction and self-reinforcement are conditioned on certain accomplishments, people are motivated to expend the effort needed to attain the desired goal, perhaps even independently of monetary gain. Walsh (1980), for example, has emphasized the expressive and psychological components of burglary. He posits that, for some burglars, the challenge of the crime is far more rewarding than the material reward. Based on interviews with victims and offenders, Walsh identifies three kinds of **expressive burglars**: (1) *the feral threat,* (2) *the riddlesmith,* and (3) *the dominator.* The feral burglar engages in destructive, malicious vandalism during the break-in by spilling things, breaking glass, smashing objects, and urinating and defecating in various areas throughout the house. This burglar may slash the clothing in the closets, and vandalize vehicles in the garage. The riddlesmith, on the other hand, tries to demonstrate his or her technical skill to the victims and investigators by setting up puzzles, mysteries, and booby traps throughout the house. The riddlesmith is inventive in the way he or she causes damage, and messages may be left on walls, floors, and mirrors. The dominator enjoys threatening or frightening victims, and therefore breaks into homes that are occupied. All three of these expressive burglars are interested in communicating to burglarized victims through a particular style or method of operating. Thus, a burglar who takes great pride in developing ingenious techniques and stumping police is even more likely to continue his illegal conduct. While external reinforcements (tangible rewards) are important, internal reinforcement may be a powerful motivating and regulating factor.

A Burglar Typology

Michael Vaughn and his colleagues (2008), using a sample of 456 adult career criminals, have empirically identified four classes of burglars: (1) young versatile, (2) vagrant, (3) drug-oriented, and (4) sexual predators. This intriguing classification system reveals the underlying motives and types of burglars, some of whom may be considered dangerous. The first group, by far the most common (60%), were young and had committed a variety of offenses. They appear to represent the types of burglars we have described thus far. The second type, the vagrant, made up 22 percent of the sample; they were often charged with various offenses primarily stemming from their transient, vagabond status. They appeared to burglarize primarily for material gain, especially during the winter months. The researchers speculated that many of these burglars may have some mental disorders and lack social skills for gaining employment. The drug-oriented group, consisting of 15 percent of the sample, had numerous drug possession and drug-trafficking offenses. They also were likely to carry weapons for protection. In most instances, these offenders tended to burglarize to support their drug habit.

The fourth group, the sexual predator burglars, was the most violent and constituted 6 percent of the sample. This group had a long criminal career, committing an assortment of offenses, including aggravated assault, robbery, rape, and prostitution/solicitation. According to Vaughn *et al.,* the burglaries committed by this group were at least partially motivated by sexual compulsion and thrills associated with entering dwellings of strangers. In some cases, these offenders were also motivated to sexually assault a person they had been stalking. Although this group represented only a small portion of the total sample, they also accounted for a large majority of the violence reported in burglary, and probably many of the reported home invasions. We will cover home invasions shortly.

The research-based typology developed by Vaughn *et al.* is an interesting one that will likely stimulate considerable research on types of burglary in the future. It also offers a sound explanation for the various types of psychological motivations for some forms of burglary. The researchers warn, however, that their sample was characterized by extensive criminal careers and may not be entirely characteristic of professional or amateur burglars who restrict their criminal activity to burglary as a way of financial survival.

Psychological Impact of Burglary

Merry and Hansent point out that, for all of us, the home is a sanctuary: "It is a special place that is central to our daily lives, a place that is at the beginning and end of most of our journeys; it is chosen and personalized" (2000, p. 36). The manner in which homes are decorated and arranged and the objects within them represent important aspects of our lives and personalities. When our homes are burglarized, therefore, it is an invasion of our intimate space and an attack on our identity, physically and symbolically. Some victims describe burglary as a rape of their home, especially when the burglar has disturbed personal photographs, letters, and diaries, leaving the feeling of having been violated or at least "touched" by the intruder (Merry & Hansent, 2000). The distress levels experienced by victims are often more pronounced when the invasion extends to private areas, such as bedrooms, closets, chests-of-drawers, bathrooms, and desks. The invasion also endangers the victims' sense of control and threatens their ability to protect their own personal territory. Many victims, after being burglarized, install security systems such as video cameras, increase and improve the locks, buy dogs, or even move to new homes. Overall, the psychological trauma caused by a burglary can be substantial for many victims, and its effects may continue for many years.

Very often, the burglar's actions are intended to produce some response from the victim. In other words, some burglars specifically tailor their styles (or signatures) to convey messages to victims and investigators, hoping to induce some strong emotional reactions from the victims. The emotional reactions of burglarized victims often run the gamut from anger and depression to fear and anxiety (Brown & Harris, 1989). In addition, the individual style utilized by the offender probably reflects something about his character and personality. According to Merry and Hansent (2000), this aspect is referred to as the interpersonal dimension of the crime. It is suggested, therefore, that the victim's feelings of fear and vulnerability are psychological losses that are translated into gains for the offender. In this sense, the burglar gains materially and psychologically from the crime. The interpersonal aspects of the burglary (i.e., the style used by the burglar) are areas that provide considerable potential for burglary profiling in future research.

Home Invasions

In about 28 percent of residential burglaries, a member of the household is present (Catalano, 2010) (see **Table 14-2**). These cases are often called **home invasions**, which refers to any crime committed by an individual unlawfully entering a residence while someone is home. Home invasion has also been used to "describe a situation where an offender forcibly enters an occupied residence with the specific intent of robbing or harming those inside" (Catalano, 2010, p. 2). In some situations, a household member may become a target either to "settle a score" or because the offender knows the person is vulnerable, such as persons with disabilities or the elderly. In other cases, the offender enters the residence mistakenly believing no one is home, or the household member returns home

TABLE 14-2	Time of Occurrence of Household Burglaries, by Presence of Household Member, 2003–2007

| | Household Member Not Present | | Household Member Present | |
Time of Day	Average Annual Number	Percent	Average Annual Number	Percent
Total	2,683,270	100.00	1,021,430	100.00
Daytime (6 a.m.–6 p.m.)	1,159,450	48.2	336,340	32.9
Nighttime (6 p.m.–6 a.m.)	697,940	26.0	626,150	61.3
Not known	825,880	30.8	58,940	5.8

Source: Data from Catalano, 2010, p. 6.

while a burglary is in process. It is perhaps misleading to refer to these last cases as home invasions, because the perpetrators did not enter the premises with the intent to do harm to the residents.

One of the most horrific and highly publicized home invasions of the past decade was the 2007 Connecticut case in which two men entered a home, beat and restrained the husband/father (who eventually escaped and ultimately survived), and sexually assaulted and killed the wife/mother, sexually assaulted at least one of the two daughters, and killed both girls. The daughters were ages 17 and 11. The family was subjected to abuse and cruelty over a lengthy period. At one point during the hours the intruders were at the home, one of them accompanied the woman to a bank and had her withdraw funds. Before leaving the home, they poured gasoline over some of the victims and set the house on fire. The two men—Steven Hayes and Joshua Komisarjevsky—were convicted and sentenced to death. Connecticut later became the 17th state to repeal the death penalty, but the repeal—signed into law by Connecticut governor Dannell Malloy in late April, 2012—did not apply to 11 inmates who were on death row, including Hayes and Komisarjevsky.

Roughly 20 percent of household burglaries result in violent victimization when the resident was at home. Unlike the Connecticut example above, simple assault was the most common form of violence in these cases. In many of these victimization cases, the burglar was a relative or intimate (current or former) (Catalano, 2010). About a third of the time, the offender was a stranger. Research to date has not allowed us to provide detailed information about the motivations of the burglars whose crimes qualify as home invasions. This is because the data have been gathered from the National Crime Victimization Survey which is not designed to determine offender motivation or intent for entering an occupied household.

LARCENY AND MOTOR VEHICLE THEFT

McCaghy (1980) refers to the larceny-theft category as a "garbage can" because it is heterogeneous and hard to classify. Larceny-theft is defined as the "unlawful taking, carrying, leading, or riding away of property from the possession or constructive possession of another" (Federal Bureau of Investigation, 1997, p. 43). It differs from burglary in that it does not involve unlawful entry. Larceny includes pickpocketing, purse snatching, shoplifting (which is discussed in a separate section), stealing from vending machines or from motor vehicles, and theft of property left outdoors (bicycles, pedigreed dogs, lawn mowers), and so on. The larceny-theft offenses in the United States during 2010 accounted for 62.9 percent of the property crime total (Federal Bureau of Investigation, 2011a).

Motor Vehicle Theft

Motor vehicle theft is defined as the theft or attempted theft of a motor vehicle, including the stealing of automobiles, trucks, buses, motorcycles, motor scooters, and snowmobiles (Federal Bureau of Investigation, 2008). The taking of a motor vehicle for temporary use by persons having lawful access is excluded from the definition (Federal Bureau of Investigation, 2005b). Of the arrests for motor vehicle theft in 2010, males accounted for 82.1 percent of those arrested (Federal Bureau of Investigation, 2011a).

Motor vehicle manufacturers have developed effective and highly sophisticated ways of preventing theft in recent years, making it increasingly difficult for thieves to steal the vehicle by traditional means. Offenders have adapted to these changes by seeking out more effective ways of obtaining keys for the vehicles (Copes & Cherbonneau, 2006). Consequently, there has been a growth in the prevalence of auto theft involving keys (Copes & Cherbonneau, 2006). In addition, obtaining keys minimizes damage done to the vehicle, which will ultimately increase its resale value. Some offenders go to great lengths to steal, find, or manipulate the keys from owners. Others are becoming skillful at manufacturing matching keys themselves.

Carjacking

Carjacking is the completed or attempted theft in which a motor vehicle is taken by force or threat of force (Klaus, 1999). It differs from other motor vehicle theft in that it involves the use of force or threat of force against the occupants of the vehicle. On average, 34,000 carjacking incidents occur each year in the United States (Klaus, 2004). Approximately a dozen homicides are associated with these carjackings each year; in other words, the driver or a passenger is killed. Recall the example in Chapter 10 in which a shooter killed patrons in a Seattle coffee shop then hijacked a car, forcing out and killing its driver. By all accounts, such murders are very rare. In about three-fourths of carjackings, the occupants face an armed offender or offenders (Klaus, 2004). In most instances, the carjacker uses a firearm. Victimization surveys indicate that the victim resisted the carjacker in two-thirds of the incidents, which resulted in about 9 percent of the victims receiving serious injury (e.g., gunshot or knife wounds, broken bones, or internal injuries).

Men tend to be victims of carjacking more than women, blacks more than whites, and Hispanics more than non-Hispanics (Klaus, 2004). This may be because carjackings are highly concentrated in particular areas and at particular times. They are highest in urban areas. They occur in parking lots and garages (24%), or in an open area, such as on the street or near public transportation (bus, subway, train station, or airport) (44%). They most often occur at night. Males committed 93 percent of the carjackings, while groups involving both males and females committed 3 percent. Women committed about 3 percent of the incidents.

Although the offense is violent, it appears to contain some elements of short-term planning and decision making and often is directed more at the object (the vehicle) than the person (Jacobs, Topalli, & Wright, 2003). Jacobs and his colleagues interviewed 28 active carjackers recruited from the streets of St. Louis, Missouri. "Active carjackers were defined as individuals who had committed two or more carjackings in the previous year" (2003, p. 675). In this study, all active carjackers were black and three were women. The interviews were semistructured and informal, allowing offenders to speak freely in their own words.

The researchers discovered that the active carjackers remain in permanent state of "alert opportunism" and ready to commit the offense if the chance came their way. Many had gotten away with carjackings in the past, and therefore believed they would succeed when the need for quick cash or quick transportation arose again. In other words, most have developed well-learned cognitive scripts for how to proceed with their offense. Moreover, each had a preference for the vehicle they sought (gold-spoked wheels, a high-performance engine, or a booming sound system), features that bring a good price on the streets. In some cases, a driver would become a victim because the carjacker interpreted him as demonstrating disrespect. Punishing the driver added an incentive to that of obtaining quick cash. Thus, the carjacking became a way to punish drivers who dare to "floss their little stuff by cruising through their neighborhoods in a disrespectful way" (Jacobs *et al.*, 2003, p. 682). For example, "flossing" might include turning the sound system up loud in the neighborhood to mark the driver's presence.

Larceny and motor vehicle theft are common and widespread offenses, but psychological research reporting specifically on these areas is rarely available. To some extent, the motivating factors that apply to burglary apply here as well. On the other hand, larceny and motor vehicle theft are more likely than burglary to be committed by the nonprofessional.

FRAUD AND IDENTITY THEFT

Crimes of fraud involve deception used for the purpose of obtaining illegal financial gain. They often involve the misrepresentation of facts and the deliberate intent to deceive with the promise of goods, services, or other benefits that either do not exist or that were never intended to be provided (Deem & Murray, 2000). Examples of fraud include identity theft, elder financial abuse, counterfeiting, mail fraud, bank fraud, and various corporate or organizational wrongdoings. In 2009, Bernard "Bernie" Madoff was convicted of operating a Ponzi scheme that has been called the largest investor fraud ever committed by a single person (Bray, 2009). The "Ponzi scheme" pulled in thousands of investors who lost an estimated $65 billion. Over the last two decades, fraud has increased in awareness with other high-profile cases, such as the savings and loan debacle of the 1980s and the massive Enron and Tyco cases of the early 2000s. In the economic crisis of 2009, corporate practices of banks, credit card companies, and other organizations were scrutinized for possible fraudulent activities. Although many of these practices were questionable and often unethical, they were not always illegal. This is an important distinction from the legal perspective, but from a psychological perspective, it still raises questions about the motives of those responsible. We discuss these issues again later in the chapter.

Identity theft occurs when one individual or a group of individuals misappropriate another person's personal identification information, such as name, Social Security number, date of birth, mother's maiden name, and uses the information to take over existing credit card or bank accounts, apply for a mortgage or car loan, make large purchases, or apply for insurance (Deem & Murray, 2000). In many instances, unsuspecting victims have no idea that anything is amiss until they receive phone calls from creditors or have difficulty applying for a job, loan, or mortgage. The National White Collar Crime Center (NW3C) has brought attention to Child Identity Theft, calling it an unanalyzed problem, and theft of the identity of deceased individuals. (See **Box 14-1** for additional discussion of these problems)

In 2007, about 7 percent of the households in the United States (8 million) had at least one member become a victim of one or more types of identity theft (Langton & Baum, 2010). Credit card theft is the most common type of identity theft. In most cases, persons discover the theft by noticing unfamiliar charges on accounts, or they are contacted by a credit card bureau

BOX 14-1

Identity Theft: Victimizing Children and the Deceased

Devout fans of the cable show *Mad Men* know Don Draper's secret. He is a successful advertising executive, but he is not *really* Don Draper. As a serviceman in the Korean War, Dick Whitman stole the identity of Draper, a fellow soldier who was scheduled to be discharged but was killed in action. Whitman took Draper's identifying documents and exchanged their dog tags. It was his opportunity to get out of the war and start life anew, escaping an unfortunate family background. Somewhat guiltily, he allowed his own family back home to believe he had been killed. The wife of the real Draper—whose picture was kept in the wallet—believed her husband never came home from the war, and perhaps had willingly disappeared.

Throughout five seasons of the show, Whitman's secret has been revealed to just a few individuals, including the wife of the real Don Draper, who agreed to give him a divorce so that he could legally marry another woman. In return for her cooperation and silence, "Draper" gave her money and helped her at regular intervals. They ultimately became good friends, and when she died, he experienced considerable grief. If this sounds like a tawdry soap opera, it is not—as avid *Mad Men* fans will attest.

Stealing the identity of a dead person is more difficult today than it was in Dick Whitman's era. Nevertheless, according to the National White Collar Crime Center (NW3C) it is not unusual. Access to Social Security numbers facilitates the process. Some thieves are acquaintances of the dead person and continue receiving their benefits or using their credit cards.

Others peruse obituaries and are able to get information, such as where the person worked. They sometimes call relatives of the deceased, pretending they are former co-workers. Armed with enough data, they can make credit card purchases or online purchases, which may not be discovered for months. The victim is deceased and cannot monitor these fraudulent activities and surviving relatives may not notice changes in the various account balances.

The NW3C also reported that—in research involving more than 40,000 children—it was discovered that Social Security numbers of approximately 10.2 percent had been used for a range of purposes, including obtaining loans or opening credit accounts. Sometimes, the fraudulent transactions are perpetrated by parents or relatives in dire economic straits, but at other times the Social Security numbers have been accessed by strangers. Children, the NW3C notes, have a blank slate, with no history of credit defaults. They have no credit file, thus transactions with their information do not lead to "fraud alerts." Children in foster care are often the targets of identity theft, because their information is broadly shared among various social service and educational institutions.

Child identity-theft may seem to be a mild form of victimization in comparison to the child abuse victimizations discussed in earlier chapters. Nevertheless, it can have repercussions many years down the line, when adolescents and young adults seek employment or apply for college and other loans. It is likely the most underanalyzed form of identity theft.

(see **Table 14-3**). The second most common type of identity theft involves the unauthorized use or attempted use of checking or debit bank accounts, or cell phone accounts (Langton & Baum, 2010). The average amount of money lost in identity theft in 2007 was $1,830. According to more recent data, identity theft has increased dramatically over the last two years. For example, in 2011, 11.6 million adults became victims of identity theft, a 13 percent increase from 2010 (Javelin Strategy & Research, 2012). Smartphones, new mobile technologies, and social media (e.g., Facebook) have probably played a major role in this increase. For example, 68 percent of people with public social media profiles shared their birthday information (with 45 percent revealing month, date, and year), 63 percent revealed their high school name, 18 percent showed their phone number, and 12 percent divulged their pet's name (Javelin Strategy & Research, 2012). These all represent prime examples of personal information that financial institutions use to authenticate a person's identity.

TABLE 14-3 Identity Theft in American Households, 2007			
Did Households Discover Identity Theft in Previous Six Months?	**Number of Households**	**Percent of Households**	**Percent of Victimized Households**
Yes	7,928,500	6.6	100.0
Unauthorized use of existing credit cards	3,894,300	3.3	49.1
Other existing accounts (such as a checking account)	1,917,000	1.6	24.1
Misuse of personal information (to obtain new accounts or loans)	1,031,200	0.9	13.0
Multiple types of theft during the same episode	1,086,100	0.9	13.6
No	108,197,000	90.5	NA
Don't know	3,378,000	2.8	NA

Source: Data from Langton & Baum (2010), p. 3.

Information on the offenders is limited at this time. However, Copes and Vieraitis (2007, 2009) interviewed 59 identity thieves incarcerated in federal prisons with respect to their backgrounds, methods, and motivations. The data revealed that offenders were a diverse group. The majority of them were between the ages of 25 and 44 years, had at least some college, and were employed in a wide range of occupations. They were motivated by the quick need for cash and perceived "identity theft as an easy, relatively risk-free way to get it" (Copes & Vieraitis, 2007, p. 2). Approximately a third of the offenders used their employment to carry out their crimes. For example, they worked for mortgage agencies, government agencies, or businesses that have access to credit card numbers and/or Social Security numbers. Many of the thieves possessed considerable knowledge about how banks and credit agencies operate. About two-thirds had prior arrests for such crimes as identity theft, drug use/sales, and property crimes. Most of the thieves utilized neutralization techniques to account for their crimes, which also encouraged them to continue offending. For instance, some denied that they caused any real harm to their victims. Others justified their crimes by claiming their actions were done to help others.

Considering the fact that the thief assumes someone else's identity, it is likely that dehumanization or denial of the victim is involved. The perpetrator does not have to see what the victim looks like, experience the victim's stress, or know anything about the victim's life, with the exception of financial data. Though we know little about the offenders, we do know that the emotional impact of identity theft—and fraud in general—on victims is substantial and should not be underestimated. In addition to having strong feelings of being victimized, feelings emerge that one should blame oneself, can no longer trust one's own ability to handle financial matters, or can no longer trust people. The experience is often described as an emotional rollercoaster, especially involving the long-drawn-out ordeal of dealing with challenged credibility, damaged credit, and the feelings of powerlessness and personal vulnerability.

SHOPLIFTING

Shoplifting, a form of larceny-theft, is a frequent and costly type of crime. Although shoplifting comprised about 17.2 percent of all arrests for larceny-theft in 2010 (Federal Bureau of Investigation, 2011a) (see **Figure 14-1**), it is obviously underreported by a large margin. In a face-to-face survey of more than 43,000 adults across the nation, Blanco *et al.* (2008) found that one in 10 Americans admitted shoplifting at some point in their lives. The survey also found that shoplifting occurs across all sociodemographic levels. In fact, it was more common among those with higher education and income, indicating that financial considerations are unlikely to be the main motivator for shoplifting.

These data are surprising in light of the rapid improvement in security measures designed to discourage and prevent the crime. For example, most sizeable retail establishments have private security officers on the premises. Furthermore, cameras now are ubiquitous in large retail stores, hidden in clocks, smoke alarms, and pushbars on fire-exit doors (Adler, 2002). However, shoplifting methods have become more sophisticated in recent years. For example, some shoplifters use "tag bags," which are hand baggage filled with materials like polyurethane and aluminum that incapacitate the electronic detection devices located at store entrances and exits (Caputo, 2004).

Comprehensive data on all economic crimes are difficult to obtain, but data acquisition for shoplifting offenses is especially difficult, since store personnel exercise wide discretion in reporting offenses. Many years ago, Hindelang (1974) found that whether charges were filed

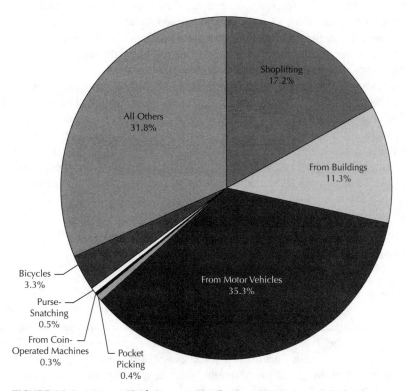

FIGURE 14-1 Larceny-Theft Percent Distribution, 2010 *Source*: Federal Bureau of Investigation (2011a).

depended on the retail value of the stolen object, what was stolen, and the manner in which it was taken, rather than demographic and personality characteristics of the shoplifter. Specifically, the offender's race did not seem to matter, nor did the offender's gender or economic status. What determined referral for arrest was whether the item was expensive, had resale value, or was stolen in a professional, skillful manner.

Later research by Davis, Lundman, and Martinez (1991) found that shoplifters are more likely to be arrested not only when they take expensive items, but also when they resist being apprehended, have no local address, and/or live in poor neighborhoods. In England, on the other hand, store managers consider the age of the shoplifter as well as the value of the stolen item (Farrington & Burrows, 1993). The British study found that, generally, store managers did not report to the police the very young (under age 17) or very old (over 60), the mentally impaired, or those shoplifters in an advanced stage of pregnancy, unless they were caught repeatedly. In a series of observational studies (also in England) by Abigail Buckle and David Farrington (1984), random samples of customers were followed by trained observers as they shopped. Approximately one in 50 was observed to steal. The amount of shoplifting, however, differed dramatically from store to store. Shoplifting characteristics in supermarkets are likely to differ significantly from those exhibited in retail department stores or hardware stores.

Buckle and Farrington (1994) conducted a replication of their 1984 study. Again, trained observers randomly followed approximately 500 customers in a small department store located in another city. The proportion of customers who shoplifted was between 1 percent and 2 percent, and a majority was male. Most of the shoplifters also purchased goods as they checked out of the store, probably to allay suspicion. In general, the items stolen were small, low-cost items. In contrast to the original study, where there was a preponderance of older shoplifters (age 55 or over), Buckle and Farrington found that most of the shoplifters were young (age 25 or less). These studies underscore the warning that estimations concerning the incidence of shoplifting must be placed within a situational, cultural, and historical context.

Apprehension statistics may tell us more about the store security personnel practices and biases than about the shoplifting population (Klemke, 1992). In fact, it is not uncommon for security personnel to claim that they have developed a "sixth sense" for picking out likely suspects. This "sixth sense" is, in some cases, a bias or stereotype against certain segments of the population more than any all-encompassing, accurate skill. For example, in one study (Dabney, Dugan, Topalli, & Hollinger, 2006) observers who received extensive training and specific instructions to ignore shopper demographics were unable to resist the power of implicit cultural stereotypes in identifying shoplifters. Specifically, the observers had a strong bias to select nonwhite adolescent males as shoplifters, whether they were or not.

Who Shoplifts?

Shoplifting is often considered a behavior that is displayed predominately by juveniles. An analysis of one million juvenile court records across nearly 2,000 jurisdictions reveals that shoplifting is the most common juvenile court referral for youths under age 15 (Kelley, Kennedy, & Homant, 2003). Shoplifting appears to decline, however, both in number of offenses and the number of those engaging in this behavior, as offenders mature and move into early adulthood (Krasnovsky & Lane, 1998; Osgood, O'Mailey, Bachman, & Johnstone, 1989). This dropping off appears to be partly due to the crystallization of moral development, as well as to the realization that a young adult is more likely to be charged with an offense than a preteen offender. In other words, the individual tempted to shoplift may believe he or she has more to lose if apprehended.

In a study designed to examine moral development and theft of clothing, Forney, Forney, and Crutsinger (2005) discovered that those juveniles who stole demonstrated a lower moral development than might be expected for someone their age. Their moral reasoning reflected the preconventional ethics of children who were much younger. The preteen juvenile offenders thought their motivations for stealing the clothing were justified. "It is okay as long as no one knows I'm stealing" or "It is okay if no one is watching." The researchers found, however, that there was a discernible shift in the moral reasoning of juvenile delinquents from preteens to teens. For example, "It is okay to steal if a friend needs the item."

There is ample evidence that adults as well as juveniles are involved in shoplifting behavior, however. Michele Tonglet (2001) found that contemporary shoplifters, both adolescents and adults, "...were significantly less likely to view shoplifting as bad, dishonest, wrong and stupid, and were less likely to be constrained by moral concerns" (p. 345). Paul Cromwell and Quint Thurman (2003) interviewed 137 apprehended shoplifters who were participants in a court-ordered diversion program for adult first offenders, and they gained interesting insights into how they justified their criminal activity. Participants were promised anonymity in answering such questions as their attitudes toward the victims, and their reasons and justifications for shoplifting. The study was primarily designed to examine the **techniques of neutralization** first proposed by Sykes and Matza (1957). According to Sykes and Matza, people try to neutralize unpleasant feelings of guilt and shame by rationalizing to themselves and others why they committed a deviant or criminal act. These techniques of neutralization basically represent different levels of moral rationalizations. For example, a shoplifter might say "I really didn't hurt anybody" or "The store can afford the hit." These two examples describe denial of any injury to the victim. We will discuss in more detail the various forms of neutralization in the white-collar and occupational crime section. The point here, however, is that Cromwell and Thurman learned that 96 percent of the shoplifters used some form of neutralization in rationalizing their criminal behavior of shoplifting. In other words, while not denying their actions, they very rarely took blame or responsibility for them.

Klemke (1992) conducted one of the first comprehensive studies on adolescent shoplifting. He collected self-report data from students in four small town high schools in the Pacific Northwest during the late 1970s. Klemke (1992) discovered that approximately three-fourths of the frequent shoplifters began shoplifting before the age of 10, but then stopped soon after their eighteenth birthday. However, Blanco and his colleagues (2008), who it will be recalled surveyed more than 43,000 adults, found that although two-thirds of the cases of shoplifting began before age 15, over a third of the shoplifters persisted after that age, many into adulthood. Blanco et al. estimate that 4 percent of the entire American adult population continues to shoplift. If we take into account the entire adult population in the United States, 4 percent represents a substantial number. Interestingly, data from college bookstores indicate that first-year students are more likely to be apprehended for shoplifting than other college students (Klemke, 1992). Readers undoubtedly can think of a variety of explanations for this, ranging from the high minded ("Sophomores, juniors, and seniors are more committed to the college community" or "Education decreases the likelihood of committing this crime") to the cynical ("Upper class students don't go near the bookstore any more").

In the Blanco et al. (2008) survey, shoplifters tended to have a higher incidence of additional antisocial behaviors than nonshoplifters. Besides shoplifting, the most common antisocial behavior in this sample was making money illegally or scamming somebody for money.

Psychological disorders were also more common among shoplifters in the Blanco et al. survey, especially those who continued to shoplift into adulthood. Although previous research often reported depression as common among shoplifters—especially female offenders—Blanco *et al.* found that depression was *not* the primary psychiatric disorder among their shoplifters. Instead, they discovered the more common disorders were problems in impulse control and self-regulation, similar to what would be reflected in pathological gambling, alcohol dependence, and substance abuse disorders. The authors concluded that "...our findings are most consistent with the understanding of shoplifting as a behavioral manifestation of impaired impulse control" (Blanco *et al.*, 2008, p. 911).

It has also been commonly assumed that shoplifting is committed largely by adolescent girls and women. The most common explanations offered for women's greater involvement are based on the belief that women have greater opportunity to steal small items from merchants than do men. As men join the ranks of frequent shoppers, however, their shoplifting rates are beginning to increase, and the gap between men and women is narrowing. In fact, the Blanco *et al.* (2008) survey discovered that shoplifting is more common among men than women. Janne Kivivuori (1998) found similar results among Finnish adolescents, and Cromwell and Thurman (2003) report similar results for apprehended adult shoplifters in Wichita, Kansas.

Baumer and Rosenbaum (1984) outline some of the psychological characteristics and behavioral patterns of shoplifters. They note that such things as extreme nervousness, aimless walking up and down the aisles, looking around frequently, glancing up from the merchandise frequently, and leaving the store and returning a number of times are some of the indicators that suggest shoplifting. These behaviors are likely to be exhibited chiefly by first-time shoplifters.

In spite of its traditional prominence in economic crime, shoplifting has received little psychological research attention. The most heavily quoted source on the subject, Mary Owen Cameron's *The Booster and the Snitch: Department Store Shoplifting* (1964), reported data accumulated long ago, in the 1940s and early 1950s. Cameron divided her shoplifters into two groups: Commercial shoplifters were "**boosters**," and amateur pilferers were "**snitches**." All of her data were subsequently explained with reference to this dichotomy. The boosters were professionals, accepted members of the criminal subculture. They stole for substantial financial gain by choosing items from preselected locations. Boosters used a wide range of techniques such as "booster boxes," packages designed for concealing items inserted through hidden slots or hinged openings, or "stalls," containers with hidden compartments (large handbags, coats with hidden pockets). As noted at the beginning of this section, these and similar methods are still used today. Snitches, on the other hand, were "respectable" persons who rarely had criminal records. They did not consider themselves thieves, and the idea that they might actually be arrested and prosecuted rarely crossed their minds. Very often, once apprehended, they claimed they stole the item on impulse and did not know what came over them.

Over the years, the term *booster* has survived, particularly in reference to people who make shoplifting a business and tend to work in small groups. "Security specialists call them 'boosting crews,' highly organized teams of thieves who sweep through supermarkets and pharmacies scooping up products such as razor blades, infant formula, meat, seafood and Tide detergent" (Seiler, 2012, p. A3). It appears that boosters have joined forces in what is now regarded as organized retail crime, and they have access to elaborate fencing operations to dispose of the goods they have taken. One local police investigator, noting that retail crime has increased over the past decade, remarked that boosters have become more sophisticated, even knowing on which days stores increase their loss prevention staff and when investigators take their lunch breaks (Seiler, 2012).

Some social science research has focused on elderly shoplifters. Feinberg (1984) found that shoplifting was neither a female-dominated offense nor undertaken for subsistence purposes. Elderly shoplifters, he notes, are neither indigent, lonely, nor victims of poor memory. He attributes their criminal offenses to changes in status that separate the elderly from mainstream society. Often, they must reevaluate their past values and try out different selves and meanings. To what extent Feinberg's research may be generalized to other age groups remains an open question.

Motives

Shoplifting behavior is influenced by a number of factors, including peer pressure, moral development, previous shoplifting experience, economic considerations, self-esteem, and perceptions of apprehension risks (Tonglet, 2001). Shoplifters differ from one another with respect to their skill, use of the stolen goods, motivations, and duration of involvement (Caputo, 2004).

A majority of shoplifters do not consider shoplifting as morally wrong, and generally feel little guilt about the theft (Tonglet, 2001). It appears that many are utilizing techniques of neutralization. These are psychological techniques people use to neutralize or turn off their conscience or "inner protest" about committing deviant behavior. When a person uses this method, it enables them to live with themselves when they do, or are about to do, something wrong or illegal. Cromwell and Thurman (2003) were able to identify nine such techniques used by shoplifters. In their study, they found only five of 137 apprehended shoplifters did not use a technique of neutralization to justify their behavior. And they didn't use these neutralizations so much to reduce their guilt as to provide themselves with the necessary justifications for their acts to others.

The motives behind commercial shoplifting may be clearer than those behind the amateur type. Whereas boosters take merchandise of value, snitches tend to take inexpensive items they can use. Some research has noted that male snitches prefer items of more value, such as stereo equipment, and jewelry. Women snitches seem to take clothing, cosmetics, and food. The boosters shoplift for the money; the snitches for more obscure reasons.

Theories concerning the intentions of snitches range from economic ones, like attempts to stretch the family budget (Cameron, 1964), to emotional ones, like attempts to satisfy needs centering around matrimonial stress, loneliness, and depression (Russell, 1973). In recent years, some have concluded that shoplifting often stems from problems with self-regulation, much like gambling and alcoholism. On the other hand, the contention that shoplifting has primarily an economic motivation seems oversimplified. Shoplifting is pursued by different people for different reasons.

Shoplifting by Proxy

Shoplifting by proxy refers to a situation in which people shoplift for someone else because that other person asks or tells them to do so (Kivivuori, 2007). In these instances, the shoplifter follows someone else's orders or suggestions in committing the crime. Essentially, the "offender is a proxy or a substitute for the instigator" (Kivivuori, 2007, p. 817). Kivivuori suggests that shoplifting by proxy can be viewed as existing along a continuum, with strong coercion or explicit threats existing at one pole, and at the other extreme, some form of subtle manipulation or suggestion. Of course, other types of crime may be committed by proxy—especially burglary and other forms of theft—but shoplifting appears to be the most common. Adults sometimes induce juveniles to commit crimes for them because the legal system often does not deal as aggressively with juveniles as with adults. For example, juveniles are more likely to be offered diversion for first-time offenses, and juvenile records are sealed in many jurisdictions.

The incidences of proxy shoplifting may be coercive or may be the result of helping or altruistic behavior. Kivivuori (2007) conducted a self-report study of 6,279 students, ages 15–16, in the Finland schools. The students were asked to respond anonymously to questions about their shoplifting behavior. Seven percent of the respondents reported having shoplifted for someone else. Males and females were equally involved in shoplifting by proxy. In the vast majority of the cases, the instigator was someone other than a family member, or a boy or girlfriend. In general, the instigator was a peer.

The most common reason provided by the offenders for shoplifting by proxy is that the instigator paid the offender to steal. In one-third of the cases, offenders shoplifted because a peer or peer group pressured them to do so. And in one quarter of the cases, the offenders said they shoplifted so that they would be popular among their peers. The most common reason given by instigators for their actions is that they did not dare to shoplift themselves or were afraid they would get caught.

To what extent other crimes by proxy are committed, such as violence or burglary, is unknown. Certainly, and as noted by Kivivuori (2007), Stanley Milgram's classical experiments on obedience (presented in Chapter 11) might illustrate some of the factors at work in more serious crimes by proxy.

Shoplifting as an Occupation

Gail Caputo and Anna King (2011) conducted qualitative research, interviewing 12 women whose primary criminal offense was shoplifting. Although the sample was extremely small, it provides some insight into shoplifting motivations and methods. The women viewed shoplifting as an occupation that paid quite well and supported their basic needs. They also admitted the practice supported their drug habit. During the early phases of their shoplifting careers, the women used a number of methods that—while not very efficient—enabled them to make enough to live on. These shoplifting methods included the "exchange for cash," and the "receipt for cash" approaches. In the first method, the shoplifter returns to the retail store with the stolen merchandise and negotiates a merchandise return for cash, indicating that they "lost" or "misplaced" the receipt. The "receipt for cash" approach was used for retailers with strict policies about returns. The shoplifter would first scour parking lots, sidewalks, and trash containers for discarded receipts, then examine the receipts and decide which merchandise on the lists would be worth shoplifting. She would enter the store, shoplift the selected items, and return to the store with the receipt for a cash refund.

Eventually, the women in Caputo and King's study sought an approach that would lead to more regular income. This required a solid customer base willing to purchase the stolen merchandise, similar to the boosting teams described above. As they learned and expanded the "trade," their customer bases became larger and more stable. Many of them also employed a "hack," which was usually a male driver who would drive them to retail establishments and wait for them. In most cases, the hack would receive about half of the proceeds.

Types of Shoplifters

Moore (1984), studying 300 convicted shoplifters referred for presentence investigation, identified five patterns of offending. Although no shoplifters were considered professional to the degree of Cameron's booster category (the professionals may have escaped detection), 11.7 percent were semiprofessional, reporting shoplifting behavior at least once a week. Their "take" amounted to approximately $1,250 a year. Other categories were the amateur, the emotionally disturbed, and the occasional.

The most frequent type of shoplifter in Moore's study was the "amateur" (56.4%) who stole small personal items when the opportunity arose. The methods used by amateurs were less sophisticated than those of the semiprofessionals, and unlike the semiprofessionals, the amateurs admitted that their behavior was morally wrong or illegal. Both types of shoplifting were premeditated, habitual, and directed toward financial gain. Persons in the amateur category were more likely to exhibit mild personality disorders or to be plagued by psychosocial stressors associated with interpersonal problems, such as family disruption.

Approximately 17 percent of Moore's offender population was impaired by mental or emotional problems. However, very few individuals (1.7%) had severe mental or emotional problems that directly "compelled" them to shoplift. The persons in this latter category were called "episodic" offenders, a subcategory of the mental impairment group.

Fifteen percent of the sample comprised "impulse" shoplifters, and another 15 percent were "occasional" offenders. Impulse shoplifters typically had seen an item that they desired but were unable to afford. They had picked it up and pocketed it or carried it around the store, often in a daze, trying to decide whether to steal it. It is likely that walking around the store in this fashion alerted store personnel. Eventually, they tried to walk out but were detected. Later, impulse shoplifters could not recall at what point they had made the decision to shoplift. Occasional offenders were less impulsive, but more likely to steal for excitement or a dare. Both impulse and occasional offenders were extremely embarrassed when detected, pleaded with officials to give them another chance, and were considered unlikely to shoplift again.

Moore found interesting differences between male and female adult offenders concerning psychological stress. More women reported being under great stress in their lives than did men (28.9% of the women compared with 13.5% of the men). However, this difference may also be due to the greater reluctance of men to report stress or other emotional problems in general.

Kleptomania: Fact or Fiction?

One thing does appear clear. Clinicians and researchers have been unable to substantiate evidence of **kleptomania**, the *irresistible* impulse to steal unneeded objects. Some have even questioned its very existence as a behavior pattern. According to the DSM-IV, the kleptomaniac "experiences a rising subjective sense of tension before the theft and feels pleasure, gratification, or relief when committing the theft" (p. 612). A strong argument against kleptomania is that shoplifters display exceedingly low recidivism rates. Once apprehended, the amateur rarely shoplifts again (Cameron, 1964; Russell, 1973), and as noted above, the same could be said of impulse and occasional offenders. Professional shoplifters, or boosters, steal for the money; their expertise at this enterprise makes it highly unlikely that irresistible impulse had anything to do with their behavior. If kleptomania were an important ingredient, we would expect the individual to steal repeatedly as the tension increases. The professional or semiprofessional steals repeatedly and is apparently "successful" at shoplifting, but he or she is unlikely to be compelled to steal; a very small percentage of Moore's population displayed compulsive behavior.

Lloyd Klemke (1992) suggests that kleptomania is a psychiatric label intended to ease the guilt of affluent women caught stealing during the turn of the twentieth century. Merchants, Klemke points out, did not want to antagonize their affluent clientele. Furthermore, affluent families wanted to keep their moral reputations untarnished and keep women at home. Nor did the courts want to convict "respectable ladies" as common criminals. Thus, kleptomania (the Greek word for "stealing madness," a term presumably coined by Esquirol in 1838) legitimized the actions of the merchants and the courts to dismiss or acquit the "afflicted" woman and excuse her from being held personally responsible for her actions.

In summary, if kleptomania does exist, it seems to be a rare phenomenon. For example, in a study conducted by Sarasalo, Bergman, and Toth (1997), 50 shoplifters (29 males, 21 females) were interviewed immediately after being caught red-handed in central Stockholm, Sweden. None of the persons interviewed fulfilled the DSM-IV criteria for kleptomania. Sarasalo *et al.*, however, did find that many of the shoplifters reported a "thrill" and challenge in connection with the crime.

Much of the literature on the causes of kleptomania focuses on its relationship to anxiety, depression, or sexual disturbances (Goldman, 1991; Sarasalo, Bergman, & Toth, 1996). Citing sexual disturbances as a cause for kleptomania is primarily based in the psychoanalytic tradition. But as Marcus Goldman (1991, p. 990) notes, "there are no modern data available to refute or confirm these earlier psychoanalytic findings."

On the other hand, research has found *depression* to be a common symptom of people who engage in "nonsensical shoplifting" (Lamontagne, Boyer, Hetu, & Lacerte-Lamontagne, 2000). This term has many similarities to kleptomania with the exception of the compulsion aspect. Yates (1986) claims that 80 percent of those who engaged in nonsensical shoplifting were depressed. McElroy and colleagues (McElroy, Pope, Hudson, Keck, & White, 1991) found that all 20 patients they studied who engaged in nonsensical shoplifting met the DSM-III-R criteria for a lifetime diagnosis of a major mood (depression) disorder. In addition, many of these patients said they engaged in nonsensical shoplifting far more often when they were depressed. It seems that some depressed people may engage in nonsensical shoplifting as a stimulating, exciting activity that moves them away from feelings of helplessness. Depression could also explain the behavior in elderly shoplifters. In fact, Goldman (1991) finds that depressive states are often reported throughout the literature as precursors to many kinds of theft that are not related to profit.

Shoplifting can be controlled to some extent by the use of electronic article surveillance (EAS) or ink tags (Eck, 2000). EAS involves attaching electronic tags on merchandise that only store clerks can remove at the time of payment. Failure to remove the tag or to scan an item sets off an alarm at the door as the customer leaves the store. Ink tags deface the merchandise if it is removed from the store without paying, thereby destroying the value of the stolen goods (Eck, 2000). Likewise, bar codes or scanners on grocery items may deter theft of food. Eck, in his review of the research literature, reports that EAS measures can reduce shoplifting 32 percent to 80 percent, and are found to be more effective than either security guards or store redesign (see Bamfield, 1994; DiLonardo, 1996; Farrington *et al.*, 1993 for more details on relevant studies). Despite these optimistic reports, shoplifters—as noted above—have found ways of overriding the electronic tags and other loss-prevention methods. The fact that shoplifting has not decreased—in fact has increased in many areas—suggests that the behavior is not well controlled.

Softlifting

Softlifting is the illegal duplication of copyrighted software by individuals for personal use (Goles *et al.*, 2008). Many people today do not consider this category a crime—of if they do, they do not believe it is a serious one. A similar attitude is displayed toward the illegal downloading of music or videos. According to most experts in the field, softlifting is a serious and costly problem for software developers and distributors. As Goles *et al.* (2008) assert, "Software is property—intellectual property, but property nonetheless—and taking another's property without compensation is stealing" (p. 482). Recent data indicated that 35 percent of all software installed on computers in 2006 were pirated versions, resulting in an estimated $11.75 billion in loss for the industry (Bhal & Leekha, 2008).

The term *piracy* of software and digital media can be divided into three major categories: (1) commercial piracy, which refers to the illegal duplication of copyrighted material for resale,

(2) corporate piracy, which refers to the illegal duplication of copyrighted material for use within an organization, and (3) illegal duplication of copyrighted material for personal use, commonly called softlifting (Goles *et al.*, 2008). This section will focus on softlifting because it is so widespread and common in society today. Although we do not discuss it here, the illegal downloading of music and videos has many similarities to softlifting.

As noted above, it is likely that most individuals do not think that softlifting is either serious or unethical. In fact, research suggests that most people consider it socially and ethically acceptable (Bhal & Leekha, 2008). In the study by Bhal and Leekha (2008), ethical considerations about software piracy were strongly influenced by the social context. Their results highlighted the role of peers and relevant others in providing socially acceptable benchmarks for acts of piracy. If friends and colleagues condoned the behavior, people were far more likely to accept the view that softlifting was acceptable. Moreover, decisions to pirate software are often made regardless of the ethical perceptions of the practice (Simpson, Banerjee, & Simpson, 1994). In other words, even if someone does consider this unethical, he or she might still pirate software.

WHITE-COLLAR AND OCCUPATIONAL CRIME

The term **white-collar crime** was coined by Edwin H. Sutherland in his presidential address to the American Sociological Society in 1939. In his speech, Sutherland urged his fellow sociologists to pay attention to the law-violating behavior of businesses, particularly large corporations. He had uncovered these violations by reviewing government files on 70 large American corporations and had learned that breaking rules was commonplace. In 1949, Sutherland published his now classic book *White-Collar Crime*, in which he detailed his findings without naming the corporations. A later edition of the book (Sutherland, 1983) did include the names.

Following Sutherland's lead, a considerable amount of pioneering research was done on white-collar crime between 1939 and 1963 (Geis, 1988). This was followed by a decade of inactivity. Since 1975, there has been a revival of interest in studying the area, although criminological literature gives far less attention to white-collar crime than to other forms of criminal behavior. The highly publicized individual and corporate scandals of recent years, like the Enron debacle and the massive fraud perpetrated by the financier Bernard Madoff have only served to illustrate that this attention is needed. Over the last decade, increasingly more examples of corporate malfeasance and the crimes of the wealthy and/or politically powerful have come to public attention. The roster of those convicted include state and federal legislators, heads of corporations, sports figures, actors, and educational officials, to name but a few professions represented in conviction statistics.

According to Sutherland (1949), "white-collar crime may be defined approximately as a crime committed by a person of respectability and high social status in the course of his occupation" (p. 9). Although Sutherland used the word *crime*, he did not intend it strictly in the legal sense. He recognized that numerous laws and regulations violated by persons of high social status carried civil rather than criminal sanctions, and he wanted these violations to be condemned. In fact, this was a critical factor to Sutherland, who saw a double standard phenomenon at work. The law-violating behavior of the poor carried criminal penalties; the law-violating behavior of the rich often did not. This was so despite the fact that "[t]he financial cost of white-collar crime is probably several times as great as the financial cost of all the crimes which are customarily regarded as 'the crime problem' " (Sutherland, 1949, p. 12).

Although Sutherland's call to study white-collar crime was heeded, his working definition produced numerous problems for subsequent criminologists. Some, most notably Paul Tappan

(1947), argued that white-collar "crime" could not really be crime unless it violated the criminal law. The terms *respectability* and *high social status* were considered vague. Over the past four decades, researchers have tried to improve on Sutherland's definition. Marshall Clinard and Richard Quinney (1980) preferred to dichotomize the concept into (1) occupational crime, committed by an individual for his or her own profit, and (2) corporate crime, committed by the corporation through its agents. This dichotomy is probably the most commonly used by criminologists today. Horning (1970) proposed a threefold division to distinguish the various behaviors that might be at issue. He reserved *white-collar crime* for acts committed by salaried employees in which their place of employment is either the victim or the locale for the commission of an illegal act from which they personally benefit. Embezzlement would be a good example of this. *Corporate crime* refers to illegal acts by employees in the course of their employment that primarily benefit the company or corporation. Illegal dumping of hazardous wastes is an example. *Blue-collar crime* refers to the whole array of illegal acts committed by nonsalaried workers against their place of employment. Thefts of machinery, tools, or paper are examples. Some criminologists also have contended that certain corporate crimes should qualify as violent crimes. James Coleman (1998), for example, cites unsafe working conditions, illegal disposal of toxic waste, and the manufacture of unsafe products as examples of violent crime.

Green's Four Categories of Occupational Crime

Gary Green (1997) made significant contributions to clarifying the definitional dilemmas associated with the term *white-collar crime* by proposing the concept of **occupational crime**. Unfortunately, Green's approach has not been widely adopted, despite its conceptual clarity. To Green, occupational crime encompasses all of the behaviors previously subsumed under white-collar crime, blue-collar crime, and their variants. Occupational crime is "any act punishable by law that is committed through opportunity created in the course of an occupation that is legal" (Green, 1997, p. 15). Green then subdivides occupational crime into four categories: (1) organizational (which includes corporate crime), (2) professional, (3) state-authority, and (4) individual (see **Table 14-4**).

In **organizational occupational crime**, a legal entity such as a company, corporation, firm, or foundation profits by the law-violating behavior. An example would be the chief financial officer of a company falsifying the company's tax records with the tacit approval of its board of directors. Other examples are antitrust violations, overcharging the government for products or services, violations of Occupational Safety and Health Administration (OSHA) standards, and bribery of public officials. **Professional occupational crime** includes illegal behavior by persons such as lawyers, physicians, psychologists, and teachers committed through their occupation. A physician's Medicaid fraud and a lawyer's suborning the perjury of a client are illustrations.

State-authority occupational crime encompasses the wide range of law violation by persons imbued with legal authority; the individual who commits state-authority occupational crime is essentially violating the public trust. Bribe taking by a public official, police brutality, and the torture of individuals held in custody are illustrative. Finally, Green uses the category **individual occupational crime** to cover all violations not included in one of the previously discussed categories. The employee who steals equipment from his employer and the person who deliberately underreports income to the IRS are covered in this category.

As evident from the earlier examples, the concept of occupational crime proposed by Green covers a wide variety of offenses, not all of which are economic in nature and not all of which are committed by persons of high social status. A therapist who sexually assaults a patient

TABLE 14-4	Summary of Green's Occupational Crime Typology
Category	**Description**
Organizational	Law-violating behavior promoted by the corporation or agency
Professional	Law-violating behavior committed as a result of being in a profession that offers the opportunity for crime
State-authority	Law-violating behavior by those in government
Individual	Law-violating behavior committed by an individual working for a company or organization, but committed for his or her own advancement or financial gain

and a correctional officer who uses excessive force against an inmate are both committing violent occupational crimes, one in the professional and one in the state authority category. Neither the therapist's nor the correctional officer's behavior would qualify as white-collar crime in its classic sense.

Green argues convincingly that his four-part division allows us to move away from the conceptual quagmire of "white-collar crime" and study a significant amount of workplace-facilitated illegal behavior in a logical, ordered manner. Although the term white-collar crime continues to be widely used, perhaps in deference to Sutherland's contributions to criminology, Green's approach offers an appealing alternative. As noted, however, the approach that seems to be preferred in the criminological literature is the "white-collar" dichotomy proposed by Clinard and Quinney, occupational and corporate crime.

The Prevalence and Incidence of Occupational Crime

Regardless of which term is used, the extent of occupationally linked illegal behavior is extremely difficult to measure. The standard methods of measuring crime discussed in Chapter 1 rarely apply. The typical UCR report, for example, does not tell us whether a reported crime or an arrest was related to the perpetrator's occupation. Fraud can be committed by a bank executive, a college student, a Fortune 500 Corporation, or a recipient of welfare benefits. Even when uncovered, the violations we have been discussing are often not reported to law enforcement and recorded in official data. Rather than publicize a theft by an employee, for example, a business might prefer to demand restitution, dismiss the employee, or force a resignation. It does not benefit the company's public image to file a criminal complaint.

When an organization is itself the violator, civil suits are often preferred to criminal charges. The plaintiff in a civil suit is more likely to get some form of restitution, in the form of damages, than the victim in a criminal case. In addition, the government regulatory process is widely acknowledged to be inefficient in preventing, uncovering, and punishing violators. When it comes to the professions, law violation is often shielded from the public, because society authorizes them to police themselves by means of standards, codes of ethics, and licensing.

Nevertheless, some attempts have been made to collect data on "white-collar" offenses, particularly those committed by individuals (Clinard & Quinney's "occupational crime" category). The National White Collar Crime Center, a nonprofit organization based in Richmond, Virginia, collects information, publishes a newsletter, and sponsors training sessions and conferences devoted to this issue. Topics that have recently come to the attention of the NW3C are Internet gambling, Internet fraud, online child pornography, insurance crime, and identity theft. Information is available at www.nw3c.org. It should be noted, though, that none of the offenses mentioned above are offenses committed by the businesses; rather they are committed by individuals. The business or its consumers may be the victims; they are not the offenders.

Without settling the difficult definitional morass associated with "white-collar crime," we will nevertheless proceed to discuss in more detail one example of this serious crime problem, specifically, crime committed by corporations and their agents. Sutherland, you will recall, focused on corporations in his original research. Following that discussion, we will consider crimes at the opposite end of the continuum, wherein individual employees victimize their employers. Although not necessarily white-collar crimes, these latter behaviors qualify as individual occupational crimes according to Green's approach.

Corporate Crime

In the 2012 election cycle, one of the presidential candidates made the statement, "Corporations are people, my friend." This statement was widely interpreted as being insensitive to the inequality between the wealth of corporations and the average citizen. Nevertheless, there was a core of truth in the statement, at least in the legal context. For example, for purposes of the criminal law, a corporation is a person. It can be charged, tried, sentenced, and punished. In addition, individuals within that organization are making decisions that render the corporate behavior a crime. Therefore, in discussing explanations for corporate crime, we will focus on the behavior of persons, despite the fact that the organizational culture as well as the economic structure of society may facilitate and reward the illegal behavior.

Corporate crime refers to any criminal offense committed by a corporation, in effect by people within it, and through which the corporation benefits. It covers offenses ranging from price fixing to failure to recall a product known to have a serious defect that could potentially cause physical harm. The offenses are so varied, in fact, that most criminologists who study corporate crime subdivide it into more manageable categories. Some of the most noteworthy categories are crimes against consumers, crimes against the environment, institutional corruption, and fiduciary fraud (Rosoff, Pontell, & Tillman, 1998); fraud and deception, manipulating the marketplace, violating civil liberties, and—as noted earlier—violent white-collar crimes (Coleman, 1998); crimes of fraud, offenses against public administration, and regulatory offenses (Albanese, 1995); and false and misleading advertising, defrauding the government, antitrust crimes, manufacture and sale of unsafe consumer products, unfair labor practices, unsafe working conditions, crimes against the environment, and political bribe giving (Green, 1997).

The estimated costs of these corporate offenses—both financial and from a human-suffering standpoint—are staggering. However, up-to-date, reliable, or accurate statistics are nearly impossible to find. Although the available research is very dated, the financial cost of corporate crime has been estimated to be between $20 and $40 billion a year (Kramer, 1984). Most scholars in this area would consider that a very conservative estimate at that time and even more so today. Kramer (1984) estimated that over 100,000 deaths a year could be attributed to occupationally related diseases, most caused by the knowing and willful violation of occupational health and safety standards by businesses and industries. Annually, 20 million serious injuries are associated with unsafe and defective consumer products, unsafe foods and drugs, and defective autos, tires, or appliances. About 110,000 of these injuries result in permanent disability, and 30,000 result in death (Schrager & Short, 1978). Obviously, not all of these accidents, injuries, and deaths are due to corporate neglect or illegal action, but the data suggest that many are (Hochstedler, 1984). Reiman (1995) has estimated that a conservative total of 90,105 Americans die every year as a result of occupational hazard and disease. Although some would argue that these deaths are not necessarily attributable to corporate malfeasance, others would say that corporations should be held responsible for the harms suffered by their workers.

Public attention to corporate crime has focused primarily on the economic crimes that have been highly publicized. These include a variety of practices that constitute fraud, including but not limited to price-fixing, false advertising, deceptive pricing, and securities fraud. Environmental and health-related crimes such as the illegal disposal of hazardous wastes and others already discussed have also attracted considerable public attention, however. In the 1990s, both the tobacco and the asbestos industry were barraged with lawsuits brought on behalf of individuals who had either died or been seriously harmed by exposure to these hazardous products.

Explanations for corporate criminality often focus on the criminogenic or crime-producing nature of the business environment; that is, in order to survive, law breaking is essential. Conklin (1977), for example, argued that law breaking in American business was normative and that executives often believe that some dishonesty or deceit has to be tolerated in the best interest of the company. In response to comments such as these, corporations proclaim that they have entered an era of social responsibility and that the extent of corporate malfeasance is exaggerated. Business schools note that business ethics courses are a requirement in virtually all programs. Gilbert Geis (1997), however, a prominent scholar in the area of white-collar crime, chastises business schools for using "lulling terms, especially 'ethics,' to camouflage what essentially are considerations of criminal behavior" (Geis, p. xii).

Justifications and Neutralizations

You may recall that in Chapter 5, we referred to strategies people use to neutralize some of their violent conduct and separate it from their personal codes. The strategies, proposed by Bandura (1978), are worth repeating here. Although they operate with reference to a wide range of reprehensible conduct, they are particularly relevant to the discussion of corporate crime. The strategies may be used individually or in combination.

One set of neutralizing strategies operates at the level of behavior. What is culpable is made honorable through moral justifications and euphemistic jargon. In other words, a normally reprehensible act becomes personally and socially acceptable when it is associated with beneficial or moral ends. "We did it in the best interest of the company, the employees and their families, and the country." Similarly, corporate decision makers may regard the laws they are violating as unfair, unjust, or simply not in keeping with good business practices. Government regulations, we are told, are tying the hands of businesses and preventing businesses from providing more jobs. Cressey (1953) called such justifications "vocabularies of adjustment." Conklin (1977) asserted that vocabularies of adjustment may play an even more crucial role in corporate crime than in juvenile delinquency, where they are frequently encountered.

A second set of neutralizing or dissociative strategies obscures or distorts the relationship between actions and their effects. In this group of strategies, people do not see themselves as personally responsible or accountable for their actions. They may disregard or deny the consequences of their actions—"It simply didn't happen the way the press reported it." Alternately, they may displace responsibility to the victim—"Consumers often don't use the appliance properly"— or diffuse the responsibility among the decision-making group—"After careful deliberation the board decided this would be the right decision."

A third set of strategies addresses the effects of the action on the recipients. Here, the dignifying qualities of the victims are removed. "Most consumers are greedy and stupid." "Third World countries are overcrowded anyway." We saw this strategy in action earlier in this text, when aggressors regarded their victims as less than human. This dehumanizing approach also seems to be a hallmark of prejudice and scapegoating. However, we also saw the strategy used in a slightly different way in property and economic crimes, like burglary and identity theft, where the perpetrator does not have to confront the "personhood" or humanity of the victim.

In sum, through cognitive restructuring supported by corporate norms, decision makers can justify and rationalize behavior that appears reprehensible to outsiders. The restructuring process prevents the manager or executive from labeling himself or herself "criminal." In fact, in some corporations, the extent to which the norms and justifying mechanisms are embraced may well determine how far up the corporate ladder one climbs.

Individual Occupational Crime

When illegal behavior is pursued for the direct benefit of the individual, and the individual is neither a professional nor someone with state authority, Green refers to it as individual occupational crime. In the Clinard-Quinney white-collar crime dichotomy referred to at the beginning of this section, the behavior would simply be "occupational" crime, distinguished from "corporate" crime. The Bernard Madoff case that came to light in 2008 and 2009 is a good example of this category. In this largely solitary pursuit, the offender is guided primarily by his or her own personal justifications and reasoning. An embezzler, for example, is operating outside organizational norms, although he may justify the behavior in much the same way as the corporate criminal may. The dissociation strategies identified by Bandura apply here as well. In other words, an embezzler may convince himself that the activity really is not a crime, since he is merely borrowing the money temporarily and will put it to good use. Later, he will reimburse the company (secretly, of course).

We should note that, with the exception of offering and taking bribes, *political* crimes are not often studied by researchers. When researchers study "white-collar crime" or offenders, they are typically focusing on individual offenses—usually within the workplace—and separate from their place in either the political or the corporate structure. That is, the white-collar offenders studied in the literature have been convicted of fraud, insider trading, antitrust violations, embezzlement, or such economic crimes. Walters and Geyer (2004) emphasized that white-collar offenders should be subdivided into those who commit only white-collar crimes and those who are versatile in their offending, committing both nonwhite-collar and white-collar offenses. In their study of criminal thinking patterns and lifestyles of these offenders, they discovered that those who committed only white-collar crimes (60% of their male sample) were older, more educated, and less likely to identify themselves as criminals than were those who were more diverse in their offending patterns. However, the white-collar-only group was also less likely to justify their behavior. Walters and Geyer's findings were replicated in a later study by Ragatz, Fremouw, and Baker (2012).

Other research has found that white-collar offenders score higher on indicators of depression and alcohol use (Benson & Moore, 1992; Poortinga, Lemmen, & Jibson, 2006) and anxiety and narcissism (Blickle *et al.*, 2006) than do nonwhite-collar offenders. However, Ragatz *et al.* (2012) did not find indication of higher alcohol use in their sample.

Some interesting research has been done examining other personality characteristics of white-collar offenders. Listwan, Piquero, and Van Voorhis (2010) found that offenders who scored high on a "neuroticism" dimension were more likely to repeat their offenses. Ragatz *et al.*

(2012) found that offenders who committed only white-collar crimes exhibited fewer criminal attitudes and were less likely to follow a criminal lifestyle compared to other offenders. They were also less likely to have problems with alcohol and other drugs. These findings are intriguing and await replication in research with larger samples and diverse groups of white-collar offenders. However, it seems that the psychological microscope is beginning to be directed at this group of offenders who traditionally have escaped study.

Employee Theft

One common type of illegal behavior in which the workplace is the victim is employee theft, which is an enormous drain on American business. An early estimate has it costing business and industry $5 to $10 billion a year (Clark & Hollinger, 1983). In a survey of employees from 47 retail, manufacturing, and service organizations, one-third admitted stealing company property (Clark & Hollinger, 1983). The property included merchandise, supplies, tools, and equipment. In addition, almost two-thirds of the employees surveyed reported other types of misconduct, such as sick leave abuse, drug or alcohol use on the job, long lunch and coffee breaks, slow and sloppy workmanship, and falsifying time sheets. Collectively, these are counterproductive behaviors. They do not involve actual removal of material goods from the organization, but they do reduce production and services.

Modern versions of employee theft involve the Internet and electronic payments. For example, the National White Collar Crime Center—first reported in 2003 that some employees were taking advantage of the Automated Clearinghouse (ACH) network to make personal purchases via the telephone or web, using the company's corporate checking account numbers that the employees obtain, often from their own paychecks. Telephone or Internet merchants often accepted the account number without verifying the account ownership. Thus, "some companies remain unaware of the fraudulent entries against their accounts for many months, leading to extended problems in regaining their funds" (*The Informant*, 2003, p. 14). Other examples of theft and fraud via use of electronic transactions abound.

Explanations for employee theft and counterproductive behaviors are multiple, but most cluster around the themes of age, dissatisfaction, and one's normative group at the workplace. The highest levels of theft and counterproductive behaviors are reported by younger, unmarried male employees (age 16 to mid-20s). Apparently, these younger employees do not feel any commitment or loyalty to the organization, probably because they do not expect to spend their lives in that situation. Many are college and high school students working only until they graduate. High levels of theft and counterproductive behaviors are also found among employees expressing dissatisfaction with some aspect of their employment, especially with their immediate supervisor. Another component of job dissatisfaction is the workers' perception of the company's attitude toward them. If the workers perceive the organization as caring little about them, job dissatisfaction and the concomitant theft and counterproductive behaviors tend to follow. In these situations, the individuals typically know that what they are doing is "wrong," and if caught, they will admit their guilt and hope for a light sentence. Interestingly, financial restitution may involve more than they actually stole. A woman who admitted to ACH debit fraud made unauthorized transactions of $6,661.08 but was sentenced to 24 months probation and restitution of $8,126.56 (*The Informant*, 2003).

While age and job dissatisfaction are highly correlated with theft and counterproductive behavior, normative support offers a viable explanation. Normative support refers to the standards, perceptions, and values the work group has established for itself, with or without the organization's implicit (or explicit) approval. In short, normative support refers to group norms. For example, the group may consider pilfered material a supplement to one's hourly wages, a fringe benefit. Vocabularies of adjustment are frequently employed. "It goes with the job." "The company expects you to take a little on the side." Another example is the work group verbally neutralizing the societal and organizational prohibitions against theft. "Everyone does it." "No one cares if we take a few things." "This is not really stealing." Sieh (1987) found that garment workers took "only what was owed them" and rarely stole items of substantial value.

Whether the group considers it acceptable to take something and where it decides a line should be drawn ("You can help yourself to ballpoint pens, but staplers are hands off"), depends on many variables. For example, the size of the organization is likely to be a factor. Smigel (1970) found that when workers were "forced" (in a questionnaire) to select an organization they would be most inclined to victimize, they first chose large businesses, then government, and lastly, small businesses. They considered large corporations and big government impersonal bureaucratic giants able to absorb losses more easily than smaller organizations.

Regardless of the explanation, employee theft seems to require some subjective justification on the part of the worker. He or she often does not perceive his or her conduct as illegal or even unethical, either because the behavior is in line with group norms, in line with internal standards, or both. From the group's or worker's perspective, the theft or the counterproductive behavior either are expected or they adjust the imbalances inherent in working for the company. It is interesting to note that employee theft diminishes when an organization clarifies for the workforce precisely what constitutes misconduct and what is expected (Clark & Hollinger, 1983). This approach, combined with working conditions that convince employees their organization cares about them, seems to be the most effective in reducing employee theft and counterproductive behavior. Furthermore, improvement in the work environment functions both ways; the worker is also expected to demonstrate loyalty and commitment to the organization, setting up appropriate models for new workers. But loyalty to a company may go too far, as when it represents a higher obligation than commitment to law and ethics. Individual blind loyalty often leads to corporate crime.

Summary and Conclusions

At first glance, the offenses discussed in this chapter appear to represent a hodgepodge of unrelated crimes, ranging from petty larceny to corporate crime that claims numerous victims. What they have in common is that they are distinct from the crimes discussed to this point, and, although there are exceptions, they are essentially committed for economic reasons. Their primary distinguishing feature from murder, assault, terrorist activities, and the sexual offenses discussed thus far is a lack of physical aggression or violence against persons. The crimes discussed in this chapter are not, by definition, violent acts. Nevertheless, there may be incidental violence—such as often occurs in home invasions—or indirect violence—such as would occur when people die as a result of a corporation's malfeasance.

The property offenses of burglary, larceny-theft, and motor vehicle theft make up the greatest proportion of the nation's Part I crime rate in any given year. Put another way, judged by reports to police, they occur far more frequently than do violent crimes. We discussed the official and victimization statistics on these crimes, as well as the effects on their victims. We have little information on the characteristics of offenders, however, with the exception of burglars who appear to be more willing than other offenders to share their secrets with researchers. In a number of studies, burglars have described how they choose victims, what tactics they use to gain access to targets, which targets they avoid, and why. Professional burglars seem to plan their offenses carefully and do not seem to consider themselves "real criminals."

In the discussion of motor vehicle theft, we included a section on carjacking, another crime that is of relatively recent origin. We covered information about the behavioral attributes or the motives of carjackers obtained from studies based on interviews with the offenders themselves. Carjackers seem motivated primarily by a need for quick money, a quick ride, or a quick thrill. Some, however, apparently wish to punish the victim of the carjacking for riding through their neighborhood in a disrespectful manner.

Home invasions are a special category of crimes that have features in common with burglary—they are usually committed for economic reasons—but they also involve direct personal encounters with their victims. In the worst form of home invasion, the perpetrators enter the home with the intention of harming its occupants. To our knowledge, no empirical, psychological research has been conducted on home invaders; those who commit violent acts are likely to possess features of aggressive behavior covered in Chapters 9 and 12. Depending on their behavior at the scene, some may possess psychopathic characteristics, such as callous-unemotional traits, discussed in Chapter 7.

Shoplifting is a nonviolent offense that presents continuing problems for commercial establishments. Individuals who shoplift do not seem to consider this behavior un-normative. Self-report data indicate that a great majority of juveniles have shoplifted at least once; surprisingly, large numbers of adults also admit to this behavior at some point during their adult lives. Today, there is more evidence of highly organized shoplifting, in which small groups of individuals plan their shoplifting strategy and have access to a network of fencing operations to dispose of their acquisitions. Research does not support the belief that kleptomania—a supposed compulsion to steal—actually exists to the extent that it would explain a significant proportion of shoplifting. While some individuals undoubtedly shoplift to gain attention, get recognition, or embarrass their family, it seems that most do so to obtain goods, go along with peers, or—in the case of some juveniles—on a dare or as initiation into a select group or gang. Furthermore, although there is some suggestion that depressed individuals may engage in "nonsensical shoplifting," the evidence that this is characteristic of large numbers of people is not persuasive.

The chapter covered briefly a number of behaviors that are facilitated by widespread use of the Internet. It is widely believed, for example, that many people today are guilty of "softlifting"—the unauthorized appropriation of computer software, an activity similar to the illegal downloading of music and videos. Identity theft and fraudulent activities associated with online banking, purchases, and payments are also more common.

We discussed white-collar crime and the difficulties in defining this concept. Green's four-part typology, although not often alluded to in the criminology literature, is helpful in considering varieties of crimes committed by individuals in the course of their legal occupations. Not all crimes mentioned by Green would be considered white-collar crime, but all are criminal offenses worthy of consideration. A display of excessive force by a police officer may be considered an aggravated assault, but the police officer's status as a person in authority suggests an additional element that should be taken into consideration in any attempt to understand this behavior. Likewise, a medical doctor's sexual assault of a female patient is still a rape, but the violations of trust and professional ethics add a dimension that render it different, from a psychological perspective, from a date rape or a stranger assault.

The traditional type of white-collar crime is the crime committed by corporations, businesses, or organizations or by individuals within those entities. One of the best explanations for this behavior lies in neutralizing techniques, in which individuals and groups convince themselves that their behavior was not really criminal or that no one was hurt, among other justifications. However, corporate crime is rarely studied by criminal psychologists, psychiatrists, or criminal justice researchers, beyond the gathering of data available from court records or government regulatory agencies. Burglars and rapists get interviewed and participate in studies. Corporate criminals are more likely to write their own books than to cooperate with professionals seeking some insight into their actions. Criminologists have, however, increased their focus on individual white-collar offenders in recent years, finding interesting personality traits, including psychopathic characteristics, and thinking patterns that may distinguish them from non-white-collar offenders.

Key Concepts

Boosters	Good burglar	Relative deprivation
Burglary	Identity theft	Repeat burglary
Carjacking	Individual occupational crime	Shoplifting by proxy
Cognitive scripts	Kleptomania	Snitches
Corporate crime	Near-repeat crimes	Softlifting
Dehumanization	Occupational crime	State-authority occupational crime
Expressive burglars	Organizational occupational crime	Techniques of neutralization
Fence	Professional occupational crime	White-collar crime

Review Questions

1. Define larceny and burglary. How are they different from each other?
2. Briefly describe Green's occupational crime typology. Give an example of each. Contrast Green's typology to that of Clinard and Quinney.
3. In what ways has shoplifting changed since it was first studied by Cameron?
4. Define *expressive burglars* and describe each type of burglary associated with the term.
5. Define kleptomania and describe the empirical support for the phenomenon.
6. Preliminary research has uncovered some characteristics, including personality features, that distinguish white-collar offenders from other offenders. Identify these characteristics.
7. Choose any two crimes covered in this chapter, and discuss them from the perspective of the psychological effects they have on their victims.

15

Violent Economic Crime and Crimes of Intimidation

CHAPTER OBJECTIVES

- Define and discuss robbery and the reasons behind the offense.
- Define and distinguish cybercrime, cyberstalking, and cyberbullying.
- Examine the literature on stalking.
- Outline hostage-taking offenses and their characteristics.
- Summarize the literature on arson, with particular emphasis on juvenile firesetting.
- Examine the psychological motives attached to serial arsons.

> *It happened in a supermarket parking lot. It was early evening and I didn't get a good look at him. I wasn't hurt, but he said he had a knife. Only my purse was taken. But he scared me to death. I don't sleep well at night and I don't go food shopping by myself any more, even in the day. It happened two years ago. (62-year-old robbery victim)*

The above may strike some readers as an overreaction to a relatively minor offense in which the victim was not injured. The woman's sleeplessness could be a result of many factors, not just her victimization, and the incident happened so long ago that she should now be able to put it behind her. Nevertheless, it cannot be denied that what occurred left a marked impression on her and affected her perceptions and her lifestyle. This can be said of all of the crimes discussed in this chapter. They often have no small impact on the people they touch.

The chapter focuses primarily on the violent economic crimes of robbery and arson, but other crimes are also considered. Of robbery and arson, the UCR program considers only robbery a violent crime; we approach both robbery and arson as violent because in both crimes, there is moderate to high level of serious injury or death to the victims, or at least the threat or possibility of such injury. However, from a psychological perspective, many robbers have little in common with those who assault, rape, or kill, because their primary intention is not to harm their victims physically. Likewise, many arsonists have no intention of harming people, even though they are responsible for deaths should they occur.

The chapter is also concerned with crimes of intimidation, such as stalking, cyberstalking, and cybercrime. Crimes of intimidation are intended to frighten, threaten, embarrass, or harass the victim or victims. Finally, hostage taking is an offense with elements of both violence and extreme intimidation, and bombing, which ends the chapter, is of course also violent. Both hostage takings and bombings have the strong potential of resulting in the deaths of the victims.

ROBBERY

Robbery is "taking or attempting to take anything of value from the care, custody, or control of a person or persons by force or violence and/or by putting the victim in fear" (Federal Bureau of Investigation, 2003, p. 303). The major distinctions between robbery and other economic crimes—such as burglary, fraud, or larceny—are the direct contact between the offender and the victim and the threat or use of force. The offender threatens bodily harm if the victim resists or impedes the offender's progress; usually, but not invariably, this threat is backed up by a clearly visible lethal weapon, such as a firearm or a knife.

There were 367,832 robberies reported in 2010, reflecting a national robbery rate of 119.1 per 100,000 people (Federal Bureau of Investigation, 2011a). Firearms were the weapons most often used in robbery (41%) followed closely by strong-arm tactics through the use of hands, feet, or fists (42%).

Interestingly, **strong-arm robbery** (without a weapon) is more likely to result in injury to the victim than is robbery with a firearm or knife. Presumably, victims are less fearful (and thus more daring) when confronted by an unarmed individual. In the absence of a gun or other weapon, the victim's resistance to losing valuable personal property is stronger, and he or she is more apt to try to resist or fight off the perpetrator. The tendency to resist, therefore, may partly account for the higher rates of victim injury in these no-weapon situations. On the other hand, the offender is likely to feel more confident, powerful, and in control of the incident when he or she has a weapon. Because of this increase in confidence, the offender is less likely to be anxious and disorganized in response patterns, and thus is better able to think clearly and evaluate the consequences of the actions.

Like many other crimes, robbery is primarily an offense committed by young adults (under the age of 25), who accounted for two-thirds of arrestees. The majority of the arrestees (approximately 90%) were males.

Robbery accounts for only about 4 percent of all arrests for economic crimes (but 35% of the violent crimes). However, because of its potential physical harm to victims, it is among the crimes most feared by the American population (Garofalo, 1977). This is especially the case for street robbery, which has an edge of desperation to it (Wright, Brookman, & Bennett, 2006). It involves a high probability of physical harm from a stranger, and it can happen to anyone. (More than half of the robberies occur on streets and highways.) (See **Figure 15-1**.) One in three victims are injured in robbery (also called stickup, holdup, mugging), and 1 in 10 so seriously that he or she requires medical attention (U.S. Department of Justice, 1988). Furthermore, robbery offenders are more likely to use weapons than other violent offenders, although as noted earlier, a surprising number use strong-arm tactics. Yet, despite its dangerousness, robbery is among the criminal offenses least studied by psychologists.

One reason for the lack of research interest on the psychology of robbery is that the crime seems so obvious and straightforward: People rob to obtain money. It is often assumed that the money will be used to buy alcohol or illegal substances, and psychologists as a group may be more interested in studying substance abuse. The process of committing a robbery is quick,

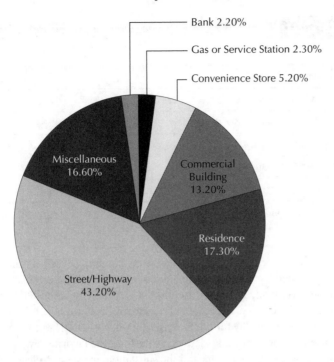

Bank 2.20%

Gas or Service Station 2.30%

Convenience Store 5.20%

FIGURE 15-1 Robbery Location, 2010 *Source:* Federal Bureau of Investigation (2011a).

and the potential returns are lucrative. Compared with burglary, however, the risks are great and the penalties substantial. Much of this may be true but, as we have seen, human behavior should not be oversimplified. The motives of offenders may be extremely varied. People behave a certain way because they have convinced themselves that is what works best for them.

Bank Robbery

"A bank robbery is indicated when the crime is robbery and the location is a financial institution" (Federal Bureau of Investigation, 2003). It accounts for 2.2 percent of all robbery in the United States (Federal Bureau of Investigation, 2011a). Although violence is rare, employees and customers are at risk of injury if the robber loses control or becomes violent. During a robbery, bank procedures are highly standardized. Tellers are instructed to comply quickly with a robber's demands and empty their cash drawers, even if no violence is threatened or weapons shown. The primary objective of banks is to ensure the safety of employers and customers. Therefore, the risk to the robber of encountering resistance is low, and consequently the robbery has a high probability of success during the early stages of the incident.

Although the principal risk to the bank robber is an eventual arrest, most are convinced they will not get caught (Erickson, 1996; Weisel, 2007). However, 15 percent of bank robbers are arrested at or near the scene, and one-third of the robberies are solved on the same day (Weisel, 2007). Overall, 60–75 percent of bank robberies are eventually solved (Federal Bureau of Investigation, 2003). Bank robberies have a high rate of being solved because they are reported quickly, have many witnesses, occur during daylight hours, and are extensively photographed by surveillance cameras.

TABLE 15-1 Bank Robberies By Establishment Robbed, 2010	
	Robberies
Commercial Banks	4,997
Mutual Savings Banks	47
Savings and Loans Associations	103
Credit Unions	396
Armored Company	3
Total	**5,546**

Source: Data from Bank Crime Statistics (2011).

According to data collected from the Bank Crime Statistics (BCS), commercial banks were the most commonly robbed bank in 2010 (see **Table 15-1**). Although clearance rates may be high, the amount of money eventually recovered is quite small, averaging about 20 percent of the total amount taken during the robbery. Bank robbery incidents are most likely to occur on Fridays. Historically, Friday has been payday for much of the nation, requiring large amounts of cash to be delivered to the various branch banks. Fridays continue to be the favorite day, even with the reduction of branch bank offices in recent years and the substantial increase in electronic banking. The time period during which most bank robberies occur is between 9:00 and 11:00 A.M.

AMATEURS AND PROFESSIONALS Most (80%) bank robberies are carried out by a single offender. A vast majority of all bank robbers are males (95%), and most are between the ages of 18 and 29. The great majority of bank robbers (80%) are amateurs who have *not* been convicted of a bank crime in the past (Federal Bureau of Investigation, 2003). An amateur tends to rob a bank on the spur of the moment without much planning, and primarily to fulfill some need, such as to pay for drugs, alcohol, or some status-enhancing goods. Basically, they tend to exhibit behavioral indicators of poor self-regulation. They are often under the influence of drugs and alcohol to fortify their nerve. Therefore, amateur bank robberies usually do not involve the meticulously planned caper carried out by a group of highly experienced criminals often portrayed in films. Amateur bank robbers are highly predictable in their behavioral patterns, as they continue to rob because the offense is so easy to carry out. Sometimes they rob other banks on the same day, employing the same *modus operandi* in successive robberies (see **Table 15-2**). They employ the same signature repeatedly, such as a distinctively worded note given to a single teller, and—if they use a disguise—they use it over and over again (Rehder & Dillow, 2003). Interestingly, about half of the amateur bank robbers do not even try to use disguises, and two-thirds are unarmed when they commit their bank robberies (Federal Bureau of Investigation, 2003). In summary, amateur bank robbers tend to commit their crime alone, unarmed, and undisguised (Weisel, 2007).

Professionals are usually armed and use multiple persons in the robbery. They also often try to disable or obscure surveillance cameras and are more likely to use disguises, such as ski masks and Halloween masks. In contrast to amateurs, who usually wait in line with customers before the robbery, try to escape on foot or by bicycle, and usually live near the bank, professionals generally use motor vehicles for escape. Banks that attract amateur bank robbers are very unlikely to attract professionals (Weisel, 2007). In addition, professionals tend to select times when there are

TABLE 15-2 Modus Operandi Used by Bank Robbers, 2010	
Modus Operandi	**Frequency**
Demand Note Used	3,142
Firearm Used	1,445
Handgun	1,394
Other Firearm	78
Other Weapon Used	126
Weapon Threatened	2,461
Explosive Device Used or Threatened	165
Oral Demand	3,096
Vault or Safe Theft	17
Depository Trap Device	1
Till Theft	91
Takeover	333

Source: Data from Bank Crime Statistics (2011).

few customers, such as at opening time and early in the week; amateurs most often select mid-day times and Fridays when bank customers are at their highest level. Professionals also select banks that are located at corner locations so that there are multiple choices for vehicle escapes. Professionals prefer to maintain as much control of the situation as possible. Therefore, the displaying of weapons and the presence of few customers increase their control over the robbery scene. They also utilize various kinds of intimidation, physical or verbal threats, and are loud and aggressive. **Table 15-3** contrasts amateur and professional bank robbers.

Some preliminary research reveals that bank workers, such as tellers, take several months to recover psychologically from the trauma of the robbery (Jones, 2002). Returning to the same environment day after day where the traumatic event took place, the victims often continue to

TABLE 15-3 Contrasting Features of Amateur and Professional Bank Robbers	
Amateurs	**Professionals**
Lone robber	Two or more robbers
Rob during high customer traffic	Rob during low traffic times
Stand in line	Control the situation, intimidate
Usually not armed	Carry and display weapons
Spur-of-the moment offending when they need money	Careful planning
Getaway by running, or use bikes	Motor vehicles for getaway

experience psychological stress associated with the incident, sometimes for longer than six months. The symptoms may be physical or emotional, and nearly anything that was present during the robbery—sights, smells, textures, sounds—may bring them on. Even bank personnel who were not directly confronted during the robbery may experience stress symptoms. The experience may also have a rippling effect that spreads to family members, friends, and coworkers. These same experiences, of course, are often experienced by victims of other types of robbery and crime in general. For example, people who have experienced workplace violence in other contexts—for example, hospitals, insurance agencies, auto plants, courthouses—may exhibit stress long after the trauma has passed.

Commercial Robbery

Approximately 15 percent of all robberies take place in commercial establishments, compared with 14 percent in residences. (Recall that entering a residence for the purpose of taking money or goods would qualify as burglary; if the residents are at home and threatened with violence, it becomes a robbery as well as a home invasion.) Convenience stores appear to be favorite commercial sites for robbery, followed by gas or service stations. Approximately 6.1 percent of all robberies take place in convenience stores, followed by gas or service stations (2.7%) (Federal Bureau of Investigation, 2005b). Most convenience stores have no robberies, but a few have many robberies (Eck, 2000). One of the debates concerning prevention of convenience store robbery is whether two or more clerks in the store, rather than one, reduce the robbery attempts. So far, the evidence is unclear, but the two-clerk experiment does not appear to discourage robberies as much as anticipated (Eck, 2000). Cameras and silent alarms do not seem to reduce convenience store robberies, but some preliminary evidence suggests that the installation of interactive CCTV (allowing communication between store personnel and security personnel watching a monitor in a remote location) may be effective in reducing store robberies by nearly one-third (Eck, 2000).

Although convenience stores have traditionally been the favorite robbery sites, America's fast-food restaurants are now becoming a preferred target. There are currently over 280,000 fast-food restaurants in the United States, compared to roughly 10,000 convenience stores (Exum, Kuhns, Koch, & Johnson, 2010). Many restaurant robberies occur at fast-food restaurants because they are open late, staffed by teenagers, full of cash, and conveniently near a highway. In describing the vulnerability of fast-food restaurants to armed robbery, Schlosser (2001, p. 84) writes, "A couple of sixteen-year-old crew members and a twenty-year-old manager are often the only people locking up a restaurant, long after midnight." About two-thirds of the robberies at fast-food restaurants involve current or former employees, and frequently, the on-duty manager suffers much of the anger and violence administered during the robbery. In 1998, more fast-food restaurant workers were murdered on the job in the United States than police officers (Schlosser, 2001).

The leading fast-food chains have tried to reduce robbery by spending millions on new security measures, including video cameras, panic buttons, drop-safes, burglar alarms, and additional lighting (Schlosser, 2001). But even the most secure restaurant remains highly vulnerable to robbery (Exum *et al.*, 2010).

Street Robbery

Overall, the greatest proportion of robberies in the United States in 2004 (42.8%) occurred on streets and highways (Federal Bureau of Investigation, 2005b). Street robbery is most common in urban areas, particularly in cities over 250,000 in population. Unlike bank and commercial robbery, however, street robbery tends to be more based on opportunity than planning. Street robbery is driven by the culture on the streets, and follows many of the characteristics of carjacking discussed in the previous chapter. Street robbers remain in a state of "alert opportunism," where the motivation to offend is always present. They are in perpetual need of money to buy status-enhancing goods, drugs, and alcohol. When an opportunity to rob occurs, there is little or no time for contemplation; otherwise the opportunity is lost forever. Still, street robbers are most likely to follow well-rehearsed cognitive scripts that have been developed and practiced through offending activities. Even though little contemplation is used when opportunity knocks, their methods and targets have developed through experimentation and tinkering of their own personal approaches or scripts. We will discuss in more detail the motivations of street robbers and situational dynamics that stimulate their criminal activity later in the section.

Professional Robbers

Assessing skilled robbery, Peter Letkemann (1973) offered pertinent remarks about the successful robber's confidence and victim "management." Contrasting the robber to the burglar, he noted that burglars do not have to be concerned with people, but professional robbers must be able to maintain control and handle their victims at all times. Bank robbers, for example, assert that the keys to a successful heist are confidence and the ability to control people under highly stressful conditions. Confidence, they believe, is reflected in the robber's tone of voice and general behavior. High levels of self-confidence are crucial if robbers are to maintain control of the situation. Successful robbers also note that the posture and physical location of the victims are deliberately designed to enhance the offender's control over them. For example, victims may be told to kneel facing a wall or lie on the floor.

According to Letkemann, professional robbers often express dismay over media treatment of robbery. For example, television and movies often downplay the seriousness of bank robbery, particularly when no one is physically hurt. The offenders therefore must work harder to convince their victims that they mean business. The entertainment media also encourage some victims to be heroes; robbers consider heroes irrational and extremely dangerous to their own safety and a threat to the successful outcome of the crime.

Motives and Cultural Influences

Some researchers view robbery as a rational choice driven primarily by the need for money and a desire to minimize the risk of detection. Other researchers believe street robbery represents a cultural pursuit in which the money and risks take second place to the psychological and social rewards toward the offender's lifestyle (Wright et al., 2006).

In a revealing study, Richard Wright and Scott Decker (1997) interviewed 86 individuals who were actively engaged in armed robbery on a regular basis in St. Louis. None of the robbers interviewed were incarcerated or otherwise under supervision of the criminal justice system (e.g., under arrest, on probation, or on parole). Most studies of armed robbery feature interviews with prisoners who either admit engaging in the offense or have been convicted of robbery.

Wright and Decker focused on determining what factors influenced the robbers as to when, how, and whom to rob. The researchers were also interested in the offenders' thoughts and actions during the commission of the crime. In addition to interviewing, the researchers took 10 of the robbers to the site of a recent holdup for which they had not been apprehended and asked them to reconstruct the crime. (This methodology may be surprising to readers; however, even if the researchers reported what they knew to police, they were not direct witnesses to the crimes and it is unlikely that their information would be of use. In comparison, the data obtained from the study itself shed considerable light on this very common crime.) The sample was overwhelmingly black, poor, male, and uneducated. Although all age groups were represented, a majority were between 18 and 29. Most of the offenders had committed numerous robberies in their lifetimes—so many in fact that they found it impossible to specify the exact number. Despite the very high number of armed robberies they said they had committed, 60 percent of the sample had never been convicted of armed robbery. Almost all the sample (96%) reported committing many other offenses, particularly theft, burglary, assault, and drug selling. A majority (85%) typically did their robbery on the street, while 12 percent preferred to rob commercial establishments (e.g., pawnshops, jewelry stores, liquor stores).

Wright and Decker found that a vast majority of the offenders did not plan the armed robbery. "The reality for many offenders is that crime commission has become so routinized that it emerges almost naturally in the course of their daily lives, often occurring without substantial planning or deliberation" (Wright & Decker, 1997, p. 30). The researchers discovered that, with few exceptions, the decision to rob was strongly influenced by a pressing need for cash to support their hedonistic, carefree lifestyle. The robbers in this sample were deeply enmeshed in the street culture where immediate gratification reigned supreme. Many robbers spent their take with reckless abandon without much thought to financial obligations or commitments. The offenders chose armed robbery as a lifestyle because it provides quick cash as the need arises. Armed robbery offered immediate cash compared with the delays inherent in disposing of hot merchandise acquired through burglary, shoplifting, and motor vehicle theft.

Although the need for cash was the overwhelming reason for armed robbery, a secondary gain expressed by some robbers was the control they held over their frightened victims, unless their victims were themselves lawbreakers. In addition, many offenders preferred to rob white victims, particularly white women, because they usually complied with their demands and did not offer much resistance. According to many of these offenders, black victims were more likely to resist and fight back. Also, many robbers in this sample reported that whites were more likely to carry credit cards and checkbooks rather than cash; the opposite was true for blacks. However, when whites did carry cash, the amounts were substantial.

One of the favorite targets of the street robbers in this sample were individuals who themselves were involved in lawbreaking, especially drug sellers and wealthy drug users. Drug dealers carry considerable amounts of cash as a result of their illegal activities. Of course, the risks are higher when targeting dealers because they are more likely to be armed, more likely to resist, and are sometimes connected to a powerful drug organization. Wealthy drug users tend to be white persons who come into a neighborhood looking to buy drugs with considerable cash. They can be easily victimized, and like other lawbreakers, they are unlikely to report the robbery to the police.

In a more focused examination of street robbery, Wright *et al.* (2006) discovered that American and United Kingdom **street culture** seem to be a very powerful social force in the commission of these crimes. "American street culture subsumes a number of powerful conduct norms, including, but not limited to, the hedonistic pursuit of sensory stimulation, disdain for conventional living, lack of future orientation and persistent eschewal of responsibility" (Wright *et al.*, 2006, p. 2). The image one presents is paramount and is one of the few sources of status available to most offenders. The same social impetus is present in U.K. street culture. As noted by Katz (1988), while the obvious reason for street robbery is money, the reasons for needing the money are far more revealing.

According to Wright *et al.* (2006), street robbery accomplishes five things, depending on the needs of the offender:

- Generates quick cash that can be spent quickly and used easily to finance gambling, drug use, and heavy drinking
- Allows purchasing nonessential, status-enhancing items (such as clothing or jewelry) to improve standing in the street culture
- Creates excitement and dominance over victims who are overpowered
- Prompts anger and eagerness to start a fight in those offenders already prone toward fighting and violence
- Achieves a certain measure of informal justice, such as debt collecting or revenge

One of the major findings of the Wright and Decker (1997) and Wright *et al.* (2006) projects is that there is little psychological mystery behind the motives of armed robbery: These offenders need cash now to support their impulsive lifestyle, and robbery provides the best route to that cash. Some also enjoy dominating their victims and frightening them, seek the "buzz" they receive from the offense, or come across as not to be messed with in the street culture, but these motives are only secondary to cash acquisition. An important point must be emphasized, however. Even though many street robberies appear to be impulsive and hold to the philosophy "strike while the iron is hot," it is highly likely the offender is following his or her favorite **cognitive script**, developed and perfected over a series of similar street crimes. Furthermore, the script has been formulated most probably through a combination of observation (social learning) and participation with a payoff (instrumental learning). When opportunity knocks, their offending cognitive script immediately comes into play. The script contains information that guides the offending behavior (Ward & Hudson, 2000). "These scripts can be enacted without conscious intention and with minimal awareness of the overall goal" (Ward & Hudson, 2000, p. 197).

Robbery by Groups

Porter and Alison (2006) investigated 116 cases of group robbery (61 commercial and 55 personal) and were able to identify a four-part typology based on the interpersonal behavior between the offenders and their victims. The researchers examined how the robbers treated the victims, and how the victims, in turn, reacted to the robbers' behavior. The four themes identified were as follows: (1) dominance, (2) submission, (3) cooperation, and (4) hostility. The interpersonal theme of dominance refers to situations in which the group of offenders attempts to control their victims completely. These offenders often use weapons and threaten the victims. In some instances, they bind and gag the victims during the robbery. Dominance is the method most preferred by professional bank robbers. In the submission theme, the offenders allow the victim to make an effort to be in control and are ultimately unsuccessful. That is, the robber group is not forceful or assertive, and the robbery becomes an attempt, with the intended victims taking over the situation. In this scenario, the victims refuse to do as they are told, may struggle with the robbers, and at the end, the robbers run away. Porter and Alison provide the example of a situation in which two youths attempted to rob a store and were physically confronted by both the owner and his wife, who chased off the offenders. "As the offenders left the premises they swore at the couple and made a two-fingered gesture towards the security camera" (Porter & Alison, 2006, p. 336).

In the cooperation theme, the behaviors of the robbers are designed to obtain cooperation from the victims. The offenders manipulate the victims to comply with their demands and to participate in the crime. Such participation involves handing over property, opening a safe, providing their PIN for the victim's cash card, filling bags with money, or making sure no additional customers enter the building. The robbers may use a single act of violence or display a weapon, but the intent here is to get cooperation from victims, rather than control them. Many victims tend to comply with the offenders' instructions rather than resist—and as mentioned above, bank employees are typically advised to cooperate. The researchers discovered that this strategy is the most frequently used in group robberies, and appears to be the most effective.

The interactional theme of hostility involves the offenders acting in an aggressive and violent manner toward the victims from the outset. In most cases, the researchers found that a hostile approach by robbers often produces a hostile reaction from victims. Many victims fight back or attempt to flee the scene. In this situation, the offenders are reckless, needlessly attacking victims with violence and verbal threats, and they often use firearms. This method is also most commonly associated with victim resistance.

Research by Porter and Alison (2006) indicated that commercial robberies were more associated with the cooperation theme than were personal robberies, and personal robberies also were more hostile than commercial robberies. Personal robberies refer to street robberies, such as at or near an ATM machine. Commercial robberies, as noted above, involve businesses like stores, gas stations, fast-food restaurants, or banks. The researchers also report that personal robbery tends to be more violent than commercial robbery because victims usually are less willing to cooperate and hand over personal property.

Recall that in Chapter 12, we discussed strategies for resisting sexual assault (e.g., Ullman, 2007) and concluded that—as a general principle—forceful resistance was least likely to result in a completed rape. When it comes to street robbery, the situation may be quite different. In that case, it is likely wiser to part with one's personal possessions than try to fend off the attacker.

CYBERCRIME

Cybercrime—a term that was hardly used 20 years ago—refers to any illegal act that involves a computer system. It is therefore also called computer crime. Cybercrime often involves traditional forms of crime, such as fraud, identity theft, distributing child pornography, stalking, and financial theft. Some of these crimes were covered in previous chapters. It can be done swiftly and perpetrated on vast numbers of potential victims (Broadhurst, 2006). "The cross-national nature of most computer related crimes has rendered many time-honoured methods of policing both domestically and in cross-border situations ineffective even in advanced nations, while the 'digital divide' provides 'safe havens' for cyber-criminals" (Broadhurst, 2006, p. 408). Advances in computer technology and increased access to personal information via the Internet have created a significant marketplace for worldwide cyber criminals to share stolen information and sophisticated criminal methods (Martinez, 2011). Some law enforcement agencies are making headway into the "digital divide," however. In 2010, the multifaceted strategies of the U.S. Secret Service to combat cybercrime led to the arrests of over 1,200 suspects for cybercrime-related violations (Martinez, 2011). The Secret Service investigations discovered over $500 million in actual fraud loss and prevented approximately $7 billion in additional losses.

The main types of financially related cybercrime are unauthorized access to computers (hacking), mischief to data (virus generation), and theft of communications (see **Table 15-4**). The development and use of malicious software has been especially worrisome for businesses and government. Malware and other computer viruses cause considerable damage to businesses, consumer networks, and governmental systems. In fact, the most recent trend in cybercrime involves the ongoing targeting of point of sale systems as well as the compromise of online financial accounts,

TABLE 15-4	Cybercrime Type Detected by American Businesses, 2005	
Type of Incident		**Percent (%)**
Cyber Theft		**16.4**
Embezzlement		3.8
Fraud		5.5
Theft of intellectual property		3.4
Theft of personal or financial data		3.7
Cyber Attack		**83**
Denial of service		18.4
Vandalism or sabotage		5.3
Computer virus		59.7

Source: Data from Rantala (2008).

usually through malware developed explicitly for that purpose. Point of sale (POS) refers to the location where a transaction occurs online, somewhat similar to an electronic cash register. POS is also called point of purchase (POP) or checkout. Malware and hacking attacks on financial systems and fraudulent transfers of electronic funds are not only becoming more prevalent but affect every sector of the world economy. In recent years, cyber criminals have concentrated on attacking small and medium-sized business, banks, and data processors as larger organizations have become more adept at developing sophisticated protections (Martinez, 2011). *Phishing* or *spoofing spam* has become increasingly popular. These terms refer to email messages with corresponding Web pages designed to appear as existing consumer or business sites. Millions of these fraudulent emails are sent to computers across the globe, claiming to come from banks, charitable organizations, individuals-in-need, lotteries, or other legitimate-sounding sites in order to persuade computer users to answer by submitting financial, personal, or password data. Most computer users are familiar with emails requesting the recipient to help in the movement of millions of dollars from a foreign country to their own personal bank account. Cybercrime offenders have developed a growing practice of buying, selling, and trading malicious malware software, credit and debit card data, personal information data, bank account information, brokerage account information, hacking services, and counterfeit identity documents (Martinez, 2011).

In 2006, an FBI agent infiltrated a cybercrime organization website called Darkmarket and was instrumental in shutting it down in 2008, resulting in numerous arrests. It had approximately 2,500 members worldwide at its peak, mostly persons involved in buying and selling stolen financial information, such as credit care data, log-in information, and equipment to carry out financial crimes (Chabinsky, 2010). Although this website was shut down, many others quickly emerged (Glenny, 2011).

Another popular cybercrime today is illegal gambling on the Internet. "Since the mid-1990s, Internet gambling operators have established approximately 1,800 e-gaming Web sites in locations outside the United States, and global revenues from Internet gaming in 2003 are projected to be $5 billion" (*The Informant,* 2003, p. 23). Given the continuing nature of gaming, it is likely that these projections were understated. Not all online gambling is illegal, however. Criminal violations occur when it is conducted from or to a location that prohibits or regulates gambling activities. Authorities stress that a major concern of Internet gambling is its tie to organized crime and to terrorist groups.

In response to the dramatic increase in computer crimes, the U.S. Congress passed the *Federal Computer Fraud and Abuse Act of 1984*, which was amended and expanded in the *Computer Abuse Amendments Act of 1994*. Computer crime is a serious problem that will continue to draw considerable attention from law enforcement agencies across the globe. In 1997, eight of the world's industrial nations joined forces to fight computer crime, particularly security intrusions and telecommunications fraud. In May 1999, the Clinton administration established a new national initiative to address the problem of Internet fraud. The initiative encouraged the FBI to join forces with the NW3C (National White Collar Crime Center, mentioned in the previous chapter) to establish the Internet Fraud Complaint Center for strategic information about and analysis of Internet fraud schemes (see **Table 15-5** for complaints of online crime over the past five years). On February 15, 2012 Senator Patrick Leahy, Chair of the Senate Judiciary Committee, introduced legislation to address the growing threat of cybercrime. The Cybercrime Protection Security Act of 2012 is designed to bolster the tools for law enforcement for preventing and prosecuting cybercrime. As with other bills introduced in Congress during 2012 (e.g., reauthorization of the Violence Against Women Act), final action has yet to be decided.

Research focusing on the psychological characteristics of cybercrime and cybercriminals is just beginning. We do know that cybercriminals are a diverse group in their talents and motivations, but usually have acquired significant computer technical skills. Some commit the crimes for the thrills of making life miserable for others, whereas others desire the monetary rewards for their efforts. Increasingly, some view themselves as businesspersons, and cybercrime is their full-time business (Chabinsky, 2010). As the level of profit increases, transnational, violent organized crime groups are becoming progressively more involved in the cybercrime enterprise (Chabinsky, 2010). These groups are beginning to shift focus away from system and personal computers to other platforms, including smart phones, tablet computers, and mobile devices.

It is likely that cybercriminals employ the same techniques of neutralizing their behavior that are employed by other offenders, particularly white-collar criminals. These were discussed in earlier chapters, and include such cognitive approaches as minimizing the extent of the harm they do.

TABLE 15-5 Complaints of Online Crime	
Year	**Complaints Received**
2010	303,809
2009	336,655
2008	275,284
2007	206,884
2006	207,492
2005	231,493
2004	207,449

Source: Data from Internet Crime Complaint Center (2008, 2011).

Cyberstalking is a serious form of cybercrime that will grow in scope and complexity as more people take advantage of the Internet and other telecommunications and digital technologies. From a psychological perspective, we are more concerned about the cyberstalker or the cyberbullier than about the individual who engages in cybercrime for economic purposes, while still recognizing that economic crimes take a great toll on their victims. A cyberstalker is able to send repeated, threatening, or harassing messages by the simple push of a button, whereas more sophisticated cyberstalkers can use programs to send messages at regular or random intervals without being physically present at the computer terminal (U.S. Department of Justice, 1999). The anonymity leaves stalkers at an advantageous position for avoiding detection. We discuss cyberstalking again in a separate section below, after reviewing research on stalking behavior in general.

STALKING

Many young adults report that they or someone they know well has experienced what they think of as stalking—such as unwelcome, persistent phone calls, text messages, or being followed on the street or into bars and nightclubs. **Stalking** is broadly defined as "a course of conduct directed at a specific person that involves repeated physical or visual proximity, nonconsensual communication, or verbal, written, or implied threats sufficient to cause fear in a reasonable person" (Tjaden, 1997, p. 2). Systematic information on stalking in the United States is limited, despite the attention it receives from the media and state and federal legislatures (Tjaden, 1997). Early research and attention focused on the stalking of famous persons, entertainment personalities, or politicians, known as "celebrity stalking." However, a substantial increase in the stalking of noncelebrities led to the passage of antistalking laws in all 50 states and the District of Columbia (Tjaden & Thoennes, 1998a).

Legal definitions of stalking vary from state to state. While most states define it as the willful, malicious, and repeated following and harassing of another person, some include such activities as lying-in-wait, surveillance, nonconsensual communication, telephone harassment, and vandalism (Tjaden & Thoennes, 1998a). Some states specify that at least two stalking events must occur before the conduct can be considered illegal.

California became the first state to enact antistalking legislation in 1990. The impetus for this legislation was not the stalking/homicide of television actress Rebecca Schaeffer as commonly believed, but rather the intractable problem of domestic violence (Lemon, 1994). A California municipal court judge initiated the development and passage of the antistalking law, following his frustration over existing laws that failed to protect four Orange County women who were killed in different incidents despite the issuance of restraining orders against their assailants. Since 1990, stalking statutes have spread rapidly to all states.

In an attempt to fill in the large gap in our knowledge about stalking, the Center for Policy Research conducted a comprehensive victimization survey of 8,000 women and 8,000 men, 18 years of age or older, on issues relating to violence (Tjaden & Thoennes, 1997). The survey revealed that 8 percent of women and 2 percent of men reported they had been stalked at some point in their lives (Tjaden, 1997). Overall, the survey indicated that approximately 1.4 million Americans are victims of stalkers every year, a surprisingly large number. More recent data indicate that in 2006, an estimated 3.4 million persons age 18 or older were victims of stalking (Baum, Catalano, & Rand, 2009). In most cases, the stalking lasted less than one year, but some people were stalked for over five years. "While individually these acts may not be criminal, collectively and repetitively these behaviors may cause a victim to fear for his or her safety or the safety of a family member" (Baum *et al.*, 2009, p. 1). It is estimated that 1 out of every 12 women and 1 out of every 45 men in the United States has been stalked during his or her lifetime (Tjaden & Thoennes, 1998a). Persons between the age of 18 and 24 experience the highest rates of stalking victimization, and the risk of victimization decreases with age (Baum *et al.*, 2009). Individuals who are divorced or separated are also at high risk of stalking victimization.

The Center for Policy Research survey (Tjaden & Thoennes) found that the motives of most stalkers were to control, intimidate, or frighten their victims. This observation was made by both male and female victims. Eighty-seven percent of the time the stalker was male, and 80 percent of the time the victim was female. In most stalking incidents, the victims (particularly women) knew their stalker. About half of the female victims were stalked by current or former marital or cohabiting partners, and a majority of these women (80%) had been physically assaulted by that partner either during the relationship, during the stalking episode, or during both. About one in ten victims were stalked by a stranger (Baum *et al.*, 2009). In about one-third of the cases, stalkers vandalized the victim's property, and about 10 percent of the time, the stalker killed or threatened to kill the victim's pet. In nearly half the cases, the stalker made overt threats to the victim. The survey dispels the myth that most stalkers are psychotic or delusional. Only 7 percent of the victims perceived their stalkers as "crazy" or abusers of drugs or alcohol.

Half of all victims reported the stalking to the police, and about one-quarter of the female victims obtained a restraining order. Not surprisingly, 70 percent of all restraining orders were violated by the assailant. About one-quarter of victims in cases where a restraining order was violated pursued prosecution. When prosecution was pursued, most cases resulted in conviction of the stalker and well over half received jail time. Although most of the stalking stopped within two years, the emotional and social effects of being stalked continued for many victims long after the incident. About one-third of the stalking victims sought psychological treatment because of the emotional and social trauma that resulted from the stalking episodes.

Meloy (1998) asserts that stalkers rarely cause serious physical injury to their victims, threaten them with weapons, or use weapons. Even so, the psychological trauma is often substantial. In a survey of 145 stalking victims (120 females, 25 males), Doris Hall (1998) reports that the experience of being stalked for months or even years is akin to psychological terrorism. A majority of the victims said their entire lives changed as a result of being stalked. "Many move or quit jobs, some change their names, others have gone underground, leaving friends and family in order to escape the terror" (Hall, 1998, p. 134). Some change their physical appearance or wear disguises. Others become exceedingly suspicious of the motives of others, often leading lonely and isolated lives. Many victims constantly worry that the stalker will find them, and that the entire experience will start all over again.

Categories of Stalking

Some researchers have identified categories or typologies of stalking. A prominent example is the four-category classification proposed by Beatty (2001): (1) simple obsession stalking, (2) love obsession stalking, (3) erotomania stalking, and (4) vengeance stalking. **Simple obsession stalking** accounts for the majority of stalking (about 60%) and often represents extensions of previous patterns of domestic violence and psychological abuse. The stalker in these cases usually seeks power and control after a failed relationship with the victim. Simple obsession stalking is perhaps the most dangerous to the victim, since it is often motivated by the stalker's conclusion that "If I can't have you, nobody will." In **love obsession stalking**, the stalker and victim are casual acquaintances or complete strangers. Stalkers in this category are characterized by low self-esteem and tend to select victims they perceive to have certain qualities they believe will raise their self-esteem. Essentially, they seek a love relationship with the object of their obsession, contrary to the wishes of their victim.

Erotomania stalking is considered delusional, and the stalker is often plagued by serious mental disorders. This type of stalker usually targets public figures or celebrities in their misguided attempts to gain self-esteem and status for themselves. Talk show host David Letterman was stalked over a number of years by a woman who believed she was his wife. The woman frequently trespassed on Letterman's property, hid in his home, and even stole his car to go grocery shopping. Tragically, the delusional woman eventually took her own life. Fortunately, erotomania stalking appears to be relatively rare, and normally the stalker is not violent. **Vengeance stalking** is quite different from the other three types because vengeance stalkers do not seek a personal relationship with their targets (Beatty, 2001). Instead, they try to elicit a particular response or change of behavior from the victims. For example, the stalker who wishes to torment those responsible for a perceived injustice or violation of their rights might follow the "guilty parties" day and night until he is fairly compensated.

Other researchers have classified stalkers according to their relationship with the victim. Studying over one thousand male and female stalkers, Mohandie, Meloy, Green-McGowan, & Williams (2006) divided them into intimate stalkers, acquaintance stalkers, public figure stalkers, and private stranger stalkers. The most violence associated with the stalking was perpetrated by intimate stalkers, with the least perpetrated by public figure stalkers. The intimate stalker resembles the simple obsession stalker described above; both are most likely to result in violence.

What terminates stalking? Some stalkers stop their activity toward the current victim when they find a new "love" interest. About 18 percent of the victims in the Center for Policy Research Survey indicated the stalking stopped when their assailant got a new spouse, partner, or boyfriend/ girlfriend. Informal law enforcement interventions also seem to help. Fifteen percent said the stalking ceased when the assailant received a warning from the police. More formal interventions such as arrest, conviction, or restraining orders do not appear to be very effective. When it comes to persistent, frightening stalking that creates risks to personal safety, the survey suggests that the most effective method may be to relocate far away from the offender. Nevertheless, this places the burden on the victim and is an unsatisfactory response to the problem created by the offender.

Cyberstalking

As mentioned above, a form of stalking that has emerged in recent years is cyberstalking, the use of the Internet or other forms of online communications to threaten or engage in unwanted advances toward another. About one in four stalking victims reported that some form of cyberstalking was used to frighten them (Baum *et al.*, 2009). Although online harassment and threats may take many forms, cyberstalking is in many ways similar to off-line stalking. In most instances, the stalkers wish to establish relationships with the victims, and are often males seeking females. In many cases, the cyberstalker and the victim had a prior relationship, and the cyberstalking begins when the victim attempts to break off the relationship (U.S. Department of Justice, 1999). Ultimately, much cyberstalking is designed to control the victim, usually through threats and harassment.

"Because e-mail is used daily by what some experts say are as many as 35 million people, and it is estimated that there are approximately 200,000 stalkers in the United States, the Internet is a perfect forum with which to terrorize their victims" (Jenson, 1996, p. 1). In the almost two decades since that statement was written, opportunities to cyberstalk have expanded dramatically. "Chat rooms," e-mail, social networking sites, and text messaging provide far-reaching and unregulated outlets for harassing unsuspecting victims. In addition, there is an enormous amount of personal information available through the Internet, and a cyberstalker can easily and quickly locate private information about a target, similar to the identity thieves discussed in Chapter 14.

One aspect of cyberstalking that should be considered is the process of deindividuation, discussed in Chapter 4. The anonymity offered by the Internet releases participants from the traditional constraints on their behavior by deindividuating them (Hinduja, 2008). Deindividuation, you will recall, reduces self-awareness and self-regulation. "Individuals who act and interact in cyberspace may feel 'hidden' or immersed among each other (and among the collective of hundreds of millions currently connected online) and more a part of a group than by oneself" (Hinduja, 2008, p. 392). Therefore, some people who cyberstalk or cyberbully may be more inclined to act in a deviant and psychologically damaging manner as a result of the anonymity the Internet provides.

Cyberbullying

Traditional bullying is defined as "systematically and chronically inflicting physical hurt or psychological distress on one or more students" (Diamanduros, Downs, & Jenkins, 2008, p. 693). As we noted in Chapter 6, bullying can take the form of physical, verbal, and nonverbal actions (Olweus, 1997; Viljoen, O'Neill, & Sidhu, 2005). **Cyberbullying** is defined as "sending or posting harmful or cruel text or images using the Internet or other digital communication devices" (Li, 2006, p. 158). Those who engage in cyberbullying often used various forms of electronic, digital media to communicate to their victims. These electronic forms of contact may include the Internet or mobile phones, most often through emails, text messaging, video/picture clips, and other social media. Even more than those who bully face to face, those who bully online can be daring, vicious, and threatening because they can remain anonymous.

Cyberbullying has become a worldwide problem among students. Estimates of the number of cyberbullied victims are difficult to obtain and have ranged from 4 percent to 72 percent of all students. There are some research projects that have been well executed and do suggest some accurate data. In Britain, for example, one in four youths between the ages of 11 and 19 said they had been cyberbullied in 2002 (Li, 2006). A similar statistic is found among Canadian youth (Li, 2006, 2007), and among American youth (Hinduja & Patchin, 2008). In a recent publication, Patchin and Hinduja (2012) report that, based on their best estimate of the research literature, about one of five school-aged youth have been victims of cyberbullying. Girls are most often the victims (Smith *et al.*, 2008). In most instances, cyberbullying is of short duration (a month or less); nevertheless, its effects on the victims can be devastating. Many of the effects of bullying discussed in Chapter 6 apply equally, if not more intensely, to cyberbullying.

In contrast with traditional bullying, cyberbullies are often anonymous. In one extensive survey of 1,211 students, approximately 40 percent of those who were cyberbullied did not know the identity of the bully, although some students had their suspects (Dehue, Bolman, & Völlink, 2008). "Cyberspace creates an illusion of invisibility because it is faceless" (Mason, 2008, p. 329). This feeling of invisibility eliminates concerns of detection, social disapproval, and punishment. In addition, cyberbullies are not personally confronted with how their victims react to their cyberbullying or the consequences of their harassments, which encourages deindividuation (Dehue *et al.*, 2008). Victims report that not knowing the person behind the cyber attacks is often discouraging and frightening; this increases their feelings of powerlessness (Vandebosch & Van Cleemput, 2008). The research literature consistently indicates that the consequences of cyber victimization include low self-esteem, poor academic performance, depression, emotional distress, and even violence and suicide (Mason, 2008).

Those who frequently cyberbully are characterized by the need to feel powerful and in control (Diamanduros *et al.*, 2008). They like to dominate, and they often select victims who are loners (Diamanduros *et al.*, 2008). In many instances, they have been bullied themselves (Barlett & Gentile, 2012; Bauman, 2010; Li, 2007). "In other words, individuals may be motivated to harm others online after receiving such harm, suggesting retaliatory motivations" (Barlett & Gentile, 2012, p. 131). Retaliatory motivations in this context refers to tendency to cyberbully either those who cyberbullied them or other individuals they know and resent. In addition, those who engage in traditional forms of bullying are the same ones who engage in a large amount of the cyberbullying (Bartlett & Gentile, 2012). For instance, Qing Li (2007) discovered that nearly one-third of the cyberbullies in her Canadian research were also traditional bullies. Li also found, however, that 60 percent of cyberbullying victims were females, and a large majority of the cyberbullies in these cases were also females. "This result supports the point that females prefer to use electronic communication medium such as chat-room and email to bully others (Li, 2007, p. 1787). A majority of the cyberbully victims and those who know about it did not report the incidents to adults. With the exception of the gender differences, Li's research indicates a close tie between bullying and cyberbullying and suggests that the many effective techniques of combating traditional bullying should also work for dealing with cyberbullying.

Legislation is pending in a number of states and in the federal government to address both cyberstalking and cyberbullying. It should be noted that most states have some type of antibullying law on the books, but not cyberbullying laws. Many states, as well as the federal government, have attempted to pass cyberbullying laws, but they must be crafted in such a way as to not infringe on first amendment protections. Bullying involves physical victimization; cyberbullying—as disturbing as it is—may impinge upon free speech.

As of April 2012, only 14 states have state cyberbullying laws on the books, and six states and the federal government have proposals for such laws on the table (Hinduja & Patchin, 2012). One federal proposal, the Megan Meier Cyberbullying Act (HR 1966), would have forbade the interstate or foreign digital or electronic communication with intent to coerce, intimidate, harass, or cause substantial emotional distress to a person. The bill died in committee, and it is unknown whether it will be revived. Megan Meier was a 13-year-old girl who committed suicide after receiving hostile messages from "Josh Evans," a "boy" she met on MySpace. Ultimately, it was learned that "Josh" was really another girl, an acquaintance of Megan's who lived down the street. The two girls had had disagreements, and the other girl's parents helped her create the fake Josh Evans identity, which she used to send distressing messages to Megan. Under existing laws, there was no way to hold the girl or her parents responsible for Megan's death. Similar suicidal incidents across the country led legislatures to craft laws that would criminalize bullying online, particularly when it led to the suicide of the bullied individual. The constitutionality of cyberbullying laws has yet to be determined.

Rather than looking to legislation, many school districts are beginning to take action in an attempt to control cyberbullying and cyberstalking. The Center for Safe and Responsible Internet Use (www.csriu.org and www.cyber-safe-kids.com) offers suggestions and help concerning problems with cyberbullying. The National Center for Victims of Crime (NCVC, 2000) has several recommendations for victims of cyberstalking. Its website (listed in the References section) also has suggestions on how to handle cyberstalking.

HOSTAGE-TAKING OFFENSES

The hostage taker holds victims against their will and uses them to obtain material gain or personal advantage. Typically, this offender threatens to take the lives of the victims if certain demands are not met within a specified time period. Included in the broad hostage-taking category are abductions and kidnappings, skyjackings, and some acts of terrorism. Recall that Chapter 11 focused on acts of international and domestic terrorism. In this chapter, the topic is discussed only as it relates specifically to hostage taking.

Instrumental and Expressive Hostage Taking

Miron and Goldstein (1978) divide hostage-taking offenses into two major categories based on the offender's primary motivation: **instrumental** and **expressive hostage taking**. In instrumental hostage taking, the offender's goal is recognizable—material gain. An example is kidnapping a child and holding him or her for ransom. The goal in expressive hostage taking is psychological: The offender wants to become significant and to take control over his or her own fate. Expressive offenders generally feel that they have little control over events in their lives. They want to become important, and they believe the media coverage accompanying their hostage taking will help them to achieve this goal. To the observer, the conduct of the expressive offender often seems senseless and even suicidal. The ex-husband who breaks into his former spouse's home and holds her and her children hostage, daring police to enter, is an example. Hostage-taking offenses sometimes begin as instrumental acts but develop into expressive ones. An offender who initially kidnaps someone for material gain may find that his demands are unrealistic and not likely to be met; in this case, the person may decide to play out the scenario for the attention, significance, and control it affords. Sometimes, both instrumental and expressive motives are clearly involved from the beginning. That is, the offender expects both material and psychological gain from the abduction.

Categories of Hostage Taking

In the 1970s, the FBI began to classify hostage takers into four broad categories: terrorists, prisoners, criminals, and the mentally disordered (Fuselier & Noesner, 1990). Research suggests that over 50 percent of all hostage-taking incidents are perpetrated by mentally disordered individuals (Borum & Strentz, 1993), thus representing the largest category. With increasing attention to terrorist activities, including hostage taking, in the twenty-first century, additional classifications have been proposed.

Call (2003) has developed a complex classification of hostage takers. He identifies six major types: the emotionally disturbed, political extremists, religious fanatics, criminals, prison inmates, and some combination of these. He further argues that there are numerous subtypes to these major categories. Although some researchers emphasize that there is no one typical hostage taker or situation (Grubb, 2010), there are similarities, such as those found in criminal and inmate hostage taking. Both are likely to be instrumental in nature. In the process of committing a bank robbery, for example, the robber may take a hostage as a human shield to assist in the getaway. Likewise, during a prison riot or escape attempt, inmates may take corrections officers or staff as hostages to help earn their way to freedom or aid in their negotiations with prison officials. Such incidents are extremely rare, and the hostages are not usually harmed, but there are exceptions. A riot in the brutal New Mexico Penitentiary in 1980 was extremely violent, and 7 of the 12 officers who were taken as hostages were seriously physically injured (Johnson, 1996). However, in the famed Attica uprising of 1971, prisoners in New York state's Attica facility held a number of officers hostage but did not harm them (Wicker, 1976). The deaths of correctional officers and inmates that are associated with that incident occurred when the prison was stormed by law enforcement officers in a controversial move to forego negotiations and end the uprising (Wicker, 1976).

Strategies for Dealing with Hostage Takers

Experienced negotiators suggest strategies for dealing with hostage takers or barricaded individuals (see **Table 15-6**), and many of these are based on psychological concepts. A **barricade situation** is one in which an individual has fortified or barricaded himself or herself in a building or residence and threatens violence, either to self or to others. First, that person should be denied the excitement and stimulation he or she hopes to initiate; this requires that a potentially chaotic situation be handled as calmly as possible, with minimum media attention. This is difficult to accomplish, because hostage-taking incidents are extremely newsworthy. As noted in Chapter 5, very high levels of arousal tend to promote disorganized response patterns and reduce internal thought processes. Under high excitement and chaos, the offender is more likely to revert to "mindless" behavior, which may include violence. The most dangerous phase in most hostage or barricade situations is the first 15–45 minutes (Noesner & Dolan, 1992). Therefore, the first officers on the scene should hold their positions until additional resources, including the negotiation team, arrive at the scene. If possible, the officers who are first on the scene should try to engage the hostage taker in conversation, emphasizing that they wish no harm to the individual. Experienced negotiators believe that conversation distracts the offender from violence and generally calms the situation, especially if the negotiator maintains a calm and steady demeanor.

Second, offenders must be allowed to feel that they are in some control of the situation. Helplessness and powerlessness may have prompted the offense in the first place. If the captors do not feel they have attained any control, they may take steps to prove the opposite, such as shooting one of the hostages.

Third, in hostage or barricade situations, time is usually a strong ally. Once the early stages of a crisis have passed and some stability and calm have been achieved, the passage of time plays a positive role. Time has several effects. After the initial high-arousal state, the body winds down

TABLE 15-6   Guidelines for Negotiation
Stabilize and contain the situation.
Take your time when negotiating.
Allow the subject to speak: It is more important to be a good listener than a good talker.
Don't offer the subject anything.
Avoid directing frequent attention to the victims; do not call them hostages.
Be as honest as possible; avoid tricks.
Never dismiss any request as trivial.
Never say "no."
Never set a deadline; try not to accept a deadline.
Do not make alternate suggestions.
Do not introduce outsiders (non–law enforcement) into the negotiation process.
Do not allow any exchange of hostages; especially do not exchange a negotiator for a hostage.

Source: Based on information from Fuselier & Noesner (1990), p. 10.

and eventually the offender begins to feel tired, sluggish, and depressed. Under these conditions, the event takes on aversive properties for the hostage taker, and the offender is likely to begin to wish the situation were over. Time also promotes, in the hostage taker, some thought processes and greater reliance on internal standards of conduct. If the offender has incorporated some values of society, he or she may begin to appreciate the ramifications of his or her behavior. However, the hostage taker may also begin to construct justifications. Either process, however, may enable the offender to accede more easily to police requests. Experienced negotiators strongly recommend that the negotiator act as spokesperson for the authorities and a conduit of information, emphasizing to the hostage taker that acceding to requests will take time. Consequently, the negotiator should not be a decision maker or in command. Otherwise, if the hostage taker is under the impression that the negotiator (or anyone in the immediate environment) has the power and decision-making authority, he or she will believe that decisions should be made quickly and directly. Under these conditions, any delay generates frustration in the captor and further increases arousal.

Time also affects the relationship with the hostage. According to social psychological research, the more familiar one is with an object or person, the more one tends to become attracted to it (e.g., Freedman, Sears, & Carlsmith, 1978). To some extent, this may happen in some hostage situations, but we must be careful in qualifying these statements. In many hostage situations, the more the victim and captor get to know one another, the more they begin to accept one another. This is not to say that the victim approves of the hostage taker; rather, some victims become less fearful of their situation as time elapses. Furthermore, if the hostage was a stranger to the captor, the hostage takes on human qualities with the passage of time.

The Stockholm Syndrome

In rare cases, an attraction develops between a victim and a captor. This phenomenon was labeled the **Stockholm syndrome**, after a hostage-taking incident in Sweden in 1973 that resulted in marriage between a female hostage and one of her abductors. Police negotiators have noted that on occasion the hostage will side with the captor in working out demands. Although this may simply reflect a wish to end the terrifying ordeal as quickly as possible, it may also signify some attraction to or identification with the abductor. When hostages act this way, experts sometimes maintain that they have been brainwashed. An alternate explanation is that they have become attracted to their captors and temporarily identified with their values and goals. In general, though, the Stockholm syndrome does not occur. According to the FBI's Hostage/Barricade System (HOBAS), a national database that contains data from over 1,200 reported federal, state, and local hostage situations, 92 percent of the victims of such incidents showed no aspect of the Stockholm syndrome (Fuselier, 1999).

Some researchers have suggested that three things must be present before the Stockholm syndrome can take place (Fuselier, 1999). First, the hostage taker and victim must be together for a significant length of time. Second, the hostage must be in direct social contact during the incident. For example, physical separation of the hostages (such as complete isolation in a separate room) from the hostage taker will likely prevent development of the effect. Third, the hostage taker must treat the hostages kindly.

Rules for Hostages to Follow

Although some experts conclude that the Stockholm effect is unusual and has minimal positive aspects, some disagree. Although strong attraction to the hostage taker is not necessary, some degree of implied sympathy with his or their motives may be helpful for surviving such a situation.

Speckhard, Tarabrina, Krasnov, and Mufel (2005) interviewed 11 of the hostages held for three days in a Moscow theater by suicide terrorists armed with bombs and firearms. The terrorists held over 800 hostages in the incident. The stand-off ended when Russian Special Forces stormed into the theater and killed the terrorists. The core question the researchers posed in their research was "Is it better to be passive and cooperate with suicide terrorist knowing they are ready and willing to die for their cause, or should one try to find ways to resist?" (Speckhard *et al.*, 2005, p. 138). According to the 11 hostages interviewed (and this is a small number, perhaps unrepresentative of the 800 who were held), those who actively resisted in this situation or were uncooperative were either shot or severely beaten. Those who were cooperative and interacted positively with the hostage takers survived. Although the sample for this study was small, the observations made by the interviewees confirm advice typically given in the event that one is ever held hostage. As emphasized by the researchers, hostage-taking events by suicide terrorists are likely to increase across the world in the future, and those who are at risk for hostage taking must be prepared. The researchers advice: "In advising an individual on how best to behave as a hostage it seems wise to teach that positive attachments and passivity are likely to arise in this terrifying state of captivity, and that if one can recognize this reaction when it is occurring and keep it within control it is likely most protective" (p. 138). That is, an individual who can act the part of a cooperative and friendly hostage while maintain some level of objective detachment is likely to survive.

The above research does not support the existence of the Stockholm syndrome captives who survived, however. Cooperating with one's captors is not the same as truly liking or identifying with them, which is what the Stockholm syndrome suggests. Moreover, in some cases a captive may "pretend" to identify with the captor or even offer to help, in the belief that this is more likely to save his or her life. Hostage takers are not likely to respond positively to the latter approach, though. Virtually all advice given to hostages is to do nothing that will antagonize the captors, including attempting to ingratiate oneself to them.

Thomas Strentz (1987) also outlines some rules to follow should a person ever be taken hostage, particularly by strangers. His suggestions are based on the psychological reactions of those hostages who survive (survivors) compared with those who do not (succumbers). **Survivors**, Strentz notes, are those "who returned to a meaningful existence with strong self-esteem, and who went on to live healthy and productive lives with little evidence of long-term depression, nightmares, or serious stress-induced illness" (p. 4). Although survivors do not ever forget the hostage experience, the experience does not prevent them from living relatively normal lives. **Succumbers**, on the other hand, are those who either did not live through the ordeal or upon release or rescue have considerable difficulty dealing with the emotional trauma caused by the ordeal. They have great trouble getting on with their lives.

Strentz emphasizes, as we did earlier, that the most dangerous phase of any hostage situation is the moment of the abduction and the early minutes thereafter. Arousal levels are extremely high for both the abductors and the hostages. Unpredictable and unforeseen things can happen. Strentz asserts that, without exception, any form of resistance is extremely dangerous and should not be tried. He recommends playing the subordinate role immediately. Furthermore, throughout the entire abduction, maintaining a positive mental attitude that things will be all right in the end is absolutely essential. Feelings of hopelessness, abandonment, and isolation can lead to serious depression. On the other hand, a mature, controlled, and stable appearance—even if one is terrified—also helps settle the hostage taker(s). Anything that calms the situation increases chances of survival for everyone.

Furthermore, hostile feelings toward one's captors must be masked as best they can, again to keep the situation calm. The hostage should not get into arguments with captors about politics, religion, social issues, or anything else. Strentz refers to the opposite strategy as the **London syndrome**, a behavioral pattern demonstrated by the Iranian press secretary, Abbas Lavasani, during a six-day hostage situation in the Iranian Embassy in London. Lavasani refused to compromise his dedication to his cause, constantly and stubbornly proclaiming his beliefs, and seemingly intent on martyrdom. Despite the pleas of his fellow hostages for silence, he kept arguing and was eventually killed by his captors. Although we should not fault Lavasani for taking this approach—he was not responsible for his own death—potential hostages should be aware of the possible consequences of forceful verbal responses to their captors.

Chances of survival improve greatly if the hostage tries to blend in with fellow captives, if there are any. The individual who stands out in the crowd "by crying, by being overly polite and helpful, or by doing more than the abductors require, is immediately setting himself or herself up as an easy mark to be exploited" (Strentz, p. 6). If a person is more comfortable in the leadership role, he or she should be prepared to take the brunt of the abuse from the captors, and may even be killed as an example to the rest of the hostages. Individuals who have experienced a hostage-taking episode also say that being able to fantasize during the many empty hours is one of the critical factors in dealing with the situation. Some imagine travel to various places or dream about what they plan to do after the episode. Also, trying to keep a normal routine as much as possible will relieve stress. Exercise, personal hygiene, writing letters, or keeping logs—if these things are possible—are examples. Finally, Strentz recommends that no matter what the circumstances, hostages should never blame themselves or ruminate about what they should have done to avoid the abduction. Rather, they should accept their status and follow the patterns described here. The possibilities of survival will be greatly enhanced.

In sum, the psychological research on hostage taking focuses more on the effects of the incident on the hostage than on the characteristics of the individual committing the crime. Strategies are offered both to the hostage, for surviving the incident, and to negotiators, for dealing with the hostage taker effectively in order to prevent escalation and to end the crisis.

ARSON

Arson is defined "as any willful or malicious burning or attempt to burn, with or without intent to defraud, a dwelling house, public building, motor vehicle or aircraft, or personal property of another" (Federal Bureau of Investigation, 2005b, p. 53). According to the UCR guidelines, only fires that law enforcement investigation determined to have been willfully or maliciously set may be classified as arson. Agencies participating in the UCR program do not report fires of suspicious or unknown origin.

Incidence and Prevalence

The U.S. Fire Administration (2009) estimates there are 210,300 fires intentionally set each year, representing 13 percent of all fires reported to fire departments. Matches (30%) and lighters (15%) are the leading heat sources of intentionally set fires. Of all reported fires in recent years, an estimated 18,100 intentionally-set fires each year involve residences. According to a recent report from the U.S. Fire Administration (2011), many communities in the United States are currently experiencing a significant increase in serial arson-related fires.

Forty-one percent of those arrested for arson in 2010 were juveniles (Federal Bureau of Investigation, 2011a). Twenty-four percent of the total arrests were under age 15. In the United Kingdom, 40 percent of those "cautioned" or arrested are under the age of 18 (MacKay, Feldberg,

Ward, & Marton, 2012). In Australia, approximately 20 percent of the arson fires are known to be set by children and adolescents (Lambie, McCardle, & Coleman, 2002). Most of the known arsonists are young males. Some studies have found that between 75 percent and 85 percent of all firesetting is done by males, with increasing percentages of females in the 13- to 17-year-old group (Federal Bureau of Investigation, 2003; Stadolnik, 2000).

In a typical year in the United States, fires set by children and youth claim the lives of approximately 250 to 300 individuals (Putnam & Kirkpatrick, 2005). Children are often the victim of these fires, accounting for 85 percent of the lives lost in the United States (U.S. Fire Administration, 2004). Next to deaths caused by motor vehicle accidents, fires are the leading cause of death among young children (Stickle & Blechman, 2002). Not all these fires, of course, were set with criminal intent or would qualify as arson.

Most fires set by youth go undetected, unreported, or unsolved (Zipper & Wilcox, 2005). It is generally acknowledged, for example, that only a small proportion of fires set by juveniles is reported, probably less than 10 percent (Adler, Nunn, Northam, Lebnan, & Ross, 1994). Zipper and Wilcox (2005) report that, of the 1,241 Massachusetts juveniles referred for counseling services because of arson, only 11 percent of the blazes these youths started were reported. No one reported these incidents, apparently because witnesses or caretakers did not consider the behavior dangerous because no loss of life or significant destruction of property occurred. In these situations, many people also worry that charging juveniles with arson will give them a criminal record that will hamper their future careers. Finally, children who set fires are often considered emotionally disturbed and thus needing treatment, not punishment. We address this perception below. Another study of youth from the third to the eighth grades in 15 school districts in Oregon found that 32 percent of the students reported setting fires outside their homes, and 29 percent said they had started fires in their own residences (Zipper & Wilcox, 2005). Because so much attention is given to the topic of firesetting among children, we focus on this in the next section.

Developmental Stages of Firesetting

Arson is the term that specifically defines the setting of fires under certain conditions as a crime. **Firesetting** is the term commonly used in the literature on child psychopathology for essentially the same behavior. It is intentional and willful behavior with an understanding of the potential consequences of that behavior. As we note below, if a four-year-old clicks on the barbecue lighter and sets the outdoor furniture alight, he is not a firesetter. If he continues to do this, though, he is at risk of becoming one. Child firesetters have attracted considerable interest among researchers in psychology.

Gaynor (1996) outlines three developmental phases related to fire: (1) fire interest, (2) fireplay, and (3) firesetting. Fascination and experimentation with fire appears to be a common feature of normal child development. Kafrey (1980) discovered that fascination with fire appears to be nearly universal in children between five and seven years old. Furthermore, this fascination with fire begins even earlier, with one in five children setting fires before the age of three (fire interest). As the child gets older, fireplay (experimentation) may take place between the ages of 5 and 9. In this stage, the child experiments with how a fire starts and what it can do. Children during this phase are especially vulnerable to the hazards of fire because of their more limited ability to understand the consequences and their lack of effective strategies for extinguishing the fire once it gets out of control (Lambie *et al.*, 2002). By age 10, and sometimes even earlier, most children have learned the dangers of fire and its consequences; if they continue to set fires at this point, they have reached the firesetting phase. These youths most often demonstrate an intention to use fires to destroy, as a form of excitement, or as a communicative device to draw attention to themselves and their problems.

The children who *continue* to set fires tend to demonstrate poor social skills, inadequate social competence, and impulsiveness compared with their peers (Kolko, 2002; Kolko & Kazdin, 1989). In a national sample of nearly five thousand 12- to 17-year-olds, Chen, Arria, and Anthony (2003) were able to conclude that children rejected by peers were more likely to set fires than those who were not rejected. In fact, in this study, a combination of aggression and peer rejection was significantly related to firesetting.

In general, persistent firesetters are more likely to demonstrate attention deficit hyperactivity disorders and poor impulse control (Forehand, Wierson, Frame, Kemptom, & Armistead, 1991), and many are considered to have "conduct problems" by their teachers. It should be noted that many studies report that conduct disorder is the most frequent diagnosis assigned to juvenile firesetters (MacKay *et al.*, 2006). Lambie *et al.* (2002) report a similar finding. From their clinical experiences, Lambie *et al.* found that firesetting is but one part of a more comprehensive set of behavior problems, the motives of which occur for a variety of reasons and typically include impulse control problems and misdirected anger and boredom. There is also some evidence that children who are consistently cruel to animals and other children also tend to engage in consistent firesetting behavior (Slavkin, 2001). Lambie *et al.* (2002) also point out that adolescent firesetters frequently commit a variety of other crimes, including rape and other sex offenses.

This range of criminal offending has been noted by other researchers as well. It seems that a very large majority of firesetters known to the juvenile justice system have committed many other serious juvenile acts besides arson (Del Bove & Mackay, 2011; Ritvo, Shanok, & Lewis, 1983; Stickle & Blechman, 2002). Stickle and Blechman (2002) found that "firesetting juvenile offenders exhibit a pattern of developmentally advanced, serious antisocial behavior consistent with an early starter or life-course-persistent trajectory" (p. 190), a finding also reported by other researchers (Becker, Stuewig, Herrera, & McCloskey, 2004; Forehand *et al.*, 1991). As might be expected, research has revealed a large portion of the persistent firesetters is boys, probably at a ratio of 9 to 1 to girls (Zipper & Wilcox, 2005).

Nearly all children who set fires beyond the normal fascination and experimental stages tend to have poor relationships with their parents and also appear to be victims of physical abuse (Jackson, Glass, & Hope, 1987) and other forms of maltreatment (Root, MacKay, Henderson, Del Bove, & Warling, 2008). The high rate of maltreatment among firesetting youth is not surprising since maltreatment has been closely associated with self-regulation, academic achievement, attachment, and social skill development (Root *et al.*, 2008). In their investigation of 205 children and youth, ages 4–17, and their caregivers, Root *et al.* (2008) determined that those who were maltreated set more fires, were more versatile regarding ignition sources and targets, and were more likely to continue to set fires. Their primary motive for firesetting was anger.

In their comprehensive review of firesetting, Kolko, Kazdin, and Meyer (1985) suggest that it may be closely associated with parental ineffectiveness and faulty or nonexistent supervision. In a retrospective study by Saunders and Awad (1991), the records of 13 adolescent girls referred to the Toronto Family Court Clinic for setting fires were examined. The authors noted,

> Reading through the 13 charts was a depressing experience even for those of us who have worked for years with families who have many problems and serious difficulties meeting their children's basic needs. These parents had a history of marital problems, separation, violence against the spouse and the children, criminal behaviour, drug and/or alcohol abuse, and inability to take care of the children. (Saunders & Awad, 1991, p. 403)

Children who continue to light fires well into adulthood tend to be less intellectually able, less assertive, have limited interpersonal skills, have less schooling, are more likely to be underemployed or unemployed, and are more prone toward depression and feelings of helplessness (Murphy & Clare, 1996). One recent study of 1,100 patients (Devapriam, Raju, Singh, Collacott, & Bhaumik, 2007) found that persistent firesetting tended to be more frequent among those individuals demonstrating intellectual disabilities. The researchers also discovered that females with intellectual disabilities were as likely to be persistent firesetters as intellectually impaired males. In general, research continually finds that as a group, arsonists are inadequate socially and interpersonally, although the exact nature of the inadequacy varies among individuals (Jackson *et al.*, 1987). Research also indicates that firesetting is used by this group as a communicative vehicle in response to conflict and stress (Day & Berney, 2001). Some researchers (e.g., Vandersall & Wiener, 1970) have found that firefighters lit fires to impress peers. Day and Berney also note that firesetting is a very common behavioral pattern for the mentally disabled. In this case, however, we must question the degree to which the behavior could be considered intentional. Interestingly, the prevalence rate of firesetting appears to be significantly higher in children referred to a clinic for psychological problems than children not referred (Kolko & Kazdin, 1989; Lambie *et al.*, 2002). Research suggests that adolescent or adult firesetters usually come from a disadvantaged group who have little or no effective means for influencing their environment and who find themselves in highly undesirable situations (Dadds, & Fraser, 2006; Jackson *et al.*, 1987). Juvenile firesetters often come from unstable homes, characterized by parental absence, indifferent or absent fathers, and abuse (Hickle & Roe-Sepowitz, 2010). Some studies describe the parents of firesetters as displaying limited affection, engaging in very little monitoring of their children's behavior, and overall, showing little involvement in their children's lives (McCarty & McMahon, 2005).

The most consistent research finding on the psychology of adult repetitive arsonists is that they, as a group, experience and perceive little control over their environment or personal lives. Consequently, the arsonist experiences worthlessness and social ineffectiveness. Some suggest setting fires may provide conditions whereby the person experiences control or, at least, some influence over the environment.

Persistent and Repetitive Firesetting Among Adults

Theoretically, repetitive firesetting may be motivated by the arsonist's attempt to take control of his or her life and gain some social recognition. For example, the firesetting seems to be precipitated by events that exacerbate the arsonist's feelings of low self-esteem, sadness, and depression (Bumpass, Fagelman, & Birx, 1983). In addition, following a firesetting, many arsonists stay at the scene of the fire, often sound the alarm, and even help fight the fire. In some cases, they take heroic action to save lives. The recognition they receive for these actions probably enhances their self-esteem and instills a sense of control in their lives. Jackson *et al.* (1987) note that most acts of firesetting by repetitive arsonists progress from small fires to large fires, and the arsonists also become increasingly involved in fighting the fire. Furthermore, repetitive arsonists set fires alone and in secret, with virtually no one aware of their actions until they are caught. If they are caught, their history of firesetting presents an additional opportunity for them to gain attention and recognition from others.

Research indicates that many persistent arsonists have a variety of mental disorders (Brett, 2004; Dickens *et al.*, 2009). In addition, they tend to come from particularly troubled backgrounds and experience difficulties in many areas of life (Lambie & Randell, 2011). Thus, firesetting may be just one component in the constellation of maladaptive behaviors displayed by these individuals. Firesetting may be among these behaviors because of previous experiences with fire. Ritvo *et al.* (1983) found that a surprisingly large number of firesetters had been burned and maltreated with fire as children. They describe how one frequent firesetter during his early childhood had his feet severely burned by his father as a punishment for lighting fires. Another boy had been beaten on his buttocks with a hot spatula by his father. Still another had his hands held over a lighted stove burner by his mother for lighting fires. Ritvo *et al.* (1983, p. 266) speculate that these punishments may have "conveyed the message that the use of fire was an acceptable mode of retaliation."

In this section, we have concentrated on the repetitive or serial arsonists who set fires primarily for psychological and social gain. This focus is not to imply that a majority of arson fires are set by these individuals. Obviously, arson is committed for a variety of reasons by a variety of offenders, although much of it is probably committed for monetary gain, such as insurance. Recent research concludes that those who persistently and repeatedly set fires are frequently involved in a wide range of other antisocial and criminal behaviors (Del Bove & Mackay, 2011; Lambie & Randell, 2011; Vaughn, *et al.*, 2010). Moreover, persistent arsonists who set multipoint fires and utilize accelerants are considered especially dangerous (Dickens *et al.*, 2009).

Motives of Arsonists

There appears to be a wide variety of motives for arson. In an effort to systematize the reasons, Boudreau and his associates (Boudreau, Kwan, Faragher, & Denault, 1977) listed six primary motives for arson:

- *Revenge, Spite, or Jealousy:* Arsonists in this category include jilted lovers, feuding neighbors, disenchanted employees, and people who want to get back at someone whom they believe cheated or abused them. In juveniles, this motive is most closely associated with maltreatment from parents and caregivers.
- *Vandalism or Malicious Mischief:* Fires set to challenge authority or to relieve boredom are by far the most common of those set by juveniles.
- *Crime Concealment or Diversionary Tactics:* At least 7–9 percent of convicted arsonists are believed to be trying to obliterate evidence of burglaries, larcenies, and murders (Inciardi, 1970; Robbins & Robbins, 1964). The offender in this category expects that the fire will destroy any evidence that a crime was committed. Usually the fire is set near the object or incident the offender wishes to conceal. In some cases, the firesetter may try to cover his or her suicide for insurance purposes. Some arsonists try to destroy records that may link them to embezzlement or other occupational crime. Arson has also been used to divert attention while the offender burglarizes another building or residence.
- *Profit, Insurance Fraud:* This is the category most likely to attract professional or semiprofessional arsonists, who generally escape detection. Consequently, there are few hard data and few statistics to support this motive. However, since the profits gained from arson of this type are so large and the probability of detection so small, actual incidence is believed to be much higher than reported statistically. The property may be residential property, businesses, or modes of transportation (vehicles, boats, planes). According to Douglas, Burgess, Burgess, and Ressler (1992, 2006), this type of arson usually has two offenders: the primary offender, who is the dominant personality in the offense, and the secondary offender, who is the "torch for hire." The torch for hire is usually male, 25–40 years of age, and unemployed. The torch is likely to have a prior arrest record for a variety of offenses, including burglary, assault, and public intoxication.

- *Intimidation, Extortion, Terrorism, Sabotage:* This category refers to fires set for the purpose of frightening or deterring. Examples are fires set by extortionists to show they mean business or by striking workers to intimidate management. Another example is the destruction of women's health clinics where abortions are performed, presumably set by antiabortionists wishing to intimidate. Members of the radical environmental activist group ELF claimed responsibility in the 1990s for the burnings of highly expensive homes built on land that the group argued should not have been developed. By most accounts, arsons in this category are extremely rare. Douglas *et al.* (1992) refer to these as extremist-motivated arsonists who are committed to further a social, political, or religious cause.

- *Pyromania and Other Psychological Motives:* **Pyromania** is a psychiatric term for an "irresistible urge" or passion to set fires along with an intense fascination with flames. Before setting the fire, the individual is said to experience a buildup of tension; once the fire is underway, he or she experiences intense pleasure or release (DSM-IV, 1994). Although the firesetting urge is believed to be uncontrollable, the individual often provides many clues about his or her intention before setting the fire. Pyromania is believed to be a motive in only a small percentage of all arsons, but we will discuss it shortly in more detail to illustrate how some crimes lend themselves well to psychoanalytical interpretation.

Douglas *et al.* (1992) suggest an additional category that is close to the pyromaniac classification: excitement-motivated (E-M) arson. Excitement-motivated arsonists set fires because they crave stimulation that is satisfied by firesetting and by watching all the excitement that accompanies the fighting of the fire. The offender often selects a location that offers a good vantage point from which to safely observe the firefighting and investigation. Sometimes he mingles with the crowd watching the fire, primarily to hear comments and feel the excitement of the crowd. This E-M arsonist is usually a juvenile or young adult, usually unemployed and living with his or her parents. Generally, the E-M arsonist is socially inadequate and has poor interpersonal skills.

Juvenile Motives

As we learned above, the primary motive for firesetting by maltreated children was anger directed at those who maltreated them. In an earlier comprehensive study of 1,016 juveniles and adults arrested for arson and fire-related crimes, Icove and Estepp (1987) discovered that vandalism was the most frequently identified motive, accounting for nearly half of the firesettings in the sample. Research (e.g., Robbins & Robbins, 1964) has consistently shown that most fires set by juveniles appear to be motivated by the wish to get back at authority or gain status or prompted by a dare or a need for excitement. Therefore, it is not surprising that the Icove–Estepp investigation revealed that the vast majority (96%) of the vandalism fires were set by juveniles, who often set the fire within a one-mile radius of their homes. Moreover, they are generally accompanied by other juveniles. About one-half of these juvenile firesetters remained at the scene. About two-thirds of the fires set by juveniles are for thrills and the excitement involved, although these fires are most often set by juveniles working alone.

Female Arsonists

Harmon, Rosner, and Wiederlight (1985) studied the psychological and demographic characteristics of 27 women arsonists that were evaluated in the Forensic Psychiatric Clinics for the Criminal and Supreme Courts of New York between 1980 and 1983. Although the sample is small and restricted to a specific geographic area, and the research is quite dated, the findings are still of interest because we have so little data on female arsonists. The researchers found these women were somewhat older than male arsonists (mid-thirties), and with a history of alcohol and drug abuse. Generally, the group was uneducated, unmarried, and relying on public assistance for support. Most often, their motivation was revenge, a consistent finding also reported by Icove and Estepp for female arsonists. In their revenge, the women tended to act impulsively, responding to a perceived wrong committed against them or a perceived threat to their persons. In their haste, they used whatever flammable material was handy to set the fire. Generally, they set fires to places they lived in—apartments or common, public spaces of their buildings.

It should be mentioned that Wachi *et al.* (2007) report similar findings among female serial arsonists in Japan. These researchers discovered that many of the female firesetters were opportunistic and impulsive acts motivated by emotional distress. Most of the Japanese female firesetters (66%), however, were motivated by revenge and involved planned and goal-directed behaviors.

In their investigation of 114 female juveniles charged with arson, Hickle and Roe-Sepowitz (2010) concluded that the typical female juvenile firesetter comes from a disorganized and unstable home environment, displays difficulties in school, has negative peer relationships, has a history of running away from home, and engages in drug abuse. Their findings are generally similar to those reported for male juvenile firesetters.

Behavioral Typology of Firesetters

Canter and Fritzon (1988) have developed a typology of firesetters based on the behavioral patterns and crime scene actions of the offender. These investigators learned that firesetting could be distinguished according to two basic behavioral and motivational features. One behavioral pattern was whether the firesetter's actions are directed at a person or persons or at objects, such as buildings or symbolic structures. A second feature—largely based on the motivation for the behavior—is concerned as to whether the actions were expressive or instrumental, much like the expressive and instrumental forms of aggression described in Chapter 5. If the firesetting is intended to draw attention to some underlying emotional distress or feeling, it is expressive. If a specific outcome is desired, such as covering up a crime scene or financial gain, then the firesetting is instrumental. The researchers combined these two features into a four-category typology: (1) expressive firesetting directed at a person (expressive person), (2) expressive firesetting directed at an object (expressive object), (3) instrumental firesetting directed at a person (instrumental person), and (4) instrumental firesetting directed at an object (instrumental object).

The **expressive-person pattern**, which is the more common type of firesetting, is often associated with mental disorders and emotional problems, such as depression and feelings of helplessness. Essentially, this firesetting is a cry for help in that the offender seeks to obtain attention from family or persons in authority, such as law enforcement or social services. Unfortunately, the offender may endanger the lives of others as well as himself or herself, but this is not the primary intent. The **expressive-object pattern** is usually characteristic of serial firesetters who set multiple fires. Fortunately, most of these serial firesetters select uninhabited objects to ignite, such as trash bins, barns, abandoned buildings, and deserted houses (Häkkänen, Puolakka, & Santtila, 2004). This suggests that they are not interested in harming or injuring others. Research suggests that these firesetters are using arson as a way of acting out and have a strong fascination with fire (Santtila, Häkkänen, Alison, & Whyte, 2003). These offenders enjoy watching the fire, the fighting activity, and the accompanying excitement.

The **instrumental-person pattern** is most often linked to failed family or ex-companion relationships and their related threats, disagreements, and arguments. In some cases, the firesetting may be directed at someone in authority such as a teacher or church personnel. The targets may be a church, a school building or something associated with school, such as the school bus. The firesetting behavior in this category is motivated by anger and revenge for a perceived wrongdoing against the offender. The overridding intent of the offender in instrumental-person arson is retaliation. The **instrumental-object pattern** is most often associated with young offenders with a serious antisocial history and is linked with covering traces of other crimes, such as burglary or murder. It may also be directly associated with financial gain, such as burning a building, motor vehicle, or house to gain insurance monies.

Pyromania

According to the *DSM-IV*, pyromania is "the presence of multiple episodes of deliberate and purposeful firesetting" (p. 614). Moreover, it is characterized by high levels of tension or emotional arousal before the act, and there is relief or reduction of this tension when setting fires, or when observing or participating in their aftermath. Pyromaniacs are believed to be regular spectators at fires in their neighborhoods and communities, even though they have not set them. They are also believed to set off false alarms and to show unusual interest in firefighting paraphernalia.

The term *pyromania* was coined in the early nineteenth century to refer to a form of "insanity" identified by the impulse to set fires without apparent motive (Schmideberg, 1953). Stadolnik (2000) believes the term originated in France in the 1833 writings of a man named Marc, who argued that firesetters were suffering from a specific mental illness he called "monomanie incendiaire." According to Stadolnik, firesetting was referred to in the literature of the nineteenth century as "pyromania of Marc." In the mid-1800s, clinicians suggested that there was a relationship between firesetting and sexual disturbances, and psychoanalytic and psychiatric literature in particular continued to promote that link throughout the twentieth century. For instance, Gold (1962, p. 416) contended that the roots of arson are "deep within the personality and have some relationship to sexual disturbance and urinary malfunction." Abrahamsen (1960, p. 129) wrote, "Firesetting is a substitute for a sexual thrill, and the devastating and destructive powers of fire reflect the intensity of the pyromaniac's sexual desires, as well as his sadism."

Orthodox psychoanalytic thinking draws a connection between pleasurable urination (urethral eroticism) and firesetting. Fenichel (1945, p. 371) concluded, "Regularly deep-seated relationship to urethral eroticism is to be found.... In the same way that there are coprophilic perversions based on urethral eroticism, perversions may also be developed based on the derivative of urethral eroticism, pleasure in fire." This theory is based in part on the presumption that many firesetters are or have been enuretic (bedwetters) (Halleck, 1967). The theory does not suggest that enuretic people are likely to be firesetters, only that firesetters have more than their share of bedwetting behavior. Whether this relationship actually exists is still very unclear from the available research.

The relationship between sexual arousal and firesetting is plausible, since, through the process of classical conditioning, virtually any object or event can become associated with sexual arousal and gratification. The fact that some arsonists have fetishes or records of previous arrests for sexual offenses (MacDonald, 1977) lends some support to this possibility. Individuals who are sexually aroused by fire may, in general, be highly able to be conditioned. That is, the sexual arousal may become associated with or linked to some object, such as clothing. Recall the discussion of conditionability in Chapter 3. We may also expect these individuals to be sexually, socially, and vocationally inadequate (as noted by Levin, 1976). Firesetting could be a way of feeling significant and resolving conflicts.

While some firesetters may obtain sexual arousal and gratification from fire, there is very little evidence that many do, however. In an extensive analysis of 68 convicted arsonists imprisoned in Florida, South Carolina, and North Carolina, sexual "abnormality" was no more in evidence than it was in a comparable group of controls (nonarsonist offenders) (Wolford, 1972). Nor is there much evidence for the diagnostic label "pyromaniac." Koson and Dvoskin (1982) were unable to find any arsonists in their sample that met the *DSM-III* criteria of pyromania. More specifically, even though 38 percent of the sample were repetitive arsonists, none qualified as exhibiting a recurrent failure to resist impulses to set fires compounded by an intense fascination with firesetting and seeing the fires burn. Doley (2003) was unable to document the evidence of pyromania in her investigations of Australia's arson population.

In their investigation of 1,016 offenders of arson and fire-related crimes in the Prince George's County area of Maryland, Icove and Estepp (1987) reported only two offenders who may have qualified as pyromaniacs. In Canada, Bradford (1982) found only 1 individual out of 34 repetitive arsonists who could even remotely qualify as a pyromaniac, and Hill and colleagues (Hill *et al.*, 1982), in another Canadian sample of 38 arsonists, found none. Rice and Harris (1991) identified only 6 out of their sample of 243 male firesetters who reported having sexual arousal in the presence of fire. Quinsey, Chaplin, and Upfold (1989) report no differences between normal subjects and firesetters' sexual arousal to fire-related stimuli. Yesavage and associates (Yesavage, Benezech, Ceccaldi, Bourgeois, & Addad, 1983) found no indications that 50 French arsonists were attracted to fire for sexual reasons. Similar findings have been reported for child firesetters (Kuhnley, Hendren, & Quinlan, 1982; Stewart & Culver, 1982). In summary, research to date has found very little empirical evidence to support the existence of pyromania.

Summary and Conclusions

The crimes discussed in the chapter are all either violent or, in most cases, have the potential of doing great physical harm to victims. Even if violence does not occur, however, the crimes typically put the victims in fear. Thus, there is great psychological impact on the victim.

We began with a discussion of robbery, its categories and its motives. Although financial gain or material gain is the primary reason for robbery, the secondary motive of controlling and instilling fear in a victim does occur, particularly in some street robberies. Bank robberies, in contrast to many depictions in the entertainment media, are rarely carried out by professionals or well planned. The typical bank robbery is the work of an amateur who undoubtedly sees this as a way of getting quick cash. Commercial robberies are usually carried out against convenience

stores or fast-food restaurants. These establishments are seen as more accessible than banks, but they produce smaller return. Nevertheless, they are considered easier targets, generally late at night, when few workers and customers are on the premises. Street robberies are rarely planned; the robber sees the opportunity with a likely target and takes it. Interestingly, the latest data show strong-arm robberies were slightly more frequent than robberies carried out with firearms or knives. Victims also are more likely to be physically harmed during a strong-arm robbery, both because they are more likely to resist and because the perpetrator has less confidence in his ability to control the victim. Professional robbers are a separate group that can conduct any of the above types of robbery but are most likely to be involved in street robbery.

Wright and Decker (1997) and Wright *et al.* (2006) interviewed robbers who had committed many robberies over a number of years but, in many cases (60%) had never been convicted. In that sense, they were professional robbers. Like the other robber categories, they seemed primarily motivated by a desire for money, drugs, or material goods; however, some did enjoy the psychological effect of control over their victims. Although most of the robberies were unplanned, it is likely that these robbers relied on their cognitive scripts to carry out their crimes. In other words, they had played out the robberies over and over in their minds, considering what tactics to use under what situation.

We gave some attention to cybercrime—or computer crime—which is becoming increasingly problematic and which challenges the resources of the law enforcement community. In addition to economically motivated cybercrime, we also discussed cyberstalking and cyberbullying. Both allow the perpetrator to harass the victim while remaining anonymous, and both qualify as crimes of intimidation. To date, we have very little research knowledge about the prevalence of the offenses or the psychological attributes of the offenders.

The most well-known crime of intimidation, stalking, has received increasing public attention since it was first reported as a problem—or first given a name—in the 1980s. It is estimated that 1 of every 12 women and 1 of every 45 men has been a victim of stalking. The perpetrator's motive is almost invariably to control, intimidate, and frighten the victim. Restraining orders, sought by about half of the victims who report the crime to police, unfortunately have had little success, since they are ignored by most stalkers. However, some do respond to the restraining order and some do cease stalking when confronted by law enforcement. We reviewed the major stalking study by Tjaden and Thoennes (1997) that provides information about the prevalence of stalking and its effect on victims. Many women who are stalked had previously experienced violence at the hands of their stalkers, and future violence is a continuing possibility. Although stalking typically stops within a two-year period, in cases where violence has occurred, the victim's best option may be to move out of the area.

We also reviewed and provided illustrations of the four major categories of stalking: simple obsession, love obsession, erotomania, and vengeance. Other researchers have classified stalking by the relationship between the stalker and the victim: intimate stalkers, acquaintance stalkers, public figure stalkers, and private stranger stalkers. The first of both classifications (the simple obsession and the intimate stalkers) are not only the most common but also the ones most likely to be accompanied by physical harm to the victim. As a group, stalkers are not typically mentally disordered. The exceptions are the erotomania stalkers and the public figure stalkers, who tend to be delusional and plagued with a variety of mental disorders.

Hostage taking is a major crime of intimidation that places its victim in great fear, even though no physical violence may result. Strategies for law enforcement negotiating with hostage takers were reviewed as were suggestions for hostages in these terrifying situations. Remaining calm, not challenging the hostage taker, and not bringing attention to oneself (in the case of multiple hostages) were among these suggestions. The Stockholm syndrome—in which the hostage identifies with and becomes emotionally close to the hostage taker—is extremely rare. There is no research evidence that this is a strong phenomenon.

The chapter ended with discussions of arson and persistent firesetting by children and adolescents. Some forms of arson are clearly economically motivated, but firesetting in the young is a conduct problem with significant psychological overtones. Considerable psychological research has studied this behavior. Although most children are fascinated by fire, particularly between the ages of 5 and 7, in a small but very problematic minority, this fascination is accompanied first by experimental firesetting and gradually by continuing and persistent firesetting behavior. Persistent firesetters are usually identified by age 10. They typically have extremely dysfunctional family backgrounds, often lacking parental supervision and plagued by physical abuse and alcohol and other drug problems. Persistent adult arsonists often began their firesetting behavior as children. We reviewed categories of these arsonists and emphasized that very few fall under the term *pyromaniac*, indicating a serious mental disorder characterized by abnormal fascination with fire.

Key Concepts

Arson	Expressive-person pattern	Robbery
Barricade situation	Firesetting	Simple obsession stalking
Cognitive script	Instrumental hostage	Stalking
Cyberbullying	taking	Stockholm syndrome
Cybercrime	Instrumental-object pattern	Street culture
Cyberstalking	Instrumental-person pattern	Strong-arm robbery
Erotomania stalking	London syndrome	Succumbers
Expressive hostage taking	Love obsession stalking	Survivors
Expressive-object pattern	Pyromania	Vengeance stalking

Review Questions

1. What is the role of street culture and cognitive scripts in the commission of opportunity crimes, such as street robbery?
2. Define cyberstalking and cyberbullying.
3. What is the difference between the Stockholm syndrome and the London syndrome?
4. Identify and briefly describe stages leading to firesetting in children.
5. Does the research literature support pyromania? Explain.
6. Describe the difference between survivors and succumbers. What advice is given to individuals who are held in a hostage situation?
7. Describe the difference between instrumental hostage taking and expressive hostage taking.
8. Define arson and describe its psychological motives.
9. What are the psychological characteristics of repetitive firesetters?

16

Substance Abuse, Alcohol, and Crime

CHAPTER OBJECTIVES

■ Summarize the effects of the psychoactive drugs that have been most connected to crime and delinquency.

■ Caution about and emphasize the many individual differences in reactions to drugs and alcohol.

■ Define and explain drug tolerance and dependence.

■ Examine closely the extent of juvenile substance and alcohol use.

■ Note the illegal drugs most commonly used by American culture.

■ Explain and discuss "club drugs."

■ Focus on the effects and extent of marijuana use, because this is the most popular illicit drug today.

■ Sketch the relationship between alcohol abuse and crime and delinquency.

■ Explain the tripartite conceptual model and experimental substance use.

Over the past 35 years, the United States has been waging a "drug war" against individuals who transport, sell, and use a wide variety of illegal substances. While other periods in history have also seen a focus on drugs, it was in the 1980s that the government began to adopt conservative policies in response to perceived epidemics in the trafficking and use of cocaine, crack cocaine, heroin, and marijuana, among others (Walker, 2001). Billions of dollars have been expended on both reducing the supply of drugs and punishing convicted individuals with long prison sentences. Although federal and some state law enforcement priorities shifted after the terrorist attacks of September 11, 2001, illicit drugs continue to be a prominent target.

Many members of the public believe the above approaches are justified. In this chapter, we review the evidence in support of or against this public perception. Others believe the drug war has been in many ways a colossal failure, neither making significant headway in interdiction nor adequately addressing the widespread problems associated with substance abuse. According to the National Council on Crime and Delinquency (NCCD), substance abuse should be considered "*primarily* [emphasis added] as a health-related problem that should reside in the public health domain" (Rosenbaum, 1989, p. 17). Increasingly, in recent years, we have heard more such calls for addressing the illegal use of drugs as at least as much a health problem as a crime problem. The increasing trend to refer substance abusers to drug courts is indication of this approach; in drug courts, defendants are monitored and provided treatment for substance abuse (Marlowe *et al.*, 2012). Legislatures in many states have decriminalized the possession of small amounts of drugs or made changes in their laws that reflect a health response to the drug problem. In 2009, for example, the State of New York revised its statutes that had called for severe sentences for drug offenders; among many other provisions, the new law emphasizes the need for treatment services for inmates with substance abuse problems.

In 2010, nearly 8 million persons (3 percent of the population) age 12 or older needed treatment for illicit drug abuse (Substance Abuse and Mental Health Services Administration, 2011). Approximately 1.5 million of these individuals received treatment at a facility specializing in problems with illicit drugs. Among youth, ages 12–17, 1.2 million needed treatment for illicit drug abuse. Approximately 98,000 of youths did receive treatment.

JUVENILE DRUG USE

Juvenile illicit drug use is widely regarded as one of today's most important social concerns (Ramirez *et al.*, 2004). Although recent surveys (e.g., Johnston, O'Malley, Bachman, & Schulenberg, 2011; Substance Abuse and Mental Health Services Administration, 2011) indicate an overall decline or leveling off in the use of drugs and alcohol nationwide, a significant proportion of youth continues to be exposed to the deleterious effects of substance abuse. However, while drug use overall has decreased, marijuana use among teens has increased significantly in recent years, and marijuana is by far the most commonly used drug among this age group (Substance Abuse and Mental Health Services Administration, 2011). For example, the Partnership Attitude Tracking Study (Partnership at DrugFree. Org, 2012) found that heavy use of marijuana increased 80 percent from 2008 among teens. One in ten teens reported using marijuana at least 20 times a month during 2011 and nearly half (47%) of all teens reported using marijuana. In addition, past month heavy marijuana users were significantly more likely than teens who are not heavy marijuana users to use cocaine/crack, Ecstasy, and prescription pain relievers.

Drug use in early adolescence is associated with serious health problems, deviant and antisocial behavior, high-risk behaviors, and poor academic performance. High-level chronic juvenile offenders are far more likely to use drugs and alcohol excessively compared with other juveniles (Wiesner, Kim, & Capaldi, 2005).

Extent of Juvenile Drug Use

A special report from the U.S. Department of Justice (Federal Bureau of Investigation, 2005b) reveals that juvenile arrests for drug abuse violations—involving all drugs—increased 22.9 percent from 1994 to 2003. However, the data also reveal that in 1994, persons under 18 accounted for 11.8 percent of the number of arrests for drug abuse. Ten years later, the juvenile proportion of arrests for drug abuse violations remained virtually identical at 11.6 percent, demonstrating that while the number of juvenile arrests for drug abuse increased, the percentage of juvenile arrests to the *total* arrests was virtually unchanged. However, the patterns of the type of drug used have changed. For example, although the number of juvenile arrests for cocaine (especially crack) has dropped during the past 10 years, the arrests for synthetic narcotics increased dramatically during those years (see **Table 16-1**). Although the data in the table are a bit dated, the important point to remember is that drug patterns among teens change about every three to five years.

TABLE 16-1 Percent Change in the Number of Estimated Drug Arrests of Juveniles by Drug Type and Arrestee's Sex: 2-, 5-, and 10-Year Comparisons

	2003/1994		2003/1999		2003/2002	
	Male	**Female**	**Male**	**Female**	**Male**	**Female**
All drug types	15.4	79.2	−0.2	22.6	5.1	10.2
Opium or cocaine	−54.8	−10.7	−30.5	−8.5	−7.0	1.5
Marijuana	54.9	97.7	2.1	16.8	7.4	10.7
Synthetic narcotics	133.6	293.6	64.9	141.3	6.7	14.7
Dangerous nonnarcotics	23.0	127.9	47.4	86.3	6.3	14.4

Source: Federal Bureau of Investigation (2005b).

The FBI Special Report defines "drug abuse" as including the sale/manufacturing or possession of the illegal drug. In this regard, the report finds that most of the arrests of juveniles for the period studied (ranging from 73.8% in 1994 to 83.7% in 2003) were for possession of drugs rather than the sale or manufacturing of illegal substances (see **Table 16-2**).

When an individual is arrested for a drug abuse violation in the United States, the arresting agency reports to the Department of Justice the type of drug involved. The types fall under one of four categories: (1) opium or cocaine and their derivatives (e.g., morphine, heroine, codeine),

TABLE 16-2 Estimated Number of Drug Arrests of Juveniles by Sale/Manufacturing and Possession by Drug Type, 2003

Drug Type	Number
Total	195,468
Sale/Manufacturing	**31,895**
Opium or cocaine	11,385
Marijuana	15,178
Synthetic narcotics	1,513
Dangerous nonnarcotics	3,820
Possession	**163,573**
Opium or cocaine	14,408
Marijuana	127,524
Synthetic narcotics	4,166
Dangerous nonnarcotics	17,474

Source: Federal Bureau of Investigation (2005b), p. 349.

(2) marijuana, (3) synthetic narcotics, and (4) dangerous nonnarcotic drugs, such as Demerol and methadone. Between 1994 and 2003, the number of arrests of juveniles for violations involving opium or cocaine declined, while arrests involving marijuana increased. Juveniles (ages 12–17) who regularly smoke cigarettes and drink alcohol are far more likely to use a variety of illicit drugs (Substance Abuse and Mental Health Services Administration, 2011).

Marijuana remains the drug associated with the highest percentage of juveniles arrested for drug abuse (see **Figure 16-1**). For example, male juveniles arrested for the sale/manufacturing and possession of marijuana combined increased from 55.1 percent of the arrests of male juveniles in 1994 to 74 percent in 2003. We review more up-to-date statistics shortly when we focus on marijuana. Arrests of juveniles for violations involving synthetic narcotics and dangerous nonnarcotics consistently accounted for the lowest percentage of juveniles arrested for drug abuse violations during the 10-year period. Furthermore, these arrests show a downward trend. The percentage of arrests of both male and female juveniles for violations involving opium or cocaine also shows a decline during the 10-year period. Arrests of male juveniles for violations involving opium or cocaine fell from 34.2 percent of the arrests of male juveniles for drugs in 1994 to 13.4 percent in 2003. These data highlight the fact that while the *prevalence* of illicit drug use remains largely the same across generations, the *type* of illicit drug used is continually changing.

The data for the 10 years covered in the FBI Special Report showed that of the number of arrests in 1994 for drug abuse violations involving juveniles under age 10, 83 percent were males

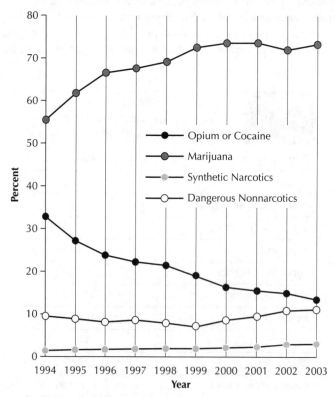

FIGURE 16-1   Percent Distribution of the Estimated Number of Drug Arrests of Juveniles by Drug Type, 1994–2003
Source: Federal Bureau of Investigation (2005b), p. 350.

and 17 percent were females. A decade later, the percentage of arrests for drug abuse violations of males under age 10 dropped to 78.9 percent, and the percentage of arrests of females increased to 21.1 percent, indicating that there may be a growing trend for female juveniles to be arrested at a younger age for drug abuse violations.

Who Is Selling to Juveniles?

In one comprehensive survey, one in nine high school students reported *selling* drugs during the past year, and most of them said they sold the drugs in school (Steinman, 2005). About 10 percent of the juveniles who bought marijuana said they purchased it at school (Substance Abuse and Mental Health Services Administration, 2005). Those students most likely to sell drugs on a *regular* basis are also more likely to engage in a variety of delinquent acts, including violence and heavy marijuana use. These youths are often hired by older dealers, especially in cities and metropolitan areas. Moreover, juveniles who sell drugs regularly do not usually have a strong relationship with family, and they prefer to associate with other deviant peers who use and sell drugs. Many are members of gangs. However, for the purposes of explaining delinquency, students who *occasionally* sell drugs to friends and relatives should not be placed in the same category as the more routine seller who distributes a variety of substances. Occasional, friend-based sellers rarely are detected by the authorities and do not usually become involved in serious delinquency.

Gender Differences in Juvenile Drug Use

Most research on drug and alcohol abuse and dependence has concentrated on males. The few studies that have focused on gender differences in alcohol and drug use among adolescents have consistently shown that males consume alcohol and drugs of various kinds more frequently and in higher quantities than females and are prone to experience more drug- and alcohol-related problems (Fothergill & Ensminger, 2006; Webb, Bray, Getz, & Adams, 2002). In addition, there is increasing evidence that males and females experience different substance abuse trajectories and consequences (Fothergill & Ensminger, 2006). Girls who show little commitment to school and academic achievement are at increased risk of later substance abuse problems (Fothergill & Ensminger, 2006).

SIX CONSISTENT RESEARCH FINDINGS ON ILLICIT DRUG ABUSE

The relationship between drugs and crime may be viewed from two perspectives: (1) the use, sale, manufacture, distribution, and possession of illegal drugs, all of which are themselves crimes, and (2) the pharmacological effects certain drugs have on a user's behavior in promoting criminal actions. Research directed at these two perspectives in recent years has reached the following six conclusions, each of which are discussed in some detail below:

1. More individuals are incarcerated or held in jails and prisons for drug offenses than for any other offense, and this has contributed to burgeoning jail and prison populations.
2. Arrestees frequently test positive for illicit drug use.
3. Arrestees and incarcerated offenders were often under the influence of illicit drugs when they committed their offenses.
4. Some offenders commit property crime to support their drug habit.
5. Drug trafficking often engenders violent crime.
6. The drug–crime relationship is difficult to identify and measure.

The first consistent finding has major implications for jail and prison crowding: More individuals are incarcerated or held in jails and prisons for drug offenses than for any other offense. In recent years many states are making serious attempts to reduce incarceration rates for drug offenders as well as accelerating their release from jails and prisons. As mentioned earlier, changes in sentencing laws relating to drug offenses are one method used to do this; another is diversion of substance abusers from standard prosecution, by offering substance abuse treatment in the community in lieu of incarceration.

According to the 2010 National Survey on Drug Use and Health, 22.6 million of Americans ages 12 and older are current illicit drug users (Substance Abuse and Mental Health Services Administration, 2011). Current drug use means use of an illicit drug during the month prior to the survey. In 2010, 1.3 million people were arrested for drug abuse violations in the United States (Federal Bureau of Investigation, 2011a) (See **Table 16-3** for information on types of drugs involved). Another 396,942 were arrested for liquor law offenses. In state courts, 195,133 people were convicted of drug trafficking in 1998, and another 119,443 were convicted of drug possession (Bureau of Justice Statistics, 2006). In 2002, one-fourth of all jail inmates were convicted of drug offenses, including 11 percent for possession and 12 percent for trafficking (Bureau of Justice Statistics, 2004).

As noted, with growing recognition that substance abuse is a serious health problem that requires intervention and treatment, many communities have established **drug courts**. Initiated in Miami, Florida, in 1989, they are designed to be a first step in diverting nonviolent offenders with drug problems into treatment and other community-based programs. Offenders who go through the drug court model often are expected to undergo long-term treatment and counseling, sanctions, incentives, and frequent court appearances. If they successfully complete their program,

TABLE 16-3 Arrests for Drug Abuse Violations by Sale/Manufacturing and Possession by Drug Type, 2010	
Drug Type	**Percent**
Total	100.0
Sale/Manufacturing	**18.1**
Heroin or cocaine (or derivatives)	6.2
Marijuana	6.3
Synthetic narcotics	1.8
Dangerous nonnarcotics	3.7
Possession	**81.9**
Heroin or cocaine (or derivatives)	16.4
Marijuana	45.8
Synthetic narcotics	4.1
Dangerous nonnarcotics	15.7

Source: Federal Bureau of Investigation (2011a).

they not only avoid jail or prison but also, in many jurisdictions, a criminal record. In 2003, there were 1,424 drug courts in existence or being planned in the United States (Office of National Drug Control Policy, 2003d). Recidivism among drug court participants ranges between 5 percent and 28 percent and is less than 4 percent for drug court *graduates* (Office of National Drug Control Policy, 2003d). Marlowe *et al.* (2012) cite six different meta-analyses conducted by independent investigators; the meta-analyses concluded "that drug courts significantly reduced criminal recidivism (typically measured by rearrest rates) by an average of 8–26 percentage points" (p. 515).

The *second* consistent finding from the research is that persons arrested for a variety of crimes frequently test positive for illicit drug use. In 2010, the Arrestees Drug Abuse Monitoring II (ADAM II) (2011) Program collected data from more than 4,700 adult male arrestees in 10 geographical locations (called sites). The ADAM II utilizes both urinalysis and self-report data to identify the level of recent drug use by the arrestees.

The ADAM II program continually finds that the level of drug use of arrestees is substantial. Fifty-two percent to 80 percent (depending on the site) tested positive for the presence of at least one drug in their system at the time of their arrest. Forty-nine percent tested positive for the presence of marijuana. Eleven to 37 percent tested positive for cocaine, and 2 to 18 percent for heroin.

The *third* consistent finding of illicit drug research findings in recent years is that arrestees and incarcerated offenders were often under the influence of illicit drugs when they committed their offenses. In 2004, nearly a third of state and a quarter of federal prisoners committed their offense under the influence of drugs (Mumola & Karberg, 2006).

Furthermore, certain professional criminal groups often prefer one drug over another. Professional pickpockets, shoplifters, and burglars, for example—when they use drugs—have a distinct preference for those that steady their nerves and provide relief from the pressures of their occupation (Inciardi, 1981). Professional pickpockets often consider opiates instrumental in furthering their careers. To some extent, this has a cyclical effect, since their material gain from their crimes is used to obtain the drug.

In reference to the *fourth* point—that some offenders commit property crime to support their drug habit—17 percent of state prisoners and 18 percent of federal prisoners said they committed their current offenses to obtain money for drugs in 2004 (See **Table 16-4**) (Mumola & Karberg, 2006). These figures are actually quite low compared with public perceptions that stealing to support a drug habit is widespread. In one recent study (Bennett, Holloway, & Farrington, 2008), the researchers found that the odds of committing a property or income producing crime

TABLE 16-4	Percent of Prisoners Who Committed Offense to Get Money for Drugs	
Most Serious Offense	**State (%)**	**Federal (%)**
Total*	16.6	18.4
Violent	9.8	14.8
Property	30.3	10.6
Drug	26.4	25.3
Public Order	6.9	6.8

*Includes offenses not shown

Source: Based on information from Mumola and Karberg (2006).

were between 3 to 4 times greater for drug users than nondrug users. In addition, the greatest odds for offending were for crack users (6 times greater), and second greatest odds were for heroin users (between 3 and 4 times greater).

The *fifth* finding of recent research is that drug trafficking often engenders violent crime. There is considerable evidence that violence accompanies drug distribution in the course of territorial disputes between rival organizations and gangs, or in conflicts between the buyer and the seller (Roth, 1996; Walker, 2001). Places where drug deals occur bring together valuable drugs, big money, weapons, and people accustomed to violence. This volatile mix creates a high potential for violence.

The *sixth* and final point is that the drug–crime relationship is difficult to identify and measure. The relationship between drugs and crimes is complicated by a fourfold interaction: (1) the pharmacological effects of the drug, which refer to the chemical impact of the drug on the body, (2) the psychological characteristics of the individual using the drug, (3) the psychosocial conditions under which the drug is taken, and (4) the interactions a particular drug has with other drugs consumed simultaneously. Discussion of pharmacological effects includes features of the nervous system, such as the amount of neurotransmitter substances within neurons, and body weight, blood composition, and other neurophysiological features that significantly influence the chemical effects of the drug. Psychological variables include the mood of the person at the time the drug is consumed, previous experience with the drug, and the person's expectancies about the drug's effects. Psychosocial variables include the social atmosphere under which the drug is taken. The people who are present and their expectations, moods, and behavior all may influence an individual's reactions to a drug. The interaction factor must be considered in any discussion of drug effects because most illegal drugs are taken in combinations, especially with alcohol. For example, it is not unusual to find teenagers and young adults consuming a variety of club drugs in combination with alcohol; more experienced users sometimes combine cocaine powder or crack with heroin (called a "speedball"). More than one-half of the arrestees in 2010 who tested positive for one drug also tested positive for another drug (ADAM II, 2011). Polydrug use is common.

In order to understand the effects of any drug, the pharmacological, psychological, psychosocial, and interacting variables all must be taken into account. Considering the fact that crime is complex to begin with, deciphering the drug–crime connection becomes very difficult, and the conclusions are necessarily that much more elusive and tentative. The relationship between drugs and crime is further complicated by the cultural, subcultural, and ethnographic aspects of drug consumption. The attitudes and perceptions of different age groups and cultures about specific drugs are often in a state of flux. Cultural preferences shift and change depending on drug availability, law enforcement priorities, and changes in cultural attitudes. In addition, demographic studies have shown that drug popularity and epidemics go through four distinct stages: incubation, expansion, plateau, and decline (Golub & Johnson, 1997). During the *incubation* stage, users experiment with the new and emerging drug, learn how to use it, and develop techniques for its use. During the *expansion* stage, prices drop, it becomes easy to use, its availability increases, and word gets around about the drug, all of which contribute to its popularity. During the *plateau* stage, there is a relatively high and constant use of the drug. But during the *decline* stage, the drug is shunned—usually by a new generation of youth—and a new drug emerges in popularity.

The Tripartite Conceptual Model

A helpful way of understanding the drug–crime relationship is the **tripartite conceptual model** proposed by Paul Goldstein (1985). Goldstein identifies three main types of drug-related crime: (1) *psychopharmacologically* driven crime, (2) *systemic* crime, and (3) *economically compulsive* crime. Goldstein's psychopharmacological component of the model presupposes that some individuals, as a result of short-term or long-term ingestion of specific drugs or chemical substances, become excitable, and/or irrational and demonstrate violent behavior. In other words, the assumption in this component is that some drugs *cause* some people (even usually nonviolent ones) to become violent and engage in a variety of criminal behaviors. The prevailing view about psychopharmacological violence, however, is that it is rare and attributable mostly to alcohol rather than illicit drugs (MacCoun, Kilmer, & Reuter, 2003).

The *systemic* component of the model hypothesizes that crime arises out of the system of drug trafficking and distribution. Examples of this component include disputes over territory between rival drug dealers and threats, assaults, and murders committed within and by drug-dealing organizations. Essentially, it refers to the violence inherent in the enterprise of drug trafficking and distribution, and is similar to the fifth observation of research noted previously.

Economically compulsive crime refers to criminal behavior that supports an expensive drug addiction. Robbery committed by drug users to support a costly drug habit is an example. Compulsive drug seeking and use is presumably an overwhelming drive, even in the face of negative health and social consequences (MacCoun *et al.*, 2003). The economically compulsive component is similar to the fourth observation discussed earlier in this section. As each of the major drug is examined in the following sections, the pharmacologically driven aspect as a cause for violence and criminal activity will be, by far, the most difficult to support.

Before entering into this discussion, it is important to stress that we do not, in this text, give more than passing attention to public policy with respect to drugs. As noted at the beginning of the chapter, there is considerable disagreement over the extent to which the government should continue on its present course of being harsh on drug offenders. The events of September 11, 2001, shifted priorities to some extent to a "war on terrorism." In 2009, with a new presidential administration, the focus again shifted to address rising unemployment rates, bank failures, and a health care crisis, although national security concerns were not ignored. Nevertheless, drug enforcement and harsh punishments continue, and the individuals who are most often affected are members of racial and economic minority groups. Although this book focuses on the individual behavior of drug users, readers also should be aware of the controversy surrounding public policy on this matter.

MAJOR CATEGORIES OF DRUGS

Four major categories of **psychoactive drugs** will be covered in the chapter: (1) hallucinogens or psychedelics, (2) stimulants, (3) opiate narcotics, and (4) sedative-hypnotics or depressants. A psychoactive drug is a chemical substance that influences a person's mood, perception, mode of thinking, and behavior. To keep the chapter within manageable limits, however, we will focus only on specific drugs within each category that represent a serious risk to public safety or that are most closely associated with criminal activity, such as the illegal manufacturing, selling, and distributing of a controlled substance. A **controlled substance** is any psychoactive drug or chemical substance whose availability is restricted, as designated by state or federal law.

The *Controlled Substances Act* (CSA), Title II of the *Comprehensive Drug Abuse Prevention and Control Act of 1970,* places all substances of potential abuse into one of five schedules. This placement is based on the substance's medical use, potential for abuse, and dependence potential (see **Table 16-5**). The purpose of the act is to control the distribution, classification, sale, and use of psychoactive drugs that have the potential for abuse. Although the term *potential for abuse* is not specifically defined in the CSA, scheduling classifications are based on available evidence that

TABLE 16-5	Formal Scheduling as Outlined by the Controlled Substances Act				
Schedule	Potential for Abuse	Accepted Medical Use in the United States	Physical Dependence	Psychological Dependence	Examples
I	High	No	High	High	Heroin, LSD, marijuana
II	High	Yes	High	High	PCP, cocaine, morphine, amphetamines
III	Medium	Yes	Moderate	High	Codeine, steroids, barbiturates
IV	Low	Yes	Low	Low	Darvon, Talwin, Valium, Xanax
V	Low	Yes	Low	Low	Cough medicines with codeine

Source: Drug Enforcement Administration (2005).

the drugs can create a hazard to health or jeopardize the safety of other individuals, or that there is a significant diversion of the drug from legitimate drug channels. Proceedings to add, delete, or change the schedule of a drug or other substance may be initiated by the Drug Enforcement Administration (DEA) or the Department of Health and Human Services (HHS), or by petition from any interested party (Drug Enforcement Administration, 2000).

The **hallucinogens** or **psychedelics**, which include LSD (lysergic acid diethylamide), mescaline, psilocybin, phencyclidine, ketamine, marijuana, and hashish, will be our first category. So called because they sometimes generate hallucinations, the hallucinogens are chemicals that lead to a change in consciousness involving an alteration of reality. In some respects, they replace the present world with an alternative one, although persons using them can generally attend to their altered state and to reality simultaneously. Marijuana, classified as a hallucinogen, is certainly a mild one for a majority who use it. Because of its widespread use and the public's tendency to mistakenly associate it with crime and bizarre behavior, it will be the main drug covered under the hallucinogens category. We will also include phencyclidine (PCP), a powerful drug that has been linked to crime during the past two decades.

Next we discuss the **stimulants**, so called because they appear to stimulate central nervous system functions. They include amphetamines, clinical antidepressants, cocaine, MDMA (Ecstasy), caffeine, and nicotine. Again, because of an alleged relationship with crime, the amphetamines, MDMA, and cocaine will be highlighted.

The third group includes the **opiate narcotics**, which generally have sedative (sleep-inducing) and analgesic (pain-relieving) effects. Heroin—a drug whose use appears to be growing at alarming rates in many communities—is featured in this section. The heroin addict appears frequently in crime statistics, since it is believed that he or she often turns to crime—particularly property crime—to finance this expensive habit.

Finally, alcohol and the "club drugs" will represent the **sedative-hypnotic compounds** that depress central nervous system functions. In most instances, the sedative-hypnotics are all capable of sedating the nervous system and reducing anxiety and tension. Examples include alcohol and the benzodiazepines.

Tolerance and Dependence

Before proceeding, we must distinguish two terms that are consistently used in the drug literature: **tolerance** and **dependence**. Drug tolerance is the "state of progressively decreased responsiveness to a drug" (Julien, 1975, p. 29). Tolerance is indicated if the individual requires a larger dose of the drug to reach the same effects he or she has previously experienced. In other words, the person has become psychologically and physiologically used to, or habituated to, the drug.

Dependence may be physical or psychological, or both. In simple terms, physical dependence refers to the physiological distress and physical pain a person suffers if he or she goes without the drug for any length of time. Psychological dependence is difficult to distinguish from physical dependence, but it is characterized by an overwhelming desire to use the drug for a favorable effect. The person is convinced that he or she needs the drug to maintain an optimal sense of well-being. The degree of psychological dependence varies widely from person to person and drug to drug. In its extreme form, the person's life is permeated with thoughts of procuring and using the drug, and he or she may resort to crime to obtain it. In common parlance, the person who is extremely psychologically and/or physically dependent is an addict.

Secondary psychological dependence may also develop. While primary dependence is associated with the reward of the drug experience (positive reinforcement), secondary dependence refers to expectancies about aversive withdrawal or the painful effects that will accompany absence of the drug. Thus, to avoid the anticipated pain and discomfort associated with withdrawal, the individual continues to take the drug (negative reinforcement).

The data reported in this chapter concerning illicit drug use and abuse were primarily gathered from the *National Household Survey on Drug Abuse* (NHSDA) (sponsored by the Substance Abuse and Mental Health Services Administration, 2011), the *2010 National Survey on Drug Abuse and Health* (the updated version of the NDSDA, also sponsored by the Substance Abuse and Mental Health Services Administration, 2011), the Office of National Drug Control Policy (sponsored by the Office of the President), the National Drug Intelligence Center (NDIC), the Bureau of Justice Statistics (BJS), the University of Michigan's 2010 *Monitoring the Future Study*, the FBI, the Drug Enforcement Administration (DEA), and the National Institute on Drug Abuse. Most of these organizations and agencies maintain up-to-date Web sites on the Internet.

THE HALLUCINOGENS

Marijuana is the most popular illegal drug used in the United States (National Institute of Drug Abuse, 2010; Substance Abuse and Mental Health Services Administration, 2011). In 2009, there were 16.7 million Americans, age 12 or older, who used marijuana at least once in the month prior to a survey (National Institute of Drug Abuse, 2010). About 16 percent are considered chronic users of the drug (used more than 300 days during the past year) (Substance Abuse and Mental Health Services Administration, 2011). Although marijuana is usually not considered a "hard" and dangerous drug, it is illegal and can lead to conviction and incarceration, and its heavy use has been linked to a range of poor health outcomes similar to those of heavy cigarette smoking (Windle & Wiesner, 2004). In 2010, 46 percent of those arrested for drug violations was for marijuana possession, and 6 percent of those arrested was for sales or manufacture of the drug (Federal Bureau of Investigation, 2011a). Incarceration for possession, however, is rare, especially for a first offense.

Marijuana is also one of the most popular illegal drugs used by juveniles, third only to alcohol and tobacco in terms of prevalence of use (Johnston *et al.*, 2011). During that same year,

11.8 percent of eighth graders, 26.7 percent of tenth graders, and 32.8 percent of twelfth grades reported using the drug during the past year. In most surveys, a substantial majority of the middle school, high school, and college students all indicated that marijuana is "fairly easy" or "very easy" to obtain. In 2005, for example, 85.6 percent of twelfth graders said it was "fairly easy" or "very easy" to get marijuana (Johnston, O'Malley, Bachman, & Schulenberg, 2006). Perhaps even more startling, in 2005, 41.1 percent of eighth graders said marijuana was relatively easy to get.

How Is Marijuana Prepared?

Marijuana, which apparently originated in Asia, is among the oldest and most frequently used intoxicants. The earliest reference to marijuana was found in a book on pharmacy written by the Chinese emperor Shen Nung in 2737 b.c. (Ray, 1972). It was called the "Liberator of Sin" and was recommended for such ailments as "female weakness," constipation, and absentmindedness. The word *marijuana* is commonly believed to have derived from "Mary Jane," Mexican slang for cheap tobacco, or from the Portuguese word *mariguano,* meaning intoxicant. Street names for the drug include pot, grass, reefer, weed, Mary Jane, and Acapulco gold.

The drug is prepared from the plant *cannabis,* an annual that is cultivated or grows freely as a weed in both tropical and temperate climates. There are at least three species of cannabis—sativa, indica, and ruderalis—each differing in psychoactive potency. The psychoactive (intoxicating) properties of the plant reside principally in the chemical Delta-9 tetrahydrocannabinol (THC), found mainly in its resin. Thus, the concentration and quality of THC within parts of the plant determine the potency or psychoactive power of the drug. Average marijuana potency has steadily increased over the past 20 years (National Drug Intelligence Center, 2009).

THC content varies from one preparation to another, partly due to the quality of the plant itself, but also due to its environment. The strain of the plant, the climate, and the soil conditions all affect THC content. For example, the resin is believed to retard the dehydration of the flowering elements and thus is produced in greater quantities in hot, tropical climates than in temperate zones. Consequently, cannabis grown in the tropics (Mexico, Columbia, Jamaica, and North Africa) presumably has greater psychoactive potential than American-grown hemp. More recent information suggests, however, that THC potency has become more a feature of the species of the cannabis plant than of geographic area or climatic conditions. Although marijuana produced in Mexico remains the most widely available in the United States, high-potency marijuana also enters the U.S. drug market from Canada (usually grown indoors). Domestically grown marijuana, either grown outdoors or indoors, also represents a substantial proportion of the U.S. drug market. Although domestically produced marijuana has substantially increased in recent years, much of the marijuana available in the United States is foreign-produced, mostly in Mexico and Canada (National Drug Intelligence Center, 2009).

The THC content for Mexican commercial-grade marijuana ranges from 4 percent to 6 percent, whereas the higher-grade sinsemilla THC content ranges from 15 percent to 22 percent (Office of National Drug Control Policy, 2003e). *Sinsemilla* is the Spanish word for "without seed." Asian criminal groups are the principal producers of high-potency marijuana in Canada (National Drug Intelligence Center, 2009).

The cannabis extracts used most commonly in the United States are marijuana and hashish. Marijuana is usually prepared by cutting the stem beneath the lowest branches, air drying, and stripping seeds, bracts, flowers, leaves, and small stems from the plant. There is evidence that the unpollinated female cannabis plant contains more THC than the male. *Hashish,* the Arabic word for "dry grass," is produced by scraping, or in some other way, extracting the resin secreted by the flowers. Therefore, hashish, which is usually sold in this country in small cubes, cakes, or even cook-ielike shapes, has more THC content than marijuana. During the 1990s, the THC content of hashish averaged around 6 percent. Hashish or hash oil is produced by repeated extractions of cannabis plant materials, a process that results in a dark, viscous liquid with a THC content as high as 20 percent (Abadinsky, 1993) but usually averaging around 15 percent (Drug Enforcement Administration, 2000). One or two drops of hash oil on a cigarette provide the same psychoactive effects as a joint. When exposed to air over a period of time, marijuana appears to lose its psychoactive potency, since THC is converted to cannabinol and other inactive compounds (Mechoulam, 1970). Cannabis extracts with higher levels of resin deteriorate more rapidly than those with lower levels.

In the United States, marijuana and hashish are usually smoked, most often in hand-rolled cigarettes called "joints," or in hollowed-out commercial cigars called "blunts." It is still popular to lace the joint or blunt with other drugs, such as phencyclidine (PCP) or crack. A common prac-tice in other countries is to consume cannabis as "tea," or mixed with other beverages or food.

The psychological effects of cannabis are so subjective and depend on such a wide range of variables that any generalizations must be accompanied by the warning that there are numerous exceptions. Reactions to cannabis, like all psychoactive drugs, depend on the complex interac-tions of both pharmacological and extrapharmacological factors. As we noted, these include the mood of the user, the user's expectations about the drug, the social context in which it is used, and the user's past experiences with the drug. The strong influence of these extrapharmacological factors, together with the widespread variation in THC content in any sample of cannabis, make it exceedingly difficult to obtain comparable research data. Essentially, the effects of cannabis are unique to each individual. Except for increases in heart rate, increases in peripheral blood flow, and reddening of the membranes around the eyes, there are few consistent physiological changes reported for all persons.

Addiction to THC does occur, but only at doses and continued use far above what is now used recreationally. Furthermore, the person who uses marijuana must learn to use the drug to reach a euphoric "stoned" or "high" state. Ray (1983) reports that a three-stage learning process is involved. First, users must inhale the smoke deeply and hold it in their lungs for approximately 20 seconds. Then they must learn to identify and control the effects. Finally, they must learn to label the effects as "pleasant."

Synthetic Marijuana

In recent years, a product known as **synthetic marijuana**, touted as legal marijuana, has reached the market. The product is sold in small packets under many brand names, including K2, Blaze, Genie, Panama Red Ball, Blueberry Haze, and Spice. On the street it may be known as serenity, wicked spice, black mamba, or fake pot or weed. It can be bought on the open market, either online, or in head shops, convenience stores, tobacco stores, or gasoline stations. Synthetic mari-juana is produced to mimic the effects of cannabis. The product usually consists of a mixture of dried leaves from herbal plants, and is often laced with synthetic cannabinoids (especially HU-210). It is believed that HU-210 may be hundreds of times more potent than THC, so even traces of the chemical in the product can be potentially effective (U.S. Drug Enforcement Administration, 2009). Some experts refer to HU-210 as "stealth marijuana."

Synthetic marijuana has been available since approximately 2006, and its popularity grew rapidly. In 2011, 11 percent of high school seniors nationwide stated they used the drug during the prior 12 months (Johnston *et al.*, 2011). Many states have banned its sale or possession, particularly by juveniles. In February 2011, the DEA declared a number of the chemicals used in the product to be Schedule I drugs, and prohibited the product's possession or sale if it contained those chemicals. The temporary federal ban will continue until the potential safety and health issues of synthetic marijuana can be investigated by the U.S. Department of Health and Human Services. If taken with alcohol the person can become very sick, and there are indications that some individuals show psychotic-like symptoms under its influence.

Cannabis and Crime

Numerous research projects directed at the effects of cannabis were launched during the 1950s, 1960s, and early 1970s. Many of these studies had methodological shortcomings and did not control for parity of dosage levels, means of administering the drug, and THC content in the drug itself. Psychological factors associated with the subjects were not considered carefully enough, and experimental settings and instructions were haphazard. At first, some of the research suggested a relationship between cannabis use and criminal behavior. However, with more sophisticated statistical analyses that controlled demographic and criminal background variables, the earlier results were found to be spurious (National Commission on Marihuana and Drug Abuse, 1972). By the beginning of the twenty-first century, no investigation had established a causal link between the use of cannabis and criminal activity (Walker, 2001). Of course, this excludes the illegal acts of producing, selling, possessing, or using the drug.

Both independent research and investigations conducted by government-sponsored commissions strongly indicate that marijuana does not directly contribute to criminal behavior. After an extensive review of available literature, the National Commission on Marijuana and Drug Abuse (1972, p. 470) came to this conclusion: "There is no systematic empirical evidence, at least that is drawn from the American experience, to support the thesis that the use of marijuana either inevitably or generally causes, leads to or precipitates criminal, violent, aggressive, or delinquent behavior of sexual or nonsexual nature." The Commission Report (p. 470) adds, "If anything, the effects observed suggest that marijuana may be more likely to neutralize criminal behavior and to militate against the commission of aggressive acts."

One of the predominant effects of THC is relaxation and a marked decrease in physical activity (Tinklenberg & Stillman, 1970). THC induces muscular weakness and inability to sustain physical effort, so that the user wishes nothing more strenuous than to stay relatively motionless. As Tinklenberg and Stillman (1970, p. 341) note, " 'being stoned' summarizes these sensations of demobilizing lethargy." It is difficult to imagine "stoned" users engaging in assaultive or violent activity. If anything, THC should reduce the likelihood of criminal activity, particularly aggressive conduct, as the Commission suggested. There is some evidence to support this conclusion.

Tinklenberg and Woodrow (1974) found that drug users who use mainly marijuana seem less inclined toward violence and aggression than their counterparts who prefer other drugs, such as alcohol or amphetamines. After examining drug usage among lower-class minority youth, Blumer and his associates (Blumer, Sutter, Ahmed, & Smith, 1967) made the same observation. In fact, they found that marijuana users deliberately shunned aggression and violence; in order to maintain one's status in the group, it was important to remain "cool" and nonaggressive, regardless of provocation.

Although the empirical evidence so far indicates that cannabis does not, as a rule, stimulate aggressive behavior or other criminal actions, whenever we deal with human behavior, there will be exceptions. Individuals familiar with the effects of cannabis have heard of occasional negative experiences produced by THC. Although the phenomenon is rare, some people do report feelings of panic, hypersensitivity, feelings of being out of contact with their surroundings, and bizarre behavior. Some individuals have experienced rapid, disorganized intrusions of irrelevant thoughts, which prompted them to feel they were losing control of their mind. Under these conditions, it is plausible that one would interpret the actions of others as threatening. It is also possible that these panicked individuals might attack those surrounding them.

However, those who investigate cannabis effects usually agree that people who act violently under the influence of the drug were probably *predisposed* to act that way, with or without the drug (National Commission on Marihuana and Drug Abuse, 1972). The evidence indicates that violent marijuana users were violent prior to using cannabis. In other words, they learned the behavioral pattern independently of cannabis. In addition, they have come to expect that the drug will "bring out" aggression or violence in them.

Summary

In summary, there is no solid evidence to indicate that cannabis contributes to or encourages violent or property crime, in spite of waning beliefs that this relationship exists. In fact, there is evidence to suggest that cannabis users are less criminally or violently prone under the influence of the drug than users of other drugs, such as alcohol and amphetamines. There are also no supportive data that cannabis is habit forming to the point where the user must get a "fix" and will burglarize or rob to obtain funds to purchase the drug. Marijuana trafficking and distribution are also not fraught with the extensive systematic violence that accompanies other drugs of abuse. However, this may change soon as large-scale Asian and Mexican drug trafficking organizations involved in cannabis cultivation and marijuana distribution are beginning to expand into the United States in increasing numbers (National Drug Intelligence Center, 2009). For most people, the primary negative effect of marijuana use is diminished psychomotor performance, thereby putting the public safety at risk when someone intoxicated with marijuana drives a motor vehicle or a boat, or operates machinery.

Marijuana certainly promotes relaxation and interferes with judgment, and probably makes people more daring and more prone to risk taking. It also alters the experience of reality and often improves mood. The drug is clearly used extensively as a recreation enhancer. As noted earlier, nearly 50 percent of individuals arrested for a variety of offenses had been using marijuana just prior to or at the time of their offense, and it is also very popular among delinquents. Most likely, arrestees and detainees used the drug to improve their sense of well-being, frequently in combination with other drugs. And the drug is classified as a Schedule I drug by the DEA. Although it is illegal to produce, possess, sell, or consume marijuana, there is little evidence that the drug propels nonviolent people to become violent or antisocial, or to engage in some kind of serious criminal behavior.

Phencyclidine (PCP)

PCP may be classified as a central nervous system depressant, anesthetic, tranquilizer, or hallucinogen. It has many effects, but most pronounced is its barbiturate-like downer effect, perceptual distortions and hallucinations, and its amphetamine-like upper effects, such as excitation and hyperactivity. An overdosed person, for example, may show signs of moving from upper to downer effects while having hallucinations.

PCP was first synthesized in 1957, but due to its psychotic and hallucinogenic reactions, it was taken off the market for human consumption in 1965 and limited to veterinary medicine as an animal immobilizing agent. Because of its serious and numerous side effects, it is no longer used even in veterinary medicine. After a decline in abuse during the late 1980s and 1990s, phencyclidine (PCP) has re-emerged as a drug of abuse (Drug Enforcement Administration, 2010). The behavior of some individuals under the influence of PCP is highly unpredictable and may lead to life-threatening situations. Under the spell of PCP psychosis, delusions of superhuman strength, persecution, and grandiosity are not uncommon. In general, PCPs are associated with a number of serious risks, and many experts believe it is one of the most dangerous illicit drugs on the streets. On occasion, individuals under the influence of PCP may use weapons to defend themselves and to commit other acts of violence.

There is wide variation in degree of purity and dosage forms of PCP manufactured in clandestine laboratories. It comes in capsules, tablets, liquids, or powders. It may be administered orally, by inhalation (snorted or smoked), and at times by intravenous injection. If it is smoked, PCP is often applied to leafy material such as mint, parsley, oregano, or marijuana. Users usually combine PCP with other drugs, particularly marijuana and alcohol. It can cause death, although the majority of fatal doses were combined with alcohol (Brunet, Reiffenstein, Williams, & Wong, 1985–1986). PCP is largely abused by young adults and high school students. According to the National Survey on Drug Use and Health reports, in 2008, 6.6 million (2.7%) individuals in the United States, ages 12 and older, reported using PCP nonmedically in their lifetime (Substance Abuse and Mental Health Services Administration, 2011). In 2008, due to PCP, there were about 37,266 confirmed vists to emergency rooms in the United States, compared to 28,035 visits in 2007 (Drug Enforcement Administration, 2010). Because of its adverse and negative effects, the reasons for its popularity remain obscure. In addition, the popularity of PCP moves in cycles. In some years, it is extremely popular, followed by limited use for a few years. The drug is marketed under a number of other names, including Angel Dust, Supergrass, Killer Weed, Embalming Fluid, and Rocket Fuel, because of its range of bizarre and volatile effects (Drug Enforcement Administration, 2005).

PCP and Crime

The available evidence clearly indicates that PCP users tend to be multiple illicit drug users (polydrug users). To what extent PCP propels a person toward a life of crime is largely unknown, but it does *not* seem likely that the PCP user regularly engages in crime to support his or her habit. PCPs are inexpensive, easily available, and only marginally addictive after chronic use. PCP users are generally polydrug users who have demonstrated a variety of types of antisocial conduct prior to PCP usage. Polydrug usage is more likely to be one symptom within a complicated matrix of other symptoms found in certain individuals habitually "going against" their environment. Currently, phencyclidine is classified as a Schedule I drug of abuse by the DEA.

THE STIMULANTS

Amphetamines

Amphetamines and cocaine are classified as central nervous system stimulants and have highly similar effects. Amphetamines are part of a group of synthetic drugs known collectively as amines. Cocaine (coke, snow, candy) is a chemical extracted from the coca plant (Erythroxylon coca), an extremely hardy plant native to Peru. The amines in particular produce effects in the sympathetic nervous system, a subdivision of the autonomic nervous system, which arouse the person to actions that might include fighting or fleeing from a frightening situation. Amphetamines are traditionally classified into three major categories: (1) amphetamine (Benzedrine), (2) dextroamphetamine (Dexedrine), and (3) methamphetamine (Methedrine or Desoxyn). Of the three,

Benzedrine is the least potent. All may be taken orally, inhaled, or injected, and all act directly on the central nervous system, particularly the reticular activating system.

Methamphetamine

In this section, methamphetamine is the focus of the amphetamine group because it is the drug most preferred by drug users, and carries the most health risks. It is a Schedule II stimulant because it has a high potential for abuse and is available only through a prescription that cannot be refilled (National Institute on Drug Abuse, 2002). Methamphetamine has traditionally been the drug of preference when the user injects the substance directly into the bloodstream. More recently, though, the preferred method of consumption is by smoking, especially the crystallized form of methamphetamine known as "ice" (Maxwell, 2004). "Ice," also known as "shard," "shabu," "tweak," "crystal," "super ice," "LA glass," or "crystal meth," is methamphetamine that has been washed in solvent such as alcohol to remove the impurities. Evaporation of the solvent produces crystals that resemble glass shards or ice shavings. Yaba is a Thai name for a colored tablet containing methamphetamine combined with caffeine, which is gaining popularity among young adults (Drug Enforcement Administration, 2010). The illegal form of the drug is manufactured in clandestine laboratories (meth labs or super labs). In recent years, Mexican drug trafficking organizations have become the primary manufacturers and distributors of methamphetamine in the United States (Drug Enforcement Administration, 2010). Methamphetamine is relatively easy to produce, and the ingredients can be purchased at local drug stores (Office of National Drug Control Policy, 2003b). Currently, methamphetamine is the primary drug of abuse in rural America (Maxwell, 2004).

Methamphetamine produces an increase in alertness and a decrease in appetite. The effects may last as long as 12 hours. In high doses, the drug can cause violent behavior, anxiety, insomnia, and symptoms of paranoid behavior, including delusions, hallucinations, and mood swings. Some chronic users develop sores on their bodies from scratching "crank bugs," bugs that, under the user's delusional state, are believed to be crawling under the skin.

Methylphenidate, a stimulant known as Ritalin, has a high potential for abuse and produces many of the same effects as methamphetamine. Many children who were diagnosed with attention deficit hyperactivity disorder take Ritalin to stabilize their behavior. Thus, Ritalin is considered easily accessible to children and adolescents who can obtain the drug from classmates or friends who have a prescription for it. In more recent years, Adderall, a mixture of amphetamine salts, has increasingly become the drug of preference for ADHD. It has traditionally been a popular drug of abuse for high school and college students, although its popularity is beginning to level out (Substance Abuse and Mental Health Services Administration, 2009, 2011).

The amphetamines are synthetic compounds, and, unlike cannabis or cocaine, can be easily produced by self-appointed chemists for large-scale illegal distribution. The manufacture of methamphetamine, for example, requires precursor drugs (drugs that are necessary in the manufacture of another) such as ephedrine or pseudoephedrine, which are widely available in Mexico and are believed to be smuggled into the United States in large quantities (Feucht & Kyle, 1996). Over-the-counter cold medicines containing ephedrine or pseudoephedrine and other materials can also be "cooked" to make methamphetamine (Office of National Drug Control Policy, 1999b). Therefore, it is exceedingly difficult to estimate the quantity of amphetamines consumed each year in the United States. The Comprehensive Methamphetamine Act of 1996 was passed, among other things, to control the sale of ephedrine and pseudoephedrine.

Khat is a flowering evergreen shrub that produces a stimulant-like effect. The drug is native to East Africa and the Arabian Peninsula where it has been used as a tradition in many social occasions. It is chewed like tobacco, and retained in the mouth, or used as tea or sprinkled on food. The common street names for the drug include Abyssinian Tea, African Salad, Catha, Chat, Kat, and Oat. Khat's health effects and potential for addiction are unknown at this time.

Cocaine and Its Derivatives

Cocaine is the second most commonly used illicit drug (following marijuana in the United States (Drug Enforcement Administration, 2011)). Approximately 2.4 million Americans use cocaine on a regular basis (Drug Enforcement Administration, 2011). Adults 18–25 years old have a higher rate of cocaine use than any other age group. Males are more likely to use the drug than females.

In general, there has been a significant decrease in the use of crack or powder cocaine among adolescents since the mid-1990s (Johnston *et al.*, 2011). Perceived risk and disapproval of the drug among this age group probably has been effective in reducing its use. Nevertheless, any use of this dangerous drug is still significant.

In the United States and Canada, cocaine is usually administered nasally (sniffing), intravenously, or by inhaling (smoking). Cocaine taken orally is poorly absorbed because it is hydrolyzed (neutralized) by gastrointestinal secretions. Slang names for powder cocaine include candy sugar, pariba, aspirin, mojo, icing, happy dust, oyster stew, and double bubble. Cocaine reached considerable popularity and extensive use during the 1980s and 1990s. Crack is produced in such a way that the cocaine ingredient can be smoked without destroying its potency. There is no safe way to use cocaine. Any route of administration can lead to toxic amounts, leading to acute cardiovascular or cerebrovascular emergencies that could lead to sudden death (National Institute on Drug Abuse, 2004).

Interestingly, it was believed that Coca-Cola contained cocaine as an active ingredient until 1903, when caffeine was substituted (Kleber, 1988). This assertion is vigorously denied by representatives of the company, who insist there is no evidence for it. However, around the turn of the century, cocaine *was* used as an important stimulant in some "soft" drinks (such as Kos-Kola, Wiseola, and Care-Cola). It was also used in cigarettes and cigars, various tonics, foods, sprays, and ointments (including hemorrhoid salves) (Smart, 1986). The famous drink "Vin Mariani," so popular among the wealthy at the time, was a combination of vintage French wine and cocaine. However, cocaine began to fall into disfavor when people became concerned about its dangerous and undesirable effects. By 1910, cocaine had become the most hated and feared drug in North America (Kleber, 1988). The Harrison Narcotics Act of 1914 in the United States, and the Propriety and Patents Medicines Act of 1908 in Canada, sharply curtailed or terminated its usage, and the popularity of cocaine correspondingly declined until the 1960s.

Psychological Effects

In small doses, both amphetamines and cocaine increase wakefulness, alertness, and vigilance; improve concentration; and produce a feeling of clear thinking. There is generally an elevation of mood, mild euphoria, increased sociability, and a belief that one can do just about anything. The duration of the stimulant's euphoric effects depends on the route of administration. The faster the absorption into the bloodstream, such as inhaling cocaine vapor into the lungs rather than snorting the powder form, the more rapid and intense the psychoactive effects. Cocaine vapor is usually produced by igniting the powder form of cocaine. In large doses, the effects may be irritability, hypersensitivity, delirium, panic aggression, hallucinations, and psychosis. Hallucinations sometimes include "coke bugs" that appear to be crawling all over the body. Injected at chronically high doses, these drugs may precipitate "toxic psychosis," a syndrome with many of the psychotic features of paranoid schizophrenia. With the metabolization and elimination of the drug, the psychotic episode usually dissipates. Cocaine, like any psychoactive drug, will engender different experiences for different individuals. Some people under the influence will exhibit violent, erratic, paranoid, or even suicidal behavior; others will display peaceful, friendly, sociable behavior.

Adverse Physical Effects

Frequent cocaine use may have some strong adverse effects, depending on how it is administered. Regularly snorting cocaine can lead to a loss of sense of smell, nosebleeds, problems with swallowing, hoarseness, and inflammation of the nasal septum (National Institute on Drug Abuse, 1999). Orally consuming cocaine can cause severe bowel gangrene because of reduced blood flow to the gastrointestinal system. Injecting cocaine can generate some serious allergic reactions, and sometimes results in death. Cocaine is usually processed with a variety of volatile solvents, such as gasoline, benzene, and kerosene, and traces of these toxic substances often remain in the powder form of cocaine.

Cocaine often has a dramatic effect on the cardiovascular system, such as disturbances in heart rhythm and heart attacks. It can adversely affect the respiratory systems, resulting in chest pain or respiratory failure. It can also cause strokes, seizures, blurred vision, nausea, fever, muscle spasms, and coma. Cocaine users who frequently inject the drug are at risk of bacterial infections and other infectious diseases. Sharing needles and using unsterilized drug paraphernalia also put users at considerable risk of HIV, hepatitis, and a variety of other viruses.

There is a potentially very dangerous drug interaction between cocaine and alcohol that should be noted. When the user ingests cocaine and alcohol at once or closely together, the drugs are converted by the body to cocethylene. Cocethylene is substantially more toxic than either drug alone, and available evidence indicates that the mixture of cocaine and alcohol is the most common two-drug combination that results in drug-related death (National Institute on Drug Abuse, 1999).

Stimulants, Cocaine, and Crime

As pointed out, heavy users of amphetamines typically prefer to inject methamphetamine directly into the bloodstream, cranking up with several hundred milligrams at one time. During these speed "runs," the user may engage in aggressive or violent behavior. However, it appears that people who behave violently under the effects of amphetamines are very often predisposed to behave violently long before they ingested amphetamines. In other words, there is little evidence to conclude that amphetamines cause people to behave violently, but they do increase the likelihood that an already prone person will behave violently.

Research sponsored by the Arrestees Drug Abuse Monitoring II (2011) program consistently reveals, however, that persons arrested frequently test positive for cocaine. Urinalysis indicated that cocaine was the second most commonly used drug by arrestees at the time of their crime in 8 out of 10 sites in 2010, ranging from 12 percent at one site (Sacramento) to 33 percent at another (Atlanta).

Both amphetamines and cocaine are considered Schedule II drugs by the DEA. In small doses, these drugs increase alertness and concentration. In large doses, they generally produce negative psychological effects. But, to date, virtually no study has shown that stimulants or cocaine facilitate either property crime or violent crime. In an exhaustive review of the literature, the Panel on the Understanding and Control of Violent Behavior concluded, "There is no evidence to support the claim that snorting or injecting cocaine stimulates violent behavior." Morgan and Zimmer (1997) also conclude that there is very little convincing evidence that cocaine, either in crack or powder form, causes a nonviolent person to suddenly become violent or dangerous to others. Nor is there any evidence to support the assumption that cocaine, especially crack, causes women to abuse their children. It is more likely the lifestyle of the parent, rather than simply the pharmacologically driven aspect of the drug, that leads to child abuse (Morgan & Zimmer, 1997).

Powder cocaine, however, can be strongly addictive, and the dependence onset can be rapid and severe. It is also expensive, and acquisition of the drug must be accomplished through organized distribution and selling. In other words, powder cocaine is one of the drugs of abuse that encourages systematic violence on a wide scale. In addition, some cocaine abusers may have a difficult time controlling their habit and may rapidly build a tolerance to the drug, requiring larger and larger amounts of the costly drug. Some cocaine users may be forced to engage in shoplifting, theft, drug dealing, and prostitution to support their habit.

Crack Cocaine

The most common method of cocaine smoking in the United States is freebasing. Freebase is prepared by dissolving cocaine hydrochloride in water, and then adding a strong base such as ammonia or baking soda to the solution (Weiss & Mirin, 1987). This cocaine freebase is generally dissolved in ether to extract the cocaine, and then the ether is removed by drying the solution. Other methods may be used that bypass the ether method by heating the mixture. The drying process produces crystalline, smokable pellets, or nuggets. The result is a product ranging from 37 percent to 96 percent purity (Weiss & Mirin, 1987).

During the 1980s, a purified, high-potency form of freebase cocaine—known as crack—exploded in popularity. It was, according to Howard Abadinsky (1993), the drug abuser's version of fast food. The drug is called "crack" because it makes a crackling sound when smoked (Abadinsky, 1993; Gold, 1984). Crack is several times more pure than ordinary street cocaine, and crack smoking generates a very rapid, intense state of euphoria, which peaks in about five minutes. The psychological and physical effects of crack are as powerful as any intravenously injected cocaine. However, the euphoria is short-lived, ending in about 10–20 minutes after inhalation, and is followed by depression, irritability, and often an intense craving for more. It is also extremely dangerous to the user and may result in a rapid and irregular heartbeat, respiratory failure, seizures, or a cerebral hemorrhage. Although most users limit themselves to one or two hits, some users seek multiple hits. Crack smokers, in order to stay high, often find a place where crack can be safely smoked, such as a crack house, because the smoke and smell are difficult to hide.

During the 1980s, crack cocaine generated much concern to local officials across the United States because of its popularity, illegal drug trafficking, and health hazards to adolescents and young adults. At one point, some experts regarded crack as the most addictive drug currently available on the street (Weiss & Mirin, 1987). This assumption has been seriously questioned by many research scientists (Morgan & Zimmer, 1997). Furthermore, it was thought that the craving for the drug might become so severe for some individuals that the user would lie, steal, or commit acts of violence in order to obtain more of the drug (Rosecan, Spitz, & Gross, 1987). Its popularity probably resided in the instantaneous psychological effects it provides, its inexpensiveness, and its wide availability throughout most major U.S. cities. The drug also provided tremendous profitability for the sellers. For a while, about one-third of all arrests made by the New York City Narcotics Division involved cocaine, and over half of them involved crack (Cohn, 1986). Because it was so inexpensive and available, it became a very popular drug for the young—including preteenagers.

Beginning in the early 1990s, the use of crack cocaine began to decline (Golub & Johnson, 1997). The reasons for the decline are multiple, but the most prominent appear to be its health risks and the changes in attitude among the new generation concerning its use. The youth today consider crack users "dumb," and "crackhead," a dirty word (Golub & Johnson, 1997). In some cities, many youths abuse crackheads or avoid them altogether. Overall, it appears that the primary users of crack cocaine who began using the drug during the 1980s continue to be the heavy users of the drug today. However, the more recent generation of youth called "Generation X" tend to avoid using the drug. Many alternatives are available.

Crack and Crime

The relationship between crack and crime remains obscure. One thing that does emerge from the research literature is that crack users, especially persistent users, are often polydrug users. Surveys indicate that virtually all crack users have been frequent users of other drugs, and most also had an extensive history of prior drug use, drug selling, and nondrug criminality (Golub & Johnson, 1997). While it is difficult at this point in our knowledge to determine which comes first, drug use or involvement in crime, the evidence does suggest that persistent offenders have engaged in a variety of illegal activities and troublesome conduct throughout their lifetimes, probably before extensive drug abuse. One thing appears clear, though: Crack use by itself does not appear to cause violent behavior in normally nonviolent people (Golub & Johnson, 1997; Morgan & Zimmer, 1997).

The association between the crack cocaine black market and systemic violence, on the other hand, is a different matter. The production, distribution, and selling of powder and crack cocaine have been associated with violence for some time, although the amount of violence fluctuates with the illicit market economy.

Ecstasy (MDMA)

MDMA or "ecstasy" is a synthetic drug (completely manufactured rather than grown or occurring naturally) that is considered a stimulant, but it also has some strong psychedelic properties similar to methamphetamine and mescaline. MDMA is an abbreviation for 3-4 methylenedioxymethamphetamine. It is sometimes confused with a similar compound 3, 4-methylenedioxyamphetamine, abbreviated MDA. The effects and pharmacological actions of MDA are similar but not identical to MDMA (Maxwell, 2004). Both MDMA and MDA are classified as Schedule I drugs. Other drugs confused with ecstasy include paramethoxyamphetamine (PMA) and p-methylthioamphetamine (MTA). These are substances packaged as ecstasy with similar psychoactive properties and associated with several deaths, especially in Europe (Maxwell, 2004).

The use of ecstasy (also known as Adam, E, X, eccie) increased sharply among teenagers during the late 1990s, reaching its peak in 2001. Since that time, there has been a steady moderate decrease in popularity. However, beginning in 2009, there has been an upswing in its popularity among teens (Johnston *et al.*, 2011).

The common psychological effects of MDMA include confusion, depression, anxiety, sleeplessness, drug cravings, and paranoia (Office of National Drug Control Policy, 2000). Its adverse physical side effects include muscle tension, involuntary clenching of the teeth, nausea, blurred vision, faintness, tremors, sweating, and chills. Baby pacifiers are often used by ecstasy users to prevent danger to or excessive grinding of the teeth. Inhalation of Vicks VapoRub is also sometimes used to enhance the drug's psychedelic effects. MDMA may also predispose users to participate in high-risk behavior (Moreland, 2000).

The drug's stimulation properties provide an "energy rush" that encourages users to stay physically active for long periods of time, such as dancing all night at rave parties. Although the drug is considered safer than many other illicit drugs, there are physical risks. At very high doses, MDMA can cause the body temperature to rise as high as 110 degrees, leading to muscle breakdown and kidney or cardiovascular failure (National Institute on Drug Abuse, 2000). Also, all-night raves and extensive dancing in crowded and overheated rooms pose the danger of producing not only high body temperatures but also dangerous levels of dehydration. Other adverse side effects of MDMA include hearing and liver damage, strokes, and long-term brain injury (National Institute of Health, 1999).

The majority of MDMA found in the United States comes from clandestine laboratories in Western Europe (primarily the Netherlands and Belgium) and Canada (Drug Enforcement Administration, 2011). MDMA is usually consumed in tablet form, which is sometimes crushed and snorted, occasionally smoked but never injected.

Stimulants and Crime

The relationship between stimulants and crime and delinquency has many facets. One thing that emerges clearly from the research literature is that heavy stimulants users, especially those who heavily use crack cocaine, are often polydrug users (National Institute on Drug Abuse, 2004). Furthermore, persistent offenders tend to be polydrug users. Although it is difficult at this point in our knowledge to determine which comes first, drug use or involvement in delinquency or crime, the evidence strongly suggests that persistent offenders have engaged in a variety of illegal activities and troublesome conduct throughout their lifetimes, most probably beginning before the onset of drug or alcohol abuse.

NARCOTIC DRUGS

The word narcotics usually prompts intense negative reactions and very often is quickly associated with crime. Like the word *dope*, it is widely misused to denote all illegal drugs. In this chapter, narcotic drugs refer only to the derivatives of or products pharmacologically similar to the products of the opium or poppy plant, *Papaver sominferum.*

The opium plant, an annual, grows to about three to five feet in height. Today, most opium is grown in Afghanistan, which produces approximately 92 percent of the world's illicit opium and opium-based narcotics (Bureau of International Narcotics and Law Enforcement Affairs, 2000; Glaze, 2007). However, the opium poppies that are of most concern to the United States are grown principally in Columbia and Mexico. Although these two countries together cultivate less than 6 percent of the world's total opium, most of the heroin found in the United States is from Columbian or Mexican suppliers. In fact, Mexico serves as the transit and distribution center for most of the drugs moving into this country.

Narcotic drugs can be divided into three major categories on the basis of the kind of preparation they require: (1) **natural narcotics**, which include the grown opium, (2) **semisynthetic narcotics**, which include the chemically prepared heroin, and (3) **synthetic narcotics**, which are wholly prepared chemically and include methadone, meperidine, and phenazocine. All are narcotics because they produce similar effects: relief of pain, relaxation, peacefulness, and sleep (*narco*, of Greek origin, means "to sleep"). The narcotics are highly addictive for some individuals; they develop a relentless and strong craving for the drug. Many heavy narcotic users, however, lead successful, productive lives, without significant interference in their daily routine. There is no single type of opium user.

Heroin

The most heavily used illegal *narcotic* in this country is heroin. Data from the 2004 National Survey on Drug Use and Health indicate that 1.4 percent of Americans (3.1 million), ages 12 and older, had used heroin at least once in their lifetime, and approximately 186,000 Americans said they had used heroin within the month preceding the survey (Office of National Drug Control Policy, 2006e). However, more complete estimates conclude that there are 980,000 heroin addicts and 1.2 million casual users in the United States (Bureau of International Narcotics and Law Enforcement Affairs, 2000).

Heroin continues to be widely available in almost all areas of the country, although its purity varies considerably from region to region. Most of the heroin east of the Mississippi River comes from Columbia, whereas most of the heroin supplied west of the Mississippi is of Mexican origin (U.S. Drug Enforcement Administration, 2012). Heroin is processed from morphine, which is extracted from the seed pod of certain varieties of poppy plants grown in Thailand, Laos, and Myanmar (Burma). High-quality heroin is processed in Afghanistan, Columbia, and Pakistan.

Despite the popularity of cocaine, heroin still reigns as the illicit or hard drug of choice in much of the world. Mexican "black tar" heroin has hit the streets in the western states of the United States in recent years. It is a dark brown substance that has the appearance of black tar and is sticky like roofing tar or, in some instances, hard like coal. The color and consistency of black tar heroin is due to the crude processing methods used to manufacture the drug. In many areas, heroin users combine heroin with cocaine powder (HCl) or with crack, and then inject the mixture. As mentioned earlier, this practice is known as "speedballing." In some regions, particularly in the West, users often mix heroin and methamphetamine and then inject. Heroin is rarely taken orally, because the absorption rate is slow and incomplete. It may be administered intramuscularly, subcutaneously ("skin popping"), or intravenously ("mainlining"), or it may be inhaled ("snorted"). Heroin inhalers usually choose to use heroin and crack simultaneously.

In the past, experienced heroin users strongly preferred mainlining because of the sensational thrill, splash, rush, or kick it provided. Injection is probably the most practical and efficient way to administer low-purity heroin. Injection works fast. Intravenous injection provides the most intense and rapid feeling of euphoria, working within seven to eight seconds after injection. Intramuscular injection is slower, taking about five to eight minutes for peak effect. However, in recent years, the dramatic increase in heroin purity has changed the preferred method of administration. The high purity of Columbian heroin available in much of the eastern United States allows the user to snort or sniff the substance like cocaine. In New York, for example, cocaine and heroin are often alternately inhaled, a practice called "criss-crossing." The quality of heroin today also allows it to be smoked.

The effects of heroin depend on the quantity taken, the method of administration, the interval between administrations, the tolerance and dependence of the user, the setting, and the user's expectations. Effects usually wear off in five to eight hours, depending on the user's tolerance. In 1999, heroin-related deaths were rising due to the decreasing price and the potency of the drug, resulting from significant increases in the purity of Columbian heroin.

Like all the narcotics, heroin is a central nervous system depressant. For many users, it promotes mental clouding, dreamlike states, light sleep punctuated by vivid dreams, and a general feeling of "sublime contentment." The body may become permeated with a feeling of warmth, and the extremities may feel heavy. There is little inclination toward physical activity; the user prefers to sit motionless and in a fog.

Heroin and Crime

No other drug group is as closely associated with crime as the narcotics, particularly heroin. The image of the desperate "junkie" looking for a fix is widespread. Furthermore, because of the adverse effects of the drug, it is assumed that the heroin user is bizarre, unpredictable, and therefore dangerous. However, high doses of narcotics produce sleep rather than the psychotic or paranoid panic states sometimes produced by high doses of amphetamines. Therefore, narcotics users rarely become violent or dangerous. Research strongly indicates that addicts do not, as a general rule, participate in violent crimes such as assault, rape, or homicide (Canadian Government's Commission of Inquiry, 1971; National Commission on Marihuana and Drug Abuse, 1973; National Institute on Drug Abuse, 1978; Tinklenberg & Stillman, 1970).

Research evidence does suggest a relationship between heroin addiction and money-producing crime. A study in Miami of 573 narcotics users found that they were responsible for almost 6,000 robberies, 6,700 burglaries, 900 stolen vehicles, 25,000 instances of shoplifting, and 46,000 other events of larceny and fraud (Inciardi, 1986). Self-report surveys find that heroin users report financing their habits largely through "acquisitive crime" (Jarvis & Parker, 1989; Mott, 1986). Parker and Newcombe (1987) studied crime patterns and heroin use in the English community of Wirral, located in northwest England. They found that many heroin users were from the poor sections of the community and were young. The researchers were also able to divide their sample into three groups: (1) the largest group, consisting of young offenders who were not known to be using heroin but were highly criminally active, (2) heroin users who engaged in considerable acquisitive crime, but were involved in this type of crime prior to their heroin addiction, and (3) heroin users who started engaging in acquisitive crime after developing their habit in order to support the habit. The Parker–Newcombe investigation suggests that some heroin addicts do support their habit through crime.

Ball, Shaffer, and Nurco (1983) found that heroin addicts committed more money-producing crime when they were addicted compared with times when they were not. Still, it may be misleading to examine the heroin–crime relationship in isolation without considering the possible interactions between polydrug use and crime, or to conclude that heroin addiction causes crime. All we can say with some confidence at this point is that those who use heroin also seem to be deeply involved in money-producing crime. Heroin users, however, may not be driven to crime by the needs of their addiction. Heroin users, particularly polydrug users, may represent a segment of society that runs counter to society's rules and expectations in multiple ways, drug use and larceny among them. It may well be that most heroin-addicted criminals were involved in crime before they became addicted. Research by Faupel (1991) does support this hypothesis. However, studies also suggest that, although many heroin users have criminal records prior to their addiction, their criminal activity increases substantially during periods of heavy drug consumption (Faupel, 1991). Furthermore, polydrug users tend to switch from drug to drug, depending on what is available and inexpensive at the time, and do not seem physiologically desperate for any one particular drug. They simply substitute one drug for the other. Overall, the relationship between heroin use and criminal behavior is a complex one and varies throughout the addict's career.

Fentanyl

Fentanyl, first synthesized in Belgium in the late 1950s (under the trade name of Sublimaze), is highly similar to heroin in its biological and psychological effects. Fentanyl is a synthetic opiate about 100 times more potent than morphine (Drug Enforcement Administration, 2009). It is normally produced as a powder, and, on the market, it is often mixed with heroin and to a lesser extent with cocaine. It may be administered by intravenous injection, smoked, or snorted, but intravenous injection is currently the preferred method. According to the Drug Enforcement Administration (2009), the drug has been officially linked to over one thousand deaths across the United States during 2005 and 2007. An intravenous dose of fentanyl hydrochloride for pain relief is about 45 micrograms, depending on the weight of the user, but careless use can lead to an overdose and possible death. Over 12 different analogues of fentanyl have been produced clandestinely and identified in the U.S. drug traffic trade.

Other Narcotic Drugs

Other drugs that are often classified as narcotics include thebaine, codeine, morphine, hydromorphone, oxycodone, and hydrocodone. Thebaine is chemically similar to both morphine and codeine, but generally produces a high rather than depressant effects. It is considered a Schedule II drug. Hydromorphone (Dilaudid) is a powerful analgesic that is sold in tablet or injectable forms as a painkiller, and may substitute for heroin or morphine. Oxycodone is similar to codeine but more powerful. It is often marketed in combination with aspirin (Percodan) or acetaminophen (Percocet) for the relief of pain. Hydrocodone is an orally active analgesic slightly less powerful than morphine.

Although oxycodone products have been illicitly abused for 30 years, the oxycodone derivative OxyContin has been used frequently in recent years. OxyContin is a prescription painkiller used to control mild to moderate pain, and is a the preferred narcotic of young adults.

OxyContin

OxyContin (oxycodone) is a narcotic that has the properties of a powerful analgesic for pain control. It is a drug that is growing in popularity with young people (Johnston *et al.*, 2006). OxyContin is classified as an opioid analgesic that is available through prescription. The drug is chemically classified as an opiate agonist because it provides pain relief by acting on opioid receptors in the spinal cord and brain. It was approved in 1995 by the Food and Drug Administration for use as an analgesic in persons with moderate to severe pain requiring several days of relief or more (Cicero, Inciardi, & Muñoz, 2005). The drug is synthesized from thebaine, a minor constituent of opium. OxyContin comes generally in tablet form, but some abusers crush the tablets and sniff the powder or dissolve the tablets in water for injection.

It usually comes in the form of a time-release tablet and acts for 12 hours, making it the longest-lasting oxycodone on the market. The pharmacological effects of OxyContin are highly similar to heroin, and consequently tend to be attractive to the same abuser population (National Drug Intelligence Center, 2001).

OxyContin abuse is by far the most prevalent and widespread abuse of all the opioids and prescription drugs in the United States, and it shows no signs of declining at this time (Cicero *et al.*, 2005). The abuse of drug is found almost exclusively by white persons (91%), especially those living in rural and suburban areas (Cicero *et al.*, 2005). Interestingly, studies have discovered an overall increase across the country in the abuse of prescription drugs in general (Cicero *et al.*, 2005). This is believed to be because prescription drugs are relatively easy to obtain compared with other illicit drugs, especially in rural areas.

OxyContin and Crime

OxyContin abuse has led to a significant increase in the number of pharmacy robberies, thefts, fraudulent prescriptions, and health care fraud incidents during the early 2000s (National Drug Intelligence Center, 2001), but in recent years, the numbers have decreased significantly. It is also obtained through what is called "doctor shopping" and improper prescription practices by physicians. Doctor shopping refers to the practice of individuals visiting numerous doctors, sometimes in several states, to acquire large amounts of the drug to use or sell to others.

THE CLUB DRUGS: SEDATIVE HYPNOTIC COMPOUNDS

Rohypnol, gamma-hydroxybutryrate (GHB), ecstasy (MDMA), ketamine, and methamphetamine have been considered the "club drugs" in recent years (Maxwell, 2004). They are called "club drugs" because they are most often consumed at teenage and young adult nightclubs, raves, or parties. Although club drugs have attracted considerable national attention, they comprise a relatively small proportion of the drug problem in the United States. Since we covered ecstasy and methamphetamine earlier in the chapter, we shall concentrate on the three sedative hypnotics in this section: ketamine, Rohypnol, and GHB.

Ketamine

Ketamine, also called "K," "Special K," "Super Acid," "LA Coke," or "cat valium," is a dissociative anesthetic with analgesic and amnestic properties. It was developed in 1962 to replace PCP in veterinary medicine. The drug was first manufactured in the United States in 1960s as Ketalar (Copeland & Dillon, 2005). Use of ketamine as a surgical anesthetic gained significant popularity on the battlefields of Vietnam (Copeland & Dillon, 2005). Much of the ketamine sold on the street in the United States is probably intended for veterinary clinics or is imported from overseas. When sold illicitly, it is often converted from a liquid to a powder—similar in appearance to cocaine and heroin—or tablets. Reports have found that ketamine is increasingly being used in social rather than medical and scientific settings in many parts of the world, especially the United Kingdom and Australia (Copeland & Dillon, 2005). It is often considered a "club drug" or "dance drug" because it is used at "raves" or dance parties, a popular scene for teenagers. Ketamine is also frequently used as a key component in fake MDMA (ecstasy) tablets.

Its chemical structure is similar to PCP but is much less potent and produces less confusion, irrationality, and violent behavior than PCP (Drug Enforcement Administration, 2005). As drug of abuse, ketamine can be administered orally, snorted, or injected. It sometimes is sprinkled on marijuana and smoked. High doses produce analgesia, amnesia, and coma.

Users report sensations ranging from a pleasant feeling of floating or being separated from their bodies (National Institute on Drug Abuse, 2005). It carries slang names such as jet, super acid, cat Valium, and honey oil. Approximately 50 percent of ketamine users have had a bad experience with the drug called the "K-hole" (Copeland & Dillon, 2005).

Ketamine is odorless and tasteless, so it can be added to beverages or food without being detected. Ketamine, along with GHB, is considered a "date rape" drug because it can be given to unsuspecting victims, inducing amnesia and a helpless physical state. Under these conditions, sexual assault can be carried out with the victim being unable to remember the incident.

Gamma Hydroxbutyrate

GHB (also known as "liquid ecstasy," "scoop," "liquid X," "grievous bodily harm," or "Georgia home boy") is a powerful and fast-acting drug most often taken by young users as a pleasure enhancer that produces a rapid state of intoxication. It is usually consumed orally, either as a grainy white- or sandy-colored powder that is often dissolved in alcohol, or as a liquid sold in small bottles. GHB is produced primarily in clandestine laboratories, and consequently there is no guarantee of quality or purity, making its psychoactive effects unpredictable. The drug can be easily produced by combining gammabutyrolactone (GBL) with either potassium hydroxide or sodium hydroxide in a container. Recipes or kits for making GHB are sold over the Internet. GHB is also marketed as an antidepressant that suppresses feelings of depression and anxiety, and is promoted and sold on the Internet as such. Prior to 1990, the drug was freely available in health food stores across the United States. However, in 1990, the Federal Drug Administration (FDA) banned GHB and does not approve the drug for any use at the present time. However, a pharmaceutical formulation of the drug is currently being developed for the treatment of cataplexy, a serious and debilitating disease.

Psychoactive effects of GHB begin to take effect within 15–30 minutes after consumption, and, depending on purity and dosage, may last as long as six hours. It is often used in conjunction with other drugs, especially alcohol. GHB has many severe and unpredictable side effects, such as nausea, drowsiness, vomiting, delusions, depression, vertigo (dizziness), hallucinations, seizures, respiratory distress, loss of consciousness, slowed heart rate, lowered blood pressure, amnesia, and coma (Office of National Drug Control Policy, 1999a). It also interferes with circulation, motor coordination, and balance, and, at higher doses (two to four grams), it produces considerable problems in motor and speech control. At these high doses, GHB usually produces a very deep sleep, resembling a coma. The drug also produces anterograde amnesia, a condition in which events that occurred during the time the drug was in effect are forgotten. In addition, the drug has increasingly been involved in poisonings, overdoses, and fatalities (National Institute on Drug Abuse, 1999).

GHB is tasteless and odorless, and mixes easily with alcohol or any nonalcoholic drink. Because it can be mixed with food and drinks without detection, and because of its ability to sedate and intoxicate unsuspecting victims, GHB has been connected to crime in recent years. It is sometimes used in the commission of sexual assault, and it often plays a role in "date rape." It is also used in some instances to pave the way for robbing heavily sedated or unconscious victims.

Because of its increasing use in sexual assaults, the Date-Rape Drug Prohibition Act of 2000 (also known as the Hillary J. Farias and Samantha Reid Date Drug Prohibition Act of 2000) was enacted in January 2000, specifically to target GHB. Congress found that the abuse of illicit gamma hydroxybutyrate acid was an imminent hazard to public safety, and moved to amend the federal *Controlled Substances Act* to include the drug as an illegal substance. The act also established a special unit of the Drug Enforcement Administration to assess the abuse of and trafficking in GHB, Rohypnol, ketamine, other controlled substances, and other so-called "designer drugs" whose use has been associated with sexual assault.

Rohypnol

The Drug Induced Rape Prevention and Punishment Act of 1996 was enacted into federal law specifically in response to the use of Rohypnol (generic name flunitrazepam), another club drug that can be used to sexually assault incapacitated individuals. It can mentally and physically incapacitate the victim. The law makes it a crime to give someone a controlled substance without his or her knowledge and with the intent to commit a crime. The law further imposes a penalty of up to 20 years for the distribution and importation of one gram or more of Rohypnol. Simple possession is punishable by up to three years in prison and a fine.

Since 1999, Rohypnol tablets have been manufactured to turn blue in a drink to increase visibility and thus more visually detectable to potential victims (Office of National Drug Control Policy, 2003a). However, the noncolored tablets continue to be on the market. Furthermore, persons who intend to commit a sexual assault may try to serve blue tropical drinks and punches so that the blue dye in the drug can be inconspicuous.

Slang names for Rohypnol include date-rape drug, circles, roofies, Mexican valium, roach-2, forget-me drug, forget pill, or wolfies. Rohypnol is popular among youth because of its low cost. Rohypnol can be ground into a powder and snorted. Similar to GHB, Rohypnol is tasteless and odorless, and can be dissolved in liquids, but not as easily as GHB, and is also sometimes used by bodybuilders for its alleged anabolic effects. It can be taken orally, snorted, or injected. It is often combined with alcohol or used as a remedy for the depression that often follows a stimulant high. The effects of Rohypnol usually begin in about 15 minutes after administration, and may last for more than 12 hours. In addition, the drug is detectable in urine for up to 72 hours after ingestion (Office of National Drug Control Policy, 2003a).

Lower doses of Rohypnol can cause muscle relaxation. In higher doses, it can cause loss of muscle control, loss of consciousness, and, when combined with alcohol, anterograde amnesia. When combined with alcohol, as is often done, it can be deadly. Chemically, the drug is similar to Valium but ten times more powerful. Rohypnol is legally manufactured in over 80 countries as a prescribed sedative for the short-term treatment of severe sleep disorders, especially in Europe, but it is neither manufactured nor approved for sale in the United States.

The benzodiazepines include chlordiazepoxide (Librium), diszepam (Valium), oxazepam (Serax), and chlorazepate dipotassium (Tranxene), all of which are marketed legally and prescribed as antianxiety tranquilizers, or to treat muscle spasms or convulsions. The most common side effects are confusion, drowsiness, and loss of coordination.

ALCOHOL

Despite the public concern over heroin, opium, marijuana, cocaine (especially crack), and the amphetamines, the number one drug of abuse has been, and continues to be, alcohol (ethanol, ethyl alcohol, grain alcohol). All 50 states have a legal drinking age of 21. However, most underage persons obtain and drink alcohol illegally. According to the Substance Abuse and Mental Health Services Administration (2005), 121 million Americans, age 12 or older, were current drinkers of alcohol in 2004, representing 50 percent of the population. About 55 million (22.8%) participated in binge drinking, defined as five or more drinks on at least one occasion in the 30 days prior to the survey (Substance Abuse and Mental Health Services Administration, 2005). And 16.7 million (6.9%) were considered heavy drinkers as defined as binge drinking on five or more days in the past month. Most of the binge and heavy drinkers were young adults between the ages of 18 and 25. Overall, alcohol is preferred by teenagers over other drugs, although marijuana use is increasing dramatically.

According to DAWN (Office of Applied Studies, 2004), 23 percent of all drug-related emergency department visits involved the effects of alcohol in persons under age 21 in 2003. Nearly one-third of the alcohol-related visits were because the youth—especially those between the ages of 12 and 17—had combined alcohol with other drugs. Marijuana (49%) and cocaine (22%) were

TABLE 16-6	Blood Alcohol Concentrations (BAC) of Drivers Involved in Fatal Accidents	

Blood Alcohol Concentration	Percent of Fatal Accidents (%)
0	58.6
0.26–0.29	4.7
0.26–0.30	1.9
0.26–0.31	2.4
0.26–0.32	17.2
0.26–0.33	9.1
0.26–0.34	3.5
0.30	2.6

Source: Data from Greenfeld (1998), p. 15.

the drugs most frequently found in combination with alcohol. Methamphetamine (8%) was also found with some frequency in these visits. There were no gender differences in alcohol-related visits to emergency departments in 2003.

Alcohol is responsible for more deaths and violence (it is the third major cause of death) than all other drugs combined. According to the National Highway Traffic Safety Administration (2005), approximately 25 percent of drivers ages 16–20 who were involved in fatal motor vehicle crashes in 2003 had been drinking alcohol.

The usual way to determine if an individual is intoxicated is by measuring his or her blood alcohol concentration, abbreviated BAC. A BAC of 0.10 percent means there are 100 milligrams of alcohol per 100 milliliters of blood. For example, a 165-pound man would reach a BAC of 0.10 percent if he drank about five drinks within one hour on an empty stomach. (A drink is defined as one-and-a-half ounces of liquor, a 12-ounce beer, or a five-ounce glass of wine.) In most states, a driver is considered intoxicated if his or her BAC is 0.10 percent, and in some states, the cutoff is 0.08 percent (e.g., California, Florida, Vermont) (see **Table 16-6** for data on BAC and fatal accidents).

Psychological Effects

The social, psychological, and psychobiological effects of excessive alcohol use can be just as destructive to the individual, his or her family, and society in general, as addictive substance abuse. Similar to the heroin addict, the alcoholic can develop a strong psychological and physical dependence on the drug. Society's attitudes toward alcohol are dramatically different from its attitudes toward other drugs of abuse, however. In virtually every part of the United States, it is legal and socially acceptable for adults to consume the drug. In public, drinking behavior is generally unregulated unless it involves heavy intoxication and correspondingly unacceptable conduct (e.g., disturbing the peace or operating a motor vehicle). In private, one can get as drunk as one wishes, a privilege technically not granted with respect to other drugs even though numerous individuals use illegal substances in nonpublic places.

The psychoactive effects of alcohol are extremely complex. Miczek and his colleagues (1994) write that the effects of alcohol depend on "a host of interacting pharmacologic, endocrinologic, neurobiologic, genetic, situational, environmental, social, and cultural determinants" (p. 382). Consequently, we can provide only a cursory review of this complicated topic here. At low doses (e.g., two or four ounces of whiskey), alcohol seems to act as a stimulant on the central nervous system. Initially, it appears to affect the inhibitory chemical process of nervous system transmission, producing feelings of euphoria, good cheer, and social and physical warmth. In moderate and high quantities, however, alcohol begins to depress the excitatory processes of the central nervous system, as well as its inhibitory processes. Consequently, the individual's neuromuscular coordination and visual acuity are reduced, and he or she perceives pain and fatigue. The ability to concentrate is also impaired. Very often, self-confidence increases, and the person becomes more daring, sometimes foolishly so. It is believed that alcohol at moderate levels begins to "numb" the higher brain centers which process cognitive information, especially judgment and abstract thought. It should be emphasized at this point that the levels of intoxication are not necessarily dependent on the amount of alcohol ingested; as for other psychoactive drugs, the effects depend on a myriad of interacting variables.

Alcohol, Crime, and Delinquency

The belief that alcohol is a major cause of crime appears to be deeply embedded in American society. Surveys, for example, suggest that over 50 percent of the population is convinced that alcohol is a major factor in crimes of violence (Critchlow, 1986). This pervasive belief appears to be based on the premise that alcohol instigates aggressive conduct in some individuals, or somehow diminishes the checks and balances of nonaggressive, nonviolent behavior.

Roizen (1997), summarizing the research on alcohol and violence, found that up to 86 percent of homicide offenders had been drinking at the time of the offense. Roizen further discovered that 60 percent of sexual offenders, 37 percent of assault offenders, 57 percent of males in marital violence, and 13 percent of child abusers had also been drinking at the time of the crime. **Table 16-7** identifies the percentage of adult offenders who admitted to drinking at the time of their offense (in 1996). Outside of public order crimes, a higher percentage of offenders reported drinking at the time of violent offenses than during the other offense categories. About seven out

TABLE 16-7   Percent of Offenders Drinking at the Time of the Offense, 1996

Offense	Adults on Probation	Convicted Offenders in Local Jails	Convicted Offenders in State Prisons	Convicted Offenders in Federal Prisons
All offenses	39.9	39.5	32.3	11.0
Violent offenses	40.7	40.6	37.5	20.4
Property offenses	18.5	32.8	31.8	8.1
Drug offenses	16.3	28.8	18.0	8.2
Public order offenses	75.1	56.0	43.0	13.1

Source: Data from Greenfeld (1998), p. 21.

of 10 alcohol-involved incidents of violence occurred in a residence, and most of the incidents (about two-thirds) are simple assaults. In addition, two-thirds of victims who suffered violence by an intimate reported that alcohol had been a factor. Ninety percent of alcohol-involved incidents of violence occur off campus (Greenfeld, 1998).

Many studies of adolescents have also concluded that alcohol use and violent behavior are linked (Swahn & Donovan, 2004). Several studies also indicate that alcohol use is more common among violent delinquents compared with nonviolent delinquents (Saner & Ellickson, 1996; Huizinga & Jakob-Chien, 1998). Dawkins (1997), on the basis of data collected on 312 youthful offenders at a public juvenile facility, reports that alcohol use is more strongly and consistently related to both violent and nonviolent offenses than is marijuana or other drugs. One study found that even after antecedent peer and family risk factors were adjusted for, young people who abused alcohol were much more likely to engage in violent offenses than those who did not misuse alcohol (Fergusson, Lynskey, & Horwood, 1996). According to Webb *et al.* (2002), alcohol use and serious delinquency are strongly associated, yet the direction of causality is unclear. Does alcohol cause violence, or do violent adolescents drink alcohol?

Furthermore, numerous other factors must be taken into account. For example, cultural differences may play a significant role in the alcohol–aggression relationship. Cognitive factors, such as a person's expectations or cognitions, also influence how he or she responds to alcohol. Alcohol serves as a cue for acting intoxicated and doing things one normally would not do. In other words, a person may act the way he or she believes alcohol makes one act. It should further be emphasized that not all adolescents who drink heavily engage in violence and aggression. Many adolescents use alcohol experimentally, sometimes frequently, and may binge drink, without engaging in antisocial, violent, or delinquent behavior.

In summary, the evidence is quite clear that approximately one-third of all offenders who commit violent crime were drinking at the time of offense, and many were highly intoxicated. In their careful review of the research literature, Reiss and Roth (1993, p. 185) conclude, "In studies of prison inmates, those classified as 'heavy' or 'problem' drinkers had accumulated more previous arrests for violent crime, and reported higher average frequencies of assaults than did other inmates." And the National Institute on Alcohol Abuse and Alcoholism (1990, p. 92) asserts, "In both animals and human studies, alcohol more than any other drug, has been linked with a high incidence of violence and aggression." However, the link does not automatically mean that alcohol causes violence. It is most likely that under the influence of alcohol, individuals prone to be aggressive, violent, and antisocial are more likely to be more aggressive, violent, and antisocial. Alcohol may *facilitate* their aggressive tendencies. The available evidence does not allow cogent conclusions that alcohol makes normally nonviolent people act violently.

Does Substance or Alcohol Abuse Lead Directly to Violence?

There is little evidence that alcohol or drug use *cause* violence in adolescent offenders (White, Moffitt, Earls, Robins, & Silva, 1990). Research indicates that aggressive and violent behavior in childhood generally *precedes* the initiation into drug and alcohol abuse, at least in boys. Aggressive behavior in the early school grades and poor school achievement are two of the best predictors of substance abuse later in adolescence and adulthood (Fothergill & Ensminger, 2006). On the other hand, serious male delinquents (including the most violent offenders) by far show the highest rates of consumption of alcohol, marijuana, and other drugs. Girls who are considered shy in early grades are more likely to have high levels of educational attainment and are at low risk of substance or alcohol abuse in adolescence or adulthood (Fothergill & Ensminger, 2006).

Many developmental psychologists contend that substance abuse often takes place in an orderly sequence, starting with tobacco use, followed by marijuana, and then hard drug use as a last step (Kandel, Yamaguchi, & Chen, 1992; White *et al.*, 1990). This gives some credence to those who consider marijuana a "gateway drug" and urge zero tolerance, even for its possession in small amounts. However, before any adolescent becomes dependent on alcohol, tobacco, or any illicit substance, he or she passes through a stage of **experimental substance use (ESU)** (Petraitis, Flay & Miller, 1995). An unknown number of youth experiment but do not continue with regular use. Events and variables that determine who experiments with substances and alcohol during adolescence and who continues are multiple, including the availability of drugs, family history, peer pressures, social attitudes concerning drug use, the social and economic context, and individual differences in biopsychological/psychological makeup. In addition, drug use and experimentation are strongly correlated with cognitions (attitudes and beliefs) about drugs. Adolescent substance and alcohol abuse is not a passive, one-dimensional process caused exclusively by social influence but is strongly influenced by subjective choice made by the youth (Getz & Bray, 2005). For example, rates of drug use are much higher in populations that do not perceive great risk of harm than in populations that do perceive great risk of harm. Thus, explanations for the sustained heavy use of marijuana in adolescents partly center around the belief that there is very little harm in the use of the drug. Due to the enormous complexity involved in ESU, many theories have been proposed to explain the phenomenon. However, very few of them have ever been empirically tested or provided cogent explanations for why some youth experiment with drugs, and others do not.

Summary and Conclusions

This chapter reviewed the relationship between crime and a number of drugs commonly associated with criminal behavior. Four major drug categories were identified: (1) the hallucinogens, (2) the stimulants, (3) the opiate narcotics, and (4) the sedative-hypnotics. Rather than discuss most of the drugs in each category, we considered only those commonly believed to be connected with criminal conduct. Moreover, we did not examine the crimes of drug distribution or possession. We are mainly concerned with whether the substance itself facilitates or instigates illegal action, especially violence, and what damage the drug does to the user. In other words, are persons under the influence of marijuana more violent than they are normally? And how does marijuana affect the health of users? Or, to what extent does alcohol directly contribute to loss of control or reduce self-regulatory mechanisms?

Because juvenile drug use is considered a major social problem, we discussed its prevalence and some of the characteristics of juvenile substance abusers early in the chapter. In addition, throughout the chapter, we distinguished between juvenile and adult drug use when data and research findings were available. Marijuana is the drug for which most juveniles are arrested, but there is troubling use and abuse by juveniles of prescription drugs, inhalants, and "club drugs" as well. There has been a 10-year decline in arrests relating to cocaine, opium, and synthetic narcotics, however. Girls are less likely than boys to have drug and alcohol problems, and their experiences with drugs differ. However, their arrest rates for drug-related behaviors are increasing, though it is still far lower than the male rate. Persistent drug use in juveniles is associated with poor academic performance, high-risk behaviors, serious health problems, and delinquency.

Cannabis, which includes marijuana and hashish, is a relatively mild hallucinogen with few psychological or physiological side effects. No significant relationship between cannabis use and crime has been consistently reported in the research literature.

If anything, marijuana seems to reduce the likelihood of violence, since its psychoactive ingredient, THC, induces muscle weakness and promotes feelings of lethargy. Nevertheless, the rise in marijuana use by teenagers is of growing concern because of the mind-altering nature of the drug, its disinhibiting effects, and possible effects on other behaviors, such as driving. Synthetic marijuana is widely available and has outpaced the laws that are intended to control it.

Amphetamines and cocaine (especially crack) represented the stimulant group. Most illegal users do not participate in crime other than the possession or sale of these drugs. Similar to marijuana, amphetamines are plentiful and inexpensive. However, there are some documented cases in which heavy users of amphetamines entered psychological states that presumably predisposed them to violence and paranoia. In addition, several studies have found correlations between violent offenders and a history of amphetamine abuse. As in all correlations, however, it is difficult to determine what contributes to what. Chronic amphetamine use has potential strong dangerous side effects if used improperly, or used in combination with other drugs of abuse. Cocaine, a natural drug that grows only in certain parts of the world, has traditionally been quite expensive. In recent years, the drug has become widely available and its cost less prohibitive. There is no strong evidence that cocaine generally renders one more violent, more out of control, or more likely to engage in property crimes, however.

We discussed heroin as the representative of the opiate narcotics. Like most other narcotics, heroin appears to be highly addictive, particularly in the sense that it creates a strong psychological dependency. Narcotics in general are so addictive and so expensive that substantial funds are needed to support a user's habit. Thus, some researchers have found a moderate correlation between narcotics and various income-generating crimes. On the other hand, others have noted that most addicts turned to drugs after they had developed criminal patterns.

Of all the drugs reviewed, alcohol—representing the sedative-hypnotic group—shows the strongest relationship with violent offenses, such as rape, homicide, and assault. At intermediate and high levels, alcohol appears to impair or disrupt the brain operations responsible for self-control. Alcohol may also impair information processing, thereby leading a person to misjudge social cues and encouraging overreactions to a perceived threat. However, it is likely that violent behavior associated with alcohol use is a joint function of pharmacological effects, cognitive expectancies, and situational influences. If the individual expects that alcohol will make him or her act aggressively, and if the social environment provides appropriate cues, aggression or violent behavior will be facilitated. The National Institute on Alcohol Abuse and Alcoholism (1997, p. 4) concluded in its extensive review of the relevant research literature that "alcohol apparently may increase the risk of violent behavior only for certain individuals or subpopulations and only under some situations and social/cultural influences." Furthermore, the National Institute noted, "intoxication alone does not cause violence" (p. 2). However, the relationship between alcohol consumption and violence is a strong one in Western civilization. The Panel on the Understanding and Control of Violent Behavior concludes, "For at least the past several decades, alcohol drinking—by the perpetrator of a crime, the victim, or both—has immediately preceded at least half of all violent events, including murders, in the sample studied by researchers" (Roth, 1996, p. 3). While the relationship between alcohol and violence clearly exists, the nature of that relationship is largely unknown. Does alcohol cause violence, or are violent people drawn to alcohol? No drug *directly causes* violence simply through its pharmacological action (Morgan & Zimmer, 1997).

In conclusion, the relationships between crime and all the drugs discussed in this chapter are complex, involving interactions among numerous pharmacological, social, and psychological variables. Research is beginning to ease some data out of the complexity, but additional studies employing well-designed methodology are greatly needed to understand the many possible influences of psychoactive drugs on human behavior, particularly criminal behavior.

At this point in our knowledge, substance abuse appears to be more of a health problem to those who use drugs than a "crime problem." On the other hand, we cannot ignore the fact that there is a drug–crime connection, as the tripartite conceptual model proposed by Goldstein (1985) indicates. Goldstein conceived of drug-related crimes as being psychopharmacologically driven, systemic, or economically compulsive. Those who advocate radical changes in government policy—such as decriminalization or legalization of certain drugs—argue that crimes characterized by the systemic and economically compulsive components would likely decrease. This conclusion reflects the continuing controversy over the "right" public policy to adopt with respect to drugs. Although this chapter has not focused on the residual effects of the nation's war on drugs—such as its effect on public health, minority groups, prison

populations, and individual civil liberties—these effects also cannot be ignored.

Relating to the psychopharmacologically driven category proposed by Goldstein, we stress that, from the psychological perspective, it is unlikely that drugs "cause" people to engage in criminal activity. On the other hand, some drugs clearly allow some people to disengage from their usual constraints against antisocial conduct, including violence. Individuals who are chronic, persistent criminals often are polydrug users, but again it is unlikely that the drugs they ingest directly cause them to engage in criminal activity. It is more likely they were criminally prone prior to and independent of polydrug use.

Key Concepts

Controlled substance
Dependence
Drug courts
Experimental substance
   use (ESU)
Hallucinogens

Natural narcotics
Opiate narcotics
Psychedelics
Psychoactive drugs
Sedative-hypnotic
   compounds

Semisynthetic narcotics
Stimulants
Synthetic marijuana
Synthetic narcotics
Tolerance
Tripartite conceptual model

Review Questions

1. What are the four main categories of drugs discussed in this chapter? List their main effects, and provide one example of a drug from each category.
2. Describe and explain briefly Goldstein's tripartite conceptual model for understanding the drug–crime relationship.
3. Briefly list the common psychological effects of any three of the following: cocaine, MDMA, heroin, alcohol, methamphetamine.
4. Describe Rohypnol and gamma hydroxybutyrate (GHB). What are they used for? What are some of the effects? How might they be involved in crime?

5. Of all the substances (drugs and alcohol) discussed in the chapter, which substance is most closely connected to crime? Why do you think this is?
6. Summarize and discuss the six main conclusions researchers have reached in recent years regarding the relationship between drugs and crime. When relevant, provide illustrations from the various categories of drugs.
7. Define and describe the three types of narcotics (based on their manufacture).
8. What are the differences between tolerance and dependence?

GLOSSARY

actuarial profiling Behavior prediction based largely on statistical methods and models.

adjudicative competence The ability to participate in a variety of court proceedings. See also, **incompetent to stand trial.**

adolescent-limited (AL) offender An individual who usually demonstrates delinquent or antisocial behavior only during his or her teen years and then stops offending during his or her young adult years.

advantageous comparison An offender's process of convincing himself that his values and ways of life are superior to those of his victims; used to explain the cognitive restructuring that occurs in terrorism.

aggression, hostile (expressive) Aggressive behavior characterized by the intent to cause the target discomfort or pain.

aggression, instrumental Aggressive behavior characterized by the intent to gain material or financial rewards from the target.

aggressive driving Reckless behavior while driving that indicates anger, hostility, or frustration as a result of a recent incident or series of incidents in the driver's life. The aggressive driving may be prompted by minor, irritating actions of another motorist but these actions are not the root cause of the reckless behavior. Should be distinguished from **road rage.**

aggressive (sadistic) pedophile An adult drawn to children for both sexual and aggressive (violent) purposes.

amnesia Complete or partial (**limited**) memory loss of an incident, series of incidents, or some aspects of life's experiences.

amygdala An almond-shaped cluster of neurons in the brain believed to be responsible for emotions and short-term memory.

anger rape A rape situation, identified by Groth, in which an offender uses more force than necessary for compliance and engages in a variety of sexual acts that are particularly degrading or humiliating to the victim.

anger-retaliation rapist A classification of rapists proposed by the Massachusetts Research Center to identify those individuals who are more motivated to humiliate the victim than to gain sexual gratification. See also **displaced anger rapist.**

antisocial behavior Clinical term reserved for serious habitual behavior, especially that involving direct harm to others.

antisocial personality disorder (APD or ASP) A disorder characterized by a history of continuous behavior in which the rights of others are violated.

arson Any willful or malicious burning or attempt to burn, with or without intent to defraud, a dwelling house, public building, motor vehicle, aircraft, or personal property of another.

assault The intentional inflicting of bodily injury on another person, or the attempt to inflict such injury.

assault, aggravated Inflicting, or attempting to inflict, bodily injury on another person, with the intent to inflict serious injury.

assault, simple The unlawful, intentional inflicting of less-than-serious bodily injury without a deadly or dangerous weapon, or the attempt to inflict such bodily injury, again without a deadly or dangerous weapon.

attachment theory A theory developed by John Bowlby, and later expanded by Mary Salter Ainsworth, which states that infants have a strong need to establish close emotional bonds with significant others in their social environments. According to the theory, the nature of this emotional bond determines the quality of social relationships later in life.

attention deficit hyperactivity disorder (ADHD) Traditionally considered a chronic neurobiological condition characterized by developmentally poor attention, impulsivity, and hyperactivity. More contemporary perspectives see the behavioral pattern as a deficiency in interpersonal skills.

authoritarian style The approach to parenting that sets a very rigid structure on the family setting and allows little decision making by the child.

authoritative style The approach to parenting that sets firm rules yet encourages the development of autonomy in the child.

authority homicide In the context of workplace violence, the killing of a supervisor or other person in authority by an employee.

autoeroticism A term coined by Havelock Ellis that refers to the self-arousal and self-gratification of sexual arousal.

availability heuristic The cognitive shortcuts that people use to make quick inferences about their world. It is the information that is most readily available to us mentally, and is usually based extensively on the most recent material we gain from the news or entertainment media.

avoidance learning A process whereby, if a person responds in time to a warning signal, he or she avoids painful or aversive stimuli.

barricade situation In hostage-taking scenarios, a situation in which an individual has fortified him or herself in a building or residence and threatens violence, typically to the hostages.

base rate Accumulated data from groups of previous offenders.

battered woman syndrome (BWS) A cluster of behavioral and psychological characteristics believed common to women who have been abused in relationships.

behavior genetics Investigates the role of genes play in the formation and development of behavior.

behaviorism A perspective that focuses on observable, measurable behavior and argues that the social environment and learning are the key determinants of human behavior.

biopsychologists Psychologists who study the biological aspects of behavior to determine which genetic and neurophysiological variables play a part. They generally see human behavior as the result of a complex interaction between the individual's physiological and social environment.

bioterrorism The category of terrorism that involves the use of bacteria, viruses, germs, and other agents.

boosters Professional shoplifters.

boot camps Military-style, short-term facilities for juveniles and adults who have not committed serious crimes; most focus on instilling discipline rather than education or treatment.

Brawner Rule A standard for evaluating the insanity defense that recognizes that the defendant suffers from a condition that substantially (1) affects mental or emotional processes, or (2) impairs behavior controls. Also called the ALI/Brawner Rule.

bump key Term for a special key that fits many different locks made by the same manufacturer. Intended for locksmiths, sets of bump keys are easily accessible to professional burglars.

burglary The unlawful entry of a structure, with or without force, with intent to commit a felony or theft.

Callous-unemotional (CU) traits Identified by Paul Frick and colleagues. Refers to a severe and chronic pattern of antisocial behavior characterized by little feeling or empathy toward others.

carjacking The completed or attempted theft in which a motor vehicle is taken by force or threat of force.

caveat paragraph A section of the ALI/Brawner Rule that excludes abnormality manifested only by repeated criminal or antisocial conduct. It was specifically designed to disallow the insanity defense for psychopaths.

child delinquents Children between the ages of 7 and 12 who have committed or are accused of committing a criminal act.

classical (Pavlovian) conditioning The process of learning to respond to a formerly neutral stimulus that has been paired with another stimulus that already elicits a response. Also called **Pavlovian conditioning.**

classic mass murder A situation in which an individual enters a public place or barricades himself or herself inside a public building, such as a fast-food restaurant, and randomly kills patrons and other individuals.

classical theory Theory of human behavior that emphasizes free will as a core concept.

clearance rate The proportion of reported crimes that have been "solved" through the arrest and turning over for prosecution of at least one person. Crimes also may be cleared through exceptional means.

clinical profiling Predictions of human behavior based largely on previous experience.

coercion theory The belief that punitive and coercive tactics employed by parents will increase the likelihood of later aggressive behavior and family violence.

cognitions The internal processes that enable humans to imagine, to gain knowledge, to reason, and to evaluate. The attitudes, beliefs, values, and thoughts that a person holds about the environment, relationships, and himself or herself.

cognitive behavior therapy An approach to therapy that focuses on changing beliefs, fantasies, attitudes, and rationalizations that justify and perpetuate antisocial or other problematic behavior. It is often used in the treatment of sex offenders.

cognitive-neoassociation model A revised theory of the frustration–aggression hypothesis proposed by Leonard Berkowitz.

cognitive processes Internal mental processes that enable humans to imagine, gain knowledge, reason, and evaluate information.

cognitive restructuring A psychological process that allows one to justify committing reprehensible actions; typically involves *moral justification, euphemistic language,* and *advantageous comparison.*

cognitive scripts Mental images of how one feels he or she should act in a variety of situations.

cognitive scripts model Rowell Huesmann's theory that social behavior in general and aggressive behavior in particular are controlled largely by cognitive scripts learned through daily experiences.

compensatory rapist An offender who rapes in response to an intense sexual arousal initiated by stimuli in the environment, often quite specific stimuli (e.g., dark-haired women). His main motive is to prove his sexual prowess.

competency to stand trial The legal requirement that a defendant is able to understand the proceedings and to help the attorney in preparing a defense. See also **incompetency to stand trial.**

concordance A term used in genetics to represent the degree to which related pairs of subjects both show a particular behavior or condition. It is usually expressed in percentages.

conduct disorder A diagnostic label used to identify children who demonstrate habitual misbehavior.

confirmation bias Tendency to look for evidence that confirms preexisting expectations or beliefs.

conformity perspective The theoretical position that humans are born basically good and generally try to do the right and just thing.

contagion effect (Copycat effect) A tendency for some people to model or copy a behavior or activity portrayed by the news or entertainment media.

controlled substance Any psychoactive drug or chemical substance whose availability is restricted, as designated by state or federal law.

corporate crime Any criminal offense committed by officers or employees in which the corporation benefits.

crime scene profiling Development of a rough behavioral or psychological sketch of an offender based on clues identified at the crime scene.

crimes of obedience Illegal acts that are committed under the order of someone in authority.

criminal homicide A term that encompasses both murder and nonnegligent homicide.

criminal or offender profiling See **profiling.**

criminal psychopath A primary psychopath who engages in repetitive antisocial or criminal behavior.

criminology The multidisciplinary study of crime.

criminology, psychiatric The branch of criminology that focuses on individual aspects of behavior, particularly internal forces and unconscious drives. Also called **forensic psychiatry.**

criminology, psychological The branch of criminology that examines the individual behavior and especially the mental processes involved in criminal behavior.

criminology, sociological The branch of criminology that examines the demographic, group, and societal variables related to crime.

crossover Refers to the extent that an offender "crosses over" to selected victims regardless of age, gender, or physical characteristics.

cultural devaluation A process that occurs when a group or culture is selected by another group as a scapegoat or an ideological enemy.

cyberbullying Sending or posting harmful or cruel text or images using the Internet or other digital communication devices. Primarily a problem with school-aged children and adolescents.

cybercrime Any illegal act that involves a computer system. Also called **computer crime.**

cyberstalking Threatening behavior or unwanted advances directed at another using the Internet or other forms of online communications.

cycle of violence The continuation of violence that may occur across generations among individuals who have experienced and witnessed violence in their families. Also pertains to the violence experienced by women in domestic violence situations.

dark figure The number of crimes that go unreported in official crime data reports.

date or acquaintance rape A sexual assault that occurs within the context of a dating relationship.

dehumanize To engage in actions that obscure the identity of the victim, such as excessive facial battery, or to see and treat victims like objects rather than human beings.

deindividuation A process by which individuals feel they cannot be identified, primarily because they are disguised or are subsumed within a group.

delusional (paranoid) disorder Mental disorder characterized by a system of false beliefs.

delusions False beliefs about the world.

dependence In substance abuse, a condition that may be physical, psychological, or both, whereby a person develops an intense craving for (and feels he or she cannot live without) a drug.

dependent variable The variable that is measured to see how it is changed by manipulations of the independent variable.

deterrence theory The theory that argues that threat of punishment will prevent crime.

developmental approach Examines the changes and influences (risk factors) across a person's lifetime that contribute to the formation of antisocial and criminal behavior or, alternately, that protect individuals with many risk factors in their lives.

developmental disability A status that is attributable to a cognitive or physical impairment.

developmental pathways In the study of criminal behavior, these are the various tracks individuals follow that lead to antisocial behavior. Researchers began by identifying two pathways but have now found evidence of more.

Diagnostic and Statistical Manual of Mental Disorders (DSM) The official guidebook or manual, published by the American Psychiatric Association, used to define and diagnose specific mental disorders. Now in its fourth revised edition (*DSM-IV-R*).

difference-in-degree The perspective of human nature that argues that humans are intimately tied to their animal ancestry in important and significant ways and differ only in the extent to which they have developed through the evolutionary process. For example, this perspective might argue that human violence is a result of innate, biological needs to obtain sufficient food supplies, territory, or mates.

difference-in-kind The perspective of human nature that humans are fundamentally different from other animals, such as in their intellectual, emotional, and spiritual capacities. Therefore, comparisons between the behavior of humans and that of other animals are unwarranted.

differential association-reinforcement (DAR) theory A theory of deviance developed by Ronald Akers that combines Skinner's behaviorism and Sutherland's differential association theory. The theory states that people learn deviant behavior through the reinforcements they receive from the social environment.

differential association theory Formulated by Edwin Sutherland, a theory of crime that states that criminal behavior is primarily due to obtaining values or messages from others, including but not limited to those who engage in crime. The critical factors include with whom a person associates, how early, for how long, how frequently, and how personally meaningful the associations are.

discriminative stimuli According to Akers, social signals or gestures transmitted by subcultural or peer groups to indicate whether certain kinds of behavior will be rewarded or punished within a particular social context.

disorganized crime scene Demonstrates that the offender committed the crime without premeditation or planning. In other words, the crime scene indicators suggest the individual acted on impulse or in rage, or under extreme excitement.

displaced aggression rapist The rapist whose attack is violent and aggressive, displaying minimum or total absence of sexual feeling. Also called **anger-retaliation rapist.**

displaced aggression theory The theory that some aggression is directed at the target as a replacement for the individual who is the real source of the provocation.

dispositions In personality theory, a term that signifies internal or personality determinants of human behavior. Dispositional theorists look to inner conflicts, beliefs, drives, personal needs, traits, or attitudes to explain behavior. See also **traits.**

disruptive behavior disorders (DBD) A pattern that generally includes conduct disorders and oppositional defiant disorders that is characterized by chronic violation of social norms and rights of others.

dissociated state A state of mind during which the person feels detached from self and surroundings.

dissociative identity disorder A psychiatric syndrome characterized by the existence within an individual of two or more distinct personalities, any of which may be dominant at any given moment. Formerly called **multiple personality disorder (MPD).**

dizygotic twins Twins who developed from two fertilized eggs and are no more *genetically* alike than nontwins. Also called **fraternal twins.**

drug courts Specialized criminal courts intended as an alternative to traditional criminal processing. Defendants are offered substance abuse counseling and are monitored closely as a condition of remaining in the community and not given jail or prison sentences.

drug treatment An approach to therapy that concentrates on reducing the targeted behavior through the use of medication.

dual system model of adolescent risk taking Developed by Laurence Steinberg, who believes that risk taking during adolescence is best explained by the dual interaction of social emotional and cognitive control systems.

Durham Rule A legal standard of insanity that holds that an accused is not criminally responsible if his or her unlawful act was the product of mental disease or defect. Also known as the **Product Rule.**

duty to protect Requirement from the *Tarasoff* case that clinicians must take steps to protect possible victims from serious bodily harm as a result of threats made by the clinicians' clients. The duty to protect does not require that the clinician contact the potential victim.

duty to warn Requirement from the *Tarasoff* case that clinicians must actively warn potential victims of threats of serious bodily harm made by their clients.

dynamic cascade model A statistical and theoretical model that sees the many risk factors in a youth's early development as affecting subsequent factors, having a snowballing effect that leads to increased antisocial behavior.

dyssocial psychopath Individual with psychopathic characteristics who is antisocial because of social learning and does not possess the features of the primary psychopath.

eldercide The killing of an older person, usually over 60.

emotional paradox The research observation that psychopaths seem to be able to talk about emotional cues but lack the ability to use them effectively in the real world.

enmeshed style A parental style in which the parent takes extraordinary control of the child's life including imposing rigid rules and seeing even trivial, minor behaviors as problematic. Typically results in harsh punishment but inconsistent discipline. Opposite of **lax style.**

equivocal death analysis See **reconstructive psychological evaluation (RPE).**

erotomania stalking In this form of stalking, the stalker usually has serious mental disorders and is considered delusional. Public figures are typically the targets.

euphemistic language Words used to make something appear more innocuous or less negative than it actually is.

evocative therapy An approach to sex offender therapy that focuses on (1) helping offenders to understand the causes and motivations of their sexual behavior, and (2) increasing their empathy for the victims of the sexual assault.

evolutionary psychology The study of the evolution of behavior using the principles of natural selection.

excitation transfer theory Theory explaining how physiological arousal can generalize from one situation to another; based on the assumption that physiological arousal, however produced, dissipates slowly over time.

executive function Higher-order mental abilities involved in goal-directed behavior. They include organizing behavior, memory, inhibition processes, and planning strategies.

expectancy theory A theory of motivation that takes into account both the expectancy of achieving a particular goal and the value placed on it.

experimental substance use (ESU) Experimentation—typically by adolescents—with various psychoactive substances before dependency or addiction to drugs occurs.

exploitative pedophile An adult who seeks children almost exclusively for sexual gratification.

exploitative rapist See **impulsive rapist.**

expressive aggression Aggression in which a person's primary aim is to hurt or do injury to another. Also called **hostile aggression,** it is the opposite of **instrumental aggression.**

expressive burglars Burglars who take considerable pride in developing ingenious techniques and skills for successful burglary.

expressive hostage taking Hostage-taking situation in which the offender's primary goal is to gain some control over his or her life.

expressive-object pattern A form of firesetting that reflects fascination with fire and its consequences. The firesetter typically does not intend to harm anyone and chooses uninhabited structures.

expressive-person pattern A form of firesetting associated with mental disorder or emotional problems; it is seen as a cry for help rather than desire to harm.

expressive sexual aggression A rape situation in which the offender's primary goal is to gain some control over his life.

extinction The decline and eventual disappearance of a conditioned or learned response when it is no longer reinforced.

extrafamilial child molester A sex abuser whose victims are outside the immediate or extended family.

Factor 1 A behavioral dimension, identified through factor analysis, representing the interpersonal and emotional aspects of psychopathy.

Factor 2 A behavioral dimension representing the socially deviant lifestyle characteristics of psychopaths.

factor analysis A statistical procedure by which underlying patterns, factors, or dimensions are identified among a series of scale items.

family mass murder A situation in which at least three family members are killed (usually by another family member).

fence An individual who accepts stolen goods and resells them.

filicide Killing of one's child older than one year.

firesetting The term used in the literature on child psychopathology for an abnormal fascination with fire accompanied by successful or unsuccessful attempts to start harmful fires.

fixated pedophile See **immature pedophile.**

forcible rape The carnal knowledge of a female, forcibly and against her will. It includes rape by force, assault to rape, and attempted rape. Although victims may be both female and male, the UCR definition limits this to female victims.

fraternal twins See **dizygotic twins.**

fratricide The killing of one's brother.

frustration An aversive internal state of arousal that occurs when one is prevented from responding in a way that previously produced rewards (or that one believes would produce rewards).

frustration–aggression hypothesis The theory that frustration leads to aggressive behavior. The theory has been revised several times, with most substantial changes coming from the work of Leonard Berkowitz.

fundamental attribution error A tendency to underestimate the importance of situational determinates and to overestimate the importance of personality or dispositional factors in identifying the causes of human behavior.

general aggression model An attempt to organize mini-theories of aggression into one unified theory.

general altercation homicide Death resulting from hostile aggression.

general theory of crime Based on the assumption that lack of self-control is the core factor in criminal behavior.

geographical profiling A type of profiling that focuses on the location of the crime and how it relates to the residence and/or base of operations of the offender.

global risk recognition failure Tendency of some women to believe they are immune to sexual assault.

good burglar Refers to the burglar who demonstrates technical skill and overall competence in burglarizing.

Guilty but Mentally Ill (GBMI) A verdict alternative in some states that allows mentally disordered defendants to be found guilty while seemingly affording them treatment for mental disorders.

hallucinations Things or events that a mentally disordered person, but no others, sees or perceives. Characteristic of schizophrenia and some forms of dementia.

hallucinogens Those psychoactive drugs that sometimes generate hallucinations and lead to changes in perceptions of reality. Also called **psychedelics.**

Hate Crime Statistics Act The first federal law requiring the FBI to collect data from law enforcement on incidents of bias crime across the U.S.

hierarchy rule In the UCR program, the rule that requires that only the most serious crime in a series be reported in the crime statistics.

hebephilia The use of young adolescent girls or boys for sexual gratification by adults, usually males.

hemisphere asymmetry An unusual or abnormal balance between the two hemispheres, both in language processing and in emotional states.

home invasion Crime in which perpetrators enter home while occupants are present; typically involves violent victimization.

hostile attribution bias The tendency to perceive hostile intent in others even when it is totally lacking.

hostile attribution model A model of aggression proposed by Kenneth Dodge, based on the finding that some individuals are prone to perceive hostile intent in others and therefore act aggressively as a result.

iatrogenic A process whereby mental or physical disorders are unintentionally induced or developed in patients by physicians, clinicians, or psychotherapists.

I-cubed theory An extension of general aggression theory.

identical twins See **monozygotic twins.**

identity theft The fraudulent use of another person's personal identification information—such as social security number, date of birth, or mother's maiden name—without that person's knowledge or permission.

imitational learning See **observational learning.**

immature pedophile A child sex abuser who demonstrates a long-standing, exclusive preference for children as both sexual and social companions. Also called **fixated pedophile.**

impulsive rapist A rapist who demonstrates neither strong sexual nor aggressive features, but engages in spontaneous rape when the opportunity presents itself. The rape is usually carried out in the context of another crime, such as robbery or burglary. Also called **exploitative rapist.**

incompetent to stand trial (IST) A judicial determination that a defendant lacks sufficient ability to understand the legal process against him or her and/or to assist a lawyer in the preparation of a defense. See also **adjudicative competence.**

independent variable The measure whose effect is being studied, and, in most scientific investigations, that is manipulated by the experimenter in a controlled fashion.

index crimes (now commonly called Part I crimes) The crimes that are of most concern, as defined by the FBI's Uniform Crime Reports, and are used to indicate the seriousness of the crime problem. The eight Part I crimes are murder and nonnegligent manslaughter, aggravated assault, robbery, forcible rape, burglary, larceny-theft, arson, and motor vehicle theft.

individual occupational crime Employee theft.

individual offender An offender prompted by a series of intense, long-lasting frustration.

infanticide Although this term literally means the killing of an infant, it has become synonymous with the killing of a child by a parent.

Insanity Defense Reform Act of 1984 A law designed to make it more difficult for defendants using the insanity defense in the federal courts to be acquitted.

instrumental aggression Aggression carried out for the primary purpose of gaining material goods or other rewards rather than for the purpose of harming the victim.

instrumental hostage taking A hostage situation in which the primary goal of the offender is material or monetary gain.

instrumental learning A form of learning in which a voluntary response is strengthened or diminished by its consequences. Also called **operant conditioning.**

instrumental object pattern A form of firesetting that is done to cover up evidence of another crime, such as a burglary or a murder; also characterizes firesetting done for direct profit, such as collecting insurance money.

instrumental-person pattern A form of firesetting motivated by anger or revenge directed at a specific person, group, or institution.

instrumental sexual aggression When the sexual offender uses just enough coercion to gain compliance from his victim.

intimate partner violence (IPV) Crimes committed against persons by their current or former spouses, boyfriends, or girlfriends.

intrafamilial child molester A child sex abuser whose victims are within the immediate or extended family.

investigative psychology The application of psychological research and concepts to the investigation of crime.

irrationality A basic ingredient of the insanity standard. Refers to the legal assumption that a person cannot be held criminally responsible for his or her actions if it is determined he or she could not understand the consequences of his or her behavior.

jail A secure facility for holding accused individuals detained before trial or convicted individuals given short sentences, typically less than a year.

just-world hypothesis A belief that one gets what one deserves in this world.

kleptomania The irresistible urge to steal unneeded objects. Whether there is such an urge is highly questionable.

language impairment Broad term for a variety of problems in expressing or understanding language.

lax style A parental style that does not respond sufficiently to problematic or antisocial behavior in children but rather allows it to occur without disciplinary action. Opposite of the **enmeshed style** and similar to the **permissive.**

learned helplessness A learned passive and withdrawing response in the face of perceived hopelessness, as theorized by Martin Seligman (1975).

learning perspective The theoretical position that humans are born basically neutral and behaviorally a blank slate. What they become as individuals depends on their learning experiences rather than innate predispositions.

life-course-persistent (LCP) offenders A term introduced by Terrie Moffitt to represent offenders who demonstrate a life-long pattern of antisocial behavior and who are resistant to treatment or rehabilitation.

limited amnesia A pathological inability to remember a specific episode, or small number of episodes, from the recent past.

London syndrome A behavioral pattern observed during a hostage situation at the Iranian Embassy in London. Refers to the explicit and consistent resistance and refusals by hostages to do what is expected by captors. This behavior often results in death or serious injury to the resistors.

Lone-wolf terrorist Terrorist who operates alone.

love obsession stalking In this form of stalking, the stalker and victim are strangers or casual acquaintances. The stalker seeks a love relationship with the object of his or her obsession.

major depressive disorder General label for symptoms that include an extremely depressed state, general slowing down of mental and physical activity, and feelings of self-worthlessness.

MAOA A gene that appears to play an important role in preventing antisocial behavior in humans.

MAOA-L Known as the "warrior gene," it appears to promote aggressive behavior in humans.

marital rape Rape that occurs within a marital relationship. These sexual assaults are rarely reflected in official crime data.

markers A term used for the neurological indicators of a particular phenomenon, such as psychopathy.

mass murder Murdering three or more persons at a single location with no cooling-off period between murders.

matricide The killing of one's mother.

mental illness or mental disorder Terms used for a vast number of mental conditions, ranging from the mild to the serious, that impede one's ability to function. Serious mental illness or disorder may, but will not necessarily, absolve an individual of criminal responsibility.

mental retardation A cognitive disability typically assessed by performance scores on standardized intelligence tests. Mental health practitioners and researchers often prefer to use the terms intellectual or developmental disability.

mixed crime scene Indicates that the nature of the crime demonstrates both organized and disorganized behavioral patterns.

M'Naghten Rule An insanity standard based on the conclusion that if a defendant has a defect of reason, or a disease of the mind, so as not to know the nature and quality of his or her actions, then he or she cannot be held criminally responsible. Also called **the right and wrong test.**

modeling See **observational learning.**

models Individuals or groups of individuals in the environment whose behavior is observed and imitated.

molecular genetics Field of biology that studies the structure and function of genes at the level of molecules.

Monitoring the Future Study (MFS) A self-report survey administered to high school students nationwide focusing on drug use and abuse.

monozygotic twins Twins who developed from one fertilized egg and share the same genes. Also called **identical twins.**

moral disengagement The process of freeing oneself from one's own moral standards in order to act against those standards. The unacceptable conduct is usually undertaken under orders from someone higher in authority or under high social pressure.

moral justification The process of convincing oneself that one's actions are worthy and have an ultimate moral and good purpose.

multiassaultive family A nuclear family (traditional or nontraditional) characterized by multiple incidents of violence involving more than one perpetrator.

multiple personality disorder (MPD) See **dissociative identity disorder.**

multisystemic therapy (MST) A treatment approach for serious juvenile offenders that focuses on the family while being responsive to the many other contexts surrounding the family, such as the peer group, the neighborhood, and the school.

Munchausen syndrome by proxy (MSBP) An unusual form of child abuse in which the parent (usually the mother), or parents, consistently bring a child for medical attention with symptoms falsified or directly induced by the parent or parents.

murder The felonious killing of one human being by another with malice aforethought. See also.

National Crime Victimization Survey (NCVS) A government-sponsored survey of victims of crime, intended to collect data from the victim's perspective on crimes both reported and not reported to police.

National Incidence Based Reporting System (NIBRS) The FBI's system of collecting *detailed* data from law enforcement agencies on known crimes and arrests. See also **Uniform Crime Reporting.**

natural narcotics Psychoactive substances classified as narcotics that require no chemical preparation.

near-repeat crimes Tendency of burglars to burglarize homes near homes that they have burglarized successfully in the past.

negative reinforcement See **reinforcement, negative.**

neglecting style Detached and unengaged parental style.

negligent manslaughter The unlawful killing of another through reckless or negligent behavior, without intention to kill.

neonaticide The killing of a newborn, usually under 48 hours.

neurotransmitters Biochemicals directly involved in the transmission of neural impulses and without which communication would not be possible. **Serotonin** is one example.

nonconformist perspective The theoretical perspective that humans will naturally try to get away with anything they can, including illegal conduct, unless social controls are imposed.

nonindex crimes (now called Part II crimes) Crimes not considered as serious as Part I crimes by the FBI and on which only arrest data are gathered for UCR purposes. Examples include simple assault, fraud, embezzlement, and vandalism.

nonnegligent manslaughter The killing of a human being without premeditation but with the intention to kill in the "heat of the moment," such as under high emotional states of anger or passion.

nonshared environments An important concept in twin studies, this refers to the living experiences that are different for each twin, such as being raised by different parents.

not guilty by reason of insanity (NGRI) A legal determination that a defendant was so mentally disordered at the time of the crime that he or she cannot be held criminally responsible for his or her actions.

nuclear/biological/chemical A form of terrorism that threatens to use nonconventional weapons (nuclear, biological, or chemical) to accomplish its goals. NBC terrorism is feared because of its potential for annihilating large numbers of people in a short period of time.

observational learning (modeling) The process by which individuals learn patterns of behavior by observing another person performing the action.

occupational crime (1) Any one of a variety of offenses committed by an individual through opportunity created by his or her occupation; see also, Green's four categories of **individual, organizational, professional,** and **state-authority** occupational crime. (2) The second category of **white-collar crime** (along with corporate) that refers to crimes committed by individuals for their own benefit.

operant conditioning See **instrumental learning.**

opiate narcotics Psychoactive drugs that have sedative (sleep-inducing) and analgesic (pain-relieving) effects.

opportunity rapist Rapist whose sexual assault is an impulsive, predatory act that is controlled by situational and contextual factors, such as a woman being present during the commission of another crime.

oppositional defiant disorder (ODD) A behavior disorder of childhood characterized by frequent disobedience and hostile behavior toward authority figures.

organized crime scene Indicates planning and premeditation on the part of the offender. In other words, the crime scene shows signs that the offender maintained control of himself or herself and of the victim, if it is a crime against a person.

organizational occupational crime Crime committed by upper level employees or directors of an organization for the benefit of the organization.

paranoid disorders See **delusional disorders.**

paraphilia The clinical term for a sexual condition exhibited in fantasies, urges, or behaviors involving nonhuman objects, suffering or humiliation of oneself or one's partner, or children or other nonconsenting persons.

parental monitoring Supervision by parents of their children's activities. Poor parental monitoring is a strong risk factor for delinquency.

parental practices Specific behaviors used by parents or caretakers in raising their children. Examples are requiring chores, spanking, or volunteering as room parent.

parental styles Seemingly nongoal-directed approaches displayed by parents, although the goals may be implicit.

parricide The killing of a parent.

Part I crime See **index crimes.**

Part II crime See **nonindex crimes.**

passive-aggressive behavior Hostile behavior that does not directly inflict physical harm, such as refusing to speak to someone against whom one holds a grudge.

patricide The killing of one's father.

Pavlovian conditioning See **classical conditioning.**

pedophile The clinical term for an adult who uses children for sexual gratification and companionship.

pedophilia The use of children by adults for sexual gratification and companionship.

permissive style a relaxed parenting style characterized by few demands, controls, or limits.

personation See **signature.**

pervasive anger type A rapist characterized by anger directed toward virtually everyone he knows.

plasticity The characteristic of the brain that allows both its structure and its function to be profoundly responsive to experiences, particularly during early life.

positive reinforcement See **reinforcement, positive.**

positivist theory Theory that argues prior experiences or influences determine present behavior.

posttraumatic stress disorder (PTSD) A cluster of behavioral patterns that result from a psychologically distressing event outside the usual range of human experience.

power rape A rape situation, identified by Groth, in which the assailant seeks to establish power and control over his victim. Thus, the amount of force and threats used depends on the degree of submission shown by the victim.

primary prevention An intervention program designed to prevent behavior or disorders before any signs of the behavioral pattern develops. Also called **universal prevention.**

primary psychopath Robert Hare's classification of the "true" psychopath. That is, the individual who demonstrates those physiological and behavioral features that represent psychopathy—in contrast to **secondary psychopaths,** who commit antisocial acts because of severe emotional problems or inner conflicts, and **dyssocial psychopaths,** who are antisocial because of social learning.

proactive aggression Similar to **instrumental aggression,** actions undertaken to obtain a specific goal. In children, refers to insensitive actions such as bullying, name-calling, and coercive actions.

professional occupational crime Illegal behavior committed by professional individuals (e.g., lawyers, doctors, engineers) as part of their occupation.

profiling The process of identifying personality traits, behavioral tendencies, and demographic variables of an offender based on characteristics of the crime.

psychedelics The category of psychoactive drugs that produce elevated mood, hallucinations, and altered states of consciousness. Also called **hallucinogens.**

psychiatric criminology See **criminology, psychiatric.**

psychoactive drugs Drugs that exert their primary effect on the brain, thus altering mood or behavior.

psychodynamic model The theoretical perspective that argues that human behavior can be best explained through the use of psychological forces and pressures. See also **hydraulic model.**

psychoeducational counseling An approach to therapy that utilizes a group or class setting to remedy deficits in social and interpersonal skills.

psychological autopsy Postmortem analysis often reserved for cases in which suicide occurred or is suspected or alleged. The psychological autopsy is frequently done to determine the reasons and precipitating factors for the death.

psychological criminology See **criminology, psychological.**

psychological signature An offender's unique way of speaking or behaving that is usually out of his or her awareness; useful to investigators seeking to identify a perpetrator.

psychometric approach The perspective that human characteristics, attributes, and traits can be measured and quantified.

psychometric intelligence (PI) A more contemporary designation of intelligence as measured by intelligence or IQ tests. However, the term is not yet widely used in comparison with "IQ."

psychopath An individual who demonstrates a distinct behavioral pattern that differs from the general population in its level of sensitivity, empathy, compassion, and guilt. See also **primary psychopath.**

Psychopathy Checklist (PCL) and Psychopathy Checklist-Revised (PCL-R). Developed by Robert Hare, currently the best-known instrument for the measurement of criminal psychopathy. Additional versions include the **Psychopathy Checklist—Screening Version,** the **P-Scan: Research Version,** and the **Psychopathy Checklist: Youth Version (PCL:YV).**

psychophysiology The study of the dynamic interactions between behavior and the autonomic nervous system.

punishment An event by which a person receives a noxious, painful, or aversive stimulus, usually as a consequence of behavior.

pyromania A psychiatric term for an irresistible urge to set fires along with an intense fascination (usually sexual) with fire. The existence of this behavioral phenomenon has been brought into serious question by the available research.

radical environmental groups Environmental activists who have used terrorist tactics to draw attention to dangers to the environment.

rape by fraud The act of having sexual relations with a supposedly consenting adult female under fraudulent conditions, such as when a physician or psychotherapist has sexual intercourse with a patient under the guise of "effective treatment."

rape myths A variety of mistaken beliefs about the crime of rape and its victims held by many men and women.

reactive aggression Spontaneous aggression, possibly in response to provocation. In children, hot-blooded aggressive acts, such as temper tantrums and emotionally driven vengeful hostility.

reactive depression A withdrawal response to negative life situations over which one perceives he or she has no control; see also, learned helplessness.

recidivism A return to criminal activity (usually measured by arrest) after being convicted of a criminal offense.

reconstructive psychological evaluation (RPE) Reconstruction of the personality profile and cognitive features (especially intentions) of deceased individuals.

reductionism A research approach that argues that in order to understand highly complex events or phenomenon, one must start examining the simplest parts first.

regressed pedophile A male who had fairly normal relationships with adults but later reverted to children for sexual and social companionship because of feelings of inadequacy.

reinforcement Anything that increases the probability of responding.

reinforcement, negative The reward received for avoiding a painful or aversive condition, or stimuli.

reinforcement, positive The acquisition of something desired as a result of one's behavior.

relapse prevention (RP) A method of treatment primarily designed to prevent a relapse of an undesired behavioral pattern.

relative deprivation A concept developed by Gresham Sykes for explaining economic crime. It refers to the perceived discrepancy between what an individual has and what he or she would like to have. It is a condition that is especially prominent when people of wealth and people of poverty live in close proximity.

repeat burglary Refers to the observation that some burglars burglarize the same place repeatedly.

residential treatment Juvenile training school or rehabilitation center where youths are incarcerated for extended periods of time. Usually considered the "last stop" for youths.

right and wrong test See **M'Naghten Rule.**

risky shift Tendency of groups to make decisions that are more extreme than if the same decisions were made by individuals.

ritualized aggression The symbolic display of aggressive intentions or strength without actual physical combat or conflict.

RNR (risk, needs, responsivity principles) A model that proposes three principles for effective treatment of offenders. The risk principle proposes that intensive treatment be provided to offenders at highest risk to reoffend. The need principle targets crime-causing needs and attitudes. The responsivity principle provides treatment in a style and mode that is responsive to the offender's learning style and ability.

road rage Anger at another motorist expressed in highly reckless driving and, in some cases, attempts to harm the other motorist. To be distinguished from **aggressive driving,** in which the actions of the other motorist are not the direct cause of the reckless behavior.

robbery The taking or attempt to take anything of value from the care, custody or control of another by force or the threat of force.

rumination The focused attention on one's own thoughts and feelings that, if excessive, can lead to aggression against others.

sadistic pedophile See **aggressive pedophile.**

sadistic rape A rape situation, identified by Groth, in which the offender experiences sexual arousal and excitement as a result of the victim's torment, distress, helplessness, and suffering. The assault usually involves bondage and torture, and the rapist directs considerable abuse and injury on various areas of the victim's body.

sadistic rapist See **sexually aggressive rapist.**

schizophrenia Mental disorder characterized by severe breakdowns in thought patterns, emotions, and perceptions.

secondary prevention An intervention program designed for individuals who demonstrate early signs or indications of behavioral problems or antisocial behavior. Also called **selective prevention.**

secondary psychopath Individual with psychopathic characteristics, but who commits antisocial acts because of severe emotional problems or inner conflicts. Distinct from **primary psychopath.**

sedative-hypnotic compounds Psychoactive drugs that depress central nervous system functioning, generally reducing anxiety and tension.

selective prevention See **secondary prevention.**

self-regulation The ability to control one's behavior in accordance with internal cognitive standards.

self-serving bias A tendency to attribute positive things that happen to us to our abilities and personalities, and to attribute negative events to some cause outside ourselves or beyond our control.

semantic aphasia A characteristic found in psychopaths whereby the words they speak are devoid of emotional sincerity.

semisynthetic narcotics See **narcotics.**

serial murder Incidents in which an individual (or individuals) kill a number of individuals (usually a minimum of three) over time.

serotonin A chemical by which nerve cells communicate with one another. Low levels of this chemical may be related to aggressive behavior.

sexual aggressive rapist A rapist who demonstrates both sexual and aggressive features in his attack. In order for him to experience sexual arousal, it must be associated with violence and pain, which excite him. Also called **sadistic rapist.**

sexual gratification rapist Rapist whose motivation is hypothesized to be sexual, marked by the presence of protracted sexual or sadistic fantasies that influence as well as sustain the rape. These offenders have in common some form of enduring sexual preoccupation.

shaken baby syndrome (SBS) A form of child abuse in which an adult (usually male) shakes a baby so hard that it causes significant brain damage or death.

shared environment An important concept in twin studies, this refers to the prenatal and life experiences that are common to both twins, such as being raised by the same biological parents.

shoplifting by proxy A person having someone else shoplift items for him or her.

siblicide The killing of one's brother or sister; **sororicide** is the killing of one's sister; **fratricide** is the killing of one's brother.

signature Any behavior that goes beyond what is necessary to commit the crime. Also called **personation.**

simple obsession stalking The form in which the stalker seeks power and control after a failed relationship with the victim; often associated with past domestic violence.

situationism A theoretical perspective that argues that environmental stimuli control behavior.

snitches Amateur shoplifters.

social control theory A theory that contends that crime and delinquency occur when an individual's ties to the conventional social order or normative standards are weak or largely nonexistent.

social learning theory A theory of human behavior based on learning from watching others in the social environment. This leads to an individual's development of his or her own perceptions, thoughts, expectancies, competencies, and values.

socialized offender A person who violates the law consistently because of learning the behavioral patterns from his or her social environment.

sociological criminology See **criminology, sociological.**

softlifting Theft of computer software

sororicide See **sibicide.**

special interest extremists Also known as single-issue terrorists, these are members of special interest groups that seek to resolve one single issue rather than seek widespread political or social change.

specific risk recognition failure Refers to tendency of some women not to recognize certain situations as high risk for sexual assault.

spree murder The killing of three or more individuals without any cooling-off period, usually at two or more locations.

staging The intentional alteration of a crime scene prior to the arrival of the police.

stalking Conduct directed at a specific person that involves repeated physical or visual proximity, nonconsensual communication, or verbal, written, or implied threats sufficient to cause fear in a reasonable person.

state-authority occupational crime Refers to a wide range of law violations by persons imbued with legal authority.

status offenses A class of illegal behavior that only persons with certain characteristics or status can commit. Used almost exclusively to refer to the behavior of juveniles. Examples include running away from home, violating curfew, buying alcohol, or skipping school.

statutory rape Rape for which the age of the victim is the crucial distinction, on the premise that a victim below a certain age (usually 16) cannot validly consent to sexual intercourse with an adult.

stereotypical child abductions Refer to abductions that are highly unusual. They often end in the death of the child, are usually committed by strangers, and receive considerable media attention.

stimulants A broad drug classification that refers to those psychoactive drugs that "stimulate" the central nervous system and elevate mood.

stimulus A person, event, or situation that elicits behavior.

Stockholm syndrome A term coined after a hostage situation in Sweden in 1973, it refers to the phenomenon of hostages becoming attracted to their captors. In the original incident, an escaped convict held four bank employees in Stockholm in the bank vault for 131 hours. One of the bank employees eventually married her hostage taker.

strain theory A prominent sociological explanation for crime based on Robert Merton's theory that crime and delinquency occur when there is a perceived discrepancy between the materialistic values and goals cherished and held in high esteem by a society and the availability of the legitimate means for reaching these goals.

street culture A variety of conduct norms, particularly in urban areas, that are conducive to robbery and other street crimes. Examples of these norms are disdain for conventional living, a hedonistic pursuit of sensory stimulation, and lack of future orientation.

strong-arm robbery A robbery in which the main weapon used is one's own body rather than guns, knives, or other weapons.

succumbers In hostage-taking situations, refers to those hostages who, after release, have considerable difficulty dealing with the aftereffects of the incident.

survivors In hostage-taking situations, refers to those hostages who are able to return to a meaningful existence with little evidence of long-term depression, nightmares, or serious stress-induced illness.

suspect-based profiling Prediction of behavioral malintent largely based on base rate data of previous offenders.

synthetic narcotics See **narcotics.**

techniques of neutralization Mental processes involved in justifying illegal behavior to oneself and others.

temperament A natural mood disposition determined largely by genetic and biological influences.

territoriality The tendency to attack violators of one's personal space.

tertiary prevention (treatment) Intervention strategy designed to reduce or eliminate behavioral problems or antisocial behavior that is fully developed in individuals. Treatment or counseling of convicted offenders is an example of tertiary prevention.

theory An integrated set of principles that describes, predicts, and explains some phenomena and that guides research.

theory verification A process whereby a scientific theory is tested through observation and analysis. If the process falsifies the theory, the theory must be revised to account for the observed events.

three-path model Proposed by Knight and Sims-Knight. Hypothesis that proposes there are three developmental paths to become a sexual offender.

tolerance In substance use, the condition in which only increasing dosages of the drug produce the desired effect.

traits Relatively stable and enduring tendencies to behave in a particular way across time and place. Traits are believed by some psychologists to be the basic building blocks of personality.

tripartite conceptual model Identifies three main categories of drug related crimes. Proposed by Paul Goldstein.

Twins' Early Development Study (TEDS) Longitudinal research on twins born in the UK in the mid 1990s, focusing on behavioral and cognitive development.

typology A classification system.

undoing A behavioral pattern found at the crime scene whereby the offender tries to psychologically "undo" the murder.

Uniform Crime Reporting (UCR) The FBI's system of gathering data from law enforcement agencies on the crimes that come to their attention and on arrests. See also **NIBRS.**

variable Any entity that can be measured.

vengeance stalkers These stalkers do not seek a relationship with their victims but rather are trying to elicit a response or change of behavior from the victim.

victimological perspective A proposal that suggests we can gain substantial amounts of knowledge on offender characteristics by also studying the nature and possibly the behavior of the victims selected by offenders.

victimology The scientific study of the causes, circumstances, individual characteristics, and social contexts associated with crime victims.

volitional prong The part of the insanity defense that requires acceptance of the possibility that a defendant could not control his or her behavior to conform to the requirements of the law. The volitional prong is not recognized in federal law or the law of many states.

weapons effect Suggestion that the mere presence of a weapon leads a witness or victim to concentrate on the weapon itself rather than other features of the crime.

white-collar crime A broad term, coined in 1939 by Edwin Sutherland, that refers to illegal acts committed by those of high social status in the process of their employment. Contemporary definitions often divide it into corporate crime and individual or occupational crime. See also **occupational crime.**

workplace aggression A term for the conduct, usually on the part of employees, that qualifies as emotional harm or minor physical harm to other employees. Distinct from workplace violence.

workplace violence The aggressive actions, including deaths, that occur at the workplace, not necessarily caused by those who work within the organization.

CASES CITED

Ashcroft v. Free Speech Coalition, 535 U.S. 234 (2002).

Baxstrom v. Herold, 383 U.S. 107 (1966).

Carter v. United States, 252 F.2d 608 (D.C. Cir. 1957).

Clark v. Arizona, 548 U.S. 735 (2006).

Cone v. Bell, 556 U.S. ____, 129 S.Ct. 1769 (2009).

District of Columbia v. Heller, 554 U.S. 570 (2008).

Durham v. United States, 214 F.2d 862 (D.C. Cir. 1954).

Dusky v. United States, 363 U.S. 402 (1960).

Foucha v. Louisiana, 51 Cr.L. 2084 (1992).

Indiana v. Edwards, 554 U.S. 208 (2008).

Jackson v. Indiana, 406 U.S. 715 (1972).

McDonald v. Chicago, 130 S.Ct. 3020 (2010).

Miller v. State, 318 N.W. 2d 673 (S.D. 1983).

M'Naghten, 10 Clark & Fin. 200, 210, Eng.Rep 718, 722 (1843).

New York v. Ferber, 458 U.S. 747 (1982).

Roper v. Simmons, 543 U.S. 551 (2005).

Sell v. United States, 539 U.S. 166 (2003).

State v. Bianchi, No. 79-10116 (Wash. Super. Ct., October 19, 1979).

State v. Felde, 422 So.2d 370 (La. 1982).

State v. Milligan, No. 77-CR-11-2908 (Franklin Co. Ohio, December 4, 1978).

State v. Rodrigues, 679 P.2d 615 (Hawaii 1984).

Tarasoff v. Regents of the University of California, 529 F.2d 553 (Cal. 1974), vac., reheard en banc, & aff'd 131 Cal. Rptr. 1, 551 P.2d 334 (1976).

Thompson v. Oklahoma, 108 S.Ct. 2687 (1989).

United States v. Brawner, 471 F.2d 969 (D.C. Cir. 1972).

United States v. Krutschewski, 509 F.Supp. 1186 (D. Mass. 1981).

United States v. Weston, 255 F.3d 873 (2001).

United States v. Williams, 553 U.S. 285 (2008).

REFERENCES

Abadinsky, H. (1993). *Drug abuse* (2nd ed.). Chicago: Nelson-Hall.

Abbey, A., Clinton-Sherrod, A. M., McAuslan, P., Zawacki, T., & Buck, P. O. (2003). The relationship between the quantity of alcohol consumed and the severity of the sexual assaults committed by college men. *Journal of Interpersonal Violence, 18*, 813–833.

Abbey, A., Zawacki, T., Buck, P. O. Clinton, A. M., & McAuslan, P. (2004). Sexual assault and alcohol consumption: What do we know about their relationship and what types of research are still needed. *Aggression and Violent Behavior, 9*, 271–303.

Abel, G. G., Barlow, D. H., Blanchard, E. B., & Guild, D. (1977). The components of rapists' sexual arousal. *Archives of General Psychiatry, 34*, 895–903.

Abel, G. G., Becker, J. V., Blanchard, E. B., & Djenderedjian, A. (1978). Differentiating sexual aggressives with penile measures. *Criminal Justice and Behavior, 5*, 315–332.

Abel, G. G., Becker, J. V., Cunningham-Rathner, J., Mittelman, M. S., & Rouleau, J. L. (1988). Multiple paraphilic diagnoses among sex offenders. *Bulletin of the American Academy of Psychiatry and the Law, 16*, 153–168.

Abel, G. G., Becker, J. V., Murphy, W. D., & Flanagan, B. (1981). Identifying dangerous child molesters. In R. B. Stuart (Ed.), *Violent behavior: Social learning approaches to prediction, management and treatment.* New York: Brunner/Mazel.

Abel, G. G., Mittelman, M., Becker, J. V., Rathner, J., & Rouleau, J. (1988). Predicting child molesters' response to treatment. In R. A. Prentky & V. L. Quinsey (Eds.), *Human sexual aggression: Current perspectives* (pp. 223–234). New York: New York Academy of Sciences.

Abrahamsen, D. (1952). *Who are the guilty?* Westport, CT: Greenwood Press.

Abrahamsen, D. (1960). *The psychology of crime.* New York: Columbia University Press.

Achenbach, T. M., & Edelbrock, C. (1983). *Manual for the child behavior checklist and revised child behavior profile.* Burlington, VT: University of Vermont.

Acoca, L., & Austin, J. (1996). *The hidden crisis: The women offenders sentencing study and alternative sentencing recommendations project.* San Francisco: National Council on Crime and Delinquency.

Acoca, L., & Dedel, K. (1998). *No place to hide: Understanding and meeting the needs of girls in the California juvenile justice system.* San Francisco: National Council on Crime and Delinquency.

ADAM II. (2011). *Annual Report: Arrestee drug abuse monitoring.* Washington, DC: Office of National Drug Control Policy.

Adams, D. (1992). Biology does not make men more aggressive than women. In K. Bjorkquist & P. Niemela (Eds.), *Of mice and women: Aspects of female aggression* (pp. 17–25). San Diego, CA: Academic Press.

Adamson, L. A., & Thompson, R. A. (1998). Coping with interparental verbal conflict by children exposed to spouse abuse from nonviolent homes. *Journal of Family Violence, 13*, 213–232.

Adler, J. (2002, February 25). The "thrill" of theft: It's not just movies stars. *Newsweek*, p. 52.

Adler, R., Nunn, R., Northam, E., Lebnan, V., & Ross, R. (1994). Secondary prevention of childhood firesetting. *Journal of the American Academy of Child and Adolescent Psychiatry, 33*, 1194–1202.

Adshead, G. (2002). Three degrees of security: Attachment and forensic institutions. *Criminal Behaviour and Mental Health, 12*, S31–S45.

Agnew, R. (1992). Foundation for a General Strain Theory of crime and delinquency. *Criminology, 30*, 47–87.

Agnew, R. (2006). General Strain Theory: Current status and directions for future research. In F. T. Cullen, J. P. Wright, & K. R. Blevins (Eds.), *Taking stock: The status of criminological theory* (Vol. 15, pp. 101–123). New Brunswick, NJ: Transaction.

Ægisdóttir, S., White, M. J., Spengler, P. M., Maugherman, L. A., Cook, R. S., Nichols, C. N., et al. (2006). The meta-analysis of clinical judgment project: Fifty-six years of accumulated research on clinical versus statistical prediction. *The Counseling Psychologist, 34*, 341–382.

Ahler, C. J., Schaefer, G. A., Mundt, I. A., Roll, S., Englert, H., Willich, S. N., et al. (2011). How unusual are the contents of paraphilias? Paraphilia-associated sexual arousal patterns in a community-based sample of men. *Journal of Sexual Medicine, 8*, 1362–1370.

Ainsworth, M. D. (1979). Infant-mother attachment. *American Psychologist, 34*, 932–937.

Ainsworth, M. D., Blehar, M. C., Waters, E., & Wall, S. (1979). *Patterns of attachment: A psychological study of the strange situation*. Hillsdale, NJ: Erlbaum.

Akers, R. L. (1977). *Deviant behavior: A social learning approach* (2nd ed.). Belmont, CA: Wadsworth.

Akers, R. L. (1985). *Deviant behavior: A social learning approach* (3rd ed.). Belmont, CA: Wadsworth.

Akers, R. L., & Cochran, J. K. (1985). Adolescent marijuana use: A test of three theories of deviant behavior. *Deviant Behavior, 6*, 323–346.

Akers, R. L., & Lee, G. (1996). A longitudinal test of social learning theory: Adolescent smoking. *Journal of Drug Issues, 26*, 317–343.

Albanese, J. S. (1995). *White-collar crime in America*. Englewood Cliffs, NJ: Prentice Hall.

Alexander, M. A. (1999). Sexual offender treatment efficacy revised. *Sexual Abuse: A Journal of Research and Treatment, 11*, 101–116.

Alison, L., Bennell, C., Ormerod, D., & Mokros, A. (2002). The personality paradox in offender profiling: A theoretical review of the processes involved in deriving background characteristics from crime scene actions. *Psychology, Public Policy, and Law, 8*, 115–135.

Alison, L. J., & Canter, D. V. (1999). Professional, legal and ethical issues in offender profiling. In D. V. Canter & L. J. Alison (Eds.), *Profiling in policy and practice*. Aldershot, UK: Ashgate.

Alison, L. J., Smith, M. D., Eastman, O., & Rainbow, L. (2003). Toulmin's philosophy of argument and its relevance to offending profiling. *Psychology, Crime & Law, 9*, 173–183.

Alison, L. J., Smith, M. D., & Morgan, K. (2003). Interpreting the accuracy of offender profiles. *Psychology, Crime & Law, 9*, 185–195.

Alison, L. J., West, A., & Goodwill, A. (2004). The academic and the practitioner: Pragmatists' views of offender profiling. *Psychology, Public Policy, and Law, 10*, 71–101.

Allen, M., Emmers, T., Gebhardt, L., & Giery, M. A. (2001). Exposure to pornography and acceptance of rape myths. *Journal of Communication, 45*, 5–53.

Allen, N. B., Lewinsohn, P. M., & Seeley, J. R. (1998). Prenatal and perinatal influences on risk for psychopathology in childhood and adolescence. *Development and Psychopathology, 10*, 513–529.

Althouse, R. (Ed.). (2010). Standards for psychology services in jails, prisons, correctional facilities, and agencies. Preamble to the Third Edition. *Criminal Justice and Behavior, 37*, 754–756.

Alvord, M. K., & Grados, J. J. (2005). Enhancing resilience in children: A protective approach. *Professional Psychology: Research and Practice, 3*, 238–245.

American Bar Association. (1979). *Juvenile justice standards project*. Chicago: Author.

American Psychiatric Association (APA). (1994). *Diagnostic and statistical manual of mental disorders* (DSM-IV). Washington, DC: Author.

American Psychiatric Association (APA). (2000). *Diagnostic and statistical manual of mental disorders—revised* (DSM-IV-R). Washington, DC: Author.

American Psychological Association. (2003). *Violence and the family: Report of the APA Presidential Task Force on Violence and the Family—executive summary*. Washington, DC: Author.

American Psychological Association. (2009). APA Board reiterates its stance on interrogations. *Monitor on Psychology, 48*, 10.

American Psychological Association. (2012). *Elder abuse and neglect: In search of a solution*. Washington, DC: Author.

Amsel, A. (1958). The role of frustrative nonreward in noncontinuous reward situations. *Psychological Bulletin, 55*, 102–119.

Andershed, H., Kerr, M., Stattin, H., & Levander, S. (2002). Psychopathic traits in non-referred youths: A new assessment tool. In E. Blauuw & L. Sheridan (Eds.), *Psychopaths: Current international perspectives*. The Hague, Netherlands: Elsevier.

Anderson, C. A. (2004). An update on the effects of playing violent video games. *Journal of Adolescence, 27,* 113–122.

Anderson, C. A., & Bushman, B. J. (2001). Effects of violent games on aggressive behavior, aggressive cognition, aggressive effect, physiological arousal, and prosocial behavior: A meta-analytic review of the scientific literature. *Psychological Science, 12,* 353–359.

Anderson, C. A., & Bushman, B. J. (2002). Human aggression. *Annual Review of Psychology, 53,* 27–51.

Anderson, C. A., & Prot, S. (2011). Effects of playing violent video games. In M. A. Paludi (Ed.), *The psychology of teen violence and victimization, Vols. 1 and 2: From bullying to cyberstalking to assault and sexual violation* (pp. 41–70). Santa Barbara, CA: Praeger.

Anderson, C. A., Sakamoto, A., Gentile, D. A., Ihori, N., Shibuya, A., Yukawa, S., et al. (2008). Longitudinal effects of violent video games on aggression in Japan and the United States. *Pediatrics, 122,* 1067–1072.

Anderson, C. A., Shibuya, A., Ihori, N., Swing, E. L., Bushman, B. J., & Sakamoto, A., Rothstein, H. R., & Saleem, M. (2010). Violent video game effects on aggression, empathy, and prosocial behavior in eastern and western countries: A meta-analytic review. *Psychological Bulletin, 136,* 151–173.

Anderson, S. W., Bechara, A., Damasio, H., Tranel, D., & Damasio, A. R. (1999). Impairment of social and moral behavior related to early damage in human prefrontal cortex. *Nature Neuroscience, 2,* 1032–1037.

Andreasen, N. C., & Carpenter, W. T. (1993). Diagnosis and classification of schizophrenia. *Schizophrenia Bulletin, 19,* 199–214.

Andrews, D. A., & Bonta, J. (1994). *The psychology of criminal conduct.* Cincinnati, OH: Anderson.

Andrews, D. A., Bonta, J., & Hoge, R. D. (1990). Classification for effective rehabilitation: Rediscovering psychology. *Criminal Justice and Behavior, 17,* 19–52.

Ansbro, M. (2008). Using attachment theory with offenders. *Probation Journal, 55,* 231–244.

Appelbaum, P. S., Jick, R. Z., Grisso, T., Givelbar, D., Silver, E., & Steadman, H. J. (1993). Use of posttraumatic stress. *Psychiatry, 150,* 229–234.

Appelbaum, P. S., Robbins, P. C., & Monahan, J. (2000). Violence and delusions: Data from the MacArthur Violence Risk Assessment Study. *American Journal of Psychiatry, 157,* 566–572.

Araji, S. (1997). *Sexually aggressive children: Coming to understand them.* Thousand Oaks, CA: Sage.

Archer, J. (2004). Sex differences in aggression in real-world settings: A meta-analytic review. *Review of General Psychology, 8,* 291–322.

Ardrey, R. (1966). *The territorial imperative.* New York: Athenum.

Arena, M. P., & Arrigo, B. A. (2005). Social psychology, terrorism, and identity: A preliminary re-examination of theory, culture, self, and society. *Behavioral Sciences & the Law, 23,* 485–506.

Arkow, P. (1998). The correlations between cruelty to animals and child abuse and the implications for veterinary medicine. In R. Lockwood & F. R. Ascione (Eds.), *Cruelty to animals and interpersonal violence: Readings in research and application.* West Lafayette, IN: Purdue University Press.

Arrestees Drug Abuse Monitoring Program II. (2011, May). *2010 annual report.* Washington, DC: Executive Office of the President, Office of National Drug Control Policy.

Arseneault, L., Tremblay, R. E., Boulerice, B., & Saucier, J-F. (2002). Obstetrical complications and violent delinquency: Testing two developmental pathways. *Child Development, 73,* 496–508.

Asbridge, M., Smart, R. G., & Mann, R. E. (2006). Can we prevent road rage? *Trauma, Violence, & Abuse, 7,* 109–121.

Ascione, R. R. (1997). *Animal welfare and domestic violence.* Logan, UT: Utah State University.

Ashford, J. B., Sales, B. D., & Reid, W. H. (2001). Introduction. In J. B. Ashford, B. D. Sales, & W. H. Reid (Eds.), *Treating adult and juvenile offenders with special needs.* Washington, DC: American Psychological Association.

Aspinwall, L. G., Brown, T. R., & Tabery, J. (2012). The double-edged sword: Does biomechanism increase or decrease judges' sentencing of psychopaths? *Science, 337* (August), 846–849.

Asscher, J. J., van Vugt, E. S., Stams, G. J. J. M., Deković, M., Eichelsheim, V. I., & Yousfi, S. (2011). The relationship between juvenile psychopathic traits, delinquency, and (violent) recidivism: A meta-analysis. *Journal of Child Psychology and Psychiatry, 52,* 1134–1143.

Associated Press. (2006, May 17). Miami flagged for worst road rage. *Albany Times Union,* p. A7.

Associated Press. (2012, May 24). Over 2,000 convicts exonerated since 1989. *Albany Times Union,* p. A5.

Au Coin, K. (2003a). Family violence against older adults. *Family violence in Canada: A statistical profile 2003.* Ottawa, ON: Canadian Centre for Justice Statistics.

Au Coin, K. (2003b). Violence and abuse against children and youth by family members. In Canadian Centre for Justice Statistics (Ed.), *Family violence in Canada: A statistical profile 2003.* Ottawa, ON: Canadian Centre for Justice Statistics.

Avery-Clark, C. A., & Laws, D. R. (1984). Differential erection response patterns of sexual child abusers to stimuli describing activities with children. *Behavior Therapy, 15,* 71–83.

Azar, B. (2010, December). Virtual violence: Researchers disagree about whether violent video games increase aggression. *Monitor in Psychology, 41,* 38–39.

Babchishin, K. M., Hanson, R. K., & Hermann, C. A. (2011). The characteristics of online sex offenders: A meta-analysis. *Sexual Abuse: A Journal of Research and Treatment, 23,* 92–123.

Babcock, J. C., Waltz, J., Jacobson, N. S., & Gottman, J. M. (1993). Power and violence: The relation between communication patterns, power discrepancies, and domestic violence. *Journal of Consulting and Clinical Psychology, 61,* 40–50.

Bacigal, R. J. (2002). Assault and battery. In K. L. Hall (Ed.), *The Oxford companion to American law.* New York: Oxford University Press.

Bagwell, C. L. (2004). Friendships, peer networks, and antisocial behavior. In J. B. Kupersmidt & K. A. Dodge (Eds.), *Children's peer relations: From development to intervention* (pp. 37–57). Washington, DC: American Psychological Association.

Baird, K. A. (2007). A survey of clinical psychologists in Illinois regarding prescription privileges. *Professional Psychology: Research and Practice, 38,* 196–202.

Bakker, E. (2006). *Jihadi terrorists in Europe, their characteristics and the circumstances in which they joined the jihad: An exploratory study.* The Hague: Clingendael Institute.

Ball, J. C., Shaffer, J. W., & Nurco, D. N. (1983). The day-to-day criminality of heroin addicts in Baltimore—a study in the continuity of offense rates. *Drug and Alcohol Dependence, 12,* 119–142.

Bamfield J. (1994). Electronic article surveillance: Management learning in curbing theft. In M. Gill (Ed.), *Crime at work: Studies in security and crime prevention.* Leiscester, UK: Perpetuity Press.

Bandura, A. (1965). Influence of models' reinforcement contingencies on the acquisition of imitative responses. *Journal of Personality and Social Psychology, 1,* 589–595.

Bandura, A. (1973a). *Aggression: A social learning analysis.* Englewood Cliffs, NJ: Prentice Hall.

Bandura, A. (1973b). Social learning theory of aggression. In J. F. Knutson (Ed.), *The control of aggression.* Chicago: Aldine.

Bandura, A. (1978). The self-system in reciprocal determinism. *American Psychologist, 33,* 344–358.

Bandura, A. (1983). Psychological mechanisms of aggression. In R. G. Geen & E. I. Donnerstein (Eds.), *Aggression: Theoretical and empirical reviews* (Vol. 1). New York: Academic Press.

Bandura, A. (1989). Human agency in social cognitive theory. *American Psychologist, 44,* 1175–1184.

Bandura, A. (1990). Selective activation and disengagement of moral control. *Journal of Social Issues, 46,* 27–46.

Bandura, A. (1991). Social cognitive theory or moral thought and action. In M. W. Kurtines & J. L. Gewirtz (Eds.), *Handbook of moral behavior and development: Vol. I. Theory.* Hillsdale, NJ: Erlbaum.

Bandura, A. (1997). *Self-efficacy: The exercise of control.* New York: Freeman.

Bandura, A. (1999). Moral disengagement in the perpetration of inhumanities. *Personality and Social Psychology Review, 3,* 193–209.

Bandura, A. (2001). Social cognitive theory: An agentic perspective. *Annual Review of Psychology, 52,* 1–26.

Bandura, A. (2004). The role of selective moral disengagement in terrorism and counterterrorism. In F. M. Moghaddam & A. J. Marsella (Eds.), *Understanding terrorism: Psychosocial roots, consequences, and interventions* (pp. 121–150). Washington, DC: American Psychological Association.

Bandura, A., Barbaranelli, C., Caprara, G. V., & Pastorelli, C. (1996). Mechanisms of moral disengagement in the exercise of moral agency. *Journal of Personality and Social Psychology, 71,* 364–374.

Bandura, A., Caprara, G. V., Barbaranelli, C., Pastorelli, C., & Regalia, C. (2001). Sociocognitive self-regulatory mechanisms governing transgressive behavior. *Journal of Personality and Social Psychology, 80,* 125–135.

Bandura, A., & Huston, A. (1961). Identification as a process of incidental learning. *Journal of Abnormal and Social Psychology, 63,* 311–318.

Bandura, A., Ross, D., & Ross, S. (1963). Vicarious reinforcement and imitative learning. *Journal of Abnormal and Social Psychology, 67,* 601–607.

Bandura, A., & Walters, R. H. (1959). *Adolescent aggression.* New York: Ronald Press.

Bank Crime Statistics. (2011). *Bank Crime Report: Final 2010.* Washington, DC: U.S. Department of Justice, Federal Bureau of Investigation.

Bank, L., & Patterson, G. R. (1992). The use of structural equation modeling in combining data from different types of assessment. In J. C. Rosen & P. McReynolds (Eds.), *Recent advances in psychological assessment* (Vol. 8, pp. 41–74). New York: Plenum Press.

Barash, J., Tranel, D., & Anderson, S. W. (2000). Acquired personality disturbances associated with bilateral damage to the ventromedial prefrontal region. *Developmental Neuropsychology, 18,* 355–381.

Bard, L. A., Carter, D. L., Cerce, D. D., Knight, R. A., Rosenberg, R., & Schneider, B. (1987). A descriptive study of rapists and child molesters: Developmental, clinical, and criminal characters. *Behavioral Sciences & the Law, 5,* 203–220.

Bardone, A. M., Moffitt, T. E., & Caspi, A. (1996). Adult mental health and social outcomes of adolescent girls with depression and conduct disorder. *Development and Psychopathology, 8,* 811–829.

Barker, M. (2000). The criminal range of small-town burglars. In D. Canter & L. Alison (Eds.), *Profiling property crimes.* Dartmouth, UK: Ashgate.

Barlett, C. P., & Gentile, D. A. (2012). Attacking others on line: The formation of cyberbullying in late adolescence. *Psychology of Popular Media Culture, 1,* 123–133.

Barnes, J. C., Beaver, K. M., & Boutwell, B. B. (2011). Examining the genetic underpinnings to Moffitt's developmental taxonomy: A behavioral genetic analysis. *Criminology, 49,* 923–954.

Baron, R. A. (1977). *Human aggression.* New York: Plenum.

Baron, R. A. (1983). The control of human aggression: An optimistic perspective. *Journal of Social and Clinical Psychology, 1,* 97–119.

Baron, R. A., & Byrne, D. (1977). *Social psychology* (2nd ed.). Boston: Allyn and Bacon.

Barry, C. T., Frick, P. J., DeShazo, T. M., McCoy, M. G., Ellis, M., & Loney, B. R. (2000). The importance of callous-unemotional traits for extending the concept of psychopathy to children. *Journal of Abnormal Psychology, 109,* 335–340.

Barry, T. D., Barry, C. T., Deming, A. M., & Lochman, J. E. (2008). Stability of psychopathic characteristics in childhood. *Criminal Justice and Behavior, 35,* 244–262.

Bartholow, B. D., Sestir, M. A., & Davis, E. B. (2005). Correlates and consequences of exposure to video game violence: Hostile personality, empathy, and aggressive behavior. *Personality and Social Psychology Bulletin, 31,* 1573–1586.

Bartol, C. R., & Bartol, A. M. (1998). *Delinquency and justice: A psychosocial approach* (2nd ed.). Upper Saddle River, NJ: Prentice Hall.

Bartol, C. R., & Bartol, A.M. (2004). *Psychology and law: Theory, research, and application* (3rd ed.). Belmont, CA: Wadsworth/Thomson.

Bartol, C. R., & Bartol, A. M. (2008). *Introduction to forensic psychology* (2nd ed.). Thousand Oaks, CA: Sage.

Bartol, C. R., & Bartol, A. M. (2013). *Criminal and behavioral profiling.* Thousand Oaks, CA: Sage.

Basile, K. C., & Smith, S. G. (2011). Sexual violence victimization of women: Prevalence, characteristics, and the role of public health and prevention. *American Journal of Lifestyle Medicine, 5,* 407–417.

Bates, J. E., & McFadyen-Ketchum, S. (2000). Temperament and parent-child relations as interacting factors in children's behavioral adjustment. In V. Molfese & D. L. Molfese (Eds.), *Temperament and personality development across the life span.* Mahway, NJ: Lawrence Erlbaum Associates.

Bates, J. E., Pettit, G. S., Dodge, K. A., & Ridge, B. (1998). Interaction of temperamental resistance to control and restrictive parenting in the development of externalizing behavior. *Developmental Psychology, 34*, 982–995.

Baum, K., Catalano, S., & Rand, M. (2009, January). *Stalking victimization in the United States.* Washington, DC: U.S. Department of Justice, Bureau of Justice Statistics.

Bauman, S. (2010). Cyberbullying in a rural intermediate school: An exploratory study. *Journal of Early Adolescence, 30*, 803–833.

Baumer, T. L., & Rosenbaum, D. P. (1984). *Combating retail theft: Programs and strategies.* Boston: Butterworth.

Baumrind, D. (1991a). Parenting styles and adolescent development. In J. Brooks-Gunn, R. Lerner, & A. C. Petersen (Eds.), *The encyclopedia of adolescence.* New York: Garland.

Baumrind, D. (1991b). The influence of parenting style on adolescent competence and substance use. *Journal of Early Adolescence, 11*, 56–95.

Beatty, D. (2001). Stalking. In G. Coleman, M. Gaboury, M. Murray, & A. Seymour (Eds.), *1999 National Victim Assistance Academy.* Washington, DC: U.S. Department of Justice.

Beauchaine, T. P., Hinshaw, S. P., & Pang, K. L. (2010). Comorbidity of attention-deficit/hyperactivity disorder and early-onset conduct disorder: Biological, environmental, and developmental mechanisms. *Clinical Psychology: Science and Practice, 17*, 327–336.

Beck, A. J., Harrison, P. M., & Guerino, P. (2010). *Sexual victimization in juvenile facilities reported by youth, 2008–2009.* Washington, DC: U.S. Department of Justice, Office of Justice Programs, Bureau of Justice Statistics.

Becker, J. V., Hall, S. R., & Stinson, J. D. (2001). Female sexual offenders: Clinical, legal and policy issues. *Journal of Forensic Psychology Practice, 1*, 29–50.

Becker, J. V., & Johnson, B. R. (2001). Treating juvenile sex offenders. In J. B. Ashford, B. D. Sales, & W. H. Reid (Eds.), *Treating adult and juvenile offenders with special needs.* Washington, DC: American Psychological Association.

Becker, K. D., Stuewig, J., Herrera, V. M., & McCloskey, L. A. (2004). A study of firesetting and animal cruelty in children: Family influences and adolescent outcomes. *Journal of the American Academy of Child and Adolescent Psychiatry, 43*, 905–913.

Beech, A. R., Mandeville-Norden, R., & Goodwill, A. (2012). Comparing recidivism rates of treatment responders/nonresponders in a sample of 413 child molesters who had completed community-based sex offender treatment in the United Kingdom. *International Journal of Offender Therapy and Comparative Criminology, 56*, 29–49.

Beike, S. M., & Zentall, S. S. (2012). "The snake raised its head": Content novelty alters the reading performance of students at risk for reading disabilities and ADHD. *Journal of Educational Psychology, 104*, 529–540.

Benda, B. B. (2005). Introduction: Boot camps revisited: Issues, problems, prospects. *Journal of Offender Rehabilitation, 40*, 1–25.

Bennell, C., & Jones, N. J. (2005). Between a ROC and a hard place: A method for linking serial burglaries using an offender's modus operandi. *Journal of Investigative Psychology and Offender Profiling, 2*, 23–41.

Bennett, D. S., Bendersky, M., & Lewis, M. (2002). Children's intellectual and emotional-behavioral adjustment at 4 years as a function of cocaine exposure, maternal characteristics, and environmental risk. *Developmental Psychology, 38*, 648–658.

Bennett, T., Holloway, K., & Farrington, D. (2008). The statistical association between drug misuse and crime: A meta-analysis. *Aggression and Violent Behavior, 13*, 107–118.

Bennett, T., & Wright, R. (1984). *Burglars on burglary: Prevention and the offender.* Brookfield, VT: Gower.

Benson, M. L., & Moore, E. (1992). Are white-collar and common offenders the same? An empirical examination and theoretical critique of a recently proposed general theory of crime. *Journal of Research in Crime and Delinquency, 29*, 251–272.

Bereczkei, T. (2000). Evolutionary psychology: A new perspective in the behavioral sciences. *European Psychologist, 5*, 175–190.

Berkowitz, L. (1962). *Aggression: A social-psychological analysis.* New York: McGraw-Hill.

Berkowitz, L. (1969). The frustration-aggression hypothesis revisited. In L. Berkowitz (Ed.), *Roots of aggression.* New York: Atherton Press.

Berkowitz, L. (1973). Words and symbols as stimuli to aggressive responses. In J. F. Knutson (Ed.), *The control of aggression.* Chicago: Aldine.

Berkowitz, L. (1983). The experience of anger as a parallel process in the display of impulsive, "angry" aggression. In R. G. Geen & E. I. Donnerstein (Eds.), *Aggression: Theoretical and empirical reviews* (Vol. 1). New York: Academic Press.

Berkowitz, L. (1989). Frustration-aggression hypothesis: Examination and reformulation. *Psychological Bulletin, 106*, 59–73.

Berkowitz, L. (1994). Guns and youth. In L. E. Eron, J. H. Gentry, & P. Schlegel (Eds.), *Reason to hope: A psychosocial perspective on violence and youth*. Washington, DC: American Psychological Association.

Berkowitz, L., & LePage, A. (1967). Weapons as aggression-eliciting stimuli. *Journal of Personality and Social Psychology, 7*, 202–207.

Berlyne, D. E. (1960). *Conflict, arousal, and curiosity*. New York: McGraw-Hill.

Bernard, F. (1975). An inquiry among a group of pedophiles. *Journal of Sex Research, 11*, 242–255.

Bernasco, W. (2006). Co-offending and the choice of target areas in burglary. *Journal of Investigative Psychology and Offending Profiling, 3*, 139–155.

Bernasco, W. (2008). Then again? Same-offender involvement in repeat and near repeat burglaries. *European Journal of Criminology, 5*, 411–431.

Bernstein, A., Newman, J. P., Wallace, J. F., & Luh, K. E. (2000). Left hemisphere activation and deficient response modulation in psychopaths. *Psychological Science, 11*, 414–418.

Berrueta-Clement, J. R., Schweinhart, L. J., Barnett, W. S., & Weikart. D. P. (1987). The effects of early educational intervention in adolescence and early adulthood. In J. D. Burhcard & S. N. Burchard (Eds.), *Prevention of delinquent behavior*. Newbury Park, CA: Sage.

Bettencourt, B. A., Talley, A., Benjamin, A. J., & Valentine, J. (2006). Personality and aggressive behavior under provoking and neutral conditions: A meta-analytic review. *Psychological Bulletin, 132*, 731–777.

Beyer, K., Mack, S. M., & Shelton, J. L. (2008). Investigative analysis of neonaticide: An exploratory study. *Criminal Justice and Behavior, 35*, 522–535.

Beyers, J. M., Bates, J. E., Pettit, G. S., & Dodge, K. A. (2003). Neighborhood structure, parenting processes, and the development of youths' externalizing behaviors: A multilevel analysis. *American Journal of Community Psychology, 31*, 35–53.

Bhal, K. T., & Leekha, N. D. (2008). Exploring cognitive moral logics using grounded theory: The case of software piracy. *Journal of Business Ethics, 81*, 635–646.

Biglan, A., Flay, B. R., Embry, D. D., & Sandler, I. N. (2012). The critical role of nurturing environments for promoting human well-being. *American Psychologist, 63*, 257–271.

Binder, A. (1988). Juvenile delinquency. *Annual Review of Psychology, 39*, 253–282.

Björkqvist, K., Lagerspetz, M. J., & Kaukianinen, A. (1992). Do girls manipulate and boys fight? Developmental trends in regard to direct and indirect aggression. *Aggressive Behavior, 18*, 117–127.

Black, H. C. (1990). *Black's law dictionary*. St. Paul, MN: West Publishing.

Blackburn, R. (1993). *The psychology of criminal conduct: Theory, research and practice*. Chichester, UK: Wiley.

Blackburn, R. (1998). Criminality and the interpersonal circle in mentally disordered offenders. *Criminal Justice and Behavior, 25*, 155–176.

Blair, C., & Raver, C. C. (2012). Child development in the context of adversity: Experiential canalization of brain and behavior. *American Psychologist, 67*, 309–318.

Blair, R. J. R., Peschardt, K. S., Budhani, S., Mitchell, D. G. V., & Pine, D. S. (2006). The development of psychopathy. *Journal of Child Psychology and Psychiatry, 47*, 262–275.

Blake, D. D., Weathers, F. W., & Nagy, L. M. (1995). The development of a clinician-administered PTSD scale. *Journal of Traumatic Stress, 8*, 75–90.

Blake, E., & Gannon, T. A. (2010). The implicit theory of rape-prone men: An information-processing investigation. *International Journal of Offender Therapy and Comparative Criminology, 54*, 895–914.

Blanchard, R., Klassen, P., Dickey, R., Kuban, M. E., & Blak, T. I. (2001). Sensitivity and specificity of the phallometric test for pedophilia in nonadmitting sex offenders. *Psychological Assessment, 13*, 118–126.

Blanchard, R., Watson, M. S., Choy, A., Dickey, R., Klassen, P., Kuban, M., & Ferren, D. J. (1999). Pedophiles: Mental retardation, maternal age, and sexual orientation. *Archives of Sexual Behavior, 28*, 111–127.

Blanco, C., Grant, J., Petry, N. M., Simpson, H. B., Alegria, A., Liu, S-M., et al. (2008). Prevalence and correlates of shoplifting in the United States: Results from the National Epideiologic Survey on Alcohol and Related Conditions (NESARC). *American Journal of Psychiatry, 155,* 905–913.

Blitstein, J. L., Murray, D. M., Lytle, L. A., Birnbaum, A. S., & Perry, C. L. (2005). Predictors of violent behavior in an early adolescent cohort: Similarities and differences across genders. *Health Education and Behavior, 32,* 175–194.

Blonigen, D. M., Carlson, S. R., Krueger, R. F., & Patrick, C. J. (2003). A twin study of self-reported psychopathic traits. *Personality and Individual Differences, 35,* 179–197.

Blonigen, D. M., Hicks, B. M., Krueger, R. F., Iacono, W. G., & Patrick, C. J. (2005). Psychopathic personality traits: Heritability and genetic overlap with internalizing and externalizing psychopathology. *Psychological Medicine, 35,* 637–648.

Blumenthal, D. R. (1999). *The banality of good and evil: Moral lessons from the Shoah and Jewish tradition.* Washington, DC: Georgetown University Press.

Blumer, H., Sutter, A., Ahmed, S., & Smith, R. (1967). *ADD center final report: The world of youthful drug use.* Berkeley, CA: University of California Press.

Boehnert, C. E. (1989). Characteristics of successful and unsuccessful insanity pleas. *Law and Human Behavior, 13,* 31–39.

Bolen, R. M., & Scannapieco, M. (1999). Prevalence of child sexual abuse: A corrective metanalysis. *Social Service Review, 73,* 281–313.

Bolt, D. M., Hare, R. D., Vitale, J. E., & Newman, J. P. (2004). A multigroup item response theory analysis of the Psychopathy Checklist—Revised. *Psychological Assessment, 16,* 155–168.

Bonanno, G. A. (2004). Loss, trauma, and human resilience: Have we underestimated the human capacity to thrive after extremely aversive events? *American Psychologist, 59,* 20–28.

Bongers, I. L., Koot, H. M., van der Ende, J., & Verhulst, F. C. (2003). The normative development of child and adolescent problem behavior. *Journal of Abnormal Psychology, 112,* 179–192.

Bonnie, R. J., & Grisso, T. (2000). Adjudicative competence and youthful offenders. In T. Grisso & R. G. Schwartz (Eds.), *Youth on trial.* Chicago: University of Chicago Press.

Bonta, J., & Andrews, D. A. (2007). *Risk-need-responsivity model for offender assessment and rehabilitation (corrections research user report no. 2007–06).* Ottawa, Canada: Public Safety Canada.

Bonta, J., Law, M., & Hanson, K. (1998). The prediction of criminal and violent recidivism among mentally disordered offenders: A meta-analysis. *Psychological Bulletin, 123,* 123–142.

Borduin, C. M. (1994). Innovative models of treatment and service delivery in the juvenile justice system. *Journal of Clinical Child Psychiatry, 23,* 19–21.

Borduin, C. M., Mann, B. J., Cone, L. T., Henggeler, S. W., Fucci, B. R., Blaske, D. M., et al. (1995). Multisystemic treatment of serious juvenile offenders: Long-term prevention of criminality and violence. *Journal of Consulting and Clinical Psychology, 63,* 569–578.

Borduin, C. M., Schaeffer, C. M., & Heiblum, N. (2009). A randomized clinical trial of multisystemic therapy with juvenile sexual offenders: Effects on youth social ecology and criminal activity. *Journal of Consulting and Clinical Psychology, 77,* 26–37.

Borum, R. (1996). Improving the clinical practice of violence risk assessment. *American Psychologist, 51,* 945–956.

Borum, R., & Fulero, S. M. (1999). Empirical research on the insanity defense and attempted reforms: Evidence toward informed policy. *Law and Human Behavior, 23,* 375–394.

Borum, R., & Gelles, M. (2005). Al-Qaeda's operational evolution: Behavioral and Organizational Perspectives. *Behavioral Sciences & the Law, 23,* 467–483.

Borum, R., & Strentz, T. (1993, April). The borderline personality: Negotiation strategies. *FBI Law Enforcement Bulletin,* 6–10.

Bottcher, J., & Ezell, M. E. (2005). Examining the effectiveness of boot camps: A randomized experiment with a long-term follow up. *Journal of Research in Crime and Delinquency, 42,* 309–332.

Boudreau, J., Kwan, Q., Faragher, W., & Denault, G. (1977). *Arson and arson investigation.* Washington, DC: USGPO.

Bourke, M. L., & Hernandez, A. E. (2009). The "Butner Study" redux: A report of the incidence of hands-on child victimization by child pornography offender. *Journal of Family Violence, 24,* 183–191.

Bourque, B. B., Cronin, R. C., Felker, D. B., Pearson, F. R., Han, M., & Hill, S. M. (1996). *Boot camps for juvenile offenders: An implementation evaluation of three demonstration programs.* Research in Brief. Washington, DC: National Institute of Justice.

Bowker, L. H. (1983). *Beating wife-battering.* Lexington, MA: Lexington Books.

Bowlby, J. (1969). *Attachment and loss: Vol. 1. Attachment.* New York: Basic Books.

Boykin, A. W. (1986). The triple quandary and the schooling of Afro-American children. In U. Neisser (Ed.), *The school achievement of minority children.* Hillsdale, NJ: Erlbaum.

Boykin, A. W. (1994). Harvesting talent and culture: African-American children and educational reform. In R. Rossi (Ed.), *Schools and students at risk.* New York: Teachers College Press.

Bradford, J. M. W. (1982). Arson: A clinical study. *Canadian Journal of Psychiatry, 27,* 188–193.

Braga, A. A., & Kennedy, D. M. (2001). The illicit acquisition of firearms by youth and juveniles. *Journal of Criminal Justice, 29,* 397–388.

Brandt, J. R., Kennedy, W. A., Patrick, C. J., & Curtain, J. J. (1997). Assessment of psychopathy in a population of incarcerated adolescent offenders. *Psychological Assessment, 9,* 429–435.

Brantley, A. G., & Kosky, R. H., Jr. (2005, January). Serial murder in the Netherlands: A look at motivation, behavior, and characteristics. *FBI Law Enforcement Bulletin,* 26–32.

Braun, J. M., Kahn, R. S., Froehlich, T., Auinger, P., & Lanphear, B. P. (2006, December). Exposure to environmental toxicants and attention deficit hyperactivity disorder in U.S. children. *Environmental Health Perspectives, 114,* 1904–1909.

Bray, C. (2009, March 12). Madoff pleads guilty to massive fraud. *The Wall Street Journal,* pp. 1, 9.

Brecklin, L. R., & Forde, D. R. (2001). A meta-analysis of rape education programs. *Violence and Victims, 16,* 303–321.

Brennan, P. A., Grekin, E. R., & Mednick, S. A. (1999). Maternal smoking during pregnancy and adult male criminal outcomes. *Archives of General Psychiatry, 56,* 215–219.

Brennan, P. A., Hall, J., Bor, W., Najman, J. M., & Williams, G. (2003). Integrating biological and social processes in relation to early-onset persistent aggression in boys and girls. *Developmental Psychology, 39,* 309–323.

Brennan, P. A., Mednick, S. A., & Hodgins, S. (2000). Major mental disorders and criminal violence in a Danish birth cohort. *Archives of General Psychiatry, 53,* 1033–1039.

Brenner, V., & Fox, R. A. (1999). An empirically derived classification of parenting practices. *The Journal of Genetic Psychology, 160,* 343–356.

Brent, D. A. (1989). The psychological autopsy: Methodological issues for the study of adolescent suicide. *Suicide and Life Threatening Behavior, 19,* 43–57.

Brett, A. (2004). 'Kindling theory' in arson: How dangerous are firesetters? *Australian and New Zealand Journal of Psychiatry, 38,* 419–425.

Brier, N. (1989). The relationship between learning disability and delinquency: A review and reappraisal. *Journal of Learning Disabilities, 22,* 546–553.

Briere, J. (1988). The long-term clinical correlates of childhood sexual victimization. In R. A. Prentky & V. L. Quinsey (Eds.), *Human sexual aggression: Current perspectives.* New York: New York Academy of Sciences.

Briere, J., Malamuth, N., & Ceniti, J. (1981). *Self-assessed rape proclivity: Attitudinal and sexual correlates.* Paper presented at APA Meeting, Los Angeles, CA.

Briggs, E. C., Thompson, R., Ostrowski, S., & Lekwauwa, R. (2011). Psychological, health, behavioral, and economic impact of child maltreatment. In J. W. White, M. P. Koss, & A. E. Kasdin (Eds.), *Violence against women and children. Vol. 1. Mapping the terrain.* (pp. 77–97). Washington, DC: American Psychological Association.

Briggs, P., Simon, W. T., & Simonsen, S. (2011). An exploratory study of Internet-initiated sexual offenses and the chat room sex offender: Has the Internet enabled a new typology of sex offender. *Sexual Abuse: A Journal of Research and Treatment, 23,* 72–91.

Broadhurst, R. (2006). Developments in the global law enforcement of cyber-crime. *Policing: An International Journal of Police Strategies and Management, 29,* 408–433.

Brodsky, S. L. (1973). *Psychologists in the criminal justice system.* Urbana, IL: University of Illinois Press.

Brodsky, S. L. (1977). Criminal and dangerous behavior. In D. Rimm & J. Somervill (Eds.), *Abnormal psychology.* New York: Academic Press.

Broidy, L. M., Nagin, D. S., Tremblay, R. E., Bates, J. E., Brame, B., Dodge, K. A., et al. (2003). Developmental trajectories of childhood disruptive behaviors and adolescent delinquency: A six-site, cross-national study. *Developmental Psychology, 39,* 222–245.

Bronfenbrenner, U. (1979). *The ecology of human development: Experiments by design and nature.* Cambridge, MA: Harvard University Press.

Brookman, F., & Nolan, J. (2006). The dark figure of infanticide in England and Wales: Complexes of diagnosis. *Journal of Interpersonal Violence, 21,* 869–889.

Brown, B. B., & Harris, P. B. (1989). Residential burglary victimization: Reactions to the invasion of a primary territory. *Journal of Environmental Psychology, 9,* 119–132.

Brown, J. S., & Farber, I. E. (1951). Emotions conceptualized as intervening variables—with suggestions toward a theory of frustration. *Psychological Bulletin, 48,* 465–495.

Brown, N. N., Connor, P. D., & Adler, R. S. (2012). Conduct-disordered adolescents with fetal alcohol spectrum disorder: Intervention in secure treatment settings. *Criminal Justice and Behavior, 39,* 770–793.

Browne, A. (1987). *When battered women kill.* New York: Free Press.

Browne, A., & Finkelhor, D. (1986). Impact of child sexual abuse: A review of the research. *Psychological Bulletin, 99,* 66–77.

Browning, K., & Loeber, R. (1999, February). Highlights of findings from the Pittsburgh Youth Study. *OJJDP Fact Sheet.* Washington, DC: U.S. Department of Justice, Office of Juvenile Justice and Delinquency Prevention.

Brownlie, E. B., Beitchman, J. J., Escobar, M., Young, A., Atkinson, L., Johnson, C., Wilson, B., & Douglas, L. (2004). Early language impairment and young adult delinquent and aggressive behavior. *Journal of Abnormal Child Psychology, 32,* 453–467.

Brunet, B. L., Reiffenstein, R. J., Williams, T., & Wong, L. (1985–1986). Toxicity of phencyclidine and ethanol in combination. *Alcohol and Drug Research, 6,* 341–349.

Bryant, J., & Zillmann, D. (Eds.). (2002). *Media effects: Advances in theory and research* (2nd ed.). Mahwah, NJ: Erlbaum.

Buckle, A., & Farrington, D. P. (1994). Measuring shoplifting by systematic observation: A replication study. *Psychology, Crime & Law, 1,* 133–141.

Bumby, K. M., & Bumby, N. H. (1997). Adolescent female sexual offenders. In J. R. Cellini & B. Schwartz (Eds.), *The sex offender: New insights, treatment innovations and legal developments* (Vol. 2). Kingston, NJ: Civil Research Institute.

Bumpass, E. R., Fagelman, F. D., & Birx, R. J. (1983). Intervention with children who set fires. *American Journal of Psychotherapy, 37,* 328–345.

Burchfield, K. B., & Mingus, W. (2008). Not in my neighborhood: Assessing registered sex offenders' experiences with local social capital and social control. *Criminal Justice and Behavior, 35,* 356–374.

Bureau of International Narcotics and Law Enforcement Affairs. (2000, March). *International narcotics control strategy report, 1999.* Washington, DC: U.S. Department of State. Available: www.state.gov/www/global/narcotics

Bureau of Justice Assistance. (2000, April). *Emerging judicial strategies for the mentally ill in the criminal caseload: Mental health courts.* Washington, DC: U.S. Department of Justice.

Bureau of Justice Statistics. (2004, July). *Profile of jail inmates, 2002.* Washington, DC: Author.

Bureau of Justice Statistics. (2006, June). *Prison statistics: Summary findings.* Washington, DC: U.S. Department of Justice, Author.

Bureau of Justice Statistics. (2012, May 3). *Number of violent victimizations, 2006–2010.* Generated using the NCVS Victimization Analysis Tool at www.bjs.gov.

Burger, J. M. (2009). Replicating Milgram: Would people still obey today? *American Psychologist, 64,* 1–11.

Burgess, A. W., Garbarino, C., & Carlson, M. I. (2006). Pathological teasing and bullying turned deadly: Shooters and suicide. *Victims and Offenders, 1*, 1–14.

Burgess, R. L., & Akers, R. L. (1966). A differential association-reinforcement theory of criminal behavior. *Social Problems, 14*, 128–147.

Burke, J. D., Waldman, I., & Lahey, B. B. (2010). Predictive validity of childhood oppositional defiant disorder and conduct disorder: Implications for the DSM-V. *Journal of Abnormal Psychology, 119*, 739–751.

Burnam, M. A., Stein, J. A., Golding, J. M., Siegel, J. M., Sorenson, S. B., Forsythe, A. B., et al. (1988). Sexual assault and mental disorders in a community population. *Journal of Consulting and Clinical Psychology, 56*, 843–850.

Busch, K G., & Weissman, S. H. (2005). The intelligence community and the war on terror: The role of behavioral science. *Behavioral Sciences & the Law, 23*, 559–571.

Bushman, B. J., & Anderson, C. A. (2001). Is it time to pull the plug on the hostile versus instrumental aggression dichotomy. *Psychological Review, 108*, 273–279.

Bushman, B. J., Bonacci, A. M., Pederson, W. C., Vasquez, E. A., & Miller, N. (2005). Chewing on it can chew you up: Effects of rumination on triggered displaced aggression. *Journal of Personality and Social Psychology, 88*, 969–983.

Bushman, B. J., & Gibson, B. (2011). Violent video games cause an increase in aggression long after the game has been turned off. *Social Psychology and Personality Science, 2*, 29-32.

Buss, A. H. (1971). Aggression pays. In J. L. Singer (Ed.), *The control of aggression and violence.* New York: Academic Press.

Buss, D. M., & Shackelford, T. K. (1997). Human aggression in evolutionary psychological perspective. *Clinical Psychology Review, 17*, 605–619.

Butler, R. A. (1954). Curiosity in monkeys. *Scientific American* (Reprint #426). San Francisco: W. H. Freeman.

Cacioppo, J. T., Berntson, G. G., Sheridan, J. F., & McClintock, M. K. (2000). Multilevel integrative analyses of human behavior: Social neuroscience and the complementing nature of social and biological approaches. *Psychological Bulletin, 6*, 829–843.

Cairns, R. B., Cairns, B. D., Neckerman, H. J., Ferguson, L. L., & Gariépy, J. L. (1989). Growth and aggression: I. Childhood to early adolescence. *Developmental Psychology, 25*, 320–330.

Caldwell, M. F. (2007). Sexual offense adjudication and sexual recidivism among juvenile offenders. *Sexual Abuse: A Journal of Research and Treatment, 19*, 107–113.

Caldwell, M. F. (2010). Study characteristics and recidivism base rates in juvenile sex offender recidivism. *International Journal of Offender Therapy and Comparative Criminology, 54*, 197–212.

California Division of Occupational Safety and Health. (1995). *Guidelines for workplace security.* San Francisco: California Department of Industrial Relations.

Call, J. (2003). Negotiating crises: The evolution of hostage/barricade crisis negotiation. *Journal of Threat Assessment, 2*, 69–94.

Callahan, L. A., McGreevy, M. A., Cirincione, C., & Steadman, H. J. (1992). Measuring the effects of guilty but mentally ill (GBMI) verdict. *Law and Human Behavior, 16*, 447–462.

Callahan, L. A., Steadman, H. J., McGreevy, M. A., & Robbins, P. C. (1991). The volume and characteristics of insanity defense pleas: An eight-state study. *Bulletin of Psychiatry and the Law, 19*, 331–338.

Cameron, M. O. (1964). *The booster and the snitch.* New York: Free Press.

Camilleri, J. A., & Quinsey, V. L. (2008). Pedophilia: Assessment and treatment. In D. R. Laws & W. T. O'Donohue (Eds.), *Sexual deviance: Theory, assessment, and treatment.* New York: Guilford.

Campbell, A. (1993). *Men, women, and aggression.* New York: Basic Books.

Campbell, A. (2006). Sex differences in direct aggression: What are the psychological mediators. *Aggression and Violent Behavior, 22*, 237–264.

Campbell, B. J. (1996). *Validity and use of evidence concerning battering and its effects in criminal trials.* Washington, DC: U.S. Department of Justice, Violence Against Women Office.

Campbell, M. A., French, S., & Gendreau, P. (2009). The prediction of violence in adult offenders: A meta-analytic comparison of instruments and methods of assessment. *Criminal Justice and Behavior, 36,* 567–590.

Campbell, M. A., Porter, S., & Santor, D. (2004). Psychopathic traits in adolescent offenders: An evaluation of criminal history, clinical, and psychosocial correlates. *Behavioral Sciences & the Law, 22,* 23–47.

Canadian Government's Commission of Inquiry. (1971). *The non-medical use of drugs: Interim report.* London: Penguin Books.

Canfield, R. L., Henderson, C. R., Cory-Slechta, A. A., Cox, C., Jusko, T. A., & Lanphear, B. P. (2003). Intellectual impairment in children with blood lead concentrations below 10 microgram per deciliter. *New England Journal of Medicine, 348,* 1517–1526.

Canter, D. (2008). Geographical profiling of criminals. In D. Canter & D. Youngs (Eds.), *Principles of geographical offender profiling* (pp. 197–219). Burlington, VT: Ashgate.

Canter, D., & Alison, L. (Eds.). (2000). *Profiling property crimes.* Burlington, VT: Ashgate.

Canter, D. V. (2000a). Offender profiling and criminal differentiation. *Legal and Criminological Psychology, 5,* 23–46.

Canter, D. V. (2000b). *Criminal shadows: The Inner Narratives of Evil.* Irving, TX: Authorlink Press.

Canter, D. V., Alison, L. J., Alison, E., & Wentink, N. (2004). The organized/disorganized typology of serial murder: Myth or model? *Psychology, Public Policy, and Law, 10,* 293–320.

Canter, D. V., & Fritzon, K. (1998). Differentiating arsonists: A model of firesetting actions and characteristics. *Legal and Criminological Psychology, 3,* 73–96.

Cantor, J. M., Blanchard, R., Robichaud, L. K., & Christensen, B. K. (2005). Quantitative reanalysis of aggregate date on IQ in sexual offenders. *Psychological Bulletin, 131,* 555–568.

Caputo, A. A., Frick, P. J., & Brodsky, S. L. (1999). Family violence and juvenile sex offending: The potential mediating role of psychopathic traits and negative attitudes toward women. *Criminal Justice and Behavior, 26,* 338–356.

Caputo, G. A. (2004). Treating sticky fingers: An evaluation of treatment and education for shoplifters. *Journal of Offender Rehabilitation, 38,* 49–68.

Caputo, G. A., & King, A. (2011). Shoplifting: Work, agency, and gender. *Feminist Criminology, 63,* 159–177.

Carbon, S. B. (2010, September 14). *Rape in the United States: The chronic failure to report and investigate rape cases.* Statement of Susan B. Carbon, Director, Office on Violence Against Women before the Subcommittee on Crime and Drugs, Committee on the Judiciary, United State Senate.

Carlson, B. E. (1991). Outcomes of physical abuse and observation of marital violence among adolescents in placement. *Journal of Interpersonal Violence, 6,* 526–534.

Carlson, M., Marcus-Newhall, A., & Miller, N. (1990). Effects of situational aggression cues: A quantitative review. *Journal of Personality and Social Psychology, 58,* 622–633.

Carnegie Council on Adolescent Development. (1995). *Great transitions: Preparing American Youth for a new century.* New York: Carnegie Corporation of New York.

Carpentier, J., & Proulx, J. (2011). Correlates of recidivism among adolescents who have sexually offended. *Sexual Abuse: A Journal of Research and Treatment, 23,* 434–455.

Carraher, T. N., Carraher, D., & Schliemann, A. D. (1985). Mathematics in the streets and schools. *British Journal of Developmental Psychology, 3,* 21–29.

Casey-Cannon, S., Hayward, C., & Gowen, K. (2001). Middle-school girls' reports of peer victimization: Concerns, consequences, and implications. *Professional School Counseling, 5,* 138–148.

Caspi, A., Wright, B. R. E., Moffitt, T. E., & Silva, P. A. (1998). Early failure in the labor market: Childhood and adolescent predictors of unemployment in the transition to adulthood. *American Sociological Review, 63,* 424–451.

Catalano, R., Haggerty, K., Oesterle, S., Fleming, C., & Hawkins, J. D. (2004). The importance of bonding to school for healthy development: Findings from the Social Development Research Group. *Journal of School Health, 74,* 252–261.

Catalano, S. M. (2005). *Crime victimization, 2004.* Washington, DC: U.S. Department of Justice, National Crime Victimization Survey.

Catalano, S. M. (2010, September). *Victimization during household burglary.* Washington, DC: U.S. Department of Justice, Bureau of Justice Statistics.

Cellini, H. R. (1995). Assessment and treatment of the adolescent sexual offender. In B. Schwartz & H. R. Cellini (Eds.), *The sex offender: Corrections, treatment and legal practice* (Vol. 1). Kingston, NJ: Civil Research Institute.

Centers for Disease Control. (2005, September 2). Mental health in the United States: Prevalence of diagnosis and medication treatment for Attention-Deficiit/Hyperactivity Disorder in the United States, 2003. Available: http://www.cdc.gov/mmwr/preview/mmwrhthl/mm5434a.2htm

Chabinsky, S. R. (2010, March 23). *The cyber threat: Who's doing what to whom? Key Note address at the GovSec/FOSE Conference.* Washington, DC: Government Security Conference.

Chaiken, J. M. (1998a, April). Learning more from national data collection programs. *National Conference on Sex Offender Registries.* Sacramento, CA: SEARCH group. Available: www.ojp.usdoj.gov/bjs/pub/

Chaiken, J. M. (1998b, April). Foreword. *National Conference on Sex Offender Registries.* Sacramento, CA: SEARCH group. Available: www.ojp.usdoj.gov/bjs/pub/

Chamberlain, P. (1996). Treatment foster care for adolescents with conduct disorders and delinquency. In P. S. Jensen & D. Hibbs (Eds.), *Psychological treatment with research with children and adolescents.* Rockville, MD: National Institute of Mental Health.

Chappell, D. (1977). *Forcible rape: A national survey of the response by prosecutors (LEAA).* Washington, DC: USGPO.

Chapple, C. L. (2003). Examining intergenerational violence: Violent role modeling or weak parental controls? *Violence and Victims, 18,* 143–159.

Chen, Y-H., Arria, A., & Anthony, J. C. (2003). Firesetting in adolescents and being aggressive, shy, and rejected by peers: New epidemiologic evidence from a national sample survey. *Journal of the American Academy of Psychiatry and Law, 31,* 44–52.

Chermak, S. M., Freilich, J. D., & Shemtob, Z. (2009). Law-enforcement training and the domestic far right. *Criminal Justice and Behavior, 36,* 1305–1322.

Chesney-Lind, M. (2002). Criminalizing victimization: The unintended consequences of pro-arrest policies for girls and women. *Criminology and Public Policy, 2,* 81–90.

Chesney-Lind, M., & Shelden, R. (1998). *Girls, delinquency, and juvenile justice* (2nd ed.). Belmont, CA: West/Wadsworth.

Child Abuse Prevention Center. (1998). *Shaken baby syndrome fatalities in the United States.* Ogden, UT: Author.

Child Welfare Information Gateway. (2012, May). *Child abuse and neglect fatalities 2010: Statistics and interventions.* Washington, DC: Children's Bureau.

ChildStats.gov. (2012). *America's children: Key national indicators of well-being, 2011.* Available: http://www.childstats.gov/americaschildren/famsoc

Chilosi, A. M., Cipriani, P., Pecini, C., Brizzolara, D., Blagi, L., Montanaro, D., et al. (2008). Acquired focal brain lesions in childhood: Effects on development and reorganization of language. *Brain & Language, 106,* 211–225.

Christiansen, K. O. (1977). A review of studies of criminality among twins. In S. Mednick & K. O. Christiansen (Eds.), Biosocial bases of criminal behavior. New York: Gardiner Press.

Christie, M. M., Marshall, W. L., & Lanthier. R. D. (1979). *A descriptive study of incarcerated rapists and pedophiles.* Ottawa, ON: Report to the Solicitor General of Canada.

Christy, A., Clark, C., Frei, A., & Rynearson-Moody, S. (2012). Challenges of diverting veterans to trauma informed care: The heterogeneity of Intercept 2. *Criminal Justice and Behavior, 39,* 461–474.

Chung, I-J, Hill, K. G., Hawkins, J. D., Gilchrist, L. D., & Nagin, D. S. (2002). Childhood predictors of offense trajectories. *Journal of Research in Crime and Delinquency, 39,* 60–90.

Cicero, T. J., Inciardi, J. A., & Muñoz, A. (2005). Trends in abuse of OxyContin˙ and other opioid analgesics in the United States: 2002–2004. *The Journal of Pain, 6,* 662–672.

Cillessen, A. H. N., & Mayeux, L. (2004). Sociometric status and peer group behavior: Previous findings and current directions. In J. B. Kupersmidt & K. A. Dodge (Eds.), *Children's peer relations: From development to intervention.* Washington, DC: American Psychological Association.

Cirincione, C., & Jacobs, C. (1999). Identifying insanity acquittals: Is it easier? *Law and Human Behavior, 23,* 487–497.

Claridge, G. (1973). Final remarks. In G. Claridge, S. Canter, & W. I. Hume (Eds.), *Personality differences and biological variations.* Oxford, UK: Pergamon Press.

Clark, J. P., & Hollinger, R. C. (1983). *Theft by employees in work organizations.* Washington, DC: USGPO.

Cleckley, H. (1976). *The mask of sanity* (5th ed.). St. Louis, MO: Mosby.

Clinard, M. B., & Quinney, E. R. (1980). *Criminal behavior systems: A typology.* New York: Holt, Rinehart & Winston.

Cochrane, R. E., Grisso, T., & Frederick, R. I. (2001). The relationship between criminal charges, diagnoses, and psychological opinions among federal defendants. *Behavioral Science & the Law, 19,* 565–582.

Cohen, D., & Strayer, J. (1996). Empathy in conduct-disordered and comparison youth. *Developmental Psychology, 32,* 988–998.

Cohen, F. (2008). *The mentally disordered inmate and the law* (2nd ed.). Kingston, NJ: Civic Research Institute.

Cohen, M., Seghorn, T., & Calmas, W. (1969). Sociometric study of the sex offender. *Journal of Abnormal Psychology, 74,* 249–255.

Cohen, M. L., Garafalo, R., Boucher, R., & Seghorn, T. (1971). The psychology of rapists. *Seminars in Psychiatry, 3,* 307–327.

Cohen, N. J., Menna, R., Vallance, D. D., Barwick, M., Im, N., & Horodezky, N. B. (1998). Language, social cognitive processing, and behavioral characteristics of psychiatrically disturbed children with previously identified and suspected language impairments. *Journal of Child Psychology and Psychiatry, 39,* 853–864.

Cohn, V. (1986). Crack use. *NIDA Notes, 1,* 6.

Coie, J. D. (2004). The impact of negative social experience on the development of antisocial behavior. In J. B. Kupersmidt & K. A. Dodge (Eds.), *Children's peer relations: From development to intervention.* Washington, DC: American Psychological Association.

Coie, J. D., Belding, M., & Underwood, M. (1988). Aggression and peer rejection in childhood. In B. Lahey & A. Kazdin (Eds.), *Advances in clinical child psychology* (Vol. 2). New York: Plenum.

Coie, J. D., Dodge, K., & Kupersmith, J. (1990). Peer group behavior and social status. In S. R. Asher & J. D. Coie (Eds.), *Peer rejection in childhood.* Cambridge, UK: Cambridge University Press.

Coie, J. D., & Miller-Johnson, S. (2001). Peer factors and interventions. In R. Loeber & D. P. Farrington (Eds.), *Child delinquents: Development, intervention, and service needs.* Thousand Oaks, CA: Sage.

Coleman, J. W. (1998). *The criminal elite* (4th ed.). New York: St. Martin's Press.

Collins, M. (2012, February 15). *Federal child pornography offenses. Testimony of Michelle Collins of the National Center for Missing & Exploited Children before the U.S. Sentencing Commission.* Washington, DC: U.S. Sentencing Commission.

Colwell, B., Villarreal, S. F., & Espinosa, E. M. (2012). Preliminary outcomes of a pre-adjudication diversion initiative for juvenile justice involved youth with mental health needs in Texas. *Criminal Justice and Behavior, 39,* 447–460.

Colwell, M. J., Pettit, G. S., Meece, D., Bates, J. E., & Dodge, K. A. (2001). Cumulative risk and continuity in nonparental care from infancy to early adolescence. *Merrill-Palmer Quarterly, 47,* 207–234.

Comer, R. J. (2004). *Abnormal psychology* (5th ed.). New York: Worth.

Committee on Preventive Psychiatry. (1999). Violent behavior in children and youth: Preventive intervention from a psychiatric perspective. *Journal of the American Academy of Child and Adolescent Psychiatry, 38,* 235–241.

Commons, M. L., & Goodheart, E. A. (2007). Consider stages of development in preventing terrorism: Does government building fail and terrorism result when developmental stages of governance are skipped? *Journal of Adult Development, 14,* 91–111.

Conduct Problems Prevention Research Group. (1999). Initial impact of the Fast Track prevention trail for conduct problems: I. The high-risk sample. *Journal of Consulting and Clinical Psychology, 67,* 631–647.

Conduct Problems Prevention Research Group. (2004). The fast track experiment: Translating the developmental model into a prevention design. In J. B. Kupersmidt & K. A. Dodge (Eds.), *Children's peer relations: From development to intervention.* Washington, DC: American Psychological Association.

Conklin, J. E. (1977). *"Illegal but not criminal."* Englewood Cliffs, NJ: Prentice Hall.

Connell, D. (1996, November). *Driver aggression.* Washington, DC: Automobile Association Group Public Policy Road Safety Unit.

Connor, D. F., Ford, J. D., Chapman, J. F., & Banga, A. (2012). Adolescent attention deficit hyperactivity disorder in the secure treatment setting. *Criminal Justice and Behavior, 39,* 725–747.

Constantine, R. J., Petrila, J., Andel, R., Givens, E. M., Becker, M., Robst, J., Van Dorn, R., Boaz, T., Teague, G., Haynes, D., & Howe, A. (2010). Arrest trajectories of adult offenders with a serious mental illness. *Psychology, Public Policy, and Law, 16,* 319–339.

Cooke, D. J., & Michie, C. (1997). An item response theory analysis of the Hare Psychopathy Checklist-Revised. *Psychological Assessment, 9,* 3–14.

Cooke, D. J., & Michie, C. (2001). Refining the construct psychopathy: Toward a hierarchical model. *Psychological Assessment, 13,* 171–188.

Cooke, D. J., Michie, C., Hart, S. D., & Clark, D. A. (2004). Reconstructing psychopathy: Clarifying the significance of antisocial and socially deviant behavior in the diagnosis of psychopathic personality disorder. *Journal of Personality Disorders, 18,* 337–357.

Cooke, D. J., Michie, C., Hart, S. D., & Hare, R. D. (1999). Evaluation of the screening version of the Hare Psychopathy Checklist—Revised (PCL:SV): An item response theory analysis. *Psychological Assessment, 11,* 3–13.

Cooper, A., & Smith, E. L. (2011, November). *Homicide trends in the United States, 1980–2008: Annual rates for 2009 and 2010.* Washington, DC: U.S. Department of Justice, Bureau of Justice Statistics.

Coordinating Council on Juvenile Justice and Delinquency Prevention. (1996). *Combating violence and delinquency: The national juvenile justice action plan.* Washington, DC: USGPO.

Copeland, J., & Dillon, P. (2005). The health and psychosocial consequences of ketamine use. *International Journal of Drug Policy, 16,* 122–131.

Copes, H., & Cherbonneau, M. (2006). The key to auto theft. *British Journal of Criminology, 46,* 1–18.

Copes, H., & Vieraitis, L. (2007, July). *Identity theft: Assessing offenders' strategies and perceptions of risks.* Washington, DC: U.S. Department of Justice, National Institute of Justice.

Copes, H, & Vieraitis, L. (2009). Understanding identity theft: Offenders' accounts of their lives and crimes. *Criminal Justice Review, 34,* 329–349.

Cornell, D. G. (1989). Causes of juvenile homicide: A review of the literature. In E. P. Benedek & D. G. Cornell (Eds.), *Juvenile homicide.* Washington, DC: American Psychiatric Press.

Cornell, D. G., Warren, J., Hawk, G., Stafford, E., Oram, G., & Pine, D. (1996). Psychopathy in instrumental and reactive violent offenders. *Journal of Consulting and Clinical Psychology, 64,* 783–790.

Corrado, R. R., Vincent, G. M., Hart, S. D., & Cohen, I. M. (2004). Predictive validity of the Psychopathy Checklist: Youth Version for general and violent recidivism. *Behavioral Sciences & the Law, 22,* 5–22.

Coscina, D. V. (1997). The biopsychology of impulsivity: Focus on brain serotonin. In C. D. Webster & M. A. Jackson (Eds.), *Impulsivity: Theory, assessment, and treatment.* New York: Guilford Press.

COT. (2007, June 7). *Lone-wolf terrorism.* The Hague, Netherlands: COT, Instituut voor Veiligheids- en Crisismanagement.

Côté, S., Zoccolillo, M., Tremblay, R. E., Nagin, D., & Vitaro, F. (2001). Predicting girls' conduct disorder in adolescence from childhood trajectories of disruptive behaviors. *Journal of the American Academy of Child & Adolescent Psychiatry, 40,* 676–684.

Cowan, P. A., & Cowan, C. P. (2004). From family relationships to peer rejection to antisocial behavior in middle childhood. In J. B. Kupersmidt & K. A. Dodge (Eds.), *Children's peer relations: From development to intervention.* Washington, DC: American Psychological Association.

Cowley, G. (1993, July 26). The not-young and the restless. *Newsweek,* pp. 48–49.

Cressey, D. R. (1953). *A study in the social psychology of embezzlement: Other people's money.* Glencoe, IL: Free Press.

Crick, N. R. (1995). Relational aggression: The role of intent attributions, feelings of distress, and provocation type. *Development and Psychopathology, 7,* 313–322.

Crick, N. R., & Grotpeter, J. K. (1995). Relational aggression, gender, and social-psychological adjustment. *Child Development, 66,* 710–722.

Crick, N. R., & Zahn-Waxler, C. (2003). The development of psychopathology in females and males: Current progress and future challenges. *Development and Psychopathology, 15,* 719–742.

Critchley, M. (1951). *The trial of Neville George Clevely Heath.* London: William Hodge.

Critchlow, B. (1986). The powers of John Barleycorn: Beliefs about the effects of alcohol on social behavior. *American Psychologist, 41,* 751–764.

Critchton, R. (1959). *The great imposter.* New York: Random House.

Critical Incident Response Group. (2001). *Workplace violence: Issues in response.* FBI Critical Incident Response Group, National Center for the Analysis of Violent Crime, Quantico, VA.

Crocker, A. G., & Hodgins, S. (1997). The criminality of noninstitutionalized mentally retarded persons: Evidence from a birth cohort followed to age 30. *Criminal Justice and Behavior, 24,* 432–454.

Cromwell, P. F., Olson, J. F., & Avary, D. W. (1991). *Breaking and entering: An ethnographic analysis of burglary.* Newbury Park, CA: Sage.

Cromwell, P. F., & Thurman, Q. (2003). The devil made me do it: Use of neutralizations by shoplifters. *Deviant Behavior, 24,* 535–550.

Crowe, R. R. (1974). An adoptive study of antisocial personality. *Archives of General Psychiatry, 31,* 785–791.

Crowe, S. L., & Blair, R. J. R. (2008). The development of antisocial behavior: What can we learn from functioning neuroimaging studies? *Development and Psychopathology, 20,* 1145–1159.

Cruise, K. R., Colwell, L. H., Lyons, P. M., & Baker, M. D. (2003). Prototypical analysis of adolescent psychopathy: Investigating the juvenile justice perspective. *Behavioral Sciences & the Law, 21,* 829–846.

Cruise, K. R., & Rogers, R. (1998). An analysis of competency to stand trial: An integration of case law and clinical knowledge. *Behavioral Sciences & the Law, 16,* 35–50.

Culberton, F. M., Feral, C. H., & Gabby, S. (1989). Pattern analysis of Wechsler Intelligence Scale for Children-Revised profiles of delinquent boys. *Journal of Clinical Psychology, 45,* 651–660.

Dabbs, J. M., Jr., Carr, T. S., Frady, R. L., & Riad, J. K (1995). Testosterone, crime, and misbehavior among 692 male prison inmates. *Personality and Individual Differences, 18,* 627–633.

Dabbs, J. M. Jr., Riad, J. K., & Chance, S. E. (2001). Testosterone and ruthless homicide. *Personality and Individual Differences, 31,* 599–603.

Dabney, D. A., Dugan, L., Topalli, V., & Hollinger, R. C. (2006). The impact of implicit stereotyping on offender profiling: Unexpected results from an observational study of shoplifting. *Criminal Justice and Behavior, 33,* 646–674.

Dadds, M. R., & Fraser, J. A. (2006). Fire interest, fire setting and psychopathology in Australian children: A normative study. *Australian and New Zealand Journal of Psychiatry, 40,* 581–586.

Dåderman, A. M., & Kristiansson, M. (2003). Degree of psychopathy: Implications for treatment in male juvenile delinquents. *International Journal of Law and Psychiatry, 26,* 310–315.

Dahlberg, L. L., & Potter, L. B. (2001). Youth violence: Developmental pathways and prevention challenges. *American Journal of Preventive Medicine, 20* (1s), 3–14.

Dalbert, C. (1999). The world is more just for me than generally: About the Personal Belief in a Just World Scale's validity. *Social Justice Research, 12,* 79–98.

Dalbert, C., & Filke, E. (2007). Belief in a personal just world, justice judgments, and their functions for prisoners. *Criminal Justice and Behavior, 34,* 1516–1527.

Damon, W. (2004). What is positive youth development? *Annals, AAPSS, 591,* 13–24.

Daniels, D. N., & Gilula, M. F. (1970). Violence and the struggle for existence. In D. Daniels, M. Gilula, & F. Ochberg (Eds.), *Violence and the struggle for existence.* Boston: Little, Brown.

Darby, P. J., Allan, W. D., Kashani, J. H., Hartke, K. L., & Reid, J. C. (1998). Analysis of 112 juveniles who committed homicide: Characteristics and a closer look at family abuse. *Journal of Family Violence, 13,* 365–375.

Darling, N., & Steinberg, L. (1993). Parenting style as context: An integrative model. *Psychological Bulletin, 113,* 487–496.

David, P. R. (1974). *The world of the burglar.* Albuquerque, NM: University of New Mexico Press.

Davies, M. (2002). Male sexual assault victims: A selected review of the literature and implications for support services. *Aggression and Violent Behavior, 7,* 203–214.

Davis, M. G., Lundman, R. J., & Martinez, R. (1991). Private corporate justice: Store police, shoplifters, and civil recovery. *Social Problems, 38,* 395–411.

Dawkins, M. P. (1997). Drug use and violent crime among adolescents. *Adolescence, 32,* 395–405.

Dawson, J. M., & Langan, P. A. (1994). *Murder in families.* Washington, DC: Bureau of Justice Statistics.

Day, K., & Berney, T. (2001). Treatment and care for offenders with mental retardation. In Ashford, J. B., Sales, B. D., & Reid, W. H. (Eds.), *Treating adult and juvenile offenders with special needs.* Washington, DC: American Psychological Association.

Day, R., & Wong, S. (1996). Anomalous perceptual asymmetries for negative emotional stimuli in the psychopath. *Journal of Abnormal Psychology, 105,* 648–652.

Deal, M. M., & Hickey, E. W. (2003). Helter-Skelter. In E. Hickey (Ed.), *Encyclopedia of murder & violent crime.* Thousand Oaks, CA: Sage.

DeAngelis, T. (2011, September). Bin Laden's death: What does it mean? *APA Monitor on Psychology,* pp. 77–78.

Decker, S. H., Pennel, S., & Caldwell, A. (1997). *Illegal firearms: Access and use by arrestees.* Washington, DC: U.S. Department of Justice, National Institute of Justice.

Decker, S. H., Wright, R., Redfern, A., & Smith, D. (1993). A woman's place is in the home: Females and residential burglary. *Justice Quarterly, 10,* 143–163.

Declercq, F., Willemsen, J., Audenaert, K., & Verhaeghe, P. (2012). Psychopathy and predatory violence in homicide, violent, and sexual offenses: Factor and facet relations. *Legal and Criminological Psychology, 17,* 59–74.

Deem, D., & Murray, M. (2000). Financial crime. In G. Coleman, M. Gaboury, M. Murray, & A. Seymour (Eds.), *1999 National Victim Assistance Academy.* Washington, DC: U.S. Department of Justice.

Dehue, F., Bolman, C., & Völlink, T. (2008). Cyberbullying: Youngsters' experiences and parental perception. *Cyberpsychology & Behavior, 11,* 217–223.

de Kemp, R. A. T., Overbeek, G., de Wied, M., Engels, R. C. M. E., & Scholte, R. H. J. (2007). Early adolescent empathy, parental support, and antisocial behavior. *The Journal of Genetic Psychology, 168,* 5–18.

Dekovic, M., Janssens, J. M. A. M., & Van As, N. M. C. (2003). Family predictors of antisocial behavior in adolescence. *Family Process, 42,* 223–235.

DeLisi, M. (2009). Introduction to special issues on biosocial criminology. *Criminal Justice and Behavior, 36,* 1111–1112.

DeLisi, M., Beaver, K. M., Vaughn, M. G., & Wright, J. P. (2009). All in the family: Gene X environment interaction between DRD2 and criminal father is associated with five antisocial phenotypes. *Criminal Justice and Behavior, 36,* 1177–1187.

Delisi, M., & Scherer, A. M. (2006). Multiple homicide offenders: Offense characteristics, social correlates, and criminal careers. *Criminal Justice and Behavior, 33,* 367–391.

DeLisi, M., Umphress, Z. R., & Vaughn, M. G. (2009). The criminology of the amygdala. *Criminal Justice and Behavior, 36,* 1231–1242.

Del Bove, G., & Mackay, S. (2011). An empirically derived classification system for juvenile firesetters. *Criminal Justice and Behavior, 38,* 796–817.

DeMatteo, D. (2005, Winter). Legal update: An expansion of Tarasoff's duty to protect. *American Psychology-Law News, 25*(2), 1, 6.

DeMatteo, D. (2007). Legal update: The Supreme Court rules on the insanity defense and capital sentencing procedures. *American Psychology-Law Society Newsletter, 27*(1), 1, 5.

Department of Health and Human Services. (2003, September). *Overview of findings from the 2002 national survey on drug use and health.* Rockville, MD: Substance Abuse and Mental Health Services, Office of Applied Studies.

Dern, H., Dern, C., Horn, A., & Horn, U. (2009). The fire behind the smoke: A reply to Snook and colleagues. *Criminal Justice and Behavior, 36,* 1085–1090.

Devapriam, J., Raju, L. B., Singh, N., Collacott, R., & Bhaumik, S. (2007). Arson: Characteristics and predisposing factors in offenders with intellectual disabilities. *The British Journal of Forensic Practice, 9,* 23–27.

Developments in the Law. (1974). Civil commitment of the mentally ill. *Harvard Law Review, 87,* 1190–1406.

Deković, M., Asscher, J. J., Manders, W. A., Prins, P. J. M., & van der Laan, P. (2012, May 7). Within-intervention change: Mediators of intervention effects during multisystemic therapy. *Journal of Consulting and Clinical Psychology.* Advance online publication: doi:10.1037/a0028482

DeWall, C. N., & Anderson, C. A. (2011). The General Aggression Model. In P. R. Shaver & M. Mikulincer (Eds.), *Human aggression and violence: Causes, manifestations, and consequences* (pp. 15–33). Washington, DC: American Psychological Association.

DeWall, C. N., Anderson, C. A., & Bushman, B. J. (2011). The General Aggression Model: Theoretical extension to violence. *Psychology of Violence, 1,* 245–258.

DeWall, C. N., Twenge, J. M., Gitter, S. A., & Baumeister, R. F. (2009). It's the thought that counts: The role of hostile cognition in shaping aggressive responses to social exclusion. *Journal of Personality and Social Psychology, 96,* 45–59.

Diamanduros, T., Downs, E., & Jenkins, S. J. (2008). The role of school psychologists in the assessment, prevention, and intervention of cyberbullying. *Psychology in the Schools, 45,* 693–704.

Diamantopoulou, S., Verhulst, F. C., & van der Ende, J. (2011). Gender differences in the development and adult outcome of co-occurring depression and delinquency in adolescence. *Journal of Abnormal Psychology, 120,* 644–655.

DiCataldo, F., & Everett, M. (2008). Distinguishing juvenile homicide from violent juvenile offending. *International Journal of Offender Therapy and Comparative Criminology, 52,* 158–174.

Dick, D. M., & Rose, R. J. (2002). Behavior genetics: What's new? What's next? *Current Directions in Psychological Science, 11,* 70–74.

Dickens, G., Sugarman, P., Edgar, S., Hofberg, K., Tewari, S., & Ahmad, F. (2009). Recidivism and dangerousness in arsonists. *Journal of Forensic Psychiatry & Psychology, 20,* 621–639.

Diener, E. (1980). Deindividuation: The absence of self-awareness and self-regulation in group members. In P. Paulus (Ed.), *The psychology of group influence.* Hillsdale, NJ: Erlbaum.

Dietrich, K. N., Ris, M. D., Succop, P. A., Berger, O. G., & Bornschein, R. L. (2001). Early exposure to lead and juvenile delinquency. *Neurotoxicology and Teratology, 23,* 511–518.

Dill, K. E., Anderson, C. A., Anderson, K. B., & Deuser, W. E. (1997). Effects of aggressive personality on social expectations and social perceptions. *Journal of Research in Personality, 31,* 272–292.

Dill, K. E., & Dill, J. C. (1998). Video game violence: A review of the empirical literature. *Aggression and Violent Behavior, 3,* 407–428.

DiLonardo, R. L. (1996). Defining and measuring the economic benefit of electronic article surveillance. *Security Journal, 7,* 3–9.

Diserens, C. M. (1925). Psychological objectivism. *Psychological Review, 32,* 121–152.

Dishion, T. J., & Andrews, D. W. (1995). Preventing escalation in problem behaviors with high-risk young adolescents: Immediate and 1-year outcomes. *Journal of Consulting and Clinical Psychology, 63,* 538–548.

Dishion, T. J., & Loeber, R. (1985). Male adolescent marijuana and alcohol use: The role of parents and peers revisited. *American Journal of Drug and Alcohol Abuse, 11,* 11–25.

Ditzler, T. F. (2004). Malevolent minds: The teleology of terrorism. In F. M. Moghaddam & A. J. Marsella (Eds.), *Understanding terrorism: Psychosocial roots, consequences, and interventions.* Washington, DC: American Psychological Association.

Dix, G. E. (1980). Clinical evaluation of the "dangerous" if "normal" criminal defendants. *Virginia Law Review, 66,* 523–581.

Dobson, V., & Sales, B. (2000). The science of infanticide and mental illness. *Psychology, Public Policy, and Law, 6,* 1098–1112.

Dodge, K. A. (1986). A social information processing model of social competence in children. In M. Perlmutter (Ed.), *The Minnesota symposium on child psychology.* Hillsdale, NJ: Erlbaum.

Dodge, K. A. (1991). The structure and function of reactive and proactive aggression. In D. J. Pepler & K. H. Rubin (Eds.), *The development and treatment of childhood aggression.* Hillsdale, NJ: Erlbaum.

Dodge, K. A. (1993). Social-cognitive mechanisms in the development of conduct disorder and depression. *Annual Review of Psychology, 44,* 559–584.

Dodge, K. A. (2001). The science of youth violence prevention: Progressing from developmental epidemiology to efficacy to effectiveness in public policy. *American Journal of Preventive Medicine, 20* (1s), 63–70.

Dodge, K. A. (2003). Do social information-processing patterns mediate aggressive behavior? In B. B. Lahey, T. E. Moffitt, & A. Caspi (Eds.), *Causes of conduct disorder and juvenile delinquency.* New York: Guilford Press.

Dodge, K. A. (2011). Social information processing patterns as mediators of the interaction between genetic factors and life experiences in the development of aggressive behavior. In P. R. Shaver & M. Mikulincer (Eds.), *Human aggression and violence: Causes, manifestations, and consequences* (pp. 165–185). Washington, DC: American Psychological Association.

Dodge, K. A., Bates, J. E., & Pettit, G. S. (1990). Mechanisms in the cycle of violence. *Science, 250,* 1678–1683.

Dodge, K. A., & Coie, J. D. (1987). Social information processing factors in reactive and proactive aggression in children's peer groups. *Journal of Personality and Social Psychology, 53,* 1146–1158.

Dodge, K. A., Greenberg, M. T., Malone, P. S., & Conduct Problems Prevention Research Group. (2008). Testing an idealized dynamic cascade model of the development of serious violence in adolescence. *Child Development, 79,* 1907–1927.

Dodge, K. A., Laird, R., Lochman, Zelli, A., & Conduct Problems Prevention Research Group. (2002). Multi-dimensional latent construct analysis of children's social information-processing patterns: Correlations with aggressive behavior problems. *Psychological Assessment, 14,* 60–73.

Dodge, K. A., Lochman, J. E., Harnish, J. D., Bates, J. E., & Pettit, G. S. (1997). Reactive and proactive aggression in school children and psychiatrically impaired chronically assaultive youth. *Journal of Abnormal Psychology, 106,* 37–51.

Dodge, K. A., & Pettit, G. S. (2003). A biopsychological model of the development of chronic conduct problems in adolescence. *Developmental Psychology, 39,* 349–371.

Doerner, W. G. (1988). The impact of medical resources on criminally induced lethality: A further examination. *Criminology, 26,* 171–179.

Doerner, W. G., & Speir, J. C. (1986). Stitch and sew: The impact of medical resources upon criminally induced lethality. *Criminology, 24,* 319–330.

Doley, R. (2003). Pyromania: Fact or fiction? *British Journal of Criminology, 43,* 797–807.

Dollard, J., Doob, L. W., Miller, N. E., Mowrer, O. H., & Sears, R. R. (1939). *Frustration and aggression.* New Haven, CT: Yale University Press.

Donnerstein, E. (1983). Erotica and human aggression. In R. G. Geen & E. I. Donnerstein (Eds.), *Aggression: Theoretical and empirical reviews* (Vol. 2). New York: Academic Press.

d'Orban, P. T., & O'Connor, A. (1989). Women who kill their parents. *British Journal of Psychiatry, 154,* 27–33.

Douglas, A-J. (2011, August). Child abductions: Known relationships are the greater danger. *FBI Law Enforcement Bulletin, 80*(8), 8–9.

Douglas, J. E., Burgess, A. W., Burgess, A. G., & Ressler, R. K. (1992). *Crime classification manual.* New York: Lexington Books.

Douglas, J. E., Burgess, A. W., Burgess, A. G., & Ressler, R. K. (2006). *Crime classification manual* (2nd ed.). San Francisco: Jossey-Bass.

Douglas, J. E., & Munn, C. (1992a). The detection of staging and personation at the crime scene. In J. E. Douglas, A. W. Burgess, A. G. Burgess, & R. K. Ressler (Eds.), *Crime classification manual.* New York: Lexington Books.

Douglas, J. E., & Munn, C. (1992b). Modus operandi and the signature aspects of violent crime. In J. E. Douglas, A. W. Burgess, A. G. Burgess, & R. K. Ressler (Eds.), *Crime classification manual.* New York: Lexington Books.

Douglas, J. E., & Munn, C. (1992c, February). Violent crime scene analysis. *FBI Law Enforcement Bulletin,* 1–10.

Douglas, J. E., Ressler, R. K., Burgess, A. W., & Hartman. C. R. (1986). Criminal profiling from crime scene analysis. *Behavioral Sciences & the Law, 4,* 401–421.

Douglas, K. S., Guy, L. L., & Hart, S. D. (2009). Psychosis as a risk factor for violence to others: A meta-analysis. *Psychological Bulletin, 135,* 679–706.

Douglas, K. S., Herbozo, S., Poythress, N. G., Belfrage, H., & Edens, J. F. (2006). Psychopathy and suicide: A multi-sample investigation. *Psychological Services, 3,* 97–116.

Douglas, V. I. (2004). Cognitive deficits in children with attention deficit hyperactivity disorder: A long-term follow up. *Canadian Psychology, 46,* 23–31.

Drug Enforcement Administration. (2000). *Drugs of abuse.* Washington, DC: U.S. Department of Justice. Available: www.usdoj.gov/dea/concern/abuse

Drug Enforcement Administration. (2005). *Drugs of abuse, 2005 edition.* Washington, DC: U.S. Department of Justice.

Drug Enforcement Administration. (2009, October). *Fentanyl.* Washington, DC: U.S. Department of Justice, Author.

Drug Enforcement Administration. (2010, April). *Phencyclidine.* Washington, DC: U.S. Department of Justice, Author.

Drug Enforcement Administration. (2011). *Drugs of abuse, 2011 edition.* Washington, DC: U.S. Department of Justice.

DSM-IV. (1994). *Diagnostic and statistical manual of mental disorders* (4th ed.). Washington, DC: American Psychiatric Association.

DSM-IV-R. (2000). *Diagnostic and statistical manual of mental disorders* (4th ed.). Washington, DC: American Psychiatric Association.

Duhaime, A., Christian, C. W., Rorke, L. B., & Zimmerman, R. A. (1998). Nonaccidental head injury in infants: The "shaken-baby syndrome." *New England Journal of Medicine, 338,* 1822–1829.

Dunn, C. S. (1976). *The patterns and distribution of assault incident characteristics among social areas.* Albany, NY: Criminal Justice Research Center, Analytic Report 14.

Durand, V. M., & Barlow, D. H. (2000). *Abnormal psychology: An introduction.* Belmont, CA: Wadsworth.

Durose, M. R., Harlow, C. W., Langan, P. A., Motivans, M., Rantala, R. R., & Smith, E. L. (2005, June). *Family violence statistics: Including statistics on strangers and acquaintances.* Washington, DC: U.S. Department of Justice, Bureau of Justice Statistics.

Duwe, G., Donnay, W., & Tewksbury, R. (2008). Does residential proximity matter? A geographic analysis of sex offense recidivism. *Criminal Justice and Behavior, 35,* 484–504.

Easterbrook, J. A. (1959). The effect of emotion on cue utilization and the organization of behavior. *Psychological Review, 66,* 183–201.

Eastman, B. J. (2004). Assessing the efficacy of treatment for adolescent sex offenders: A cross-over longitudinal study. *Prison Journal, 84,* 472–485.

Eastvold, A., Suchy, Y., & Strassberg, D. (2011). Executive function profiles of pedophilic and nonpedophilic child molesters. *Journal of the International Neuropsychological Society, 17,* 295–307.

Eaton, J., & Polk, K. (1961). *Measuring delinquency.* Pittsburgh, PA: University of Pittsburgh Press.

Ebert, B. W. (1987). Guide to conducting a psychological autopsy. *Professional Psychology: Research and Practice, 18,* 52–56.

Eccles, J., & Robinson, D. N. (1984). *The wonder of being human: Our brain and our mind.* New York: Free Press.

Eck, J. (2000). Preventing crime at places. In L. W. Sherman, D. Gottfresson, D. MacKenzie, J. Eck, P. Reuter, & S. Bushway (Eds.), *Preventing crime: What works, what doesn't, what's promising.* A Report to the United State Congress. Available: www.ncjrs.org/works

Eddy, J. M. (2003). *Conduct disorders: The latest assessment and treatment strategies.* Kansas City, MO: Compact Clinicals.

Edens, J. F., Campbell, J., & Weir, J. (2007). Youth psychopathy and criminal recidivism: A meta-analysis of the psychopathy checklist measures. *Law and Human Behavior, 31,* 53–75.

Edens, J. F., Guy, L. S., & Fernandez, K. (2003). Psychopathic traits predict attitudes toward a juvenile capital murderer. *Behavioral Sciences & the Law, 21,* 807–828.

Edens, J. F., Petrila, J., & Buffington-Vollum, J. K. (2001). Psychopathy and the death penalty: Can the Psychopathy Checklist-Revised identify offenders who represent "a continuing threat to society?" *Journal of Psychiatry and Law, 29,* 433–481.

Edens, J. F., Skeem, J. L., Cruise, K. R., & Cauffman, E. (2001). Assessment of "juvenile psychopathy" and its association with violence: A critical review. *Behavioral Sciences & the Law, 19,* 53–80.

Edleson, J. L. (1999). Children's witnessing of adult domestic violence. *Journal of Interpersonal Violence, 14,* 839–870.

Edwards, S. (1983). Sexuality, sexual offenses, and conception of victims in the criminal justice process. *Victimology: An International Journal, 8,* 113–128.

Efran, M. G., & Cheyne, J. A. (1974). Affective concomitants of the invasion of shared space: Behavioral, physiological, and verbal indicators. *Journal of Personality and Social Psychology, 29,* 219–226.

Eisenberg, N., & Fabes, R. A. (1998). Prosocial development. In W. Damon (Series Ed.) & N. Eisenberg (Vol. Ed.), *Handbook of child psychology: Vol 3. Social, emotional and personality development* (5th ed.). New York: Wiley.

Elhai, J. D., Grubaugh, A. L., Kashdan, T. B., & Frueh, B. C. (2008). Emprical examination of a proposed refinement to DSM-IV posttraumatic stress disorder symptom criteria using the National Comorbidity Survey Replication data. *Journal of Clinical Psychiatry, 69,* 597–602.

Elliott, D. S. (1989). Criminal justice procedures in family violence crimes. In L. Ohlin & M. Tonry (Eds.), *Family violence* (Vol. 11). Chicago: University of Chicago Press.

Elliott, D. S., Dunford, T. W., & Huizinga, D. (1987). The identification and prediction of career offenders utilizing self-reported and official data. In J. D. Burchard & S. N. Burchard (Eds.), *Prevention of delinquent behavior.* Newbury Park, CA: Sage.

Elliott, D. S., & Menard, S. (1996). Delinquent friends and delinquent behavior: Temporal and developmental patterns. In J. D. Hawkins (Ed.), *Delinquency and crime: Current theories.* New York: Cambridge University Press.

Ellis, C. A., & Lord, J. (2001). Homicide. In G. Coleman, M. Gaboury, M. Murray, & A. Seymour (Eds.), *1999 National Victim Assistance Academy.* Washington, DC: U.S. Department of Justice.

Ellis, L. (1998). Why some sexual assaults are not committed by men: A biosocial analysis. In P. Anderson & C. Struckman-Johnson (Eds.), *Sexually aggressive women.* New York: Guilford.

Else-Quest, N. M., Hyde, J. S., Goldsmith, H. H., & Van Hulle, C. A. (2006). Gender differences in temperament: A meta-analysis. *Psychological Bulletin, 132,* 33–72.

Emery, R. E., & Laumann-Billings, L. (1998). An overview of the nature, causes, and consequences of abusive family relationships. *American Psychologist, 53,* 121–135.

Erhardt, D., & Hinshaw, S. P. (1994). Initial sociometric impressions of attention-deficit hyperactivity disorder and comparison boys: Predictions from social behaviors and from nonbehavioral variables. *Journal of Consulting and Clinical Psychology, 62,* 833–842.

Erickson, R. (1996). *Armed robbers and their crimes.* Seattle, WA: Athena Research Corporation.

Ericson, N. (2001, June). *Addressing the problem of juvenile bullying.* Washington, DC: U.S. Department of Justice, Office of Juvenile Justice and Delinquency Prevention.

Eron, L. D., & Huesmann, L. P. (1984). The relation of prosocial behavior to the development of aggression and psychopathology. *Aggressive Behavior, 10,* 201–211.

Eron, L. D., & Slaby, R. G. (1994). Introduction. In L. D. Eron, J. H. Gentry, & P. Schlegel (Eds.), *Reason to hope: A psychosocial perspective on violence and youth.* Washington, DC: American Psychological Association.

Eskridge, C. W. (1983). Prediction of burglary: A research note. *Journal of Criminal Justice, 11,* 67–75.

Eslea, M., Menesini, E., Morita, Y., O'Moore, M., Mora-Merchán, J. A., Pereira, B., et al. (2003). Friendship and loneliness among bullies and victims: Data from seven countries. *Aggressive Behavior, 30,* 71–83.

Evans, G. W. (2004). The environment of childhood poverty. *American Psychologist, 59,* 77–92.

Ewing, C. P. (1990). Psychological self-defense: A proposed justification for battered women who kill. *Law and Human Behavior, 14,* 579–594.

Exum, M. L., Kuhns, J. B., Koch, B., & Johnson, C. (2010). An examination of situational crime prevention strategies across convenience stores and fast-food restaurants. *Criminal Justice Policy Review, 21,* 269–295.

Eysenck, H. J. (1967). *The biological basis of personality.* Springfield, IL: Charles C Thomas.

Fagan, J. (1989). Cessation of family violence. In L. Ohlin & M. Tonry (Eds.), *Family violence* (Vol. 11). Chicago: University of Chicago Press.

Falkenbach, D. M. Poythress, N. G., & Heide, K. M. (2003). Psychopathic features in a juvenile diversion population: Reliability and predictive validity of two self-report measures. *Behavioral Sciences & the Law, 21*, 787–805.

Fantuzzo, J. W., Boruch, R., Abdullahi, B., Atkins, M., & Marcus, S. (1997). Domestic violence and children: Prevalence and risk in five major U.S. cities. *Journal of American Academy of Child and Adolescent Psychiatry, 36*, 116–122.

Fantuzzo, J. W., DesPaola, L. M., Lambert, L., Martino, T., Anderson, G., & Sutton, S. (1991). Effects of interparental violence on the psychological adjustment and competencies of young children. *Journal of Consulting and Clinical Psychology, 59*, 258–265.

Farrell, A. L., Keppel, R. D., & Titterington, V. B. (2011). Lethal ladies: Revisiting what we know about female serial murderers. *Homicide Studies, 15*, 228–252.

Farrell, G., Phillips, C., & Pease, K. (1995). Like taking candy, why does repeat victimization occur? *British Journal of Criminology, 35*, 384–399.

Farrington, D. P. (1991). Childhood aggression and adult violence: Early precursors and later life outcomes. In D. J. Pepler & K. H. Rubin (Eds.), *The development and treatment of childhood aggression*. Hillsdale, NJ: Erlbaum.

Farrington, D. P. (1995). Crime and physical health: Illnesses, injuries, accidents, and offending in the Cambridge study. *Criminal Behaviour and Mental Health, 5*, 278.

Farrington, D. P. (2005a). The importance of child and adolescent psychopathy. *Journal of Abnormal Child Psychology, 33*, 489–497.

Farrington, D. P. (2005b). Family background and psychopathy. In C. J. Patrick (Ed.), *Handbook of psychopathy*. New York: Guilford.

Farrington, D. P., Bowen, S., Buckle, A., Burns-Howell, T., Burrows, J., & Speed, M. (1993). An experiment on the prevention of shoplifting. In R. V. Clarke (Ed.), *Crime prevention studies* (Vol. 1). Monsey, NY: Criminal Justice Press.

Farrington, D. P., & Burrows, J. N. (1993). Did shoplifting really decrease? *British Journal of Criminology, 33*, 57–59.

Farrington, D. P., Ttofi, M. M., & Coid, J. W. (2009). Development of adolescence-limited, late-onset, and persistent offenders from age 8 to age 48. *Aggressive Behavior, 35*, 150–163.

Farris, C., Treat, T. A., Viken, R. J., & McFall, R. M. (2008). Sexual coercion and the misperception of sexual intent. *Clinical Psychology Review, 28*, 48–66.

Farris, C., Viken, R. J., Treat, T. A., & McFall, R. M. (2006). Heterosocial perceptual organization: Application of the choice model to sexual coercion. *Psychological Science, 17*, 869–875.

Faupel, C. E. (1991). *Shooting dope: Career patterns of hard-core heroin users*. Gainesville, FL: University of Florida Press.

Federal Bureau of Investigation. (1985, August). Crime scene and profile characteristics of organized and disorganized murders. *FBI Law Enforcement Bulletin, 54*, 18–25.

Federal Bureau of Investigation. (1992). *Killed in the line of duty: A study of selected felonious killings of law enforcement officers*. Washington, DC: U.S. Department of Justice.

Federal Bureau of Investigation. (1997). *Uniform Crime Reports—1996*. Washington, DC: U.S. Department of Justice.

Federal Bureau of Investigation. (2002). *Uniform Crime Reports—2001*. Washington, DC: U.S. Department of Justice.

Federal Bureau of Investigation. (2003). Special report: Bank robbery in the United States. *Uniform Crime Reports—2002*. Washington, DC: U.S. Department of Justice.

Federal Bureau of Investigation. (2005a). *Serial murder: Multi-disciplinary perspectives for investigators*. Washington, DC: Behavioral Analysis Unit-2, National Center for the Analysis of Crime.

Federal Bureau of Investigation. (2005b). *Crime in the United States 2004: Uniform Crime Reports*. Washington, DC: U.S. Department of Justice.

Federal Bureau of Investigation. (2008). *Crime in the United States 2007: Uniform Crime Reports*. Washington, DC: U.S. Department of Justice.

Federal Bureau of Investigation. (2011a). Crime in the United States 2010: Uniform Crime Reports. Washington, DC: U.S. Department of Justice.

Federal Bureau of Investigation. (2011b). Hate crime statistics 2010. Washington, DC: U.S. Department of Justice.

Federal Interagency Forum on Child and Family Statistics. (2005). *America's children: Key national indicators of well-being 2005.* Washington, DC: Author.

Fehrenbach, P. A., & Monastersky, C. (1988). Characteristics of female sexual offenders. *American Journal of Orthopsychiatry, 58,* 148–151.

Fehrenbach, P. A., Smith, W., Monastersky, C., & Deisher, R. W. (1986). Adolescent sexual offenders: Offender and offense characteristics. *American Journal of Orthopsychiatry, 56,* 225–233.

Feinberg, G. (1984). Profile for the elderly shoplifter. In E. S. Newman, D. J. Newman, & M. L. Gewirtz (Eds.), *Elderly criminals.* Cambridge, MA: Oelgeschlager, Gunn & Hain.

Feldman, R., & Klein, P. S. (2003). Toddler's self-regulated compliance to mothers, caregivers, and fathers: Implications for theories of socialization. *Developmental Psychology, 39,* 680–692.

Fenichel, O. (1945). *The psychoanalytic theory of neurosis.* New York: W. W. Norton.

Ferguson, C. A., Rueda, S. M., Cruz, A. M., Ferguson, D. E., Fritz, S., & Smith, S. M. (2008). Violent video games and aggression: Causal relationship or byproduct of family violence and intrinsic violence motivation? *Criminal Justice and Behavior, 35,* 311–332.

Fergusson, D. M., Boden, J. M., Horwood, L. J., Miller, A., & Kennedy, M. A. (2012). Moderating role of the MAOA genotype in antisocial behaviour. *British Journal of Psychiatry, 200,* 116–123.

Fergusson, D. M., Lynskey, M. T., & Horwood, L. J. (1996). Factors associated with continuity and change in disruptive behavior patterns between childhood and adolescence. *Journal of Abnormal Child Psychology, 24,* 533–553.

Ferro, C., Cermele, J., & Saltzman, A. (2008). Current perceptions of marital rape: Some good and not-so-good news. *Journal of Interpersonal Violence, 23,* 764–779.

Feshbach, S. (1964). The function of aggression and the regulation of aggressive drive. *Psychological Review, 71,* 257–272.

Festinger, L., Pepitone, A., & Newcomb, T. (1952). Some consequences of de-individuation in a group. *Journal of Abnormal and Social Psychology, 47,* 382–389.

Feucht, T. W., & Kyle, G. M. (1996, November). Methamphetamine use among adult arrestees: Findings of the DUF program. *NIJ Research in Brief.* Washington, DC: U.S. Department of Justice.

Fields, G. (2006, September 26). Police are changing how they confront the mentally ill. *The Wall Street Journal,* pp. A1, A11.

Fierro, I., Morales, C., & Álvarez, F. J. (2011). Alcohol use, illicit drug use, and road rage. *Journal of Studies on alcohol and drugs, 72,* 185–193.

Finckenauer, J. O., & Schrock, J. (2000). *Human trafficking: A growing criminal market in the U.S.* Washington, DC: National Institute of Justice, International Center. Available: www.ojp.usdoj.gov/nij/international/ht.html

Finkelhor, D. (1979). *Sexually victimized children.* New York: Free Press.

Finkelhor, D. (2011). Prevalence of child victimization, abuse, crime, and violence exposure. In J. W. White, M. P. Koss, & A. E. Kasdin (Eds.), *Violence against women and children. Vol. 1. Mapping the terrain.* (pp. 9–29). Washington, DC: American Psychological Association.

Finkelhor, D., & Araji, S. (1986). Explanations of pedophilia: A four factor model. *The Journal of Sex Research, 22,* 145–161.

Finkelhor, D., & Dziuba-Leatherman, J. (1994). Children as victims of violence: A national survey. *Pediatrics, 94,* 413–420.

Finkelhor, D., Hammer, H., & Sedlak, A. J. (2002, October). *Nonfamily abducted children: National estimates and characteristics.* Washington, DC: U.S. Department of Justice.

Finkelhor, D., & Lewis, I. A. (1988). An epidemiologic approach to the study of child molestation. In R. A. Prentky & V. L. Quinsey (Eds.), *Human sexual aggression: Current perspectives.* New York: New York Academy of Sciences.

Finkelhor, D., Ormrod, R. K., & Turner, H. A. (2007). Poly-victimization: A neglected component in child victimization trauma. *Child Abuse & Neglect, 31,* 7–26.

Finkelhor, D., Ormrod, R., Turner, H., & Hamby, S. L. (2005). The victimization of children and youth: A comprehensive, national survey. *Child Maltreatment, 10,* 5–25.

Finkelhor, D., Turner, H. A., Ormrod, R., & Hamby, S. L. (2009). Violence, abuse, and crime exposure in a national sample of children and youth. *Pediatrics, 124,* 1411–1423.

Firestone, P., Bradford, J. M., Greenberg, D. M., & Larose, M. R. (1998). Homicidal sex offenders: Psychological, phallometric, and diagnostic features. *Journal of the American Academy of Psychology and Law, 26,* 537–552.

Fishbein, D. (2001). *Biobehavioral perspectives in criminology.* Belmont, CA: Wadsworth/Thomson Learning.

Fite, P. J., Stoppelbein, L., & Greening, L. (2009). Proactive and reactive aggression in a child psychiatric inpatient population: Relations to psychopathic characteristics. *Criminal Justice and Behavior, 36,* 481–493.

Flannery, D. J., Williams, L. L., & Vazsonyi, A. T. (1999). Who are they with and what are they doing? Delinquent behavior, substance abuse, and early adolescence after school time. *American Journal of Orthopsychiatry, 69,* 247–253.

Flor-Henry, P. (1973). Psychiatric syndromes considered as manifestations of lateralized temporal-limbic dysfunction. In L. V. Latiner & K. E. Livingston (Eds.), *Surgical approaches in psychiatry.* Lancaster, UK: Medical and Technical Publishing.

Flor-Henry, P., & Yeudall, L. T. (1973). Lateralized cerebral dysfunction in depression and in aggressive criminal psychopathy. *International Research Communications, 7,* 31.

Flynn, E. E. (1983). Crime as a major social issue. *American Behavioral Scientist, 27,* 7–42.

Fontaine, N., Carbonneau, R., Vitaro, F., Barker, E. D., & Tremblay, R. E. (2009). Research review: A critical review of studies on the developmental trajectories of antisocial behavior in females. *Journal of Child Psychology and Psychiatry, 50,* 363–385.

Fontaine, R. G. (2008). Reactive cognitive, reaction emotion: Toward a more psychologically-informed understanding of reactive homicide. *Psychology, Public Policy, and Law, 14,* 243–261.

Fontaine, R. G., & Dodge, K. A. (2006). Real-time decision making and aggressive behavior in youth: A heuristic model of response evaluation and decision (RED). *Aggressive Behavior, 32,* 604–624.

Forbes, G. B., Adams-Curtis, L. E., & White, K. B. (2004). First- and second-generation measures of sexism, rape myths and related beliefs, and hostility toward women. *Violence Against Women, 10,* 236–261.

Forehand, R., Wierson, M., Frame, C. L., Kemptom, T., & Armistead, L. (1991). Juvenile firesetting: A unique syndrome or an advanced level of antisocial behavior? *Behavioral Research and Therapy, 29,* 125–128.

Forney, W. S., Forney, J. C., & Crutsinger, C. (2005). Developmental stages of age and moral reasoning as predictors of juvenile delinquents' behavioral intention to steal clothing. *Family and Consumer Sciences Research Journal, 34,* 110–126.

Forrstrom-Cohen, B., & Rosenbaum, A. (1985). The effects of parental marital violence on young adults: An exploratory investigation. *Journal of Marriage and Family, 47,* 467–472.

Forth, A. E., & Burke, H. C. (1998). Psychopathy in adolescence: Assessment, violence, and developmental precursors. In D. J. Cooke, A. E. Forth, & R. D. Hare (Eds.), *Psychopathy: Theory, research and implications for society.* Boston: Kluwer Academic.

Forth, A. E., Kosson, D. S., & Hare, R. D. (2003). *Psychopathy Checklist-Youth Version: Technical manual.* Toronto, ON: Multi-Health Systems.

Fothergill, K. E., & Ensminger, M. E. (2006). Childhood and adolescent antecedents of drug and alcohol problems: A longitudinal study. *Drug and Alcohol Dependence, 82,* 61–76.

Fox, J. A., & Levin, J. (2003). Mass murder: An analysis of extreme violence. *Journal of Applied Psychoanalytic Studies, 5,* 47–64.

Franke, D. (1975). *The torture doctor.* New York: Avon.

Frederick, R. I. (2000). Mixed group validation: A method to address the limitations of criterion group validation in research on malingering detection. *Behavioral Sciences & the Law, 18,* 693–718.

Freedman, J. L., Sears, D. O., & Carlsmith, J. J. (1978). *Social psychology* (3rd ed.). Englewood Cliffs, NJ: Prentice Hall.

Freeman, N. J., & Sandler, J. C. (2008). Female and male sex offenders: A comparison of recidivism and risk factors. *Journal of Interpersonal Violence, 23,* 1394–1413.

Freilich, J. D., Chermak, S. M., & Caspi, D. (2009). Critical events in the life trajectories of domestic extremist white supremacist groups: A case study analysis of four violent organizations. *Criminology and Public Policy, 8,* 497–530.

Frick, P. J. (1998). Callous-unemotional traits and conduct problems: Applying the two-factor model of psychopathy to children. In D. J. Cooke, A. E. Forth, & R. D. Hare (Eds.), *Psychopathy: Theory, research and implications for society.* Boston: Kluwer Academic.

Frick, P. J. (2006). Developmental pathways to conduct disorder. *Child and Adolescent Psychiatric Clinics of North America, 15,* 311–331.

Frick, P. J. (2009). Extending the construct of psychopathy to youth: Implications for understanding, diagnosing, and treating antisocial children and adolescents. *Canadian Journal of Psychiatry, 54,* 803–812.

Frick, P. J., Barry, C. T., & Bodin, S. D. (2000). Applying the concept of psychopathy to children: Implications for the assessment of antisocial youth. In C. B. Gacono (Ed.), *The clinical and forensic assessment of psychopathy* (pp. 3–24). Mahwah, NJ: Erlbaum.

Frick, P. J., Bodin, S. D., & Barry, C. T. (2000). Psychopathic traits and conduct problems in community and clinic-referred samples of children: Further development of the psychopathy screening device. *Psychological Assessment, 12,* 382–393.

Frick, P. J., & Hare, R. D. (2001). *The Antisocial Process Screening Device.* Toronto, ON: Multi-Health Systems.

Frick, P. J., & Morris, A. S. (2004). Temperament and developmental pathways to conduct problems. *Journal of Clinical Child and Adolescent Psychology, 33,* 54–68.

Frick, P. J., O'Brien, B. S., Wootton, J., & McBurnett, K. (1994). Psychopathy and conduct problems in children. *Journal of Abnormal Psychology, 103,* 700–707.

Friel, A., White, T., & Hull, A. (2008). Posttraumatic Stress Disorder and criminal responsibility. *The Journal of Forensic Psychiatry & Psychology, 19,* 64–85.

Frieze, I. H., & Browne, A. (1989). Violence in marriage. In L. Ohlin & M. Tonry (Eds.), *Family violence* (Vol. 11). Chicago: University of Chicago Press.

Frintner, M., & Rubinson, L. (1993). Acquaintance rape: The influence of alcohol, fraternity membership and sports team membership. *Journal of Sex Education and Therapy, 19,* 272–284.

Fung, M. T., Raine, A., Loeber, R., Lynam, D. R., Steinhauser, S. R., Venables, P. H., & Stouthamer-Loeber, M. (2005). Reduced electrodermal activity in pychopathy-prone adolescents. *Journal of Abnormal Psychology, 114,* 187–196.

Funk, J. B., Baldacci, H. B., Pasold, T., & Baumgarnder, J. (2004). Violence exposure in real-life, video games, television, movies, and the internet: Is there desensitization? *Journal of Adolescence, 27,* 23–39.

Furby, L., Weinrott, M. R., & Blackshaw, L. (1989). Sex offender recidivism: A review. *Psychological Bulletin, 105,* 3–30.

Fuselier, G. D. (1999, July). Placing the Stockholm syndrome in perspective. *FBI Law Enforcement Bulletin,* 9–12.

Fuselier, G. D., & Noesner, G. W. (1990, July). Confronting the terrorist hostage taker. *FBI Law Enforcement Bulletin,* 6–11.

Gabrielli, W. F., & Mednick, S. A. (1983). Genetic correlates of criminal behavior. *American Behavioral Scientist, 27,* 59–74.

Gacono, C. B., Nieberding, R. J., Owen, A., Rubel, J., & Bodholdt, R. (1997). Treating conduct disorder, antisocial, and psychopathic personalities. In J. B. Ashford, B. D. Sales, & W. H. Reid (Eds.), *Treating adult and juvenile offenders with special needs.* Washington, DC: American Psychological Association.

Gacono, C. B., Nieberding, R. J., Owen, A., Rubel, J., & Bodholdt, R. (2001). Treating conduct disorder, antisocial, and psychopathic personalities. In J. B. Ashford, B. D. Sales, & W. H. Reid (Eds.), *Treating adult and juvenile offenders with special needs.* Washington, DC: American Psychological Association.

Galovski, T. E., & Blanchard, E. B. (2002). The effectiveness of a brief psychological intervention on court-referred and self-referred aggressive drivers. *Behavior and Research Therapy, 40,* 1385–1402.

Ganley, A. L., & Schechter, S. (1996). *Domestic violence: A national curriculum for children's protective services.* San Francisco: Family Violence Prevention Fund.

Gannon, T. A., & Polaschek, D. L. L. (2006). Cognitive distortions in child molesters: A re-examination of key theories and research. *Clinical Psychology Review, 26,* 1000–1019.

Gannon, T. A., & Rose, M. R. (2008). Female child sexual offenders: Towards integrating theory and practice. *Aggression and Violent Behavior, 13,* 442–461.

Gannon, T. A., Ward, T., & Collie, R. (2007). Cognitive distortions and child molesters: Theoretical and research developments over the past two decades. *Aggression and Violent Behavior, 12*, 402–416.

Gao, Y., Glenn, A. L., Schug, R. A., Yang, Y., & Raine, A. (2009). The neurobiology of psychopathy: A neuro-developmental perspective. *The Canadian Journal of Psychiatry, 54*, 813–823.

Garbarino, J. (1989). The incidence and prevalence of child maltreatment. In L. Ohlin & M. Tonry (Eds.), *Family violence* (Vol. 11). Chicago: University of Chicago Press.

Garbarino, J., & Asp, C. E. (1981). *Successful schools and competent students.* Lexington, MA: Lexington Books.

Garcia, M. M., Shaw, D. S., Winslow, E. B., & Yaggi, K. E. (2000). Destructive sibling conflict and the development of conduct problems in young boys. *Developmental Psychology, 36*, 44–53.

Garcia-Retamero, R., & Dhami, M. K. (2009). Take-the-best in expert-novice decision strategies for residential burglary. *Psychonomic Bulletin & Review, 16*, 163–169.

Gardner, T. J. (1985). *Crime law: Principles and cases.* St. Paul, MN: West Publishing.

Garofalo, J. (1977). *Public opinion about crime: The attitudes of victims and nonvictims in selected cities.* Washington, DC: USGPO.

Garside, R. B., & Klimes-Dougan, B. (2002). Socialization of discrete negative emotions: Gender differences and links with psychological distress. *Sex Roles: A Journal of Research, 14*, 115–129.

Gaynor, J. (1996). Firesetting. In M. Lewis (Ed.), *Child and adolescent psychiatry: A comprehensive textbook.* Baltimore, MD: Williams & Wilkins.

Geis, G. (1988). From Deuteronomy to deniability: A historical perlustration on white-collar crime. *Justice Quarterly, 5*, 7–32.

Geis, G. (1997). Preface. In G. Green, *Occupational crime* (2nd ed.). Chicago: Nelson-Hall.

Gelles, R. J. (1982). Domestic criminal violence. In M. E. Wolfgang & N. A. Weiner (Eds.), *Criminal violence.* Beverly Hills, CA: Sage.

Gelles, R. J. (1997). *Intimate violence in families.* Thousand Oaks, CA: Sage.

Gendreau, P., Little, T., & Goggin, C. (1996). A meta-analysis of the predictors of adult offender recidivism: What works! *Criminology, 34*, 575–607.

Gentile, D. A., & Walsh, D. A. (2002). A normative study of family media habits. *Journal of Applied Developmental Psychology, 23*, 157–178.

George, W. H., & Marlatt, G. A. (1989). Introduction. In D. R. Laws (Ed.), *Relapse prevention with sex offenders.* New York: Guilford Press.

Gerbner, G., Gross, L., Morgan, M., & Signorielli, N. (1981). Health and medicine on television. *The New England Journal of Medicine, 305*, 901–904.

Gerler, E. R., Jr. (2007). What the Amish taught us. *Journal of School Violence, 6*, 1–2.

Getz, J. G., & Bray, J. H. (2005). Predicting heavy alcohol use among adolescents. *American Journal of Orthopsychiatry, 75*, 102–116.

Gibbons, D. C. (1977). *Society, crime and criminal careers* (3rd ed.). Englewood Cliffs, NJ: Prentice Hall.

Gibbons, D. C. (1988). Some critical observation on criminal types and criminal careers. *Criminal Justice and Behavior, 15*, 8–23.

Giddan, J. J., Milling, L., & Campbell, N. B. (1996). Unrecognized language and speech deficits in pre-adolescent psychiatric patients. *American Journal of Orthopsychiatry, 66*, 85–92.

Gidycz, C. A., McNamara, J. R., & Edwards, K. M. (2006). Women's risk perception and sexual victimization: A review of the literature. *Aggression and Violence Behavior, 11*, 441–456.

Gini, G. (2006). Social cognition and moral cognition in bullying: What's wrong? *Aggressive Behavior, 32*, 528–539.

Glaze, J. A. (2007, October). *Opium and Afghanistan: Reassessing U.S. counternarcotics strategy.* Calisle, PA: U. S. Army War College, Strategic Studies Institute.

Glenny, M. (2011). *Darkmarket: Cyberthieves, cybercops, and you.* New York: Knopf.

Glueck, S., & Glueck, E. (1950). *Unraveling juvenile delinquency.* New York: Harper & Row.

Goetting, A. (1993). Patterns of homicide among children. In A. V. Wilson (Ed.), *Homicide: The victim/offender connection.* Cincinnati, OH: Anderson.

Gogtay, N, & Thompson, P. M. (2010). Mapping gray matter development: Implications for typical development and vulnerability to psychopathology. *Brain and Cognition, 72,* 6–15.

Gold, M. S. (1984*). 800-cocaine.* New York: Bantam.

Golding, S. L., Skeem, J. L., Roesch, R., & Zapf, P. A. (1999). The assessment of criminal responsibility: Current controversies. In I. B. Weiner & A. K. Hess (Eds.), *Handbook of forensic psychology* (2nd ed.). New York: Wiley.

Goldman, M. J. (1991). Kleptomania: Making sense of the nonsensical. *American Journal of Psychiatry, 148,* 986–995.

Goldstein, J. H. (1975). *Aggression and crimes of violence.* New York: Oxford University Press.

Goldstein, N. E., Arnold, D. H., Rosenberg, J. L., Stowe, R. M., & Ortiz, C. (2001). Contagion of aggression in day care classrooms as a function of peer and toddler responses. *Journal of Educational Psychology, 93,* 708–719.

Goldstein, P. J. (1985). The drugs-violence nexus: A tri-partite conceptual framework. *Journal of Drug Issues, 15,* 493–506.

Goles, T., Jayatilaka, B., George, B., Parsons, L., Chambers, V., Taylor, D., et al. (2008). Softlifting: Exploring determinants of attitude. *Journal of Business Ethics, 77,* 481–499.

Golub, A. L., & Johnson, B. D. (1997, July). *Crack's decline: Some surprises across U.S. cities.* NIJ Research in Brief. Washington, DC: U.S. Department of Justice.

Goodwill, A. J., Alison, L. J., & Beech, A. R. (2009). What works in offender profiling? A comparison of typological, thematic, and multivariate models. *Behavioral Sciences & the Law, 27,* 507–529.

Gooren, E. M. J. C., van Lier, P. A. C., Stegge, H., Terwogt, M. M., & Koot, H. M. (2011). The development of conduct problems and depressive symptoms in early elementary school children: The role of peer rejection. *Journal of Criminal Child & Adolescent Psychology, 40,* 245–253.

Gordon, R. (1983). An operational definition of prevention. *Public Health Reports, 98,* 107–109.

Gorman-Smith, D., & Loeber, R. (2005). Are developmental pathways in disruptive behaviors the same for girls and boys? *Journal of Child and Family Studies, 14,* 15–27.

Gorman-Smith, D., Tolan, P. H., Huesmann, L. R., & Zelli, A. (1996). The relation of family functioning to violence among inner-city minority youths. *Journal of Family Psychology, 10,* 115–129.

Gottfredson, G. D., Gottfredson, D. C., Payne, A. A., & Gottfredson, N. C. (2005). School climate predictors of school disorder: Results from a national study of delinquency prevention in schools. *Journal of Research in Crime and Delinquency, 42,* 412–444.

Gottfredson, M., & Hirschi, T. (1990). *A general theory of crime.* Stanford, CA: Stanford University Press.

Gottman, J. M. (2001). Crime, hostility, wife battering, and the heart: On the Meehan *et al.* (2001) failure to replicate the Gottman *et al.* (1995) typology. *Journal of Family Psychology, 15,* 409–414.

Gove, W. R., & Crutchfield, R. D. (1982). The family and delinquency. *Sociological Quarterly, 23,* 301–319.

Grafman, J., Schwab, K., Warden, D., Pridgen, A., Brown, H. R., & Salazar, A. M. (1996). Frontal lobe injuries, violence and aggression: A report of the Vietnam Head Injury Study. *Neurology, 46,* 1231–1238.

Grann, M. (2000). The PCL-R and gender. *European Journal of Psychological Assessment, 16,* 147–149.

Grant, V. (1977). *The menacing stranger.* New York: Dover.

Green, G. S. (1997). *Occupational crime* (2nd ed.). Chicago: Nelson-Hall.

Greendlinger, V., & Byrne, D. (1987). Coercive sexual fantasies of college men as predictors of self-reported likelihood to rape and overt sexual aggression. *Journal of Sex Research, 23,* 1–11.

Greenfeld, L. A. (1996, March). *Child victimization: Violent offenders and their victims.* Washington, DC: U.S. Department of Justice, Bureau of Justice Statistics.

Greenfeld, L. A. (1997, February). *Sex offenses and offenders: An analysis of data on rape and sexual assault.* Washington, DC: U.S. Department of Justice, Bureau of Justice Statistics.

Greenfeld, L. A. (1998, April). *Alcohol and crime: An analysis of national data on the prevalence of alcohol involvement in crime.* Washington, DC: U.S. Department of Justice.

Greenhouse, L. (2008, May 20). Supreme Court upholds child pornography law. *New York Times, 157,* pp. 54–316.

Gregorie, T. (2000). Workplace violence. In G. Coleman, M. Gaboury, M. Murray, & A. Seymour (Eds.), *1999 National Victim Assistance Academy.* Washington, DC: U.S. Department of Justice.

Gretton, H. M., McBride, M., Hare, R. D., O'Shaughnessy, R., & Kumka, G. (2001). Psychopathy and recidivism in adolescent sex offenders. *Criminal Justice and Behavior, 28,* 427–449.

Grimes, T., & Bergen, L. (2008). The epistemological argument against a causal relationship between media violence and sociopathic behavior among psychologically well viewers. *American Behavioral Scientist, 51,* 1137–1154.

Grisso, T. (1986). *Evaluating competencies: Forensic assessments and instruments.* New York: Plenum.

Grossman, D., & DeGaetano, G. (1999). *Stop teaching our kids to kill: A call to action against TV, movie and video game violence.* New York: Crown Publishing Group.

Groth, A. N. (1978). Patterns of sexual assault against children and adolescents. In A. W. Burgess, A. N. Groth, L. L. Holmstrom, & S. M. Sgroi (Eds.), *Sexual assault of children and adolescents.* Lexington, MA: Lexington Books.

Groth, A. N. (1979). *Men who rape: The psychology of the offender.* New York: Plenum.

Groth, A. N., & Burgess, A. W. (1977). Motivational intent in the sexual assault of children. *Criminal Justice and Behavior, 4,* 253–271.

Groth, A. N., Hobson, W. F., & Gary, T. S. (1982). The child molester: Clinical observation. *Journal of Social Work and Human Sexuality, 1,* 129–144.

Grubb, A. (2010). Modern day hostage (crisis) negotiation: The evolution of an art form within the policing arena. *Aggression and Violent Behavior, 15,* 341–348.

Guerra, N. G., Huesmann, L. R., Tolan, P. H., Van Acker, R., & Eron, L. D. (1995). Stressful events and individual beliefs as correlates of economic disadvantage and aggression among urban children. *Journal of Consulting and Clinical Psychology, 63,* 518–528.

Guerra, N., Tolan, P. H., & Hammond, W. R. (1994). Prevention and treatment of adolescent violence. In L. R. Eron, J. H., Gentry, & P. Schlegel (Eds.), *Reason to hope: A psychological perspective on violence and youth.* Washington, DC: American Psychological Association.

Gunter, B. (2008). Media violence: Is there a case for causality? *American Behavioral Scientist, 51,* 1061–1122.

Gurley, J. R. (2009). A history of changes to the criminal personality in the DSM. *History of Psychology, 4,* 285–304.

Gurley, J. R., & Marcus, D. K. (2008). The effects of neuroimaging and brain injury on insanity defenses. *Behavioral Sciences & the Law, 26,* 85–97.

Guymer, A. C., Mellor, D., Luk, E. S., & Pearse, V. (2001). The development of a screening questionnaire for childhood cruelty to animals. *Journal of Child Psychology and Psychiatry, 42,* 1057–1063.

Haapasalo, J., & Petäjä, S. (1999). Mothers who killed or attempted to kill their child: Life circumstances, childhood abuse, and types of killing. *Violence and Victims, 14,* 219–239.

Häkkänen, H., & Laajasalo, T. (2006). Homicide crime scene behaviors in a Finnish sample of mentally ill offenders. *Homicide Studies, 10,* 33–54.

Häkkänen, H., Puolakka, P., & Santtila, P. (2004). Crime scene actions and offender characteristics in arsons. *Legal and Criminological Psychology, 9,* 197–214.

Hald, G. M., Malamuth, N. M., & Yuen, C. (2010). Pornography and attitudes supporting violence against women: Revisiting the relationship in nonexperimental studies. *Aggressive Behavior, 36,* 14–20.

Hall, D. M. (1998). The victims of stalking. In J. R. Meloy (Ed.), *The psychology of stalking: Clinical and forensic perspectives.* San Diego, CA: Academic Press.

Hall, G. C. N. (1995). Sexual offender recidivism revisited: A meta-analysis of recent treatment studies. *Journal of Consulting and Clinical Psychology, 63,* 802–809.

Hall, G. C. N., Proctor, W. C., & Nelson, G. M. (1988). Validity of physiological measures of pedophilic sexual arousal in a sexual offender population. *Journal of Consulting and Clinical Psychology, 56,* 118–122.

Halleck, S. L. (1967). *Psychiatry and the dilemmas of crime.* New York: Harper & Row.

Hallett, B. (2004). Dishonest crimes, dishonest language: An argument about terrorism. In F. M. Moghaddam & A. J. Marsella (Eds.), *Understanding terrorism: Psychosocial roots, consequences, and interventions.* Washington, DC: American Psychological Association.

Hämäläinen, T., & Haapasalo, J. (1996). Retrospective reports of childhood abuse and neglect among violent and property offenders. *Psychology, Crime & Law, 3,* 1–13.

Hammond, W. R., & Yung, B. (1994). African Americans. In L. D. Eron, J. H. Gentry, & P. Schlegel (Eds.), *Reason to hope: A psychosocial perspective on violence and youth.* Washington, DC: American Psychological Association.

Hampson, J. E., Rahman, M. A., Brown, B., Taylor, M. E., & Donaldson, C. J. (1998). Project SELF: Beyond resilience. *Urban Education, 33,* 6–33.

Haney, C., & Zimbardo, P. (1998). The past and future of U.S. prison policy: Twenty-five years after the Stanford prison experiment. *American Psychologist, 53,* 709–727.

Haney, C. W. (1983). The good, the bad, and the lawful: An essay on psychological injustice. In W. S. Laufer & J. M. Day (Eds.), *Personality theory, moral development, and criminal behavior.* Lexington, MA: Lexington Books.

Hanfland, K. A., Keppel, R. D., & Weis, J. G. (1997, May). *Case management for missing children homicide investigation.* Washington, DC: U.S. Department of Justice, Office of Justice Programs.

Hanson, R. K. (2001). *Age and sexual recidivism: A comparison of rapists and child molesters.* Ottawa, ON: Solicitor General Canada.

Hanson, R. K. (2009). The psychological assessment of risk for crime and violence. *Canadian Psychology, 50,* 172–182.

Hanson, R. K., Bourgon, G., Helmus, L., & Hodgson, S. (2009). The principles of effective correctional treatment also apply to sexual offenders: A meta-analysis. *Criminal Justice and Behavior, 36,* 865–891.

Hanson, R. K., & Morton-Bourgon, K. E. (2005). The characteristics of persistent sexual offenders: A meta-analysis of recidivism studies. *Journal of Consulting and Clinical Psychology, 73,* 1154–1163.

Harbin, H. T., & Madden, D. J. (1979). Battered parents: A new syndrome. *American Journal of Psychiatry, 136,* 1288–1291.

Hare, R. D. (1965a). A conflict and learning theory analysis of psychopathic behavior. *Journal of Research in Crime and Delinquency, 2,* 12–19.

Hare, R. D. (1965b). Acquisition and generalization of a conditioned-fear response in psychopathic and nonpsychopathic criminals. *Journal of Psychology, 59,* 367–370.

Hare, R. D. (1968). Psychopathy, autonomic functioning, and the orienting response. *Journal of Abnormal Psychology, 73,* 1–24.

Hare, R. D. (1970). *Psychopathy: Theory and research.* New York: Wiley.

Hare, R. D. (1976). Anxiety, stress and psychopathy. In G. Shean (Ed.), *Dimensions in abnormal psychology.* Chicago: Rand McNally.

Hare, R. D. (1980). A research scale for the assessment of psychopathy in criminal populations. *Personality and Individual Differences, 1,* 111–119.

Hare, R. D. (1991). *The Hare Psychopathy Checklist-Revised.* Toronto, ON: Multi-Health Systems.

Hare, R. D. (1993). *Without conscience: The disturbing world of the psychopaths among us.* New York: Pocket Books.

Hare, R. D. (1996). Psychopathy: A clinical construct whose time has come. *Criminal Justice and Behavior, 23,* 25–54.

Hare, R. D. (1998). Emotional processing in psychopaths. In D. J. Cooke, R. D. Hare, & A. Forth (Eds.), *Psychopathy: Theory, research, and implications for society.* The Netherlands: Kluwer Academic Publishers.

Hare, R. D. (2003). *The Hare Psychopathy Checklist—Revised* (2nd ed.). Toronto, ON: Multi-Health Systems.

Hare, R. D., Clark, D., Grann, M., & Thornton, D. (2000). Psychopathy and the predictive validity of the PCL-R: An international perspective. *Behavioral Sciences & the Law, 18,* 623–645.

Hare, R. D., & Connolly, J. F. (1987). Perceptual asymmetries and information processing in psychopaths. In S. A. Mednick, T. E. Moffitt, & S. A. Stack (Eds.), *The causes of crime: New biological approaches.* Cambridge, UK: Cambridge University Press.

Hare, R. D., & Craigen, D. (1974). Psychopathy and physiological activity in a mixed-motive game. *Psychophysiology, 11,* 197–206.

Hare, R. D., Forth, A. E., & Stachan, K. E. (1992). Psychopathy and crime across the life span. In R. D. Peters, R. J. McMahon, & V. L. Quinsey (Eds.), *Aggression and violence throughout the life span.* Newbury Park, CA: Sage.

Hare, R. D., Hart, S. D., & Harpur, T. J. (1991). Psychopathy and the DSM-IV criteria for antisocial personality disorder. *Journal of Abnormal Psychology, 100,* 391–398.

Hare, R. D., & McPherson, L. M. (1984). Violent and aggressive behavior by criminal psychopaths. *International Journal of Law and Psychiatry, 7,* 35–50.

Hare, R. D., & Neumann, C. S. (2008). Psychopathy as a clinical and empirical construct. *Annual Review of Clinical Psychology, 4,* 217–246.

Hare, R. D., & Neumann, C. S. (2010). The role of antisociality in the psychopathy construct: Comment on Skeem and Cooke (2010). *Psychological Assessment, 22,* 446–454.

Hare, R. D., & Quinn, M. (1971). Psychopathy and autonomic conditioning. *Journal of Abnormal Psychology, 77,* 223–239.

Harenski, C. L., Harenski, K. A., Kiehl, K. A., & Shane, M. S. (2010). Aberrant neural processing of moral violations in criminal psychopaths. *Journal of Abnormal Psychology, 119,* 863–874.

Harmon, R. B., Rosner, R., & Wiederlight, M. (1985). Women and arson: A demographic study. *Journal of Forensic Sciences, 10,* 467–477.

Harpur, T. J., Hakstian, A., & Hare, R. D. (1988). Factor structure of the Psychopathy Checklist. *Journal of Consulting and Clinical Psychology, 56,* 741–747.

Harrell, E. (2011, March). *Workplace violence, 1993–2009.* Washington, DC: U.S. Department of Justice, Bureau of Justice Statistics.

Harris, A. J., Fisher, W., Veysey, B. M., Ragusa, L. M., & Lurigio, A. J. (2010). Sex offending and serious mental illness: Directions for policy and research. *Criminal Justice and Behavior, 37,* 596–612.

Harris, A. J., Lobanov-Rostovsky, C., & Levenson, J. S. (2010). Widening the net: The effects of transitions to the Adam Walsh Act's federally mandated sex offender classification system. *Criminal Justice and Behavior, 37,* 503–519.

Harris, A. J., & Lurigio, A. J. (2010). Special issue: Sex offenses and offenders: Toward evidence-based public policy. *Criminal Justice and Behavior, 37,* 503–519.

Harris, D. A., Mazerolle, P., & Knight, R. A. (2009). Understanding male sexual offending: A comparison of general and specialist theories. *Criminal Justice and Behavior, 36,* 1051–1069.

Hart, C. H., Nelson, A. A., Robinson, C. C., Olsen, S. F., & McNeilly-Choque, M. K. (1998). Overt and relational aggression in Russian nursery-school-age children: Parenting style and marital linkages. *Developmental Psychology, 34,* 687–697.

Hart, S. D., Cox, D. N., & Hare, R. D. (1995). *The Hare Psychopathy Checklist: Screening Version.* Toronto, ON: Multi-Health Systems.

Hart, S. D., & Dempster, R. J. (1997). Impulsivity and psychopathy. In C. D. Webster & M. A. Jackson (Eds.), *Impulsivity: Theory, assessment and treatment.* New York: Guilford.

Hart, S. D., & Hare, R. D. (1997). Psychopathy: Assessment and association with criminal conduct. In D. M. Stoff, J. P. Maser, & J. Breiling (Eds.), *Handbook of antisocial behavior.* New York: Wiley.

Hart, S. D., Hare, R. D., & Forth, A. E. (1993). Psychopathy as a risk marker for violence: Development and validation of a screening version of the Revised Psychopathy Checklist. In J. Monahan & H. Steadman (Eds.), *Violence and mental disorder: Development in risk assessment.* Chicago: University of Chicago Press.

Hastings, P. D., Zahn-Waxler, C., Usher, B., Robinson, J., & Bridges, D. (2000). The development of concern for others in children with behavior problems. *Developmental Psychology, 36,* 531–546.

Hawes, D. J., & Dadds, M. R. (2005). The treatment of conduct problems in children with callous-unemotional traits. *Journal of Consulting and Clinical Psychology, 73,* 737–741.

Hawkins, D. L., Pepler, D. J., & Craig, W. M. (2001). Naturalistic observations of peer interventions in bullying. *Social Development, 10,* 512–527.

Hawkins, S. R., Graham, P. W., Williams, J., & Zahn, M. A. (2009, January). *Resilient girls: Factors that protect against delinquency.* Washington, DC: U.S. Department of Justice, Office of Justice Programs.

Hebb, D. O. (1955). Drives and the C.N.S. (Conceptual Nervous System). *Psychological Review, 62,* 243–254.

Heckel, R. V., & Shumaker, D. M. (2001). *Children who murder: A psychological perspective.* Westport, CT: Praeger.

Heide, K. (1993). Adolescent parricide offenders: Synthesis, illustration and future directions. In A. V. Wilson (Ed.), *Homicide—the victim/offender connection.* Cincinnati, OH: Anderson.

Heide, K. M. (2003). Youth homicide: A review of the literature and blueprint for action. *International Journal of Offender Therapy and Comparative Criminology, 47,* 6–36.

Heide, K. M., Roe-Sepowitz, D., Solomon, E. P., & Chan, H. C. (2012). Male and female juveniles arrested for murder: A comprehensive analysis of U.S. data by offender gender. *International Journal of Offender Therapy and Comparative Criminology, 56,* 356–384.

Heide, K. M., Solomon, E. P., Sellers, B. G., & Chan, H. C. (2011). Male and female juvenile homicide offenders: An empirical analysis of U.S. arrests by offender age. *Feminist Criminology, 6,* 3–31.

Heilbrun, K., DeMatteo, D., Yasuhara, K., Brooks-Holliday, S., Shah, S., King, C., DiCarlo, A. B., Hamilton, D., & LaDuke, C. (2012). Community-based alternatives for justice-involved individuals with severe mental illness: Review of the relevant research. *Criminal Justice and Behavior, 39,* 351–419.

Heilbrun, K., Douglas, K. S., & Yasuhara, K. (2009). Violence risk assessment: Core controversies. In J. L. Skeem, K. S. Douglas, & S. O. Lilienfeld (Eds.), *Psychological science in the courtroom: Consensus and controversies* (pp. 333–357). New York: The Guilford Press.

Hellmich, C. (2008). Creating the ideology of Al Qaeda: From hypocrites to Salafi-Jihadists. *Studies in Conflict & Terrorism, 31,* 111–124.

Hemphill, J. F., & Hare, R. D. (2004). Some misconceptions about the Hare PCL-R and risk assessment: A reply to Gendreau, Goggin, and Smith. *Criminal Justice and Behavior, 31,* 203–243.

Hemphill, J. F., Hare, R. D., & Wong, S. (1998). Psychopathy and recidivism: A review. *Legal and Criminological Psychology, 3,* 139–170.

Hendricks, N. J., Ortiz, C. W., Sugie, N., & Miller, J. (2007). Beyond the numbers: Hate crimes and cultural trauma within Arab American immigrant communities. *International Review of Victiminology, 14,* 95–113.

Henggeler, S. W. (1996). Treatment of violent juvenile offenders—we have the knowledge. *Journal of Family Psychology, 10,* 137–141.

Henggeler, S. W. (2011). Efficacy studies to large-scale transport: The development and validation of multi-systemic therapy programs. *Annual Review of Clinical Psychology, 7,* 351–381.

Henggeler, S. W., & Borduin, C. M. (1990). *Family therapy and beyond: A multisystemic approach to treating the behavior problems of children and adolescents.* Pacific Grove, CA: Brooks/Cole.

Henggeler, S. W., Letourneau, E. J., Chapman, J. E., Borduin, C. M., Schewe, P. A., & McCart, M. R. (2009). Mediators of change for multisystemic therapy with juvenile sex offenders. *Journal of Consulting and Clinical Psychology, 77,* 451–462.

Henggeler, S. W., Melton, G. B., & Smith, L. A. (1992). Family preservation using multisystemic therapy—an effective alternative to incarcerating serious juvenile offenders. *Journal of Consulting and Clinical Psychology, 60,* 953–961.

Henggeler, S. W., Melton, G. B., Smith, L. A., Schoenwald, S. K., & Hanley, J. (1993). Family preservation using multisystemic therapy: Long-term follow-up to a clinical trial with serious juvenile offenders. *Journal of Child and Family Studies, 2,* 283–293.

Henker, B., & Whalen, C. K. (1989). Hyperactivity and attention deficits. *American Psychologist, 44,* 216–244.

Henn, F. A., Herjanic, M., & Vanderpearl, R. H. (1976a). Forensic psychiatry: Profiles of two types of sex offenders. *American Journal of Psychiatry, 133,* 694–696.

Henn, F. A., Herjanic, M., & Vanderpearl, R. H. (1976b). Forensic psychiatry: Diagnosis of criminal responsibility. *The Journal of Nervous and Mental Disease, 162,* 423–429.

Henry, B., Caspi, A., Moffitt, T. E., & Silva, P. A. (1996). Temperament and familial predictors of violent and nonviolent criminal conviction: Age 3 to age 18. *Developmental Psychology, 32,* 614–623.

Henry, B. C., & Sanders, C. E. (2007). Bullying and animal abuse: Is there a connection? *Society and Animals, 15,* 107–126.

Hepburn, L. M., & Hemenway, D. (2004). Firearm availability and homicide: A review of the literature. *Aggression and Violent Behavior, 9,* 417–429.

Hepworth, W., & Towler, A. (2004). The effects of individual differences and charismatic leadership on workplace aggression. *Journal of Occupational Health Psychology, 9,* 176–185.

Herpertz, S. C., & Sass, H. (2000). Emotional deficiency and psychopathy. *Behavioral Sciences & the Law, 18,* 567–580.

Hetherington, E. M., & Parke, R. D. (1975). *Child psychology: A contemporary viewpoint.* New York: McGraw-Hill.

Hewitt, C. (2003). *Understanding terrorism in America: From the Klan to al Qaeda.* New York: Routledge.

Hickey, E. (1991). *Serial killers and their victims.* Pacific Grove, CA: Brooks/Cole.

Hickey, E. W. (1997). *Serial murderers and their victims* (2nd ed.). Belmont, CA: Wadsworth.

Hickey, E. W. (2006). Serial murderers and their victims (9th ed.). Belmont, CA: Thomson/Wadsworth.

Hickey, E. W. (2010). *Serial murderers and their victims* (5th ed.). Belmont, CA: Wadsworth/Cengage Learning.

Hickle, K. E., & Roe-sepowitz, D. E. (2010). Female juvenile arsonists: An exploratory look at characteristics and solo and group arson offences. *Legal and Criminological Psychology, 15,* 385–399.

Higgins, G. E., Piquero, N. L., & Piquero, A. R. (2011). General Strain Theory, peer rejection, and delinquency/crime. *Youth & Society, 43,* 1272–1297.

Hill, H. M., Soriano, F. I., Chen, S. A., & LaFromboise, T. D. (1994). Sociocultural factors in the etiology and prevention of violence among ethnic minority youth. In L. D. Eron, J. H. Gentry, & P. Schlegel (Eds.), *Reason to hope: A psychosocial perspective on violence and youth.* Washington, DC: American Psychological Association.

Hill, L. G., Lochman, J. E., Coie, J. D., & Geenberg, M. T. (2004). Effectiveness of early screening for externalizing problems: Issues of screening accuracy and utility. *Journal of Consulting and Clinical Psychology, 72,* 809–820.

Hill, N. E., Castellino, D. R., Lansford, J. E., Nowlin, P., Dodge, K. A., Bates, J. E., et al. (2004). Parent-academic involvement as related to school behavior, achievement, and aspirations: Demographic variations across adolescence. *Child Development, 75,* 1491–1509.

Hill, P. (1960). *Portrait of a sadist.* New York: Avon.

Hill, R. W., Langevin, R., Paitich, D., Handy, L., Russon, A., & Wilkinson, L. (1982). Is arson an aggressive act or a property offense? *Canadian Journal of Psychiatry, 27,* 648–654.

Hillbrand, M., Alexandre, J. W., Young, J. L., & Spitz, R. T. (1999). Parricide: Characteristics of offenders and victims, legal factors, and treatment issues. *Aggression and Violent Behavior, 4,* 179–190.

Hindelang, M. J. (1974). Decisions of shoplifting victims to invoke the criminal justice process. *Social Process, 21,* 580–593.

Hinduja, S. (2008). Deindividuation and Internet software piracy. *Cybercrime and Behavior, 11,* 391–398.

Hinduja, S., & Patchin, J. (2008). Cyberbullying: An exploratory analysis of factors related to offending and victimization. *Deviant Behavior, 29,* 129–156.

Hindujua, S., & Patchin, J. (2012). *A brief review of state cyberbullying laws and policies.* Cyberbullying Research Center. Available: www.cyberbullying.us

Hinshaw, S. P. (1992). Externalizing behavior problems and academic underachievement in childhood and adolescence: Causal relationships and underlying mechanisms. *Psychological Bulletin, 111,* 127–155.

Hirschi, T. (1969). *Causes of delinquency.* Berkeley: University of California Press.

Hirschi, T., & Hindelang, M. J. (1977). Intelligence and delinquency. *American Sociological Review, 42,* 571–587.

Hochstedler, E. (Ed.). (1984). *Corporations as criminals.* Beverly Hills, CA: Sage.

Hockenbury, D. H., & Hockenbury, S. E. (2004). *Discovering psychology* (3rd ed.). New York: Worth.

Hodgins, S. (2001). The major mental disorders and crime: Stop debating and start treating and preventing. *International Journal of Law and Psychiatry, 24,* 427–446.

Hodgins, S., Cree, A., & Mak, T. (2008). From conduct disorder to severe mental illness: Associations with aggressive behaviour, crime and victimization. *Psychological Medicine, 38,* 975–987.

Hoeve, M., Smeenk, W., Loeber, R., Stouthamer-Loeber, M., van der Laan, P. H., Gerris, J. R. M., **et al.** (2007). Long-term effects of parenting and family characteristics on delinquency of male young adults. *European Journal of Criminology, 4*, 161–194.

Hoffman, B. (1993). *"Holy terror": The implications of terrorism motivated by a religious imperative* (RAND Research Paper P-7834). Santa Monica, CA: RAND.

Hoffman, B. (2002). Rethinking terrorism and counterterrorism since 9/11. *Studies in Conflict and Terrorism, 25*, 303–316.

Hoffman, K. L., Kiecolt, K. J., & Edwards, J. N. (2005). Physical violence between siblings: A theoretical and empirical analysis. *Journal of Family Issues, 26*, 1103–1130.

Hoge, C. W., Terhakopian, A., Castro, C. A., Messer, S. C., & Engel, C. C. (2007). Association of posttraumatic stress disorder with somatic symptoms, health care visits, and absenteeism among Iraq war veterans. *American Journal of Psychiatry, 164*, 150–153.

Hoge, S. K., Poythress, N., Bonnie, R., Eisenberg, M., Monahan, J., Feucht-Haviar, T., & Oberlander, L. (1996). Mentally ill and non-mentally ill defendants' abilities to understand information relevant to adjudication: A preliminary study. *Bulletin of the American Academy of Psychiatry and the Law, 24*, 187–197.

Hoge, S. K., Poythress, N., Bonnie, R., Monahan, J., Eisenberg, M., & Feucht-Haviar, T. (1997). The MacArthur adjudicative competence study: Diagnosis, psychopathology, and competence-related abilities. *Behavioral Sciences & the Law, 15*, 329–345.

Holder, E. (2012, January). Attorney General Eric Holder announces revisions to the Uniform Crime Report's definition of rape. *FBI National Press Release*, Washington, DC.

Hollinger, R. (1986). Acts against the workplace: Social bonding and employee deviance. *Deviant Behavior, 7*, 53–75.

Hollister-Wagner, G. H., Foshee, V. A., & Jackson, C. (2001). Adolescent aggression: Models of resilience. *Journal of Applied Social Psychology, 31*, 445–466.

Holmes, C. T. (1989). Grade level retention effects: A meta-analysis of research studies. In L. A. Shepard & M. L. Smith (Eds.), *Flunking grades: Research and policies on retention*. Philadelphia: Falmer Press.

Holmes, S. T., Hickey, E., & Holmes, R. M. (1991). Female serial murderesses: Constructing differentiating typologies. *Journal of Contemporary Criminal Justice, 7*, 245–256.

Holt, S. E., Meloy, J. R., & Stack, S. (1999). Sadism and psychopath in violent and sexual violent offenders. *Journal of the American Academy of Psychiatry and Law, 27*, 23–32.

Holtzworth-Monroe, A., & Stuart, G. L. (1994). Typologies of male batterers: Three subtypes and the differences among them. *Psychological Bulletin, 116*, 476–497.

Homant, R. J., & Kennedy, D. B. (1998). Psychological aspects of crime scene profiling: Validity research. *Criminal Justice and Behavior, 25*, 319–343.

Home Office. (1986). *Criminal statistics: England and Wales 1985*. London: HMSO.

Honomichl, R. D., & Donnellan, M. B. (2012). Dimensions of temperament in preschoolers predict risk taking and externalizing behaviors in adolescents. *Social Psychological and Personality Science, 3*, 14–22.

Horgan, J. (2005). *The psychology of terrorism*. London: Routledge.

Horning, D. N. M. (1970). Blue-collar theft: Conceptions of property, attitudes toward pilfering, and work group norms in a modern industrial plant. In E. O. Smigel & H. L. Ross (Eds.), *Crimes against bureaucracy*. New York: Van Nostrand Reinhold.

Hornung, C. A., McCullough, B. C., & Sugimoto, T. (1981). Status relationships in marriage: Risk factors in spouse abuse. *Journal of Marriage and the Family, 43*, 675–692.

Hotaling, G. T., & Straus, M. A. (1989). Intrafamily violence, and crime and violence outside the family. In L. Ohlin & M. Tonry (Eds.), *Family violence* (Vol. 11). Chicago: University of Chicago Press.

Hubbard, J. A., Dodge, K. A., Cillessen, A. H. N., Coie, J. D., & Schwartz, D. (2001). The dyadic nature of social information processing in boys' reactive and proactive aggression. *Journal of Personality and Social Psychology, 80*, 268–280.

Hudson, M. I. (1986). Elder maltreatment: Current research. In K. A. Pillemer & R. S. Wolf (Eds.), *Elder abuse: Conflict in the family*. Dover, MA: Auburn House.

Huesmann, L. R. (1988). An information processing model for the development of aggression. *Aggressive Behavior, 14,* 13–24.

Huesmann, L. R. (1997). Observational learning of violent behavior: Social and biosocial processes. In A. Raine, P. A. Brennan, D. P. Farrington, & S. A. Mednick (Eds.), *Biosocial bases of violence.* New York: Plenum.

Huesmann, L. R. (1998). The role of social information processing and cognitive schema in the acquisition and maintenance of habitual aggressive behavior. In R. G. Geen & E. Donnerstein (Eds.), *Human aggression: Theories, research, and implications for social policy.* San Diego, CA: Academic Press.

Huesmann, L. R. (2007). The impact of electronic media violence: Scientific theory and research. *Journal of Adolescent Health, 41,* Supplement, S6–S13.

Huesmann, L. R., Dubow, E. F., & Boxer, P. (2011). The transmission of aggressiveness across generations: Biological, contextual, and social learning processes. In P. R. Shaver & M. Mikulincer (Eds.), *Human aggression and violence: Causes, manifestations, and consequences* (pp. 123–142). Washington, DC: American Psychological Association.

Huesmann, L. R., Moise-Titus, J., Podolski, C., & Eron, L. D. (2003). Longitudinal relations between children's exposure to TV violence and their aggressive and violent behavior in young adulthood: 1977–1992. *Developmental Psychology, 39,* 201–221.

Hughes, H. M. (1988). Psychological and behavioral correlates of family violence in child witnesses and victims. *American Journal of Orthopsychiatry, 58,* 77–90.

Hughes, H. M., & Barad, S. J. (1983). Psychological functioning of children in a battered women's shelter: A preliminary investigation. *American Journal of Orthopsychiatry, 53,* 525–531.

Hughes, H. M., Parkinson, D., & Vargo, M. (1989). Witnessing spouse abuse and experiencing physical abuse: A "double whammy"? *Journal of Family Violence, 4,* 197–209.

Huizinga, D., & Jakob-Chien, C. (1998). The contemporaneous co-occurrence of serious and violent juvenile offending and other problem behaviors. In R. Loeber & D. P. Farrington (Eds.), *Serious & violent juvenile offenders: Risk factors and successful interventions.* Thousand Oaks, CA: Sage.

Hunter, J. A., & Becker, J. V. (1999). Motivators of adolescent sex offenders and treatment perspectives. In J. Shaw (Ed.), *Sexual aggression.* Washington, DC: American Psychiatric Press.

Hunter, J. A., & Figueredo, A. J. (1999). Factors associated with treatment compliance in a population of juvenile sex offenders. *Sex Abuse: A Journal of Research and Treatment, 11,* 49–67.

Hunter, J. A., Figueredo, A. J., Malamuth, N. M., & Becker, J. V. (2003). Juvenile sex offenders: Toward the development of a typology. *Sexual Abuse: A Journal of Research and Treatment, 15,* 27–48.

Hutchings, B., & Mednick, S. A. (1975). Registered criminality in the adoptive and biological parents of registered male criminal adoptees. In R. R. Fieve, D. Rosenthal, & H. Brill (Eds.), *Genetic research in psychiatry.* Baltimore, MD: Johns Hopkins University Press.

Icove, D. J., & Estepp, M. H. (1987, April). Motive-based offender profiles of arson and fire-related crime. *FBI Law Enforcement Bulletin,* 17–23.

Inciardi, J. A. (1970). The adult firesetter, a typology. *Criminology, 3,* 145–155.

Inciardi, J. A. (1981). Crime and alternative patterns of substance abuse. In S. E. Gardner (Ed.), *Drug and alcohol abuse.* Rockville, MD: National Institute on Drug Abuse.

Inciardi, J. A. (1986). *The war on drugs: Heroin, cocaine, crime and public policy.* Palo Alto, CA: Mayfield Publishing.

The Informant. (2003). Newsletter of National White Collar Crime Center (August issue). Richmond, VA: National White Collar Crime Center.

Ingram, G. L., Gerard, R. E., Quay, H. C., & Levison, R. B. (1970). An experimental program for the psychopathic delinquent: Looking in the "correctional wastebasket." *Journal of Research in Crime and Delinquency, 7,* 24–30.

Internet Crime Complaint Center. (2008). *Annual report on Internet crime.* Available: www.Ic3.gov

Internet Crime Complaint Center. (2011). *Annual report on Internet crime.* Washington, DC: U.S. Department of Justice.

Ishikawa, S. S., & Raine, A. (2004). Prefrontal deficits and antisocial behavior: A causal model. In B. B. Lahey,

T. E. Moffitt, & A. Caspi (Eds.), *Causes of conduct disorder and juvenile delinquency.* New York: Guilford.

Ishikawa, S. S., Raine, A., Lencz, T., Bihrle, S., & Lacasse, L. (2001). Autonomic stress reactivity and executive functions in successful and unsuccessful criminal psychopaths from the community. *Journal of Abnormal Psychology, 110,* 423–432.

Jackson, C., & Foshee, V. A. (1998). Violence-related behaviors of adolescents: Relations with responsive and demanding parenting. *Journal of Adolescent Research, 13,* 343–359.

Jackson, H. F., Glass, C., & Hope, S. (1987). A functional analysis of recidivistic arson. *British Journal of Clinical Psychology, 26,* 175–185.

Jackson, R. L., Neumann, C. S., & Vitacco, M. J. (2007). Impulsivity, anger, and psychopathy: The moderating effect of ethnicity. *Journal of Personality Disorders, 21,* 289–304.

Jackson, R. L., Rogers, R., Neumann, C. S., & Lambert, P. L. (2002). Psychopathy in female offenders: An investigation of its underlying dimensions. *Criminal Justice and Behavior, 29,* 692–704.

Jacobs, B. A., Topalli, V., & Wright, R. (2003). Carjacking, streetlife and offender motivation. *British Journal of Criminology, 43,* 673–688.

Jacobs, G. D., & Snyder, D. (1996). Frontal brain asymmetry predicts affective style in men. *Behavioral Neuroscience, 110,* 3–6.

Jaffee, S. R., Caspi, A., Moffitt, T. E., Dodge, K. A., Rutter, M., Taylor, A., et al. (2005). Nature x nurture: Genetic vulnerabilities interact with physical maltreatment to promote conduct problems. *Development and Psychopathology, 17,* 67–84.

Jaffee, S. R., Strait, L. B., & Odgers, C. L. (2012). From correlates to causes: Can quasi-experimental studies and statistical innovations bring us close to identifying the causes of antisocial behavior. *Psychological Bulletin, 136,* 279–295.

James, D. J., & Glaze, L. E. (2006, September). *Mental health problems of prison and jail inmates.* Washington, DC: U.S. Department of Justice, Bureau of Justice Statistics.

James, J. (1978). The prostitute as victim. In J. R. Chapman & M. Gates (Eds.), *The victimization of women.* Beverly Hills, CA: Sage.

Jarvis, G., & Parker, H. (1989). Young heroin users and crime. *British Journal of Criminology, 29,* 175–185.

Javelin Strategy & Research. (2012, February 22). *2011 Identity Fraud Survey Report.* Pleasanton, CA: Author.

Jeffrey, C. R. (1965). Criminal behavior and learning theory. *Journal of Criminal Law, Criminology and Police Science, 56,* 294–300.

Jenkins, P. (1988). Serial murder in England 1940–1985. *Journal of Criminal Justice, 16,* 1–15.

Jenkins, P. (1993). Chance or choice: The selection of serial murder victims. In A. V. Wilson (Ed.), *Homicide: The victim/offender connection.* Cincinnati, OH: Anderson.

Jenson, B. (1996 May). *Cyberstalking: Crime, enforcement and personal responsibility in the on-line world.* Available: www.law.ucla.edu/Classes/Archive.S96/340/cyberlaw.htm

Johns, J. H., & Quay, H. C. (1962). The effect of social reward on verbal conditioning in psychopathic military offenders. *Journal of Consulting Psychology, 26,* 217–220.

Johnsen, M. (2008, October 20). Pinched by economy retail crime on the rise. *Drug Store News,* pp. 1, 6, 42.

Johnson, R. (1996). *Hard time: Understanding and reforming the prison* (2nd ed.). Belmont, CA: Wadsworth.

Johnson, W. (2007). Genetic and environmental influences on behavior: Capturing all the interplay. *Psychological Review, 114,* 424–440.

Johnson, W., Turkheimer, E., Gottesman, I. I., & Bouchard, T. J. Jr. (2009). Beyond heritability: Twin studies in behavioral research. *Current Directions in Psychological Science, 18,* 217–220.

Johnston, L. D., O'Malley, P. M., Bachman, J. G., & Schulenberg, J. E. (2006). *Monitoring the future national results on adolescent drug use: Overview of key findings, 2005.* Bethesda, MD: National Institute on Drug Abuse.

Johnston, L. D., O'Malley, P. M., Bachman, J. G., & Schulenberg, J. E. (2011, December). *Monitoring the future: National results on adolescent drug use: Overview of key findings 2011.* Bethesda, MD: National Institute on Drug Abuse.

Joiner, T. E. (1994). Contagious depression: Existence, specificity to depressed symptoms, and the role of reassurance seeking. *Journal of Personality and Social Psychology, 67,* 287–296.

Joint, M. (1995, March). *Road rage.* Washington, DC: Automobile Association Group Public Policy Road Safety Unit.

Jolliffe, D., & Farrington, D. P. (2006). Examining the relationship between low empathy and bullying. *Aggressive Behavior, 32,* 540–550.

Jolliffe, D., & Farrington, D. P. (2007). Examining the relationship between low empathy and self-reported offending. *Legal and Criminological Psychology, 12,* 265–286.

Jones, C. A. (2002). Victim perspective of bank robbery trauma and recovery. *Traumatology, 8,* 191–204.

Jones, A. P., Laurens, K. R., Herba, C. M., Barker, G. J., & Viding, E. (2009). Amygdala hypoactivity to fearful faces in boys with conduct problems and callous-unemotional traits. *American Journal of Psychiatry, 166,* 95–102.

Jones, C., & Aronson, E. (1973). Attribution of fault to a rape victim as a function of respectability of the victim. *Journal of Personality and Social Psychology, 26,* 415–419.

Jones, J. G., Butler, H. L., Hamilton, B., Perdue, J. D., Stern, H. P., & Woody, R. C. (1986). Munchausen syndrome by proxy. *Child Abuse and Neglect, 10,* 33–40.

Jones, S., Cauffman, E., Miller, J. D., & Mulvey, E. (2006). Investigating different factor structures of the Psychopathy Checklist: Youth Version (PCL:YV) confirmatory factor analytic findings. *Psychological Assessment, 18,* 33–48.

Julien, R. M. (1975). *A primer of drug action.* San Francisco: W. H. Freeman.

Julien, R. M. (1992). *A primer of drug action* (6th ed.). New York: W. H. Freeman.

Junger, M., West, R., & Timman, R. (2001). Crime and risk behavior in traffic: An example of cross-situational consistency. *Journal of Research in Crime and Delinquency, 38,* 439–459.

Kafrey, D. (1980). Playing with matches: Children and fire. In D. Canter (Ed.), *Fires and human behaviour.* Chichester, UK: Wiley.

Kahn, R. E., Frick, P. J., Youngstrom, E., Findling, R. L., & Youngstrom, J. K. (2012). The effects of including a callous-unemotional specifier for the diagnosis of conduct disorder. *Journal of Child Psychology and Psychiatry, 53,* 271–282.

Kahn, T. J., & LaFond, M. A. (1988). Treatment of the adolescent sex offender. *Child and Adolescent Social Work, 5,* 135–148.

Kandel, D., Yamaguchi, K., & Chen, K. (1992). Stages of drug involvement from adolescence to adulthood: Further evidence for the gateway theory. *Journal of Studies on Alcohol, 53,* 447–457.

Kandel, E., Mednick, S. A., Kirkegaard-Sorenson, L., Hutchings, B., Knop, J., Rosenberg, R., & Schulsinger, F. (1988). IQ as a protective factor for subjects at high risk for antisocial behavior. *Journal of Consulting and Clinical Psychology, 56,* 224–226.

Kanin, E. J. (1984). Date rape: Unofficial criminals and victims. *Victimology, 9,* 95–108.

Karmen, A. (1996). *Crime victims: An introduction to victimology* (3rd ed.). Belmont, CA: Wadsworth.

Karmen, A. (2009). *Crime victims: An introduction to victimology* (7th ed.). Florence, KY: Cengage Learning.

Kazdin, A. E. (1987). Treatment of antisocial behavior in children: Current status and future directions. *American Psychologist, 48,* 127–141.

Kazdin, A. E. (1989). Developmental psychopathology: Current research, issues, and directions. *American Psychologist, 44,* 180–187.

Kelleher, M. D. (1997). *Profiling the lethal employee: Case studies of violence in the workplace.* Westport, CT: Praeger.

Kelleher, M. D., & Kelleher, C. L. (1998). *Murder most rate: The female serial killer.* Westport, CT: Dell Publishing.

Kelley, T. M., Kennedy, D. B., & Homant, R. J. (2003). Evaluation of an individualized treatment program for adolescent shoplifters. *Adolescence, 38,* 725–733.

Kelman, H. C., & Hamilton, V. L. (1989). *Crimes of obedience: Toward a social psychology of authority and responsibility.* New Haven, CT: Yale University Press.

Kendall, P. C., & Hammen, C. (1995). *Abnormal psychology.* Boston: Houghton Mifflin.

Kendler, K. S., Prescott, C. A., Myers, J., & Neale, M. C. (2003). The structure of genetic and environmental risk factors for common psychiatric and substance use disorders in men and women. *Archives of General Psychiatry, 60,* 929–937.

Kerlinger, F. (1973). *Foundations of behavioral research* (2nd ed.). New York: Holt, Rinehart & Winston.

Kerns, K. A., Aspelmeier, J. E., Gentzler, A. L., & Grabill, C. M. (2001). Parent-child attachment and monitoring in middle childhood. *Journal of Family Psychology, 15,* 69–71.

Kessler, R. C., Adler, L., Barkley, R., Biedereman, J., Conners, C. K.., Demler, O., et al. (2006). The prevalence and correlates of adult ADHD in the United States: Results from the National Comorbidity Survey Replication. *American Journal of Psychiatry, 163*(4), 716–723.

Kiehl, K. A. (2006). A cognitive neuroscience perspective on psychopathy: Evidence for paralimbic system dysfunction. *Psychiatry Research, 142,* 107–128.

Kiehl, K. A., Smith, A. M., Hare, R. D., Mendrek, A., Forster, B. B., Brink, J., et al. (2001). Limbic abnormalities in affective processing by criminal psychopaths as revealed by functional magnetic resonance imaging. *Biological Psychiatry, 50,* 677–684.

Kilgore, K., Snyder, J., & Lentz, C. (2000). The contribution of parental discipline, parental monitoring, and school risk to early-onset conduct problems in African American boys and girls. *Developmental Psychology, 36,* 835–845.

Kilmann, P. R., Sabalis, R. F., Gearing, M. L., Bukstel, L. H., & Scovern, A. W. (1982). The treatment of sexual paraphilias: A review of the outcome research. *Journal of Sex Research, 18,* 193–252.

Kilpatrick, D. G., Best, C. L., Saunders, B. E., & Veronen, L. J. (1988). Rape in marriage and in dating relationships: How bad is it for mental health? In R. A. Prentky & V. L. Quinsey (Eds.), *Human sexual aggression: Current perspectives.* New York: New York Academy of Sciences.

Kilpatrick, D. G., Resnick, H. S., Ruggiero, K. J., Conoscenti, L. M., & McCauley, J. (2007, February). *Drug-facilitated, incapacitated, and forcible rape: A national study.* Charleston, SC: Medical University of South Carolina.

Kilpatrick, D. G., Whalley, A., & Edmunds, C. (2000). Sexual assault. In A. Seymour, M. Murray, J. Sigmon, M. Hook, C. Edmunds, M. Gaboury, & G. Coleman (Eds.), *2000 National Victim Assistance Academy.* Washington, DC: U.S. Department of Justice.

Kilpatrick, D. G., Whalley, A., & Edmunds, C. (2002). Sexual assault. In A. Seymour, M. Murray, J. Sigmon, M. Hook, C. Edmunds, M. Gaboury, & G. Coleman (Eds.), *2002 National Victim Assistance Academy.* Washington, DC: U.S. Department of Justice.

Kim-Cohen, J., Caspi, A., Taylor, A., Williams, B., Newcombe, R., Craig, I. W., & Moffitt, T. E. (2006). MAOA, maltreatment, and gene-environment interaction predicting children's mental health: New evidence and a meta-analysis. *Molecular Psychiatry, 11,* 903–913.

Kim-Cohen, J., & Gold, A. L. (2009). Measured gene-environment interactions and mechanisms promoting resilient development. *Current Directions in Psychological Science, 18,* 138–142.

Kimonis, E R., Skeem, J. L., Cauffman, E., & Dimitrieva, J. (2011). Are secondary variants of juvenile psychopathy more reactively violent and less psychosocially mature than primary variants? *Law and Human Behavior, 35,* 381–391.

Kinports, K. (2002). Sex offenses. In K. L. Hall (Ed.), *The Oxford companion to American law.* New York: Oxford University Press.

Kinscherff, R. (2012, January). *A primer for mental health practitioners working with youth involved in the juvenile justice system.* Washington, DC: Technical Assistance Partnership for Child and Family Mental Health.

Kinsey, A. (1948). *Sexual behavior in the human male.* Philadelphia: Saunders.

Kinsey, A., Pomeroy, W., Martin, C., & Gebhard, P. (1953). *Sexual behavior in the human female.* Philadelphia: Saunders.

Kivivuori, J. (1998). Delinquent phases: The case of temporally intensified shoplifting behaviour. *British Journal of Criminology, 38,* 663–680.

Kivivuori, J. (2007). Crime by proxy: Coercion and altruism in adolescent shoplifting. *British Journal of Criminology, 47,* 817–833.

Klassen, D., & O'Connor, W. (1988). Crime, inpatient admissions, and violence among male mental patients. *International Journal of Law and Psychiatry, 11,* 305–312.

Klassen, D., & O'Connor, W. (1990). Assessing the risk of violence in released mental patients: A cross-validation study. *Psychological Assessment: A Journal of Consulting and Clinical Psychology, 1,* 75–81.

Klaus, P. (1999, March). *Carjackings in the United States, 1992–1996.* Washington, DC: U.S. Department of Justice, Bureau of Justice Statistics.

Klaus, P. (2000, January). *Crimes against persons age 65 or older, 1992–97* (NCJ 176352). Washington, DC: U.S. Department of Justice, Bureau of Justice Statistics.

Klaus, P. (2004, July). *Carjacking, 1993–2002.* Washington, DC: U.S. Department of Justice, National Crime Victimization Survey.

Kleber, H. D. (1988). Epidemic cocaine abuse: America's present, Britain's future. *British Journal of Addiction, 83,* 1359–1371.

Klemke, L. W. (1992). *The sociology of shoplifting: Boosters and snitches today.* Westport, CT: Praeger.

Klinteberg, B., Magnusson, D., & Schalling, D. (1989). Hyperactive behavior in childhood and adult impulsivity: A longitudinal study of male subjects. *Personality and Individual Differences, 10,* 43–50.

Knight, R. A. (1988). A taxonomic analysis of child molesters. In R. A. Prentky & V. L. Quinsey (Eds.), *Human sexual aggression: Current perspectives.* New York: New York Academy of Science.

Knight, R. A. (1989). An assessment of the concurrent validity of a child molester typology. *Journal of Interpersonal Violence, 4,* 131–150.

Knight, R. A. (1999). Validation of a typology for rapists. *Journal of Interpersonal Violence, 14,* 303–330.

Knight, R. A., Carter, D. L., & Prentky, R. A. (1989). A system for the classification of child molesters: Reliability and application. *Journal of Interpersonal Violence, 4,* 3–23.

Knight, R. A., & Prentky, R. A. (1987). The developmental antecedents and adult adaptations of rapist subtypes. *Criminal Justice and Behavior, 14,* 403–426.

Knight, R. A., & Prentky, R. A. (1990). Classifying sexual offenders: The development and corroboration of taxonomic models. In W. L. Marshall, D. R. Laws, & H. E. Barbaree (Eds.), *The handbook of sexual assault: Issues, theories, and treatment of the offender.* New York: Plenum.

Knight, R. A., & Prentky, R. A. (1993). Exploring characteristics for classifying juvenile sex offenders. In H. E. Barbaree, W. L. Marshall, & S. M. Hudson (Eds.), *The juvenile sex offender.* New York: Guilford.

Knight, R. A., Rosenberg, R., & Schneider, B. A. (1985). Classification of sexual offenders: Perspectives, methods, and validation. In A. W. Burgess (Ed.), *Rape and sexual assault.* New York: Garland.

Knight, R. A., & Sims-Knight, J. E. (2003). The development of antecedents of sexual coercion against women: Testing alternative hypotheses with structural equation modeling. *Annuals of the New York Academy of Science, 989,* 72–85.

Knight, R. A., & Sims-Knight, J. E. (2004). Testing an etiological model for male juvenile sexual offending against females. *Journal of Child Sexual Abuse, 13,* 33–55.

Knight, R. A., & Sims-Knight, J. (2011). Risk factors for sexual violence. In J. W. White, M. R. Koss, & A. F. Kazdin (Eds.), *Violence against women and children. Vol. 1. Mapping the terrain.* (pp. 125–150). Washington, DC: American Psychological Association.

Knight, R. A., Warren, J. I., Reboussin, R., & Soley, B. J. (1998). Predicting rapist type from crime-scene variables. *Criminal Justice and Behavior, 25,* 46–80.

Knoll, J. L. (2008). The psychological autopsy, Part I: Applications and methods. *Journal of Psychiatric Practice, 14,* 393–397.

Knoll, J. L. (2009). The psychological autopsy, Part II: Toward a standardized protocol. *Journal of Psychiatric Practice, 15,* 52–59.

Knopp, F. H., Rosenberg, J., & Stevenson, W. (1986). *Report on nationwide survey of juvenile and adult sex-offender treatment programs and providers.* Syracuse, NY: Safer Society Press.

Kochanska, G., Friesenborg, A. E., Lange, L. A., & Martel, M. M. (2004). Parents' personality and infants' temperament as contributors to their emerging relationship. *Journal of Personality and Social Psychology, 86,* 744–759.

Kocsis, R. N., Cooksey, R. W., & Irwin, H. J. (2002). Psychological profiling of offender characteristics from crime behaviors in serial rape offenses. *International Journal of Offender Therapy and Comparative Criminology, 46,* 144–169.

Koenen, M. A., & Thompson, J. W. (2008). Filicide: Historical review and prevention of child death by parent. *Infant Mental Health Journal, 29,* 61–75.

Kofler, M. J., McCart, M. R., Zajac, K., Ruggiero, K. J., Saunders, B. E., & Kilpatrick, D. G. (2011). Depression and delinquency covariation in an accelerated longitudinal sample of adolescents. *Journal of Consulting and Clinical Psychology, 79,* 458–469.

Kohlberg, L. (1976). Moral stages and moralization: The cognitive development approach. In T. Licona (Ed.), *Moral development and behavior*. New York: Holt, Rinehart, & Winston.

Kohlberg, L. (1977). The child as a moral philosopher. In CRM, *Readings in developmental psychology today*. New York: Random House.

Koivisto, H., & Haapasalo, J. (1996). Childhood maltreatment and adulthood in psychopathy in light of file-based assessments among mental state examinees. *Studies on Crime and Crime Prevention, 5*, 91–104.

Kokko, K., & Pulkkinen, L. (2005). Stability of aggressive behavior from childhood to middle age in women and men. *Aggressive Behavior, 31*, 485–497.

Kolko, D. (Ed). (2002). *Handbook on firesetting in children and youth*. Boston: Academic Press.

Kolko, D. J., & Kazdin, A. E. (1989). The children's firesetting interview with psychiatrically referred and nonreferred children. *Journal of Abnormal Child Psychology, 17*, 609–624.

Kolko, D. J., Kazdin, A. E., & Meyer, E. C. (1985). Aggression and psychopathology in childhood firesetters: Parent and child reports. *Journal of Consulting and Clinical Psychology, 53*, 377–385.

Kolko, D., & Pardini, D. A. (2010). ODD dimensions, ADHD, and callous-emotional traits as predictors of treatment respond in children with disruptive behavior disorders. *Journal of Abnormal Psychology, 119*, 713–725.

Kornhauser, R. R. (1978). *Social sources of delinquency*. Chicago: University of Chicago Press.

Koson, D. F., & Dvoskin, J. (1982). Arson: A diagnostic study. *Bulletin of the American Academy of Psychiatry and the Law, 10*, 39–49.

Koss, M. P., & Dinero, T. E. (1988). Predictors of sexual aggression among a national sample of male college students. In R. A. Prentky and V. L. Quinsey (Eds.), *Human sexual aggression: Current perspectives*. New York: New York Academy of Sciences.

Kosson, D. S. (1998). Divided visual attention to psychopathic and nonpsychopathic offenders. *Personality and Individual Differences, 24*, 373–391.

Kosson, D. S., Smith, S. S., & Newman, J. P. (1990). Evaluating the construct validity of psychopathy in black and white male inmates: Three preliminary studies. *Journal of Abnormal Psychology, 99*, 250–259.

Kosson, D. S., Suchy, Y., Mayer, A. R., & Libby, J. (2002). Facial affect recognition in criminal psychopaths. *Emotion, 2*, 398–411.

Kovacs, M. (1996). Presentation and course of major depressive disorder during childhood and later years of the life span. *Journal of the American Academy of Child and Adolescent Psychiatry, 35*, 705–715.

Kozol, H. L., Boucher, R. L., & Garofalo, P. F. (1972). The diagnosis and treatment of dangerousness. *Crime and Delinquency, 8*, 371–392.

Kraemer, G. W., Lord, W. D., & Heilbrun, K. (2004). Comparing single and serial homicide offenses. *Behavioral Sciences & the Law, 22*, 325–343.

Krahé, B. (2005). Predictors of women's aggressive driving behavior. *Aggressive Behavior, 31*, 537–546.

Krahé, B., & Möller, I. (2004). Playing violent electronic games, hostile attributional style, and aggression-related norms in German adolescents. *Journal of Adolescence, 27*, 53–69.

Kramer, R. C. (1984). Corporate criminality: The development of an idea. In E. Hochstedler (Ed.), *Corporations as criminals*. Beverly Hills, CA: Sage.

Krasnovsky, T., & Lane, R. (1998). Shoplifting: A review of the literature. *Aggression and Violence Behavior, 3*, 219–235.

Kratzer, L., & Hodgins, S. (1999). A typology of offenders: A test of Moffitt's theory among males and females from childhood to age 30. *Criminal Behavior and Mental Health, 9*, 57–73.

Krebs, C. P., Lindquist, C. H., Warner, T. D., Fisher, B. S., & Martin, S. L. (2007, December). *The Campus Sexual Assault (CSA) study: Final report*. Washington, DC: National Institute of Justice.

Kreider, R. M. (2008). *Current population reports: Living arrangements of children: 2004*. Washington, DC: U.S. Department of Commerce, Economics and Statistics Administration, U. S. Census Bureau.

Krisberg, B. (1992). Youth crime and its prevention: A research agenda. In I. M. Schwartz (Ed.), *Juvenile justice and public policy*. New York: Lexington Books.

Krisberg, B. (1995). The legacy of juvenile corrections. *Corrections Today, 57*, 122–126.

Krisberg, B., & Howell, J. C. (1998). The impact of the juvenile justice system and prospects for graduated sanctions in a comprehensive strategy. In R. Loeber & D. P. Farrington (Eds.), *Serious & violent juvenile offenders: Risk factors and successful interventions.* Thousand Oaks, CA: Sage.

Krisberg, B., & Schwartz, I. (1983). Rethinking juvenile justice. *Crime and Delinquency, 29,* 333–364.

Krohn, M. D., Akers, R. L., Radosevich, M. J., & Lanza-Kaduce, L. (1982). Norm qualities and adolescent drinking and drug behavior: The effects of norm quality and reference group on using and abusing alcohol and marijuana. *Journal of Drug Issues, 4,* 343–360.

Krueger, R. F., Caspi, A., Moffitt, T. E., White, J., & Stouthamer-Loeber, M. (1996). Delay of gratification, psychopathology, and personality: Is low self-control specific to externalizing problems? *Journal of Personality, 64,* 107–129.

Kruesi, M. J. P. (1979). Cruelty to animals and CSF 5HIAA. *Psychiatry Research, 28,* 115–116.

Kruesi, M. J. P., & Jacobsen, T. (1997). Serotonin and human violence: Do environmental mediators exist? In A. Raine, P. A. Brennan, D. P. Farrington, & S. A. Mednick (Eds.), *Biological bases of violence.* New York: Plenum.

Kruesi, M. J. P., Rapoport, J., Hamburger, S., Hibbs, E., Potter, W., Levane, M., et al. (1990). Cerebrospinal fluid monoamine metabolites, aggression, and impulsivity in disruptive behavior disorders of children and adolescents. *Archives of General Psychiatry, 47,* 419–426.

Kruger, T. H. C., & Schiffer, B. (2011). Neurocognitive and personality factors in homo- and heterosexual pedophiles and controls. *Journal of Sexual Medicine, 8,* 1650–1659.

Kruglanski, A. W., & Fishman, S. (2006). The psychology of terrorism: "Syndrome" versus "tool" perspectives. *Terrorism and Political Science, 18,* 193–215.

Kuhnley, E. J., Hendren, R. L., & Quinlan, D. M. (1982). *Journal of the American Academy of Child Psychiatry, 21,* 560–563.

Kulka, R. A., Schlenger, W. E., Fairbank, J. A., Jordan, B. K., Hough, R. L., Marmar, C. R., et al. (1991). Assessment of post-traumatic stress disorder in the community: Prospects and pitfalls from recent studies of Vietnam veterans. *Psychological Assessment: A Journal of Consulting and Clinical Psychology, 4,* 547–560.

Laajasalo, T., & Häkkänen, H. (2006). Excessive violence and psychotic symptomatology among homicide offenders with schizophrenia. *Criminal Behaviour and Mental Health, 16,* 242–253.

Lacourse, E., Nagin, D., Tremblay, R. E., Vitaro, F., & Claes, M. (2003). Developmental trajectories of boys' delinquent group membership and facilitation of violent behaviors during adolescence. *Development and Psychopathology, 15,* 183–197.

Lahey, B. B., Loeber, R., Hart, E. L., Frick, P. J., Applegate, B., Zhang, Q., Green, S. M., & Russo, M. (1995). Four-year longitudinal study of conduct disorder in boys: Patterns and predictors of persistence. *Journal of Abnormal Psychology, 104,* 83–93.

Lahey, B. B., & Waldman, I. D. (2003). A developmental propensity model of the origins of conduct problems during childhood and adolescence. In B. B. Lahey, T. E. Moffitt, and A. Caspi (Eds.), *Causes of conduct disorder and juvenile delinquency.* New York: Guilford.

Laird, R. D., Jordan, K., Dodge, K. A., Pettit, G. S., & Bates, J. E. (2001). Peer rejection in childhood, involvement with antisocial peers in early adolescence, and the development of externalizing problems. *Development and Psychopathology, 13,* 337–354.

Laird, R. D., Pettit, G. S., Bates, J. E., & Dodge, K. A. (2003). Parents' monitoring—relevant knowledge and adolescents' delinquent behavior: Evidence of correlated developmental changes and reciprocal influences. *Child Development, 74,* 752–768.

Laird, R. D., Pettit, G. S., Dodge, K. A., & Bates, J. E. (2005). Peer relationship antecedents of delinquent behavior in late adolescence: Is there evidence of demographic group differences in developmental processes. *Development and Psychopathology, 17,* 127–144.

Lamb, H. R., Weinberger, L. E., & Gross, B. H. (2004). Mentally ill persons in the criminal justice system: Some perspectives. *Psychiatric Quarterly, 75,* 107–126.

Lambie, I., McCardle, S., & Coleman, R. (2002). Where there's smoke there's fire: Firesetting behaviour in children and adolescents. *New Zealand Journal of Psychology, 31,* 73–79.

Lambie, I., & Randell, I. (2011). Creating a firestorm: A review of children who deliberately light fires. *Clinical Psychology Review, 31*, 307–327.

Lamontagne, Y., Boyer, R., Hetu, C., & Lacerte-Lamontagne, C. (2000). Anxiety, significant losses, depression, and irrational beliefs in first-offence shoplifters. *Canadian Journal of Psychiatry, 45*, 63–66.

Landy, D., & Aronson, E. (1969). The influence of the character of the criminal and his victim on the decisions of simulated jurors. *Journal of Experimental Social Psychology, 5*, 141–152.

Langan, P. A., Schmitt, E. L., & Durose, M. R. (2003, November). *Recidivism of sex offenders released from prison in 1994*. Washington, DC: U.S. Department of Justice, Bureau of Justice Statistics.

Lang, S., af Klinteberg, B., & Alm, P.-O. (2002). Adult pschopathy and violent behavior in males with early neglect and abuse. *Acta Pschiatrica Scandinavica, 106*, 93–100.

Langer, E. J., & Miransky, J. (1983). Burglary (non) prevention. In E. J. Langer (Ed.), *The psychology of control*. Beverly Hills, CA: Sage.

Langevin, R. (1983). *Sexual strands*. Hillsdale, NJ: Erlbaum.

Langton, C. M. (2012). Introduction to the special issue: Treatment considerations for aggressive adolescents in secure settings. *Criminal Justice and Behavior, 39*, 685–693.

Langton, L., & Baum, K. (2010, June). *Identity theft reported by households, 2007—statistical tables*. Washington, DC: U.S. Department of Justice, Bureau of Justice Statistics.

Langton, L., & Planty, M. (2011). *Hate crime, 2003–2009: Special Report*. Washington, DC: U.S. Department of Justice, Office of Justice Programs, Bureau of Justice Statistics.

Lansford, J. E., Deater-Deckard, K., Dodge, K. A., Bates, J. E., & Pettit, G. S. (2004). Ethnic differences in the link between physical discipline and later adolescent externalizing behaviors. *Journal of Child Psychology and Psychiatry, 45*, 801–812.

Lansford, J. E., Dodge, K. A., Pettit, G. S., Bates, J. E., Crozier, I., & Kaplow, J. (2002). Long-term effects of early child physical maltreatment on psychological, behavioral, and academic problems in adolescence: A 12-year prospective study. *Archives of Pediatrics and Adolescent Medicine, 156*, 824–830.

Lanyon, R. I. (1986). Theory and treatment in child molestation. *Journal of Consulting and Clinical Psychology, 54*, 176–182.

Larkin, R. W. (2009). The Columbine legacy: Rampage shootings as political acts. *American Behavioral Scientist, 52*, 1309–1326.

Law, D. R., Hudson, S. W., & Ward, T. (2002). Remaking relapse prevention with sex offenders: A sourcebook and practice standards and guidelines for members of the Association for the Treatment of Sexual Abusers (ATSA). *Journal of Psychiatry and Law, 30*, 285–292.

Leach, E. (1973). Don't say "boo" to a goose. In A. Montagu (Ed.), *Man and aggression* (2nd ed.). London: Oxford University Press.

Leary, M. R., Kowalski, R. M., Smith, L., & Phillips, S. (2003). Teasing, rejection, and violence: Case studies of the school shootings. *Aggressive Behavior, 29*, 202–214.

Le Blanc, M., & Loeber, R. (1998). Developmental criminology updated. In M. Tonry (Ed.), *Crime and justice: A review of research* (pp. 115–198). Chicago: The University of Chicago Press.

Lee, J. K. P., Jackson, H. J., Pattison, P., & Ward, T. (2002). Developmental risk factors for sexual offending. *Child Abuse and Neglect, 26*, 73–92.

Leiner, A. S., Kearns, M. C., Jackson, J. L., Astin, M. C., & Rothbaum, B. O. (2012). Avoidant coping and treatment outcome in rape-related posttraumatic stress disorder. *Journal of Consulting and Clinical Psychology, 80*, 317–321.

Lemon, N. K. D. (1994, December). *Domestic violence & stalking: A comment on the Model Anti-Stalking Code proposed by the National Institute of Justice*. Duluth, MN: Battered Women's Justice Project.

Lenhart, A., Kahne, J., Middaugh, E., Macgill, A. R., Evans, C., & Vitak, J. (2008). *Teens, video games, and civics*. (Report No. 202-415-4500). Washington, DC: Pew Internet and American Life Project.

Lerner, M. J. (1980). *The belief in a just world: A fundamental delusion*. New York: Plenum.

Lerner, M. J., & Miller, D. T. (1978). Just world research and the attribution process: Looking back and ahead. *Psychological Bulletin, 85*, 1030–1051.

Lerner, M. J., & Simmons, C. H. (1966). Observer's reaction to the "innocent victim": Compassion or rejection? *Journal of Personality and Social Psychology, 4,* 203–210.

Lesch, K. P., & Merschdorf, U. (2000). Impulsivity, aggression, and serotonin: A molecular psychobiological perspective. *Behavioral Sciences & the Law, 18,* 581–604.

Letkemann, P. (1973). *Crime as work.* Englewood Cliffs, NJ: Prentice Hall.

Letourneau, E. J., & Miner, M. H. (2005). Juvenile sex offenders: A case against the legal and clinical status quo. *Sexual Abuse: A Journal of Research and Treatment, 17,* 293–312.

Levant, R. F. (2002). Psychology responds to terrorism. *Professional Psychology: Research and Practice, 33,* 507–509.

Levant, R. F., Barbanel, L., & DeLeon, P. H. (2004). Psychology's response to terrorism. In F. M. Moghaddam & A. J. Marsella (Eds.), *Understanding terrorism: Psychosocial roots, consequences, and interventions.* Washington, DC: American Psychological Association.

Leve, L. D., & Chamberlain, P. (2004). Female juvenile offenders: Defining an early-onset pathway for delinquency. *Journal of Child and Family Studies, 13,* 439–452.

Levin, B. (1976). Psychological characteristics of firesetters. *Fire Journal, 70,* 36–41.

Levine, N. (2000). *CrimeStat: A spatial statistics program for the analysis of crime incident locations.* Annadale, VA: Ned Levine & Associates; Washington, DC: National Institute of Justice.

Levine, N. (2002). *CrimeStat II: A spatial statistics program for the analysis of crime incident locations.* Houston, TX: Ned Levine & Associates.

Lewis, C. F., Baranoski, M. V., Buchanan, J. A., & Benedek, E. P. (1998). Factors associated with weapon use in maternal filicide. *Journal of Forensic Sciences, 43,* 613–618.

Lewis, C. F., & Bunce, S. C. (2003). Filicidal mothers and the impact of psychosis on filicide. *Journal of the American Academy of Psychiatry and the Law, 31,* 459–470.

Lewis, D. O., Lovely, R., Yeager, C., Ferguson, G., Friedman, M., Sloane, G., et al. (1988). Intrinsic and environmental characteristics of juvenile murderers. *Journal of the American Academy of Child and Adolescent Psychiatry, 27,* 582–587.

Lewis, D. O., Moy, E., Jackson, L. D., Aarsonson, R., Restifo, N., Serra, S., et al. (1985). Biopsychological characteristics of children who later murder: A prospective study. *American Journal of Psychiatry, 142,* 1161–1167.

Li, Q. (2006). Cyberbullying in schools: A research on gender differences. *School Psychology International, 27,* 157–170.

Li, Q. (2007). New bottle but old wine: A research of cyberbullying in schools. *Computers in Human Behavior, 23,* 1777–1791.

Lidzba, K., & Staudt, M. (2008). Development and (re) organization of language after early brain lesions: Capacities and limitation of early brain plasticity. *Brain & Language, 106,* 165–166.

Lightsey, O. R., Jr. (2006). Resilience, meaning, and well-being. *Counseling Psychologist, 34,* 96–107.

Lilienfeld, S. O., Gershon, J., Duke, M., Marion, L., & de Waal, F. B. M. (1999). A preliminary investigation of the construct of psychopathic personality (psychopathy) in chimpanzees (*Pan troglodytes*). *Journal of Comparative Psychology, 113,* 365–375.

Linedecker, C., & Burt, W. (1990). *Nurses who kill.* New York: Pinnacle Books.

Lingren, H. G. (2001). *Dating violence and acquaintance assault.* Lincoln, NE: Nebraska Cooperative Extension, University of Nebraska.

Lipsey, M. W., & Wilson, D. B. (1998). Effective interventions with serious juvenile offenders: A synthesis of research. In R. Loeber & D. P. Farrington (Eds.), *Serious and violent juvenile offenders: Risk factors and successful intervention.* Thousand Oaks, CA: Sage.

Lipton, D. N., McDonel, E. C., & McFall, R. M. (1987). Heterosocial perception in rapists. *Journal of Consulting and Clinical Psychology, 55,* 17–21.

Lisak, D., Gardinier, L., Nicksa, S. C., & Cote, A. M. (2010). False allegations of sexual assault: An analysis of ten years of reported cases. *Violence Against Women, 16,* 1318–1334.

Lisak, D., & Miller, P. M. (2002). Repeat rape and multiple offending among undetected rapists. *Violence and Victims, 17,* 73–84.

Listwan, S. J., Piquero, N., & Van Voorhis, P. (2010). Recidivism among a white-collar sample: Does personality matter? *The Australian and New Zealand Journal of Criminology, 43*, 156–174.

Litwack, T. R., & Schlesinger, L. B. (1999). Dangerous risk assessments: Research, legal, and clinical considerations. In A. K. Hess & I. B. Weiner (Eds.), *The handbook of forensic psychology* (2nd ed.). New York: Wiley.

Liu, J., Raine, A., Venables, P. H., & Mednick, S. A. (2004). Malnutrition at age 3 years and externalizing behavior at ages 8, 11, and 17 years. *American Journal of Psychiatry, 161*, 2005–2013.

Lizotte, A., & Sheppard, D. (2001, July). *Gun use by male juveniles: Research and prevention.* Washington, DC: U.S. Department of Justice, office of Juvenile Justice and Delinquency Prevention.

Lochman, J. G., & Conduct Problems Prevention Research Group. (1995). Screening of child behavior problems for prevention programs at school entry. *Journal of Consulting and Clinical Psychology, 63*, 549–559.

LoCicero, A., & Sinclair, S. J. (2008). Terrorism and terrorist leaders: Insights from developmental and ecological psychology. *Studies in Conflict & Terrorism, 31*, 227–250.

Loeber, R. (1990). Development and risk factors of juvenile antisocial behavior and delinquency. *Clinical Psychology Review, 10*, 1–41.

Loeber, R., Farrington, D. P., & Petechuk, D. (2003, May). Child delinquency: Early intervention and prevention. *Child Delinquency Bulletin Series.* Washington, DC: U.S. Department of Justice, Office of Juvenile Justice and Delinquency Prevention.

Loeber, R., Farrington, D. P., Stouthamer-Loeber, M., & Van Kammen, W. B. (1998). *Antisocial behavior and mental health problems: Explanatory factors in childhood and adolescence.* Mahmah, NJ: Lawrence Erlbaum.

Loeber, R., Lahey, B. B., & Thomas, C. (1991). The diagnostic conundrum of oppositional defiant disorder and conduct disorder. *Journal of Abnormal Psychology, 100*, 379–390.

Loeber, R., Pardini, D., Homish, D. L., Wei, E. H., Crawford, A. M., Farrington, D., et al. (2005). The prediction of violence and homicide in young men. *Journal of Consulting and Clinical Psychology, 73*, 1074–1088.

Loeber, R., & Stouthamer-Loeber, M. (1998). Development of juvenile aggression and violence: Some common misconceptions and controversies. *American Psychologist, 53*, 242–259.

Loehlin, J. C. (1992). *Genes and environment in personality development.* Newbury Park, CA: Sage.

Lombardo, V. S., & Lombardo, E. F. (1991). The link between learning disabilities and juvenile delinquency: Fact or fiction? *International Journal of Biosocial and Medical Research, 13*, 112–117.

Longo, R. F., Bird, S., Stevenson, W. F., & Fiske, J. A. (1995). *1994 nationwide survey of treatment programs and models.* Brandon, VT: Safer Society Program and Press.

Lonsway, K. A., & Fitzgerald, L. F. (1994). Rape myths: In review. *Psychology of Woman Quarterly, 18*, 133–164.

Looman, J., Gauthier, C., & Boer, D. (2001). Replication of the Massachusetts Treatment Center child molester typology in a Canadian sample. *Journal of Interpersonal Violence, 16*, 753–767.

Lorber, M. F. (2004). Psychophysiology of aggression, psychopathy, and conduct problems: A meta-analysis. *Psychological Bulletin, 130*, 531–552.

Lord, W. D., Boudreaux, M. C., & Lanning, K. V. (2001, April). Investigating potential child abduction cases: A developmental perspective. *FBI Law Enforcement Bulletin*, 1–10.

Lorenz, A. R., & Newman, J. P. (2002). Deficient response modulation and emotion processing in low-anxious caucasian psychopathic offenders: Results from a lexical decision task. *Emotion, 2*, 91–104.

Lorenz, K. (1966). *On aggression.* New York: Harcourt Brace Jovanovich.

Lösel, F., & Schmucker, M. (2005). The effectiveness of treatment for sexual offenders: A comprehensive meta-analysis. *Journal of Experimental Criminology, 1*, 117–146.

Loukas, A., Zucker, R. A., Fitzgerald, H. F., & Krull, J. L. (2003). Developmental trajectories of descriptive behavior problems among sons of alcoholics: Effects of parent psychopathology, family conflict, and child under control. *Journal of Abnormal Psychology, 112*, 119–131.

Lubenow, G. C. (1983, June 27). When kids kill their parents. *Newsweek*, pp. 35–36.

Lucia, S., & Killias, M. (2011). Is animal cruelty a marker of interpersonal violence and delinquency? Results of a Swiss national self-report study. *Psychology of Violence, 1*, 93–105.

Lumley, V. A., McNeil, C. B., Herschell, A. D., & Bahl, A. B. (2002). An examination of gender differences among young children with disruptive behavior disorders. *Child Study Journal, 32*, 89–100.

Lykken, D. T. (1955). *A study of anxiety in the sociopathic personality* (Doctoral dissertation, University of Minnesota). Ann Arbor, MI: University Microfilms, No. 55–944.

Lykken, D. T. (1957). A study of anxiety in the sociopathic personality. *Journal of Abnormal and Social Psychology, 55*, 6–10.

Lykken, D. T. (1978). The psychopath and the lie detector. *Psychophysiology, 15*, 137–142.

Lykken, D. T., & Venables, P. H. (1971). Direct measurement of skin conductance: A proposal for standardization. *Psychophysiology, 8*, 856–872.

Lynam, D. R. (1997). Pursuing the psychopath: Capturing the fledgling psychopath in a nomological net. *Journal of Abnormal Psychology, 106*, 425–438.

Lynam, D. R. (1998). Early identification of the fledgling psychopath: Locating the psychopathic child in the current nomenclature. *Journal of Abnormal Psychology, 107*, 566–575.

Lynam, D. R., Caspi, A., Moffitt, T. E., Loeber, R., & Stouthamer-Loeber, M. (2007). Longitudinal evidence that psychopathy scores in early adolescence predict adult psychopathy. *Journal of Abnormal Psychology, 116*, 155–165.

Lynam, D. R., Charnigo, R., Moffitt, T. E., Raine, A., Loeber, R., & Stouthamer-Loeber, M. (2009). The stability of psychopathy across adolescence. *Developmental and Psychopathology, 21*, 1133–1153.

Lynam, D. R., Moffitt, T., & Stouthamer-Loeber, M. (1993). Explaining the relation between IQ and delinquency: Class, race, test motivation, school failure, or self control? *Journal of Abnormal Psychology, 102*, 187–196.

Maccoby, E. E. (1986). Social groupings in childhood. In D. Olweus, J. Block, & M. Radke-Yarrow (Eds.), *Development of antisocial and prosocial behavior: Research, theories, and issues.* New York: Academic Press.

MacCoun, R., Kilmer, B., & Reuter, P. (2003, July). *Research on drugs-crime linkages: The next generation. NIJ Special Report: Toward a drug and crime research agenda for the 21st century.* Washington, DC: National Institute of Justice.

MacDonald, J. M. (1977). *Bombers and firesetters.* Springfield, IL: Charles C Thomas.

MacKay, S., Feldberg, A., Ward, A. K., & Marton, P. (2012). Research and practice in adolescent firesetting. *Criminal Justice and Behavior, 39*, 842–864.

MacKay, S., Henderson, J., Del Bove, G., Marton, P., Warling, D., & Root, C. (2006). Fire interest and antisociality as risk factors in the severity and persistence of juvenile firesetting. *Journal of the American Academy of Child and Adolescent Psychiatry, 45*, 1077–1084.

MacKenzie, D. L., & Hebert, E. (Eds.). (1995). *Correctional boot camps: A tough intermediate sanction.* Washington, DC: National Institute of Justice.

MacKenzie, D. L., Layton, D., Soural, C., Sealock, M., & Bin Kashen, M. (2001). Effects of correctional boot camps on offending. *The Annals of the American Academy of Political and Social Sciences, 78*, 126–143.

Maeder, E., Dempsey, J., & Pozzulo, J. (2012). Behind the veil of juror decision-making: Testing the effects of Muslim veils and defendant race in the courtroom. *Criminal Justice and Behavior, 39*, 666–678.

Maikovich, A. K. (2005). A new understanding of terrorism using cognitive dissonance principles. *Journal for the Theory of Social Behaviour, 35*, 373–397.

Maker, A. H., Kemmelmeier, M., & Peterson, C. (1998). Long-term psychological consequences in women witnessing parental physical conflict and experiencing abuse in childhood. *Journal of Interpersonal Violence, 13*, 574–589.

Malamuth, N. M. (1981). Rape proclivity among males. *Journal of Social Issues, 37*, 138–157.

Malamuth, N. M. (1989). The attraction to sexual aggression scale: Part one. *Journal of Sex Research, 26*, 26–49.

Malamuth, N. M., & Check, J. V. P. (1981). The effects of violent-sexual movies: A field experiment. *Journal of Research in Personality, 15*, 436–446.

Malamuth, N. M., Check, J. V. P., & Briere, J. (1986). Sexual arousal in response to aggression: Ideological, aggressive, and sexual correlates. *Journal of Personality and Social Psychology, 50,* 330–340.

Malamuth, N. M., Haber, S., & Feshbach, S. (1980). Testing hypothesis regarding rape: Exposure to sexual violence, sex differences, and the "normality" of rape. *Journal of Research in Personality, 14,* 121–137.

Malamuth, N. M., Heim, M., & Feshbach, S. (1980). The sexual responsiveness of college students to rape depictions: Inhibitory and disinhibitory effects. *Journal of Personality and Social Psychology, 38,* 399–408.

Malamuth, N. M., Huppin, M., & Paul, B. (2005). Sexual coercion. In D. M. Buss (Ed.), *The handbook of evolutionary psychology* (pp. 394–418). Hoboken, NJ: Wiley.

Mann, C. R. (1993). Maternal filicide of preschoolers. In A. V. Wilson (Ed.), *Homicide: The victim/offender connection.* Cincinnati, OH: Anderson.

Mann, R. E., Zhao, J., Stoduto, G., Adlaf, E. M., Smart, R. G., & Donovan, J. E. (2007). Road rage and collision involvement. *American Journal of Health Behavior, 31,* 384–391.

Margolin, G., & Vickerman, K. A. (2011). Posttraumatic stress in children and adolescents exposed to family violence: Overview and issues. *Couple and Family Psychology: Research and Practice, 1,* 63–73.

Marleau, J. D., Millaud, F., Auclair, N. (2003). A comparison of parricide and attempted parricide: A study of 39 psychotic adults. *International Journal of Law and Psychiatry, 26,* 269–279.

Marlowe, D. B., Festinger, D. S., Dugosh, K. L., Benasutti, K. M., Fox, G., & Croft, J. R. (2012). Adaptive programming improves outcomes in drug court: An experimental trial. *Criminal Justice and Behavior, 39,* 514–532.

Marques, J. K., Wiederanders, M., Day, D. M., Nelson, C., & Van Ommeren, A. (2005). Effects of a relapse prevention program on sexual recidivism: Final results from California's Sex Offender Treatment and Evaluation Project (SOTEP). *Sexual Abuse: A Journal of Research and Treatment, 17,* 79–107.

Marsella, A. J. (2004). Reflections on international terrorism: Issues, concepts, and directions. In F. M. Moghaddam & A. J. Marsella (Eds.), *Understanding terrorism: Psychosocial roots, consequences, and interventions.* Washington, DC: American Psychological Association.

Marshall, C. E., Benton, D., & Brazier, J. M. (2000). Elder abuse: Using clinical tools to identify clues of mistreatment. *Geriatrics, 55,* 42–53.

Marshall, L. A., & Cooke, D. J. (1999). The childhood experiences of psychopaths: A retrospective study of familial and societal factors. *Journal of Personality Disorders, 13,* 211–225.

Marshall, W. L. (1988). The use of sexually explicit stimuli by rapists, child molesters, and nonoffenders. *Journal of Sex Research, 25,* 267–288.

Marshall, W. L., & Barbaree, H. E. (1988). An outpatient treatment program for child molesters. In R. A. Prentky and V. L. Quinsey (Eds.), *Human sexual aggression: Current perspectives.* New York: New York Academy of Sciences.

Marshall, W. L., Barbaree, H. E., & Fernandez, M. (1995). Some aspects of social competence in sexual offenders. *Sexual Abuse, 7,* 113–127.

Marshall, W. L., & Christie, M. M. (1981). Pedophilia and aggression. *Criminal Justice and Behavior, 8,* 145–158.

Marshall, W. L., & Mazzucco, A. (1995). Self-esteem and parental attachments in child molesters. *Sexual Abuse, 7,* 229–285.

Martin, E. K., Taft, C. T., & Resick, P. A. (2007). A review of marital rape. *Aggression and Violent Behavior, 12,* 329–347.

Martinez, P. A. (2011, September 7). *Cybercrime: Updating the computer fraud and abuse act to protect cyberspace and combat emerging threats.* Comments of Pablo A. Martinez, Deputy Special Agent in Charge, Criminal Investigative Division, U.S. Secret Service, before the U.S. Senate Committee on the Judiciary. Available: http://www.dhs.gov/ynews/testimony/20110907-Martinez-cybercrime-computer-fraud.shtm

Maslow, A. H. (1954). *Motivation and personality.* New York: Harper.

Mason, K. L. (2008). Cyberbullying: A preliminary assessment for school personnel. *Psychology in the Schools, 45,* 323–348.

Matheny, A. P. (1989). Children's behavioral inhibition over age and across situations: Genetic similarity for a trait during change. *Journal of Personality, 57,* 215–235.

Matthews, J. K., Hunter, J. A., & Vuz, I. (1997). Juvenile female sexual offenders: Clinical characteristics and treatment issues. *Sexual Abuse: A Journal of Research and Treatment, 9,* 187–199.

Maughan, B., Rowe, R., Messer, J., Goodman, R., & Meltzer, H. (2004). Conduct disorder and oppositional defiant disorder in a national sample: Developmental epidemiology. *Journal of Child Psychology and Psychiatry, 45,* 609–621.

Maxwell, C. D., Robinson, A. L., & Post, L. A. (2003). The nature and predictors or sexual victimization and offending among adolescents. *Journal of Youth and Adolescence, 32,* 465–478.

Maxwell, J. C. (2004). *Patterns of club drug use in the U.S., 2004.* Austin, TX: The Center for Excellence in Drug Epidemiology, The Gulf Coast Addition Technology Transfer Center, University of Texas.

Mayes, L. C. (1999). Developing brain and in utero cocaine exposure: Effects on neural ontogeny. *Development and Psychopathology, 11,* 685–714.

Mazerolle, P., Brame, R., Paternoster, R., Piquero, A., & Dean, C. (2000). Onset age, persistence, and offending versatility: Comparisons across gender. *Criminology, 38,* 1143–1172.

Mazulis, A. H., Hyde, J. S., & Clark, R. (2004). Father involvement moderates the effect of maternal depression during a child's infancy on child behavior problems in kindergarten. *Journal of Family Psychology, 18,* 575–588.

McArdle, M. (1993, October 12). Guns at home. Washington Post health section, *Washington Post,* pp. 12–15.

McCabe, K. M., Hough, R., Wood, P. A., & Yeh, M. (2001). Childhood and adolescent onset conduct disorder: A test of the developmental taxonomy. *Journal of Abnormal Child Psychology, 29,* 305–316.

McCabe, K. M., Rodgers, C., Yeh, M., & Hough, R. (2004). Gender differences in childhood onset conduct disorder. *Development and Psychopathology, 16,* 179–192.

McCaghy, C. H. (1967). Child molesters: A study of their careers as deviants. In M. Clinard & R. Quinney (Eds.), *Criminal behavior systems: A typology.* New York: Holt, Rinehart & Winston.

McCaghy, C. H. (1980). *Crime in American society.* New York: Macmillan.

McCarty, C. A., & McMahon, R. J. (2005). Domains of risk in the developmental continuity of fire setting. *Behavior Therapy, 36,* 185–195.

McClearn, G. E., & DeFries, J. C. (1973). *Introduction to behavioral genetics.* San Francisco: W. H. Freeman.

McClosky, L. A., Figueredo, A. J., & Koss, M. P. (1995). The effects of systemic family violence on children's mental health. *Child Development, 66,* 1239–1261.

McCord, D. (1987). Syndromes, profiles and other mental exotica: A new approach to the admissibility of non-traditional psychological evidence in criminal cases. *Oregon Law Review, 66,* 19–108.

McCord, W., McCord, J., & Zola, I. K. (1959). *Origins of crime: A new evaluation of the Cambridge-Somerville Youth Study.* New York: Columbia University Press.

McDermott, R., Tingley, D., Cowden, J., Frazzetto, G., & Johnson, D. D. P. (2009). Monoamine oxidase A gene (MAOA) predicts behavioral aggression following provocation. *Proceedings of the National Association of Sciences, 106,* 2118–2123.

McElroy, S. L., Pope, H. G., Hudson, J. I., Keck, P. E., & White, K. L. (1991). Kleptomania: A report of 20 cases. *American Journal of Psychiatry, 148,* 652–657.

McGinley, H., & Paswark, R. A. (1989). National survey of the frequency and success of the insanity plea and alternate pleas. *Journal of Psychiatry and Law, 17,* 205–221.

McKee, G. R., & Shea, S. J. (1998). Maternal filicide: A cross-national comparison. *Journal of Clinical Psychology, 54,* 679–687.

McKenzie, C. (1995). A study of serial murder. *International Journal of Offender Therapy and Comparative Criminology, 39,* 3–10.

McKnight, L. R., & Loper, A. B. (2002). The effect of risk and resilience factors on the prediction of delinquency in adolescent girls. *School Psychology International, 23,* 186–198.

McMahon, R. J., Witkiewitz, K., Kotler, J. S., & The Conduct Problems Prevention Research Group. (2010). Predictive validity of callous-emotional traits measured in early adolescence with respect to multiple antisocial outcomes. *Journal of Abnormal Psychology, 119,* 752–763.

McShane, D. A., & Plas, J. M. (1984a). Response to a critique of the McShane & Plas review of American Indian performance on the Wechsler Intelligence Scales. *School Psychology Review, 13,* 83–88.

McShane, D. A., & Plas, J. M. (1984b). The cognitive functioning of American Indian children: Moving from the WISC to the WISC-R. *School Psychology Review, 13*, 61–73.

Meadows, S. (2006, July 17). Murder on their minds. *Newsweek*, pp. 28–29.

Mechoulam, R. (1970). Marihuana chemistry. *Science, 168*, 1159–1166.

Mednick, S. A., Gabrielli, W. F., & Hutchings, B. (1984). Genetic influences in criminal convictions: Evidence from an adoption cohort. *Science, 234*, 891–894.

Mednick, S. A., Gabrielli, W. F., & Hutchings, B. (1987). Genetic factors in the etiology of criminal behavior. In S. A. Mednick, T. E. Moffitt, & S. A. Stack (Eds.), *The causes of crime: New biological approaches*. Cambridge, UK: Cambridge University Press.

Megargee, E. I. (1982). Psychological determinants and correlates of criminal violence. In M. E. Wolfgang & N. A. Weinder (Eds.), *Criminal violence*. Beverly Hills, CA: Sage.

Meier, M. H., Slutske, W. S., Heath, A. C., & Martin, N. G. (2009). The role of harsh discipline in explaining sex differences in conduct disorder: A study of opposite-sex twin pairs. *Journal of Abnormal Child Psychology, 37*, 653–664.

Meloy, J. R. (1998). The psychology of stalking. In J. R. Meloy (Ed.), *The psychology of stalking: Clinical and forensic perspectives*. San Diego, CA: Academic Press.

Melton, G. B., Petrila, J., Poythress, N. G., & Slobogin, C. (Eds.). (2007). Psychological evaluations for the courts: A handbook for mental health professionals and lawyers (3rd ed.). New York: Guilford Press.

Mercy, J., & Salzman, L. (1989). Fatal violence among spouses in the United States, 1986–1987. *American Journal of Public Health, 79*, 595–599.

Merry, S., & Hansent, L. (2000). Intruders, pilferers, raiders, and invaders: The interpersonal dimension of burglary. In D. Canter & L. Alison (Eds.), *Profiling property crimes*. Dartmouth, UK: Ashgate.

Merton, R. K. (1957). *Social theory and social structure* (Rev. ed.). New York: The Free Press.

Merz-Perez, L., Heide, K. M., & Silverman, I. J. (2001). Childhood cruelty to animals and subsequent violence against humans. *International Journal of Offender Therapy and Comparative Criminology, 45*, 556–573.

Messner, S., & Rosenfeld, R. (1994). *Crime and the American dream*. Belmont, CA: Wadsworth.

Meyer, C. L., & Oberman, M. (2001). *Mothers who kill their children: Understanding the acts of moms from Susan Smith to the "prom mom."* New York: University Press.

Meyer, T. P. (1972). The effects of sexually arousing and violent films on aggressive behavior. *Journal of Sex Research, 8*, 324–333.

Miczek, K. A., DeBold, J. F., Haney, M., Tidey, J., Vivian, J., & Weerts, E. M. (1994). Alcohol, drugs of abuse, aggression, and violence. In A. J. Reiss & J. A. Roth (Eds.), *Understanding and preventing violence. Vol. 3. Social influences*. Washington, DC: National Academy Press.

Milgram, S. (1963). Behavioral study of obedience. *Journal of Abnormal and Social Psychology, 67*, 371–378.

Milgram, S. (1974). *Obedience to authority*. New York: Harper & Row.

Milgram, S. (1977). *The individual in a social world*. Reading, MA: Addison-Wesley.

Miller-Johnson, S., Coie, J. D., Maumary-Gremaud, A., Bierman, K., & the Conduct Problems Prevention Research Group. (2002). Peer rejection and aggression and early starter models of conduct disorder. *Journal of Abnormal Child Psychology, 30*, 217–230.

Miller, L. (2006). The terrorist mind I: A psychological and political analysis. *International Journal of Offender Therapy and Comparative Criminology, 50*, 121–138.

Miller, M., Hennenway, D., & Solop, D. (2002). Road rage in Arizona: Armed and dangerous. *Accident Analysis and Prevention, 34*, 807–814.

Miller, N., Pedersen, W. C., Earleywine, M., & Pollack, V. E. (2003). A theoretical model of triggered displaced aggression. *Personality and Social Psychology Review, 7*, 75–97.

Miller, P. A., & Eisenberg, N. (1988). The relation of empathy to aggressive and externalizing antisocial behavior. *Psychological Bulletin, 103*, 324–344.

Miller, R. D. (2003). Hospitalization of criminal defendants for evaluation of competence to stand trial or for restoration of competence: Clinical and legal issues. *Behavioral Sciences & the Law, 21*, 369–391.

Miron, M. S., & Goldstein. A. P. (1978). *Hostage*. Kalamazoo, MI: Behaviordelia.

Mirrless-Black, C. (1999). *Domestic violence: Findings from a new British crime survey self-completion questionnaire.* London: Great Britain Home Office Research Development and Statistics Directorate.

Mischel, W. (1976). *Introduction to personality* (2nd ed.). New York: Holt, Rinehart & Winston.

Mitchell, K. J., Wolak, J., & Finkelhor, D. (2005). Police posing as juveniles online to catch sex offenders. Is it working? *Sexual Abuse: A Journal of Research and Treatment, 17,* 241–267.

Mizell, L. (1995). *Aggressive driving.* Washington, DC: AAA Foundation for Traffic Safety.

Moffitt, T. E. (1990a). The neuropsychology of juvenile delinquency: A critical review. In M. Tonry & N. Morris (Eds.), *Crime and justice: A review of research.* Chicago: University of Chicago Press.

Moffitt, T. E. (1990b). Juvenile delinquency and attention deficit disorder: Boys' developmental trajectories from age 13 to age 15. *Child Development, 61,* 893–910.

Moffitt, T. E. (1993a). Adolescence-limited and life-course-persistent antisocial behavior: A developmental taxonomy. *Psychological Review, 100,* 674–701.

Moffitt, T. E. (1993b). The neuropsychology of conduct disorder. *Development and Psychopathology, 5,* 135–151.

Moffitt, T. E. (2003). Life-course-persistent and adolescent-limited antisocial behavior: A 10-year research review and research agenda. In B. B. Lahey, T. E. Moffitt, and A. Caspi (Eds.), *Causes of conduct disorder and juvenile delinquency.* New York: Guilford.

Moffitt, T. E. (2005a). The new look of behavioral genetics in developmental psychopathology: Gene-environment interplay in antisocial behaviors. *Psychological Bulletin, 131,* 533–534.

Moffitt, T. E. (2005b). Genetic and environmental influences on antisocial behaviors: Evidence from behavioral-genetic research. *Advances in Genetics, 55,* 41–104.

Moffitt, T. E. (2006). Life-course-persistent versus adolescence-limited antisocial behavior. In D. Cicchetti & D. J. Cohen (Eds.), *Developmental psychopathology. Vol. 3: Risk, disorder, and adaptation* (2nd ed.). Hoboken, NJ: Wiley.

Moffitt, T. E., Arseneault, L., Jaffee, S. R., Kim-Cohen, J., Koenen, K. C., Odgers, C. L., et al. (2008). Research review: DSM-V conductor disorder: Research needs for an evidence base. *Journal of Child Psychology and Psychiatry, 49,* 3–33.

Moffitt, T. E., & Caspi, A. (2001). Childhood predictors differentiate life-course persistent and adolescence-limited antisocial pathways among males and females. *Development and Psychopathology, 13,* 355–375.

Moffitt, T. E., Caspi, A., Dickson, N., Silva, P., & Stanton, W. (1996). Childhood-onset versus adolescent-onset antisocial conduct problems in males: Natural history from age 3 to age 18. *Development and Psychopathology, 8,* 399–424.

Moffitt, T. E., Caspi, A., Fawcett, P., Brammer, G. L., Raleigh, M., Yuwiler, A., et al. (1997). Whole blood serotonin and family background relate to male violence. In A. Raine, P. A. Brennan, D. P. Farrington, S. A. Mednick (Eds.), *Biological bases of violence.* New York: Plenum.

Moffitt, T. E., Caspi, A., Harrington, H., & Milne, B. J. (2002). Males on the life-course-persistent and adolescence-limited antisocial pathways: Follow-up at age 26 years. *Development and Psychopathology, 14,* 179–207.

Moffitt, T. E., Caspi, A., Rutter, M., & Silva, P. A. (2001). *Sex differences in antisocial behaviour: Conduct disorder delinquency, and violence in the Dunedin Longitudinal Study.* New York: Cambridge University Press.

Moffitt, T. E., Lynam, D. R., & Silva, P. A. (1994). Neuropsychological tests predicting persistent male delinquency. *Criminology, 33,* 111–139.

Moffitt, T. E., & Silva, P. A. (1988). Self-reported delinquency, neuropsychological deficit, and history of attention deficit disorder. *Journal of Abnormal Child Psychology, 16,* 553–569.

Moghaddam, F. M., & Marsella, A. J. (2004a). Preface. In F. M. Moghaddam & A. J. Marsella (Eds.), *Understanding terrorism: Psychosocial roots, consequences, and interventions.* Washington, DC: American Psychological Association.

Moghaddam, F. M., & Marsella, A. J. (2004b). Introduction. In F. M. Moghaddam & A. J. Marsella (Eds.), *Understanding terrorism: Psychosocial roots, consequences, and interventions.* Washington, DC: American Psychological Association.

Mohandie, K., Meloy, J. R., Green-McGowan, M., & Williams, J. (2006). The RECON typology of stalking: Reliability and validity based upon a large sample of

North American stalkers. *Journal of Forensic Sciences, 51*, 147–155.

Molina, B. S. G., Pelham, W. E., Cheong, J. W., Marshal, M. P., Gnagy, E. M., & Curran, P. J. (2012). Childhood Attention-Deficit/Hyperactivity Disorder (ADHD) and growth in adolescent alcohol use: The roles of functional impairments, ADHD symptom persistence, and parental knowledge. *Journal of Abnormal Psychology*, Advance online publication. DOI: 10.1037/a0028260.

Monahan, J. (1976). The prevention of crime. In J. Monahan (Ed.), *Community mental health and the criminal justice system*. New York: Pergamon Press.

Monahan, J. (1981). *Predicting violent behavior*. Beverly Hills, CA: Sage.

Monahan, J. (1984). The prediction of violent behavior: Toward a second generation of theory and policy. *American Journal of Psychiatry, 141*, 10–15.

Monahan, J. (1992). Mental disorder and violent behavior: Perceptions and evidence. *American Psychologist, 47*, 511–521.

Monahan, J. (1996). Violence prediction: The past twenty years and the next twenty years. *Criminal Justice and Behavior, 23*, 107–120.

Monahan, J. (2011). The individual risk assessment of terrorism. *Psychology, Public Policy, and Law*. Advanced online publication DOI: 10.1037/a0025792.

Monahan, J., Steadman, H. J., Silver, E., Appelbaum, P. S., Robbins, P. C., Mulvey, E. P., et al. (2001). *Rethinking risk assessment: The MacArthur study of mental disorder and violence*. New York: Oxford University Press.

Monahan, J., Steadman, H., Robbins, P.C., Appelbaum, P., Banks, S., Grisso, T. Heilbrun, K., Mulvey, E. P., Roth, L., & Silver, E. (2005). An actuarial model of violence risk assessment for persons with mental disorders. *Psychiatric Services, 56*, 810–815.

Monahan, J., & Walker, L. (1990). *Social science and law: Cases and materials* (2nd ed.). Westbury, NY: Foundation Press.

Monahan, J., & Walker, L. (1994). *Social science and law: Cases and materials* (3rd ed.). Waterbury, NY: Foundation Press.

Monahan, T. P. (1957). Family status and the delinquent child: A reappraisal and some new findings. *Social Forces, 35*, 250–258.

Montagu, A. (1973). *Man and aggression* (2nd ed.). London: Oxford University Press.

Montagu, A. (1976). *The nature of human aggression*. New York: Oxford University Press.

Moore, R. H. (1984). Shoplifting in middle America: Patterns and motivational correlates. *International Journal of Offender Therapy and Comparative Criminology, 28*, 53–64.

Morawetz, T. H. (2002). Homicide. In K. L. Hall (Ed.), *The Oxford companion to American law*. New York: Oxford University Press.

Moreland, J. (2000). Toxicity of drug abuse—amphetamine designer drugs (ecstasy): Mental effects and consequences of a single dose. *Tox Letters*, 147–152.

Morgan, A. B., & Lilienfeld, S. O. (2000). A meta-analytic review of the relation between antisocial behavior and neuropsychological measures of executive function. *Clinical Psychology Review, 20*, 113–146.

Morgan, J. P., & Zimmer, L. (1997). The social pharmacology of smokeable cocaine: Not all it's cracked up to be. In C. Reinarman & H. G. Levine (Eds.), *Crack in America: Demon drugs and social justice*. Berkeley, CA: University of California Press.

Morris, D. (1967). *The naked ape*. New York: McGraw-Hill.

Morris, N., & Miller, M. (1985). Prediction of dangerousness. In M. Tonry & N. Morris (Eds.), *Crime and justice: An annual review of research*. Chicago: University of Chicago Press.

Morrissey, T. W. (2009). Multiple child-care arrangements and young children's behavioral outcomes. *Child Development, 80*, 59–76.

Morse, S. J. (1978). Behavior, morals, and science: An analysis of mental health law. *Southern California Law Review, 51*, 527–654.

Morse, S. J. (1985). Excusing the crazy: The insanity defense reconsidered. *Southern California Law Review, 58*, 777–836.

Morse, S. J. (1986). Why amnesia and the law is not a useful topic. *Behavioral Sciences & the Law, 4*, 99–102.

Moskowitz, A. (2004). Dissociation and violence: A review of the literature. *Trauma, Violence, & Abuse, 5*, 21–46.

Mott, J. (1986). Opioid use and burglary. *British Journal of Addiction, 81,* 671–677.

Mounts, N. S. (2002). Parental management of adolescent peer relationships in context: The role of parenting style. *Journal of Family Psychology, 16,* 58–69.

Mulder, R. T., Wells, J. E., Joyce, P. R., & Bushnell, J. A. (1994). Antisocial women. *Journal of Personality Disorders, 8,* 279–287.

Müller, J. L., Sommer, M., Wagner, V., Lange, K., Taschler, H., Röder, C. H., et al. (2003). Abnormalities in emotion processing within cortical and subcortical regions in criminal psychopaths: Evidence from a functional magnetic resonance imaging study using pictures with emotional content. *Biological Psychiatry, 54,* 152–162.

Mulvey, E. P. (2011). Highlights from *Pathways to Desistance: A longitudinal study of serious adolescent offenders.* (Fact Sheet). Washington, DC: U.S. Department of Justice. Office of Justice Programs. Office of Juvenile Justice and Delinquency Prevention.

Mulvey, E. P., Arthur, M. W., & Reppucci, N. D. (1993). The prevention and treatment of juvenile delinquency: A review of the research. *Clinical Psychology Review, 13,* 133–167.

Mulvey, E. P., Schubert, C. A., & Chassin, L. (2010). *Substance use and offending in serious adolescent offenders.* Washington, DC: U.S. Department of Justice, Office of Justice Programs, Office of Juvenile Justice and Delinquency Prevention.

Mumley, D. L., Tillbrook, C. E., & Grisso, T. (2003). Five year research update (1996–2000): Evaluations for competence to stand trial (adjudicative competence). *Behavioral Sciences & the Law, 21,* 329–350.

Mumola, C. J., & Karberg, J. C. (2006, October). *Drug use and dependence, state and federal prisoners, 2004.* Washington, DC: U.S. Department of Justice, Bureau of Justice Statistics.

Munetz, M. R., & Griffin, P. A. (2006). Use of the sequential intercept model as an approach to decriminalization of people with serious mental illness. *Psychiatric Services, 57,* 544–549.

Murphy, G. H., & Clare, C. H. (1996). Analysis of motivation in people with mild learning disabilities (mental handicap) who set fires. *Psychology, Crime, & Law, 2,* 153–164.

Murray, J. B. (1997). Munchausen syndrome/Munchausen syndrome by proxy. *The Journal of Psychology, 131,* 343–350.

Murray, J. P. (2008). Media violence: The effects are both real and strong. *American Behavioral Scientist, 51,* 1212–1230.

Murrie, D. C., Boccaccini, M. T., McCoy, W., & Cornell, D. G. (2007). Diagnostic labeling in juvenile court: How do descriptions of psychopathy and conduct disorder influence judges? *Journal of Clinical Child and Adolescent Psychology, 36,* 228–241.

Murrie, D. C., & Cornell, D. G., Kaplan, S., McConville, D., & Levy-Elkon, A. (2004). Psychopathy scores and violence among juvenile offenders: A multi-measure study. *Behavioral Sciences & the Law, 22,* 49–67.

Myers, D. G. (1996). *Social psychology* (5th ed.). New York: McGraw-Hill.

Myers, W. C. (1992). What treatments do we have for children and adolescents who have killed. *Bulletin of the American Academy of Psychiatry and Law, 20,* 47–58.

Myers, W. C. (1994). Sexual homicide by adolescents. *Journal of the American Academy of Child and Adolescent Psychiatry, 33,* 962–969.

Myers, W. C. (2004). Serial murder by children and adolescents. *Behavioral Sciences & the Law, 22,* 357–374.

Myers, W. C., & Mutch, P. J. (1992). Language disorders in disruptive behaviour disordered homicidal youth. *Journal of Forensic Sciences, 37,* 919–922.

Myers, W. C., & Scott, K. (1998). Psychotic and conduct disorder symptoms in juvenile murderers. *Homicide Studies, 2,* 160–175.

Myers, W. C., Scott, K., Burgess, A. W., & Burgess, A. G. (1995). Psychopathology, biopsychosocial factors, crime characteristics, and classification of 25 homicidal youths. *Journal of the American Academy of Child and Adolescent Psychiatry, 34,* 1483–1489.

Nachshon, I. (1983). Hemisphere dysfunction in psychopathy and behavior disorders. In M. Myslobodsky (Ed.), *Hemisyndromes: Psychobiology, neurology, psychiatry.* New York: Academic Press.

Nachshon, I., & Denno, D. (1987). Violent behavior and cerebral hemisphere function. In S. A. Mednick, T. E. Moffitt, & S. A. Stack (Eds.), *The causes of crime: New biological approaches.* Cambridge, UK: Cambridge University Press.

Nagin, D. (2007). Moving choice to center stage in criminological research. *Criminology, 45,* 259–272.

Nagin, D. S., & Land, K. C. (1993). Age, criminal careers, and population heterogeneity: Specification and estimation of a nonparametric mixed Poisson model. *Criminology, 31,* 163–189.

Narag, R. E., Pizarro, J., & Gibbs, C. (2009). Lead exposure and its implications for criminological theory. *Criminal Justice and Behavior, 36,* 954–973.

National Cable Television Association. (1998). *National Television Violence Study* (Vol. 3). Thousand Oaks, CA: Sage.

National Center for Juvenile Justice. (2003, July). *Juvenile court statistics 1999.* Washington, DC: U.S. Department of Justice, Office of Juvenile Justice and Delinquency Prevention.

National Center for Victims of Crime (NCVC). (2000). *Cyberstalking.* Available: www.ncvc/special/cyber_stk.htm

National Center on Child Abuse and Neglect. (2000). *Study findings: National study of the incidence and severity of child abuse and neglect.* Washington, DC: U.S. Department of Health and Human Services.

National Center on Elder Abuse. (1999). *Types of elder abuse in domestic settings.* Washington, DC: Author.

National Commission on Marihuana and Drug Abuse. (1972). *Marihuana: A signal of misunderstanding.* (Appendix, Vol. 1). Washington, DC: USGPO.

National Commission on Marihuana and Drug Abuse. (1973). *Drug use in America: Problem in perspective* (2nd report). Washington, DC: USGPO.

National Counterterrorism Center. (2009, April 30). *2008 Report on Terrorism.* Washington, DC: Office of the Director of National Intelligence.

National Drug Intelligence Center. (2001, January). *OxyContin diversion and abuse.* Washington, DC: Author.

National Drug Intelligence Center. (2009, July). *Domestic cannabis cultivation assessment: 2009.* Washington, DC: U.S. Department of Justice.

National Highway Traffic Safety Administration. (2005, March). *Alcohol involvement in fatal motor vehicle traffic crashes, 2003.* Springfield, VA: Author.

National Information Support and Referral Service. (1998). Available: www.ojp.usdoij.gov/nisrs

National Institute of Health. (1999, June). *NIDA news release: Long-term brain injury from use of "ecstasy."* Rockville, MD: National Institute of Drug Abuse. Available: www.nida.nih.gov/MedAdv/99/NR-614b.html

National Institute on Alcohol Abuse and Alcoholism. (1990). *Alcohol and health: Neuroscience.* Rockville, MD: USGPO.

National Institute on Alcohol Abuse and Alcoholism. (1997, October). *Alcohol, violence, and aggression. Alcohol Alert.* Rockville, MD: USGPO.

National Institute on Drug Abuse. (1978). Drug abuse and crime. In L. D. Savitz & N. Johnson (Eds.), *Crime in society.* New York: Wiley.

National Institute on Drug Abuse. (1999, May). *Cocaine: Abuse and addiction.* Rockville, MD: USGPO. Available: www.nida.nih.gov/researchreports/cocaine/cocaine.html

National Institute on Drug Abuse. (2000, June). *Epidemiologic trends in drug abuse.* Rockville, MD: USGPO. Available: www.nida.gov/CEWG/AdvancedRep/6_20ADV/0600adv.html

National Institute on Drug Abuse. (2002). *Methamphetamine: Abuse and addiction.* Rockville, MD: U.S. Department of Health and Human Services.

National Institute on Drug Abuse. (2004, November). *Cocaine: Abuse and addiction.* Rockville, MD: U.S. Department of Health and Human Services.

National Institute on Drug Abuse. (2005). *Hallucinogens and dissociative drugs.* Rockville, MD: U.S. Department of Health and Human Services.

National Institute of Drug Abuse. (2010, November). *Marijuana.* Rockville, MD: U.S. Department of Health and Human Services.

Naudts, K., & Hodgins, S. (2005, December 29). Neurobiological correlates of violent behavior among persons with schizophrenia. *Schizophrenia Bulletin,* 1–11.

Nee, C., & Taylor, M. (1988). Residential burglary in the Republic of Ireland: A situational perspective. *Howard Journal, 27,* 105–116.

Needleman, H. L., McFarland, C., Ness, R. B., Fienberg, S. E., & Tobin, M. J. (2002). Bone lead levels in adjudicated delinquents: A case control study. *Neurotoxicology and Teratology, 24,* 711–717.

Neighbors, C., Vietor, N. A., & Knee, C. R. (2002). A motivational model of driving anger and aggression. *Personality and Social Psychology Bulletin, 28,* 324–335.

Neisser, U., Boodoo, G., Bouchard, T., Boykin, A. W., Brody, N., Ceci, S. J.*, et al. (1996). Intelligence: Knowns and unknowns. *American Psychologist, 51,* 77–101.

Nelson, C. A., & Bloom, F. E. (1997). Child development and neuroscience. *Child Development, 68,* 970–987.

Nelson, D. R., Hammen, C., Brennan, P. A., & Ullman, J. B. (2003). The impact of maternal depression in adolescent adjustment: The role of expressed emotion. *Journal of Consulting and Clinical Psychology, 71,* 935–944.

Nettler, G. (1984). *Explaining crime* (3rd ed.). New York: McGraw-Hill.

Neugebauer, R., Hoek, H. W., & Susser, E. (1999). Prenatal exposure to wartime famine and development of antisocial personality disorder in early adulthood. *Journal of the American Medical Association, 4,* 479–481.

Neuman, J. H., & Baron, R. A. (1998). Workplace violence and workplace aggression: Evidence concerning specific forms, potential causes, and preferred targets. *Journal of Management, 24,* 391–419.

Neumann, C. S., & Hare, R. D. (2008). Psychopathic traits in a large community sample: Links to violence, alcohol use, and intelligence. *Journal of Consulting and Clinical Psychology, 76,* 893–899.

Neumann, C. S., Hare, R. D., & Newman, J. P. (2007). The superordinate nature of Psychopathy Checklist-Revised. *Journal of Personality Disorders, 21,* 102–107.

Neumann, C. S., Kosson, D. S., Forth, A. E., & Hare, R. D. (2006). Factor structure of the Hare Psychopathy Checklist: Youth Version (PCL:YV) in incarcerated adolescents. *Psychological Assessment, 18,* 142–154.

Newcomb, A. F., Bukowksi, W. M., & Pattee, L. (1993). Children's peer relations: A meta-analytic review of popular, rejected, neglected, controversial and average sociometric status. *Psychological Bulletin, 113,* 99–128.

Newman, J. P., Curtin, J. J., Bertsch, J. D., & Baskin-Sommers, A. R. (2010). Attention moderates the fearlessness of psychopathic offenders. *Biological Psychiatry, 67,* 66–70.

Newman, J. P., Schmitt, W. A., & Voss, W. D. (1997). The impact of motivationally neutral cues on psychopathic individuals: Assessing the generality of the response modulation hypothesis. *Journal of Abnormal Psychology, 106,* 563–575.

Nicholls, T. L., Ogloff, J. R. P., Brink, J., & Spidel, A. (2005). Psychopathy in women: A review of its clinical usefulness for assessing risk for aggression and criminality. *Behavioral Sciences & the Law, 23,* 779–802.

Nicholls, T. L., & Petrila, J. (2005). Gender and psychopathy: An overview of important issues and introduction to the special issue. *Behavioral Sciences & the Law, 23,* 729–741.

Nicholson, R. A., & Kugler, K. E. (1991). Competent and incompetent criminal defendants: A quantitative review of comparative research. *Psychological Bulletin, 109,* 355–370.

Nietzel, M. T. (1979). *Crime and its modification: A social learning perspective.* New York: Pergamon.

Nigg, J. T., & Huang-Pollock, C. L. (2003). An early-onset model of the role of executive functions and intelligence in conduct disorder/delinquency. In B. B. Lahey, T. E. Moffitt, and A. Caspi (Eds.), *Causes of conduct disorder and juvenile delinquency.* New York: Guilford.

Nisbett, R. E. (2005). Heredity, environment, and race differences in IQ. *Psychology, Public Policy, and Law, 11,* 302–310.

Noesner, G. W., & Dolan, J. T. (1992, August). First responder negotiation training. *FBI LawEnforcement Bulletin,* 1–4.

Nordström, A., Dahlgren, L., & Kullgren, G. (2006). Victim relations and factors triggering homicides committed by offenders with schizophrenia. *Journal of Forensic Psychiatry & Psychology, 17,* 192–203.

Norris, J., Nurius, P. A., & Graham, T. L. (1999). When a date changes from fun to dangerous: Factors influencing women ability to distinguish. *Violence Against Women, 5,* 230–250.

Nurius, P. S. (2000). Risk perception for acquaintance sexual aggression: A social-cognitive perspective. *Aggression and Violent Behavior, 5,* 63–78.

Nurius, P. S., Norris, Young, D. S., Graham, T. L., & Gaylord, J. (2000). Interpreting and defensively responding to threat: Examining appraisals and coping with acquaintance sexual aggression. *Violence and Victims, 15,* 187–298.

Obeidallah, D. A., & Earls, F. J. (1999). *Adolescent girls: The role of depression in the development of delinquency.* Washington, DC: National Institute of Justice.

Odgers, C. L., Moffitt, T. E., Broadbent, J. M., Dickson, N., Hancox, R. J., Harrington, H., et al. (2008). Female and male antisocial trajectories: From childhood origins to adult outcomes. *Development and Psychopathology, 20,* 673–716.

Odgers, C. L., Reppucci, N. D., & Moretti, M. M. (2005). Nipping psychopathy in the bud: An examination of the convergent, predictive, and theoretical utility of the PCL-YV among adolescent girls. *Behavioral Sciences & the Law, 23,* 743–763.

O'Donnell, J., Hawkins, J. D., & Abbott, R. D. (1995). Predicting serious delinquency and substance abuse among aggressive boys. *Journal of Consulting and Clinical Psychology, 63,* 529–537.

Office of Applied Studies. (2004). *Drug abuse warning network, 2003.* Rockville, MD: U.S. Department of Health and Human Services.

Office of Justice Programs. (2011, October). *Bullying. OJP fact sheet.* Washington, DC: Author.

Office of National Drug Control Policy. (1999a, November). *Gamma hydroxybutyrate (GHB).* Washington, DC: Executive Office of the President. Available: www.whitehousedrugpolicy.gov

Office of National Drug Control Policy. (1999b, May). *Methamphetamine.* Washington, DC: Executive Office of the President. Available: www.whitehousedrugpolicy.gov

Office of National Drug Control Policy. (1999c, April). *Drug data summary.* Available: www.whitehousedrugpolicy.gov

Office of National Drug Control Policy. (2000, June). *MDMA.* Washington, DC: Executive Office of the President. Available: www.whitehousedrugpolicy.gov

Office of National Drug Control Policy. (2003a, February). *Rohypnol.* Washington, DC: Executive Office of the President. Available: www.whitehousedrugpolicy.gov

Office of National Drug Control Policy. (2003b, November). *Methamphetamine.* Washington, DC: Author.

Office of National Drug Control Policy. (2003c, November). *Drug data summary.* Washington, DC: Author.

Office of National Drug Control Policy. (2003d, October). *Marijuana.* Washington, DC: Author.

Office of National Drug Control Policy. (2005, November). *Marijuana.* Washington, DC: Author.

Office of National Drug Control Policy. (2006a, July). *Marijuana.* Washington, DC: Author.

Office of National Drug Control Policy. (2006b, July). *Methamphetamine.* Washington, DC: Author.

Office of National Drug Control Policy. (2006c, June). *Cocaine.* Washington, DC: Author.

Office of National Drug Control Policy. (2006d, June). *MDMA.* Washington, DC: Author.

Office of National Drug Control Policy. (2006e, May). *Heroin.* Washington, DC: Author.

Office of National Drug Control Policy. (2006f, July). *OxyContin.* Washington, DC: Author.

Office of National Drug Control Policy. (2006g, July). *Club drugs.* Washington, DC: Author.

Offord, D. R., Boyle, M. C., & Racine, Y. A. (1991). The epidemiology of antisocial behavior in childhood and adolescence. In D. J. Pepler & K. H. Rubin (Eds.), *The development and treatment of childhood aggression.* Hillsdale, NJ: Erlbaum.

Offord, D. R., Chmura Kraemeer, H., Kazdin, A. E., Jensen, P. S., & Harrington, R. (1998). Lowering the burden of suffering from child psychiatric disorder: Trade-offs among clinical, targeted, and universal interventions. *Journal of the American Academy of Child & Adolescent Psychiatry, 37,* 686–694.

Ogloff, J. R., & Wong, S. (1990) Electrodermal and cardiovascular evidence of a coping response in psychopaths. *Criminal Justice and Behavior, 17,* 231–245.

Ohlin, L. E., & Tonry, M. (1989). Family violence in perspective. In L. Ohlin & M. Tonry (Eds.), *Family violence* (Vol. 11). Chicago: University of Chicago Press.

Oliver, B. R., & Plomin, R. (2007). Twins' early development study (TEDS): A multivariate, longitudinal genetic investigation of language, cognition and behavior problems from childhood through adolescence. *Twin Research and Human Genetics, 10,* 96–105.

Olson, C. K. (2004). Media violence research and youth violence data: Why do they conflict? *Academic Psychiatry, 28,* 144–150.

Olson, S. L., Sameroff, A. J., Kerr, D. C. R., Lopez, N. L., & Wellman, H. M. (2005). Developmental foundations of externalizing problems in young children: The role of effortful control. *Development and Psychopathology, 17,* 25–45.

Olweus, D. (1997). Bully/victim problems in school: Facts and intervention. *European Journal of Psychology of Education, 12,* 495–510.

Ondrovik, J., & Hamilton, D. (1991). Credibility of victims diagnosed as multiple personality: A case study. *American Journal of Forensic Psychology, 9,* 13–17.

O'Neill, M. L., Lidz, V., & Heilbrun, K. (2003). Adolescents with psychopathic characteristics in a substance abusing cohort: Treatment process and outcomes. *Law and Human Behavior, 27,* 299–313.

Orne, M. T., Dinges, D. F., & Orne, E. C. (1984). On the differential diagnosis of multiple personality in the forensic context. *International Journal of Clinical and Experimental Hypnosis, 32,* 118–169.

Osgood, W. D., O'Malley, P. M., Bachman, G. G., & Johnstone, L. D. (1989). Time trends and urge trends in arrests and self-reported illegal behavior. *Criminology, 27,* 389–415.

Osofsky, M. J., Bandura, A., & Zimbardo, P. G. (2005). The role of moral disengagement in the executive process. *Law and Human Behavior, 29,* 371–393.

O'Toole, M. E. (2000). *The school shooter: A threat assessment perspective.* Quantico, VA: Critical Incident Response Group, National Center for the Analysis of Violent Crime.

Paciello, M., Fida, R., Tramontano, C., Lupinetti, C., & Caprara, G. V. (2008). Stability and change of moral disengagement and its impact on aggression and violence in late adolescence. *Child Development, 79,* 1288–1309.

Pagani, L. S., Tremblay, R. G., Nagin, D., Zoccolilo, M., Vitaro, F., & McDuff, P. (2004). Risk factor models for adolescent verbal and physical aggression toward mothers. *International Journal of Behavioral Development, 28,* 528–537.

Pagelow, M. D. (1989). The incidence and prevalence of criminal abuse of other family members. In L. Ohlin & M. Tonry (Eds.), *Family violence* (Vol. 11). Chicago: University of Chicago Press.

Pardini, D., & Byrd, A. L. (2012). Perceptions of aggressive conflicts and others' distress in children with callous-unemotional traits: 'I'll show you who's boss, even if you suffer and I get in trouble'. *Journal of Child Psychology and Psychiatry, 53,* 283–291.

Pardini, D., Lochman, J. E., & Powell, N. (2007). The development of callous-unemotional traits and antisocial behavior in children: Are there shared and/or unique predictors. *Journal of Clinical Child and Adolescent Psychology, 36,* 319–333.

Pardini, D., & Loeber, R. (2008). Interpersonal callousness trajectories across adolescence: Early social influences and adult outcomes. *Criminal Justice and Behavior, 35,* 173–196.

Parent, G., Guay, J-P., & Knight, R. A. (2011). An assessment of long-term risk of recidivism by adult sex offenders: One size doesn't fit all. *Criminal Justice and Behavior, 38,* 188–209.

Parents Television Council. (2007, January). *Dying to entertain: Violence on prime time broadcast television 1998 to 2006.* Lost Angeles, CA: Author.

Parker, H., & Newcombe, R. (1987). Heroin use and acquisitive crime in an English community. *British Journal of Sociology, 38,* 331–350.

Parker, J. G., & Asher, S. R. (1987). Peer relations and later personal adjustment: Are low-accepted children at risk? *Psychological Bulletin, 102,* 357–389.

Patchin, J. W., & Hinduja, S. (2012). Cyberbullying: An update and synthesis of the research. In J. W. Patchin & S. Hinduaj (Eds.), *Cyberbullying Prevention and Response: Expert Perspectives* (pp. 13–35). New York: Routledge.

Patrick, C. J., Bradley, M. M., & Lang, P. J. (1993). Emotion in the criminal psychopath: Start reflex modulation. *Journal of Abnormal Psychology, 102,* 82–92.

Patrick, C. J., Zempolich, K. A., & Levenston, G. K. (1997). Emotionality and violent behavior in psychopaths: A biosocial analysis. In A. Raine, P. A. Brennan, D. P. Farrington, & S. A. Mednick (Eds.), *Biosocial bases of violence.* New York: Plenum.

Patterson, G. R. (1982). *Coercive family processes.* Eugene, OR: Castalia Press.

Patterson, G. R. (1986). Performance models for antisocial boys. *American Psychologist, 41,* 432–444.

Patterson, G. R., Forgatch, M. S., & DeGarmo, D. S. (2010). Cascading effects following intervention. *Development and Psychopathology, 22,* 949–970.

Patterson, G. R., & Yoerger, K. (2002). A developmental model for early- and late-onset delinquency. In J. B. Reid, G. R. Patterson, & J. J. Snyder (Eds.), *Antisocial behavior in children and adults: A developmental analysis and the Oregon model for intervention*. Washington, DC: American Psychological Association.

Paull, D. (1993). *Fitness to stand trial*. Springfield, IL: Charles C Thomas.

Paus, T. (2010). Growth of white matter in the adolescent brain: Myelin or axon. *Brain and Cognition, 72*, 26–35.

Pearl, P. T. (1995). Identifying and responding to Munchausen syndrome by proxy. *Early Child Development and Care, 106*, 177–185.

Penfield, W. (1975). *The mystery of the mind*. Princeton, NJ: Princeton University Press.

Penrod, S. (1983). *Social psychology*. Englewood Cliffs, NJ: Prentice Hall.

Pepler, D. J., & Slaby, R. G. (1994). Theoretical and development perspectives on youth and violence. In L. D. Eron, J. H. Gentry, & P. Schlegel (Eds.), *Reason to hope: A psychosocial perspective on violence and youth*. Washington, DC: American Psychological Association.

Pereda, N., Guilera, G, Forns, M., & Gómez-Benito, J. (2009). The prevalence of child sexual abuse in community and student samples: A meta-analysis. *Clinical Psychology Review, 29*, 328–338.

Pérez-Fuentes, G., Olfson, M., Villegas, L., Morcillo, C., Wang, S., & Blanco, C. (2012). Prevalence and correlates of child sexual abuse: A national study. *Comprehensive Psychiatry*. DOI: 10.1016

Perilla, J. L., Lippy, C., Rosales, A., & Serrata, J. V. (2011). Prevalence of domestic violence. In J. W. White, M. P. Koss, & A. E. Kasdin (Eds.), *Violence against women and children. Vol. 1. Mapping the terrain*. (pp. 199–220). Washington, DC: American Psychological Association.

Perkins, C. A. (2003). *Weapon use and violent crime*. Washington, DC: U.S. Department of Justice, Bureau of Justice Statistics.

Peters, S. D., Wyatt, G. E., & Finkelhor, D. (1986). Prevalence. In D. Finkelhor (Ed.), *Sourcebook on child sexual abuse*. Beverly Hills, CA: Sage.

Petraitis, J., Flay, B. R., & Miller, T. Q. (1995). Reviewing theories of adolescent substance abuse: Organizing pieces in the puzzle. *Psychological Bulletin, 117*, 67–86.

Petras, H., Schaeffer, C. M., Ialongo, N., Hubbard, S., Muthén., Lambert, S. F., Poduska, J., & Kellam, S. (2004). When the course of aggressive behavior in childhood does not predict antisocial behavior outcomes in adolescence and young adulthood: An examination of potential explanatory variables. *Development and Psychopathology, 16*, 919–941.

Pettit, G. S., Laird, R. D., Bates, J. E., & Dodge, K. A. (1997). Patterns of after-school care in middle childhood: Risk factors and developmental outcomes. *Merrill-Palmer Quarterly, 43*, 515–538.

Pfiffner, L. J., McBurnett, K., Rathouz, P. I., & Judice, S. (2005). Family correlates of oppositional and conduct disorder in children with attention deficit/hyperactivity disorders. *Journal of Abnormal Child Psychology, 33*, 551–563.

Pharo, H., Sim, C., Graham, M., Gross, J., & Hayne, H. (2011). Risky business: Executive function, personality, and reckless behavior during adolescence and emerging adulthood. *Behavioral Neuroscience, 125*, 970–978.

Piaget, J. (1948). *The moral judgment of the child*. New York: Free Press.

Piazza, J. A. (2009). Is Islamist terrorism more dangerous? An empirical study of group of ideology, organization, and goal structure. *Terrorism and Political Violence, 21*, 62–88.

Pillemer, K., & Finkelhor, D. (1988). The prevalence of elder abuse: A random sample survey. *Gerontologist, 28*, 51–57.

Pillemer, K., & Suitor, J. J. (1988). Elder abuse. In V. B. van Hasselt, R. L. Morrison, A. S. Morrison, A. S. Bellak, & M. Hersen (Eds.), *Handbook of family violence*. New York: Plenum.

Pillmann, F., Rohde, A., Ullrich, S., Draba, S., Sannemueller, U., & Marnerous, A. (1999). Violence, criminal behavior, and the EEG: Significance of left hemispheric focal abnormalities. *Journal of Neuropsychiatry & Clinical Neurosciences, 11*, 454–457.

Pinizzotto, A. J. (1984). Forensic psychology: Criminal personality profiling. *Journal of Police Science and Administration, 12*, 32–40.

Pinizzotto, A. J., & Finkel, N. J. (1990). Criminal personality profiling: An outcome and process study. *Law and Human Behavior, 14*, 215–234.

Pirelli, G., Gottdiener, W. H., & Zapf, P. A. (2011). A meta-analytic review of competency to stand trial research. *Psychology, Public Policy, and Law, 17*, 1–53.

Pithers, W. D., Beal, L. S., Armstrong, J., & Petty, J. (1989). Identification of risk factors through clinical interviews and analysis of records. In D. R. Laws (Ed.), *Relapse prevention with sex offenders.* New York: Guilford.

Pithers, W. D., Kashima, K. M., Cumming, G. F., Beal, L. S., & Buell, M. M. (1988). Relapse prevention of sexual aggression. In R. A. Prentky & V. L. Quinsey (Eds.), *Human sexual aggression: Current perspectives.* New York: New York Academy of Sciences.

Pithers, W. D., Marques, J. K., Gibat, C. C., & Marlatt, G. A. (1983). Relapse prevention with sexual aggressives. In J. G. Greer & I. R. Stuart (Eds.), *The sexual aggressor: Current perspectives on treatment.* New York: Van Nostrand Reinhold.

Pleck, E. (1989). Criminal approaches to family violence, 1640–1980. In L. Ohlin & M. Tonry (Eds.), *Family violence* (Vol. 11). Chicago: University of Chicago Press.

Plomin, R. (1986). *Development, genetics, and psychology.* Hillsdale, NJ: Erlbaum.

Plummer, D. L., & Graziano, W. G. (1987). Impact of grade retention on the social development of elementary school children. *Developmental Psychology, 23*, 267–275.

Podnieks, E., Pillemer, K., & Nicolson, J. P. (1990). *National survey on abuse of the elderly in Canada: Final report.* Toronto, ON: Ryerson Polytechnic Institute.

Poortinga, E., Lemmen, C., & Jibson, M. D. (2006). A case control study: White-collar defendants compared with defendants charged with nonviolent theft. *Journal of the American Academy of Psychiatry and the Law, 34*, 82–89.

Pope, C. E. (1977). *Crime-specific analysis: The characteristics of burglary incidents (LEAA).* Washington, DC: USGPO.

Popper, K. R. (1968). *The logic of scientific discovery.* New York: Harper & Row.

Porter, C. L., Hart, C. H., Yang, C., Robinson, C. C., Olsen, S. F., Zeng, Q., et al. (2005). A comparative study of child temperament and parenting in Beijing, China and the western United States. *International Journal of Behavioral Development, 29*, 541–551.

Porter, L. E., & Alison, L. J. (2006). Behavioural coherence in group robbery: A circumplex model of offender and victim interactions. *Aggressive Behavior, 32*, 330–342.

Porter, S., Birt, A. R., & Boer, D. P. (2001). Investigation of the criminal and conditional release histories of Canadian federal offenders as a function of psychopathy and age. *Law and Human Behavior, 25*, 647–661.

Porter, S., Fairweather, D., Drugge, J., Herve, H., Birt, A. R., & Boer, D. (2000). Profiles of psychopathy in incarcerated sexual offenders. *Criminal Justice and Behavior, 27*, 216–233.

Porter, S., Woodworth, M., Earle, J., Drugge, J., and Boer, D. (2003). Characteristics of sexual homicides committed by psychopathic and nonpsychopathic offenders. *Law and Human Behavior, 27*, 459–470.

Porter, T., & Gavin, H. (2010). Infanticide and neonaticide: A review of 40 years of research literature on incidence and causes. *Trauma, Violence, & Abuse, 11*, 99–112.

Portzky, G., Audenaert, K., & van Heeringen, K. (2009). Psychological and psychiatric factors associated with adolescent suicide: A case-control psychological autopsy study. *Journal of Adolescence, 32*, 849–862.

Posner, J. K., & Vandell, D. L. (1999). After-school activities and the development of low-income urban children: A longitudinal study. *Developmental Psychology, 35*, 868–879.

Post, J. M., & Gold, S. N. (2002). The psychology of the terrorist: An interview with Jerrold M. Post. *Journal of Trauma Practice, 1*, 83–100.

Post, L. A., Biroscak, B. J., & Barboza, G. (2011). Prevalence of sexual violence. In J. W. White, M. P. Koss, & A. F. Kazdin (Eds.), *Violence against women and children. Vol. 1. Mapping the terrain* (pp. 101–123). Washington, DC: American Psychological Association.

Postmes, T., & Spears, R. (1998). Deindividuation and antinormative behavior: A meta-analysis. *Psychological Bulletin, 123*, 238–259.

Potoczniak, M. J., Mourot, J. E., Crosbie-Burnett, M., & Potoczniak, D. J. (2003). Legal and psychological perspectives on same-sex domestic violence: A multisystematic approach. *Journal of Family Violence, 17*, 252–259.

Poulin, F., & Boivin, M. (2000). Reactive and proactive aggression: Evidence of a two-factor model. *Psychological Assessment, 12,* 115–122.

Powers, R. (2002, March). Apocalypse of adolescence. *Atlantic Monthly,* pp. 58, 60–65.

Prentky, R. A., Harris, B., Frizzell, K., & Righthand, S. (2000). An actuarial procedure of assessing risk in juvenile sex offenders. *Sexual Abuse: A Journal of Research and Treatment, 12,* 71–93.

Prentky, R. A., & Knight, R. A. (1986). Impulsivity in the life style and criminal behavior of sexual offenders. *Criminal Justice and Behavior, 13,* 141–164.

Prentky, R. A., Knight, R. A., & Lee, A. F. S. (1997). *Child sexual molestation: Research issues.* NIJ Research Report. Rockville, MD: National Criminal Justice Reference Service. Available: www.ncjrs.org/txtfiles/163390.txt

President's Commission on Law Enforcement and Administration of Justice. (1967). *The challenge of crime in free society.* Washington, DC: USGPO.

PRIDE Surveys. (2003). *2002–2003 PRIDE surveys national summary, grades 6 through 12.* Bowling Green, KY: Author.

Prinstein, M. J., Boergers, J., & Vernberg, E. M. (2001). Overt and relational aggression in adolescents: Social-psychological adjustment of aggressors and victims. *Journal of Clinical Child Psychology, 30,* 479–491.

Prinstein, M. J., & La Greca, A. M. (2004). Childhood peer rejection and aggression predictors of adolescent girls' externalizing and health risk behaviors: A 6-year longitudinal study. *Journal of Consulting and Clinical Psychology, 72,* 103–112.

Protection of Children from Sexual Predators Act. (1998, October 30). United States Congress, Pub. L. No. 105-314 § & 701. Washington, DC: U.S. Government Printing Office.

Putnam, C. T., & Kirkpatrick, J. T. (2005, May). Juvenile firesetting: A research overview. *Juvenile Justice Bulletin* (NCJ 207606). Washington, DC: U.S. Department of Justice, Office of Juvenile Justice and Delinquency Prevention.

Puzzanchera, C. M. (2009, April). *Juvenile arrests 2007.* Washington, DC: U.S. Department of Justice, Office of Juvenile Justice and Delinquency Prevention.

Puzzanchera, C. M., & Adams, B. (2011, December). *Juvenile arrests, 2009. National Report Series Bulletin.* Washington, DC: U.S. Department of Justice, Office of Juvenile Justice and Delinquency Prevention.

Puzzanchera, C., Adams, B., & Sickmund, M. (2011). *Juvenile Court Statistics, 2008.* Pittsburgh, PA: National Center for Juvenile Justice.

Puzzanchera, C. M., Stahl, A. L., Finnegan, T. A., Tierney, N., & Snyder, H. N. (2004, December). *Juvenile court statistics 2000.* Washington, DC: Office of Juvenile Justice and Delinquency Prevention, National Center for Juvenile Justice.

Quattrocchi, M. R., & Schopp, R. F. (2005). Tarasaurus Rex: A standard of care that could not adapt. *Psychology, Public Policy, and Law, 11,* 109–137.

Quay, H. C. (1965). Psychopathic personality: Pathological stimulation-seeking. *American Journal of Psychiatry, 122,* 180–183.

Quay, H. C. (1987). Intelligence. In H. C. Quay (Ed.), *Handbook of juvenile delinquency.* New York: Wiley.

Quayle, E., & Jones, T. (2011). Sexualized images of children on the Internet. *Sexual Abuse: A Journal of Research and Treatment, 23,* 7–21.

Quinet, K. (2007). The missing missing: Toward a quantification of serial murder victimization in the United States. *Homicide Studies, 11,* 319–339.

Quinet, K. (2011). Prostitutes as victims of serial homicide: Trends and case characteristics, 1970–2009. *Homicide Studies, 15,* 74–100.

Quinsey, V. L., Chaplin, T. C., & Upfold, D. (1989). Arsonists and sexual arousal to firesetting: Correlation unsupported. *Journal of Behaviour Therapy and Experimental Psychiatry, 20,* 203–209.

Quinsey, V. L., Harris, G. T., Rice, M. E., & Cormier, C. (2006). *Violent offenders: Appraising and managing risk* (2nd ed.). Washington, DC: American Psychological Association.

Quinsey, V. L., & Marshall, W. L. (1983). Procedures for reducing inappropriate sexual arousal: An evaluation review. In J. G. Greer & I. R. Stuart (Eds.), *The sexual aggressor.* New York: Van Nostrand Reinhold.

Quinsey, V. L., Rice, M. E., & Harris, G. T. (1995). Actuarial prediction of sexual recidivism. *Journal of Interpersonal Violence, 10,* 85–105.

Quinsey, V. L., Skilling, T. A., Lalumière, M. L., & Craig, W. M. (2004). *Juvenile delinquency: Understanding the origins of individual differences.* Washington, DC: American Psychological Association.

Rabkin, J. G. (1979). Criminal behavior of discharged mental patients: A critical appraisal of the research. *Psychological Bulletin, 86,* 1–27.

Rabrenovic, G. (2007). Introduction: Responding to hate violence: New challenges and solutions. *American Behavioral Scientist, 51,* 143–148.

Ragatz, L. L., Fremouw, W., & Baker, E. (2012). The psychological profile of white-collar offenders: Demographics, criminal thinking, psychopathic traits, and psychopathology. *Criminal Justice and Behavior, 39,* 978–997.

Rainbow, L., & Gregory, A. (2011). What behavioural investigative advisers actually do. In L. Alison & L. Rainbow (Eds.), *Professionalizing offender profiling* (pp. 18–34). London: Routledge.

Raine, A. (1993). *The psychopathology of crime: Criminal behavior as a clinical disorder.* San Diego, CA: Academic Press.

Raine, A. (2002). Biosocial studies of antisocial and violent behavior in children and adults: A review. *Journal of Abnormal Child Psychology, 30,* 311–326.

Raine, A. (2008). From genes to brain to antisocial behavior. *Current Directions in Psychological Science, 17,* 323–328.

Raine, A., Brennan, P., & Mednick, S. A. (1997). Interaction between birth complications and early maternal rejection in predisposing individuals to adult violence: Specificity to serious, early-onset violence. *American Journal of Psychiatry, 134,* 1265–1271.

Raine, A., Buschsbaum, M., & LaCasse, L. (1997). Brain abnormalities in murderers indicated by positron emission tomography. *Biological Psychiatry, 42,* 495–508.

Raine, A., Venables, P. H., & Williams, M. (1995). High autonomic arousal and electrodermal orienting at age 15 years as protective factors against criminal behavior at age 29 years. *American Journal of Psychiatry, 152,* 1595–1600.

Raine, A., Venables, P. H., & Williams, M. (1996). Better autonomic arousal and faster electrodermal half-recovery time at age 15 years as possible protective factors against crime at age 29 years. *Developmental Psychology, 32,* 624–630.

Ramirez, D., McDevitt, J., & Farrell, A. (2000, November). *A resource guide on racial profiling data collection systems: Promising practices and lessons learned.* Boston: Northeastern University Press. Available: www.usdoj.gov

Ramirez, J. M. (2003). Hormones and aggression in childhood and adolescence. *Aggression and Violent Behavior, 8,* 621–644.

Ramirez, J. R., Crano, W. D., Quist, R., Burgoon, M., Alvaro, E. M., & Grandpre, J. (2004). Acculturation, familism, parental monitoring, and knowledge as predictors of marijuana and inhalant use in adolescents. *Psychology of Addictive Behavior, 18,* 3–11.

Rantala, R. R. (2008, September). *Cybercrime against businesses, 2005.* Washington, DC: U.S. Department of Justice, Bureau of Justice Statistics.

Räsänen, P., Tiihonen, J., Isohanni, M. Rantakallio, P., Lehtonen, J., & Moring, J. (1998). Schizophrenia, alcohol abuse, and violent behavior: A 26-year follow-up study of an unselected birth cohort. *Schizophrenia Bulletin, 24,* 432–441.

Rasche, C. (1993). Given reason for violence in intimate relationships. In A. Wilson (Ed.), *Homicide.* Cincinnati, OH: Anderson.

Raskin, D. C., & Hare, R. D. (1978). Psychopathy and detection of deception in a prison population. *Psychophysiology, 15,* 126–136.

Ray, O. (1972). *Drugs, society and human behavior.* St. Louis, MO: C. V. Mosby.

Redlich, A. D., Kulish, R., & Steadman, H. J. (2011). Comparing true and false confessions among persons with serious mental illness. *Psychology, Public Policy, and Law, 17,* 394–418.

Redlich, A. D., Liu, S., Steadman, H. J., Callahan, L., & Robbins, P. C. (2012). Is diversion swift? Comparing mental health court and traditional criminal justice processing. *Criminal Justice and Behavior, 39,* 420–433.

Redlich, A. D., Summers, A., & Hoover, S. (2010). Self-reported false confessions and false guilty pleas among offenders with mental illness. *Law and Human Behavior, 34,* 79–90.

Rehder, W., & Dillow, G. (2003). *Where the money is: True tales from the bank robbery capital of the world.* New York: Norton.

Reid, J. B. (1993). Prevention of conduct disorder before and after school entry: Relating interventions to developmental findings. *Development and Psychopathology, 5,* 243–262.

Reid, J. B., & Eddy, J. M. (2002). Preventive efforts during the elementary school years: The linking the interests of families and teachers (LIFT) project. In J. B. Reid & G. Patterson (Eds.). *Antisocial behavior in children and adolescents: A developmental analysis* (pp. 219–333). Washington, DC: American Psychological Association.

Reiman, J. (1995). *The rich get richer and the poor get prison* (4th ed.). Needham Heights, MA: Allyn & Bacon.

Reiss, A. J., & Roth, J. A. (Eds.) (1993). *Understanding and preventing violence.* Washington, DC: National Academy Press.

Reitzel, L. R. (2003, January). Sexual offender update: Juvenile sexual offender recidivism and treatment effectiveness. *Correctional Psychologist, 35*(1), 3–4.

Rengert, G., & Wasilchick, J. (1985). *Suburban burglary: A time and place for everything.* Springfield, IL: Charles C Thomas.

Rengert, G. F., & Groff, E. (2011). *Residential burglary: How the urban environment and our lifestyles play a contributing role* (3rd ed.). Springfield, IL: Charles C Thomas.

Rennison, C. M. (2002, August). *Rape and sexual assault: Reporting to police and medical attention, 1992–2000.* Washington, DC: U.S. Department of Justice, Bureau of Justice Statistics.

Rennison, C. M. (2003, February). *Intimate partner violence, 1993–2001* (NCJ 197838). Washington, DC: U.S. Department of Justice, Bureau of Justice Statistics.

Rennison, C. M., & Rand, M. R. (2003, August). *Criminal victimization, 2002.* Washington, DC: U.S. Department of Justice, Bureau of Justice Statistics.

Rennison, C. M., & Welchans, S. (2000, May). *Intimate partner violence.* Washington, DC: U.S. Department of Justice.

Resnick, P. J. (1969). Child murder by parents. *American Journal of Psychiatry, 126,* 325–334.

Resnick, P. J. (1970). Murder of the newborn: A psychiatric review of neonaticide. *American Journal of Psychiatry, 126,* 1414–1420.

Resnick, P. J. (1995). Guidelines for the evaluation of malingering in posttraumatic stress disorder. In R. I. Simon (Ed.), *Posttraumatic stress disorder in litigation guidelines for forensic assessment* (pp. 309–329). Washington, DC: American Psychiatric Association.

Revitch, E., & Schlesinger, L. B. (1988). Clinical reflections on sexual aggression. In R. A. Prentky & V. L. Quinsey (Eds.), *Human sexual aggression: Current perspectives.* New York: New York Academy of Sciences.

Revitch, G., & Weiss, R. G. (1962). The pedophiliac offender. *Diseases of the Nervous System, 23,* 73–78.

Rhee, S. H., & Waldman, I. D. (2002). Genetic and environmental influences on antisocial behavior: A meta-analysis of twin and adoption studies. *Psychological Bulletin, 128,* 490–529.

Rhee, S. H., & Waldman, I. D. (2011). Genetic and environmental influences on aggression. In P. R. Shaver & Mario Mikulincer (Eds.), *Human aggression and violence: Causes, manifestations, and consequences* (pp. 143–163). Washington, DC: American Psychological Association.

Rice, M. E., & Harris, G. T. (1991). Firesetters admitted to a maximum security psychiatric institution. *Journal of Interpersonal Violence, 6,* 461–475.

Rice, M. E., & Harris, G. T. (2002). Men who molest their sexually immature daughters: Is a special explanation required? *Journal of Abnormal Psychology, 111,* 329–339.

Rice, M. E., Harris, G. T., & Cormier, C. A. (1992). An evaluation of a maximum security therapeutic community for psychopaths and other mentally disordered offenders. *Law and Human Behavior, 16,* 399–412.

Rich, T., & Shively, M. (2004, December). *A methodology for evaluating geographic profiling software.* Cambridge, MA: Abt Associates.

Richard, A. (1999, November). *International trafficking in women to the United States: A contemporary manifestation of slavery and organized crime.* Washington, DC: Center for the Study of Intelligence.

Richards, H., Casey, J., & Lucente, S. (2003). Psychopathy and treatment response to incarcerated female substance abusers. *Criminal Justice and Behavior, 30,* 251–276.

Righthand, S., & Welch, C. (2001, March). *Juveniles who have sexually offended: A review of the professional literature.* Washington, DC: Office of Juvenile Justice and Delinquency Prevention.

Riley, S. (1998). Competency to stand trial adjudication: A comparison of female and male defendants. *Journal of the American Academy of Psychiatry and the Law, 26,* 223–240.

Ritvo, E., Shanok, S. S., & Lewis, D. O. (1983). Firesetting and nonfiresetting delinquents. *Child Psychiatry and Human Development, 13,* 259–267.

Robbins, E., & Robbins, L. (1964). Arson with special reference to pyromania. *New York State Journal of Medicine, 2,* 795–798.

Robers, S., Zhang, J., Truman, J., & Snyder, T. D. (2012, February). *Indicators of school crime and safety: 2011.* Washington, DC: National Center for Educational Statistics, Bureau of Justice Statistics.

Robers, S., Zhang, J., Truman, J., & Snyder, T. D. (2012, February). *Indicators of School Crime and Safety: 2011.* Washington, DC: U.S. Department of Education, U.S. Department of Justice Office of Justice Programs.

Roberts, A. R. (2002). Preface. In A. R. Roberts (Ed.), *Handbook of domestic violence intervention strategies: Policies, programs, and legal remedies.* New York: Oxford University Press.

Roberts, A. R., Zgoba, K. M., & Shahidullah, S. M. (2007). Recidivism among four types of homicide offenders: An exploratory analysis of 336 homicide offenders in New Jersey. *Aggression and Violent Behavior, 12,* 493–507.

Roberts, L., & Indermaur, D. (2005). Boys and rage: Driving-related violence and aggression in Western Australia. *Australian & New Zealand Journal of Criminology, 38,* 361–380.

Robinson, M., McLean, N. J., Oddy, W. H., Mattes, E., Bulsara, M., Li, J., & Newnham, J. P. (2010). Smoking cessation in pregnancy and the risk of child behavioural problems: A longitudinal perspective. *Journal of Epidemiology and Community Health, 64,* 622–629.

Roche, P. Q. (1958). *The criminal mind: A study of communication between criminal law and psychiatry.* New York: Grove Press.

Rodman, H., & Grams, P. (1967). *Juvenile delinquency and the family: A review and discussion.* Task Force

Report: Juvenile delinquency and youth crime. Washington, DC: USGPO.

Roesch, R., Zapf, P. A., Golding, S. L., & Skeem, J. L. (1999). Defining and assessing competency to stand trial. In A. K. Hess & I. B. Weiner (Eds.), *The handbook of forensic psychology* (2nd ed.). New York: Wiley.

Roe-Sepowitz, D. (2007). Adolescent female murderers: Characteristics and treatment implications. *American Journal of Orthopsychiatry, 77,* 489–496.

Rogers, P., & Davies, M. (2007). Perceptions of victims and perpetrators in a depicted child sexual abuse case: Gender and age factors. *Journal of Interpersonal Violence, 22,* 566–584.

Rogers, R. (1997). *Clinical assessment of malingering and deception* (2nd ed.). New York: Guilford.

Rogers, R. (2000). The uncritical acceptance of risk assessment in clinical practice. *Law and Human Behavior, 24,* 595–605.

Rogers, R., Blackwood, H. L., Fiduccia, C. E., Steadham, J. A., Drogin, E. Y., & Rogstad, J. E. (2012). Juvenile Miranda warnings: Perfunctory rituals or procedural safeguards? *Criminal Justice and Behavior, 39,* 229–249.

Rogstad, J. E., & Rogers, R. (2008). Gender differences in contributions of emotion to psychopathy and antisocial personality disorder. *Clinical Psychology Review, 28,* 1472–1484.

Roizen, J. (1997). Epidemiological issues in alcohol-related violence. In M. Galanter (Ed.), *Recent developments in alcoholism* (Vol. 13). New York: Plenum.

Romer, D. (2010). Adolescent risk taking, impulsivity, and brain development: Implications for prevention. *Developmental Psychobiology, 52,* 263–276.

Romer, D., Betancourt, L. M., Brodsky, N., Giannetta, J. M., Yang, W., & Hurt, H. (2011). Does adolescent risk taking imply weak executive function? A prospective study of relations between working memory performance, impulsivity, and risk taking in early adolescence. *Developmental Science, 14,* 1119–1133.

Root, C., MacKay, S., Henderson, J., Del Bove, G., & Warling, D. (2008). The link between maltreatment and juvenile firesetting: Correlates and underlying mechanisms. *Child Abuse & Neglect, 32,* 161–176.

Rose, A. J., Swenson, L. P., & Waller, E. M. (2004). Overt and relational aggression and perceived popularity: Developmental differences in concurrent and prospective relations. *Developmental Psychology, 40,* 378–387.

Rosecan, J. S., Spitz, H. I., & Gross, B. (1987). Contemporary issues in the treatment of cocaine abuse. In H. I. Spitz & J. S. Rosecan (Eds.), *Cocaine abuse: New directions in treatment and research.* New York: Brunner/Mazel.

Rosenbaum, D. P., Lurigio, A. J., & Davis, R. C. (1998). *The prevention of crime: Social and situational strategies.* Belmont, CA: West/Wadsworth.

Rosenbaum, M. (1989). *Just saw what? An alternative view on solving America's drug problem.* San Francisco: National Council of Crime and Delinquency.

Rosenfeld, B., & Ritchie, K. (1998). Competence to stand trial: Clinician reliability and the role of offense severity. *Journal of Forensic Sciences, 43,* 151–157.

Rosenthal, D. (1970). *Genetic theory and abnormal behavior.* New York: McGraw-Hill.

Rosenthal, D. (1971). *Genetics of psychopathology.* New York: McGraw-Hill.

Rosoff, S. M., Pontell, H. N., & Tillman, R. (1998). *Profit without honor: White-collar crime and the looting of America.* Upper Saddle River, NJ: Prentice Hall.

Ross, M. P., & Bachar, K. J. (2002). Rape. In D. Levinson (Ed.), *Encyclopedia of crime and punishment* (Vol. 3). Thousand Oaks, CA: Sage.

Rossmo, D. K. (1997). Geographic profiling. In J. L. Jackson & D. A. Bekerain (Eds.), *Offender profiling: Theory, research, and practice.* Chichester, UK: Wiley.

Roth, J. A. (1996). *Psychoactive substances and violence.* Washington, DC: U.S. Department of Justice. Available: www.ncjrs.org/txtfile/psycho.txt

Rothman, D. (1971). *The discovery of the asylum.* Boston: Little, Brown.

Rowe, D. C., & Gulley, B. (1992). Sibling effects on substance abuse and delinquency. *Criminology, 35,* 217–233.

Rowe, D. C., Rodgers, D. C., & Meseck-Bushey, S. (1992). Sibling delinquency and the family environment: Shared and unshared influences. *Child Development, 63,* 57–67.

Roza, S. J., Verburg, B. O., Jaddoe, V. W. V., Hofman, A., Mackenbach, J. P., Steegers, E. A. P., & Tiemeier, H. (2007). Effects of maternal smoking pregnancy on prenatal brain development: The Generation R Study. *European Journal of Neuroscience, 25,* 611–617.

Rubin, B. (1972). Predictions of dangerousness in mentally ill criminals. *Archives of General Psychiatry, 27,* 397–407.

Rubin, K. H., Bukowski, W., & Parker, J. G. (1998). Peer interactions, relationships, and groups. In W. Damon (Series Ed.) & N. Eisenberg (Vol. Ed.), *Handbook of child psychology: Vol. 3. Social, emotional, and personality development* (5th ed.). New York: Wiley.

Rubin, K. H., Burgess, K. B., Dwyer, K. M., & Hastings, P. D. (2003). Predicting preschoolers' externalizing behaviors from toddler temperament, conflict, and maternal negativity. *Developmental Psychology, 39,* 164–176.

Rubinsky, E. W., & Brandt, J. (1986). Amnesia and criminal law: A clinical overview. *Behavioral Sciences & the Law, 4,* 27–46.

Rubinstein, M., Yeager, C. A., Goodstein, C., & Lewis, D. O. (1993). Sexually assaultive male juveniles: A follow-up. *American Journal of Psychiatry, 150,* 262–265.

Ruby, C. L. (2002). Are terrorists mentally deranged? *Analyses of Social Issues and Public Policy, 2,* 15–26.

Ruchkin, V. (2002). Family impact on violent youth. In R. R. Corrado, R. Roesch, S. D. Hart, & J. K. Gierowski (Eds.), *Multi-problem violent youth: A foundation for comparative research on needs, interventions, and outcomes.* Amsterdam: IOS Press.

Ruffolo, M. C., Sarri, R., & Goodkind, S. (2004). Study of delinquent, diverted, and high-risk adolescent girls: Implications for mental health intervention. *Social Work Research, 28,* 237–245.

Russell, A., Hart, C. H., Robinson, C. C., & Olsen, S. F. (2003). Children's sociable and aggressive behaviour with peers: A comparison of the US and Australia, and contributions of temperament and parental styles. *International Journal of Behavioral Development, 27,* 74–86.

Russell, D. (1973). Emotional aspects of shoplifting. *Psychiatric Annals, 3,* 77–86.

Rutter, M. (1997). Individual differences and levels of antisocial behavior. In A. Raine & P. A. Brennan (Eds.), *Biological bases of violence.* New York: Plenum.

Rutter, M. (2005). Commentary: What is the meaning and utility of the psychopathy concept? *Journal of Abnormal Child Psychology, 33,* 499–503.

Rutter, M., Giller, H., & Hagell, A. (1998). *Antisocial behavior by young people.* Cambridge, UK: Cambridge University Press.

Ryan, G., Miyoshi, T. J., Metzner, J. L., Krugman, R. D., & Fryer, G. E. (1996). Trends in a national sample of sexually abusive youths. *Journal of the American Academy of Child and Adolescent Psychiatry, 33,* 17–25.

Sageman, M. (2004). *Understanding terrorist networks.* Philadelphia: University of Pennsylvania Press.

Sagovsky, A., & Johnson, S. D. (2007). When does repeat burglary victimization occur? *Australian and New Zealand Journal of Criminology, 40,* 1–26.

Salekin, R. T. (2002). Psychopathy and therapeutic pessimism: Clinical lore or clinical reality? *Clinical Psychology Review, 22,* 79–112.

Salekin, R. T. (2010). Treatment of child and adolescent psychopathy: Focusing on change. In R. T. Salekin & D. R. Lyman (Eds.), *Handbook of child and adolescent psychopathy* (pp. 343–373). New York: Guilford.

Salekin, R. T., Brannen, D. N., Zalot, A. A., Leistico, A-M, & Neumann, C. S. (2006). Factor structure of psychopathy in youth: Testing the applicability of the new four-factor model. *Criminal Justice and Behavior, 33,* 135–157.

Salekin, R. T., & Frick, P. J. (2005). Psychopathy in children and adolescents: The need for a developmental perspective. *Journal of Abnormal Child Psychology, 33,* 403–409.

Salekin, R. T., Leistico, A-M. R., Trobst, K. K., Schrum, C. L., & Lochman, J. E. (2005). Adolescent psychopathy and personality theory—the interpersonal circumplex: Expanding evidence of a nomological net. *Journal of Abnormal Child Psychology, 33,* 445–460.

Salekin, R. T., & Lochman, J. E. (2008). Child and adolescent psychopathy: The search for protective factors. *Criminal Justice and Behavior, 35,* 159–172.

Salekin, R. T., & Lynam, D. R. (Eds.). (2010). *Handbook of child and adolescent psychopathy.* New York: Guilford Press.

Salekin, R. T., Rogers, R., & Machin, D. (2001). Psychopathy in youth: Pursuing diagnostic clarity. *Journal of Youth and Adolescence, 30,* 173–195.

Salekin, R. T., Rogers, R., & Sewell, K. W. (1997). Construct validity of psychopathy in a female offender sample: A multitrait-multimethod evaluation. *Journal of Abnormal Psychology, 106,* 576–585.

Salekin, R. T., Rogers, R., Ustad, K. L., & Sewell, K. W. (1998). Psychopathy and recidivism among female inmates. *Law and Human Behavior, 22,* 109–128.

Salekin, R. T., Ziegler, T. A., Larrea, M. A., Anthony, V. L., & Bennett, A. D. (2003). Predicting psychopathy with two Millon Adolescent Psychopathy scales. The importance of egocentric and callous traits. *Journal of Personality Assessment, 80,* 154–163.

Salisbury, E. J., & Van Voorhis, P. (2009). Gendered pathways: An empirical investigation of women probationers' paths to incarceration. *Criminal Justice and Behavior, 35,* 541–566.

Saltaris, C. (2002). Psychopathy in juvenile offenders: Can temperament and attachment be considered as robust developmental precursors? *Clinical Psychology Review, 22,* 729–752.

Sameroff, A. J., Peck, S. C., & Eccles, J. S. (2004). Changing ecological determinants of conduct problems from early adolescence to early childhood. *Development and Psychopathology, 16,* 873–896.

Sampson, R. (2011, August). *Acquaintance rape of college students: Problem-oriented guides for police problem-specific guides, No. 17.* Washington, DC: Office of Community Oriented Policing Services, U.S. Department of Justice.

Sampson, R. J., & Lauritsen, J. L. (1994). Violent victimization and offending: Individual, situational and community-level risk factors. In A. T. Reiss Jr. & J. Roth (Eds.), *Understanding and preventing violence: Social Influences* (Vol. 3). Washington, DC: National Academy Press.

Sampson, R. J., Morenoff, J. D., & Gannon-Rowley, T. (2002). Assessing neighborhood effects: Social processes and new directions in research. *Annual Review of Sociology, 28,* 443–478.

Sandler, J. C., & Freeman, N. J. (2007). Typology of female sex offenders: A test of Vandiver and Kercher. *Sex Abuse, 19,* 73–89.

Saner, H., & Ellickson, P. (1996). Concurrent risk factors for adolescent violence. *Journal of Adolescent Health, 19,* 94–103.

Santa Clara Criminal Justice Pilot Project. (1972). *Burglary in San Jose.* Springfield, VA: U.S. Department of Commerce.

Santiago, G. B. (2002). Latina battered women: Barriers to service delivery and cultural considerations. In A. R. Roberts (Ed.), *Handbook of domestic violence intervention strategies: Policies, programs, and legal remedies.* New York: Oxford University Press.

Santtila, P., Häkkänen, H., Alison, L., & Whyte, C. (2003). Juvenile firesetters: Crime scene actions and offender characteristics. *Legal and Criminological Psychology, 8,* 1–20.

Sarangi, S., & Alison, L. (2005). Life story accounts of left wing terrorists in India. *Journal of Investigative Psychology and Offender Profiling, 2,* 69–86.

Sarasalo, E., Bergman, B., & Toth, J. (1996). Personality traits and psychiatric and somatic morbidity among kleptomaniacs. *Acta Psychiatrica Scandinavica, 94,* 358–364.

Sarasalo, E., Bergman, B., & Toth, J. (1997). Kleptomania-like behaviour and psychosocial characteristics among shoplifters. *Legal and Criminological Psychology, 2,* 1–10.

Sarbin, T. R. (1979). The myth of the criminal type. In T. R. Sarbin (Ed.), *Challenges to the criminal justice system: The perspective of community psychology.* New York: Human Services Press.

Satterfield, J. H., Swanson, J., Schell, A., & Lee, F. (1994). Prediction of antisocial behavior in attention-deficit hyperactivity disorder boys from aggression/defiance scores. *Journal of the American Academy of Child and Adolescent Psychiatry, 33,* 185–191.

Saulnier, K., & Perlman, D. (1981). The actor-observer bias is alive and well in prison: A sequel to Wells. *Personality and Social Psychology, 7,* 559–564.

Saunders, E. B., & Awad, G. A. (1991). Adolescent female firesetters. *Canadian Journal of Psychiatry, 36,* 401–404.

Savage, J. (2008). The role of exposure to media violence in the etiology of violent behavior: A criminologist weighs in. *American Behavioral Scientist, 51,* 1123–1136.

Savage, J., & Yancey, C. (2008). The effects of media violence exposure on criminal aggression: A meta-analysis. *Criminal Justice and Behavior, 35,* 772–791.

Sawyer, A. M., & Borduin, C. M. (2011). Effects of multisystemic therapy through midlife: A 21.9-year follow-up to a randomized clinical trial with serious and violent juvenile offenders. *Journal of Consulting and Clinical Psychology, 79,* 643–652.

Scaret, D., & Wilgosh, L. (1989). Learning disabilities and juvenile delinquency: A causal relationship? *International Journal for the Advancement of Counselling, 12,* 113–123.

Schachter, S., & Latané, B. (1964). Crime, cognition, and the autonomic nervous system. In M. R. Jones (Ed.), *Nebraska symposium on motivation.* Lincoln, NE: University of Nebraska Press.

Schauer, E. J., & Wheaton, E. M. (2006). Sex trafficking into the United States: A literature review. *Criminal Justice Review, 31,* 146–169.

Schacter, D. L. (1986). On the relation between genuine and simulated amnesia. *Behavioral Sciences & the Law, 4,* 47–64.

Schaeffer, C. M., & Borduin, C. M. (2005). Long-term follow-up to a randomized clinical trial of multisystemic therapy with serious and violent juvenile offenders. *Journal of Consulting and Clinical Psychology, 73,* 445–453.

Schaffer, M., Clark, S., & Jeglic, E. L. (2009). The role of empathy and parenting style in the development of antisocial behaviors. *Crime & Delinquency, 55,* 586–599.

Scherer, D. G., Brondino, M. J., Henggeler, S. W., Melton, G. B., & Hanley, J. H. (1994). Multisystemic family preservation therapy: Preliminary findings from a study of rural and minority serious adolescent offenders. *Journal of Emotional and Behavioral Disorders, 2,* 198–206.

Schiffer, B., & Vonlaufen, C. (2011). Executive dysfunctions in pedophilic and nonpedophilic child molesters. *Journal of Sexual Medicine, 8,* 1975–1984.

Schlosser, E. (2001). *Fast food nation: The dark side of the all-American meal.* Boston: Houghton Mifflin.

Schmideberg, M. (1953). Pathological firesetters. *Journal of Criminal Law, Criminology and Police Science, 44,* 30–39.

Schmucker, M., & Lösel, F. (2008). Does sexual offender treatment work? A systematic review of outcome evaluation. *Psicothema, 20,* 10–19.

Schneider, J. L. (2005). Stolen-goods markets. *British Journal of Criminology, 45,* 129–140.

Schrager, L., & Short, J. (1978). Toward a sociology of organizational crime. *Social Problems, 25,* 407–419.

Schuller, R. A., & Vidmar, V. (1992). Battered woman syndrome evidence in the courtroom: A review of the literature. *Law and Human Behavior, 16,* 272–292.

Schulsinger, F. (1972). Psychopathy: Heredity and environment. *International Journal of Mental Health, 1,* 190–206.

Schuster, M. A., Stein, B. D., Jaycox, L. H., Collins, R. L., Marshall, G. N., & Elliott, M. N. (2001). A national survey of stress reactions after the September 11, 2001, terrorist attacks. *New England Journal of Medicine, 345,* 1507–1512.

Schwartz, I. M. (1989). (In) *justice for juveniles: Rethinking the best interests of the child.* Lexington, MA: Lexington Books.

Schwartz, J. P., Hage, S. M., Bush, I., & Burns, L. K. (2006). Unhealthy parenting and potential mediators as contributing factors to future intimate violence: A review of the literature. *Trauma, Violence, & Abuse, 7,* 206–221.

Sciarra, D. (1999). Assessment and treatment of adolescent sex offenders: A review from a cross-cultural perspective. *Journal of Offender Rehabilitation, 28,* 103–118.

Scott, E. S., & Steinberg, L. (2008). Adolescent development and regulation of youth crime. *The Future of Children, 18,* 15–33.

Scott, M. S. (2004, January). *Burglary of single-family houses in Savannah, Georgia.* Washington, DC: U.S. Department of Justice.

Scully, D., & Marolla, J. (1984). Convicted rapists' vocabulary of motive: Excuses and justifications. *Social Problems, 31,* 530–544.

Seagrave, D., & Grisso, T. (2002). Adolescent development and measurement of juvenile psychopathy. *Law and Human Behavior, 26,* 219–239.

Sears, R., Maccoby, E., & Levin, H. (1957). *Patterns of child rearing.* Evanston, IL: Row, Peterson.

Seeley, K., Tombari, M. L., Bennett, L. J., & Dunkle, J. B. (2011). *Bullying in schools: An overview.* Washington, DC: U.S. Department of Justice, Office of Justice Programs, Office of Juvenile Justice and Delinquency Prevention.

Séguin, J. R., Nagin, D., Asaad, J-M., & Tremblay, R. E. (2004). Cognitive-neuropsychological function in chronic physical aggression and hyperactivity. *Journal of Abnormal Psychology, 113,* 603–613.

Seiler, C. (2012, June 6). Bills would fight 'shoplifting on steroids.' *Albany Times Union,* p. A3.

Seligman, M. E. (1975). *Helplessness: On depression, development, and death.* San Francisco: W. H. Freeman.

Selkin, J. (1987). *Psychological autopsy in the courtroom.* Denver, CO: Author.

Sellbom, M., & Verona, E. (2007). Neuropsychological correlates of psychopathic traits in a non-incarcerated sample. *Journal of Research in Personality, 41,* 276–294.

Sellin, T. (1970). A sociological approach. In M. E. Wolfgang, L. Savitz, & N. Johnson (Eds.), *The sociology of crime and delinquency* (2nd ed.). New York: Wiley.

Serin, R. C., & Amos, N. L. (1995). The role of psychopathy in the assessment of dangerousness. *International Journal of Law & Psychiatry, 18,* 231–238.

Serin, R. C., Peters, R. D., & Barbaree, H. E. (1990). Predictors of psychopathy and release outcome in a criminal population. *Psychological Assessment, 2,* 419–422.

Serin, R. C., & Preston, D. L. (2001). Managing and treating violent offenders. In J. B. Ashford, B. D. Sales, & W. H. Reid (Eds.), *Treating adult and juvenile offenders with special needs.* Washington, DC: American Psychological Association.

Seto, M. C. (2008a). *Pedophilia and sexual offending against children: Theory, assessment and intervention.* Washington, DC: American Psychological Association.

Seto, M. C. (2008b). Pedophilia: Psychopathology and theory. In D. R. Laws & W. T. O'Donohue (Eds.), *Sexual deviance: Theory, assessment, and treatment* (2nd ed.). New York: Guilford.

Seto, M. C. (2012). Is pedophilia a sexual orientation. *Archives of Sexual Behavior, 41,* 231–236.

Seto, M. C., & Barbaree, H. E. (1999). Psychopathy, treatment behavior, and sex offender recidivism. *Journal of Interpersonal Violence, 14,* 1235–1248.

Seto, M. C., & Hanson, R. K. (2011). Introduction to special issue on Internet-facilitated sexual offending. *Sexual Abuse: A Journal of Research and Treatment, 23,* 3–6.

Seto, M. C., Hanson, R. K., & Babchishin, K. M. (2011). Contact sexual offending by men with online sexual offenses. *Sexual Abuse: A Journal of Research and Treatment, 23,* 124–145.

Seto, M. C., & Lalumière, M. L. (2010). What is so special about male adolescent sexual offending? A review and test of explanations through meta-analysis. *Psychological Bulletin, 136,* 526–575.

Seto, M. C., Maric, A., & Barbaree, H. E. (2001). The role of pornography in the etiology of sexual aggression. *Aggression and Violent Behavior, 6,* 35–53.

Sevecke, K., Pukrop, R., Kosson, D. S., & Krischer, M. K. (2009). Factor structure of the Hare Psychopathy Checklist: Youth Version in German female and male detainees and community adolescents. *Psychological Assessment, 21,* 45–56.

Seymour, A. (2001). Victimization of the elderly. In G. Coleman, M. Gaboury, M. Murray, & A. Seymour (Eds.), *1999 National Victim Assistance Academy.* Washington, DC: U.S. Department of Justice.

Shah, N. R., & Bracken, M. B. (2000). A systematic review and meta-analysis of prospective studies on the association between maternal cigarette smoking and preterm delivery. *American Journal of Obstetrics and Gynecology, 182,* 465–472.

Shain, R., & Phillips, J. (1991). The stigma of mental illness: Labeling and stereotyping in the news. In L. Wilkins & P. Patterson (Eds.), *Risky business: Communicating issues of science, risk, and public policy.* Westport, CT: Greenwood Press.

Shaver, P. R., & Mikulincer, M. (2011). Introduction. In P. R. Shaver & M. Mikulincer (Eds.), *Human aggression and violence: Causes, manifestations, and consequences* (pp. 3–11). Washington, DC: American Psychological Association.

Shaw, D. S., Gilliom, M., Ingoldsby, E. M., & Nagin, D. S. (2003). Trajectories leading to school-age conduct problems. *Developmental Psychology, 39,* 189–200.

Shaw, D. S., Owens, E. B., Giovannelli, J., & Winslow, E. B. (2001). Infant and toddler pathways leading to early externalizing disorders. *Journal of the American Academy of Child and Adolescent Psychiatry, 40,* 36–43.

Shneidman, E. S. (1994). The psychological autopsy. *American Psychologist, 49,* 75–76.

Short, J. F., & Nye, I. (1957). Reported behavior as a criterion of deviant behavior. *Social Problems, 5,* 207–213.

Shover, N. (1972). Structures and careers in burglary. *Journal of Criminal Law, Criminology and Police Science, 63,* 540–548.

Showers, J. (1999). *Never never never shake a baby: The challenges of shaken baby syndrome.* Alexandria, VA: National Association of Children's Hospitals and Related Institutions.

Shufelt, J. L., & Cocozza, J. J. (2006). *Youth with mental health disorders in the juvenile justice system: Results from a multi-state prevalence study.* Delmar, NY: National Center for Mental Health and Juvenile Justice.

Shulman, E. P., Cauffman, E., Piquero, A. R., & Fagan, J. (2011). Moral disengagement among serious juvenile offenders: A longitudinal study of the relations between morally disengaged attitudes and offending. *Developmental Psychology, 47,* 1619–1632.

Shumaker, D. M., & Prinz, R. J. (2000). Children who murder: A review. *Clinical Child and Family Psychology Review, 3,* 97–115.

Sickmund, M. (2004, June). *Juveniles in corrections.* (NCJ 202885). Washington, DC: U.S. Department of Justice, Office of Juvenile Justice and Delinquency Prevention.

Sickmund, M. (2009, June). *Delinquency cases in juvenile court, 2005.* Washington, DC: U.S. Department of Justice, Office of Juvenile Justice and Delinquency Prevention.

Siegel, A., & Kohn, L. (1959). Permissiveness, permission, and aggression: The effect of adult presence or absence on aggression in children's play. *Child Development, 30,* 131–141.

Siegel, J. A., & Williams, L. M. (2001, July). *Risk factors for violent victimization of women: A prospective study.* Washington, DC: U.S. Department of Justice.

Siegel, J. M., Sorenson, S. B., Golding, J. M., Burnam, M. A., & Stein, J. A. (1987). The prevalence of childhood sexual assault: The Los Angeles Epidemiological Catchment Area Project. *American Journal of Epidemiology, 126,* 1141–1153.

Sieh, E. W. (1987). Garment workers: Perceptions of inequity and employee theft. *British Journal of Criminology, 27,* 174–190.

Siever, L. J. (2008). Neurobiology of aggression and violence. *American Journal of Psychiatry, 165,* 429–442.

Silberman, E. K., & Weingartner, H. (1996). Hemispheric lateralization of functions related to emotion. *Brain and Cognition, 5,* 322–353.

Silke, A. (2003). The psychology of suicidal terrorism. In A. Silke (Ed.), *Terrorists, victims and society: Psychological perspectives on terrorism and its consequences.* Chichester, UK: Wiley.

Silke, A. (2008). Holy warriors: Exploring the psychological processes of Jihadi radicalization. *European Journal of Criminology, 5,* 99–123.

Silver, E. (2006). Understanding the relationship between mental disorder and violence: The need for a criminological perspective. *Law and Human Behavior, 30,* 685–706.

Silvern, L., Karyl, J., Waelde, L., Hodges, W. F., Starek, J., Heidt, E., et al. (1995). Retrospective reports of parental partner abuse: Relationships to depression, trauma symptoms and self-esteem among college students. *Journal of Family Violence, 10,* 177–202.

Silverthorn, P., & Frick, P. J. (1999). Developmental pathways to antisocial behavior: The delayed-onset pathway in girls. *Development and Psychopathology, 11,* 101–126.

Sim, D. J., & Proeve, M. (2010). Crossover and stability of victim type in child molesters. *Legal and Criminological Psychology, 15,* 401–413.

Simon, R. J. (1983). The defense of insanity. *Journal of Psychiatry and Law, 11,* 183–201.

Simon, R. J., & Aaronson, D. E. (1988). *The insanity defense.* New York: Praeger.

Simon, R. J., & Cockerham, W. (1977). Civil commitment, burden of proof, and dangerous acts: A comparison of the perspectives of judges and psychiatrists. *Journal of Psychiatry and Law, 5,* 571–594.

Simonelli, C. J., Mullis, T., & Rohde, C. (2005). Scale of negative family interactions: A measure of parental and sibling aggression. *Journal of Interpersonal Violence, 20,* 792–803.

Simons, D. A., Wurtele, S. K., & Durham, R. L. (2008). Developmental experiences of child sexual abusers and rapists. *Child Abuse & Neglect, 32,* 549–560.

Simons, R. L., Lin, K. H., & Gordon, L. C. (1998). Socialization in the family of origin and male dating violence: A prospective study. *Journal of Marriage and the Family, 60,* 467–478.

Simourd, D. J., & Hoge, R. D. (2000). Criminal psychopathy: A risk-and-need perspective. *Criminal Justice and Behavior, 27,* 256–272.

Simpson, P. M., Banerjee, D., & Simpson, C. L., Jr. (1994). Softlifting: A model of motivating factors. *Journal of Business Ethics, 13,* 431–438.

Singer, M. I., Miller, D. B., Guo, S., Flannery, D. J., Frierson, T., & Slovack, K. (1999). Contributors to violent behavior among elementary and middle school children. *Pediatrics, 104,* 878–884.

Sipe, R., Jensen, E. L., & Everett, R. S. (1998). Adolescent sexual offenders grown up: Recidivism in young adulthood. *Criminal Justice and Behavior, 25,* 109–124.

Sitnikova, T., Goff, D., & Kuperberg, G. R. (2009). Neurocognitive abnormalities during comprehension of real-world, goal-directed behaviors in schizophrenia. *Journal of Abnormal Psychology, 118,* 256–277.

Skeem, J. L., & Cauffman, E. (2003). Views of the downward extension: Comparing the youth version of the Psychopathy Checklist with the Youth Psychopathic Traits Inventory. *Behavioral Sciences & the Law, 21,* 737–770.

Skeem, J. L., & Cooke, D. J. (2010a). Is criminal behavior a central component of psychopathy? Conceptual directions for resolving the debate. *Psychological Assessment, 22,* 433–445.

Skeem, J. L., & Cooke, D. J. (2010b). One measure does not a construct make: Directions toward reinvigorating psychopathy research—reply to Hare and Neuman (2010). *Psychological Assessment, 22,* 455–459.

Skeem, J. L., Edens, J. F., Camp, J., & Colwell, L. H. (2004). Are there ethnic differences in levels of psychopathy? A meta-analysis. *Law and Human Behavior, 28,* 505–527.

Skeem, J. L., Edens, J. F., & Colwell, L. H. (2003, April). Are there racial differences in levels of psychopathy? A meta-analysis. *Paper presented at the 3rd annual conference of the International Association of Forensic Mental Health Services,* Miami, FL.

Skeem, J. L., Edens, J. F., Sanford, G. M., & Colwell, L. H. (2003). Psychopathic personality and racial/ethnic differences reconsidered: A reply to Lynn (2002). *Personality and Individual Differences 35*, 1439–1462.

Skeem, J. L., Emke-Francis, P., & Louden, J. L. (2006). Probation, mental health, and mandated treatment: A national survey. *Criminal Justice and Behavior, 33*, 158–184.

Skeem, J. L., Monahan, J., & Mulvey, E. P. (2002). Psychopathy, treatment involvement, and subsequent violence among civil psychiatric patients. *Law and Human Behavior, 26*, 577–603.

Skeem, J. L., Poythress, N., Edens, J., Lilienfeld, S., & Cale, E. (2003). Psychopathic personality or personalities? Exploring potential variants of psychopathy and their implications for risk assessment. *Aggression and Violent Behavior, 8*, 513–546.

Skilling, T. A., Quinsey, V. L., & Craig, W. M. (2001). Evidence of a tax on underlying serious antisocial behavior in boys. *Criminal Justice and Behavior, 28*, 450–470.

Skinner, B. F. (1964). Behaviorism at fifty. In T. W. Wann (Ed.), *Behaviorism and phenomenology*. Chicago: University of Chicago Press.

Skogan, W. G. (1977). Dimensions of the dark figure of unreported crime. *Crime and Delinquency, 23*, 41–50.

Slavkin, M. L. (2001). Enuresis, firesetting, and cruelty to animals: Does the ego triad show predictive validity? *Adolescence, 36*, 461–467.

Slobogin, C. (1985). The guilty but mentally ill verdict: An idea whose time should not have come. *George Washington Law Review, 53*, 494–580.

Slobogin, C. (1999). The admissibility of behavioral science information in criminal trials: From primitivism to *Daubert* to voice. *Psychology, Public Policy, and Law, 5*, 100–119.

Slotter, E. B., & Finkel, E. J. (2011). I³ theory: Instigating, impelling, and inhibiting factors in aggression. In P. R. Shaver & M. Mikulincer (Eds.), *Human aggression and violence: Causes, manifestations, and consequences* (pp. 35–52). Washington, DC: American Psychological Association.

Slovenko, R. (1989). The multiple personality: A challenge to legal concepts. *The Journal of Psychiatry and Law, 17*, 681–719.

Smallbone, S. W., & Wortley, R. K. (2004). Criminal diversity and paraphilic interests among adult males convicted of offenses against children. *International Journal of Offender Therapy and Comparative Criminology, 48*, 175–188.

Smart, R. G. (1986). Cocaine use and problems in North America. *British Journal of Criminology, 28*, 109–128.

Smart, R. G., Asbridge, M., Mann, R. E., & Adlaf, E. M. (2003). Psychiatric distress among road rage victims and perpetrators. *Canadian Journal of Psychiatry, 48*, 681–688.

Smigel, E. O. (1970). Public attitudes toward stealing as related to the size of the victim organization. In E. O. Smigel & H. L. Ross (Eds.), *Crimes against bureaucracy*. New York: Van Nostrand Reinhold.

Smith, B. L., & Morgan, K. D. (1994). Terrorists right and left: Empirical issues in profiling American terrorists. *Studies in Conflict and Terrorism, 17*, 39–57.

Smith, D. (2002, June). Helping mentally ill offenders. *Monitor on Psychology, 33*, 64.

Smith, E. J. (2006). The strength-based counseling model. *The Counseling Psychologist, 34*, 13–79.

Smith, G. A., & Hall, J. A. (1982). Evaluating Michigan's guilty but mentally ill verdict: An empirical study. *Michigan Journal of Law Reform, 16*, 75–112.

Smith, P. K., Mahdavi, J., Carvalho, M., Fisher, S., Russell, S., & Tippett, N. (2008). Cyberbullying: Its nature and impact in secondary school pupils. *Journal of Child Psychology and Psychiatry, 49*, 376–385.

Smith, S. S., & Newman, J. P. (1990). Alcohol and drug abuse-dependence disorder in psychopathic and non-psychopathic criminal offenders. *Journal of Abnormal Psychology, 99*, 430–439.

Smithey, M. (1998). Infant homicide: Victim-offender relationship and causes of death. *Journal of Family Violence, 13*, 285–287.

Smithey, M. (2002). Infanticide. In D. Levinson (Ed.), *Encyclopedia of crime and punishment* (Vol. 2). Thousand Oaks, CA: Sage.

Snider, J. F., Hane, S., & Berman, A. L. (2006). Standardizing the psychological autopsy: Addressing the Daubert standard. *Suicide and Life-Threatening Behavior, 36*, 511–518.

Snook, B., Cullen, R. M., Bennell, C., Taylor, P. J., & Gendreau, P. (2008). The criminal profiling illusion: What's behind the smoke and mirrors? *Criminal Justice and Behavior, 35*, 1257–1276.

Snook, B., Dhami, M. K., & Kavanagh, J. M. (2011). Simply criminal: Predicting burglars' occupancy decisions with a simple heuristic. *Law and Human Behavior, 35*, 316–326.

Snook, B., Eastwood, J., Gendreau, P., Goggin, C., & Cullen, R. M. (2007). Taking stock of criminal profiling: A narrative review and meta-analysis. *Criminal Justice and Behavior, 34*, 437–453.

Snyder, H. N. (2000). *Sexual assault of young children as reported to law enforcement: Victim, incident, and offender characteristics.* Washington, DC: U.S. Department of Justice, Bureau of Justice Statistics.

Snyder, H. N. (2001). Epidemiology of official offending. In R. Loeber & D. P. Farrington (Eds.), *Child delinquents: Development, intervention, and service needs.* (pp. 25–46). Thousand Oaks, CA: Sage.

Snyder, H. N. (2006, December). *Juvenile arrests 2004.* Washington, DC: U.S. Department of Justice, Office of Juvenile Justice and Delinquency Prevention.

Snyder, H. N. (2008, August). *Juvenile arrests 2005.* Washington, DC: U.S. Department of Justice, Office of Juvenile Justice and Delinquency Prevention.

Snyder, H. N., Espiritu, R. C., Huizinga, D., Loeber, R., & Petechuk, D. (2003, March). Prevalence and development of child delinquency. *Child Delinquency Bulletin Series* (NCJ193411). Washington, DC: U.S. Department of Justice, Office of Juvenile Justice and Delinquency Prevention.

Snyder, H. N., Sickmund, M., & Poe-Yamagata, E. (2000). *Juvenile transfer to criminal court in the 1990s: Lessons learned from four studies.* Washington, DC: Office of Juvenile Justice and Delinquency Prevention.

Snyder, J., & Patterson, G. (1987). Family interaction and delinquent behavior. In H. C. Quay (Ed.), *Handbook of juvenile delinquency.* New York: Wiley.

Snyder, J., Reid, J., & Patterson, G. (2003). A social learning model of child and adolescent antisocial behavior. In B. B. Lahey, T. E. Moffitt, & A. Caspi (Eds.), *Causes of conduct disorder and juvenile delinquency.* New York: Guilford.

Sorenson, S. B., Stein, J. A., Siegel, J. M., Golding, J. M., & Burnam, M. A. (1987). The prevalence of adult sexual assault: The Los Angeles Epidemiological Catchment Area Project. *American Journal of Epidemiology, 126*, 1154–1164.

Southerland, M. D., Collins, P. A., & Scarborough, K. E. (1997). *Workplace violence.* Cincinnati, OH: Anderson.

Spaccarelli, S., Coatsworth, J. D., & Bowden, B. S. (1995). Exposure to serious family violence among incarcerated boys: Its association with violent offending and potential mediating variables. *Violence and Victims, 10*, 163–182.

Spain, S. E., Douglas, K. S., Poythress, N. G., & Epstein, M. (2004). The relationship between psychopathic features, violence, and treatment outcomes: The comparison of three youth measures of psychopathic features. *Behavioral Sciences & the Law, 22*, 85–102.

Spallone, P. (1998). The new biology of violence: New geneticisms for old? *Body and Society, 4*, 47–65.

Sparr, L. F. (1996). Mental defenses and posttraumatic stress disorder: Assessment of criminal intent. *Journal of Traumatic Stress, 9*, 405–425.

Speckhard, A., Tarabrina, N., Krasnov, V., & Mufel, N. (2005). Stockholm effects and psychological responses to captivity in hostages held by suicide terrorists. *Traumatology, 11*, 121–140.

Sperry, R. (1983). *Science and moral priority.* New York: Columbia University Press.

Spinelli, M. G. (2001). A systematic investigation of 16 cases of neonaticide. *American Journal of Psychiatry, 158*, 811–813.

Spinrad, T. L., Eisenberg, N., & Bernt, F. (2007). Introduction to the special issues on moral development: Part I. *The Journal of Genetic Psychology, 168*, 101–104.

Stadolnik, R. F. (2000). *Drawn to the flame: Assessment and treatment of juvenile firesetting behavior.* Sarasota, FL: Professional Resources Press.

Stagg, V., Wills, G. D., & Howell, M. (1989). Psychopathology in early childhood witnesses of family violence. *Topics in Early Childhood Special Education, 9*, 73–87.

Staller, J. A. (2006). Diagnostic profiles in outpatient child psychiatry. *American Journal of Orthopsychiatry, 76*, 98–102.

Stanger, C., Achenbach, T. M., & Verhulst, F. C. (1997). Accelerated longitudinal comparisons of aggressive versus delinquent syndromes. *Development and Psychopathology, 9,* 43–58.

Stark, C., Paterson, B., Henderson, T., Kidd, B., & Godwin, M. (1997). Counting the dead. *Nursing Times, 93,* 34–37.

Stark, E. (2002). Preparing for expert testimony in domestic violence cases. In A. R. Roberts (Ed.), *Handbook of domestic violence intervention strategies: Policies, programs, and legal remedies.* New York: Oxford University Press.

Statistics Canada. (2011). *Family violence in Canada: A statistical profile.* Ottawa, ON: Canadian Centre for Justice Statistics.

Stattin, H., & Klackenberg-Larsson, I. (1993). Early language and intelligence development and their relationship to future criminal behavior. *Journal of Abnormal Psychology, 102,* 369–378.

Stattin, H., & Magnusson, D. (1991). Stability and change in criminal behaviour up to age 30. *The British Journal of Criminology, 31,* 327–346.

Staub, E. (2001). Genocide and mass killing: Their roots and prevention. In D. J. Christie, R. V. Wagner, & D. D. Winter (Eds.), *Peace, conflict, and violence: Peace psychology for the 21st century.* Upper Saddle River, NJ: Prentice-Hall.

Staub, E. (2004). Understanding and responding to group violence: Genocide, mass killing, and terrorism. In F. M. Moghaddam & A. J. Marsella (Eds.), *Understanding terrorism: Psychosocial roots, consequences, and interventions.* Washington, DC: American Psychological Association.

Steadman, H. J. (1976). Predicting dangerousness. In D. J. Madden & J. R. Lion (Eds.), *Rage • hate • assault • and other forms of violence.* New York: Spectrum Publishers.

Steadman, H. J., & Cocozza, J. J. (1974). *Careers of the criminally insane.* Lexington, MA: Lexington Books.

Steadman, H. J., McGreevy, M. A., Morrissey, J. P., Callahan, L. A., Robbins, P. C., & Cirincione, C. (1993). *Before and after Hinckley: Evaluating insanity defense reform.* New York: Guilford Press.

Steadman, H. J., Mulvey, E. P., Monahan, J., Robbins, P. C., Appelbaum, P. S., Grisso, T., et al. (1998). Violence by people discharged from acute psychiatric inpatient facilities and by others in the same neighborhoods. *Archives of General Psychiatry, 55,* 393–401.

Steffan, J. S., & Morgan, R. D. (2005, February). Meeting the needs of mentally ill offenders: Inmate service utilization. *Corrections Today,* pp. 38–43.

Steinberg, L. (2004). Risk-taking in adolescence: What changes, and why? *Annals of the New York Academy of Sciences, 1021,* 51–58.

Steinberg, L. (2007). Risk-taking in adolescence: New perspectives from brain and behavioral science. *Current Perspectives in Psychological Sciences, 16,* 55–59.

Steinberg, L. (2008). A social neuroscience perspective on adolescent risk taking. *Developmental Review, 28,* 78–106.

Steinberg, L. (2010a). A dual system model of adolescent risk taking. *Developmental Psychobiology, 52,* 216–224.

Steinberg, L. (2010b). A behavioral scientist looks at the science of adolescent brain development. *Brain and Cognition, 72,* 160–164.

Steinberg, L., Cauffman, E., Woolard, J., Graham, S., & Banich, M. (2009). Are adolescents less mature than adults? *American Psychologist, 64,* 583–594.

Steinman, K. J. (2005). Drug selling among high school students: Related risk behaviors and psychosocial characteristics. *Journal of Adolescent Health, 36,* 71–79.

Steinmetz, S. K. (1981). A cross-cultural comparison of sibling violence. *International Journal of Family Psychiatry, 2,* 337–351.

Stern, K. R. (2001, May). A treatment study of children with attention deficit hyperactivity disorder. *OJJDP Fact Sheet.* Washington, DC: U.S. Department of Justice, Office of Juvenile Justice and Delinquency Prevention.

Sternberg, R. J. (2003). A duplex theory of hate: Development and application of terrorism, massacres, and genocide. *Review of General Psychology, 7,* 299–328.

Stevens, M. J. (2005). What is terrorism and can psychology do anything to prevent it? *Behavioral Sciences & the Law, 23,* 507–526.

Stewart, M. A., & Culver, K. W. (1982). Children who set fires: The clinical picture and a follow-up. *British Journal of Psychiatry, 140,* 357–363.

Stickle, T., & Blechman, E. (2002). Aggression and fire: Antisocial behavior in firesetting and nonfiresetting juvenile offenders. *Journal of Psychopathology and Behavioral Assessment, 24,* 177–193.

Stoltenborgh, M., van Ijzendoorn, M. H., Euser, G. M., Bakermans-Kranenburg, M. J. (2011). A global perspective on child sexual abuse: Meta-analysis of prevalence around the world. *Child Maltreatment, 16,* 79–101.

Stone, A. (1975). *Mental health law: A system in transition.* Washington, DC: USGPO.

Stone, M. H. (1998). Sadistic personality in murders. In T. Millon, E. Simonsen, M. Burket-Smith, & R. Davis (Eds.), *Psychopathy: Antisocial, criminal, and violent behavior.* New York: Guilford.

Stouthamer-Loeber, M., Loeber, R., Wei, E., Farrington, D., & Wilkström, P. H. (2002). Risk and promotive effects in the explanation of persistent serious delinquency in boys. *Journal of Consulting and Clinical Psychology, 70,* 111–123.

Stouthamer-Loeber, M. Wei, E., Loeber, R., & Masten, A. S. (2004). Desistence from persistent serious delinquency in the transition to adulthood. *Development and Psychopathology, 16,* 897–918.

Strassberg, D. S., Eastvold, A., Kenny, J. W., & Suchy, Y. (2012). Psychopathy among pedophilic and nonpedophilic child molesters. *Child Abuse & Neglect, 36,* 379–382.

Straus, M. (1991). Discipline and deviance: Physical punishment of children and violence and other crime in adulthood. *Social Problems, 38,* 133–154.

Straus, M. A., & Gelles, R. J. (1990). *Physical violence in American families.* New Brunswick, NJ: Transaction Publishers.

Strentz, T. (1987, November). A hostage psychological survival guide. *FBI Law Enforcement Bulletin,* pp. 1–7.

Stretesky, P. B., & Lynch, M. J. (2001). The relationship between lead exposure and homicide. *Archives of Pediatrics and Adolescent Medicine, 155,* 579–582.

Stretesky, P. B., & Lynch, M. J. (2004). The relationship between lead and crime. *Journal of Health and Social Behavior, 45,* 214–219.

Strickland, S. M. (2008). Female sex offenders: Exploring issues of personality, trauma, and cognitive distortions. *Journal of Interpersonal Violence, 23,* 474–489.

Suarez, E., & Gadalla, T. M. (2010). Stop blaming the victim: A meta-analysis on rape myths. *Journal of Interpersonal Violence, 25,* 2010–2035.

Substance Abuse and Mental Health Administration. (2005, September). *2004 National Survey on Drug Abuse and Mental Health.* Rockville, MD: U.S. Department of Health and Human Services, Author.

Substance Abuse and Mental Health Administration. (2006, March). *State estimates of substance use from the 2003–2004 national surveys on drug use and health.* Rockville, MD: U.S. Department of Health and Human Services, Author.

Substance Abuse and Mental Health Administration. (2009, April). *Nonmedical use of Adderall among full-time college students.* Rockville, MD: U.S. Department of Health and Human Services, Author.

Substance Abuse and Mental Health Administration. (2011, September). *Results from the 2010 National Survey of Drug Use and Health: Summary of national findings.* Rockville, MD: U.S. Department of Health and Human Services, Author.

Sunstein, C. R. (2008). Adolescent risk-taking and social meaning: A commentary. *Developmental Review, 28,* 145–152.

Surette, R. (1999). *Media, crime, and criminal justice* (2nd ed.). Belmont, CA: West/Wadsworth.

Sutherland, E. H. (1947). *Principles of criminology* (4th ed.) Philadelphia: Lippincott.

Sutherland, E. H. (1949). *White-collar crime.* New York: Holt, Rinehart & Winston.

Sutherland, E. H. (1983). *White-collar crime: The uncut version.* New Haven, CT: Yale University Press.

Sutherland, E. H., & Cressey, D. R. (1974). *Criminology* (9th ed.). Philadelphia: Lippincott.

Sutherland, E. H., & Cressey, D. R. (1978). *Criminology* (10th ed.). Philadelphia: Lippincott.

Sutherland, E. H., Cressey, D. R., & Luckenbill, D. F. (1992). *Principles of criminology* (11th ed.). Dix Hills, NY: General Hall.

Sutker, P. B., Uddo-Crane, M., & Allain, A. N. (1991). Clinical and research assessment of posttraumatic stress disorder: A conceptual overview. Psychological Assessment: *A Journal of Consulting and Clinical Psychology, 3,* 520–530.

Sutton, R. M., & Douglas, K. M. (2005). Justice for all, or all for me? More evidence of the importance of the self-other distinction in just-world beliefs. *Personality and Individual Differences, 39,* 637–645.

Sutton, S. K., Vitale, J. E., & Newman, J. P. (2002). Emotion among women with psychopathy during picture perception. *Journal of Abnormal Psychology, 111,* 610–619.

Swahn, M. H., & Donovan, J. E. (2004). Correlates and predictors of violent behavior among adolescent drinkers. *Journal of Adolescent Health, 34,* 480–492.

Sykes, G. M. (1956). *Crime and society.* New York: Random House.

Sykes, G. M., & Matza, D. (1957). Techniques of neutralization: A theory of delinquency. *American Sociological Review, 22,* 664–670.

Syngelaki, E. M., Moore, S. C., Savage, J. C., Fairchild, G. E., & Van Goozen, S. H. M. (2009). Executive functioning and risky decision making in young male offenders. *Criminal Justice and Behavior, 36,* 1213–1227.

Tappan, P. W. (1947). Who is the criminal? *American Sociological Review, 12,* 100–110.

Tarolla, S. M., Wagner, E. F., Rabinowitz, J., & Tubman, J. G. (2002). Understanding and treating juvenile offenders: A review of current knowledge and future directions. *Aggression and Violent Behavior, 7,* 125–143.

Taylor, D. M., & Louis, W. (2004). Terrorism and the quest for identity. In F. M. Moghaddam & A. J. Marsella (Eds.), *Understanding terrorism: Psychosocial roots, consequences, and interventions.* Washington, DC: American Psychological Association.

Taylor, J., Iacono, W. G., & McGue, M. (2000). Evidence for a genetic etiology of early-onset delinquency. *Journal of Abnormal Psychology, 109,* 634–643.

Taylor, M., & Nee, C. (1988). The role of cues in simulated residential burglary. *British Journal of Criminology, 28,* 396–401.

Taylor, P. J., Leese, M., Williams, D., Butwell, M., Daly R., & Larkin, E. (1998). Mental disorder and violence: A special (high security) hospital study. *British Journal of Psychiatry, 172,* 477–484.

Tedeschi, R. G., & Kilmer, R. P. (2005). Assessing strengths, resilience, and growth to guide clinical interventions. *Professional Psychology: Research and Practice, 36,* 230–237.

Tengström, A., Hodgins, S., Grann, M., Långström, N., & Kullgren, G. (2004). Schizophrenia and criminal offending: The role of psychopathy and substance use disorders. *Criminal Justice and Behavior, 31,* 367–391.

Teplin, L. (1984). Criminalizing mental disorder. *American Psychologist, 39,* 794–803.

Teplin, L. (2000, October). Psychiatric disorders in youthful offenders. *National Institute of Justice Journal,* 30–32.

Terrorism Research Center. (1997). *The basics: Combating terrorism.* Alexandria, VA: Author.

Terry, K. J. (2008). Stained glass: The nature and scope of child sexual abuse in the Catholic church. *Criminal Justice and Behavior, 35,* 549–569.

Terry, K. J., & Tallon, J. (2004). *Child sexual abuse.* New York: John Jay College Research Team, John Jay College of Criminal Justice.

Testa, M., Hoffman, J. H., & Livingston, J. A. (2010). Alcohol and sexual risk behaviors as mediators of the sexual victimization-revictimization relationship, *Journal of Consulting and Clinical Psychology, 78,* 249–259.

Testa, M., VanZile-Tamsen, C., & Livingston, J. A. (2007). Prospective prediction of women's sexual victimization by intimate and nonintimate male perpetrators. *Journal of Consulting and Clinical Psychology, 75,* 52–60.

Tewksbury, R. (2005). Collateral consequences of sex offender registration. *Journal of Contemporary Criminal Justice, 21,* 67–81.

Thakker, J., Collie, R. M., Gannon, T., & Ward, T. (2008). Rape: Assessment and treatment. In D. R. Laws & W. T. O'Donohue (Eds.), *Sexual deviance: Theory, assessment, and treatment.* New York: Guilford.

Thomas, A., & Chess, S. (1977). *Temperament and development.* New York: Brunner/Mazel.

Thompson, R. A. (1998). Early sociopersonality development. In W. Damon & N. Eisenberg (Eds.), *Handbook of child psychology. Vol. 3. Social, emotional, and personality development* (5th ed.). New York: Wiley.

Thompson, R. A., & Nelson, C. A. (2001). Developmental science and the media: Early brain development. *American Psychologist, 56,* 5–15.

Thorley, G. (1984). Review of follow-up and follow-back studies of childhood hyperactivity. *Psychological Bulletin, 96,* 116–132.

Thornberry, T. P., & Burch, J. H. H. (1997). *Gang membership and delinquent behavior.* Washington, DC: U.S. Department of Justice, Office of Juvenile Justice and Delinquency Prevention.

Thornberry, T. P., Huizinga, D., & Loeber, R. (1995). The prevention of serious delinquency and violence: Implication from the program of research on the causes and correlates of delinquency. In J. C. Howell, B. Krisberg, J. D. Hawkins, & J. Wilson (Eds.), *Sourcebook on serious violent and chronic juvenile offenders.* Thousand Oaks, CA: Sage.

Thornberry, T. P., & Krohn, M. D. (2005). Applying interactional theory to the explanation of continuity and change in antisocial behavior. In D. P. Farrington (Ed.), *Integrated developmental and life-course theories of offending.* New Brunswick, NJ: Transaction.

Thornberry, T. P., Krohn, M., Lizotte, A. J., & Chard-Wierschem, D. (1993). The role of juvenile gangs in facilitating delinquent behavior. *Journal of Research in Crime and Delinquency, 30,* 55–87.

Tighe, A., Pistrang, N., Casdagli, L., Baruch, G., & Butler, S. (2012). Multisystemic therapy for young offenders: Families' experiences of therapeutic processes and outcomes. *Journal of Family Psychology, 26,* 187–197.

Tinklenberg, J. R., & Stillman, R. C. (1970). Drug use and violence. In D. Daniels, M. Gilula, & F. Ochberg (Eds.), *Violence and the struggle for existence.* Boston: Little, Brown.

Tinklenberg, J. R., & Woodrow, K. M. (1974). Drug use among youthful assaultive and sexual offenders. In S. H. Frazier (Ed.), *Aggression.* Baltimore, MD: Williams & Wilkins.

Tittle, C. R. (1980). *Sanctions and social deviance: The question of deterrence.* New York: Praeger.

Tjaden, P. (1997, November). *The crime of stalking: How big is the problem?* NIJ Research Preview. Washington, DC: U.S. Department of Justice.

Tjaden, P., & Thoennes, N. (1997). *Stalking in America: Findings from the National Violence Against Women Survey.* Denver, CO: Center for Policy Research.

Tjaden, P., & Thoennes, N. (1998a). *Stalking in America: Findings from the National Violence Against Women Survey.* Washington, DC: U.S. Department of Justice.

Tjaden, P., & Thoennes, N. (1998b). *Prevalence, incidence, and consequences of violence against women: Findings from the National Violence Against Women Survey.* Washington, DC: U.S. Department of Justice.

Tjaden, P., & Thoennes, N. (2000, November). *Full report of prevalence, incidence, and consequences of violence against women: Findings from National Violence against Women Survey.* Washington, DC: National Institute of Justice.

Tjaden, P., & Thoennes, N. (2006, January). *Extent, nature, and consequences of rape victimization: Findings from the National Violence Against Women Survey.* Washington, DC: U.S. Department of Justice.

Toch, H. (2008). (Ed.), Special issue: The disturbed offender in confinement. *Criminal Justice and Behavior, 35.*

Tolan, P. H., Gorman-Smith, D., & Henry, D. B. (2003). On developmental ecology of urban males' youth violence. *Developmental Psychology, 39,* 274–279.

Tolan, P. H., & Thomas, P. (1995). The implications of age of onset for delinquency II: Longitudinal data. *Journal of Abnormal Child Psychology, 23,* 157–169.

Tomarken, A. J., Davidson, R. J., Wheeler, R. E., & Doss, R. C. (1992). Individual differences in anterior brain asymmetry and fundamental dimensions of emotion. *Journal of Personality and Social Psychology, 62,* 676–687.

Tonglet, M. (2001). Consumer misbehaviour: An exploratory study of shoplifting. *Journal of Consumer Behaviour, 1,* 336–354.

Torres, A. N., Boccaccini, M. T., & Miller, H. A. (2006). Perceptions of the validity and utility of criminal profiling among forensic psychologists and psychiatrists. *Professional Psychology: Research and Practice, 37,* 51–58.

Tran, H., & Weinraub, M. (2006). Child care effects in context. Quality, stability, and multiplicity in non-maternal child care arrangements during the first 15 months of life. *Developmental Psychology, 42,* 566–582.

Tremblay, R. E. (2003). Why socialization fails: The case of chronic physical aggression. In B. B. Lahey, T. W. Moffitt, & A. Caspi (Eds.), *Causes of conduct disorder and juvenile delinquency* (pp. 182–226). New York; Guilford.

Tremblay, R. E., & Craig, W. (1995). Developmental crime prevention. In M. Tonry & D. P. Farrington (Eds.), *Building a safer society: Strategic approaches to crime prevention.* Chicago: University of Chicago Press.

Tremblay, R. E., LeMarquand, D., & Vitaro, F. (1999). The prevention of oppositional defiant disorder and conduct disorder. In H. C. Quay & A. F. Hogan (Eds.), *Handbook of disruptive behavior disorders.* New York: Kluwer Academic/Plenum Publishers.

Tremblay, R. E., Vitaro, F., Gagnon, C., Piche, C., & Royer, N. (1992). A prosocial scale for the Preschool Behaviour Questionnaire: Concurrent and predictive correlates. *International Journal of Behavioral Development, 15,* 227–245.

Trentacosta, C. J., & Shaw, D. S. (2009). Emotional self-regulation, peer rejection, and antisocial behavior: Developmental associations from early childhood to early adolescence. *Journal of Applied Developmental Psychology, 30,* 356–365.

Trouton, A., Spinath, F. M., & Plomin, R. (2002). Twins Early Development Study (TEDS): A multivariate, longitudinal genetic investigation of language, cognitions and behavior problems in childhood. *Twin Research, 5,* 444–458.

Truman, J. L. (2011, September). *National Crime Victimization Survey: Criminal Victimization, 2010.* U.S. Department of Justice, Bureau of Justice Statistics.

Tsang, J. (2002). Moral rationalization and the integration of situational factors and psychological processes in immoral behavior. *Review of General Psychology, 6,* 25–50.

Tucker, D. M. (1981). Lateral brain function, emotion and conceptualization. *Psychological Bulletin, 89,* 19–46.

Turchik, J. A., & Edwards, K. M. (2011). Myths about male rape: A literature review. *Psychology of Men & Masculinity, 12,* 1–16.

Turrell, S. C. (2000). A descriptive analysis of same-sex relationship violence for a diverse sample. *Journal of Family Violence, 15,* 281–293.

Turvey, B. E. (2008). *Criminal profiling: An introduction to behavioral evidence analysis* (3rd ed.). San Diego, CA: Elsevier.

Turvey, B. E. (2012). *Criminal profiling: An introduction to behavioral evidence analysis* (4th ed.). San Diego, CA: Elsevier.

Tuvblad, C., Eley, T. C., & Lichtenstein, P. (2005). The development of antisocial behaviour from childhood to adolescence: A longitudinal twin study. *European Child and Adolescent Psychiatry, 14,* 216–225.

Tyler, J., Darville, R., & Stalnaker, K. (2001). Juvenile boot camps: A descriptive analysis of program diversity and effectiveness, *Social Science Journal, 38,* 445–460.

Ullman, A., & Straus, M. A. (2003). Violence by children against mothers in relation to violence between parents and corporal by parents. *Journal of Comparative Family Studies, 34,* 41–64.

Ullman, S. E. (1997). Review and critique of empirical studies of rape avoidance. *Criminal Justice and Behavior, 24,* 177–204.

Ullman, S. E. (1999). Social support and recovery from sexual assault: A review. *Aggression and Violent Behavior: A Review Journal, 4,* 343–358.

Ullman, S. E. (2007). A 10-year update of "Review and critique of empirical studies of rape avoidance." *Criminal Justice and Behavior, 34,* 411–429.

Ullman, S. E., & Knight, R. A. (1993). The efficacy of women's resistance strategies in rape situations. *Psychology of Women Quarterly, 17,* 23–38.

Ullman, S. E., & Najdowski, C. J. (2011). Vulnerability and protective factors for sexual assault. In J. W. White, M. R. Koss, & A. F. Kazdin (Eds.), *Violence against women and children. Vol. 1. Mapping the terrain.* (pp. 151–163). Washington, DC: American Psychological Association.

Ullrich, S., Farrington, D. P., & Coid, J. W. (2008). Psychopathic personality traits and life-success. *Personality and Individual Differences, 44,* 1162–1171.

Underwood, R. C., & Patch, P. C. (1999). Siblicide: A descriptive analysis of sibling homicide. *Homicide Studies, 3,* 333–348.

UNFPA. (2009). *Programming to address violence against women: 8 case studies.* New York: Author.

U.S. Bureau of the Census. (2001). *2000 census of population and housing.* Washington, DC: USGPO.

U.S. Bureau of the Census. (2002). *Who's minding the kids? Child care arrangements.* Washington, DC: USGPO.

U.S. Conference of Majors. (1998). *A status report on hunger and homelessness in America's cities: 1998.* Washington, DC: Author.

U.S. Department of Defense. (2009, March). *Report on sexual assault in the military, FY 2009.* Washington, DC: U.S. Department of Defense, Sexual Assault and Response Office.

U.S. Department of Health and Human Services. (2003, April 1). *Child abuse prevention: An overview.* Washington, DC: Author.

U.S. Department of Justice. (1988). *Report to the nation on crime and justice: The data* (2nd ed.). Washington, DC: USGPO.

U.S. Department of Justice. (1989). *Criminal victimization in the United States, 1987.* Washington, DC: USGPO.

U.S. Department of Justice. (1999). *Cyberstalking: A new challenge for law enforcement and industry.* Washington, DC: Author. Available: www.usdoj.gov/criminal/cybercrime/cyberstalking.htm

U.S. Department of Justice. (2000a). *Terrorism in the United States–1998.* Washington, DC: Author.

U.S. Department of Justice. (2000b). *The structure of family violence: An analysis of selected incidents.* Washington, DC: Author.

U.S. Department of Justice. (2002a, October). *Highlights from the NISMART Bulletin.* Washington, DC: U.S. Department of Justice, Office of Juvenile Justice and Delinquency Prevention.

U.S. Department of Justice. (2002b, October). *Nonfamily abducted children: National estimates and characteristics.* Washington, DC: U.S. Department of Justice, Office of Juvenile Justice and Delinquency Prevention.

U.S. Drug Enforcement Administration. (2009, March). "Spice"—plant material(s) laced with synthetic cannabinoids or cannabinoid mimicking compounds. *Microgram Bulletin.* Washington, DC: Author.

U.S. Drug Enforcement Administration. (2012). *Drugs of abuse 2011 edition: A DEA resource guide.* Washington, DC: Author.

U.S. Fire Administration. (2004). *Arson and juveniles: Responding to the violence.* Washington, DC: Federal Emergency Management Agency, National Fire Data Center.

U.S. Fire Administration. (2009, November). Intentionally set fire. *Topical Fire Report Series, 9*(5), 1–8.

U.S. Fire Administration. (2011, March 11). *USFA announces the 2011 arson awareness week theme.* Emmitsburg, MD: Author.

University of Iowa Injury Prevention Research Center. (2001). *Workplace violence: A report to the nation.* Iowa City: Author.

Vachon, D. D., Lynam, D. R., Loeber, R., & Stouthamer-Loeber, M. (2012). Generalizing the nomological network of psychopathy across populations differing on race and conviction status. *Journal of Abnormal Psychology, 121,* 263–269.

van Beijsterveldt, C. E. M., Bartels, M., Hudziak, J. J., & Boomsma, D. I. (2003). Causes of stability of aggression from early childhood to adolescence: A longitudinal genetic analysis in Dutch twins. *Behavior Genetics, 33,* 591–605.

Vandebosch, H., & Van Cleemput, K. (2008). Defining cyberbullying: A qualitative research into the perceptions of youngsters. *Cyberpsychology & Behavior, 11,* 499–503.

Vandell, D. L., & Posner, J. K. (1999). Conceptualization and measurement of children's after-school environments. In S. L. Freidman & T. D. Wachs (Eds.), *Measuring environment across the life-span: Emerging methods and concepts.* Washington, DC: American Psychological Association.

VandenBos, G. R. (Ed.). (2007). *APA dictionary of psychology.* Washington, DC: American Psychological Association.

Vandersall, T. A., & Wiener, J. M. (1970). Children who set fires. *Archives of General Psychology, 22,* 63–71.

Vandiver, D. M., & Kercher, G. (2004). Offender and victim characteristics of registered female sexual offenders in Texas: A proposed typology of female sexual offenders. *Sexual Abuse: A Journal of Research and Treatment, 16,* 121–137.

Vandiver, D. M., & Walker, J. T. (2002). Female sex offenders: An overview and analysis of 40 cases. *Criminal Justice Review, 27,* 284–300.

van Lier, P. A. C., Vuijk, P., & Crijen, A. M. (2005). Understanding mechanisms of change in the development of antisocial behavior: The impact of a universal intervention. *Journal of Abnormal Psychology, 33,* 521–533.

van Lier, P. A. C., Wanner, B., & Vitaro, F. (2007). Onset of antisocial behavior affiliation with deviant friends and childhood maladjustment: A text of the childhood- and adolescent-onset models. *Development and Psychopathology, 19,* 167–185.

van Wijk, A., van Horn, J., Bullens, R., Bijleveld, C., & Doreleijers, T. (2005). Juvenile sex offenders: A group on its own? *International Journal of Offender Therapy and Comparative Criminology, 49,* 25–36.

Vaughn, M. G., DeLisi, M., Beaver, K. M., & Howard, M. O. (2008). Toward a quantitative typology of burglars: A latent profile analysis of career offenders. *Journal of Forensic Sciences, 53,* 1387–1392.

Vaughn, M. G., DeLisi, M., Beaver, K. M., & Wright, J. P. (2009). DAT1 and 5HTT are associated with pathological criminal behavior in a nationally representative sample of youth. *Criminal Justice and Behavior, 36,* 1113–1124.

Vaughn, M. G., Fun. Q., DeLisi, M., Wright, J. P., Beaver, K. M., Perron, B. E., & Howard, M. O. (2010). Prevalence and correlates of fire-setting in the United States: Results from the National Epidemiological Survey on Alcohol and Related Conditions. *Comprehensive Psychiatry, 51,* 217–233.

Veenstra, R., Lindenberg, S., Oldehinkel, A. J., De Winter, A. F., & Ormel, J. (2005). Bullying and victimization in elementary schools: A comparison of bullies, victims, bully/victims, and uninvolved preadolescents. *Developmental Psychology, 41,* 672–682.

Veenstra, R., Lindenberg, S., Oldehinkel, A. J., De Winter, A. F., & Ormel, J. (2006). Temperament, environment, and antisocial behavior in a population sample of preadolescent boys and girls. *International Journal of Behavioral Development, 30,* 422–432.

Vega, V., & Malamuth, N. M. (2007). Predicting sexual aggression: The role of pornography in the context of general and specific risk factors. *Aggressive Behavior, 33,* 104–117.

Veneziano, C., & Veneziano, L. (2002). Adolescent sex offenders: A review of the literature. *Trauma, Violence, & Abuse, 3,* 247–260.

Verlinden, S., Hersen, M., & Thomas, J. (2000). Risk factors in school shootings. *Clinical Psychology Review, 20,* 3–56.

Verona, E., Joiner, T. E., Johnson, F., & Bender, T. W. (2006). Gender specific gene-environment interactions on laboratory-assessed aggression. *Biological Psychology, 71,* 33–41.

Verona, E., Patrick, C. J., & Joiner, T. E. (2001). Psychopathy, antisocial personality, and suicide risk. *Journal of Abnormal Psychology, 110,* 462–470.

Vetter, H. J., & Silverman, I. J. (1978). *The nature of crime.* Philadelphia: W. B. Saunders.

Victoroff, J. (2005). The mind of the terrorist: A review and critique of psychological approaches. *Journal of Conflict Resolution, 49,* 3–42.

Viding, E., Blair, R., James, R., Moffitt, T. E., & Plomin, R. (2005). Evidence for substantial genetic risk for psychopathy in 7-year-olds. *Journal of Child Psychology and Psychiatry, 46,* 592–597.

Viding, E., & Larsson, H. (2010). Genetics of child and adolescent psychopathy. In R. T. Salekin & D. R. Lynam (Eds.), *Handbook of child and adolescent psychopathy* (pp. 113–134). New York: Guilford Press.

Vien, A., & Beech, A. R. (2006). Psychopathy: Theory, measurement, and treatment. *Trauma, Violence, & Abuse, 7,* 155–174.

Viljoen, J. L., Elkovitch, N., Scalora, M. J., & Ullman, D. (2009). Assessment of reoffense risk in adolescents who have committed sexual offenses: Predictive validity of the ERASOR, PCL:YV, YLS/CMI, and Static-99. *Criminal Justice and Behavior, 36,* 981–1000.

Viljoen, J. L., MacDougall, E. A. M., Gagnon, N. C., & Douglas, K. S. (2010). Psychopathy evidence in legal proceedings involving adolescent offenders. *Psychology, Public Policy, and Law, 16,* 254–283.

Viljoen, J. L., O'Neill, M. L., & Sidhu, A. (2005). Bullying behaviors in female and male adolescent offenders: Prevalence, types, and association with psychosocial adjustment. *Aggressive Behavior, 31,* 521–536.

Viljoen, J. L., & Wingrove, T. (2007). Adjudicative competence in adolescent defendants: Judges' and defense attorneys' views of legal standards for adolescents in juvenile and criminal court. *Psychology, Public Policy, and Law, 13,* 204–229.

Vincent, G. (2006). Psychopathy and violence risk assessment in youth. *Child and Adolescent Psychiatric Clinics of North America, 15,* 407–428.

Vincent, G. M., Odgers, C. L., McCormick, A. V., & Corrado, R. R. (2008). The PCL:YV and recidivism in male and female juveniles: A follow-up into young adulthood. *International Journal of Law and Psychiatry, 31*, 287–296.

Vincent, K. R. (1991). Black/white IQ difference? *Journal of Clinical Psychology, 47*, 266–270.

Vitacco, M. J., Neumann, C. S., & Jackson, R. L. (2005). Testing a four-factor model of psychopathy and its association with ethnicity, gender, intelligence, and violence. *Journal of Consulting and Clinical Psychology, 73*, 466–476.

Vitacco, M. J., Van Rybroek, G. J., Rogstad, J. E., Erickson, S. K., Tripp, A., Harris, L., et al. (2008). Developing services for insanity acquittees conditionally released into the community: maximizing success and minimizing recidivism. *Psychological Services, 5*, 118–125.

Vitale, J. E., Newman, J. P., Serin, R. C., & Bolt, D. M. (2005). Hostile attributions in incarcerated adult male offenders: An exploration of diverse pathways. *Aggressive Behavior, 31*, 99–115.

Vitale, J. E., Smith, S. S., Brinkley, C. A., & Newman, J. P. (2002). The reliability and validity of the Psychopathy Checklist-Revised in a sample of female offenders. *Criminal Justice and Behavior, 29*, 202–231.

Vitaro, F., & Brendgen, M. (2005). Proactive and reactive aggression: A developmental perspective. In R. E. Tremblay, W. W. Hartrup, & J. Archer (Eds.), *The developmental origins of aggression*. New York: Guilford.

Vitaro, F., Brendgen, M., & Barker, E. D. (2006). Subtypes of aggressive behaviors: A developmental perspective. *International Journal of Behavioral Development, 30*, 12–19.

Vitaro, F., & Tremblay, R. P. (1994). Impact of a prevention program on aggressive children's friendships and social adjustment. *Journal of Abnormal Child Psychology, 22*, 457–476.

Vold, G. B. (1958). *Theoretical criminology*. New York: Oxford University Press.

Vossekuil, B., Fein, R., Reddy, M., Borum, R., & Modzeleski, W. (2002). *The final report and findings of the Safe School Initiative: Implications for the prevention of school attacks in the United States*. Washington, DC: U.S. Secret Service and Department of Education.

Waaktaar, T., Christie, H. J., Borge, A. I. H., & Torgerson, S. (2004). How can young people's resilience be enhanced? Experiences from a clinical intervention project. *Clinical Child Psychology and Psychiatry, 9*, 167–183.

Wachi, T., Watanabe, K., Yokota, K., Suzuki, M., Hoshino, M., Sato, A., et al. (2007). Offender and crime characteristics of female serial arsonists in Japan. *Journal of Investigative Psychology and Offender Profiling, 4*, 29–52.

Wagner, R. V., & Long, K. R. (2004). Terrorism from a peace psychology perspective. In F. M. Moghaddam & A. J. Marsella (Eds.), *Understanding terrorism: Psychosocial roots, consequences, and interventions*. Washington, DC: American Psychological Association.

Waite, D., Keller, A., McGarvey, E. L., Wieckowski, E., Pinkerton, R., & Brown, G. L. (2005). Juvenile sex offender re-arrest rates for sexual, violent nonsexual, and property crimes. *Sexual Abuse: A Journal of Research and Treatment, 17*, 313–331.

Wakschlag, L. S., & Hans, S. L. (2002). Maternal smoking during pregnancy and conduct problems in high-risk youth: A developmental framework. *Development and Psychopathology, 14*, 351–369.

Walker, K. L., & Chestnut, D. (2003). The role of ethnocultural variables in response to terrorism. *Cultural Diversity and Ethnic Minority Psychology, 9*, 251–262.

Walker, L. E. (1979). *The battered woman*. New York: Harper Colophon Books.

Walker, S. (2001). *Sense and nonsense about crime and drugs* (5th ed.). Belmont, CA: Wadsworth/Thomson Learning.

Wallace, H. (1996). *Family violence: Legal, medical, and social perspectives*. Boston: Allyn & Bacon.

Wallace, H., & Seymour, A. (2001). Domestic violence. In G. Coleman, M. Gaboury, M. Murray, & A. Seymour (Eds.), *1999 National Victim Assistance Academy*. Washington, DC: U.S. Department of Justice.

Wallerstein, J. S., & Wyle, J. (1947). Our law-abiding law breakers. *Probation, 25*, 107–112.

Walsh, A. (2005). African Americans and serial killing in the media. *Homicide Studies, 9*, 271–291.

Walsh, D. (1980). *Break-ins: Burglary from private homes.* London: Constable.

Walters, G. C., & Grusec, J. E. (1977). *Punishment.* San Francisco: W. H. Freeman.

Walters, G. D. (2003). Predicting institutional adjustment and recidivism with the Psychopathy Checklist factor scores: A meta-analysis. *Law and Human Behavior, 27,* 541–558.

Walters, G. D., Deming, A., & Elliott, W. N. (2009). Assessing criminal thinking in male sex offenders with the Psychological Inventory of Criminal Thinking Styles. *Criminal Justice and Behavior, 36,* 1025–1036.

Walters, G. D.., & Geyer, M. D. (2004). Criminal thinking and identity in male white-collar offenders. *Criminal Justice and Behavior, 31,* 263–281.

Ward, T. (2000). Sexual offenders' cognitive distortions as implicit theories. *Aggression and Violent Behavior, 7,* 53–68.

Ward, T., & Hudson, S. M. (2000). Sexual offenders' implicit planning: A conceptual model. *Sexual Abuse: A Journal of Research and Treatment, 12,* 189–202.

Ward. T., Hudson, S. M., Marshall, W. L., & Siegert, R. (1995). Attachment style and intimacy deficits in sexual offenders: A theoretical framework. *Sexual Abuse: A Journal of Research and Treatment, 7,* 317–335.

Wareham, J., & Dembo, R. (2007). A longitudinal study of psychological functioning among juvenile offenders: A latent model analysis. *Criminal Justice and Behavior, 34,* 259–273.

Warren, J. I., Burnette, M. L., South, S. C., Chauhan, P., Bale, R., Friend, R., et al. (2003). Psychopathy in women: Structural modeling and comorbidity. *International Journal of Law and Psychiatry, 26,* 223–242.

Warren, J. I., Rosenfeld, B., Fitch, W. L., & Hawk, G. (1997). Forensic mental health clinical evaluation: An analysis of interstate and intersystemic differences. *Law and Human Behavior, 21,* 377–390.

Wasserman, G. A., & Seracini, A. M. (2001). Family risk factors and interventions. In R. Loeber & D. P. Farrington (Eds.), *Child delinquents: Development, intervention, and service needs* (pp. 165–190). Thousand Oaks, CA: Sage.

Watson, R. I. (1973). Investigation into deindividuation using a cross-cultural survey technique. *Journal of Personality and Social Psychology, 25,* 342–345.

Webb, J. A., Bray, J. H., Getz, J. G., & Adams, G. (2002). Gender, perceived parental monitoring, and behavioral adjustment: Influences on adolescent alcohol use. *American Journal of Orthopsychiatry, 72,* 392–400.

Weiler, B. L., & Widom, C. S. (1996). Psychopathy and violent behaviour in abused and neglected young adults. *Criminal Behaviour and Mental Health, 6,* 253–271.

Weis, J. G. (1989). Family violence methodology and design. In L. Ohlin & M. Tonry (Eds.), *Family violence* (Vol. 11). Chicago: University of Chicago Press.

Weis, J. G., & Sederstrom, J. (1981). *The prevention of serious delinquency. What to do?* Washington, DC: U.S. Department of Justice.

Weis, R., & Toolis, E. E. (2008). Military style residential treatment for disruptive adolescents: A critical review and look to the future. In A. M. Columbus (Ed.), *Advances in psychology research* (Vol. 56). Hauppauge, NY: Nova Science Publishers.

Weisbrot, D. M. (2008). Prelude to school shooting? Assessing threatening behaviors in childhood and adolescence. *Journal of the American Academy of Child & Adolescent Psychiatry, 47,* 847–852.

Weisel, D. L. (2007, March). *Bank robbery.* Washington, DC: U.S. Department of Justice, Office of Community Oriented Policing Services.

Weiss, R. D., & Mirin, S. M. (1987). *Cocaine.* Washington, DC: American Psychiatric Press.

Wenk, E. A., Robison, J. O., & Smith, G. W. (1972). Can violence be predicted? *Crime and Delinquency, 18,* 393–402.

Wheatman, S. R., & Shaffer, D. R. (2001). On finding for defendants who plead insanity: The crucial impact of dispositional instructions and opportunity to deliberate. *Law and Human Behavior, 25,* 167–183.

Wheeler, R. W., Davidson, R. J., & Tomarken, A. J. (1993). Frontal brain asymmetry and emotional reactivity: A biological substrate of affective style. *Psychophysiology, 30,* 82–89.

Whitcomb, D. (2001). Child victimization. In G. Coleman, M. Gaboury, M. Murray, & A. Seymour (Eds.), *1999*

National Victim Assistance Academy. Washington, DC: U.S. Department of Justice.

White, J. L., Moffitt, T. E., Earls, F., Robins, L., & Silva, P. A. (1990). How early can we tell? Predictors of childhood conduct disorder and delinquency. *Criminology, 28,* 507–533.

White, J. L., Moffitt, T. E., & Silva, P. A. (1989). A prospective replication of the protective effects of IQ in subjects at high risk for juvenile delinquency. *Journal of Consulting and Clinical Psychology, 57,* 719–724.

White, J. W., Koss, M. P., & Kazdin, A. E. (Eds.). 2011. *Violence against women and children. Vol 1. Mapping the terrain.* Washington, DC: American Psychological Association.

Wicker, T. (1976). *Time to die.* New York: Ballatine.

Widom, C. S. (1978). A methodology for studying non-institutionalized psychopaths. In R. D. Hare & D. Schalling (Eds.), *Psychopathic behavior: Approaches to research.* Chichester, UK: Wiley.

Widom, C. S. (1992, September). The cycle of violence. *Research in Brief.* Washington, DC: U.S. Department of Justice.

Widom, C. S. (2000, January). Childhood victimization: Early adversity, later psychopathology. *National Institute of Justice Journal,* 3–9.

Wiesner, M., Kim, H. K., & Capaldi, D. M. (2005). Developmental trajectories of offending: Validation and prediction to young adult alcohol use, drug use, and depressive symptoms. *Development and Psychopathology, 17,* 251–270.

Wiesner, M., & Windle, M. (2004). Assessing covariates of adolescent delinquency trajectories: A latent growth mixture modeling approach. *Journal of Youth and Adolescence, 33,* 431–432.

Wilczynski, A. (1997). Mad or bad? Child-killers, gender, and the courts. *British Journal of Criminology, 37,* 419–436.

Wike, T. L., & Fraser, M. W. (2009). School shootings: Making sense of the senseless. *Aggression and Violent Behavior, 14,* 162–169.

Williams, F. P., & McShane, M. D. (2004). *Criminological theory* (4th ed.). Upper Saddle River, NJ: Prentice Hall.

Williams, J. E., & Holmes, K. A. (1981). *The second assault: Rape and public attitudes.* Westport, CT: Greenwood Press.

Williamson, S., Hare, R. D., & Wong, S. (1987). Violence: Criminal psychopaths and their victims. *Canadian Journal of Behavioral Science, 19,* 454–462.

Willoughby, T., Adachi, P. J. C., & Good, M. (2011, October 31). A longitudinal study of association between violent video game play and aggression among adolescents. *Developmental Psychology.* Advance online publication. Doi: 10.1037/a0026046.

Wilson, J. K., Brodsky, S. L., Neal, T. M. S., & Cramer, R. J. (2011). Prosecutor pretrial attitudes and plea-bargaining behavior toward veterans with Posttraumatic Stress Disorder. *Psychological Services, 8,* 319–331.

Wilson, J. Q., & Herrnstein, R. J. (1985). *Crime and human nature.* New York: Simon & Schuster.

Windle, M., & Wiesner, M. (2004). Trajectories of marijuana use from adolescence to young adulthood: Predictors and outcomes. *Development and Psychopathology, 16,* 1007–1027.

Wolak, J., Finkelhour, D., & Mitchell, K. (2005). *Child pornography possessors and the Internet: A national study.* Arlington, VA: National Center for Missing & Exploited Children.

Wolf, B. C., & Lavezzi, W. A. (2007). Paths to destruction: The lives and crimes of two serial killers. *Journal of Forensic Science, 52,* 199–203.

Wolf, R. S. (1992). Victimization of the elderly: Elder abuse and neglect. *Reviews in Clinical Gerontology, 2,* 269–276.

Wolfe, D. A., Jaffe, P. G., Wilson, S. K., & Zak, L. (1985). Children of battered women: The relation of child behavior to family violence and maternal stress. *Journal of Consulting and Clinical Psychology, 53,* 657–665.

Wolford, M. R. (1972). Some attitudinal, psychological and sociological characteristics of incarcerated arsonists. *Fire and Arson Investigator, 16,* 8–13.

Wong, S. (2000). Psychopathic offenders. In S. Hodgins & R. Muller-Isberner (Eds.), *Violence, crime and mentally disordered offenders: Concepts and methods for effective treatment and prevention.* New York: Wiley.

Wood, J. J., Cowan, P. A., & Baker, B. L. (2002). Behavior problems and peer rejection in preschool boys and girls. *Journal of Genetic Psychology, 163,* 72–89.

Woodworth, M., & Porter, S. (2001). Historical foundations and current applications of criminal profiling in violent crime investigations. *Expert Evidence, 7,* 241–264.

Woodworth, M., & Porter, S. (2002). In cold blood: Characteristics of criminal homicides as a function of psychopathy. *Journal of Abnormal Psychology, 111,* 436–445.

Worling, J. R. (1995). Adolescent sibling incest offenders: Differences in family and individual functioning when compared to adolescent nonsibling sex offenders. *Child Abuse & Neglect, 19,* 633–643.

Worling, J. R., & Langton, C. M. (2012). Assessment and treatment of adolescents who sexually offend: Clinical issues and implications for secure settings. *Criminal Justice and Behavior, 39,* 814–841.

Wright, J., & Hensley, C. (2003). From animal cruelty to serial murder: Applying the graduation hypothesis. *International Journal of Offender Therapy and Comparative Criminology, 47,* 71–88.

Wright, J. C., Huston, A. C., Vandewater, E. A., Bickman, D. S., Scantlin, R. M., Kotler, J. A., et al. (2001). American children's use of electronic media in 1997: A national survey. *Applied Developmental Psychology, 22,* 31–47.

Wright, J. D., & Rossi, P. H. (1994). *Armed and considered dangerous: A survey of felons and their firearms.* New York: Aldine De Gruyter.

Wright, J. P., & Boisvert, D. (2009). What biosocial criminology offers criminology. *Criminal Justice and Behavior, 36,* 1228–1240.

Wright, R., Brookman, F., & Bennett, T. (2006). The foreground dynamics of street robbery in Britain. *British Journal of Criminology, 46,* 1–15.

Wright, R. T., & Decker, S. (1997). *Armed robbers in action: Stickup and street culture.* Boston: Northeastern University Press.

Xie, H., Farmer, T. W., & Cairns, B. D. (2003). Different forms of aggression among inner-city African-American Children: Gender, configurations, and school social networks. *Journal of School Psychology, 41,* 355–375.

Yang, Y., Raine, A., Lencz, T., Bihrle, S., LaCasse, L., & Colletti, P. (2005). Volume reduction in prefrontal gray matter in unsuccessful criminal psychopaths. *Biological Psychiatry, 57,* 1103–1108.

Yates, E. (1986). The influence of psychosocial factors on nonsensical shoplifting. *International Journal of Offender Therapy and Comparative Criminology, 30,* 203–211.

Yesavage, J. A., Benezech, M., Ceccaldi, P., Bourgeois, M., & Addad, M. (1983). Arson in mentally ill and criminal populations. *Journal of Clinical Psychiatry, 44,* 128–130.

Yoshikawa, H., Aber, J. L., & Beardslee, W. R. (2012). The effects of poverty on the mental, emotiona, and behavioral health of children and youth: Implications for prevention. *American Psychologist, 67,* 272–284.

Young, S., Fox, N. A., & Zahn-Waxler, C. (1999). Relations between temperament and empathy. *Developmental Psychology, 35,* 1189–1197.

Youstin, T. J., Nobles, M. R., Ward, J. T., & Cook, C. L. (2011). Assessing the generalizability of the near repeat phenomenon. *Criminal Justice and Behavior, 38,* 1042–1063.

Yu, J., Evans, P. C., & Perfetti, L. (2004). Road aggression among drinking drivers: Alcohol and non-alcohol effects on aggressive driving and road rage. *Journal of Criminal Justice, 32,* 421–430.

Zahn, M. A., Brumbaugh, S., Steffensmeier, D., Feld, B. C. Morash, M., Chesney-Lind, M., et al. (2008, May). *Violence by teenage girls: Trends and context.* Washington, DC: U.S. Department of Justice, Office of Juvenile Justice and Delinquency Prevention.

Zahn, M. A., Day, J., Mihalic, S. F., & Tichavsky, L. (2009). Determining what works for girls in the juvenile justice system: A summary of evaluation evidence. *Crime & Delinquency, 55,* 266–293.

Zahn, M. A., Hawkins, S. R., Chiancone, J., & Whitworth, A. (2008, October). *The Girls Study Group—Charting the way to delinquency prevention for girls.* Washington, DC: U.S. Department of Justice, Office of Juvenile Justice and Delinquency Prevention.

Zapf, P. A., Golding, S. L., & Roesch, R. (2006). Criminal responsibility and the insanity defense. In I. B. Weiner & A. K. Hess (Eds.), *The handbook of forensic psychology* (3rd ed., pp. 332–363). Hoboken, NJ: Wiley.

Zawitz, M. W., & Strom, K. J. (2000, October). *Firearm injury and death from crime, 1993–1997.* Washington, DC: U.S. Department of Justice.

Zigler, E., Taussig, C., & Black, K. (1992). Early childhood intervention: A promising prevention for juvenile delinquency. *American Psychologist, 47,* 997–1006.

Zillmann, D. (1971). Excitation transfer in communication-mediated aggressive behavior. *Journal of Experimental Social Psychology, 7,* 419–434.

Zillmann, D. (1979). *Hostility and aggression.* Hillsdale, NJ: Erlbaum.

Zillmann, D. (1983). Arousal and aggression. In R. G. Geen & E. I. Donnerstein (Eds.), *Aggression: Theoretical and empirical reviews* (Vol. 1). New York: Academic Press.

Zillmann, D. (1988). Cognitive-excitation interdependencies in aggressive behavior. *Aggressive Behavior, 14,* 51–64.

Zimbardo, P. G. (1970). The human choice. Individuation, reason, and order versus deindividuation, impulse, and chaos. In W. J. Arnold & D. Levine (Eds.), *Nebraska symposium on motivation 1969.* Lincoln, NE: University of Nebraska Press.

Zimbardo, P. G. (1973). The psychological power and pathology of imprisonment. In E. Aronson & R. Helmreich (Eds.), *Social psychology.* New York: Van Nostrand.

Zipper, P., & Wilcox, D. K. (2005, April). The importance of early intervention. *FBI Law Enforcement Bulletin, 74,* 3–9.

Zkireh, B., Ronis, S. T., & Knight, R. A. (2008). Individual beliefs, attitudes, and victimization histories of male juvenile sexual offenders. *Sexual Abuse: Journal of Research and Treatment, 20,* 323–351.

Zorza, J. (1991). Woman battering: A major cause of homelessness. *Clearinghouse Review, 25*(4), 421–429.

Zucker, R. A., Fitzgerald, H. E., Refior, S. K., Puttler, L. I., Pallas, D. M., & Ellis, D. A. (2000). The clinical and social ecology of childhood for children of alcoholics: Description of a study and implications for a differentiated social policy. In H. E. Fitzgerald, B. M. Lester, & B. S. Zuckerman (Eds.), *Children of addiction: Research, health, and public policy issues.* New York: RoutledgeFalmer.

AUTHOR INDEX

Note: The 'f' and 't' followed by the locator refers to figures and tables respectively.

SUBJECT INDEX

Note: The letter 'b', 'f', and 't' followed by the locator refers to boxes, figures, and tables respectively.